AMERICAN PASSAGES

AMERICAN
PASSAGES

A History of the United States

Fourth Edition

ADVANTAGE EDITION

Edward L. Ayers
University of Richmond

Lewis L. Gould
University of Texas at Austin, Emeritus

David M. Oshinsky
University of Texas at Austin

Jean R. Soderlund
Lehigh University

WADSWORTH
CENGAGE Learning™

Australia • Brazil • Japan • Korea • Mexico • Singapore • Spain • United Kingdom • United States

WADSWORTH
CENGAGE Learning™

American Passages: A History of the United States, Advantage Edition, Fourth Edition
Edward L. Ayers, Lewis L. Gould, David M. Oshinsky, and Jean R. Soderlund

Publisher: Suzanne Jeans

Senior Sponsoring Editor: Ann West

Assistant Editor: Megan Curry

Editorial Assistant: Megan Chrisman

Senior Media Editor: Lisa Ciccolo

Senior Marketing Manager: Katherine Bates

Marketing Coordinator: Lorreen Pelletier

Marketing Communications Manager: Christine Dobberpuhl

Project Manager, Editorial Production: Jane Lee

Senior Art Director: Cate Rickard Barr

Senior Print Buyer: Becky Cross

Senior Rights Acquisition Account Manager: Katie Huha

Production Service: Pre-PressPMG

Senior Photo Editor: Jennifer Meyer-Dare

Cover Image: Edward Hopper, 1882–1967, *Yonkers*, 1916. Oil on canvas 24-1/4 × 29-1/8 in. Credit: Whitney Museum of American Art, New York; Josephine N. Hopper bequest, 70.1215. Photograph by Geoffrey Clements.

Compositer: Pre-PressPMG

For product information and technology assistance, contact us at **Cengage Learning Customer & Sales Support, 1-800-354-9706**

For permission to use material from this text or product, submit all requests online at **www.cengage.com/permissions**
Further permissions questions can be emailed to **permissionrequest@cengage.com**

Library of Congress Control Number: 2009934261

Student Edition:

ISBN-13: 978-0-547-16646-9

ISBN-10: 0-547-16646-X

Wadsworth
20 Channel Center Street
Boston, MA 02210
USA

Cengage Learning is a leading provider of customized learning solutions with office locations around the globe, including Singapore, the United Kingdom, Australia, Mexico, Brazil, and Japan. Locate your local office at: **international.cengage.com/region**

Cengage Learning products are represented in Canada by Nelson Education, Ltd.

For your course and learning solutions, visit **www.cengage.com**

Purchase any of our products at your local college store or at our preferred online store **www.ichapters.com**

Printed in the United States of America
3 4 5 6 7   13 12 11 10

Brief Contents

Contents

3

CRISIS AND CHANGE, 1675–1720

55

6

TOWARD A MORE PERFECT UNION, 1783–1788

144

16

**RECONSTRUCTION:
ITS RISE AND FALL,
1865–1877**

401

17

**AN ECONOMY
TRANSFORMED:
THE RISE OF BIG
BUSINESS,
1877–1887**

432

22

OVER THERE AND OVER HERE: THE IMPACT OF WORLD WAR I, 1914–1921

568

23

THE AGE OF JAZZ AND MASS CULTURE, 1921–1927

597

26

THE SECOND WORLD WAR, 1939–1945

679

30

CRISIS OF CONFIDENCE, 1969–1980

795

Preface

Like other teachers of history, we have seen our students intrigued by the powerful stories of this nation's past. But textbooks often bear little resemblance to our favorite works of history or to the best kinds of teaching. Textbooks tend to replace the concrete with the abstract, the individual with the aggregate, the story with the summary. They can remove entire regions and ethnic groups from the flow of American history and relegate them to separate chapters, isolated and frozen in time. They can give away the end of the story too easily, squandering drama.

We believed that we could write a book that captured what we love most and what explains the most about history. We decided to write the first U. S. history text in which time stood front and center. Time is what makes history History rather than sociology, anthropology, or economics. Time—and the dramatic pace of events—is what most textbooks have sacrificed in the name of convenience and false clarity. In short, we set out to write a more *historical* history text.

Now in its fourth edition, *American Passages* is unique in its insistence, in every part of every chapter, that time, with the characteristics of sequence, simultaneity, and contingency, is the *defining nature* of history. Sequence shows how events grow from other events, personalities, and broad changes. Political, social, and cultural history naturally intertwine, and simultaneity shows how apparently disconnected events were situated in larger shared contexts. Contingency shows how history suddenly pivots, how it often changes course in a moment.

ORGANIZATION AND PEDAGOGY

American Passages is written to convey the excitement and uncertainty of this nation's past—to see it whole.

Each chapter in the text contains a wealth of review material to help students keep track of major events, important people, and larger movements. "Identification" terms appear in boldface throughout the chapters. At the end of every chapter, chapter summaries review key points, and "Making Connections" sections guide students backward and forward to place the current chapter's content in perspective.

CHANGES TO THE FOURTH EDITION

For this fourth edition we made a series of significant changes designed to make the book more attractive to students and easier for them to use. We adopted a new one-column design, the format students tell us they prefer. This also allowed us to interweave the images, art, and maps more fully into the text narrative. We considered every word and whether it was needed to tell a clear, compelling story; when it didn't, we took it out. About 40 percent of the photographs are new, and many are larger so that students can better see important details. We added new Picturing the Past features throughout both volumes.

In additon to the changes in formatting and appearance, we have carefully reviewed each chapter for clarity and new scholarship and incorporated revisions and updates throughout. We are grateful to the reviewers who provided many helpful suggestions as well. Specific revisions include:

In Chapters 1–8, there are new Picturing the Past features on Native American women in New France, Education and Gender in colonial British America, Abigail Adams during the Revolutionary period, and the first federal census of 1790. Special attention was given to tightening up the end of Chapter 8 ("The New Republic Faces a New Century, 1800–1815") to allow for a smoother transition into chapter 9, which covers the period following the War of 1812.

Chapters 15 and 16 have been reworked so that 15 focuses solely on the Civil War and 16 covers Reconstruction only. New Picturing the Past topics in Chapters 9–16 include *Cherokee Nation v. Georgia,* Southern industrialization and industrial slavery, Manifest Destiny, the Lincoln Family, Confederate Nationalism, and the Rise and Fall of the Copperheads.

In Chapters 17–24, we have new Picturing the Past topics include Jim Thorpe and the 1912 Olympics and Aimee Semple McPherson.

In Chapters 25–32, most changes relate to popular culture, science, and medicine. There is a longer and more detailed section on the growth and impact of television and sports and a section on how wonder drugs and other discoveries have increased our life span. There is new material relating to the story behind the Iwo Jima Flag Raising ("Flags of Our Fathers"), the impact of Soviet spying (the Rosenberg case, specifically), the Cuban Missile Crisis, the importance of Cesar Chavez, and the legacy of Watergate (including the self-identification of Deep Throat). Chapter 32 takes the story up to 2008, with expanded coverage of Native American activism and new discussions of the subprime loan crisis, the debate over the definition of marriage, and deepening debates over climate change.

About the Authors

EDWARD L. AYERS is President and Professor of History of the University of Richmond. Named National Professor of the Year in 2003, Ayers has written and edited ten books. *The Promise of the New South: Life After Reconstruction* (1992) was a finalist for both the National Book Award and the Pulitzer Prize. *In the Presence of Mine Enemies, Civil War in the Heart of America* (2003) won the Bancroft Prize for distinguished writing in American history and the Beveridge Prize for the best book in English on the history of the Americas since 1492. Ayers created *The Valley of the Shadow: Two Communities in the American Civil War,* a website that has attracted millions of visitors.

LEWIS L. GOULD is the Eugene C. Barker Centennial Professor in American History *emeritus* at the University of Texas, where he won awards for both undergraduate and graduate teaching. He is currently the editor of the Modern First Ladies series with the University Press of Kansas and the general editor of the Documentary History of the John F. Kennedy Presidency with LexisNexis. His recent books include *The Modern American Presidency* (2003); *Grand Old Party: A History of the Republicans* (2003); *The Most Exclusive Club: A History of the Modern United States Senate* (2005); and *Four Hats in the Ring: The 1912 Election and the Birth of Modern American Politics* (2008).

JEAN R. SODERLUND is Professor of History and Deputy Provost for Faculty Affairs at Lehigh University. Her book *Quakers and Slavery: A Divided Spirit* won the Alfred E. Driscoll Publication Prize of the New Jersey Historical Commission. Soderlund was an editor of three volumes of the *Papers of William Penn* (1981–1983) and co-authored *Freedom by Degrees: Emancipation in Pennsylvania and Its Aftermath* (1991). She has written articles and chapters in books on the history of women, African Americans, Native Americans, Quakers, and the development of abolition in the British North American colonies and early United States. She is currently working on a book-length study titled, *Violence and Peace on the Delaware: The Evolution of Liberal Society in Colonial New Jersey and Pennsylvania.*

DAVID M. OSHINSKY is the Jack S. Blanton Chair in History at the University of Texas at Austin and a Distinguished Scholar in Residence at New York University. Among his publications are *"A Conspiracy So Immense": The World of Joe McCarthy* (1983), which was voted one of the year's "notable books" by the *New York Times,* and won the Hardeman Prize for the best work about the history of the U.S. Congress; and *Worse Than Slavery* (1996), which won both the Robert F. Kennedy Book Award for the year's most distinguished contribution to human rights, and the American Bar Association's Scribes Award for distinguished legal writing. His most recent publication, *Polio: An American Story* (2005), won both the Pulitzer Prize for History and the Hoover Presidential Book Award.

Contact, Conflict, and Exchange in the Atlantic World, to 1590

When the Italian navigator Christopher Columbus sighted the Caribbean island of San Salvador on October 12, 1492, Native Americans were living in cities and towns throughout the Americas. Columbus called the Native Americans *Indios*, or Indians, because he thought he had reached islands in Asia. Although Columbus was not the first European to reach the Western Hemisphere, his landfall initiated the conquest of two continents whose vast extent and wealth were previously unknown to Europeans.

For Native Americans, these white men and their sailing ships spelled demographic catastrophe. Their great cities were destroyed, and within 150 years, the Indian population was reduced by 90 percent. For Europeans, Columbus's unexpected "discovery" brought unimaginable new opportunities. And for Africans, European colonization sparked the transatlantic slave trade, which over the next four centuries transported at least 10 million Africans to the Americas.

Yet contact among Native Americans, Europeans, and Africans involved more than conquest, enslavement, and death. Together the three groups created new traditions and societies. Although the Europeans won the contest for power, the American colonies were shaped by the exchange of knowledge, culture, and work among all participants. Three major cultural traditions came together in the New World. This chapter explores Native American, European, and African societies at the time of contact; European exploration; and Spain's initial colonization in Central and South America.

THE FIRST AMERICANS

Estimates of the number of Native Americans in 1492 vary widely, from 8 million to more than 100 million. They possessed widely divergent cultures, ranging from the Inuit who hunted seal and walrus along the shores of the Arctic Ocean, to the Aztecs of central Mexico and Incas of the Peruvian Andes who lived in state-level agricultural societies. In the geographic area that now encompasses the United States, they included mound-building farmers of the Mississippi valley, the pueblo-dwelling Hopi and Zuñi Indians and nomadic Apaches of the Southwest, and the Iroquois and Algonquians of the eastern woodlands. Their culture diverged with adaptation to the many different habitats of the Americas.

Native American Societies Before Contact

Some Native Americans believe that their ancestors have always lived in the Western Hemisphere. However, archaeological evidence in North and South America supports a theory that the first Americans migrated by boat from Asia or crossed the Bering land bridge from Siberia to Alaska more than 10,000 years ago. As glaciers from the last Ice Age receded, groups migrated throughout the hemisphere, adapting to the widely varied environments. Initially they hunted game, fished, and collected berries, seeds, and nuts.

Ancient Americans began cultivating crops and developing settled societies in Mesoamerica—present-day Mexico and northern Central America—and in Peru. Of greatest importance was the development of maize, or Indian corn, probably from the grass *teosinte*, which grew in dry areas of Mexico and Guatemala. Mesoamericans also domesticated beans, squash, chili peppers, and avocado. Higher yields spurred population growth, a greater division of labor, and the emergence of cities.

Between 1200 B.C. and Columbus's arrival, a series of great civilizations emerged in Mesoamerica and the central Andes. Ancient Americans built cities and extensive trade networks and developed systems of religion and knowledge, art, architecture, and hierarchical social classes. Two of the best-known civilizations of precontact America were the people of the Valley of Mexico and the Maya, located on the Yucatán peninsula. The people of the Valley of Mexico built the city of Teotihuacán east of Lake Texcoco. Its population of about 200,000 depended on intensive farming of nearby irrigated lands. The grid-patterned Teotihuacán held at its core the Pyramid of the Sun and the Pyramid of the Moon. Even after the city's decline, it retained religious significance for later Mexicans. The **Maya**, at their height from 300 to 900 A.D., built cities of stone pyramids, temples, and palaces, with populations ranging to more than 60,000. Maya kings, considered divine, extended their empire to more than fifty states and maintained trade with distant peoples. The Maya had a numeral system based on units of twenty, hieroglyphics, knowledge of astronomy, and several calendars.

The **Aztecs** settled in the Valley of Mexico around 1200. Their capital, Tenochtitlán, founded in 1325, was built on two islands in Lake Texcoco, which they connected to the shore by causeways. They cultivated intensively the marshlands surrounding their island and built a militaristic state. By the time the Spanish arrived in 1519, the Aztecs controlled territory from the Pacific to the Gulf Coast. The Aztecs required tribute from the people they conquered: gold, feathers, turquoise, food, cotton, and human beings for sacrifice. They believed that every day they had to feed human hearts to the sun god, Huitzilpochtli, to prevent the world from coming to an end.

This icon will direct you to interactive activities and study materials on the American Passages website: www.cengage.com/history/ayers/ampassages4e

CHAPTER TIMELINE

38,000–12,000 B.C.	Migration of ancient hunters to the Americas
300–900 A.D.	Height of Mayan civilization in Yucatan
300–1600 A.D.	Succession of empires, Ghana, Mali, and Songhay, in West Africa
700–1450 A.D.	Mississippian people build Cahokia and other urban centers in North America
c. 1000 A.D.	Leif Eriksson establishes Viking colony on Newfoundland
c. 1300 A.D.	Aztecs settle in Valley of Mexico
1420	Prince Henry of Portugal initiates search for ocean route to Asia
1440s	Portuguese mariners take Africans as slaves
c. 1452	Portugal begins sugar production on Madeira
c. 1460–1500	European improvements in navigation and ships
1487	Bartholomeu Dias of Portugal rounds Cape of Good Hope
1492	Christopher Columbus crosses Atlantic Ocean
1494	Treaty of Tordesillas establishes Line of Demarcation
1497–1498	Vasco da Gama reaches India for Portugal
1517	Martin Luther challenges the Church of Rome
1519–1521	Hernán Cortés conquers the Aztecs
1519–1522	Magellan's expedition circumnavigates the world
1528–1536	Cabeza de Vaca's adventures in Florida and Texas
1534	Act of Supremacy separates England from the Church of Rome
1539–1542	Hernando de Soto explores the region from Florida to the Mississippi River
1540–1542	Coronado explores the American Southwest
1541	Cartier establishes Charlesbourg-Royal in Canada
1556	Philip II of Spain takes the throne
1558	Elizabeth I becomes queen of England
1564	French Huguenots build Fort Caroline in northern Florida
1577–1580	Francis Drake circumnavigates the globe
1585	English attempt colonization at Roanoke Island
1588	English defeat the Spanish Armada

To the north of the Valley of Mexico, the first mainly agricultural societies developed in the deserts of the present-day American Southwest. The Hohokam cultivated Indian corn, cotton, squash, and beans in Arizona and northern Sonora, built irrigation canals to draw water from nearby rivers. In what is now northern Ods and New Mexico, Colorado, and Utah, Anasazi farmers relied on rain ʸon, to water their crops. One of their settlements was Pueblo Bonito in C ded by which housed perhaps a thousand people in eight hundred roor ʸon cliffs high walls; another was the complex of rock dwellings built hig at Mesa Verde. Descendants of the Anasazi—the Hopi and Zuñi Indians—were called Pueblo (meaning "village" or "people") Indians by the Spanish for the adobe villages with large apartment dwellings in which they lived.

Farther east, in a large area drained by the Mississippi River, by 1000 B.C. early Americans developed civilizations characterized by large earthen burial mounds, some sixty feet high. These mounds entombed the dead and such grave goods as copper spoons and beads made from seashells. The Adena-Hopewell people, who built the Great Serpent Mound located in southern Ohio, lived in small villages along rivers, hunted game, fished, and raised squash, Indian corn, sunflowers, and gourds. Their trading network extended from the Gulf Coast (shells) to Lake Superior (copper). By 800 A.D., people in the Mississippi Valley had constructed large towns, including Cahokia, near present-day St. Louis, Missouri. At the center of these towns stood large rectangular mounds topped by temples and mortuaries in which members of the upper class were buried. By 1450, the region's population had declined, perhaps as a result of illness spread by urban crowding.

Peoples of the Eastern Woodlands Along the Atlantic seaboard and extending inland to the Appalachian Mountains lived Native Americans of two major language groups: the Algonquian and the Iroquois. In most areas of the eastern woodlands, fertile soil and moderate rainfall and temperatures supported agriculture and many kinds of game, fish, and wild plants. Algonquian-speaking people dominated the Atlantic coast from Canada to Florida; they included the Micmacs and Algonquin in Canada, the Pequots in New England, the Lenapes of the middle Atlantic region, and members of the Powhatan confederacy in what became Virginia. Many of the Iroquois lived in the Finger Lakes area of central New York State. They belonged to five tribes: the Mohawks, Oneidas, Onondagas, Cayugas, and Senecas, from east to west, who banded together in the Iroquois confederacy.

Indians of the eastern woodlands had much in common. They held land cooperatively, not as individuals or families. Except in parts of Canada and far northern New England, Indians had a mixed economy of agriculture, gathering, fishing, and hunting. Women were responsible for raising corn, squash, beans, and, in the Chesapeake region especially, tobacco. They also gathered nuts and fruit, built houses, made clothing, took care of the children, and prepared meals, while men cleared land, hunted, fished, and protected the village from enemies. The combination of corn, squash, and beans enriched the soil, providing high yields from small plots of land; eaten together, these foods were high in protein. The Native Americans cleared land by girdling the large trees (removing a strip of bark around the trees about three feet from the ground). When the trees died, the Indians removed them, burned the underbrush, and sowed crops among the stumps. Eastern woodlands people used nets and weirs to catch fish, and to ensure good hunting, they periodically burned underbrush from sections of forest. The burning stimulated the growth of lush grass, providing fodder for deer and other game. The fires allowed some sunlight to penetrate the forest, promoting the growth of strawberries, raspberries, and blackberries.

Indian religions were widely diverse in many ways yet incorporated a common worldview. The peoples of the eastern woodlands believed that the earth formed a spiritual realm of which they were a part, but not the masters. Spirits filled the earth and could be found in plants, animals, rocks, or clouds.

Great Serpent Mound

This is an aerial photograph of the Great Serpent Mound in southern Ohio, which was probably built by the Adena or Hopewell people sometime between 500 B.C. and 500 A.D. The Hopewell people had trade networks extending to the Gulf Coast, Rocky Mountains, and Lake Superior. Archaeologists digging at Hopewell sites have recovered copper, quartz, shark and grizzly bear teeth, and silver from distant areas. Artisans created jewelry, smoking pipes, musical pan-pipes, and other art from these materials.

The Great Serpent Mound, more than one-quarter mile long from the tri-angular tip to the tail, demonstrates the knowledge of astronomy of these ancient people. According to anthropologist William F. Romain in *Mysteries of the Hopewell* (2000), the mound is oriented to true astronomical north, and its measurements conform to the standard Hopewell 1,053-foot unit of length. The large oval and serpent's head almost precisely face the setting sun on June 21, the summer solstice; the serpent's body is aligned to the rising and setting moon.

(Courtesy, National Museum of the American Indian, Smithsonian Institution #P18523)

Each spirit, or *manitou*, could become the guardian of a young Indian man (less often a young woman), who, in search of a manitou, went into the woods alone, without eating or sleeping perhaps for days. If the spirit made itself known, it would provide h and counsel to the individual for the rest of his or her life. These Native Am also believed in a Master Spirit or Creator who was all-powerful and all-kn whose presence was rarely felt. Religious leaders called *shamans* perfo influence the weather or ward off danger. They were usually me munities the shaman was a woman. Indians believed that sha interpret dreams, bring good weather, and predict the fut

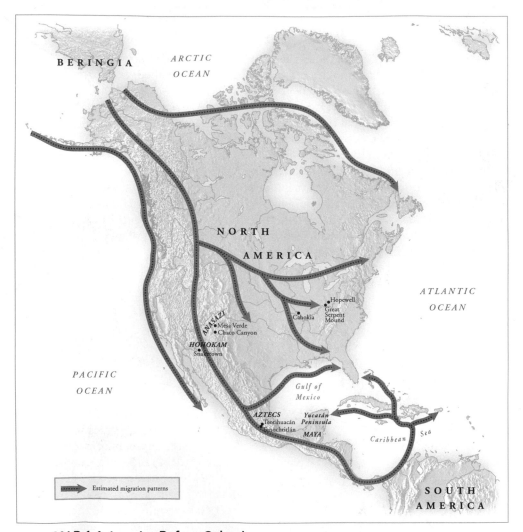

MAP 1.1 America Before Columbus.

The first inhabitants of North America probably migrated from Asia by boat and across the Bering land bridge (Beringia), which was created when sea levels dropped during the last Ice Age. Archaeological evidence along the Pacific coast and from sites such as Cahokia and Mesa Verde provide important information about Native American societies before 1492.

The kinship group, or extended family, formed the basis of Native American society. The heads of kinship groups chose the band's chief leaders, called *sachems*, who with advice assigned fields for planting, decided where and when to hunt, managed trade and diplomacy, and judged whether to go to war. Among Algonquian-speaking ~ves, most heads of extended families were men, as were the sachems they chose. Iroquois culture, women served as clan leaders and therefore had a share of ~ower. Iroquois society was matrilineal, with family membership passing from ~ildren, and matrilocal, as the husband left his native family to live with his ~lders could not speak publicly at tribal councils or serve as sachems,

Woman and Girl of Pomeioc

The Englishman John White painted this watercolor in 1585, during his stay in the Roanoke colony on the coast of what is now North Carolina. It is one of a series of illustrations, also including *Secotan Village* and *Man with Body Paint*, that provide some of the best evidence about the Algonquians of eastern North America in the late sixteenth century.

The label at the top states that this is the wife of a chief of Pomeioc and her daughter, who is aged eight or ten years. White tried to present the Indians' appearance faithfully, including their hairstyles, jewelry, and clothing. The chief's wife is dressed like other women of the eastern woodlands during the summer and is carrying a container for liquids. The girl has an English doll that Thomas Harriot, another colonist, said Indian children enjoyed. Algonquian women in North Carolina and Virginia cared for children and raised crops including corn and tobacco.

© Woman and Child of Pomeioc (w/c on paper), White, John (fl.1570–93)/British Museum, London, UK/The Bridgeman Art Library International

DOING HISTORY ONLINE

Native American Oral Traditions

Read documents 1 to 3 and consider: What are some of the advantages and disadvantages of relying on written transcriptions of oral traditions?

www.cengage.com/
history/ayers/
ampassages4e

but they chose these political leaders and advised them on such matters as waging war.

Thus, in 1492, highly complex and differentiated societies existed in North and South America. Dense populations inhabited parts of South, Central, and North America. Throughout the hemisphere, Indian people had distinctive cultures tied to the resources of their environment. Despite this wide variety of languages and cultures, most Europeans adopted the single name that Columbus mistakenly employed: Indians. An alternative the colonists used was "savages." The view of many Europeans that Native Americans had undifferentiated, uncivilized societies justified conquest and the seizure of their lands.

BEGINNING OF EUROPEAN OVERSEAS EXPANSION

Like the peoples of the Americas, Europeans spent most of their energy producing food. They farmed wheat, rye, and other crops; raised livestock; and gathered nuts and berries. In contrast to Native Americans, Europeans could own land individually and thus had the right to sell, fence, plant, erect buildings, hunt, fell timber, and exclude others from their property.

European societies were patriarchal: men were the heads of their families, and political power was nearly always in the hands of men. Although women occasionally inherited the throne, as did Isabella of Spain and Elizabeth I of England, men controlled government, the church, and the military. Married women were considered subordinate to their husbands. Under English common law, a married woman was a *feme covert*, or "covered woman." She could not own or manage property, make a contract, write a will, take custody of her children, own a business, or sue in court without her husband's permission. An unmarried woman or widow, in legal terms a *feme sole*, was not subject to these restrictions.

In the fifteenth century, the pope headed a united Catholic church in western and central Europe. At the same time, monarchs were consolidating national power in Portugal, Spain, France, and England, providing financial support and a greater sense of national identity to fuel European expansion. In turn, wealth from distant empires and trade funded wars among these emerging nations.

Trade with the East When Columbus sailed out into the Atlantic Ocean in 1492, he expected to establish a new trade route with Asia. In the fifteenth century, eastern trade was a chief source of riches, for affluent Europeans wanted spices that would not grow in Europe, such as black pepper, cinnamon, and cloves, for preserving and flavoring their food. Merchants commanded high prices for transporting spices, silk, cotton cloth, and jewels from India, the East Indies, and other parts of East Asia.

Before 1500, Arab and Italian merchants dominated the eastern trade. Arabs controlled eastern trading centers and carried goods to the Red Sea and Persian Gulf. From there, caravans took cargoes to Mediterranean ports for purchase by Italian merchants. The Italians then distributed the spices and other goods throughout Europe by pack trains and coastal shipping. European cities developed to handle the exchange of valued products from the East in return for silver, gold, woolen and linen cloth, furs, and leather. Centers of trade and banking included Venice, Genoa, Paris, Lyons, Amsterdam, London, Barcelona, Cadiz, and Lisbon. The rise of great cities accompanied the growth of unified political states. Merchants provided funding for kings to consolidate small feudal states into nations. In Portugal, Spain, France, and England, commercial interests supported unification to obtain social order, commercial monopolies, and standardized codes of law.

Portugal Explores the West African Coast, 1424–1450 Early in the fifteenth century, **Prince Henry of Portugal** (1394–1460), called "the Navigator," decided to challenge the Arab and Italian hold on commerce with the East. He also hoped to increase Portugal's power by adding territorial possessions, promote trade with Africa, and spread Christianity.

In 1420, cartographers knew a great deal about the Mediterranean Sea and had produced highly accurate charts, called *portolano*, of its shorelines and harbors. But European sailors knew nothing of the West African coast south of Cape Bojador. Seamen had heard that monsters and perhaps even Satan dwelled in the waters beyond Cape Bojador; other stories told that the ocean boiled at the equator. Prince Henry challenged current wisdom by sending ships down Africa's coast to find a route to the East.

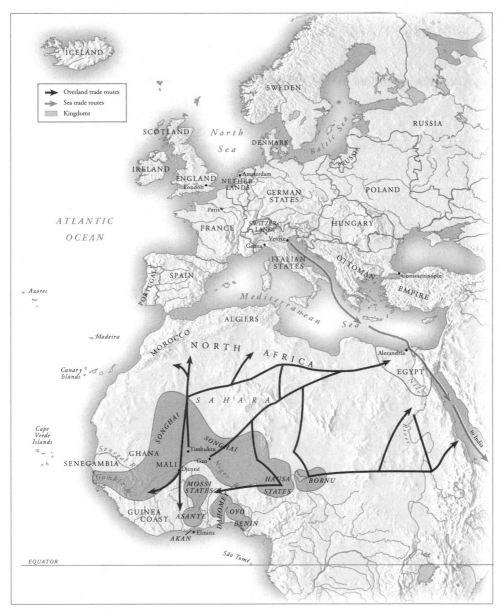

MAP 1.2 Europe, Africa, and Southwest Asia, c. 1500.

Advances in navigational technology and ship design made the Portuguese voyages of exploration possible. Compasses had been in use since at least the thirteenth century, but not until about 1460 did Europeans develop the means of determining latitude (distance north or south from the equator). Sea captains used an astrolabe or a quadrant to determine the angle of the sun from the horizon, then consulted astronomical tables that Abraham Zacuto compiled in 1478.

The Portuguese developed a new ship for their ocean voyages, the small but sturdy *caravel*. The first European oceangoing ships were large and square-rigged. To increase maneuverability along jagged coastlines, Portuguese seafarers designed the caravel with lateen (triangular) sails. The most successful Portuguese ship for long voyages was the square-rigged caravel, developed late in the fifteenth century, which combined square sails on two masts for speed with a lateen sail on the third mast for agility. The Portuguese mounted artillery on the caravels and by 1500 introduced the practice of broadside fire. They changed nautical warfare by sinking enemy vessels with gunfire instead of boarding them with foot soldiers.

Portuguese ships were cramped and uncomfortable places to live on a voyage that might last months or even years. Only the senior officers had regular sleeping quarters; the rest of the seamen slept on deck, or below in bad weather. Their shipmates included rats and cockroaches. The sailors ate hard bread, beans, salt pork, and beef, and drank mostly wine, since their casked water quickly became foul.

AFRICA AND THE ATLANTIC SLAVE TRADE

The Portuguese explorers ventured farther and farther down the West African coast, finally sailing past Cape Bojador in 1434. Within a few years the Portuguese established a lucrative coastal trade in slaves, gold, and malaguetta pepper in the Senegal region and farther south and east to the Gold Coast and Benin. Merchants now began investing in expeditions. Between the 1440s and 1505, Portuguese traders transported forty thousand Africans to perform domestic labor in Portugal and Spain and to work on the sugar plantations of the Azores, Madeira, and Canary Islands.

West African Cultures From before 300 A.D. to 1600, a succession of empires—Ghana, Mali, and Songhai—dominated western Africa. These empires had large armies, collected tribute over vast distances, and traded with Europeans and Arabs. West Africans were predominantly agricultural people. By 1100, Ghana had declined as a result of droughts that dried up several rivers. Mali then took control, as its monarchs regulated the all-important gold trade. The Mali kings were followers of Islam: one of the most famous, Mansa Kankan Mussa, made a pilgrimage to Mecca in 1324 to fulfill his religious duty as a Muslim. His caravan is said to have included more than sixty thousand people and eighty camels carrying gold.

Mali provided stable government over a wide area until the fifteenth century, when **Songhai** successfully challenged its dominance. Songhai was centered at Gao. Under Sonni Ali, who ruled from 1468 to 1492, Songhai captured Timbuktu, an important trading and cultural center of Mali. Askia Mohammed, who ruled from 1493 to 1528, expanded the empire even farther. He strengthened ties with other Muslims and reformed government, banking, and education. He adopted Islamic law and encouraged intellectual growth. After his reign, however, Songhai declined, and Moroccans conquered Timbuktu in 1593.

Beyond these empires, along the West African coast lay smaller states with highly developed cultures. Although influenced by Islam, they retained much of their traditional religions. Divine kings governed many of the coastal states. Like Native Americans and Europeans, the people of Africa kept religion central to their lives and endowed their leaders with both political and religious authority.

Most important in traditional African religions was a single all-powerful God, the Creator. Beneath the Creator were lesser gods, including gods of rain, thunder, and lightning; of rivers and lakes; of animals, trees, and hills. These gods could be benevolent or harmful, so people sought positive relationships through rituals, sacrifice, and prayer. Africans also believed that their ancestors watched over the extended family, with power over fertility, health, and even life. When the eldest father, or patriarch, of a kinship group died, his spirit became a god. All family members paid respect to the deceased, whose burial was delayed until distant relatives could arrive. Before his death, the patriarch had been the extended family's priest; he communicated with its ancestors through prayer and the sacrifice of animals such as chickens and sheep. The patriarch also served as political leader. Thus, in many African societies, the state, religion, and family united under a single hierarchical structure.

Kinship in West Africa varied from one culture to another; extended families could be either patrilineal or matrilineal. In all cases, however, a child belonged to only one kin group. In patrilineal societies, descent flowed from father to child. In matrilineal groups, descent proceeded from mother to child, but it was the mother's brother, not the mother, who assumed responsibility for her children. When a woman married, she usually went to live with her husband's family. The husband compensated her family for the loss of her services with a payment called bride wealth. Polygyny, or having more than one wife, was generally reserved to men of high status. When men had more than one wife, each woman lived with her children in a separate house.

The extended family held land in common and assigned plots to individual families. Women and men worked in fields growing crops such as rice, cassava, wheat, millet, cotton, fruits, and vegetables. They kept livestock, including cattle, sheep, goats, and chickens. Families produced food for their own use and for the market, where women were the primary traders. Artisans were skilled in textile weaving, pottery, basketry, and woodwork. They also made tools and art objects of copper, bronze, iron, silver, and gold. As in the case of Native Americans, West Africans had experienced

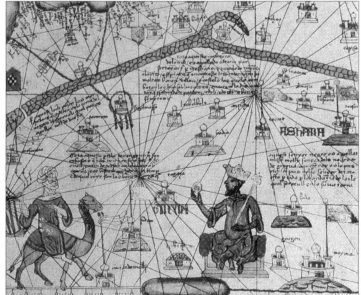

European Map of Northwest Africa.

This 1375 European map of northwest Africa shows an Arab trader approaching Mansu Musa of Mali, who is holding a large nugget of gold.

(The Granger Collection, New York)

the rise and fall of empires and had developed diverse, complex cultures by the time Europeans arrived on their shores.

The Atlantic Slave Trade Begins   Over the course of four centuries, beginning in the 1440s, Africa lost more than 10 million people to the **Atlantic slave trade**. Slavery had existed in Africa and throughout the Mediterranean for centuries before the Portuguese arrived on the West African coast. African slavery was different, however, from the institution that developed in the Americas. Most African slaves were prisoners of war; others had committed some offense that caused their kinfolk to banish them. The primary function of slavery in West Africa was social rather than economic: to provide a place in society for people cut off from their families. Although trans-Saharan traders transported a few Africans for sale to wealthy Europeans, most slaves remained in West Africa, where they became members of a household, married, and had children. Enslaved Africans could be transferred from one owner to another at will, but their children could not be sold and were frequently emancipated.

The plantation slave system that became dominant in America began near Africa. Portugal began growing sugar as early as 1452 on the island of Madeira, off West Africa. Planting, tending, and harvesting sugar cane required large amounts of menial, strenuous labor in a hot climate. To supply Madeira, Portuguese merchants purchased black slaves from Muslim trans-Saharan traders and from Africans along the coast. When sugar proved an extraordinarily profitable commodity, the Portuguese colonized the small islands in the Gulf of Guinea—São Tomé, Príncipe, and Fernando Po—to create new sugar plantations. The mortality rate was high and the demand for laborers great, spurring growth of the slave trade on the Gold Coast. By the end of the fifteenth century, before European settlement in America, Portugal developed both the plantation system and the commercial mechanism for purchasing human beings from African traders. The growth of slavery and the slave trade in America after 1500 represented an expansion of these earlier developments.

SPAIN AND PORTUGAL DIVIDE THE GLOBE

Once Portugal had established trade on the West African coast, Spanish merchants tried to participate. Prince Henry appealed to the pope, who in 1455 gave Portugal sole possession of lands to the south and east toward India. The pope's decision gave Portugal a monopoly on the Atlantic slave trade. Spain and Portugal affirmed the decision with the Treaty of Alcaçovas (1479), in which Spain recognized Portugal's sphere of interest in Africa and Portugal acknowledged Spain's claim to the Canary Islands.

As the Portuguese sailed south, they came to recognize the vastness of the African continent. They made rapid progress sailing around the continent only after 1482, when King John II of Portugal stepped up the program of discovery. In 1487 Bartholomeu Dias rounded the Cape of Good Hope. The Portuguese now knew that a sea route to India existed.

Columbus Sails West, 1492–1493   The Spanish had to find another route to the Far East. Thus, the Spanish monarchs Isabella and Ferdinand decided to fund

Christopher Columbus, despite their skepticism of his calculation of the distance to Asia. A native of Genoa, Italy, Columbus relocated to Portugal and sailed on merchant voyages to Iceland, Ireland, and the West African coast. In 1484, he sought patronage from John II of Portugal for a voyage west across the Atlantic in the belief that Asia was within reach. When John turned him down, Columbus sought support from Isabella and Ferdinand. They finally approved his request in January 1492. Competition for Asian markets and goods and, desire for gold, power, fame, and missionary zeal all contributed to the drive to find a new route to the East.

In August 1492, Columbus sailed west from the Canaries, taking advantage of the favorable current and trade winds. When the ships reached San Salvador in the Bahamas in October, Columbus thought they had located the East Indies. Hoping to establish trade, Columbus sailed southward to Cuba, then touched Hispaniola, where Native Americans offered gold in return for the trade goods he brought. The Spanish lost their flagship *Santa Maria* on a coral reef and used its timbers to build a fort on Hispaniola.

Leaving a small contingent of men at the fort, Columbus set out for home in January 1493; he again found favorable winds, but encountered a violent storm and sought shelter in Portugal. King John II, whose explorers had not yet reached India by sailing around Africa, refused to believe that Columbus had located Asia. The lands he had found, the king claimed, lay within Portugal's sphere.

Spanish and Portuguese "Spheres," 1493–1529

Isabella and Ferdinand rejected Portugal's argument for claiming lands, and they petitioned Pope Alexander VI, who was Spanish, to grant them dominion over the newly discovered lands. After negotiations with John II, the pope established a Line of Demarcation, giving all lands "discovered or to be discovered" west of the line to Spain and all lands east of the line to Portugal. The **Treaty of Tordesillas** (1494) located the line 370 leagues (about 1,100 miles) west of the Azores and expanded the principle of spheres of influence, by which European nations sought to dominate most of the world. Portugal retained its rights to the Atlantic slave trade and the sea route around Africa to India. Spain received permission to explore, conquer, and Christianize all lands and people to the west. The question of where Portuguese and Spanish spheres should be divided in the Far East was left unresolved until 1529, when the Treaty of Saragossa established a line seventeen degrees to the east of the Moluccas (Spice Islands), thus placing most of Asia within Portugal's sphere.

Between 1493 and 1529, Portugal and Spain sent out expeditions to explore their spheres. Columbus made three more voyages to the west: in November 1493 he sailed with seventeen ships to the Lesser Antilles, Puerto Rico, and Hispaniola. Later he explored the coasts of South and Central America. Meanwhile, the Portuguese completed their efforts to reach India. In 1497–1498, Vasco da Gama rounded the Cape of Good Hope and sailed across the Indian Ocean, returning to Portugal with a cargo of pepper and cinnamon. In 1500, Portugal instructed Pedro Álvares Cabral to find the Cape of Good Hope by sailing west. Instead, he touched the coast of Brazil, further convincing the Portuguese that this was not Asia. On the basis of Cabral's expedition and because a section of Brazil lay east of the Line of Demarcation, Portugal claimed that part of South America. The Italian captain Amerigo Vespucci made two separate voyages, in 1499 and 1501, for Spain and Portugal, respectively. He explored much of the Atlantic coast of South America, demonstrating that it was a huge land mass that had to be

Columbus Taking Possession of New Country. *A late nineteenth-century image of Columbus's first contact with Native Americans in the Bahamas.*

circumnavigated to reach Asia. In recognition of his insight, the German cartographer Martin Waldseemüller applied Vespucci's first name, Amerigo, not that of Columbus, to the newly "discovered" continents.

An Expanding World   Europeans continued to search for a western sea route to Asia. Ferdinand Magellan convinced King Charles I of Spain that he could sail around the cape of South America and claim the Molucca Islands. Magellan was Portuguese, but his own country gave him no support because it already had a profitable sea route to the East. With five ships, in 1519 Magellan set out on an expedition that would take three years. The voyagers faced shipwreck, a harrowing passage through the straits subsequently named for Magellan, and starvation. The Pacific was so much wider than anticipated that the mariners had to eat ship rats and leather. When inhabitants of the Philippines killed Magellan, Sebastian del Cano took command, returning to Spain with one surviving ship, laden with cloves. Together Magellan and del Cano commanded the first circumnavigation of the globe. In doing so, however, they demonstrated that the southwest passage through the Strait of Magellan was much more difficult than they had envisioned.

England and France ignored the pope's division of the world between Spain and Portugal and decided to seek a northerly route, the "northwest passage," to the East. During the fifteenth century (before Columbus's landfall), seafarers from England and France had caught fish in the Grand Banks off the coast of Newfoundland. Some sailors had camped ashore, where they traded with Native Americans. King Henry VII of England sent the Italian navigator John Cabot (Giovanni Caboto) in search of a northwest passage in 1497. Cabot's expedition reached Newfoundland and possibly Nova Scotia, but when he returned the following year, most of his ships were lost, and he died at sea. Although Cabot had failed to find the northwest passage, his efforts supported England's later claim to land in North America.

A generation after Cabot, the French entered the search for a route to Asia. In 1524, King Francis I sent another Italian sea captain, Giovanni da Verrazano, to look for the elusive passage. Landing at Cape Fear (now North Carolina), Verrazano sailed north along the Atlantic seaboard to Newfoundland, finding no evidence of a waterway through the continent. In expeditions in 1534 and 1535, Jacques Cartier hoped to find the route by way of the gulf and river of St. Lawrence. Although neither Verrazano nor Cartier found a northwest passage, they established France's claim to part of the continent.

THE SPANISH EMPIRE IN AMERICA, 1519–1590

Because England and France showed only occasional interest in America before 1560 and Portugal focused on Asian trade and Brazil, the Spanish had little interference from other Europeans in exploring and colonizing the New World. By 1543, Spanish settlements extended south to Chile and north through Mexico. Spanish explorers had crossed North America from Florida to California in what is now the southern United States. Spanish conquistadores advanced from island to island in the Caribbean, then moved through Mexico and Central America. The conquistadores expected to make their fortune in America and retire to Spain. In contrast, the Spanish Crown had a more complicated set of goals in colonizing America: to enlarge its power among European nations, exploit the wealth of the New World, and convert the Native Americans to Christianity.

Spanish Invasion, 1519–1538

When the Spanish found little gold on Hispaniola, they enslaved its inhabitants and expropriated the land. Many natives died when forced to work on plantations and tend livestock. European diseases and cruel treatment had taken their toll. As a result, the colonists sent slave-raiding parties to other islands and to the mainland. The conquistadores who explored Cuba and Puerto Rico were seeking slaves and gold. Juan Ponce de León, known for his search in 1513 for the legendary "fountain of youth" in Florida and Yucatan, sought Indian slaves. The same year Vasco Núñez de Balboa led explorers across the Isthmus of Panama; they became the first Europeans to see the Pacific Ocean. Alonso Álvarez de Pineda, in 1519–1520, sailed the coastline of the Gulf of Mexico from Florida to Mexico.

As Spanish explorers became aware of the vastness of the Americas, they organized militarily to subdue the natives living there. Despite the small size of their armies, the Spanish prevailed thanks to their superior weaponry and the impact of European diseases such as smallpox. The most famous of the conquerors was **Hernán Cortés** who launched an expedition against the Aztecs in 1519. With an army of only six hundred, Cortés persuaded the Totonacs, Tlaxcalans, and other enemies of the Aztecs to join him. He marched to Tenochtitlán without opposition and seized the emperor, Moctezuma. When Cortés outlawed human sacrifice and made incessant demands for gold, the Aztecs rebelled. They killed Moctezuma and forced the Spanish and their allies to retreat, slaying a third of Cortés's troops as they tried to escape across the causeways linking Tenochtitlán with the shore of Lake Texcoco.

By 1521, however, smallpox had ravaged the Aztec capital, and Cortés returned. With thousands of Indian allies, the Spanish built small ships to cross Lake Texcoco, took control of the causeways, and after a long siege destroyed Tenochtitlán building by building. They rebuilt the city as Mexico City, the capital of New Spain. Cortés then sent troops to take Guatemala; rival conquistadores seized Honduras. Francisco Pizarro advanced to the south, preceded by smallpox. After a difficult struggle, he defeated the Incas of Peru by 1538. Others expanded into Argentina and Chile.

Exploration of Florida and the American Southwest, 1528–1542

In 1528, Pánfilo de Narváez led an expedition to Florida that opened the way to later exploration of territories that became the southern United States. Narváez and his men landed at Tampa Bay, where they met Native Americans who warned them to return to the sea. When the Europeans refused and spoke of their search for silver and gold, the Indians directed them to "Apalachen," near the present site of Tallahassee. The Spanish marched northward through insect- and snake-infested terrain. Soon discouraged, they made the mistake of kidnapping a chief of the Apalachees. The Indians attacked, convincing the Spanish to return to New Spain immediately. The soldiers constructed barges to carry them across the Gulf of Mexico. When storms separated the craft, most of the explorers, including Narváez, were lost at sea.

Two barges crossed the gulf intact, beaching their occupants on the Texas coast. The native Karankawas captured the survivors. After several years, one of the Spaniards, Álvar Núñez Cabeza de Vaca, who had become an Indian priest and healer, escaped with three others, including an African slave named Esteban. They hoped to reach New Spain but lacked maps or instruments to find their way. For several years they lived with Native American peoples, learning their languages and customs. The Spanish earned the Indians' friendship and respect with seemingly miraculous cures. When they finally reached Mexico City in 1536, de Vaca told the Spanish viceroy about their journey.

De Vaca's report excited interest in exploring lands north of Mexico. When he refused to head an expedition, the viceroy sent Esteban with a Franciscan missionary, Fray Marcos de Niza, along with several Indians. When Esteban was killed by Zuñis, Fray Marcos returned to Mexico City with extravagant claims that the land flowed with riches.

In 1540, an army of 336 Spanish and about 1,000 Indians marched north under the command of Francisco Vásquez de Coronado, with Fray Marcos as their guide. The explorers intended to conquer the cities of gold (the so-called Seven Cities of Cibola) but were disappointed. The "golden" city that Fray Marcos had spotted was actually a Zuñi Indian pueblo. The Zuñis unsuccessfully resisted the intruders, then informed the Spanish that the cities of gold lay to the west. Another Indian told stories about great wealth in the country to the east. Over the next year, Coronado's troops explored in both directions. They encountered the Hopi of northeastern Arizona and buffalo-hunting Indians of the Great Plains, saw the Grand Canyon, and traveled as far east as Kansas. They found no gold or silver but left descriptions of a substantial part of what became the American Southwest.

Unknown to Coronado, an expedition led by Hernando de Soto, governor of Cuba, came within a few hundred miles of his own company at about the same time. In 1539, de Soto and about six hundred troops landed in Tampa Bay. Over the next three years they trekked through the Southeast, exploring lands hitherto unknown to the Spanish. They plundered the towns of the Apalachees and other Florida Indians who were part of the Mississippian cultures, with temple mounds and long-range trading networks. Stealing food, taking Indians as slaves, and killing those who resisted, de Soto's men marched north from the Florida peninsula, through central Georgia to the Carolinas, then west across the Appalachians into the Tennessee River valley. They followed the Tennessee River south into Alabama, then traveled west toward the Mississippi River. Despite heavy losses when Chickasaws burned their camp and supplies, de Soto crossed into Arkansas. After he died of a fever in 1542, the three hundred survivors of his expedition safely reached New Spain by boat.

In 1542, the initial period of Spanish expansion throughout the Americas came to a close. Without discovery of precious metals, the Spanish had little reason to push farther into North America. Instead they focused their colonizing efforts on Mexico, Peru, and Bolivia, where the richest silver deposit in the Americas was discovered in 1545.

> ### DOING HISTORY ONLINE
>
> **Images of the New World**
>
> Examine documents 4, 5, 10, 12, and 13. What do the images suggest about European expectations and impressions of the New World?
>
> www.cengage.com/history/ayers/ampassages4e

Demographic Catastrophe and Cultural Exchange

Contact among Europeans, Native Americans, and Africans after 1492 changed societies in both hemispheres. This process, called the *Columbian exchange*, included transmission of disease, knowledge about food and technology, and culture.

Disease was the chief ally of the Spanish in their drive through Central and South America. Smallpox was most lethal; other killers included measles, bubonic plague, chicken pox, influenza, whooping cough, and diphtheria. These diseases were particularly deadly because the microbes were new to America and the Indians lacked immunity. Native populations declined as much as 90 percent, as whole tribes were eliminated and others weakened severely. Illness spread from one native population to another, infecting the people of North America even before the English and French established colonies along the Atlantic coast. Some regions of the continent seemed uninhabited to European latecomers because of prior contact with disease.

The Columbian exchange also included livestock and crops that diversified cultures across continents. European settlers imported horses, sheep, cattle, pigs, and chickens for transportation, clothing, and food. Some Indians, especially on the Plains, adopted horses and became skilled riders; others raised pigs and fowl. Problems resulted, however, because Europeans often allowed their animals to roam. Cattle and pigs trampled native fields and helped spread disease and the seeds of aggressive European plants that forced out native species.

Indians introduced the Europeans and Africans to crops that soon circled the globe and had a major impact on the growth of world populations: Indian corn (or maize), tomatoes, potatoes, peppers, beans, chocolate, pumpkins, and tobacco. The white potato of South America became a major staple in Europe; the sweet potato and Indian corn were important throughout the world. New crops also came to America from Europe and Africa, including cultivated rice, wheat, oats, sugar cane, bananas, onions, peaches, and watermelon. And while Europeans brought firearms and iron tools, Native Americans showed them how to build canoes and catch fish using weirs.

Native Americans generally resisted assimilation to Spanish culture. They retained their languages, clothing, housing, agricultural methods, and, to a considerable extent, religion. The degree to which they blocked acculturation depended largely on class. The Spanish focused their attention on local Indian leaders (*caciques*) and their sons, with whom they interacted most frequently. Many caciques learned to speak Spanish, converted to Christianity, and adopted Spanish-style clothing. Their sons attended schools where they learned Latin and other advanced subjects. The common Indians avoided some Spanish ways of living and accepted others. They raised and ate chickens but grew wheat primarily to pay as tribute. They abhorred cattle, but groups like the Apaches quickly accepted the horse. Natives favored their digging sticks over the European plow, which required the use of draft animals and alteration in the assignment of fields.

RELIGION

The complexity of interaction between the Spanish and Native Americans can be seen most vividly in religion. The Europeans had a mandate from the pope to convert the "pagans" of America to Christianity. The missionaries believed that it was an act of humanity to introduce the Indians to Catholicism. The Spanish eliminated human sacrifice and destroyed temples and relics, but for the most part avoided forcing conversion on the natives. At first, missionaries expected most Native Americans to accept Spanish religious practice without change, as many Indians consented to baptism and voluntarily built churches in every town. But most Indians merged the European faith with rituals and beliefs of their traditional religions, resulting in *syncretism*, the blending of two faiths. For example, some natives added the Christian God to their polytheistic system; others focused on the saints or the Trinity of Father, Son, and Holy Spirit rather than one god. Indians organized their own societies to raise money for church functions and festivals and at times asserted independence from the Spanish church authority.

The retention of native beliefs and practices disappointed many Spanish priests, who would accept nothing less than complete submission to Catholicism. Nevertheless, missionaries worked for humane treatment of Indians. Colonists often justified enslaving Indians because they had "inferior" cultures and religion. A number of priests, including **Bartolomé de las Casas**, condemned Spanish policies. In his *A Short Account of the Destruction of the Indies*, written in 1542, las Casas described atrocities in one colony after another, informing the king of "the excesses which this New World has witnessed, all of them surpassing anything that men hitherto have imagined even in their wildest dreams."

Spanish Colonial Government The goal of the colonial government was to control and convert Native Americans and use their labor to exploit the wealth of the New World. The Spanish were only partly successful in imposing their rule over the Indians. The colonial government was most effective in central Mexico and the Andes, where the Spanish could substitute their rule for that of the Aztecs and Inca. Native Americans in northern Mexico, Florida, Arizona, New Mexico, and central Chile, who had never been subject to outside control, evaded Spanish rule. Many in the fringe areas, such as the Apaches, avoided Spanish domination altogether because their bands were highly mobile and autonomous.

The Spanish colonial administration was hierarchical and tied closely to Spain. **Sovereignty**, or supreme political power, rested in the monarch. The Spanish, like other Europeans at the time, believed that God had vested such power in the Crown. Directly below the monarch was the Council of the Indies, located in Spain and composed of men who knew little about the New World. The council regulated trade, appointed officials, made laws, and determined who should be allowed to emigrate. The highest officials residing in America were the **viceroys**. In the sixteenth and seventeenth centuries, the Spanish empire consisted of two viceroyalties: New Spain, with its capital in Mexico City, and Peru, with its capital in Lima. The viceroyalties were divided into provinces, ruled by governors and *audiencias*, who advised the governors and functioned as courts. The audiencias could appeal all decisions to the king, thus limiting the wide powers of the viceroys and governors. Neither Spanish colonists nor Indians had much say in making and enforcing laws. The right of subjects to appeal official decisions to the king, however—along with delays caused by distance, corruption, and inefficiency—introduced flexibility into the governmental structure.

In central Mexico and Peru, the Spanish viceroys, governors, and audiencias took power away from the ruling native elite. At the local level, however, native leaders often retained their positions. These caciques headed the Indian towns, collected tribute from households, and recruited forced laborers on demand of the Spanish authorities.

Spanish Mercantilism The Crown regulated commerce through the Casa de la Contratación, a government-controlled trading house founded in 1503 in Seville. Spain pursued the economic policy of **mercantilism**, which held that nations had monopolistic rights to trade with their colonies. Under mercantilism, the primary goal of economic activity was to achieve a favorable balance of trade and the acquisition of specie (gold and silver). Colonies were to serve as markets for goods from the home country and provide raw materials, gold, and silver to increase its wealth. All merchants desiring to send ships to Spanish America needed permission from the Casa, as did anyone wishing to emigrate. The Casa denied leave to persons of Jewish ancestry, for example, though in fact many found passage to America without official permission. To the monarch, a crucial function of the Casa was registration of imports of precious metals, because the king received one-fifth, called the **royal fifth**, of all silver and gold. Colonists had to obtain permission to build plantations and mines. In return they paid taxes to the king and, if they found precious metals, the royal fifth.

When Columbus obtained gold from the inhabitants of Hispaniola, he raised expectations of great wealth. However, the explorers at first met disappointment. Even the Aztecs failed to satisfy the Spanish thirst for gold, so most colonists turned to agriculture to make their fortunes. Then, in the 1540s, the Europeans located two immensely rich silver mines, one at Potosí in present-day Bolivia and the other at Zacatecas in Mexico. Between 1500 and 1650, about 181 tons of gold and 16,000 tons of silver officially reached Europe from the Americas. Production of silver expanded greatly in the 1570s with the introduction of mercury to the refining process.

The Spanish organized their silver trade to outwit privateers of other nations, especially France and England. In 1565, the Spanish founded St. Augustine in Florida as a base to fight the buccaneers and reinforce Spain's claim to North America. They devised a convoy system to protect their fleets. Two convoys left Spain from Seville each year, carrying wine, books, oil, grain, clothing, and other luxuries: one left in May headed for Mexico, and the other departed in August for the Isthmus of Panama, from which mules carried the goods to Peru. Both convoys stayed the winter with the intention of meeting in Cuba by early summer so they could return to Spain together before the hurricane season.

For Spain, the discovery of rich mines fulfilled its dreams in the New World. Spanish kings used the bullion to pay for their European wars. American silver and gold helped to create inflation throughout Europe, as the immense supply depressed their value and the prices of other goods increased. Merchants depended on the bullion to pay for luxuries from the East. Goods worth about one-half the value of the metals were returned to the colonies.

Forced Labor Systems

Because Spanish immigrants were few in number and had no intention of working in the mines or fields, they adopted ways to compel Native Americans to work. In 1550, the white colonists remained a small percentage of New World inhabitants, with a population of about 100,000 in New Spain alongside an estimated 2.6 million Native Americans in central Mexico alone. But if some European settlers hoped to have millions of Christianized Indian workers do their bidding, they were disappointed.

When the first explorers on Hispaniola tried to consign the native Arawaks to slavery, most of the Indians died. In 1500, the Spanish Crown ruled that only Indians captured in a "just war" could be forced into perpetual bondage. This judgment had little impact because conquistadores could define as hostile any natives who resisted capture. In 1513, the government drew up a document called the *Requerimiento* (or Requirement), which explorers read when they entered an Indian town for the first time. The Requerimiento informed the natives that they must accept the Catholic faith and Spanish rule. If they did, they would become Spanish subjects in peace; if they did not, the soldiers would "make war against you . . . take you and your wives and your children and . . . make slaves of them . . . and shall do to you all the harm and damage that we can."

By the time Spain outlawed most Native American slavery in 1542, the Arawaks of the West Indies had been destroyed. The Spanish had expropriated their lands for sugar plantations, replacing the Indians with enslaved Africans. On the mainland, the Spanish government established two forms of forced Indian labor. With the *encomienda* system, Indians living on specified lands had to pay tribute to individual colonists and sometimes provide labor for which they received minimal wages. At first, the system included no transfer of land to the colonists, but as the numbers of Native Americans declined and Spanish increased, the colonists took Indian property for farms and ranches. By the seventeenth century, grazing livestock replaced Indian farms on vast stretches of Spanish America.

In 1600, only about 1 million Indians survived in central Mexico, a dramatic decrease from their population of 2.6 million in 1550. Since the Spanish still depended on the natives for food and labor, the government devised the *repartimiento* system: Indians could now be forced to work in mines, agriculture, or public works for several weeks, months, or even a year. For example, natives labored for year-long stints at the Potosí silver mines in Bolivia. At

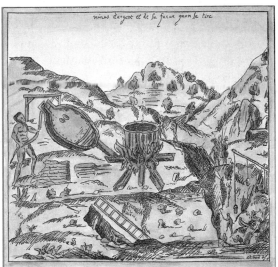

nines d'argent et de sa façon qu'on le tire

(The Granger Collection, New York)

Silver Mining, 1600. *Drawing of Indians working in a silver mine, from Samuel de Champlain's* Narrative of a Voyage to the West Indies and Mexico.

Potosí, workers assigned as carriers had to climb some six hundred feet through tunnels about as wide as a man's body with heavy loads of silver ore on their backs. Those who worked in refining were exposed to mercury poisoning when they walked with bare legs through a slurry of mercury, water, and ore. As the Indian population continued to decline, the Spanish attempted to increase the length and frequency of work periods. Indians resisted these changes, sometimes successfully.

As early as 1502 on West Indies plantations, the Spanish had looked to Africa to meet their insatiable labor demands. They had already purchased Africans from Portuguese traders to work in Spain and on the sugar plantations of the Canary Islands. The government set up a system of licenses for merchants to supply certain numbers of slaves. During the sixteenth century, ships transported approximately seventy-five thousand Africans to Spanish America, with perhaps an equal number dying en route, either in Africa or at sea. The Spanish imported Africans to work on sugar plantations in the West Indies and coastal areas of the mainland where most Native Americans had died. Severe work regimes and rampant disease also resulted in high death rates among imported blacks.

PROTESTANT NORTHERN EUROPEANS CHALLENGE CATHOLIC SPAIN

In the sixteenth century, French and English activity in America was tentative and sporadic. Although fishing expeditions regularly visited the North American coast and private groups initiated trade and settlement, the English and French governments did not support permanent colonies. But religious and political change in Northern Europe provided the impetus to test Spain's domination of the New World. In the age of Reformation and religious wars, America became both a refuge for religious dissidents and a battlefield on which European nations fought for wealth, glory, and power.

The Protestant Reformation, 1517–1598 When the German monk **Martin Luther** launched the **Protestant Reformation** in 1517, the Catholic church was the dominant faith in western and central Europe. Luther believed the church had become corrupt and saw the sale of indulgences, which were supposed to reduce the amount of time a deceased person spent in purgatory before moving to heaven, as an example of moral decline. Luther believed that Christians received salvation as a gift from God in return for faith ("justification by faith") rather than for good works: making pilgrimages, giving money to the church, or attending mass, for example. Luther also challenged the authority of priests, arguing for a "priesthood of all believers." Christians should seek the word of God in the Bible, which he translated into German to make it accessible to laypeople. Luther contended that the Bible recognized only two sacraments, baptism and communion, not the seven authorized by the Catholic church. He also opposed the requirement of celibacy for priests, and he married Katharina von Bora, a former nun.

Luther's teachings led to the division of Western Christianity, as common people and princes alike adopted his beliefs. In Germany, composed of many individual states, some princes accepted Lutheranism and others remained Catholic, requiring their subjects to follow their example. Lutheranism spread through northern Germany and into Scandinavia. Luther inspired other critics of Catholicism to offer variant Protestant doctrines, including the Mennonites, Hutterites, and Swiss Brethren, all called Anabaptists because they required adult baptism.

The most influential of the systems of belief that Lutheranism spawned was that of **John Calvin** (1509–1564), a native of France, who attempted to create a model society in Geneva, Switzerland. Followers of Calvin established churches in what became known as the Reformed tradition, including the French Huguenots, English Puritans, Scottish Presbyterians, and Dutch and German Reformed. Calvin went further than Luther in arguing that humans could do nothing to save themselves. According to his concept of **predestination**, God alone determined who would be saved (the "elect"). Through communion with God, the elect learned that they were saved; they strove to live blamelessly to reflect their status.

Calvin and his followers convinced the city council and churches of Geneva to adopt many Reformed doctrines, stripping the churches of decoration, images, and colorful rituals. The Bible, as interpreted by Calvin, became the basis for law. The civil government punished moral offenders and nonbelievers identified by the church elders. The Calvinists disciplined individuals for dancing, wearing fancy clothes, and insubordination. They forced one man to walk through the city wearing only a shirt because he criticized Calvin and burned another at the stake for heresy. Calvin came close to establishing a theocracy, in which the church fathers ruled in the name of God.

The Reformation in England, 1534–1588

In England, opposition to the Catholic church—its bishops, taxes, monasteries, and rituals—had surfaced years before Luther. Thus, Henry VIII found sympathy for his own break with Rome. Henry wanted to marry Anne Boleyn, whom he hoped would provide a male heir, but the pope refused to allow an annulment of his marriage to Catherine of Aragon. To solve the problem, Henry prevailed on the English Parliament to pass the Act of Supremacy (1534), mandating that the king be "taken, accepted, and reputed the only supreme head in earth of the Church of England." The Crown dissolved the monasteries and confiscated their property. Henry was no Lutheran, however, for the Six Articles (1539) that formed the theological basis of Anglicanism confirmed Catholic beliefs on priestly celibacy, the mass, confession, and sacraments. But because the Six Articles were ambiguous on many points, the Church of England from its inception allowed a fairly wide range of doctrine. In 1552, under Henry's son, Edward VI, the revised Anglican prayer book incorporated many Protestant beliefs. After Edward's death in 1553, however, Henry's daughter Mary I attempted to force England back to the Catholic church. Her persecution of Protestants earned her the name "Bloody Mary"; her marriage to the staunch Catholic Philip II of Spain inspired an English nationalism that fused loyalty to church and state. When Mary died in 1558, her half-sister, **Elizabeth I**, the daughter of Anne Boleyn, became queen, ending the immediate threat that England would return to Catholicism. The new English monarch and a large proportion of her subjects saw Spain as a threat to their national church, now Protestant, and their independence as a nation.

Under Elizabeth, the English confronted Spain on a number of fronts. England became a dominant Protestant power, supported the Dutch revolt against Philip II, and challenged Spain's claims to the New World. Although pragmatic and more interested in power than theology, Elizabeth confirmed England's break with the pope and approved earlier moderate Protestant reforms. The Act of Uniformity (1559) required adherence to the Anglican Book of Prayer. The queen suppressed resistance from both Calvinists, who wanted further reforms, and supporters of Rome. Some Catholics turned to Elizabeth's cousin, Mary, queen of Scots, a Roman Catholic and the heir to the English throne. In 1587, after several unsuccessful plots on Elizabeth's life, Mary was tried as a conspirator and beheaded.

One of the most fervent supporters of Mary, queen of Scots, was Philip II of Spain. Throughout Europe he strove to wipe out the Protestant heresy. When many of his Dutch subjects adopted Calvinism, Philip retaliated with his Inquisition, executing thousands. The Dutch rebelled. In 1581, the northern part of the Netherlands, composed of seven provinces, including Holland, declared its independence as the United Provinces. When Elizabeth sent aid to the United Provinces in 1585, she was in effect declaring war on Spain. In 1588, Philip sent his mighty armada of 130 ships and thirty thousand men to invade England. The English defeated the armada, preserving their national sovereignty and religion.

French Huguenots and English Sea Dogs

In France, persecution led some Protestant Huguenots to look to America as a refuge. In 1555, a group of wealthy Frenchmen sent Huguenot settlers to Brazil. When disputes occurred among the colonists, some returned to France; the Portuguese, who claimed Brazil, killed or enslaved the majority who remained. In 1562, Huguenots tried again, establishing Charlesfort on the South Carolina coast, in part to attack the Spanish silver fleet as it headed home. When the Spanish moved against the small French colony in 1564, they found it already abandoned. But the Huguenots attempted another settlement that year, this one at Fort Caroline on the St. Johns River in northern Florida. The Spanish quickly destroyed it, murdering most of the settlers.

The English "sea dogs"—privateers unofficially supported by the Crown—learned a great deal about the New World from the Huguenots. With Elizabeth I's ascension to the throne in 1558, seafarers and colonizers like John Hawkins, **Francis Drake**, Humphrey Gilbert, and Walter Raleigh gained favor and support. Hawkins visited Fort Caroline in 1565; other Englishmen gained knowledge of the North American coast from the French.

The English took their time before attempting an American colony. The Spanish remained a serious threat. Thus, for two decades, until the 1580s, English adventurers sought wealth by sea. In 1562, John Hawkins took three hundred Africans to Hispaniola without a license. The local Spanish officials allowed him to exchange the slaves for sugar and hides because the colony needed labor. Hawkins made a second voyage, earning another handsome profit, this time mostly in silver. When the Spanish authorities protested, Elizabeth forbade further expeditions, but in 1567, she reversed her decision. On his third voyage, Hawkins was conducting business in the harbor of San Juan de Ulúa, Mexico, when the annual fleet arrived from Spain several weeks early and destroyed three of his ships. Hawkins and his cousin Francis Drake escaped with two badly damaged vessels. Their crews nearly starved on the return to England.

Hawkins stopped interloping in Spanish trade, but other English privateers followed. The most famous was Francis Drake, who in 1572, with the help of Native Americans and runaway African slaves, intercepted the mule train carrying Potosí silver across Panama. Five years later, he set out to circumnavigate the globe. Following Magellan's route through the straits, he attacked Spanish towns along the Pacific coast, explored the North American coast for evidence of a northwest passage, and returned to England in 1580 by way of Asia and the Cape of Good Hope. Six years later, when England and Spain were formally at war, Drake attacked Spanish ports in America, including St. Augustine in Florida, which he looted and burned.

While Drake was making his fortune through piracy, other sea dogs hoped to make their mark by starting colonies. They decided to ignore Spain's claim to North America. On the basis of Cabot's voyage of 1497, Elizabeth granted a charter to Humphrey Gilbert, who sailed to Newfoundland in 1583. He assumed ownership for the English Crown. Nothing came of Gilbert's colony, however, as he was lost at sea on his return to England.

Walter Raleigh then attempted a settlement farther south, in the land named for the "virgin" queen, Elizabeth I. In 1585, the first group of settlers arrived at **Roanoke Island**, in what is now North Carolina. After their ships returned home leaving them with short supplies, the colonists tried to force neighboring Indians to provide food. Quickly a pattern of hostility emerged between the English and

Native Americans. Francis Drake saved the Roanoke colonists from starvation, carrying them home in 1586. A year later, Raleigh sent out another expedition. This time the war with Spain prevented ships from returning to Roanoke until 1590, when all that was left of the colony was the word "Croatoan" carved on a tree. The colonists may have moved to nearby Croatoan Island or farther inland to live with Native Americans, but the fate of this "Lost Colony" has never been determined. The English did not colonize successfully in North America until the founding of Jamestown in 1607.

CONCLUSION

By 1590, the Spanish had created an empire that extended from South America through the West Indies and Mexico. They funded their European wars to extinguish Protestantism with American silver and gold. The Portuguese, united under the Spanish Crown in 1580, had developed the Atlantic slave trading system that sent enslaved Africans to Brazil and New Spain.

The irony of colonization in America was that European nations at war in the Old World emulated one another in the New World. The Spanish and Portuguese provided the model for later colonizers in expropriating land and labor from Indians and Africans. Europeans justified their behavior toward the people of America and Africa by emphasizing religious and cultural differences, ignoring much that they had in common. Although European nations organized colonization in various ways, all sought mercantilistic ends.

In the early seventeenth century, when the English, French, and Dutch settled in North America, their goals were very similar to those of Spain. They hoped to locate precious metals, find the elusive northwest passage, exploit Indian labor, extend Christianity to America, and expand the power of the state.

CHAPTER REVIEW, PREHISTORY TO 1590

- When Europeans made contact with Native American and West African cultures in the fifteenth century, they found many diverse, complex societies with sophisticated political and social systems and extensive trade networks.
- Portuguese traders' arrival in West Africa triggered the development of the Atlantic slave trade, to which Africa would lose more than 10 million people over the course of four centuries.
- Seeking a trade route to Asia, Christopher Columbus landed in the Americas in 1492, opening the New World to European conquest and settlement.
- In the wake of the Spanish conquest of America, approximately 90 percent of the Native American population died as a result of disease, war, and exploitative working conditions.
- In the mid-sixteenth century, Britain, France, and Holland began to challenge Spanish dominance in America. Like Spain, these nations sought to expand their national power, exploit native labor, establish new trade routes, and spread Christianity.

◀️▌▌▌ *Looking Back*

Chapter 1 examines the cultures of the people of North and South America, Africa, and Europe at the time Europeans began exploring and colonizing other parts of the world. The chapter considers the impetus for exploration and its initial consequences.

1. In what ways were the cultures of Native Americans, Africans, and Europeans similar?
2. In what ways were their cultures different?
3. What were the positive and negative results of interactions among these three groups?
4. Why did the Portuguese and Spanish explore the globe? How did their goals change over time?
5. What was the process by which the Spanish took control of Mexico and other parts of Central and South America?

Looking Ahead ▌▌▌▶️

Spain's empire in America and Portugal's Atlantic slave trade established models of exploitation for other European nations. In Chapter 2, we examine how England, France, and the United Provinces (Netherlands) joined the contest for American colonies.

1. What impelled the English, French, and Dutch to become colonizers?
2. What was the significance of England's defeat of the Spanish Armada in 1588?
3. Why do you think the English emulated so much of the Spanish pattern of colonization despite their religious animosity and war?

Go to the American Passages website at www.cengage.com/history/ayers/ampassages4e for additional review materials.

Colonization of
North America,
1590–1675

In 1590, the only permanent European settlement in what is now the United States was St. Augustine, the struggling Spanish town in Florida that the English privateer Francis Drake had burned four years earlier. Spain was much more concerned with its silver mines and West Indies plantations than in colonizing along the Atlantic coast, yet it wanted to prevent intrusion by other nations, for good reason. In the late sixteenth century, buccaneers from France and England thought the best way to get rich was by looting the Spanish silver fleet and ports.

Although Spain expanded in Florida and New Mexico in the 1600s, the English defeat of the Spanish Armada and the Dutch surge in overseas trade eroded Spanish control of the New World. France, England, the Netherlands, and Sweden all established colonies in North America by 1638, hoping to duplicate Spain's success. While none found gold or an easy route to Asia—and the Swedes and Dutch soon lost their toeholds in the Delaware and Hudson valleys altogether—Europeans prospered from the West Indies sugar boom, Canadian fur trade, and Chesapeake tobacco. In addition, New England offered a haven for Puritan dissenters.

By 1675, the English held a string of settlements along the Atlantic coast. Unlike the Spanish, England's colonization proceeded with little regulation from the Crown, resulting in a variety of social, economic, and political structures. The English government helped to create the diversity by granting different kinds of charters to individuals and groups.

The expansion of European settlement in North America changed the countryside forever. Cheap, even free, land and developing commerce offered opportunity to men and women of all economic classes who were willing to risk their lives by crossing the Atlantic. Their farms destroyed Indian hunting lands, altering the ecological balance of plants and animals. Although many Native Americans resisted the European invasions, disease seriously undermined their power. The fur trade also changed the cultural values of many Indians, drawing them into Atlantic commerce and tempting them to overhunt. For Native Americans from New Mexico to Canada, European colonization was a disaster.

THE SPANISH IN NORTH AMERICA

After Francisco Vásquez de Coronado and Hernando de Soto failed to locate cities of gold, Spain abandoned further exploration in North America. Then Francis Drake's voyage along the Pacific coast raised alarms of foreign interest in the region north of Mexico. To strengthen Spain's hold on the area, in 1581, the viceroy of New Spain gave **Franciscan priests** permission to establish missions among the Pueblo Indians of the Rio Grande Valley. The friars named the area San Felipe del Nuevo México. The missionaries described the Pueblos as friendly and numerous: thousands could be converted to Christianity and forced to labor for Hispanic colonists. But by the time a party arrived in 1582 to escort the Franciscans back to Mexico, the missionaries had been killed by the Native Americans.

Settlement of New Mexico   Despite this setback, the Spanish remained interested in the region. Conquistadores needed permission from the Crown to invade new lands, however, for the king had issued Orders for New Discoveries (1573), which more strictly regulated colonization, in part to protect Native Americans from the atrocities Bartolomé de las Casas had described decades before. When one would-be conqueror led an illegal expedition into New Mexico in 1590, he was arrested and returned to Mexico City in chains.

The Spanish government delayed appointing a governor of New Mexico until 1595, when the viceroy authorized **Juan de Oñate** to undertake settlement with his own funds. Oñate, a native of Mexico, inherited great wealth and obtained even more by marrying Isabel Tolosa Cortés Moctezuma, a descendant of both Cortés and the Aztec emperor. The expedition proved expensive as delays increased costs. Finally, in 1598, 129 soldiers, their families, servants, and slaves, and seven thousand livestock headed north. Ten Franciscan missionaries accompanied the colonists. Oñate expected his investment to yield an empire. As he wrote to King Philip II, "I shall give your majesty a new world, greater than New Spain." The governor envisioned mines of silver and gold and a water passage through the continent. He believed his province would extend from the Atlantic to the Pacific.

Upon arrival in New Mexico, Oñate declared Spanish sovereignty over Pueblo lands. In a ritual complete with trumpets and high mass, he promised peace and prosperity to those who cooperated. The Spanish asserted that the Pueblos acquiesced "of their own accord." The Franciscans founded missions in the largest pueblos and supervised construction of a church in the Tewa pueblo, Yungé, which the Spanish designated as their capital, San Gabriel.

For some months, the Spanish and the Indians coexisted without serious incident. The colonists moved into the Pueblos' apartments in San Gabriel, forcing the inhabitants to depart. Soon the Indians tired of providing food, which they had intended as

This icon will direct you to interactive activities and study materials on the American Passages website: www.cengage.com/history/ayers/ampassages4e

CHAPTER TIMELINE

1598	Spanish expedition into New Mexico
1599	Destruction of Ácoma by the Spanish
1603	James I takes the English throne
1605	French establish Port Royal
1607	English found colony at Jamestown
1608	French establish Quebec
1609	Henry Hudson explores for the Dutch East India Company
1609–1614	Anglo-Powhatan War in Virginia
1616–1618	Plague epidemic decimates eastern New England natives
1619	Africans arrive in Virginia • Virginia Company establishes a representative assembly
1620	Separatists found the Plymouth colony
1622	Native Americans attack the Virginia colony
1624	Virginia Company loses charter • Virginia becomes a royal colony • Dutch West India Company establishes New Netherland
1625	Charles I becomes king of England
1630	Massachusetts Bay colony founded by Puritans
1634	The Ark and the Dove arrive in Maryland
1636	Founding of Connecticut and Rhode Island
1637	Massachusetts and Connecticut troops destroy the Pequots • Anne Hutchinson is tried for heresy
1642–1648	English Civil War
1649	Charles I of England is beheaded
1651	English Parliament passes first Navigation Act
1660	Charles II of England becomes king
1663	Carolina proprietors receive charter
1664	English forces conquer New Netherland • New York and New Jersey are founded
1673	Dutch recapture New York, then return the colony to England with the Treaty of Westminster (1674)

gifts but the Spanish considered tribute. The soldiers resorted to murder and rape to obtain supplies. The crisis came in December 1598 when a Spanish troop demanded provisions from the people of **Ácoma,** a pueblo high atop a mesa west of the Rio Grande. One of Coronado's party had described Ácoma as "the greatest stronghold ever seen in the world." The Pueblos refused to give flour to the soldiers and killed eleven men when they attempted to take the food by force. Oñate moved swiftly, his small army laying siege to Ácoma with several cannons, as native men and women defended the town with arrows and stones. The Spanish killed approximately five hundred men and three hundred women and children and took the survivors prisoner. They leveled the town. Everyone was sentenced to servitude, and each man over age twenty-five had one foot cut off. The Ácomas would not rebuild their town until the late 1640s.

With this harsh action, Oñate only temporarily prevented further opposition among the Pueblos, for another town resisted the following year. The colonists also complained of food shortages and the governor's mismanagement; many returned to Mexico. The Franciscans charged that Oñate's cruelty to the Indians made conversion difficult. Oñate was removed as governor, tried, and found guilty of mistreating the Native Americans and some of his settlers. He was banished from New Mexico but sailed to Spain, where he received a knighthood and position as the Crown's chief inspector of mines.

After Oñate's departure, New Mexico became a royal province. Pedro de Peralta, the next governor, established a new capital at Santa Fe in 1610. As late as 1670, only twenty-eight hundred Spanish colonists inhabited the Rio Grande Valley. They lived on farms and ranches along the river, exploiting the Pueblos' labor through the encomienda system to produce hides, blankets, sheep, wool, and pine nuts for sale in Mexico.

Spanish Missions in New Mexico and Florida　The Franciscan missionaries, who assumed a major role in colonizing the Spanish borderlands, were members of the Catholic religious order that Francis Bernardone of Assisi had founded in Italy in 1209. The friars vowed not to engage in sexual relations or acquire property, and they lived on the gifts of others. Unlike other religious brotherhoods, which remained in seclusion, the Franciscans operated in the world among ordinary Christians. The Orders for New Discoveries of 1573 gave primary responsibility to the friars for "pacifying" the Indians of New Mexico and Florida.

During the first part of the seventeenth century, many Pueblos seemed to accept the Franciscans' message. The friars initially offered gifts of food, metal tools, beads, and clothing. Placing some confidence in the priests, the natives agreed to build convents and churches. Women built the walls, while men did carpentry. The priests decorated the sanctuaries with paintings, statues, and silver chalices. They created missions by imposing their influence over existing Indian towns, backed by threat of military force. In New Mexico, the Spanish started more than fifty churches by 1629; in Florida, missions extended west from St. Augustine to the Gulf Coast and north into Georgia (or Guale, as the region was called).

The Native Americans who came under Spanish control in theory could choose whether to accept Christian baptism, but they recognized that soldiers supported the priests. The Franciscans expected the natives to learn the catechism and enough of the Castilian (Spanish) language to communicate and to adopt European dress, food, and farming methods. Many Indians embraced Catholicism, but in doing so, they modified the religion. Even in the twentieth century, the Pueblos preserved both native and Catholic religious practices. Christian Indians in Florida continued to play a ball game during the 1600s until the missionaries realized it had religious significance and abolished the game, calling the pole used as a target the "ballpost of the devil."

In merging Indian gods with the Christian Trinity and adding Catholic holidays to native celebrations, Native Americans altered Spanish Catholicism. With the "Lady in Blue," they created a religious tradition that both the Indians and Spanish accepted. In the 1620s, Plains Indians reported that a nun appeared to them, telling them in their language to become Christians. Although the woman remained invisible to the missionaries, they believed the stories. On a trip to Spain, one priest discovered that a Franciscan nun, María de Jesús de Agreda, claimed to have made flights to America with the help of angels. Her claims and the Indians' visions together created the resilient legend of the Lady in Blue.

THE ENGLISH INVADE VIRGINIA

New Mexico and Florida remained marginal outposts in the Spanish empire. Spain's control was tenuous because its military forces were small and its cultural influence was weak. After the defeat of the Spanish Armada, Philip II's government could not keep other European nations out of North America. During the first decade of the seventeenth century, the English, French, and Dutch sent expeditions to fish, search for a northern passage to the East, trade for furs, and establish colonies.

English Context of Colonization Seventeenth-century England was an intensely hierarchical society in which the king claimed divine right, or God-given authority, and the nobility and gentry dominated Parliament. But it was a society undergoing turmoil and change. Elizabeth I's successor was her cousin, James I, who governed from 1603 until 1625, when he died and his son, Charles I, took the throne. Both James and Charles had strife-torn reigns marked by power struggles with Parliament, culminating in Charles's loss of the English Civil War and his beheading in 1649.

Parliament was composed of two houses: the House of Lords, made up of nobles and high church officials, and the House of Commons, whose representatives from the counties and boroughs were elected by male landowners, an estimated 15 to 30 percent of all Englishmen. The members of Parliament in the Commons were country gentry, government officials, and lawyers. By imposing levies without Parliament's consent, James I and Charles I challenged Parliament's prerogative to approve or reject new taxes. For their part, the legislators tried to whittle away at royal powers. The fundamental issue concerning the balance of power between the king and property holders, as represented in Parliament, remained unsettled until the Glorious Revolution of 1688.

Economic developments loosened English society, giving individuals greater opportunity to change from one social class or occupation to another. Many found it necessary to move geographically as the woolen industry expanded, causing landowners to raise more sheep. In what has been called the **enclosure movement,** landlords ended leases for tenant farmers living on their lands, confiscating common fields that peasant communities had shared for grazing their livestock and raising crops. The landowners enclosed the commons with fences and hedges. In 1500, peasants had farmed 70 percent of arable land in England; by 1650, they farmed only 50 percent. Thus, many tenants were forced from the land. Some went to London, where the population expanded from 55,000 in 1520 to 475,000 in 1670. Others signed up as colonists for America.

A developing economy meant dislocation for poor tenants. For merchants, however, it spelled opportunity. They found it first in the woolen trade with Antwerp, in what is now Belgium. When this trade declined after 1550, they looked for alternative investments, which they found as war with Spain increased the demand for coal, lead, glass, ships, salt, iron, and steel. Investors formed **joint stock companies** to explore trade routes and establish new markets. The companies obtained capital by selling stocks. These investments were risky, for shareholders were liable for all company debts. The stocks could also be immensely profitable, as in the case of Francis Drake's circumnavigation of the globe, which brought a 4,600 percent profit from silver and gold captured from Spanish ships.

Joint-stock companies provided capital for the first permanent English colonies in America. Unlike the Spanish monarchy, the English Crown had little role in funding, or even governing, its first New World settlements. In 1606, James I granted a charter to the **Virginia Company** with rights to settle colonies in North America. The Virginia Company had two groups: one in London and the other in Plymouth, in the west of England. The groups received overlapping claims, with the Plymouth group obtaining lands from what is now Maine to Virginia and the London group receiving Connecticut to the Carolinas. Either could settle in the overlapping area, but initial colonies had to be at least a hundred miles apart.

Jamestown   In 1607, the Virginia Company of London funded the first permanent English colony at **Jamestown.** The initial 104 settlers arrived in May 1607 after an exhausting winter crossing. The native inhabitants watched them select a site on the James River, chosen for safety from Spanish attack, but next to malarial swamps. The Native Americans called their territory Tsenacommacah, or "densely inhabited land." They were Algonquian-speaking Indians; most belonged to a confederacy that **Powhatan,** head sachem of the Pamunkey tribe, had forged in eastern Virginia. Before the arrival of the English, the chief unifying force among the bands of the Powhatan confederacy was the threat from powerful enemies, the Manahoacs and the Monacans, who controlled lands to the west. The leaders of tribes subject to Powhatan were supposed to pay tribute and provide military assistance, but they sometimes refused.

One of Powhatan's brothers was **Opechancanough,** described as having "large Stature, noble Presence, and extraordinary Parts" and being "perfectly skill'd in the Art of Governing." Historical evidence suggests that he was born around 1544, and at about age sixteen, he was taken by a Spanish ship to Spain, where he received instruction in the Castilian language and took the name Don Luis de Velasco, after the viceroy of New Spain. The new Don Luis stayed with the Spanish until 1570, when he accompanied several missionaries to his homeland on Chesapeake Bay. He broke with the priests when they criticized him for taking several wives and murdered the priests the next year. If Opechancanough and Don Luis were the same man, as seems likely, he was well prepared with knowledge of Europeans when the Jamestown settlers arrived.

The English colony's first decade was a struggle. The company ran Virginia as a business enterprise, keeping control of government, land, and trade. Settlers were company employees, not landholders. To satisfy investors, the company instructed the colonists to search for gold and silver mines, find a passage to Asia, and establish industries and trade that would offer handsome returns. The company had chosen individuals for these purposes, not people who were willing to grow crops. Among the first Jamestown settlers were many gentlemen, who by definition avoided manual labor. They were adventurers who expected to strike it rich and return to England. The others, nearly all men, included the gentlemen's personal servants, a jeweler, a goldsmith, a perfumer, carpenters, blacksmiths, and some laborers. Not one of them described himself as a farmer.

When the colonists failed to locate mines or a passage to the East, their lives became aimless. Rather than plant crops or even hunt and fish, they expected the company and neighboring Indians to provide food. When sufficient provisions failed to arrive, the settlers starved. One of the leaders, a young officer named **John Smith,** took control in 1608, stabilizing the colony briefly by making everyone work. When criticism of his strict discipline reached company officials the next year, they removed him from command. During the particularly bitter winter of 1609–1610, one man killed his pregnant wife and chopped her up, planning to eat her body. Some of the colonists dug up graves to eat the corpses. By spring 1610, only sixty colonists remained of at least six hundred who had come to Jamestown in three years. Although some had returned to England or escaped to live with the Indians, the majority died of starvation and disease.

In 1609, the Virginia Company hoped to salvage its investment by exploiting the land. To recruit farmers, the company offered each emigrant one share of stock and a parcel of land after seven years of service. The settlers remained employees of the company in the meantime, with assigned tasks and the obligation to buy all supplies and ship all products through the company store.

Still, the Jamestown settlers refused to work. When Sir Thomas Dale arrived as governor in May 1611, he found nothing but a few gardens planted and the inhabitants at "their daily and usual work, bowling in the streets." He established his Laws Divine, Morall and Martiall, which were mostly martial. The men received military ranks, were divided into work gangs, and proceeded from home to work—and to church twice daily—at the beat of a drum. Laws prescribed death for a variety of crimes, including rape, adultery, theft, lying, slander against the company, blasphemy, and stealing an ear of corn. For taking two or three pints of oatmeal, one man had a large needle thrust through his tongue, then was chained to a tree until he starved. For the first offense of failing to work regular hours, an idler was tied neck to heels all night. The punishment for a second offense was whipping and for a third offense, death. Although the required hours of work were reasonable—five to eight hours per day in the summer and three to six in the winter—the punishments specified in **Dale's Laws** became a scandal in England, discouraging prospective emigrants. In the words of John Smith, "No man will go from [England] to have less liberty there."

The Struggle for Virginia   The Jamestown adventurers had expected to put the Indians to work in silver mines and fields, as in New Spain, but the inhabitants proved both too few in number for an adequate work force yet too powerful for the wretched gang of settlers to conquer. During the early years at Jamestown, the English seemed irrational in their dealings with the Native Americans. To many colonists, the natives were barbarians. Some settlers did attempt to trade for food, but others burned Indian villages and crops.

In 1608–1609, Captain John Smith tried to force the sachems to provide food. The Indians had spared his life several times; nevertheless, he kidnapped two men, obligating Opechancanough to beg for their release. Next, he entered the Pamunkey village with soldiers demanding food, which the Indians refused to give, and again he humiliated the tall sachem: in Smith's words, he did "take this murdering Opechancanough. . . . by the long lock of his head; and with my pistol at his breast, I led him [out of his house] amongst his greatest forces, and before we parted made him [agree to] fill our bark with twenty tuns of corn." Otherwise, Smith warned, he would load the ship with their "dead carkases." Opechancanough probably never forgot this scene. Between 1609 and 1614, full-scale war existed between the Virginia colonists and the Powhatan confederacy. Eventually the English, with reinforcements from the Virginia Company, defeated Powhatan, taking control of the James River.

John Smith Threatening Opechancanough.
John Smith threatening Opechancanough in 1608, with images in the background of skirmishes between colonists and Indians that took place at other times, not on this occasion. From Smith's Generall Historie of Virginia.

C. Smith taketh the King of Pamavnkee prisoner. -1608.

(North Wind Picture Archives)

In contrast to Spain, the English Crown failed to take responsibility for protecting any rights of Native Americans. When colonists had sufficient power, they enslaved Indians, sending them away from their homelands to prevent escape. The English justified expropriation of native lands with the belief that the king of England, as the Christian monarch, received sovereignty over North America from God. Thus, the Virginia Company obtained rights to land from the Crown, not the Indians. Another basis for taking native territory was the legal concept of *vacuum domicilium*, which meant that lands not occupied could be taken. To the English, "occupation" meant improving the land with buildings, fences, and crops; they did not recognize Indian sovereignty over the vast stretches of hunting lands that extended beyond small villages and fields. Even when the English purchased land from the Indians, their contrasting concepts of ownership caused grave misunderstanding. Whereas the colonists believed in private property, the natives thought they were selling the rights to use lands for hunting, fishing, and communal farming. They expected to continue using the territory they had "sold" for these purposes. Conflicts resulted when, for example, a settler's cattle trampled Indian crops or when a native killed a colonist's cow, mistaking it for a deer.

Tobacco Boom   Demand for land became paramount in Virginia after 1617, when the colonists discovered tobacco as a staple crop. Though James I called smoking "a custom loathsome to the eye, hateful to the nose, harmful to the brain, dangerous to the lungs, and in the black stinking fumes thereof, nearest resembling the horrible stygian smoke of the pit that is bottomless," the habit soon consumed England. The mercantilist advantages were clear. With production in Virginia, the English could acquire tobacco from its own colony rather than pay premium prices to foreign countries, and they could generate an industry to process the leaves. For Virginians, the tobacco trade meant capital to purchase clothing and other supplies from home. Tobacco became the first staple crop in England's colonial mercantilist system, followed by sugar, after 1640, in the West Indies.

In 1619, the Virginia Company updated the land policy, granting "headrights" of 100 acres of land to those who came before 1616 and 50 acres to those who came after. Settlers who paid their own way received land immediately; those who immigrated at the company's expense received land after seven years of service. Virginia settlers thus fell into two categories: freeholders who paid for their own transportation, and servants whose way the Virginia Company or someone else financed. Recipients of headrights did not pay for the land, but owed quitrents, annual payments to the company, of 1 shilling per year for each 50 acres. Also in 1619, the Virginia Company relaxed its hold on the government of Virginia by establishing an assembly of elected delegates. The governor, who was appointed by the company, retained the right to veto all laws; the company's General Court in London could also disallow any decision. The Virginia Company also adopted English common law to replace the martial law under which the colony had operated.

Although the revised land policy and the assembly gave settlers a greater stake in society, the cultivation of tobacco ensured Virginia's ultimate success. During the 1620s, tobacco drew high prices—as much as three shillings per pound. Virginia became the first North American boom town, as settlers threw all of their energies into growing tobacco. Between 1617 and 1623, approximately 5,000 new immigrants arrived. Because the amount of the crop a planter could grow depended largely on the number of workers, those with capital eagerly paid to transport servants. The Virginia Company imported servants too, but it still failed to show a profit, partly because company officials diverted many to their own plantations.

Africans in Early Virginia   English servants provided most of the labor in the colony until late in the seventeenth century. But Virginia planters needed as much labor as they could afford to strike it rich from tobacco, so they also purchased Africans, probably even before 1619 when a Dutch ship brought about twenty blacks. Though some Africans became servants with terms shorter than lifetime bondage, others probably were slaves. Little is known of their status during the early decades. In 1625, Africans numbered twenty-three of 1,200 Virginia colonists. Fifteen were the property of two men: Abraham Peirsey, the wealthiest man in the colony, and George Yeardley, who had served as governor. In 1660, about nine hundred blacks and twenty-four thousand Europeans lived in the Chesapeake Bay area.

In contrast, by 1660, Africans outnumbered whites in Barbados, the richest of the English West Indies. Founded in 1627, Barbados quickly turned to sugar production, importing Africans to raise and process the crop. The white islanders created a harsh slave regime to prevent organized rebellion and force the rapidly growing black population to perform hard, repetitive labor.

Until the 1660s, conditions for Africans remained less rigid in Virginia than in the West Indies. Some Virginia blacks achieved freedom and married, and a few acquired land. For example, by the 1650s, free blacks Anthony and Mary Johnson owned a 250-acre plantation on Virginia's eastern shore and, like neighboring whites, protected their property by going to court. Even so, most Africans remained in bondage, as Virginians adopted the practice from the Portuguese, Spanish, and Dutch. In purchasing people from slave traders, the white colonists bought into the Atlantic slave system.

Early Virginia documents distinguished consistently between white servants and blacks, always with the suggestion that Africans were subordinate. In a 1627 will, Governor Yeardley bequeathed his "goode debts, chattels, servants, negars, cattle or any other thing" to his heirs. Censuses of the 1620s also point to the lower regard for Africans: English settlers were listed with full names, while most Africans were enumerated simply with a first name or designated as "negar" or "Negro." For example, Anthony and Mary Johnson were called "Antonio a Negro" and "Mary a Negro Woman" in early records. The Virginia tax law of 1643 further demonstrated that the colonists viewed Africans as different from themselves. Everyone who worked in the field was to be taxed—all men and black women. White women apparently were not expected to tend tobacco. Virginia also excepted blacks, but not white servants, from the obligation to bear arms.

DOING HISTORY ONLINE

Life in Virginia

Examine documents 2, 3, and 4. How do these items relate to one another? What do they reveal about life in Virginia during the first years of English settlement?

 www.cengage.com/history/ayers/ampassages4e

The Colony Expands

The colonists had found the way to economic success by growing tobacco, but Virginia faced difficulty for many years. Because mortality remained high and settlers had few children, the population grew slowly despite immigration that averaged about a thousand people per year. From 1619 to 1640, the population rose from seven hundred to about eight thousand, though approximately twenty thousand English immigrants had arrived during that time. Young men and women who left England to become servants in Virginia gambled with their lives to obtain land that they could not gain at home. Dysentery, typhoid fever, and malaria took their toll on new settlers who suffered a period of "seasoning" after their arrival in Virginia. Men were much more likely to migrate to the colonies than women. A 1625 census indicated that more than three-quarters of the Virginia colonists were male, and less than one-fifth were children. Many people came as servants, which meant that they could not legally marry and have children until their terms expired years later. The census also provided ample evidence of high rates of mortality and family disruption, as many of the married couples were childless, in part because of high infant and childhood mortality. And with short life expectancy for adults, more than half of the colony's children had lost one parent, and one-fifth apparently had no relatives in Virginia at all.

By 1621, Opechancanough and a prophet named Nemattanew, whom the colonists called "Jack of the Feathers" because he wore clothes covered with plumes, recognized the threat of increased immigration. Now that the English had tobacco, they were not going to leave. Nemattanew inspired a nativist religious revival among the Powhatans, rejecting Christianity and European customs. Opechancanough organized a military offensive to push the English back into the sea. At the same time, he used diplomacy to convince the settlers to lower their guard. When several whites killed Nemattanew in 1622, Opechancanough rallied his troops, slaying one-fourth of the settlers before the colony could react. A ten-year war followed in which each side tried to annihilate the other but failed, and in 1632 both sides agreed to peace.

Although the bankrupt Virginia Company lost its charter in 1624, immigration to the colony continued. Its economic promise helped convince the English Crown to claim it as a royal colony. Desire for new tobacco lands placed constant pressure on the Powhatans, so in 1644, Opechancanough launched another attack. After two years of war, the Powhatans submitted, and Opechancanough was captured and murdered by a guard. The 1646 treaty required the Native Americans to live on lands north of the York River and, to symbolize their subordination, pay an annual tribute of twenty beaver skins. Colonists expanded rapidly north and south of the James River and to the eastern shore.

FISHING, FURS, AND SETTLEMENTS IN THE NORTH

While settlers and Native Americans struggled for Virginia, European adventurers explored and colonized the region to the north. By 1600, groups of fishermen monopolized specific waters, such as the French who caught walrus in the Gulf of St. Lawrence. The beaver furs that Europeans obtained in petty trade with Native Americans became popular in Europe for making felt hats, exciting merchants in France, the Netherlands, and England to seek more permanent arrangements. All three nations claimed the northern territories as their own, ignoring the Indians' prior ownership.

Indians of New France, 1701.
A pen-and-ink drawing, c. 1701, attributed to Charles Becard de Granville.

(The Granger Collection, New York)

New France In North America, French traders focused on furs. When a French ship sent to North America in 1582 returned with a cargo of furs earning a 1,500 percent profit, merchants enthusiastically organized more voyages. In 1605, **Samuel de Champlain** planted a temporary base at Port Royal on the Bay of Fundy in Canada. He sailed south to Cape Cod looking for a permanent site, but decided in 1608 to retain Port Royal and establish a main settlement on the St. Lawrence River. The French chose

Quebec, which means "the place where the river narrows" in Algonquian, an ideal location for controlling the Canadian interior.

For two decades, Port Royal and Quebec remained little more than trading posts. The French had already traded with the Micmacs of the coastal region and Algonquins of the St. Lawrence Valley. Champlain strengthened these ties and made new alliances with several groups: the Montagnais, who lived in the region north of the St. Lawrence River and like the Algonquins and Micmacs were Algonquian; and the Hurons, who were Iroquoian and lived north of Lake Ontario. Their location enabled the Hurons to link French outposts with the interior, the source of the most valuable furs. In 1609, to demonstrate allegiance to his allies, Champlain helped them fight a group of Iroquois from what is now New York, thus making the Five Nations enemies of New France. He also explored the watershed of the St. Lawrence River and lands as far west as Lake Huron.

In 1627, Quebec was still essentially a trading post with about a hundred French inhabitants, including a few women. Cardinal Richelieu, who for all practical purposes ruled France, organized the Company of One Hundred Associates to spur colonization. The company received a charter for territory from the Arctic Circle to Florida and from the Atlantic to the Pacific, with a monopoly on the fur trade. The company also pledged to send missionaries to the Indians and grant them the status of "natural French" when they were baptized. The priests established missions in Indian villages and learned their languages, looking for similarities between the two cultures in an effort to make the Indians part of French society (see Picturing the Past: Canadian Women at Work).

Because the company focused on the fur trade and considered transporting settlers too expensive, by 1663 just three thousand French settlers lived in the colony. The Crown revoked the company's charter, making New France a royal province. Nevertheless, population growth remained slow. From the beginning, the government refused to allow Protestants, the most likely immigrants, to settle there; it wanted to maintain control of the society through the Catholic church. Further, New France developed under feudal land tenure, in which wealthy lords received large manors, or seigniories, along the St. Lawrence River. Ordinary settlers

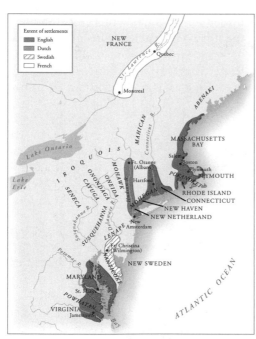

MAP 2.1 Eastern North America, 1650.

By the mid-seventeenth century, northern European nations established colonies along the Atlantic coast from French Quebec and Montreal in the St. Lawrence Valley to the English settlements on Chesapeake Bay. Although at this date all of the colonies were relatively small, New England and the Chesapeake were expanding agricultural societies, while the French, Dutch, and Swedes concentrated on trade.

on these manors became tenants rather than independent farmers. Lacking the opportunity to improve their status in the New World, French peasants were reluctant to make the dangerous transatlantic voyage.

The fur trade and small population made French relations with the Native Americans different from those of New Spain and Virginia, where labor demands and white expansion put greater pressure on the Indians. The most efficient way to obtain furs was to offer desirable products from Europe, including textiles, guns, metal tools, pots, and alcohol, not to drive trading partners from the land or exploit their labor. One French priest reported that, at least for a while, the Montagnais thought they were getting the better deal: "I heard my [Indian] host say one day, jokingly, Missi picoutau amiscou, 'The Beaver does everything perfectly well, it makes kettles, hatchets, swords, knives, bread; and in short, it makes everything.' He was making sport of us Europeans . . .[and said], showing me a beautiful knife, 'The English have no sense; they give us twenty knives like this for one Beaver skin.'"

Nevertheless, the French arrival had tragic effects on the Indians of Canada, who succumbed to disease in large numbers. The demand for furs altered cultural attitudes and intensified hostility among Indian nations. In keeping with their religion, Indians had taken only what they needed from nature and little more; they generally used entire animals, the meat as well as the skins. With the fur trade, natives killed animals just for their furs and in numbers far greater than before. As a result, the balance of nature that the Native Americans had maintained was broken. They had to reach farther and farther back into the continent as they exterminated the deer, beaver, and other fur-bearing animals.

New Netherland In the first decade of the seventeenth century, the Dutch too challenged the dominance of Spain in the New World. The seven northern United Provinces had declared independence from Spain in 1581 and remained at war until 1609, when they signed a twelve-year truce. With its expiration, the war resumed and continued as part of the Thirty Years' War, which ended in 1648 with the Treaty of Münster, recognizing Dutch independence.

Despite this ongoing struggle, Dutch commerce flourished. Because land was scarce and high-priced in the Netherlands and agriculture insufficient, affluent individuals put their capital into trade. In 1602, merchants formed the United East India Company, which six years later had 160 ships around the globe. In 1609, the company sent out Henry Hudson, an Englishman, to search for the long-sought northwest passage through North America. He sailed up the river that later bore his name, in what is now New York State, trading for furs with the Native Americans. The pelts brought a good return in Holland, so the company dispatched traders, who set up a post near the present site of Albany and explored Long Island Sound and the Connecticut River. In 1621, the Dutch government chartered another group, the **Dutch West India Company,** to establish commerce and colonies in America. Like the East India Company, it received broad powers, including the rights to make war and sign treaties. During the seventeenth century, the Dutch muscled their way to control a large part of international commerce, including the Atlantic slave trade and routes to Asia.

In 1624, working for the Dutch West India Company, Cornelius Jacobsen May founded New Netherland to provide a base for trade in the Hudson River region. The first colonists were mostly Protestant refugees from the Spanish Netherlands.

Canadian Women at Work

This drawing of two Indian women grinding corn with an infant on a cradleboard appeared in Father François Du Creux's *Historiæ Canadensis, sev Novæ Franciæ* (Paris, 1664). Du Creux based his history, which covered the period 1625 to 1658, on the *Jesuit Relations,* the reports that Jesuit missionaries sent back to France about their efforts to convert Native Americans to Christianity. Du Creux also interviewed Jesuits who returned from Canada, but he never himself visited New France.

(Image from 1644 edition of *Historiae Canadensis*, Lehigh University, Special Collections)

Du Creux characterized the Indian women as "at once servants, slaves, workmen, and beasts of burden," who did most of the work, ranging from cooking, preserving food, and making clothes and moccasins, to fishing, setting up wigwams, and repairing canoes. In addition, he emphasized, the women cared for the children. "Instead of our European cradles," he wrote, "the women suspend a wooden frame from the forehead by a broad strap and carry their burden on their shoulders."*

* Father François Du Creux, *History of Canada or New France,* trans. Percy J. Robinson and ed. James B. Conacher (Toronto: Champlain Society, 1951, reprt. New York: Greenwood Press, 1969), 1:84–85.

They established their primary settlement, called New Amsterdam, on Manhattan Island, and maintained trading posts at Fort Orange (near what is now Albany) and on the Delaware and Connecticut rivers. As in Jamestown, the first settlers were employees of the company who received no land of their own. The company paid for their transportation, tools, livestock, and two years' worth of supplies, assigning them company land on which to farm. The colonists were expected to trade only with the company. The government consisted of appointed company officers headed by a director-general, or governor, with wide powers. The colonists could not elect an assembly or any of their officials.

With good soil, the lucrative fur trade, and lumbering, the colony prospered economically, though its population grew slowly. Brewing became the second most important industry; in 1638, New Amsterdam residents complained that they were losing sleep from the singing of drunken sailors. People of many nationalities and religions arrived to take advantage of the Dutch policy of religious freedom, but few Dutch could be convinced to emigrate. In 1629, the company attempted to spur population growth by offering huge manors, called patroonships, to any member of the company who transported fifty persons to work his land. On the Hudson River, each patroonship extended for miles along one or both banks. Similar to New France, the settlers were tenants of the manor. This arrangement attracted few settlers, however; in fact, it discouraged immigration because the manors tied up large tracts that might otherwise go to small farmers.

At first, New Netherland had good relations with the Indians because the colony grew slowly and depended on the fur trade. In the famous 1626 purchase, director-general Peter Minuit exchanged goods worth about 60 guilders for Manhattan Island. Upriver, the Dutch bought furs from the Iroquois, the enemies of the Algonquians and Hurons who supplied the French, thus contributing to the devastating warfare among tribes. By the late 1640s, the Iroquois, with help from epidemics, destroyed the Hurons, a nation of about twenty thousand people. At the same time, constant warfare and disease seriously debilitated the Iroquois as well.

In the region surrounding New Amsterdam, relations began to deteriorate between the whites and the Indians around 1638. As with the English, the Dutch and natives had different conceptions of landownership. Although the Indians understood that they had sold rights to share the land and intended to continue using it themselves, the Dutch believed they had bought exclusive rights. Violence erupted as the settlers' cattle destroyed the Indians' corn, and dogs belonging to Native Americans attacked Dutch livestock. Beginning in 1640, the Dutch and Indians of the lower Hudson Valley fought a series of damaging wars that ended only in 1664, when the English took control of New Netherland and made peace with the Native Americans.

RELIGIOUS EXILES FROM ENGLAND

While the colonizers of Virginia, New France, and New Netherland had primarily economic motives, the English founders of Plymouth, Massachusetts Bay, and Maryland sought places where they could practice their religion free from persecution and at the same time earn a decent living. Seventeenth-century England was rife with religious controversy. The government required attendance at Anglican worship and financial support of ministers. Dissenters who refused to obey and held separate services could be imprisoned and fined. Roman Catholics could also be stripped of their property and jailed for life if they refused to take the oath of supremacy to the king, which denied the authority of the pope. The search for freedom of worship became a major impetus for crossing the Atlantic.

English Calvinists By 1603, when James I took the throne, two strains of English Calvinism, or **Puritanism,** had developed. One group included the Separatists, or Pilgrims, who founded the Plymouth colony in 1620; the others, known as Puritans, established the Massachusetts Bay colony ten years later. Both groups charged that the Anglican church needed to be "purified" of its rituals, vestments, statues, and bishops. They rejected the church hierarchy, believing each congregation should govern itself. The Separatists started their own congregations, abandoning all hope that the church could be reformed. The Pilgrims' decision to begin a colony in America was the ultimate expression of this separatism. The Puritans hoped to reform the Church of England from within. Their purpose in founding

Massachusetts Bay was to develop a moral government that they hoped the people of England would someday make their own.

The Plymouth Colony

The Pilgrims were a small band who had originated in Scrooby, England, where they established a separate congregation. In 1607, when some were jailed as nonconformists, they decided to leave England for the Netherlands, which offered freedom of worship. The Pilgrims settled in Leyden but were unhappy there, so they made an agreement with a group of London merchants who obtained a patent for land from the Virginia Company. In exchange for funding to go to America, the Pilgrims promised to send back fish, furs, and lumber for seven years.

Thirty-five of the Leyden congregation chose to emigrate. Sailing first to England, they joined sixty-seven others, of whom many were not Separatists. In September 1620, the *Mayflower* departed Plymouth, England, crowded with 102 passengers, about 20 crew members, and assorted pigs, chickens, and goats. Headed for Virginia, the ship reached Cape Cod on November 9. In shallow waters, fearing shipwreck, the exhausted travelers built their colony at **Plymouth.** They were outside the jurisdiction of the Virginia Company and therefore lacked a legal basis for governing themselves or claiming land. The first problem was more urgent because some of the colonists questioned the authority of the Pilgrim leaders. The group avoided a revolt by drafting and signing the **Mayflower Compact,** a social compact by which they agreed to form a government and obey its laws. The London merchants eventually solved the second problem by obtaining title to the land.

The settlers' first years at Plymouth were difficult, though they found unused supplies of corn left by Indians struck recently by epidemic disease and chose the site of a deserted Patuxet village with relatively clear fields. Over the first winter they built houses, but half of the colonists died of illness and exposure to the cold. In the spring of 1621, they planted corn with the help of **Squanto,** perhaps the lone surviving Patuxet, and other crops. Squanto and neighboring Pokanokets helped the Plymouth colony despite earlier problems with Englishmen. In 1614, Squanto and about twenty other Patuxets had been kidnapped by an English sea captain, who intended to sell them as slaves in Spain. Saved from bondage by Spanish priests, Squanto made his way to England, where he learned the language, then to Newfoundland, and finally back to Patuxet in 1619. There he found the unburied bodies of many of his people who had perished in the epidemic. One Englishman described the scene: "Their bones and skulls made such a spectacle. . . . it seemed to me a new found Golgotha."

At harvest in 1621, the Indians and colonists celebrated together for three days. Soon after their feast, the ship *Fortune* arrived with thirty-five new settlers, for whom no food was available until the next year's crop. After the colonists filled the *Fortune* with furs and lumber in hopes of starting to repay their debt to the London merchants, the French captured the ship.

By 1623, though, the Plymouth colony was well established and growing as new immigrants arrived. The community solved the problem of food supply by assigning individual plots to families. Still, the hard-working colonists had trouble fulfilling their bargain with the merchants. During a trading voyage, the crew mutinied. On one fishing trip, the ship sank; when it was raised and sent out again, the Spanish captured it. The London merchants gave up and in 1626 agreed to sell the land to the colonists for a large sum, which they paid by 1645, receiving a patent of ownership. Although

Plymouth's economic fortunes improved, the colony remained small and self-consciously separate from the larger group of English dissenters who streamed into New England.

Massachusetts Bay The Puritan migration to Massachusetts Bay was much larger and more tightly organized than the Plymouth settlement. During 1630, the first year, seven hundred women, men, and children arrived in eleven ships. Though at least two hundred died during the first winter, the colony grew quickly as about twelve thousand people went to Massachusetts during the 1630s. From King Charles I, the Massachusetts Bay Company obtained a charter specifying its government and the colony's boundaries. When most of the company officials emigrated, taking the charter with them, they greatly strengthened the colony's independence from the Crown and the Anglican church.

Thus, the Massachusetts Bay colonists did not answer to London merchants who expected handsome profits. The Puritans themselves financed colonization; they included wealthy investors as well as many middling families who could pay their own way. As a result, the founders devoted much of their energy to creating a model society. In the words of leader John Winthrop, the colony would be "as a Citty upon a Hill, the Eyes of all people are uppon us; soe that if wee shall deale falsely with our god in this worke wee have undertaken and soe cause him to withdrawe this present help from us, wee shall be made a story and a byword through the world." The Puritans believed that in addition to their charter from the king, they had a covenant with God that bound them to create a moral community. As Calvinists, they held that individuals were saved from eternal damnation by faith rather than by good works. Men and women could seek to avoid sin and work hard throughout their lives, but unless they were among God's chosen, or the "elect," they would go to hell. Under the covenant, the elect were responsible for the behavior of unsaved members of their community. The Puritan leaders were responsible to God. They thought that if they maintained a moral society, the Lord would help it prosper.

In Massachusetts, the Puritans restructured the company government to create their version of a godly commonwealth. According to the Massachusetts Bay charter, the company officials were a governor, deputy governor, and executive board of eighteen "assistants," to be elected by "freemen" (stockholders) who would meet in a general assembly called the General Court. These officers could make laws and regulations, appoint lower officials, grant lands, and punish lawbreakers. The colony's leaders changed the rules to allow all male church members (the male elect), not just stockholders in the company, to become freemen. In theory, every freeman would be a member of the General Court,

Massachusetts Bay Company Seal. *The seal of the Massachusetts Bay Company, 1629, shows an Indian calling to the English, "Come over and help us."*

(Courtesy of the Massachusetts Historical Society)

or colonial legislature. But as the population grew and towns formed quickly, freemen voted in town meetings for representatives to the assembly.

With the governor and assistants, the General Court drew up a law code for the colony, which after several revisions was published as the *Laws and Liberties of Massachusetts* (1648). The code was a combination of biblical law, English common law, and statutes tailored specifically to colonial needs. It protected the liberties of individuals by upholding trial by jury and due process of law, including the rights of the accused to receive a prompt public trial and call witnesses. It also prohibited feudal tenure of lands and outlawed slavery, "unlesse it be lawfull captives, taken in just warrs, and such strangers as willingly sell themselves or are solde to us." This provision limited the possibility that whites would be enslaved but had little effect on black bondage. The *Laws and Liberties* prescribed the death penalty for fewer crimes than in England but included as capital offenses blasphemy and adultery (in cases where the woman was married), which under the English common law were lesser crimes. Children could be put to death for failing to respect their parents, and fornicators were required to marry and be whipped or fined. The code enabled judges to extend the terms of negligent servants and send back to England any married persons who arrived in Massachusetts without their spouses. Although these terms may seem harsh, the colony did not actually impose the death penalty for blasphemy or abuse of parents by children, and it executed only two people for adultery. The magistrates evidently wanted to instill fear in the hearts of potential offenders rather than mete out harsh punishments.

The Puritans attempted to create a government operated according to God's will, as determined by the colony's leaders. The Puritan government was composed of members of the elect; ministers advised the magistrates but could not serve officially. The government required all inhabitants to attend Puritan churches. Persons who disagreed with orthodox doctrines could be expelled, whipped, fined, and even executed. The church was the center of each town, with all property owners paying taxes for its support. Though the Puritans had suffered persecution for their beliefs in England, they refused to allow freedom of worship in Massachusetts. Instead, they replaced one established church with another.

DOING HISTORY ONLINE

Plan for a Massachusetts Town, 1636

According to document 14, what issues were the settlers of Springfield most concerned about at the time of its founding? How do these issues compare to the concerns of the early Virginia settlers?

 www.cengage.com/ history/ayers/ ampassages4e

New England Society   Unlike the Jamestown settlers, a large proportion of Puritan immigrants came in families. Many originated from Norfolk, Suffolk, and Essex (together called East Anglia). Located directly across the North Sea from the Netherlands, East Anglia was the center of both the wool trade and Puritanism. By 1630, its residents had kept contact with European Calvinists for almost a century; entire congregations, ostensibly part of the Church of England, adopted Puritan ways. For decades they had worshipped freely, protected by the local Puritan gentry. Then during the 1620s and 1630s, the Puritans faced a series of hardships, including a depressed market for woolen cloth, poor harvests, and bubonic plague. Charles I and the Anglican church hierarchy, notably Archbishop William Laud, enforced laws against nonconformists, removing Puritan ministers from their pulpits. Many families migrated to Massachusetts, where they could make a new start under a congenial government. Some entire communities accompanied their minister.

The Puritan notion of an ideal community defined the ways in which the Puritans acted toward one another and toward outsiders. If the model society were to succeed, everyone had to have a place in the family, church, and commonwealth. Like other English, the Puritans kept a hierarchical social order. In the family, the husband was superior to the wife, but together they ruled the children and servants. In the church, the minister and elders dominated the congregation. In the community or common-wealth, the officials led the people. Ideally this hierarchy required little coercion: people saw themselves as part of the community and worked for the common good, or "weal" (hence "commonwealth"), rather than for their own benefit. They understood that all humans were equal spiritually but accepted social inequality as the will of God.

Most Puritan women accepted a subordinate place in their society without com-plaint. They viewed themselves as part of a community and a family, with duties determined by their sex and age, not as individuals with rights equal to those of men. Women raised children; kept the house and garden; preserved fruits and vegetables; made beer, cider, cheese, and butter; tended livestock and poultry; spun and wove cloth; sewed clothing; cared for the sick; and supervised the training of daughters and servants. Women often specialized in certain trades, such as spinning, weaving, poul-try raising, or medicine; they conducted trade among themselves, separate from the commercial networks of their husbands. Men had responsibility for raising grain such as wheat, Indian corn, and rye; cutting firewood; and maintaining the fences, build-ings, and fields. In addition to farming, many followed a trade or profession such as fishing, carpentry, shopkeeping, overseas trade, medicine, or the ministry. Only men could vote in church and town meetings, serve as government officials, or become ministers. Only when a man became incapacitated or was away from home was his wife expected to take his place at work or represent the family in legal matters or dis-putes. She temporarily assumed the role of "deputy husband," then yielded it when he became well or returned. Puritans recognized women's ability in public matters, but expected them normally to confine themselves to accepted women's tasks.

The role of Puritan women in the church was indicative of their place in society. On the one hand, women were the spiritual equals of men and held responsibility for the religious education of their children. On the other hand, the Puritans emphasized the inheritance of Eve, who, they believed, had led Adam to sin in the Garden of Eden. Women were expected to keep quiet in the church. They could not preach or vote on church business, though they could exert informal influence on their husbands. The Puritans, like other Christians of the time, embraced Saint Paul's instruction to the Corinthians: "Let your women keep silence in the Churches. . . . And if they will learn anything, let them ask their husbands at home."

In this patriarchal society, children deferred to their fathers, assuming a subservi-ent role until they were able to establish households of their own. Though some New England colonists held servants and a few owned enslaved Africans, sons and daugh-ters were the majority of the work force. Families on average had five children who reached adulthood. They worked for their parents until marriage—longer in the case of sons who inherited the family farm. Unlike seventeenth-century Virginia, living conditions in Massachusetts promoted patriarchy, for life expectancy was long. Persons who survived childhood diseases often lived past age sixty or even seventy. Thus, eldest sons could be middle-aged before their fathers died and willed them control of the family homestead. Younger sons, who had little hope of receiving the farm, often moved away from their parents, settling in the new towns that developed throughout New England. Parents usually attempted to give all of their children a start in life, with a farm, apprenticeship, money, or college tuition to sons and personal property or cash to daughters.

Connecticut and New Haven

Connecticut was an early destination of people looking for good land. The first Puritans went there to trade with Native Americans, but when news of attractive land in the Connecticut Valley arrived in Massachusetts, many settlers decided to move. The earl of Warwick owned the rights to the land at the mouth of the Connecticut River, which he ceded to a group of Puritan noblemen. To build a trading post and settlement, they sent John Winthrop, Jr., who convinced Thomas Hooker, the minister of Newtown, Massachusetts, to lead some of his congregation there. With another group that left from Dorchester, they founded Connecticut in 1636. Lacking a charter from the king, the founders agreed on the Fundamental Orders of Connecticut, which created a General Assembly of representatives from each town. In most respects, the Connecticut government resembled that of Massachusetts, with the exception that freemen, or voters, did not have to be church members. The assembly elected a governor, who could serve only one year at a time, and a group of magistrates who functioned as the upper house of the assembly. As in Massachusetts, Puritanism was the only recognized religion and received tax support.

As white settlement expanded, relations between the Puritans and Native Americans deteriorated. Like other English, the Puritans believed that the Indians worshiped the devil and had barbarous customs. The settlers justified expropriation of native lands on the basis of *vacuum domicilium*. Even more, the Puritans considered the Indians "strangers," who could have no role in building the model society. They were dispensable and dangerous, presenting a dual threat because their customs could corrupt the holy commonwealth and because they resented their loss of lands.

The 1637 war against the Pequots of eastern Connecticut showed the lengths to which the New England settlers could go. The Pequots, a powerful tribe, attempted to unite New England Indians against the English. In May 1637, troops from Massachusetts and Connecticut, with their Indian allies, the Narragansetts, attacked a Pequot village on the Mystic River before dawn, killing hundreds of sleeping women, children, and old men. The Pequots who escaped this massacre, mostly young men absent from the town, were later executed or enslaved. The Treaty of Hartford (1638) declared their nation dissolved.

Shortly after the Pequot War, in 1638, a group of staunch Puritans established New Haven. Persecuted in England, Reverend John Davenport took his flock first to Boston, but decided to move on to the Long Island Sound west of the Connecticut colony. They had no charter for New Haven, so the freemen made the Bible their law, eliminating trial by jury, for example, because it had no scriptural basis. Only male church members could vote. The colony grew as the settlers built towns farther west along the sound and on Long Island. Together the towns agreed on a government comprising a governor, magistrates, and a representative assembly.

Pequot War Diagram

This engraving of the attack on the Pequots at Mystic River in 1637 by the English and Narragansetts was published in Captain John Underhill's *News from America* (1638).

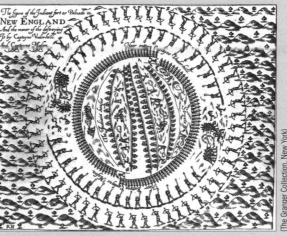

(The Granger Collection, New York)

According to labels on the entrances to the palisade, Underhill's troops entered the Pequot town on one side while Captain John Mason's soldiers entered on the other. The engraver shows English warriors shooting inhabitants, some of them unarmed, between rows of houses. Outside the palisade are rings of soldiers with muskets and Narragansetts with bows and arrows.

The English killed the Pequots and burned the town to the ground. The Narragansetts, who had nearly ended their long-standing conflict with the Pequots before the attack, were shocked by the slaughter. According to Underhill, the Narragansetts were pleased with the conquest but cried, "Mach it, mach it; that is, it is naught, it is naught, because it is too furious, and slaies too many men."

Exiles to Rhode Island

The founding of Rhode Island resulted from another kind of emigration from Massachusetts, that of people who refused to submit to the Puritan magistrates. The first was **Roger Williams,** an independent-minded minister who had studied divinity at Cambridge University, where he became a vocal Separatist. In 1631, he immigrated to Massachusetts Bay, where he accused the government of holding fraudulent title to its territory because the king had no authority to give away Indian lands. He said the colony should send the charter back to the king for correction; the settlers should return to England if they could not obtain rights from the true owners of the land. The Puritan officials ordered him to be quiet; he refused, soon broaching the issues of religious freedom and separation of church and state. "Forced worship stinks in God's nostrils," he proclaimed. "There is no other prudent, Christian way of preserving peace in the world, but by permission of differing consciences." He attacked the laws requiring church attendance and tax support of Puritan churches. Williams believed that government would pollute the church, not that giving legal preference to one religion was unfair. He opposed laws regulating religion to protect the church from state interference.

When the General Court banished Williams from Massachusetts for challenging the government in 1636, he went south to Narragansett Bay. There he purchased land from the Narragansett Indians, establishing Providence Plantation at the Great Salt

River. With the sympathizers who joined him, he created a society based on religious toleration, separation of church and state, and participation in government by all male property owners.

Another exile from Massachusetts was **Anne Hutchinson,** a midwife and nurse who in 1634 arrived in Boston with her husband, merchant William Hutchinson, and children. As Hutchinson assisted women in childbirth and sickness, she became convinced that Bostonians placed too much emphasis on good works and not enough on faith. She was a follower of one of Boston's ministers, the influential John Cotton, who stressed the importance of the individual's relationship with God over the obligation to obey laws. Hutchinson went further than Cotton, coming close to suggesting that if a person were saved it did not matter how she or he behaved, a belief known as the Antinomian heresy.

To the orthodox Puritan faction led by Governor John Winthrop, Hutchinson was a threat for several reasons. She emphasized individual judgment over communal authority, thus questioning the rule of colonial leaders. She told the Puritan patriarchs that God spoke to her directly, so she did not need the assistance of magistrates and ministers in interpreting God's will. Furthermore, Hutchinson went outside the accepted role of women by taking a public stand on religion. Most serious, she became the standard-bearer for a group that contested power with the Winthrop faction. In 1637, Winthrop's government put Hutchinson on trial for defaming ministers and exiled her from the colony. With her family and supporters, she founded a colony at Portsmouth on Narragansett Bay.

Following the settlement of Williams and Hutchinson on Narragansett Bay, several other dissenters established colonies there. William Coddington, a supporter of Hutchinson, started the town of Newport, and Samuel Gorton founded Warwick. The four leaders had trouble cooperating, but knew they needed a charter from the English government to avoid annexation by Massachusetts. Roger Williams went to England for that purpose during the Civil War. The 1644 Rhode Island charter, which Parliament granted, united the four settlements under one representative assembly, which could pass statutes consistent with the laws of England. The Rhode Island colonists based their government on Williams's principles of freedom of worship, separation of church and state, and wide participation in government.

The Proprietary Colony of Maryland

In 1632, Charles I granted a charter for Maryland to George Calvert, the first Lord Baltimore, who had served in high office until he converted to Catholicism. Although Calvert was forced to resign, he remained a royal favorite and requested a grant in America to build a haven for Catholics. He also expected to support his family by selling the land. He died before actually obtaining the charter, so his son, Cecilius Calvert, the second Lord Baltimore, became lord proprietor of Maryland. The colony was carved out of the northern part of Virginia. Calvert received ownership of the soil and was sovereign in government, subject only to the king.

Calvert spent £40,000 for two ships, the *Ark* and the *Dove,* with supplies to send the first settlers, who arrived in Maryland in 1634. The proprietor planned a feudal system in which manorial lords received large tracts depending on the number of tenants they transported. For example, a person who brought five laborers to Maryland at a total cost of £20 received a manor of two thousand acres.

Though Maryland settlers suffered no "starving time" as had settlers in Virginia and had a cash crop in tobacco, the colony grew slowly. Mortality was high and immigration sluggish. By 1642, Calvert had granted rights for only sixteen manors, mostly to wealthy Catholic friends. To improve his income, Calvert distributed farms to less wealthy immigrants, who had to pay annual quitrents. Over the seventeenth century, rich investors acquired sixty manors, but by far most settlers were small landowners.

The extension of landownership beyond Calvert's circle of loyal supporters created problems for the lord proprietor. Under the charter, he was obligated to call together an assembly of freemen, or landowners, to enact laws. Calvert interpreted this to mean that they should approve legislation he prepared, but the freemen, meeting first in 1635, claimed the right to draft the code of laws. Calvert refused to accept their draft, so for three years the colony operated without a code. In 1638, they reached a compromise, with the proprietor and assembly each drafting some of the bills. The colony finally had a legal basis for governing and punishing crime.

But the struggle for power between the proprietor and freemen continued. The ordinary planters, who formed the majority of freemen and were mostly Protestant, resented the power of the Catholic elite and had little sympathy for Calvert's vision of a society in which all Christians could worship freely. Religious and political strife became most acute in Maryland during the English Civil War and the Puritan Commonwealth, from 1642 to 1660.

The Impact of the English Civil War Over two decades, the English Civil War transformed the political situation in England. The war resulted from a contest for power between Parliament and Charles I, who imprisoned opponents without due process and launched a crusade to force all his subjects, even those in Presbyterian Scotland and Catholic Ireland, to conform to the Anglican church. In 1642, war broke out between the "Cavaliers," or royalists, and the "Roundheads," or parliamentary forces, of whom many were Puritans. Oliver Cromwell led the Roundheads to victory in 1648; the following year they beheaded the king.

The revolutionaries attempted to rule through an elected Parliament, but conflicting factions of Puritans and radical sects undermined their plans. Some radical theorists wanted an entire restructuring of society—in the words of one contemporary, "a world turned upside down." They called for extension of the vote to all men and redistribution of land. The gentry and wealthy merchants who had led Parliament to victory utterly rejected these ideas. In 1653 they named Cromwell the Lord Protector of the Commonwealth of England, Scotland, and Ireland. He ruled alone, backed by the army, until his death in 1658. An attempt failed to make his son Richard the successor, and two years later, the monarchy was restored. The accession of Charles II did not mean a complete reversal to the time of his father, however. The king confirmed Parliament's right to approve taxes and abolished the royal courts that had punished opponents of the Crown. But the Restoration brought the Cavaliers back into power, making the Anglican church the state religion once again.

The struggle for power during the Civil War and its aftermath had repercussions in the colonies. Initially the rebellion of English Puritans against the king raised hopes among New Englanders that English society would be reformed. Of more practical importance to the colonies was the lack of English military protection. Plymouth, Massachusetts, Connecticut, and New Haven counted among their enemies the French,

Dutch, Native Americans, and Rhode Island. In 1643, they formed the New England Confederation, agreeing to share the cost of war, provide soldiers in proportion to population, and make no treaties without each colony's consent. The New England Confederation was the only successful league of colonies in English North America before the Revolutionary War. In assuming power to conduct war and make treaties, it went beyond colonial rights. The English government, in the midst of civil war, was too preoccupied to react.

In the Chesapeake colonies of Virginia and Maryland, the civil war and its aftermath were more disruptive. In 1652, the English Commonwealth removed the royalist Virginia governor, William Berkeley, because he had proclaimed Charles II the king upon his father's execution. In Maryland, the parliamentary revolt weakened the position of Lord Baltimore, whose authority came directly from the king. Protestants, especially Puritans, opposed Lord Baltimore, even though he had encouraged them to migrate from Virginia, where they had suffered Governor Berkeley's persecution. Calvert had approved the Act Concerning Religion (1649), which guaranteed freedom of religion to all Christians. Nevertheless, in 1654, the Maryland Puritans established a commonwealth. Their assembly deposed the proprietor's government, restricted the right of Catholics to worship, and created a Puritan code of behavior, including laws against swearing, drunkenness, and breaking the Sabbath. Calvert appealed to Oliver Cromwell, who confirmed his proprietorship, but Lord Baltimore regained control of the colony only in 1657, after a period of local civil war.

ENGLISH COLONIZATION AFTER 1660

The accession of Charles II in 1660 initiated a new phase of colonization, in which the English government paid more attention to its colonies than it had before the civil war. In 1662, the Crown granted Connecticut a charter, and the following year it confirmed the charter Rhode Island had received from Parliament. To tighten colonial administration, the king and Parliament approved a series of navigation acts that formed the basis of a mercantilist colonial policy.

Navigation Acts   The English Commonwealth, recognizing the growing economic value of the colonies, had passed the Navigation Act of 1651. The law required that goods brought to England or its colonies from Asia, Africa, or America be carried on English ships (including those of English colonies). Goods from European nations had to be transported on either English ships or those of the country of origin. The chief purposes of the act were to encourage growth of England's merchant marine and challenge Dutch ascendancy on the seas and in colonial ports. The Commonwealth went further between 1652 and 1654, with the first Anglo-Dutch War, by attacking Dutch vessels in the English Channel and North Sea.

The Navigation Acts of 1660, 1663, and 1673 confirmed the 1651 restrictions on transport and created a list of "enumerated articles"—major colonial products including tobacco, sugar, indigo, cotton, ginger, and dyewoods—that could be shipped only to England or another English colony. The colonists could not sell these goods directly to other nations. The "articles" first went to England, where they were taxed and reexported by English merchants, who benefited from the business. Conversely, with some exceptions, goods shipped from other nations to the English colonies had to go to England first. The colonists considered these laws detrimental because English middlemen added charges to products going in both directions. The English government created a colonial administration to enforce the acts, but the results were complicated and inefficient. Colonial governors lacked the resources (and in many cases the will) to eliminate smuggling.

Carolina　Charles II was penniless when he ascended the throne and owed substantial debts to his supporters. Expansion of the colonial empire permitted him to repay these creditors and at the same time advance England's commerce and national power. Carolina became the first post-Restoration colony on the North American mainland after England obtained Spain's concession of lands north of present-day Charleston with the Treaty of Madrid (1670). The chief promoters of Carolina were Anthony Ashley Cooper, Governor William Berkeley of Virginia, and John Colleton, a West Indies planter. They obtained help from five men who were close to the king; together the eight associates became proprietors of Carolina. They obtained a charter like Maryland's and received wide latitude in matters of religion. They drew up the Fundamental Constitutions of Carolina, creating a complicated feudal society with nobles and lords, a scheme the ordinary settlers of Carolina refused to accept.

Two colonies developed in Carolina. Small planters from Virginia built the first, which later became North Carolina. As early as 1653, people had settled on the shores of Albemarle Sound, where they raised tobacco, corn, and livestock. In 1664, Berkeley sent William Drummond to organize a council and assembly. The Albemarle settlement, which remained poor, was a haven for pirates and difficult to govern. In 1691, the Carolina proprietors effectively established North Carolina by appointing a separate governor.

In 1670, Anthony Ashley Cooper organized the second Carolina colony at Charles Town. Many of its early settlers came from the West Indies island of Barbados, which had run out of vacant land. The Barbadian planters had money to develop plantations in South Carolina and owned African slaves to do the work. The proprietors offered generous acreages to household heads for each person brought to the colony. A planter with his own family and several enslaved blacks could qualify for hundreds of acres. From the colony's founding, a large proportion of South Carolinians were African slaves. They produced food, livestock, firewood, and barrel staves for Barbados.

New York and New Jersey　To control eastern North America, the English next had to seize New Netherland. With a series of outposts, the Dutch held the region between Connecticut and Maryland, including New Amsterdam and lands on the Delaware River that Sweden had settled in 1638 and the Dutch had captured in 1655. The English justified their attack in 1664 against New Netherland on several grounds, including John Cabot's 1497 voyage to the region and Dutch illegal trade with English colonies. Settlers from New England living under Dutch jurisdiction reported that Dutch military defenses were weak. James, the duke of York, Lord High Admiral of the Navy, urged his brother, Charles II, to send a fleet. The king granted James a proprietary charter for lands between the Connecticut and

Delaware rivers, as well as Long Island, Nantucket, Martha's Vineyard, and part of present-day Maine. The charter gave the duke wide governmental powers, even dispensing with an assembly. The duke could write his own legal code as long as it conformed to the laws of England.

With charter in hand, James quickly forced out the Dutch. In 1664, his deputy governor, Richard Nicolls, took New Amsterdam without a fight. The second Anglo-Dutch War (1665–1667) in part resulted from this action. Assuming ownership, James called his colony New York, but granted the land between the Delaware and lower Hudson rivers to John Lord Berkeley and Sir George Carteret, who named the area New Jersey.

Despite his extensive powers, James realized that he had to make New York attractive to inhabitants. He gave residents the choice of keeping their Dutch citizenship or becoming naturalized as English subjects. In 1665, he issued a legal code, called the Duke's Laws, which guaranteed freedom of religion, recognized preexisting titles to land, and allowed New Englanders on Long Island to form town governments. The New York government consisted of a governor and council appointed by the duke but no legislature.

When England and the Netherlands continued their rivalry in the third Anglo-Dutch War (1672–1674), the Dutch easily recaptured New York. After sixteen months, they returned the colony to England as part of the Treaty of Westminster (1674). Receiving a new charter, James resumed possession of New York and reconfirmed his grants to New Jersey, which had been divided into two colonies. Carteret held East New Jersey, while Berkeley sold West New Jersey to a Quaker, Edward Byllinge, who then transferred title to a group of coreligionists, including William Penn.

CONCLUSION

During the first three-quarters of the seventeenth century, the English, French, and Dutch ended Spain's mastery of the New World. By 1675, the English held colonies along the Atlantic coast from New England to the Carolinas. The French controlled Canada and had explored the Great Lakes and the upper Mississippi Valley. The Dutch established, but then lost, New Netherland. Spain retained its borderland outposts in New Mexico and Florida. Everywhere the Europeans colonized, the Indians died from epidemic disease. Their relations with the white invaders depended a great deal on the numbers of Europeans who arrived, their attitudes, and goals of settlement.

From the beginning, the English colonies were diverse—in their form of government, degree of stability, relations with Native Americans, and economic base. The Crown fostered this variety by granting charters to an assortment of companies and individuals, including Puritan and Catholic opponents of the established church. Virginia and Maryland prospered from tobacco but battled persistent high mortality. Nevertheless, in the mid-seventeenth century, the Chesapeake was "the best poor man's country" for English people willing to take risks. Most New Englanders came primarily to start a model society based on their Calvinist beliefs. They enjoyed a healthier climate than the people of the Chesapeake but inferior soil. They supported themselves modestly by fishing and mixed farming, developing trade with the West Indies to pay for English imports.

In New Mexico, Spanish colonists exploited the Pueblos' labor to support their trade with Mexico, while Catholic missionaries tried to claim the Indians' souls. In all three areas—New England, the Chesapeake, and New Mexico—pressures between Europeans and Native Americans, and within the colonial societies, would soon erupt in war.

CHAPTER REVIEW, 1590–1675

- British, French, and Dutch expansion ended Spanish dominance of North America during the seventeenth century. Spain retained land-holdings in Central and South America and the borderland territories of New Mexico and Florida.
- The nature of interactions between white colonizers and Native Americans depended on colonizers' goals, the number of white settlers, and European attitudes toward native peoples.
- Contact between Native Americans and Europeans inevitably caused the devastating spread of epidemic disease among Native American populations.
- Many English settlers were drawn to the colonies by the prospect of economic opportunity and religious freedom. New England became a refuge for religious dissidents, in particular, the Puritans.
- Drawn to the New World primarily by economic considerations, many French and Dutch settlers became involved in the fur trade. While French relations with neighboring Native Americans were relatively amicable, Dutch interactions were frequently violent.
- The 1660 restoration of Charles II to the British throne resulted in founding the Carolinas and a series of wars between the British and the Dutch over the territory of New Netherland.

◀▌▌▌ *Looking Back*

Chapter 2 discusses the colonization of North America by the Spanish, French, Dutch, and English during the seventeenth century. While the colonies varied in political organization, economic development, labor, religion, and relations with Native Americans, we can also determine common patterns.

1. What were the economic goals of the adventurers who founded each of the following colonies: New Mexico, Jamestown, New France, New Netherland, and Massachusetts?
2. What was the significance of religion in the development of each of these colonies?
3. How did the settlement of Rhode Island compare with the founding of Massachusetts Bay?
4. How did the English Civil War affect the colonies?
5. Why were the relations of the English with Native Americans in Virginia different from Indian–French interaction in Canada?

Looking Ahead ▌▌▌▶

After 1660, with restoration of the English monarchy, the government began tightening administration of the colonies. This included enforcement of the Navigation Acts, which restricted colonial trade. Chapter 3 considers internal conflicts and wars that the colonists faced as their societies matured and as they participated more fully in the expanding empire. Also significant after 1675 was the shift to enslaved African labor in the southern colonies.

1. Why did the English Crown expand the Navigation Act, which the Commonwealth initiated in 1651?
2. What changes did the English government make in colonial administration after 1675?
3. What was the importance of the African slave trade to colonial development in North America?

 Go to the American Passages website at www.cengage.com/history/ayers/ampassages4e for additional review materials.

Crisis and Change, 1675–1720

3

In February 1676, Narragansett Indians burned Lancaster, Massachusetts, killing many of the English settlers and taking others prisoner, including Mary White Rowlandson, a minister's wife, and her three children. The Narragansetts had joined the Wampanoags and other New England Algonquians to destroy the European settlements. Their leader was the Wampanoag sachem, Metacom, called King Philip by the colonists. In the Indians' words, according to Rowlandson in *The Narrative of the Captivity and Restoration of Mrs. Mary Rowlandson,* "they would knock all the Rogues in the head, or drive them into the Sea, or make them flie the Country."

Though Rowlandson began her captivity with hatred toward the Indians, whom she called "Barbarous Creatures," she came to respect some as individuals and to appreciate aspects of their culture. She was most impressed, she said, that while the Algonquians had little corn, "I did not see (all the time I was among them) one Man, or Woman, or Child, die with Hunger." They ate "Ground-nuts . . . also Nuts and Acorns, Hartychoaks, Lilly-roots, Ground-beans, and several other weeds and roots that I know not." Desperately hungry, Rowlandson ate unfamiliar foods too, surviving to rejoin her husband in Boston.

King Philip's War, as the English settlers called it, was just one of the crises that afflicted colonial America in the last quarter of the seventeenth century. In Virginia, a comparatively minor skirmish between Indians and whites escalated into Bacon's Rebellion, a civil war among the English settlers. In New Mexico, the Pueblos expelled the Spanish for thirteen years. Following closely on King Philip's War and Bacon's Rebellion, William Penn intended to avoid conflict with the Indians in founding Pennsylvania. An unstable English government disrupted politics in the colonies when James II, a Roman Catholic, succeeded his brother King Charles II in 1685. James's attempt to make sweeping changes in both the home and colonial governments met strong resistance. The Glorious Revolution quickly ended his reign. In 1689, settlers in Massachusetts, New York, and Maryland overthrew his provincial governments, declaring allegiance to the new king and queen, William and Mary. In Massachusetts, the impact of years of political uncertainty helped spread witchcraft hysteria from Salem to other towns.

From 1689 to 1713, European wars spilled into North America, fueling hostilities in Florida and Canada among Native Americans, English, French, and Spanish. The French moved south through the Mississippi Valley and founded Louisiana, while the English pushed south into Florida, west across the Appalachian Mountains, and north into Maine. As the English colonies expanded and matured, their economies and labor systems diverged, particularly with the entrenchment of slavery. Despite revolutions and wars, planters built successful staple crop economies in the southern colonies, while northerners profited from networks of trade with England, Europe, and the West Indies.

REBELLIONS AND WAR

The wars of 1675 to 1680 in New England, Virginia, and New Mexico resulted from pressures that had been building for decades. In Massachusetts, the spread of settlement forced Native Americans to defend their homes. In Virginia, demands of former servants for good land precipitated a civil war, and in New Mexico, severe droughts deepened opposition to forced labor, impelling the Pueblos to rid themselves of Spanish overlords. After the upheavals, elites in each settlement made changes that avoided further serious revolt.

Decline of New England Orthodoxy In 1675, Massachusetts seemed to have lost sight of the goals of its first settlers. When the Indians attacked, Puritan ministers warned the sons and daughters of the founding generation that God was punishing them for their faithlessness and sin.

In fact, Puritan church membership had declined since 1650, especially among men. After midcentury, women became a large proportion of the "elect," comprising 60 percent, and in some congregations 75 percent, of newly admitted members. The ministers believed that men were becoming more worldly, thus undermining the church's social and political authority. A related problem was that the children of nonchurch members could not be baptized. In 1662, the clergy devised an alternative to full church membership, the **Halfway Covenant**, which permitted adults who had been baptized but who were not yet saved to be "halfway" members. In congregations that accepted this innovation (not all churches did), people could assume partial status by showing that they understood Christian principles and would strive to obey God. As unconverted members, they were not entitled to take communion, but they could have their children baptized.

The growth of competing religions in New England also proved to Puritan ministers that their model society had failed. Believing theirs to be the only true religion, Puritans rooted out dissent. After 1650, the Quakers and Baptists threatened religious unity. The **Society of Friends**, or Quakers, was a radical Protestant sect born in the turmoil of the English Civil War. Like the Puritans, they were reformers who believed that the Church of England was corrupt and should be purified of its rituals, decorations, and hierarchy. But the Quakers went even further: they claimed that the Puritans also practiced false doctrine by paying ministers to preach, relying too much on the Bible as the word of God, and retaining the sacraments of baptism and

This icon will direct you to interactive activities and study materials on the American Passages website: www.cengage.com/history/ayers/ampassages4e

CHAPTER TIMELINE

1675	Appointment of English Lords of Trade
1675–1676	King Philip's War • Bacon's Rebellion
1678	Charles II demands renegotiation of Massachusetts charter
1680	Popé's Rebellion
1681	William Penn receives Pennsylvania charter
1682	La Salle claims the Mississippi Valley for France
1683	Iroquois of New York defeat New France
1684	Revocation of Massachusetts charter
1685	James II becomes king of England • Dominion of New England created
1688–1689	Glorious Revolution in England • William and Mary ascend throne
1689	Revolutions in Massachusetts, New York, and Maryland
1689–1697	King William's War
1690	Spanish settlements in Texas
1691	Massachusetts receives its new charter
1691–1692	Salem witchcraft hysteria
1693	Spanish regain control of New Mexico
1696	Board of Trade and Plantations replaces Lords of Trade
1698	Royal African Company loses slave trade monopoly
1699	French establish Louisiana
1701	Iroquois treaty of neutrality
1702–1713	Queen Anne's War
1704	South Carolina defeats Spanish Florida
1712	Slave revolt in New York City
1715	Calverts regain Maryland government • Yamassee War in South Carolina

communion. The Friends believed that God communicated directly with individuals through the "Spirit" or "Light." They worshipped by gathering in plain meetinghouses to "wait upon the Lord." In worship services, they had no Bible reading, prepared sermon, music, or ritual. Rather, they waited in silence for the Spirit to inspire one or several of the congregation to communicate God's message. Ministers, who included women as well as men, regularly received inspiration to speak. They required no advanced learning because their words were supposed to come straight from God, not from a prepared text.

Appalled by these Quaker teachings, Puritan leaders tried to prevent their spread by deporting the traveling missionaries. The Friends were stubborn, however, and they repeatedly returned to Massachusetts. They interrupted Puritan church services, preached in the streets, and made some converts among the people. The Puritan magistrates arrested and whipped them, even cropping their ears. In 1658, the General Court prescribed the death penalty for Quakers who returned after banishment.

A Quaker Woman Preaching

The Quakers were unique among English religions in the seventeenth century in recognizing women as ministers. Women were among the earliest followers of George Fox of England, considered the founder of Quakerism around 1650. Female missionaries then traveled through the British Isles, Europe, and America. They believed that God spoke through them, and they hoped to convince others of the "Light."

QUAQUERESSE qui preche.

(Courtesy of Special Collections, University Research Library, University of California at Los Angeles)

In New England, these women ministers challenged both the Puritan faith and expectations of female subordination. When Quaker missionaries interrupted church services and gained followers, Massachusetts leaders banished them and threatened to execute those who returned to the colony. Several were hanged, including Mary Dyer in 1660, who had determined to "look their bloody laws in the face." This illustration was published somewhat later, in J. F. Bernard's *The Ceremonies and Religious Customs of the Various Nations of the Known World . . .* (1733–1739), when Quakers had become less controversial and worshipped openly in Massachusetts.

The hangings of several Quaker missionaries caused consternation on both sides of the Atlantic. When Charles II demanded an explanation, the Puritans ended the executions. The magistrates continued to persecute nonconformers, but over the decades following 1660, they realized that their policy of intolerance had failed. Rhode Island served as a base for Quaker missionaries to evangelize in the Puritan colonies, further supporting the colony's reputation among Puritans as "the sewer of New England." The Baptists, whose objection to infant baptism was their chief disagreement with orthodox Puritans, increased in numbers after approval of the Halfway Covenant, which they vehemently opposed. They believed that a church should include only the saved—indeed that only the saved should be baptized. Despite persecution, dissenters successfully formed congregations throughout New England.

King Philip's War, 1675–1676 The unceasing expansion of white settlers into the frontier destroyed the relative peace between the Algonquians and the settlers of New England. By 1675, more than fifty thousand whites inhabited the region. The colonists had large families of sons and daughters who desired farms of their own. These settlers occupied more and more of the hunting, fishing, and agricultural lands of the Indians.

Since the massacre of the Pequots in 1637, the Puritans and Native Americans of New England had managed an uneasy peace. The colonists traded for furs with local nations and with the Mohawks, the closest nation of Iroquois in New York. Some Puritan ministers, of whom John Eliot is best known, convinced several local tribes who were greatly diminished by disease and loss of lands to dwell in **praying towns**. In these villages, adjacent to but separate from the towns of white settlers, the Indians were supposed to adopt English customs and learn the fundamentals of Puritan religion. By 1674, Eliot had organized fourteen praying towns of Native Americans who took the first steps toward giving up their traditional ways.

Many New England Indians, including Wampanoags and Narragansetts, did not form praying towns, but even so remained allies of the Puritan governments for many years. Trouble began in 1671 when the Plymouth government attempted to force the

MAP 3.1 New England at the Time of King Philip's War, 1675–1676.

The Indians and English destroyed and damaged each other's towns throughout Plymouth, Rhode Island, and Massachusetts. The Narragansetts, who lived in Rhode Island and had assisted the Puritan governments against the Pequots in 1637, entered King Philip's War after an English army invaded their territory.

Wampanoags to surrender their firearms and obtain permission to sell land. **Metacom** (or King Philip) built a league with neighboring tribes. When John Sassamon, an Indian educated at Harvard College, informed the Plymouth government of impending attack and was murdered, the white authorities hanged three Wampanoags for the deed.

In 1675, Metacom mobilized Algonquians throughout New England, attacking fifty-two English towns. White refugees fled to Boston. But by the end of summer 1676, with the help of the Mohawks, the colonial governments turned back the attack, as disease, hunger, and a weapons shortage weakened Metacom's troops. The war took a heavy toll on both sides, for the Algonquians destroyed twelve towns, killed many colonists, and took others prisoner, as described earlier. White frontier settlement would not return to its 1675 limits for another forty years.

For the Indians of southern New England, the war was calamitous. Thousands died, and many others were enslaved. Even bands that supported the English lost autonomy. At the outbreak of war, the colonists had forced residents of the praying towns to live on desolate Deer Island in Boston Harbor, where they lacked sufficient food and shelter. Some of the Indian men later fought in the colonial militia against Metacom, but when the war was over, all Native Americans in southern New England had to live in praying towns, where they worked as servants or tenant farmers for neighboring whites. Metacom was killed, his head paraded before the white settlements and kept on a pole in Plymouth for twenty years; his wife and son were sold as slaves.

War in the
Chesapeake

Just as New England struggled over land in King Philip's War, Virginia faced a similar crisis in **Bacon's Rebellion**. The Chesapeake uprising involved civil war among the English as well as Indian–white conflict. But at its root, the chief issue was land: How could the competing interests of landless immigrants and dispossessed natives be resolved? Since the 1640s, the white population of Virginia and Maryland had grown quickly. By 1670, approximately forty thousand colonists lived in the Chesapeake, including native-born sons and daughters of early settlers as well as more recent arrivals. Among the new immigrants were servants who expected to obtain land on completing their terms. In the 1670s, however, many Virginians discovered that the combination of low tobacco prices and high land prices blocked their dream of obtaining plantations. They received headrights, or individual rights to land, but could find no good vacant tobacco acreage to claim.

Part of the problem, these landless freemen believed, was that the Indians held too much territory. Specifically, the 1646 treaty between the Virginia government and the Powhatans designated the area north of the York River for Native Americans. This agreement had been acceptable to whites in the 1640s when space south of the York seemed ample, but was unsatisfactory thirty years later, when white settlement was pushing north. It was also true, many freemen recognized, that wealthy planters, powerful in government, speculated in large acreages that they left empty while others starved for land.

The first flames of war occurred in July 1675, when some Doeg Indians attempted to take hogs as payment for a settler's unpaid debt. After people on both sides were killed, the Susquehannocks got involved. When they attacked frontier settlements, a thousand-man army of Virginia and Maryland colonists marched against their village on the Potomac River. Vastly outnumbered, several Susquehannock sachems agreed to negotiate, but when they left their stockade, the colonists murdered them. During the winter of 1675–1676, the Susquehannocks retaliated, raising fears that King Philip's

DOING HISTORY ONLINE

Royal Description of Nathaniel
Bacon, c. 1676

Read documents 1 through 7,
on Bacon's Rebellion. How
persuasive is the description of
Nathaniel Bacon provided in the
official report? Are there reasons
to doubt its accuracy?

www.cengage.com/
history/ayers/
ampassages4e

War had spread south. Discontented and venge-
ful colonists responded indiscriminately, killing
friendly neighboring Indians rather than those
who were actually attacking the frontier.

The landless freemen found a leader in
Nathaniel Bacon. Only twenty-nine years old,
Bacon had come to Virginia with enough money
to purchase a large plantation. Governor Berkeley
nominated him to the Virginia council, despite
his youth. Nevertheless, Bacon evidently saw his
opportunity to challenge Berkeley for leadership of the colony by mobilizing freemen and
small planters against the Indians. The settlers
knew that the natives were weak, just a fraction of their pre-1607 population, were weak.
Bacon's supporters also demanded a greater voice in the Virginia government.

Governor Berkeley declared Bacon a traitor and sent troops to end his forays against
the Indians. He also called new elections that brought many Bacon supporters into the
House of Burgesses. The delegates passed measures that extended suffrage to landless
freemen, taxed provincial councilors, and placed limits on the terms and fees of local
officials. These efforts failed to end the rebellion, as Bacon's army burned Jamestown.
For months, Virginians plundered the plantations of neighbors who took the other
side. Few white fatalities occurred, however; rebels vented most of their frustration by
killing Indians. The rebellion finally ceased with Bacon's death, probably of dysentery,
in October 1676. The war marked a serious defeat for the Indians of the Chesapeake,
who lost the protection of the 1646 treaty and gradually surrendered their lands.

Bacon's Rebellion awakened the Virginia elites to the dangers of a large class of landless freemen but resulted in no substantive political change. A new assembly in 1677
reversed the reform acts of the 1676 House of Burgesses, including the law extending
the vote to landless freemen. A commission appointed by the Crown to end the rebellion also opposed expanding popular power, stating that to grant suffrage to unpropertied men was "repugnant to the Lawes of England and to the Lawes and Peace of the
Colony." The commission did call for taxing "the great Ingrossers of Lands" who caused
"misery and mischiefs" by "occasioning the Planters to straggle to such remote distances
when they cannot find land nearer to seat themselves but by being Tenants which in a
Continent they think hard," but nothing was done. Rather than create a society in which
power and wealth were distributed more evenly, in which Virginia once again would
offer opportunity to poor Englishmen, the planter elite began importing more enslaved
Africans. Bound for life and restricted by laws, black slaves could not demand farms
or a voice in government. With settlement in New Jersey, Carolina, and Pennsylvania
during the 1670s and 1680s, immigrants had better options than Virginia.

**The Pueblo Revolt,
1680 1693**   Four years after Bacon's Rebellion, across the continent in
New Mexico, the Pueblos drove out the Spanish—and kept
them out for thirteen years. The Pueblos, who lived along the
Rio Grande had the advantage of a much smaller white population in New Mexico—
twenty-eight hundred—than in New England or the Chesapeake. The Spanish hold

(© South West Museum, Los Angeles, CA/The Bridgeman Art Library)

Madonna.   *Pueblo Indian hide painting of a Christian Madonna, 1675.*

over the missions was tenuous, for native fighting men greatly outnumbered Spanish troops. Nevertheless, the Hispanic settlers and priests demanded forced labor and strict adherence to Christianity. A number of Indian towns had rebelled during the previous half-century, but most failed to win autonomy.

The Pueblos became more desperate during the 1670s, when New Mexico endured severe drought. As famine persisted, they faced Apache and Navajo attacks. The Pueblos became convinced that the root of their troubles lay in their rejection of ancient gods, the *katsina*. To bring rain and renewed prosperity, some presented gifts to the katsina and performed dances that the Spanish had outlawed. When punished for abandoning Catholicism, the Indians felt even greater resentment, and they finally revolted.

The leader of the 1680 rebellion was **Popé**, a shaman of the village of San Juan, north of Santa Fe. When the katsina told him that the Spanish must be driven from the land, he organized a general insurrection, sending knotted ropes to allied villages, indicating when the uprising should start. On August 10, 1680, the Pueblos launched a full-scale attack, killing four hundred colonists and twenty-one priests. Strategically, the Indians confiscated or destroyed the settlers' chief means of transportation: their horses and mules. When Santa Fe fell to the rebels on September 21, the whites escaped south, settling in the area of present-day Ciudad Juárez, Mexico. Some Spaniards explained the revolt as God's punishment for their sins, whereas others blamed the harsh labor and efforts to repress native religions. As Popé supervised, the Pueblos destroyed churches, broke up church bells, and burned images of Christ and the saints. According to one witness, "In order to take away their baptismal names, the water, and the holy oils, [the Indians] were to plunge into the rivers and wash themselves."

Several times during the next few years, the Spanish attempted unsuccessfully to retake New Mexico. The rebellion spread south into northern Mexico, where Native Americans demolished settlements and missions. But by 1692, as famine continued, the Pueblo alliance fell into disarray. The new Spanish governor of New Mexico, Don Diego de Vargas, marched north to Santa Fe with 160 troops. Though many Indians resisted, the Spanish reestablished control over the province. In December 1693, after a three-day siege, Vargas's troops took Santa Fe, killing all of the Indian men and making slaves of the women and children. The Spanish subsequently retained a foothold in New Mexico but not without further struggle. The Pueblos rejected the Franciscan missionaries, revolting once again in 1696. Some Pueblos fled from New Mexico; others submitted as Vargas systematically conquered the Indian towns once again. After 1696, the Spanish and Pueblos lived together in relative peace, but only because the Hispanics eased requirements for tribute, forced labor, and adherence to Christianity.

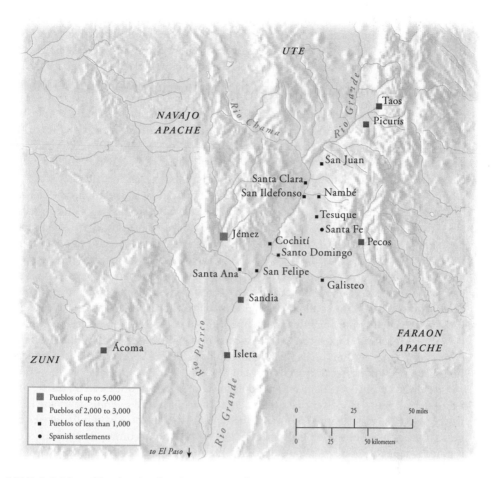

MAP 3.2 New Mexico in the Seventeenth Century.
The Spanish had established their colony in 1598 by sending soldiers, their families, and Franciscan missionaries north through the Rio Grande Valley. In 1680, at the time of the Pueblo Revolt, the Spanish population remained small and centered in the capital, Santa Fe.

WILLIAM PENN'S "HOLY EXPERIMENT"

In England, the Quaker leader **William Penn** approached Charles II with a petition to establish a new colony in America, one that would avoid bloodshed by dealing justly with the Indians. Although the Pueblos had not yet driven out the Spanish, Penn knew of King Philip's War and Bacon's Rebellion. He was determined to do things differently in Pennsylvania.

Plans for Pennsylvania	Penn had inherited a £16,000 debt owed to his father by the king but had little hope for repayment in cash, so he requested

a colony on the west bank of the Delaware River. The king approved Penn's request in 1681, granting him a charter for Pennsylvania that was more restrictive than Lord Baltimore's, in part because the English government was attempting to assert greater control over its colonies and in part because Penn was a Quaker. The new proprietor received the right to enact laws and impose taxes with the consent of the freemen but was required to submit all laws for approval to the home government within five years of passage. And to protect the status of the Church of England, the charter stipulated that twenty Anglican inhabitants could request a minister from the bishop of London.

In establishing Pennsylvania, Penn hoped to provide a haven for Quakers, who faced persecution in England because they would not pay tithes for church support or attend Anglican services. Friends also refused to give oaths, so they could not legally pledge allegiance to the king. A Quaker ideal was to live according to the doctrine that all were equal in the eyes of God; thus they rejected certain customs, such as removing one's hat in the presence of superiors. For practicing their faith, they were jailed and fined, and when they refused to pay, local English officials took their property.

William Penn conceived of his colony as a "holy experiment," a place where Quakers could exercise their beliefs without interference and the government would operate like a Quaker meeting, acting in unison as it followed God's will. Penn also intended to pay the Lenape Indians for tracts of land and to set up arbitration panels of Native Americans and colonists to resolve conflicts peacefully. He paid the Lenapes a much lower price than he in turn charged the settlers, however, and assumed the Indians would leave after they sold their land.

Like Lord Baltimore, Penn intended to make a fortune from Pennsylvania, summing up his goals: "The service of God first, the honor and advantage of the king, with our own profit." Despite Penn's strong Quaker convictions, which for some suggested a simple life, he appreciated fine food, drink, and accommodations. He possessed large landholdings in southern England and Ireland, retained many servants, and enjoyed such delicacies as salmon, partridges, saffron, and chocolate. Urgently needing money, he thought the sale of millions of acres in America would solve his financial problems.

Penn spent a great deal of time planning the colony. His scheme of government established an assembly with two houses, both elected by the freemen, defined as adult males who owned at least fifty acres of land or paid taxes on other property. During the early decades, when servants received fifty acres at the end of their term of service, nearly every man in Pennsylvania could vote. Penn did not extend that right

Wampum Belt, 1682. *Wampum belt, which, according to legend, the Lenape gave to William Penn in 1682. It has become a symbol of Penn's efforts to preserve peace with the Indians of Pennsylvania.*

© Atwater Kent Museum of Philadelphia, Courtesy of Historical Society of Pennsylvania Collection/The Bridgeman Art Library)

to women or alter the common law restrictions on married women. Though female Friends took an active role in their meetings as ministers, missionaries, and supervisors of discipline, their legal status in the Quaker commonwealth was similar to that in other colonies. Penn's laws stood out in another respect, however: it required capital punishment for just two offenses: treason and murder.

The proprietor's planning went beyond politics, for he also drew up specifications for his capital city. In designing **Philadelphia**, and thus taking on the role of city planner, Penn was unique among early English colonizers. He conceived the city as a large "green country town," with wide streets in a grid pattern, public parks, ample lots, and brick houses. He failed to fulfill his plan completely because he could not obtain enough acreage to build Philadelphia as he wanted. Dutch and Swedish residents already owned the land along the Delaware River, so Penn decided to buy a site of just twelve hundred acres between the Delaware and Schuylkill rivers. His proposal remained orderly, with the grid design and parks, but with smaller lots than he originally planned. To maintain a constant income from the colony, landowners would pay annual quitrents, or fees paid on land based on the number of acres. Quitrents were a holdover from the feudal system and replaced labor obligations to the feudal lord.

A Diverse Society

Penn sold land briskly: six hundred people bought 700,000 acres within four years. Most of the buyers were Quaker farmers, merchants, artisans, and shopkeepers from England, though many also originated from Scotland, Ireland, Wales, Europe, the West Indies, Maryland, and New York.

Penn's settlers moved into an area inhabited by the Lenapes, who welcomed the newcomers, and by Swedes, Finns, and Dutch, who served as intermediaries with the Indians. The Lenapes, or Delawares as the colonists later called them, had conducted trade with the Dutch as early as 1610 and yielded land to the whites. Because Dutch and Swedish settlements remained small, relatively few violent incidents occurred. By the time Penn arrived with thousands of colonists, the Lenapes had declined significantly in size from disease. As they sold their lands, some moved to northern or western Pennsylvania, while others remained on marginal tracts in the Delaware Valley.

The European "old residents" integrated with the new arrivals, though not without friction. Some earned money by selling land and provisions or by serving as guides and interpreters. One local Swede, Captain Lasse Cock, in 1682 translated for the Indians and English, and traveled to the Susquehanna and Lehigh rivers as Penn's emissary. The Swedes, Dutch, and Finns continued to worship in their own congregations but became naturalized as English subjects; some served in the assembly and local government. The old residents made up a large part of the population in the Lower Counties (later Delaware), leading to conflict as the different interests of the Lower Counties and Pennsylvania became clear. In 1704, after two decades of wrangling, the three southern counties obtained their own separate Delaware assembly.

Pennsylvania got a boost from its late arrival on the colonial scene because its merchants could tap existing networks in the Atlantic economy. Substantial traders came from New York, the Chesapeake, and the West Indies, bringing their connections and capital to build breweries, tanneries, warehouses, wharves, and ships. Farmers found a market for wheat, livestock, and lumber in the West Indies. By 1700, Philadelphia had become a thriving port town, with seven hundred houses and more than three thousand people.

But for William Penn, his colony was deeply disappointing: land sales reaped smaller profits than he had hoped, and the costs of administering the colony soared. When purchasers refused to send him quitrents, he went more seriously into debt. Penn traveled to his colony twice but stayed a total of only four years. Although the province became prosperous and quite successful as a tolerant, diverse society, he reckoned it a failure.

THE GLORIOUS REVOLUTION AND ITS AFTERMATH

The founding of Pennsylvania coincided with the Crown's effort to tighten colonial government. Compared with the Spanish empire, English administration was a hodge-podge. The Privy Council at first appointed temporary committees to address colonial concerns, then in 1675 formed a permanent committee, the Lords of Trade, which met sporadically. Even after 1696, when the more formalized **Board of Trade and Plantations** was established, this body could gather information and give advice, but lacked authority to appoint colonial officials or enforce laws. These powers belonged to a host of governmental offices, including the secretary of state, the Treasury, and the War Office.

Dominion of New England While experimenting with these committees, the Crown made other efforts to rein in the colonies. Most vulnerable was the Massachusetts Bay colony, for its unrestrictive charter and the perceived intransigence of Puritan leaders. In 1678, Charles II required Massachusetts to send agents empowered to renegotiate the charter. He specifically wanted the New Englanders to comply with the Navigation Acts and apologize for having coined their own money. The colonists delayed action, though they sent regrets for having passed laws contrary to the laws of England. They offered to renounce any "except such as the repealing whereof will make us to renounce the professed cause of our first coming hither."

Impressed by neither the Puritans' arguments nor the speed of their response, the English government brought legal proceedings against the Massachusetts Bay Company for "usurping to be a body Politick" and revoked the charter in 1684. The colony's assembly, the General Court, was prohibited from meeting. In February 1685, before a royal governor could be appointed, Charles died, and his brother James became king. James II quickly took advantage of events to move toward centralizing the colonies. With the Privy Council's consent, in 1685, he combined Massachusetts, New Hampshire, and Maine under the **Dominion of New England**; he added Plymouth, Rhode Island, and Connecticut in 1686 and New York and New Jersey in 1688. Apparently James's plan for the colonies was to create two large dominions, one north of the fortieth degree of latitude (the approximate location of Philadelphia) and one to the south. These dominions would supersede colonial charters, eliminating the confusing diversity of laws and political structures. Representative government would end.

For Massachusetts Puritans, the Dominion of New England was a disaster. James's governor-general, **Sir Edmund Andros**, made sweeping changes that undercut the

Puritan notion of a covenanted community. He levied taxes without the approval of a representative assembly, restricted the power of town meetings, mandated religious toleration, and confiscated a Boston church for use by Anglicans. Andros enforced the Navigation Acts, favored his own cronies over the Puritan elite in distributing patronage, required landowners to obtain new land titles from the Crown, demanded payment of quitrents, and took control of common lands. A number of colonists who rebelled by refusing to pay taxes without a voice in their passage were jailed and fined.

Revolutions
of 1689

Governor Andros managed to avoid serious revolt until the spring of 1689, when news of James's removal from the throne reached Massachusetts. The king's rule had been as heavy-

handed in England as in the colonies. A Roman Catholic, he installed his friends in office and defied Parliament. Protestants feared James would make England a Catholic nation under authoritarian rule. Thus, parliamentary leaders forced him into exile in France, inviting his Protestant daughter, Mary, and her husband, William of Orange, the leader of the Dutch, to take the throne. The **Glorious Revolution**, though bloodless, had long-lasting results in England: it permanently limited the king's power by establishing parliamentary control of taxation, supremacy of law, and autonomy of the courts.

On the morning of April 18, 1689, many of Boston's populace formed companies with the militia. Numbering more than a thousand by afternoon, the insurgents, who included several Puritan ministers and some wealthy merchants, deposed the dominion government. They interpreted the revocation of the charter and James's illegal taxation and expropriation of lands as part of a "popish plot" that Protestant New England must help destroy.

With the dominion gone, Plymouth, Rhode Island, and Connecticut reactivated their charters, but Massachusetts, which had lost its charter under Charles II, had to negotiate a new one. The colonists' arguments for the charter were based less on the old covenant theory than on the fundamentals of the Glorious Revolution, especially the right of English people to representative government. The resulting 1691 Massachusetts charter, which annexed Plymouth to the Bay colony, established a royal province with an elected assembly and a governor appointed by the king. The charter required freedom of worship and forbade religious restrictions on voting.

Revolutions also took place in New York and Maryland in the wake of James II's loss of power. New York fell into turmoil with news of William and Mary's ascent to the throne in England and the revolt in Boston. The reports unleashed opposition to Lieutenant Governor Francis Nicholson, who headed the dominion's government in New York. Again the struggle was defined in religious terms as a crusade to destroy the "papist" threat.

In the city of New York, insurgents included merchants and artisans who had been denied economic privileges to trade and mill flour under James's government. In 1689, led by **Jacob Leisler**, a German-born merchant and militia captain, they forced Nicholson back to England and elected a Committee of Safety to replace James's council. When Henry Sloughter, the new governor appointed by William and Mary, arrived in 1691, however, he reinstalled James's councillors and executed Leisler for treason. Despite Leisler's early proclamation of the new monarchs in 1689, his enemies had better connections in London.

In Maryland, simmering resentment of Protestants against the Roman Catholic proprietor, Charles, Lord Baltimore, erupted in the summer of 1689. Baltimore's troubles intensified when his nephew, George Talbot, president of the provincial council, murdered the king's customs collector, "with a dagger newly prepared and sharpened," aboard a royal ship. This event rocked the colony, so Baltimore sent a man he thought would provide strong leadership as governor, William Joseph, a Roman Catholic and adherent of James II. Upon arrival in 1688, Joseph proceeded to alienate Maryland's assemblymen, calling them adulterers and drunks. When he required them to renew their oaths of fidelity to the proprietor, they refused.

In July 1689, a handful of Maryland leaders formed the Protestant Association. Aroused by rumors that Catholics were plotting with the Indians to destroy the Protestants, the association raised troops, defeating the proprietary government without a shot. The rebels obtained articles of surrender that banned Catholics from provincial offices; sent a message to William and Mary informing them of the takeover and requesting a Protestant government; and elected an assembly, the "Associators' Convention," that ruled Maryland for the next two and one-half years.

The three provincial revolutions of 1689, in Massachusetts, New York, and Maryland, had similarities to England's Glorious Revolution in the relative absence of bloodshed and the recurring theme of "popish plots." They failed, however, to bring about permanent change in the constitutional relationship between England and its colonies. The provincials, lacking delegates in Parliament, continued to endure taxation and mercantilist regulation without their assent. The colonial revolts of 1689 resembled Bacon's Rebellion of 1676; they too mobilized out-of-power elites against those who controlled the colonial governments. In 1676, the insurgents in Virginia had manipulated landless discontents by appealing to hatred against Native Americans as well as grievances against Berkeley's government. In 1689, the leading rebels employed the twin specters of authoritarianism and Catholicism, with rumors of impending French and Indian attack, to gain support from the populace.

Witchcraft in New England   When Governor William Phips arrived in Boston Harbor with the new Massachusetts charter in May 1692, he found the colony in disarray. Symptomatic of the turmoil was the **witchcraft hysteria** that had erupted months earlier in Salem Village, a farming community north of Boston. Since 1675, the Bay colony had faced one crisis after another: King Philip's War, loss of the charter, Andros's dominion, the Revolution of 1689. Accompanying this turmoil were structural changes in the society, as traditional religious authority yielded to elites whose power rested on mercantile wealth. The Salem witch mania was a tragic holdover from a passing culture. Its fury was aggravated by the psychological reaction of traditionally minded folk to the new, more commercial, secular society of turn-of-the-century New England.

Belief in witchcraft was embedded in European and Anglo-American culture, though, ironically, it was losing force by the time of the Salem outbreak. The colonists, like their contemporaries in the Old World, believed that both God and Satan influenced everyday events. When something bad happened that they could not explain, they turned to supernatural explanations, including the possibility that an individual had aligned with the devil to do evil deeds. In England, witchcraft had been a capital offense since the time of Henry VIII in the early sixteenth century; colonial governments followed suit in condemning those who gave "entertainment to Satan." Over the seventeenth century, the Puritan governments charged many more men and women with witchcraft than did other English colonies: 350 New Englanders were accused between 1620 and 1725. Of these, the Salem episode accounted for almost 200. The southern and middle colonies, in contrast, tried few accused witches and executed none.

The witchcraft cases of Salem in 1691–1692 at first resembled those in other places and times. Several girls experimented with magic, aided by a slave woman, Tituba, and her husband, John, who together baked a "witch cake" of rye meal and urine and fed it to a dog. The girls started having fits, presumably caused by witches. According to one report, the girls began "getting into holes, and creeping under chairs and stools, and to use sundry odd postures and antic gestures, uttering foolish, ridiculous speeches." Apparent possession spread to other village girls, leading to the arrest of three women as witches: Tituba; a poor beggar, Sarah Good; and an ailing elderly woman, Sarah Osborne.

These three alleged witches were the sort of people traditionally prosecuted for the crime. Generally in witchcraft cases, the accused were women past menopause who in various ways deviated from expected roles. But while the Salem craze commenced in the time-worn pattern, it soon engulfed people of all social levels. Accusations descended on prosperous church members, a minister, a wealthy shipowner, and several town officials. Hysteria spread from Salem to adjacent towns. Of those executed, fourteen women and five men were hanged on "Witches Hill" and another man was crushed to death with stones.

Governor Phips, supported by influential clergymen, had allowed the prosecutions to proceed after his arrival but put a stop to them when the accusers pointed to people at the highest levels of society, including his own wife, Mary. It had become clear, to many besides the governor, that the situation was out of control, that the evidence presented by the possessed was unreliable and quite likely the work of the devil. After Salem, witchcraft accusations no longer assumed its earlier importance in New England society.

DOING HISTORY ONLINE

Salem Witchcraft

The accusations of witchcraft in Salem involved a number of social and cultural institutions for which the Massachusetts Bay colony and New England have become famous. Read documents 8 through 13 on the trial of Bridget Bishop. Which institutions played a role in the crisis? What role did each play?

www.cengage.com/
history/ayers/
ampassages4e

WARS AND RIVALRY FOR NORTH AMERICA

From 1680 to 1713, the Spanish, English, French, and many Indian nations battled for territory in North America. Despite the political and social turmoil of the 1680s and early 1690s, the English settlements were the most populous and dynamic European colonies on the continent. By the mid-1680s, New France had approximately ten thousand settlers, compared with more than seventy thousand in New England alone. Spanish Florida consisted chiefly of missions, run by forty Franciscan priests, and the fortified town of St. Augustine, which held about fourteen hundred Spanish, African, and Indian residents. Despite declining populations, many Native American peoples remained powerful in eastern North America, in particular the Five Nations of the Iroquois in New York.

In the late seventeenth century, the three primary areas of dispute on the continent were Florida and Guale (later Georgia), Louisiana and Texas, and Canada. Conflict occurred against the backdrop of two long European wars, the War of the League of Augsburg, 1689–1697, and the War of the Spanish Succession, 1702–1713 (respectively known as King William's War and Queen Anne's War to the English colonists).

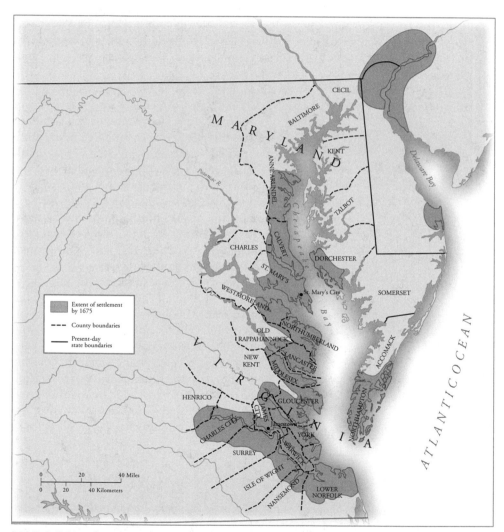

MAP 3.3 North America in 1700.

Significant change had occurred in North America since the early 1600s. Along the Atlantic coast, the English now had settlements from Maine (part of Massachusetts) to South Carolina. As the English population expanded, Native Americans declined, with many groups absorbed into other nations, such as the Catawbas of South Carolina.

Florida and
Guale

Beginning in 1680, the English colonists of South Carolina decided to take advantage of smoldering unrest among the mission
Indians of Guale and Florida to attack the Spanish colony. The
Native Americans had rebelled against forced labor and efforts to stamp out their traditional religions. They had killed Spanish missionaries and destroyed property, but
had not closed the missions altogether. The Carolinians raided Guale and Florida with
no humanitarian motives to assist the Indians. In fact, a chief reason for attacking the
Spanish missions was to capture Native Americans to sell as slaves in the West Indies.
The English also wanted to control the deerskin trade in the Southeast.

By 1686, the Carolinians had thrust the missionaries out of Guale. Then in 1704,
during Queen Anne's War, an army under former Carolina governor James Moore
crushed the missions in Apalachee. The Carolinians obtained help from their trading partners, the Yamassees, and from many of the mission Indians, who resented
Spanish oppression. Moore's troops inflicted brutal torture, burning people alive. The
surviving Apalachees dispersed, losing their identity as a nation. The Spanish retained
St. Augustine and a fort they built at Pensacola in 1698, but lost control of Guale and
most of Florida.

Louisiana and
Texas

The Spanish erected their fort at Pensacola Bay in response to
French efforts to establish a colony in Louisiana. At risk, the
Spanish knew, were their silver mines in Mexico and domina-
tion of the Gulf of Mexico. In 1682, René Robert Cavelier, **Sieur de La Salle**, had explored the Mississippi River from New France to the gulf, naming the territory
Louisiana in honor of King Louis XIV. La Salle sailed to France, then returned to set
up a colony. However, he miscalculated the location of the Mississippi, instead building Fort St. Louis in Texas, near Matagorda Bay. The colony quickly dissolved from
disease, loss of ships, and attacks by Karankawa Indians; in 1687, La Salle's own men
murdered him.

The French incursion in the Gulf of Mexico inspired the Spanish to expand their
settlements in the borderlands. In 1690, they founded missions among the Caddo people of eastern Texas and western Louisiana, from whom they took the Caddo word
Tejas or *Texas,* meaning "friends." Three years later, when the Caddos blamed the
friars for bringing smallpox, the friars fled. The Spanish abandoned Texas until the
French once again entered the area.

In 1699, Pierre LeMoyne, Sieur d'Iberville, resumed the French search for
the mouth of the Mississippi River, which was difficult to locate in the muddy
Mississippi Delta. Iberville found the river's mouth by accident, then built forts at
Biloxi Bay and on the Mississippi to establish French possession. Spain might have
forced the French out of Louisiana with quick action, but in 1700, the grandson of
French King Louis XIV took the Spanish throne; the two nations became allies against
the English, Dutch, and Austrians in the War of the Spanish Succession.

Although the French–Spanish alliance gave Louisiana a chance to develop without interference from New Spain, the colony grew slowly. In 1708, about a hundred
white soldiers and settlers lived in Louisiana. They obtained food, deerskins, and the
right to occupy the land from local Native Americans by exchanging firearms and
other goods. Relations between the French and Indians were not trouble free, however.
In 1715, for example, after Natchez Indians killed four French traders, the colonists

literally demanded the assassins' heads. When the Natchez failed to execute all of the perpetrators, the French murdered Indian hostages and required the Natchez to accept a fortified trading post on their land.

Canada   Conflict developed in the north when the Iroquois confederation attacked New France to stop French fur trading in the Ohio Valley and Illinois. The Iroquois defeated New France in 1683, but war continued as the English, French, and Native Americans struggled over trade routes and territory. The outbreak of King William's War in 1689 fueled the contest, as the Five Nations attacked settlements in Canada, while the French and their Indian allies destroyed English frontier outposts from New York to Maine. New England troops took Port Royal in Acadia but failed to conquer Quebec. Though the European belligerents agreed in the Peace of Ryswick (1697) to return to prewar status in North America, the Canadians won an important victory over the Iroquois and their English allies. The Five Nations signed a neutrality treaty in 1701. Frustrated by New York's failure to provide reinforcements, they ended their alliance with the English. New France then developed trade, religious missions, and agricultural settlements in the Great Lakes and Illinois Territory.

The renewal of hostilities between the English and French in 1702 with Queen Anne's War again brought raids on the New England frontier. In 1704, the Canadians and Native Americans attacked Deerfield, Massachusetts, burning houses and barns, killing inhabitants, and taking many captives. The English once again took Port Royal but called off an attack on Quebec when they lost nine hundred men in storms on the St. Lawrence River. This time, however, the peace treaty gave the victory to England (which had joined with Scotland in 1707 to form Great Britain). In North America, the **Treaty of Utrecht** (1713) ceded Nova Scotia (formerly Acadia), Newfoundland, and control of the Hudson Bay territory to the British. Yet they had failed to oust France from North America.

THE ENTRENCHMENT OF SLAVERY IN BRITISH AMERICA

Despite wars, rebellions, and witch hysteria, the most significant development in British North America during the late seventeenth and early eighteenth century was large-scale investment in enslaved Africans. The decisions of thousands of individual colonists to purchase men, women, and children who had been seized from their homelands in Africa left an indelible imprint on American society and culture. The slave buyers could not foretell the monumental effects of their actions. They responded to economic conditions: their need for workers, the declining availability of white servants, and the developing Atlantic slave trade.

Adopting   How could people who increasingly prized their own freedom—
Slavery   who had braved a treacherous ocean voyage to find opportunity
                           in a new land—deprive other human beings of liberty, and often
life itself? The answer lies in traditional English culture and the colonists' perceived economic needs.

The English, like other Europeans, believed that hierarchies existed in human society and, indeed, all of nature. Humans were superior to animals, Christians superior to "heathens." English language and culture also differentiated sharply between white and black, with whiteness suggesting purity and good, blackness imbued with filth and sin. The English compared their light skin with the Africans' darker brown color, and judged the latter to be inferior. In African religion, social customs, dress, and political organization, the Europeans found serious deficiencies, just as they had found deficiencies among Native Americans. The people of sub-Saharan Africa, the English thought, were lower on the scale of humanity than they were and could justifiably be enslaved. The example of the Portuguese, Spanish, and—most recently—the Dutch, who had fabricated the Atlantic slave trade over the previous two centuries, made the decision to buy Africans seem natural. The mainland English colonists could also look to their countrymen in the West Indies, where thousands of African slaves, outnumbering whites, toiled in sugar fields.

Despite this cultural context, colonists viewed their investment in slaves as an economic decision. In Virginia and Maryland, planters purchased Africans because they needed large numbers of workers to grow tobacco. Chesapeake settlers had learned that Native Americans, who easily escaped enslavement and died in catastrophic numbers, would not fill their labor needs. White servants filled the gap until about 1675. Many young Englishmen, and fewer women, had willingly signed up to work for three or more years in return for passage and rights to fifty acres of land. In the last quarter of the century, however, the supply of English servants declined in Maryland and Virginia. Economic conditions improved in England, while good tobacco land became scarce. Bacon's Rebellion taught Chesapeake elites the danger of importing thousands of white servants under these circumstances. With the founding of the Carolinas, New Jersey, and Pennsylvania, where land was plentiful, servants had a wider range of options.

Chesapeake planters searching for an alternative labor supply turned to African slaves. Population figures for Virginia and Maryland demonstrate graphically the result of individual decisions. In 1660, only nine hundred blacks resided in the Chesapeake, some of whom had come as servants and were free. Two decades later, their number had grown to forty-three hundred; by 1720, blacks composed one-fifth of the population. A similar increase occurred in the Carolinas (primarily South Carolina), where 38 percent of the residents in 1720 were African slaves. The situation was different in New England, where only 2 percent of the population was enslaved, and in the middle colonies (New York, New Jersey, Pennsylvania, and Delaware), where about one resident in ten suffered perpetual bondage.

The Slave Trade   English entry into the Atlantic slave trade helped spur the transition to an African work force. Though smugglers like John Hawkins had interloped earlier in the Spanish trade, England officially became involved in selling human beings in 1663. Charles II granted a monopoly to supply captives to the English colonies first to the Company of Royal Adventurers, then in 1672 to the **Royal African Company**. When the companies could not meet the demand of labor-hungry colonists, smugglers got involved, so in 1698, the Crown abandoned the monopoly, opening the slave trade to any English merchant who wanted to participate.

As a result, the supply of Africans in the English colonies soared and slave prices declined, thus encouraging colonists to invest in even more black labor.

The experience of enslavement and transit across the Atlantic Ocean was dehumanizing and perilous. Probably half of those sold into slavery died while still in Africa before transport or during the Atlantic passage. Approximately three-quarters of those taken to English North America came from the area of West Africa between Senegambia and the Bight of Biafra, with the remainder coming mostly from Angola. As European sea captains made successive trips to the coast, African traders had to reach farther and farther into the continent to find enough people to enslave. Some captives marched five hundred miles or more to the sea in "coffles," the term given to the files of shackled prisoners. On the coast, they were confined in enclosures called barracoons, often exposed to the sun for long periods without adequate food and drink. When a ship arrived, according to a Dutch trader, Willem Bosman, in 1700, the Africans were lined up on shore,

> where, by our surgeons . . . they are thoroughly examined, even to the small-est member, and that naked both men and women, without the least distinction or modesty. Those that are approved as good, are set on one side; and the lame or faulty are set by as invalids, which are here called *mackrons*: these are such as are above five and thirty years old, or are maimed in the arms, legs or feet; have lost a tooth, are grey-haired, or have films over their eyes; as well as all those which are affected with any venereal distemper, or several other diseases.

For the Africans chosen for transport, the horror had only begun. The Europeans branded them with the insignia of the company—for example, slaves of the Royal African Company had their skins burned with the letters "DY," for James, duke of York. Then followed the voyage across the Atlantic, called the **middle passage**, which could take from three weeks to more than three months, depending on the weather and destination. Ships normally carried rations for three months, so severe weather could mean starvation. Weather permitting, the captives spent their days on deck— the men in chains, the women and children unrestrained. At night, and around the clock in bad weather, slaves occupied spaces about the size of coffins in the hold of the ship, where temperatures could soar. Disease was often rampant. Some slaves attempted suicide by jumping overboard or refusing to eat: the latter was so common that traders invested in a tool called the speculum oris to force open a person's mouth.

Africans also rebelled violently, attacking the white captain and crew and occa-sionally taking over the ship. Because they were unfamiliar with ocean navigation, mutineers had the best hope of success when the ship was still in African waters and large numbers could carry out the revolt, escaping to shore. When rebels failed, pun-ishment was swift and brutal. The slave trader Bosman described an incident when a sea captain placed an extra anchor in the ship's hold. The enslaved Africans,

> unknown to any of the ship's crew, possessed themselves of a hammer, with which, in a short time they broke all their fetters in pieces upon the anchor:
>
> > After this, they came above deck, and fell upon our men, some of whom they grievously wounded, and would certainly have mastered the ship, if a French and English ship had not very fortunately happened to lie by us; who perceiving by our firing a distressed-gun, that something was in disorder on board, immediately

came to our assistance with shallops and men, and drove the slaves under deck: notwithstanding which, before all was appeased, about twenty of them were killed. The Portuguese have been more unlucky in this particular than we; for in four years they lost four ships in this manner.

Upon arrival in America, the Africans faced the ordeal of sale by auction or pre-arranged contract. They were stripped naked once again and examined for disease and physical defects. Because the greatest need was for strong field hands who would provide years of labor, plantation owners paid the highest prices for healthy young men in their prime. Buyers paid less for women, children, and older men. For both the Africans and their owners, the year following debarkation was most critical. During this period of seasoning, Africans endured serious illness and high mortality from the new disease environment.

Systems of Slavery in British North America As more and more Africans arrived, colonial assemblies instituted **black codes** to define slavery and control the black population. Before 1660, Maryland had officially sanctioned perpetual bondage, but Virginia moved more slowly. Enough flexibility existed in Virginia society to allow black servants to gain freedom, earn their livelihoods, and in some cases acquire land. In the 1660s, however, Virginia joined Maryland in enacting laws that recognized differences in the terms of white servants and African slaves. By law, slavery lasted a person's lifetime, descended from mother to child, and was the normal status of blacks but never whites.

In the late seventeenth and early eighteenth centuries, Virginia and Maryland created clearly articulated caste systems based on perceptions of race. Skin color denoted status: all Africans and their descendants encountered severe discrimination, whether enslaved or free. The Virginia assembly ruled that any master who killed a slave during punishment was not guilty of a felony. Conversely, no black person, slave or free, could strike a white, even in self-defense. Virginia lawmakers made emancipation difficult to obtain. Evolving black codes banned interracial marriage, forbade owners from releasing their slaves except in special cases, and restricted enslaved blacks from traveling without permission, marrying legally, holding property, testifying against whites, or congregating in groups. Over the course of the eighteenth century, other British colonies passed similar codes that ranged from fairly moderate New England laws to a harsh regime in Carolina, keyed in large part to the density of the black population.

In the life of an African slave, these laws had force, but more direct was the power of the master over work and family. To be a slave meant that someone else possessed your body and could command your daily activities. The owner chose your job; he or she decided whether your children would stay with you or be sold. During off-hours, however, Africans generally maintained autonomy in religion, social customs, and family life.

The work Africans and native-born African Americans performed varied by region. In the Chesapeake and Carolina, most slaves spent long hours planting, weeding, and harvesting tobacco, corn, and rice. A farm's production depended largely on the number of workers tending the crop. Over time, as the southern black population increased naturally and importation continued, the supply of labor became more plentiful. Plantation owners assigned slaves to different tasks, though most still raised the staple crop. Some men became drivers and artisans; some women served as nurses, cooks, and spinners. Both women and men performed domestic service. At the same time, female slaves were responsible for the household needs of their own families, including food preparation, laundry, and sewing.

Agricultural production in the middle colonies and New England centered on grains and livestock, which demanded less labor than tobacco or rice, so most parts of the northern countryside had relatively few slaves. Exceptions included New York and neighboring eastern New Jersey, which had difficulty attracting European immigrants; thus, well-to-do farmers purchased large numbers of Africans to work their land. The largest slaveholder in New Jersey was probably Colonel Lewis Morris of Shrewsbury, who employed more than sixty slaves at his plantation and ironworks. In Rhode Island's Narragansett region, some plantation owners held as many as fifty blacks. Most northern slaves lived in the port towns, however, where women worked as cooks and household servants and men labored at crafts, domestic service, and as shipbuilders and sailors. Boston, New York, and Philadelphia merchants imported Africans as part of the West Indies trade. In New York City, blacks were about one-fifth of the population and in Boston and Philadelphia about one-tenth.

A source of comfort to slaves who had lost their African homelands and kin was to establish new families in America. Slaves achieved some autonomy from their masters by creating families and kinship networks. All knew, however, that owners could destroy loving relationships by selling away spouses, children, brothers, and sisters. The ability of blacks to form families changed over time and varied from one region to another. High mortality and a skewed sex ratio prevented many African-born men from marrying and having children. In the disease-ridden West Indies and northern cities like Philadelphia, mortality was so high that colonists had to keep importing Africans to avoid population decline. In the Chesapeake colonies, however, natural population growth began with the first generation of native-born slaves. African American women had more children than their African mothers had, creating communities of slaves on large plantations. Whereas most of the first Africans dwelled in white households with just a few blacks, their offspring, known as "country-born" slaves, lived with parents, brothers, and sisters. The third generation lived with grandparents and cousins as well.

Resistance and Rebellion   For many slaves, family and kin helped to reduce their feelings of despair; for others, nothing relieved the pain of lifetime bondage. Many resisted their masters' power by staging slowdowns; pretending illness; destroying crops and tools; or committing theft, arson, assault, or murder. Newly arrived Africans were especially likely to rebel against their new status, often by running away. Slaves who were sold away from their families frequently escaped to rejoin them. Men ran away in greater numbers than women, who, as mothers, found it difficult to escape with children in tow.

Although slaves in the English West Indies often rebelled, blacks in the mainland colonies rarely took the ultimate step of armed insurgency, primarily because they were so outnumbered by whites. Before 1713, West Indian blacks staged seven full-scale revolts; their large population made success seem possible. In Barbados in 1675, for example, conspirators planned to take over the island, installing an elderly slave, Cuffee, as king. When whites got wind of the plot, they burned alive or beheaded thirty-five blacks. On mainland North America, just one slave revolt occurred by the early 1700s. In New York City in 1712, about twenty slaves set fire to a building, attacking the white men who came to extinguish it. Nine whites were killed, and terror spread up and down the Atlantic coast. As in the case of later slave revolts and conspiracies, the revenge wreaked on the black community surpassed any violence the rebels had committed. In the wake of the New York revolt, thirteen slaves were hanged, three burned at the stake, and one tortured on the wheel (an instrument used to stretch and disjoint its victims), and another starved to death in chains; six committed suicide to avoid execution.

Early Abolitionists As slavery became entrenched in North America, a few white colonists questioned its morality. They feared slave rebellions and abhorred the violence needed to enslave Africans, transport them to the colonies, and keep them in bondage. Slavery was morally repugnant, they believed, because all humans are equal in the eyes of God. One of the American opponents of perpetual bondage was Samuel Sewall, a Boston judge, who wrote in 1700, "It is most certain that all Men, as they are the Sons of Adam . . . have equal Right unto Liberty, and all other outward Comforts of Life."

Quakers also spoke out publicly against the institution. Certainly not all Friends were abolitionists—in Pennsylvania and New Jersey before 1720, a large proportion of the Quaker elite owned slaves—but a few interpreted Quaker ideals to mean that human bondage reeked with sin. According to John Hepburn of New Jersey, for example, slavery violated the Golden Rule to do unto others as you wish others to do unto you. Whereas owners got rich without physical labor, wore fine-powdered wigs and great-coats, and their wives and children similarly lived well, slaves endured beatings, wore rags, and slept in the ashes of the fire. In the context of rising importation throughout the colonies, however, the protests of Sewall, Hepburn, and a few other critics had little effect.

ECONOMIC DEVELOPMENT IN THE BRITISH COLONIES

Despite differences in agriculture, labor, and commerce from one region to another, the mainland colonies were all part of the Atlantic economy, dominated by the staple crops of sugar, tobacco, and rice. The developing mercantile economies of New England and the mid-Atlantic region depended heavily on the slave system, because their chief market was providing food for the multitudes of blacks laboring on West Indies sugar plantations.

Northern Economies Family farms and dependence on the sea characterized New England's economy. When agriculture failed to provide a lucrative staple crop, traders turned to fishing and shipping. With rocky, generally poor soil and a cool climate, the region could not grow a profitable commercial crop like tobacco or sugar, so rural New England families raised livestock, wheat, rye, Indian corn, peas, other vegetables, and fruit. They ate most of what they produced—a fairly monotonous diet of brown bread, boiled or baked peas, boiled meat and vegetables, and dark beer or apple cider—within their families and communities.

Fishing and shipping developed as important industries during the seventeenth century. The New England fishers initially sold their catch, in return for manufactured goods such as shoes, textiles, glass, and metal products, to London merchants, who sent the fish to Spain, Portugal, and the Wine Islands, off the coast of Africa

The fishing industry spurred the growth of maritime trade, as New England merchants recognized even greater profits to be made by trading directly with the Wine Islands and the West Indies. They formed partnerships among themselves and with English merchants, encouraging a local shipbuilding industry. The New Englanders exported fish, barrels, and other wood products. They imported wine, fruit, and salt from the Wine Islands, and rum, molasses, sugar, dyes, and other goods from the Caribbean. Soon, aided by the Navigation Acts, they were the chief carriers of goods along the North American coast, exchanging enslaved Africans and rum distilled from West Indies molasses for Pennsylvania wheat and livestock, Chesapeake tobacco, North Carolina tar and turpentine, and South Carolina rice. The credits they earned in shipping were as significant as the value of New England products sold in the trade.

The economy of the middle colonies resembled New England's in a number of ways but was much more prosperous agriculturally. With plenty of good land, farmers raised wheat and livestock commercially, purchasing servants and some slaves to supplement family labor. The region had two ports: one at New York City and the other at Philadelphia. Though neither city matched Boston in population or commercial importance before 1750, both quickly surpassed the Massachusetts seaport after that date. New York merchants maintained links with Amsterdam, the Dutch West Indies, and New Spain even after the English takeover in 1664. Philadelphia Quakers exploited their connections with Friends in other ports, especially in England and the West Indies.

Life in the Seaports

Maritime trade encouraged the development of port cities in the British provinces: Boston, New York, Philadelphia, and Charleston. Until 1750, merchants of Boston and other seaport towns in Massachusetts and Rhode Island dominated colonial trade. The ports thrived because they forged commercial links between farmers and external dealers, housing the markets through which imports and exports flowed. The maritime industry itself created demand for shipbuilders, suppliers of provisions, rope and sail makers, carters, dockworkers, and sailors.

Commercial growth brought social change, distinguishing an urban lifestyle from the countryside. Some merchants became fabulously wealthy from transatlantic and coastal trade. They spent their income conspicuously, building costly mansions, purchasing enslaved Africans as household servants, and wearing expensive clothes. They lived comfortably, with servants and slaves to do their menial chores. Other city dwellers were much less fortunate because they earned minimal wages or lacked employment. Port cities stimulated both affluence and dire poverty. They attracted many people who hoped to make their fortunes, or at least a decent living, but died with little more than the clothes on their backs. Maritime commerce frequently suffered disruption from war, bad weather, and economic downturns. Seamen and artisans, dependent on overseas trade, could expect little work during the winter, when few ships sailed. City folk were also at greater risk of death than those who lived in the country: some arriving ships spread smallpox and other diseases to the dense urban populations. The towns lacked adequate sanitation facilities, so garbage and waste cluttered streets, polluting the water supply.

As trade expanded, sailors became an important segment of the labor force. They were a varied lot. Some went to sea only part time, to supplement the income of their farms. Others chose seafaring as a career, dividing their time between shipboard and the taverns and boardinghouses of port towns along the Atlantic coast. Some had no choice in the matter, for they were enslaved Africans whose masters purchased them to work on the ships.

Sailors led a difficult and dangerous life. Crews on ordinary merchant ships were small, so seamen worked long hours loading and unloading the ship, maintaining the rigging and sails, and pumping water from the bilge, a backbreaking job. The organization of labor on board was hierarchical, with power descending from the captain to mates, to specialists like ship carpenter and surgeon, to seamen. Discipline could be harsh. The crewmen had little hope of moving up through the ranks, for captains were generally from affluent families, often merchants and part-owners of their ships. Instead, the more common fate of an ordinary "Jack Tar" was early death or disability from shipwreck, combat with enemies or pirates, and such occupational hazards as falling overboard, broken bones, scurvy, rheumatism, and hernias (the "bursted belly" as they called it).

When conditions on ship became insufferable, the seamen rebelled, sometimes deserting the ship at the next port. Most radically, they mutinied and, if successful, sometimes became pirates. As pirates, they plundered merchant vessels and port towns, sharing the proceeds evenly among themselves, electing officers, and recruiting much larger crews than could be found on merchant ships. With eighty or more men on a pirate ship of average size, compared with fifteen on a comparable merchant vessel, each had much less work to do. One pirate, Joseph Mansfield, admitted in 1722 that "the love of Drink and a Lazy Life" were "Stronger Motives with him than Gold."

Plantation Economies in the Chesapeake and South Carolina From 1675 to 1720, tobacco remained king in Maryland and Virginia, and planters increasingly purchased enslaved Africans instead of white servants. The wealth of plantation owners grew with each child born to a slave mother. At the same time, the richest planters bought up the land of small farmers who found it difficult to compete with the slaveholders. The wealthiest man in early-eighteenth-century Virginia was Robert Carter of Lancaster County, called "King" Carter. A slave trader and land speculator, he parlayed his inheritance of £1,000 and 1,000 acres into an estate of £10,000 in cash, 300,000 acres of land, and more than seven hundred slaves. Carter, with his relatives and friends, formed a tightly knit group of Chesapeake gentry.

In 1720, and throughout the rest of the century, Chesapeake society was hierarchical. At the bottom of the social structure were African and country-born slaves who owned no property and had little hope for freedom. Above them were the non-landholding whites, perhaps 40 to 50 percent of white families, who rented land and owned a horse or two, some cows, a few pigs, tools, and some household goods, but rarely held bound servants or slaves. They lived in shanties and ate from wooden dishes rather than from pottery. Their incomes from tobacco were so meager that they had trouble paying taxes and rent. Often they were in debt to the local merchant-planter for needed manufactured goods, such as ammunition, fabric, shoes, and tools.

Maryland Planter's House

This is a reconstruction of a typical Chesapeake colonist's house at the Godiah Spray tobacco plantation at historic St. Mary's City, Maryland. Most dwellings in the seventeenth-century Chesapeake were impermanent structures of wood. Many had only one room, without glass windows or wooden floors. They decayed quickly from the hot, humid climate and insects. Scholars have used archaeological evidence and historical documents to determine the size and construction of these cabins.

(Courtesy of Historic St. Mary's City)

Despite the growth of large plantations in Virginia and Maryland between 1675 and 1720, more than one-third of white families lived in small cabins and rented rather than owned land. The men who supported Nathaniel Bacon came from this group. They rarely owned servants or slaves to help grow tobacco. They possessed some livestock and agricultural tools, but most used wooden rather than pottery dishes, and lacked bed and table linens, knives, forks, spices, and books.

Next up in the hierarchy were small landholders whose incomes allowed them to live more comfortably, with pottery, more furniture, and nicer (though still quite small) homes. If they owned several slaves, which few did before 1720, they worked alongside them in the fields and house.

In the upper 5 percent were the gentry, who owned many slaves, held large acreages, and usually acted as merchants as well. They served as intermediaries for smaller planters, selling tobacco abroad and importing manufactured goods. In this way, they became creditors of their poorer neighbors, who often owed them substantial debts. In Maryland and Virginia, the merchant-planters conducted trade without the development of port cities. Ships docked at their plantations along the many tributaries of the Chesapeake Bay to load casks of tobacco and unload imported goods. Tobacco required relatively little processing: workers dried the leaves in sheds, removed large fibers, and packed the tobacco in casks made by local coopers. Merchant-planters and rural artisans, including slaves, provided goods and services for the community without centralizing their activities in towns. Even the two capitals, Williamsburg and Annapolis, remained small throughout the colonial period.

Situated in a semitropical climate, South Carolina developed a plantation economy that was linked to, and in many ways resembled, the West Indies. Most early settlers in South Carolina, both black and white, came from the English colony of Barbados, where land was in short supply and almost entirely devoted to sugar cultivation. White planters claimed Carolina headrights, then sold corn, salt beef, salt pork, barrel staves, firewood, and Native American slaves to the islands. South Carolinians enslaved the Indians they captured in raids throughout the American Southeast and obtained them from native traders in exchange for guns, ammunition, and cloth. Native Americans also supplied deerskins, which found a ready market in England, though they were not valued quite so highly as Canadian furs.

As with the northern fur trade between Europeans and Indians, the Carolinians used English trade goods to establish alliances with native groups. Such major trading partners as the **Yamassees**, however, quickly discovered that white merchants used theft, violence, rum, and false weights to gain unfair advantage. In 1715, in league with the Creeks, the Yamassees attacked white settlements, nearly destroying the colony. The whites saved themselves by getting help from the Cherokees. The Yamassees and Creeks were defeated, their people killed, enslaved, or forced to migrate from the coastal area. White South Carolinians then expropriated their lands.

The settlers wanted the new territory because they had found an export that became much more lucrative than provisions, enslaved Indians, or deerskins. Planters had experimented with a variety of crops—tobacco, cotton, sugar, silk, wine grapes, and ginger—but rice proved most successful in the wet lowlands of the Carolina coast. Also significant were the skills in rice production that many Africans brought to America. Rice exports expanded rapidly in South Carolina, reaching 1.5 million pounds per year by 1710 and nearly 20 million pounds by 1730. The chief markets for rice were Europe and the West Indies. Carolinians first sent their crop directly to Portugal, but in 1705 Parliament added rice to the list of enumerated products that had to be shipped to England first, taxes paid, and then reexported to Europe. The colonists argued that in the case of southern Europe, this detour made their crop arrive too late for Lent, when much of it was consumed. In response, Parliament allowed South Carolina after 1731 to trade directly with Spain, Portugal, and Mediterranean Europe, but the larger share of the rice crop, which went to northern Europe, still required transit through Britain.

The conversion to rice transformed South Carolina society, affecting the black population with special force. Before planters adopted full-scale rice production, slaves had performed a variety of jobs in crafts, timber, livestock, and agriculture. Their workloads were moderate, especially in comparison with the West Indies. Rice monoculture changed this situation altogether, and planters imported thousands of Africans. In the coastal areas north and south of Charleston, blacks reached 70 percent of the population in the 1720s. With high importation and harsher working conditions, death rates surged. As in the Chesapeake, wealthy planters bought up neighboring farms while investing heavily in slaves. They created large rice plantations, worked by growing numbers of African slaves. Small planters moved to the periphery, where they raised grain and livestock for the rice district and the Caribbean. The rice planters found the Carolina lowlands isolated and unhealthy, so they left their plantations part of the year. However, the Carolinians supervised their plantations directly—unlike British West Indian sugar planters who fled to England, leaving management in the care of overseers.

Charleston, where the rice planters spent at least several weeks each year, was the fourth largest city in the British colonies. The port channeled the trade in provisions, deerskins, rice, slaves, and English manufactures. Charleston remained smaller than Boston, Philadelphia, and New York because British and New England shippers controlled its trade. Without a strong merchant community, the South Carolina seaport lacked the impetus for shipbuilding and associated crafts.

CONCLUSION

Between 1675 and 1720, the people of North America shed blood over territory, trade, and political autonomy. As English, French, and Spanish settlers expanded into new regions, they established commerce, but also spread smallpox and fostered conflict among the Indians. The Narragansetts and Wampanoags of New England waged a costly war in 1675-1676, while the Pueblos successfully, though temporarily, expelled the Spanish from New Mexico. Native Americans throughout the continent, weakened by disease and war, yielded to the Europeans. During Bacon's Rebellion and the Revolutions of 1689, governments in Virginia, Massachusetts, New York, and Maryland faced challenges from rival elites and their discontented, lower-class allies.

By the turn of the eighteenth century, the Spanish had reconquered New Mexico and infiltrated Texas, France had moved into the Great Lakes region and Louisiana, and the English had pushed out in many directions. To develop their economies, the British colonists imported Africans in large numbers. With the growth of plantation slave economies in the South and maritime commerce in the North, British North America developed distinctive regional characteristics. Yet in 1720, the Atlantic seaboard colonies had much in common: their settlement by enterprising men and women, regard for English rights of property and representation, and governance within the British imperial system. During the next half century, the importance of these commonalities would become clear.

CHAPTER REVIEW, 1675–1720

- The period between 1675 and 1720 was characterized by white expansion in North America. The French established settlements in the Great Lakes region and Louisiana, and Quaker William Penn founded the colony of Pennsylvania as a "holy experiment" in peaceful Native American–white relations.
- European expansion generated widespread Native American resistance to white encroachment and sparked armed conflicts such as King Philip's War and the Pueblo Revolt.
- The late seventeenth century was a time of great domestic turmoil; the colonies witnessed uprisings such as Bacon's Rebellion and hysteria during the Salem witch trials.
- James II's assumption of the British throne sparked resistance to royal control and, in the case of Protestant colonists, against Catholic rule.
- The institution of slavery became entrenched in colonial society as trade in enslaved people and staple crops became central to both northern and southern economies

◀︎꜍ Looking Back

Chapter 3 looks at how the English colonies expanded in population between 1675 and 1720 by approximately 400 percent; they faced challenges from Native Americans, settler unrest, and efforts by the Crown to consolidate authority. At the same time, the British provinces became full participants in the Atlantic trading system, importing thousands of enslaved Africans to work on southern plantations and in northern cities.

1. Why did New England Indians wage King Philip's War?
2. Why did Virginia freemen rise up in Bacon's Rebellion?
3. Were the revolutions of 1689 in Massachusetts, New York, and Maryland related or separate events?
4. Why did the English North American colonists adopt slavery?
5. What was the impact of European wars on North America?

Looking Ahead ꜍▶︎

Chapter 4 pursues the development of North America through the Seven Years' War, a time when the British colonies achieved greater political and economic maturity. Expansion of settlement put even greater pressure on Native Americans, and economic development entrenched slavery more firmly. Intellectual and religious trends such as the Enlightenment and Great Awakening crossed colonial boundaries, helping to create a shared American culture.

1. How did settler–Indian relations evolve after 1720?
2. How did Scots-Irish and German immigration in the eighteenth century compare with English settlement before 1700?
3. What was the impact of the Enlightenment on colonial thought and culture?

Go to the American Passages website at www.cengage.com/history/ayers/ampassages4e for additional review materials.

4

The Expansion of Colonial British America, 1720–1763

I n 1721, smallpox hit Boston viciously, infecting about six thousand residents and killing 844. Business stopped for several months, as almost every family battled the contagion. In many respects, this epidemic was unremarkable in the British American colonies: settlers and Native Americans alike had previously experienced the ravages of disease. But this time, one Puritan minister took an unprecedented step. Cotton Mather, who thirty years earlier had helped aggravate the Salem witch hysteria, encouraged a Boston doctor, Zabdiel Boylston, to test **inoculation**. Mather had learned from Onesimus, his African slave, and from English scientific papers that inoculation was used in Africa and Turkey to prevent smallpox epidemics. An experiment would be risky, for the procedure involved introducing the smallpox virus into the body, thereby giving the person what was usually (but not always) a mild case of the disease. Many doctors, as well as much of Boston's populace, condemned the proposal. Nevertheless, Dr. Boylston inoculated about 250 persons over the course of a year. Those who submitted to the procedure had a much lower death rate than Bostonians who contracted the disease naturally.

Mather was far ahead of his time in advancing the theory that disease was caused by an invasion of the body by viruses, which he called invisible "worms." Significantly, it was a minister, rather than a physician or scientist, who advanced this hypothesis. During the eighteenth century, science lacked the rigid boundaries of complexity and specialization that would later separate it from other fields of intellectual endeavor. American theologians and philosophers, as well as doctors, naturalists, and astronomers, read the latest scientific literature from England and Europe. The great divide between science and religion did not yet exist. Like many other theologians, Mather understood epidemics as God's punishment for sin. But he also believed inoculation was a divine gift, that people should use any means available to combat disease.

Mather's support for inoculation has been called the greatest contribution to medicine by an American during the colonial period. Certainly it represented change. The **Enlightenment**, a new intellectual movement, was spreading from Britain to the

CHAPTER TIMELINE

1720	Theodore Jacob Frelinghuysen begins revivals in New Jersey
1721–1722	Smallpox inoculation in Boston
1732	Founding of Georgia • Hat Act
1733	Molasses Act
1734	Jonathan Edwards starts revivals in Northampton, Massachusetts
1737	Walking Purchase in eastern Pennsylvania
1739	Stono Uprising in South Carolina
1739–1740	George Whitefield tours northern colonies
1739–1744	War of Jenkins' Ear
1740	James Oglethorpe leads invasion of Florida
1741	British attack on Cartagena
1744–1748	King George's War
1745	New Englanders conquer Louisbourg
1747	Boston riot against impressment
1750	Iron Act
1754	Defeat of Virginia militia at Fort Necessity • Albany Congress proposes plan for colonial unity
1754–1763	Seven Years' War
1755	Braddock's defeat near Fort Duquesne
1758	British capture Louisbourg
1760	British conquer Montreal, seizing control of Canada
1763	Pan-Indian war begins in Ohio Valley and Great Lakes region • Proclamation of 1763 outlaws white settlement west of the Appalachians • Paxton Boys revolt in Pennsylvania

colonies and bringing important changes. During the years 1720 to 1763, the British provinces experienced intellectual, religious, and social ferment as they continued to expand through North America. As new knowledge, beliefs, and consumer goods arrived from Europe, colonists from Maine to Georgia (founded in 1732) increasingly lived within a common cultural framework. With rising wealth, colonial elites supported colleges and purchased books and luxury goods. This common culture had important ties to England, yet was not altogether English, for immigrants from Scotland, Ireland, and the continent of Europe and slaves from Africa brought ideas and practices from their native lands. Immigration into the British colonies also promoted regional diversity, as the newcomers from Europe settled on the frontier from Pennsylvania to Georgia, and the numbers of enslaved Africans grew to 40 percent of the southern population. The Europeans came looking for land: when they set up farms in contested territory,

This icon will direct you to interactive activities and study materials on the American Passages website: www.cengage.com/history/ayers/ampassages4e

they provoked conflicts with the Native Americans, French, and Spanish, resulting in a series of wars that lasted a quarter-century. When the Seven Years' War ended in 1763, the British colonies took a great deal of pride in their contribution to the victory, offering it as evidence of their economic and political maturity within the empire.

INTELLECTUAL TRENDS IN THE EIGHTEENTH CENTURY

The willingness of Mather and Boylston to try inoculation showed important changes in the way people viewed their world. The Puritan clergyman's personal journey from witch-hunter in 1692 to medical investigator in 1721 reflected the growing inclination to find natural rather than supernatural causes for unexplained events. The Enlightenment blossomed first in Europe and then in America, encompassing political theory and philosophy as well as science. Though primarily intellectual, the Enlightenment had far-reaching effects, inspiring new technology as well as new concepts of human freedom. For Americans, its greatest significance lay in the acceptance of natural rights philosophy, which paved the way for independence and republican government.

Impact of Newton and Locke   In the late seventeenth century, two English theorists, **Isaac Newton** and **John Locke**, had challenged traditional notions that humans had no role in determining their fate, that they could only trust in God to rule the universe. They confronted this older view without denying the existence of God. Newton discovered universal laws that predictably govern the motion of planets, moons, and comets; the motion of falling bodies on earth (gravity); and the ebb and flow of tides. His work demonstrated that the universe operates according to fixed principles, which humans are capable of detecting and understanding. Locke built on Newton's breakthrough in his *Essay Concerning Human Understanding* (1690). Locke argued against the accepted belief in innate knowledge— that infants are born with ideas implanted by God in their minds. He contended that all knowledge is gained by experience, not preordained at birth. Humans are born with the ability to learn, to use their acquired knowledge to benefit society.

Locke, and the Enlightenment thinkers he inspired, believed in freedom and the possibility of human progress, in the right of people to improve the conditions in which they live. Science, of course, was an important means of such improvement. The English philosopher also had a major impact on eighteenth-century politics, in particular providing a theoretical basis for the American Revolution and the U.S. Constitution. In *Two Treatises on Civil Government* (1690), he argued that humans, according to natural law, had rights to life, liberty, and property. By social contract, they formed governments to guarantee those rights. If a state failed in its obligation, the people had the duty to rebel and establish a new government.

Education in the British Colonies   Throughout British North America, formal education beyond basic reading, writing, and arithmetic was rare, so few had read the works of Locke and Newton directly. After 1720, however, as newspapers became more available and reprinted articles from London, provincial readers gained greater familiarity with Enlightenment thought. Many colonists learned to read, though boys and girls spent much of their time learning the

Education and Gender

In colonial British America, the education of children varied by gender. Although most people in New England learned to read, colonists considered writing a separate skill (not linked to reading as it is today) and less crucial for everyone. Many people could not write even their signature, so they made a mark on legal documents; someone else then wrote the name next to the mark. According to a study of New England wills in 1660, 40 percent of men and 70 percent of women were unable to sign their names. By the time of the American Revolution, almost all New Englanders wrote a signature rather than a mark.

Throughout the British colonies, girls received less academic education than boys. In addition to reading, girls commonly learned sewing and knitting. Boys who planned to enter college attended grammar school from about age seven to fourteen, studying Latin, elementary Greek, and sometimes Hebrew. Latin was necessary for the professions: law, medicine, and the ministry.

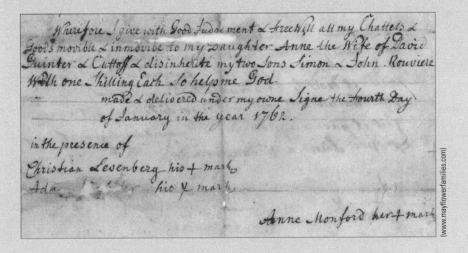

(www.mayflowerfamilies.com)

occupations they would pursue as adults. The availability of formal schooling varied widely by region, class, and gender. Nowhere did a system of universal, free, public education exist, though New England had some tax-supported schools. Everywhere, schools emphasized moral behavior and used religious texts.

New England made the greatest effort of the British colonies to educate its populace. In 1642, the Massachusetts legislature required parents and ministers to teach all children to read so they could obtain direct understanding of the Bible and the colony's laws. In 1647, the assemblymen ordered towns with at least fifty families to establish petty (elementary) schools, and those with one hundred or more families to maintain Latin grammar (secondary) schools. Connecticut and Plymouth passed similar legislation. Although some towns ignored the laws, most New England children learned to read, whether from their parents, at the town school, or at dame schools, where women in their homes taught young girls and boys for a fee.

South of New England, colonial governments did not require town schools. In the middle colonies, churches and private teachers offered instruction. Affluent Quaker and Anglican boys were most likely to obtain formal education, though after 1750, girls and poor boys, including African Americans, had better access to schools than previously. In the Chesapeake, with dispersed settlement, neither Maryland nor Virginia had many schools. Upper-class boys and girls had private tutors, while middling families in some localities pooled their resources to establish schools. Large numbers of poor whites obtained no education at all. Very few slaves learned to read and write, for owners thought these skills would breed discontent and enable slaves to forge passes, facilitating escape.

New England also surpassed other regions in higher education; the Puritans established Harvard College in Massachusetts in 1636 and Yale College in Connecticut in 1701. William and Mary, founded in Virginia in 1693, was the only other college in the British colonies before the 1740s. None of the colonial colleges admitted women. The Puritans intended Harvard to preserve classical learning and civilization, provide liberal education to the region's male elite, and ensure a supply of well-educated ministers. Harvard offered a curriculum of ethics, religion, logic, mathematics, Greek, Hebrew, rhetoric, and natural history (biology and geology). Most early graduates became clergymen; others went into medicine, public service, teaching, commerce, and agriculture.

The Growth of Science

After 1720, influenced by Scottish universities that quickly absorbed Enlightenment thinking into their curricula, American colleges expanded their course work to include French, English literature, philosophy, and science. They offered mathematics and what was then called **natural philosophy**—astronomy, physics, and chemistry. The colleges hired some of their faculty from Scotland and purchased scientific apparatus, including telescopes, sextants, clocks, and orreries, which demonstrate the motion of planets and moons within the solar system.

American professors of natural philosophy were part of a larger community of scholars centered in the prestigious Royal Society of London, which published *Philosophical Transactions,* a journal offering the latest scientific ideas and knowledge. This transatlantic community included academics like John Winthrop of Harvard College, as well as largely self-taught men like Benjamin Franklin and John Bartram. More than thirty colonists belonged to the Royal Society. Scientists took from the Enlightenment a commitment to experiment and observe natural phenomena to obtain information that would lead to human progress.

John Winthrop was the most renowned professor of natural philosophy in British America, with research interests in such wide-ranging subjects as sunspots, mathematics, earthquakes, and the weather. In 1761, he participated in an important international scientific effort to calculate the distance between the Earth and the sun, made possible by the transit of the planet Venus across the face of the sun. Venus had last crossed the sun in 1639, when no useful measurements had been made. Winthrop journeyed to Newfoundland to observe the transit. His data, combined with observations from the Cape of Good Hope, were inexact, but eight years later, scientists— including Winthrop—had another chance. This time, at least part of the transit could be viewed in the mainland British colonies. The stakes were high because another transit would not occur for 105 years. The data were again imprecise, but when combined with measurements from around the globe, they yielded results very close to the accepted distance of 93 million miles between the Earth and sun.

Other colonists contributed to understanding the physical world. Perhaps best known for his diplomacy and political leadership during the Revolutionary era, **Benjamin Franklin** has become a symbol of the American Enlightenment for his efforts to improve society through science, inventions, and civic organizations. Franklin was born in Boston, ran away at age seventeen from an apprenticeship with his older brother, and arrived in Philadelphia nearly penniless. He built a highly successful printing business, publishing a newspaper, books, and *Poor Richard's Almanack,* which gained a wide readership. Throughout his life, Franklin put the Enlightenment ideal of human progress into action. He founded a debating club to discuss politics, morals, and natural philosophy, and he helped establish the first American lending library, a hospital, and the College of Philadelphia. Franklin's experiments in electricity yielded information about its properties, including the basic concepts of "plus" and "minus." His inventions, which applied scientific principles to improving daily life, included bifocal eyeglasses, the lightning rod, and an iron stove that was more efficient than colonial fireplaces.

John Bartram, also of Pennsylvania, was the most energetic of American naturalists; his chief contribution to science was collecting specimens of New World plant life. In return for a yearly pension from the king and payment for seeds he sent to wealthy collectors in England, Bartram traveled up and down the eastern seaboard searching for new plants and animals. His efforts greatly expanded botanical knowledge of the Western Hemisphere, for he sent specimens to such scholars as Carl Linnaeus, the Swedish author of the modern classification system.

Another prominent American naturalist was Cadwallader Colden, a Scot who immigrated to the colonies after receiving his medical degree. Like many other well-educated doctors, Colden had broad interests in science. While serving as surveyor-general and lieutenant-governor of New York, he collected and classified plants in the neighborhood of his estate. He corresponded with European botanists, sending them specimens and descriptions. As their demands became overwhelming, Colden taught his daughter, Jane, how to classify according to Linnaeus's scheme. Her accurate descriptions and drawings earned high praise from Linnaeus, Bartram, and other naturalists.

Changes in Medical Practice

Just as Colden and other university-trained doctors were interested in many scientific fields, the practice of medicine itself attracted people of widely different backgrounds. Medicine was beginning to develop as a profession. During the colonial period, men with formal medical education comprised a small proportion of the people who provided care for disease, physical injury, and childbirth. Having completed formal course work abroad—the first medical school in the British colonies, located in Philadelphia, did not open until 1766—educated physicians were at the top of their profession and charged the highest fees. Consequently, they practiced primarily in cities. Below them were men who learned their craft as apprentices; though they assumed the title of doctor in the colonies, they were actually akin to the surgeon-apothecaries of Great Britain. As surgeons, they performed emergency procedures such as setting bones, amputating limbs, and removing superficial tumors but no major surgery. As apothecaries, they prepared and prescribed drugs for a variety of illnesses.

Female **midwives** traditionally attended at childbirth, treated the ill, and prescribed herbal remedies. Having learned their skills through informal apprenticeships and from witnessing the childbirths of neighbors and relatives, they received payment for their services. During the colonial period, childbirth was the province of women. As an expectant mother's labor began, she called together a group of women, presided over by the midwife, who assisted in the birth. In the early stages of her labor, the woman provided special refreshments, called "groaning beer" and "groaning cakes." The attendants helped her walk around and offered herbal teas or liquor to relieve the pain. In normal deliveries, the mother squatted on a "midwife's stool" or remained standing while supported by several women. If complications occurred, the midwife manipulated the infant manually but would not perform a cesarean section. In the worst cases, the midwife had to kill the child; sometimes the mother died. Without modern antibiotics, women faced the constant threat of infection during pregnancy and in the weeks following delivery.

In the last half of the eighteenth century, the practice of obstetrics changed. In 1762, **Dr. William Shippen, Jr.**, returned from studying medicine in England and Scotland to give lectures in anatomy to Philadelphia midwives and doctors. Soon he accepted only male students. Shippen established an obstetrical practice of his own, quickly attracting well-to-do patients who expected a higher level of care than they received from midwives. Affluent urban women were convinced that the male physicians offered a better chance for a safe, less painful delivery. The doctors' obstetrical training and their use of opiates and instruments such as forceps spelled progress to these women, inducing them to abandon the traditional woman-dominated rituals of childbirth. That the new obstetrics brought improvement is doubtful. The male doctors, faced with taboos against observing the private parts of ladies, attended their clients in darkened rooms, with the women lying in bed under covers. The physicians also lacked the means to prevent infection, and their use of bloodletting and opium could impede safe delivery. In any case, midwives continued to attend the great majority of women, those who lived in rural areas and the poor who could not afford the doctors' fees.

THE GREAT AWAKENING

As Enlightenment ideas gained sway, many Protestant ministers embraced Christian rationalism, a theology that stressed moral, rational behavior and the free will of individuals to lead their lives and achieve salvation. Some rationalists spoke of an impersonal God who had long ago created the universe to operate according to natural laws, rather than a loving or angry God who controlled a person's daily life. For many, the rationalist religion was comforting, because it included in the church all who tried to live decent Christian lives, not just those who believed they were saved. To others, however, Christian rationalism was heretical, for it rejected the Calvinist belief that salvation came from grace, as the gift of God, and that people must be saved to be full members of the church.

From the 1720s to the 1760s, ministers from various denominations called for the renewal of these beliefs in a series of religious revivals known as the **Great Awakening**. Several of the most important Awakeners brought the impetus for revival from Europe and Great Britain. Religious ferment convulsed British North America, spreading from the churches to threaten social and political authority.

Religious Diversity Before the Great Awakening
In 1720, the British provinces varied widely in religious and ethnic makeup. New England was the most homogeneous, for Massachusetts, New Hampshire, and Connecticut remained predominantly Puritan and of English descent. The established Puritan churches received tax support, but Anglicans, Baptists, and Quakers could also worship freely. Rhode Island, which still embraced the principles of religious liberty and separation of church and state, was home to various denominations, including Quakers, Baptists, and Separatists.

From their founding, the middle colonies offered an open door to people of various backgrounds. In the late seventeenth century, according to one report, residents of New York City spoke eighteen languages. In eastern New Jersey, Scottish Presbyterians, Dutch Reformed, New England Puritans, Baptists, and Quakers settled towns and plantations, and farther south, on both sides of the Delaware River, Native Americans, Dutch, Swedes, and Finns met the Quakers who accompanied William Penn. Philadelphia and its environs in the 1720s boasted organized meetings of many denominations. Though disputes occasionally arose between churches, the Quaker government upheld liberty of conscience throughout the colonial period.

With few towns in the Chesapeake, the established Anglican church suffered from southern rural conditions, and ministers in Virginia faced serious obstacles in meeting the spiritual needs of their scattered congregations. Only half of the Anglican churches had regular preachers. Few planters were interested in converting their African slaves, who kept—and passed on to their children—many traditional African beliefs. The colony's laws against nonconformity prevented most dissent, so only a few Presbyterians and Quakers worshipped openly. In Maryland, many Quakers and Roman Catholics retained their faith but suffered legal disabilities. The established Church of England in South Carolina was in better condition than in Virginia; some prosperous parishes could afford to pay their well-trained clergy adequately. Even so, Presbyterians, Baptists, Huguenots, and Quakers worshipped freely, for the proprietors had actively recruited dissenters to increase population and obtain their political support.

DOING HISTORY ONLINE

The Enlightenment and the Great Awakening

Based on Documents 1 through 4, in what ways do you think the Enlightenment and the Great Awakening complement each other? Do you see them as antagonistic toward each other at all? How?

 www.cengage.com/history/ayers/ampassages4e

The Great Awakening shattered the existing church structure of the colonies, as congregations wakened to the teachings and vigorous preaching style of revivalist, or New Light, ministers. Religious diversity grew in provinces where established churches, with government support, dominated religious life—especially Puritan churches in Connecticut and Massachusetts and the Anglican establishment in Virginia. As a result of the revivals, religious life in these colonies became more like that in Rhode Island, New York, and Pennsylvania.

Early Revivals in the Middle Colonies and New England

In 1720, New Jersey felt the first stirrings of the Great Awakening when Theodore Jacob Frelinghuysen emigrated from Holland to serve four churches in the Raritan Valley. He had been educated in Dutch Reformed pietism, which emphasized the importance of conversion and personal religious experience (or piety). Using an emotional, revivalist preaching style, he led many people to experience salvation. But Frelinghuysen created a split in the Dutch Reformed churches of New Jersey between his followers, who believed a person must experience God's saving grace before participating in church sacraments, and his opponents, who thought that a commitment to living a godly life was sufficient.

Next, revivals engulfed Presbyterian churches in New Jersey, as they adopted doctrines preached by Gilbert and John Tennent, the sons of William Tennent, a Scots-Irish immigrant and Presbyterian minister. The younger Tennents took pulpits in New Brunswick and Freehold, close to Frelinghuysen's congregations. Impressed by the Dutch Reformed pastor's style of preaching, they inspired revivals of their own. Meanwhile, in Neshaminy, Pennsylvania, the elder Tennent established a seminary, called the "Log College" by his critics, where many New Light ministers received training.

(The Granger Collection, New York)

George Whitefield. *George Whitefield, the itinerant English evangelist, had a spellbinding effect on his listeners, as portrayed here by John Wollaston.*

In Massachusetts, revivals began in 1734, when minister Jonathan Edwards of Northampton preached a series of sermons on salvation, inclining many of his parishioners to believe they were saved. They went through the process of self-judgment—first feeling despair as sinners who were damned to hell, then rejoicing in the conviction that God rescued them from this fate. Edwards wrote to a colleague that "this town never was so full of Love, nor so full of Joy, nor so full of distress as it has lately been." Over the next few years, the revival spread to other towns along the Connecticut River.

Revivalism Takes Fire

Beginning in 1739, the Great Awakening gained strength throughout the British mainland colonies after a young Anglican minister, **George Whitefield**, arrived from England to tour the middle colonies. Called the Grand Itinerant, he had a magnificent voice, ranging from a whisper to a roar, that could be heard by large crowds in fields and city streets. Benjamin Franklin calculated that twenty-five thousand people could easily hear the spectacular preacher at one time.

Whitefield found adherents across denominational lines and among native-born Americans and immigrants alike. In 1740, Jonathan Edwards invited Whitefield to Northampton, prompting the itinerant to travel through New England, where he attracted crowds as large as eight thousand in Boston. Other New Light ministers followed, including Gilbert Tennent and James Davenport, a Puritan preacher of Southold, Long Island.

Davenport took the Awakening to extremes, harshly attacking other pastors as "unconverted." In 1743, he instigated the burning of books written by well-known clergymen; a year later he repented this excess.

The full force of the Awakening hit the South later than New England and the Middle Atlantic states. During the 1740s, Presbyterian missionaries—men who received their education at Tennent's Log College—set up churches on the southern frontier. The new settlements were a fertile field for the revivalists because few regular clergy had migrated west. The more explosive Baptist revivals began in the 1750s, when itinerants traveled through Virginia and North Carolina making converts and forming churches. The Baptists believed that individuals should be saved before they were baptized. With their emotional religious style and challenge to the Anglican establishment in Virginia, they appealed particularly to ordinary white farm families and enslaved African Americans. Followers called each other "Sister" and "Brother," whether slave or free, affluent or poor. They refused to attend their local parish services and condemned many aspects of gentry culture, including horseracing, cockfights, elegant dress, and entertaining on Sunday. Lacking formal churches, Baptists met in fields and homes. The ministry was open to all, even women and slaves, with no requirement for college training.

The Awakening's Impact   The revivals proved to be socially divisive, and many communities split into two groups: the "New Lights" and the "Old Lights." The style of most New Light preachers was to give impassioned, extemporaneous sermons that contrasted dramatically with the closely reasoned sermons of their opponents, the rationalist Old Light ministers. New Lights believed that salvation was more important than religious training; they required a "saved" ministry, with a dynamic preaching style. Congregations responded by fainting, shrieking, and shedding tears. Old Light clergymen, who defended their advanced education in theology, Greek, Hebrew, and ethics, resented accusations that they were unsaved. In turn, they charged the revivalists with being unlearned.

As congregations broke apart, bitter disputes ensued over church property and tax support, spilling what had begun as a religious controversy into the courts and politics. Where strong established churches existed—as in Massachusetts, Connecticut, and Virginia—the New Lights challenged political as well as religious authority. In response, the Connecticut Assembly, for example, passed the Anti-Itinerancy Act, which made it illegal for a clergyman to preach in another's parish without his permission and repealed the 1708 law permitting religious dissent.

Higher education in the British colonies also felt the flames of revivalistic fervor. Yale College was at the center of the intense religious and political battles in

Connecticut. When the New Haven church separated, a large number of students, many of them studying for the ministry, followed the New Lights. They skipped classes to attend revivals, challenged Yale's curriculum, and questioned whether their teachers were saved. To suppress the student rebellion, Thomas Clap, head of the college, obtained permission from the Connecticut Assembly to expel any student who attended New Light services. Clap's opposition to the Awakening was not permanent, however, for by 1753, he himself had become a New Light. As in many other congregations, people eventually found ways to heal the bitterness and division that the Great Awakening had caused.

A more lasting effect of the revivals was the founding of new colleges. Until the mid-1740s, only Harvard, William and Mary, and Yale—all with ties to established churches—existed in the British colonies. The revivals created a need for different ministerial training. Between 1746 and 1769, the revivalists founded the College of New Jersey (now Princeton), the College of Rhode Island (Brown), Queen's College (Rutgers) in New Jersey, and Dartmouth College in New Hampshire. Anglicans established King's College (Columbia) in New York City, and a group of civic leaders, headed by Benjamin Franklin, started the College of Philadelphia (University of Pennsylvania) on a nonsectarian basis. Though each of these new schools except the College of Philadelphia was tied to a specific religious denomination, all accepted young men of various faiths. These new colleges taught traditional subjects, but also adopted the new curricula in mathematics, science, and modern languages.

CULTURAL DIVERSITY AND EXPANSION

Between 1720 and 1760, the population of British North America grew from 472,000 to 1.6 million. Much of this growth came from natural increase, but new arrivals also spurred population growth, as thousands of Germans and Scots-Irish immigrated and slave traders continued to import blacks.

The newcomers brought ideas, religious beliefs, skills, and ways of life that significantly altered the cultural mix of the British colonies. Some played important roles in spreading the Enlightenment; others helped start the Great Awakening. The immigrants from the European continent and the British Isles sought a new beginning in "the best poor man's country": many disembarked in the middle colonies, traveling west to settle the backcountry from Pennsylvania south through the Shenandoah Valley to the Carolinas. Others went directly to Georgia, which reformers started in 1732 as a haven for the poor. The population explosion and demand for new lands brought the British colonists face to face with the Spanish in Florida, the French in Canada and the Ohio Valley, and Native Americans all along the frontier.

German and Scots-Irish Immigrants More than 100,000 Germans left their homelands for America during the century after 1683; most of them immigrated between 1727 and 1756. Some were forced out by religious persecution, oppressive regulations, and war; others sought economic opportunity. Promoters called **newlanders** told Germans of cheap fertile land and moderate government in the British colonies. Many immigrants paid their own passage. Those who could not signed on as "redemptioners," the equivalent of indentured servants, whose labor would be sold for a number of years upon arrival. Immigrants went to ports from New York to Georgia, with most entering the Delaware Valley. Some Germans remained in Philadelphia, but the majority headed for the Pennsylvania hinterland and south through the backcountry of Maryland, Virginia, and the Carolinas.

German-speaking immigrants found the freedom they sought in North America, congregating in distinct communities, building separate churches and schools, and maintaining German language and culture. Pennsylvania was the heart of German America, as the colony's religious freedom allowed a multitude of sects and churches to flourish: the Mennonites, Amish, Brethren, Moravians, Schwenkfelders, Lutheran, and Reformed.

Cultural exchange between the Germans and English enriched American society. German churches installed organs and introduced the sophisticated choral music of their homelands. The printer Christopher Saur reprinted German hymnals along with his German-language newspaper and almanac. Congregations founded schools in which children learned both German and English. Immigrants retained the old tongue in their churches and homes, but used English in business, the courts, and politics. German American decorative arts proliferated by the 1740s, in house ornaments, furniture, and elaborately illustrated documents, such as marriage certificates, with gothic Fraktur lettering. German farm women did much heavier fieldwork than most English wives but otherwise played a similar role in maintaining domestic culture.

Large numbers of Scots, Scots-Irish, and Irish Catholics also came during the eighteenth century, settling in New York, Pennsylvania, Delaware, western Maryland, and the southern backcountry. Most were Ulster Scots (or **Scots-Irish**, as they were called in America)—Presbyterians whose families had migrated during the 1600s from Scotland to northern Ireland in search of economic opportunity. There they had combined tenant farming and weaving until the early eighteenth century, when their leases expired. Because landlords raised rents exorbitantly, many Ulster Scots left with their families for the colonies. The first large wave of immigrants departed during 1717–1718; poor harvests and downturns in the linen industry impelled successive groups toward America.

In the colonies, the Scots-Irish achieved a reputation as tough defenders of the frontier. As relatively late arrivals, they had to stake out farms on the edges of existing white settlements. The combination of agriculture and linen manufacture was a distinctive contribution of the Ulster Scots to the colonial economy. As frontier inhabitants, the Scots-Irish came into frequent contact with Native Americans, often with violent results. The new settlers often marked out their farms on Indian hunting lands without negotiating a sale. One Pennsylvania frontiersman, not recognizing the Indians' rights, echoed the early Puritans when he argued that it was contrary to "the laws of God and nature, that so much land should be idle, while so many Christians wanted it to labor on, and to raise their bread."

The Founding of Georgia

The last of the British mainland colonies, Georgia lured many German and Scots-Irish immigrants, as well as Scots and English. Animated by Enlightenment ideals of human progress and freedom, **James Oglethorpe** and John Viscount Percival, members of the Associates of the Late Doctor Bray, a philanthropic society, sought a charter for the colony. They were convinced that something had to be done to help the poor. They also argued that the settlement could serve as a buffer between Spanish Florida and

South Carolina. The English had craved the region since the late seventeenth century when Carolinians destroyed the Spanish missions of Guale. George II granted the charter, placing control of the colony in the hands of trustees, or proprietors, who could neither receive financial benefits from the province nor own land within its boundaries.

The double function of Georgia as a haven for the poor and a military outpost shaped the terms under which settlers immigrated. The trustees intended to create a peaceful, moral society of small farmers in which all except indentured servants worked for themselves. The proprietors wanted to avoid duplicating lowland South Carolina, where large plantation owners lived off the toil of their slaves. The Georgia Trustees, led by Oglethorpe, set three significant policies: they prohibited importation of hard liquor, banned slaveholding, and limited landownership to five hundred acres or less. Each free male immigrant was granted land at no charge, but no one could buy or sell real estate, and only men could inherit land. The trustees hoped to keep Georgia as a refuge for small farmers who, coincidentally, would defend the southern frontier.

In February 1733, the ship *Anne* with approximately one hundred passengers arrived at a site on the Savannah River. Here they built the first town, Savannah, on a high bluff overlooking the river. Oglethorpe purchased land from the Native Americans and pledged to prevent price gouging in trade, a significant complaint of the Indians against South Carolina merchants. He established alliances with Lower Creeks, Cherokees, and Chickasaws against Spanish Florida, not least because English traders offered better merchandise than their rivals.

Many settlers in Georgia believed that the prohibitions on liquor, land sales, and slavery were unreasonable, but they could do little to change the colony's direction because they lacked a representative assembly. The embargo on rum, a major Caribbean commodity, prevented expansion of trade with the West Indies, a ready market for their abundant lumber. The bans on slavery and large landholdings were also unpopular with many settlers, who coveted the grander lifestyle of planters north of the Savannah River, in South Carolina.

In consequence, some settlers left almost immediately, and so Georgia grew slowly. The trustees gradually recognized their failure, and they allowed the importation of rum in 1742 and land sales and slavery in 1750. Preparing to turn the colony over to the Crown, in 1751 they called together Georgia's first elected assembly, which obtained legislative powers three years later when the royal government took control. The Georgia population swelled as South Carolinians migrated across the Savannah River, transforming Georgia into a slave society. By 1773, the province had thirty-three thousand inhabitants, of whom 45 percent were enslaved blacks. Despite its halting start before 1750, Georgia attracted settlers of a variety of nationalities and religions. The colony tapped the eighteenth-century flow of European immigrants, including Spanish and German Jews and German-speaking Lutherans.

The Growth of the African American Population

The failure of the trustees to create a free society in Georgia was symptomatic of the entrenchment of slavery in America. Like the Germans and Scots-Irish, Africans helped diversify the American population and shape its culture. Although the number of African Americans grew naturally in many places, slave traders imported more than 200,000 people between 1720 and the Revolution, most from West and Central

Africa. In 1750, blacks were one-fifth of the population of the mainland colonies, including about 40 percent in the Chesapeake and the Lower South.

As the number of African Americans increased and slave societies matured, blacks created patterns of community, work, and culture. Extended kinship networks structured community life on large plantations, and even in places where slaves lived in small households, such as in northern cities, family ties remained paramount. Blacks were most successful in perpetuating African language and customs in regions where they were most numerous, particularly the South Carolina low country and, later, Georgia. Because they came from hundreds of societies in Africa, with many different cultural attributes, they had difficulty keeping traditional ways intact. They melded African and European forms together and, in the process, influenced evolving mainstream cultures, especially in the South.

The opportunity of slaves to engage in independent activities varied with the amount of time they had to spend working for their master. In South Carolina, blacks labored by the task; each slave received a certain amount of work to perform each

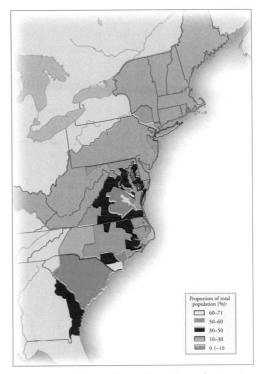

MAP 4.1 African American Population in Colonial British America, c. 1760.

A much higher concentration of enslaved African Americans lived in colonies south of Pennsylvania. Notice, however, that the percentage of slaves in parts of New York and New Jersey was as high as in portions of the Chesapeake region and North Carolina. Uniform data for South Carolina mask the fact that the population of African Americans was much larger along the seacoast than in the up country.

day—a field to hoe, thread to spin, a fence to build. Those who completed their assignments quickly had time to raise their own crops and livestock. Consequently Carolina slaves participated in trade, selling their production at the "Negro market" in Charleston on Sundays. As in Africa, women were responsible for marketing the family's goods. In the Chesapeake, most slaves on plantations labored for a specified number of hours rather than by the task. They planted, weeded, or harvested in gangs until the overseer told them to stop. As a result, they had little time to work for themselves.

The persistence of African culture was conspicuous in language, food, music, dance, and religion. Some newly arrived Africans knew Dutch, Spanish, Portuguese, French, or English from former contacts in Africa or the West Indies, but to communicate with other slaves and with Europeans, most adopted Creole speech, a combination of English and African languages. In the Lower South, for instance, the Creole tongue known as **Gullah** evolved from English and various languages from southern Nigeria, the Gold Coast, Angola, and Senegambia. African Americans retained black dialect from

Creole. For example, most blacks used the word *buckra,* from the African word meaning "he who governs," to refer to white men. Africans also influenced white speech patterns, and white children and immigrants sometimes adopted African American dialect. One British traveler complained that plantation owners allowed "their children . . . to prowl amongst the young Negroes, which insensibly causes them to imbibe their manners and broken speech." Some African words became part of American vocabulary, including *cola, yam, goober* (peanut), and *toting* (carrying) a package.

Blacks contributed to the food and material culture of British America, popularizing new foods such as okra, melons, and bananas. They made clay pipes, pottery, and baskets with African designs, and carved eating utensils, chairs, and other useful objects from wood. They built houses on African rather than European models. In music, they introduced the use of percussion instruments—cymbals, tambourines, and drums—to British military bands. Although masters discouraged Africans from drumming because of the potential to call others to revolt, whites enjoyed the music of black fiddlers. Slaves helped create the Virginia jig, a fusion of African and European elements, accompanied by banjos and fiddles.

Along with whites during the Great Awakening, Africans shaped the forms of worship in southern Baptist churches. Blacks retained traditional African concepts of the hereafter, where the deceased reunited with ancestors, combining these beliefs with European views of heaven. Funerals remained important to African Americans throughout the colonies; mourners buried the dead facing Africa, with traditional rituals, music, and dance. In Philadelphia, for example, the blacks' burial ground was the focus of community activities; they gathered there on Sundays and holidays, "dancing after the manner of their several nations in Africa, and speaking and singing in their native dialects." Blacks also passed down African medical practice, a combination of physical and psychological treatment including magic. More African American women than men were doctors, practicing midwifery as well as nursing and providing cures.

Despite cultural exchange and indications of human understanding, the antagonism and economic exploitation inherent in slavery poisoned relationships among whites and blacks. Whites believed that African Americans were an inferior race, and masters used their power in the slave system to control their human property with harsh punishments. Nevertheless, blacks refused to accept their subordinate position; increasing numbers ran away or were truant for weeks at a time.

Some enslaved Africans took more violent means, killing their masters or setting fire to fields and homes. In 1739, a group of more than fifty bondmen revolted near the Stono River in South Carolina. For most of a day, they marched with drums and banners from one plantation to another, killing about twenty whites. When armed planters defeated the rebels in battle, some of the slaves regrouped and headed for St. Augustine, Florida. But the South Carolina militia pursued the insurgents, putting to death everyone suspected of being involved. The **Stono uprising** sent shock waves throughout the American colonies. The South Carolina legislature enacted a harsh slave code in an effort to prevent future revolts and limited slave importation for a decade. Most of the core group who planned the Stono rebellion were African-born slaves who hoped to escape to Florida, where Spanish authorities offered them religious sanctuary and freedom. By 1740, about a hundred former Carolina slaves had built the village of Gracia Real de Santa Teresa de Mose, called Mose, two miles north of St. Augustine.

Native American Worlds in the Mid-Eighteenth Century As the British colonies grew, Native Americans chose strategies to maintain their communities and cultures. Those who remained within the British provinces were called by white Americans "settlement Indians," "domestic Indians," or "little Tribes." Many lived among European Americans and worked as servants, slaves, day laborers, mariners, artisans, and tenant farmers, assimilating some parts of English culture but rejecting others. Others, such as the Mashpees in Massachusetts, Lenapes (or Delawares) in New Jersey, and Catawbas in South Carolina, lived on remnants of traditional lands. They continued to hunt, fish, gather berries and wood, and raise corn while also trading with neighboring whites. Indians peddled venison and turkeys to the colonists or crafted baskets and brooms for sale. The Lenapes of central New Jersey farmed parcels of land through the eighteenth century: they pursued their traditional seasonal economy by hunting in Pennsylvania, fishing at the Jersey shore, and gathering berries and wood for baskets in the Pine Barrens.

Dr. Alexander Hamilton, a recent immigrant from Scotland, recorded many encounters with Indians in 1744 as he traveled through the settlements from Maryland to Maine. The Native Americans he met varied greatly in status, from an Indian sachem who had established himself as a wealthy planter to those on the margins, who tried to hold on to native traditions within an alien culture. In Rhode Island, he approached the large plantation of

> an Indian King named George . . . upon which he has many tennants and has, of his own, a good stock of horses and other cattle. The King lives after the English mode. His subjects have lost their own government policy and laws and are servants or vassals to the English here. His queen goes in a high modish dress in her silks, hoops, stays, and dresses like an English woman. He educates his children to the belles letters and is himself a very complaisant mannerly man. We pay'd him a visit, and he treated us with a glass of good wine.

During worship in a Boston church, Hamilton sat near several Native Americans. He met an Indian at Princeton, New Jersey, who saluted him with, "How' s't ni tap," and, in New York, he watched "about ten Indians fishing for oysters . . . stark naked" near his tavern. Although most native people who stayed in white settled areas had given up political autonomy, they had not surrendered all of their traditions. Many spoke English in addition to their native language but did not learn to read and write.

Native Americans who intended to preserve their political independence moved west, a strategy that worked temporarily. From 1660 to the 1740s, for example, Iroquois, Shawnees, and Lenapes relocated in the eastern part of the Ohio Valley, from Pennsylvania and western New York to west-central Ohio. Wyandots inhabited the lands to the west, at Sandusky and near the French fort at Detroit. Some of the Lenapes left the East as a result of the Walking Purchase of 1737, when two of William Penn's sons, the proprietors, used an alleged 1686 deed to cheat the Indians out of their territory on the Pennsylvania side of the Delaware River. The deed, of which only a copy survived, ceded lands as far as a man could walk in one and a half days. Coerced by an alliance between the Penns and the Iroquois, the Lenapes agreed to comply. The Penns sent runners in relay to cover more than sixty miles of land in a day and a half, a deception the Lenapes could not fail to remember; in 1754, with the outbreak of war on the Pennsylvania frontier, many sought revenge.

The Ohio Valley became the focus of conflict in the 1740s as the British and French competed for trade. Following the Lenapes and Shawnees west, some Pennsylvania traders took up residence in the multi-ethnic towns such as Chiningue (or Logstown), where Iroquois, Lenapes, Shawnees, Ottawas, and other Indians lived. The Ohio Valley, as one Indian leader said, was "a country in between" the English and the French, unfortunately a country that the Europeans craved. From 1754 to 1814, the Native Americans fought the British and Americans to keep their lands and native religions, forging pan-Indian alliances to meet the Anglo threat.

WARS FOR EMPIRE, 1739–1765

For a quarter century beginning in 1739, the British colonies took part in conflicts between Great Britain and Spain, France, and Native Americans. The War of Jenkins' Ear (1739–1744) against Spain; King George's War (1744–1748) against France; the Seven Years' War, called the French and Indian War in the colonies (1754–1763); and the Indian war for autonomy in the Ohio Valley (1763–1765) all required British colonists to participate more actively in defending the empire.

The Southern Frontier

The colonies along the southern tier—British South Carolina and Georgia, Spanish Florida, French Louisiana, and Spanish Texas and New Mexico—competed for trade with Native Americans and control of territory. Except for war between Georgia and Florida in the early 1740s, the most important battles along the southern rim were commercial, a competition the British traders often won because they had more plentiful and cheaper goods. They exchanged tools, clothing, scissors, guns, ammunition, and rum in return for slaves, deerskins, and furs from the Indians. In comparison with the English provinces, the Spanish and French colonies remained small and badly supplied by their parent nations. In 1760, Florida had approximately three thousand Spanish settlers, Texas had twelve hundred, and New Mexico about nine thousand; Louisiana counted four thousand whites and five thousand enslaved Africans. In contrast, in the same year, South Carolina and Georgia had a population of about forty-five thousand whites and fifty-nine thousand black slaves.

Governor James Oglethorpe of Georgia tried to use the outbreak of the War of Jenkins' Ear to eject the Spanish from Florida. As part of the 1713 Treaty of Utrecht, Britain had obtained the *asiento,* the right to sell a specified number of African slaves and commodities to the Spanish provinces. This opening led to British smuggling, which the Spanish countered with heavy-handed searches of British ships. Accounts of Spanish brutality inflamed the British public, especially when Captain Robert Jenkins displayed one of his ears, which he claimed the Spanish cut off when they caught him smuggling. In 1740, Oglethorpe attacked Florida with seven ships and two thousand troops. They captured several Spanish forts and Mose, the village of escaped Carolina blacks, but failed to conquer Fort San Marcos, where the residents of St. Augustine and Mose took cover. A large percentage of Florida residents were soldiers to guard Atlantic shipping lanes. When Spanish and black soldiers slipped out of the fort and recaptured Mose, and then the fort was resupplied by Cuba, Oglethorpe retreated.

In 1741, a force of thirty-six hundred colonists participated in the British expedition against the Spanish fort at Cartagena, in what is now Colombia. The campaign ended bitterly, with heavy losses from battle and smallpox. The following year, the Spanish took revenge for the invasion of Florida by attacking St. Simon's Island, Georgia, but withdrew before conquering it. After some minor skirmishes, both sides gave up, bringing calm to the Georgia–Florida border.

King George's War, 1744–1748   The British avoided further conflict with Florida because they began hostilities with France in 1744, in the War of the Austrian Succession, known to the colonists as King George's War. The war began in Europe, but spilled into North America when, provoked by French attacks on Nova Scotia, Governor William Shirley of Massachusetts launched an attack on Louisbourg, which controlled access to the St. Lawrence River. In April 1745, four thousand New England farmers and fishermen assaulted the French garrison, which held out against the badly organized offensive until June but then surrendered. New Englanders considered Louisbourg a great victory, even after many of their troops succumbed to disease. The war degenerated into a series of debilitating border raids. The Canadians and their Indian allies ravaged Saratoga, New York, and northern New England. In spring 1746, a fleet of seventy-six ships left France to retake Louisbourg, but after fighting disease and Atlantic storms for three months, they returned to France empty-handed.

Despite this reprieve, New Englanders had little to celebrate, for they faced another threat—this one from their own imperial navy. During the war, Parliament had permitted naval officers to impress sailors without the permission of colonial authorities. The Royal Navy used impressment, or involuntary recruitment, because many seamen fled the harsh conditions on naval vessels. In 1747, several thousand Bostonians protested when a British press gang from the fleet of Admiral Charles Knowles swept up men along the waterfront. The mob surrounded the governor's house and burned a British barge in his courtyard. When the governor called up the militia, the troops refused to move. Knowles threatened to shell the town, but after negotiations lasting several days, he released the impressed men instead.

As the colonists became more involved in imperial politics, they learned that their interests held little sway. To their shock, the British government restored Louisbourg to the French in the Treaty of Aix-la-Chapelle (1748), and the combatants agreed to return all North American territories seized during the war. Despite heavy human and financial costs, the war brought no change in the power balance between Great Britain and France in North America.

The Seven Years' War, 1756–1763   During King George's War, the British and Iroquois had evicted French traders from the Ohio Valley. The Canadians returned, however, backed by a government determined to force out the British colonists. The Ohio Company of Virginia, which had received the rights to half a million acres from the British government, in 1749 made preparations to sell land in the region of present-day Pittsburgh, Pennsylvania, where the Monongahela and Allegheny rivers combine to form the Ohio River. Virginia's claim to the territory dated from its charter. In response, the French constructed forts to stop the incursion of Anglo-American traders and Virginia's land speculators. In 1754, the governor of

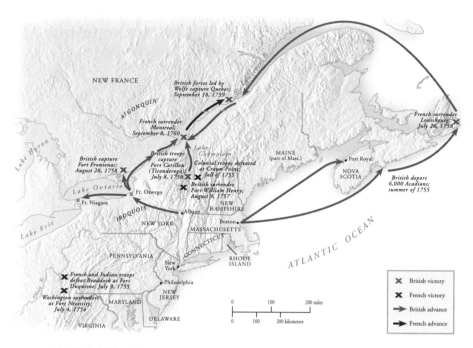

MAP 4.2 The Seven Years' War in North America, 1754–1760.

The war began in the Ohio Valley, an area Virginians claimed and hoped to sell to settlers. To do so, they had to force out the French, who sent troops to establish ownership; defeat the Delawares and Shawnees, who had built towns along the Allegheny and Ohio rivers; and prevail over Pennsylvania's competing charter claims. The English captured Quebec in 1759 and Montreal in 1760, defeating France in North America.

Virginia sent a young militia officer, George Washington, with about 160 troops to erect a stronghold to defend the colony's interests. When hostilities resulted, the Virginians were defeated at the inadequate structure they had built, Fort Necessity, by a superior force of French and Indians.

Recognizing that war was imminent, seven colonies sent delegates to a congress at Albany, New York, where they negotiated unsuccessfully with the Iroquois for an alliance against the French. The Albany Congress also amended and adopted the **Albany Plan** devised by Benjamin Franklin to unite the colonies for common defense. The plan for an intercolonial government empowered to tax, pass laws, and supervise military defense needed endorsement by each colony and the Crown. When the delegates returned home with the proposal, not one of the provincial assemblies approved it.

The British decided to destroy French forts even before a formal declaration of war. In early 1755, Major General Edward Braddock landed in the colonies with two British regiments. Joined by hundreds of provincial soldiers, the army marched through the Virginia backcountry to capture Fort Duquesne (now Pittsburgh). The British troops were unprepared for frontier fighting. Ten miles short of Fort Duquesne, the French and allied Indians ambushed Braddock's army, killing or wounding two-thirds of the British force. The general himself was mortally wounded. George Washington, his uniform ripped by bullets, led the retreat.

Benjamin Franklin's "Snake Device." *Benjamin Franklin published his "Snake Device" just before the Albany Congress in 1754. Considered the first political cartoon in the colonies, it later became an important symbol of American resistance to Britain.*

JOIN, or DIE.

(The Historical Society of Pennsylvania)

The 650 Native Americans who fought with the French included their traditional allies and some Delawares and Iroquois of the Ohio Valley who had previously supported the British. By 1754, some Ohio Indians were convinced that Britain and its colonies posed the greater threat to their lands; with the defeat of Braddock, many more joined the French. Between 1755 and 1757, Delawares, Shawnees, Iroquois, and many others attacked the white frontier from Pennsylvania to Virginia, burning settlements and killing or capturing thousands of colonists.

Help for the westerners was slow in coming. In 1756, the struggle in North America became part of the larger European conflict known as the Seven Years' War, in which Great Britain supported Prussia against Austria, Russia, and France. The French penetrated into New York, seizing Fort William Henry and two thousand soldiers at Lake George. The tide changed after the British statesman **William Pitt** took command of the war effort. He poured money and men into the American theater, expecting colonial legislatures to do the same. The new generals, Jeffery Amherst and **James Wolfe**, with an army of almost ten thousand men, captured Louisbourg in July 1758. The French then pulled their troops out of the Ohio Valley to protect Quebec and Montreal, allowing the British to take control of the west. Without French supplies and devastated by smallpox, the Native Americans ended their war on the frontier.

DOING HISTORY ONLINE

The French and Indian War

Read Documents 11 through 16. If you were a young white man living in Virginia or Massachusetts, what motivation would you have for joining the British forces to fight the French and Indians?

 www.cengage.com/history/ayers/ampassages4e

In 1759, the British and provincial armies had even greater success, leading some of the Iroquois of New York to abandon neutrality to join their side. The British reestablished control of New York, while from Louisbourg, General Wolfe sailed up the St. Lawrence to Quebec, where after several months his forces pierced the defenses of the well-fortified city. The next year, Amherst's army seized Montreal, thus ending French control of Canada.

While the defeat of Canada marked the cessation of war in North America, the Seven Years' War continued off the coast of France, in India, and in the West Indies. The British military took a number of French sugar islands, including the richest, Guadeloupe. When Spain entered the conflict as France's ally in 1762 in return for the promise of lands west of the Mississippi River, the British captured Manila in the Philippines and Havana, Cuba.

During the Seven Years' War, thousands of colonists joined the British army, and many more served in the provincial forces. Ordinary settlers came into close contact with the imperial authorities—and many loathed the experience. The British army contained professional soldiers drilled rigorously in military tactics, cleanliness, and order. Women served in the field, generally soldiers' wives who cooked, washed, and nursed. British officers, from the upper classes, maintained discipline with punishments of death for major offenses such as desertion and up to a thousand lashes—which could also kill—for lesser crimes. The British officers disdained the colonial units, which were accustomed to much lighter discipline and sometimes elected their superiors. Because the provincials failed to keep their camps and clothing clean, many died from disease. For their part, some colonial soldiers thought the British regulars were immoral, profane men who needed to be controlled with brutal discipline.

The British colonists welcomed the Treaty of Paris in 1763, which finally ended the war. Under the treaty, France lost all of its territory in North America but retrieved the valuable sugar islands of Guadeloupe and Martinique. Spain relinquished Florida to get back Cuba and the Philippines and, because the British lacked interest in the region, acquired French territory west of the Mississippi and New Orleans, located on the east side of the river. The Treaty of Paris gave the British colonists security from France and Spain; the home government received two unprofitable colonies, Canada and Florida. The provincials celebrated the victory with patriotic fervor: New York City raised a statue of George III, who had taken the throne in 1760 at age twenty-two. Many colonists, especially New England ministers, had interpreted the war as a fight against Catholicism and tyranny. They viewed the victory as a sign that God favored Britain and its colonies. One Massachusetts clergyman preached,

> Safe from the Enemy of the Wilderness, safe from the gripping Hand of arbitrary Sway and cruel Superstition; Here shall be the late founded Seat of Peace and Freedom. Here shall our indulgent Mother [Britain], who has most generously rescued and protected us, be served and honoured by growing Numbers, with all Duty, Love and Gratitude, till Time shall be no more.

The Indians Renew War in the Ohio Valley, 1763–1765   The Treaty of Paris seriously undermined the position of Native Americans east of the Mississippi whether they had fought for the British or French or had remained neutral. The defeat of France worsened the situation of native people in the Ohio Valley, for they could no longer play one European nation off the other. The British alone supplied European goods, so they could set prices and the terms of trade. They ended the custom of giving annual presents, charged high prices, stopped selling rum, and reduced the amount of ammunition sold. Furthermore, with the end of the Seven Years' War, white settlers streamed west into Indian lands, as wealthy land speculators and poor squatters alike ignored treaties that colonial governments had made with the Native Americans.

The altered British trade policies and land grabbing drove many Delawares, Shawnees, Iroquois, and others to renew the fighting. They gained spiritual unity from the Delaware prophet **Neolin**, one of a line of spiritual leaders among the Delawares and Shawnees who preached that Indians must reject Christianity and European goods, particularly rum, and revitalize their ancient culture. Neolin called on Native Americans to drive the Europeans out, demanding: "Whereupon do you suffer the whites to dwell upon your lands? Drive them away; wage war against them. I love them not." He warned his followers, "If you suffer the English among you, you are dead men. Sickness, smallpox, and their poison will destroy you entirely."

Many Indians throughout the Ohio Valley adopted Neolin's strategy, boycotting the fur trade by hunting only for their own food and personal needs. The Delaware councils called for a gradual return to military skills with bow and arrow and adopted a ritual tea, which caused vomiting, to cleanse themselves of the "White people's ways and Nature." In 1763, Native Americans from western Pennsylvania through the Great Lakes region launched a pan-Indian assault on British garrisons, often called Pontiac's War. A follower of Neolin and leader of the Ottawas, Pontiac laid siege unsuccessfully to the British fort at Detroit. Other Indians defeated thirteen British outposts, though not Forts Niagara or Pittsburgh. Although the British army established military dominance in the Ohio Valley by the end of 1763, fighting continued for two more years.

In addition to armed force, the British government tried to end the war by keeping white settlers out of the Ohio Valley. The king issued the **Proclamation of 1763**, requiring colonists to stay east of a line drawn along the crest of the Appalachian Mountains from Maine to Georgia. Colonial governors were instructed to prohibit surveys or land grants west of the proclamation line; only authorized agents of the Crown could buy lands from the Indians for future settlement. The proclamation failed in its purpose, however, as land speculators continued their operations and immigrants demanded farms. The British government, weighed down by debt from the Seven Years' War, failed to supply manpower to enforce the law, withdrawing troops from the Ohio Valley and Great Lakes region.

THE BRITISH PROVINCES IN 1763

The end of the Seven Years' War brought pivotal changes in British North America. For more than a century and a half, Europeans had crossed the ocean to trade with the Native Americans, build farms and businesses, and develop networks of Atlantic commerce. The colonies had dealt with crises, from economic slumps to rebellions, becoming ever more confident of their position as semi-independent societies. During the last quarter-century, with greater involvement in imperial affairs and rising importation of consumer goods, the provincials felt more a part of the British empire—more English—even as they created a separate identity as Americans. Most important, they believed that they were equal to the residents of Great Britain and possessed the rights of English people.

The Economy   In 1763, the mainland provinces still operated within the system of British mercantilism, which consisted of regulations on colonial trade and manufactures. For mercantilism to work to Britain's benefit, the colonies

Atlantic Trade Patterns

By 1750, the Atlantic economy had matured, as each of the British mainland colonies developed products for sale in Great Britain, Europe, Africa, and the West Indies. Patterns of trade were much more complicated than the notion of a triangular trade route in which England sold manufactured goods in Africa in exchange for slaves who were sent to America where they produced sugar, tobacco, and rice destined for Europe. Although this exchange was important, other trade patterns sustained colonial economies as well: shipment of fish and lumber from New England to the West Indies and mid-Atlantic flour and meat to southern Europe and the West Indies. The fur trade linked Native Americans to the Atlantic economy. West Indies sugar—and the rum that New England and Philadelphia distillers manufactured from it—found markets everywhere. Because the Navigation Acts allowed American ships to carry goods, the shipping trade itself became a significant source of income.

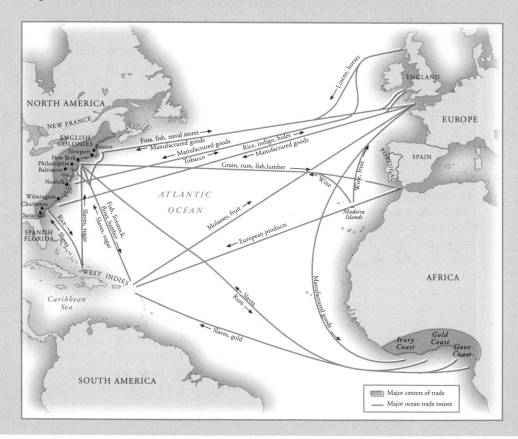

had to produce raw materials and agricultural staples needed by the home economy and serve as a market for its manufactured goods. Such colonial products as sugar, molasses, tobacco, cotton, certain wood products, copper, and furs were "enumerated," meaning that they could be shipped only to Britain or British colonial ports, not to foreign countries such as France and Spain. The basic laws establishing the British mercantilist system were the seventeenth-century Navigation Acts, which Parliament supplemented from time to time. Although most colonial trade conformed to the law by the eighteenth century, smuggling occurred often enough to prompt demands within the British government for strict enforcement. In particular, colonial shippers bribed customs officials to ignore the Molasses Act (1733), which levied prohibitive duties on foreign sugar products, including a tax of sixpence per gallon on molasses. The British West Indies planters had pushed for the act to create a monopoly for themselves, lowering the cost of provisions and raising the price of their exports. If the Molasses Act had been enforced, it would have severely damaged the economies of New England and the middle colonies, which traded with the French, Spanish, and Dutch West Indies, as well as the British islands.

Other laws passed by Parliament prior to 1763 had a significant but uneven impact on colonial economic growth. British legislation, combined with lack of investment capital, limited the development of most manufactures. The Woolen Act (1699) and the Hat Act (1732) banned the export of American-produced woolen products and hats from one colony to another. Other laws prohibited the export of machinery and the migration of skilled craftsmen from Britain to America. The Iron Act (1750) allowed duty-free import of colonial bar iron into Britain but forbade fabrication of iron goods in the colonies. Nevertheless, crude iron production received substantial investment, as did shipbuilding and rum distilling. Unhampered by mercantilist regulation, North American shipbuilders produced nearly 40 percent of vessels in the British-owned merchant fleet.

Despite these laws, the wealth of the British colonies increased between the 1720s and 1760, as trade flourished with the West Indies and, after 1750, with southern Europe, where crop failures and population growth swelled demand for wheat and flour. The middle colonies, already expanding with German and Irish immigration, were well situated to supply new markets. Philadelphia became the largest city in the British colonies: its wealthy merchants invested in ships, built mansions, purchased coaches and other luxuries, and speculated in western lands from the profits of trade. Artisans, shopkeepers, and farmers prospered. To the south, large planters in the Chesapeake and Carolinas accumulated great estates, while ordinary farmers more modestly improved their standard of living. All along the eastern seaboard, after 1740, white families indulged in what has been called a "consumer revolution." Not only could they purchase cloth, clothing, carpets, paper, gloves, mirrors, clocks, silverware, china tea sets, pottery, and books but they also had more choices in the specific kind of cloth or paper or gloves they could buy. In New York City in the 1750s, for instance, merchants advertised gloves of various colors—purple, orange, white, and flowered—as well as different sizes and materials, including chamois, silk, "Maid's Lamb Gloves," and "Men's Dog Skin Gloves."

The colonies became major markets for textiles, metalware, and other items, which under the Navigation Acts they could import only from Britain. The consumer revolution made the British more attentive to their North American provinces; at the same time, the imports helped to create a more standardized English culture in America. Affluent colonists became aware of the latest fashions in England and complained when they received out-of-date merchandise. The young George Washington groused in 1760, for example, "that instead of getting things good and fashionable in their several kinds we often have Articles sent Us that coud only have been usd by our Forefathers in the days of yore."

The economic upswing of the 1750s gave way to a depression after 1760, as the Seven Years' War moved to the Caribbean and military spending dropped. The seaport towns, having attracted workers during the wartime boom, faced deepening poverty and rising demands for relief. With depressed wages and long periods of unemployment, families found survival difficult. The resumption of immigration from Europe after the war intensified economic hardships and contributed to unrest in the backcountry.

Politics

In late 1763, after months of Indian attacks in the Ohio country, a band of western Scots-Irish Pennsylvanians used violence to force the Quaker-dominated assembly to provide military protection. The "Paxton Boys" of Lancaster County murdered a number of Christian Indians at Conestoga, then marched on Philadelphia. By the time the rebels reached the capital, the legislature

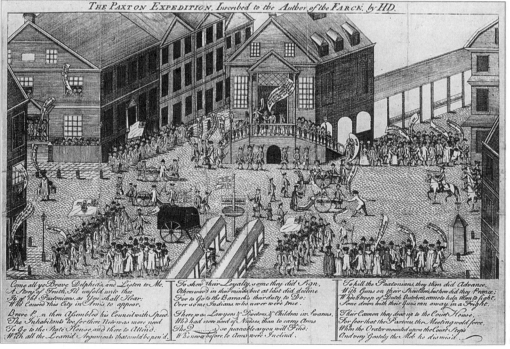

Paxton Expedition. *The Paxton Expedition, by Henry Dawkins, depicts the threat by western "Paxton Boys" against Philadelphia, demanding frontier defense during Pontiac's War.*

(The Library Company of Philadelphia)

had passed a bill raising a thousand troops to defend the frontier. The westerners returned home without attacking the city. At the heart of their revolt was the belief that they were poorly represented in the provincial government. As the backcountry population exploded, eastern politicians guarded their power by allotting fewer assembly seats to outlying counties than they deserved.

The revolt by the Paxton Boys signaled the end of an era of political stability that had prevailed since the late 1720s in the British mainland provinces. As part of Britain's empire, the eighteenth-century colonists believed themselves among the most fortunate people on earth. The Glorious Revolution of 1688–1689, which removed James II, had ended the long, bitter contest between king and Parliament. The monarch's power was subsequently limited by the national legislature, composed of the House of Lords, which represented the aristocracy, and the House of Commons, which in theory represented everyone else. As a result of the 1689 settlement, Parliament's consent was necessary for taxes, new courts, raising an army in peacetime, and foreign invasions. Parliament gained control over its own meetings, and after 1707, the Crown lost veto power over legislation.

The balance of powers, political theorists argued, prevented domination by a single segment of society, the monarch, aristocracy, or common people. Thus, the British avoided forms of government considered destructive of liberty: rule by a single despot (tyranny), corrupt and self-serving rule by a group of aristocrats (oligarchy), and uncontrolled rule by the mob (democracy). In their provincial governments, the British colonists expected to find a similar balance, one that would protect their rights. Indeed, the prevailing structure of governor, appointed council, and elected lower house of the assembly reflected the English model.

The British provinces were the only European settlements in North America where ordinary people could vote for representative legislatures. An estimated 50 to 75 percent of white men were qualified to vote in the British colonies, the result of much broader property ownership than in England, where about 15 to 30 percent of adult males had the franchise. According to English political theory, a person needed a "stake in society," a certain amount of property, to vote or hold office. Servants, slaves, children, and unpropertied men were beholden to someone else, so they could not make independent decisions. Giving them suffrage would award their owner, father, or employer another vote, the theorists claimed, especially in many places where people voted orally, in public. By tradition, women also lacked the franchise, whether or not they owned property or were married. Denial of the vote to all females arose from the belief that they were intellectually and morally inferior to men and thus should have no formal role in government.

The colonists favored direct representation, requiring their legislators to live in the area from which they were elected and to advocate the interests of their constituents, unlike England, where members of the House of Commons did not have to reside in their electoral districts. The British believed that Parliament represented all of the people of the empire whether they elected delegates or not, a concept known as virtual representation.

Beyond suffrage, English political theory also recognized the right of common people to resort to crowd action to withstand tyranny and require authorities to protect them from harm. The people theoretically had this right as long as violence was limited—directed at property rather than at persons. At various times, colonial mobs protested to prevent grain from being exported when food was in short supply, destroy houses of prostitution, and stop the British navy from impressing men into the king's service, as with the 1747 Knowles riot in Boston.

The most important and sustained political development in British America during the first half of the eighteenth century was the rise of the elected lower houses of assembly. The legislatures acquired greater power and assumed more functions—most significant, the right to initiate bills to raise taxes and disburse public funds, that is, the power of the purse. They also gained the authority to initiate other legislation, choose their own leadership, and settle disputed elections.

The political stability and rise of the assemblies that marked the mid-eighteenth century resulted from a number of factors, including the long period of economic growth that began in the 1720s. Prosperity supported the formation of cohesive elites—mostly second-, third-, and fourth-generation Americans with inherited wealth, large estates, and enslaved Africans or servants to meet their domestic needs, and (consequently) sufficient leisure time for politics. They formed a class of skilled politicians—men who had learned from their fathers how to govern and then elaborated the art. Many studied the law: the growth of the colonial bar accompanied the professionalization of politics. Economic prosperity inclined ordinary whites to defer to the elites as long as opportunity was good and they had crops to tend or other work to do. Their deference to social and economic superiors became most visible after 1725, when participation at the polls declined among eligible voters, and incumbent assemblymen won reelection year after year.

The provincial elites also benefited after 1720 from the British decision to administer the colonies with a light touch, allowing royal governors to accommodate the assemblies. And although riots occurred during the 1740s and 1750s over land claims and impressment, none threatened social disorder on the level of the seventeenth-century rebellions. Indeed, most ordinary whites feared attacks by Native Americans and slave revolts more than misuse of governmental power by elites.

CONCLUSION

By the end of 1763, the British colonists of North America had reason to be optimistic about their future, despite the pan-Indian assaults in the Ohio Valley and postwar economic downturn. The British army had withstood the worst attacks in the West, and colonists could expect a return to prosperity. After a quarter-century of war, they celebrated the withdrawal of Spain and France east of the Mississippi and looked forward to peace and semi-autonomy within the empire. Free colonists appreciated the benefits of being British—their liberties and right to participate in government, as well as access to advanced learning and consumer goods. At the same time, the Americans were creating societies quite different from the English, with greater ethnic and religious diversity, dependence on enslaved labor, and wider opportunity to acquire land (even if it meant pushing out the Indians). After 1763, the London government shocked the American colonists with its effort to rein in the empire, to make them surrender some of their accumulated rights. In turn, the British were unprepared for the coordinated fury with which the thirteen mainland provinces greeted their "reforms."

CHAPTER REVIEW, 1720–1763

- In the colonies, the Enlightenment created new educational opportunities, promoted scientific research, and encouraged the development of new political theories.
- Between 1720 and 1760, the Great Awakening, a series of religious revivals that emphasized emotionalism and personal salvation, swept across British America.
- The population of the colonies became increasingly diverse as the African American population grew, through both natural increase and increased importation, and from a significant influx of German and Scots-Irish immigrants.
- Between 1744 and 1765, colonists participated in a series of wars waged by Britain against Spain, France, and their Native American allies. By the end of these conflicts, France had withdrawn from the North American mainland.
- Involvement in British wars and integration into Atlantic trade networks fostered among many colonists a strong sense of English identity and feelings of entitlement to the rights of Englishmen.

◀◀◀ *Looking Back*

Chapter 4 shows that between 1720 and 1763 the thirteen British provinces underwent considerable change as a result of German and Scots-Irish immigration, the intellectual challenges of the Enlightenment, religious developments of the Great Awakening, and economic expansion within the Atlantic world.

1. What kind of education could young Americans receive in the early eighteenth century?
2. What contributions did Americans make to science?
3. How did the Great Awakening affect colonial society?
4. In what ways did Native Americans respond to the expansion of British America?
5. What economic restrictions did the British government place on the colonies prior to 1763?

Looking Ahead ▶▶▶

Chapter 5 looks at how the year 1763 marked a major change in British government policy toward its North American colonies, a change that led to revolution a dozen years later.

1. Why did London impose the series of "reforms" beginning with the Sugar and Currency acts?
2. Why was Boston the center of colonial resistance?
3. How did events in the Spanish borderland colonies of Louisiana, Texas, and New Mexico compare with the unfolding crisis in the British provinces?

Go to the American Passages website at www.cengage.com/history/ayers/ampassages4e for additional review materials.

5

Wars for Independence, 1764–1783

The treaty of 1763 that ended the Seven Years' War forced Spain and Great Britain to reassess their North American colonies. Both nations had relatively new kings: Charles III had taken Spain's throne in 1759, and George III had become the British monarch in 1760. For the Spanish, the borderlands in North America were of secondary importance, serving as a buffer to protect the Mexican silver mines. For Britain, however, the mainland provinces had become increasingly significant as a source of revenue and market for consumer goods. The Seven Years' War marked Britain's ascendancy to world power, but it resulted in a national debt of £130 million. Annual interest payments alone amounted to £4.5 million, equal to more than half of the government's yearly expenditures prior to the war.

When Parliament imposed levies on the American colonies to help pay expenses, the colonists protested vehemently that they should not be taxed without their consent. They complained that they had no representatives in Parliament and that only their elected provincial assemblies could constitutionally tax them. Beginning in 1764, the Americans petitioned, rioted, boycotted British goods, destroyed tea, and ultimately defied George III and parliamentary leaders when they sent troops. The colonists' belief that they possessed the same rights as the English was something for which many were willing to fight. Nevertheless, the consensus to declare independence did not come quickly, nor was the war to defend independence easily won. Americans who disagreed that the British actions warranted insurrection remained loyal to the king. These **loyalists**, also called Tories after the pro-monarchy faction in England, tried to subvert the Revolutionary governments and formed loyalist militia units to fight alongside British troops. They found allies in many Native Americans and African Americans who conducted wars of independence of their own. Other colonists remained neutral, whether from principled opposition to violence or from sheer indifference. The Revolution touched everyone: Native Americans, women, and enslaved blacks, as well as the white men who served as military and civilian leaders and served in most of the armed forces. The cause of the patriots—or

CHAPTER TIMELINE

1764	Sugar and Currency Acts • St. Louis founded
1765	Stamp Act provokes widespread colonial protest • Stamp Act Congress
1766	Parliament repeals Stamp Act, passes Declaratory Act • Spanish governor arrives in Louisiana
1766–1771	North Carolina Regulator movement
1767	Passage of Townshend Act • John Dickinson publishes "Farmer" letters
1767–1769	South Carolina Regulator movement
1768	Massachusetts assembly sends "circular letter" • Non-importation movement against Townshend duties • British troops stationed in Boston • Louisianans expel Spanish governor
1769	Spanish reestablish control of Louisiana
1770	Boston Massacre • Partial repeal of Townshend Act
1772	Burning of Gaspée
1772–1773	Committees of Correspondence established
1773	Boston Tea Party
1774	Passage of Coercive Acts; port of Boston closed • Quebec Act • First Continental Congress • Congress organizes Continental Association
1775	Battles of Lexington and Concord • Second Continental Congress • Battle of Bunker Hill • Congress authorizes invasion of Canada • Lord Dunmore's proclamation to servants and slaves
1776	Thomas Paine publishes Common Sense • British evacuation of Boston • Declaration of Independence • Cherokee War on the southern frontier • Americans defeated on Long Island; British occupation of New York City • Battle of Trenton
1777	Battle of Princeton • British occupy Philadelphia after defeating Washington at Brandywine • Battle of Germantown • Burgoyne surrenders to Americans at Saratoga • Congress approves Articles of Confederation; sends document to states for ratification
1778	Alliance with France • Iroquois and loyalist attacks in New York and Pennsylvania • British withdraw from Philadelphia • Whig frontiersmen take settlements in the Illinois country • British invade Georgia
1780	Americans surrender at Charleston • Battle of Camden
1781	Battle of Cowpens • Articles of Confederation ratified • Battle of Guilford Courthouse • Southern army reconquers most of South Carolina and Georgia • Surrender of Cornwallis at Yorktown
1782	Massacre at Gnadenhutten
1783	Signing of Treaty of Paris

This icon will direct you to interactive activities and study materials on the American Passages website: www.cengage.com/history/ayers/ampassages4e

Whigs, as the American revolutionaries called themselves, after the English party that had led opposition to the Crown—depended on the efforts of many people: those who supplied and supported the troops, as well as those who fought, played vital roles.

REALIGNMENTS IN THE SPANISH BORDERLANDS

The peace of 1763 required Spain to withdraw from Florida, assume the government of Louisiana, and rethink its defenses in Texas and New Mexico. With Britain's enhanced power, safeguarding the Mexican silver mines took high priority. The Spanish also considered the soaring population of the British colonies a threat to their American empire.

Florida and
Louisiana

Spain ordered all of its subjects to leave Florida when Britain took control. Although the British promised religious freedom to the Catholic Floridians, some 200 Christian Indians, 79 free African Americans, 350 slaves, and nearly all of the 3,000 Spanish departed. They sold their property at a loss to British bargain hunters. The free blacks of Mose, near St. Augustine, could expect enslavement by the English, so they accepted Spain's offer of homesteads in Cuba. They received some tools and money from the government but faced hard times because they never received adequate compensation for their property in Florida.

Acquisition of Louisiana, including all French territory west of the Mississippi River and New Orleans on the east bank, gave Spain an extensive region to administer. The Spanish needed to win the loyalties of French inhabitants and Native Americans and hoped to keep the British colonists out. The concern about British expansion became all too real as interlopers spanned the Mississippi River to trade with Indians on the Great Plains. Indeed, within a decade, four thousand British colonists and their fifteen hundred African American slaves were living on the Gulf Coast and eastern shore of the Mississippi.

The more immediate challenge for Spanish authorities in Louisiana, however, was asserting political control of the province. For several years, the French government remained; even after the first Spanish governor, **Antonio de Ulloa**, arrived in 1766, he tried to govern jointly with the last French governor. Adhering to Charles III's instructions, Ulloa left the French administration and legal system intact, even allowing the French flag to fly over the capitol.

Ulloa did not extend this leniency to commerce, however. He tried to stop business with France and Great Britain and restricted the Native American trade to certain dealers. New Orleans merchants feared loss of markets and lower prices for their tobacco, indigo, sugar, deerskins, and lumber. Like the thirteen British provinces on the Atlantic coast, and at about the same time, the merchants protested the new restrictions, then in October 1768 issued a declaration of loyalty to the king of France. With few Spanish troops at his disposal, Governor Ulloa left for Cuba. When the French refused to intervene, the colony became independent, but only for a year.

The Spanish regained Louisiana when General Alexander O'Reilly arrived in 1769 with more than two thousand soldiers. An Irishman with a successful career in the Spanish army, O'Reilly arrested the rebels; he put five of them to death but pardoned most who had participated in the uprising. He raised the Spanish flag and within a year ended the French government, changed the legal system, made Castilian the official language, and outlawed trade with other nations. Despite the merchants' fears, the economy flourished as smuggling continued with Britain, and Spanish markets welcomed their goods. St. Louis, established in 1764, became the thriving center of trade for beaver, buffalo, and deerskins with Native Americans of the Illinois and Missouri countries. Louisiana remained culturally French, as the numbers of French settlers far surpassed the Spanish.

Fortifying the Southwest
With ownership of Louisiana, the Spanish could alter their defenses along the frontier in Texas and New Mexico. They removed several forts from East Texas. By the 1760s, the most immediate danger in the Southwest came from the Apaches and Comanches, who defended their freedom from Spanish slave catchers and attempted to drive the Spanish back into Mexico. Skillfully adopting the European horse and gun, they refused to submit to Spanish rule or Christianity. Spain gave up trying to convert them through missions, emphasizing military defense instead. The Apaches and Comanches raided settlements and pack trains, and they stole horses, mules, cattle, and supplies, killing Pueblos and white settlers alike.

During the 1760s and 1770s, in the face of constant Indian assaults, Spain tried to reform its administration and improve the colonies' defenses. From 1766 to 1768, the Marqués de Rubí, a high-level military official from Spain, inspected the fortifications and missions of the Southwest. He discovered badly located **presidios** (or forts) and soldiers suffering from lack of food and clothes because of their commanders' greed. At one Texas presidio, Rubí found sixty troops without shoes or uniforms, and among them, only two muskets that worked. He recommended building new presidios and relocating others to create an orderly cordon of military bases situated about a hundred miles apart. The presidios would extend from the Gulf of California to the Gulf of Mexico, along a line that was close to today's boundary between the United States and Mexico. Small numbers of Spanish troops would hold garrisons at Santa Fe and San Antonio, north of the cordon, to help defend Hispanics and allied Indians in New Mexico and Texas. The borderlands officials also received more autonomy to deal with local problems, but they lacked sufficient troops to conquer the Apaches and Comanches.

THE BRITISH COLONIES RESIST IMPERIAL REFORM, 1764–1775

In Britain's colonies, which experienced few restrictions before 1763, trouble began when George III appointed George Grenville as first minister, with responsibility for solving the debt crisis that resulted from the Seven Years' War. Grenville decided that Americans should pay more taxes because they benefited from the war and continued to drain the government's budget for administrative and military costs. Because the British at home were highly taxed, Grenville's plan to make the colonies pay their way seemed reasonable to many Britons. The Americans saw it differently, however, and quickly moved to the brink of revolt.

The Sugar and Currency Acts of 1764
Grenville began his program in 1764 with the **Sugar Act**, which initiated a new policy of charging duties primarily to raise revenue rather than to regulate trade. It reduced the duty on foreign molasses from sixpence (under the Molasses Act of 1733) to threepence per gallon, which was further reduced to one penny in 1766.

Grenville assumed merchants would pay the lower tariff rather than go to the risk of smuggling and bribery, as they had been doing. The law also added timber, iron, and hides to the list of enumerated goods. To make smuggling more hazardous, the act gave increased powers to the vice-admiralty courts. Because these courts lacked juries, the government expected easy convictions for smuggling. In addition, the law expanded the use of **writs of assistance** (search warrants), empowered the Royal Navy to inspect ships, and required endless bureaucratic paperwork from colonial shippers. Parliament also passed the Currency Act (1764), which had the potential to cause further hardship by forbidding colonies from issuing paper money, thus creating a shortage of currency.

Coming in the midst of an economic depression, this legislation stirred up colonial protest. Provincial assemblies sent petitions to England requesting relief. Merchants feared that if imports of foreign molasses were cut off, their provision trade to the Spanish and French West Indies would be lost. Without foreign credits, they could not pay for British manufactures. The Americans cut back their orders from Britain and encouraged home industry, arousing opposition to Grenville's policies from English businessmen.

The Stamp Act, 1765	Passed by Parliament in 1765, the **Stamp Act** provoked an even greater storm of protest. The law departed entirely from the confines of mercantilist policy, for its purpose was to raise

an internal revenue, which would be used to pay troops in the colonies. The act required individuals to purchase stamps for official documents and published papers, including deeds, liquor licenses, bills of lading, court documents, wills, passports, playing cards, newspapers, and pamphlets. All publications and official transactions were to be subject to this special tax, which increased with the value of a land sale or the size of a pamphlet. The tax could be paid only in specie, an onerous requirement because colonists generally used paper money and credit instead of the scarce gold and silver. The vice-admiralty courts would enforce the act, confiscating any land or property involved in transactions conducted without the stamps.

Colonists of all walks of life found the Stamp Act offensive. Everyone who engaged in public business, whether to buy a newspaper or sell property, would have to pay the tax. Because Parliament, not their own provincial assemblies, passed the act, Americans considered it a violation of their rights as British subjects. As they understood the British constitution, the people must consent to taxes through their representatives. The provinces could not send delegates to Parliament, so that body should not tax them to raise revenue. As one Philadelphia merchant said succinctly, "The point in dispute is a very Important one, if the Americans are to be taxed by a Parliament where they are not nor can be Represented, they are no longer Englishmen but Slaves." Only tariffs to regulate trade such as the 1733 duty on molasses, many colonists believed, were constitutionally valid.

Recognizing Parliament's attack on their powers, provincial assemblies protested the Stamp Act. In the Virginia House of Burgesses, the newly elected **Patrick Henry**, only twenty-nine years old, introduced fourteen resolves against the tax. The Virginia assembly refused to accept all of Henry's proposals, but in June 1765 approved the more moderate resolutions that defended the colonists' right to tax themselves.

When newspapers spread word of Virginia's action, other provinces responded. Rhode Island instructed its officials to ignore the stamp tax; Massachusetts,

Connecticut, New York, New Jersey, Pennsylvania, Maryland, and South Carolina passed resolves similar to Virginia's. In October 1765, representatives from nine colonies traveled to New York City to attend the Stamp Act Congress. In resolutions and petitions to Parliament, the congress upheld the power of representative assemblies, not Parliament, to tax the colonists. Further, the congress defended trial by jury, which the expanded authority of the vice-admiralty courts threatened. By issuing resolves and organizing the Stamp Act Congress, the colonial elite challenged British efforts to assert control.

Ordinary colonists joined the challenge. They drew on the tradition of the mob to protest what they considered tyranny. The anti–Stamp Act riots began in Boston on August 14, 1765, when a group who called themselves the Loyal Nine organized a demonstration to hang in effigy the appointed stamp collector for Massachusetts, Andrew Oliver. The crowd destroyed a partially constructed building they thought he intended as his stamp office, then damaged his home. Oliver resigned his commission. Twelve days later, a Boston mob attacked the houses of several other officials, gutting the mansion of Lieutenant Governor Thomas Hutchinson.

Protesters all along the Atlantic seaboard mobilized to prevent stamp distribution, scheduled to begin November 1. News of Oliver's resignation prompted anti–Stamp Act mobs in other cities to demand the same from their appointed stampmen. In some colonies, rioters forced stamp officials to relinquish their commissions. In others, just the threat of disorder was effective. By the end of 1765, distributors in every colony except Georgia had resigned.

The men who led the crowds called themselves **Sons of Liberty**. They were mostly propertied men—small merchants, shopkeepers, and craftsmen. These people who needed documents to conduct business would regularly feel the pinch of the stamp tax. The Sons of Liberty also established networks to organize boycotts of British goods. Merchants and retailers in New York City, Philadelphia, and Boston signed pacts to stop imports until Parliament repealed the act. By early 1766, the Sons of Liberty had coerced customs officials and judges to open the ports and resume court business without stamps. To Thomas Hutchinson, it appeared that "the authority of every colony is in the hands of the sons of liberty." In truth, the American resistance aimed to expunge the stamp tax, not end British authority. The movement achieved success in 1766, when Parliament repealed the Stamp Act after British businessmen from more than twenty cities had petitioned for relief. Suffering from postwar economic depression and unemployment, the British textile industry faced even worse times with an American boycott. British merchants clearly understood the growing significance of the colonial market.

DOING HISTORY ONLINE

The Stamp Act

Read Documents 1 to 7 on reactions to the Stamp Act. What specifically upset the colonists so much? Did they overreact to the act?

 www.cengage.com/ history/ayers/ ampassages4e

Protest Widens in the Lower South In the Carolinas, the Stamp Act resistance spawned revolts against colonial elites. To blacks, the radicals' oft-spoken argument that the English government intended to deprive white Americans of freedom—to make them slaves—seemed ironic. Yet such statements also gave them hope, for the Revolutionary movement spotlighted the institution of slavery and its immorality and injustice. In January 1766 in Charleston, fourteen hundred seamen and a group of black slaves threatened serious disorder. The sailors became restless because the customs agents refused to release ships from port without stamped documents. The people of Charleston were even more concerned, however, when a group of enslaved men marched through the town shouting "Liberty!" The city armed itself against a slave revolt, and the South Carolina assembly became so frightened that it restricted slave imports for three years.

The North Carolina Regulator movement also began in 1766, inspired by the uproar against the Stamp Act, but it targeted the colonial elite, not Britain. Six thousand western farmers demanded confirmation of land titles and the end of speculators' monopoly of the best land. The **Regulators** also protested corrupt local officials, excessive court fees and taxes, and lack of adequate representation for ordinary backcountry farmers in the North Carolina legislature. They called for a secret ballot to reduce the influence of wealthy planters in assembly elections. The North Carolina Regulators refused to pay taxes and closed several courts. In 1771, when the government sent the eastern militia, two thousand Regulators met them at Alamance Creek but were dispersed.

Most of the grievances of the South Carolina Regulators were different from the grievances of the North Carolina Regulators, except that they too lacked fair representation in the provincial government. They were planters who wanted to bring order—"to regulate" the backcountry. The South Carolina legislature had failed to create local government for the westerners, so they had no courts or jails. Westerners had to travel to Charleston to conduct legal business, but even worse, bandits roamed freely, stealing horses and cattle, destroying property, and sometimes torturing and killing their victims. The frontier robbers were mostly propertyless whites and some free blacks and escaped slaves; one report in the *South-Carolina Gazette* noted "a Gang of Banditti, consisting of Mulattoes—Free Negroes, and notorious Harbourers of run away Slaves." The Regulators resorted to vigilante "justice," capturing and whipping suspected felons, taking some to jail in Charleston, and evicting others from the colony. They finally ceased their activities in 1769 when the legislature established a circuit court system for the entire province.

The Townshend Revenue Act, 1767   In other British mainland colonies, attention focused on imperial tensions rather than on regional disputes. The British government and American radicals emerged from the Stamp Act crisis with conflicting views: the Americans celebrated the Stamp Act's repeal, but the British yielded no authority. In the Declaratory Act, passed with the repeal in March 1766, Parliament affirmed its power "to make laws and statutes of sufficient force and validity to bind the colonies and people of America, subjects of the crown of Great Britain, in all cases whatsoever." The act generated little response in the colonies but should have, for it laid the basis for subsequent restrictions.

In June 1767, Parliament passed three more laws affecting the Americans: an act establishing the American Board of Customs Commissioners to enforce legislation against illegal trade, the New York Restraining Act, and the **Townshend Revenue Act**. The Restraining Act threatened to dissolve the New York Assembly for refusing adequate supplies to British soldiers stationed in the province. Instead, the New York legislators gave in, pledging additional funds for the troops. The Townshend Revenue

Act was conceived by Charles Townshend, the British chancellor of the exchequer, who wanted the Americans to contribute, over time, an increasing percentage of imperial expenses in North America. The Townshend Act, which placed duties on tea, glass, paper, lead, and paint, would be just the beginning, for they would raise less than one-tenth of the colonial administrative and military costs. The revenues would pay the salaries of governors and judges, thus removing their dependence on the provincial legislatures. The act also required colonial courts to provide customs officials with writs of assistance to search houses and businesses for smuggled merchandise.

To American Whigs, the Townshend Act was dangerous for two reasons: it raised revenue without the approval of colonial assemblies and removed royal officials from the lawmakers' control. If the king rather than the legislatures paid provincial governors, the colonies lost a powerful negotiating tool for obtaining consent to the laws they wanted. Whereas the British saw the Townshend Act as an appropriate way to force the Americans to begin paying their share, the colonists believed it was a step toward tyranny.

At first, colonial reaction to the Townshend Act was restrained. Then, in December 1767, a few weeks after the act went into effect, John Dickinson, a Philadelphia lawyer and owner of a Delaware plantation, began publishing a series of twelve letters signed "A Farmer." Soon reprinted by newspapers throughout the thirteen colonies and published in pamphlet form as *Letters from a Farmer in Pennsylvania* (1768), Dickinson's arguments galvanized opposition to the Townshend duties. He rejected the position that the colonists should accept external taxes (duties) but not internal taxes (like the stamp tax), stating that only elected representatives could legally impose any revenue tax. He believed that Parliament could collect duties in the colonies if the purpose was to regulate trade (as with the Molasses Act of 1733), but not to raise revenue. Further, the purpose of the funds collected under the Townshend Act was oppressive, for it eliminated the power of the colonial legislatures over Crown officials. Dickinson predicted, "If we can find no relief from this infamous situation . . . we may bow down our necks, with all the stupid serenity of servitude, to any drudgery which our lords and masters shall please to command." Dickinson urged the colonies to petition for repeal; if that failed, they should once again boycott British goods.

Massachusetts responded to the Townshend Act first. In early 1768, its assembly petitioned George III for redress and then dispatched a "circular letter," or communication, to the other twelve colonies suggesting they do the same. The new English secretary of state for the colonies, Lord Hillsborough, realized that the circular letter was a call to unified resistance. Denouncing Dickinson's pamphlet as "extremely wild," he ordered the Massachusetts assemblymen to rescind their circular letter. They refused. When he directed colonial governors to dissolve assemblies that responded to the letter, most legislatures sent petitions and were disbanded.

Simultaneously, Hillsborough reassigned military units from the Ohio Valley to Florida, Nova Scotia, Quebec, and the mid-Atlantic region, where they could be called on to control the defiant provinces. In June 1768, he sent British regiments to Boston when the customs commissioners demanded protection against rioters. As the troops disembarked in October, they heard cries of protest but met no armed resistance.

During 1768, Boston residents signed a nonimportation agreement, using the same strategy against the Townshend Act that had proved successful against the Stamp Act. Most of the city's merchants pledged to stop importing goods from Great Britain after January 1, 1769, unless the Townshend duties were repealed. The nonimportation movement soon spread to New York City, where artisans supported the merchants by agreeing to boycott any retailer who imported British goods. Traders in Philadelphia, New Haven, and other northern ports delayed action, however, because they would face economic loss. They waited until 1769 for the imperial government to respond to their petitions and then approved nonimportation. In Virginia, George Washington supported the boycott. He wrote, "At a time when our lordly masters in Great Britain will be satisfied with nothing less than the deprivation of American freedom, it seems highly necessary that some thing should be done to avert the stroke and maintain the liberty which we have derived from our Ancestors."

The boycotts, which were unofficial agreements without the force of law, met uneven success. Between 1768 and 1769, American imports from England declined by 38 percent. As the months passed, however, importers wavered as their incomes fell. In contrast, craftspeople—beyond their concern for liberty—often benefited from the boycott because it created a demand for their products. Some artisans organized into street groups to threaten merchants and customs officials who tried to undermine the nonimportation pacts.

Women participated as both purchasers of goods and producers. Many "Daughters of Liberty" gave up imported tea and clothing, signing agreements to avoid the banned goods. Throughout New England, women organized spinning bees to produce woolen yarn. In Boston, some impoverished women profited from the temporary demand for American-made cloth, when William Molineaux, a merchant and radical Whig, contracted with local artisans to build four hundred spinning wheels, which he distributed to women to spin yarn in their homes. With this "putting-out" system, Molineaux and the spinners responded to both their patriotism and economic needs.

Crisis in Boston   During the years 1769 to 1775, Boston became the powder keg of the Revolution. Violence broke out in the summer of 1769 between the Bostonians and British redcoats, whose chief responsibilities were to protect the despised customs commissioners and help them collect duties. The soldiers became even more unpopular when they took jobs at low pay during their off-duty hours, thus throwing city laborers out of work.

The first serious incident occurred in July 1769, when a redcoat, John Riley, was jailed for hitting a local butcher who had insulted him. A near riot followed as twenty of Riley's comrades tried to rescue him from jail. Such episodes continued into early 1770. On March 2, the violence escalated when soldiers seeking revenge for an insult attacked workers at John Gray's ropeworks. Street fights intensified over the next few days.

On March 5, the bloodiest incident occurred, the so-called **Boston Massacre**. A young apprentice taunted the British sentry at the Customs House, who hit the boy with his gun. When a crowd gathered, shouting at the sentry, "Kill him, kill him, knock him down," Captain Thomas Preston led seven soldiers in his defense. The crowd grew larger, throwing snowballs, ice, and sticks at the soldiers and threatening them with clubs. Then someone hit a redcoat with a club, knocking the gun out of his hands. Preston's men fired, killing five townspeople and wounding six. The dead became martyrs, with March 5 commemorated as "Massacre Day" in the years ahead. The incident crystallized the colonists' opposition to standing armies. Nevertheless, when Captain Preston and six soldiers were tried for murder, the jury found two soldiers guilty of manslaughter and cleared the others. The radical Whig lawyer **John Adams** defended them, saying that all Englishmen should have a fair trial.

Just as the crisis in Boston came to a head in spring 1770, the British government decided on partial repeal of the Townshend Act, removing its duties except that on tea. The duties had raised less than £21,000 in revenues, but they had cost hundreds of thousands of pounds sterling in trade as a result of the nonimportation movement. As in the case of the Stamp Act, British officials backed away from a specific revenue measure without abandoning their right to levy taxes. Following Parliament's action, merchants in New York City and other colonial ports, eager to resume trade, cancelled their boycotts except on tea. Imports into the thirteen colonies from England rebounded over the next several years, increasing from £1.3 million in 1769 to £4.2 million in 1771.

The *Gaspée* Incident, 1772   For two years, the conflict between Great Britain and the colonies abated, but in 1772, it flared again. The trouble began this time in Rhode Island, when more than a hundred men burned the British schooner *Gaspée* and wounded its commander, William Dudingston. Avidly enforcing the Sugar Act, the *Gaspée* had harassed merchant vessels sailing

(Courtesy of the Rhode Island Historical Society, Neg. #RHi [x4]1)

Burning of Gaspée, by Charles De Wolf Brownell. *The seizure and burning of the British customs ship Gaspée by Rhode Island merchants in June 1772 moved the colonies closer to revolution.*

through Narragansett Bay. The Crown named a Commission of Inquiry to locate the perpetrators and send them to England to be tried for high treason. Although the commission identified none of the *Gaspée*'s attackers, colonists viewed the policy of taking defendants to England for trial as a serious threat to their constitutional rights.

In response, the Virginia assembly appointed a Committee of Correspondence to monitor British policy and facilitate communication among the provinces. Within a year, Committees of Correspondence in all colonies coordinated opposition to Britain's restraints.

The Coercive Acts, 1773–1774
The final showdown began in 1773 when Parliament passed the Tea Act to bail out the nearly bankrupt East India Company. Although some colonists purchased British tea, the boycott on the product was still in effect, and many purchased cheaper, smuggled Dutch tea. To sell the company's huge surplus, the government dropped a heavy import duty into England on tea headed for America, but it retained the Townshend duty, which Lord North insisted on keeping to uphold Parliament's power to tax the colonies. The company also received a monopoly in the colonies, with the right to choose certain provincial merchants as agents. The company selected consignees in the ports of Charleston, Philadelphia, New York, and Boston, to whom it promptly dispatched nearly 600,000 pounds of tea. While the tea agents in the other cities resigned, the consignees in Boston refused, thus inciting strong resistance from militants.

For the British, the Boston Tea Party required stern action. London decided that steps must "be taken to secure the Dependence of the Colonies" and, in particular, "to mark out Boston and separate that Town from the rest of the Delinquents." George III believed that the Americans must be forced to submit, because they increasingly assumed the "independency which one state has of another, but which is quite subversive of the obedience which a colony owes to its Mother Country." In 1774, Parliament passed four **Coercive Acts**: they closed the port of Boston until residents paid for the destroyed tea and altered the provincial charter to limit the power of town meetings and create a Crown-appointed, instead of elected, provincial council. Further, the acts expanded the governor's control over the courts, allowed the removal of trials of royal officials to England or to another colony, and permitted quartering of troops in private buildings if a colony failed to provide suitable barracks. The Crown appointed General Thomas Gage, commander of the British army in North America, as Massachusetts governor, thus threatening the colonists with military force.

Americans also considered the Quebec Act (1774) intolerable, though London did not intend it to punish the Bostonians. The Quebec Act helped keep the loyalty of French Canadians by confirming religious freedom to Roman Catholics in the province, allowing them to hold public office. It denied Canadians an elected assembly, however, designating an appointed governor and council to make laws. Residents of the thirteen colonies abhorred the act because it extended rights to "papists" and undermined representative government. It also gave control of the Ohio Valley to the Quebec government, thus curbing the ambitions of speculators in other colonies.

The First Continental Congress, 1774
Although the British government expected the Coercive Acts to isolate Boston and convince other provinces to be obedient, the policies actually pushed Americans toward more unified

resistance. After the port of Boston closed, residents faced severe unemployment and food shortages. Neighboring towns provided supplies and harbored refugees looking for work. Sam Adams and the Boston Committee of Correspondence called for an immediate boycott of British trade. Instead the other provinces favored a Continental Congress to consider what action to take. The Massachusetts assembly proposed a meeting in Philadelphia on September 1, 1774, to which all of the thirteen colonies except Georgia sent delegates. The fifty-five representatives included Richard Henry Lee, Patrick Henry, and George Washington of Virginia; Sam and John Adams of Massachusetts; and John Dickinson and Joseph Galloway of Pennsylvania.

The primary purpose of the First Continental Congress was to obtain repeal of the Coercive Acts and other restrictions. The Congress wanted Parliament to recognize the rights of Americans but was not ready to declare independence. Some of its leadership, notably Galloway (who later became a loyalist), argued for a moderate course, but the Congress was committed to action. It confirmed the Suffolk County Resolves forwarded to Philadelphia by a local Massachusetts convention. The resolves blasted the Coercive Acts as "gross infractions of those rights to which we are justly entitled by the laws of nature, the British constitution and the charter of this province." The laws should "be rejected as the attempts of a wicked administration to enslave America." Everyone qualified to fight should learn "the art of war as soon as possible, and . . . appear under arms at least once a week." By endorsing these resolves, the Congress took a militant stance.

Further, the Continental Congress passed nonimportation, nonexportation, and nonconsumption resolutions, ending all trade with Great Britain and Ireland and exports to the West Indies. It also banned importation of slaves. If the British had hoped to divide the colonies by closing Boston, expecting other cities to pick up its trade, the plan backfired when all of the colonies closed their ports. The boycott would continue until repeal of the Coercive Acts. Congress set up the Continental Association to enforce the ban on trade through elected local committees, called Committees of Observation and Inspection or Committees of Safety. The groups would expose violators of the boycott as "enemies of American liberty," publicizing their names and interrupting their business. Almost every town and county in the colonies elected these committees, which soon took on other functions of local government, including raising militias and collecting taxes. This transfer of authority from colonial governments to the Committees of Observation was revolutionary: Americans were now vesting sovereignty in themselves rather than in Parliament.

RESISTANCE BECOMES A WAR FOR INDEPENDENCE, 1775–1776

Over the winter of 1774–1775, the rift widened between the thirteen colonies and Great Britain. George III and his ministers considered the colonies in rebellion, yet the colonists themselves were unprepared to declare independence.

Lexington and Concord   The British government instructed General Gage to take forceful action. Headquartered in Boston, he decided to seize the patriots' stores of food and ammunition at Concord, twenty miles to the west, which he had learned about from an informer. Militant

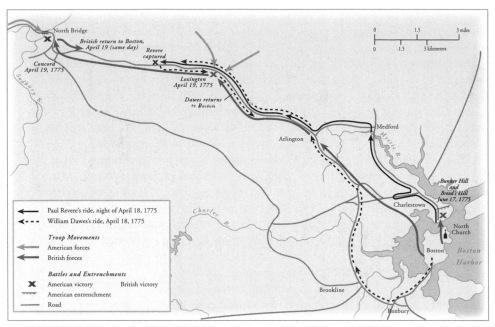

MAP 5.1 Battles in Eastern Massachusetts, April–June 1775.

Paul Revere and William Dawes left Boston during the night of April 18, 1775, to alert colonial leaders that the British troops were marching to destroy military supplies at Concord. The map also shows the location of the Battle of Bunker Hill two months later.

Bostonians discovered Gage's plan from their own spies, so they were ready to spread the alarm on the night of April 18, 1775, when seven hundred redcoats mustered on Boston Common. Paul Revere and William Dawes escaped the city to raise the colonial militia and alert leaders Sam Adams and John Hancock, who were staying at Lexington, on the route to Concord. The Massachusetts Provincial Council, just a few weeks before, had resolved to resist any advance by Gage's troops.

As the British marched toward Concord, they heard church bells and saw lights in windows. Soon after sunrise on April 19, they reached Lexington, where they met about seventy armed militia, nearly half of the town's adult males. The Lexington company, led by Captain John Parker, had formed only a few weeks earlier, so its training was incomplete. But the men were willing to defend, in the words of their town meeting, their "natural, constitutional and chartered rights." In the face of six companies of British infantry, Captain Parker attempted to disperse his troops. The British officer, Major John Pitcairn, wanted to disarm the Americans, not engage in battle. But as the British advanced, a shot rang out, then several more and a British volley. Pitcairn tried to stop his troops, but the shooting continued for fifteen to twenty minutes, leaving eight Lexington men dead and ten wounded. Only one British soldier was wounded and none killed.

The British reached Concord at about eight o'clock in the morning, long after the patriots had hidden most of their military stores. Following a brief skirmish in which the Americans inflicted more casualties than the British did, the redcoats headed back to Boston in a harrowing flight for their lives. Hundreds of colonial militia from

Battle of Lexington.   Battle of Lexington, *engraving by C. Tiebout after the drawing by E. Tisdale. The artist evokes the confusion and shock of the first battle of the Revolution.*

throughout the Massachusetts countryside had rushed to battle. These farmers used guerrilla tactics, shooting from behind trees, walls, rocks, and buildings. The British countered by sending advance parties to clear houses along the route. Using their famed skills with the bayonet, the redcoats killed the occupants and set fire to the homes. By the end of the day, British losses totaled seventy-three dead and two hundred wounded or missing, and Massachusetts counted forty-nine killed and forty-three wounded and missing.

In the days that followed the battles of April 19, New England went to arms. More than twenty thousand volunteers streamed to Cambridge, across the river from Boston. A large proportion of these soldiers soon returned home, but many stayed, expecting their wives, mothers, and sisters to work the family farms and defend the towns. One group of about thirty-five women, dressed in men's clothes and armed with muskets and pitchforks, guarded a bridge on the route British reinforcements might travel from Canada.

The Second Continental Congress   On May 10, 1775, the Second Continental Congress met in Philadelphia. Although the delegates remained unwilling to support independence, they were disappointed by Parliament's refusal to change its course. They faced the prospect of executing a war already in progress, convinced that British troops had fired the first shots and committed atrocities. To ensure that all of the colonies backed the war and to place the military under the control of Congress, they appointed George Washington of Virginia as commander in chief of the Continental army. Designating a southerner to head the military, which in June 1775 consisted primarily of New Englanders, broadened the appeal of the Massachusetts cause. At the same time, Washington was himself a delegate to Congress and steadfastly committed to civilian control of the armed forces. Despite his limited military experience, Washington

Abigail Adams

Abigail Adams (1744–1818) of Massachusetts wrote frequently to her husband, John Adams, while he served as delegate to the Continental Congress in Philadelphia. Like the wives of other Revolutionary leaders and soldiers, she managed the family farm during John's absence, including negotiating with laborers and buying land. Abigail Adams wrote during the 1775 battles in eastern Massachusetts that women were ready to defend their homes: "We are in no wise dispirited here. If our men are all drawn off and we should be attacked, you would find a race of Amazons in America." In 1776, as Congress developed a plan of government, she echoed Whig rhetoric in arguing that women must receive increased legal and political rights. "I desire you would Remember the Ladies," she wrote, for "we are determined to foment a Rebellion, and will not hold ourselves bound by any Laws in which we have no voice, or Representation."

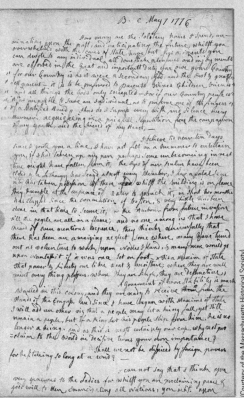

(Courtesy of the Massachusetts Historical Society)

(The Granger Collection, New York)

proved to be an excellent choice. His military bearing, determination, dignity, physical stamina, and ability to learn from his mistakes suited his role as commander in chief.

"An Open and Avowed Rebellion" Before Washington could arrive in Massachusetts, his troops engaged in the Battle of Bunker Hill. Learning that the British planned to seize the hills overlooking Boston, a detachment of the patriot army began to fortify the Charlestown Heights. By mistake, the men built defenses on Breed's Hill rather than on the higher and less exposed Bunker Hill.

This lapse might have isolated the detachment from the rest of the army had the British moved more quickly. Instead of attacking immediately, however, General Gage and the man who would soon replace him as commander of British forces, William Howe, foolishly allowed the Americans to complete their fortifications and obtain reinforcements. The British regulars lined up in proper European formation to storm Breed's Hill, and Boston residents climbed to their roofs to watch. While the redcoats shot as they advanced up the hill—to little effect—the patriots waited until the enemy was within range of their guns. The redcoats failed on their first two assaults, losing many officers and troops; then reinforcements took the hill when the Americans' ammunition gave out. The patriots retreated, pounded by artillery from British ships. Although the British won the battle, their losses were staggering: more than 40 percent of their combatants were killed or wounded.

During the year following Bunker Hill, many colonists became Whigs. The lives lost on battlefields in eastern Massachusetts undercut advocates of restraint. Still, given opposition from many delegates, the Continental Congress could not declare independence. During the summer of 1775, Congress asked the king for peace while preparing for war. In July, it approved a petition to George III, called the Olive Branch Petition, asking that he resolve the dispute with Parliament. Upon receipt of the petition in August, outraged by the colonists' armed resistance, the king proclaimed the thirteen provinces in "an open and avowed rebellion." In December, Parliament cut off all trade with the colonies, making American ships and any vessels engaging in commerce with the mutinous provinces subject to confiscation. For many Americans, these actions proved that the British government meant to crush the colonies militarily and economically.

The Continental Congress further alienated the British by ordering General Philip Schuyler to invade Canada. The congressmen hoped to make Canada the fourteenth British colony in rebellion. They expected to obtain help from French Canadians and perhaps even France itself, but even more, they wanted to prevent a northern attack. The American invasion of Canada was a failure from the start. Schuyler, suffering from illness and indecision, assembled troops and provisions too slowly, wasting valuable summer days. In September, much too late, Brigadier General Richard Montgomery took charge and moved the army north via Lake Champlain.

Concurrently Washington dispatched a small army led by Benedict Arnold and Daniel Morgan over a rugged route through Maine. Their march took so much longer than predicted that the men resorted to eating their dogs and soap. When the combined American forces finally attacked Quebec in a blinding December snowstorm, they were defeated with heavy casualties; Montgomery was among the dead, and Arnold was wounded. The army remained in Canada until May 1776, when British reinforcements arrived, pushing the patriots back into New York. For Congress, the campaign was a major error. The colonies lost five thousand troops to battle, desertion, and disease, and an enormous amount of supplies.

Taking Sides   The deepening conflict forced colonists to decide whether to support the Revolutionary Whigs. Some people remained neutral, either because they cared little about the issues or because, like the pacifist Quakers, they were opposed to violence on religious grounds. Loyalists rejected the Revolution for a variety of motives. Some believed that the king and Parliament had reason to expect the colonists to pay their share toward imperial administration. During the course of the war, about eighty thousand loyalists departed for Britain or other British colonies. Many more, perhaps several hundred thousand, continued to live among their patriot neighbors. Tories included Crown officials, Anglican clergy, and merchants with close ties to Britain. Some of the best-known loyalists were wealthy gentlemen and officeholders: Governor Thomas Hutchinson and Chief Justice Peter Oliver of Massachusetts; Joseph Galloway, Speaker of the Pennsylvania Assembly; and Frederick Philipse, landlord of a fifty-thousand-acre manor in New York.

Not all Tories were rich or intimately tied to Great Britain, for the Revolution became a power struggle within American society, not just one between the colonies and London. The tenants of New York manors, for example, took the opposite side of their landlords. Thus, residents of Frederick Philipse's manors became Whigs, whereas tenants of the patriot Livingstons and Schuylers supported the British. In Maryland, the loyalists gained widespread backing in counties on Chesapeake Bay's Eastern Shore, where farmers, suffering from economic decline and lack of political power, regarded the patriot elite as their enemies. The South Carolina backcountry divided along economic lines drawn during the 1760s, with the more affluent former Regulators supporting the Whigs and their opponents, the "lower sort," casting their lot with the British.

Of considerable concern to white Americans were the loyalties of enslaved African Americans. Of the 2.5 million people in the thirteen colonies in 1775, about 500,000 were blacks. As the rhetoric of revolution reached African American slaves, increasing numbers escaped. On Maryland's Eastern Shore, loyalist whites made common cause with the bondpeople of Whig planters: in fall 1775, a Dorchester County committee reported that "the insolence of the Negroes in this county is come to such a height, that we are under a necessity of disarming them. . . . The malicious and imprudent speeches of some among the lower classes of whites have induced them to believe that their freedom depended on the success of the King's troops."

A chief source of unrest, the patriots believed, was the November 1775 proclamation of Lord Dunmore, royal governor of Virginia, declaring "all indented [sic] servants, Negroes, or others [owned by rebels] free, that are able and willing to bear arms, they joining His Majesty's Troops." Whigs considered this proclamation foul play, an attempt to start an insurrection. They increased slave patrols and warned of harsh punishments to those who ran away or took up arms against their masters. The penalty for slave rebellion, of course, was death. Nevertheless, African Americans aided the British by joining the army and employing their firsthand knowledge of the Chesapeake Bay. Some served as pilots along its tributaries; others delivered fresh provisions to the British ships by foraging plantations at night.

African Americans also supported the Revolution, but they received little welcome from the Whigs. As the Americans created an army from volunteer forces besieging Boston, they excluded slaves and even free blacks from participating. From 1775 through much of 1776, when white enlistments seemed adequate, the patriot leaders, many of them slave owners, were unwilling to grant freedom in exchange for military service. By 1777, however, when recruiters found it difficult to fill their quotas, the states north of Virginia began accepting free blacks and slaves. Officially Virginia took only free African Americans, but some masters sent slaves as substitutes for themselves. An estimated five thousand African Americans served in the Continental army and state militias or at sea on American privateers. At the end of their service, many of the enslaved African Americans who fought for independence received freedom.

Some masters who had pledged liberty to their slaves if they served as substitutes broke the promises after the war.

Estimates of the total number of Americans who joined the Whig forces range from 100,000 to 250,000. Most signed up for tours of duty lasting several months or a year, not for the duration of the war. An ardent Boston patriot, for example, a poor shoemaker named George Robert Twelves Hewes, served at least six stints for a total of twenty months. Ordinary people like Hewes did their best to support both the patriotic cause and their families. Thus, Washington and his generals constantly faced the problem of expiring enlistments, a condition that severely hampered execution of the war. The inability of Congress to pay soldiers adequately also hindered recruitment and retention of troops. As time went on, the American troops became better trained and disciplined, but they came from less privileged rungs of society. By 1778, most of the states had to adopt conscription to fill their quotas. Men were drafted by lottery but could pay a fine or hire a substitute, loopholes that contributed to disproportionate service by the poor.

Women took part in the American war effort by operating farms and businesses in their husbands' absence, defending their homes and families against marauding enemy soldiers, supplying food and clothing for the troops, and even joining the army. Perhaps several hundred women put on uniforms to become soldiers. These troops included Deborah Sampson of Massachusetts, who enlisted under the name Robert Shurtleff. She fought in battle but was discovered when she received a wound; after the war, she collected an army pension. Others performed unofficial short-term service as spies. The most substantial contribution of women to the American military was that of the **Women of the Army**, as George Washington called them. Numbering perhaps twenty thousand over the course of the war, they served as nurses, cooks, laundresses, and water carriers. They were regular members of the army who drew rations and were subject to military discipline. Some saw action in battle, particularly women in artillery crews who carried water to swab out the cannon after each firing. The legend of "Molly Pitcher" evolved from women like Mary Hayes of Carlisle, Pennsylvania, who took the place of fallen soldiers.

> ### DOING HISTORY ONLINE
> #### Women in the Revolution
> Drawing on Documents 7, 14, 16, and 17, describe the range of female wartime experience. What other perspectives or experiences can you imagine that are not represented in these documents?
>
> www.cengage.com/history/ayers/ampassages4e

| Independence and Confederation, 1776 | During the winter and spring of 1776, fighting continued between Great Britain and the thirteen colonies. Although the Canada campaign was a disaster, the Americans met success in their siege of Boston. |

They sledged the heavy guns from Fort Ticonderoga about three hundred miles, installing them in March 1776 on the Dorchester Heights overlooking Boston. Instead of storming the artillery, the British withdrew from the city, sailing to Nova Scotia in preparation for an invasion of New York City.

In 1776, London undertook a huge effort to put down the revolt. It sent across the Atlantic Ocean 370 transports with supplies and thirty-two thousand troops, of whom many were German mercenaries (called Hessians, because the largest proportion came from the principality of Hesse-Cassel). The British intended these soldiers to join General William Howe's ten thousand troops from Nova Scotia, take New York City, and destroy Washington's army. The British navy, with seventy-three warships and thirteen thousand sailors in American waters, would bombard seaports and wreak havoc on colonial shipping.

As the British military descended on New York in midsummer 1776, the Continental Congress finally declared independence. The force of events propelled most moderate delegates to cast their vote for a complete break. In January 1776, Thomas Paine, a recent immigrant from England, had published **Common Sense** to argue the case for independence. Paine used language that appealed to ordinary Protestant Americans, employing biblical arguments that churchgoing farmers and craftspeople could appreciate and avoiding Latin phrases and classical references. He wanted to demonstrate that the time for compromise had passed, that the proper course was to shed the British monarchy and aristocracy to create an American republic. "We have it in our power to begin the world over again," he wrote. The bloodshed that began at Lexington justified rejection of the king: "No man was a warmer wisher for a reconciliation than myself, before the fatal nineteenth of April, 1775, but the moment the event of that day was made known, I rejected the hardened, sullen-tempered Pharaoh of England for ever." Pragmatically, Paine argued that the colonists must break their ties with London if they expected aid from France and Spain. He pointed out the importance of American exports, which "will always have a market while eating is the custom in Europe." He exclaimed, "TIS TIME TO PART . . . there is something very absurd, in supposing a continent to be perpetually governed by an island." Although his arguments were familiar to Congress and readers of political tracts, Paine convinced the American public of the need for independence. *Common Sense* sold more than 100,000 copies within a few months, reaching hundreds of thousands of people as copies changed hands and many listened to Paine's words read aloud.

Through the spring of 1776, sentiment for independence increased. News that the British had engaged German mercenaries heated the debate. The provincial assemblies of Georgia, South Carolina, and North Carolina gave their delegates in Congress permission to support the break, and Rhode Island declared independence on its own. Virginia proposed that Congress separate from Britain, taking measures "for forming foreign alliances and a confederation of the colonies." But in June, the New York, Pennsylvania, Delaware, and Maryland assemblies, controlled by moderate factions, were still not ready to condone a split. Nevertheless, Congress appointed a committee to draft the **Declaration of Independence**, of which Thomas Jefferson, a wealthy thirty-three-year-old Virginia planter and lawyer, was the principal author. A graduate of the College of William and Mary and a serious intellectual, he had been an active opponent of British policies since first elected to the Virginia assembly in 1769.

The declaration set forth Congress's reasons for separating from the government of George III; the revolutionaries focused on the king's offenses because they had already denied the sovereignty of Parliament. It held "these truths to be self-evident: That all men are created equal; that they are endowed by their Creator with certain unalienable rights; that among these are life, liberty, and the pursuit of happiness." Employing the philosophy of John Locke and other Enlightenment writers, Jefferson continued, "That, to secure these rights, governments are instituted among men, deriving their just powers from the consent of the governed; that whenever any form of government becomes destructive of these ends, it is the right of the people to alter or to abolish it, and to institute new government." Congress placed the blame for the breach on the king, listing his misdeeds: refusing to approve necessary laws passed by the colonial assemblies, dissolving legislatures and courts, stationing a standing army, interrupting trade, and imposing taxes without colonial consent. Most recently, the Continental Congress announced to the world, George III had declared "us out of his protection and wag[ed] war against us. He has plundered our seas, ravaged our coasts, burned our towns, and destroyed the lives of our people. He is at this time transporting large armies of foreign mercenaries to complete the works of death, desolation, and tyranny already begun." In reference to Lord Dunmore's proclamation, the congressmen accused the king of exciting "domestic insurrection among us." For these reasons and more, the Continental Congress declared the thirteen colonies, now to be called the United States of America, "free and independent states" having "full power to levy war, conclude peace, contract alliances, establish commerce, and do all other acts and things which independent states may of right do."

On July 2, 1776, all delegations to the Continental Congress approved independence except New York's, which had not received new instructions and so was forced to abstain. Completing revisions two days later, the Continental Congress adopted the Declaration of Independence. For many Americans, independence ended the problem of fighting a government that they continued to recognize as sovereign. When the Continental troops heard the Declaration read on July 9, they cheered, as did civilians throughout the states. However, the battles to defend this independence still lay ahead. General Washington cautioned "every officer and soldier . . . that now the peace and safety of his Country depends (under God) solely on the success of our arms."

To mount sufficient military force to win the war, the states needed unity. In mid-July 1776, the Continental Congress began debating the **Articles of Confederation**, a plan for permanent union, which it approved and sent to the states for ratification more than a year later. The chief disagreement among the congressmen was one that remained central to American politics for two centuries: the power of the national government versus that of individual states. The Articles permitted less centralized authority than would the Constitution, which was drafted a decade later. Under the Articles, Congress had responsibility to conduct foreign affairs, make war and peace, deal with Native Americans residing outside the states, coin and borrow money, supervise the post office, and negotiate boundary disputes between states. The "United States" meant thirteen sovereign states joined together by a Congress with specific functions. Article 1 established the "confederacy" to be called the United States of America, not a sovereign nation. Article 2 held that "each State retains its sovereignty, freedom and independence, and every power, jurisdiction, and right, which is not by this confederation expressly delegated to the United States, in Congress assembled." The Congress could neither tax nor raise troops, but could only assess quotas on the states, a serious disadvantage in time of war. Even so, the Articles of Confederation were not ratified until 1781, when the last of the states finally approved them. Conflict over state claims on western lands held up ratification. In the meantime, Congress attempted to govern within the limits of the unratified Articles of Confederation, but its inability to raise revenue and draft troops obstructed the American war effort, creating huge shortages of supplies and men.

CHAPTER 5

WAR IN THE NORTH, 1776–1779

For the American patriots, the Revolution was a defensive war. It lasted eight years, from 1775 to 1783, longer than any other in U.S. history until the Vietnam War. The Continental army was often outmatched, for it remained smaller than General Washington wanted; his troops constantly needed training as veterans left and new recruits arrived. But as the theater of war moved from one region to another, American generals obtained reinforcements from state militias and local volunteers. The British, despite considerable assistance from Tories, lacked enough reserves to subdue the rebellious North American seaboard. The sheer expanse of the thirteen states and the three thousand miles distance from England made the British army's task extremely difficult, despite its formal training and Britain's larger population and wealth.

Invasions of New York To conquer New York, and thus divide New England from the rest of the states, British troops landed on Staten Island in July 1776. In August, they attacked Washington's army at Brooklyn Heights. The redcoats defeated the Americans soundly, pushing them back to Manhattan Island and then to White Plains. But they failed to take advantage of Washington's mistakes, which could have allowed them to surround his troops. In November, however, the British did hand Washington a humiliating defeat by capturing the twenty-nine hundred defenders of Manhattan's Fort Washington.

The Continental army retreated across New Jersey with the British and their German allies at its heels. The patriots crossed the Delaware River into Pennsylvania, allowing the British to occupy New Jersey towns. The British gathered Tory support by offering a pardon to anyone who would take a loyalty oath within sixty days. For the Whigs, as Thomas Paine wrote, these were "times that try men's souls." The army was in retreat, and the New Jersey government had dispersed; citizens who were skeptical of Washington's abilities rallied to the British.

Before the end of the year, however, fortunes changed. British plundering across New Jersey turned indifferent farmers into radical Whigs, who became guerrillas, ambushing the enemy and stealing supplies. Meanwhile, Washington devised a plan that bought him time, acting before the enlistments of a large proportion of his army would expire on December 31. He attacked fourteen hundred Hessians at Trenton on Christmas night, in the midst of a winter storm. Taking the enemy by surprise, the Americans captured more than nine hundred men. In early January, Washington took the offensive once again, having convinced many of his soldiers to extend their terms for six weeks. Pennsylvania and New Jersey militia, inspired by the victory at Trenton, reinforced his troops. Washington eluded a superior British army under Lord Cornwallis, then defeated a smaller force at Princeton. General William Howe withdrew most of his army to New York. In the words of one British officer, the Americans had "become a formidable enemy."

In 1777, as the British made plans to suppress the rebellion once and for all, their strategy for the upcoming campaign became confused. General Howe intended to take Philadelphia not by crossing New Jersey, but by means of his brother Admiral Richard Howe's fleet. At the same time, London organized an invasion from Canada to win back Fort Ticonderoga and divide the states. The campaigns were not coordinated, and neither started before June, when British General "Gentleman Johnny"

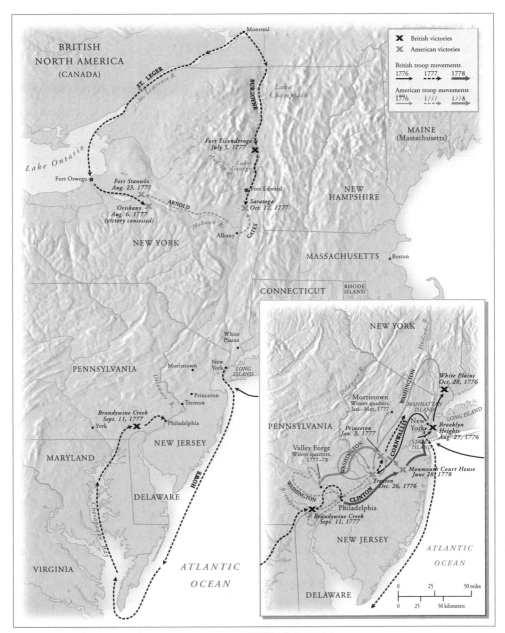

MAP 5.2 The War in the North, 1775–1778.

The major Revolutionary battles of these years took place in New York, New Jersey, and Pennsylvania. In 1776, British invaded Long Island and New York City, pushing Washington's troops across New Jersey until they won crucial battles at Trenton and Princeton. In 1777, the British were defeated at Saratoga, New York, but captured Philadelphia.

Burgoyne led his force of more than seven thousand British regulars, German mercenaries, Native Americans, and Canadians by boat down Lake Champlain. True to his reputation, Burgoyne overburdened his troops with baggage, including cartloads of personal clothing and champagne. Burgoyne easily took Fort Ticonderoga, then headed for Albany. But the American forces under Philip Schuyler had felled trees and rolled boulders into the path of Burgoyne's heavy column. Covering twenty-three miles of terrain that was difficult even without American sabotage took the British army twenty-four days. Short on supplies and horses, Burgoyne sent eight hundred troops to Bennington, Vermont, where General John Stark and his militia ambushed them by pretending to be Tories. Troops under British officer Barry St. Leger returned to Canada when they heard that Benedict Arnold was headed west to intercept them. The rebel forces burgeoned with volunteers as British soldiers pillaged the countryside. In September, near Saratoga, Burgoyne encountered the American army under General Horatio Gates, who had replaced Schuyler. The Americans surrounded the enemy, firing on them day and night. Burgoyne sent for help from New York City, but Howe had long since sailed with most of his troops to Philadelphia. Burgoyne's fifty-eight-hundred-man army surrendered at Saratoga on October 17, 1777.

The British Occupy Philadelphia As Burgoyne marched toward disaster in New York, General Howe more successfully reached Philadelphia. In July, his thirteen thousand soldiers departed from New York City aboard a fleet of 260 ships, but instead of disembarking within a week along the Delaware River, they sailed south to the Virginia capes, then up the Chesapeake Bay to Head of Elk. Their voyage lasted more than a month, costing Howe valuable time that might have permitted him to assist Burgoyne. Washington tried unsuccessfully, with an army of eleven thousand at Brandywine, to block Howe's advance through southeastern Pennsylvania. The British occupied Philadelphia, dividing their forces between Germantown and the capital. On October 4, 1777, Washington attacked the British encampment at Germantown, inflicting serious damage, though he was once again defeated.

Even so, in 1777, the British had failed to put down the American rebellion during yet another season of war. Upon hearing that Burgoyne's army had surrendered, the Howe brothers resigned. General Henry Clinton became the new commander of British forces in North America. The redcoats wintered in relative comfort at Philadelphia while Washington's troops nearly starved and froze to death at Valley Forge, to the west of the city. In February 1778, Continental soldiers lacked adequate clothing and received just three pounds of bread and three ounces of meat to last a week. Some ate only "fire cakes," baked from a paste of flour and water. Nevertheless, they became a disciplined army at Valley Forge under the Prussian officer Baron von Steuben, who rigorously trained the Americans in the European art of war.

Alliance with France, 1778 Although February 1778 brought despair to the Americans, it also brought hope—in the form of an alliance with France. Already supporting the United States with economic and military assistance, the French government hoped to recoup the international status it had lost during the Seven Years' War. Convinced by the victory at Saratoga that the former colonies could win the war, the French signed two pacts with the United States. The first was the Treaty of Amity and Commerce, in which France recognized American independence and both nations pledged "a firm, inviolable and universal peace." The second was the military Treaty of Alliance, in which they agreed to fight Great Britain jointly until the Americans had won independence, pledged not to negotiate a separate peace, and confirmed their defensive alliance "forever." France renounced claims to its former colonies in North America but could retain any of the British West Indies that it conquered.

In supporting the Americans, the French renewed their long struggle with Great Britain that had been suspended in 1763. France's entry widened the war, placing greater focus on the West Indies, whose sugar production made them more valuable than the North American mainland to the British. The following year, Spain allied with France but refused to recognize or assist the American insurgents beyond providing limited financial aid. Unlike France, which denied interest in North America, the Spanish viewed the Americans as potentially dangerous competitors.

| The Wartime Economy | Despite significant economic assistance from France and a much smaller contribution from Spain, the United States had grave economic problems during the war. The loss of British |

markets devastated farmers, merchants, and fishermen, because the embargo closed crucial ports in the West Indies and British Isles. The Royal Navy attacked and blockaded American harbors and ravaged ships at sea. On land, the armies laid waste to farms and towns.

For Congress, the chief economic problem was paying for the war. Without the power to tax, it printed money—a total of almost $200 million in paper bills by 1779. The states printed a similar amount, despite their ability to tax, primarily because printing money was easier than trying to collect revenues from a financially strapped populace. However, as the war continued year after year, the demand for military equipment, food, medical supplies, clothing, and soldiers' wages persisted. This extraordinary demand for provisions, coupled with the continuing emission of paper money, sent prices soaring. By 1779, the paper money was nearly worthless, inspiring the slogan "not worth a Continental."

The depreciation of currency resulted in popular unrest, and a group of Philadelphia militia in 1779 demanded a more equitable military draft and regulation of food prices. They were angry that the burden of militia service fell disproportionately on the poor because those who were better off could pay fines to avoid the draft. At the same time, the prices of food and firewood skyrocketed. In just two months, August and September 1779, the price of beef, flour, and molasses rose by more than 80 percent. The protesters, according to one broadside posted along the streets, blamed "a few overbearing Merchants, a swarm of Monopolizers and Speculators, an infernal gang of Tories" for the spiraling costs.

In the so-called Fort Wilson Incident, armed members of the Philadelphia militia met at Burns's Tavern on October 4, planning to capture and exile from the city four suspected Tories. Several hundred militiamen marched their prisoners through the streets to the fife and drum of the Rogue's March, ordinarily played by the military when a soldier was discharged dishonorably.

The militia was ridiculing the reputed Tories, all four of them wealthy citizens. When rumors raced through the capital that the militia planned to arrest others, about thirty gentlemen who thought they might be targets armed themselves and gathered

Continental Currency

The Continental Congress, which acted under the Articles of Confederation throughout the war, lacked the ability to tax. Because the states were reluctant to raise money through taxation to support the war, Congress funded military spending through loans and printed money. Before the Revolution, colonies had printed paper currency. For example, New York and Pennsylvania issued paper money as loans, thus putting needed money into circulation and obtaining public revenue from the interest.

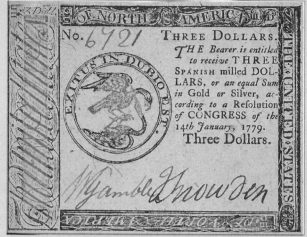

(Courtesy American Antiquarian Society)

Continental money, as noted in this example, promised the bearer the equivalent in Spanish dollars. Congress thus rejected the English system of pounds, shillings, and pence to adopt the Spanish denomination. This was a logical step because Spanish coins manufactured from Mexican and South American silver and gold had commonly circulated in colonial British America despite the official English currency. Unfortunately, Continental dollars quickly lost value as Congress printed millions to fund the war. By April 1781, $168 Continental was the equivalent of one silver dollar.

at the house of lawyer James Wilson. Although a member of Congress, Wilson was suspect because he opposed price regulation. The militia marched past "Fort Wilson" and gave three cheers. Then shots rang out. Although it is unknown who shot first, both sides subsequently exchanged fire. After cavalry broke up the battle, six people lay dead and seventeen wounded, the majority of them militia.

The Fort Wilson Incident terrified many people because lower-class patriots had directed armed force against the Whig elite, protesting the policies of their own government. Henry Laurens, a wealthy South Carolina merchant and member of the Continental Congress, wrote, "We are at this moment on a precipice, and what I have long dreaded and often intimated to my friends, seems to be breaking forth—a convulsion among the people."

THE WAR MOVES WEST AND SOUTH

The failure of the British army to defeat Washington's troops and the entry of France into the war led the imperial government to rethink its military strategy. Protection of Caribbean sugar islands from the French navy gained top priority. With redeployment of forces to the West Indies, British General Clinton had to consolidate his army, so in June 1778, he pulled his occupation forces out of Philadelphia, marching across New Jersey toward New York. Washington's army caught up with Clinton at Monmouth Courthouse, where the battle, fought in traditional European style with soldiers in rank and file, was indecisive. The British escaped to New York.

The Frontier War In the West, from New York to Georgia, fighting devastated the backcountry. When the Revolution broke out, many Indians supported the British, who still held garrisons in the West and had more gunpowder and provisions than the patriots did. Yet Native Americans responded in various ways to "this dispute between two brothers," as neutral Iroquois called the Revolution in 1775. "The quarrel seems to be unnatural," they said; "you are two brothers of one blood." Just as colonists divided among radical Whigs, Tories, and neutrals, so did the Native Americans. Even within some tribes, factions separated those who favored the British or the Americans or wanted to avoid any involvement. The militant Indians who sided with Great Britain considered the threat of white settlers crossing the Appalachians as most dangerous to their future. Many attempted to form pan-Indian alliances to fight their own wars of independence against land grabbers from the East.

Beginning in 1776, Indians attacked Anglo-Americans from the Georgia frontier to the Great Lakes. The Cherokees raided the southern backcountry and planned a major assault on Whig militia in Tennessee, but they ran short of gunpowder and were defeated in fall 1776. Many Cherokees, Choctaws, Creeks, Shawnees, Iroquois, and others did not give up, however, but rather planned in 1779 "a general invasion of the Frontiers" coordinated by Henry Hamilton, the British lieutenant governor of the Illinois country. **George Rogers Clark**, a surveyor, heard of plans for the Indian and British offensive. To Patrick Henry, he wrote, "The Case is Desperate but Sir we must Either Quit the Country or attack Mr. Hamilton." In 1779, Clark assaulted Fort Vincennes with a small force and obtained the British surrender, thus ending the pan-Indian campaign.

Despite Clark's victory at Vincennes, the Kentucky–Ohio frontier remained embattled throughout the war. The same was true of Pennsylvania and New York, where after 1777, most Iroquois and Delawares abandoned their neutrality to ally with the British. In 1778 and 1779, Major John Butler, his son, Captain Walter Butler, and the Mohawk leader, Theyendanegea, also known as Joseph Brant, led Tory and Native American forces against white settlements. The loyalists and Iroquois burned houses, barns, fields, and orchards; ran off livestock; and killed or captured settlers over a swath of frontier ranging from fifty to a hundred miles wide. In summer 1779, General Washington sent General John Sullivan with four thousand troops, who retaliated by burning Iroquois villages, orchards, and fields of corn. At Newtown, New York, Sullivan defeated a contingent of about seven hundred loyalists and Indians. His scorched-earth policy seriously damaged most of the Iroquois towns, displacing Indians, who suffered through the winter of 1779–1780 on short rations. But the next spring they renewed their assaults.

Because many Anglo-Americans had trouble distinguishing between Indian friends and foes, Native Americans who allied with the United States or remained neutral throughout the war often fared little better with the Whigs than those who sided with the British. In March 1782, frontier militia massacred ninety-six pacifist Indian men, women, and children at the Moravian mission of Gnadenhutten in Ohio. The Mahicans of Stockbridge in western Massachusetts, who fought in the American army, returned home to find that whites had taken over their land. The Catawbas of South Carolina were better treated. They performed extensive service for the patriots, searching for loyalists and escaped slaves, supplying food to the rebels, fighting the Cherokees in 1776, and battling the British, who destroyed their town in retaliation. After the war, the South Carolina assembly compensated them for their loyalty and livestock, refusing to abet the governor's plan to lease out their reservation.

The Southern Campaigns

Although the Revolution ravaged the frontier, the main theater of war remained east of the Appalachians, where the British inaugurated a new strategy in 1778. Retaining troops in New York City, they invaded the South, counting on loyalist support in Georgia, the Carolinas, and Virginia to restore colonial governments to the Crown. The British also expected the large numbers of enslaved African Americans in the South to weaken patriot defenses. In November 1778, General Clinton sent thirty-five hundred troops under Lieutenant Colonel Archibald Campbell to Georgia, where they joined two thousand soldiers from Florida. They captured Savannah and Augusta, but had trouble conquering the backcountry. Then, with ten thousand troops, the British turned to Charleston, where in May 1780 they compelled the American general Benjamin Lincoln to surrender fifty-five hundred men. The British fanned out through South Carolina, as many residents pledged their loyalty to the king. In July 1780, the American general Horatio Gates arrived to build a new southern army. Disaster struck once again, when Gates placed too much responsibility on untrained militia in action against Lord Cornwallis at Camden, South Carolina. The battle was a rout; even the regular Continentals were dispersed, and Gates, the hero of Saratoga, was disgraced.

The tide turned after General Nathanael Greene replaced Gates as commander of the southern army. The British contributed to the turnaround, as they became more insistent in demanding oaths of allegiance from Carolinians who preferred to keep out of the fray. This provoked a backlash, particularly because the British army stretched itself so thin that it withdrew protection from the people who took the oaths, thus exposing them to punishment by the Whigs. The redcoats and Tories also plundered, outraging many southerners and pushing them into the American camp. Most notorious was Banastre Tarleton's Tory Legion, which executed prisoners of war and destroyed houses and fields, leaving many families homeless. "Bloody" Tarleton created new revolutionaries, who joined Greene's army or the smaller irregular brigades led by Thomas "The Gamecock" Sumter, Colonel Andrew Pickens, and Francis Marion, "the Swamp Fox." During 1780 and 1781, Greene rebuilt the southern army using both traditional and guerrilla forces.

Although African American slaves were not welcome as soldiers in South Carolina and Georgia, they played an important role in the southern campaigns, acting as spies and counterspies for each side. One man, Antigua, received freedom by act of the South Carolina assembly for himself, his wife, Hagar, and their child in reward for "procuring information of the enemy's movements and designs." Throughout the South, African Americans provided much of the supporting labor for both armies: they built fortifications, worked in lead mines, constructed and repaired roads, produced arms and ammunition, and drove wagons. American officers complained about the chronic shortage of black laborers, because Whig slave owners jealously guarded their strongest and most talented slaves to work on their plantations. Further, thousands of

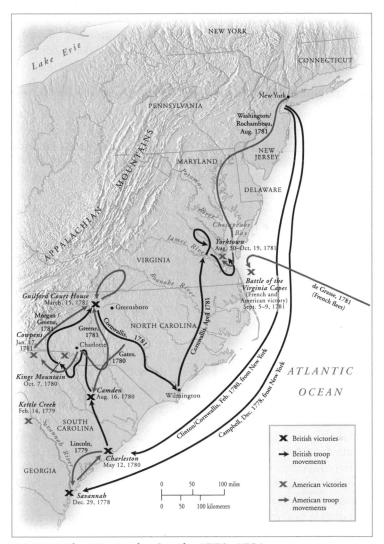

MAP 5.3 The War in the South, 1778–1781.

In late 1778, the British decided to invade the South, where they were no more successful in ending the war. They agreed to peace after their defeat by the Americans and French at the Battle of Yorktown in Virginia.

African Americans took advantage of General Clinton's 1779 proclamation offering freedom to those who joined the king's service.

A practice of rebel leaders that highlighted their ability to dissociate their own fight for liberty from the plight of enslaved African Americans was to offer recruits enlistment "bounties" in slaves, much as other states promised bounties in land. In South Carolina, Thomas Sumter offered one African American bondman or bondwoman to each private who would enlist for ten months. A colonel would receive three mature blacks and one child. The practice was adopted by Andrew Pickens as well and supported by General Greene, who expected to pay the bounties from slaves confiscated from loyalist estates. Because sufficient numbers of African Americans owned by Tories were lacking, regiments reported "pay" in arrears, some with grotesque precision. One payroll noted a deficit of 93 3/4 mature slaves and "Three Quarters of a Small Negro."

In fall 1780, Lord Cornwallis decided to head north, believing that since the British had destroyed two American armies and taken control of South Carolina and Georgia, the time had come to conquer the entire South. As his forces marched toward North Carolina, however, they met heavy resistance. In several battles, the conflict became a civil war as Americans fought on both sides. In October 1780, just to the south of the state line at King's Mountain, Whig frontier units defeated an enemy force, of which only Patrick Ferguson, the commander of the loyalists, was British. In January 1781, at Cowpens, General Daniel Morgan crushed Tarleton's Tory Legion by making the most of his sharpshooting frontiersmen. Morgan lined up the riflemen in front of his disciplined Continentals. The sharpshooters fired several volleys at Tarleton's troops, then withdrew to back up the regulars, who took the brunt of the fighting.

When Cornwallis learned that Tarleton's legion was lost, he chased the Americans into North Carolina, abandoning most of his equipment and supplies to move quickly. In March, Cornwallis met Greene at the Guilford Courthouse, where the American general used Morgan's Cowpens tactics, though less effectively because his successive lines of irregulars and Continentals were spread too far apart. Although the battle ended indecisively, one-fourth of Cornwallis's troops lay wounded or dead. Having discarded tents, medical equipment, and food—and cut off from his base in South Carolina—the British general withdrew to the North Carolina coast, where he sought naval support.

Meanwhile, Greene moved south to regain South Carolina and Georgia, where the British still had eight thousand men in arms. Because these troops were spread out in numerous towns and forts, Greene's fifteen hundred Continental soldiers and the guerrilla brigades of Sumter, Pickens, and Marion could pick off the garrisons one by one. Greene wrote to Washington in May 1781 that if the enemy "divide their force, they will fall by detachments, and if they operate collectively, they cannot command the country." By July, the Americans had pushed the redcoats and Tories back to a narrow strip of territory between Charleston and Savannah, which the British held until their evacuation the next year. Despite initial disastrous defeats, the Whigs prevailed in the Carolinas and Georgia by recruiting irregular forces and employing them strategically. The great sweep of territory controlled by the former colonies proved impossible for the British army to subdue.

The surrender of Cornwallis at Yorktown in October 1781 effectively ended the war. The general had moved into Virginia in April 1781, replacing Benedict Arnold as commander of the British forces there. Arnold, the former American officer, had turned traitor, joined the British army, and most recently captured Richmond. With an army of about eight thousand men, Cornwallis intended to concentrate on British military efforts in Virginia, so he requested more troops from New York. General Clinton refused. Their squabbling and delay allowed the Americans and the French to surround Cornwallis's camp on the Virginia peninsula by land and sea. Several times before, the French forces had collaborated with the Americans, but their joint efforts had resulted in failure. This time, soldiers under the Comte de Rochambeau and French fleets commanded by the Comte de Grasse and Comte de Barras played a decisive role in defeating Cornwallis at the Virginia capes. Washington's army marched south from New York to join American and French troops assembled in Virginia. With seventeen thousand men and heavy artillery, the American and French forces won the British surrender, finally placing the seal on American independence.

The Peace Settlement, 1783 In negotiating the peace, the United States had to reckon with both its adversary, Great Britain, and its ally, France, which in turn was beholden to Spain. American peace commissioners Benjamin Franklin, John Jay, and John Adams, whom Adams called "militia diplomats," shrewdly worked one European nation against the other to obtain a desirable settlement. They ignored Congress's instructions to take advice from France because they understood that French and Spanish goals were different from their own. France had little interest in a strong American nation; Spain particularly feared its territorial expansion. Thus, in violation of the 1778 treaty with France, the American diplomats negotiated separately with the British, obtaining recognition of independence and most other provisions they requested.

The British and American peacemakers approved preliminary articles of peace on November 30, 1782; the **Treaty of Paris** signed on September 3, 1783, was essentially unchanged. The new nation would extend from approximately the present-day U.S.–Canada boundary on the north, to the Mississippi River on the west, to the thirty-first parallel on the south (today's Georgia–Florida state line and due west). The American diplomats also secured fishing rights off Newfoundland and the St. Lawrence River, of particular interest to New Englanders. Further, the British agreed to evacuate their troops promptly from the United States "without causing any destruction or carrying away any Negroes or other property of the American inhabitants." For its part, Congress would urge state governments to return confiscated property to the loyalists. Prewar debts owed by citizens of each country to citizens of the other would be honored: they should "meet with no lawful impediment to the recovery of the full value in sterling money."

The treaty was a success on paper for the United States, but left France and Spain dissatisfied and pro-British Native Americans "thunderstruck." In coming decades, the Americans would struggle to enforce its provisions. The French gained little from the war except the separation of the mainland colonies from Great Britain. The Spanish had wanted to keep the Americans out of the Mississippi Valley and hoped to obtain the return of Gibraltar from the British. They instead accepted East and West Florida and the Mediterranean island of Minorca. Native Americans were furious that their British allies had signed away their lands.

While U.S. possession of the trans-Appalachian region remained disputed for decades, the provision that most immediately caused trouble was the one dealing with enslaved African Americans. Even before the final treaty was signed, American slave owners claimed that the British military forces were taking their "property." The situation was complicated, for thousands of African Americans had fled behind British lines to find freedom, and some had fought against their former masters. The British ruled that blacks who sought refuge before the signing of the provisional treaty in November 1782 could not be considered the property of Americans because they were already free, but slaves who escaped after that date would be returned to their masters. General Washington, Congress, and state governments tried but failed to convince the British to return all blacks to their former masters. At least twenty thousand African Americans, including those who accompanied loyalist owners as well as the ex-slaves of Whigs, left with the British military. Some went to Nova Scotia, where they received a generally unfriendly welcome from white residents; many others were transported to Florida and the West Indies. In the Sugar Islands most of the newly freed blacks were quickly reenslaved.

CONCLUSION

The War of Independence was a success: American Whigs cast off a monarchy to create a new government in which the people, not a king and nobility, held power. They rejected as tyranny British efforts to impose revenue taxes without approval of representative assemblies and to curb rights such as trial by jury. The patriots used a variety of tactics, including economic boycotts, riots, mass meetings, and petitions, as well as outright warfare. Their local associations assumed governmental authority, providing the basis for republican rule.

Against many odds, including opposition from large numbers of loyalists, the thirteen British colonies won independence, created a confederation of sovereign states, and obtained claims to the vast trans-Appalachian territories. French financial aid and military support were crucial to victory. The Whigs avoided military dictatorship, preserved individual rights for white Americans, and established the framework for a future democratic society. Yet not all Americans reaped immediate benefits. While wartime ideology challenged slavery in the North, the vast majority of African Americans remained enslaved. And though the Revolution offered women new, temporary roles in the economy and military—and more permanent educational opportunities after the peace—their political and legal status was essentially unchanged. The Treaty of Paris ignored the territorial rights of Native Americans.

Of immediate importance to the nation's leaders was establishing a stable government. The 1780s presented a series of challenges to the new republic.

CHAPTER REVIEW, 1764–1783

- Discontent with British rule arose among colonists primarily because of British efforts to impose taxation without representation in Parliament. To resist British policy, colonists boycotted British goods, circulated petitions, held meetings, and participated in riots.
- Colonial resistance culminated in the Boston Tea Party. In response to this act of rebellion, Britain passed the unpopular Coercive Acts, which further exacerbated tensions between the colonies and the mother country.
- The Revolutionary War began in 1775. Despite Britain's superior military strength, the colonies, with crucial support from the French, won their independence in 1783.
- After gaining independence, Americans created a confederation of sovereign states, claimed vast lands in the trans-Appalachian territories, and built a society that granted new rights and freedoms to propertied white men.
- Not all members of society benefited equally from American independence. Under the new government, Native American land rights were not respected, the institution of slavery became more firmly entrenched, and white women remained legally disempowered.

⬅︎▦ *Looking Back*

Chapter 5 focused on the period from 1764 to 1783, when the thirteen colonies moved from relatively peaceful resistance to outright war against the British government's "reform" program of new taxes and regulations.

1. Why did the colonists oppose the Sugar, Currency, and Stamp acts when they had posed no political complaint against the Molasses Act?
2. What was the role of African Americans during the Revolution?
3. How did the patriots achieve the unity necessary to wage the War for Independence?
4. How significant was the loyalist opposition?
5. What was the impact of the Revolution on Native Americans?

Looking Ahead ▦➡︎

In Chapter 6 we examine the problems facing the new United States under the Articles of Confederation and the steps that nationalists took to remedy what they perceived to be the government's ills.

1. What were the chief economic problems of the new nation?
2. How, if at all, did the status of women change after the Revolution?
3. Did the Constitution of 1787 fulfill the promise of the Revolution? Why or why not?

Go to the American Passages website at www.cengage.com/history/ayers/ampassages4e for additional review materials.

6

Toward a More Perfect Union, 1783–1788

The American patriots had won victory on the battlefield and, at least on paper, in negotiating the peace. The new country soon discovered, though, that independence brought severe tests as well as opportunities. In 1786, Dr. Benjamin Rush of Philadelphia summarized in a pamphlet the tasks facing the United States:

> There is nothing more common than to confound the terms of the American revolution with those of the late American war. The American war is over: but this is far from being the case with the American revolution. On the contrary, nothing but the first act of the great drama is closed. It remains yet to establish and perfect our forms of government; and to prepare the principles, morals, and manners of our citizens, for those forms of government.

Having fought for liberty and self-government, Americans now had to create an effective political framework to protect those rights. Their first government was a confederation of small republics in which property-holding white men elected representatives. But questions remained about how to avoid the opposite evils of tyranny and anarchy—questions that inspired fiery debates and even rebellion during the 1780s.

American leaders had understood since 1776 that the task of creating a workable government lay before them. They were less prepared for other problems that arose soon after the war ended. With limited powers under the Articles of Confederation, the Congress faced challenges in demobilizing the army, conducting trade outside the confines of British mercantilism, paying the war debt, coexisting with Spanish colonies in Louisiana and Florida, dealing with Native Americans, and supervising white settlement in the West. Despite Congress's competent action on some of these issues, the need for a more powerful central government became clear. In 1787, just four years after the conclusion of the war, delegates from the states met in Philadelphia to draft the new

CHAPTER TIMELINE

1783	Protest of Continental army officers at Newburgh, New York • Great Britain closes British West Indies to American ships • Massachusetts Supreme Court finds slavery unconstitutional
1784	Rhode Island and Connecticut pass gradual abolition laws • Spain closes port of New Orleans to Americans • Spain signs treaty of alliance with the Creeks • United States forces Iroquois to cede rights in Northwest Territory with Treaty of Fort Stanwix
1785	Native Americans yield lands in Ohio with Treaty of Fort McIntosh • Congress passes land ordinance for the Northwest Territory
1786	Shawnees sign Treaty of Fort Finney • Country party takes control of Rhode Island assembly • Virginia statute for religious liberty • Annapolis convention fails • Western Confederacy rejects treaties ceding lands in the Northwest Territory • Massachusetts farmers close county courts
1787	Shaysites attack the federal arsenal at Springfield, Massachusetts • Constitutional Convention meets in Philadelphia • Congress passes Northwest Ordinance • Constitution signed and sent to the states for ratification
1787–1788	Publication of The Federalist essays • Ratification of the Constitution by eleven states

Constitution, which became law on ratification in 1788. This Constitution has endured, with relatively few amendments, for more than two centuries.

POLITICS AND CHANGE IN THE NEW REPUBLIC

In contrasting "the American revolution" with "the late American war," Rush made a distinction that many people have debated since the 1780s. Rush thought the revolution had to continue because the government was not yet "perfect"—the states had too much power relative to the nation, leading to disunity and inertia. Others have framed the question in a different way: To what extent did the War of Independence bring about basic changes in politics and society? The war was revolutionary for propertied white men, but less so for women, African Americans, religious minorities, and the poor.

Republican Politics Under the Articles of Confederation, the United States consisted of thirteen sovereign states rather than one nation. In framing the Confederation, representatives from the states had refused to transfer sovereignty to a central government. Only state assemblies, elected by the voters, could impose taxes; the central government, or Congress, would be an agent of the states. This decision was based on republican theory, which held that only in a small republic could representatives act according to the will of its citizens. If the territory were large,

This icon will direct you to interactive activities and study materials on the *American Passages* website: www.cengage.com/history/ayers/ampassages4e

(c) Bettmann/CORBIS

Great Seal of the United States. *The Great Seal of the United States, adopted by Congress in 1782, incorporated as symbols of the new nation the thirteen stars and stripes, the eagle with the olive branch of peace and arrows of war, and the motto E Pluribus Unum, Latin for "Out of Many, One."*

the interests and desires of the people would be too diverse, making harmony impossible. Furthermore, state officials, guarding their power, feared that a strong national government would be dominated by factions with interests opposite their own. Each state had an equal vote in Congress and sent delegates "appointed in such manner as the legislature of each State shall direct." The U.S. Congress had responsibility to conduct foreign affairs, declare war and peace, and coin money, but it could not levy taxes or raise troops. During the 1780s, its dependence on the states for funds brought the Confederation to a standstill. For years, Congress sought an amendment of the Articles of Confederation to permit a national tax but failed to obtain the required unanimous consent of the states.

The structure of the state governments reflected their framers' concept of republicanism. Most of the state constitutions resembled the old colonial governments but incorporated changes that made them more responsible to the people. Most had two-house legislatures and a governor but gave the largest share of power to the lower house of assembly, elected annually by the voters. The Pennsylvania constitution of 1776, more democratic than others, included no governor or upper house of assembly (senate), which was designed to represent the wealthier segment of society. Georgia also excluded the upper house and denied its governor any power. Even states that retained the governor eliminated his veto over legislation or allowed the assembly to override with a two-thirds vote. All of the states produced written constitutions as a protection against the kind of changes they believed the British had made in their unwritten constitution before the Revolution.

During the late 1770s and 1780s, as Americans formulated and revised state constitutions, they also developed the method by which frames of government were written and approved—the **Constitutional Convention**. Pennsylvania radicals called the first state convention in 1776, explaining that its members would be "invested with powers to form a plan of government only, and not to execute it after it is framed." Then, in 1780, Massachusetts voters demanded a convention to write a new constitution rather than accept a document their assemblymen had prepared. The constitution was ratified by the people (voters), who thus claimed to be sovereign—the ultimate source of political power—because the frame of government originated with them. Within a few years, other states adopted the same process, recognizing that a constitution should not be written by a governmental body—the legislature—that the constitution created. As one theorist argued, "Conventions . . . are the only proper bodies to form a Constitution, and Assemblies are the proper bodies to make Laws agreeable to that Constitution." Remarkably, in Massachusetts in 1780, every free man, even those without property, could vote on the new constitution. However, the document they approved limited suffrage to propertied men.

State constitutions also provided some protection for the liberties many Americans had defended in the Revolution. Virginia included a model Declaration of Rights that other states copied loosely. Most state constitutions offered freedom of worship, required search warrants, and banned excessive fines and quartering of troops in private dwellings. Only some of the states, however, guaranteed trial by jury and the rights of free speech, press, and assembly. A few opposed monopolies and imprisonment for debt.

The state constitutions were radical in the context of eighteenth-century politics because they vested power in the voters and lower houses of assembly. Nevertheless, the definition of who was qualified to cast ballots and hold office remained traditional. John Adams spoke for most politicians of his time when he wrote that only property holders should be counted among the sovereign people who could choose and serve as magistrates because the purpose of government was to safeguard property. "It is dangerous," Adams wrote, ". . . to alter the qualifications of voters. There will be no end to it. New claims will arise. Women will demand a vote. Lads from 12 to 21 will think their rights not enough attended to, and every man, who has not a farthing, will demand an equal voice." Voters, according to republican theory, must have a stake in society. Wives, slaves, servants, and unpropertied laboring men were dependent on others and thus unqualified for suffrage. Yet in most places, women and free African Americans who owned property were also barred from voting by law or by informal pressure. One exception was New Jersey, where the 1776 state constitution extended the vote to "all free inhabitants" who held sufficient property; in 1807, the legislature fell into line with other states by disenfranchising all women and blacks.

The Question of Abolishing Slavery   The revolutionary rhetoric of freedom and self-determination unleashed a public debate over the legitimacy of slavery. African Americans fueled the discussion by escaping to the British and serving in the American army. In doing so, African Americans made whites more aware of the hypocrisy of fighting a war of independence while they kept other human beings in chains.

In the North, the first significant opposition to slavery had developed among Pennsylvania and New Jersey Quakers well before the Revolution. Since the seventeenth century, individual members of the Society of Friends had argued that black bondage violated basic Christian concepts, particularly the belief that all humans are equal in the eyes of God. For decades, these Quaker abolitionists failed to convince their meetings that slavery was wrong because many wealthy, powerful Friends held slaves. But after 1750, the Society of Friends became the first American religion to denounce perpetual bondage as a sin and to prohibit members from holding slaves. The Quakers then spearheaded an emancipation movement that gained strength among other whites in the 1770s and 1780s, contributing, along with escapes by African Americans, to the growth of free black communities in Philadelphia, New York, and other northern towns and cities. In addition, by the 1780s, slavery was less important economically in northern states than in the South. Thus, the combination of religious conviction, natural rights concepts of liberty and equality, and pressure by African Americans undercut its viability in the North. Prospective owners, already sensitized by guilt, grew wary of purchasing slaves, who were likely to demand emancipation or run away. Instead, northern employers hired workers from among the growing numbers of free laborers, including many African Americans.

In Pennsylvania and New England, state governments acted against slavery by the mid-1780s. The Pennsylvania assembly passed the first abolition law in 1780, its preamble reflecting the ideas that inspired many abolitionists of the revolutionary era:

> When we contemplate our abhorrence of that condition to which the arms and tyranny of Great Britain were exerted to reduce us, when we look back on the variety of dangers to which we have been exposed, [we are grateful for] the manifold blessings which we have undeservedly received. . . . We conceive that it is our duty, and we rejoice that it is in our power, to extend a portion of that freedom to others.

The act was less comprehensive than its heartiest supporters wished. As a result of compromises required for passage, the Pennsylvania act abolished slavery gradually—so gradually that under its provisions, no black Pennsylvanian would achieve freedom until 1808. The law provided that children born to slave mothers after March 1780 would be freed when they reached age twenty-eight. Slaves who had been born before that date would remain in bondage.

The Pennsylvania act was more effective than expected because many enslaved blacks, exasperated that the law failed to free them, escaped their masters. Hundreds of slaveholders conformed to the spirit of the law by manumitting (freeing) their slaves, regardless of birth date, at about age twenty-eight. Although these owners benefited from the labor of African Americans during their prime years, the manumissions helped hasten the end of slavery in the state. Also significant was the work of the **Pennsylvania Abolition Society**, which tested the limits of the 1780 abolition act by providing legal counsel to African Americans to defend their liberty. The number of slaves in Pennsylvania declined from almost 7,000 in 1780 to 795 in 1810.

Elsewhere in the North, the Massachusetts Supreme Court in 1783 decided that slavery was incompatible with the state's 1780 constitution, which said all men are free and equal, though it did not specifically outlaw perpetual bondage. As blacks sued for freedom, the courts ruled on their behalf, and so by 1790 Massachusetts reported no slaves on the federal census. The Connecticut and Rhode Island legislatures in 1784 followed Pennsylvania's example by passing gradual abolition laws, and Vermont and New Hampshire also banned the institution. New York and New Jersey passed gradual abolition acts in 1799 and 1804, respectively.

During the 1780s, considerable support for abolition developed in the Chesapeake region, though enslaved African Americans composed almost 40 percent of the population. Southern states, like their northern counterparts, continued the First Continental Congress's prohibition of the slave trade. Some people expected cessation of the trade to result in the gradual death of slavery in Virginia and Maryland—a mistake because the African

DOING HISTORY ONLINE

Gradual Abolition of Slavery in the North

Read Document 2 (Pennsylvania Act for the Gradual Abolition of Slavery) and Document 5 (essay by Anthony Benezet). According to Section I of the Pennsylvania act, for what reasons did the Pennsylvania Assembly enact gradual abolition? How did their rationale compare with Benezet's reasoning against slavery?

www.cengage.com/
history/ayers/
ampassages4e

Pennsylvania Abolition Society Broadside

In 1775, ten Philadelphia men founded the first abolition society in America. They were mostly Quaker craftsmen and shopkeepers who were determined to sway public opinion against slavery and liberate enslaved people through legal and political action. Interrupted by the American Revolution, they reorganized in 1784, after Pennsylvania passed its gradual abolition act of 1780. Pennsylvania Abolition Society members then focused on enforcing its provisions, in particular making sure that free African Americans were not reenslaved.

The abolition society distributed this diagram of a slave ship as part of a broadside against the international slave trade. The illustration shows the lower deck, with compartments (starting from the left) for men, boys, women, and girls. The text of the 1789 tract described the situation of the enslaved Africans, "packed, side by side, almost like herrings in a barrel, and reduced nearly to the state of being buried alive."

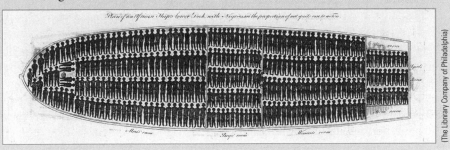

(The Library Company of Philadelphia)

American population there grew naturally by reproduction. Involuntary bondage would persist without positive action for abolition.

Thomas Jefferson exemplified the troubled and confused state of mind of many white Americans about slavery. Although he remained a slaveholder throughout his life and held racist beliefs, Jefferson claimed to support a strategy for gradual abolition in Virginia. The plan, never considered by the assembly, would have freed and educated African American children born after the law went into effect and, when they became adults, removed them to a separate territory. Relocation of blacks would ensure that whites would keep political power after emancipation.

Efforts for general abolition failed south of Pennsylvania, yet some progress occurred when Virginia (in 1782), Delaware (in 1787), and Maryland (in 1790) made private manumission easier. New laws permitted slaveholders who were inspired by antislavery beliefs to free their slaves. A private abolition movement took fire in areas of the Upper South, where Quakers and Methodists were numerous and planters were changing from tobacco to wheat as their chief crop, thus requiring fewer field hands. Slaveholders had the choice of whether to emancipate or sell their bondpeople. A market for slaves existed in the Carolinas and Georgia, where abolitionist sentiment had little impact.

The rise in the number of free African Americans in the Upper South was a measure of opposition to slavery. The free black population in Delaware rose to more than eight thousand by the end of the century; in Maryland there were twenty thousand free blacks, and in Virginia nearly thirteen thousand. Even with impressive numbers of manumissions, however, emancipated blacks in 1800 were just 8 percent of all African Americans in the region.

Defining Religious Liberty
The issue of religious freedom also confronted the architects of the new state governments. Revolutionary ideals led many to challenge laws that forced people to attend and financially support an established church. Before the Revolution, the colonies had varied widely in the relationship of church and state. Congregational churches were tax supported in Massachusetts, New Hampshire, and Connecticut; the Church of England (Anglican) was established in the Carolinas, Virginia, Maryland, and New York. In contrast, Rhode Island, New Jersey, and Pennsylvania protected a great diversity of religions, giving none of them public funds. All of the colonies, however, limited service in political office to members of certain religions.

The break with Great Britain had the greatest impact on the established Church of England, called the Protestant Episcopal church in the United States after the Revolution. With independence, some of its parishes dissolved as missionaries departed because the church hierarchy in England stopped paying their salaries. Many Anglican clergymen and laypeople in New England and the mid-Atlantic region had been loyalists, which helped fuel the Whig movement for disestablishment. Upon independence, all of the states in which the Anglican church was established promptly ended government support except Virginia, which finally acted in 1786. Its assembly passed Thomas Jefferson's **statute for religious freedom**, stating, "No man shall be compelled to frequent or support any religious worship, place or ministry whatsoever, nor shall be enforced, restrained, molested, or burthened in his body or goods, nor shall otherwise suffer on account of his religious opinions or belief."

Nevertheless, the movement to end discrimination stalled, and in the 1780s, religious tests for political office remained common. Most Americans, who were overwhelmingly Protestant, thought that only Christian men, preferably Protestants, should govern. State and local laws required observance of the Sabbath, outlawed gambling and other entertainments, and proclaimed days of thanksgiving and prayer. The states most resistant to disestablishment were the old Puritan strongholds in New England. Massachusetts, New Hampshire, and Connecticut required tax support for Protestant churches well into the nineteenth century.

CHALLENGES TO THE CONFEDERATION

Despite the dominance of the states, the Confederation Congress had important functions that required far more unity and power than it possessed. Of all Congress's difficulties, the inability to tax was most damaging, resulting in the Confederation's quick demise.

Military Demobilization
One of the most remarkable aspects of the American revolutionary experience—in the light of revolutions since that time—was the absence of a serious military challenge to civilian control. George Washington was committed to popularly elected government and

thus ignored suggestions that he become a military ruler. Even so, the United States faced two problems concerning the armed forces. During the war, Congress failed to pay or supply the army properly, but it had promised generous pensions and bounties to entice men to sign up for the duration of the war. The second question confronting Congress was whether to establish a peacetime army, an issue that had both ideological and financial significance.

For two years after the Battle of Yorktown in 1781, the Continental army continued to exist, with Washington encamped at Newburgh, New York, where his troops monitored the British army still in New York City. American officers and enlisted men voiced grievances because they needed food, clothing, and wages. Soldiers rioted and insulted their officers, while many simply went home with no compensation except their weapons. Officers at Newburgh drew up a list of complaints for Congress, demanding as much of their back pay as possible and a full reckoning of the entire sum they were owed. The officers suggested that they receive lump sums instead of the promised pensions of half-pay for life. They seemed so disgruntled that Washington remained at Newburgh instead of going home to Mount Vernon as he had planned.

The officers' discontent became more threatening when several politicians who favored a strong central government recognized an opportunity to pressure the states into giving Congress the power to tax. In what became known as the Newburgh conspiracy, **Robert Morris** of Philadelphia and Gouverneur Morris and Alexander Hamilton of New York hatched a plan to use the officers' protests to strengthen the Confederation. Washington would not cooperate, stating that the army was a "most dangerous instrument to play with," even to obtain a national tax. In early 1783, rumors spread that the officers were ready to take "manly" action against the government unless their demands were met. The crisis ended when Washington pledged to negotiate for their back pay and pensions and the officers swore their loyalty to Congress. For its part, Congress agreed to pay troops three months' wages at discharge, and officers would receive pensions of five years' full pay in government bonds. A group of eighty enlisted men stationed at Lancaster, Pennsylvania, found the offer unacceptable, so they mutinied and marched on Philadelphia, barricading the State House where Congress met. Although the soldiers backed down without violence, the frightened congressmen fled to Princeton.

Restitution of military pensions, back wages, and bounties took until the 1790s because Congress lacked the funds to discharge its debts. Soldiers who had been promised land bounties in the West had to wait fifteen years for surveys, in large part because Native Americans refused to give up the territory. By the 1790s, most veterans had long since sold their rights to speculators for a fraction of their worth.

The issue of a **standing army** squared revolutionary ideology against the need for defense. One of the chief causes of the Revolution had been the peacetime quartering in New York and Boston of the British army, which patriots called a "MONSTER of a standing ARMY." But now the United States faced threats from the Spanish in Florida and Louisiana, the British in Canada, and Native Americans everywhere along the frontier. In April 1783, Congress appointed a committee to consult Washington and other generals on military requirements. The commander in chief argued that the United States had to be prepared against its enemies. He suggested retaining twenty-six hundred Continentals in one artillery and four infantry regiments. He also advised Congress to organize a national citizens' militia that would stay in training for ready defense. In 1784, Congress dismissed Washington's plan, stationing a total of eighty men at two forts in New York and Pennsylvania. For reasons of principle and finances, the Confederation government virtually disbanded the army during an interval of peace, a pattern the nation would follow well into the twentieth century.

Economic Troubles The Confederation Congress failed to solve the problem of its war debt, which by 1790 amounted to an estimated $10 million owed to other countries and $40 million owed to Americans. During the war, the government had issued **paper currency** to pay for goods and services. It abandoned this policy because of rampant inflation. Congress turned to the states, which refused to contribute sufficient funds, and then borrowed from France and from American merchants and farmers for military provisions. As mentioned above, it also deferred payment on soldiers' wages. As the principal and interest mounted on these promissory notes and bonds, Congress requested an amendment to the Articles of Confederation to permit a national duty of 5 percent on all imports. The legislators tried for five years to obtain the necessary unanimous agreement of the states but failed on each attempt.

One long-lasting consequence of the war's inflationary crisis was conflict between urban and rural interests over public finance. The spiraling cost of food and fuel in the late 1770s had hurt city residents much more than farmers. In public debate over currency and credit, farmers wanted access to government loans based on the value of their land and its production, similar to the colonial land banks that had allowed them to use real estate as collateral for loans. Although the provincial currency issued by the land banks had been fairly stable, merchants and urban artisans in the 1780s recalled the more recent inflation of the Revolution. They believed that paper currency based on real estate would send prices soaring. At the same time, merchants knew that the economy would stagnate if specie (gold and silver) were required for every transaction, so they embraced an alternative method of generating paper currency, the bank.

The first bank in the United States was the **Bank of North America**, created in 1781 in Philadelphia. Robert Morris proposed the institution, based on the Bank of England, as a way to help solve the wartime fiscal crisis. Morris obtained support from Alexander Hamilton, Thomas Paine, and a committee of Congress for his plan; both the Congress and state of Pennsylvania chartered the institution. Instead of issuing paper currency through a land office, as farmers wanted, the bank issued currency in the form of short-term loans to merchants. These bank notes were backed by gold and silver plate and coins that investors deposited in return for a share of the bank's profits. The attraction for stockholders was that formerly idle gold and silver assets could now earn interest. The Bank of North America earned regular profits during its first two decades, beginning with an 8.74 percent dividend to investors in 1782. If people doubted the security of the bank, they could redeem their bank notes. Bank advocates believed that once a few people tested its soundness and received specie, others would trust the bank and accept the bank notes as currency.

In fact, the Bank of North America followed a conservative course that kept it solvent financially but made it unpopular with many people. The bank's manager, Thomas Willing, lent money only to good credit risks in the mercantile community, thus angering artisans and farmers who viewed the bank as a monopoly created by

Congress to benefit the commercial elite. Also, Willing refused to liberalize the bank's loan policy as confidence in the bank's strength increased. Instead of expanding the money supply as later banks did, the Bank of North America made loans only up to the amount of specie in its vaults.

Despite its flaws, the Bank of North America helped the mercantile community through a time of uncertainty. Commerce had suffered in the period immediately preceding and during the Revolution as merchants lost connections with trading partners in Great Britain and the British West Indies. In 1783, Americans expected to reestablish those ties as well as enter new markets in Europe and the French and Spanish colonies. With their newly won independence, they gained release from the restrictions of British mercantilism.

But being part of the mercantilist system had brought advantages as well as constraints. The British closed the ports of the British West Indies to American ships, a sharp blow for New England and the Middle Atlantic states, which before the war had found a major market in the islands for exports of fish, grain, flour, lumber, and livestock. To Great Britain and its colonies, the United States was now a foreign country. Americans could sell provisions in the islands and purchase rum, sugar, and molasses, but everything had to be carried on British ships. West Indies planters complained because this resulted in higher prices; American ship owners had to find new routes. For its part, Britain was eager to purchase tobacco from the Chesapeake and sell to Americans all the manufactures they would buy. U.S. merchants had access by treaty to ports in France and the French colonies but were barred from trading in New Spain. Gradually Americans developed trade with Germany, the Netherlands, Scandinavia, and even China. By the end of the 1780s, U.S. exports recovered to approximately their pre-Revolutionary level.

The road to recovery was rocky, however, because in the immediate postwar years, American demand for British manufactures far outstripped exports. During the Revolution, American artisans had attempted to supply metal goods and textiles, but had been unable to match British quality and prices. With peace, British manufacturers extended generous credit to American consumers for clocks, watches, furniture, textiles, clothing, mirrors, and other goods. When depression hit in fall 1783 because of the loss of the West Indies market, American farmers, merchants, and shopkeepers found themselves seriously in debt. In New England, for example, the balance of trade with Great Britain was so uneven that exports covered only 13 percent of imports. Although the economy improved after mid-1785, many farmers had difficulty escaping from debt.

Indeed, estimates of the gross national product suggest that the Revolution had an extended negative impact on the American economy. Data available for 1774 and 1790 indicate that income declined by more than 40 percent, close to the decrease Americans experienced during the Great Depression of the 1930s.

Foreign Affairs   Though the United States had won the war, its leaders soon learned that they received little respect among European nations. Despite the boundary provisions of the Treaty of 1783, Spain and Great Britain took advantage of the Confederation's weakness to trespass on territory in the West. The Spanish and English gained allies among Native Americans who were losing their lands to the steady stream of white settlers crossing the Appalachians.

North America in 1783

The peace treaty ending the American Revolution gave the United States most of the territory from the Atlantic Ocean to the Mississippi River, south of the St. Lawrence River and Great Lakes, and north of Spanish Florida. The new nation obtained claims to the region west of the Appalachians primarily because Great Britain, France, and Spain had more urgent goals. The treaty left several borders vague, however, and the United States had difficulty enforcing several provisions. Spain refused to recognize the thirty-first parallel as Florida's northern border and closed the Mississippi River to American trade. Problems with Britain were more long-lived. Until 1796, the British refused to evacuate nine military posts, including Michilimackinac, Detroit, and Niagara. Britain controlled the West through these forts, both militarily and through diplomatic alliances with the region's Native Americans. The imprecise border between Maine and Canada nearly caused war between the United States and Britain two generations later, but the boundary dispute was resolved diplomatically in 1842.

MAP 6.1 North America in 1783.

 This icon will direct you to interactive activities and study materials on the *American Passages* website: www.cengage.com/history/ayers/ampassages4e

During the 1780s, Spain tried to restrict expansion of the United States. The Spanish government had refused to accept the treaty boundaries granting the region between the Appalachians and the Mississippi River to the United States. With settlers rapidly filling the area, Spain feared for its control of Louisiana and East and West Florida. It wanted to extend its territory north from West Florida to the Ohio River and pursued this objective in a number of ways. It retained forts north of the thirty-first parallel, which the United States claimed as its southern border. Then in 1784, the Spanish government closed the port of New Orleans to Americans, apparently hoping to detach from the United States the region that later became Kentucky and Tennessee. Settlers in the trans-Appalachian region protested vigorously because they needed access to the New Orleans market for their goods. Some threatened to secede from the United States unless Congress convinced Spain to reverse its decision; a few, including James Wilkinson, a former Continental army officer, negotiated directly with the Spanish. Reporting on a journey in the West, George Washington wrote, "The western settlers (I speak now from my own observation) stand as it were upon a pivot; the touch of a feather would turn them any way."

Congress directed **John Jay**, the secretary of foreign affairs and a New Yorker, to negotiate with Spain to reopen the port. The Spanish diplomat Diego de Gardoqui refused to budge, instead offering to open other Spanish ports to U.S. commerce if Americans would relinquish demands for free navigation on the lower Mississippi. With the permission of Congress, Jay agreed to a treaty that provided commercial advantages for eastern merchants but closed New Orleans to westerners for a generation. The West and South erupted in opposition, blocking approval of the Jay-Gardoqui Treaty. The lower Mississippi River remained closed until 1788, when the Spanish permitted Americans to use New Orleans on payment of duties.

The Spanish government also cooperated with Native Americans to slow the influx of Anglo-American settlers into contested territory. Spanish colonists in the Floridas remained few, so they depended on good relations with the Creeks, Choctaws, and Chickasaws who controlled the region. Groups of Creeks who had migrated to Florida, and were called Seminoles by the British, could mobilize at least twice as many soldiers as the Spanish. Contrary to Spain's traditional policy of considering Native Americans as subjects to the Crown, its colonial officials in 1784 signed written treaties of alliance with the Indians.

Most threatening of these pacts to the United States was the one with the Creeks, which their leader, **Alexander McGillivray**, arranged. The son of a Scottish trader and a French-Creek woman and educated in Charleston, McGillivray could negotiate his way in both European and Indian societies. To protect Creek lands from settlers streaming in from Georgia, he offered the Spanish "a powerful barrier in these parts against the ambitious and encroaching Americans" in return for an alliance and weapons. The Creeks called the invading Georgians "Ecunnaunuxulgee," or "people greedily grasping after the lands of the red people." With Cherokees and Shawnees to the north, the Creeks battled Anglo-Americans through the 1780s, thus slowing settlement on the southwest frontier.

The Confederation government also had difficulty establishing its claims against the British and the Indians of the Ohio Valley. In the Treaty of 1783, the British had promised to remove their troops from forts in the Great Lakes region. Through the 1780s, however, they refused to withdraw, hoping for return of the territory.

They barred American ships from the Great Lakes and allied with Native Americans who wanted to halt white settlement. British diplomats justified these actions with the excuse that Americans had failed to pay prewar debts to British creditors and return confiscated loyalist property.

Great Britain's neglect of its Indian allies in negotiating the peace led the U.S. government to treat them as a conquered people. With great bravado, considering the Confederation's small army, American commissioners said to the Ohio Indians, "You are mistaken in supposing that . . . you are to become a free and independent nation, and may make what terms you please. . . . You are a subdued people." Other officials announced, "We claim the country by conquest." Under threat of arms, a group of Iroquois yielded rights in the Northwest with the Treaty of Fort Stanwix (1784); Wyandots, Delawares, and others ceded Ohio lands in the Treaty of Fort McIntosh (1785); and Shawnees gave up territory in the Treaty of Fort Finney (1786). Many Native Americans refused to recognize these treaties because their negotiators lacked authority and had been forced to sign.

Soon frontier warfare made U.S. officials realize that they were the ones who were "mistaken" in presuming that the Indians had been "subdued." Theyendanegea (Joseph Brant), the pro-British Mohawk leader, rallied Indians against white settlement in the Northwest. In 1786, he urged potential allies, "The Interests of Any One Nation Should be the Interests of us all, the Welfare of the one Should be the Welfare of all the others." Their resistance convinced Secretary of War Henry Knox that the United States must change its tactics or risk a general Indian war. He suggested that Congress return to the policy of purchasing lands instead of demanding them by conquest. The congressmen agreed, incorporating into the Northwest Ordinance of 1787 the futile promise that the Indians' land "shall never be taken from them without their consent."

The Northwest Ordinances of 1785 and 1787   Despite war with the Indians and the presence of British troops, the Confederation Congress moved forward with legislation to create the Northwest Territory. The issue of western lands had divided the thirteen states even during the Revolution. Some states claimed territories from their colonial charters; others, such as Maryland and New Jersey, had never possessed such claims. Titles stood in conflict with one another, as in the case of the region north of the Ohio River, which Virginia claimed in its entirety and Connecticut and Massachusetts claimed in part. States lacking rights to western lands believed that all should be ceded to the Confederation because together the states had won the trans-Appalachian territory in the Revolution. Virginia, whose charter rights were oldest, resolved the issue in 1781 by agreeing to transfer to the United States the region north and west of the Ohio River, the area that later became the states of Ohio, Indiana, Illinois, Michigan, Wisconsin, and part of Minnesota. Virginia offered cession on the condition that the territory eventually be divided into states that would join the Confederation on an equal basis with the original thirteen. The trans-Appalachian lands south of the Ohio River remained temporarily under the control of Virginia, North Carolina, and Georgia.

Congress passed three ordinances to establish guidelines for distributing land and governing the Northwest Territory. Wealthy speculators who had purchased rights from Native Americans had significant influence over the shape these ordinances took. Thomas Jefferson was principal author of the first ordinance, which passed Congress in 1784. This law gave settlers a great deal of autonomy in establishing a territorial government. The Northwest would be divided into seven districts, with the settlers of each to govern themselves by choosing a constitution and laws from any of the existing states. When any district reached the population of the smallest of the original thirteen states, it would be admitted as a state to the Confederation on equal terms. Congress retained responsibility for selling the public lands.

The second ordinance, passed in 1785, set the rules for distributing lands. The influence of speculators was apparent, for the minimum price of a lot was $640, payable in specie or its equivalent, a sum far beyond the means of many potential settlers. All property would be surveyed before sale, laid out in townships 6 miles square. Each lot would contain 640 acres, sold at a minimum of $1 per acre, with better land offered at a higher price. The government retained lots for public schools and for distribution to Revolutionary War veterans. Because of the relatively high cost, Congress found few individual buyers. In fact, many land-hungry squatters simply set up their farms without government approval, sometimes purchasing rights from neighboring Indians, sometimes not. So Congress accepted a deal offered by a group of New England speculators, the Ohio Company, agreeing to sell them 1.5 million acres for $500,000 in depreciated bonds, or less than ten cents per acre in hard money. Given the Confederation's debt, the sale was welcome.

Congress further cooperated with the Ohio Company in drafting the **Northwest Ordinance of 1787**. In response to speculators' demands, the law established firmer congressional control over the territory, providing settlers less self-government than under the 1784 ordinance. Initially a governor, secretary, and three judges appointed by Congress would administer the government. When five thousand adult males resided in the territory, they could elect an assembly, but the governor held a veto over its actions. Men were eligible to vote if they owned at least fifty acres of land. Three to five states would be created from the Northwest Territory, with each state qualified to enter the Union when its population reached sixty thousand. New states would have equal status with the original thirteen. The ordinance of 1787 also included provisions for individual rights that the Congress and the Ohio Company hoped would attract purchasers from New England. The ordinance protected private contracts, religious liberty, trial by jury, and habeas corpus (protection against illegal imprisonment). It prohibited slavery from the region forever. Thus, while catering to the interests of speculators, the Northwest Ordinance also extended rights won during the Revolution to new settlers in the West. Further, it limited the spread of slavery and determined that western territories would achieve the status of states rather than remain colonies.

POLITICAL AND ECONOMIC TURMOIL

Political strife under the Articles of Confederation disappointed Americans who had high hopes for their republic. Instead of harmony, economic interests clashed; the states failed to satisfy everybody. Many elites thought the United States was becoming too democratic and anarchic. As farmers revolted, government failed to control the violence, and some legislatures approved the insurgents' demands.

Creditors Versus
Debtors

As a result of the postwar depression, farmers throughout the United States faced economic hardship. Many had eagerly purchased British manufactures, expecting to pay for the new clothes and consumer goods by selling their grain and livestock to the West Indies. British merchants offered easy credit to stimulate sales; American merchants and shopkeepers passed the credit on to farm families, who would pay with the fall crop.

This house of cards collapsed when the British government closed the West Indies to American ships. English mercantile houses called in their debts in specie only, starting a chain of default that extended from London to the frontier. Americans lacked the gold and silver that the British demanded, but merchants refused to accept payment in farm products because they had no market for the goods. So they took farmers to court: in many places, the number of debt cases rose dramatically. For example, in Hampshire County, Massachusetts, the court heard three thousand debt cases between 1784 and 1786. Almost one-third of the county's adult males were prosecuted for insolvency.

State governments aggravated the situation by imposing taxes to repay war bonds in full, a policy that worked to the advantage of wealthy speculators who had bought up the bonds from farmers and artisans at a large discount. The Massachusetts government particularly favored mercantile interests, levying on farmers high taxes that also had to be paid in specie. When farmers defaulted, the courts sold their land and cattle, often at only one-third to one-half value. If their assets failed to cover the debts and back taxes, the farmers were imprisoned until they or someone else paid the sum. Often men sat in crowded jails with insufficient ventilation, heat, or food because they owed small debts. Ordinary folk became angry as they feared imprisonment and the loss of their farms.

Farmers Demand Reform Protesters mobilized as they had in the pre-Revolutionary period, at first meeting in county conventions to draw up petitions to the state assembly. In Massachusetts, they demanded changes in the state constitution to make the government more responsive to their needs and less costly to run. They wanted abolition of the state senate, which represented the commercial elite; lowering of property qualifications to hold office; and transfer of the capital from Boston to a more central location. Inland towns found it difficult to send representatives to the assembly because expenses were so high. The farmers also demanded paper money and tender laws, the latter enabling them to settle debts and taxes with goods rather than specie. Both would ease the credit crisis. During the Revolution, the yeomen had benefited from inflation and were able to pay off prewar debts with cheap dollars. While they stopped short of demanding a return to high inflation, they hoped for a gentle upswing in prices and a larger money supply to help them settle their debts.

When state legislatures emitted paper money or passed tender laws, as in Rhode Island, North Carolina, New York, and Georgia, little unrest ensued. In Rhode Island, political parties channeled conflict, for after the Country Party ousted the Mercantile Party in spring 1786, the new assembly issued paper money with stiff fines for creditors who refused to accept it. Elites elsewhere referred to "Rogue Island," even suggesting that the state be abolished and divided between Massachusetts and Connecticut. In other states, mercantile factions maintained control of the government. They detested paper money because debtors would pay in depreciated bills; they opposed tender laws because of the lack of a market for grain and livestock. Merchants argued that paper currency issued as loans on farm property (rather than as notes based on gold and silver deposited in banks) was immoral because it would lose value, allowing debtors to violate contracts by paying back less than they had borrowed. Creditors asserted that their property rights were at risk.

Shays's Rebellion, 1786–1787   When state governments failed to help, debtors in New England, New Jersey, Pennsylvania, Maryland, Virginia, and South Carolina protested militantly. Events moved furthest in Massachusetts. In fall 1786, armed Massachusetts farmers closed down county courts to prevent further hearings for debt. Perhaps one-fourth of potential soldiers in the state were involved, calling themselves the "Regulators," after the Carolina insurgents of the 1760s. Their opponents first labeled the rebels "Green Bushers" because they wore a sprig of evergreen—the Massachusetts symbol for liberty—and later called **Shaysites** when Daniel Shays, a forty-year-old veteran of Bunker Hill and Saratoga, emerged as their leader. The government frantically requested aid from Congress, which complied by requisitioning $530,000 and 1,340 soldiers from the states. When the states failed to cooperate, the powerlessness of the Confederation was clear.

The Massachusetts government acted on its own, taking measures that further alienated angry farmers. The assembly passed the Riot Act, which prohibited armed groups from gathering in public and permitted sheriffs to kill rioters who refused to disband. The legislature also suspended habeas corpus, allowing officials to jail suspected insurgents without showing cause. The farmers refused to back down; one warned, "I am determined to fight and spill my blood and leave my bones at the courthouse till Resurrection." They protested that the suspension of habeas corpus was "dangerous if not absolutely destructive to a Republican government." Nevertheless, in November 1786, the state government sent three hundred soldiers to arrest rebel leaders. When that failed to stop the farmers from closing the courts, Boston merchants raised private funds to outfit forty-four hundred troops. Residents of Boston and coastal towns who feared the inflationary consequences of paper money filled the ranks. Revolutionary general **Benjamin Lincoln** commanded the army; in January 1787, they marched to Worcester to protect the county court.

Lincoln's army forced the Shaysites to choose between submission and armed rebellion, for a middle ground of petitions and court closings was no longer viable. The farmers amassed their own troops, estimated at twenty-five hundred men, with Shays in charge of one regiment. They unsuccessfully attacked the federal arsenal at Springfield for weapons to assault Boston, then regrouped to await the merchants' army. Shays was convinced that their cause was just; in a newspaper interview, he confidently stated that he "knew General Lincoln was coming against him, but as he would bring with him nobody but shopkeepers, lawyers, and doctors, he could easily defeat him." Lincoln attacked Shays by surprise in a blizzard, dispersing the rebels within half an hour.

The aftermath of Shays's defeat was more divisive and bloody than the engagements between the armies. The assembly declared a state of "open, unnatural, unprovoked, and wicked rebellion," giving the governor the power to treat the Shaysites as enemies of the state. The legislators passed the Disqualification Act, which barred people implicated in the revolt from voting and holding office for three years, teaching school, or keeping inns and taverns. Many of the insurgents escaped to New York and

Vermont. Others, including individuals who had not been involved, were imprisoned. Militant Shaysites prolonged the conflict by raiding homes and kidnapping people who had sided with the government. As a result of the uprising and repression, voter turnout skyrocketed in the April 1787 election. A much greater number of western Massachusetts towns sent delegates to the legislature than they had in previous years, making the new assembly somewhat more responsive to rural debtors. While refusing to approve paper money, it enacted a tender law and quickly restored the civil rights of the insurgents.

THE MOVEMENT FOR CONSTITUTIONAL REFORM

The Confederation's helplessness in response to spreading armed rebellion strengthened the hand of nationalists like Robert Morris and Alexander Hamilton, who had been arguing for a more powerful central government. By 1787, Congress had lost much of its authority, and representatives stopped attending, often preventing action for lack of a quorum. Because it had failed to obtain a national tax and could not force the states to send requisitioned funds, the Confederation was broke. In 1785, Congress stopped interest payments on the French debt and in 1787 ended those on the principal. Nor could it reimburse American creditors. In 1787, Congress transferred responsibility for the national debt to the states.

The Philadelphia Convention

In September 1786, when Shays's Rebellion was still gathering steam, representatives gathered for a convention in Annapolis, Maryland, to discuss amending the Articles to give Congress power to regulate trade. The convention failed when only five state delegations arrived on time. Several of the delegates, including Alexander Hamilton, **James Madison**, and John Dickinson, called for another convention to meet in May 1787 at Philadelphia to consider a more thorough revision of the Articles. By early 1787, the disorder in Massachusetts and the growing concern about state emission of paper money built support for constitutional reform. In February, Congress endorsed a change in the Articles. Twelve states—all but Rhode Island, where farmers controlled the legislature—sent delegates to Philadelphia.

Although the appointed day was May 14, 1787, the convention failed to start until May 25, when enough representatives finally arrived. State legislatures had delayed choosing their delegations, and travel was slow. Among the first to arrive were Virginia's representatives, who used the extra time for planning. James Madison, a thirty-six-year-old planter, slaveholder, and intellectual who had served in the Virginia assembly and Congress, came to the convention well prepared. A shy man who avoided public speaking, Madison nevertheless took a dominant role in the proceedings, for which he was later called the Father of the Constitution. Propelled by the breakdown of Congress and the problems he witnessed in state government, Madison wanted to reform the Confederation to create a stronger central government. He believed that state constitutions with powerful assemblies were too democratic, giving too much influence to the common people. As a consequence, these legislatures collaborated with debtors by circulating paper money, which Madison considered an attack on property. The common people should be represented adequately, Madison thought, but their power must be constrained. The United States needed a new constitution that would place authority in the hands of well-educated, propertied men. Another Virginia delegate was George Washington, whose popularity and prestige made his support for the convention crucial. He presided over the proceedings but participated little in the debates.

Fifty-five men served at the Constitutional Convention between opening day and adjournment four months later. Twenty-one were practicing lawyers, another thirteen had been educated in the law, seven were merchants, and eighteen were farmers or planters; nineteen owned African American slaves. Most were relatively young men under the age of fifty, and many had served in the Revolution and had held political office. Benjamin Franklin, now eighty-one years old and ailing, was a member of the Pennsylvania delegation. Several heroes of the Revolution were absent, including Thomas Jefferson and John Adams, who were serving as ministers to France and Great Britain, respectively. Samuel Adams was not chosen as a delegate, and Patrick Henry refused to participate because he "smelt a rat." Most of the delegates supported a plan to place more power in the national government.

The Great Compromise
The convention can be divided into two periods. During the first seven weeks, the matter overshadowing all discussion was the power of large versus small states. After this issue was resolved, delegations formed blocs in new ways, according to concerns about the executive, slavery, and commerce. The basic question that the convention avoided debating at length was whether to amend the Articles of Confederation or write an entirely new constitution. Madison, who thought the Confederation beyond repair, moved the convention along with a document he had drafted in advance, called the **Virginia Plan**, which scrapped the Articles. Madison was able to set the convention's agenda because at the outset, no delegate had prepared an alternate design.

The Virginia Plan proposed a powerful central government, dominated by the National Legislature of two houses (bicameral). The lower house would be elected by qualified voters and would choose the members of the upper house from nominations by state legislatures. The number of delegates from each state would depend on population. This bicameral National Legislature would be empowered to appoint the executive and judicial branches of the central government and to veto state laws.

Several states opposed the Virginia Plan because it gave greater representation in the National Legislature to states with large populations. Delaware, Maryland, New Jersey, and Connecticut feared the power of Virginia, Pennsylvania, and Massachusetts, which together contained almost one-half of the American people. If the Virginia Plan were adopted, just four states could dominate the legislature. In dividing on this issue, states considered the possibility of future population expansion as well as existing size. Thus, states with unsettled territories mostly sided with the large states, while those without room for growth chose the opposite camp.

The small states preferred a constitution that retained the structure of the Confederation Congress but expanded its powers. In mid-June, William Paterson introduced the **New Jersey Plan**, which proposed a one-house, or unicameral, Congress in which the states had equal representation. Congress would appoint an executive council, which would choose a supreme court. As in the Virginia Plan, the authority of Congress was much enlarged, with powers to tax, regulate commerce, and compel states to obey its laws. The large states objected to this plan, arguing that Delaware (population 59,000) should not have as much power as Virginia (population 748,000).

The debate over representation in Congress brought the convention to an impasse. It made little progress toward a new constitution until the issue of state representation was resolved. The large states had a majority of the votes in the convention but knew that ratification would be impossible if the Virginia Plan prevailed. The Delaware delegation threatened to walk out until Connecticut formally proposed what has become known as the **Great Compromise**. The plan established a bicameral Congress, with representation in the lower house based on population. This body, called the House of Representatives, would be elected directly by the voters every two years and have the sole right to initiate revenue bills. Thus, the idea that all people with a stake in society should elect the representatives who taxed them was incorporated into the document. In the upper house, called the Senate, states would have equal representation; each state legislature would choose two senators for six-year terms. The bicameral Congress resolved the division between the small and large states and also satisfied those who wanted to limit the influence of ordinary voters. Senators were expected to come from the wealthier, more established segments of society; their long terms and appointment by state legislators would shield them from public opinion and thus provide a stabilizing influence. Both houses of Congress had to approve legislation.

The compromise between the large and small states created a government that was both national and federal. It was national because the House of Representatives was popularly elected, with not more than one representative per thirty thousand people. Upon ratification, the United States would become a single nation rather than a confederacy of states. By expanding legislative powers, the sovereign people vested more authority in the central government. Congress received the powers to tax, coin and borrow money, regulate commerce, establish courts, declare war, and raise armed forces. States were specifically forbidden from keeping troops without the permission of Congress, making treaties, coining money, and issuing paper currency. At the same

(Independence National Historical Park)

***Signing of the Constitution* by Thomas Prichard Rossiter, c. 1872.** *This painting of the Constitutional Convention of 1787 by Thomas Prichard Rossiter shows George Washington presiding. Because the convention met in secrecy, the artist used his imagination to paint the scene.*

time, the new Constitution established a federal government—one in which the states retained rights, including equal representation in the Senate. Congress was forbidden from giving one state preference over another when levying taxes and regulating trade, and it could not impose export duties, prohibit the slave trade until 1808, or carve a new state from any state's territory without permission. Approval by three-fourths of the states would be necessary to amend the Constitution. But despite these provisions, many Americans believed that the states—the small republics—had lost too much power. The struggle for ratification would revolve in large part around this issue.

The Executive, Slavery, and Commerce

Once the question of state representation was solved with the great compromise, the convention made greater headway. Factions within the convention shifted from one debate to the next.

The power of the executive was a concern to people living in a world dominated by kings and princes. Delegates wanted to ensure that their government remained a republic, that it would not become a monarchy or dictatorship. At the same time, they believed that the executive branch should serve as a check on the legislature. The convention debated several questions affecting the executive's power. Should there be a single president or an executive board? While some argued that a plural executive could prevent one person from usurping power, the convention chose a single president, expecting to limit his authority in other ways. Length of term also stimulated discussion, for the longer the term, the greater a president's autonomy. The convention reached agreement on a four-year term, without specifying the number of times the president could be reelected.

The question of how the president would be chosen was divisive, with some preferring direct election by the people and others wanting Congress or the state legislatures to make the choice. Once again, the issue of states' rights reared its head. A committee appointed by the convention devised an ingenious but complicated formula to satisfy all sides: an **electoral college** was empowered to elect the president and vice president, with each state allotted as many votes as it had representatives and senators. Thus, even the smallest state received three votes and the large states were represented according to population. The state legislatures could determine how to choose the electors. The electoral college would never meet together as a group. The electors of each state gathered within their states to cast votes, which they sent to Congress for counting. If no candidate received a majority, the House of Representatives made the selection from among the five candidates with the most votes.

Of the Philadelphia convention's decisions on the executive, most crucial to the endurance of the Constitution was the balance of power between the executive and legislative branches. The convention gave the president

TABLE 6.1 Enslaved Population in the United States, 1790

	Total	Slaves
New England	1,009,206	3,763
Middle Atlantic	1,017,087	45,210
Maryland and Virginia	1,067,338	395,663
Lower South	726,626	237,141

Source: U.S. Bureau of the Census, *A Century of Population Growth from the First Census of the United States to the Twelfth, 1790–1900* (Government Printing Office, 1909), 57, 133.

a veto power over laws passed by Congress. The legislators could override the veto if two-thirds of both houses approved. Congress also had authority to remove the president by impeachment and trial for treason, bribery, and "other high Crimes and Misdemeanors." Whereas Congress received power to declare war and raise troops, the president served as commander in chief. Only with the "advice and consent" of the Senate could the chief executive negotiate treaties and appoint ambassadors, Supreme Court justices, and other officials.

Slavery was a major factor in the convention's deliberations, though the words *slavery, slave,* and *slave trade* appeared nowhere in the 1787 Constitution. African American bondage affected the debates on representation in Congress, the election of the president, and the regulation of commerce. The southern states wanted to include slaves in a state's population when computing delegates to the House of Representatives and votes in the electoral college. Since slaves made up significant portions of the population in southern states, northerners protested that this would give white southerners an unfair advantage. They argued that slaves should not be counted because they could not vote. As part of the Great Compromise, the convention decided that five enslaved Americans would count as three free persons for apportioning representation and direct taxes among the states. Since three-fifths of slaves living in the Chesapeake and Lower South numbered 380,000 people, the power of white voters south of Pennsylvania was significantly increased by this compromise.

Political bargaining resulted in additional provisions that upheld slavery. The convention approved a **fugitive slave clause**, which prevented free states from emancipating slaves who had escaped from masters in other states. The delegates also adopted a provision that forbade Congress from prohibiting slave importation for twenty years (with no requirement that it ban the slave trade after that time). North and South Carolina and Georgia demanded the option of importing people from Africa because they expected settlement to continue into western Georgia and what are now the states of Alabama, Mississippi, and Tennessee.

Northern delegates did almost nothing to promote the abolition of slavery. Instead, they made the regulation of commerce their priority. The New England delegates agreed to the twenty-year protection of the slave trade in return for a compromise on international trade. The southern states suspected that the national government, if dominated by northerners in the future, would place heavy taxes on tobacco, rice, and indigo—the South's main exports. Southerners thought that navigation laws could also work to their detriment because northern merchants owned most American shipping. If Congress passed legislation requiring that all exports be transported in American ships, southerners would lose the choice of using a foreign, perhaps cheaper, carrier. Northerners, for their part, wanted Congress to have the authority to negotiate trade agreements on an equal basis with other nations. Congress could then retaliate if a country imposed restrictions such as closing ports. The convention settled these matters, first by forbidding Congress from imposing export duties, then with a deal that empowered Congress to regulate commerce. In return for South Carolina's vote for the latter provision, New England agreed to extend the slave trade for twenty years.

The Philadelphia convention created a Constitution that shifted important powers to a national government but still vested a great deal of authority in the states. The framers painstakingly created checks and balances among the branches of government. They required direct popular election of only the House of Representatives, giving that body the right to initiate taxes. The convention incorporated flexibility into the document, which had been absent in the Articles of Confederation, by permitting amendment with approval of two-thirds of both houses of Congress and three-fourths of the states.

The document shielded some individual rights, though critics argued that many were omitted. The Constitution protected trial by jury in criminal cases and habeas corpus. It banned religious tests for holding office under the United States, ex post facto (retroactive) laws, and bills of attainder, which extinguished a person's civil rights on sentence of death or as an outlaw. While codifying the principles of self-government and individual liberties, however, the convention denied them to almost one-fifth of the American population by embedding slavery within the fabric of the new government.

DOING HISTORY ONLINE

The Constitution

Read Documents 8 to 12 and 15 to 16. Why were Virginia and New York so important to the ratifying process and the "more perfect union"?

www.cengage.com/
history/ayers/
ampassages4e

Ratification, 1787–1788

After the delegates to the Philadelphia convention signed the Constitution on September 17, 1787, they quickly sent it to the Confederation Congress, which forwarded it to the states after little debate. One congressman from Virginia, Richard Henry Lee, tried to bury the document by adding amendments, but he was overruled. Article 7 of the document required **ratification** by nine state conventions. States refusing to ratify could remain independent or unite under another frame of government. Advocates of ratification knew that prompt action was necessary to forestall an effective opposition movement.

The group favoring ratification was not particularly well organized but had two advantages over its opponents. One advantage came from the choice of a name, the Federalists, for it undercut the ground on which their adversaries stood. James Madison, Alexander Hamilton, John Jay, and other supporters of the Constitution argued in favor of the federalist provisions that reserved powers to the states as well as the nationalist elements of the prospective government. While others denounced the

The Federal Pillars. *The Federal Pillars, from the Centinel* (Boston, Massachusetts), August 2, 1788, illustrates ratification of the Constitution of 1787.

Constitution because it transferred too much power to the national government from the states, the Federalists claimed the document provided balance. The critics were obliged to take the negative name of Antifederalists, which misrepresented their position in favor of states' rights.

The second advantage of those favoring ratification was that many advocates of a strong central government resided in the coastal cities and towns, where public opinion was easier to mobilize than in outlying areas. Most newspapers supported the Constitution. For example, in New York, where the ratification battle became intense, Hamilton, Madison, and Jay published in the newspapers a series of eighty-five essays that provided a detailed argument in favor of the Constitution. The essays also gained wide attention outside New York, and in spring 1788, the authors published them in book form as *The Federalist*, which is still considered a major work in American political theory.

Most Federalists gained their livelihoods as merchants, shopkeepers, professionals, artisans, and commercial farmers. As creditors and consumers, many favored the Constitution because it stopped state emission of paper currency. Federalists desired a government that would foster the growth of a market economy and facilitate trade with other countries. They believed a national government would provide the stability and strength that were lacking under the Confederation, enabling the United States to gain stature among the nations of Europe. Some frontier settlers, seeking military defense against Native Americans, also supported the Constitution.

The Federalists, who viewed commercial development more favorably than the Antifederalists did, thought the purpose of government was to arbitrate among opposing interests. They believed that society benefited when people pursued their own individual goals. They considered elusive the republican ideal of a community in which citizens could reach a consensus because they had similar needs. Madison argued in Federalist No. 10 that people possess different interests because they have unequal abilities and thus varying success in accumulating property. People by nature also have "different opinions concerning religion, concerning government, and many other points." In a free society, they form factions on the basis of their conflicting ideologies and "the various and unequal distribution of property." Madison wrote:

> A landed interest, a manufacturing interest, a mercantile interest, a moneyed interest, with many lesser interests, grow up of necessity in civilized nations, and divide them into different classes, actuated by different sentiments and views. The regulation of these various and interfering interests forms the principal task of modern legislation, and involves the spirit of party and faction in the necessary and ordinary operations of the government.

Madison claimed that the Constitution would be beneficial because a large republic contained more safeguards than a small one. In an extended polity, so many factions exist that the ability of a single interest to monopolize power is reduced. With the national government, "You take in a greater variety of parties and interests; you make it less probable that a majority of the whole will have a common motive to invade the rights of other citizens."

Antifederalists disagreed with this analysis, both because they favored small republics and because they feared the actions of men who would likely dominate the central government. Small farmers, many of them debtors who considered the mercantile elite their enemies, wanted nothing to do with this Constitution. At the core of their opposition was the belief that power should remain in the states. The Antifederalists understood that despite equal representation in the Senate, the new government was fundamentally different from that under the Articles. They argued that a republic must be geographically small with a homogeneous population in order to meet the needs of its people. They believed the new central government would be too large and too remote, that the interests of citizens of the thirteen states were too diverse. A congressman could never know the will of thirty thousand constituents; with so few persons elected to Congress and such large electoral districts, affluent, well-known candidates would have the advantage over ordinary men who ran for office. Thus, even the House of Representatives, the institution closest to the people, would become the domain of the rich. To the Antifederalists, the Constitution lacked sufficient barriers against corruption and abuse of power. At the least, term limits on the president and senators were required to prevent these officials from keeping their offices for life. Annual elections (instead of every two years) would make the House of Representatives more responsive to the voters.

Antifederalists also pointed to the omission of a bill of rights as cause for rejecting the Constitution. They advocated freedom of speech, press, assembly, and religion; jury trials for civil cases; judicial safeguards such as the right to a speedy trial and to confront accusers and witnesses; and prohibitions against unwarranted searches and

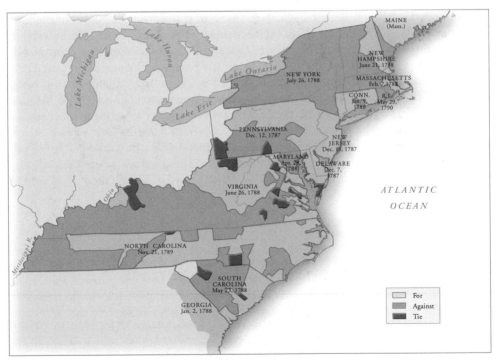

MAP 6.2 Ratification of the Constitution, 1787–1790.

The pattern of support by relatively small states is visible in the votes of Delaware, New Jersey, Georgia, and Connecticut. In Pennsylvania, Massachusetts, and New York, the more populated urban areas supported ratification.

seizures. The Federalists answered that a bill of rights would be superfluous because state constitutions offered these protections (some did, but in no case was protection comprehensive), and because a bill of rights was needed against a powerful king, not when the people themselves were sovereign. This latter argument ignored the vulnerability of the individual to the will of the majority. The Federalists used poor judgment in failing to incorporate a bill of rights into the 1787 Constitution, for the Antifederalists gained momentum as a result. Omitting these rights, for which the patriots had fought, turned many Americans against the proposed frame of government.

Nevertheless, ratification proceeded rapidly at first as state legislatures called elections for the state ratifying conventions. Delaware was the first to ratify when its convention approved the Constitution unanimously on December 7, 1787. In Pennsylvania, where resistance was potentially heavy in the backcountry, Federalists moved quickly, securing approval by a two-to-one margin. New Jersey and Georgia then ratified unanimously. When Connecticut accepted the new government in January 1788 by a three-to-one vote, five states had joined the Union. All of these states except Pennsylvania were relatively small and recognized the advantages of joining a union in which they had equal representation in the Senate.

Then the conventions became more acrimonious. North Carolina and Rhode Island rejected the document outright, and New Hampshire put off its decision. Maryland and South Carolina ratified easily, but the vote in Massachusetts was close, as animosities from Shays's Rebellion colored the debate. Turnout for the Massachusetts convention was huge because farmers in the central and western regions of the state believed the Constitution represented the interests of the eastern elite. The convention barely ratified the document by a vote of 187 to 168, recommending a series of amendments to protect individual rights and limit the powers of Congress. In June 1788, New Hampshire finally acted, becoming the ninth state to ratify, the number required to establish the new government. Nevertheless, two states remained crucial: Virginia and New York, whose size and economic importance made their approval necessary if the Constitution were to succeed. Virginia ratified in late June after a fierce debate, recommending to the first Congress a series of amendments, including a bill of rights. New York approved in late July, also with recommended changes, after New York City threatened to secede from the rest of the state if rural districts failed to accept the document.

CONCLUSION

The period from 1783 to 1788 was a crucial time for the United States as the country fixed the limits of revolutionary change and established a new government. Americans initially tried a political framework of thirteen small republics in which assemblies held the power to tax. All of the states (except New Jersey) restricted the vote—and political sovereignty—to propertied white men. "Republican motherhood" defined women's political role in the new nation. And despite a robust antislavery movement in the North, most African Americans remained enslaved.

The Congress, with little power under the Articles of Confederation, failed to solve its most pressing problems: the national debt, trade, and protection of U.S. borders against Spain and Great Britain. Even Congress's chief success, the legislation for governing and distributing land in the Northwest Territory, was marred by high land prices, delays in surveying, settlement by squatters, favoritism toward speculators, and conflict with Native Americans. When national government came to a halt and farmers rose in armed rebellion, nationalists demanded a constitution in which educated, propertied men like themselves would determine national economic policy and foreign affairs. These nationalists, who assumed the name Federalists, crafted the Constitution of 1787 to shift power from the states to a central government. The Antifederalists fought the new Constitution despite the Great Compromise, which provided states equal representation in the Senate regardless of their size. The lack of a bill of rights intensified opposition. The Federalists prevailed, however, and with ratification by eleven states by July 1788, the United States began a new experiment in republican government.

CHAPTER REVIEW, 1783–1788

- The United States based its new government on the republican principles of small government and the sovereignty of independent property owners.
- The Articles of Confederation created a weak central government that proved unable to raise money, repel border challenges from Britain and Spain, or resolve land disputes with Native Americans.
- The young republic suffered from a postwar economic depression that caused the proliferation of paper money, widespread debt, and economically motivated uprisings such as Shays's Rebellion.
- The Constitutional Convention was characterized by contentious debates over states' rights, proportional representation and slavery, and the proper powers of the national government.
- Opposition to the Constitution of 1787 arose from doubts about the new powers the document gave to the central government and the lack of a bill of rights.

◀◀▥ *Looking Back*

In 1783 the American patriots had won independence from Great Britain and achieved a favorable treaty, yet they faced many problems in establishing the new nation. The Articles of Confederation failed to provide the framework by which the thirteen states could pay the war debt and provide national defense.

1. What were the chief problems facing the Confederation Congress in 1783?
2. Why did Massachusetts farmers rise in Shays's Rebellion?
3. Should the Northwest Ordinance of 1787 be considered a success of the Confederation Congress? Why or why not?
4. Why has James Madison been called the Father of the Constitution?
5. What were the most important differences between the Articles of Confederation and the Constitution of 1787?

Looking Ahead ▥▶▶

Chapter 7 examines the process by which the Federalists created the national government as required by the Constitution. Although the election of George Washington as president offered stability, many issues remained unresolved. Differences within the ranks of former revolutionaries and supporters of the Constitution resulted in political parties.

1. How did Washington's administration address the problem of the Revolutionary War debt?
2. What was the new government's policy toward Native Americans?
3. Why did former allies such as Alexander Hamilton and James Madison create opposing political parties?

Go to the *American Passages* website at www.cengage.com/history/ayers/ampassages4e for additional review materials.

The Federalist Republic, 1789–1799

After ratification of the Constitution, the Federalists took leadership in creating the new government. Everyone expected George Washington to become president. The three authors of *The Federalist*, Alexander Hamilton, James Madison, and John Jay, who had been so important in the creation and ratification of the Constitution, went on to play a central role in making it work. John Adams and Thomas Jefferson, who were serving as ministers to Great Britain and France during the convention, returned home to become, respectively, vice president and secretary of state.

Although many Federalists disagreed with specific parts of the Constitution, they accepted compromise and knew the weak Confederation had to be replaced. In the flush of victory over the Antifederalists, they set to the task of remedying the nation's ills. Differences soon became clear, however, between Hamilton on the one side and Madison and Jefferson on the other, as the first administration tackled the national debt and foreign policy. Out of their conflicts over policy, varying interpretations of the Constitution, and competition for power, the nation's first political parties developed.

THE NEW GOVERNMENT, 1789–1790

The first national elections went well from the Federalist point of view, considering the strong Antifederalist opposition to the Constitution. The great majority of representatives and senators in the first Congress were **Federalists**. They fulfilled Madison's image of well-to-do men of national reputation and experience in politics. Many had served in the Constitutional Convention and signed the document. Most had military or political experience during the Revolution and Confederation period; just a few came from lower-class backgrounds. Although the first congressmen were revolutionaries, they were also elites who believed that the country's interests coincided with their own. They wanted a stable government to foster economic growth.

George Washington Becomes President

The choice of George Washington as president was a forgone conclusion, though he would have preferred to stay at his Mount Vernon estate in northern Virginia. In February 1789, members of the electoral college met in their state capitals to cast unanimous votes for the former commander in chief. Washington's leadership during the war, his dignity and character, and his support for republican government made him the obvious choice. He might have tried to grasp power during the shaky Confederation, like a Napoleon or Stalin, but he did not. The first president's commitment to the success of the Constitution ensured the nation's survival during the early years. John Adams, elected vice president, received fewer than half as many votes as Washington.

The president-elect's trip from Mount Vernon to New York City, the temporary federal capital, became an eight-day triumphal march. In large and small towns along his way—Alexandria, Baltimore, Wilmington, Philadelphia—crowds of people, troops of infantry and cavalry, and local officials feted him with ceremonies, cannon fire, and banquets. Philadelphia citizens erected a Roman arch, crowning the Revolutionary hero with a laurel wreath. In New Jersey, throngs saluted his military victories at Trenton and Princeton. On April 23, 1789, Washington crossed into Manhattan on a festooned barge, welcomed by thousands of cheering New Yorkers. He took the oath of office a week later.

The president and Congress, aware that they were setting precedent, initially placed a great deal of emphasis on titles and the comportment of officials. In this republic, in a world of monarchies, how should they be addressed? Should the president keep his door open to the public or remain detached? Although the questions may seem trivial, they indicate the novelty of this republican experiment. Adams, with diplomatic experience in Europe, urged Congress to adopt titles like those of other nations. A Senate committee suggested, for example, that Washington be called "His Highness the President of the United States of America, and Protector of their Liberties." After much debate, Congress dropped the notion of titles, preferring a more republican style. Washington and his successors have been addressed simply as "Mr. President."

For his part, the president wondered how to dignify his office and accomplish his work. He could easily have spent all of his time meeting with visitors, entertaining, and dining out. But he did not want complete separation from the people. Washington's personality tended toward aloofness. He decided to hold a one-hour reception once a week, invite a few visitors to dinner, and sometimes attend the theater.

Washington also developed, by trial and error, the way in which the chief executive would deal with Congress. Early in his administration, in advance of negotiating a treaty with the Creek Indians, he attended the Senate to request their "advice and consent," as the Constitution seemed to direct. The senators were unprepared to discuss Washington's proposal, leading to embarrassment on both sides. The president resolved never to consult in formal session again. Instead, he set the precedent of private informal meetings with members of Congress. Instead of the president attending congressional hearings, the heads of executive departments, such as the secretary of the treasury, would do so. And in the case of treaties, the executive would seek the Senate's consent after negotiations were complete, not advice—at least formally—beforehand.

 This icon will direct you to interactive activities and study materials on the American Passages website: www.cengage.com/history/ayers/ampassages4e

CHAPTER TIMELINE

1789	First Congress meets • Inauguration of George Washington as president • French Revolution begins • Judiciary Act of 1789
1790	Site on Potomac River chosen for permanent capital • Congress approves the funding and assumption plans • Samuel Slater builds first water-powered textile mill in the United States • First national census • Nootka Convention
1791	Bank of the United States is established • Native Americans of the Ohio Valley destroy Arthur St. Clair's army • Ratification of Bill of Rights
1793	France declares war on Great Britain and Spain • Washington begins second term • Proclamation of Neutrality • Genêt Affair • Britain seizes U.S. merchant fleet • Eli Whitney invents cotton gin
1794	Battle of Fallen Timbers • Whiskey Rebellion
1795	Senate approves the Jay Treaty • Treaty of Greenville • Treaty of San Lorenzo
1797	John Adams becomes second president
1798	XYZ Affair becomes public • Congress passes Alien and Sedition Acts • Kentucky and Virginia Resolutions
1798–1800	Quasi-War with France
1799	The Fries Rebellion • Napoleon takes power in France

Beyond titles and modes of operating, Congress and the president needed to establish executive departments and courts, and draw up a bill of rights, to fill gaps in the written Constitution. In creating executive departments, which included War, Treasury, State (foreign affairs), and the attorney general, the most crucial constitutional question concerned who would be able to remove the heads of departments from office. Some senators hoped to restrict the president's power by requiring Senate approval before officeholders could be fired, thus making them more accountable to the legislature. In rejecting this proposal, Congress clarified one aspect of the Constitution's balance of powers.

With the **Judiciary Act of 1789**, Congress put some flesh on the skeleton outlined in Article III of the Constitution, which stated that the "judicial power of the United States shall be vested in one Supreme Court, and in such inferior courts as the Congress may from time to time ordain and establish." Congress might have created a full-blown national court system, but supporters of states' rights opposed such enhancement of national power. Thus, the Judiciary Act, the result of compromise, established a Supreme Court of six justices and a system of federal inferior courts, which were few in number and restricted primarily to consideration of federal crimes. State courts retained original jurisdiction in most civil and criminal cases, with the U.S. Supreme Court taking appeals from the highest state courts. John Jay became the first chief justice.

The Bill of Rights   During its first months, Congress took up the question of amending the Constitution to satisfy criticisms voiced during ratification that basic rights were not protected, objections that by the summer of 1789

George Washington in New York City

Although ratification of the Constitution provided the political institutions to move forward as a republic, the nation lacked a unifying political culture. George Washington, hero of the Revolution, became a symbol of unity for all Americans, perhaps especially for those who could not vote or participate in government. He journeyed throughout the country, welcomed with triumphal arches and celebrations. An observer noted that if "every individual personally [were] consulted as to the man whom they would elect to fill the office of President of this rising empire, the only reply from New Hampshire to Georgia, would be Washington."

As suggested in this illustration, thousands greeted George Washington on his arrival in New York City for inauguration as president. The broad participation in such festivities—though not in actual suffrage and politics—is seen in the portrayal of Native Americans, African Americans, and women among the crowd. Other parades and pageants, most important the annual celebration of July 4, helped to bond voters and nonvoters alike to the new nation.

(The Granger Collection, New York)

still kept North Carolina and Rhode Island out of the Union. More than the original document, the first ten amendments, called the **Bill of Rights**, represented the will of the American people.

The ratification campaign had elicited a mountain of proposals for amending the Constitution. Opponents offered two major grounds for altering the document or abandoning it altogether. Antifederalist leaders believed it took too much power from the states and from themselves as leaders of state and local governments; popular opinion feared the loss of personal freedoms to a strong national government.

James Madison became the chief proponent of the Bill of Rights in Congress despite his earlier advocacy of the Federalist position that the amendments were unnecessary. In order to get elected to the House of Representatives, he had promised his Virginia constituents to obtain the safeguards. Madison took his vow seriously, pushing his reluctant Federalist colleagues to the task. Antifederalist leaders, who wanted to scrap the Constitution entirely, now denied support to the Bill of Rights because they knew protection of individual freedoms would garner popular support.

After much negotiation between the Senate and the House, on September 25, 1789, Congress sent to the states for ratification a total of twelve amendments. By December 15, 1791, three-quarters of the states had approved the ten amendments known as the Bill of Rights, thus putting them into effect. Of the two amendments not approved at the time, one was a rule concerning congressional salaries that was not ratified for two centuries, until 1992, and the other was a complicated formula for computing representation in Congress that was never adopted. Of the Bill of Rights, Articles 1 through 8 enumerated basic individual rights, while the intention of Article 9 was to protect any personal freedoms omitted from this list. Article 10 directed that "powers not delegated to the United States by the Constitution, nor prohibited by it to the States, are reserved to the States respectively, or to the people." It addressed concerns that the national government might assume powers that were not mentioned in the Constitution. Passage of the Bill of Rights by Congress attracted enough support to bring in the two remaining states; North Carolina ratified the Constitution in November 1789, and Rhode Island followed suit in May 1790.

The First Census, 1790   Congress promptly ordered a census of the American population, which the Constitution required within three years of Congress's first meeting and every ten years subsequently. The census, the founders expected, would provide an accurate enumeration for apportioning delegates to the House of Representatives and electoral college. Congress set August 1790 as the date of the first census, appointing marshals to complete their work within nine months, which actually stretched to eighteen.

Although it was sketchy and incomplete, the **U.S. Census of 1790** served as a baseline for measuring the growth of a dynamic, expanding people. President Washington reported to Congress a total of 3.9 million people, of whom 60,000 were free blacks and almost 700,000 were slaves. The census covered the territory included in the thirteen original states and also Vermont, Kentucky, and Tennessee, which became states respectively in 1791, 1792, and 1796. It did not encompass the area north of the Ohio River, where at least 4,000 white settlers had taken up land.

During the 1780s, the white population of the country had swelled by an extraordinary 44 percent, mostly through reproduction; in the 1790s, the increase remained high, at 36 percent. After the Treaty of Paris, European immigrants once again began crossing the Atlantic Ocean, with the majority coming from Ireland. From 1783 to 1799, 156,000 Europeans entered the United States: 69 percent were Irish; 14 percent were English, Scottish, or Welsh; and 6 percent were German. The African American population also grew quickly during the 1780s and 1790s, at a rate of 32 percent per decade.

Especially striking in the 1790 census are the small numbers of enslaved African Americans in New England and Pennsylvania compared with the southern states, the result in part of northern abolition. This sectional difference would grow in the nineteenth century as the North focused more on commerce and developed a manufacturing sector, while the South cast its fate with agriculture, adopting cotton as its major crop.

First Federal Census, 1790

The Congress moved quickly to fulfill the constitutional requirement to conduct a census of the American population. The first census asked just six questions: name of head of household and numbers of free white males aged sixteen years and over, free white males under age sixteen, free white females, other free persons (mostly African Americans but also some Native Americans), and slaves. The separate listing of enslaved persons was required by the constitutional clause counting three-fifths of slaves for representation and taxes. The distinction between free whites and blacks came from cultural values rather than some practical use. The census did not include Native Americans who lived outside areas settled by whites. The 1790 census remains an important resource for historians of the early U.S. republic. Later decennial censuses are more informative, with details such as the name, birthplace, occupation, and literacy of residents.

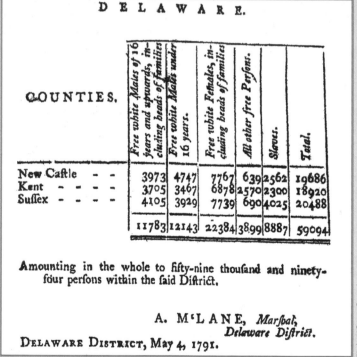

DELAWARE.

COUNTIES.	Free white Males of 16 years and upwards, including heads of families.	Free white Males under 16 years.	Free white Females, including heads of families.	All other free Persons.	Slaves.	Total.
New Castle - -	3973	4747	7767	639	2562	19686
Kent - - - -	3705	3467	6878	2570	2300	18920
Suffex - - - -	4105	3929	7739	690	4025	20488
	11783	12143	22384	3899	8887	59094

Amounting in the whole to fifty-nine thousand and ninety-four persons within the said District.

A. M'LANE, Marshal,
Delaware District.

DELAWARE DISTRICT, May 4, 1791.

(National Census Bureau)

OPPOSING VISIONS OF AMERICA

Almost immediately during Washington's first administration, political divisions arose between sides favoring commerce versus agriculture. Two divergent conceptions of the nation's future emerged among supporters of the Constitution. During the early 1790s, two political parties developed, though leaders avoided calling them that because public opinion considered parties detrimental to unified republican government. As events unfolded in foreign and domestic affairs, the two parties contested one issue after another.

Hamilton Versus Jefferson

Alexander Hamilton, appointed by Washington as secretary of the treasury, saw the future greatness of the United States in commerce and manufacturing. Born in the West Indies, Hamilton attended King's College in New York City, then served as Washington's aide-de-camp during the Revolution. Highly intelligent, full of energy and enthusiasm, he was a major proponent of the new Constitution. Appointment to the treasury allowed Hamilton to promote his concept of a strong nation modeled on Great Britain, but his efforts to foster commerce and manufacturing aroused resistance among former allies, particularly Madison and Jefferson, leading to bitter partisan disputes.

Hamilton's party took the name Federalist, which in the late eighteenth century referred to the power of the states. The Federalists were really nationalists, however; they favored commercial development, a national bank, high tariffs to spur manufacturing, and a strong central government based on a loose interpretation of the Constitution, which allowed expansive powers to Congress and the president. The Federalists favored the British, abhorred the French Revolution after 1792, and were generally suspicious of power wielded by ordinary folk. They were somewhat critical of slavery, however, and gained the allegiance of free blacks. Because their power base lay in New England and the Middle Atlantic states, the Federalists had little enthusiasm for western expansion and sometimes supported the right of Native Americans to retain their lands.

DOING HISTORY ONLINE

Development of Political Parties

Using the textbook and Documents 5 and 6, determine what major issues contributed to party development

 www.cengage.com/history/ayers/ampassages4e

The **Republican Party**, in contrast, favored a strict interpretation of the Constitution, opposing a strong central government and federal privileges for manufacturing and commerce. It thought Hamilton's plans for funding the national debt, the bank, and protective tariffs infringed on states' rights and helped the "few" at the expense of the "many." It disdained the British model and charged Hamilton with advocating a return to monarchy. With their power base in the South, the West, and northern cities, the Republicans rejected efforts to abolish slavery and were ardent expansionists on the frontier. They had little sympathy for Indian rights.

Thomas Jefferson became the chief spokesman for the Republican Party, though James Madison collaborated in its growth. Jefferson, a wealthy planter and slaveholder, author of the Declaration of Independence, former minister to France, and now Washington's secretary of state, argued that Hamilton wanted too much national power. He believed the root of Britain's effort to destroy American liberty in the 1760s and 1770s had been commercial speculation and greed. Manufacturing in cities created poverty, dependency, and political corruption. Instead, the United States, with limitless land, should foster an agrarian society of small producers. A virtuous republic was one made up of small farmers whose goal was to produce enough to support their families. Commerce should exist primarily to allow them to sell their surplus in Europe and purchase manufactured goods in return. The farmers should be educated to participate wisely in republican government. Their self-sufficiency and education would encourage them to act for the good of society rather than solely for their own gain.

Paradoxically a large proportion of the Republicans were not small farmers. Many of the leaders were southern plantation gentry like Jefferson and Madison or old Antifederalist elites. The party drew together people who had opposed ratification of the Constitution as well as those who favored it but abhorred the government's direction under Washington and Hamilton. The Republicans received solid backing from farmers, especially in the South and West, and from urban craftsmen and small traders who watched wealthy speculators and merchants benefit from Hamiltonian policies.

Funding the National Debt

As secretary of the treasury, Alexander Hamilton's primary challenge was the Revolutionary War debt. A strong nationalist, he viewed the debt more as an opportunity to enlarge national power than as a financial hurdle. The United States owed $10 million to foreigners, particularly to the French, and $40 million to Americans. The states also owed $25 million in domestic debts. To continue the War of Independence when funds were depleted, Congress and the states had issued certificates to merchants, artisans, and farmers for supplies and to soldiers for wages. After the war, many ordinary folks could not wait for the government to pay—or lost hope that the money was forthcoming—so they sold their certificates to wealthy speculators for a fraction of face value. Often the sellers received only 10 to 15 percent, rates that reflected the risk speculators were taking during the shaky Confederation period.

In his **Report on Public Credit** of January 1790, Hamilton formulated a plan by which the U.S. government would honor at face value all Revolutionary War debts, including those of the states. His funding proposal was to exchange new federal securities for the old debt certificates. He planned to pay off foreign creditors as soon as possible but retain the domestic debt, paying only interest and a small amount of the principal each year. A customs duty on imports and an excise tax on whiskey would cover the interest; post office income would gradually reduce the principal. Hamilton's funding plan would tie wealthy Americans to the new government through their continuing investment. His assumption plan, by which the federal government assumed state war debts, expanded this strategy by reorienting the loyalty of investors from the states to the nation.

Congress eventually passed Hamilton's proposal, though with great opposition. Many people, including Madison, thought that repaying the domestic debt at face value was unfair because speculators would receive a windfall at the expense of the poor. The split between Hamilton and Madison began over this issue. Critics argued that funding allowed the "few" to benefit from the hardships of the "many," who had lost money when they sold their war bonds and who would pay again through import duties and the excise tax. Opponents also feared the expansion of national power and became convinced that the treasury secretary was upsetting the balance between the central government and the states. Assumption raised additional questions because some states had more debt remaining than others. Massachusetts and South Carolina were keen on having the federal government assume their large debts, whereas Virginians opposed the plan because they had satisfied most of their state's debt. Despite these divisions, the funding and assumption program passed Congress in July

1790 as part of a bargain struck by Hamilton, Jefferson, and Madison to situate the nation's permanent capital on the Potomac River, in Maryland and Virginia.

Planning Washington, D.C. The choice of the Potomac for the nation's capital was controversial. Although everyone agreed that a central location was necessary, regional interests surfaced as congressmen recognized its potential economic and political benefits. They also debated the question of the temporary capital. Should New York City or Philadelphia host the federal government until the permanent site was ready? The complicated negotiations over funding and assumption resulted in moving the temporary capital from New York to Philadelphia, as well as locating the new city on the Potomac.

President Washington and his fellow Virginians supervised the development of the capital. The Residence Act of 1790 gave the president authority to select a 10-mile-square location somewhere along the Potomac; he chose land on both sides of the river that included Alexandria in Virginia and Georgetown in Maryland. The federal city would be built in neither of those towns, but on open land on the east bank of the river. Washington appointed a surveyor, three commissioners to manage the project, and **Pierre Charles L'Enfant** to design the layout of the capital and its major buildings. L'Enfant's grandiose street plan and Greek and Roman architecture expressed an exalted vision of the republic. The commissioners named the federal city "Washington" and the entire district "Columbia."

The president expected to finance construction by selling lots in the capital, thinking that land prices would skyrocket as citizens valued proximity to the seat of government. Instead, land sold poorly, and lack of money undermined the project. At one of the failed auctions, even the participation of the president and a parade of two brass bands and an artillery troop could not foster sales. When the commissioners suspended construction temporarily for insufficient funds, L'Enfant protested and was fired. His plan for grand boulevards, public squares, fountains, and imposing buildings was retained, but its execution would wait. For a decade, the enterprise limped along, saved by grants from Maryland and Virginia. In 1800, when the government moved to Washington, the president's mansion was still unfinished, and only one wing of the Capitol had been built.

The National Bank The cornerstone of Hamilton's new commercial order was a national bank, to be patterned after the Bank of England. The **Bank of the United States** and its branches would hold the federal government's funds and regulate state banks. The chief purpose of the national bank was to expand the money supply, thereby encouraging commercial growth.

The Bank of the United States, which Congress chartered in 1791 for twenty years, would have assets of $10 million, including $2 million in government deposits. Private investors could purchase the remaining $8 million in stock. As the bank prospered, stockholders would receive dividends on their funds. Thus, Hamilton created a way for wealthy Americans, who had just profited from funding the Revolutionary War debt, to benefit further. Because the government was a major stockholder, it also received dividends that could be used to pay off the national debt. The bank made loans to merchants beyond the value of its stock of gold and silver (specie), thus increasing the supply of money, a critically important move for an economy short of specie. The bank notes circulated as currency; the federal government supported their value by accepting them for taxes. To Hamilton and his commercial backers, the Bank of the United States was essential for economic growth. The majority of the House of Representatives agreed, by a vote of 39 to 20, but the tally indicated important regional differences that fueled growth of political parties. Among northern congressmen, 33 voted for the bank and 1 against, whereas only 6 southern delegates supported and 19 opposed Hamilton's bill.

The plan had many opponents, who variously considered the bank immoral, monopolistic, or unconstitutional. Some believed that all paper money should be based on gold and silver. "Every dollar of a bank bill that is issued beyond the quantity of gold and silver in the vaults," John Adams said, "represents nothing, and is therefore a cheat upon somebody." The wild frenzy to purchase the bank's stock—in which twenty-five thousand shares sold in two hours and then the shares were bid up to 1,300 percent of their face value—reinforced fears that the national bank would undermine republican virtue. Jefferson called the bank's stock "federal filth." Others charged the bank with monopoly, complaining that merchants could secure short-term loans to finance their commercial ventures, but farmers and artisans could not obtain mortgages for purchasing property or making improvements.

In Congress, Madison opposed the national bank on the constitutional grounds that the federal government lacked the power to create corporations, a strict interpretation of the Constitution. In particular, Madison said, the Tenth Amendment would deny the central government any power not expressly given. Hamilton and his supporters countered that some powers of the federal government are implied. In the case of the bank, for example, the Constitution delegated to Congress and the president the power to lay and collect taxes, pay debts, regulate commerce, and coin and regulate money. It also provided the authority to "make all laws which shall be necessary and proper for carrying into execution the foregoing powers." Hamilton argued that the bank was a method by which the United States could fulfill its functions, and because some means were necessary, the power to establish the bank was implied. Though President Washington was initially unsure, he accepted Hamilton's reasoning and approved the bill.

Jefferson, like Madison, was convinced that the national bank was unconstitutional. By 1791, the secretary of state realized the political and economic consequences of the funding act—channeling more power to the federal government and more money to the rich—and thought the bank could only further these trends. He said he had been "duped" by Hamilton and "made a tool for forwarding his schemes" in accepting the assumption of state debts in return for the capital on the Potomac. He now believed that the treasury secretary's program "flowed from principles adverse to liberty," as Jefferson told the president. It was "calculated to undermine and demolish the republic." Hamilton chafed at this criticism, stating "that Mr. Madison, cooperating with Mr. Jefferson, is at the head of a faction decidedly hostile to me and my administration; and actuated by views, in my judgment, subversive of the principles of good government and dangerous to the Union, peace, and happiness of the country."

Technology and Manufacturing   Although the treasury secretary won congressional support for the bank and funding the national debt, he was much less successful in his plan for industry. In the 1790s, U.S. manufacturing remained on a small scale. Americans appreciated the quality of British imports; what they did not import, they produced themselves or purchased from neighboring artisans. Industry could not be stimulated overnight, for it required technology and the willingness of businessmen to invest time and capital for the long term. Although some master craftsmen enlarged their shops and hired more workers, mechanized factories with mass production still lay in the future.

During the colonial and revolutionary periods, urban entrepreneurs had attempted large-scale textile manufacturing to provide employment for poor women and independence from British imports, but these efforts were short-lived and not mechanized. The "factories" had consisted of workhouses in which large numbers of impoverished widows produced thread and yarn at traditional spinning wheels. Other businessmen used a "putting-out" system, whereby they distributed flax and wool for spinning at home.

In 1788, the Pennsylvania Society for the Encouragement of Manufactures and the Useful Arts introduced spinning jennies, or multispindled machines, to their textile factory in Philadelphia. The jennies threatened to displace home spinners by producing cheaper yarn and thread. In 1790, however, the factory and its wooden jennies went up in flames, as did other early textile mills in the Delaware Valley. The promoters believed that home spinners were sabotaging the factories, but the mills were highly flammable so fires may well have been accidental.

Samuel Slater, a twenty-two-year-old millworker and recent immigrant from Great Britain, instituted a new phase in American cloth production in 1790 by building a textile mill in Pawtucket, Rhode Island, using water power to run the spinning machines. From memory he constructed a spinning frame, a machine that produced stronger threads than the jenny produced. He had left Britain illegally; to keep its advantage in textile making, the government prohibited emigration of craftworkers or export of drawings of the machines. No satisfactory power loom yet existed, so Slater's mill performed only the first two steps of cloth production: carding, or preparing the cotton fibers for spinning, and spinning the thread. Slater then used the putting-out system of distributing the thread to families, who produced the cloth on looms at home. Though Slater established additional mills in Rhode Island and Massachusetts, his work force stayed fairly small, with about one hundred millworkers in 1800.

The United States made some progress during the 1790s toward industrialization. In 1790, Congress passed patent legislation, giving inventors exclusive rights to their work for seventeen years, and Slater initiated water-powered textile manufacture, as described above. Then, in 1793, while visiting a Georgia plantation, **Eli Whitney**, a New Englander, built the cotton engine, or gin. The device, which separated cotton fibers from husks and seeds, greatly increased the productivity of cotton cultivation, swelling the demand for African American slaves and fertile land in the Southwest and spurring cloth production in the North. Because the gin could be duplicated easily, Whitney failed to make a fortune from the machine. In 1798, he further laid the basis for industrial growth by attempting to manufacture guns with interchangeable parts. After receiving a government contract for ten thousand weapons, he specified that each part be made identical to its counterparts so that it could be exchanged from one rifle to another, allowing less-skilled workers to build and repair the firearms. At this early date, however, such rigid standards were impossible to meet, and as a result, parts needed filing to fit together smoothly.

In 1772, at age seventeen, Delaware-born artisan **Oliver Evans** heard that the Scottish inventor James Watt had improved the steam engine a few years earlier. Evans began building his own model but, for lack of money, thirty years passed before he actually installed a high-pressure steam engine in his gypsum fertilizer factory in Philadelphia. This was the first application of steam power to an industrial setting. In the meantime, in the 1780s, Evans also developed the idea of automating mills. He devised water powered machinery for large grist mills that allowed one worker instead of three to supervise all the steps of producing flour. Evans obtained exclusive rights from the states of Pennsylvania and Maryland for his system of automated elevators, conveyors, and hoppers. With insufficient capital, however, he was unable to pursue many of his designs, including steam carriages and trucks, a machine gun, refrigeration, central heating, and gas lighting.

EXPANSION AND CONFLICT IN THE WEST

While Alexander Hamilton's financial policies aided commerce in the East, dynamic growth also occurred in the West. The westward movement of settlers challenged the ability of the new government to keep their loyalty. In particular, Hamilton's excise tax on whiskey weighed heavily on westerners. The young nation also contended with Native Americans who were losing lands to the settlers; the British military, who kept forts in the Northwest; and the Spanish, who contested U.S. territorial claims and rights to navigate the Mississippi.

Kentucky and Tennessee   During the 1780s, the region west of the Appalachians and south of the Ohio River developed quickly as families left Virginia and North Carolina in search of fertile land and lower taxes. Even before the Revolution ended, settlers crossed the mountains in large

Model of Eli Whitney's Cotton Gin. *In 1794, Eli Whitney was awarded one of the first U.S. patents for the cotton gin. He used models like this in court cases to defend his rights to the invention against manufacturers who were selling similar machines.*

(National Museum of American History, Smithsonian Institution)

numbers: the area that became Kentucky swelled from 150 settlers in 1775 to 61,000 whites and 12,500 enslaved blacks in 1790; Tennessee reported 32,000 whites and 3,500 slaves in 1790.

White settlement of Kentucky and Tennessee proceeded quickly as state governments, speculators, and frontiersmen defeated the Cherokees, who claimed ancestral rights to the territory. Believing that they were renting the land out rather than selling it, in 1775 a group of Cherokee leaders, including Attakullaculla and Oconostota, had traded twenty-seven thousand square miles to Richard Henderson and his associates for a cabin of consumer goods. Called Henderson's Purchase, the sale involved most of Kentucky and was illegal in Indian and English law. With the outbreak of the Revolution, most Cherokees joined the British, fighting for return of their lands. Receiving little help from Britain, the Cherokees were defeated in 1777 and forced to sign away even more territory.

Young militants led by Dragging Canoe, Bloody Fellow, and others, assisted by loyalist whites who intermarried and became members of the tribe, rejected these land cessions. In the 1780s and early 1790s, the militant Cherokees, called **Chickamaugas**, allied with Creeks and Shawnees against settlers along the frontier from Kentucky to Georgia. On both sides, fighting was vicious, with men, women, and children burned, scalped, and shot; and as in so many other cases, the whites failed to distinguish between enemy Indians and those who wanted peace.

The Washington administration attempted to end the hostilities with the Treaty of Holston in 1791, but it gave responsibility for negotiating with the Cherokees to **Governor William Blount** of the Tennessee Territory, a land speculator the Indians called "dirt king" for his greed after land. Blount ignored Washington's promise to the Cherokees that if they ceded territory on which the whites had settled, the United States would guarantee their remaining lands. Instead, Blount required a cession of more than four thousand square miles in return for an annual payment of $1,000 and no guarantee. When Blount surveyed the border without Cherokee witnesses, the treaty fell apart and war continued. In 1794, after Dragging Canoe died and the Spanish stopped supplying the Indians because of war in Europe, the Chickamaugas met defeat.

By the end of the war, parts of Kentucky and Tennessee had passed the initial stages of settlement. Early on, groups of settlers had gathered in frontier stations consisting of two-story log houses connected by a high wall to create a fort against Indian attack. As the population grew and the threat from Native Americans declined, families moved away from the stations. In the early years, all family members worked to provide food, clothing, shelter, and a few amenities such as soap and rough-hewn furniture. They needed to become familiar with their new environment. One Kentucky pioneer described how "the women the first spring we came out, wo'd follow their cows to see what they ate, that they might know what greens to get. My Wife and I had neither spoon, dish, knife, or any thing to do with when we began life. Only I had a butcher knife." The settlers grew corn, tobacco, hemp, cotton, vegetables, and fruits; raised cattle, sheep, horses, and pigs; and hunted and fished. Soon they produced a surplus to trade for necessities they could not make themselves, such as nails, rifles, ammunition, needles, tools, and salt, as well as to pay taxes and fees. They sold furs, ginseng, agricultural produce, and livestock. As fertile lands such as Kentucky's Bluegrass region yielded bountiful crops, farmers sought markets by way of the Mississippi River and the port of New Orleans. But transporting crops overland through the mountains was much more difficult and expensive than sending them downstream, so southwestern farmers demanded that the federal government convince Spain to end its restrictions on lower Mississippi shipping.

Although the population increased and a market economy developed in the 1790s, the trans-Appalachian region had few schools or church buildings. Most children, if taught at all, learned reading and arithmetic at home. In towns where schools existed, boys might attend for a few months, but girls did not. The exception was the children of wealthy families, who entered academies with secondary school curricula. One man remembered the experience of most residents of Kentucky in the 1790s: "Our preachers and teachers were, in general, almost as destitute as the people at large, many of whom could neither read nor write, did not send their children to school, and of course, kept no books in the house."

Religion was the frontier's chief cultural institution. Throughout the region, Presbyterian, Baptist, and Methodist ministers held services in private homes. Baptist lay ministers farmed beside their neighbors through the week, then led services on Sunday. Methodist circuit riders traveled from one congregation to another, conducting worship services, baptisms, marriages, and prayer meetings. The churches expected members to avoid sin, including fighting, excessive drinking, adultery, and even celebrating the Fourth of July. If members committed offenses and failed to express regret, they were expelled, a serious consequence for people who had few social outlets. In addition to church, social activities included barn raisings, corn huskings, and log rollings. These events caused trouble when whiskey and frivolity led church members astray, as with one couple whom a Kentucky Methodist church expelled for "Disorderly Conduct." Another man was "Excluded from this Church for Fighting & Drinking to Excess."

The Ohio Country　White settlement moved more slowly north of the Ohio River, partly because the U.S. government kept tighter control in the Northwest Territory, but more because Native Americans resisted strongly. Delawares, Shawnees, Iroquois, and many others refused to cede lands that the federal government wanted to sell to land-hungry easterners. In the 1780s, the United States obtained a series of cessions, but from just some of the people who owned the land. Indians who were not party to the agreements rejected them. Forming a confederacy to withstand U.S. invasion, Ohio Indians attacked whites who risked settling in the region. This northern Indian confederacy allied with the Chickamaugas and Creeks in the South, establishing a pan-Indian defensive that gained help from the Spanish in the South and the British in the North. At one meeting in 1787, the Native Americans agreed to merge their forces "for a general defense against all Invaders of Indian rights."

In the early 1790s, President Washington challenged the northern confederacy by sending two expeditions, both of them unsuccessful. Arthur St. Clair, governor of the Northwest Territory, led the second invasion in 1791, in which six hundred of his fourteen hundred men died. Washington believed that the disaster resulted from the use of militia, so he instructed General Anthony Wayne to raise five thousand regulars. Wayne trained the troops for two years, and on August 20, 1794, he defeated the Native Americans decisively at the Battle of Fallen Timbers. Though the British had customarily given aid to the Ohio tribes, this time they closed the gates to Fort Miami, denying refuge to the retreating Indians. A year later, when it became clear to the

Native Americans that their alliance with the British had ended, they signed the Treaty of Greenville, ceding to the United States the land south and east of the treaty line, most of it in present-day Ohio.

| The Whiskey | In 1794, the Washington administration also sent troops against |

The Whiskey Rebellion, 1794

In 1794, the Washington administration also sent troops against western Pennsylvania farmers, who since 1791 had resisted the whiskey tax. Washington and Hamilton decided to take advantage of the unrest to demonstrate the power of the new central government. Farmers throughout the West resented the tax on spirits, for distilling whiskey from grain made their produce less bulky, and thus less expensive to transport to eastern markets. They also used the whiskey instead of cash and consumed a good portion of it themselves. In much of the trans-Appalachian region, officials failed to collect the excise at all.

The administration found willing officials in western Pennsylvania, however, and there proceeded to enforce the law. The Pittsburgh area farmers held protest meetings and refused cooperation with the collectors. In what became known as the **Whiskey Rebellion**, the farmers tarred and feathered collaborators, burned barns, and destroyed stills of people who paid the tax. The rebels charged that the tax favored large distillers and was collected unevenly. They left notes signed "Tom the Tinker" to warn distillers who registered for the tax that their stills would be "fixed" (that is, ruined) unless they joined the revolt. The insurgents understood their fight as a struggle for "the virtuous principles of republican liberty." But the whiskey tax was only one of the farmers' complaints, which included failure to open up the Ohio country and removal of Spanish trade restrictions on the Mississippi.

Events came to a climax in July 1794. When officials continued to collect the tax and arrest resisters, five hundred men surrounded the excise inspector's home, exchanged gunfire that killed several people, and burned the house. The official and his family escaped. In the days that followed, rebels set more buildings on fire, raised liberty poles, attacked collectors, and rumored secession. The uprising spread to central Pennsylvania, Virginia, Maryland, and Ohio. Washington sent commissioners to obtain oaths of submission, but when the insurrection continued, he called up thirteen thousand eastern militia, who marched west with the president briefly in command. By the time the soldiers reached western Pennsylvania, the revolt was over, as the show of force intimidated the rebels. The administration had demonstrated that armed resistance to federal policies would not be tolerated.

DOING HISTORY ONLINE

Rebellion and Government

Using your book and Documents 2, 7–10, and 13, compare the official responses to Shays's Rebellion and to the Whiskey Rebellion. What does the comparison reveal about the Articles of Confederation and the Constitution and the evolution of the national government?

 www.cengage.com/history/ayers/ampassages4e

The Spanish Frontier

As settlers from the United States migrated across the Appalachians and traders extended their commercial networks, they came into contact with the Spanish. The 1790s marked the high point of Spain's control in North America, its provinces extending from East Florida across the Gulf Coast to Louisiana, Texas, New Mexico, and California (refer next page to Map 7.1). The

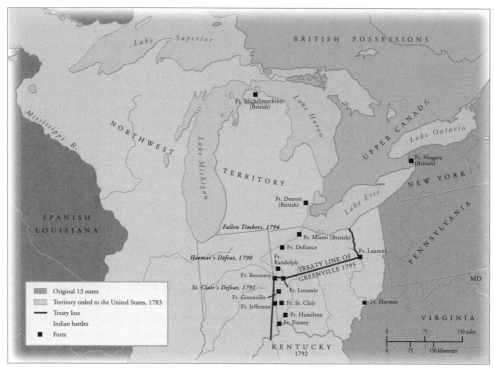

MAP 7.1 Conflict in the Northwest Territory, 1790–1796.

Native Americans continued to resist U.S. settlement in the Ohio region. They defeated U.S. forces in 1790 and 1791 but lost the Battle of Fallen Timbers in 1794. British forts in the Northwest Territory supported the Ohio Indians until that time.

Spanish government continued to view these borderlands of their empire as a buffer against American and British designs on Mexican silver. Spanish officials recognized the phenomenal population growth of the United States. One warned that Americans were "advancing and multiplying . . . with a prodigious rapidity," and another took a dim view of the American frontier people, whom he considered "nomadic like Arabs and . . . distinguished from savages only in their color, language, and the superiority of their depraved cunning and untrustworthiness."

Nevertheless, the Spanish decided to open their territory to Americans, hoping to bolster the small settler populations. Spain offered free land in the Floridas and Louisiana, and even changed official policy to allow Protestants to keep their religion as long as they took an oath of allegiance to the Crown and had their children baptized Catholic. Because Spain could not provide desired consumer goods or adequate markets, it also relaxed mercantilist restraints, allowing plantation owners in the borderlands to sell their sugar, cotton, and indigo in the United States. These new immigration and economic policies facilitated later U.S. acquisition of the Floridas and Louisiana. Jefferson said prophetically, in 1791, that Spain had provided "the means of delivering to us peaceably, what may otherwise cost us a war."

Farther west in New Mexico, the Spanish finally achieved peace with the Comanches and Apaches. Abandoning the attempt to make them subjects of the Crown, Spain signed a treaty recognizing their sovereignty. The Indians had forced the Spanish to set aside the goal of complete domination and to provide such gifts as guns, ammunition, clothing, mirrors, paint, tobacco, and sugar. Still, the Spanish sent prisoners of war to Cuba as forced laborers and settled other Apaches on reservations called *establecimientos de paz,* or peace establishments. Many Apaches refused to live on the reservations, however, steadfastly maintaining their independence. But the fighting stopped, making Texas, New Mexico, and Arizona safer for travel and economic development. Finally, settlers could journey directly between San Antonio, Santa Fe, and Tucson without fear of attack.

For several decades, fearing Russian and British incursions along the Pacific coast, Spain had expanded settlement in California. The government sent missionaries and soldiers north from Baja California in 1769 to set up missions and presidios along the coast from San Diego to San Francisco. José de Gálvez organized the effort, enlisting **Junípero Serra**, a zealous Franciscan priest, to establish the missions. Though fewer than a thousand Hispanics lived in California by 1790, the missions controlled most of the arable land along the Pacific. With military force and by conversion, they put thousands of California Indians to work on mission lands. Before Spanish colonization, the region's native people possessed neither firearms nor horses; they lived in small villages with neither elaborate political structures nor much experience with war. In the earliest years after Spanish settlement, the natives lacked unity to avenge the crimes of Spanish soldiers or to refuse to serve as agricultural laborers. In 1775, however, one group burned the San Diego mission, followed by rebellions of other coastal Indians.

As elsewhere in North America, the California Indians declined sharply in population after contact with Europeans. People who went to work in the missions lived an average of ten to twelve years; their high death rate probably resulted from close quarters and exposure to disease. According to one missionary, "they live well free but as soon as we reduce them to a Christian and community life . . . they fatten, sicken, and die." The native population in the mission region along the Pacific coast declined from approximately sixty thousand in 1769 to thirty-five thousand at the end of the century.

The Spanish also looked to the Pacific Northwest, which they explored in 1774, four years earlier than the British explorer Captain James Cook. After Cook publicized the trade for sea otter furs, however, British and American merchants sailed to Nootka Sound,

California Indians.   *California Indians are lined up at the Spanish mission in Carmel to greet French visitors.*

(Courtesy of the Bancroft Library, University of California, Berkeley)

at Vancouver Island, challenging the Spanish claim to the area north of San Francisco. The traders made huge profits by purchasing the silky black otter pelts from the Tlingit, Haida, Nootka, and Chinook peoples, to sell in China for tea, porcelain, and silk. The Indians had formerly hunted the sea otter on a limited basis for fine clothing and food. When the Spanish seized two British ships, England threatened war. Spain signed the Nootka Convention (1790), yielding its sole claim to the Pacific Northwest and returning the confiscated vessels. Over the next several years, the two countries tried but failed to negotiate a northern boundary of California. Of more concern to Spain, Great Britain, and the United States during the 1790s was the outbreak of war in Europe and the Atlantic, in the wake of revolution in France.

FOREIGN ENTANGLEMENTS

In 1789, the United States rejoiced when the French abolished noble privileges and formed a constitutional monarchy. Americans believed that France had followed their example, for during the first phase of the French Revolution, its moderate leaders included friends of the United States, notably the Revolutionary War hero the marquis de Lafayette. In 1792, however, radicals took control; they executed King Louis XVI the next year. The international situation became perilous when the French Republic declared war on Britain and Spain. The king's execution and thousands of deaths by guillotine during the second phase of the French Revolution cost the French support in the United States, particularly among Federalists, who feared the consequences of ordinary people, "the mob," taking power. Republicans did not defend the excesses, but they remained sympathetic toward France because they hated monarchical Britain more.

Neutrality   The European war presented Americans with a tricky situation, for they had potentially dangerous connections with both France and Britain. The U.S.–France commercial and military alliance of 1778 remained in force. It did not require the United States to enter the war, but the French Republic expected favorable trade policies and informal military assistance. Though Secretary of State Jefferson favored France and despised Britain, he agreed that neutrality was essential. American commerce was closely tied with Britain, whose navy could sweep U.S. ships from the sea.

Hamilton was particularly concerned that British imports remain high because tariffs paid the lion's share of interest on the national debt. With all of this in mind, President Washington made the only reasonable decision, issuing his Proclamation of Neutrality in April 1793. The message warned citizens to avoid hostile acts against either side, including sale of weapons and privateering. Washington sought the belligerents' recognition of the U.S. right to trade in nonmilitary goods.

American neutrality quickly hit shoals with the activities of **Edmond Genet**, the new minister from France. Citizen Genet, as he was called in republican France, had arrived in Charleston several weeks before Washington proclaimed neutrality. He enlisted American mercenaries to man privateers and obtained ships to sail under the French flag against British shipping. The privateers, with largely American crews, seized British vessels, taking them to U.S. ports. There the French consuls sold the ships and their cargoes, paying the mercenaries with part of the proceeds. The French claimed this right under the 1778 alliance. The Washington administration, fearful of British reprisals and outraged by this violation of U.S. sovereignty, closed the ports to Genet's privateers and requested his recall. The government prohibited foreign belligerents from arming vessels in U.S. ports and recruiting U.S. citizens in American territory, set the limit of U.S. territorial waters at three miles, and forbade foreign consuls from holding admiralty courts in U.S. cities to auction confiscated ships.

The Washington administration had greater success protecting the nation's sovereignty from French designs than from those of the British. The American republic's weakness became all too clear when the Royal Navy began impressing—recruiting by force—U.S. citizens from merchant ships. Then in November 1793, the British ordered a total blockade of the French West Indies: any ship intending to trade there would be confiscated. The blockade was timed to coincide with their invasion of St. Domingue, or Haiti, where enslaved blacks had risen up against their French masters in 1791. The British kept the blockade a secret until after U.S. ships headed for the Caribbean. Over the winter, their navy seized more than 250 American vessels, whether they were aimed for French, British, or neutral ports. The British impounded ships, cargoes, and even the sailors' possessions. Because international correspondence was so slow, Washington received no intelligence of the blockade and confiscations until March 1794.

The United States and Britain seemed headed for war. Exacerbating the crisis was the British refusal to vacate their forts and their aid to Native Americans in the Ohio country. Britain also helped Native Americans resist settlement in the West. In fact, in 1794 the governor of Canada, Lord Dorchester, told a group of Indians that they could expect war to break out between the United States and Britain within a year. With British victory, Dorchester promised, the Native Americans could reclaim the lands they had lost north of the Ohio River.

The Jay Treaty, 1795   The crisis abated when the British ended their total blockade of the French islands, permitting Americans to trade foodstuffs and consumer goods but not war material. Rather than take retaliatory action, the president sent John Jay, chief justice of the Supreme Court, as special envoy to England. Jay's instructions were to convince the British to evacuate their forts in the West, pay for African American slaves who had left with their army after the Revolution, end impressment, open the British West Indies trade to American ships, and compensate recent shipping losses in the Caribbean.

Jay was unable to secure compensation for slaves, convince the British to stop impressment, or obtain recognition of all the neutral rights that Americans demanded. He did gain British withdrawal from the western forts by June 1, 1796, payment for confiscated ships in the Caribbean, and the opening of trade in the British West Indies to American vessels of 70 tons or less. He agreed, however, that American shippers would not export from the United States certain tropical products, including cotton, molasses, sugar, coffee, and cocoa, and that Americans would repay British creditors for pre-Revolutionary debts.

Washington received the **Jay Treaty** in March 1795, keeping its contents secret until the Senate debate in June. The Federalists struck the provision forbidding U.S. merchants from exporting tropical crops. If they had agreed to this section, American trade would have faced a serious obstacle, particularly with the development of cotton.

Twenty Federalist senators voted to ratify, while ten Republicans refused. Thus, the Senate approved the treaty by exactly the two-thirds needed and sent it to the president, who signed the treaty as amended.

When Jay's treaty became public, Republicans flew into a rage. Their opposition in large part was political: they abhorred any treaty with the British and privately bemoaned Jay's success on important issues. Publicly they complained about his failures on impressment, neutral rights, and compensation for slaves. The Jay Treaty greatly hastened the growth of political parties, as Republicans gained support from former Federalists, particularly in the South. Whereas Hamilton defended the treaty, opponents roared that it surrendered American independence to the former imperial tyrant. John Jay was burned in effigy; mass meetings, petitions, and demonstrations protested the treaty throughout the country.

By spring 1796, however, the tumult was over, in part because news arrived that Thomas Pinckney had concluded an agreement with Spain the previous October. The Treaty of San Lorenzo opened the Mississippi River to free navigation, allowed Americans to use the port of New Orleans without charge, and fixed the boundary between the United States and West Florida at the thirty-first parallel as specified in the Treaty of Paris.

Washington Retires

With the threat of war temporarily eased, the West open for settlement and trade, and a flourishing economy, the success of the republic seemed more certain than before. General Wayne's defeat of the Ohio Indians, the Jay Treaty, and Pinckney's diplomatic success gave westerners—and westward-looking Americans—resolution of their major problems: cession of lands in Ohio, removal of the British from the forts, free access to the Mississippi, and the right of deposit at New Orleans. Eastern merchants and farmers benefited from the lifting of trade restrictions in the British West Indies. Wartime demand for provisions in Europe and the Caribbean drove up farm prices and stimulated production. By the end of the century, American exports and shipping profits were almost five times their 1793 level. As a major neutral maritime nation, the United States was assuming a greater place in world trade. With increased transportation profits, merchants invested more heavily in ships. The shipbuilding boom created demand for lumber, rope, and other supplies; wages for craftsmen and laborers rose, though so did the cost of living. Americans took advantage of their new-found prosperity to buy British imports, which in turn paid tariff income toward the national debt. Hamilton's funding plan was a success—the nation's credit was firm—despite resistance to the whiskey tax.

As the election of 1796 approached, George Washington announced his retirement, raising the question of his successor. The president had served two terms, his health had declined, and the battle over the Jay Treaty had left him exhausted and angry. In his Farewell Address, Washington surveyed the accomplishments of his administration and gave the nation advice. The United States should avoid as much as possible becoming entwined in international affairs, he counseled. The European war demonstrated how perilous such involvement could be and how difficult it was to escape. "The great rule of conduct for us in regard to foreign nations is, in extending our commercial relations to have with them as little *political* connection as possible," Washington urged. His other major argument concerned factions. The outgoing president warned against parties based on sectional differences—North against South or

East against West. And he cautioned against parties more generally that the "disorders and miseries which result [from factionalism] gradually incline the minds of men to seek security and repose in the absolute power of an individual." In lamenting "the spirit of party," Washington blamed the Republicans for failing to support his administration. They had undercut his authority and the ideal of a consensual republic.

THE ADAMS PRESIDENCY, 1797–1801

Although Washington's successors appreciated the wisdom of his "great rule" of foreign policy, they had less enthusiasm for his advice on factions. In 1796, the parties lacked full-scale national organization, and candidates did not campaign. But the contest was very much alive: Federalists supported the policies of Hamilton and Washington, and Republicans opposed them.

Election of 1796   In the third presidential election under the Constitution, both parties had sufficient cohesion to offer national tickets: the Federalist candidates were John Adams for president and Thomas Pinckney for vice president; the Republicans put up Thomas Jefferson for president and Aaron Burr, a senator from New York, for the second spot. The results of the electoral college vote were close: Adams 71, Jefferson 68, Pinckney 59, Burr 30, and a number of other candidates totaling 48. As specified by the Constitution, Adams became president and Jefferson vice president. Americans quickly realized the problem of this procedure for electing the executive, because the president represented one party and the vice president the other. In any event, the Federalists kept control of the presidency, though barely, and they increased their votes in Congress by a small margin, to sixty-four Federalists versus fifty-three Republicans.

For many Americans, John Adams possessed credentials from service in the Revolution and the new republic that made him a worthy heir to Washington. He had contributed to pre-Revolutionary agitation in Boston, served as a delegate to the Continental Congress, promoted the Continental navy, and assisted Jefferson in drafting the Declaration of Independence. He had helped negotiate the 1783 Treaty of Paris, and in 1785 he became the first U.S. minister to Great Britain. Adams was a skilled diplomat, an avid student of government, and entirely honest, but he lacked Washington's charisma, military bearing, and understanding of executive leadership. As a lawyer, Adams's style was more intellectual and independent. He preferred to make decisions on his own, without consulting the cabinet or congressional leaders.

Like Washington, Adams denounced parties. He began his administration with the hope, soon abandoned, that he might bridge the gulf between Federalists and Republicans. Jefferson rebuffed the chief executive's peace overture and directed the Republican opposition from his post as vice president. After the first few days of the Adams administration, the president and vice president never consulted one another.

"Quasi-War" with   The second president inherited an international situation that
France   had worsened by the time he assumed office in March 1797. The French, now ruled by a dictatorial executive board called the Directory, declared that the Jay Treaty revoked the 1778 alliance with the United

States. They confiscated American merchant ships and cut off diplomatic relations. Once again, the United States seemed headed for war.

Called into special session in May 1797 by Adams, Congress authorized the mobilization of eighty thousand militia, completion of three war vessels, and fortification of harbors. Adams also appointed a commission of three men to negotiate with France: John Marshall of Virginia, Elbridge Gerry of Massachusetts, and Charles Cotesworth Pinckney of South Carolina. Their assignment was to prevent war, stop the confiscation of American ships carrying nonmilitary cargoes, and obtain compensation for recent losses. In France, the commission corresponded with French Foreign Minister Talleyrand through three intermediaries, who later became known to the American public as X, Y, and Z. The French agents told the commissioners that, like other petitioners to the Directory, they must pay a bribe even to be heard. The amount specified in this case was $250,000. The Directory also required an apology from Adams for criticizing France, a huge loan, and assumption by the U.S. government of any unpaid debts owed by France to American citizens. The commission refused these conditions and returned home. Their experience became known as the **XYZ Affair**.

In spring 1798, Adams received delayed correspondence that his envoys had been rebuffed. When he called for additional troops and warships, Congress responded by giving him more than he requested. Jefferson denounced the military buildup as "insane"; Republicans demanded to see evidence of France's treachery. When Adams made the commission's dispatches public, war fever engulfed the nation. The cry in the 1798 congressional elections became, "Millions for defense, but not a cent for tribute." Two patriotic songs, "Adams for Liberty" and "Hail Columbia," were widely sung, the latter serving as the unofficial national anthem. Congress expanded the regular army and war fleet, established the Department of the Navy, authorized naval vessels to protect American merchant ships, suspended commerce with France, and revoked the French alliance. George Washington assumed command of the army, with Alexander Hamilton in charge of field operations. To pay for all of this, Congress levied a direct tax of $2 million on dwelling houses, land, and slaves.

Without declaring war, the United States engaged France in hostilities from 1798 to 1800. In what was known as the Quasi-War, the U.S. navy dominated the French, defeating their warships and sinking privateers. The British navy helped by protecting U.S. carriers. Although some congressmen feared a French invasion and thereby justified further military preparations, French naval losses to Great Britain and the United States quickly removed that threat.

The Alien and Sedition Acts of 1798

The Federalists rode the crest of patriotism in 1798, using their majority in Congress to pass a series of acts that limited the rights of immigrants and critics of the administration. Congressional sponsors argued that the laws were necessary wartime measures. Their practical purpose, however, was to destroy the Republicans by undermining popular support and closing newspapers. The Federalists tried to take advantage of the Quasi-War to link their opponents with the enemy. This strategy worked in the short term, as the pro-French Republicans lost votes in the 1798 congressional election, but it proved suicidal for Adams's party after the fear of invasion had passed.

The Federalist design resulted in four restrictive laws. The Naturalization Act of 1798 lengthened the period of residence needed for citizenship from five to fourteen years. The legislation was intended to stop the flow of Irish immigrants who, because they were anti-British and pro-French, swelled the number of Republican voters. The Alien Enemies Act established procedures in the event of declared war or invasion for jailing and deporting citizens of the enemy nation who were considered likely to spy or commit sabotage. The Alien Act, which had a term of two years, allowed the president to deport any non–U.S. citizens "he shall judge dangerous to the peace and safety of the United States, or shall have reasonable grounds to suspect are concerned in any treasonable or secret machinations against the government thereof." Like the Naturalization Act, this law potentially threatened Irish immigrants, but Adams refrained from using it.

The fourth law, the Sedition Act, made it illegal for "any persons [to] unlawfully combine or conspire together, with intent to oppose any measure or measures of the government of the United States" or to interfere with the execution of a law. Nor could a person "write, print, utter or publish . . . any false, scandalous and malicious writing or writings against the government of the United States, or either house of the Congress . . . or the President." In effect, this law permitted imprisonment and fines for criticizing the government, an obvious infringement on freedom of speech and freedom of the press. The term of the law lasted until March 3, 1801, the day before the next president would be inaugurated. Thus, the Federalists ensured that if the next chief executive were a Republican, he would not be able to retaliate without obtaining a new statute.

The administration enforced the law with serious results. Adams believed that the Sedition Act was constitutional, that people who censured his policies threatened the future of the republic. The prime targets for prosecution were Republican newspapers, including the *Philadelphia Aurora,* edited by Benjamin Franklin's grandson, Benjamin Bache, who was one of Adams's most powerful critics. The official authorized to administer the act was Secretary of State Timothy Pickering, a staunch Federalist who methodically reviewed the Republican papers for actionable offenses. He even ordered an inquiry into the private correspondence of a Republican congressman who reputedly called Adams a traitor; however, the investigation was dropped. Under the law, the Federalists indicted and tried at least seventeen people for sedition. They timed the cases to reach court in the fall of 1799 or the following spring, with the goal of silencing the Republican press during the 1800 election. Some papers folded and others closed temporarily while their editors were imprisoned. All but one of the cases were prosecuted in New England and the Middle Atlantic states, where the Federalists controlled the courts and could pack juries.

The Republican Opposition Grows, 1798–1799   Passage of the Alien and Sedition acts and the jailing of Republican spokesmen shifted the political winds. In late 1798, the Kentucky and Virginia legislatures approved resolutions that protested the acts on the grounds that they were unconstitutional. The Kentucky and Virginia resolutions, drafted anonymously by Thomas Jefferson and James Madison, respectively, argued that these laws violated the First Amendment and granted powers to the national government not delegated by the Constitution. The Virginia assembly resolved that "in case of a deliberate, palpable, and dangerous exercise of other powers, not granted by the [Constitution], the states . . . have the right, and are in duty bound, to interpose, for arresting the progress of the evil." Virginia and Kentucky sent their resolutions to other legislatures, none of which agreed that states could declare a federal law unconstitutional. Rhode Island, for example, responded that the federal courts held the power to determine constitutionality; "that for any state legislature to assume that authority would be . . . Hazarding an interruption of the peace of the states by civil discord, in case of a diversity of opinions among the state legislatures." Nevertheless, the resolutions contributed toward a theory of "nullification," the idea that a state had the right to veto a federal law it considered unconstitutional. This theory was based on the strict interpretation of the Constitution that denied, as in the controversy over the national bank, implied powers to the central government.

With the Alien and Sedition acts, the Federalists had made a strategic error. Where formerly the Republicans could be branded as a faction creating animosity and disunity, they now became seen as legitimate defenders of Revolutionary principles. The Republican Party justified its opposition by warning that the Federalists were on the road to tyranny. The Sedition Act, the Virginia Resolutions argued, impeded free investigation of the actions of government officials and "free communication among the people thereon, which has ever been justly deemed the only effectual guardian of every other right."

The administration fanned the flames of indignation with its heavy-handed reaction to a tax rebellion among German Americans in eastern Pennsylvania, a group who had previously favored the Federalists or stayed out of politics entirely. The Republicans took advantage of the rural Pennsylvanians' aversion to the 1798 federal property tax to win their votes in the congressional election. They circulated petitions against the tax, the defense buildup, and the Alien and Sedition laws, petitions that Congress ignored. By early 1799, the people of Northampton and Bucks counties held public meetings and stopped tax assessors from doing their work. In March, after the U.S. marshal jailed eighteen suspected tax resisters in Bethlehem's Sun Tavern, John Fries, a fifty-year-old auctioneer of upper Bucks County, led a band of 140 armed men to release the prisoners.

The Fries Rebellion ended quickly, as the rebels considered the magnitude of their offense. Fries announced that he would pay the tax and would even welcome the assessor to his house for dinner. Nevertheless, the president decided to make an example of the episode. He dispatched troops that failed to march until almost four weeks after the resistance had ceased. The army descended on the countryside, entering houses and arresting sixty men. One army officer wrote "that every hour's experience confirms me more and more that this expedition was not only unnecessary, but violently absurd." Contrary to the Judiciary Act of 1789, the prisoners were taken to Philadelphia for trial. Fries and two others were found guilty of treason by a Federalist court and sentenced to hang but were subsequently pardoned by the president. The Republicans added the administration's unwarranted use of force to their arsenal of charges against the Federalists.

CONCLUSION

George Washington had warned in his Farewell Address that "the spirit of Party . . . agitates the Community with ill founded jealousies and false alarms, kindles the animosity of one part against another, foments occasionally riot and insurrection. It opens the door to foreign influence and corruption." He invoked the ideal of consensual community, challenging his fellow citizens to work together for the good of their country. The flaw in this conception was that Americans could not agree on which policies were best for everyone. The interests of farmers, merchants, and artisans, and of residents of the North, South, and West, often diverged. The Federalist and Republican parties grew out of different visions of the nation's future. During the 1790s, the Federalists retained control of the central government, confident that their vision was correct. They denounced parties, identifying their government with the republic as a whole. When they tried to eliminate factions by silencing their adversaries with the Sedition Act, ironically they legitimized the party system in the eyes of many Americans.

CHAPTER REVIEW, 1789–1799

- After the ratification of the Constitution, Americans worked to create a new government. Members of the electoral college unanimously elected George Washington to be the nation's first president. Congress and the states amended the Constitution with a Bill of Rights designed to protect individuals against government abuses of authority.
- During the 1790s, two opposing factions arose within American politics, one led by Alexander Hamilton, which favored strong central government and commerce, the other led by Thomas Jefferson, which favored weak national government and agriculture.
- Increased expansion into the West caused tensions between white settlers and the Spanish and Native American peoples who already inhabited these territories.
- The new republic attempted to remain neutral in the conflicts that raged between Britain and France between 1793 and 1815. The 1778 alliance between the United States and France, however, and ongoing trade relations with both nations, made neutrality impossible to maintain.
- John Adams's administration was characterized by an increase in partisan feeling, growth in sentiment against the Federalists, the buildup of the military, and the passage of the unpopular Alien and Sedition acts.

◀▥▥ *Looking Back*

Within the context of world history, with governments that regularly rise and fall, the longevity of the American republic is remarkable. As discussed in Chapter 7, the decade following ratification of the Constitution was critical. Despite conflicts such as the Whiskey and Fries Rebellions, growing opposition from the Republicans, and the Sedition Act, the Washington and Adams administrations established strong precedents for constitutional rule.

1. What were the most important challenges that George Washington faced as he assumed the presidency?
2. What fueled the acrimony between Alexander Hamilton and Thomas Jefferson?
3. Why did James Madison spearhead the effort to approve a bill of rights?
4. How did international affairs, particularly the war between Great Britain and France, affect U.S. domestic politics?
5. Was Hamilton's plan for an economy based on manufacturing realistic in 1790? Why or why not?

Looking Ahead ▥▥▶

In Chapter 8, we will see that the year 1800 marked a watershed in American politics because the Federalists lost control of the federal government and declined in power. For most Americans, however, national politics held little importance as they focused on building communities and churches and pursued their daily lives.

1. Why were the Republicans, under Thomas Jefferson, able to win the election of 1800?
2. To what extent did Jefferson adhere to his vision of an agrarian republic?
3. How did the Jefferson administration deal with the continuing foreign entanglements of war between Great Britain and France?

Go to the American Passages website at www.cengage.com/history/ayers/ ampassages4e for additional review materials.

The New Republic Faces a New Century, 1800–1815

Americans confronted the nineteenth century with a variety of fears. For the Federalists, the growing Republican opposition warned that the evils of democracy and anarchy stood ready to take control. For the Republicans, the Alien and Sedition acts and Federalist repression of the whiskey rebels and John Fries underscored the need for change. Both parties, still members of the revolutionary generation, thought in terms of the ideals for which they had fought against the British. They also measured events against what was transpiring elsewhere in the world. By 1800, the excesses of the French Revolution and Napoleon Bonaparte's rise to power dismayed Americans. The never-ending European war threatened to involve the United States for twenty years, and it finally did in 1812. The 1791 revolt by slaves in the French West Indies horrified southern slave owners.

Although Thomas Jefferson's presidency would prove to be less revolutionary than many Federalists feared, the new century brought indelible changes to American politics and society. The Federalist Party shriveled and died, the Louisiana Purchase expanded the nation's territory to the Rocky Mountains and beyond, slavery became more firmly embedded in the southern economy, and the republic fought once more against Great Britain. The Second Great Awakening, the series of religious revivals that began in the late 1790s and gained steam after the turn of the century, influenced the ways in which many people interpreted these events.

RELIGION IN AMERICAN SOCIETY

During the first decade of the nineteenth century, religion absorbed the energies of many different groups: frontier settlers and Native Americans caught up in revivals, organizations to provide welfare relief in towns and cities, new sects like the Shakers, and free African Americans who built separate churches as the cornerstone of their communities. Many people believed that renewed emphasis on religion would transform the nation through individual faith and communal action.

CHAPTER TIMELINE

1800	Washington, D.C., becomes national capital • Gabriel's rebellion • Convention of 1800 with France • Jefferson's election as president • Rise of Handsome Lake as a Seneca prophet
1801	Adams's "midnight appointments" • John Marshall becomes chief justice • Tripolitan War • Cane Ridge, Kentucky, camp meeting
1802	Judiciary Act of 1801 repealed
1803	Marbury v. Madison case • Great Britain and France resume war • Louisiana Purchase
1804	Lewis and Clark expedition departs from St. Louis • Aaron Burr kills Alexander Hamilton • Twelfth Amendment ratified • Haiti founded • Reelection of Jefferson as president
1805	Essex decision in Britain
1806	Non-Importation Act
1807	Burr tried for treason • Leopard-Chesapeake affair • Embargo Act
1808	Federal ban on importation of slaves • Madison elected as president
1809–1811	Tecumseh organizes pan-Indian resistance to land cessions
1809	Giles's Enforcement Act • Embargo repealed; replaced with Non-Intercourse Act • Treaty of Fort Wayne
1810	Annexation of West Florida
1811	Charter of national bank expires • Battle of Tippecanoe
1812	U.S. declares war on Great Britain • Hull surrenders Detroit • Madison elected to second term
1813	Perry defeats British navy on Lake Erie • Battle of the Thames
1814	Battle of Horseshoe Bend • British burn public buildings in Washington, D.C. • Americans repel invasion on Lake Champlain • Hartford Convention • Treaty of Ghent

The Second Great Awakening

As the century began, people throughout the country sought spiritual renewal. Among New England Congregationalists, the revivals spread from one town to another between 1797 and 1801. The national Methodist conference of 1800 held in Baltimore witnessed an outpouring of religious fervor. These flames heralded a series of revivals—the **Second Great Awakening**—which lasted into the 1830s. In accepting the message of revival, large numbers of Americans embraced evangelicalism—the belief that they must take their message of salvation to others. They expected to create a more godly nation through conversion and good works.

In particular, eastern clergy worried that people on the frontier, where there were few churches, would let sin take control of their lives. Americans streamed west across the Appalachians; by 1810, Ohio had 230,000 settlers, Kentucky and Tennessee had 668,000, and the Mississippi and Louisiana territories had 117,000. Evangelical ministers feared

This icon will direct you to interactive activities and study materials on the American Passages website: www.cengage.com/history/ayers/ampassages4e

for the nation because so many westerners were unchurched. The clerics expressed their dread in terms of millennialism, the belief that the millennium—Christ's second coming—was at hand, as foretold in Revelation, the last book of the Bible. Pastors urged their congregations to prepare for the millennium by supporting missionary efforts in the West. They believed that Americans throughout the country must embrace Christianity and convert Native Americans and the people of other lands.

Circuit preachers and missionaries traveled throughout the frontier; the churches they started were often the first social organizations in new communities. The great western revivals of 1800–1815, which built on this work, began when several Presbyterians summoned the first camp meeting, a religious gathering held outside over the course of several days. People came together, miles from their homes, to hear revivalist preachers. The most famous of the early camp meetings took place in August 1801 at Cane Ridge, Kentucky, where Presbyterian, Methodist, and Baptist clergy preached for about a week to a throng numbering about twenty thousand. From wagons and crude tents, the crowds listened to the message that Jesus Christ could save all people from their sins. People reacted emotionally and physically to this message, some jerking their heads or entire bodies, others falling to the ground in a faint.

Reminiscent of the Great Awakening in the South during the 1750s and 1760s, the camp meetings spread through Kentucky, Tennessee, and southern Ohio, gathering new congregations. The Methodist and Baptist churches, which placed less importance on the fine points of religious doctrine and a well-educated clergy than did the Presbyterians, benefited most from the revivals. They saw extraordinary growth among ordinary people. As one minister wrote, "the illiterate Methodist preachers actually set the world on fire, (the American world at least) while [pastors of other denominations] were lighting their matches!"

Religion was also important to black Americans, whether they remained enslaved or had achieved freedom. In the South, African Americans responded enthusiastically to revivalist preachers. The Methodists and Baptists welcomed free and enslaved blacks into their congregations as equals in spirit though not in governing the church. In hostile northern cities, free black communities depended on separate churches for leadership and communal fellowship.

Growth of Sects   The period around 1800 witnessed the expansion of several dissenting sects: the Shakers, the Society of the Public Universal Friend, and the Universalists. They are called *sects,* rather than *denominations,* because they were new and fairly small. They held distinctive beliefs that set them apart from mainstream religions yet had a significant influence on intellectual and social movements of their times.

The Shakers, whose official name was the United Society of Believers in Christ's Second Coming (the Millennial Church), came to America in 1774, when Mother **Ann Lee** arrived from Britain with eight disciples. They left England to escape mob attacks and imprisonment. The group grew slowly at first, but expanded after Lee's death in 1784 as they reaped followers from revivals, especially Baptists. The sect offered an avenue for people who had been spiritually reborn in the Awakening and sought a distinctive way to represent that rebirth in their lives.

From visions, Mother Lee believed that she embodied Christ's Second Coming, that the millennium had already arrived. Because Christ had appeared as a man, and Lee (called Mother of the New Creation) came as a woman, God had both male and female elements. The Shakers believed in salvation by confession of sin, equality regardless of sex or race, opposition to slavery and war, and assistance to the poor. They abstained from sexual relations. In Shaker communities, which by 1809 existed from Maine to Kentucky, men and women ate, slept, and worked separately. They followed a strict discipline and aspired to economic self-sufficiency. Shakers sat on straight-backed chairs, cut their food into square pieces, and walked along paths laid out in right angles. But in religious worship, they abandoned this right-angle order. In a large open space without pulpit or pews, worshippers danced, shouted, and sang. The Shakers influenced other groups to organize communal, utopian experiments during the years after 1815.

A similar but smaller sect was the Society of the Public Universal Friend, founded by Jemima Wilkinson of Rhode Island. Disowned by Quakers in 1776 for joining the Baptists, Wilkinson became ill, believed that she died, and then returned to life as the Public Universal Friend. Her mission was to convince others to repent their sins and prepare for the millennium. Like Mother Lee, Wilkinson preached celibacy, peace, and opposition to slavery. She traveled sidesaddle on horseback, attracting a coterie of believers in New England and Pennsylvania. As one convert said, Wilkinson was "the Messenger of Peace . . . Travelling far & wide to spread the glad tidings & news of Salvation to a lost and perishing & dying World who have all gone astray like Lost Sheep." In 1788, on gathering more than two hundred Universal Friends, she organized a community called Jerusalem in western New York. The Universal Friends neither organized a communal economy like the Shakers nor continued to seek new members. Nevertheless, the community survived well past Wilkinson's death in 1819.

Another sect, the **Universalists**, rejected the Calvinist belief that only a minority of people, the elect, could attain salvation. They preached that "it is the purpose of God, through the grace revealed in our Lord Jesus Christ, to save every member of the human race from sin." The American Universalist church, established in 1779 by an Englishman, John Murray, found a sympathetic audience among ordinary people caught up in the Second Great Awakening in New England and on the frontier. Its message of universal salvation had wide influence, though the Universalist Church itself remained small.

Revivalism Among Native Americans   While the Second Great Awakening and dissenting sects claimed the imagination and souls of white and black Americans, a new wave of revivals drew together Native Americans. Among the Iroquois living on reservations in western New York and the Shawnees, Creeks, Cherokees, and other nations retaining lands in the trans-Appalachian region, prophets warned of imminent doom unless people changed their ways. Native Americans had continued to lose lands to whites throughout the area from the Appalachians to the Mississippi; by 1812, settlers in the region dwarfed the Indian population by seven to one. Decline in the numbers of fur-bearing animals caused economic hardship, and conflict over whether to cooperate with the United States created political factions within tribes.

Like the Delaware prophet Neolin in the 1760s, the new nativists blamed loss of land and power on the Indians' failure to maintain traditional rituals and on their adoption of practices from the whites such as drinking rum. Among many prophets, **Handsome Lake** of the Senecas (a nation of the Iroquois) and **Tenskwatawa** of the Shawnees wielded the greatest influence in the first decade of the nineteenth century.

Handsome Lake, a respected warrior and leader of the Allegany Senecas, fell ill in 1799, seemed to die, and then came back to life saying that he had had a vision in

Tenskwatawa, the Shawnee Prophet

With his brother Tecumseh, Tenskwatawa organized pan-Indian resistance to white settlement in the Great Lakes region. He was one of a series of nativist prophets who challenged their followers to reject alcohol and European American customs. The Shawnee Prophet and Tecumseh opposed accommodationist leaders who sold Indian land, and during the War of 1812, the brothers unsuccessfully allied with Great Britain against the United States.

George Catlin painted this portrait of Tenskwatawa in 1830, nineteen years after the Battle of Tippecanoe. It is one of many paintings produced by Catlin and other artists in the 1830s of individual Native American leaders and scenes demonstrating Indian customs, such as dances and the hunt. Unlike many other Indians of the time, the prophet is wearing skins rather than a cloak. He has silver earrings, armbands, and a gorget at his throat, but not a peace medal indicating alliance with the U.S. or British government, as appeared in the portraits of other Native Americans at the time.

(Smithsonian American Art Museum, Washington, DC/Art Resource, NY)

which messengers told him to become a prophet. In a series of revelations over several years, Handsome Lake received a message of impending catastrophe and a means to salvation. He told his people to stop drinking alcohol and practicing witchcraft; instead they should perform their ancestral rituals. The prophet also advocated peace. He embraced the U.S. acculturation policy by which Quakers tried to convince the Iroquois to adopt white farming methods and gender roles, but he opposed further large-scale land cessions, the whiskey trade, social dancing by couples, and gambling with cards. Other Indians opposed acculturation, which required women to leave the fields and take up spinning and men to farm rather than hunt. They viewed the policy, accurately, as a way to justify further expropriation of hunting lands.

Handsome Lake served as a political leader of the Iroquois only briefly, from 1801 to 1803, but his spiritual message remained strong in the years that followed. Most influential was his drive against liquor. A former heavy drinker himself, the Seneca prophet advised, in the words of a white observer, that "the Whiskey is the great Engine which the bad Spirit uses to introduce Witchcraft and many other evils amongst Indians." Many Iroquois abstained from hard drink. One Quaker visitor "noted with satisfaction that in the course of our travels among all the Indians on the Allegheny River . . . we have not seen a Single individual the least intoxicated with Liquor—which perhaps would be a Singular Circumstance to Observe in traveling among the same number of white Inhabitants."

Also influential was Tenskwatawa, called the Shawnee Prophet, who became prominent among the people of the Great Lakes and Ohio Valley. With his brother, Tecumseh, he inspired a nativist movement to resist the U.S. government's acculturation policy and land grabbing. To avoid fiery destruction, Tenskwatawa warned, Indians must revitalize their traditional ceremonies, avoid liquor, and reject new gender roles. One of the prophet's visions promised that the whites would be destroyed if his people obeyed these instructions.

AFRICAN AMERICANS

As slavery ended in the North, free blacks faced discriminatory practices that kept the racial caste system in place, including segregation in churches and schools and restriction from politics and many occupations. Despite this racism, northern blacks created new lives, institutions, and communities that offered a potent draw to African Americans in the South. Southern blacks also considered more violent means to end bondage, as in the case of Gabriel's revolt in Virginia.

Free Blacks in the North   By 1800, Pennsylvania, New York, and all of New England had passed gradual abolition acts or ended slavery outright. New Jersey in 1804 became the last northern state to pass a law for gradual emancipation, which, like those of other states, freed children henceforth born to slave mothers but retained slaves born before that date in perpetual bondage. The black children who benefited from the law would be required to serve their mother's owner, much like indentured servants, until a certain age—in New Jersey, twenty-five for males and twenty-one for females.

Despite the gradual nature of these emancipation laws, slavery declined rapidly in the northern states. Responding to their slaves' requests for freedom and to the spirit of the abolition acts, many owners freed people whom the laws left in bonds. Masters usually required some additional years of service for the promise of freedom. Frequently blacks negotiated agreements for themselves or family members. In 1805, a New York slave, Margaret, obtained her owner's pledge of freedom in eight years if she behaved "as she always has done in an orderly manner as a servant ought to do." A New Jersey man promised to pay his owner $50 per year for four years in return for his release. When masters proved recalcitrant, blacks often forced the issue by running away.

The northern cities became magnets for escaped slaves. Humanitarian concerns touched some southern

TABLE **8.1 Free Black Population in Northern Cities**

	1790	1800	1810
Pennsylvania	1,849	6,028	8,942
New York City	1,078	3,499	8,137
Boston	761	1,174	1,464

Source: Gary B. Nash and Jean R. Soderlund, *Freedom By Degrees: Emancipation in Pennsylvania and its Aftermath* (New York: Oxford University Press, 1991), 18; U.S. Bureau of the Census, *A Century of Population Growth from the First Census of the United States to the Twelfth 1790–1900* (Washington: Government Printing Office, 1909), 84; Leonard P. Curry, *The Free Black in Urban America 1800–1850* (University of Chicago Press, 1981), 250.

masters, including George Washington, who freed his slaves in his will. Some owners in Delaware and the Chesapeake region, who held more slaves than they needed, emancipated their slaves and then sold them as indentured servants in the North. Between 1790 and 1810, the free black population of Philadelphia and New York City soared, while that of Boston also grew, though more slowly.

Philadelphia and New York City became centers of free African American culture, with churches fostering autonomous community growth. In Philadelphia, responding to hostility from whites, freed men and women organized separate black congregations in the 1780s and 1790s. Reverend **Richard Allen**, for example, led black worshippers from St. George's Methodist Episcopal Church when whites insisted on segregated seating. Allen described the scene as they were forced to move during prayer:

> We had not been long upon our knees before I heard considerable scuffling and loud talking. I raised my head up and saw one of the trustees, H_____ M_____, having hold of the Rev. Absalom Jones, pulling him off his knees, and saying, "You must get up, you must not kneel here." . . . We all went out of the church in a body, and they were no more plagued by us in the church.

Allen purchased a blacksmith's shop and converted it into a church, calling it Bethel. By 1803, the black Methodist church had 457 members, the result of revivals and Allen's fervent preaching. But while the evangelical message of Methodism appealed to African Americans, and "Mother" Bethel grew, the congregation found relations with the hierarchy of the white Methodist church difficult. In the early decades of the nineteenth century, black Methodists in Philadelphia, Baltimore, Wilmington, and New York struggled against white control, finally seceding to form separate denominations. In 1816, Philadelphia's Bethel became the first congregation of the African Methodist Episcopal church.

Urban black churches provided mutual aid, fellowship, and avenues for leadership. One benefit of belonging to a New York congregation became obvious to an eighty-year-old woman after a fire destroyed her home. When asked where she would find shelter, she answered, "O a sister in the church has promised to take me in." Shunned by white organizations, effectively barred from politics, and lacking equal opportunity for employment, African Americans created alternatives through the church.

Like white urban residents, freed men and women formed mutual benefit societies. The names African Americans chose for these organizations demonstrated pride in their African heritage, though many of the founders were two, three, or even four generations removed from ancestral lands. Philadelphians, for example, formed the Free African Society, Daughters of Ethiopia, Angola Society, Sons of Africa, and many others. The official purpose of these societies was to collect dues to provide relief to poor widows and children, but just as important, the groups facilitated community involvement.

With little money or access to capital, few African Americans, perhaps one in ten, scraped together the funds to purchase a house, shop, or farm. In the first decades of the nineteenth century, many blacks were still completing terms of servitude; others, though free, lived and worked in white households as domestic servants. Even if they established their own households, women generally washed clothes or performed domestic service for others. Most men were mariners or common laborers.

The African Episcopal Church of St. Thomas

As the free African American population grew in Philadelphia, churches became central to the developing community. Black Philadelphians founded separate churches for several reasons, including the discrimination they experienced in white congregations and the desire for black leadership. Many of the African American community's key leaders were ministers, including the Rev. Richard Allen, founder of the

(Historical Society of Pennsylvania [Bb 882 B756 44])

Bethel African Methodist Church, and Rev. Absolem Jones, leader of the African Church of Philadelphia, which affiliated with Episcopalians to become St. Thomas's. The African Episcopal Church of St. Thomas, shown in this view by David Kennedy and William Lucas, was founded in 1794 and had 427 members the next year. Increasingly, black Philadelphians attended the separate churches. In explaining why former slaves sought their own institutions, Absolem Jones wrote, "to arise out of the dust and shake ourselves, and throw off that servile fear, that the habit of oppression and bondage trained us up in."

The African American community provided additional opportunity by employing its own. Residents supported black shoemakers, carpenters, food retailers, hucksters, barbers, hairdressers, seamstresses, tailors, cooks, bakers, schoolteachers, and ministers. In Philadelphia, a few African Americans achieved considerable wealth and fame. By 1807, James Forten employed thirty men—blacks and whites—to produce sails for the city's shipbuilders. Robert Bogle developed the idea of catering parties, weddings, and funerals, and Frank Johnson became the city's premier musician. He performed on trumpet and violin, composed dance music and songs, and organized a band that played at balls and public events.

African Americans in northern cities also knew of recent struggles by slaves in St. Domingue and elsewhere; a large number of blacks in Philadelphia and New York City had come from the French island with their masters who had fled the black revolt. During the 1790s, blacks on **St. Domingue** led by Toussaint L'Ouverture, a former slave, had defeated local whites and the French, Spanish, and British armies. In 1802, Napoleon tried to regain control of the island but failed when disease decimated his forces. In 1804, the victorious rebels of St. Domingue established Haiti as an independent nation. Most white Americans dreaded the importation of black revolt. Thomas Jefferson opposed trade with the island, stating, "We may expect therefore black crews, and supercargoes and missionaries thence into the southern states. . . . If this combustion can be introduced among us under any veil whatever, we have to fear it."

Slave Rebellion in the South With more than 850,000 enslaved blacks in the American South in 1800, one-third of the population, whites had reason to be concerned about slave insurgency. After St. Domingue erupted, Georgia and the Carolinas declared black émigrés from the West Indies a threat, prohibiting their entry. South Carolina, in reopening its international slave trade in 1803, made every effort to avoid admitting rebels. The state excluded blacks from the West Indies and South America and any who had ever lived in the French West Indies. Every man imported from another state needed a certificate indicating that he had not "been concerned in any insurrection or rebellion."

In August 1800, the worst fears of white southerners were nearly realized when an enslaved blacksmith named Gabriel organized an armed march against the capital of Virginia. With about six hundred supporters from Richmond and surrounding counties, Gabriel planned a full-scale insurrection. His strategy included seizing guns from an arsenal, taking Governor James Monroe hostage, and forcing concessions from town officials. Gabriel expected poor whites to join him because they, like slaves, lacked political power. The attack failed when a torrential rainstorm washed out bridges, making travel impossible. Efforts to try again another day collapsed when two informers passed word of the conspiracy to authorities, who rounded up suspects. Although Gabriel eluded capture for more than three weeks, he was arrested and hanged, as were twenty-six others implicated in the plot.

White Americans still held the revolutionary belief that all men and women desired freedom, masters took seriously the threat of slave revolt. After Gabriel's rebellion, Governor Monroe observed about enslaved African Americans, "Unhappily while this class of people exists among us we can never count with certainty on its tranquil submission." In 1802, Virginians discovered additional conspiracies, with rumors of more violence heightening tensions. In 1805, after four whites had been poisoned in North Carolina, officials burned a slave woman alive, hanged three other slaves, and whipped and cut off the ears of another. Gabriel's plot, the St. Domingue uprising, and what appeared to be an upsurge of murders and arson by blacks convinced southern lawmakers to enact more stringent slave codes. South Carolina and Georgia tightened requirements for slave patrols and defined as treason any collaboration in slave rebellion. Hardening attitudes toward slavery snuffed out southern antislavery societies that were already faltering. On a more positive note, as the twenty-year constitutional restriction on prohibiting the slave trade expired, Congress officially banned the importation of slaves after January 1, 1808.

JEFFERSON'S REPUBLIC

In 1800, the federal government moved from the nation's cultural capital in Philadelphia to an unfinished village on the Potomac: Washington, D.C. The ruling party also changed, as voters voiced their dissatisfaction with the Federalists by electing Thomas Jefferson and a Republican Congress. Jefferson's promise of reduced government and taxes appealed to a populace concerned about other things besides national politics—their finances, their souls, and local communities. Events prevented the young nation from wrapping itself in isolation, however, for its economic prosperity depended a great deal on international commerce, a trade severely hampered by the ongoing European war.

The Election of 1800

Shortly before the election, the United States had been involved in the Quasi-War with France, in which the French navy initially ravaged the American merchant fleet. Congress had expanded the army, authorized the U.S. Navy to protect commercial ships, and revoked unilaterally the American-French treaty of 1778. The Federalists had swept the congressional elections of 1798 on the crest of anti-French fervor and had tried to use war fever against the Republicans through the Alien and Sedition acts. Instead, the backlash of concern about civil liberties swelled the opposition.

As the 1800 election approached, many Federalists expected to take advantage of the unresolved difficulties with France in continuing to paint the Jeffersonian Republicans as pro-French, and hence un-American. Nevertheless, President John Adams moved to end hostilities. He nominated a three-man commission—William Vans Murray (minister to the Netherlands), Chief Justice Oliver Ellsworth, and Governor William R. Davie of North Carolina—to make peace with France. The commission received instructions that proved impossible to fulfill: its mission was to obtain French agreement that the 1778 alliance had ended and indemnities for confiscated American ships. In March 1800, Murray, Ellsworth, and Davie met with Napoleon, who had no intention of paying compensation. The commissioners reached an accord only by ignoring their instructions. The **Convention of 1800**, signed in France in October and ratified reluctantly by the U.S. Senate in February 1801, echoed provisions of the 1778

MAP 8.1 The Election of 1800.

The election Thomas Jefferson called "the revolution of 1800" was close, with Jefferson receiving 73 votes to John Adams's 65. The Federalist ticket, headed by Adams and Charles Cotesworth Pinckney, obtained considerable support from the Carolinas and the mid-Atlantic states, as well as New England.

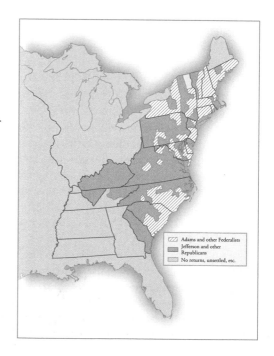

commercial treaty in calling for "a firm, inviolable, and universal peace," but it voided the defensive alliance of 1778, eliminating the French claim to U.S. support against Great Britain. The pact also included a vague confirmation by the French of neutral rights in international trade, but it provided no restitution to American shippers, a failing that opponents said made the convention worthless. In fact, it had value in normalizing relations between the two countries.

The chief beneficiary of reduced tensions with France was Thomas Jefferson, named in May 1800 as Republican nominee for president, with Aaron Burr of New York for vice president. John Adams received the Federalist nomination for reelection, with Charles Cotesworth Pinckney of South Carolina as his running mate. Many Federalists opposed Adams for making peace with France. When the electoral votes were tallied, Jefferson and Burr each received 73 votes, Adams 65, Pinckney 64, and John Jay 1. In lining up votes in the electoral college, the Republicans had failed to take account of the constitutional election procedures that lacked provision for party slates. The Constitution directed that each elector cast two votes, with the candidate receiving the highest number elected president and the runner-up vice president. The electors had no way of designating which candidate they supported for president and which for vice president. The Federalists avoided the difficulty by having one elector vote for John Jay, thus giving Pinckney one fewer vote than Adams.

If Burr had simply yielded to Jefferson, the problem would have been resolved without complication. Instead, the tie sent the election to the House of Representatives, which had a Federalist majority from the previous election. Each state delegation received one vote. Some of the Federalists hatched a plan to support Burr, thinking that they might be able to control him as president. Hamilton opposed the plot vigorously, contending that "Burr loves nothing but himself; thinks of nothing but his own aggrandizement, and will be content with nothing, short of permanent power in his own hands." The former secretary of the treasury advised his party to make a deal with Jefferson to keep the system of public credit and the navy, retain Federalist appointees in office, and remain neutral in the war between Britain and France. The House of Representatives required thirty-six ballots over six days before the Federalist delegate from Delaware, James A. Bayard, shifted his position from Burr to Jefferson to break the tie. Jefferson became president and Burr vice president.

JEFFERSON'S "REVOLUTION"

The third president assumed a conciliatory stance toward the Federalists as he took office. On March 4, 1801, Jefferson delivered his inaugural address to the new Congress, which the Republicans now dominated in the House by 69 votes to 36 and in the Senate by 18 to 13. He gave the address almost in a whisper, for he was not a good public speaker. The speech reflected his Republican beliefs: emphasis on the power of state governments, freedom of religion and the press, majority rule but protection of minority rights, low government expenditures, and reduction of the federal debt. Jefferson upheld the Convention of 1800 with France implicitly by stating that he desired amity and trade with foreign nations and "entangling alliances with none." His most famous statement, "We are all republicans, we are all federalists," attempted to get beyond the partisan battles that had bedeviled his two predecessors. He later described his election as "the revolution of 1800" that "was as real a revolution in the principles of our government as that of 1776 was in its form; not effected indeed by the sword, as that, but by the rational and peaceable instrument of reform, the suffrage of the people." Despite bitter political enmity, American leaders had created a party system by which power could be contested in elections rather than through bloodshed. With the election of 1800, the Constitution passed a crucial test, with peaceful transfer of power from one party to its opponents.

The new president worked to put his principles into action and create an agrarian republic in which the federal government kept its role to a minimum. The location in Washington, D.C., seemed the ideal setting for a weak government. In 1800, the town had fewer than four hundred dwellings, which one government official described as mostly "small miserable huts." The Capitol was incomplete, with wings for the Senate and House but no center. What existed was poorly constructed: the acoustics were dreadful, the roof leaked, and the heating was "noxious." The president's house was not yet finished in 1814 when the British burned it. Construction materials littered the grounds during Jefferson's administration to the extent that, according to one guest, "in a dark night instead of finding your way to the house, you may, perchance, fall into a pit, or stumble over a heap of rubbish." Cows grazed on what later became the Mall; hogs ran through the city's streets.

Washington, D.C., remained a village in part because the federal government was small and Jefferson had no interest in seeing it grow. In 1802, federal personnel throughout the country numbered under ten thousand, of whom sixty-five hundred served in military posts. Of the nonuniformed officials, fewer than three hundred worked in the capital. The president and Supreme Court each had one clerk, Congress employed thirteen, and the attorney general had none. The central government had relatively little to do, for state and local governments or voluntary associations took primary responsibility for keeping law and order, maintaining roads and bridges, supervising the militia, and providing welfare relief and schools.

Jefferson's lack of attention to building Washington, D.C., revealed his approach to the presidency. In contrast to Federalist efforts to reflect the grandeur of European courts and capitals, he adopted informality and frugality. Jefferson dealt with members of Congress and foreign diplomats personally, inviting small groups for dinner and conversation. He avoided making speeches, instead sending written messages to Congress. With only one clerk, he handled many documents himself.

The change of political power from the Federalists to the Republicans raised questions about office holding and political spoils. At the highest level of executive appointments, the cabinet, Jefferson assumed his right to appoint trusted supporters. He named James Madison of Virginia, his closest ally, as secretary of state and Albert Gallatin of Pennsylvania as secretary of the treasury. Other members of the cabinet were Levi Lincoln of Massachusetts as attorney general, Henry Dearborn of Massachusetts as secretary of war, and Robert Smith of Maryland as secretary of the navy.

The question of whether to retain bureaucrats was more difficult. Jefferson supported the idea of a civil service in which public officers held their positions on the basis of merit; during the election crisis, he suggested that he would allow most officeholders to keep their jobs. When he learned that Washington and Adams had appointed only six Republicans to about six hundred positions, however, the new president replaced about half of the Federalists with Republicans. Most infuriating to Jefferson were the "**midnight appointments**," as Jefferson characterized them—the appointments Adams made as a lame duck after he knew that the election was lost. In February 1801, the Federalist Congress had passed a new Judiciary Act creating these additional judgeships and other offices, all of which Federalists received. Jefferson called on the new Republican Congress to repeal the law.

Jefferson and Gallatin placed high priority on decreasing government expenditures, taxes, and the national debt. Gallatin opposed all spending by the federal government, including the military. With the support of the Republican Congress, the administration cut the defense budget in half. It repealed all excise taxes, including that on whiskey, relying primarily on import duties for income.

Jefferson's plan to reduce the navy and remain clear of international conflicts hit a snag when Yusuf Karamanli, the leader of Tripoli in North Africa, demanded payments from the United States to "protect" American merchant carriers from pirates. To end this extortion, in 1801 Jefferson sent naval vessels to blockade Tripoli and protect shipping. The United States experienced a major loss when the ship *Philadelphia* ran aground while pursuing pirates, but when a small force of U.S. Marines and Arab mercenaries seized the port city of Derna, the Tripolitans agreed to peace. The war had propelled military expenditures upward, however, and convinced Jefferson of the navy's value, thus hindering somewhat the administration's plans for reduced government spending.

The Judiciary

Although the Republicans had captured the presidency and Congress in 1800, the judiciary remained firmly in the hands of the Federalists. Adams and the outgoing Congress had tried to solidify their party's power in the courts with the Judiciary Act of 1801, which amended the Judiciary Act of 1789. By appointing additional federal judges, the new law ended the onerous requirement for Supreme Court justices to ride from state to state to convene circuit courts twice a year. The act also reduced the number of justices on the Court from six to five, thereby denying Jefferson the opportunity to make an appointment when a seat became vacant. The Republican Congress repealed this law in early 1802, reinstating the Judiciary Act of 1789, thus forcing some federal judges out of their jobs and the Supreme Court back to the circuit.

Jefferson's bitter relationship with the Supreme Court resulted in part from his antipathy toward Chief Justice **John Marshall**, his distant cousin, whom Adams had named to the bench in early 1801. Like Jefferson, Marshall was tall, informal in manner, and a native of Virginia. He had joined the patriot forces in 1775, serving until 1781. He attributed his nationalism to that service, saying he became "confirmed in the habit of considering America as my country, and congress as my government." Marshall began a successful law practice after the war, served as a Virginia assemblyman, supported ratification of the Federal Constitution, then became the leading Federalist in his state. In the legal environment of the new republic, many colleagues appreciated his originality in building cases on logic and natural law rather than depending on English precedent. On the Supreme Court, too, Marshall followed his own lights, creating the legal basis on which the power of the Court still rests. During his long, illustrious career, which lasted until 1835, Marshall solidified the authority of the judicial branch of the federal government.

Marshall's most important decision, *Marbury v. Madison* (1803), commenced in a suit by William Marbury, nominated by Adams as a justice of the peace but not commissioned by the Jefferson administration. Marbury sued under the Judiciary Act of 1789, which granted the Supreme Court the power to require Secretary of State

Madison to hand over Marbury's commission. Given the partisanship involved, most observers expected Marshall and his Federalist court to direct Madison to comply. Instead, the chief justice said that he could not remedy Marbury's situation, though he wished to do so, because the Congress had erred in giving the Court such authority. Marshall declared the provision of the 1789 Judiciary Act unconstitutional, thus establishing the Supreme Court's power of judicial review.

Jefferson decided that the federal judiciary, still dominated by Federalists and growing in power under Marshall, had to be controlled. Because federal judges constitutionally held their seats for life, "during good behavior," the president suggested to congressional Republicans that they start impeachment proceedings against objectionable Federalists. The Republicans impeached John Pickering, an official of the federal district court of New Hampshire, who was an alcoholic and insane but who had not to anyone's knowledge committed any high crimes. The Senate found him guilty anyway and removed him from his position. Next, in January 1805, the House of Representatives impeached Samuel Chase of Maryland, an associate justice of the Supreme Court and extreme Federalist who had castigated Jefferson's administration. But the prosecution failed to convince two-thirds of the Senate that Chase should be expelled from office for misconduct and other charges. Some moderate Republicans refused to adopt Jefferson's strategy to eject troublesome opponents. Thus ended Congress's attempt to remove Federalists from the bench by impeachment.

Domestic Politics Jefferson and the Republicans gained in popularity as they steered a course more moderate than the "revolution" of 1800 had promised. The president had reduced taxes and attempted to limit the judiciary, but did not dismantle the Federalist edifice of national power, including the military and the national bank. He mixed republican theory, based on a nation of small farmers, with practical politics aiding commerce. His policies, combined with booming exports, steadily increased Republican support, as many Federalist voters switched parties. In the election of 1802, the Republicans won 102 seats to the Federalists' 39 in the House of Representatives; the Republican margin in the Senate was 25 to 9.

Looking forward to the next presidential election, Congress acted promptly to avoid the deadlock that had occurred in 1800. The Republicans wanted a formal way to keep the Federalists from conspiring once again to elevate the Republican candidate for vice president to the presidency. The **Twelfth Amendment** to the Constitution, which required the electors to draw up distinct lists for president and vice president, was ratified by September 1804.

The election of 1804 demonstrated the demise of the Federalists as an effective national party. Jefferson defeated the Federalist presidential candidate, Charles Cotesworth Pinckney, by 162 electoral votes to 14.

Jefferson had replaced Aaron Burr as his running mate with George Clinton, also of New York, thus keeping the ticket balanced geographically. For his part, Burr ran for governor of New York against the Republican candidate, Morgan Lewis, but lost by a landslide. Alexander Hamilton played a decisive role in the defeat by publicly denouncing his long-time enemy. Burr challenged Hamilton to a duel. When the two faced each other at Weehawken, New Jersey, in July 1804, Burr shot Hamilton to death. In doing so, the vice president ended his own political career, as well as the life of one of the architects of the American nation-state.

THE LOUISIANA PURCHASE

Jefferson had boosted his popularity prior to the 1804 election with the **Louisiana Purchase**, which marked the greatest success of his presidency. In pursuing the deal with France, he deviated from one of his beliefs—in limited power of the central government—to obtain land for his agrarian republic. Long interested in the West, he scored a diplomatic coup that doubled the size of the United States and reduced Spain's dominance west of the Mississippi River.

The Bargain with Napoleon, 1803 The chain of events leading to the Louisiana Purchase began in 1800, when France signed a secret treaty with Spain to recover the lands in western North America it had ceded to Spain in 1763. When Jefferson and Madison heard in 1801 of the impending transfer, they sent the new U.S. minister to France, Robert R. Livingston, with instructions to prevent the exchange or at least obtain West Florida. The Americans wanted to prevent France from controlling the Mississippi Valley; the dilapidated Spanish empire had caused trouble enough. In October 1802, the Spanish suspended once again the right of Americans to deposit goods for export at New Orleans. The Americans thought, incorrectly, that Napoleon was behind the ban. Many wanted to take New Orleans by force. Jefferson wrote to Livingston, "The day that France takes possession of N. Orleans . . . we must marry ourselves to the British fleet and nation." Jefferson pushed for negotiations, however, not war.

In response to Livingston's overtures, Napoleon decided to sell the entire Louisiana Territory to the United States. The French leader's zeal to construct an American empire had cooled with the loss of his army in St. Domingue. In documents dated April 30, 1803, the United States agreed to pay France $15 million, respect the rights of the French and Native Americans living in the territory, and recognize the French residents as American citizens. Spain was furious because Napoleon had promised not to sell the region to the British or the Americans. Jefferson ignored the Spanish objections but worried, as a strict constructionist, that the Louisiana Purchase was unconstitutional because the federal government had no specific power to acquire territory. He put aside these concerns, confident that it was right to avoid war and add vast lands for expansion of the American republic. "By enlarging the empire of liberty," the president argued, the nation could maintain its agrarian foundations and thus avoid descent into vice, luxury, and decay. A successful republic was dependent on broad property holding, for virtuous, independent, middling farmers made ideal citizens. The Louisiana Purchase, Jefferson believed, would extend the life of the republic by providing space for generations of ordinary planters. Although some Federalists disagreed, most Americans celebrated the end of friction over the Mississippi River and New Orleans. Western farmers could get their products to market while eastern merchants prospered from the trade.

DOING HISTORY ONLINE

Jefferson and the Louisiana Territory, 1804

Based on his letter to Governor Claiborne (Document 2), what appear to be Jefferson's concerns regarding governance of the Louisiana Territory?

 www.cengage.com/history/ayers/ampassages4e

Disputes with Spain When U.S. officials gained formal possession of Louisiana in December 1803, the Spanish had only recently transferred control to the French. The ceremonies took place in New Orleans, a city of eight thousand that had been reconstructed in Spanish style since several great fires a decade earlier. With a cathedral, theater, impressive city hall, and mansions, New Orleans served as the cultural and economic center of the lower Mississippi Valley. In population, it was larger than other towns of the Spanish borderlands. The entire white population of the Louisiana Territory—French, Spanish, Germans, English, and Americans—was approximately fifty thousand.

Beyond Spain's objection to the U.S. purchase of Louisiana, the two nations also disputed the territory's boundaries because the treaties transferring ownership were vague. Thomas Jefferson pushed for the most generous interpretation for the United States. He demanded West Florida, with an eastern boundary at the Perdido River, the boundary today between Alabama and the Florida panhandle. The president also thought his new acquisition extended in the Southwest to the Rio Grande, incorporating all of Texas and part of New Mexico, and in the Northwest to the Rocky Mountains. Spain, however, said the Louisiana Territory included only a constricted region along the west bank of the Mississippi from northern Missouri to the Gulf of Mexico.

In 1804, Jefferson sent troops to West Florida, hoping to convince Spain by threat of force to give up or sell the province. Americans already outnumbered Spanish residents in the territory, which later contained parts of Mississippi, Alabama, and Louisiana. Jefferson also wanted East Florida. He decided not to attack and instead attempted to purchase the Floridas over the next several years, but failed.

The Lewis and Clark Expedition, 1804–1806 To strengthen U.S. claims to the West, Jefferson sponsored an exploratory mission to the Pacific Ocean. Several times since 1783, he had tried to organize expeditions for scientific knowledge and promote American interests in the region. As president, he now had the authority and financial resources to support this major undertaking. By the early nineteenth century, however, others had surveyed parts of the territory. In 1792, an American sea captain, Robert Gray, explored the Columbia River, and George Vancouver, a British naval officer, sailed the Northwest coast. A few years later, fur traders working for the Spanish government ascended the Missouri River to present-day North Dakota, and British traders from Canada began moving west.

Even before buying Louisiana, the president had decided to send an expedition west; the purchase gave the project greater urgency. He appointed his private secretary, **Meriwether Lewis**, captain of the enterprise. Jefferson selected Lewis for his scientific interests as well as his wilderness experience. The president wanted "a person who to courage, prudence, habits & health adapted to the woods, & some familiarity with the Indian character, joins a perfect knoledge of botany, natural history, mineralogy & astronomy." Lewis chose his friend William Clark to be his partner. Lewis and Clark had served in the army together in the Old Northwest, so both were familiar with frontier conditions.

Jefferson had a long list of goals for his explorers. They were to travel to the source of the Missouri River to find the elusive Northwest Passage, fill in huge blanks in geographic knowledge of the West, and bring back descriptions of species of plants and animals thus far unknown. He also hoped they would make peaceful contact

Meriwether Lewis. *A portrayal of Meriwether Lewis during the western expedition. C.B.J. F. de Saint-Memin produced the print in 1816, after the explorer's death.*

with Native Americans to expand commercial networks for fur traders. Lewis and Clark more than fulfilled their assignment, keeping daily journals of their experiences, including descriptions of Indian societies and culture, systematic weather records, and observations of flora and fauna, as well as a detailed map of their journey. Their relations with the people of the Northwest were for the most part amicable.

Lewis and Clark received commissions as army officers to lead the Corps of Discovery of about forty men who departed from St. Louis in May 1804. During that summer and fall, they traveled up the Missouri River, using poles and tow ropes against the current. They battled the hot sun, diarrhea, and mosquitoes; several men deserted, and one died, the only member of the group to perish during the entire trip. The adventurers met with the leaders of Indian nations along the way, telling them that the United States had taken possession of the territory from the Spanish. They arrived in the Mandan and Hidatsa villages of what is now North Dakota, where they spent the winter of 1804–1805.

In April 1805, the Lewis and Clark expedition set out with a Shoshone woman, **Sacagawea,** and her French husband and infant son. They proceeded up the Missouri River, made an arduous crossing of the Rockies, and reached the mouth of the Columbia River before winter. On the way back, the Corps of Discovery divided in two, with Clark leading a party southeast along the Yellowstone River and Lewis taking a northern route through Montana. They joined forces once again in North Dakota and returned to St. Louis by September 1806. They had been away so long that many assumed they had been killed by the Spanish or Native Americans.

Spies and Infiltrators

Spanish officials in fact had tried to intercept Lewis and Clark, whom they correctly suspected of making allies for the United States among the western Indians. General James Wilkinson, commander of U.S. troops in the West, governor of the Louisiana Territory, and a double agent known to the Spanish as "Agent 13," had tipped off New Spain about the expedition. The governor of New Mexico sent out search parties but failed to find Lewis and Clark. They did stop the mission of Thomas Freeman and Peter Custis, who in 1806 had started from Louisiana to find the source of the Red River. Another Spanish party nearly intercepted Zebulon Pike, whom Wilkinson had dispatched to explore and spy in the region that is now Kansas, Colorado, and New Mexico. When Pike became lost in the southern Rockies, he was rescued by Spanish soldiers, who arrested, and then released, him.

The United States and Spain knew they were playing for high stakes. The United States could use exploration of the West and alliances with Native Americans to help confirm its claims to broad boundaries of the Louisiana Territory. The Spanish had by far superior documentation for Texas, New Mexico, Arizona, California, and western Colorado. But they also denied American rights to what is now western Louisiana. Jefferson sent General Wilkinson with troops to the undefined boundary between Louisiana and Texas; the Spanish dispatched Lieutenant Colonel Simón de Herrera to defend eastern Texas. The two officers avoided fighting by establishing a neutral zone until diplomats could negotiate the border.

Still concerned about protecting their silver mines in Mexico, the Spanish took steps to increase settlement in Texas. They welcomed Indian exiles—Cherokees, Choctaws, and Alabamas—from lands overrun by American settlers east of the Mississippi, but the Hispanic population failed to grow significantly. New Spain officials specifically barred U.S. citizens from Texas, under threat of arrest and imprisonment. The Americans, one Spanish official feared, "are not and will not be anything but crows to pick out our eyes." Anglo-American traders continued to infiltrate Texas, however, to trap animals and bargain for horses with the Comanches and other Indians.

The Burr Conspiracy

While Lewis and Clark were reconnoitering the Far Northwest, Aaron Burr, who in 1804 had mortally wounded Alexander Hamilton in a duel and was estranged from Jefferson, conceived a plot to create a separate nation in the West. He contacted the double agent James Wilkinson, various unhappy politicians, and representatives of foreign governments. Burr suggested a variety of plans to those who would listen, including an invasion of New Spain, an attack on Washington, D.C., and secession of the West. Wilkinson cooperated with Burr at first, then turned informer when the conspiracy became public knowledge. Jefferson ordered Burr's arrest for treason, while applauding Wilkinson's "fidelity." Burr tried to escape to Europe but was captured and taken to Richmond, Virginia, where he was tried in 1807.

The Burr conspiracy case, presided over by Chief Justice Marshall and involving three prosecutors and six defense lawyers, might have been called the trial of the century. An unbiased jury could not be found; one juror said before the case was heard that Burr should be hanged. The principal actors in the trial were Marshall, who ignored his responsibility as an impartial judge to favor the defense, and Jefferson, who directed the prosecution from afar. Because Marshall upheld a definition of treason that required actual gathering of troops, not just conspiracy, the case against Burr collapsed. Jefferson blamed Marshall and considered trying to impeach him, but he found insufficient congressional support.

MORE FOREIGN ENTANGLEMENTS

The renewal of war in 1803 between Great Britain and France portended trouble for the United States. American merchants flourished as they took advantage of neutrality and wartime demand for provisions in Europe and the West Indies. But their ships became vulnerable to the British navy and French privateers.

A Perilous Neutrality

Great Britain and France each wanted to prevent the United States from provisioning the other. In particular, the British intended to stop American traders from carrying foreign sugar, coffee, and other tropical products to Europe, even though the merchants conformed technically to British guidelines by taking the goods first to U.S. ports, then reexporting. In the *Essex* case of 1805, British courts stiffened their rules, stating that merely carrying Spanish and French goods to U.S. soil for reexport was insufficient; only commodities originally meant for sale in the United States, then subsequently redirected to Europe, would be considered exempt from seizure. Few reexported cargoes met the new guidelines. With the *Essex* rule, the Royal Navy stepped up its confiscations of American ships. Then, in 1806 and 1807, the British and French blockaded each other's harbors, in combination eliminating neutral trade with Europe and the British Isles. The British insisted that neutral ships sail to Britain first for inspection and licensing before trading in Europe. Napoleon's Berlin and Milan Decrees banned trade with Britain and threatened neutrals who obeyed the British rules with seizure.

After the British destroyed the French and Spanish navies in 1805 at Trafalgar, off the coast of Spain, the British restrictions and impressment of sailors were by far the more troublesome to Americans. Many Federalists and some Republicans cried for war. But Jefferson and the congressional majority looked for ways to avoid hostilities. With a trimmed federal budget and small military, the Republicans were unprepared for war. Congress passed the Non-Importation Act (1806) banning specified British goods, and the president opened negotiations with Great Britain to end impressment and recognize neutral trading rights. No agreement satisfactory to both sides could be reached. Then in June 1807, the British ship *Leopard* fired on the American frigate *Chesapeake* for refusing to submit to a search for British deserters. The *Chesapeake*, hit twenty-two times, managed to respond with only a single shot. The *Leopard* boarded her, impressing four men.

The Embargo of 1807   As Americans clamored for war in response, Jefferson closed U.S. ports and territorial waters to British vessels and recalled American ships from the Mediterranean, where they would have been trapped had war begun. The British refused to stop impressing American sailors, and they challenged Jefferson's port closure by firing on coastal towns in Maine and sailing into Chesapeake Bay. The president resisted a declaration of war but placed military posts and gunboats on alert. He chose economic warfare instead. Unfortunately, this policy destroyed the commercial boom that had meant high prices for farmers and employed thousands of sailors.

At the urging of President Jefferson and Secretary of State Madison, Congress passed the **Embargo Act** in December 1807, which prohibited exportation to all other countries. The administration hoped in particular to defang the former parent country by withholding provisions to the British Isles and West Indies. A by-product of nonexportation would be a severe drop in imports of British manufactures. Jefferson and Madison argued that the boycott would hurt all warring parties but Britain the worst. During 1808, the administration faced difficulty enforcing the embargo because ships, especially from New England, left harbor pretending to sail to American coastal ports but headed for foreign destinations instead. The trade with the British West Indies continued illegally. Federal agents also had little success in preventing smuggling into Canada. In January 1809, the government resorted to an extreme measure, Giles's Enforcement Act, which empowered the president to use the militia against smugglers. The act effectively ended trade.

The embargo had considerable impact on the U.S. economy. Agricultural prices declined, leading to farm foreclosures. According to official records, exports declined by 80 percent in 1808, though smuggling certainly cushioned the effect. The U.S. Treasury suffered a loss in customs revenue, its chief source of income. However, the embargo stimulated further technological development of the textile industry, particularly in weaving cotton cloth with power looms.

With stern enforcement of Giles's Act, New Englanders became strident in their demands for termination of the embargo. Jefferson became convinced that civil war was possible, but he refused to support repeal. Republicans in Congress moved anyway, replacing on March 1, 1809, the embargo with the Non-Intercourse Act, which reopened trade with all countries except Great Britain and France. If either of the two belligerents changed its policy to favor neutral rights, the United States would resume commerce with that nation as well. Although the new law banned trade with major markets, loopholes offered generous opportunities for smuggling.

Congress made this shift just days before the close of Jefferson's presidency. Jefferson thus ended his administration without solving the nation's international troubles, which Americans increasingly defined as an effort by Britain to subjugate its former colonies. As he returned to Monticello, however, the president could reflect favorably on the goals he had achieved: lower taxes and national debt, smaller government, open doors to immigrants, and peace. He also took pride in an accomplishment he had not foreseen in 1801: the purchase of the Louisiana Territory. Jefferson's administration was remarkable for what it did—and for what it did not do, considering his opposition to Hamiltonian policies in the 1790s. Under Jefferson, the Republicans left intact the national bank, the federal administrative structure, and the armed forces. Considering the war-torn world in which the young nation found its way, however, the Republican commitment to minimal government left the United States militarily unprepared.

MADISON AND THE WAR OF 1812

When Britain continued to impress American sailors and seize ships, the United States was faced with two choices: accept humiliation or declare war on Great Britain. The British argued that they acted from necessity, as Napoleon conquered Europe. Americans upheld their rights as neutrals to sell provisions to both sides. They considered British impressment of six thousand seamen as a violation of national sovereignty and human rights. Between 1809 and 1812, these conflicts developed into war.

The Election of 1808   Despite the embargo, Jefferson retained enough popularity to win a third term, had he chosen to run. Instead, he declined and designated James Madison, the secretary of state, as his successor. James Monroe, who had served as governor of Virginia and minister to Great Britain, challenged Jefferson's choice, but congressional Republicans endorsed Madison. Dissenting Republicans, called the Tertium Quids (meaning a third alternative), gave Monroe some support, but his candidacy died quickly. George Clinton accepted renomination for vice president. The Federalists put up Charles C. Pinckney and Rufus King, hoping that the effects of the embargo might reverse their party's decline.

The Federalists improved on their performance in 1804 and 1806, gaining twenty-four seats in Congress, but they still had much less than a majority. The electoral vote for president was 122 for Madison and 47 for Pinckney. Although Americans suffered from the embargo, most were unprepared to desert the Republicans. In electing the new president, citizens ratified Jefferson's political philosophy and policies, which Madison had helped formulate. The third and fourth presidents had jointly founded and nurtured the Republican party; together they had adjusted their ideals to meet the practical needs of the expanding nation. The country could expect a continuation of Jeffersonian policies, though the retiring president withdrew entirely from decision making.

In another way, however, the new administration represented a real departure. Madison brought his elegant wife, Dolley Payne Madison, with him to the executive mansion, which was still unfinished when they arrived. They made a remarkable couple, as one observer noted:

> Mr. Madison was a very small man in his person, with a very large head—his manners were peculiarly unassuming; and his conversation lively, often playful. . . . Mrs. Madison was tall, large and rather masculine in personal dimensions; her complexion was so fair and brilliant as to redeem this objection, in its perfectly feminine beauty. . . . There was a frankness and ease in her deportment, that won golden opinions from all, and she possessed an influence so decided with her little Man.

The first lady transformed the president's house into a proper executive mansion. She served as hostess to frequent teas and dinner parties, inviting Federalists and Republicans to socialize together.

Heading for War   After Madison's election, the European struggle continued to embroil the United States. Although both Britain and France were hostile to free trade, the British dominated the seas, and as a consequence they had substantial impact on U.S. commerce. Over the period to 1812, as Napoleon pushed across Europe, invaded Russia, and met defeat, he became inconsequential as a threat to the Americans. Indeed, his attempt to install his brother Joseph Bonaparte as king of Spain in 1808 undermined Spanish control in the New World. In West Florida, Anglo-Americans, who had earlier pledged allegiance to Spain, in 1810 commandeered the Spanish fort at Baton Rouge, declared independence, and petitioned Madison for annexation by the United States. The president promptly claimed West Florida as part of the Louisiana Purchase, and U.S. troops occupied Baton Rouge. When Louisiana became a state in 1812, it included the western part of West Florida from Baton Rouge to the Pearl River.

In 1811, Madison appointed James Monroe, his former rival for the presidency, as secretary of state. Monroe took office hoping to reach an accord with the British, but he soon decided that they wanted nothing less than to put the United States back into its colonial yoke. Great Britain adhered to its Order in Council that American exports go to England before shipment to Europe; the Royal Navy continued to impress American seamen. When Napoleon partially lifted his blockade in 1811, the United States resumed trade with France. Madison tried to convince the British to drop their restrictions as well, but instead they pounced on American ships headed for French ports.

Events in the West also intensified anger toward Britain, because Anglo-Americans believed that the British in Canada were stirring up Native American discontent. In fact, whereas some Indians traded with the British, many natives distrusted the whites of both Canada and the United States. An alliance between militant Indians and the British took time to evolve, as each group moved independently toward war with the Americans. The nativist message of Tenskwatawa, the Shawnee Prophet, and his brother **Tecumseh** found widespread support as a result of the Louisiana Purchase, expanding white settlement, and sales by accommodationist Indian leaders of a large proportion of native lands still remaining east of the Mississippi.

The nativists were spurred into action by the Treaty of Fort Wayne (1809), which turned over 2.5 million acres to the United States. Tecumseh met with **William Henry Harrison**, governor of the Indiana Territory, to request that the treaty be annulled. Failing that, the Indian leader went south to seek support from the Creeks, Cherokees, and Choctaws. He found allies among militant factions of Creeks and Seminoles. These factions, called the Red Sticks, opposed the accommodationists among their own people who sold land to the United States and adopted Anglo-American ways of life. Tecumseh's effort to create a pan-Indian movement throughout the trans-Appalachian West ultimately failed, however, because by 1811, large white populations in Tennessee, Kentucky, and Ohio formed a barrier between northern and southern Indians.

In November 1811, William Henry Harrison decided to cut short Tecumseh's efforts for unity. The governor did not believe the Indian leader's assurance that whites were "unnecessarily alarmed at his measures—that they really meant nothing but peace—the United States had set him the example by forming a strict union amongst all the fires that compose their confederacy." Harrison led a force against Prophetstown, a village Tenskwatawa had founded several years before on the Tippecanoe River. Before Harrison struck, the prophet attacked the encamped soldiers at night, but suffered casualties and withdrew. Harrison also lost men, but burned the town and claimed victory in what became known as the Battle of Tippecanoe. The nativists subsequently rebuilt their settlement; Harrison's action had little effect except to drive them closer to the British.

The War of 1812 Begins

When news of the battle reached Washington, many officials interpreted it as evidence that a British–Indian alliance already existed. The outcome, they mistakenly believed, showed that the British were weak, incapable of sustaining their allies. "War Hawks" in Congress, including the newly elected Speaker of the House, Henry Clay of Kentucky, and Representative John C. Calhoun of South Carolina, advocated preparations for war. They represented a new generation who had not participated in the Revolutionary War and perceived Britain's actions as attempts to restore colonial status. In Calhoun's words, his generation had to prove to "the World, that we have not only inherited that liberty which our Fathers gave us, but also the will and power to maintain it." By April 1812, President Madison agreed. The Federalists, only one-fourth of Congress and primarily from New England, opposed conflict with Great Britain in part to obstruct administration policy, in part for commercial interests. The Republicans were divided. Opponents claimed that Madison intended to wage war for territorial expansion in Canada and Florida.

The nation was ill prepared when Madison issued his war message on June 1. Military

---

DOING HISTORY ONLINE

The United States Enters the War of 1812

Based on your reading of Documents 8 and 9, what effect did the foreign crises of the early 1800s, culminating in the War of 1812, have on Americans' sense of nationhood?

 www.cengage.com/ history/ayers/ ampassages4e

funding would prove difficult because the charter of the Bank of the United States had been allowed to expire in 1811 due to politics and state banking interests, leaving state banks but no central agency as a source of loans. Lack of federal taxes beyond import duties, which fell sharply when the British blockaded the Atlantic coast, further limited the country's resources. The failure of New England leaders to provide their share of funds—indeed, some merchants provisioned the enemy, and some New Englanders pressed for a separate peace—severely hampered the war effort. The governors of Massachusetts and Connecticut refused to send their militia. Not everyone in New England opposed the war, however, for the majority of representatives from Vermont, New Hampshire, and Maine (still part of Massachusetts) voted in favor of the June 1812 declaration of war. Large numbers of the region's young men enlisted in the army.

Despite military deficiencies and lack of national unity, the Madison administration pushed forward into battle. Madison offered an armistice if the British stopped impressment, but they refused. Canada, with only five thousand regular soldiers, seemed the logical target. The redcoats there had little hope for reinforcements as long as Napoleon marched through Europe.

U.S. military leaders planned three advances: one from Lake Champlain to Montreal, a second at the Niagara River, and the third from Fort Detroit east through Upper Canada. With American victories, they hoped, Canada would fall, forcing Britain to recognize U.S. rights. The Americans moved first in the West, where they expected more support from local militia than from New England. Both the Canadians and the United States needed control of the Great Lakes to retain access to lands farther west. General William Hull received orders to lead about two thousand troops against Fort Malden, opposite Detroit, under the command of British General Isaac Brock and reinforced by Tecumseh and his men. Hull dawdled long enough to allow more British soldiers to arrive. He failed to take Fort Malden and surrendered Detroit. The British and Native Americans then took control of much of the region by capturing Fort Michilimackinac, to the north, and Fort Dearborn, at the present site of Chicago. Another blow came for the United States in October when the army lost the Battle of Queenston, opposite Fort Niagara, after the New York militia refused to leave American soil to assist the regular troops. William Henry Harrison, commissioned a general, reinforced Fort Wayne against Indian attack. The Americans held Fort Harrison (Terre Haute, Indiana) and other points along a line from Sandusky, Ohio, to St. Louis, and undermined Tecumseh's war effort by destroying Indian towns and cornfields in Ohio, Indiana, and Illinois.

During the frustrating campaign against Canada, James Madison stood for reelection. Some critics claimed that he had started the conflict to win another term. His opponent was DeWitt Clinton, a New York Republican who ran as a Federalist. Clinton tried to gain support from both political parties by advocating peace to the Federalists while telling the Republicans that Madison had failed to prosecute the war hard enough. However, in contrast to the army's failures in 1812, the tiny U.S. fleet had surprising success against the mighty Royal Navy. The *Constitution* sank the British *Guerrière* in August; two months later. the United States, captained by Stephen Decatur, took the *Macedonian*; in December the *Constitution* destroyed the *Java*. The American defeats of an enemy considered master of the seas greatly bolstered public opinion. The president won by an electoral tally of 128 to 89; he obtained substantial Republican majorities in the House and Senate.

(Courtesy of the U.S. Naval Academy Museum)

Constitution and Guerrière. Constitution and the Guerrière, *by Thomas Birch, depicts an important victory of the* USS Constitution *early in the War of 1812.*

Victories and Losses, 1813–1814 Despite the naval successes, on land 1813 began with another disaster for the Americans: the British and Native Americans killed or captured nearly an entire force of nine hundred troops at Frenchtown, south of Detroit. The United States managed to hold Fort Meigs and Fort Stephenson in northern Ohio. But to destroy British control of Lake Erie and territory to the west, the army needed naval support. The United States began building ships at Presque Isle, Pennsylvania (now Erie), and on September 10, 1813, Oliver Hazard Perry defeated the British squadron at Put-in-Bay, establishing American dominance of the lake. This naval victory cleared the way for General Harrison to attack Fort Malden, from which the British and Indians hastily retreated toward Niagara. The Americans caught up with them at Moraviantown on October 5, winning a decisive victory known as the Battle of the Thames. Tecumseh died on the battlefield; his brother Tenskwatawa continued to fight alongside the British during the rest of the war, but with little success. To the east, the U.S. Army had burned York (Toronto), the capital of Upper Canada. But the Americans met defeat in an offensive against Montreal and lost Fort Niagara.

In the Mississippi Territory, the nativist Red Sticks waged civil war against Creek leaders who accommodated Anglo-American demands for land. The fratricidal conflict became a war against the United States in July 1813 when 180 American militia struck a much smaller group of Red Sticks. A month later, the nativists killed about 250 settlers who had taken cover in a stockade called Fort Mims. The Red Sticks, with four thousand warriors but lacking adequate arms, faced overwhelming odds against the combined forces of U.S. troops, accommodationist Creeks, and Cherokee allies. Three armies entered Red Stick territory, destroying homes and dispersing families.

The turning point came in March 1814 when General **Andrew Jackson**, with three thousand militia and Indian allies, defeated a thousand Red Sticks in the Battle of Horseshoe Bend, killing eight hundred of them. The surviving militants escaped to Florida, where they joined nativist Seminoles and continued to fight. Despite the fact that accommodationist Creeks assisted Jackson's troops in the battle, the United States forced them to cede more than 20 million acres of land, including much of what was to become Alabama and a fifth of present-day Georgia.

In the summer of 1814, the British turned greater attention to the war in America, having defeated Napoleon in April. They sent ten thousand experienced redcoats to Canada, threatening New York until the American naval victory on Lake Champlain in September cut short the British invasion. Britain also sent forces to Chesapeake Bay, where in August they attacked the nearly defenseless Washington, D.C. Redcoats burned the Capitol and the president's mansion shortly after the Madison household fled, saving official documents and the Gilbert Stuart portrait of George Washington. The enemy promptly left the capital, and the U.S. government returned.

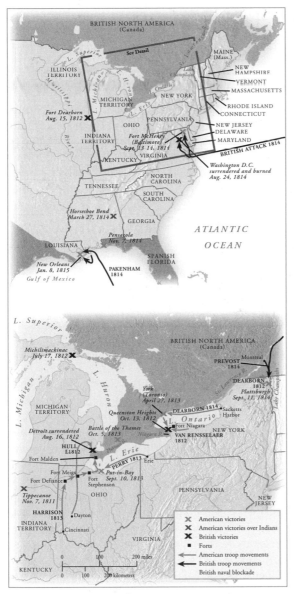

MAP 8.2 The War of 1812.

Many of the battles occurred in the Great Lakes region, on the U.S.–Canadian border. In 1814, the British failed in their attempt to defeat the United States by taking Washington, D.C. Their attack on New Orleans occurred after the Treaty of Ghent.

The British then assaulted Baltimore. Despite heavy bombardment of Fort McHenry by the Royal Navy, the redcoats failed to take the city. James Monroe, by then secretary of war as well as secretary of state, took credit for Baltimore's stand. Francis Scott Key memorialized the scene of flaming rockets and exploding bombs in his poem "The Star

Spangled Banner," which was later set to the tune of a popular English song and became the national anthem in the early twentieth century. The British sailed south to the Gulf Coast, intending to block off the Mississippi River. In late 1814, Andrew Jackson captured Pensacola, Florida, and then organized the defense of New Orleans.

The Hartford Convention, 1814   Over the course of the war, sentiment had grown in New England for secession as the British tightened their blockade of the region and occupied the Maine coast. The Massachusetts governor secretly contacted the British about a separate peace. In late 1814, a group of Federalists organized the **Hartford Convention** to find a more moderate course to remedy their loss of power within the Union. The convention issued a report supporting the right of states to declare federal laws unconstitutional (similar to the Virginia and Kentucky Resolutions of 1798) and arguing that states should be responsible for their own defense. The Hartford delegates called for significant amendments to the Constitution: removal of the three-fifths clause that counted slaves in apportioning delegates in the House of Representatives and electoral college; a two-thirds majority in Congress to declare war and admit new states; a one-term limit on the president and ban on residents from the same state succeeding one another in the office (obviously targeted at Virginia); and prohibition of naturalized citizens, who were largely Republican, from federal positions. These proposals, calculated to damage Republican power bases in the South and West and among new immigrants in the cities, fell on deaf ears when news of a peace treaty arrived from Europe.

The Treaty of Ghent, 1814   Peace came as both the British and the United States recognized that the end of the twenty-year struggle in Europe had eliminated the rationale for war in America. The defeat of Napoleon removed Britain's need to regulate neutral trade and impress seamen. Both sides could also see that they had little hope of victory. Britain might continue its blockade and smother U.S. commerce, but to what purpose? Conquest of the former colonies, now expanded into the West, would require huge expenditures of manpower and funds. British victory at New Orleans would plug the Mississippi, but in late 1814 success was still uncertain. As the British considered terms for peace, news arrived that the Americans had repelled the offensives at Lake Champlain and Baltimore. Although some Britons desired revenge, more wanted to resume trade.

Madison authorized John Quincy Adams, Albert Gallatin, Henry Clay, and two others to meet a British peace delegation in August 1814 at Ghent, in what is now Belgium. After several months of stalemate, the negotiators agreed on Christmas Eve, 1814, to return to the status quo at the outbreak of war. The British dropped their demands for part of Maine and an independent Indian territory north of the Ohio River, and the Americans stopped insisting that the British renounce impressment, which had ceased.

Battle of New Orleans, 1815   Bad weather in the Atlantic delayed the ship bringing news of the Treaty of Ghent until February. In the meantime, British forces prepared to move against the Gulf Coast. A fleet of sixty ships and fourteen thousand men planned to attack Mobile, seize control of the coast and the rivers, and then move against New Orleans.

For Americans unaware of the peace treaty, such a plan posed a serious threat. New Orleans, distant and disconnected from the cities of the East Coast, lay vulnerable to invasion. Once the British established a foothold there, troops could move up the Mississippi River. Moreover, a British invasion threatened to bring free and enslaved African Americans, French and Spanish settlers, Native Americans, and even pirates into the conflict throughout the Gulf territories, igniting rebellions against white farmers and traders.

The commander in charge of the American forces, Andrew Jackson, was especially sensitive to the dangers settlers to the Gulf Coast. A Tennessee lawyer, planter, and militia leader, he had defeated the Red Sticks at Horseshoe Bend. He repelled the British at Mobile, then raced to New Orleans before the British troops could arrive. The Americans got there first, in December 1814. When six hundred free blacks volunteered to help defend the city, Jackson gratefully accepted their offer.

A series of attacks by the British damaged the American forces but did not take New Orleans. The British general in charge, Sir Edward Pakenham, unleashed a frontal assault on January 8, 1815. Two Congreve rockets, launched by the British to signal the beginning of the assault and frighten their opponents, screamed into the air. Jackson's troops, dug in behind earthworks, fired directly into the charging British troops; wave after wave of the onslaught fell as American troops took turns firing and reloading. In less than an hour, it was over: Pakenham and two of his generals lay dead, along with more than two thousand of their troops. The Americans suffered only thirteen dead and a few dozen wounded or missing. Nearly a month later, word of Jackson's remarkable success reached the nation's capital. "ALMOST INCREDIBLE VICTORY!!!" headlines trumpeted. Nine days later word of the Treaty of Ghent, ratified two weeks before the Battle of New Orleans, arrived in Washington.

CONCLUSION

With its simple provision to reinstate the status quo ante bellum, the Treaty of Ghent might appear to have made the War of 1812 meaningless. The lost lives and dollars, and disaffection of New England, all seemed to make the victory hollow. Yet most Americans celebrated the peace, knowing they had withstood Britain's attempt to treat them as colonials. A second generation of Americans had proven they could survive a struggle with what was probably the world's most powerful nation. In addition, the United States had defeated Tecumseh's pan-Indian movement in the West, effectively ending Native American power east of the Mississippi.

Much had changed from 1800 to 1815. The Federalists transformed themselves from the architects of the national government in the 1790s to advocates of narrow sectional interests. Thomas Jefferson and James Madison, who had upheld states' rights, moved in the opposite direction during their administrations. Without denying their commitment to limited government, a skeleton military, low taxes, and republican principles, they expanded "the empire of liberty" by purchasing Louisiana and forcing Native Americans from their lands. Jefferson and Madison used every means short of armed conflict to protect commerce, then went to war when all else failed. In purchasing Louisiana, Jefferson relaxed his philosophy of strict interpretation of the Constitution in hope that the additional territory would extend the life of his agrarian republic. Madison facilitated the growth of nationalism by exacting respect from Great Britain. With the Atlantic world at peace once again, residents from Maine to Louisiana concentrated on making money and building their communities, all with a greater sense that they belonged to an American nation.

CHAPTER REVIEW, 1800–1815

- In the late eighteenth and early nineteenth centuries, African Americans established their own churches, new Christian sects such as the Shakers were founded, and Native Americans and whites experienced religious revivals.
- Free African Americans developed distinctive cultural institutions and networks in northern cities. In the South, slave rebellions caused widespread anxiety among the white population and led to the development of harsher slave codes.
- In 1800, Thomas Jefferson was elected president. Although committed to the republican ideal of limited government, Jefferson relaxed his strict construction of the Constitution to extend the republic's landholdings through the Louisiana Purchase.
- The impressment of American men into the British navy caused tensions between the two nations, which Americans sought to diffuse through economic sanctions such as the Embargo of 1807.
- Between 1812 and 1815, Britain and America engaged in the War of 1812. Although the war did not bring significant gains to either side, it inspired nationalism in the United States.

◀▬ɪɪɪ *Looking Back*

Chapter 8 considered the religious context in which Americans—native whites, African Americans, new immigrants, and Indians—shaped their communities and interpreted political affairs. The Republican administrations of Thomas Jefferson and James Madison, while taking action for national expansion and defense, reflected the desire of many Americans for limited government.

1. Why was religion so important to Americans on the frontier and in developing cities?
2. Was Jefferson's administration consistent with the Republican principles he had stated prior to his election? Why or why not?
3. Why did the Federalists decline?
4. Did Madison make the right decision to go to war against Great Britain? Why or why not?
5. What was the significance of the Hartford Convention?

Looking Ahead ɪɪɪ▬▶

With the War of 1812 behind them, Americans expanded westward, building turnpikes and canals to facilitate trade. As will be discussed in Chapter 9, under President James Monroe, the government entered a period of reduced factionalism.

1. What was the impact of U.S. expansion on Native Americans during the period from 1815 to 1828?
2. Why were the years of Monroe's administration known as the "Era of Good Feelings"?
3. How did the Supreme Court assist economic development?

Go to the American Passages website at www.cengage.com/history/ayers/ampassages4e for additional review materials.

Exploded
Boundaries,
1815–1828

T he sudden climax of the War of 1812 surprised everyone. The leaders of the United States had wondered whether a large and lightly governed republic could survive in the rough-and-tumble world of international conflict. When the new country held its own in the war against England, the most powerful military force on earth, Americans gained a new confidence.

James Monroe, another in a long line of Virginia Republican presidents, easily won the national election of 1816. He bore the reputation of being an honest and dependable man, though less intellectually distinguished than Jefferson or Madison. Monroe and his wife set a new tone for the presidency, with greater emphasis on etiquette, style, and entertaining, on embodying and celebrating the new national stature of the United States. The Monroes had the executive mansion painted a brilliant white to cover the smoke stains from its burning during the war with England; the residence became known as the "White House." Newly secure, the United States entered a period of territorial expansion and economic growth no one could have foreseen just a few years earlier.

NEW BORDERS

The borders of the United States had been fluid and in doubt throughout the nation's brief history. In every direction, other nations and peoples contested American boundaries. To the north, English power loomed in Canada. To the west, American Indians resisted efforts by whites to buy or seize their ancestral lands. To the south, the Spanish held on in Florida. Moreover, many states had little economic dealing with one another, trading instead with England, Europe, and the Caribbean. As a result, states defended sharply conflicting policies, and their economies did not connect with one another very effectively. The peace after 1815 provided an opportunity for the United States to establish its borders more securely and to integrate itself more fully.

Native Peoples President Monroe worked to establish clearer borders for the young nation. He succeeded in his dealing with Great Britain when the two countries clarified the boundaries between the United States and Canada. The Rush-Bagot Treaty of 1817 calmed conflict on the Great Lakes, and the Convention of 1818 fixed the border with Canada at the **forty-ninth parallel**.

Relations with Native Americans proved much more challenging. By the early nineteenth century, many Native Americans had lived in contact with European culture for more than two hundred years. They had long combined their ancient practices with newer ones. Commercial hunting expeditions covered ever-expanding territory, tracking animals to exchange with white trading partners. Trade networks stretched over thousands of miles.

Native American clothing reflected the combination of cultures, combining moccasins with woolen breeches, imported cloth turbans, and jewelry made of melted silver coins. The intermingling worked both ways, for considerable numbers of English and Scots traders lived among native peoples or their trading partners. Many men of European background adopted Native American dress and language and married into native families. African Americans, too, often took refuge with the Creeks and **Seminoles**.

The removal of the British troops after the War of 1812 dealt a strong blow to the hopes of the Native Americans. Their alliances with the British, both actual and threatened, had helped hold back white Americans. Now that the alliance with England had been destroyed, the United States quickly sought to exert firm control over the eastern half of the continent. Andrew Jackson, triumphant general in the war, was placed in charge of negotiating with the Creek, Cherokee, Chickasaw, and Choctaw nations of Alabama, Florida, and Mississippi after the peace of 1815. Jackson used heavy-handed treaties to force Native Americans from their former lands. Many resisted the removal, objecting that the treaties Jackson had extracted had been signed by leaders who had no authority to make such concessions.

The various native peoples identified themselves by the location of their villages, their languages, and their traditional enemies, and they often fought with one another, but whites nevertheless insisted on lumping these diverse people into groups that could be more easily dealt with. Jackson and other officials relied on particular Native Americans as allies in war but then deliberately punished all the tribes in the region regardless of earlier promises. Such policies weakened the power of native leaders and left their people little choice but to accept bribes and annual grants of money in return for their lands. As soon as Jackson managed to secure lands from the Creeks, Cherokees, and Chickasaws, white settlers rushed into the territories, hungry for the fertile land and the fortunes it could build. Such incursions occurred across millions of acres in North Carolina, Kentucky, and Tennessee, as well as in Alabama, Mississippi, and Georgia; in each state, the native peoples were pushed to the hilly and mountainous lands least desirable for farming. The U.S. government made it easy for white settlers to buy land and sold about 1 million acres a year throughout the next decade. Not surprisingly, tensions steadily mounted between the ancient residents of the land and those who now claimed it.

This icon will direct you to interactive activities and study materials on the American Passages website: www.cengage.com/history/ayers/ampassages4e

CHAPTER TIMELINE

1815	Battle of New Orleans • Enterprise first steamboat from New Orleans to Pittsburgh
1816	Monroe elected president: "Era of Good Feelings" begins • Clay calls for "American System" • Second Bank of the United States chartered • Indiana admitted to the Union
1817	Mississippi admitted to the Union
1818	Jackson invades Florida • Erie Canal begun • Illinois admitted to the Union • National Road completed
1819	Transcontinental (or Adams-Onís) Treaty with Spain • Dartmouth College v. Woodward and McCulloch v. Maryland • Financial panic and depression • Alabama admitted to the Union • Auburn penitentiary established
1820	Missouri Compromise • Monroe elected president • Maine admitted to the Union
1821	Missouri admitted to the Union
1822	Denmark Vesey Rebellion, Charleston
1823	Monroe Doctrine announced
1824	Contested election of John Quincy Adams • Lafayette's visit • Gibbons v. Ogden
1825	Completion of Erie Canal
1826	Kidnapping of William Morgan

As in the South, white settlement in the Northwest was made possible by the subjugation of the native peoples. After northern Native Americans' disastrous losses in the War of 1812, they posed little threat to white settlers. The U.S. government quickly established a series of forts throughout the Northwest to intimidate any Native Americans in the area and to make sure that the British did not regain a foothold. The growing numbers of white farmers made it difficult for Native Americans to hunt for a living. Whites who moved to the Northwest confronted only scattered remnants of native peoples, trading with white merchants for food and sometimes begging from homesteaders.

Native Americans strove to adapt to white ways while maintaining native identities; the Cherokees, in particular, won praise for their customs that whites considered "civilized." One Cherokee, Sequoyah, devised an alphabet in his people's language in 1821. The wealthiest Cherokees purchased African American slaves and built substantial cotton plantations. No matter what accommodations they made, however, they suffered repeated conflicts with whites, who relied on sheer numbers, trickery, violence, and the law to dispossess them of their land claims.

The Spanish in Florida

Like the Native Americans, the Spanish who remained in Florida after 1815 had become vulnerable. Without the assistance of the British, they found it nearly impossible to resist American incursions into their territory. White Americans, for their part, felt they had

Expanding Borders

What now seem the natural boundaries of the continental United States were by no means obvious in 1815. As it stood, somewhat surprised in its victory over the powerful British in the War of 1812, the United States still had poorly defined and dangerous borders in almost every direction. The boundaries of Maine, the enormous area west of the Great Lakes, and Oregon remained contested with Great Britain in the North. Although we now think of the relationship between the United States and Canada as the very model of peaceful coexistence, at the time many people worried about this British territory as it loomed over the United States. To the south, Spain (and runaway slaves and the Seminoles) controlled Florida and much of the Gulf Coast. The territory, so close to the booming areas of the South, posed a threat to slavery as well as to the territorial ambitions of the United States. To the west, the territory that would become Mexico remained contested, still in the process of defining its own nationhood. In the five years after the peace of 1815, the United States eagerly negotiated treaties with Great Britain and Spain to clarify and stabilize the young nation's borders. The settlement of the treaties helped create the conditions for rapid growth and economic development.

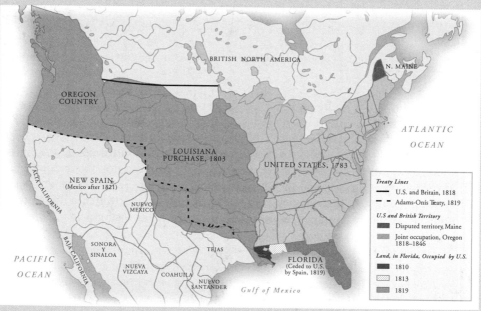

MAP 9.1 Redrawing the Nation's Boundaries.

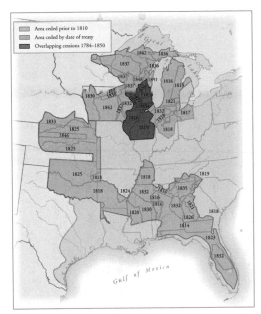

MAP 9.2 Lands Ceded by Native Americans.

The United States negotiated one treaty after another with Native Americans in the decades after 1815, acquiring land and pushing the natives of these areas to the west.

a right, even an obligation, to drive the Spanish from the mainland, in part because Anglo Protestants had a long tradition of distrusting the Catholic, monarchical Spanish. Many Americans thought it inevitable that Florida and Mexico would become part of the United States. To make relations even more volatile, sixty miles from the southern border of the United States stood the so-called Negro Fort near Pensacola, occupied by runaway slaves and their Indian allies.

In the spring of 1816 Jackson warned the Spanish commandant of Pensacola that the stronghold was "occupied by upwards of two hundred and fifty negros many of whom have been enticed away from the service of their master—citizens of the United States." Spain was eager, in fact, to be rid of the fort as well, but it did not have the military power to overthrow it. The Spanish feared that Jackson would use the refuge as a pretext to invade Florida. Indeed, the Americans sent an expedition against the fort; a projectile hit a powder magazine, killing 270 men, women, and children inside.

In 1818, Jackson's forces also punished groups of Seminoles, who, with their Creek allies, had launched raids against white settlers in south Georgia and then fled into Florida. Although his authorization from Washington was doubtful, Jackson invaded Spanish territory, executed a Creek prophet and two British men he accused of abetting the Indian cause, and overran the weak Spanish presence in the most important outposts. Some in Congress wanted to punish Jackson for what they considered his unauthorized attack. Jackson rushed to Washington to defend himself. The congressional hearings on Jackson's behavior in the war had little effect except to make Jackson suspicious of the men in power in Washington.

Meanwhile, American and Spanish officials negotiated. The U.S. delegation was led by the brilliant and tenacious John Quincy Adams, son of the former president. With Jackson's military victories giving force to his words, Adams held out until the Spanish, in return for $5 million in compensation for private claims, ceded to the United States all territories east of the Mississippi River. In this, the **Adams-Onís Treaty** of 1819, the Spanish kept the vast territory from Texas to present-day California, while the United States claimed a northern border that ran unbroken to Oregon and the Pacific Ocean. Adams called his handiwork the Transcontinental Treaty, for it stretched the borders of the United States from the Atlantic to the Pacific.

BUILDING A NATIONAL ECONOMY

Leading members of the Republican Party, long known for their opposition to federal power, began to view the central government more favorably after the victory over Britain in 1815. Young Republicans such as **Henry Clay** of Kentucky and **John C. Calhoun** of South Carolina urged Congress and the president to encourage the growth of enterprise with the aid of the government, creating roads, canals, a strong navy, and a national bank. In their eyes, the war with Great Britain had shown the dangers of a sprawling American nation, its resources scattered and its defenses thin. The future of the country, Clay and Calhoun believed, lay in commerce and industry. The government should ally itself with the forces of trade. These nationalists called their vision the **American System**.

Adopting some ideas of the American System, President Monroe urged Congress to use protective tariffs to protect American manufacturing, build roads to tie the newly expanded markets and farms together, and connect the abundant rivers and lakes in the United States with a system of canals.

Banks, Corporations, and Law

No other country needed credit more than the United States. Because far too little cash spread across its vast and growing territory, much business within the country rested on nothing more than trust and promises. Credit relations became tangled and fragile; the fall of one borrower could bring down a chain of lenders. Throughout the years before and during the War of 1812, states had chartered banks to help alleviate the problems caused by a shortage of cash. More than two hundred such banks had been founded by 1815 and nearly four hundred by 1818, issuing notes that served as currency in cash-starved areas.

Many influential men, including the recently elected President Monroe, supported a new national bank to stabilize the economy and distribute scarce money more uniformly. Advocates of the bank argued that the notes of state banks varied far too much in soundness and value, making the economic system dangerously unstable. The expanding country's economic system needed a central institution to coordinate the flow of money. Accordingly, in 1816 Congress chartered the **Second Bank of the United States**. Based in Philadelphia, it was authorized to establish branches wherever it wished. The new national bank was an amalgam of public and private enterprise: the federal government deposited its funds in the bank and appointed a fifth of the directors, but the bank ran as a private business. For the privilege of being the only such institution authorized to operate on a national basis, the bank handled the funds of the federal treasury without fees. The bank pumped large amounts of paper currency into the system in an attempt to feed the voracious hunger of the postwar economy, especially in the new states of the West, where speculation in land fueled demands for access to easier credit.

The local, state, and federal courts also encouraged the growth of business after the peace of 1815. Those who wanted to dam rivers for factories or build roads enjoyed increasing precedence over farmers and landowners threatened by floods, fires, or disruption caused by development. The courts assumed that the public good from the growth of business outweighed the stability favored by older notions of justice. Because many people bitterly protested this shift in emphasis, state legislatures sometimes sought to curb the power of business interests.

The Supreme Court under Chief Justice **John Marshall** issued a number of important decisions following the War of 1812 that also hastened economic development. Marshall was more concerned with establishing the power of the federal government than with developing the economy, but by creating a more uniform legal environment that transcended the restrictions of particular states, the Court accelerated the growth of business. One decision of 1819 made bankruptcy laws more uniform across the country; another, *Dartmouth College v. Woodward*, sheltered corporations from legislative interference; and yet another, **Gibbons v. Ogden**, limited the rights of states to interfere in commerce with either special favors and monopolies or restrictive laws. "In all commercial regulations," Marshall pronounced, "we are one and the same people." In **McCulloch v. Maryland**, which established the constitutionality of the Bank of the United States and protected it from state taxation, the Supreme Court ruled that the laws of the federal government "form the supreme law of the land." In this new legal environment, increasingly emulated by state courts and legislators, business flourished.

Roads and Canals

Americans threw themselves into a frenzy of road and turnpike building after 1815. Investors, states, and even the federal government built thousands of miles of private roads, called turnpikes, that charged tolls to offset the roads' notoriously high maintenance costs. In 1818, the U.S. government opened the **National Road**, connecting the Potomac River at Cumberland, Maryland, with Wheeling, Virginia (now West Virginia), on the Ohio River. The road was the best that technology could provide at the time, with excellent bridges and a relatively smooth stone surface. It attracted so much business, however, that traffic jams slowed movement to a crawl, and the road quickly fell into poor condition. Even on good roads, it often cost more to move bulky items such as corn or wheat than the price the products could bring at market.

Private corporations and state governments began to plan dependable canals with controllable locks and a steady flow of water. Fortunately for New York, a passage broke through the Appalachian Mountains within the state's borders. New Yorkers believed that a canal through this area, connecting the Hudson River to Lake Erie, would far surpass any other kind of transportation at that time. Such a canal would be ten times longer than any other canal then in existence: 364 miles through swamps and solid rock, through places where virtually no white settlers had bothered to migrate.

Year after year, the canal edged toward Lake Erie, transforming the countryside along the way. As soon as workers completed a segment, boats crowded on its waters, the tolls they paid financing the portions yet unfinished. The **Erie Canal** was completed in 1825, and by 1834, approximately nine boats passed through its major locks each minute.

Steamboats

Canals were certainly useful, but they reached only a limited part of the vast North American continent. Rivers, especially the Mississippi, Missouri, and Ohio, offered faster and cheaper travel. But their limitations were obvious as well. The rivers could be dangerously fast in some seasons and so slow as to be impassable in others. They often froze for months in the winter. Strong currents ran in only one direction. Those who wanted to transport goods northward had to push their boats upstream against the current. Others simply sold their craft for scrap in New Orleans and walked back to Ohio or Illinois, a long and arduous trip.

Steamboat Popularity

Steamboats began to ply the Mississippi River and other major waterways in the 1810s and 1820s, accelerating trade and fueling the growth of cities such as St. Louis, pictured here, along the way. The technology of the steamboat had been known before the War of 1812, but the end of the war opened the rivers of the United States to a rapidly increased trade. Although steamboat technology steadily improved so that steamboats became safer, larger, and more comfortable, they remained dangerous by their very nature. Built light and carrying large tanks under extreme pressure, steamboats were vulnerable to submerged obstacles and often exploded without warning and without obvious cause.

Smithsonian American Art Museum, Washington, DC/Art Resource, NY

Not surprisingly, people dreamed of using steam engines to drive riverboats. Robert Fulton's steamboats had traversed the quieter waters of the Northeast since 1807, but Fulton did not manage to build one for the rigors of the Mississippi until 1811. Dozens of other craft soon joined his, competing with one another. In 1817, the journey from New Orleans to Louisville had been reduced from several months to twenty-five days and, in 1819, fourteen days. "If any one had said this was possible thirty years ago," a journalist marveled, "we should have been ready to send him to a mad-house."

The increasing speed and frequency of the steamboats encouraged the growth of villages and towns along the rivers. Huge stacks of wood carted in from the countryside appeared wherever the steamboats regularly stopped for fuel; new stores sold the goods transported on the river; muddy villages dreamed of becoming major cities such as Louisville, Pittsburgh, and Cincinnati.

REGIONAL GROWTH

As the American economy grew, different parts of the country specialized economically. Enslaved people in the South produced cotton that fueled the growth of the Northeast's textile factories and provided a large market for the farms of Ohio, Illinois, and Indiana.

The Creation of the Cotton South

The demand for cotton in England took off after the War of 1812, when cotton became, for the first time, the clothing of choice for large numbers of the world's people. Cotton clothes were cheaper, easier to create, and more comfortable in warm weather than those made from wool or linen. No other place in the world was as prepared to supply the burgeoning demand for cotton as the American South. Small farmers as well as planters from the older states of the southern seaboard saw opportunity in the new states of Alabama and Mississippi. Many white farmers also moved to western Tennessee and parts of Louisiana. The steamboat and the cotton gin gave planters in the **Cotton South** powerful new tools, while slaves could clear and cultivate land for new plantations far more quickly than would have been possible otherwise. Slave owners in the older states of the Atlantic seaboard, faced with what they considered a surplus of labor, eagerly sold slaves to planters moving to the "new" lands. As a result, the price of slaves, which had been stagnant or declining before 1815, began to rise. Hundreds of thousands of slaves endured forcible migration to the new states of the Old Southwest in the 1810s and 1820s. Some moved in groups along with their owners to new plantations, but many were sold as individuals to slave traders in the East, who then shipped or marched them to slave markets in New Orleans, Mobile, and other cities in the Southwest. The families of many enslaved African Americans were broken apart as slave traders eagerly bought those in their teens for the hard work of clearing land for plantations from virgin forest. This domestic trade, a complex network of traders, provisioners, and insurers, constituted as much as 13.5 percent of the total southern economy.

The movement west was not a simple march from the East, but rather it followed the geographic and political contours of areas recently acquired from Native Americans. The first settlements began along the rivers that made it possible to transport cotton to market and in those places where the Creeks and other Native Americans exercised no claims. The new plantation districts were disconnected from one another, centering on Montgomery in Alabama, Jackson in Mississippi, and Memphis in Tennessee, all areas taken from the natives of the region since 1814. Small farmers occupied the land farthest from the rivers, supporting themselves with hunting and foraging as well as with growing small amounts of cotton. Young lawyers and newspaper editors headed out for the Southwest as well, eager to make their mark in the river towns and county seats growing up across Alabama

DOING HISTORY ONLINE

The Rise of the Market Economy

Read Documents 2, 6, and 11. What do they say about cotton and the economy? What social and economic changes do the authors attribute to the cotton boom?

www.cengage.com/
history/ayers/
ampassages4e

and Mississippi. The combined population of Alabama, Mississippi, and Louisiana more than tripled between 1810 and 1820.

Some ambitious young men from northern states also moved to the new cotton lands, the place in the United States where it seemed the greatest fortunes could be made in the shortest amount of time. Virgin land could produce a cotton crop in only one year; in two years, a plantation could be in full production. But most of the new residents came from older plantation states. Young southern men were especially eager to move and make their mark. Their wives, mothers, and daughters were often much less enthusiastic about migrating to Mississippi or Alabama, for it meant leaving the kin who gave those women much of their happiness and social standing. But the lure of the Southwest overrode concerns husbands might have felt for their wives' opinions, for the new states offered a chance at the independence they considered synonymous with manliness. They sought to build a world as much as possible like those of Virginia or Carolina, only more prosperous.

Emergence of the Old Northwest
The area west of the Appalachians, north of the Ohio, and east of the Mississippi—the Old Northwest—was growing even faster than the Southwest. "Old America seems to be breaking up, and moving westward," one man wrote in 1817 as he watched people move down the Ohio River. In the first two decades of the new century, the trans-Appalachian population grew from about 300,000 inhabitants to more than 2 million. This immigration in the North bore considerable similarities to its southern counterpart. Many of the settlers to the Old Northwest came from the states of the Upper South; large parts of southern Ohio, Indiana, and Illinois were settled by people from Virginia, Kentucky, Tennessee, and North Carolina. Some southern migrants to the North professed themselves eager to move out of states with slavery, while others merely followed the easiest routes to good land. People from New England and New York filled the towns and farms of the northern parts of the new states. As in the Southwest, settlers to the Northwest did not move in a simple westward wave, but rather traveled up the rivers and spread from there, sometimes back toward the East. People often emigrated in family or community groups.

Most white settlers proved dissatisfied with the first land they claimed, for about two out of three migrants moved again within a few years. Rumors always circulated about richer land a bit farther west, about a new town certain to develop into a major city, about opportunity just over the horizon. Many people who had moved once found it easy to move again. Those who remained in a community became its leading citizens, consolidating land into larger farms, setting up gristmills and sawmills, running for office, establishing the small towns that served as county seats and trading centers. In many cases, storekeepers were among the first to arrive and among those whose fortunes flourished best. Storekeepers became the bankers and wholesalers of their communities, often buying considerable amounts of land along the way, boosting the towns growing around the stores, churches, and schoolhouses. Courthouses were built early on to formalize land sales and taxation.

Farm and Factory in the Northeast
While the economies of the West and the South were being transformed by settlers and slaves, the economy of the East underwent its own fundamental change. Since the colonial years, people outside the major cities—more than nine out of ten Americans—had

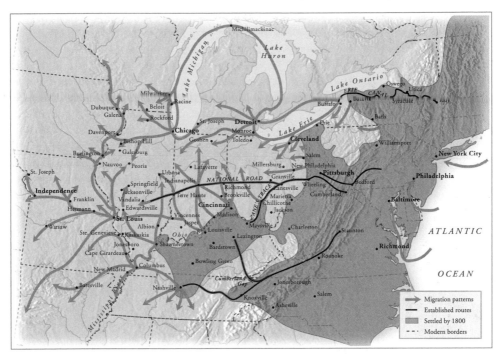

MAP 9.3 Migration Patterns in the Old Northwest, 1800–1850.

As in the South, northern migrants wove their way to the West. New Englanders and New Yorkers followed a northerly path, while other people traveled from the South, all of them following rivers, canals, and major roads.

made in their own homes much of what they needed. This local production grew stronger when trade dried up during the war with England; in the war's wake, more than two-thirds of the clothes Americans wore were made in their own homes. Household manufacturing peaked in 1815. Local blacksmiths, tailors, cobblers, and other artisans supplied what families could not produce for themselves, and local gristmills and sawmills processed crops and lumber.

Farms averaged a little over a hundred acres, about half cultivated and the other half occupied by wood lots for fuel and timber. Forests often dominated the farms of younger families, while mature families proudly claimed large areas of cultivation, the products of years of labor. Women and men, children and adults shared and divided the work among themselves. Farm families cleared their fields at spring thaw, manuring, plowing, and planting as soon as danger of frost passed. Livestock and poultry needed constant attention; sheep had to be washed and sheared and geese plucked in the spring. Farm families reaped flax in June, enjoyed a brief respite in August, and then pushed hard for the fall harvest. In winter, men and boys cut wood, while women and girls spun thread and wove cloth for clothes. The garden and dairy for the family's use and local sale were the responsibility of women and girls, the major cash crops the responsibility of men. Farmers, chronically short of cash, bartered among themselves and with merchants.

DOING HISTORY ONLINE

Improving Female Education

Read Documents 1, 3, 5, and 13. How does Emma Willard justify education for women? What are some of the rights and responsibilities of women, according to Huntington, Crocker, and Willard? How do they justify education for women? What limitations do they see on women's political and intellectual involvement?

 www.cengage.com/
history/ayers/
ampassages4e

After 1815, the farms in many parts of New England, New York, and Pennsylvania would be tied ever more tightly to the economies of the towns and cities. Farm families produced more cash crops and bought more goods with money rather than through barter. Women, especially widows and other single females, worked in their homes to produce palm hats, portions of shoes, or articles of clothing that merchants from nearby cities gathered and had assembled in workshops. These women added such **piecework** to their farm work, laboring in the evenings and throughout the winters. With so many young men leaving New England for the West, many communities found themselves with considerable numbers of young women who might never marry, as well as older women who could not count on the support of sons. Piecework offered these women a chance to add scarce cash to their household economies. It was important to everyone in their families that wage-earning women did not have to leave home to earn those wages.

The expanding cash economy thus overlapped and conflicted with an older, more self-contained economy. Families sought opportunity in new jobs and new markets, even as they feared that the increasingly dense networks of trade would depress the value of their crops, make seasonal farm labor even more difficult to acquire, entice young people from the farm, alter women's roles, and undermine local artisans. Although it would be generations before cities and factories dominated the economies of the Northeast, farms, towns, and small factories grew ever more interconnected.

The textile industry of New England stood as the most dramatic example of industrial growth. The cost of cotton clothing fell faster than the cost for any other product as machinery and cheaper cotton lowered the price. Francis Cabot Lowell of Boston designed a power loom in 1813, recreating from memory a machine he had seen on a recent trip to England. The same year, Lowell and a partner, Nathan Appleton, spent more than $400,000 to open the first factory in the United States that could integrate all the steps of making cloth under a single roof: the Boston Manufacturing Company, in Waltham, Massachusetts, where a waterfall with a ten-foot drop offered free power. An expanded group of investors in the enterprise—the Boston Associates, they were called—pooled the resources of the city's most prominent merchant families.

Unlike earlier factories, the Boston Associates used unskilled labor and machines even for weaving, the most expensive part of the process. Lowell and Appleton, concerned that the introduction of factories into the United States might create the same alienated and despised working class they saw in England, recruited young New England farm women and girls as operatives. Young females had experience in producing yarn and cloth at home, and they would work hard for low wages. Many were eager to earn money for themselves for a time, to move out of crowded homes, and to send money back to their families. Combining plentiful water power and plentiful people eager to work for wages, factories spread across the Northeast.

Early Textile Mills. *Young women who were familiar with fabrics and thread were considered especially suited to work in textile mills. Although the work was exhausting and often dangerous, women's wages gave them a measure of independence and helped support families back home.*

The operatives, unlike British laborers, considered millwork a three- or four-year commitment before they married and began families of their own. They worked fourteen hours a day, six days a week. When they signed a contract with agents, who received a dollar a head for each worker they could recruit, the young women agreed to stay with the mill for at least twelve months; if they did not, they would be put on a blacklist that would prevent them from getting a job elsewhere. The factory was unlike anything the young women had ever confronted. "You cannot think how odd everything seemed," one mill girl recalled; even those who had spun and woven for years could not be prepared for the "frightful" sight of "so many bands, and wheels, and springs in constant motion."

CONSEQUENCES OF EXPANSION

The enlarged boundaries of the American nation, as exciting and promising as they seemed, brought troubles almost immediately. The newly integrated economy proved vulnerable to fluctuations in currency and outside pressure. The rapid spread of slavery in the South threatened northerners, who did not want to see the institution expand into new territories in the West. The resulting political fight over the future of slavery inspired slaves to launch a revolt in South Carolina. The leaders of the United States came to feel that their new status in the world called for an emboldened foreign policy, one that proclaimed an enlarged role for the United States in its hemisphere. In all these ways, the explosive growth of the country in the fifteen years after 1815 brought consequences few could have imagined.

The Panic of 1819   In 1819, a series of events abroad and at home combined to bring a sudden halt to some of the economic growth in the United States. Prices for cotton lands in the Southeast skyrocketed as world demand for cotton cloth increased every year. Southern cotton prices rose to such an extent that in 1818 and 1819, British manufacturers turned to other cotton sources, especially India, and as they did, American cotton prices tumbled, along with the value of the land that produced it. The panic of 1819 had begun.

The panic proved a sudden and sobering reminder of just how complicated and interdependent the economy of the nation was becoming. The cities were hit the hardest. About half a million workers lost their jobs as business ground to a halt. Americans shuddered to see "children freezing in the winter's storm—and the fathers without coats and shoes." In the streets where new goods had been piled, people now wandered without homes or food. Charitable groups opened soup kitchens. Wherever they could, families who had moved to towns and cities returned to the countryside to live with relatives. Things were not much better in the country, however, where the failure of banks meant that apparently prosperous farmers saw household goods, farm animals, and the people they held as slaves sold in humiliating auctions.

Many people, including congressmen, began to call for the revocation of the charter of the Second Bank of the United States. States had chafed throughout the two years of the bank's life at what they considered its dictatorial power. Several states tried to limit that power by levying extremely high taxes on the branches of the bank in their states, but they were overruled by the Supreme Court in *McCulloch v. Maryland.*

Despite the panic, James Monroe was reelected to the presidency in 1820 in one of the quietest and most lopsided elections in the nation's history. The Federalist Party, fatally crippled by its opposition to the War of 1812, offered no effective opposition. Neither did Monroe face an organized contest from others within his own party, which was divided along sectional lines. He received every electoral vote but one. Most Americans seemed to blame someone other than President Monroe for the panic of 1819 and the lingering hard times that followed it. The **Era of Good Feelings,** so called for the near-absence of party politics, somehow managed to survive in the White House—though, it turned out, not in the halls of Congress.

The Missouri   The recent admission of the new states of the Southwest and
Compromise, 1820   Old Northwest had left a precarious balance in the Senate
                   between slave states and free, though northern states held a strong, and growing, preponderance in the House of Representatives. The Missouri Territory posed a special challenge to the balance. Slavery had quickly spread in Missouri, stretching along the richest river lands. If Missouri were admitted with slavery, as its territorial legislature had decreed, then the slave states would hold a majority in the Senate. Slavery in Missouri, an area of the same latitude as much of Illinois, Indiana, and Ohio, seemed to violate the assumption long held by many people in the North that slavery, if it grew at all, would expand only to the south.

The three-fifths clause of the Constitution, northerners complained, gave the slave states twenty more members of Congress and twenty more electors for the presidency than they would have if only white populations were counted. The South seemed to be getting extra representation unfairly.

The debates over slavery in Missouri in 1819 and 1820 were not between fervent abolitionists in the North and fervent proslavery advocates in the South. Neither of those positions had yet been defined. Instead, white northerners and southerners of all political persuasions agreed that as many blacks as possible should be sent to Africa. White Americans who could come together on little else about slavery did agree that blacks and whites could not live together in the United States once slavery had ended. That was the message of the American Colonization Society, founded in 1816 and based in Washington, D.C. The society bought land in Africa, naming the new country "Liberia," and sent about twelve thousand free African Americans there over the next fifty years. Disease in Liberia took a terrible toll, however, and many died. As time went by, fewer African Americans migrated. In Philadelphia, many even staged protests against the notion of **colonization**.

In the meantime, slavery caused problems for the political system. A New York congressman, James Tallmadge, Jr., introduced an amendment to the bill that would admit Missouri as a state only if it admitted no more slaves and if those slaves in the territory were freed when they became twenty-five years old. More than eighty of the North's congressmen supported the Tallmadge amendment and only ten opposed it. In the Senate, though, the slave states prevailed by two votes. A deadlocked Congress adjourned in March 1819, to meet again in December.

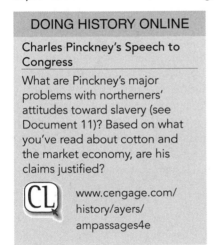

DOING HISTORY ONLINE

Charles Pinckney's Speech to Congress

What are Pinckney's major problems with northerners' attitudes toward slavery (see Document 11)? Based on what you've read about cotton and the market economy, are his claims justified?

www.cengage.com/history/ayers/ampassages4e

During the months in between, politicians worked behind the scenes to prepare for the debates and decisions of December. The Union, so celebrated and expansive in the wake of the war with Britain, so peaceful for whites since the Creeks, Seminoles, and Cherokees had been quelled, now seemed in danger of breaking apart from within. Both northern and southern politicians talked openly of ending the Union if need be. Simmering northern resentment, held in check for decades, was suddenly announced, even celebrated. Southerners felt betrayed. In their eyes, slavery was something they had inherited, for which they bore no blame. White southerners thought northerners irresponsible and unrealistic to attack it as the proposed Tallmadge amendment did. The denial of Missouri statehood seemed to southerners nothing less than an assault on their character.

In northern states, where antislavery societies had been relatively sedate, people suddenly announced the depth of their distaste for the institution. Furious meetings erupted in towns and cities across the North, turning out petitions and resolutions in large numbers. Slavery, these petitions thundered, was a blot on the nation, a violation of the spirit of Christianity, an abomination that must not spread into places it had not already ruined. The antislavery advocates of the 1820s expected colonization and abolition to occur simultaneously and gradually. But they were also determined to stop the spread of slavery toward the northern part of the continent.

After weeks of debate, the **Missouri Compromise** emerged from the Senate: Missouri, with no restriction on slavery, should be admitted to the Union at the same time as Maine, thereby ensuring the balance between slave and free states. Slavery would be prohibited in all the lands acquired in the Louisiana Purchase north of the southern border of Missouri at 36°30' latitude. Such a provision excluded the Arkansas territory, where slavery was already established, but closed to slavery the vast expanses of the Louisiana Territory—the future states of Iowa, Minnesota, Wisconsin, the Dakotas, Nebraska, and Kansas. Any slaves who escaped to the free states would be returned. Many northern congressmen who voted for the measure found themselves burned in effigy back home and defeated when it came time for reelection. Southerners were no more satisfied than the northerners; they were furious to hear themselves vilified in the national capital they had long dominated.

Northern and southern politicians had become wary and distrustful of one another as they had never been before. In a real sense, the debates over slavery in Missouri created "the North" and "the South," uniting the new states of the Northwest with the states of New England, New York, and Pennsylvania, and forging a tighter alliance among the new states of the Southwest and Virginia, the Carolinas, and Georgia. Accusations of greed, corruption, and hypocrisy flew. The country became polarized geographically.

In Charleston, South Carolina, the heart of South Carolina's richest plantation district, a free black man named **Denmark Vesey** had followed in the papers the debates over the Missouri controversy. What he read there reinforced what he had seen in the Bible and the documents of the American Revolution: slavery was immoral. Vesey, a middle-aged man of large stature who had bought his freedom twenty years earlier, stood as a commanding presence among the African American people of the Low Country. A skilled carpenter and preacher, Vesey traveled up and down the coast and into the interior, berating blacks who accepted racial insult. Many African Americans were attracted to him, but most were afraid to oppose him regardless.

Vesey drew not only on his own strengths but on those of a powerful ally, Gullah Jack. This man, an Angolan, had arrived in South Carolina near the turn of the century, one of the forty thousand slaves brought into the state right before the end of the legal slave trade in 1807. With huge whiskers, tiny arms, and unusual gestures, Gullah Jack projected an aura of spiritual authority.

Vesey, Gullah Jack, and their followers conspired to seize the city's poorly protected guardhouse, stores, and roads before the whites could gather themselves in opposition. House slaves would kill their white owners. Once Charleston was secure, the rebels, Vesey planned, would sail to Haiti, where Toussaint L'Ouverture had staged a black rebellion decades earlier and where slavery had been abolished. But a house servant alerted Charleston whites to the danger only two days before the revolt planned for June 16, 1822. The governor ordered out five military companies, and Vesey called off the attack. Over the next two months, white authorities hanged thirty-five alleged conspirators and banished thirty-seven more from the state. Few of the rebels would reveal the names of their allies, going to their deaths with the secrets of the revolt secure. Denmark Vesey was one of those executed.

Charleston's mayor, James Hamilton, bragged, "There can be no harm in the salutary inculcation of one lesson, among a certain portion of our population, that there is nothing they are bad enough to do, that we are not powerful enough to punish." Despite such boasts, white southerners blamed Vesey's rebellion on the agitation against slavery by northern congressmen in the Missouri debate. "The events of 1822," a leading South

Carolinian observed, "will long be remembered, as amongst the choicest fruits of the agitation of that question in Congress."

The Monroe Doctrine, 1823 The instability of the Spanish regime in Europe, exacerbated by the Napoleonic Wars, sent aftershocks into the colonies in the New World. Throughout the first and second decades of the nineteenth century, one struggle after another disrupted Latin America. Seeing Spain vulnerable in Europe and abroad, leaders in the colonies of the Western Hemisphere—Simón Bolívar in Venezuela, José de San Martín in Argentina, and Miguel Hidalgo in Mexico—pushed ahead with their long-simmering plans for national independence. By 1822, Chile, Mexico, Venezuela, and the Portuguese colony of Brazil had gained independence.

Neither the United States nor Great Britain wanted to see France or Russia fill the vacuum left by Spain in the New World. Accordingly, in March 1822, President Monroe urged Congress to recognize the new republics of Latin America. Throughout the next year, as the French army invaded Spain, the U.S. minister in England proposed that the United States and England jointly declare that neither country would annex any part of Spain's tottering empire or permit any other power to do so. Encouraged by former presidents Jefferson and Madison, Monroe wanted to make the joint declaration, but Secretary of State John Quincy Adams persuaded him that it would be more fitting and dignified for the United States to declare its policy independently instead of coming "in as a cock-boat in the wake of the British man o'war." Adams's policy was directed more against outside intervention in Latin America than in favor of the new republics, which he considered weak and unlikely to endure an attack by a major power.

In December 1823 the president used his annual message to Congress to announce what would eventually become known as the **Monroe Doctrine**: "The American continents, by the free and independent conditions which they have assumed and maintained, are henceforth not to be considered as subjects for future colonisation by any European power." The North American republic had exerted its first claim to recognition by the great powers of the world, making a show of acting independently even though Great Britain was the real power. The Russians and Spanish denounced the American policy as "blustering," "arrogant," "indecent," and "monstrous," meriting only "the most profound contempt." They tolerated the doctrine because the European powers, exhausted by wars among themselves, had little desire to expand their involvement on the other side of the world. The leaders of the Latin American revolts welcomed the warning to the European powers, but they were less certain about the intentions of the United States toward Latin America. The Monroe Doctrine, after all, did not say that the United States would not interfere in the Western Hemisphere, only that it would not permit European countries to do so.

THE REINVENTION OF POLITICS, 1824–1828

Few eligible voters had bothered to cast a ballot when James Monroe was reelected in 1820 virtually without opposition. But bitter debates over slavery and the role of the national government that followed set off a new era of political partisanship. The election of 1824 showed that Americans had become far more divided than had seemed possible only four years earlier.

The Election of 1824 With five strong contenders eying the presidency in 1824, politicians and observers expected a more interesting contest than four years earlier. Many thought the next president would be William Crawford, secretary of the treasury, a Georgian and apparent heir to the Virginia dynasty. Others focused on John Quincy Adams, an experienced statesman, a New Englander, and the secretary of state—the office from which several presidents had come, including his father. Others looked to John C. Calhoun of South Carolina, an impressive secretary of war and advocate of a strong national government. Yet others placed their bets on Henry Clay of Kentucky, Speaker of the House of Representatives for many years and one of the most visible members of Congress. Finally, Andrew Jackson of Tennessee hoped to parlay the widespread fame he had won in the wars against the English and the Indians into the presidency.

Several of these men realized they did not command sufficient national support to win the election outright. They hoped, however, to prevail if the election went into the House of Representatives, where the top three candidates would vie if no candidate won a majority in the electoral college. Cliques spread rumors, and alliances of convenience flourished. Openly partisan newspapers sang the praises of their man and published lacerating rumors about his opponents. The most novel was John Henry Eaton's successful press campaign to portray Jackson as a patriotic soldier, quietly tending his farm while Washington politicians schemed to block his election by ordinary voters because of his lack of polish and his incorruptible character.

Many American voters seemed disenchanted with the crass politicking, though, and relatively few voted in 1824. Jackson's popular vote nearly equaled that of Adams and Crawford combined, but the election was thrown into the House of Representatives because no candidate received a plurality in the electoral college. The House could choose among the top three candidates: Jackson, Adams, and Crawford.

Since his fourth-place finish put him out of the running, Clay, the Speaker of the House, sought to strike the best deal he could with the other candidates, assuring himself of maximum power, visibility, and opportunities in subsequent elections. Clay, considering Jackson unworthy of the post and a potential military despot, discussed his future with Adams. When the vote came to the House of Representatives in early 1825, Adams won the presidency, taking the three states Clay had won in the electoral college. Two weeks later, Henry Clay received the appointment of secretary of state. "So you see," Andrew Jackson fumed, "the Judas of the West has closed the contract and will receive the thirty pieces of silver." Throughout the muddy little city of Washington, people speculated about the promises the upright John Quincy Adams had made to win the presidency. People often mentioned the cold sweat that broke out on his face when he received word of his election.

Adams wanted a stronger national government, internal improvements, and a tariff to protect American industry. But he could not mobilize support for his positions, either within Washington or among the voters. Adams refused to use patronage to persuade or coerce people to go along with his plans. His administration bogged down into factionalism and paralysis, with his supposed "corrupt bargain" with Clay darkening his reputation.

New York politicians sought to harness ambition into useful and organized forms in the 1820s, pioneering the development of the party system. Aaron Burr converted a simple patriotic club in New York City, the Society of Saint Tammany, into the beginnings of a major political machine. DeWitt Clinton invented the "spoils system," in which it became the expectation that an incoming officeholder would remove those appointed by his predecessor and put his own supporters in their place. Martin Van Buren, a young lawyer and politician from New York, nicknamed the "Little Magician," combined the city machine and the spoils system into a powerful statewide organiza- tion. He used newspapers in Albany and New York City to spread the word of the party to the fifty small newspapers he controlled throughout the state, which also published vast numbers of handbills, posters, and ballots at election time. He built a large network of party men, many of them lawyers, who traveled widely in the state and knew many of their counterparts. Van Buren's goal was to combine party unity with personal advancement for party members, creating a powerful and self-reinforcing cycle.

Van Buren opposed John Quincy Adams in the presidential contest of 1824 because Adams's nationally sponsored canals, roads, education, and other services would cut into the power of state government, elevating what Van Buren saw as dan- gerous federal power over power closer to home. Partly for this reason, Van Buren cast his lot in 1824 and the years thereafter with Andrew Jackson, who shared Van Buren's preference for localized power. As the next presidential election came closer, Van Buren, now a senator, worked ever more energetically for Jackson, hoping to spread the model of New York politics to the nation as a whole.

The Adams Twilight The second half of John Quincy Adams's administration proved as unhappy and unproductive as the first. Neither Adams's talents nor his devotion to the Union had faded, but the public mood seemed little interested in either. The "corrupt bargain" still hung over the White House in 1827. In the eyes of many, Adams had proven himself unfit for office, not only with his reputed bargain but also, false rumor persisted, by procuring a young American girl for the Russian czar when Adams had served as a fourteen-year-old member of the U.S. diplomatic corps in St. Petersburg. The president's elite education and even his purchase of a billiard table and chess set for the White House were disparaged by opponents as symbols of "aristocracy."

Supporters of Andrew Jackson of Tennessee, John C. Calhoun of South Carolina, and William Crawford of Georgia gradually joined forces in anticipation of the elec- tion of 1828, when they hoped to unseat Adams and his vision of an active and cen- tralized government. The struggle, Calhoun wrote to Jackson, was between "power and liberty." The champion of power had had his turn, Adams's opponents believed; now it was time for the champions of liberty to step forward. After some jockeying, Andrew Jackson emerged as the man to challenge Adams.

Adams's supporters warned of the dangers of electing a raw and rough "military chieftain" such as Andrew Jackson to the presidency. Jackson's opponents distributed a handbill marked with eighteen coffins, each one representing a man Jackson had sup- posedly killed in a duel or ordered executed under his military command. The most incendiary charge, however, was that Jackson had married a woman married to another man, leading her to commit both bigamy and adultery in the process. The facts of the case were unclear—it appears that Rachel Jackson was a religious woman, trapped in a bad marriage, who thought she had received a divorce when she married Jackson—but the anti-Jackson forces made the most of any suspicions to the contrary.

The Anti-Masons Organize
Charges of conspiracy and corruption raged throughout American politics in the 1820s. Some of the suspicions seemed confirmed by events in New York. As the economy of that state prospered along with the Erie Canal, so did fraternal organizations of every sort. The Ancient Order of Masons did especially well, claiming almost 350 lodges in the state. The Masons' exclusive society, surrounded by elaborate ritual and strict secrecy, many non-Masons felt, contradicted American ideals of democracy and openness. Since Masons were obliged to show business or political preference to a brother over "any other person in the same circumstances," many feared Masonic influence.

Suspicion of the Masons exploded when a brother named William Morgan turned against the order and published its secret rituals. Local Masonic leaders used their influence with county officials to harass and jail Morgan, who disappeared in September 1826. Many said he had been murdered. The investigation soon stalled, however, as Masonic law enforcement officers and others dragged their feet. Despite twenty trials and three special prosecutors, only a few convictions resulted, and those convictions brought only minor jail terms. Congregations split and communities divided into warring factions over the Masons. Alleged Masonic skullduggery proved a convenient way to explain personal and political setbacks.

By 1827, nearly a hundred "Morgan committees" had met and formed in New York and began to spread across the entire northern half of the country, attracting men of reputation and prestige. Within two years, the "Anti-Masons" had established more than a hundred newspapers. They held public meetings and launched lobbying campaigns, bypassing local elites and inventing new means of pressuring legislatures directly. They devoted themselves to changing public opinion, to mobilizing people against a powerful entrenched force. They succeeded: masonry lost more than half its members and created virtually no new lodges for the next fifteen years.

Birth of the Democrats
Even while the struggle over the Masons unfolded, Martin Van Buren traveled throughout the United States, hammering out a new coalition of ambitious state politicians willing to back Andrew Jackson. The members of the coalition called themselves "Democratic Republicans," eventually shortened to "Democrats." Their candidates did extremely well in the off-year congressional elections of 1827, exploiting people's disapproval of the ineffectual Adams administration. The Democrats controlled both the House and the Senate.

In preparation for Jackson's contest with Adams, Van Buren and the other party leaders organized voters as they had never been organized before. Although Jackson himself was a prominent Mason, Van Buren adopted techniques not unlike those pioneered by the Anti-Masons in these same years. Using every strategy at their disposal—bonfires, speeches, barbecues, parades, professional writers, and the first campaign song—these Jacksonians claimed that they had found a true man of the people to strip the office from the aristocratic Adams. In towns across the country, "Old Hickory"—Jackson was supposedly as hardy as that toughest of trees—was celebrated with hickory poles, brooms, sticks, and trees. The National Republicans, as Adams's supporters became known, sniffed at what they considered the unseemly display that diverted attention from real issues, but they could not deny the power of the new methods to win voters' attention.

In the meantime, American politics became more democratic and inclusive. Most legislatures across the Union lowered property requirements for voting and made judicial offices elective rather than appointed. Citizens seemed restless, hungry for someone to give direction and force to public life. As a result, voter turnout in 1828 was double that of the 1824 election. The dramatic confrontation of men and styles contributed to widespread voter interest, and politicians at every level and on both sides made sure voters went to the polls. Jackson's supporters wanted no repeat of the last electoral controversy or chance for victory to be stolen by insider politics.

Jackson won easily over Adams, winning 178 of the 261 electoral votes, capturing the critical mid-Atlantic states and all the states of the South except Louisiana and Kentucky. The election proved bittersweet for Jackson, though: his wife died soon afterward. Jackson blamed the slanderers of the other party for Rachel's death, for she had fallen ill after seeing an editorial denouncing her. The president-elect passed the weeks before his inauguration in sadness and bitterness.

To sweep the Augean Stable.

FOR PRESIDENT,
Andrew Jackson.

FOR VICE-PRESIDENT,
JOHN C. CALHOUN.

Hickory Broom. *If elected, "Old Hickory's" supporters promised to sweep away the political corruption they associated with the Adams administration. Ironically, Jackson himself was soon accused of corruption in distributing the newly available political posts. (Library of Congress)*

CONCLUSION

The decade after 1815 saw two powerful tendencies warring with each other in the United States. On one hand, restless Americans surged to the West after the defeat of the British in the War of 1812 removed a major barrier to territorial growth. On the other hand, many other Americans feared what such ceaseless movement might mean for families, churches, morals, and politics. The tension between growth and the consequences of that growth defined the events of this turbulent decade.

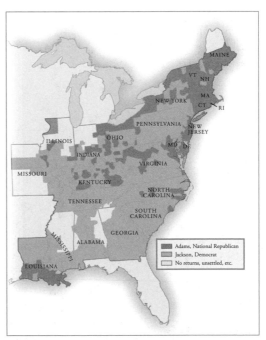

MAP 9.4 The Election of 1828.

Andrew Jackson overwhelmed John Quincy Adams almost everywhere except in Adams's native New England.

The expansion of the United States was not simply the story of hardy pioneers marching toward the West. The lands they came to occupy had been occupied for generations by Creeks, Cherokee, and Chickasaw peoples. The Indians' lands came into American hands through war, trickery, and bribery, as well as through treaties and purchase. Many white settlers did not much care about the means through which the lands entered the United States, for those settlers and their political leaders considered the land the rightful property of those who would convert it to profitable use.

As soon as the lands became available for settlement, white Americans surged there to establish farms, plantations, and towns. The rich land supported cotton in endless quantities—cotton produced by tens of thousands of enslaved African Americans. In what was then called the Northwest—what we now consider the Midwest—hungry white families did the work themselves on the rich but raw land they rushed to occupy. In the Northeast, new factories arose to provide clothing and shoes for the restless American population.

At the same time that Americans elbowed their way into territories and created new states, political leaders struggled to contain the consequences of unconstrained growth. The first great crisis over slavery, triggered by the admission of Missouri in 1819, made many people wonder whether the United States would be able to control the forces pulling it apart. The North and the South became ever more distinct as they expanded across the continent, and the area dominated by slavery grew as quickly as the area ruled by free labor. The burgeoning economy posed deep challenges to long-established ways of doing business. Well-funded corporations and partnerships flourished in the heightened competition for resources and markets. At the same time, charges of political corruption widened divisions between geographic regions and political parties.

CHAPTER REVIEW, 1815–1828

- Treaties established new borders of the United States to the north, west, and south.
- A newly integrated national economy emerged, based on improved roads, canals, and steamboats.
- The first major financial panic shook the entire country.
- Cotton drove the aggressive expansion of slavery across the South.
- Factories developed in the Northeast.
- The Missouri Compromise redefined the relationship between the North and the South.
- The first major national political party, the Democrats, was forged by Martin Van Buren and Andrew Jackson.

◀▮▮▮ *Looking Back*

Chapter 9 shows that the expansion of the United States after the War of 1812 unleashed a series of unanticipated challenges to the new nation. This raises a number of questions:

1. Could the spread of slavery into the southern territories have been avoided? Explain your reasoning.
2. How might relations between the U.S. government and Native Americans have followed a different path?
3. What role did governments play in the growth and spread of the economy?

Looking Ahead ▮▮▮▶

Chapter 10 will show how the compromises and reforms of the 1820s, designed to balance conflicting political interests, would shape political and economic development in future years.

1. Why did lawmakers believe that the Missouri Compromise could offer a long-term solution to conflicts between the North and the South? Were they right?

Go to the American Passages website at www.cengage.com/history/ayers/ ampassages4e for additional review materials.

10

The Years of Andrew Jackson, 1829–1836

Tumultuous change came to the United States in the years Andrew Jackson served as president. Elections became sweeping public events that involved men of every class. Voters and leaders hotly debated and contested the role of government in American life. Religious revivals swept up entire communities in devotion and prayer. Working people created labor unions, and abolitionists launched a bold crusade against slavery.

Growing democracy was not the full story of these years, however. The people of the Creek, Choctaw, Cherokee, Seminole, Sac, and Fox nations were driven from their homes in the South and in the Old Northwest. A crisis threatened to ignite a military struggle between South Carolina and the federal government. The revolt of Nat Turner and debates over slavery in Virginia unleashed a proslavery reaction throughout much of the South. The defeat of Mexico by the Republic of Texas opened a vast new territory to slavery as well as to the settlement of free Americans. Few other decades in American history have witnessed such important and fundamental changes.

Accompanying this rapid expansion of boundaries of every sort was considerable anxiety that American society threatened to spin out of control. The government held little power, and people worried that many Americans had moved beyond the influence of church, family, school, or employer. Some Americans began to suggest ways to contain the consequences of change. They offered political compromise, reform societies, and new ideals of the home as ways to counteract what they saw as threatening chaos.

ANDREW JACKSON TAKES CHARGE

Andrew Jackson, still wearing black after the recent death of his beloved wife, Rachel, traveled by steamboat from Nashville, Tennessee, to Washington in the winter of 1829 to begin his presidency. The entire nation watched to see what sort of changes this new kind of leader might make, what sort of America he might help create.

The People's President
Once he arrived in Washington, Jackson began to assemble his cabinet, balancing North, South, and West. Martin Van Buren, the leader of Jackson's successful 1828 campaign, became secretary of state, a position traditionally reserved for the man next in line for the presidency. Vice President John C. Calhoun, ambitious for the presidency himself, chafed at the appointment but could do little to change it; he and his wing of the party had to satisfy themselves with the appointment of one of their number as secretary of the treasury. The most controversial appointment, however, proved volatile for reasons that had little to do with political partisanship. Jackson wanted a close friend in the cabinet, someone in whom he could confide, and he chose an old Tennessee associate and influential newspaper editor, John Eaton, as his secretary of war.

Eaton, a widower in middle age, had married Peggy O'Neal Timberlake, an attractive and witty twenty-nine-year-old daughter of a well-known innkeeper in Washington. She was rumored to have driven her last husband to suicide, forcing him to defraud the government to pay debts she had run up. She was also rumored to have had sex with Eaton before their marriage—along with, one contemporary smirked, "eleven doz. others!" Eaton had asked Jackson's opinion of the marriage beforehand, receiving the old general's blessing; the president liked outspoken women and knew from bitter experience the power that unfounded rumors could hold. Jackson, in a gesture of friendship and support as the gossip flew, offered Eaton the cabinet position, apparently hoping he would decline. Unfortunately for Jackson, Eaton accepted. The decision electrified Washington.

Despite his rambunctious youth, Jackson disdained official Washington's fondness for strong drink, endless banquets, and overheated social life. He had witnessed that high life during his time as senator from Tennessee and held it in contempt when he returned to the capital; he preferred to attend the city's churches. Jackson considered himself an outsider despite his power and popularity, an outsider determined to reform Washington and make the city worthy of the nation it was supposed to serve.

As the inauguration day of March 4 neared, Washington's population doubled as men who considered themselves important in General Jackson's election arrived in the city to claim their fair share of glory, excitement, and jobs. They drank all the whiskey the city had to offer, slept five to a bed, and generally offended the more genteel residents of the capital. At the inauguration, thirty thousand people crowded in to see the new president. They surged into the White House, spilling barrels of orange punch, standing with muddy boots on expensive chairs to get a better look at the proceedings, and smashing thousands of dollars worth of china. Servants attracted the mob outside by moving the liquor. Jackson, suffocated by admirers and disgusted by the scene, climbed out a rear window and went for a steak at his boardinghouse.

This icon will direct you to interactive activities and study materials on the American Passages website: www.cengage.com/history/ayers/ampassages4e

CHAPTER TIMELINE

1828	Tariff of Abominations • Calhoun's Exposition • Election of Jackson
1829	David Walker's Appeal • Mexico tries to abolish slavery in Texas
1830	Indian Removal Act • The Book of Mormon • Finney's revivals begin in Rochester • Anti-Masonic party holds first national party convention
1831	Nat Turner's rebellion • Garrison's The Liberator • Jackson reorganizes cabinet, Van Buren over Calhoun • Mormons migrate from New York to Ohio
1832	Bank War begins • Nullification Crisis • Virginia debates over slavery • Jackson reelected
1833	Formation of American • Anti-slavery Society • Force Bill against South Carolina • Compromise Tariff • Slavery abolished in British Empire
1834	Whig party organized • National Trade Union formed
1835	Arkansas admitted to the Union • Revolution breaks out in Texas • Abolitionists' postal campaign • War against Seminoles and runaway slaves in Florida
1836	Congress imposes gag rule • Battle of the Alamo • Texas Republic established • Treaty of New Echota • Election of Martin Van Buren

Jackson and the Spoils System

Many people in Washington were as appalled at the events that followed the inauguration as they were with the inauguration itself. As the new administration got under way, Jackson and his advisers cleaned house in the federal government, removing officials whose competence, honesty, or loyalty to Jackson and the Democrats was suspect. Although such a policy had become established practice in several major states, including Van Buren's New York, Jackson was the first president to make such sweeping changes on the federal level. He envisioned himself purging an arrogant bureaucracy of corruption and establishing the democratic practice of rotation in office. As officeholders quaked and fretted, Jackson's lieutenants decided which customhouses and federal offices would be cleansed. Some of the incumbents clearly deserved to lose their jobs, having served jail terms, embezzled funds, or succumbed to drink, but others were guilty only of being active partisans for the other side in the recent election.

Jackson further infuriated opponents by appointing partisan newspaper editors to important posts, leading to charges that Jackson was corrupting, rather than cleansing, American government. Over the course of Jackson's two terms, he replaced only about 10 percent of all officeholders, not many more than his predecessors had, but Jackson also recognized the power of the postal system to aid partisan political aims. He elevated the postmaster general to a cabinet-level position and worked to appoint friendly editors as local postmasters where they solicited subscriptions to Democratic publications. These allies were frequently accused of misrouting or destroying rivals' pamphlets and newspapers.

Jackson removed about nine hundred of ten thousand men from their offices and did so in an especially brash spirit. One Jackson supporter unwisely announced to the

(The Granger Collection, New York)

Peggy Eaton. *The young wife of Secretary of War John Eaton became the center of a scandal that rocked Washington during Andrew Jackson's first term.*

Senate that the Jacksonians saw "nothing wrong in the rule that to the victors belong the spoils of the enemy." This proclamation gave an enduring notoriety to what from then on would be called the **spoils system**, a system that Jackson envisioned as reform, not cynical politics.

The festering conflict within the administration over the so-called Eaton affair proved just how important matters of symbolism could be. The wives of the other cabinet members, Vice President Calhoun's wife, and even Emily Donelson—Jackson's daughter-in-law and hostess of the White House—refused to be in the same room with **Peggy Eaton**. But Jackson would not be swayed in his support for John and Peggy Eaton. The new cabinet found itself bitterly divided between pro-Eaton and anti-Eaton factions. Jackson labored to mend fences, calling an influential pastor to the White House and trying to find evidence to prove Mrs. Eaton's virtue. Nothing proved effective, though, and Jackson decided that the real villain of the story was Vice President Calhoun and his unbending wife, Floride. By contrast, Martin Van Buren, a widower, cemented his friendship with the president by treating Mrs. Eaton with ostentatious respect. Jackson, embittered by the refusal of his other advisers to stand by Mrs. Eaton, largely abandoned his official cabinet and relied instead on an informal group of advisers, his so-called Kitchen Cabinet, and on Van Buren, the only winner in the Eaton episode.

STRUGGLES OVER SLAVERY

Several issues surrounding slavery came to a head in the years around 1830. Leaders in the southern states, worried about the rapidly growing population and power of the North, sought to define the limits of federal power. Feeling themselves neglected and abused by northern interests, South Carolina's leaders tried to secure greater autonomy. At the same time, free blacks in both the North and the South worked to replace the colonization movement with a campaign to end slavery and create freedom for African Americans in the United States. Even as these struggles unfolded, one of the largest slave revolts in the history of the United States erupted in Virginia. Combined, these events demonstrated that slavery and the issues on which it touched would bedevil the confident and boisterous young country.

The Tariff of Abominations, Nullification, and States' Rights, 1828–1833

Before the election of 1828, Martin Van Buren and other Democrats had sought to broaden support for Jackson, whose strength lay in the South, by passing a tariff favorable to the economic interests of New Englanders and westerners. After elaborate deal making, the Democrats enacted a major tariff. But it came with a high cost: southerners were furious with what they called this "tariff of abominations," for it raised the price they would have to pay for manufactured items and threatened markets for southern cotton abroad. John C. Calhoun, like other South Carolina planters, feared not only that the tariff would bleed the state dry economically but that it would set a regulatory precedent for anti-slavery forces, who might gain control of the federal government at some future date.

Accordingly, in the summer and early fall of 1828, a few months before he would take office as Jackson's vice president, Calhoun sought to find a principled way to reconcile his national ambitions and his local concerns. Rather than argue only against the tariff itself, Calhoun asserted the general rights of individual states within the Union. To do so, he returned to what he called "the primitive principles of our government," the foundations on which everything else rested. Calhoun insisted that interests had become so diverse in the United States that laws appropriate for one state or section might well harm another. Rather than merely letting the majority run roughshod over the minority, Calhoun believed, it made more sense to let a state "nullify" a national law within its own borders. Such **nullification** was constitutional, he said, because the federal system did not locate sovereignty in any one place, but rather divided it among the states and the nation. Should three-fourths of the states agree that a law must apply to all the country, then that clear majority could overrule the nullification. Calhoun thought he was finding a way to preserve order in an increasingly contentious Union. The document in which he laid out his ideas, the *South Carolina Exposition*, appeared in December 1828; the pamphlet was published anonymously because it was too politically dangerous for the vice president of the United States to be publicly on record for nullification.

South Carolina planters persuaded themselves that they would have to do something soon. They watched with growing alarm as newspapers told of the success of British abolitionists in ending slavery in the British West Indies—the place from which many elite white South Carolina families had come generations earlier. With the memory of Denmark Vesey's plan of 1822 and an 1829 revolt in the Low Country still fresh in their memory, white South Carolinians felt they could display no weakness on the slavery issue. Unlike other southern states, where stark geographic differences between Low Country and hill country often divided voters and encouraged party differences, there was broad agreement among the South Carolina electorate on this crucial issue. Throughout the state, raucous crowds gathered to call for a fight against the federal government on the tariff. South Carolinians who favored a more conciliatory stance toward the federal government could not generate nearly as much support for their position.

President Jackson had no sympathy for nullification, and the leaders of the movement in South Carolina were surprised and disappointed that they enjoyed no support from other southern states in resisting federal authority. After all, Jackson, like them, was a planter and slaveholder and would suffer economically along with the South Carolinians. Jackson considered the tariff to be for the good of the nation as a whole. The tariff provided money for defense and prevented federal debt. The South Carolina challenge would limit the power of the U.S. government to make law for the country in matters that transcended state boundaries. Jackson did not believe the United States could afford to permit such divisiveness to impair its strength in the world of nations. Jackson, the old general, would tolerate no opposition on such matters. Congress passed a "force bill" to permit him to use military power to keep South Carolina in line and collect the tariff duties.

Congress twisted and turned on nullification, not wanting South Carolina to get its way but unwilling to see Jackson use arms against fellow Americans. After much debate, Congress, under the leadership of Henry Clay, offered a compromise in early 1833: the tariff would be slowly but steadily lowered over the next decade, giving northern manufacturers time to adapt. South Carolina, secretly relieved, declared itself the victor and accepted the compromise tariff.

Free Blacks and African American Abolitionism   Even as the white leaders of South Carolina struggled to define the extent of their powers within the Union, free blacks and slaves struggled to define their freedom. Communities of several thousand free blacks lived in every major northern city, establishing their own churches, newspapers, schools, and lodges. More numerous still were free African Americans in the Upper South slave states, especially Maryland and Virginia, and in all major cities on the Atlantic and Gulf coasts of the South. These free blacks stayed in contact with African Americans in the North through newspapers, letters, and word passed by the many black sailors who plied the eastern seaboard.

Free blacks throughout the country debated the merits of leaving the United States altogether, as many whites encouraged them to do. The colonization movement struggled in the 1820s because few black Americans were willing to be shipped to a place they had never seen; only about fourteen hundred black Americans went to Liberia in the 1820s. Moreover, African Americans came to see in colonization an attack on their hard-won accomplishments in the United States, insisting that people of color had earned a place in this country. Rather than spending moral energy and money on removing black people, they argued, Americans should work instead on making the United States a fairer place.

David Walker proved to be an important figure in this movement that sought to improve the plight of black Americans. Walker had lived in Charleston at the time of Denmark Vesey's conspiracy in 1822 and was familiar with the long tradition of revolt and resistance in the Carolina Low Country. After the suppression of Vesey, Walker moved to Boston. There, he established a used-clothing store, one of the few businesses open to African Americans in the North. Walker did well in the business, bought a home, joined the African Methodist church, and became a black Mason, an organization that fought against slavery and the slave trade. He gave his support to

Freedom's Journal, an anticolonization paper published by black people in Boston and New York City between 1827 and 1829.

In 1829, Walker released his *Appeal . . . to the Colored Citizens of the World*. Americans, whatever their skin color, had never read such a document. Walker denied that slaves felt or owed any bond to their masters. He called for black spiritual self-renewal, starting with African Americans' recognition of just how angry they were with their lot in the United States. They needed to channel that anger with God's love, Walker urged, making a group effort to end slavery immediately. He called for black Americans to be full Americans in both government and the economy. Walker accused those supporting colonization of concocting a "plan to get those of the colored people, who are said to be free, away from those of our brethren whom they unjustly hold in bondage, so that they may be enabled to keep them the more secure in ignorance and wretchedness. . . . For if the free are allowed to stay among the slaves, they will have intercourse together, and . . . the free will learn the slaves *bad habits*, by teaching them that they are MEN . . . and certainly *ought* and *must* be FREE."

Within weeks of its publication, Walker's *Appeal* appeared in Savannah, where it was seized, then in Georgia's capital, Milledgeville, and then in Virginia, North Carolina, South Carolina, and New Orleans. The *Appeal* created panic and repression wherever it appeared. Southern whites worried at this evidence of invisible networks of communication and resistance among the slaves, free blacks, and, perhaps, sympathetic whites in their midst. Events in Virginia bore out their worst suspicions.

The Crisis of Slavery in Virginia, 1831–1832

Nat Turner was a field hand, born in 1800, who felt that God had called him for more than the lot of a slave. Well known even in his youth for his intellectual abilities and his effectiveness as a preacher, on Sundays Turner traveled throughout the countryside around Southampton County, Virginia, coming to know most of the slaves and free black people who lived there. Praying and fasting, Turner saw visions: drops of blood that formed hieroglyphics on leaves, black shadows across the white moon. These things, he became certain, foretold a slave revolt, of the time "fast approaching when the first should be last and the last should be first." Turner, unlike Gabriel in Richmond in 1800 and Vesey in Charleston in 1822, chose to build his revolt around a small group of select lieutenants rather than risk spreading the word broadly. Their plan was to begin the rebellion on their own and then attract compatriots along the way.

On August 22, 1831, Turner and his band began their revolt. They moved from one isolated farmhouse to the next, killing all the whites they found inside, including children, and then taking the horses and weapons there. Turner rode at the end of the group, praying for guidance on what plan they should follow. As the night wore on, Turner's men killed about seventy people, starting with the family of Turner's master. By morning, word had rushed to Richmond of the unimaginable events in Southampton. Whites huddled together in Jerusalem, the county seat, and troops arrived to put down the revolt. Blacks, many of whom had no connection with the rebellion, were killed by infuriated and frightened whites hundreds of miles away from Southampton. Turner's troops were all captured or killed, but Turner managed to escape and hide in the woods for two months. Once captured, he narrated a remarkable "confession" in which he told of his visions and prophecies. He had no regrets and no doubts that God would stand in judgment of the people who held other people in slavery. At his hanging in November, he showed no signs of remorse.

White southerners saw in Nat Turner their worst nightmares. Here was a literate slave, allowed to travel on his own, allowed to spread his own interpretation of the Bible to dissatisfied slaves eager to listen to Turner's prophecies. The crackdown was not long in coming: delegates to the state assembly gathered in Richmond a month after Turner's execution. In a series of remarkable debates, these white Virginians, some of them sons and grandsons of Thomas Jefferson, John Marshall, and Patrick Henry, openly admitted the debilitating effect of slavery on Virginia. They worried most about slavery's influence on whites, worried that slavery kept the economy from developing as it did in the North. Delegates from western Virginia, where relatively few slaves lived, expressed their misgivings most freely, but even large slaveholders from the East admitted slavery had negative effects. Petitions flowed into Richmond urging the legislators to take a decisive step to rid Virginia of slavery. Defenders of slavery warned that the **Virginia slave debates**, published in the newspapers and discussed on the streets and in shops and homes across the state, might result in more revolts. Enslaved Virginians were not an "ignorant herd of Africans," one delegate warned, but an "active, intelligent class, watching and weighing every movement of the Legislature, with perfect knowledge of its bearing and effect."

Some delegates urged that the state purchase all slaves born after a certain date—1840 was proposed—and colonize them in Africa or sell them to plantations farther south. Others argued that the state could not afford such a step, that the Virginia economy would collapse without slavery, that slaves born before the date of freedom would revolt, that property rights guaranteed in the Constitution made it ridiculous to talk about taking slaves from their owners. Others went much further, arguing that slavery was not wrong at all but rather God's plan for civilizing Africans otherwise lost to heathenism and barbarism. The disparate regions of Virginia found themselves in deep conflict; some discussed separating themselves from the rest of the state if one policy or another were followed. The lawmakers, starkly divided, ultimately decided that it was "inexpedient" to take any step at all against slavery at that time, that it would be left for subsequent legislatures to begin the process that would free Virginia from slavery. In the meantime, they passed harsher laws to limit the movement and gathering of free blacks and slaves.

POLITICAL TURMOIL AND THE ELECTION OF 1832

Andrew Jackson made fervent enemies as well as devoted followers throughout his presidency. No one could be neutral about him, for he seemed to touch everything in American life. The election of 1832 saw voters and leaders mobilize in opposition to or support of Jackson, latching on to a wide range of issues: the economy, states' rights, and morality. The president, furious at any resistance, lashed out, determined that his work not be wasted. The nation had never seen such political conflict.

Taking Sides   In September 1830, the first national political convention in U.S. history met in Baltimore, convened by the Anti-Masons. Despite their origins and their name, the Anti-Masons were concerned with the state of American politics in general, not merely with the threat posed by the Masons. They attracted an impressive list of ambitious and accomplished young men to their convention, including many who believed that Jackson, a Mason, was too prosouthern and too

The Bank of the United States as a Monster

This elaborate cartoon conveyed a simple message but with many subtleties that informed people at the time could have decoded. Each of the heads of the "hydra" is labeled with the name of a state, representing the way the "monster" of the Bank of the United States had slithered its way into every corner of the nation. The largest head at the center of the hydra, that of Nicholas Biddle, is labeled "Penn" for Pennsylvania. The soldier on the right has dropped his axe, discovering that splitting one of the heads of the hydra only reveals another inside.

GENERAL JACKSON SLAYING THE MANY HEADED MONSTER.

(The Granger Collection, New York)

President Jackson, elderly and yet still vigorous and determined, wields a sword labeled "veto," killing with a manly thrust a frightening opponent that seemed too formidable for anyone else to conquer. Vice President Martin Van Buren seems to be trying to help, albeit ineffectually. He contributes mainly by exclaiming, "Well done general!"

callous toward Native Americans. The Anti-Masons promised to become a powerful third party, a wild card in an already tumultuous American politics.

Economic resentment also fueled the conflict of the early 1830s. As prices and rents rose more quickly than wages, urban working people found themselves falling behind. These working men and women felt their contributions slighted in the new economy. Workers formed unions to defend their rights in cities from New York to Kentucky. They sponsored newspapers, lobbied legislatures, and supported one another during strikes. By the mid-1830s, between 100,000 and 300,000 men and women belonged to unions. Some unions became deeply engaged in politics and put forward their own candidates. Although union members generally liked Andrew Jackson's blows against monopoly, they believed he pulled up short in his attack on economic privilege.

The Bank War, 1832–1834   Despite the tariffs intended to serve their interests, most people in the Northeast felt they had received little from Andrew Jackson's first term. They viewed him with distrust and growing anger, perceiving in Old Hickory an enemy to moral and commercial progress, a defender of the backward South and West against the East. The fate of the Second Bank of the United States stood as the key issue in easterners' frustration. Many merchants and businessmen, worried about stabilizing the American economy, supported the Bank of the United States and its president, Nicholas Biddle. The bank ensured that state banks kept plenty of metal currency—specie—on hand with which to pay the national bank when asked to do so. Such rules kept the state banks from putting out too

DOING HISTORY ONLINE

Jackson Takes Office

Based on your readings of the text and Documents 4 to 8, what kind of president did Americans expect Andrew Jackson to be? Were those expectations fulfilled? Did Jackson's eight years in the presidency hold surprises for his supporters?

  www.cengage.com/
history/ayers/
ampassages4e

many notes, inflating the currency with paper money unsupported by gold or silver. When the economy fell into trouble, Biddle and the Bank of the United States would lessen their demands on the state banks, preventing panics and deflation.

While businessmen appreciated this role of the bank, many other Americans distrusted it. In their eyes, this largely private institution enjoyed far too much power for its own good or the good of the country. Why should privileged stockholders in the bank, they asked, profit from the business of the federal government? Why should the national notes be allowed to depress the value of state notes, with their origins closer to home?

For many voters, objections to the Bank of the United States were as much objections to banking and commerce in general as to any specific policies of the national bank. The whole business of banking seemed suspect, with its paper money, its profits seemingly without labor, its government-supported monopolies, its apparent speculation with public money. Andrew Jackson shared these feelings of mistrust: he disliked monopoly, he disliked paper money, and he disliked the Bank of the United States.

Jackson initiated what became known as the "**Bank War**," vetoing a re-chartering of the bank and proclaiming that the bank was "unauthorized by the constitution, subversive of the rights of the States, and dangerous to the liberties of the people." He moved all federal funds from the Bank of the United States to state banks. The Bank of the United States, deprived of government support, began a slow death.

Jackson's opponents saw the president, not the bank, as the usurper of American rights. How dare he single-handedly overturn what the people, in the form of Congress, had declared to be their will? Henry Clay and other opponents argued that his action posed a far greater threat to the American people than did the bank. If the president could force his way into the lawmaking process, the division of powers laid out in the Constitution would be violated and the Union would risk falling under the despotic rule of a president who would be king.

"King Andrew the First." *Fearing the president's growing power, Whigs began referring to Jackson as "King Andrew I."*

(Library of Congress)

In the election of 1832, Jackson portrayed himself as the champion of the common man fighting against a bloated aristocracy of privilege and monopoly. Clay, the candidate of the National Republicans, portrayed himself as the defender of the Union against an arrogant and power-hungry president; Clay characterized Jackson as a man who had disregarded morality and justice in his dealing with Native Americans, had corrupted the government with the spoils system, and had attacked the national bank. William Wirt, the candidate of the Anti-Masons, declared himself the opponent of all conspiracies, corruptions, and subversions.

Jackson won by a considerable margin. Emboldened by his majority at the polls, the president went on the offensive. Those opposed to Jackson began to call themselves "Whigs." Like their British namesakes, the American Whig party saw itself as the counterbalance to otherwise unchecked monarchical power—in this case "King Andrew I," "the most absolute despot now at the head of any representative government on earth."

THE INDIAN PEOPLES AND THE MEXICAN NATION

Andrew Jackson's administration focused much of its energy on the native peoples of North America. Native Americans held immense areas of the South and the West when Jackson took office—land that many whites wanted and demanded. The southwestern border of the United States remained tantalizingly ambiguous as well. Mexico governed its northern provinces loosely, and many white Americans coveted that land.

Jackson and the American Indians   Andrew Jackson had announced, and acted on, his attitudes toward Native Americans years before he took office as president. The steady pressing of white population onto the rich lands of the Cherokees, Chickasaws, Creeks, Seminoles, and Choctaws, he thought, left the people of those nations with two choices: become "industrious Citizens" who accepted the sovereignty of the states that claimed the lands on which they lived, or "remove to a Country *where* they can retain their ancient customs, so dear to them, that they cannot give up in exchange for regular society." Their only other choice, Jackson thought, was extinction.

White people had mixed feelings about Native Americans. Americans of European descent considered native peoples admirable in many ways, dignified and free, able to learn and prosper. Not a few "white" and "black" families were proud to claim some native ancestry. Many white Americans, including some in Congress, had long contributed time and money to the Native Americans, helping to build and staff schools, sending seed and agricultural implements to ease the transition to farming.

By the late 1820s, the "civilized tribes" had adapted themselves to the dominant society. Many of the tribes were led by chiefs of mixed descent—leaders who lived in cabins, houses, and even mansions. Men such as **John Ross** negotiated land settlements and profited from such deals but also attempted to create systems of political representation and law. Ross joined the Methodist church and courted any political party he believed best advanced Cherokee interests. The wealthiest Native Americans, especially the Cherokees, bought African American slaves. The children of the Native American leaders and others went to schools established by white missionaries, who

Cherokee Nation v. Georgia

In 1831 the Cherokees, led by Chief John Ross, appealed to the Supreme Court for protection against Georgia's Indian policies. They argued that the Constitution defined Indian tribes as foreign nations and thus not subject to any state's authority. At stake were issues of states' rights as well as U.S.–Indian relations. Chief Justice John Marshall dismissed the case, ruling that Native Americans were "domestic dependent nations" rather than foreign nations. "Their relation to the United States resembles that of a ward to his guardian," Marshall wrote, a decision that the United States quickly seized on to disregard Indian treaties. His decision in *Worcester v. Georgia* a year later upheld tribal sovereignty against state governments, however, prompting Andrew Jackson to declare caustically, "John Marshall has made his decision; now let him enforce it." U.S. soldiers soon forced the Cherokees off their lands.

(Library of Congress)

persuaded a considerable number of Native Americans to convert to Christianity. The Cherokees published a newspaper that included articles in both their own language and in English.

Despite their many adaptations, the Native Americans of the Southeast in the late 1820s showed no desire to leave the land on which they lived. In their view, they had already given up more land than they should have—millions of acres over the preceding twenty years—and were determined to hold on to what remained. "We would not receive money for land in which our fathers and friends are buried," they declared. Most whites, especially those who lived nearby and coveted the rich cotton lands under the Native Americans' control, bristled at the continuing presence of the native inhabitants.

Jackson told the Native Americans he was their friend, even their "father," but that he could do nothing to stop their mistreatment except to move them beyond the Mississippi River, where, he promised, they would be safe. The Native Americans and their supporters, mostly religious people in the North, responded bitterly to such claims, arguing that the rights of the Constitution should certainly extend to people who had lived in North America since time immemorial. But the Jacksonians quickly pushed through the **Indian Removal Act** of 1830. Two Supreme Court decisions in favor of the Cherokees, in 1830 and in 1832, *Cherokee Nation v. Georgia* and *Worcester v. Georgia*, proved to be without effect, since they depended on the federal government to implement them and Jackson had no intention of doing anything of the sort.

In the face of the impending removal, most of the native peoples split into pro-assimilation, "progressive," factions and anti-assimilation, "conservative," factions. They debated fiercely and sometimes violently among themselves. Agents, some of mixed blood, swindled the Native Americans as they prepared for the removal. The Choctaws, the first to move, underwent horrific experiences, suffering greatly and dying in large numbers as they traveled in the worst winter on record with completely inadequate supplies. The Creeks too confronted frauds and assaults.

The Native Americans who moved sold whatever they could not take with them, usually at a great loss. Wagons and carts carried the old and the sick, while women and children drove livestock along the trail. Soldiers usually accompanied the Indians, along with an agent to hand out whatever support the government provided. "To see the remnant of a once mighty people fettered and chained together forced to depart from the land of their fathers into a country unknown to them," an Alabama newspaper admitted, "is of itself sufficient to move the stoutest heart."

The Cherokee removal was the most prolonged. After years of negotiating, the government struck a bargain with a small and unrepresentative number of Cherokees in the Treaty of New Echota in 1836. While groups of several hundred at a time left, including some of the wealthiest, seventeen thousand refused to leave by the deadline. General Winfield Scott then led seven thousand troops against them, driving people from their homes empty-handed, marching them to stockades, and shipping them out by rail and water. About a quarter of all eastern Cherokees died on what they called the **Trail of Tears**. Some Cherokees remained in the mountains of North Carolina and Tennessee, but the power of the eastern Indians was destroyed.

The Seminoles fought against removal as long as they could. Led by **Osceola**, the son of an English trader and the husband of an escaped slave, the Seminoles tried to break the will of the whites by killing soldiers and civilians and burning their crops and homes. The Second Seminole War launched by the federal government to remove the five thousand Native Americans began in 1835 and dragged on for nearly seven years. The conflict proved both unpopular and unsuccessful. Of the thirty-six thousand or so U.S. soldiers who fought, fifteen hundred died, and many more suffered debilitating disease. The federal government spent $20 million in the fight, even though few white people wanted to settle on the Seminoles' land. The United States captured Osceola only by deception at a supposed peace conference. He died in captivity a few months later, after which some Seminoles finally migrated to Oklahoma. But most of the Seminole people, able to live in the swampy landscape, were never driven out of Florida.

Fighting also erupted in the Illinois Territory between white settlers and the Sac and Fox natives. These people, under the leadership of Black Hawk, saw their lands along the Mississippi River taken over by whites while the Native Americans were on a hunting expedition in 1832. The whites burned the Native Americans' huts and plowed under their fields. In retaliation, the Sac and Fox destroyed white settlements. A large contingent of volunteers (including a young Abraham Lincoln), regular troops, and allied Native Americans set out after Black Hawk and his people, who also had allies from other native nations. Eventually the whites outnumbered Black Hawk and overran his camp, killing nearly five hundred as they tried to cross the

The Trail of Tears. *The Cherokee called their forced migration to Oklahoma the Trail of Tears. About 4,000 of the 15,000 Indians forced to move died along the way, as did more than 25,000 of the 100,000 southeastern Indians who were driven from their homes in these years.*

Mississippi River. Taken prisoner, Black Hawk refused to repent, telling his captors that he "has done nothing for which an Indian ought to be ashamed. He has fought for his countrymen, the squaws and papooses, against white men who came, year after year, to cheat them and take away their land." Black Hawk's words and deeds, widely reported in the newspapers of the country, attracted considerable sympathy among whites in the East. Andrew Jackson met with Black Hawk and pardoned him; the warrior's autobiography became a best-seller.

Conflict with
Mexico

In the wake of the panic of 1819, speculators and settlers from the United States emigrated to Mexican Texas, where large swaths of Mexican land could be had on far better terms than the U.S. government offered. Prospective immigrants simply had to swear allegiance to the Mexican government, become (at least nominally) Catholic, and present letters testifying to their good character. Mexico began inviting American settlers into its vulnerable northern border region in hopes of populating Texas, but soon clashed with the settlers over the issue of slavery. Mexico attempted to outlaw slavery at various times but found that Mexico City was too far from Texas to exercise effective control over the region.

A key leader in the American migration was **Stephen F. Austin**, a Virginia-born entrepreneur who first arrived in Mexico in 1821 on the heels of Mexican independence. Throughout the 1820s, Austin, negotiating with the changing Mexican governments, allotted and registered land grants and oversaw the settlement of hundreds of Americans.

Most of these settlers came from the U.S. South, and while a significant number were not slaveholders most agreed that slavery would be crucial for the development of Texas.

General **Antonio López de Santa Anna** began consolidating power in Mexico during the early 1830s. His attempts to centralize control in Mexico City led to revolts throughout Mexico, including the Yucatan, Zacatecas, and Texas. Settlers increasingly came into conflict with the Mexican government when provincial officials attempted to collect tariffs and slow immigration into the province. Austin and others petitioned the Mexican government to let them become a separate Mexican state under its own administration, but they were rebuffed when Santa Anna took control. In Santa Anna's eyes, the Texans were clearly inviting an expansionist United States to take this province away from Mexico; he sent in troops to meet the threat.

In 1835, a convention of Texans created a provisional government, with Sam Houston as commander of the army, to fight against Santa Anna for their rights as Mexican citizens outlined in the Constitution of 1824. For many Texans, this was not a vote for independence; those seeking immediate independence were voted down thirty-three to fifteen. Austin was sent east, offering large parcels of land to all who would fight in the struggle.

During the Texas Revolution, volunteers and money flowed from the United States to Texas; southern states in particular sent hundreds of men. Nevertheless, Texas army enlistments were greatly outnumbered by the Mexicans. When the Mexican army occupied San Antonio in early 1836, about two hundred rebels—including David Crockett of Tennessee, famous for his frontier exploits—took refuge in an old mission called the Alamo. Most of the people inside were American or European immigrants, but they were joined by *Tejanos* (Mexicans native to Texas) who allied themselves with the rebellion against Santa Anna. The defenders of the Alamo held out against nearly three thousand Mexican soldiers for two weeks, until the Mexicans finally stormed the mission and killed all inside except three white women, two white children, and an African American slave. On orders of Santa Anna, the Mexican army stripped the bodies of the insurrectionists and burned them. In the aftermath of the Alamo, Texans committed themselves to creating an independent state. Support for the rebellion grew rapidly in the United States, where it came to be seen as a moral struggle between the forces of freedom and the forces of autocracy.

Santa Anna stood on the verge of destroying the Texas rebellion until Sam Houston's army surprised the larger Mexican force at San Jacinto in April 1836. A force of nine hundred Texans with *Tejano* cavalry commanded by **Juan Seguín** stormed Santa Anna's troops, winning decisively in only eighteen minutes. Santa Anna, captured a day after the battle, signed treaties removing Mexican troops from Texas, granting Texas its independence, and recognizing the Rio Grande as the boundary. The Mexican Congress, on hearing of this capitulation, renounced the treaty on the grounds that Santa Anna had signed under penalty of death.

Texans, and many Americans elsewhere, urged the U.S. government to annex the new republic before it could be reconquered by Mexico. The question of annexation unleashed a heated and protracted debate between advocates of U.S. expansion and those who thought such a step would be immoral and impolitic. Much of the debate raged between southerners, who saw Texas as a vast new empire, and northerners, especially abolitionists, who opposed annexation because it would lead to slavery's expansion. The fate of Texas would remain a central political issue for the next decade.

RELIGION AND REFORM

The power and influence of Protestant churches surged to a new level in the Jacksonian era. Far more than in any previous generation, the churches took leading roles in every facet of life and in every part of the Union. Revivals pulled in scores of new members. Many of those who experienced the spiritual rebirth of the revivals sought to bring others closer to God through religious education and social reform. A radical new movement against slavery gathered force with stunning speed. Other Americans worked to reform asylums, orphanages, and penal institutions. Still others sought purer forms of religion itself, listening to prophets who spoke of new churches and new possibilities.

Revivalism   Since the late eighteenth century, revivals led by the major Protestant denominations had periodically inflamed the United States. In those revivals, people who had never before declared their faith or had fallen away from the church made public expressions of their faith. Thousands of people gathered across the nation and along the frontier, in town and countryside, to pray and hear ministers tell them of God's love and forgiveness. Hearing of these gifts and aware of their own sinfulness, men and women sometimes fell to the ground as if stricken. Others cried and screamed. The churches that devoted themselves to spreading the Gospel periodically experienced revivals, or "awakenings," when numbers of people expressed or renewed their faith. This revivalism burst out again in the mid-1820s.

As Americans looked about them in the 1820s, they became concerned that little seemed to be holding their society together. People had moved far beyond the reach of government and beyond the eyes of their parents and communities. Men and women married at younger ages and left home far earlier than their parents had. The opening of land in the West undermined one of the principal forms of control exercised by fathers in earlier generations: the promise of passing on land to sons who stayed and worked at home. Now sons could acquire land in the West with or without the support of their parents. Daughters might marry earlier, begin families of their own, and move far away. The American population skyrocketed as so many young families established themselves.

The new economy also caused concern for many. Increasingly men and women seemed pulled in different directions, away from a sole focus on the family farm or family artisan shop. Men found new opportunities in town, in businesses and shops in a central area. Young men often worked for wages for a number of employers rather than serving for many years with one master. Young women might move to mill towns, where they too lived among strangers, away from parental control. Revivals and reform movements responded to these dislocations and uncertainties.

Many ministers and churches across the country were swept up in the religious awakening of the 1820s, but one man embodied its new and aggressive spirit: **Charles Grandison Finney**. Finney, a young attorney from Utica, New York, who had not regularly attended church until encouraged to do so by his fiancée, suddenly found himself struck with the power of God's love. "An overwhelming sense" of his wickedness brought Finney to his knees. "I wept aloud like a child [and] the Holy Spirit descended upon me in a manner that seemed to go through me body and soul," he recalled. "I could feel the impression like a wave of electricity, going through and through me." Finney spread the word of the Bible in the plain and straightforward language of everyday life. He told people that they had it within their power to take the first step toward God and that God would listen.

Finney found in the new cities of western New York a receptive audience among young men, on their own in a rapidly changing America, and among women of every age. The churches, these people believed, had grown cold in the hands of the established ministry and needed a revival of spirit. They wanted a Christianity of activity, of prayer meetings, of spreading the word any way they could. Finney's influence grew in strength and numbers as women prayed with one another. The district of upstate New York that lay along the path of the Erie Canal became known as "the burned-over district," as one revival after another blazed through its towns and farms.

The revivals took on a new scale and urgency in 1830 as they ignited Rochester, New York. Like other rapidly growing towns and cities along the Erie Canal, Rochester was ripe for revival. Many people of the young city worried that they barely knew one another and that husbands and wives, workers and employers, rich and poor, were drifting apart. Politics appeared a morass of selfishness; alcohol seemed to drown hopes of social progress and family happiness; men seemed more concerned with their businesses, lodges, and politics than with their souls. When Finney came to town in 1830, he was met by people hungry for a new message.

Women's prayer groups met daily and traveled from home to home in efforts to bring the word of Jesus. Women pleaded with their husbands to listen to the Reverend Finney. Employers made it clear to the men who worked under them that it would be noticed whether they attended the revival. These efforts, combined with Finney's masterful sermons and hopeful message, brought hundreds of people into the church who had not come before and reclaimed many who had strayed. All the Protestant denominations worked together, setting aside for a while their doctrinal differences.

Such a powerful revival seemed evidence to many people that America could be changed by faith. As they watched saloons shut down, families brought together, and shops and stores closed while the revival was in progress, it appeared that the way was being prepared for God's kingdom on earth. If the United States could be adequately reformed, these people believed, the day of redemption could be hastened. It was up to Americans themselves to purge their country of sin, to make themselves better, and then to help others see the way as well. Such faith bred a demand for immediate reforms.

The Birth of Mormonism

Like many other American families of these years, that of **Joseph Smith** could not find a secure place. His father, who dreamed of bringing his family out of poverty, moved them from one community to another. Young Joseph, like hundreds of other people in upstate New York, sought his fortune by looking for treasure rumored to have been buried long ago in the mountains; but he also watched with concern for his soul as revivals came and went without his conversion. Smith reported that he felt the presence of an angel, however, who told him "that God had work for me to do, and that my name should be for good and evil among all nations, kindreds, and tongues. He said there was a book hidden, written upon gold plates, giving an account of the former inhabitants of this continent, and the source from which they sprang. He also said that the fullness of the everlasting Gospel was contained in it." Smith claimed that the angel directed him to the location of the sacred writings.

Smith began to transcribe what he had found; sitting in a tent divided by a partition, he read the plates to an assistant on the other side. *The Book of Mormon* took shape, telling of a struggle between the chosen ones and their persecutors, of a promised land reserved for the righteous. North America, the book said, had been visited by Jesus in the distant past, but the people had lost their way and fallen into disputation. Those people had been cursed by God for their sins and marked with dark skins; their descendants were Native Americans, who had forgotten their lost paradise.

After 1830 Joseph Smith and several followers traveled throughout New York selling copies of what they called the "Gold Bible." They were met with hostility virtually everywhere they went, but they slowly gathered converts to their Church of Jesus Christ of Latter-Day Saints. Many of the new members were poor, including some free blacks, but others had considerable resources. The most important converts were two brothers, Brigham and Joseph Young. As the movement gathered momentum, hundreds of people joined the church; entire congregations of churches of other faiths joined the Mormons and contributed everything they owned to the church's common fund. The faithful moved first to Ohio and then to what Smith believed to be the original Eden: Missouri. But other settlers made no secret of their disapproval of the Mormons: they fired shots, threw stones through windows, and burned the crops of the Latter-Day Saints. The Mormons found no peace for the next decade. They were constantly harassed by non-Mormons who feared the growing number of converts and the local economic power that came from the church members' pooled resources and hard work.

| Women at Home and Beyond | Americans looked to the new churches for guidance, but they also turned to families, and especially middle-class women, to create virtuous children and husbands. The lives of these |

middle-class women underwent a dramatic shift, especially in the towns and cities of the Northeast. Bakeries, butcher shops, clothiers, and candlemakers began to offer, more easily and cheaply than ever before, some of the things that women had long labored to produce at home. Schools and academies became more common, providing a place for children to receive education beyond the bounds of the home. Young women from poorer backgrounds came into cities looking for jobs as maids and laundresses, taking away some of the household burden for women well off enough to hire them. Families in towns and cities had fewer children with each passing decade.

As ministers, journalists, and other opinion makers looked at the changing households, they began to articulate an ideal of what has been called "domesticity." Women, they said, should put their minds to higher purposes, nurturing their children in spirit and mind as well as in body. Women would become the moral center of the household, the guardians of good thoughts, clean living, providers of a sense of safety for children and husbands. While the world beyond the household seemed increasingly threatening and disorienting, women could make the home a place of refuge and renewal.

Many middle-class women welcomed this message and this mission, which fit well with their own experiences and their own aspirations. In a time when public life made almost no provisions for female participation and when women found virtually no well-paying jobs open to them, the elevation of the home promised an elevation of women's role. Men believed what they said: they thought women naturally better than themselves—more moral and feeling, more intuitive and spiritual. Men worried about the coarseness and callousness of the tumultuous marketplace even as they enjoyed the sense of freedom, excitement, and possibility that it offered.

Domesticity asked something of men as well. If the home were to be a haven, the center of society, men would have to make a greater investment in those homes than had their fathers. Men needed to acknowledge the feelings of their wives more, speaking in tones of respect and affection, respecting their wishes about sex and children. Fathers were expected to spend more time with their children, providing a firm male model to accompany the softer nurture of their wives. Drinking and cursing had no place in the home.

This ideal, however, remained beyond the reach of many Americans. Women who had to work for others all day had little time to devote to their own families, and men who could not be certain of their next day's wages could not afford to keep children out of the work force into their late teens. Slave families struggled to stay together in any way they could. Nevertheless, this middle-class ideal was elaborated and celebrated in print and sermons across the growing young nation.

An Eruption of Reform Movements The same Americans who promoted the Christian middle-class home as their ideal looked to other institutions and reforms in the 1820s to help remake American society. They sought to extend the ideals of character, self-control, and education to those who seemed to fall beyond the good effects of family and household. They worried about hungry children, desperate fathers, and distraught mothers. They noticed increasing numbers of women selling themselves on the city streets. They decried bulging jails and streets full of people without homes.

Groups of reform-minded people mobilized themselves to counter these problems. Some of their efforts grew out of the churches, while others grew out of the ideals of the American Revolution and the marketplace. The American Bible Society launched an ambitious drive to put Bibles in every American home, pioneering steam presses and national systems of distribution, and ultimately issuing over 32 million Bibles.

The American Sunday School Union wrote and published materials for children to be used in Sunday schools across the country. Those schools, although based in churches, taught reading and writing as well as religion. The American Tract Society, which was formed in 1825, produced millions of short inspirational pamphlets to reach those who might not set foot in a church or pick up a Bible. The new organizations prided themselves on being national in reach, extending to the Northwest and Southwest, knitting Americans together with a common faith. They preached nothing controversial, claiming only to spread the good news of the Protestant Christian faith. They depended on the hard work of women, who filled the membership rolls and helped raise funds.

Reformers created a new kind of institution—the "penitentiary"—in these years for those apparently most in need of reform: criminals. In a penitentiary, unlike a common jail, criminals would be locked in individual cells, free from the contamination of others, alone with their consciences and the Bible. There, reflecting on their crimes, they would become "penitent" and would emerge as better people. They would undergo some of the moral nurture they had obviously missed as children and would be ready to take their place in the economy of wages, self-discipline, and delayed gratification growing in the

United States. Americans were proud of their penitentiaries, among the first in the world, holding them up as examples of what the enlightened new nation could do.

Alongside penitentiaries, asylums for the deaf and blind, for the insane, for orphans, and for the poor began to appear in the 1820s, replacing more informal kinds of care. **Dorothea Dix** became famous throughout the United States for her often lonely crusade on behalf of people otherwise forgotten. Dix lobbied ceaselessly for the construction of cleaner, healthier, and more hopeful kinds of institutions for those who could not care for themselves. Each institution placed its faith in strict order, moral teaching, and faith in the inherent goodness of human nature.

Abolitionism

Two hundred antislavery societies emerged in the early 1830s. Ground that had been prepared by the evangelical crusades of the preceding few years proved fertile for the antislavery cause. Some northern church members argued that it was the duty of good Christians to cast out slaveholders and work for immediate emancipation, to use the enormous power of the church as a force for freedom. These "immediatists" called for slaveholders to recognize the truth of what the abolitionists were saying, to free their slaves immediately, hire them as free workers, and help repay the former slaves for their years of unpaid toil. These early abolitionists hoped to convert slaveholders by persuasion and prayer, by church and newspaper—not by law and force.

DOING HISTORY ONLINE

Newspapers

African Americans began publishing a newspaper in 1827 and the Cherokees did so in 1828. Just over a decade later, women working in New England factories started a number of papers, such as the *Factory Girl*, the *Voice of Industry*, the *Wampanoag and Operatives' Journal*, and the *Lowell Offering*. Based on Documents 2, 3, and 12, why did these groups turn to newsprint?

 www.cengage.com/
history/ayers/
ampassages4e

In the late 1820s, **William Lloyd Garrison**, the young editor of a prohibition newspaper, attended antislavery meetings held by African Americans, including the group that published the first antislavery newspaper, *Freedom's Journal*. Garrison suddenly saw the limitations of the colonization movement as he witnessed the passion of people such as David Walker. In 1831, the balding and bespectacled young Garrison launched a paper of his own: *The Liberator*. It called for the immediate start toward emancipation, explicitly rejecting colonization. In its first year, the paper had only six subscribers, but it had acquired fifty-three, most of them African American, by the following year. "I *will* be as harsh as truth," Garrison announced, "and as uncompromising as justice. On this subject, I do not wish to think, speak, or write, with moderation. . . . I am earnest—I will not equivocate—I will not excuse—I will not retreat a single inch—AND I WILL BE HEARD." He was. *The Liberator* spread the news of abolition to many whites who had never seen a newspaper edited by black people. Ironically, Garrison's argument was spread even further by newspaper editors who denounced him.

The American Anti-Slavery Society formed in Philadelphia in 1833. Looking to the example of Great Britain, where the major denominations supported the antislavery movement that was at that moment triumphing over slavery in the British West Indies, the members of the society expected American church leaders to take the lead against American slavery. The North would have to be converted before it could expect the South to follow. To convert the North, antislavery organizations held out the prospect of a free South, where 2 million freed slaves would constitute an "immense market" for the products of Northern "mechanics and manufacturers." These abolitionists expected the former slaves to remain in the South; they spoke little of the competition the freed people might provide to the workers of the North. Similarly, the antislavery people believed a free South would prosper, with planters and free whites flourishing as they had never before; the South, they claimed, would "exhibit the flush of returning health, and feel a stronger pulse, and draw a freer breath."

The antislavery organizations proved volatile inside as well as out. Far more than any other organizations in the United States at this time, the antislavery cause brought together male and female, black and white, patrician and working class, Quaker and Unitarian, Baptist and Methodist, radical and moderate, political and antipolitical people. Each of these groups had its own vision of how the abolitionists should spend their energies and influence. Black abolitionists, in particular, wanted the

(The Library Company of Philadelphia)

SLAVERY AND THE SLAVE TRADE AT THE NATION'S CAPITAL.

HAIL COLUMBIA!!

View of the Capitol at Washington.

One would think that slavery and the slave trade were the last things to have a legal and protected existence in the capital of a boasted free nation. But there they are—unpaid toil, whips, chains, dungeons, separations, murders, and all!

The Slave Trade and the Capitol. *Abolitionists pointed to the irony of the slave trade taking place within sight of the U.S. capitol, the symbol of "a boasted free nation."*

organizations to do more to help black communities in the North. Black women such as Maria W. Stewart published pamphlets that cried out that it "is of no use for us to wait any longer for a generation of well educated men to arise. . . . Let every colored man throughout the United States, who possesses the spirit and principles of a man, sign a petition to Congress, to abolish slavery in the District of Columbia, and grant you the rights and privileges of common free citizens."

The antislavery societies used pamphlets, leaflets, and other literature as their major weapons. Rapid innovations in printing lowered the cost of producing such materials, which flooded post offices and streets. The postal campaign reached its peak in 1834 and 1835, when a million pieces went out through the mail, much of it to the South, where the abolitionists hoped to appeal directly to ministers and others who might be willing to listen to their pleas. That literature, white southerners furiously protested, virtually invited slaves to follow Nat Turner's example. Georgia slaveholders offered a $12,000 reward for the capture of wealthy merchant Arthur Tappan, who, along with his brother Lewis, funded much of the postal campaign against slavery. Arthur received a slave's severed ear in the mail. Mobs in Charleston seized sacks of mail from northern cities and burned them in the streets.

The pamphlets infuriated people in much of the North as well. Mobs, led by some of the wealthiest merchants of northern towns but constituted in large part by white working people, rose up violently against the abolitionists. In 1835 mobs destroyed the home of African Americans, pelted antislavery speakers, and dragged William Lloyd Garrison through the streets of Boston at the end of a rope. The leaders of that mob announced that they had assaulted Garrison "to assure our brethren of the South that we cherish rational and correct notions on the subject of slavery." Many white northerners believed the abolitionists to be hypocrites who cared nothing for the United States and everything for their own sanctimonious souls. Antislavery speakers risked a mob every time they spoke; one man counted over 150 attacks made on him. Abolitionists' churches were blown up and their school buildings dragged into swamps.

The persecution, ironically, strengthened the abolitionist cause. Denunciation and harassment only made the abolitionists more certain of the need for their efforts, of the moral decay caused by slavery. The two hundred antislavery societies of 1835 grew to more than five hundred in 1836. The reformers flooded Congress with petitions calling for the end of slavery in the District of Columbia, sending more than three hundred petitions signed by forty thousand people. The acceptance of these petitions by the House, southerners argued, besmirched slaveholders' honor and threatened to incite slaves to rebellion; the southerners said the petitions should be rejected out of hand. Congress sought to avoid conflict by merely tabling the petitions, but the compromise pleased no one.

Over the next decade, northerners of even a mild antislavery bent chafed at this **gag rule**, which they saw as a clear violation of American freedom in the interests of slavery. Former President John Quincy Adams fought back in 1837 by attempting to present a petition from twenty-two slaves. Representatives from Georgia and Alabama demanded that Adams be expelled and the petition "taken from the House and burnt or the southern states would withdraw from the House." In their fury to squelch any petitions to Congress on the subject of slavery, southern representatives failed to notice that the petition from the slaves did not advocate abolition. Angered and embarrassed at Adam's trickery, one Mississippian decried this "outrage that has no parallel in parliamentary history" and condemned Adams as one who "rejoiced in the alarm and excitement he occasions like the midnight incendiary who fires the dwelling of his enemy, and listens with pleasure to the screams of his burning victims."

CONCLUSION

Few other peacetime eras in American history have seen greater changes than the years between 1829 and 1836. The seeds for many of the major events of the next several generations were planted during these years. Westward migration and an increasingly complex economy and society changed the nature of everyday life.

The political system, feeling its way during the first generations of nationhood, aligned into the forms it would follow into the twenty-first century: highly mobilized and antagonistic parties that extended their reach into every community in the nation. Andrew Jackson solidified the Democrats around his power, patronage, and popular appeal. His embrace of the spoils system gave political identity a concrete and immediate meaning for the thousands of officeholders across the United States. His defeat of the Bank of the United States showed what a determined president could do with the authority of his office.

Native Americans, who had struggled for more than two centuries with the consequences of European colonization and growth, were finally driven from their ancestral lands in the early 1830s. Andrew Jackson, dedicated to expanding opportunity for white men, oversaw the forced removal of many thousands of Creeks, Choctaws, Cherokees, and Chickasaws to reservations on the western side of the Mississippi River. Since much of this land lay in the South, this displacement also opened the way for the spread of plantation slavery to some of the richest lands in North America.

African Americans, who had glimpsed freedom during the era of the American Revolution and its afterglow, saw their hopes diminish in the wake of increased surveillance and repression following Nat Turner's rebellion in Virginia and the frantic expansion of slave-based plantations throughout the Gulf States. The Virginia legislature walked to the brink of emancipation in the early 1830s, only to pull back at the last minute.

Determined and purposeful, African Americans launched a campaign to begin the immediate end of slavery. Starting within free black communities, these men and women organized themselves to denounce colonization to Africa and to demand that the United States embrace their black residents as full citizens and as full participants in American life. David Walker's *Appeal* electrified those who read it—and those who read it included enslaved men and women all along the Atlantic seaboard.

William Lloyd Garrison of Boston, hearing and understanding the new black message of immediate emancipation—abolition—threw himself into the crusade for African American freedom. White southerners and others opposed to his challenge to slavery gave Garrison a wide notoriety and helped galvanize other supporters for abolitionism.

Abolitionism found a ready audience in part because Christian Americans, who had seen their churches dislocated by the churning movement of the young nation's population in the decades after the Revolution, experienced a rebirth. With revivals emerging across the United States, Christians felt themselves, their communities, and their nation prepared to help bring forth a more nearly perfect society. While some focused on alcohol and others on spreading the word through distributing Bibles, others decided to focus on what they considered the worst American sin: slavery.

The slave states, faced with this new opposition, struggled to define their relationship to the federal government so that local power would not be diminished. South Carolina, the most unified slave state, defied federal power in the nullification crisis, focusing on the issue of the tariff to test the boundaries of authority. Under Andrew Jackson's strong leadership, the federal government stared South Carolina down and made it clear that efforts to defy the power of Washington would bring sharp consequences.

But the slave states, under attack from enslaved people, abolitionists, and President Jackson, provoked another kind of victory. The United States sided with American insurrectionists who sought to take Texas from Mexico. Southern slaveholders viewed Texas jealously and coveted the rich lands of the Mexican province. The conflict they started would soon grow into a full-fledged war.

CHAPTER REVIEW 1829–1836

- Andrew Jackson became the most active president the United States had yet seen.
- Slaves were involved in revolts in South Carolina and Virginia.
- Slavery generated a debate over nullification in South Carolina and wide-ranging debate over the future of the institution in Virginia.
- The Bank of the United States became a major focus of political conflict.
- President Jackson led a determined and successful effort to remove eastern Native Americans to west of the Mississippi River.
- The Second Great Awakening shook the nation.
- A movement for the immediate abolition of slavery emerged in the North.

◀▌▌▌ Looking Back

Chapter 10 describes a series of dramatic changes that burst on the American scene during the early 1830s. During these years the forces of democracy came into direct conflict with the forces of slavery.

1. Why did the U.S. government finally decide to remove Native Americans from the eastern part of the country after they had lived alongside whites for so many generations?
2. Why did the abolitionist movement suddenly come into prominence, when white Americans had lived with slavery for so long?
3. Why did so many people, both male and female, look to women as the moral guardians of American society? How could the idea of the moral superiority of women both improve and hinder women's public roles? Their private lives?

Looking Ahead ▌▌▌▶

Chapter 11 shows that the two-party system would prove to be a permanent part of the United States. It came into being by accident and at first had little to do with the major problem that would face the nation over the next two generations: the place of slavery in America.

1. What would be the consequences of having political power exercised by two distinct and highly mobilized parties in every county in the United States?
2. What could be done to slow the spread of slavery without abolishing it?

Go to the American Passages website at www.cengage.com/history/ayers/ ampassages4e for additional review materials.

Panic and Boom, 1837–1845

In 1837, the largest financial panic and depression the nation had ever experienced descended on the United States. The hard times shaped reform, literature, politics, slavery, and foreign policy. The hard times in the East drove westward expansion. These were the years in which the mass migration to the Pacific began, as pioneers pushed across the West to Oregon and California. Politics churned as citizens worried over the consequences of rapid territorial growth.

It was not surprising that economic troubles stimulated political conflict, but the reform spirit also flowered during these hard years. Men and women championed public education, abstinence from alcohol, antislavery, and a host of other improvements to American life. The popular press burgeoned, along with art, photography, and literature. A few leading thinkers articulated a bold and distinctive American philosophy, one that bore the marks of its tumultuous time.

ECONOMIC CRISIS AND INNOVATION

The late 1830s and early 1840s produced a surprising mixture of bad and good economic news. The economy fell into prolonged depression, but at the same time courts and legislatures fostered an environment favorable to business, and inventors and investors plunged ahead despite the failures they saw all around them. In fact, the most important economic development of the entire century, the railroad, emerged from these years of turmoil.

Panic and Depression

Andrew Jackson sought to leave a comfortable legacy to his handpicked successor, **Martin Van Buren**, but within weeks of Van Buren's inauguration, the American economy hit stormy waters. An unprecedented amount of silver poured into American banks in the mid-1830s from abroad, fueling overheated speculation. Britain's economy expanded rapidly, increasing the demand for cotton, encouraging southern planters to buy land and slaves on credit, and boosting foreign investment in American projects such as canals and turnpikes. British investors bought up state bonds and securities, and British exporters offered generous credit to purchase a wide array of manufactured goods. American merchants, land speculators, and state governments indulged in a feast of easy credit and seemingly endless profits.

Unfortunately, poor harvests in Britain disrupted the American economy when British firms, facing a cash shortage at home, demanded repayment of loans at just the time that prices for American cotton declined because of record production and reduced English demand. As a result, a major New Orleans cotton broker failed when it could not make its payments to British banks or pay debts in excess of $1 million. The collapse triggered panic. As a city official noted, "Everybody will fail—all Hell will fail." Desperate merchants and creditors tried to extract cash from debtors, credit evaporated, and thousands lost their jobs.

Despite the role of international trade in bringing on the crisis, many people blamed the problems on Jackson's banking policy, especially the practice of accepting only specie, not paper money, for the purchase of public lands. They looked to Van Buren to lead the repeal of this strategy, but Jackson made it clear to Van Buren that he did not want to see his work undone. Delegations of merchants came to the White House to plead with Van Buren, but to no avail. A run began on the banks: customers withdrew $1 million in specie in only two days in early May. The **Panic of 1837** had begun and soon spread to every city and region of the country.

The panic quickly affected working people as well as the rich. Jobs dried up, and many urban families had no idea of where they would get their next meal. In New York City, a poster warned that "Bread, Meat, Rent, Fuel—Their Prices Must Come Down. The Voice of the People Shall Be Heard, and Will Prevail." Thousands of people gathered for a public meeting in the freezing weather. Told that a nearby warehouse held fifty thousand barrels of flour, the protesters stormed the building; they took what they could and broke open hundreds of barrels. The riots continued for days until the police managed to restore order.

A second panic came in 1839, and the economy suffered until 1843. Labor unions weakened as workers grew afraid to risk their jobs. States' plans to finance canals, roads, and other public projects crashed. Nine states defaulted on the bonds they intended to use to finance those improvements, leading furious European investors to shun American investments. Governors and legislators found themselves under attack from voters angry that the states had permitted themselves to go so far into debt.

Van Buren admitted that allowing state banks to hold federal funds had apparently fueled the speculation, but he would not even consider reinstating a national bank. Instead he proposed what came to be known as the Sub-Treasury Plan or the Independent Treasury Plan. In that system, public funds would be disbursed by the secretary of the treasury as the economy seemed to dictate, and banks would be kept out of the picture. It would be two more years before the plan passed, but by then it could not do the country, the Democrats, or Martin Van Buren much good. The Whigs quickly won state-level offices and looked forward to harvesting more.

 This icon will direct you to interactive activities and study materials on the American Passages website: www.cengage.com/history/ayers/ampassages4e

CHAPTER TIMELINE

1837	Financial panic • Charles River Bridge v. Warren Bridge decision • Grimké sisters lecture to mixed audiences • Elijah P. Lovejoy murdered in Alton, Illinois • Horace Mann becomes first secretary of Massachusetts State Board of Education • Ralph Waldo Emerson, "The American Scholar"
1838	John Quincy Adams successfully defeats attempt to annex Texas
1839	Depression worsens • Daguerreotypes introduced to the United States
1840	Congress passes Independent Treasury Act • Harrison elected president • Frederick Douglass escapes from slavery • American Antislavery Society splits • Washingtonian temperance movement emerges • James G. Birney runs for president as candidate for Liberty party
1841	Harrison dies; John Tyler becomes president • Brook Farm founded • California sees arrival of first wagon train • Oregon fever • P. T. Barnum opens the American Museum • Amistad case heard before the Supreme Court
1842	Edgar Allan Poe, "The Murders in the Rue Morgue"
1843	Oregon sees arrival of first wagon trains
1844	Methodist Episcopal church divides over slavery • James K. Polk claims the United States's claim to "all Oregon" • Baltimore-Washington telegraph line • Samuel F. B. Morse patents the telegraph • Edgar Allan Poe, "The Raven"
1845	Texas and Florida admitted to the Union • Baptist church divides over slavery

The *Charles River Bridge* Case, 1837   Even as the panic unfolded, some basic issues raised by the economic changes worked their way through the American court system. American law still embodied many assumptions from the centuries before corporations and far-flung economic enterprises challenged local power.

The Charles River Bridge of Boston, for example, had been granted a franchise by the state legislature in 1785, and the owners of the bridge charged a toll for everyone who crossed. As the population of Boston and Charlestown grew rapidly, so did the traffic and the tolls on the bridge. The bridge, which had cost about $70,000 to build and improve, was bringing in $30,000 a year by the late 1820s. Another bridge also chartered by the state, the Warren Bridge, went up across the Charles, only 260 feet away. No sooner was the new bridge built than the traffic on the older bridge declined by more than half. The managers of the Charles River Bridge sued in court, claiming that their original charter implied a monopoly that the state had violated by building a competing bridge. Throughout the 1830s, *Charles River Bridge v. Warren Bridge* proceeded to the U.S. Supreme Court and was heard in 1837.

The chief justice of the Supreme Court, Roger B. Taney, shared the Jacksonian animosity against monopolies. His decision in the **Charles River Bridge case** held that a state charter did not imply monopoly. Should old charters be permitted to hinder modern improvements, the country "would be obliged to stand still." The charters had perhaps been necessary in the past, he admitted, but by the 1830s, such props no longer seemed necessary to attract capital investment. Taney's decision in the *Charles River Bridge* case reflected a growing consensus among Democrats and Whigs that older forms of economic privilege had to make way for innovation and investment.

Railroads

By the 1830s, Americans had devised several means for dealing with the vast spaces of their continent. Thousands of miles of canals cut across the East, and steamboats plied the waters of the North and South. Such means of transport, while cheap and dependable, remained relatively slow and limited in their reach. Inland cities longed for fast overland connections with the outside world, and they knew of experiments with railroads in England and the United States over the past decade. When New Jersey sponsored a bold rail and canal connection between New York and Philadelphia in 1831, it ordered a custom-built locomotive from an English company: the John Bull. The railroad became an immediate success, carrying more than 100,000 passengers in 1834. Ralph Waldo Emerson rode an early train and marveled that "men & trees & barns whiz by you as fast as the leaves of a dictionary."

By 1841, ten American railroad shops had opened to meet the growing demand. Those shops soon began changing the English designs, making the engines more powerful and the rails cheaper. Railroad companies quickly grew into some of the largest and most complex American businesses. Employing hundreds of people, they pioneered management and engineering innovations.

Railroads almost immediately became the key form of transportation in the United States. Rail transport grew cheaper as the network expanded, and trains could run when canals had frozen over. By 1840, American companies and states had spent $75 million to build thirty-three hundred miles of track, surpassing Great Britain; by 1850, the country claimed nearly nine thousand miles of railroad. New industries rose to serve the trains as iron, coal, and steel manufacturing burgeoned with the railroads' demand. The railroads consumed enormous amounts of wood for their ties, trestles, and boilers.

Railroads appeared in every region of the United States but not in a uniform network. Beginning from many different entrepreneurial efforts and adapting to widely

(The First Railroad Train on the Mohawk and Hudson Road, E. L. Henry, Albany Institute of History & Art)

Early Locomotive. *This locomotive in New York State, like its other early counterparts, pulled passenger cars based on old-fashioned carriages. The technology evolved quickly in the 1840s, however, and the United States played an important role in that evolution.*

varying terrain, railroads did not adapt a standard distance between the rails (the gauge). As a result, trains could not travel rapidly across the nation; cargo had to be unloaded and reloaded. Trains connected coastal cities with inland plantations and farms in the South, while in the North and West, railroads ran from city to city, knitting together a network of economic development that benefited a wider area. In this way, railroads accelerated the growth of differences between the South and the rest of the country.

Telegraph poles marched alongside the railroads, their wires carrying news of train locations on single-track lines and preventing gruesome crashes while also speeding the flow of information just as the railroads sped the flow of people and goods. Like the locomotive, the telegraph was the product of inventors in several countries, but it received a major impetus from America. **Samuel F. B. Morse** patented his version of the electronic telegraph in 1840. Morse struggled with the invention for more than ten years, devising the code of dots and dashes that bears his name, as well as devising ways to make the current travel farther. In 1842, he received $30,000 from Congress to run an experimental line from Washington to Baltimore. Following its success, the telegraph spread across the country with great speed. In the four years after its initial test in 1844, more than five thousand miles of wire had been strung, with another three thousand under construction.

LIFE IN THE NEW SLAVE SOUTH

The South, increasingly dominated by slavery, remained an integral part of the United States. Southern cotton drove national economic growth, and southern politicians controlled much of the nation's government. The South was a prosperous place for white people, whose average per capita incomes exceeded those of almost every other society in the world and were catching up to those in the North.

Thanks to the rapid expansion of newspapers and the telegraph, white southerners took part in all the national conversations about race, slavery, and politics. As northerners and southerners read the critical words often aimed across the Mason-Dixon line, though, distrust between the regions grew. The single profound difference between the North and South, slavery, became ever more significant as it grew ever stronger.

African Americans and the South   By the 1830s, slavery had spread over an area stretching from Maryland to Texas. The domestic slave trade expanded at a feverish rate during the decade as the new planters of Mississippi, Alabama, and Louisiana eagerly imported slaves to clear land and plant cotton. American slavery became ever more diverse as it expanded. Enslaved people worked in hemp, wheat, rice, corn, sugar, and tobacco fields, as well as cotton fields. They worked with livestock and racehorses, practiced trades such as carpentry and blacksmithing, and labored in factories and on the docks and in the shipyards of southern ports. Some knew the white people among whom they lived quite well; others belonged to absolute strangers. Some worked in large groups of black people; others worked alone or beside whites.

Southern culture mixed English, African, Scots-Irish, Caribbean, French, Indian, and Hispanic influences into a rich and complex blend. Language, food, music, and religion took on new shapes as black and white cultures interacted. In the meantime,

Paths of the Slave Trade

The slave trade grew into a vast business in the years before the Civil War. Many people, including those who did not own slaves themselves, made their livings from supplying slave traders with food, shelter, transportation, insurance, and banking. As Map 11.1 shows, the trade ran strongly from the Upper South to the Lower South, from east to west.

Although slavery remained firmly entrenched in states such as Virginia, Kentucky, and North Carolina, the demand for slave labor was so strong in the new plantation districts of Alabama, Mississippi, and Louisiana that slaveholders sold off "surplus" slaves to the traders who came through their counties each year. Traders gathered slaves in the cities of the Chesapeake, especially Alexandria, Virginia, to ship them around the Florida Keys to New Orleans and other ports on the Gulf Coast. Meanwhile, other slaves were sold "down the river" from places close to the border with the North to the plantations surrounding Vicksburg, Natchez, and Baton Rouge. Other slaves were forced to walk or take trains across the middle of the South. Throughout this period, even more slaves were bought and sold within states, being moved from one county to another in ways that do not appear on this disheartening map.

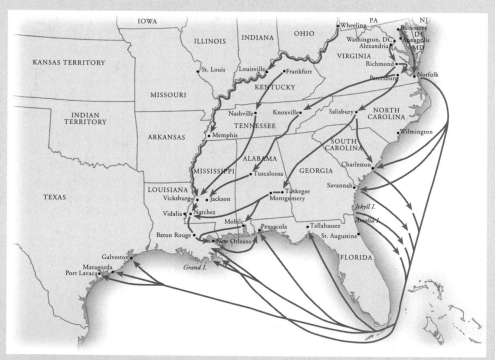

MAP 11.1 Paths of the Slave Trade, 1840–1860.

FIGURE 11.1 Patterns of Black Population in the South. *Most black people lived on large plantations with more than ten other enslaved people, even while others were scattered on much smaller farms and in towns and cities.*

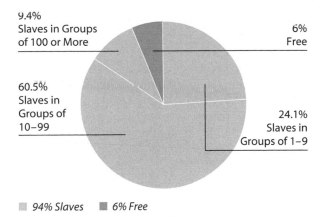

9.4%
Slaves in Groups of 100 or More

6%
Free

60.5%
Slaves in Groups of 10–99

24.1%
Slaves in Groups of 1–9

▨ *94% Slaves* ▪ *6% Free*

African Americans prided themselves on the stories, songs, and dances they knew to be particularly their own; on the styles of the baskets, quilts, and clothes they sewed; and on the way they carried themselves. Black culture remained distinct and vibrant, even as it influenced the larger American culture.

African American families, often split apart by sale, tended to rely on a broader range of kin than did white families. Grandparents, aunts, and uncles often played significant roles in child rearing in black families. When people of blood relation were unavailable, southern slaves created "fictive kin," friends and neighbors given honorary titles of "brother" or "aunt" and treated as relatives. These arrangements permitted slave families considerable resiliency and variety. African Americans often found wives or husbands on nearby farms, visiting one another on evenings and weekends.

Plantations and Farms

Most slave owners in the American South lived on the same farms as their slaves, but wealthier owners, particularly those from the unhealthy regions of the Gulf and Atlantic coasts, put day-to-day control of their plantations in the hands of professional overseers. These overseers were often ambitious young men of middling background who used the position as a steppingstone to purchasing their own plantations. Slaves could and did appeal to their owners if they thought the overseers unfair. Since a master might trust a well-known slave more than a new overseer, the overseer's position involved tact as well as brute force.

On larger plantations, where slaves often worked in groups called gangs, trusted male slaves served as "drivers." Such drivers tended to be especially strong and skilled, commanding respect from whites as well as blacks. Although whites held the ultimate threat of force, they much preferred to keep the work moving smoothly, minimizing both potential conflict and their own exposure to heat and weather. The driver could help both sides, protecting fellow slaves from abuse and ensuring that the work got done efficiently. Drivers frequently found themselves caught between the two competing sets of demands, however, and slaves often resented or even hated drivers.

Slavery and Industrialization

The 1830s and 1840s saw not only the spread of agricultural slavery, but also efforts by proslavery advocates to adapt slavery to southern industrial enterprise. In Richmond, Virginia, slaves worked in flour mills and tobacco-processing factories. Joseph Reid Anderson experimented with slave labor at Richmond's Tredegar Ironworks, pictured here, one of the foremost industrial enterprises in the South. "Eventually all iron establishments in a slave state must come to the employment of slaves," he predicted confidently. Far from dying out, as many drafters of the Constitution had hoped it would, slavery proved to be remarkably adaptable to the demands of a modernizing economy.

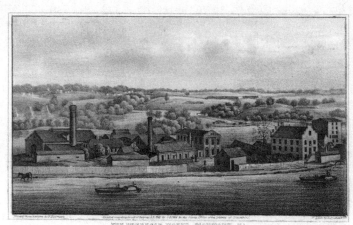

THE TREDEGAR WORKS, RICHMOND, VA.

(Boston Athenaeum)

About three out of four enslaved people were field hands, though almost all enslaved people went to the fields during the peak times. Women and men also served in white households as cooks and domestics. Slaves were well known for controlling the pace of work, reporting their tools broken or "lost" when they were forced to work too fast or too long. They traditionally had Sundays to garden for themselves, do their domestic chores, or hunt.

Slaves' lives were by no means simple. Lines of power often became complicated and tangled on plantations and farms, with slave owners, their children, overseers, and drivers claiming authority. Slaves tended to work at several different jobs over the course of the year. Some slaves were respected as purveyors of healing or religious knowledge from Africa; some were admired for their musical ability; others won recognition for their ability to read and preach the Gospel. These abilities did not always correspond with the opinions of whites, who frequently underestimated the abilities and character of the people among whom they lived.

Whites told themselves that they provided "their people" a better life than they would have known in Africa. Indeed, southern masters explained the justice of slavery to themselves and to the North by stressing their Christian stewardship for the slaves. As one clergyman wrote to his fellow slaveholders in the early 1840s, slaves "were placed under our control . . . not exclusively for our benefit but theirs also."

Most masters would not permit their slaves to learn to read, but they did arrange to have Bible selections read to their slaves. Although many slaves eagerly accepted the Gospel in the white-dominated churches, others resented the obvious and shallow uses the masters made of the sermons, telling the slaves to accept their lot and refrain from stealing food. Such slaves displayed their deepest religious feelings only in their own worship, in secret meetings in brush arbors and cabins in the slave quarters.

Largely oblivious to the lives their slaves led beyond their sight, masters pointed to the physical condition of the slaves as evidence of their concern. Compared with slaves elsewhere in the hemisphere, it was true that those of the American South were relatively healthy. Although they lived with monotonous diets, ineffective or dangerous health care, continual fear of violence and sale, small and drafty houses, and rough clothing, they managed to survive.

Many slave owners did not refrain from having their slaves whipped on small provocation, branded, shackled, or locked up in sweltering enclosures; female slaves especially suffered sexual abuse. Partly because expectant mothers were often kept in the fields until labor began, about a third of all black babies died before they reached their first birthday. American slavery was a harsh institution.

The Politics of the White South   White men in the South took their politics seriously and built much of it around slavery. America's commitment to slavery was grounded in a cold social and economic calculus. In southern cities such as Natchez, Mississippi, whites enjoyed among the highest per capita incomes in the nation, the finest homes, and access to music, theater, and public entertainment that rivaled any city in the country. In the South as in the North, the Whigs portrayed themselves as the party of progress and prosperity, appealing to lawyers, editors, and merchants, as well as to large planters on the richest lands and farmers in the mountains of the Upper South who wanted to expand connections to outside markets.

The Democrats found their strongest supporters among the middling farmers and aspiring planters of the South. These men tended to resent taxes on their lands and slaves. They admired the Democrats' aggressive approach to western expansion and removing the American Indians. Southerners distrustful of northern reformers and financial speculators found the small-government pronouncements of the Democrats appealing.

In the South, both the Whigs and the Democrats declared themselves the friends of southern slavery, but they differed in their emphases. Democrats pledged that they would protect slavery by extending the power of the federal government as little as possible. Whigs argued that the best way to protect slavery was for the South to develop its region's economy and build strong economic and political bridges to the North and Europe.

REFORM TAKES ROOT

The wild economic swings of the 1830s, added to religious reform impulses, further drove Americans to improve their society. They could see dangers all around them, but they could also glimpse how things could be better. The news machinery of railroads, telegraphs, and printing presses held out exciting new possibilities for spreading reforms to wider audiences than ever before.

Some Americans took practical routes to progress, focusing their efforts on schools and the prohibition of alcohol, whereas others explored philosophy and literature. Some used the new printing machinery of the age for entertainment, whereas others turned it to the fight against social evils.

Public Schools   Many Americans had become dissatisfied with the way young people were schooled. No state had a statewide school system, and local districts ran their own affairs, often wretchedly. The rich attended private schools or employed tutors, whereas the parents of poorer children had to sign oaths declaring themselves "paupers" before their children could benefit from charity schools. Parents from the middle classes, charged a fee according to the number of children they had, sent their offspring to schools often taught by untrained teachers. Hundreds of districts, especially in the South and West, created no schools at all. Many American children never went to school in the 1820s and 1830s, and those who did often attended for only a short time, interrupted by the demands of family and farm.

Reformers argued that unequal and inadequate education would not suffice in America, a country dependent on an informed democracy. These reformers wanted free schools. Taxes and other state support would make it possible for all children to go to public schools. The rich would be more likely to send their children to such schools, reformers reasoned, if their tax dollars were supporting them; the poor would be more likely to send their children if they were not stigmatized as paupers. Buildings and teachers could be improved with the increased support.

A Massachusetts lawyer and Whig politician, **Horace Mann** worked relentlessly to make rich citizens, especially manufacturers, see that a tax in support of schools was a wise investment. Think how much better workers would be, he argued, if they could read and calculate. Think to what good use women could be put as teachers, he argued, instilling future citizens with their virtues of cooperation and peacefulness. Mann gradually persuaded influential people in Massachusetts of the practicability of common schools. In 1837, he became the first secretary of the Massachusetts Board of Education.

When Mann took over, many schools were in session for only a couple of months a year. He transformed that system during his tenure. The minimum school year stretched to six months, buildings and teacher training improved significantly, and teachers' pay increased by more than half.

Women teachers became common in the Northeast and Midwest. Females attended new "normal schools" that provided teacher training; they read educational journals, received professional supervision, and taught with uniform textbooks. These standards spread throughout the North and West in the 1840s and 1850s, as did McGuffey's Readers. These books, which sold an astonishing 9 million copies between 1836 and 1850, celebrated Christian piety, the virtues of hard work, and patriotism.

The Dangers of Drink

In this popular image, viewers could trace the devastating effects of drinking on a young man and his family. Everyone knew the excuses people told themselves about drinking. At first, in the lower left corner, the very young man shares a drink with a friend. He then proceeds to make weak excuses, such as drinking to "keep the cold out." From there, it is a short step to losing control, having "a drink too much," and becoming "riotous." At the "summit," the star of the story has become a "confirmed drunkard," wasting his life with equally drunken friends. His drinking leads quickly to poverty and then to desperate crime in order to support the habit. Finally, despairing, he turns to suicide as the only way out. Meanwhile, an abandoned wife and child, homeless, suffer on their way to the poorhouse. This was America's first war on drugs, and it struck many of the same themes as those of later crusades.

(Library of Congress)

The Washingtonians Americans had long waged campaigns against intemperance, but the fight against drink took on a new urgency in the depression years of the late 1830s and early 1840s. Many people, religious and otherwise, saw alcohol as the scourge of American life. Men drank at work, farmers routinely turned their surplus grain into whiskey, and rum was a major part of New England commerce. Americans aged fifteen or older consumed an annual average of forty gallons of beer, spirits, and wine per capita.

The **Washingtonian temperance movement**, named in honor of George Washington, gave great force and visibility to a crusade against alcohol. Whereas earlier temperance movements had mainly enlisted those who were already opposed to alcohol, the new movement marked an effort by drinkers to reform themselves. Older reform attempts had been largely the efforts of men, but now women became active.

The Washingtonians began in Baltimore in 1840, when six drinkers pledged to one another to quit drinking and persuade other drinkers to do the same. Word of the new movement quickly spread up the eastern seaboard, and by 1843 the Washingtonians claimed millions of adherents. Unlike earlier temperance efforts led by upper-class or religious leaders, Washingtonians prided themselves on an egalitarian ethos. Partly as a result of the new organization and partly from the growing stigma attached to drunkenness, Americans' consumption of alcohol plummeted in the 1840s.

Women's "Martha Washington" societies grew rapidly, challenging the men's movement in both size and in fervor. These female temperance advocates were not well-to-do ladies stooping to help the fallen, but rather the wives of artisans and small businessmen. They helped families in distress get back on their feet. They also provided a new edge to the temperance crusade, reminding men that drunkenness was more often than not a male failing and that it was the wives and children of drunkards who suffered most from their neglect, cruelty, and financial irresponsibility. Where a farm family might weather an alcoholic husband through consumption of their own produce and local bartering, city families needed a man's wages to pay for the rent, fuel, and food necessary for survival.

DOING HISTORY ONLINE

Age of Reform

Historians have long tried to explain the flurry of reform efforts during the 1830s and 1840s. Based on your reading of Documents 5 to 7, 11, and 12 and the textbook, in this and other chapters, what explanation would you offer?

 www.cengage.com/
history/ayers/
ampassages4e

Abolitionism Strengthened and Challenged

By the late 1830s, the American Anti-Slavery Society claimed more than a quarter of a million members, primarily in the Northeast and Midwest. The first female abolitionist speakers, **Angelina and Sarah Grimké**, were prize recruits into the antislavery ranks, for they were the daughters of a prominent South Carolina slave-owning planter. By relating their own own experiences with slavery to New England audiences, the Grimkés held a credibility that white northern abolitionists could not match. In 1837, the Grimkés decided to exert their power in a new forum by lecturing to mixed audiences of men and women. Although some people strenuously objected to such an elevation of women in the public sphere, the Grimkés spoke to more than forty thousand people in nine months in 1837 and 1838. "*All moral beings have essentially the same rights and the same duties,* whether they be male or female," Angelina Grimké admonished an audience. The female slaves of the South, who "now wear the iron yoke of slavery in this land of boasted liberty and law . . . are our countrywomen— *they are our sisters.*"

As it grew stronger, the antislavery cause met with more determined opposition. When abolitionist editor **Elijah P. Lovejoy** offended readers of his religious paper in St. Louis—denouncing a local judge who prevented the trial of a mob who had burned a black man alive—citizens of Alton, Illinois, invited Lovejoy to move to their town.

Alton prided itself on being a progressive place, but soon some prominent members of the community, angered at Lovejoy's paper for its dissemination of "the highly odious doctrines of modern Abolitionism," held a public meeting demanding that he quit printing such ideas. Lovejoy only intensified his attacks on slavery. Mobs destroyed two of his presses and vowed to tar and feather him, but he persisted. A mayoral candidate in Alton whipped a mob to a frenzy to destroy a replacement press as it was offloaded from the train in September. In November 1837, as his fifth press arrived, a battle erupted, and Lovejoy was killed as he and his assistants fought the crowd. The mob shattered his press, and local law officers arrested the defenders of Lovejoy for inciting the violence.

Abolitionists debated the proper response to such opposition. William Lloyd Garrison, editor of the antislavery newspaper *The Liberator,* counseled his allies to offer no resistance to violence. He and his supporters renounced all allegiance to the established parties and churches, which had long since shown themselves tolerant of slavery. Other abolitionists, by contrast, used whatever means they could to bring slavery to an end, including political parties.

The differences among the abolitionists came to a head at the annual meeting of the American Anti-Slavery Society in 1839. They differed most visibly in their attitudes toward the role of women. Women constituted perhaps half of all members of the antislavery organizations, but some male abolitionists sought to keep females in a subordinate role and prevent women members from voting, speaking publicly, or serving on committees with men. Unable to resolve their differences, the abolitionists split. The more conservative group, based in New York, created the **Liberty Party** to run a candidate for president in the upcoming election of 1840. Garrison's organization maintained a more radical stance on the role of women and mocked those who sought "to sustain and propagate those eternal, immutable principles of liberty, justice, and equality" by denying "woman her right as a human being to speak and act with brethren on the anti-slavery platform."

Whatever their differences, abolitionists barraged Congress with petitions demanding that slavery be ended in the District of Columbia. Former President John Quincy Adams, now a congressman from Massachusetts, used all his parliamentary skill to fight the gag rule that prevented Congress from recognizing antislavery petitions; he finally succeeded in getting it overthrown in 1845. Adams also successfully defended Africans who had seized a slave ship, the *Amistad*, bound for Cuba and landed it in Connecticut. Supported by a large network of abolitionists, Adams took the case before the U.S. Supreme Court and in 1841 won not only the acquittal of the Africans for murdering the ship's captain but their freedom as well.

Black antislavery speakers greatly strengthened the antislavery cause. Abolitionists such as Henry Brown, Henry Bibb, Solomon Northup, Sojourner Truth, **Harriet Tubman**, and Ellen Craft electrified audiences. Slavery, they made clear, was nothing like the benign institution portrayed by its defenders. Public speakers such as Henry Highland Garnet urged listeners to "strike for your lives and liberties. Let every slave throughout the land do this, and the days of slavery are numbered. Rather die freemen than live to be slaves. Remember that you are FOUR MILLIONS! . . . Let your motto be resistance! resistance! RESISTANCE!"

Although white abolitionists valued the contributions of their black compatriots, they urged black speakers not to make too much of a fuss when confronted with the insults and indignities black people faced in the North African American abolitionists chafed under the restrictions they faced from fellow reformers and enemies alike; they demanded greater rights for northern as well as southern blacks. Their experiences showed the extent to which race was a national problem.

One of the most remarkable Americans of the nineteenth century burst into visibility in the early 1840s. **Frederick Douglass** had grown up in Maryland. Like other places in the Upper South, Maryland's economy was diversifying in the 1830s and 1840s as commerce intensified and railroads spread. Douglass learned to read from his mistress, though it was against the law for her to teach him. He carried with him a copy of Webster's *Spelling Book* and *The Columbian Orator,* a book of speeches, including a slave's persuasive argument with his master to set him free.

Sent to Baltimore by his owner, Douglass worked in the shipyards, continued to read widely, and plotted his escape to freedom. After several attempts, Douglass finally borrowed the papers of a free black sailor and rode a train to freedom in 1840. Douglass found himself in New York City, alone and without any notion of what he should do. A runaway slave might be hunted down by a slave catcher for a reward. Fortunately for Douglass, he met a black man who introduced the young runaway to the New York Anti-Slavery Society. After white abolitionists saw the skill with which he spoke, they sent Douglass to lecture throughout the North with William Lloyd Garrison.

DOING HISTORY ONLINE

Slavery

Read Document 13. Why do you imagine a fugitive slave would correspond with his or her former master? Why might it be risky to contact a former master?

www.cengage.com/ history/ayers/ ampassages4e

DEVELOPMENT OF AN AMERICAN CULTURE

European visitors had long scoffed at the failure of the United States to create anything they considered culture, stimulating defensiveness and resentment among Americans. During the first desperate decades of the nation's experience, filled with war, economic panic, and political conflict, few Americans found opportunity to write novels, produce ambitious paintings, or carve sculptures. But in the 1830s and 1840s, the new country experienced a sudden outburst of creativity in everything from the most elevated philosophy to the most popular amusements.

Transcendentalism, Romanticism, and the American Landscape

Leading thinkers saw the possibilities of improvement everywhere, not just in education or reform. Several of those thinkers came out of Unitarianism, a form of liberal Christianity especially strong in New England. Unitarianism encouraged people to emphasize feeling rather than dogma. Several young people raised within the Unitarian church took these ideas further than their elders intended, rejecting much Christian doctrine. A belief in the literal truth of the Bible, these youthful critics argued, trapped religion in the past. Better to appeal directly to the heart from the very beginning. These thinkers wanted religion to transcend the limits of churches and denominations. In turning to nature for inspiration, they also sought a balance to the dangers and dislocations of American progress.

Women played an active role in the effort to create a tradition of American philosophy, with Margaret Fuller becoming especially important. Fuller, raised in the Unitarian church in Cambridge, Massachusetts, received a fine education. But she felt herself adrift, full of "unemployed force," after her male classmates went on to college. She read widely and taught school with two other important figures in the revolt against Unitarianism: Elizabeth Peabody and Bronson Alcott. These three, like Horace Mann, believed that children were innately good and that education should be designed to let that goodness flourish. They argued that school, like church, should not be permitted to get in the way of people's natural connection with nature and with one another.

They soon took their lead from **Ralph Waldo Emerson,** who had grown up near Concord, Massachusetts. Though descended from a distinguished ministerial family, he was raised by a widowed mother and forced to work his way through Harvard College. Uncomfortable as a minister and dissatisfied as a schoolteacher, Emerson set out for Europe, where he met exciting English intellectuals whose stirring ideas influenced him deeply: Samuel Coleridge, Thomas Carlyle, and William Wordsworth. These writers, caught up in European romanticism with its rejection of the austere logic of the Enlightenment and search for inspiration in nature, provided Emerson with a perspective far removed from the cool Unitarianism on which he had been raised. Emerson perceived humankind as deeply tied to nature, filled with its rhythms and longings. He published such ideas in his first book, *Nature* (1836), which gained him considerable attention from the like-minded young people of New England.

> ### DOING HISTORY ONLINE
>
> Ralph Waldo Emerson on the American Scholar, 1837
>
> Read the excerpted passages from Ralph Waldo Emerson's "The American Scholar" (Document 2) and Horace Mann's report to the Massachusetts Board of Education (Document 7). Why did each consider education so important for all Americans?
>
> www.cengage.com/history/ayers/ampassages4e

But it was Emerson's address before the Phi Beta Kappa initiates at Harvard in 1837 that announced his arrival to a larger audience. Emerson worried over the state of the nation after the panic of 1837. The panic directly touched one of Emerson's friends in Concord, Henry David Thoreau, who graduated from Harvard in the panic year and could find no decent job.

In his speech, "The American Scholar," Emerson argued that the scholar should be a man of action, a man of nature, a man of risk and endeavor. Books and poetry held tremendous power, Emerson admitted, but it was in activity, in striving, that the scholar became truly American. It was time to set the teachings of Europe aside long enough to find America's own voice, Emerson told the graduates.

Echoes of these ideas were also heard in the South. **William Gilmore Simms**, a leading essayist, novelist, poet, and proslavery advocate from South Carolina, lectured and wrote on diverse topics such as "Americanism in Literature" and "The Philosophy of History." Americans anxiously promoted their political and economic independence, Simms wrote, yet "our people have taken too little interest in the productions of the American mind. . . . A nation . . . must do its own thinking as well as its own fighting" or risk falling "a victim to that genius of another, to which she passively defers."

Speakers developed these ideas throughout the late 1830s, enjoying growing fame and influence through public lectures. Railroads made it feasible for the first time for speakers to cover a large amount of territory. Public speaking generally paid much better than any kind of writing. The growth of newspapers and other printing facilitated advertising, getting word of the lectures out beforehand, and spreading summaries of the lectures to those unable to attend. In the lecture hall, Emerson exulted, "everything is admissible, philosophy, ethics, divinity, criticism, poetry, humor, fun, mimicry, anecdotes, jokes, ventriloquism." People flocked to the lectures for personal improvement and social camaraderie.

Emerson's home in Concord became the gathering place for a group who came to be called the **transcendentalists**: they sought to "transcend" the mundane into the mystical knowledge that every human possessed if he or she would listen to it. Margaret Fuller became the editor of the *Dial,* the transcendentalist magazine, and Elizabeth Peabody opened a bookstore catering to the interests of the group. Bronson Alcott and about eighty others founded Brook Farm, one of the many utopian experiments of the 1830s and 1840s. Brook Farm put people to work in the fields in the morning and on their books in the afternoon. The community produced both crops and an impressive weekly newspaper, and its schools stood as examples of enlightened education. The experiment failed economically after a few years, but for a while, Brook Farm offered the possibility of combining intellectual excitement, physical work, and social responsibility in a way the transcendentalists craved.

Since the transcendentalists believed that people should establish a close connection to nature, Henry David Thoreau decided to conduct an "experiment in human ecology." He wanted to see—and show—how a modern man could live in harmony with nature. In 1845, he built an isolated house in the woods near Concord's Walden Pond, where he strove to be self-sufficient and self-contained. Thoreau published reflections on his experience as *Walden: Life in the Woods* (1854).

The transcendentalists were not alone in their search for spiritual intensity through connection with nature. American painters, sculptors, and writers found an increasing audience for their works in the 1830s. Thomas Cole, a key figure in the emergence of American painting, was born in England and moved to the Ohio frontier as a small child. Cole taught himself to paint but went to England and Italy to perfect his art. He returned to New York's Hudson River Valley in the late 1830s and early 1840s to paint its dramatic and uniquely American landscapes. Soon younger painters, such as Asher Durand and Frederick Edwin Church, joined Cole in their fascination with the stirring American landscape, creating what became known as the **Hudson River School**.

Cole also turned to richly symbolic allegorical painting. His journey to Europe had struck him by its contrasts—"both the ruined towers that tell of outrage, and the gorgeous temples that speak of ostentation." He believed America, by contrast, "to be the abode of virtue." He embodied his notions of the cycles of civilization and personal life in two powerful allegorical series, *The Course of Empire* and *The Voyage of Life.* Engravings of these series became popular fixtures in American homes.

Other important artists followed their own paths through the American landscape. Beginning in the 1830s, George Catlin lived among the Native Americans of the Great Plains, making hundreds of drawings and paintings. As a young man he was moved by the sight of a Native American delegation visiting Philadelphia and vowed that "nothing short of the loss of my life shall prevent me from visiting their country and becoming their historian." In Catlin's paintings, easterners thought they might catch the last glimpse of a noble and disappearing people.

Audiences could also view vanishing wildlife in the remarkable watercolors of John James Audubon. Audubon, born in Haiti and educated in France, settled on the Kentucky frontier as a merchant after he married. He loved the American wilderness too much to stay in his shop, though, and he launched out on daunting journeys to record the environment and appearance of the birds of the young nation. After ten years of work, Audubon produced *The Birds of America, from Original Drawings, with 435 Plates Showing 1,065 Figures* in four immense volumes, completing the project in 1838.

The most popular artistic production of antebellum America, however, was a statue: Hiram Powers's *The Greek Slave,* completed in 1846. Powers grew up in the raw country of Ohio but moved to Italy as he prospered. There, he sculpted his statue of a nude young woman bound in chains. The young woman represented, Powers said, a Greek girl captured by the Turks in the Greco-Turkish war. As such, she represented Christianity and whiteness, unbowed by the evil and darkness surrounding her. *The Greek Slave* served as the model for hundreds of miniature copies that appeared in the drawing rooms of the finest homes.

Emergence of a Popular Culture

The same drawing rooms also began to display a novelty of the age: daguerreotypes. This form of photography developed in France but arrived in the United States in 1839 soon after its creation. Within a few years, more than eighty young photographers practiced their craft in New York City alone, and by 1850 as many as ten thousand daguerreotypists had set up shop. This early photography was cumbersome and required long periods of sitting still before the camera, but Americans nevertheless flocked to studios to have their portraits done.

Engravings based on paintings and photographs soon filled the publications coming off the presses. For the first time, illustrations could be produced cheaply. Etched metal plates replaced crude woodcuts for the mass production of lithographs of popular subjects such as Bible stories, sporting events, shipwrecks, and railroad disasters. Magazines, incorporating short stories and illustrations, became tailored to children, farmers, women, sportsmen, and other specialty audiences.

Seeing the opportunity afforded by this emergence of a popular audience for print, American writers worked hard to fill the hunger. One especially gifted author, Edgar Allan Poe, skillfully navigated between the market and his art. Poe wrote short stories, the kind of writing most in demand, but he brought to the form a kind of self-consciousness few had demonstrated before. Poe tapped into a widespread fascination with the occult, crime, séances, and ghosts, filling his work with ruins, shadows, and legends. Throughout the 1840s, Poe published stories such as "The Masque of the Red Death," "The Pit and the Pendulum," and "The Tell-Tale Heart" and poetry such as "The Raven." Plagued by ill health, however, Poe did not survive the decade.

P. T. Barnum also exploited public fascination with the macabre and fanciful when he opened his American Museum in New York in 1841. Barnum displayed oddities that strained the limits of belief but that could not be completely disproved. He displayed an aged black woman who, he claimed, was 161 years old and had been George Washington's nurse. Thousands turned out to gaze at her infirm body and hear her tales of "dear little George." Unlike earlier museum curators, Barnum frankly offered entertainment, including magicians and midgets such as the famous Tom Thumb and the Feejee Mermaid, actually a monkey torso attached to the body of a large fish. The fact that the "curiosities" were often attacked as fakes by scientists did not seem to deter visitors: Barnum's American Museum flourished for the next twenty years and habituated Americans to a culture of celebrity and publicity stunts.

The Transformation of American Politics, 1840–1842

Popular politics had expanded in the United States since the 1820s, when Andrew Jackson electrified the electorate and states lowered the obstacles to political participation. The two major parties, the Democrats and the Whigs, had experimented with ways to mobilize voters and retain the power they won. The system grew throughout the 1830s, but no one was prepared for what happened in 1840.

The Election of 1840

The **election of 1840** should have offered an easy contest for the Whigs. Much of the nation remained mired in depression. Democratic President Van Buren offered little effective leadership during the economic crisis, and many people held him to blame for the hard times. But the Whigs were not as strong as they might have been. Their party had been built piece by piece in the 1830s in reaction to Andrew Jackson. As a result, it was a crazy quilt of interests and factions. In 1836, the party had permitted three candidates to run against Van Buren because no one man could command the party's full allegiance. Party leaders vowed that they would not make the same mistake in 1840.

The Whigs were determined to find a candidate who stood for the common beliefs that unified Whigs beneath their surface differences. Those beliefs turned around faith in commerce, self-control, Protestantism, learning, and self-improvement. Most important, the Whigs wanted to make an active response to the depression plaguing the nation by putting money in circulation, building internal improvements, and strengthening banks. The trick was to find a candidate who embodied their beliefs without appearing to be "aristocratic" or hungry for power.

The Whig Party found such a man in William Henry Harrison. Harrison had made his name as a general in the Old Northwest—most notably for his defeat of an Indian confederacy in the Battle of Tippecanoe in 1811—and later served in the House of Representatives and the Senate. He had won fame without gathering many political liabilities and was identified with no particular position.

Seeking to balance their ticket, the Whigs chose Senator John Tyler of Virginia. Tyler shared few beliefs with his fellow Whigs, but his embrace of slavery helped mollify southerners. Moreover, his name made a nice pairing in the phrase that soon became famous: "Tippecanoe and Tyler, Too."

The Democrats were relieved that the Whigs had nominated Harrison. Democrats considered the old general a nonentity; one reporter commented sarcastically that if Harrison were merely given some hard cider and a small pension, he would contentedly sit out the rest of his days in a log cabin. (He actually lived in a mansion and was a rich man.) The sarcasm backfired, though, for many Americans, still living in rural homesteads, saw log cabins and home-brewed cider as evidence of American virtue and

The Election of 1840. *Democrats warned that the log cabin and hard cider imagery of the Whigs were mere traps to snare voters against their true wishes.*

FEDERAL BANK WHIG MOTTO.

"WE STOOP TO CONQUER."

FEDERAL-ABOLITION-WHIG TRAP.

TO CATCH VOTERS IN.

(Library of Congress)

self-reliance. The Whigs, long frustrated at their reputation as snobs and elitists, seized on hard cider and log cabins as symbols of their party's loyalty to the common American.

All over the country, Whig speakers displayed paintings, signs, flags, and models of log cabins at huge outdoor rallies while freely dispensing cider to thirsty crowds. Harrison himself went out on the campaign trail, the first presidential candidate to do so. A new kind of American political style was being forged. For the first time, women became prominent at these rallies, encouraging their husbands, fathers, and suitors with smiles, waving kerchiefs, and riding in parades with pro-Harrison banners they had sewn. The Whigs embraced causes many women supported, such as temperance and church attendance.

The Democrats had no idea of how to respond to the hard cider and log cabin campaign. Martin Van Buren proved an easy target for a Whig campaign that emphasized homespun values. The president's portly figure and penchant for silk vests and doeskin gloves made the Democrats' long-standing claims of representing the common man look hypocritical. Andrew Jackson himself came out to campaign, firing the same charges against the Whigs that had worked so well in the past, charges of elitism, hostility to slavery, and softness on the bank issue. Even these charges failed. Harrison won nineteen of the twenty-six states, bringing about half a million new voters to the Whigs. Voter turnout surged to a level almost unimaginable just a decade earlier: eight of every ten eligible voters went to the polls. After 1840, electoral success would demand the same combination of active campaigning, potent symbols, and boisterous public displays.

Tyler, Webster, and Diplomacy   The Whig celebration did not last long. Harrison, determined to prove his fitness despite his age, expounded the longest inaugural speech in American history in March 1841, in bitterly cold weather. He contracted pneumonia and died exactly a month after taking office. John Tyler had become president even though he shared few of the prevailing ideals of the Whigs in Congress. Efforts on the part of Whig leaders to expand the

MAP 11.2 The Election of 1840.

Although William Henry Harrison won resoundingly in the electoral college, Whig and Democratic support balanced each other among voters in most states. National leaders had to appeal to both proslavery and antislavery voters if they were to remain in power.

power and reach of government with tariffs, banks, and internal improvements proved fruitless in the face of Tyler's opposition. Whig leaders in Congress responded by gathering in the Capitol gardens and excommunicating him from the party. Whig newspapers denounced him as "His Accidency" and the "Executive Ass." All but one member of the cabinet Tyler inherited from Harrison resigned in protest.

The only member to stay on, Secretary of State Daniel Webster, did so because he feared his rival Henry Clay's ascendancy if he resigned and did not think it proper to step down until important negotiations with England were complete. Conflicts between the two countries had broken out over the boundary between the United States and Canada. In 1837, armed men had fought along the border as Americans aided a rebel movement trying to overthrow British control of Canada; later, Canadian militia burned an American steamboat carrying supplies for the insurgents, generating intense anger in the northern United States. Armed battle also erupted in the "Aroostock War" over the disputed boundary between Maine and New Brunswick.

Conflict had also long been building between the British and the Americans over the African slave trade. Great Britain insisted that its vessels be permitted to search American ships off the coast of Africa to prevent the transportation of slaves to British colonies, where slavery had ended in 1832. Americans resented the intrusion in its affairs and refused. The issue threatened to explode in 1841, when American slaves seized a slaving ship, the *Creole*, which was taking them from Virginia to New Orleans. The slaves steered the vessel to the Bahamas and claimed their freedom under British law. Much to the anger of southern whites, the British gave sanctuary to the slaves.

Daniel Webster met with the British representative, Lord Ashburton, to settle these issues before they flamed up into a war that neither nation wanted. After extensive debate, the United States and Great Britain decided on a new boundary that gave each about half of what each had claimed in Maine and in the area to the west of Lake Superior. The Webster-Ashburton Treaty also established joint American-British patrols to intercept ships carrying slaves from Africa. Although the treaty stipulated that the United States must maintain a minimum presence totaling eighty guns along the African coast, Tyler's secretary of the navy undercut American effectiveness by sending only four large and slow ships instead of schooners better suited for the task of coastal patrolling. In 1850, while the U.S. Navy had captured only seven slavers since beginning the patrols, the British had captured more than five hundred ships and freed more than thirty-eight thousand Africans.

THE CHALLENGE OF THE WEST

Americans kept their eyes to the West. Railroads, telegraphs, canals, and roads strained in that direction, and population restlessly flowed there. But thoughtful people recognized that the lack of borders and limits posed threats as well as opportunities.

The "Wests" The hard times in the East made moving west seem an increasingly attractive option. Horace Greeley, the most influential newspaper editor of the day, warned people looking for jobs in the midst of the depression not to come to the city but rather to "go to the Great West." To people in New England, migration to the West in the 1840s often meant migration to the lands of the northern plains and surrounding the Great Lakes. To people from Virginia and Kentucky, migration to the West might mean heading to the free states of Ohio, Indiana, or Illinois or, more often, to Mississippi, Louisiana, and Texas. For people from the cities of the East, the destination might be a booming new city such as Indianapolis, Chicago, or Detroit.

One "West" that captured the imagination of Americans in these years lay in Oregon and Mexican California, word of whose beauty and wealth had slowly filtered east throughout the preceding decade. Although many people considered it nothing less than suicide to attempt to cross the Rockies and what was considered "The Great American Desert," a growing stream of families decided to take the chance.

Most of those who moved to the Pacific coast gathered in northern Missouri or southern Iowa. They set out in early May across undulating plains, with water and fuel easy to find, their wagons pulled by oxen. The settlers gradually ascended to Fort Laramie, at the edge of the Rockies. By July, they had reached the Continental Divide, the point at which rivers on one side flowed to the east and those on the other flowed to the west. On the trail for more than three months by this point, the settlers had covered two-thirds of the distance of their journey.

From the divide, the settlers heading to California split off from those going to Oregon. Both faced enormous difficulties in the remainder of their trip. They raced the weather, for early mountain snowstorms could be deadly. Some of the mountainous areas were so steep that wagons had to be dragged up one side and let down the

MAP 11.3 Population Expansion, 1850.

The population of the United States moved steadily westward at the same time that the Northeast became ever more densely settled. The population of the South remained thinner because plantations did not concentrate people as the family farms and towns of the North did.

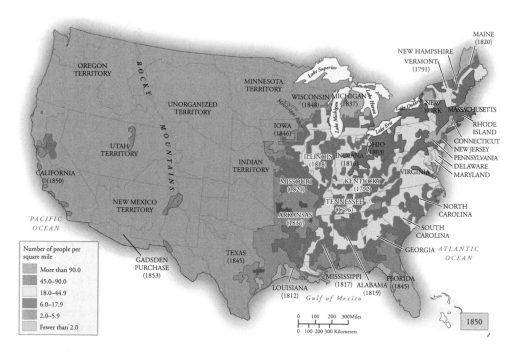

other with ropes, chains, and pulleys. Finally, by October, two thousand miles and six months after they had left Missouri or Iowa, the settlers crossed one last ridge and looked down on the sparkling valleys of Sacramento or the Willamette River.

Migration to the Pacific began slowly, with only a few dozen families making the treacherous journey between 1840 and 1842. The numbers mounted between 1843 and

1845, when more than five thousand people passed through Utah on their way to Oregon and California. Throughout the 1840s, the great majority of migrants chose Oregon over Mexican California as their destination. Oregon came to seem a respectable place for literate and upright Protestant families to settle, whereas California seemed a gamble, attractive mainly to single men willing to take their chances in a foreign country.

Manifest Destiny In 1842, the Great United States Exploring Expedition returned from an ocean journey of 87,780 nautical miles. It had circumnavigated the globe, located Antarctica, and explored the Pacific coast. The captain of the expedition reported that Oregon was a treasure trove of "forests, furs, and fisheries."

Catlin, The Female Eagle-Shawano. In his paintings, George Catlin sought to convey the dignity and individuality of his vanishing American Indian subjects.

If the United States did not use its military to occupy the territory all the way to the 54°40′ boundary, it would be risking much more than the Oregon Territory itself. California might throw off the light Mexican rule under which it rested and join with an independent Oregon to create a nation "that is destined to control the destinies of the Pacific." The Tyler administration sought to downplay this report, not wanting to disrupt negotiations still pending on the boundary of Maine and Wisconsin.

The forces of expansion proved too strong for the administration to contain, however. In 1845, newspaper editor John Louis O'Sullivan announced that it was the "**manifest destiny**"—the clear and unavoidable fate—of the United States "to overspread the continent allotted by Providence for the free development of our yearly multiplying millions." In other words, God intended white Protestant Americans to fill in every corner of the continent, pushing aside Native Americans, Mexicans, English, and anyone else.

The Democrats in Congress and President Tyler supported this expansion, focusing first on Texas. If the United States did not quickly annex Texas, Democrats contended, it might fall under the sway of the British and become not only a barrier to further American migration but also a bastion of antislavery. If, by contrast, the United States acted quickly, Texas could attract not only slaveholders and their slaves but also emancipated slaves, keeping them away from the North and the other attractive lands such as California and Oregon. Midwestern Democrats, for their part, agreed that westward expansion was essential to the American future. The country simply could not afford to have major ports and potential markets sealed off. These Democrats had their eye on Oregon.

Politics in Turmoil, 1844–1845   In 1844, James K. Polk, a former governor of Tennessee, received the Democratic nomination for president after an acrimonious convention and nine ballots. The Democrats appealed to both northerners and southerners with a program of aggressive expansion, attempting to counter fears of slavery's growth not by rejecting Texas but by embracing Oregon as a free territory.

The Whigs nominated Henry Clay for president on a platform opposed to expansion. The apparently clear-cut choice between Clay and Polk soon became complicated, however. Clay announced that he would not oppose Texas annexation if it could be done peacefully and by consensus. His strategy backfired, attracting few advocates of expansion but alienating antislavery advocates and opponents of expansion.

At the same time, the abolitionist Liberty Party won sixty-two thousand votes in 1844. In New York, in fact, the Liberty Party's strong showing took enough votes from Clay to give the state to Polk. And those electoral votes proved the difference in the national election. Although Polk won only 49.6 percent of the vote, hardly a ringing endorsement of aggressive expansionism, he entered office with a clear vision of annexing large areas of Mexican territory, Texas, and Oregon.

Even before Polk took office, the Senate voted to annex Texas, an independent republic since 1836, as soon as Texas consented. Texas gave its approval in the fall of 1845 and won its vote for annexation in Washington at the end of that year. The Democrats sought to quiet concerns among northerners by simultaneously annexing Oregon as a free territory. Although Americans, including some northern Democrats in Congress, clamored for all of Oregon to its northernmost boundary with Russian territory, chanting "Fifty-Four Forty or Fight," Polk secretly negotiated with Britain to set the boundary at the forty-ninth parallel, an extension of the northern U.S. boundary from the east. Northern Democrats who had supported Polk on

MAP 11.4 Oregon Boundary Dispute.

Although many Americans called for "54°40′ or Fight," the United States and Great Britain agreed to establish the border at 49°, an extension of the boundary farther east.

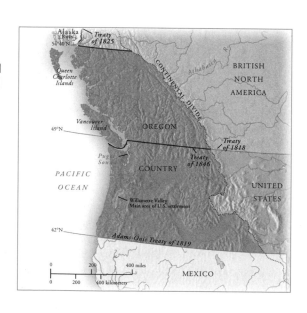

Texas felt betrayed and cheated by this southern conspiracy to "strangle Oregon." Their resentment of Polk's handling of Oregon would smolder, ready to flare again.

Meanwhile, the early 1840s witnessed bloody battles over religion. A growing stream of immigrants from Ireland, the great majority of them Catholic, flowed into northern cities. In Protestant eyes, the Roman Catholic church, with an undemocratic hierarchy, posed a direct threat to American institutions. Catholics would obey the pope rather than act as loyal Americans. In 1844, the largest anti-Catholic riot of antebellum America broke out in Philadelphia; several Catholic churches burned to the ground while local firemen, rather than fight the blaze, simply hosed down the surrounding buildings to prevent the fire from spreading. Because the Democrats proved far more sympathetic to the Irish than did the largely Protestant Whigs, the political differences between the parties now became inflamed with religious and ethnic conflict.

Slavery too led to **religious schisms**. In 1844, the Methodist church divided over slavery, and the Baptists split the following year. Southern church leaders were angry that many of their northern brethren refused to believe that American slavery was part of God's plan and bitterly resented their northern brethren's passage of a clause demanding no communion with slaveholders. Five hundred thousand southerners formed the Methodist Episcopal Church, while Baptists from nine southern states created the Southern Baptist Convention. Questions about slavery moved beyond laws and the Constitution into debates about sin, evil, and God's plan for the nation.

CONCLUSION

The years around 1840, like other eras in American history, were relatively quiet in terms of obvious events we might think of as "history"; there was no major war, for example. Instead, this period was marked by a far more common occurrence: a sharp slowdown in the nation's economy. The "panic," as a crisis in banking and investment was known, and the subsequent loss of jobs, decline in prices, and loss of property—what we would now call a "recession"—presented people with some sharp choices. Would they uproot their families and move to another county, state, or territory? Would they reject the political leaders who had apparently led the country astray? Would they join with other people to make fundamental changes in American society during these times of apparent failure? For many people, the answer to each of these questions was yes.

The panic and the hard times that followed touched virtually every American, rich and poor. People of wealth suddenly saw investments fail and property disappear. Laboring people found their jobs had vanished when their employers no longer had the money with which to pay them. Even enslaved people could feel the effects of the panic as hard-pressed owners might decide to sell a parent, child, or sibling to bring in extra cash. The economy was the one part of American life that touched everyone, regardless of gender or skin color.

People in trouble confronted widely differing options. There was nothing a slave could do when faced with sale. A free family could decide that things must be better somewhere else and could load all they owned into a wagon and head west, looking for land on which to settle. The poorest working people in cities did not have this option: they had no money with which to buy a wagon, oxen, and provisions. They could only somehow make it to another town or city and hope they could find a job that would put food in their mouths.

Some people, when confronted with such deep challenges, sought to make serious changes in their society. The most obvious recourse was to remove the political party in power at the time of the economic troubles, and that is what happened in 1840—as it has in many decades since. The Whigs, newly aggressive with their log cabin and cider campaign, replaced Martin Van Buren with a relatively obscure former general, William Henry Harrison. It was no accident that these symbols of a simpler, more secure time proved powerful when the increasingly sophisticated American economy suddenly crashed.

Perhaps too it was no accident that the late 1830s and early 1840s generated the most active period of social reform the United States had seen to date. The hard times presented many reasons to change people's lives. A working man without a job could not afford to drink: his family counted on him to bring every dime home. Therefore, for the first time, poorer people mobilized themselves to limit drinking in their midst with the Washingtonian movement. Other people, better off, developed a growing sympathy with those who lived in want all of the time: the enslaved people of the South. Men and women who had not seen slavery firsthand imagined what it would be like to have no freedom as well as no economic security.

Not everything that happened in these years was the direct result of the hard times. Railroads and telegraphs spread relentlessly despite the evaporation of investment money, and they flourished as prosperity returned. Artists such as Cole, Audubon, and Powers painted pictures and carved sculptures despite the economic conditions, and authors such as Emerson and Poe set their eyes on subjects far removed from the immediate present. But even these people lived in their times, taking advantage of growing towns, railroads, and printing presses of the early 1840s to create new audiences for their work. Both long-term and short-term changes in American life shaped everything that people who lived in these years experienced.

CHAPTER REVIEW, 1837–1845

- The United States experienced the largest economic depression it had ever seen.
- Railroads began to spread over large parts of the country.
- The Washingtonian movement against alcohol gathered momentum.
- Abolitionism spread, but so did a violent reaction against abolitionists.
- Major figures of philosophy emerged in the transcendentalist movement, and the United States saw its first original artists.
- The election of 1840 redefined electoral politics.
- Many Americans followed trails to the Pacific Coast.

◄▬ Looking Back

As Chapter 11 shows, the years surrounding 1840 presented Americans of all descriptions with the biggest economic challenge the country had yet seen, combining a sharp panic with long-term changes in the fundamental structures of the American economy.

1. How did the business cycle shape people's lives in ways they may not have been perceived at the time?
2. How much did reform movements grow from optimism and how much from fear of social disorder? Why did they tend to be stronger in the North than in the South?

Looking Ahead ▬►

Chapter 12 will show that after the hard times of the early 1840s, the United States entered a period of rampant expansion, political mobilization, and economic growth.

1. How did the election of 1840 influence every campaign that followed? Were those changes positive, negative, or mixed?
2. What legacy did the major cultural events of the late 1830s and early 1840s leave on American culture?

Go to the American Passages website at www.cengage.com/history/ayers/ampassages4e for additional review materials.

12

Expansion and Reaction, 1846–1854

The years of territorial expansion, population growth, and prosperity that followed victory in a war with Mexico also proved to be years of unprecedented foreboding for the United States. Positive changes came accompanied with discouraging consequences. Heightened expectations of a transcontinental American empire led to bitter political fighting; the immigration of working people from Europe fueled social conflict; and writers, reformers, and ordinary Americans grappled with the questions raised by these upheavals.

THE MEXICAN–AMERICAN WAR, 1846–1848

The immense Spanish territory to the south and west of the United States had been a major concern for generations. Throughout the 1820s, American leaders had struggled with Mexican independence; throughout the 1830s and 1840s, Americans had aided Texans in their fight against the Mexican army and fought with each other over the **annexation of Texas** to the Union. Americans longed for the territories Mexicans controlled in western North America, but Mexico pledged to keep those lands. No one could be at all certain that the United States could defeat Mexico in a large-scale war, but President Polk seemed determined to find out.

The United States at War The Mexican government had never recognized the independence of Texas, which Texans claimed as a result of their victory over Santa Anna in 1836. President James K. Polk raised the stakes by insisting that the border between Texas and Mexico lay at the Rio Grande, not at the Nueces River farther north, the accepted southern border of Texas. Even before the formal annexation of Texas was ratified in July 1845, Polk ordered American troops under the command of General **Zachary Taylor** to cross the Nueces.

Mexico, already furious over annexation, claimed that the decision to move U.S. troops across the Nueces constituted an invasion of Mexican territory. With four major factions struggling for control of the Mexican government, no leader could ignore the U.S. advance. Yet the army lacked funds, effective weapons, and training. Mexican president José Joaquín de Herrera ordered troops to assemble on the south side of the Rio Grande and wait.

Polk had his eyes not only on the border with Texas but on larger prizes still: California and New Mexico. Polk ordered John C. Frémont, leading an army expedition to map rivers within U.S. borders, to California. Frémont, acting on instructions to seize California "in the event of any occurrence," supported the "Bear Flag Rebellion," an armed struggle in 1846 by American settlers against the Mexican government. Disrupted, Polk hoped the Mexican provinces might be sacrificed more easily and more cheaply to the United States.

The president prepared for war in Texas, seizing on a skirmish in April 1846 between Mexican and American troops north of the Rio Grande as a convenient excuse. He declared that Mexico had started a war when it "invaded our territory and shed American blood on the American soil." Although northern Whigs continually denounced the war and its motives, Whig congressmen believed they had to support appropriations for the soldiers in the field. The final vote for war was overwhelming, with only fourteen Whig congressmen and two senators opposing the president. While unpopular in New England, the war stirred widespread support in the South and West, where residents hoped a victory over Mexico would open new land for American settlement. Enough volunteers to fill fourteen regiments swamped recruiters in Illinois, and thirty thousand men responded in Tennessee, earning the state the nickname the "Volunteer State."

The war with Mexico unfolded across an enormous area. Sixteen hundred American troops under the leadership of Colonel Stephen Kearny took Santa Fe in New Mexico with no casualties late in the summer of 1846. California proved to be a greater struggle, partly because Mexican settlers there put up more of a fight and partly because Frémont—now commanding a volunteer unit of Indian mercenaries, Bear Flaggers, and sharpshooters—provoked fights and stimulated enraged Californios to drive the Americans from Los Angeles. Nevertheless, with seizure of the territory's ports, the American forces won control of California a few months after they had taken New Mexico. The U.S. Army, under Zachary Taylor and Winfield Scott, achieved a startling series of victories in Mexico itself in 1846 and 1847, including an impressive amphibious landing at Vera Cruz by Scott's forces in 1847 that ended in the conquest of Mexico City and "the halls of Montezuma."

The regular U.S. forces enjoyed impressive leadership from their officer corps. The Mexican-American War familiarized Americans with names like Ulysses S. Grant, Jefferson Davis, and Robert E. Lee. These well-trained leaders commanded something less than a polished army, however. As many as 40 percent of recruits were recent immigrants, and 35 percent were illiterate. Conditions of service were harsh, with savage discipline, irregular pay, and poor supply. At any period during the Mexican–American War, one-third of the men on the muster rolls had deserted, the highest rate of desertion among American wars.

 This icon will direct you to interactive activities and study materials on the American Passages website: www.cengage.com/history/ayers/ampassages4e

CHAPTER TIMELINE

1846	Mexican War begins; Stephen Kearny occupies Santa Fe; Zachary Taylor takes Monterey • Border between Canada and United States established at 49th parallel • Wilmot Proviso ignites sectional conflict • Bear Flag Republic in California proclaimed • Hiram Powers completes statue The Greek Slave
1847	Taylor defeats Santa Anna at Buena Vista; Winfield Scott captured • Veracruz and Mexico City • Mormons reach Great Salt Lake Valley
1848	Gold discovered in California • Treaty of Guadalupe Hidalgo • Attempts to buy Cuba from Spain • Free-Soil party runs Van Buren for president • Zachary Taylor elected president • Seneca Falls Convention • Oneida community established • Regular steamship trips between Liverpool and New York City • Mormons settle in Great Basin
1849	California seeks admission to Union • "Forty-niners" race to California • Cotton prices invigorate South • Cholera epidemic returns
1850	Nashville Convention attempts to unify South • Fugitive Slave Law • Taylor dies; Millard Fillmore becomes president • Compromise of 1850 • Nathaniel Hawthorne, *The Scarlet Letter* • First land-grant railroad: Illinois Central • John C. Calhoun dies
1851	Herman Melville, *Moby-Dick* • Maine adopts prohibition • Woman's rights convention in Akron, Ohio • Indiana state constitution excludes free blacks
1852	Franklin Pierce elected president • Harriet Beecher Stowe, Uncle Tom's Cabin • Daniel Webster and Henry Clay die
1853	Gadsden Purchase • Nativism increases
1854	Know-Nothings win unexpected victories • Whig party collapses • Republican party founded • Kansas-Nebraska Act • Ostend Manifesto encourages acquisition of Cuba • Henry David Thoreau, *Walden* • High-point of immigration • Railroad reaches Mississippi River

The Consequences of War   Many northerners worried about the expansion of slavery and southern political power that might accompany victory over Mexico. To put such concerns to rest, David Wilmot, a first-term Pennsylvania Democrat in favor of the war, made a bold move: when a bill to appropriate $2 million to end the war and purchase California and Mexican territory north of the Rio Grande came before Congress in 1846, Wilmot offered a "proviso," or condition, that declared slavery could not be established in any territory the United States might win from Mexico as a result of the war. Still smarting over perceived mistreatment of their interests in Oregon by Polk and aware of growing rejection of slavery's expansion among their section's voters, northern Democrats saw the proviso as "our declaration of independence from southern dictation, arrogance, and misrule." It passed the House by a vote of 83 to 64, with congressmen, with few exceptions, voting along sectional rather than party lines. The Wilmot Proviso eventually went down to defeat in

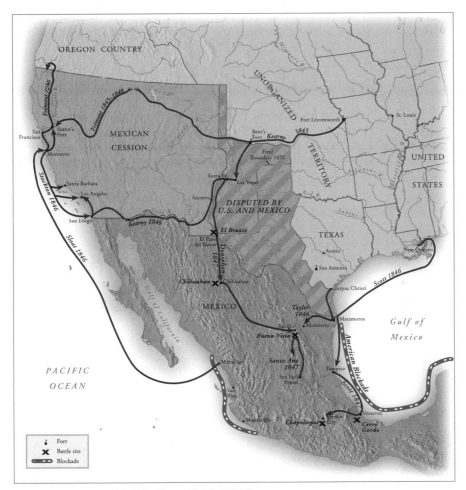

MAP 12.1 War with Mexico, 1846–1848.

The war between the United States and Mexico ranged over an enormous territory, though the main battles occurred deep within Mexico. While the navy blockaded Mexican coastlines, General Winfield Scott landed at Vera Cruz, marched more than two hundred miles inland, and seized the capital, Mexico City, forcing a negotiated settlement to the war.

the Senate and the war proceeded, but from 1846 on, the opponents of slavery's expansion increasingly distrusted Polk, and southern political leaders doubted northern Democrats' reliability on the defense of slavery.

The war with Mexico limped to a conclusion in late 1847 and early 1848. American troops controlled Mexico City, the Gulf Coast, and all the northern provinces claimed by the United States, but the Mexican government refused to settle on terms of peace. President Polk, General Winfield Scott, and peace commissioner Nicholas Trist bickered over the treaty. Some Americans urged Polk to lay claim to all of the conquered country, others insisted that the United States should seize no territory at all from the war, and

The Battle of Cerro Gordo

After seizing the coastal town of Vera Cruz in late March 1847, American forces under the command of Winfield Scott prepared to march overland to Mexico City. President Polk hoped that if Scott captured the Mexican capital, he could compel Mexico to accept Texas annexation and negotiate the sale of California and New Mexico.

Realizing that yellow fever season would soon arrive in the coastal lowlands, Mexican General Antonio López de Santa Anna tried to trap Scott there by blocking a rugged mountain pass near the town of Cerro Gordo. On April 18, Scott ordered a frontal attack against the Mexican-held heights, while the main body of his army followed a small trail discovered by Captain Robert E. Lee to seize the road behind Santa Anna and secure access to Mexico City. Mexicans' outdated weapons proved ineffective against the Americans' modern artillery and long-range rifles; threatened with encirclement, Santa Anna fled. Scott's forces inflicted some one thousand casualties on the Mexican troops and took another three thousand captive, while losing just over four hundred of their own.

On hearing the news from Cerro Gordo, one Mexican legislator wrote, "Everything is lost. Absolutely nothing was saved; not even hope." Discredited by his defeat, Santa Anna's attempts to recruit additional troops were largely unsuccessful, and he was forced to face the U.S. army, itself ravaged by disease and desertion, with ever-dwindling troops at subsequent battles between Cerro Gordo and Mexico City.

(Library of Congress)

many, such as Senator John C. Calhoun, driven by racial fears, wanted to limit seized territories to the sparsely settled regions to prevent "the fatal error of placing these colored races on an equality with the white race." Trist, on his own in Mexico, finally signed a treaty in Guadalupe Hidalgo that brought the negotiations to an end in February 1848.

Mexico, for $15 million and the abandonment of American claims against the Mexican government and its people, agreed to sell California, New Mexico, and all of Texas above the Rio Grande. When the treaty finally appeared before Congress for ratification the following month, many doubted that it would pass. Declining popular support for the war derailed plans to send an additional thirty thousand troops to occupy northern Mexico. The various factions, however, swallowed their disagreements long enough to ratify the treaty in March. A prominent newspaper pronounced the treaty "a peace which every one will be glad of, but no one will be proud of." The Mexicans signed the treaty in May, and the war finally closed, with Mexico surrendering nearly 600 million acres of territory to the United States.

War and Politics: The Election of 1848

James K. Polk did not seek reelection in 1848. The Democrats, scrambling to find someone to unite the northern and southern branches of the party, decided on Lewis Cass of Michigan. Cass, a rather colorless man except for his red wig, spoke for the majority of northern Democrats who sympathized with white southerners in their determination to keep black people enslaved. He called for **popular sovereignty**, allowing people in the territories to make their own policies on slavery. Antislavery Democrats walked out of the Democratic convention and called their own convention in Buffalo, New York, where they nominated former president Martin Van Buren as the Free-Soil candidate for the presidency.

Abolitionists who had earlier supported the failed Liberty Party were intrigued to see a candidate who might win a substantial number of votes. Antislavery "Conscience Whigs" also threw their support behind Van Buren. These various groups forged a working alliance for the election of 1848, declaring their solidarity behind the name of the **Free-Soil Party** and its stirring motto: "fight on and fight forever" for "free soil, free speech, free labor, and free men." Opposition to slavery's expansion into the West fractured old party loyalties developed in the Jacksonian era.

The mainstream Whigs found themselves in an awkward spot, for they had fervently opposed the Mexican War but now sought to capitalize on the popularity of General Zachary Taylor, whom they nominated for the presidency. Taylor, a Virginian, had several advantages as a candidate. He had no troubling political past. Though he was a slaveholding planter, he had opposed the war with Mexico before he had been sent there to lead American troops. Just what he thought about anything was unclear, but with his lack of connection to recent bitter party squabbles, Taylor appealed to voters in both sections who desired a less partisan style of political leadership.

Taylor won the election in the electoral college, but the popular vote revealed little consensus. Taylor, with 1.36 million votes, won eight slave states and seven free ones. Cass won eight free states and seven slaveholding ones, with 1.22 million votes. Although the Free-Soilers' prospects as a third party appeared bleak, Van Buren came in second in several important states, and his vote total was large enough to gain the notice of northern Democrats and send twelve men to Congress.

MAP 12.2 The Election of 1848.

The balanced strength of the two-party system across the entire country was demonstrated by the 1848 election, in which Taylor and Cass won northern and southern states in almost equal numbers.

AMERICANS ON THE MOVE

Americans moved in massive numbers in the years around 1850. As the economy improved, transportation developed, boundaries became settled, and gold beckoned, people flooded to the states of the Old Northwest and the Old Southwest as well as to Texas, Oregon, and California. The suffering of Ireland and political conflict within Germany drove millions across the Atlantic, filling the cities and farms of the East.

Rails, Sails, and Steam

In the late 1840s and early 1850s, the United States had the fastest-growing rail lines and the fastest ships in the world. Private investors poured tens of millions of dollars into rail expansion, and the federal government aided railroads with free surveys and vast grants of land. The major cities of the eastern seaboard competed against one another to attract as many rail lines as possible. Owners of mines and factories subsidized new railroads, as did Wall Street speculators and investors from Great Britain.

Railroads proved more important for some parts of the country than for others, especially areas where canals and roads became impassable in winter. Railroads flourished in New England and New York, where the density of population and manufacturing permitted the new technology to work most efficiently. Midwestern states such as Ohio, Illinois, and Indiana also showed themselves well suited to the railroads, flat and fertile. Chicago had no railroads at all in 1850, but by 1860 twelve lines converged in the city.

Rural areas as well as cities immediately felt the effects of the railroad. Farmers now found it profitable to ship their produce to cities a hundred miles away. Previously crops spoiled or were weather damaged in transit, or the cost and hazards of the journey eliminated the profit. Farmers began to specialize, becoming dairymen, vegetable growers, or fruit producers. Corn, wheat, hogs, and cattle flowed out of Ohio, Illinois, Indiana, and Wisconsin. The older farms of New England, New York, and Pennsylvania turned to specialty products such as cheese, maple sugar, vegetables, and cranberries. These products rode the railroad tracks to market, tying countryside and city together.

In the South, still recovering from failed improvement schemes and loan repudiation after the economic crises of the late 1830s, railroad building trailed off in the 1840s. While spending levels did not match those of the North, states such as Virginia aggressively pursued rail construction beginning in 1847 and had spent more than $15 million by 1860 in loans to corporations and the building of two state-owned lines. North Carolina reversed decades of opposition to state-supported improvements in 1849, building a major line and subsidizing plank roads, private rail lines, and navigational aids. Despite this progress with railroads, most southern commerce and passengers relied instead on the steamboats that plied the Mississippi and other major rivers. The riverboats grew in size, number, and ornateness throughout the period. The 1850s marked the glory days of these riverboats, with cotton bales stacked on every square inch of deck.

Elsewhere, packet steamships carried mail, freight, and passengers up and down the eastern seaboard, over the Great Lakes, and as far west as the rivers allowed. Over 57 million newspapers, pamphlets, and magazines and nearly 48 million letters crisscrossed the nation in 1847. Beginning in 1848, Americans could count on regular steam-powered travel between New York and Liverpool, England. These innovations in transportation, exciting as they were, came at a steep cost. Accidents were frequent on the new railroads and steamboats. "I never open a newspaper that does not contain some account of disasters and loss of life. This world is going on too fast. Oh, for the good old days of heavy post-coaches," one diarist observed.

Clipper ships enjoyed a brief but stirring heyday in the late 1840s and early 1850s. Clippers used narrow hulls and towering sails to attain speeds unreached by any other sailing vessels their size. They sailed from New York to San Francisco, all the way around South America, in less than a hundred days. Although they were to be displaced after 1855 by uglier and more efficient steamships, for a few exciting years the clipper ships thrived on the high prices, small cargoes, long voyages, and desperate need for speed fueled by remarkable discoveries in California.

The Gold Rush

The natives of California had long known of the gold hidden in the rocks and creeks of that vast territory. White American settlers too had found gold deposits in the early 1840s. But it was a discovery in January 1848 that changed everything.

In 1839, John Sutter emigrated from Switzerland to the area that became Sacramento, where he established a large fort, trading post, and wheat farm. Sutter hired a carpenter named James Marshall to build a mill on the American River. While working on the project, Marshall happened to notice "something shining in the bottom of the ditch." He realized that the nugget, about half the size of a pea, was gold. Sutter, Marshall, and the other men on the place tried to keep the find a secret, but word leaked to San Francisco. There, sailors abandoned their ships, soldiers deserted their barracks, and clerks left their shops to look for gold along the American River. Newspapers stopped publishing and local governments shut down as Mexicans, Native Americans, and white Americans in California rushed to the foothills. By the end of 1848, these men had gathered nuggets and dust worth about $6 million.

Back east, people remained calm, even skeptical, about the discovery until 230 ounces of almost pure gold went on display in the War Department in Washington, D.C., and the president confirmed, in his State of the Union address in December 1848, that "the accounts of the abundance of gold in that territory are of such extraordinary character as would scarcely command belief." The gold rush began: "The coming of the Messiah, or the dawn of the Millennium could not have excited anything like the interest," one newspaper marveled. By the end of 1849, more than seven hundred ships carrying more than forty-five thousand easterners sailed to California. Some of the ships went around South America; others transported their passengers to the Isthmus of Panama, which they crossed by foot and canoe.

About fifty-five thousand settlers followed the overland trails cut across the continent. Some traveled alongside the continuing stream of settlers to Oregon; others followed trails directly to the goldfields from destinations as far south as Mexico. Whether they went by sea or land, participants in the gold rush were quite different from other immigrants to the West. The **forty-niners** tended to be either single men or groups of men from the same locality. Most of the men who flooded into California had little interest in settling there permanently: they intended to find their share of the gold and move on. Once in California, men of all classes, colors, and nations worked feverishly alongside one another in the streams and mountainsides. Disease, violence, and miserable living conditions hounded them, sending thousands to their deaths.

(The Granger Collection, New York)

Chinese Gold Miners. *A diverse population of men rushed to the California goldfields in 1849. Recent immigrants from China worked alongside Native American, white, and African American miners.*

When some Chinese men returned home from California flush with American riches and stories of the "Golden Mountain," the fever spread in Asia. About

70 percent of the Chinese immigrants came from Guangdong Province, where many peasants and artisans had become impoverished and desperate enough to undertake the dangerous journey to California. Young men, in particular, thought California might offer a way to attain the wealth they needed to acquire a farm and a wife back in China. Migrants could buy tickets from brokers on credit, with high interest. Upon their arrival in California, the Chinese immigrants discovered that they had to borrow yet more money from Chinese merchants in San Francisco to be transported to the goldfields. The miners worked continuously in hopes of paying off that debt.

California held hope for African Americans too. Most of the black migrants to California left from the coastal cities of New England. California beckoned with the promise of an American West where color might not matter so much. Although abolitionists, black and white, warned that even California might not be safe for black migrants, several thousand African Americans decided to take the chance.

Whatever their race, few miners discovered a fortune. The average miner in 1848 found about an ounce of gold a day, worth around $20, or about twenty times what a laborer back east made with a daily wage. As the number of competing miners skyrocketed over the next few years, however, the average take declined until it reached about $6 a day in 1852. Mining became more mechanized, and soon the biggest profits went to companies that assaulted the riverbeds and ravines with battalions of workers, explosives, and crushing mills.

Although miners of every background went bust, California as a whole flourished. Towns appeared wherever people gathered to look for gold. Men who were tired of mining turned instead to farming, teaching school, or building houses. The largest fortunes were made supplying the miners: Levi Strauss, a dry goods salesman from New York, created tough denim jeans, and Collis P. Huntington, later founder of the Central Pacific Railroad, met arriving ships and bought all the shovels on board for marked-up sale to miners. San Francisco was the big winner: by 1850, it had grown into a brash and booming city of thirty-five thousand diverse residents.

The Mormon Migration

A different kind of westward movement was already in full force as the California gold rush got under way. These migrants were members of the Church of Jesus Christ of Latter-Day Saints, or Mormons. In the face of relentless persecution, Joseph Smith, the founder of the church, had led his flock to Illinois. There they established the town of Nauvoo, which by the mid-1840s had become the largest city in Illinois, with more than fifteen thousand people. But conflict erupted among his followers when Smith decreed that polygamy was God's will and that leading men within the church would marry several wives. He created the Nauvoo Legion, an armed force to protect his followers. When Smith ordered the destruction of a Mormon press that printed a poster condemning polygamy, the paper's owners signed warrants for his arrest. In June 1844, a mob of non-Mormons broke into the jail where Smith was being held and killed him and his brother.

After a struggle among the elders, **Brigham Young**, a young loyalist of Joseph Smith, emerged as the new leader of the Mormons. Young decided to move to a place beyond the reach of the Mormons' many enemies. He knew about the Great Salt Lake, a place cut off from the east by mountains and from the west and south by deserts.

The Mormons abandoned Nauvoo in the spring of 1846 as anti-Mormons pounded the town with cannon, destroying the Great Temple. In a well-coordinated migration, fifteen thousand Mormons moved in stages to the Great Salt Lake. When they arrived in 1847, the valley presented a daunting picture of rock and sagebrush, but the settlers irrigated the land, turning it into a thriving community.

When frosts, insects, and drought ruined much of the crop in the spring of 1848, Young announced that the Mormons would pool their labor and their resources even more than before. They designed an ambitious city with wide streets surrounding a temple that would "surpass in grandeur of design and gorgeousness of decoration all edifices the world has yet seen." Young concentrated control of the city and its farms in his own hands and in those of his fellow church leaders.

As some non-Mormons settled at the Great Salt Lake, Young decided that a form of government other than the church must be established. He oversaw the creation of a state called "Deseret," a Mormon term meaning "honeybee." The Mormons began a successful campaign to attract new converts from Europe, Asia, and Latin America. In 1849, the residents of Deseret, with Brigham Young as territorial governor, petitioned Congress for admission into the Union as a new state—a status it was not to achieve for another half-century because of conflict over polygamy.

Although polygamy was practiced by no more than 15 percent of Mormons, the church decreed in 1852 that plural marriage was a fundamental church doctrine. The pronouncement provoked outrage across the country and led President Buchanan to order the military to prepare for an attack on Salt Lake City.

The High Tide of Immigration Even as Americans moved west, a vast immigration from Ireland surged into the eastern United States. Irish immigration was not new; about a million people had left Ireland for the United States between 1815 and 1844. But the situation in Ireland changed much for the worse beginning in 1845, when a blight struck healthy potato fields, turning the leaves black almost overnight and filling the air with "a sickly odor of decay." This, the Great Potato Famine, which would last for nearly a decade, destroyed the basic food for most of the Irish people. More than 1 million people died; another 1.8 million fled to North America. In all, about a fourth of the island's population departed, with more people leaving in the eleven years after 1845 than in the preceding 250 years combined.

The Irish immigrants tended to be young, single, poor, unskilled, and Catholic; they came over in the dead of winter, with virtually no money or property. Although some spread throughout North America, most congregated in the cities of the North and Midwest. They lived from day to day on whatever money they could earn. Most men worked on docks, others in canal and railroad construction; women worked as domestics and as unskilled laborers in textile mills.

The high tide of Irish immigration occurred just before the peak of German immigration. Over 1 million Germans came to America between 1846 and 1854, many of them dislocated by a failed revolution in Germany in 1848. The Germans tended to be farmers who brought some money with them and established farms in the Midwest. They, more than the Irish, were divided by wealth, generation, politics, regional background, and religion. Combined, the Irish and German immigrants accounted for almost 15 percent of the population of the United States in the 1850s.

THE QUEST FOR PERFECTION

Although the late 1840s and early 1850s were relatively peaceful and prosperous, reformers continued working to mitigate the evils they saw in American society. Some became so disenchanted that they established utopian communities where they could experiment with alternative ways of organizing labor, power, and sexuality. Others, building on the ideas of the abolitionist movement, launched a crusade for woman's rights.

Perfect Communities

Most of the hundred or so utopian communities created in the United States between the Revolutionary War and the Civil War were founded in the 1840s. Some communities were secular in origin and some religious. Like the Transcendentalists at Brook Farm, they all insisted that people truly dedicated to social improvement had to flee corruption and compromise.

The most notorious American communal experiment emerged in 1848, when John Humphrey Noyes and his 250 followers created the **Oneida Association** in upstate New York. Like other religious thinkers of the day, Noyes had become convinced that it was possible for humans to be "perfected," that is, made free of sin. More controversial, he argued that people in a state of perfection should not be bound by conventional monogamous marriages; all belonged to one another sexually in "complex marriage." He gathered a small group of disciples around him who put such beliefs into action, practicing birth control by having males withdraw during intercourse.

Oneida experimented not only with sex but also with economic cooperation. Everyone performed the full range of labor. The women of the group cut their hair short, wore pantaloons rather than skirts, and played sports with their male compatriots. Unlike other utopian communities, Oneida focused its energies on manufacturing rather than farming. The community produced an improved and profitable steel animal trap. Later, Oneida transformed itself into a profitable business corporation specializing in silverware.

The utopian communities testified to the freedom the United States offered. People took advantage of the isolation offered by the enormous space of the young country to experiment with communities based on religious, sexual, or philosophical principles. The proliferation of such communities also revealed, however, how full of longing many Americans seemed for communal relations in a society changing from the influences of immigration, technological advances, and political conflict.

Women's Rights

The seeds for the organized movement for women's rights in the United States had been planted in 1840 when women attending the World's Anti-Slavery Convention in London, England, found themselves consigned to seats in a separate roped-off area. One of the delegates was **Elizabeth Cady Stanton**. Listening to the debates over the place of women in antislavery, Stanton felt "humiliated and chagrined, except as these feelings were outweighed by contempt for the shallow reasoning of the opponents and their comical pose and gestures." Stanton discovered an important ally at the London meeting: Lucretia Mott, a devout Quaker and feminist. The two women vowed that they would start a movement back in the States for women's rights, but they did not soon find the opportunity they sought.

Sojourner Truth. *Sojourner Truth, a former slave from New York, embodied for many people the pride and strength of black women, for she spoke out for both her gender and her race.*

(The Granger Collection, New York)

Stanton devoted her time to raising her family in Boston. In 1847, she moved with her family to Seneca Falls, New York.

While living in Seneca Falls, Stanton grew frustrated with the narrowness of life in a small town and the limitations placed on women there. Meeting with Lucretia Mott again, Stanton told her friend how miserable she had become. The two women joined with three of Mott's Quaker friends to plan a convention in July in Seneca Falls, although only Mott had had any experience in organizing a reform meeting. Stanton recalled that they "felt as helpless as if they had been suddenly asked to construct a steam engine."

Casting about for a way to express their grievances most effectively, they decided to model their "Declaration of Rights and Sentiments" on the Declaration of Independence. The document demanded women's right to vote and insisted on women's full equality with men in every sphere of life, including property rights, education, employment, divorce, and in court. The organizers worried about how many people might attend the meeting—held in an obscure town during a busy season for farmers—but more than a hundred people came, including a considerable number of men. Of those men, the most prominent was Frederick Douglass, whose newspaper, the *North Star*, was one of the few papers to give the convention a positive notice.

The organizers of the **Seneca Falls Convention** succeeded in their major role: getting Americans to talk about women's rights. Word of the declaration spread among the many women's groups working in other reform organizations. Stanton, Mott, and their allies determined that they would hold a convention each year to keep the momentum going.

At the Akron meeting in 1851, a black woman spoke. She had escaped slavery in New York in 1827 and supported her family by working as a domestic. In 1843, she had a vision in which she was commanded to carry the word of God; she renamed herself "**Sojourner Truth**." In Akron, Truth celebrated women. "I have plowed and reaped and husked and chopped and mowed, and can any man do more than that?" she asked. The campaign for women's rights developed a complex relationship to abolition and to African Americans. The movement might have offered a rare opportunity for women such as Sojourner Truth to be heard, but white women's rights advocates generally phrased their demands for equal rights in terms of education and refinement that neglected black women and their needs.

Not all activist women dedicated themselves to woman's suffrage. More conservative women, usually from middle- or upper-class families, devoted their energies to acquiring public funds for orphanages or shelters for "fallen" women and the poor, using their connections to important men in state legislatures, on city boards, and in prosperous businesses to raise money and garner support. They asked for laws to criminalize seduction and change property laws, oppose Indian removal, restrict slavery, support colonization of free blacks to Africa, and stop the sale of liquor. Southern women in particular rejected the cause of woman's suffrage, in part because it was linked so closely to abolitionism. Woman "has no need to make her influence felt by a stump speech, or a vote at the polls," fumed Louisa S. McCord. "The woman must *raise* the man, by helping, not by rivalling, him." These women often achieved success through indirect means of influencing powerful men, and they saw little need to agitate for the vote.

DOING HISTORY ONLINE

Frances Gage Remembers Sojourner Truth Appearing at the Akron Convention, 1851

What evidence is there in this piece (Document 9) that Frances Gage, like other white women's rights activists of the day, held a condescending attitude toward black women like Sojourner Truth?

 www.cengage.com/history/ayers/ampassages4e

POPULAR CULTURE AND HIGH CULTURE

The ever-growing acceleration of printing presses and railroads in the 1850s meant that Americans enjoyed increasing access to books, newspapers, plays, and lectures every year. People hungered for education and entertainment of all sorts. Performances of Shakespeare became widely popular, for example, as audiences flocked by the thousands to see *Hamlet* and *King Lear*. Other products of popular culture reflected—sometimes in lurid detail—concerns about immigration, alcohol consumption, and women's contributions to society.

Mass Appeal

Several authors, now forgotten, reached remarkably large audiences with their writing. Some achieved success by playing on the nativism and anti-Catholicism of these years with polemics such as *Maria Monk's Awful Disclosures,* supposedly by one Maria Monk of a nunnery of Montreal. That titillating volume, imagining sordid behavior by priests and nuns, sold more than 300,000 copies in the first twenty-five years after its publication in 1836. George Lippard composed a serialized melodrama, *The Quaker City; or the Monks of Monk Hall, A Romance of Philadelphia Life, Mystery, and Crime,* which sold sixty thousand copies in 1844 and at least ten thousand copies annually for ten years. Lippard paraded the worst aspects of the criminal poor and dissolute rich to appeal to middle-class vanity and desires for reform.

Other authors used the new capacities of mass printing to produce an ever-growing flood of self-help books. Catherine Beecher reprinted an edition of her *Treatise on Domestic Economy* every year in the 1840s and into the 1850s. The book offered a comprehensive guide to women on how to live their lives in the new domestic world, providing tips on topics as diverse as etiquette and how to wash feathers (carefully). The book was more than a how-to compilation, however; it told women that their work stood at least equal in importance to the work their husbands did outside the home.

One of the most influential books of the era bore the intriguing title of *Ten Nights in a Bar-Room.* In that book, first published in 1854 and eventually selling more than 400,000 copies, Timothy Shay Arthur described how the weakness of drink dragged down not only the main characters, who wasted their nights in a bar, but also their families, their neighborhoods, and even "a nation of drunkards." Temperance societies adapted the book into traveling plays and skits to highlight the evils of alcohol.

In their popular reading, Americans showed themselves both excited and frightened by the large social changes through which they were living. Whether the books fed fear and suspicion or offered strategies for dealing with the new challenges—or both—Americans liked stories told in bold colors.

Hawthorne, Melville, and Whitman

While popular authors dealt with the changes around them in melodramatic and obvious ways, more enduring writers also captured key elements of the American mood in the 1850s. Nathaniel Hawthorne's *The Scarlet Letter* (1850) and Herman Melville's *Moby Dick* (1851) were ironic, dark, and complex allegories, but Walt Whitman's *Leaves of Grass* (1855) evoked a hopeful vision. Their lives as well as their work bore the unmistakable marks of the times in which they lived.

Nathaniel Hawthorne of Massachusetts, fascinated by the lingering consequences of sin, turned to the history of New England as the setting for his best work, finding there an allegory for the struggles of his own age. Hawthorne wrote for Democratic newspapers and won a patronage post in the Salem customhouse, but his Whig opponents tried to remove him from his job and charged him with corruption. Perhaps not coincidentally, Hawthorne wrote *The Scarlet Letter,* a story about revenge and its costs, at this point in his life. Though set in the colonial era, the novel opened with a biting portrayal of the Salem customhouse and its petty Whig politicians. The novel propelled Hawthorne into literary fame.

After the arrival of Hawthorne's long-delayed prosperity, he and his family moved to Lenox, Massachusetts. There he met a younger writer, one who admired Hawthorne for his willingness to write complicated stories of guilt. The young author, **Herman Melville**, had left school at the age of fifteen and tried his hand at writing, but he was in need of work that paid better and more certainly, and he went to sea. His experiences gave him the subjects for most of his writing.

Melville's masterpiece, about a ship captain's search for the great white whale named Moby-Dick, created a peculiarly American idiom: part Old Testament, part adventure story, part how-to book, part encyclopedia. Good and evil swirled together in *Moby-Dick.* Unlike *The Scarlet Letter, Moby-Dick,* published in 1851, did not do well on the market. Melville, disenchanted, made his work more cynical and biting. His novel *The Confidence-Man,* published six years after *Moby-Dick,* dwelled on the swindling, corruption, and self-deception that seemed at the heart of the United States in the 1850s. Few people at the time noticed Melville's bold experiments, and he gradually fell silent.

A bit farther south, in Brooklyn, **Walt Whitman** labored on an epic work, *Leaves of Grass,* throughout the early 1850s. This collection of poems reflected America at midcentury in all its diversity, roughness, innocence, and exuberance. This poetry included everything and everyone, speaking in a language stripped of classical allusion and pretension. As Whitman wrote in the preface to this book, anyone who would be a poet in the mid-nineteenth century must "flood himself with the immediate age."

Whitman took the raucous city of New York as his subject. Working as a partisan Democratic journalist, he ran a shop, worked as a building contractor, spent days in the public library, moved from one editing job to another, and attended boisterous political meetings—all the while jotting notes for a new kind of epic poetry taking shape in his head. Whitman invented a poetical style to match his kaleidoscopic vision of American life. Both his life and his poem would be "A Song of Myself." Whitman's book was literally self-made; in 1855, he set some of the type and hired friends—printers of legal work—to publish the book for him.

Leaves of Grass came out to no public recognition whatsoever. Whitman sent a few copies to people he admired, however, including Ralph Waldo Emerson. The reply could not have been more heartening: "I find it the most extraordinary piece of wit and wisdom that America has yet contributed." But most readers of the book, including several leading literary figures who read it on Emerson's recommendation, considered it vulgar, even obscene, shapeless, and crude. The hopeful words of *Leaves of Grass* soon became lost in years when a darker vision of the United States prevailed.

SLAVERY AND A NEW CRISIS IN POLITICS

The 1850s began with many signs of change and progress as the economy kicked into high gear. People flooded to the recently acquired territories of California and Oregon while clipper ships, steamships, and railroads tied the nation together even more tightly. Yet a persistent undercurrent of anxiety wore at even the most privileged Americans when they read their newspapers.

The Crisis of 1850   Some of Americans' worry emanated from the new golden land of California, where lawlessness became rampant. The men who had left everything back east or in Europe to come to the goldfields showed little respect for the property rights—or even the lives—of the Mexicans, Native Americans, and white men who were there before them, or for each other. In the eyes of many, anarchy threatened if California could not form a government quickly. As gold fever spread, the military governor urged the president to grant the territory a government as soon as possible. A territorial convention created such a government in 1849, helping to restore order, but one of the provisions of the new constitution created great disorder of another kind back in the United States. The new constitution declared that "neither slavery nor involuntary servitude . . . shall ever be tolerated in this state."

This straightforward statement exacerbated conflicts that had been brewing in Washington ever since the Wilmot Proviso three years earlier. White southerners of both parties considered the admission of a free California a grave threat to their own status in the Union, giving the Senate a free-state majority. John C. Calhoun, the most vocal and extreme spokesman for the South, urged his fellow white southerners to band together. If they did not cooperate, Calhoun argued, they would be overwhelmed by the numbers and the energy of the free states of the North and the West. Southern congressmen talked of commercial boycotts, even of secession.

Southern Whigs had supported Zachary Taylor for the presidency in 1848, assuming that as a southerner himself, he would support the expansion of slavery. To the disbelief and disgust of southerners, however, Taylor urged that California be admitted as it wished to be admitted, without slavery. Taylor's support of the proposed California constitution unleashed a bitter debate in Congress. Southerners in Washington argued that to deny the South an equal representation in the Senate was to risk war between North and South. To give in on California was to lose the sectional balance on which their very safety rested. The most aggressive white southerners wanted to go on the offensive before northerners in Congress had time to act; in October 1849, they called a convention of the southern states to meet in Nashville in June 1850.

A fabled session of Congress occurred as a result. In January 1850, the three most famous legislators of the first half of the nineteenth century—John C. Calhoun, Henry Clay, and Daniel Webster—assumed leading roles in the great national drama. Calhoun played the role of the southern protagonist, delivering fiery warnings and denunciations on behalf of the white South; Clay reprised the role of the Great Compromiser that had made him famous in the Missouri controversy thirty years earlier; Webster played the role of the conciliator, persuading the angry North to accept, in the name of the Union, the South's demand for respect. Clay and Webster rehearsed their lines in a private meeting before Clay presented his bill to Congress.

Clay's bold plan addressed in one inclusive "omnibus" bill all the issues tearing at the United States on the slavery issue. Balance the territory issue, he suggested, with other concerns that angered people about slavery. Keep slavery legal in the District of Columbia, but abolish the slave trade there. Provide a stronger law to capture fugitive slaves in the North, but announce that Congress had no power to regulate the slave trade among the states. Admit California as a free state, but leave undetermined the place of slavery in the other territories won from Mexico.

MAP 12.3 The Compromise of 1850.

The Compromise of 1850, the result of elaborate and bitter negotiation, brought California into the Union as a free state, leaving the territories of Utah and New Mexico open to the (slight) possibility of slavery.

Advocates on both sides hoped the compromise would buy time for passions to cool, but the arguments went on for months. In March, Webster, trying to put the conflict to rest, claimed to speak "not as a Massachusetts man, nor as a northern man, but as an American." He was widely denounced in the North as a traitor, buckling under to the slave mongerers. President Taylor—like Clay and Webster, a Whig—refused to support the compromise.

The Nashville Convention of southern states, meanwhile, turned out to be still-born, because six states sent no representatives and the representatives who did come disagreed on a course of action. Although a South Carolinian argued that "unite, and you shall form one of the most splendid empires in which the sun ever shone," most delegates still believed slavery was best preserved by remaining in the Union. In nine days of deliberations, the convention took no stand on the pending compromise; the representatives waited to see its provisions.

Although the omnibus bill in Congress appeared doomed, a series of unanticipated events brought compromise. Both Calhoun and Taylor died a few months apart. Millard Fillmore, now president, supported the omnibus bill. Webster resigned to serve as Fillmore's secretary of state, and the elderly Clay, after seventy addresses to the Senate defending the omnibus bill, left Washington to recover. Younger, less prominent, members of Congress steered the various components of the compromise through committees and votes. The compromisers were led by **Stephen A. Douglas**, a promising young Democrat of Illinois. The majority of northern and southern senators and representatives tenaciously voted against one another, but each part of the compromise passed because a small group of conciliatory congressmen from each side crafted shifting coalitions large enough to pass each section. By September the various components of the **Compromise of 1850** had become law.

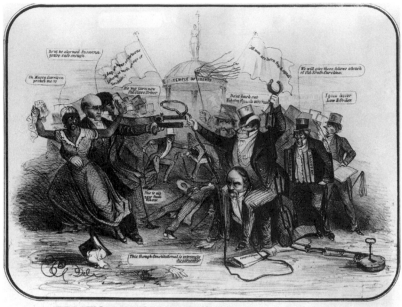

PRACTICAL ILLUSTRATION OF THE FUGITIVE SLAVE LAW.

(© CORBIS)

Fugitive Slave Law. *This cartoon ridicules the Fugitive Slave Law that required northerners to help capture and return runaway slaves. It glorifies William Lloyd Garrison but assails Daniel Webster, who voted in favor of the law as part of the Compromise of 1850.*

The problem of slavery, of course, would not go away merely because of a political compromise. The fugitive slave component of the Compromise of 1850 proved especially troubling. The **Fugitive Slave Act** directly implicated white northerners in the capture of runaway slaves. Marshals and sheriffs could force bystanders, including abolitionists, to help capture accused fugitives. The commissioners who decided the fate of black Americans accused of being runaway slaves received $10 if an accused fugitive were returned to his or her master but only $5 if freed. The alleged runaway could not testify in his or her own defense or call witnesses. And no matter how long it had been since slaves had escaped, no matter how settled or respectable they had become, they could be captured and sent back into bondage. Most of the two or three hundred alleged fugitives prosecuted under the law were ruled to be runaways and sent south.

Abolitionists raged at the Fugitive Slave Law, and they were not alone. Armed opposition to the slave catchers immediately arose in cities across the North; mobs broke into jails to free ex-slaves; one slave owner who came north to claim his property was shot. The Fugitive Slave Law, far from calming the conflict between North and South, made it more bitter.

African Americans and the White North
In the years surrounding the crisis of 1850, minstrel shows reached their peak of popularity. The traveling troupes of minstrels offered the strange ritual of white men in blackface simultaneously ridiculing and paying homage to the creativity of African American culture. Although white people of all classes and backgrounds

Minstrelsy

White men in blackface mimicked southern slaves for white audiences in the era, acting out ambivalent feelings of contempt and envy. Minstrelsy centered on comedy, dance, skits, and song. On the eighteenth- and nineteenth-century stage, black characters normally were played by whites who painted their faces black and danced, mimed, and parodied exaggerated sexuality and foppishness to amuse white audiences, many of whom were recent immigrants. Crude racist humor combined with idealized plantation scenes of abundance and sloth to portray blacks as simultaneously foolish and sly, responding to their oppression with bemusement and a dance step. Ironically, black dance styles drawn from Africa would evolve into complex tap routines that became a staple of the American stage. These shows were wildly popular in all sections of the country and created stereotypes of black behavior and comic style that persisted well into the twentieth century in movies, radio, and television.

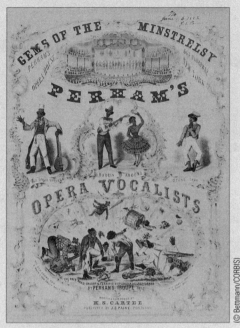

© Bettmann/CORBIS

attended the minstrel shows, the quick-paced, humorous, and flashy skits and songs held special appeal for members of the white working class. Over the preceding decades, native-born workers had seen the value of their labor eroded by mechanization and immigration, while immigrants had struggled to find their way in an unfamiliar culture and economy. For both groups, the minstrel shows offered a comforting dramatization of white racial superiority and a way to associate imaginatively with carefree and fun-loving "black" people.

White northerners revealed ambivalence about African Americans in other ways. Those who argued for "free soil" in the new territory of the West frequently insisted on the exclusion of free blacks. Ohio, Indiana, Illinois, and Oregon passed laws barring free blacks from entering or settling within their boundaries. The great majority of northern whites showed little interest in attending abolition rallies.

Harriet Beecher Stowe's *Uncle Tom's Cabin or Life Among the Lowly* helped change some of these white attitudes toward African Americans. In 1849, Stowe's infant son died of cholera in Cincinnati; the next year she moved back to New England. There, people talked angrily of the new Fugitive Slave Law.

Stowe put her objections to the law and its effects into a story printed serially in a moderate antislavery newspaper, the *National Era,* beginning in June 1851. She based her portrayals of black people on the African Americans she had known in Cincinnati, where they worked for her as domestic servants. They told Stowe of the terrors of being sold south to Louisiana, of their vulnerability to sexual exploitation. Stowe also drew on firsthand narratives of escape. She switched the usual roles of the freedom narratives, however, making a woman—Eliza—the active heroine and a man—Uncle Tom—the one left behind to endure slavery. The love of a mother for her children drove the story. The image of Eliza crossing the partially frozen Ohio River, baby in her arms, grew into one of the most powerful and familiar scenes of American culture.

The novel's 300,000 copies drove eight steam presses night and day to meet the demand in 1852 alone; eventually more than 6.5 million copies sold in the United States and around the world. It was the best-selling novel of the nineteenth century. *Uncle Tom's Cabin* became the subject of the most popular play in American history. Readers and theatergoers were shocked at stories of cruelty, violence, and sexual abuse. Stowe used techniques commonly found in domestic novels—the sanctity of the family, the power of religion, the triumph of endurance—to dramatize the moral argument against slavery.

That *Uncle Tom's Cabin* and minstrel shows reached their peak of popularity at the same time gives some idea of the confusion and ambivalence with which white northerners viewed African Americans in the early 1850s. Stowe's story was based on an antislavery message, but thousands of whites laughed at other whites in blackface acting out crude racial stereotypes.

Politics in Chaos, 1852–1854

The high tide of immigration in the early 1850s unleashed a political backlash as nativists organized themselves against the newcomers from Ireland and Germany. Meanwhile, the booming economy drove other Americans to lust for expanded territory beyond the bounds of the continental United States. Movement to the West triggered the most violent conflict the nation had yet seen between the forces of slavery and antislavery.

The Know-Nothings Franklin Pierce, the Democratic candidate for president in 1852, was a northerner friendly to the white South. Pierce's Whig opponent, Winfield Scott, proved to be unimpressive despite his fame as a general in the war with Mexico. Pierce crushed Scott in every state except four. "General opinion seems to be that the Whig party is dead and will soon be decomposed into its original elements," one diarist commented in the wake of the election.

Many influential Whigs took the 1852 election as a sign that the Democrats would always succeed by appealing to the lowest common denominator. The issues that had originally shaped the two parties—banks, the tariff, and internal improvements—no longer distinguished them from one another. Neither did slavery and sectional issues sharply define the two parties, for each tried to appease voters in both the North and the South. Even the broader cultural orientation of the two parties had blurred in 1852, as the Whigs appealed to the burgeoning foreign-born vote.

In the eyes of many white Protestants, the new arrivals, especially from Ireland, appeared impossible to assimilate. "They increase our taxes, eat our bread, and encumber our street," commented one American diarist. The immigrants threatened to drive down wages because they were willing to work for so little. They often received the right to vote in state and local elections soon after they landed, with Irish Catholics supporting the Democratic Party and opposing the prohibition of alcohol, while English, German, and Irish Protestants supported the Whigs and frequently voted in favor of prohibition. The conflict over alcohol became even more volatile in 1851 when Maine became the first state to enact statewide prohibition.

In the face of such challenges to their values and power, "native Americans" organized against the immigrants. The most powerful manifestation of nativism appeared in New York City in 1849, when Charles Allen founded the Order of the Star Spangled Banner, its membership restricted to native-born white Protestants sworn to secrecy. When asked about the order by outsiders, members were instructed to say "I know nothing"—and thus they became popularly known as the "Know-Nothings." The order grew slowly at first, but its appeal to deeply held and deepening prejudices grew as existing political parties seemed too corrupt to stem the flood-tide of immigration.

The **Know-Nothings** moved into politics in 1854 in a way few expected. Mobilizing as many as 1.5 million adherents, they did not announce their candidates beforehand but wrote them in on the ballots, taking incumbents by complete surprise. In Massachusetts, the Know-Nothings won virtually all the seats in the legislature, the governor's chair, and the entire congressional delegation with this strategy. By 1855, they dominated much of New England and displaced the Whigs as the major opponents to the Democrats through the Middle Atlantic states, in much of the South, and in California. Democrat and Whig leaders denounced "the 'Know Nothing' fever" that disrupted the campaigns and strategies of the parties.

No one in the major parties had anticipated such a turn of events. The Whigs, after all, had long attracted the nativists, fervent Protestants, and temperance advocates to whom the Know-Nothings now appealed. The Know-Nothings offered a revitalized political party, one more receptive than the Whigs to the anti-Catholic and anti-immigrant desires of its constituents and one that would attack problems rather than compromise on them. Many rural districts voted heavily for the Know-Nothings as a way to get back at the cities that had dominated the major parties for so long. Voters blamed standing politicians for corruption and sought a new organization free from the control of the "wire pullers" who ran campaigns from smoke-filled backrooms.

The appearance of the Know-Nothings reflected a deep-seated change in the American political system. The party system began disintegrating at the local and state level, with the Whigs fading in some states as early as 1852 and in others not until three years later. Voters defected from the Whigs and Democrats to both the Know-Nothing and Free-Soil parties.

A Hunger for Expansion   The same forces of commerce and transportation that tied together the vastly expanded United States in the late 1840s and early 1850s pulled Americans into world affairs. American ships set out for South America, Asia, Australia, New Zealand, and Tahiti, as well as Europe. The ships carried lumber and hides, tea and silks, missionaries and scientists. American whaling ships patrolled the South Pacific, stopping for fuel and food at islands scattered over a vast territory. Some entrepreneurs, such as the American Guano Company, rushed to mine two hundred foot-high mountains of bird droppings piled up on remote Pacific islands. The droppings, called guano, offered a nitrogen-rich fertilizer much in demand on the farms and plantations of the eastern United States. American traders eager to break into the Asian market appeared in Japanese ports.

Some well-placed Americans gazed at yet more Mexican territory with covetous eyes, urging the Pierce administration to acquire Baja California and other parts of northern Mexico. Mexico was not interested. Proponents of expansion had to settle for much less than they had wanted: after long wrangling, in 1853 the United States paid $15 million for a strip of Mexico to use as a route for a southern transcontinental railroad. This was the **Gadsden Purchase**, named for the American diplomat who negotiated it. The purchase defined the final borders of the continental United States.

Cuba seemed the most obvious place for further expansion. Many Americans believed that Cuba should be part of the United States. It was rich from sugar production, its slave trade flourishing even after the slave trade to the United States had ended. Abolitionists and others talked of freeing Cuba from both slavery and the Spanish, whereas white southerners talked of adding this jewel to the slave empire.

The United States offered to buy Cuba from Spain in 1848 but met a rude rebuff. Franklin Pierce, pressured by the southerners in his party and in his cabinet, renewed the effort to "detach" Cuba from Spain in the early 1850s. American diplomats in Europe created a furor in October 1854 when they clumsily wrote the "Ostend Manifesto," a statement of the policy they wanted the administration to follow: gain Cuba peacefully or by force. When the "manifesto" was leaked to the press, the Pierce administration was widely vilified. London newspapers derided the manifesto as the "pursuit of dishonorable objects by clandestine means." Pierce publicly renounced any intention of taking over Cuba. The movement to expand the United States into the Caribbean came to a temporary halt.

Kansas-Nebraska Lets Loose the Storm, 1854   As the Cuban episode revealed, Franklin Pierce proved to be an ineffectual president and a weak leader. The best hope for the Democrats, according to Senator Stephen A. Douglas, was to deflect attention to the West. Douglas called for two kinds of action: organizing the territories of the West, especially the Kansas and Nebraska area, and building a railroad across the continent to bind together the expanded United States with the route running through his home state of Illinois. The two actions were interrelated, for the railroad could not be built through unorganized territory. Partly to get southern votes for the territorial organization and partly because he believed that slavery would not survive in the northern territories, Douglas wrote a bill invalidating the Missouri Compromise line. He proposed that the people of the new territories decide for themselves whether their states would permit slavery. Adopting the phrase others had used to describe such territorial self-determination, "popular sovereignty," Douglas put it forward in the **Kansas-Nebraska Bill**.

Douglas's plan unleashed political and sectional resentments that had been bottled up by prior compromises. Six prominent Free-Soil senators, including Salmon P. Chase, Charles Sumner, and Joshua Giddings, denounced the plan as a plot by a "Slave Power" to make Nebraska a "dreary region of despotism, inhabited by masters and slaves." Northern ministers publicly protested the pending legislation in their sermons, and newspapers throughout the North scornfully attacked the proposal. Despite the widespread opposition, however, the opponents of the Kansas-Nebraska Bill could not coordinate their efforts sufficiently to stop its passage.

The fight over the Kansas-Nebraska Bill inflamed northern resentment as never before. Many northerners determined that they could no longer trust southerners to keep a bargain and that northerners were no longer obligated to enforce the Fugitive Slave Act because the Kansas-Nebraska Bill had nullified the Compromise of 1850. Attempts to arrest and extradite Anthony Burns, a fugitive slave in Boston, created such a turmoil that the mayor called out fifteen hundred militia to line the streets along the route between the courthouse and the ship that was to take Burns back to slavery in Virginia.

The Kansas-Nebraska Bill sparked a chain reaction: it divided the Democratic Party across the North; provided a set of common concerns and language to unite disgruntled northern Whigs, Democrats, Free-Soilers, and abolitionists; and upset the fragile balance of power between North and South in Congress. Northern voters punished Democrats who had supported the Kansas-Nebraska Act; the party lost sixty-six of the ninety-one free-state House seats it had gained in 1852. As northern Democrats lost seats, southerners gained control of the party, fueling further resentment of southern dominance. Know-Nothings took advantage of the widespread disillusionment with the two major parties to campaign against Catholics, immigrants, and corruption—issues apparently unrelated to slavery.

Over the next two years the northern political system lurched along as voters looked for a party that would reflect their concerns and also have a chance of winning power. The Know-Nothings began to fade almost as quickly as they had emerged. They came to seem just another political party led by ambitious politicians who exploited patronage for personal gain. Violent gangs that terrorized immigrants under the Know-Nothing banner alienated many voters, and Know-Nothing legislators proved unable to restrict Catholic influence as they had promised.

In 1854, a party was founded in Wisconsin to unite disgruntled voters. The new party appealed to former Whigs, Free-Soilers, Know-Nothings, and even Democrats fed up with their pro-southern party. This new party called itself the "Republican" Party. Its platform announced that it would not permit slavery in the territories or in new states. People wondered whether the new party could finally unite the North against the South.

CONCLUSION

The late 1840s and early 1850s do not have a catchy name. Perhaps these years saw too many contradictory changes to fall under one convenient label. In many ways, things had never been better in the United States. In other ways, the danger had never been greater. The promise and the threat proved to be parts of the same situation.

The United States, dissatisfied with the status of Texas and with Mexico's ownership of much valuable North American territory, pushed into war. Combining West Point leadership with tens of thousands of volunteers, the United States waged impressive military campaigns in California, Texas, and the heart of Mexico itself. Support for the war ran strong in most of the country, but bitter opposition grew in New England and among many Whigs, who saw the war against Mexico as a war on behalf of slavery.

The political events that followed the conclusion of the war confirmed the worries of those who argued that the vast new territories would throw into disarray the balance between slave and free states that had prevailed since the Missouri Compromise of 1820. The Compromise of 1850, so elaborately constructed by Democrats and Whigs, northerners and southerners, began to fall apart almost as soon as it was completed.

The Fugitive Slave Law turned many white northerners against the South; the South returned the ill feelings.

Despite the political turmoil, the economy, driven by railroads and clipper ships, flourished as never before. Cotton prices soared, as did the price of slave labor. The population of the new country, fed by millions of immigrants from Ireland and Germany, grew at an astonishing rate, filling cities and farms from coast to coast. Throwing more fuel on the roaring blaze of the economy, the California gold rush ignited the dreams of young men across the United States and sent them on journeys across the continent. The gold rush gave hope, too, to desperate young men in China, who came across the Pacific in hopes of making enough money for a prosperous return home.

The combination of a raging economy, millions of immigrants, and political instability proved too much for the Whig Party. Weakened by a series of unsuccessful presidential candidates and factionalism between the North and the South, the Whigs began to fracture and fragment. In the vacuum left by the Whigs' decline, a nativist party, the Know-Nothings, rushed in. Playing on the resentment native-born white men felt against immigrants and the political power they wielded, the Know-Nothings secretly coordinated campaigns to elect their own men. The result was a weakening of the Democrats and the demise of the Whigs. The party system that had held the United States together through the turmoil of the preceding twenty years was unraveling, and no one knew what would take its place.

The Kansas-Nebraska Bill brought political conflict and economic motives together. The bold and self-interested act of a leading northern Democrat, Stephen A. Douglas, the Kansas-Nebraska Bill sought to use western economic development to distract voters from the volatile political situation in Washington. With everyone focused on the possibilities of a transcontinental railroad, the Democrats hoped, slavery would become less of an issue. Instead, just the opposite happened: the promise of enormous territorial gains and senatorial seats drove the North and South farther apart than ever before. Slavery never seemed to matter more than when glittering new possibilities for expansion beckoned over the horizon. Economic success would not be a substitute for national harmony. In fact, economic prosperity seemed only to exacerbate divisions between the North and the South.

CHAPTER REVIEW, 1846–1854

- The United States went to war with Mexico, winning enormous territory as a consequence.
- A gold rush in California drove hundreds of thousands of people to the West.
- Mormons moved to the Great Salt Lake.
- Movements for women's rights emerged.
- American authors produced the first great novels and poetry of the young nation.
- The Compromise of 1850 and the Kansas-Nebraska Act galvanized the politics of the nation.
- A nativist movement won much support throughout the country.

◀▮▮ Looking Back

Chapter 12 shows that in the years following the war with Mexico the United States found itself pulled apart by the forces of economic growth, massive immigration, territorial expansion, and conflict over slavery.

1. Could the United States have avoided war with Mexico? Explain your answer.
2. Under what conditions might the Whig party have been able to survive the 1850s?
3. Why did slavery seem such an issue in the North in the early 1850s?

Looking Ahead ▮▮▶

In Chapter 13 we will see that many Americans hoped that the crisis of 1850, and the resulting compromise, would put an end to the bitter fight over slavery. In fact, it did just the opposite.

1. Did the Kansas-Nebraska Bill make it a certainty that the North and the South would collide repeatedly over slavery, or was there hope that things might die down once that crisis had passed?
2. What role did *Uncle Tom's Cabin* play over the years that followed its publication in mobilizing white northerners against slavery?

Go to the American Passages website at www.cengage.com/history/ayers/ampassages4e for additional review materials.

13

Broken Bonds, 1855–1861

The United States had never seemed stronger than at the beginning of 1855. The economy was booming, settlers pushed into the West, railroads spread at a relentless rate, and immigrants streamed into American farms and factories. Churches, schools, and reform organizations grew faster than ever.

But the danger signs were not hard to see. The conflict to control the national future grew more bitter with each passing political crisis. Every year brought a clash more divisive than the one before. Disputes broke out in the Kansas Territory, in the village of Harpers Ferry, and finally in the contest for president. Parties and politicians, weakened by nativism and loss of faith by voters, seemed powerless to stop the disintegration.

NORTH AND SOUTH COLLIDE, 1855–1857

Conflict had been a staple of American politics for decades before 1855. Territories proved a persistent problem, but Americans also argued over tariffs, nominees for high office, and the role of religion. The arguments grew hot, but eventually calmed down until the next outbreak. Events of the late 1850s, however, broke the pattern. New crises came before the old ones could cool. The crises suddenly engulfed every political, economic, moral, and practical difference among Americans. Citizens were under pressure to prove their loyalties and defend their vision of America's future course—slave or free. The time for compromises and moderation was over.

The White South Fortifies Itself Slavery had never been stronger in the United States than it was in the 1850s. The 3.5 million slaves of the South extended over a vast territory stretching from Delaware to Texas and north to Missouri. Theorists devised ever more elaborate and aggressive defenses of slavery, no longer depicting it merely as a necessary evil or an unfortunate inheritance from the English. Rather, they claimed, slavery was an instrument of God's will, a means of civilizing and Christianizing Africans otherwise lost to barbarism and heathenism. Southern physicians went to great lengths to "prove" that Africans and their descendants were physically and intellectually inferior to whites.

Some defenders of slavery argued that slavery was more humane and Christian than free labor. If the hypocritical and self-righteous men of the North would admit it, white Southerners argued, free labor exacted a great cost. Men, women, and children went hungry when unemployment, ill health, or old age struck. In the South, by contrast, slaveholders cared for their slaves even when those slaves had grown too old or feeble to work. The South's relative lack of schools, orphanages, asylums, and prisons, the defenders of the region insisted, testified not to backwardness but to a personalized society where individual responsibility replaced impersonal institutions.

Some white Southerners in the late 1850s argued for the expansion of American territory in Cuba or Central America, where slavery could flourish. William Walker, a young Tennessean, dreamed of personal glory and a new territory for slavery. After several attempts at **filibustering**, or small-scale military efforts, in Mexico, Walker took advantage of a civil war to seize power in Nicaragua in 1855 and 1856. President Pierce granted diplomatic recognition of Walker's government, but Central American leaders united against him, cholera wiped out his dwindling, poorly supplied army, and Cornelius Vanderbilt, furious at Walker's revocation of Vanderbilt's Nicaraguan steamship charter, cut off his support from Washington. White Southerners enthusiastically supported several attempts by Walker in the late 1850s to take Nicaragua, but he failed repeatedly, and finally he was executed by a firing squad in Honduras in 1860.

Despite the agitation of a few editors and politicians for reopening the African slave trade, most white Southerners wanted above all to keep and protect what they had, not jeopardize slavery by brashly expanding it. Not only would a renewed slave trade with Africa ignite the opinion of the world against the South, but it would also drive down slave prices and create new problems of discipline and revolt. The white South prided itself on having created a stable and prosperous society during its two and a half centuries of slavery and did not want to endanger that society.

Moreover, the slave economy boomed in the late 1850s. Planters took advantage of improved cotton gins, riverboats, railroads, and new kinds of seed to double, in the 1850s alone, their production of cotton. The claim of Southern politicians that "Cotton Is King" proved no empty boast. Even though Northern factories and farms grew rapidly in the 1850s, cotton accounted for a growing proportion of U.S. exports—more than half in 1860. Without cotton, many thousands of Northern and British workers would have had no jobs.

The prosperity created by the cotton boom resonated throughout the Southern economy. Slaves proved to be adaptable to both factories and cities. Southern cities grew quickly, attracting immigrants and businesses. Although the South could not keep up with the North, it actually did quite well by international standards. Considered as a separate economy, the South stood second in the world in the number of miles of railroad, sixth in cotton textile factories, and eighth in iron production. Nevertheless, the South was not urbanizing or industrializing nearly as quickly as the North. It did not create a large class of entrepreneurs or skilled workers, nor did the region invest much money in machinery to make its farms and plantations more efficient. The Southern plantation economy, in effect, was too profitable for its own good. The short-term gains of the 1850s,

 This icon will direct you to interactive activities and study materials on the American Passages website: www.cengage.com/history/ayers/ampassages4e

CHAPTER TIMELINE

1855	Proslavery and free-soil forces clash in Kansas • Massachusetts desegregates public schools
1856	John Brown's raid in Kansas • James Buchanan elected president • Congressman Preston Brooks canes Senator Charles Sumner
1857	Financial panic and depression • Dred Scott decision • Lecompton Constitution • Baltimore–St. Louis rail service completed • Hinton R. Helper, The Impending Crisis of the South • Mass revivals
1858	Lincoln-Douglas debates • Frederick Law Olmsted begins design for Central Park in New York City
1859	John Brown's raid on Harpers Ferry • Vicksburg convention calls for reopening of African slave trade • Kansas ratifies free-soil constitution
1860	Democratic convention divides • Abraham Lincoln elected president • South Carolina secedes from the Union
1861	Mississippi, Florida, Alabama, Georgia, Louisiana, and Texas secede • Montgomery Convention creates Confederate States of America • Lincoln inaugurated • Firing on and surrender of Fort Sumter

reflected in the escalating value of slaves, dissuaded wealthy Southerners from investing in businesses that might have held greater potential for long-term development.

Critics of the South argued that slavery victimized not only slaves but also "poor whites." In the antislavery portrayal, the **Slave Power's** domination began at home, where haughty self-proclaimed aristocrats lorded over ignorant whites, bullying them into supporting parties and policies that worked against their own interests. Antislavery advocates charged that slaves degraded white labor in the South and substituted a cheap sense of racial superiority for actual accomplishment.

Most Southern whites, however, saw slavery as an avenue for their own advancement, not a hindrance. Many men and women bought a slave before they bought land. Slave owners included women, shopkeepers, industrialists, lawyers, ministers, and even a few free blacks. No investment seemed to offer a more certain return than a slave, especially in the 1850s when slave prices rose rapidly. Although that rise in

FIGURE 13.1 Cotton and the American Economy.

Even as the economy of the entire nation boomed, cotton accounted for an ever-growing proportion of American exports to the rest of the world.

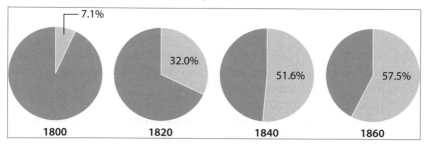

A Yeoman Farm

Nonslaveholding whites in the antebellum South, living on farms such as this one in Texas, comprised approximately 75 percent of the white population. Most owned small plots of land they farmed themselves with the aid of family and local networks of kin and community for access to market goods. They are frequently referred to as **yeoman** farmers, an ideal of the self-sufficient farm household as one of the cornerstones of American democracy.

Access to arable land and the prospects to purchase slaves became issues of increasing concern through the 1850s. Land exhausted by tobacco or cotton or that was tied up in large holdings of wealthier farmers raised the stakes of access to western lands. In many areas back east in Virginia and the Carolinas, poorer white families and younger sons found themselves unable to move from being laborers and farm tenants to landownership. While many Southern yeomen families migrated to southern Illinois, Indiana, and Missouri to break ground in areas without slavery, many others considered the opportunity to own slaves part of their political birthright and supported slavery's expansion even if they owned no slaves themselves.

(Carl G. Von Iwonski, *Blockhouse in New Braunfels*, Daughters of the Republic of Texas Library)

prices meant that a growing proportion of white people would be unable to afford a slave, many Americans' livelihoods depended on servicing the slave trade, through insurance, manufacture of slave shoes and clothing, medical care, and transport. Often Southerners who could not afford to purchase slaves or did not need slave labor year-round hired slaves to do specific tasks. The slave trade generated tens of millions of dollars in the antebellum economy.

Politics reinforced the sense among Southern white men that they lived in a fair and democratic society. Although many nonslaveholders in mountainous districts across the South voted against the large slaveholding districts, most Southern white men voted in concert with the richest men in their immediate neighborhoods. In the eyes of the poorer men, their wealthy neighbors could act as spokesmen and brokers for the community in the state capital.

Southern whites identified themselves most of all as white people, tied to other whites by blood and heritage. Whites held black people in contempt, despite their knowledge that many African Americans were more intelligent, hard-working, and Christian than many whites. To be white was to be the inheritor of all the accomplishments of the ancients, of Christendom and of the modern world. Such attitudes were reinforced at every level, from the daily rituals of life to the writings of leading thinkers from Europe.

Despite the solidarities of racial thinking, important political differences divided Southerners. At one extreme were the so-called **fire-eaters**, virulent defenders of the South and slavery. These men were diverse. Some lived in cities, others on plantations. Some, such as J. D. B. DeBow, wanted to make the South more industrial and modern, whereas others rejected such development as a Yankee blight on the rural South. Whatever their differences, these men argued that the abolitionists and their Republican supporters intended to destroy the South. The only sane response, they believed, was to agitate the slavery issue constantly, to refuse to yield an inch in the territories or anywhere else.

At the other end of the political spectrum in the South were the former Whigs and Know-Nothings, men who considered themselves a "thoughtful, sedate, constitution-abiding, conservative class of men." They considered the Democrats, especially the fire-eaters, great threats to the future of the South and slavery. The many Unionists in the Upper South, in cities, and in some of the richest plantation districts of the cotton South warned that those who boasted of slavery's power would unify the white North against slavery. Caution and compromise, these men argued, were the best friends of slavery.

Bleeding Kansas, 1855–1856

The Kansas-Nebraska Act declared that settlers would decide for themselves, by "popular sovereignty," what kind of society they would create. But partisans from both the North and the South determined to fill the territory with settlers of their own political persuasion.

The Massachusetts Emigrant Aid Company announced that it planned to raise $5 million to aid and encourage settlement in Kansas to ensure that the embattled territory became a free state. Proslavery advocates in Missouri, for their part, flooded across the border to vote in support of the proslavery candidates for the territorial legislature, casting roughly thirty-four hundred more ballots than there were eligible voters. This action by the **border ruffians**, as the Northern press quickly labeled them, was not necessary, for Southerners already accounted for six of every ten men settled in Kansas by 1855. The proslavery forces took control of the territorial legislature in Lecompton and passed a series of aggressive laws against free-soil advocates. Forbidding antislavery men to serve on juries or hold office, the legislature also decreed the death penalty for any person who assisted a fugitive slave.

Antislavery Kansans decided that their only recourse was to establish a rival government. They worked through the summer and fall of 1855 in Topeka to write a constitution of their own. Over the winter, the free-soil advocates "ratified" their constitution and elected their own legislature and governor. Antislavery forces in New England and New York sent rifles to Kansas to arm what they saw as the side of righteousness. These arms became nicknamed "Beecher's Bibles" because Henry Ward Beecher's congregation, at his urging, funded part of their cost. Southerners, in turn, organized an expedition of three hundred young men to reinforce their comrades.

Not surprisingly, this volatile situation soon exploded into violence. On May 21, 1856, a group of slave-state supporters marched into the free-soil stronghold of Lawrence, Kansas, to execute warrants from the proslavery territory court against free-state leaders and two newspapers. They threw printing presses into the river, fired cannon at the Free State Hotel, and burned the hotel to the ground. Free soilers labeled the episode the "sack of Lawrence."

The next day, in Washington, D.C., Representative Preston Brooks of South Carolina searched out Senator **Charles Sumner** of Massachusetts. Sumner had delivered a series of bitter speeches against slavery, attacking Brooks's relative and fellow South Carolinian, the elderly Senator Andrew P. Butler, for taking "the harlot, slavery" as his "mistress." As Sumner wrote letters at his Senate desk, Brooks, defending the honor of his family and his state, struck Sumner repeatedly about the head with a heavy rubber cane. By attacking with a cane, a punishment usually reserved for servants or slaves, Brooks implied that Sumner was unworthy of a gentleman's challenge to a duel. Because of the severity of his injuries, Sumner did not return to his seat for two and a half years, and his empty seat became a symbol in the North of Southern brutality.

The next day, an event back in Kansas intensified the conflict. The episode swirled around **John Brown**, a free-soil emigrant to Kansas. Brown had been a supporter of abolitionism since 1834 and followed five of his sons to Kansas in 1855. There, he became furious at the proslavery forces. He accompanied a group of free-staters to defend Lawrence, but they heard of the hotel's destruction before they arrived. Brown persuaded four of his sons and a son-in-law, along with two other men, to exact

SOUTHERN CHIVALRY — ARGUMENT versus CLUB'S.

(The Granger Collection, New York)

Caning of Sumner. *Preston Brooks's attack on Charles Sumner in the U.S. Senate electrified the nation in the spring of 1856—even though this artist apparently did not have an image of Brooks from which to work.*

revenge for the defeat. The band set out for Pottawatomie Creek. There, acting in the name of the "Army of the North," they took five men from three houses and split their skulls with broadswords. The men had been associated in some way with the territorial district court, but no one was sure of Brown's precise motives. He was never punished for the killings.

In the wake of the "sack of Lawrence," the caning of Sumner, and the "Pottawatomie massacre"—exploding in just a three-day period in May 1856—the territory became known as **Bleeding Kansas**. The legitimacy of the territorial government remained an issue of heated contention, and the symbolic value of Bleeding Kansas would long endure.

The Republicans Challenge the South: The Election of 1856

Democrats were still divided in the wake of their stunning losses in the congressional elections of 1854. Northern Democrats knew that too open a submission to Southern interests could cost them reelection. To many Southerners, the Democrats seemed a mere tool of Stephen Douglas and his Northern allies; to many Northerners, it seemed that Douglas's call for popular sovereignty was a cover for slaveholder dominance. President Franklin Pierce seemed incapable of leadership. The Democrats, needing someone who had not been tarnished by the events of the preceding two years, turned to **James Buchanan** to run for president in 1856. As minister to England, Buchanan had conveniently been out of the country during the Kansas-Nebraska crisis.

Although Know-Nothings were able to agree at the local and state levels on issues of corruption and anti-Catholicism, slavery split them as they attempted to organize a presidential campaign and develop consensus on sectional issues. In February 1856, Know-Nothing unity ended in a controversy over a proslavery platform when fifty Northern delegates from eight states walked out of the National Council and called for a separate convention of Northerners in June. Southerners who had voted with the Know-Nothings had nowhere to turn but to the Democrats, but Northern Know-Nothings were attracted to the new Republican Party. The Republicans bypassed their most outspoken antislavery men for the 1856 nomination and turned to **John C. Frémont**, famed as an explorer of the West. He had taken almost no public positions and had accumulated almost no political experience. The Republicans thought they had found just the sort of vague candidate who would give few potential voters a reason to vote against him.

The new Republican Party was antislavery but not pro-black; Republicans avoided talking about race. What they did talk about was the goodness of the North, which, they argued, was everything the South was not: a place where hard-working white men could build a life for their families free from competition with powerful slaveholders. They denied any intention of ending slavery in the South and even resurrected talk of colonization, the movement abolitionists had abandoned twenty-five years earlier. The Republicans, although better than the pro-Southern Democrats, still dissatisfied the abolitionists.

The Republicans talked of the "Slave Power," a political conspiracy by slaveholders to dominate the national government. Republicans saw everything from the three-fifths clause to the bloodshed in Kansas as the fruit of the Slave Power. How else to explain the long list of Southern victories at a time when the North grew more populous and wealthy? Kansas and the caning of Sumner showed that the Slave Power, a Cincinnati paper raged, "cannot tolerate free speech anywhere, and would stifle it in Washington with the bludgeon and the bowie-knife, as they are now trying to stifle it in Kansas."

Many Republicans attacked Catholics, repeating the charges that nativists had made for decades about the undemocratic power of the pope, priests, and nuns. Ironically, rumors that Frémont was a Catholic quickly surfaced and refused to subside. Moreover, Frémont refused to give direction to the national campaign. To make matters worse, former president **Millard Fillmore** ran under the banner of the American Party, as the Know-Nothings called themselves in a vain attempt to resurrect themselves as a national party. Fillmore hoped that the three-way election would split the electorate so that the final decision would rest with the House, where he would appear as a compromise candidate.

On election day in 1856, 83 percent of the eligible voting men went to the polls, one of the highest turnouts of the era. Although Buchanan won all of the South except Maryland, he received only 45 percent of the popular vote in the country as a whole. A difference of a few thousand votes in a few states would have denied Buchanan the

MAP 13.1 The Election of 1856.

By 1856, none of the national political parties proved able to bridge the growing sectional divide. Buchanan won all Southern states except Maryland, although Fillmore's American Party also made a strong showing throughout the South. The newly formed Republican Party dominated much of New England and the Upper North.

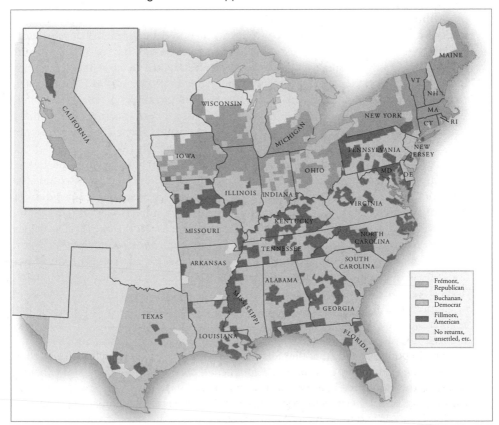

election. The Democrats had won, but they were filled with anxiety; the Republicans had lost, but they were filled with confidence. It was clear to everyone that the American political system was in flux and transition.

Observers of all political persuasions believed that James Buchanan had it within his power to strengthen the Democrats in both the North and the South. His party, after all, still controlled the Senate. The Republicans, moreover, had drawn much of their power from the chaos in Kansas. Once Kansas had peacefully entered the Union as a free state under the banner of popular sovereignty, Democrats happily observed, no other territory awaited in which similar conflicts might be expected. Slavery, everyone seemed to agree, had no chance in Oregon, Nebraska, Minnesota, Washington, Utah, or New Mexico. The territorial issue that had torn at the country since 1820 might finally die down.

Dred Scott, 1857   In his inaugural address, James Buchanan mentioned a case pending before the Supreme Court, a case regarding a slave. Dred Scott, born a slave in Virginia around 1800, had in the 1830s been taken by his master, an army surgeon named John Emerson, to territories far in the Upper Midwest. Scott had married Harriet Robinson, the slave of a federal Indian agent. Dr. Emerson bought Harriet and thus owned the two daughters she bore with Scott. When Emerson died in 1843, Scott and his family became the property of Emerson's widow, who moved to St. Louis. In 1846 the Scotts petitioned for their freedom, claiming that their residence in the free territory entitled them to free status.

A long series of postponements and delays dragged the case on into the early 1850s, when the legal environment had become especially divided by political controversy over slavery. Democratic judges and lawyers worked to deny the Scotts their freedom on the grounds that such a precedent would undermine the right of Southerners to take slaves into the territories. A Republican lawyer agreed to carry the Scotts' case before the Supreme Court to counter the Democrats' aggressive claims. Unfortunately for the Republicans and the Scotts, five Southern Democrats sat on the Court, along with two Northern Democrats, one Northern Whig, and one Northern Republican. Presiding was Chief Justice **Roger B. Taney** (pronounced "tawney"), an eighty-year-old Marylander appointed to the Court by Andrew Jackson in 1835.

The ***Dred Scott* case** came before the Supreme Court during the superheated months of 1856, when Kansas, the Brooks/Sumner affair, and the presidential election commanded the country's attention. Although the case could have been decided on relatively narrow grounds, the Democratic members of the Court wanted to issue a sweeping pronouncement that would settle once and for all the question of slavery in the territories. President-elect Buchanan pressured a fellow Pennsylvanian on the Court to side with the Southerners. Two days after Buchanan took office in March 1857, the Court announced its decision in the *Dred Scott* case. It took Chief Justice Taney two hours to read the opinion.

Taney spent half his time denying that Scott had the right to bring a case in the first place. Black people, Taney decreed, could not become citizens of the United States because "they were not included, and were not intended to be included, under the word 'citizens' in the Constitution." Taney declared that at the time the Constitution was written, throughout the "civilized and enlightened portions of the world," members of the "negro African race" were held to be "altogether unfit to associate with the white race . . . and so far inferior, that they had no rights which the white man was bound to respect." Therefore, Dred Scott had never been a citizen of Missouri and had no right to sue his mistress. Taney also decreed that Congress had never held a constitutional right to restrict slavery in the territories and that therefore the Missouri Compromise of 1820 was invalid. Two justices dissented from the majority's opinion, but the decision stood as the law of the land.

Southerners and many Northern Democrats exulted that they had been vindicated by the *Dred Scott* decision, that the Republicans' demand for territories free of slavery was simply unconstitutional. Republicans, however, sneered at the decision, which they saw as one more corrupt act by the Slave Power designed to turn the nation into "one great slave pen." They reprinted the dissenting opinions in the *Dred Scott* case and denounced the decision in the state legislatures they controlled throughout the North. They argued that the founding fathers had never intended slavery to be a permanent part of the United States and merely tolerated bondage because they expected it to die of its own weight. If the *Dred Scott* decision were followed to its logical conclusion, they warned, the United States would reopen the slave trade with Africa and even extend slavery into northern states, where it had been banned. Republicans recognized that outrage over the decision would strengthen their own party.

AMERICAN SOCIETY IN CRISIS, 1857–1859

The American economy boomed in the mid-1850s. Not only did cotton do well, but so did the farms, factories, railroads, and cities of the North and West. People cheered the laying of a telegraphic cable across the Atlantic Ocean, an incredible feat that triggered celebrations in towns across the nation, including wild fireworks in New York City that set city hall ablaze. Currier and Ives prints became the rage, brightening homes around the country with charming scenes of American life. The sale of newspapers, books, and magazines surged. Working people's organizations staged a comeback. Churches and schools spread with remarkable speed. The mileage of railroads tripled to more than thirty thousand miles.

But underlying this prosperity ran a deep current of unease. Some people worried that Americans were growing soft and self-indulgent. Others felt guilt that as the economy boomed, slavery became stronger. Others despaired at the state of American politics, which seemed in disarray. The conflict between the North and the South embodied all these anxieties, giving them concrete shape.

Financial Panic and Spiritual Revival, 1857 Late in the summer of 1857, people warned that there had been too much speculation recently, that companies and individuals had borrowed too much money. The end of the Crimean War in Europe seemed ominous for the United States, for now the countries of the Old World could turn their energies toward growing their own food, undermining the heavy demand for American farm products that had buoyed the economy for several years. When a major insurance company went under in 1857, a panic spread among New York banks, and railroad stocks plummeted along with western land values. Soon banks and companies across the country began to fail.

Working people of all ranks lost their jobs. Not only did unskilled laborers, domestics, and millworkers find themselves without work, but so did educated bookkeepers

The Panic of 1857

New York City symbolized for many Americans the consequences of the high living and corrupt practices that brought on the panic of 1857. "With fifty-seven suspended banks . . . hundreds and thousands of bankrupt merchants, importers, traders, and stock jobbers . . . with her rotten bankruptcies permeating and injuring almost every solvent community in the nation," raged one New Orleans newspaper, New York stood as "the center of reckless speculation, unflinching fraud and downright robbery." This cartoon dramatizes the moral corruption that many people believed lay at the heart of the panic.

The panic had more immediate and concrete causes. The end of the Crimean War in Europe triggered a decline in overseas demand for American agricultural products and reduction in specie flows into the nation from European investors. A wave of bankruptcies caused bank closures as cash became scarce and banks shut their doors when cash supplies ran out. Small businessmen and managers, with no prospects of sales, laid off workers or offered them payment in kind instead of wages. Ironically, the Southern cotton economy rebounded sooner, as European demand for cotton recovered by 1858, but Northern and midwestern grain farmers faced low prices for the next two years.

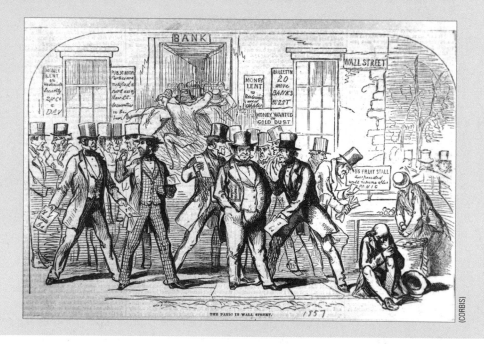

and clerks. Across the North, hundreds of thousands of people had no income, and many were forced to rely on charity to feed and clothe themselves. Workers tried to organize, but employers shut down the mills and factories. As winter approached, many people wondered whether their families would survive through the cold months.

Southerners blamed northern financiers for bringing on the **Panic of 1857**. Though the white and free black working people of southern cities suffered along with their counterparts in the North, white Southerners bragged that their region quickly recovered from the panic. They also boasted that their slaves, unlike white workers, never starved or went without a roof over their heads.

A wave of religious revivals that emerged in response to the panic lasted for over a year, sweeping back and forth across the country. Unlike earlier revivals, the religious spirit emerged not in rural districts but in the largest cities of the Northeast. Unlike earlier revivals, too, those of 1857 attracted a conspicuously large number of men as well as women. In contrast to earlier revivals in rural areas, middle-class men in the commercial districts of larger cities met for daily prayer meetings. The Young Men's Christian Association expanded rapidly during this time, providing young single clerks a venue for creating a "businesslike piety."

It seemed to many people that the revivals were the most heartening and significant in American history, showing that the people in the forefront of modern America were trying to change their ways.

The Agony of Kansas	Most of the settlers who arrived in Kansas in 1856 and 1857 were nonslaveholding migrants from the Upper South and did not appear eager to establish slavery in Kansas. An open elec-

tion therefore would likely install a constitutional convention in favor of free soil at the time Kansas became a state. The proslavery legislature elected in the earliest days of the territory, however, still controlled Kansas in 1857. That legislature had to produce a constitution that the U.S. Congress would accept before Kansas could become a state. The draft they wrote permitted voters to choose between the constitution with slavery or without slavery. In either case, slave owners already in Kansas would be permitted to keep their slaves.

This "Lecompton Constitution" unleashed serious problems for Democrats across the country. Northern members of the party could not support it without appearing too sympathetic to the South; they could not oppose it without alienating the Southern Democrats who made up the bulk of the party's strength. President Buchanan knew well that 112 of his 174 electoral votes had come from the South and that 100 of the 165 Democrats in both houses of Congress were Southerners.

Stephen Douglas refused to endorse the Lecompton Constitution because it was a violation of popular sovereignty, but President Buchanan urged its adoption. The president persuaded himself that the constitution was a moderate compromise, letting Kansas enter the Union as a free state in the long run while protecting the slaveholders who were already there. Once Kansas was a state, Buchanan reasoned, its legislature could decide what to do with those slaves. Most Northerners saw the matter differently: though it was obvious that the great majority of Kansans wanted to enter the Union as a free state, antislavery Kansans would be forced to accept slavery.

Republicans could hardly believe that Buchanan had handed them such an easy way to portray him as a tool of the South. And moderate Southern and Northern Democrats warned that the South was destroying its only hope for continued success: a strong Democratic Party in the North. When Kansas voters overwhelmingly rejected the Lecompton Constitution in 1858, they rejected Buchanan and the South as well. The Democrats suffered widespread defeat in the state elections that spring and lost control of the House. Northern Democrats, still weak from the loss of seats after the 1854 elections, lost again as only thirty-two of fifty-three free-state Democrats survived the 1858 contest and twelve of those were opposed to the Lecompton Constitution. Stephen Douglas faced a tough election battle, and Buchanan did everything he could to destroy this rival in his own party. Running against a promising Republican candidate, **Abraham Lincoln**, Douglas needed all the help he could get.

The Lincoln-Douglas Debates, 1858

Abraham Lincoln was very much the underdog in the Illinois senatorial race of 1858. As a Whig in a heavily Democratic state, Lincoln had not found it easy to win or hold office in the 1840s and 1850s. He had lost repeatedly, occupying national office for all of two years: elected to the House of Representatives in 1846, Lincoln lasted only one term and was sent back to his law office in Springfield. There, he made a good living as a lawyer, drawing on his own abilities and the connections that came with his marriage to Mary Todd, a member of a prominent family. Lincoln's modest beginnings on the Kentucky and Illinois frontier lay comfortably in the past. Still, he longed for a major public office.

Though the short, portly, pragmatic, and famous Stephen Douglas seemed the opposite of the tall, thin, inexperienced, principled, and obscure Abraham Lincoln, the two men shared their constituents' moderate positions on most national issues.

Illinois's population was composed of many New England migrants in the northern half of the state, upcountry Southern migrants in the lower half, and German and Irish immigrants in Chicago. Both the factories and the farms of Illinois prospered in the 1850s, as did abolitionists, Know-Nothings, Whigs, and Southern-leaning Democrats. The Illinois senatorial election of 1858 promised to throw all these groups into contention. At stake was this question: Could the Democrats survive as a national party, with Douglas as their leader, or were they doomed to become a party of the South?

Douglas traveled by private railroad car from Chicago to Springfield, the state capital and Lincoln's base. All along the way, he gave speeches to thousands of people, telling them that he was the voice of experience, principled compromise, and popular sovereignty. He also told them that Lincoln held "monstrous revolutionary doctrines" of abolitionism. To Douglas's great annoyance, Lincoln followed the senator to rebut his arguments and charges, sometimes appearing in the crowd, sometimes arriving the next day. Douglas, though reluctant to give the relatively unknown Lincoln a share of attention, finally agreed to hold seven joint debates in the late summer and early fall.

Lincoln was far from an abolitionist, refusing to join the antislavery Liberty and Free-Soil parties and staying with the Whigs longer than many of the men who became Republicans. He repeatedly brought up the *Dred Scott* decision from the previous year, however, arguing that it would permit slavery to spread into lands where Illinois men or their sons would otherwise migrate. The West must remain a region where "white men may find a home . . . where they can settle upon some new soil and better their condition in life." Douglas offered what he saw as practical, commonsense responses to such charges, arguing that slavery would not spread anywhere the majority of the white population did not want it to. A far greater and more immediate threat, Douglas argued, was that the Republicans would force the South into desperate acts by dragging moral issues into political contexts. Let the sovereign white people of each state decide for themselves whether they would have slavery, Douglas counseled. Douglas did not defend slavery, but he declared, "I care more for the great principle of self-government, the right of the people to rule, than I do for all the negroes in Christendom."

Lincoln charged that Douglas's strategy merely postponed an inevitable reckoning between the slave states and the free states. He argued that "a house divided against itself cannot stand. . . . Either the opponents of slavery will arrest the further spread of it, . . . or its advocates will push it forward till it shall become alike lawful in all the States, old as well as new." Notwithstanding Douglas's efforts to dismiss the morality of slavery as beside the point, that morality repeatedly surfaced in the debates. Lincoln argued that he, not Douglas, was the one defending true self-government. Douglas's policy permitted the forces of slavery to grow stronger and more aggressive, whereas Lincoln's would place slavery on the path toward "ultimate extinction." It would likely be several generations before that extinction occurred, Lincoln believed, but the process could begin in 1858. Lincoln took the offensive, making Douglas appear more of a defender of slavery than at heart he was.

The election was close, but the state legislature, which elected U.S. senators in these decades, went to the Democrats, and they returned Douglas to Washington. But Lincoln had become identified as the spokesman for a principled yet restrained antislavery. All across the North, in fact, the Republicans made impressive gains in 1858. In every state, many people wanted the nation to find some compromise. But the political environment did not have a chance to calm in 1859, for it was then that John Brown returned to the national scene.

John Brown and Harpers Ferry, 1859

John Brown had become famous in the three years since he had burst into prominence in Bleeding Kansas in 1855. Antislavery people back east, assured by journalists that Brown had not personally killed anyone at Pottawatomie, admired the hard man for his firsthand opposition to slaveholders. Thus, as he toured New England in search of funds to carry on the cause, he found willing listeners and open hands. Antislavery advocates were eager to contribute to the fight against slavery in Kansas, not realizing they were contributing to a fight against slavery much closer to home. Brown wrote letters to wealthy abolitionists requesting assistance for "an important measure, in which the world has a deep interest." Throughout 1857 and 1858, Brown planned an attack on the federal arsenal at **Harpers Ferry**, Virginia. He had a thousand iron pikes forged to arm the slaves he believed would rise in rebellion once he and his men triggered the revolt. He tried to win the support of Frederick Douglass, who, while sympathetic, thought the plan doomed. But Brown pressed on.

The assault on Harpers Ferry started in earnest in the summer of 1859, when Brown rented a farm seven miles away and assembled his men and munitions. To his disappointment, he could recruit only twenty-one men, five of them African Americans. The raid began easily enough on Sunday, October 16, as Brown's men quickly seized the arsenal and a rifle-manufacturing plant. Brown and his men remained in the small armory building, waiting for word to spread among the slaves of Virginia that their day of liberation had come. The word spread instead among local whites, who quickly surrounded Brown's men, killing or capturing eight of them. Militia from Virginia and Maryland arrived the next day, followed soon after by federal troops that rushed the armory. Ten of the abolitionist force were killed, five (including Brown) wounded, and seven escaped. Brown was tried within two weeks and found guilty. He was sentenced to be hanged exactly a month later, on December 2.

The entire episode, from the raid to Brown's execution, took only about six weeks to unfold. Yet during those six weeks, opinion in both the North and the South changed rapidly. Public opinion, mixed at first, crystallized into sharply opposing viewpoints. Even Northerners who were appalled at the violence were shocked at the speed with which Brown was tried and condemned. Even Southerners who read with reassurance early denunciations of Brown in the North were appalled when they realized that many Northerners refused to condemn the raid. The many people of moderate sympathies on both sides watched, dismayed, as common ground eroded beneath their feet.

THE NORTH AND SOUTH CALL EACH OTHER'S BLUFF, 1860–1861

Everyone knew the election of 1860 held enormous meaning for the United States, but no one could be sure what that meaning might be. Would this be the election that brought all to their senses? Would the border states be able to control the election? Would Northern voters suddenly realize the South meant what it said? The actual events proved far more complex than most Americans had believed possible.

The Election of 1860

White Southerners automatically linked John Brown with the Republican Party, though leading Republicans explicitly denied any connection. Not only had any Southern base of support disappeared, but the execution of John Brown and Southern exultation at his death made the Republicans more attractive among Northern voters than before.

The Democrats also felt the effects of Brown's raid. Meeting in Charleston in April 1860 to decide on their presidential nominee for the fall election, the Northern Democrats nominated Stephen Douglas in what they saw as a compromise with the South. But Southern Democrats demanded that the party explicitly uphold the rights of slaveholders to take their slaves into the territories as stated in the *Dred Scott* decision. Northern Democrats could not afford to make that concession and still have a chance to win back home. The Southerners proved heedless of this plea, however, and they walked out of the convention. Several weeks later, the Democrats met in Baltimore and nominated Douglas. Southerners, walking out once again and declaring themselves the "purified" Democratic party, nominated **John C. Breckinridge** of Kentucky.

Before the Democratic convention met again in June, Unionists in both the North and the South tried to avert catastrophe by nominating a compromise candidate. Calling themselves the Constitutional Union Party, they settled on **John Bell** of Tennessee. Many of these Unionists were former conservative Whigs and Know-Nothings who no longer had a political home. They advocated an end to agitation over slavery, "the Union as it is, the Constitution unchanged," to safeguard the "priceless heritage of our fathers." They counted on the other candidates to create a deadlock that would have to be settled in the House of Representatives. There, the Unionists hoped, legislators would gratefully turn to their compromise candidate.

As the Democrats tore themselves apart, the Republicans met in Chicago. There, in efforts to put Southern concerns at rest, the Republicans announced their belief in

Gender and Antislavery in the Election of 1860

By 1860, Republicans sought to extend their appeal to political moderates. In this portrait, the Lincoln family embodies the ideal of Northern middle-class domesticity. Abraham, the affectionate father, reads to his sons, while Mary plays a traditional maternal role, her political engagement restricted to helping her husband nurture and educate future voters. Given the Republicans' connection to antislavery and women's rights causes, reassurances such as these were particularly important to moderate voters. For many Americans, women's political participation represented a threat to both masculinity and the nation's families. The tasteful furnishings, art, flowers, and books in this scene attest to Mary's refinement and the Lincolns' commitment to domestic harmony. At the same time, a toy cannon in the lower left-hand corner suggests that Abraham is training his sons in the ways of traditional masculinity—and that by extension, he himself will face conflicts "manfully."

(Library of Congress)

the right of each state to decide for itself whether it would have slavery. The Republicans cemented their appeal to voters unconcerned with the slavery issue by calling for protective tariffs, internal improvements, and free homesteads for anyone who would settle the West. The Republicans were much stronger than they had been only four years earlier. Party strategists calculated that they need only win Pennsylvania and one other state they had lost to the Democrats in 1856 to wrap up the election. The states they needed to take were Illinois, Indiana, or New Jersey—all of them on the border with the South and all of them far more moderate on the slavery question than states farther east or north. Thus, the Republicans turned to a moderate who was a favorite son of one of the crucial states: Abraham Lincoln of Illinois.

People in 1860 did not know that the way they voted would bring on a civil war, or even secession. Although Stephen Douglas constantly warned of such a danger, both Breckinridge and Lincoln downplayed such dire consequences. Ironically, all the years of conflict had persuaded both the North and the South that the other talked tougher than it would act. The parties staged loud and raucous political events that proved long on emotion and short on clearly defined positions. Lincoln said nothing and stayed close to home while his party leaders displayed split fence rails and touted his honesty.

The election of 1860 was actually two separate elections: one in the North and one in the South. Lincoln made no attempt to explain himself to the South; Breckinridge made little attempt in the North. They never met face to face. Bell spoke mainly to the already converted. Douglas, breaking with tradition, spoke from New England to Alabama, trying to warn people what could happen if they voted along sectional lines. While campaigning across the Deep South, he endured having rotten fruit thrown at him, insults, and injuries from a collapsed platform. Few men were willing to believe their opponents would have the nerve to act on their threats.

On election day, November 6, Lincoln won in every Northern state except New Jersey, which divided between Douglas and Lincoln. Douglas won outright only in Missouri. Breckinridge won the entire South except the border states of Virginia, Tennessee, and Kentucky, which went with Bell. Even at this late stage of sectional division, voters did not fit into easy categories. It was hardly a contest between a rural South and an industrial urban North, for Northern cities tended to vote for compromise candidates, not for Lincoln. Similarly, over half of Southerners voted for Bell or Douglas, supporting the Union over the South.

Once the election returns were in, these complications seemed to evaporate. Although Lincoln won only in the North, the election was not even close in the electoral college, where Lincoln won 180 electoral votes to Breckinridge's 72, Bell's 39, and Douglas's 12. In Southern eyes, the North had arrogantly placed its own interests above those of the Union, insisting on electing a man who did not even appear on Southern ballots. In Northern eyes, the South, walking out of nominating conventions and talking of disunion, was to blame. The election of 1860 completed the estrangement of North and South.

The South Debates Independence

The fire-eaters declared Abraham Lincoln's 1860 victory a sign that the North valued neither the Union nor the Constitution on which it was based. The South, they said, had every right, every incentive, to leave the Union. Although the Republicans claimed to work within the political system, Lincoln's supporters had violated an honored tradition of compromise.

Even though the Democrats still controlled the Senate and the Supreme Court, Southerners believed that Lincoln would use the patronage of the federal government to install Republican officials throughout the South and possibly entice nonslaveholders with their free labor doctrines. Such officials could undermine slavery from within, eroding the authority of slave owners. For years, Lincoln had talked of "a house" that had to be unified, of a nation that had to be all slave or all free. Would he not act to undermine slavery now that he was in power?

The nation's eyes turned to South Carolina. Influential men there, after all, had talked of secession since the nullification crisis nearly thirty years earlier. They believed that the same states that had created the Union could also dissolve that Union when it no longer served their purposes. The South Carolina legislature met on the day after Lincoln's election but did not secede immediately. Its members called for an election two months later to select delegates who would then decide the course the state should follow. In the meantime, they hoped, support for secession would grow. The next day, a local paper blustered, "The tea has been thrown overboard; the revolution of 1860 has been initiated."

States of the Deep South quickly lined up behind South Carolina. Carolina leaders, heartened by the response, seceded earlier than they had planned, on December 20. Southerners serving in Buchanan's cabinet began resigning, and by the administration's annual New Year's Day reception, the Southerners in attendance refused to shake Buchanan's hand or acknowledge the president. By February 1, Mississippi, Florida, Alabama, Georgia, Louisiana, and Texas had joined the secession movement. On February 4, delegates from these states met in Montgomery, Alabama, and created a provisional constitution, similar to that of the United States except in its explicit guarantee of slavery and states' rights. On February 18, the convention inaugurated a provisional president, Jefferson Davis of Mississippi, and a vice president, Alexander H. Stephens of Georgia. Davis was a strong states' rights advocate but not a fervent secessionist. With an eye toward opinion in the crucial states of Virginia, North Carolina, Kentucky, and Tennessee, these leaders of the new Confederacy portrayed themselves as a calm and conservative people, not wild-eyed revolutionaries.

The advocates of secession knew they had to strike before Lincoln took office. Two bad things could happen if they waited to see what the new president did once in office: he might either attack the South by force, or he might prove to be as moderate as he claimed to be. In the latter case, secessionists feared, white Southerners would let the moment pass.

Many thousands of white Southerners resisted secession. Some argued that secession was treason. Others warned that the South was committing suicide. A few argued that the Southern states should wait until they could cooperate with one another more formally and fully. By presenting a united front to the North, these "cooperationists" insisted, the South would not need to secede at all. The North, recognizing that the South was not bluffing, would grant concessions protecting slavery forever.

The arguments against immediate secession appealed to a large portion of Southerners. Even in the Southern states that rushed to secede in January 1861, almost half of all votes went to delegates who had not supported immediate secession. The opposition to secession proved stronger still in the Upper South. Upper South moderates warned that their states would bear the brunt of any conflict between the Lower South and the North. And voters listened: more than a month after the first seven states seceded, secession lost in Virginia by a two-to-one margin. The secessionists were also stymied in Tennessee, North Carolina, and Arkansas. The leaders of these border states believed they could bargain between the Gulf Confederacy and the North, winning the concessions the South wanted while maintaining the Union.

Recognizing the need to convince the border states to join the secession movement, five states from the Lower South dispatched agents to the Upper South to advocate and justify disunion. These commissioners wrote numerous letters to local politicians and spoke to legislatures, public meetings, and private gatherings of community leaders in their efforts to cajole and persuade. These conversations among Southerners emphasized the importance of race and slavery as the foundation of the states' rights argument. Delegates warned that the Republican Party's future vision of America "destroys the property of the South, lays waste her fields, and inaugurates all the horrors of a San Domingo servile insurrection, consigning her citizens to assassinations and her wives and daughters to pollution and violation."

Northerners too remained quite divided at the beginning of 1861. Many recent immigrants viewed the conflict as none of their business. Northern Democrats called for conciliation with the South. Many black Northerners warned that a war for the Union alone did not deserve black support. A war to end bondage would be worth fighting, they argued, but in 1861 only the most aggressive white abolitionists spoke of such a cause.

People had plenty of opportunity to air their opinions, for events did not move quickly after Lincoln's election. After the first flush of secessionist victory at the beginning of 1861, people throughout the nation watched and waited to see what would happen when the new president officially assumed office on March 4. In the meantime, no one appeared to be in charge. James Buchanan, as lame-duck president, could not do much, and neither could the lame-duck Congress.

Most Republicans, including Lincoln, viewed the rhetoric and even the votes for Southern secession as negotiating strategies rather than actual steps toward dissolving the Union. The Republicans showed no inclination to bargain with the South over what remained the key issue: federal support for slavery in the territories. The tensions that had built up in the 1850s, Lincoln thought, could no longer be avoided. "The tug has to come," he argued, "and better now, than any time hereafter." If the North postponed action, Lincoln and other Republicans thought, the South would step up its efforts to gain new slave territories in the Caribbean and Central America, dragging the United States into war.

THE FIRST SECESSION, 1861

In the winter of 1861, the center of the conflict between the North and the South gradually shifted to two obscure forts in the harbor of Charleston, South Carolina. A Kentucky-born U.S. Army officer, Major Robert Anderson, worried that secessionists would attack his small federal force at Fort Moultrie in Charleston. Determined to avoid a war, Anderson moved his small garrison from Fort Moultrie to **Fort Sumter** on December 26, a facility occupying a safer position in the center of the Charleston harbor. When South Carolina guns drove away a ship President Buchanan had sent with supplies for Anderson and his men, Buchanan chose not to force the issue. Meanwhile, South Carolina troops strengthened their position around the Charleston harbor.

Lincoln Becomes President Men from both the North and the South worked frantically, but fruitlessly, to find a compromise during these weeks. Some urged the passage of a new constitutional amendment that would permit slavery forever; some urged the purchase of Cuba to permit slavery to expand; some urged that war be declared against another country to pull the United States together again. All the compromises were designed to placate the South. Abolitionists viewed such maneuvering with disgust and told their countrymen to let the South go. "If the Union can only be maintained by new concessions to the slaveholders," Frederick Douglass argued, "then . . . let the Union perish." Such views were not popular. Mobs attacked antislavery advocates throughout the North.

On February 11, Abraham Lincoln began a long and circuitous railway trip from Illinois to Washington, covering nearly 2,000 miles and using twenty separate rail lines, pausing frequently along the way to speak to well-wishers. At first, he downplayed the threat of secession: "Let it alone," he counseled, "and it will go down of itself." But as the train rolled on and the Confederate convention in Montgomery completed its provisional government, Lincoln became more wary. Warned of attempts on his life, he slipped into Washington under cover of darkness.

Lincoln assembled his government under the growing shadow of war. He sought to balance his cabinet with men of various backgrounds. The two most formidable cabinet members were Secretary of State William H. Seward, a moderate Republican, and Secretary of the Treasury Salmon P. Chase, a radical Republican inclined to take a harder line with the South. Fort Sumter stood as the most pressing issue facing the new administration. Any show of force to reclaim the fort from South Carolina, Southern Unionists warned, and the secessionists would sweep border states such as Virginia into the Confederacy.

Lincoln, with Seward's advice, toned down the speech he delivered at his inauguration in March. He told the South that he had no intention of disturbing slavery where it was already established, that he would not invade the region, that he would not attempt to fill offices with men repugnant to local sensibilities. But he also warned that secession was illegal. It was his duty to maintain the integrity of the federal government, and to do so he had to "hold, occupy, and possess" federal property in the states of the Confederacy, including Fort Sumter. Lincoln pleaded with his countrymen to move slowly and let passions cool.

People heard in Lincoln's inaugural what they chose to. Republicans and Unionists in the South thought it a potent mixture of firmness and generosity. Skeptics focused on the threat of coercion at Fort Sumter. If Lincoln attempted to use force of any kind, they warned, war would be the inevitable result. Lincoln did not plan on war; he was trying to buy time, hoping that compromisers in Washington would come up with a workable strategy.

The Decision at Fort Sumter, April 12–14, 1861   There was less time than Lincoln realized. On the very day after Lincoln's speech, Major Anderson reported to Washington that he would be out of food within four to six weeks. Initially unsure as to the wisdom of retaining the fort, Lincoln finally decided that he had to act: he would send provisions but not military supplies to Fort Sumter. By doing so, Lincoln would maintain the balance he promised in his inaugural speech, keeping the fort but not using coercion unless attacked first.

Jefferson Davis and his government had decided a week earlier that any attempt to reprovision the fort would be an act of war. Davis believed that no foreign power would respect a country, especially one as new and tenuous as the Confederate States of America, if it allowed one of its major ports to be occupied by another country. The Union's resupply of the fort would mean the Union still controlled it.

The Confederate government decided that its commander in Charleston, P. G. T. Beauregard, should attack Fort Sumter before the relief expedition had a chance to arrive. The leaders understood the risks. The Confederate secretary of state, Robert Toombs, warned Jefferson Davis that the attack would "lose us every friend at the North" and "wantonly strike a hornet's nest which extends from mountains to ocean, and legions, now quiet, will swarm out and sting us to death. It is unnecessary; it puts us in the wrong; it is fatal." Nevertheless, on April 12, at 4:30 in the morning, Beauregard opened fire on the Union garrison. The shelling continued for thirty-three hours.

Anderson held out for as long as he could, but when fire tore through the barracks and his ammunition ran low, he decided the time for surrender had come. Northerners agreed that the events in South Carolina could not go unanswered. Lincoln issued a call for seventy-five thousand volunteers to defend the Union. Southerners agreed that they would have no choice but to come to that state's aid if the North raised a hand against their fellow Southerners.

CONCLUSION

> ### DOING HISTORY ONLINE
>
> **Broken Bonds, 1855–1861**
>
> After reading Documents 1 to 18, evaluate the following statement: the Civil War was a conflict that was inevitable, a struggle that was bound to occur.
>
> www.cengage.com/ history/ayers/ ampassages4e

The North and the South had long been on a collision course. Ever since the framing of the Constitution, slavery had defined the contrast between the regions. Sometimes that difference seemed to fade in importance to white Americans; at other times it burst into a central role in the nation's understanding of itself. Years of relative quiet passed between episodes such as the Missouri Compromise and Nat Turner's Rebellion and the Mexican-American War. But in the late 1850s, events piled on top of one another, delivering blows so quickly that the nation did not have time to regain its balance.

Kansas became a hothouse for the sectional conflict. Proslavery men and antislavery men fought over the future of slavery in Kansas. The caning of Senator Charles Sumner of Massachusetts by Representative Preston Brooks of South Carolina in the halls of Congress carried the violence into the very heart of the nation. With a weak president in the White House, no one seemed to be in charge.

Although both the North and the South prospered economically in the 1850s, both claimed to see weakness in the other, especially when the panic of 1857 hit. Southerners pointed to the unemployed masses in the North's cities as evidence of the superiority of slavery; Northerners pointed to the speed with which their economy recovered as evidence of its fundamental soundness. A national religious revival testified to a sense among Americans that they were losing their way both publicly and privately. John Brown's raid unleashed a disgust that many Americans had rarely before expressed about each other.

In the meantime, the election of 1860 loomed. With the new Republican Party having done so well in the 1856 election and with the Democrats spending most of their energy squabbling with one another, voters throughout the country realized that the election in 1860 would be a crucial test for the United States.

Party leaders worked furiously in the summer and fall of 1860 to steer the election in their direction. John Bell and Stephen Douglas pleaded with their countrymen not to vote for men they portrayed as purely regional candidates: Abraham Lincoln in the North and John Breckinridge in the South. On election day, many voted for the candidates of compromise, especially in states along the border between the North and the South. But more men voted for candidates who stood for clear purpose and even defiance. The North's burgeoning population gave the region the power to elect a Republican who was not on the ballot in most Southern states, and they did: Abraham Lincoln became president.

As soon as the election results were announced, South Carolina began the process of seceding from the Union. Other states in the Lower South joined South Carolina, and by early 1861, before Lincoln had even taken office, the Confederate States of America had begun to take form.

The question now was whether the slave states of Virginia, North Carolina, Tennessee, Kentucky, Maryland, and Missouri, on the border between the North and the South, would join the new Confederacy or remain in the United States. When the food ran out in Fort Sumter, however, and when the cannons boomed over Charleston, everyone realized that time had run out.

CHAPTER REVIEW, 1855–1861

- Bleeding Kansas and the *Dred Scott* decision fed the growth of the new Republican Party.
- Abraham Lincoln and Stephen Douglas engaged in famous debates that sharply defined the place of slavery in American politics.
- John Brown's raid horrified the South and mobilized the North in response.
- The election of 1860 pitched four candidates against each other, and Abraham Lincoln emerged victorious because of his victories across the North.
- The states of the Gulf South formed the Confederate States of America and then fired on Fort Sumter in Charleston.

◀▦ Looking Back

As Chapter 13 shows, in the late 1850s and early 1860s, voters in the United States faced the most important elections in the country's history. Those elections turned around the meaning that slavery held for white Americans.

1. Why did the sectional crisis peak when it did?
2. Were there times when events could have taken a different turn and the United States could have avoided secession? When might that have happened?
3. Did long-term economic and social changes push the United States toward war, or were the causes located firmly in political events?

Looking Ahead ▦▶

Chapter 14 will show how the events of 1860 quickly spun out of control and began what would become a vast war.

1. What kind of conflict would Americans in both the North and the South have predicted lay ahead of them when South Carolina seceded in December 1860?
2. Why were both Northerners and Southerners so confident in 1860?

Go to the American Passages website at www.cengage.com/history/ayers/ ampassages4e for additional review materials.

14

Descent into War, 1861–1862

At the beginning of 1861, Americans could not imagine anything like the war that would soon consume their nation. Events piled on one another in ways that no one could have anticipated. The men who voted for Lincoln did not think the South would secede, the architects of secession did not think the North would resist, and neither side thought the other would or could fight for long. Events proved no more predictable once the war began. Last-minute reinforcements and retreats changed the outcome of battles; news from the battlefield shaped every political and diplomatic decision.

WAR BEGINS: APRIL TO JULY 1861

Neither the Union nor the Confederacy was ready for conflict in the spring of 1861. A number of states had yet to declare their loyalties; other states, communities, and families were divided against themselves. In a matter of months, both the North and the South had to prepare for war.

Lincoln Calls for Troops, April 15, 1861

Two days after the Confederate flag went up over Fort Sumter on April 15, President Lincoln declared South Carolina in rebellion against the United States and called for seventy-five thousand militiamen to help put the rebellion down. The president sought to appear restrained in his response. He demanded that forces gathering from the states of the Lower South "disperse and retire peacefully." He still hoped that Unionists in Southern states besides South Carolina would rally to the nation's defense if he showed that he was no extremist. Lincoln also acted cautiously because he had not received the approval of Congress, which would not convene until July.

Lincoln's attempt to blend firmness and conciliation failed. Southern states saw the call to the militia as an act of aggression against South Carolina and state sovereignty. The Upper South states replied with defiance to Lincoln's requests for their troops on April 15, 1861. One Virginia representative responded to the president, "I have a Union constituency which elected me by a majority of one thousand, and I believe now that there are not ten Union men in that county today." Virginia seceded two days later. Although many people in Virginia still clung to hopes of avoiding war, two delegates to every one voted for secession on April 17. These Virginians, like white Southerners of all inclinations and temperaments, refused to supply soldiers to confront another slaveholding state. Recognizing the importance of moving President **Jefferson Davis** and his government closer to their armies, the Confederacy immediately voted to move its capital to Richmond in May 1861.

In the North, even in areas like New York City, which had opposed Lincoln's election, 250,000 people filled the streets in a Unionist rally in response to Southern aggression. Democrat Stephen Douglas addressed a tumultuous Chicago crowd. "There are only two sides to the question," he proclaimed. "Every man must be for the United States or against it. There can be no neutrals in this war, only patriots—or traitors."

The States Divide   Arkansas, Tennessee, and North Carolina quickly followed Virginia's example and joined the new Confederacy. North Carolinians, who over the winter rioted against secession and shot Confederate flags from their staffs, considered Lincoln's actions a call to arms for Southern men that "as by a stroke of lighting, . . . made the South wholly South." The Oklahoma Territory, too, aligned itself with the Confederacy. There, leaders of the Five Civilized Tribes, slaveholders themselves, used the opportunity to fight against the U.S. government that had dispossessed them from their homes three decades earlier. As leaders of other Indian nations sided with the Union, however, conflict spread within and among tribes to control the Indian Territory.

State leaders elsewhere frantically struggled with one another. In Maryland, rioters attacked Massachusetts troops as they marched through Baltimore two days after the secession of neighboring Virginia—spilling the first blood of the war when twelve civilians and four Union soldiers died in the gunfire. Maryland was bitterly divided: the southern portion of the state sympathized with the Confederacy while Baltimore, where free blacks outnumbered slaves by eleven to one, and the western portion generally supported the Union. Should the United States lose Maryland, the District of Columbia would be completely surrounded by Confederate territory. Accordingly, Lincoln acted quickly to keep Maryland in line, jailing secession advocates and suspending the **writ of habeas corpus**, which allowed prisoners to petition against unlawful detention, so they could not be released.

Kentucky, after months of determined attempts to remain neutral, decided for the Union in September after Confederate troops entered the state. Missouri officially remained in the Union but was ravaged from within by brutal violence for the next four years. Dissension took a different form in the mountains of western Virginia. In June, delegates from fifty counties met in Wheeling to renounce the Virginia secession convention, begin the gradual abolition of slavery, and declare their loyalty to the Union. Lincoln recognized these breakaway counties as the legal government of Virginia, and their legislative delegations were seated in July 1861. After a complicated series of conventions and elections, the state of West Virginia came into being in 1862 and joined the Union the following year.

This icon will direct you to interactive activities and study materials on the American Passages website: www.cengage.com/history/ayers/ampassages4e

CHAPTER TIMELINE

1861	April 15	Lincoln calls for 75,000 militia
	April 17–May 20	Arkansas, Tennessee, Virginia, and North Carolina secede
	May 29	Richmond becomes capital of Confederacy
	July 21	Confederate victory at Bull Run (Manassas)
	July 25	Frémont takes command in the West
	July 27	McClellan takes command of Union forces near Washington
	August 30	Frémont declares martial law, and frees slaves, in Missouri
	September 6	Kentucky remains in the Union
	November 1	McClellan assumes command of all Union armies
	November 6	Jefferson Davis elected president of Confederacy with six-year term
	November 7	Union capture of Port Royal, South Carolina
	November 8	Union navy seizes Confederate commissioners Mason and Slidell from British ship *Trent*
	November 19	Halleck replaces Frémont as Union commander in West
	December 26	Union government releases Mason and Slidell
	December 30	Suspension of specie payments
1862	February 6	Union captures Fort Henry on Tennessee River
	February 16	Confederates surrender Fort Donelson to Grant
	February 22	Inauguration of Jefferson Davis
	February 25	Legal Tender Act in North authorizes "greenbacks"
		Confederates evacuate Nashville
	February 27	Confederate Congress authorizes martial law and suspends habeas corpus
	March 8–9	*Virginia v. Monitor* in Hampton Roads, Virginia
	March 17	McClellan begins move to James River Peninsula
	April 5	McClellan begins siege of Yorktown
	April 6–7	Grant wins dramatic victory at Shiloh
	April 16	Confederacy passes Conscription Act
	April 25	New Orleans surrenders to Admiral Farragut
	May 8–9	Jackson's Shenandoah Valley Campaign
	May 20	Homestead Act passed by Union Congress
	May 31	Lee takes command of Army of Northern Virginia
	June 6	Confederates evacuate Memphis
	June 26	Lee drives McClellan from Richmond in Seven Days' Battles
	July 11	Halleck appointed general-in-chief of Union armies
	July 12	Border states reject Lincoln plan for gradual emancipation
	July 17	Second Confiscation Act

CHAPTER TIMELINE

July 22	Cabinet hears Lincoln's draft of Emancipation Proclamation
August 3	Union decides to evacuate McClellan's troops from peninsula
August 29–30	Confederate victory at Second Bull Run (Manassas)
September 4–6	Lee invades Maryland
September 17	Battle of Antietam (Sharpsburg)
September 22	First Emancipation Proclamation
October 3–4	Union victory at Corinth
November 7	Burnside replaces McClellan as commander of Army of the Potomac
	Republicans lose widely in mid-term elections in North
December 13	Lee overwhelms Burnside at Fredericksburg
December 16–20	Crisis in Lincoln's cabinet
December 27–29	Sherman defeated near Vicksburg

As it turned out, the Union and the Confederacy divided about evenly. Virginia, Tennessee, North Carolina, and Arkansas all joined the Confederacy only after Lincoln requested their troops to assist in suppressing insurrection in the Lower South. Had they remained in the Union, the Confederacy would have had little hope of sustaining a successful war against the North. Those states accounted for half of all manufacturing and half of all food production in the Confederacy. Maryland, Kentucky, and Missouri might well have joined the Confederacy; had they done so, the Union cause would have been weakened, perhaps fatally. Kentucky and Missouri occupied crucial positions along the major rivers that led into the South and linked the western Confederacy to the East. Even the dissidents balanced: eight states along the border provided 235,000 white and 85,000 black troops to the Union and 425,000 white troops to the Confederacy.

Although Abraham Lincoln was criticized from every angle in these months, he managed to bring into the Union the states he had to win. Had he lost these struggles, he might well have failed in all the other struggles that awaited him.

The Numbers In retrospect, the cards seemed heavily stacked in the North's favor. The Union, after all, had vastly greater industrial capacity, railroads, canals, food, draft animals, ships, and entrepreneurial experience, all the things a mid-nineteenth-century war required. The Union could also claim four times as many white residents as the South. And although the 3.5 million enslaved people who lived in the Confederacy were extraordinarily valuable to the South, everyone recognized that the slaves could become equally valuable allies for the North.

Since the South acknowledged the North's advantages, many people then and since assumed that the Confederates must have been driven by either irrational rage or heedless bravery. Neither the Confederates nor the Unionists, however, expected the secession crisis to turn into a full-fledged war, much less a four-year war. When Lincoln called for the seventy-five thousand militia, he called them for only ninety days' service. When Southern boys and men rushed to enlist for the Confederacy in the spring of 1861, they assumed they would be back home in time to harvest their crops in the autumn.

Southerners considered themselves natural soldiers, caricaturing their new enemies as clerks and factory workers. Although the Union did have more city men and immigrants than the South, most Northerners, like Southerners, were young men raised on farms. Since both sides believed that their opponents were weak and divided, Northerners and Southerners thought the conflict would likely come to a swift, and peaceful, resolution. Commanders on each side recognized their lack of experience. Lincoln calmed General Irvin McDowell: "You are green, it is true, but they are green also, you are all green alike." In such a struggle, sheer numbers did not seem nearly as important as they eventually became.

The Strategies

The military strategies of both sides sought to minimize actual fighting. The South saw itself as purely on the defensive; it would wait for Northern armies to invade and then defeat them. The North, for its part, counted on General Winfield Scott's **Anaconda Plan**, named after the large snake of that name that slowly engulfs and squeezes its prey to death. That plan depended on sending an overpowering force down the Mississippi River in the fall, dividing the South in two. At the same time, the Union navy would seal off the South from outside supplies. Ground troops and land battles would be kept to a minimum.

The Confederacy possessed considerable military advantages. It occupied an enormous area, larger than today's United Kingdom, France, Italy, and Spain combined. It possessed dozens of harbors and ports, connected by an excellent system of rivers and an adequate network of railroads. The Confederacy's long border with Mexico made it difficult to seal off outside supplies. The Confederacy could wage a defensive war, moving its troops internally from one point to another, whereas the Union had to move around the perimeter. The many country roads of the South, known only to locals, would provide routes for Confederate surprise attacks or strategic retreats.

For a model of how such a defensive plan might work, Southerners looked to the American Revolution. Like the American colonies eighty years earlier, the Confederates did not have to win every battle or conquer Northern territory. Southerners thought they had only to keep fighting long enough for the North's political, economic, regional, and ethnic divisions to overwhelm its temporary unity. Indeed, the Confederacy enjoyed advantages the American colonies had not enjoyed. The new Southern nation covered twice as much territory as had the colonies, and the North possessed nowhere near the military power of the British at the time of the Revolutionary War.

Leadership   There was also the matter of leadership. In 1861, many observers would have given the advantage to the Confederates in this regard. Abraham Lincoln, after all, had held public office for only two years before he assumed the presidency, and his only military service had been a brief service in the militia during Black Hawk's War. Jefferson Davis, by contrast, had distinguished himself in the war with Mexico. He had been secretary of war under Franklin Pierce and had served in the U.S. Senate. Davis, unlike Lincoln, directed his forces' military strategy with the confidence born of firsthand knowledge and experience.

At the beginning of the war, it appeared that the South had the better generals. The Southern leaders certainly had more experience: the average age of the Union generals in 1861 was thirty-eight; of Confederate generals, forty-seven. **Robert E. Lee** of Virginia had served as an engineer, an officer in the Mexican War in the 1840s, and superintendent of West Point in the late 1850s. He resigned his U.S. military commission and accepted command of Virginia's forces. By abandoning the United States, Lee made the same decision about two-thirds of Southern-born officers made when secession finally came.

Military experience and ability did not always prove to be the major considerations in the appointment of generals. Given the small size of the Federal armed forces before the war, the creation of two hostile armies resulted in a shortage of trained military leaders on both sides. Lincoln chose generals from the ranks of various constituencies he needed to appease: Republicans, abolitionists, Democrats, the Irish, Germans, and powerful politicians from across the North. Jefferson Davis did the same to bind ambitious politicians from the various states to the new Confederacy. About a third of Union generals and half their Confederate counterparts had not been professional soldiers, though most had some military training; overall, the North and the South placed roughly similar proportions of professional soldiers in command.

Neither the Union nor the Confederacy enjoyed a clear advantage in civilian leadership. Both Lincoln and Davis assembled cabinets that balanced geography, political faction, personality, and expertise. The Confederates had to create a government from scratch, including the design of flags, stamps, and money. Davis ran through several secretaries of war and secretaries of state before finding the two men on whom he felt he could rely, James A. Seddon and Judah P. Benjamin, respectively.

The Union enjoyed a head start in such matters, but the Republicans had many problems to iron out. Office seekers besieged Washington at the very time Lincoln was trying to keep the South in the Union; he felt like an innkeeper, he said, faced with customers demanding rooms in one wing while he tried to put out a fire in another. Lincoln's cabinet ended up containing men whom he barely knew and on whom he was not always sure he could rely.

The First Conflicts   Battles began before anyone was ready. On the day following Lincoln's call for troops in April, Federal officers in charge of the arsenal at Harpers Ferry and the naval yard in Norfolk, Virginia, sought to destroy the supplies and weapons under their command before secessionists could seize them. Despite their efforts, Virginia troops managed to recover valuable gun-making machinery, artillery, naval stores, and ships for the Confederate cause. A few weeks later, battles broke out along the B&O Railroad in what would become West Virginia, with Robert E. Lee, the new general for Virginia, leading an unsuccessful series of

Confederate Recruiting.
Broadsides such as this appeared across the Confederacy, calling on men to defend their wives and daughters from the Yankee's "hired and ruffian soldiers."

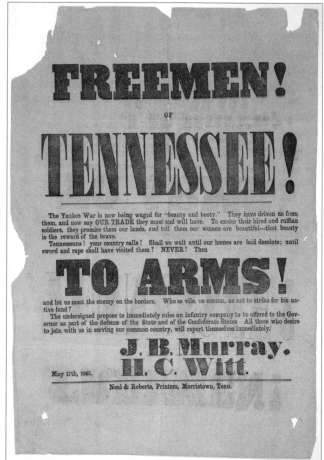

(Library of Congress)

attacks that damaged his reputation and led a Richmond newspaper to dub him "Granny Lee." Meanwhile, nearly four thousand Confederates, most of them from Texas, pushed into New Mexico. They hoped to win the mineral riches discovered in Colorado in 1857, and perhaps even those of California, for the Southern cause.

All these struggles showed both sides to be far from ready to fight a war in 1861. Not only were guns and uniforms scarce, but so was combat experience. Even men who had attended West Point had learned more about engineering than they had about tactical maneuvers or logistics. The U.S. Army contained only about sixteen thousand men, and nearly twelve thousand of them were scattered across the vast territory west of the Mississippi River. The militia who first responded to the calls of the Union and Confederacy had scarcely been trained at all.

Mobilization

Both sides took immediate steps to create new armies, organized within local communities and led by local men. The Confederate Congress authorized 400,000 volunteers in May 1861. In its special session beginning in July 1861, the Union Congress authorized 500,000 troops, each signing on for three years; 700,000 eventually enlisted under this authorization. Much mobilization took place on the local level. Prominent citizens often supplied uniforms, guns, and even food for the troops from their localities. Units elected their own officers. States competed to enlist the largest numbers of men.

Some Northerners wondered whether the many divisions among classes, occupations, religions, and ethnic groups would hinder the Union war effort. Such doubters took heart at the response to the crisis of 1861. Both workingmen and wealthy men eagerly signed up. Members of ethnic groups took pride in forming their own units; the Irish and Germans supplied more than 150,000 men each, with the total of foreign born in service totaling nearly half a million. Northerners congratulated themselves that patriotism and self-sacrifice had not been killed, as many feared, by the spirit of commerce so strong in the land. Editor Horace Greeley sketched the transformation of Northerners from "a sordid, grasping money-loving people" to one in whom the "fires of patriotic devotion" still burned.

Southerners too found reason to be proud in 1861. The leaders of the South had secretly worried that when push came to shove, the nonslaveholders would not fight for a cause that many identified with the defense of slavery. But Southern boys and men were activated by the same impulses that drove their Northern counterparts: dreams of glory, youthful self-confidence, and a burning desire to impress family, friends, and young women with their bravery. At this point in the war, white Southerners talked less about slavery than they had before or they would later. In their eyes, they fought to defend their farms and homes from "foreign" invaders.

DOING HISTORY ONLINE

Mobilization

Read the documents in this module. In order to sufficiently mobilize for the war, what special demands may have been made on the Southern states?

 www.cengage.com/ history/ayers/ ampassages4e

Editors, politicians, and citizens of both the North and the South demanded that the conflict be wrapped up immediately. "ON TO RICHMOND" ran the headline in Northern papers while General Beauregard informed Jefferson Davis of his troops' readiness "to meet the enemies of our country under all circumstances." Confident of victory, they itched for the fight that would settle things once and for all. Only a few, such as William T. Sherman, dissented. This "is to be a long war—very long—much longer than any politician thinks."

The First Battle, July 21, 1861

Northerners soon grew impatient with the passive Anaconda Plan of cutting the South off from the outside. With so many men eagerly signing on to fight, Northerners thought they should get the war over early, before the South had time to consolidate its forces. The Union already had thirty-five thousand men poised in northern Virginia, about 25 miles away from a Confederate force of twenty thousand under the command of **P. G. T. Beauregard**. Beauregard's troops protected the rail junction at Manassas, along Bull Run (a "run" is a stream). Confederate and Union troops also watched one another warily in the Shenandoah Valley, about 50 miles to the west.

These troop deployments reflected a primary goal of each side in the early stages of the war: capturing the capital of its enemy. Union leaders thought that if they could

Confederate Nationalism

As the Southern states seceded, their leaders struggled to create a sense of national identity to unify slaveholders and nonslaveholders and to justify their cause to an international audience. Portraying themselves as the true heirs of the American Revolution,

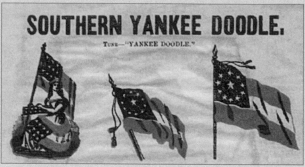

SOUTHERN YANKEE DOODLE.

Tune—"YANKEE DOODLE."

(Special Collections Department, Z. Smith Reynolds Library, Wake Forest University, Winston-Salem, North Carolina)

Southerners appropriated familiar Revolutionary symbols to embody their struggle. Engravings of George Washington appeared on Confederate postage stamps and the national seal; cruder likenesses were printed on broadsides for popular distribution. The "Stars and Bars," the official flag of the Confederacy, deliberately invoked the pattern of the familiar "Stars and Stripes," with one star for each state in the Confederacy.

Suffering from paper shortages, more than 85 percent of the South's newspapers ceased operation during the war. In this context, music and sermons took on added importance in fueling nationalist sentiment. Preaching to their congregations during nine national days of humiliation and prayer, Confederate ministers invoked biblical support for slavery and a war they viewed as just and defensive. New lyrics to "Yankee Doodle" and "The Star Spangled Banner" could be memorized easily and sung by soldiers and civilians alike. These songs often commemorated battles and rallied Confederates around new military heroes. Robert E. Lee, in particular, became a powerful focus for Confederate nationalism.

Although the sacrifices demanded by four years of war took their toll on military and civilian morale, the sense of a unified white national identity persisted after the defeat of the Confederate nation itself. This identity served as a powerful appeal to white voters in the Reconstruction era.

win Richmond—the industrial, commercial, and administrative center of the South— the rest of the Confederacy would soon follow. Confederate leaders thought that if they could conquer the capital of the United States, forcing Lincoln and his cabinet to flee, European powers would recognize the Confederacy's sovereignty and legitimacy. As a result, the Northern will to fight would be broken.

Officers of both the Union and the Confederacy had learned strategy at West Point, although few had ever commanded units above the regimental level. These officers usually attempted to concentrate their forces in hopes of overwhelming the enemy at the point of attack. The Union tried to take advantage of its greater numbers of men and resources; the Confederacy sought to use its interior lines, knowledge of the Virginia landscape, and aggressive maneuvers to gain an advantage. Educated with the same texts and serving together in peace and war, leaders on both sides knew what the others hoped and planned to do.

In the first major battle of the war, the South's advantages outweighed the North's. Both sides attempted to coordinate their troop movements near Washington and in the **Shenandoah Valley**. The valley had long served as a major corridor between the North and the South. If that corridor was left unprotected by the Union, Confederate forces could rush up the valley and capture Washington. But if too many troops protected the valley, the North would tie up men and resources that could be used more effectively elsewhere. The Confederacy employed cavalry, under the command of the flamboyant young colonel James E. B. (Jeb) Stuart, to move quickly up and down the valley, keeping the North off balance.

The Union, under the command of General Irvin McDowell, tried to concentrate most of its forces at Manassas by moving them from the valley. On July 21, the Northern troops were finally ready to attack. Congressmen and other spectators drove their carriages out from Washington to "see the Rebels get whipped." Union troops flooded over the battlefield, fording the creeks, flanking the strongest points in the Confederate lines. The Southern forces fell back to more defensible positions. When it looked as if the Confederates were to be routed, a Southern general pointed out **Thomas J. Jackson** to his men, "There is Jackson standing like a stone wall! Rally behind the Virginians!" "Stonewall Jackson," until recently an undistinguished mathematics professor at the Virginia Military Institute, had been christened.

The Confederate reinforcements who poured off the train at Manassas gave Beauregard a renewed spirit. The Union forces suffered confusion when the lack of a common uniform led some Northerners to mistake Confederates for their own troops. They began to pull back and then to run. Some civilian carriages got caught in the panicked flood of troops rushing back to Washington; the Confederates gleefully captured a New York congressman hiding in the woods and held him for the next six months in Richmond as a prisoner.

The South had claimed its first victory. Each side had engaged about eighteen thousand soldiers, making Bull Run by a considerable margin the largest battle ever waged in the United States up to that time. Both the North and the South lost about six hundred men. Nevertheless, the humiliating rout confirmed the Confederate belief that one Rebel could whip ten Yankees.

Key parts of Confederate lore emerged from Bull Run as well: the Rebel yell and the Confederate battle flag. The yell was not merely a scream or a roar, but a high wail, unnerving and strange, and it served as the rallying cry for Southern troops for the rest of the war. The first flag of the Confederacy, the Stars and Bars, looked a great deal like that of the United States, leading to confusion in the heat of battle. After Bull Run, Beauregard designed a new flag—a square banner, red with a blue cross and white stars—to ensure that Southern troops did not fire on one another. It was that battle flag, never the official flag of the Confederacy, that later generations came to consider synonymous with the South.

Each side called this first great battle of the war by different names. Northern forces generally named battles after physical features such as rivers and mountains; thus, they deemed this the Battle of Bull Run. Southerners usually named battles after nearby towns or villages; they called this one Manassas.

Women and War   Women had avidly followed the debates being waged in the newspapers. They had expressed their opinions in private conversation, at home, in their letters, and in their diaries. Many had listened to the speeches on all sides. They had counseled their sons and husbands, sometimes urging their men on to join others of their community. They had worn cockades displaying their loyalties and had sung the latest songs. Once the speeches, songs, and toasts had come to an end and the fighting had begun, women became even more active. Within two weeks of the war's beginning, women on the two sides had formed twenty thousand aid societies, which devoted themselves to supplying the armies' needs, especially clothing and medical supplies. One such organization in Alabama provided, in just one month, "422 shirts, 551 pairs of drawers, 80 pairs of socks, 3 pairs of gloves, 6 boxes and one bale of hospital supplies, 128 pounds of tapioca, and a donation of $18 for hospital use."

With the first battles, women claimed positions as nurses, even though previously only men had served as military nurses. **Dorothea Dix**, long known as the champion of the mentally ill and other neglected people in the antebellum era, took matters in hand for the North. She became superintendent of nurses for the Union army, the highest executive appointment for a woman to date, organizing three thousand women who volunteered to serve. Concerned both about the effectiveness and propriety of women ministering to young male strangers, Dix decreed that she wanted only "plain" women, women over thirty years old, and women who would dress in brown and black.

Women's efforts soon became legendary. They labored until they could no longer stand, until their long dresses trailed blood from amputations and wounds. Kate Cumming and Phoebe Pember played leading roles in the Confederacy, and Clara Barton took her aid to the front lines of the Union and later founded the American Red Cross. Most women stayed closer to home, working in factories, doing piecework in their households, or tilling fields. As Northern farmers departed for the military, observers in the Midwest saw "more women driving teams" and more "at work in fields than men."

WAR ESCALATES: AUGUST 1861 TO MARCH 1862

The war spread across the continent in the fall, winter, and spring of 1861–1862. Generals consolidated command and launched campaigns thousands of miles from their respective capitals. Governments transformed their economies, invented or expanded navies, conducted diplomacy, and cemented the loyalties of those at home. Families steeled themselves for a war longer than they had been willing to imagine.

McClellan Assumes Control   The North, while embarrassed at Bull Run, took from that defeat a determination to fight more effectively. Volunteers flooded into recruitment offices. Lincoln removed the leaders responsible for that battle and replaced them with **George B. McClellan**. Although short of stature and only thirty-four years old, McClellan, known as the "young Napoleon," exuded great authority. He had distinguished himself in the Mexican War and had studied military tactics in Europe. Moreover, he had already frustrated Confederate forces under Robert E. Lee in western Virginia. He now threw himself into reorganizing and reenergizing the Union troops under his command.

The press lavished praise on the young general. Already inclined toward grandiose visions of his abilities, McClellan developed an exalted sense of himself. The cocky commander considered Lincoln an "idiot" and his cabinet incompetent "geese," and he ignored, avoided, and insulted them at every opportunity. He wanted to make his army perfectly prepared before he risked it, and his reputation, in battle against Confederates whose numbers his spies consistently exaggerated. Meanwhile, months dragged by. Lincoln and newspaper editors became furiously impatient, but McClellan would not be moved.

The War in the West Begins

There was to be no waiting in the West. Four days after the battle at Bull Run, the Union installed a new commander in charge of the forces in Missouri: John C. Frémont, the "pathfinder of the West" and former Republican presidential candidate. Whereas the situation in Virginia unfolded slowly, the situation in Missouri burst into chaos in July and August 1861. Guerrilla forces raged throughout the state. Confederate armies built up on the southern border, ready to attack in both the eastern and western parts of the state. Frémont decided that he had to protect the Mississippi River in the East and therefore left a weak force in the West. That force, outnumbered by the Confederates, staged a desperate attack, with terrible losses, at Wilson's Creek. As at Bull Run, the lack of a standard uniform color created deadly confusion. The Northern units fell into ragged retreat, exposing Missouri to Confederate incursions.

With the populace of Missouri so divided in its loyalties, Frémont, who, a contemporary noted, had "all of the qualities of genius except ability," did not know whom to trust. Frantic, he declared the entire state under martial law, decreed the death penalty for captured guerrillas, and seized the slaves and other property of all Confederate sympathizers. Slaveholders in the border states of Kentucky and Maryland threatened to throw their allegiances to the South if Lincoln did not overrule Frémont.

The president, desperate to keep the border states within the Union, advised the general that his emancipation proclamation angered loyal slave owners and requested him to revoke his order. When Frémont resisted, demanding a public order overruling him, Lincoln felt that he had no choice but to remove Frémont from his post.

Events on the battlefield in the earliest stages of the war proved to be a poor guide to the long term. Although the North had been shaken by Bull Run and Missouri, it had lost neither Washington nor the border states. And although the South had apparently won at Bull Run, the Confederate forces, exhausted and bogged down in mud, had not taken advantage of the situation to attack the Union capital. Although slaveholders in the border states fumed at the Union government and military leaders, they remained in the Union. As a result, the South was deprived of a key strategic advantage: access to the Ohio River and a defensible border with the North. With the Union army able to move up and down the Ohio at will, the Confederates had to defend a vast, vague, and shifting border in Kentucky and Tennessee. The war was not to be won by a decisive battle within a few months of the war's start. Instead, slower and less dramatic processes proved decisive.

Paying for War

The Civil War, involving so many men over such an enormous territory, immediately became breathtakingly expensive. It was by no means clear how either side was going to pay. Although the Union and the

Confederacy were rich societies by any international standard, neither had ever supported a large army or an active government. Taxes on imported goods and the sale of apparently endless public lands paid for what government there was. Ever since the Bank War of the 1830s, the federal and state governments had done little to manipulate the currency. As a result, when the war came, the men responsible for paying for it had only a few options: loans, new taxes, or the creation of paper money.

Loans met the least resistance in both the North and the South, but this borrowing could provide only a third of the cost of the war. Taxes proved even less effective. The Confederacy quickly decided that it had no choice but to turn to paper money. As soon as it could find adequate engravers and printing presses, the South began producing millions of dollars in the new currency. Catastrophic inflation began to grow as early as the winter of 1861–1862.

The situation was not quite as bad in the North, where taxes and bonds carried much more of the burden of financing the war, but the Union too was forced to issue paper money by the first winter of the war. People hoarded gold in anticipation of the deprivations a widened war would cause. New York banks felt compelled to suspend specie payments in December 1861. In February 1862, the Union Congress reluctantly decided to create paper money. The Legal Tender Act of that month permitted the treasury to release up to $10 million of the new currency, quickly dubbed **greenbacks**. Over $450 million in paper notes circulated during the war, replacing the earlier system of state bank notes with the first unified national currency.

The Confederate Home Front

Southerners watched helplessly as armies stripped their farms of food and livestock. They ministered to the bleeding young men dragged into their parlors and bedrooms. The residents of places where both Unionists and Confederates remained strong—such as Missouri and eastern Tennessee—became caught in internal civil wars that pitted roving gangs of thugs against one another. Governors received letters from women, their husbands and sons gone, who worried that they faced starvation if they did not get help soon.

Inflation ate away at the Confederacy like a cancer. The rapid rise in prices made currency worth less every day. The government issued war bonds that paid 8 percent interest per year at a time when inflation reached 12 percent per month in 1861. Speculators could make money simply by buying up supplies and holding them while prices escalated. Farmers faced the temptation to grow cotton despite the needs of the armies. Cotton stored well and everyone believed that it would fetch a high price after the war, no matter who won. As a result, land and labor that could have grown food bent under the weight of cotton. A Georgia newspaper blamed speculators, for "a conscienceless set of vampires . . . are determined to make money even if one-half of the people starve."

Confederate leaders worried that the plantations could not produce the food the armies so desperately needed if white men did not force the slaves to work. African Americans wanted to hunt, fish, or work for themselves and their own families rather than to labor for the white people. Plantation mistresses often discovered that slaves would not work when the master—and the whips and guns he wielded—no longer hung over them. Accordingly, under pressure from plantation owners, the Confederate Congress passed laws exempting from the draft white men to supervise slaves on larger plantations. That a government in such need of every available soldier felt compelled to write such laws revealed how central slavery remained even in the midst of war.

To many poorer Southerners, the law was another in a growing list of grievances. Resentment against wealthy men and women—mediated during peacetime by family ties, common church membership, and democratic politics—quickly came to the surface in the context of war. Common people were quick to notice when plantation slaves labored over cotton rather than corn, when the well-to-do hoarded gold, received draft exemptions, or dodged taxes. Wealthy young men sometimes entered the Confederate army as privates, but others considered an officer's commission their just due as gentlemen. Scions of plantation fortunes often did little to disguise their disgust or amusement at the speech or clothing of the poorer men alongside whom they fought. The poorer soldiers and their wives noticed the insults.

Navies

The Union enjoyed a great initial advantage in its number of ships, but many of those ships were scattered around the globe, and it took months to bring them home. Moreover, most of the Union's vessels were deep-sea ships that could not navigate harbors and rivers. With remarkable speed, however, the Union naval department built new craft and deployed them against the South. In the first months of the war, the Navy Department armed merchant ships and sent them to blockade Southern ports. By the end of 1861, over 260 vessels patrolled the coasts, and the skilled workers of the shipbuilding towns of the East Coast had 100 more under construction, including the North's first ironclad ships.

The South had virtually no ships at the beginning of the war, but the Confederate navy seized, acquired, or built roughly 125 ships each year, including more than 400 steam-powered vessels. The Confederacy immediately contracted with large shipbuilding companies in England. Jefferson Davis authorized sailors to attack Northern ships on the high seas and turn them in for a share of the booty. For a few months, these privateers preyed on any unguarded ship they could find, but the Union navy quickly shut them down. The Confederates then attempted to sink rather than claim enemy ships. One intrepid officer, Raphael Semmes, escaped through the blockade in 1861 and seized eighteen Union ships before he was trapped at Gibraltar and forced to sell his ship and escape to England.

In the meantime, the North pushed its advantage. Larger ships began to blockade 189 harbors and ports from Virginia to Texas, patrolling 3,500 miles of coastline. Such enormous territory obviously proved difficult to control, especially because Northern ships periodically had to travel to ports hundreds of miles away for supplies and fuel. When Union craft left for such journeys, Southern **blockade runners** rushed into the unprotected ports. The Union navy decided to seize several Southern ports for use as supply stations and prevent their use by Confederate blockade runners.

The Federal ships moved first, in August, at Cape Hatteras in North Carolina, shelling the forts there and cutting off the supplies that dozens of blockade runners had brought into the Confederacy. The Northern navy also took a station near Biloxi, Mississippi, from which it could patrol the Gulf of Mexico. The most valuable seizure was Port Royal, South Carolina. Not only did that place offer an excellent harbor, but it stood midway between the major Southern ports of Charleston and Savannah.

The seventy-seven ships and sixteen thousand sailors and soldiers dispatched to Port Royal were the largest combined force yet assembled in American warfare.

Diplomacy and the *Trent* Affair, November 8, 1861–January 1, 1862 On the day after the capture of Port Royal, a Union ship stopped a British mail packet, the *Trent*, as it traveled from Cuba to St. Thomas. The *Trent* carried James Mason and John Slidell, Confederate commissioners sailing to London and Paris to negotiate for the support of the British and French governments. The captain of the Union ship, Charles Wilkes, after firing two shots across the bow of the British vessel, boarded it and seized the Confederate emissaries. When Wilkes arrived in Boston to deposit Mason and Slidell in prison, he met with a hero's welcome. Congress ordered a medal struck in his honor.

The excitement began to wane, however, when people realized the possible repercussions of Wilkes's actions. Despite the growth of the Union navy, Great Britain still ruled the oceans. British newspapers and politicians called for war against the arrogant Americans, warning that the British navy "with little difficulty could blow to the four winds their dwarf fleet."

The ***Trent* affair** reflected the uneasy state of international relations created by the war. The Confederacy hoped that England or France, or even both, would come to its aid. The importance of cotton in the international marketplace was such, Southerners argued, that the industrial powers of Europe could not long afford to allow the Northern navy to enforce its blockade.

The situation in the winter of 1861–1862 proved more complicated than people had expected, however. International law did not offer a clear ruling on whether Captain Wilkes had acted legally. And neither did self-interest offer a clear guide as to whether England should declare war on the United States or aid the Confederacy. British factories had stockpiled cotton in expectation of the war; industrialists had also begun investing heavily in Egyptian cotton production. Thus, British manufacturers did not clamor for intervention as Southerners had hoped. Anger over the *Trent* affair was balanced by resentment of Southern assumptions about British dependence on cotton. Confederates who "thought they could extort our cooperation by the agency of king cotton" would be disappointed, British leaders warned. France and England watched one another warily, neither country eager to upset the fragile balance of power between themselves by taking the first step in America.

Public opinion within England and France divided, for it was by no means clear to most Europeans which side had the better claim to their sympathies. Lincoln repeatedly declared that the war was not a war to end slavery. That declaration, Lincoln believed, was necessary to cement the support of the border states, but it undercut the support of English and European abolitionists for the Union cause. The Confederates claimed to be fighting for self-determination, a cause with considerable appeal in Europe, but potential supporters often viewed Southern slaveholding with disgust and distrust. Both the English and the French waited for events on the battlefields of North America to clarify issues.

The *Trent* affair was settled through diplomatic evasion and maneuvering, but the international situation remained tense throughout the war. Leaders of both the North and the South could imagine situations in which England or France would intervene with weapons and supplies. Foreign intervention—and the legitimacy that foreign recognition would give the South—loomed as a fervent hope for the Confederacy and a great fear of the North.

Confederate Ships Under Construction in England

The Confederacy depended on English shipyards, such as this one in Liverpool, to construct vessels to run the Union blockade, attack Union ships on the seas, and defend its ports. English willingness to construct and equip Southern ships waned as battlefield defeats reduced the prospect of Confederate victory. The most effective arm of the Confederate navy consisted of commerce raiders, which destroyed roughly 255 Union ships and doubled the cost of marine insurance for Northern merchants. Two of the most successful, the *Alabama* and the *Shenandoah*, built at the Laird shipyards in Liverpool, were hybrid sail and steam-powered ships that disrupted Northern commerce and destroyed merchant ships in the Atlantic and Pacific oceans. The *Shenandoah* fired the last official shot of the war across the bows of a whaler in the Bering Sea on June 28, 1865, as part of a month-long campaign that resulted in the capture of twenty-four whaling ships. Not until August 2 did her captain, James Waddell, learn the war had ended. Fearing prosecution for piracy, Waddell sailed the *Shenandoah* warily back to England, arriving off the Irish coast on November 5, 1865.

(Williamson Art Gallery and Museum, Birkenhead, England)

The Rivers of the West

The Union felt starved for victories at the beginning of the hard winter of 1862. Northern troops remained bogged down in the eastern theater, but Union generals in the West moved aggressively. Deprived of control of the Ohio River when Kentucky sided with the Union, the Confederates under Albert Sidney Johnston desperately needed to stop the Union in the West. Troops under the command of **Ulysses S. Grant**, a relatively obscure general from

Illinois, confronted a Confederate line of defense across southern Kentucky. Employing the Union's new river gunboats to great effect, Grant pushed down both the Tennessee and the Cumberland Rivers across the Kentucky border into Tennessee.

Important Confederate forts stood on both these rivers, but Grant hoped to overwhelm them by combined attacks on water and land. He assaulted Fort Henry on the Tennessee River in early February, easily overcoming the fort's defenses with the big guns on his river craft. The Union now commanded a river that flowed all the way through Tennessee into northern Alabama. Grant sent his boats steaming back up the Tennessee River to the Cumberland while he marched his men overland to Fort Donelson. There, the Confederates fought desperately, destroying several of the gunboats. Despite the Confederates' efforts, however, Grant pressed his advantage and overwhelmed Southern troops who attempted to break out of the fort and retreat to nearby Nashville.

When the Confederate general in charge of the thirteen thousand troops who remained in the fort attempted to negotiate with Grant (an old friend) for their surrender, Grant brusquely responded: "No terms except an unconditional and immediate surrender can be accepted. I propose to move immediately upon your works." Grant's phrase

MAP 14.1 Campaigns in the West in 1862.

While Lee and McClellan remained immobilized in Virginia, U.S. Grant boldly pushed to the Mississippi border.

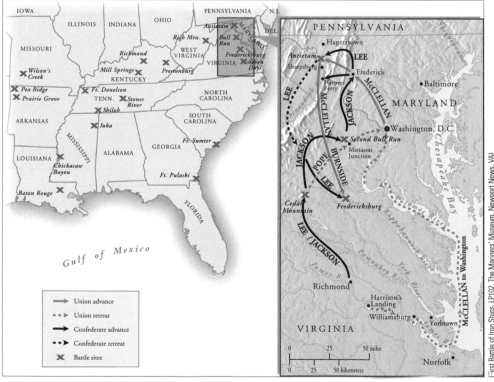

(First Battle of Iron Ships, LP102, The Mariners' Museum, Newport News, VA)

soon echoed through Northern newspapers, jokes, and even mildly risqué love letters. Grant's first two initials, Northern newspapers crowed, actually stood for Unconditional Surrender. Within days, Union troops pushed into nearby Nashville, the capital of Tennessee, making it the first great conquest of the war.

The *Monitor* and the *Virginia*, March 9, 1862

Even as Grant's troops seized their victories on the rivers of Tennessee, the Union navy continued its relentless attack on the eastern seaboard of the Confederacy. A well-planned amphibious assault allowed the Northern navy to consolidate its control of the North Carolina coast. The blockade steadily tightened.

Despite the Union's success, the Southern navy had reason for hope in early 1862. Confederate Secretary of the Navy Stephen Mallory had created an effective and innovative department, and he sought to take advantage of recent developments in shipbuilding and naval warfare such as steam power, the screw propeller, and armor. The Confederacy eagerly experimented, too, with mines in their harbors and developed the world's first combat submarine, the C.S.S. *Hunley*.

Most important, the South examined the possibilities of iron-plated ships. In the years immediately preceding the Civil War, the French and British had been experimenting with such vessels, but the United States remained far behind. The Confederacy began building an ironclad almost from the very beginning of the war, adding walls of 2-foot-thick solid oak, covered with 2-inch-thick iron plate, to the hull of a Union frigate scuttled in Norfolk in April 1861. Engineers installed an iron ram on the front to rip through the wooden hulls of enemy ships and armed the ship with ten heavy guns. The Confederacy changed the ship's name from the U.S.S. *Merrimack* to the **C.S.S. *Virginia***.

The Union, for its part, hired a Swiss inventor to design a different kind of ironclad; his innovative plan called for a shallow-draft ship that would be mostly submerged except for a rotating turret on top. It was by no means clear how such a craft—condemned as a "cheesebox on a raft"—might work in battle. No one was even sure it would stay afloat, much less fight effectively with its two guns. It was called the ***Monitor***.

On March 8, 1862, the Confederates decided the time had come to unleash their new weapon. The *Virginia* attacked several Union ships occupying the harbor at Hampton Roads, Virginia. The ironclad sank two wooden ships and drove three others aground; their guns proved useless against the heavy iron sheathing.

In one of the more dramatic episodes of the young war, however, the Union happened to be sending its own ironclad to another Virginia port 30 miles away on the morning after the *Virginia* launched its attack. As soon as the sound of the guns in Hampton Roads reached the *Monitor*, it steamed down. The two vessels pounded one another for hours. Although neither iron ship actually won the battle of March 9, the advantages of the Northern *Monitor* quickly became evident. Not only did that craft provide a much smaller target and a more maneuverable set of guns, but the *Monitor* required only half as much water in which to operate. The *Virginia* proved too big to retreat into rivers and too unwieldy for open seas. The imposing Southern ironclad had been neutralized, and the blockade would continue. The Union began a crash campaign to build as many ironclads as possible, using the *Monitor* as its model.

THE UNION ON THE OFFENSIVE: MARCH TO SEPTEMBER 1862

The Union strategy had long pivoted around the effort to take Richmond. With apparently unlimited resources, Northerners expected to make quick work of Virginia. Although the Confederacy had put up a surprisingly effective campaign, the Union believed it would win the war in the spring and summer of 1862. As with all other things in this war, however, events followed directions no one could foresee.

The Peninsular Campaign Begins On the very day that the C.S.S. *Virginia* emerged at Hampton Roads, Abraham Lincoln gave his approval of General George McClellan's long-delayed plan to win the war in the East. Rather than fighting in northern Virginia, McClellan would attack Richmond from the south, using the peninsula between the James and York rivers as an invasion route and relying on the Chesapeake Bay as a supply route. By moving the war away from Washington, McClellan argued, he would lessen the threat to the nation's capital.

Four hundred watercraft of every description began transferring Union soldiers to the tip of the peninsula at Fort Monroe, about 70 miles from Richmond. The transfer of 100,000 men took weeks to unfold. McClellan, with his usual methodical style, required several more weeks to arrange them in preparation for what he expected to be his triumphant march into Richmond.

The Battle of Shiloh, April 6–7, 1862 In the meantime, U.S. Grant and his fellow general William T. Sherman pushed their troops ever deeper into Tennessee. The Confederates, under Albert Sidney Johnston, had retreated to Corinth, Mississippi, where they regrouped and joined with other units arriving by train from throughout the Confederacy. They planned to attack Grant to regain momentum, if not the enormous territory and strategic rivers they had lost at Fort Henry and Fort Donelson. Grant established his own base of operations only 20 miles away, at Pittsburgh Landing, Tennessee. To the surprise of the Union, Johnston attacked the larger Union force at Shiloh Church on April 6.

The scattered woods and rough terrain around Shiloh turned the battle into a series of brutal fights among desperate groups of scattered men with little coordinated leadership. Johnston, killed leading an attack, was replaced by Beauregard, who succeeded in pushing the Union men back 2 miles. The Confederates' dominance proved short-lived, however, for twenty-five thousand Northern reinforcements arrived overnight. The Southerners received no new men. The next day saw Grant and his army regain the ground they had lost, driving the Confederates back to Corinth. Though the Southern forces had been badly hurt, the Northern forces were too exhausted and shaken to pursue.

The carnage at Shiloh exceeded anything anyone had ever seen. The bloodiest battle in the hemisphere up to that point, Shiloh exacted a horrible toll: about seventeen hundred killed and eight thousand wounded on each side. About two thousand of the wounded men in both the Union and the Confederacy forces would soon die. Newspapers and generals debated the outcome of the battle for months, trying to decide the hero and the loser, but it eventually became clear that the Southern attempt to halt Northern momentum in the Mississippi Valley had failed. Frustrated with McClellan's inertia, Lincoln turned aside criticism of Grant: "I can't spare this man, he fights."

The Capture of New Orleans, April 18–May 1, 1862 Yet another drama played itself out in New Orleans. There, a Union naval force under David Farragut determined to do what Confederates considered impossible: overwhelm their largest city and largest Gulf port. Confederates recalled that the mighty British of 1815 had failed to take New Orleans and fully expected the same fate to befall the Yankees. The city lay under the protection of two forts claiming 115 guns as well as a river blocked with logs, barges, and thick cables. So safe did they consider New Orleans that Confederate troops abandoned the city to fight at Shiloh, leaving the port protected only by militiamen.

Farragut had his own weapons, however: 20 mortar boats, 17 ships with 523 guns, and 15,000 soldiers. The Union navy pounded the forts for days with the mortars, unsuccessfully. Finally, before dawn on April 24, Farragut audaciously led his ships, single file, through a gap opened in the cables past the forts and past Confederate ships that tried to ram the Union craft or set them on fire with flaming rafts. Once they

MAP 14.2 Eastern Battles of 1862.

George McClellan's long-awaited campaign to take Richmond, Virginia, the capital of the Confederacy, began in March 1862. The vast maneuver unfolded over many months and ended with the brutal stalemate of the Seven Days' Battles. Stonewall Jackson's Valley Campaign kept the Union forces divided.

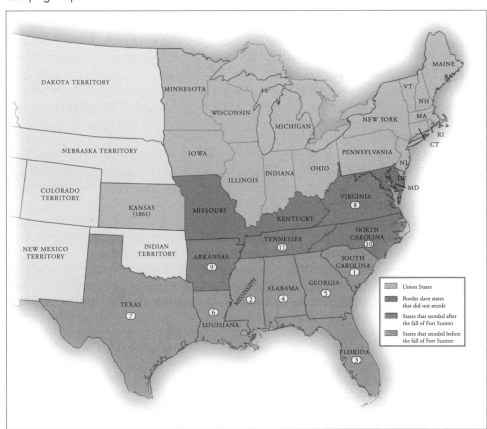

had run this gauntlet, the Union ships had clear sailing right up to the docks of New Orleans. There, they confronted no resistance as four thousand Confederate troops withdrew from the city.

Troops under the command of Benjamin Butler occupied New Orleans while Farragut continued to drive up the Mississippi River. He took Baton Rouge and Natchez, but **Vicksburg** held Farragut off. Armed riverboats coming from the north soon took Memphis as well, giving the Union control of all the Mississippi River except the area near Vicksburg. Northern forces used the river as a major supply route. Rather than a highway uniting the Upper and Lower South, the Mississippi became a chasm separating one half of the Confederacy from the other.

The Confederate Draft

The end of April 1862 seemed to promise the early end to the war that people had expected at its outbreak. Although many of the battles had been close that spring, they all seemed to turn out in favor of the North. The first year-long enlistments in the Confederate army were running out in April, and many soldiers left for home. The Confederate Congress, fearful that its armies would be short of men as the Union stepped up its attacks, decided that it had no choice but to initiate a compulsory draft. All white men between the ages of eighteen and thirty-five were required to fight for three years. If men enlisted or reenlisted within the thirty days following passage of the law, they could choose which unit they wanted to fight with.

Although the Confederacy eventually abolished substitution, a policy that allowed men with enough money to pay a substitute to fight in their place, it still permitted men from many occupations, such as teachers and apothecaries, to claim an exemption from military service. Governors appointed many men to positions in their state governments and militia so that they would be exempted from the draft. In Georgia and North Carolina, the state and counties aided the families of poor soldiers by taxing slaves and large property owners.

The Confederacy also exempted one white man for every twenty slaves he supervised with passage of the "**twenty negro law.**" That law, like the draft in general, necessary though it was, divided Southerners more profoundly than anything else in the Civil War. A Mississippi private deserted to return home, refusing to "fight for the rich men while they were at home having a good time."

The Seven Days' Battles, June 25– July 1, 1862

"Every blow tells fearfully against the rebellion," a New York newspaper declared at the end of May. "It now requires no very far reaching prophet to predict the end of this struggle." From the viewpoint of the battlefields in Tennessee and Mississippi, the war did indeed seem to be nearing its end. And in Virginia, George McClellan's troops, the pride of the Union and 100,000 strong, had pushed their way up the peninsula toward Richmond. By the end of May, only 5 miles separated them from their destination.

It would not be easy for the Union troops to take Richmond. The river assaults that had worked so well two months earlier in Tennessee failed in Virginia. The Confederates were able to attack the river gunboats from the heights of Drewry's Bluff. Even the *Monitor* proved ineffectual when faced with an enemy a hundred feet above. Moreover, the Confederates had established imposing defenses around Richmond and concentrated many of their troops in the vicinity.

Defensive positioning proved more important in the American Civil War than in any prior conflict. Defenders gained their advantage from a new kind of weapon: the rifle. A rifle, unlike a musket, used a spiral groove in the barrel to put spin on a bullet, like a football pass, giving the bullet much greater stability and accuracy. A musket had been accurate at only about 80 yards, but a rifle could hit a target at four times that distance. Although the benefits of rifling had long been recognized, it was not until the 1850s that a French inventor, Charles Minié, devised a way to make it possible for a rifled gun to fire without requiring the grooves to be cleaned. Although the rifles still had to be loaded from the end of the barrel, preventing even the most skillful soldiers from firing more than three times a minute, rifles nevertheless made it much more difficult for attacking troops to overwhelm a defense.

Lincoln and McClellan believed that Washington faced a direct threat from Confederate troops in the Shenandoah Valley under the command of the increasingly impressive Stonewall Jackson. For three months in the spring of 1862, Jackson maneuvered his men up and down the valley, creating the impression that his forces were larger than they were and that they could attack anywhere and at any time. As a result, the Union divided its forces, depriving McClellan's invasion of tens of thousands of soldiers that otherwise would have been available for the assault on Richmond.

The Union and the Rebel forces tested one another around Richmond in May and June, inflicting heavy casualties in battles that settled nothing. Robert E. Lee replaced Joseph Johnston, wounded in battle, as general of the Confederate forces in Virginia. Lee quickly proved himself aggressive and daring. He almost immediately planned an attack against the larger force under McClellan's command. Lee sent out J. E. B. Stuart, his cavalry leader, who rode all the way around McClellan's troops, reconnoitering their position and stealing their supplies. Stuart reported that part of McClellan's troops were vulnerable to attack. Lee brought Jackson and his men to join in an assault.

The resulting prolonged conflict, which became known as the Seven Days' Battles, did not distinguish either side. Thirty thousand men had been killed and wounded. The Confederates' offensive did not work as planned, and Jackson failed to carry out his part of the assault. For the North's part, McClellan, though possessing far more troops than his opponents' 90,000, believed himself outnumbered, wiring Lincoln that he faced 200,000 Confederates and "if this [army] is destroyed by overwhelming numbers . . . the responsibility cannot be thrown on my shoulders." Despite military successes, McClellan abandoned the attempt to take Richmond.

Slavery Under Attack

By the summer of 1862, the war seemed to have reached a stalemate. Both the Union and the Confederacy believed a decisive battle could still win the war. The North took heart because Union ships controlled the coasts and rivers on the perimeter of the South even as Union troops pushed deep into Tennessee and Mississippi. The Confederacy took comfort because vast expanses of rich Southern farmland and millions of productive slaves remained beyond the reach of Union control.

President Lincoln, while detesting slavery personally, feared that a campaign against bondage would divide the North. As the war dragged into its second year, however, even Northerners who did not oppose slavery on moral grounds could see that slavery offered the South a major advantage: slaves in the fields meant more white Southerners on the battlefields.

More important, black Southerners themselves pressed slavery as a problem on the Union armies. Wherever those armies went, slaves fled to the Federals as refugees. The Union called the black people who made their way to the Union ranks **contrabands,** a shortened form of the term "contraband of war," used to describe property that could be used in a war effort and was thus subject to confiscation. Although some Union officers returned the slaves to their owners, other officers seized the opportunity to strike against slavery and use former slaves to further their war aims. Union and Confederate commanders employed these slaves as local guides, camp laborers, and to construct defensive earthworks for the military.

Northern leaders confronted such issues most directly near **Port Royal,** South Carolina. When the Union forces overran the Sea Islands along the coast in 1861, the relatively few whites who lived there fled, leaving behind ten thousand slaves. Almost immediately, various groups of Northerners began to vie for the opportunity to reshape Southern society. The Sea Islands claimed some of the largest and richest plantations in the South, growing rare and expensive long-staple cotton. With the question of emancipation still undecided, abolitionists felt it crucial that freed slaves prove they would work willingly and effectively. Ministers and schoolteachers journeyed from the Northeast to educate the freedmen, while other abolitionists arrived to demonstrate that plantations run on the principles of free labor could be both productive and humane. Politicians, ministers, and newspapermen reported the conditions and progress made at Port Royal as a measure of what the end of slavery would mean for blacks and for the South.

The former slaves valued the opportunity to learn to read and write and wanted land of their own, but they did not always appreciate lessons from the newcomers about religion and agriculture. Many former slaves associated cotton with servitude and refused to plant it. Not only in South Carolina but wherever else the Union army penetrated, officers and civilians sought to control black labor and rich land. Sometimes Federal officials decreed that the freed people could sign contracts with whomever they chose—but they had to sign contracts with someone. In other times and places, Union leaders permitted black people to take responsibility for some of the land they had worked as slaves. Some white Northerners proposed seizing land from former slaveholders to give to the former slaves.

General David Hunter, a man of abolitionist sympathies, took advantage of his position in Port Royal in late spring 1862 to organize a number of black military units and declare slavery abolished in South Carolina, Georgia, and Florida. Hunter stated that Union soldiers would not act "as a police force for the protection of property." Lincoln, however, revoked Hunter's proclamation. Lincoln did not envision the immediate emancipation decreed by Hunter, with no compensation to slaveholders and with former slaves living alongside their former masters. Lincoln thought that slavery must end gradually, with payments to the slaveholders for their loss of property. Ideally, Lincoln argued, the former slaves would be colonized beyond the borders of the United States, perhaps in Haiti or Liberia.

Lincoln also resisted those members of his party and his cabinet who thought that black men should be enlisted into the Union army. Such Republicans, often called "Radicals" for their support of black rights, passed laws that forbade Northern commanders to return refugee slaves to their former masters, and they ended slavery in the District of Columbia (albeit gradually and with compensation).

Many Northern Democrats firmly opposed such expansion of the war's purposes and means, warning that abolition would only embitter and embolden the Confederates.

MAP 14.3 Campaigns in Virginia and Maryland, 1862.

As Union troops moved from the peninsula below Richmond to an area closer to Washington in August, Lee and Jackson used the opportunity to go on the offensive. Over the next several months, they clashed with Union forces at Manassas and Antietam in Maryland.

McClellan, a strong opponent of Radical Republicans, believed emancipation would "disintegrate our present armies." Democrats sympathetic to the South, called **Copperheads** by their opponents, marched under the motto, "The Constitution as it is and the Union as it was." They wanted slavery to remain in place so that the South would come back into the nation, and they were deeply hostile to ideas of racial equality.

Lincoln sought to steer a course between the Radicals and the Copperheads. But in the summer of 1862, he moved closer to an assault on slavery. The Union army had strengthened its position in Kentucky and Missouri, and it no longer appeared that the border states could effectively align themselves with the Confederates. Similarly, Lincoln came to see that the Southern Unionists, far fewer in number than he had believed, could not or would not organize effective opposition to the Confederacy from within. Lincoln decided that to win the war, he would have to hit slavery. Responding to a Southern Unionist, the president wrote, "This government cannot much longer play a game in which it stakes all, and its enemies stake nothing. Those enemies must understand that they cannot experiment for ten years trying to destroy the government, and if they fail still come back into the Union unhurt."

On July 22, 1862, Lincoln and his cabinet authorized Federal military leaders to take whatever secessionist property they needed and to destroy any property that aided the Confederacy. That meant that Union officers could protect the black men and women who fled to Northern camps, using them to work behind the lines. Lincoln decided to wait for a victory on the battlefield before announcing the most dramatic part of his plan: that as of January 1, 1863, he would declare all slaves in areas controlled by the Confederates free. Although this proclamation would free no slaves under Union control in the border states, it ruled out compromise that would end the war and bring the South back into the Union with slavery. Knowing that this announcement would unleash harsh criticism in the North, Lincoln wanted to wait until the North was flush with confidence before he announced this preliminary Emancipation Proclamation. When and where that victory might occur, however, was by no means clear in July 1862.

The Battles of Second Manassas and Antietam, August 29–30 and September 17, 1862 Confidence actually ran higher in the Confederacy than in the Union during the second summer of the war. The Union, after all, could draw little solace from McClellan's sluggish performance in the ferocious Seven Days' Battles outside Richmond in June. Lincoln placed Henry Halleck, who advocated a more aggressive stance toward Southern civilians and their slaves, in charge of all Union troops. The president put John Pope, who had been fighting in the West, in charge of the new Army of Virginia. McClellan still commanded troops, but his role had been restricted. Pope issued a series of orders that signaled a new, harder tone to the conflict: troops would forage as needed, no longer guard Southern property, and hold local civilians responsible for damages caused by Confederate guerrillas.

The new Union leaders decided to remove McClellan's troops from the peninsula of Virginia and consolidate them, under the joint command of Pope, with troops from the Shenandoah Valley. The forces began to move from the peninsula in August, creating a temporary opportunity for the Confederacy. Lee decided to attack Pope's troops while McClellan's were withdrawing. He hoped to occupy as much territory as possible, resting and resupplying his troops while complicating Union efforts to unify their forces.

Lee's plan worked better than he could have expected. Stonewall Jackson attacked Pope's men and pillaged a large Federal supply depot at Manassas. Pope then fell under attack by James Longstreet's troops, who drove the new Yankee commander back into Washington. With McClellan no longer threatening Richmond and Pope posing no danger to northern Virginia, Lee decided to push into Maryland. He believed that large numbers of Marylanders would rush to the Confederate cause. Lee had another audience in mind as well: England and France. In the wake of Union indecision and defeat in the summer of 1862, leaders in both countries were leaning toward recognition of the Confederacy. A major victory in Northern territory, Lee felt certain, would prove that the South deserved the support of the major powers.

Lee acted so confidently because he knew he would face George McClellan again. On September 17, the two old adversaries fell into battle once more, this time at Antietam Creek, near Sharpsburg, Maryland. The Confederates had thirty-five thousand men to McClellan's seventy-two thousand, but the Southerners held the defensive ground. The terrible battle ended in confusion and stalemate. More men were killed, wounded, or declared missing on this day than on any other day in the Civil

Missionaries at Port Royal

In Union hands since 1861, the Sea Islands of South Carolina attracted slaves from the mainland who joined the ten thousand slaves who remained when their masters fled the Federal army. These islands quickly became a testing ground for Northern ideals. Abolitionists realized that these slaves could help disprove theories of black inability to adapt to a free labor society. Societies formed in Boston, New York, and Philadelphia to organize financial and educational support for the newly liberated men and women on the islands. Among the fifty-three missionaries and teachers who traveled to the Sea Islands in March 1862 were twelve women. Others, including abolitionist Laura M. Towne and Charlotte Forten, a free black woman from Philadelphia, arrived later in the year. By publishing accounts of their experiences and meeting with Union officials in Washington, Towne and others served as advocates for full emancipation and federal protection of the freedmen's interests.

While efforts to prove the profitability of cotton grown by free labor were frequently dogged by graft, abuse, and mutual mistrust between local freedmen and Northern superintendents, teachers in Port Royal found a ready reception from the former slaves. As many as two hundred young scholars regularly crowded one church where classes were held. Adult freedmen attended classes at night. Towne's Penn School became one of the most successful legacies of the Port Royal Experiment, training African American teachers in the Sea Islands until the 1940s.

(The Western Reserve Historical Society, Cleveland, Ohio)

War: thirteen thousand for the Confederacy and twelve thousand for the Union. Lee had lost nearly a third of his army; McClellan, despite his numerical advantage, had been unable to shatter the enemy.

Neither side could be satisfied with the battle's outcome. The Confederacy decided that it would pull back into Virginia to fight another day. Lincoln, making the best of the situation, decided that **Antietam** represented enough of a victory to justify his announcement of the preliminary Emancipation Proclamation. The European powers decided that they would withhold their support for the Confederacy for the time being.

Things could have turned out very differently at this juncture. Had McClellan destroyed Lee's army, the Confederacy might have given up its claims for independence before slavery had been ended. Had Lee merely held his ground in Virginia after driving McClellan away from Richmond and Pope back into Washington, England and France might have offered mediation—and the North might well have accepted, again without the end of slavery. As it was, however, both the North and the South would fight again and again.

Stalemate   While Northerners and Southerners slaughtered one another in Maryland with no decisive advantage gained by either side, Southern forces under the command of Braxton Bragg pushed far into Kentucky, determined to regain ground lost early in the war. Confederates believed that Kentuckians would rush to the Southern flag if given a chance. But Kentuckians had little confidence that the Confederates could prevail in Kentucky and did not want to risk all they had in support of a losing cause. Although the Confederates never suffered sharp defeat in Kentucky, they had too few men to occupy the state, and they retreated after the Battle of Perryville. Rather than risk losing his army, Bragg pulled his men into a more defensible position in Tennessee.

By the summer and fall of 1862, many men had died to little apparent purpose. Lincoln decided that generals in both the East and the West must be removed; George McClellan and Don Carlos Buell seemed too slow to react. Lincoln replaced Buell with William S. Rosecrans and replaced McClellan with Ambrose E. Burnside, an appealing man uncertain that he was qualified for the job. His doubts proved to be well founded.

In November, Burnside decided to establish a new base for yet another assault on Richmond. He moved his troops to Fredericksburg, Virginia, and launched an attack on a virtually impregnable Confederate position at Marye's Heights. With Southerners able to fire down on them at will from protected positions, more than twelve thousand Union soldiers were killed, wounded, or missing. Observing the suicidal Union charges, Robert E. Lee remarked to General Longstreet, "It is well that war is so terrible—we should grow too fond of it." At battle's end, both armies remained where they had been at the battle's beginning.

The North fell into mourning, humiliation, and anger at this sacrifice. Officers as well as enlisted men made no secret of their loss of faith in Burnside. Despondent, Lincoln responded to defeat at Fredericksburg, "If there is a worse place than Hell, I am in it." In Tennessee, Rosecrans felt that he had to move against Bragg to demonstrate Union resolve and power. The two armies clashed on the last day of 1862 at Stones River near Murfreesboro. The two sides, losing about a third of their men each, fought to a virtual draw.

The winter of 1862–1863 saw the North and the South precariously balanced, both against one another and within their own societies. Military victories would decide whether the South or the North would break first.

CONCLUSION

Eighteen months after Lincoln had begun his journey to Washington to become president, war had become a way of life.

The boundaries between the Union and the Confederacy had been firmly drawn. After agonizing months of debate, Virginia, North Carolina, Tennessee, and Arkansas had cast their lot with their fellow slave states. After similar debates, Maryland, Kentucky, and Missouri—other slave states—cast their lot with the United States. The balance of power between North and South meant that the war they began in 1861 would not be settled quickly. Both sides claimed crucial advantages: whereas the North had more men, machinery, and money, the South was fighting on the defensive and on its home ground.

The governments of both sides had begun to function effectively. The Lincoln and Davis administrations both improvised desperately, piecing together the resources to put vast armies in the field in a matter of months. The tiny peacetime army of the United States ballooned in size as volunteers rushed to fight under the minority of officers trained at West Point. Most officers in both armies were elected by their fellow volunteers with most more popular than skilled. The nonexistent army of the Confederate States coalesced around its own West Pointers who swore allegiance to the new nation rather than to the nation they had been trained to defend. The North put its faith in George B. McClellan at the outset; the South, taking longer to locate its leaders, decided on Stonewall Jackson and Robert E. Lee.

The first volunteer units of both armies had been mobilized. Men of all descriptions rushed to arms: poor and rich, urban and rural, foreign born and native born. They signed on at first for three months, then found themselves fighting for much longer as the war proved harder to win than either side thought possible at the war's beginning.

Both the South and the North had claimed military victories. The Confederacy recalled the battle at Manassas with pride, but then watched as the Union took New Orleans, Nashville, and its Atlantic port cities. The United States gloried in its naval victories, but then watched as its soldiers lost in the Shenandoah Valley and on the peninsula that led to Richmond. Clarity did not come as the months passed. Even though the South won at Second Manassas, the North rebuffed the enemy at Antietam. The debacle at Fredericksburg in December 1862 horrified a United States that seemed incapable of mounting a successful campaign against Robert E. Lee. The waste of young lives on the hills below Marye's Heights made many question the conduct of the war.

In the midst of all this suffering, President Lincoln sought to define a greater purpose for the war. Even while the Union army was stalled outside Richmond in the summer of 1862, Lincoln drafted an emancipation proclamation. He had come to realize that the Confederacy could not be defeated unless slavery, its bedrock, were destroyed. In the wake of Antietam, enough of a victory to call a victory, Lincoln announced the end of slavery in all areas held by the Confederacy by January 1. Denounced throughout the South and in much of the North as well, Lincoln tried to strike a death blow against the surprisingly strong enemy. He knew as well as anyone else, however, that without victories on the battlefield, nothing else would matter. He entered 1863 hoping the victories would come soon.

CHAPTER REVIEW, 1861–1862

- The states of the Upper South divided, with Virginia, North Carolina, Tennessee, and Arkansas going to the Confederacy and Kentucky, Maryland, and Missouri staying in the Union.
- The United States and the Confederacy built vast armies and mobilized their entire societies to wage war.
- The Battle of Bull Run, a Confederate victory, showed that neither side was ready to fight.
- The United States won early and crucial victories on the rivers of Tennessee and Louisiana.
- The Confederacy managed to hold off the United States in Virginia, and the United States turned the Confederacy back in Maryland.

◀▦▮ *Looking Back*

In Chapter 14 we see that a series of now-familiar events shook the United States in 1861 and 1862, all of them unbelievable at the time.

1. What would have changed had the Union forces won at Manassas in July 1861?
2. What did the Confederacy need to accomplish in order to claim victory in the Civil War?
3. Are you struck at the speed or the slowness with which Abraham Lincoln turned the war into a war against slavery?

Looking Ahead ▮▮▶

Chapter 15 shows that as 1862 came to an end, no one could know that the war would devastate the nation for two more years and hundreds of thousands more deaths.

1. What seemed the likely outcome of the war as 1863 began?
2. Which society, the North or the South, seemed more likely to suffer internal conflict as the years of the war passed?

Go to the American Passages website at www.cengage.com/history/ayers/ampassages4e for additional review materials.

Blood and Freedom, 1863–1865

The Civil War enveloped the entire nation, home front and battlefield alike. The outcome of a battle could win an election or trigger a riot, while events at home affected the leaders' decisions of when and where to fight. In the North, the strong political opposition to Abraham Lincoln and his policies exerted a constant pressure on his conduct of the war. In the South, slaves abandoned plantations, and white families' hardships led soldiers to rethink their loyalties.

The outcome of the Civil War was not predetermined by the North's advantages of population and resources. Deep into the war, events could have taken radically different turns. Slavery might have survived the conflict had the Confederacy won at particular junctions or, what would have been more likely, had the United States lost the will to push the devastating war to the South's full surrender and the immediate abolition of slavery. Even with the war's end, the future course of the nation remained in doubt as Americans confronted the greatest rupture in their history.

PEOPLE AT WAR: SPRING 1863

Both Northerners and Southerners expected the spring of 1863 to bring the climax of the Civil War. Yet while generals and armies determined the result of battles, the women, slaves, workers, bureaucrats, draft dodgers, and politicians behind the lines would determine the outcome of the war.

Life in the Field

Soldiers eventually adjusted to the miseries of sleeping on the ground, eating poorly cooked food, and marching through driving rain and endless mud. They learned to adapt to gambling, drinking, cursing, and prostitution, either by succumbing to the temptations or by steeling their resolve against them. They could toughen themselves to the intermittent mails and the arrival of bad news from home. Men recalled their initial mortification and humiliation of discovering the entire company infested with lice, a shame that turned to indifference when the sharper horror of wounds descended.

CHAPTER TIMELINE

1863	January	Second Emancipation Proclamation
	March	Union Congress passes Conscription Act • Confederate Congress passes Impressment Act
	April	Bread riot in Richmond
	May	Culmination of Lee's victory over Hooker at Chancellorsville
	June	Lee's army crosses Potomac
	July	Union victory at Gettysburg • Vicksburg surrenders to Grant • Port Hudson surrenders to Union • Lee retreats across Potomac into Virginia • New York City draft riots • Black troops fight at Fort Wagner, South Carolina
	October	Grant assumes control of Union forces in West
	November	Lincoln's Gettysburg Address • Union victory at Chattanooga
1864	March	Grant assumes command of all Union forces
	May	Battle of the Wilderness in Virginia
	July	Union failure at Battle of the Crater near Petersburg
	September	Sherman captures Atlanta • Sheridan's victories in Shenandoah Valley
	November	Lincoln reelected president • Beginning of Sherman's march from Atlanta to the Atlantic
1865	February	Columbia, South Carolina, burned; Confederates evacuate Charleston
	March	Congress creates Bureau of Refugees, Freedmen, and Abandoned Lands (Freedmen's Bureau) • Lincoln's second inauguration • Confederate army authorizes recruitment of slaves into army
	April	Fall of Richmond to Union • Lee surrenders to Grant at Appomattox Court House • Lincoln assassinated
	May	Jefferson Davis captured • Former Confederate states hold constitutional conventions through December; pass "black codes" • African Americans hold conventions in South
	December	Thirteenth Amendment to Constitution ratified, abolishing slavery

Even the most stalwart of soldiers could not adapt, however, to the constant threat of diseases such as diarrhea, dysentery, typhoid, malaria, measles, diphtheria, and scarlet fever. As bloody as the battles were, disease killed twice as many men as those who died from the guns of the enemy. Many doctors of the Civil War era used the same instruments of surgery on soldier after soldier, unwittingly spreading disease and

This icon will direct you to interactive activities and study materials on the American Passages website: www.cengage.com/history/ayers/ampassages4e

infection. After every battle, screams filled the night as surgeons sawed off legs and arms, feet and hands, in often vain hopes of stopping gangrene.

Purposes

The North announced that it fought for the Union; the Confederacy announced that it fought for the right of self-determination. Yet soldiers acted courageously not only because they believed in the official political purposes for which they were fighting but also because they wanted to be admired by the people at home, because they wanted to do their part for their comrades, because they wanted to bring the war to a quicker end, and because they grew to hate the enemy.

Many men fought alongside their brothers, uncles, and cousins. A steady stream of letters flowed back and forth between the units and the families and neighbors back home. Gossip, praise, and condemnation flourished. Any soldier who planned to return home knew that his deeds in the war would live with him the rest of his life. As a result, even fearful or halfhearted soldiers might throw themselves into battle to demonstrate their courage.

Courage developed, too, out of hatred. People on both sides spread the worst stories and rumors about one another. Newspapers printed exaggerated or fabricated atrocity reports about the enemy. The longer the war went on, the more people felt they had to hate one another to justify so much bloodshed.

The sermons men heard in the camps told them they were fighting on the side of the right. The Old Testament afforded rich imagery and compelling stories of violence inflicted for good causes. Many Americans believed that God's will was enacted directly in human affairs. As the war ground on, the leaders, the soldiers, and the civilians of both sides came to feel that events were more than the product of human decision or even courage. Surely, they told themselves, so much suffering and sacrifice had to be for a larger purpose.

The Problems of the Confederate Government

Convinced that greedy merchants were holding supplies of flour until shortages and inflation drove prices even higher, in the spring of 1863 poor women in Richmond broke open the stores of merchants accused of hoarding the precious staple and took what they needed. After President Davis climbed on a wagon and threw coins at the crowd, he ordered a militia unit to prepare to fire on them. The threat of violence and of arrest, as well as the promise of free supplies, broke up the **bread riot**, but similar events occurred in several other Southern cities such as Atlanta, Columbus, and Augusta. No one could tell when even larger riots might erupt again. Fearing the consequences for morale, military officers in Richmond ordered the press and telegraph office to suppress news of the riot, but word of the riot soon spread.

The rioters were not the only ones who took what they needed. Confederate officers in the field forced reluctant farmers to accept whatever prices the army offered, in an increasingly worthless currency. In the spring of 1863, the Confederate government attempted to curb the worst abuses of this practice in the **Impressment Act**. If a farmer did not think the prices he or she received were fair, the case could be appealed before local authorities. In practice, however, this cumbersome system failed.

Farmers hid their produce from officers and were resentful when they were forced to sell. North Carolina's governor denounced impressments to the War Department in Richmond: "If God Almighty had yet in store another plague . . . I am sure it must have been a regiment or so of half-disciplined Confederate cavalry."

The Southern government could not afford to lose civilian support. Although the absence of political parties initially appeared to be a sign of the South's consensus, that absence eventually undermined what original consensus the Confederacy had enjoyed. Jefferson Davis, without a party mechanism to discipline those who spoke out against him, could not remove enemies from office. Davis's own vice president, Alexander Stephens, became a persistent and outspoken critic of the Confederate president's "tyrannical" policies, actively undermining support for Davis and even allying with avowed enemies of Davis and his policies.

(Courtesy of the Library of Virginia)

Richmond Bread Riots. *This Northern portrayal of the Richmond bread riots imagined the rioters as fearsome, gaunt amazons; other accounts emphasized their respectability. In either case, they behaved in ways quite remarkable for any women in nineteenth-century America.*

The Confederate government faced a fundamental dilemma. The whole point of secession had been to move political power closer to localities, protecting slavery in particular and self-determination in general. The government of the Confederacy, however, had to centralize power. If the armies were to be fed and clothed, if diplomats were to make a plausible case for the Confederacy's nationhood, if soldiers were to be mobilized, then the Confederate government had to exercise greater power than its creators had expected or intended. Jefferson Davis continually struggled with this tension. For every Southerner who considered Davis too weak, another considered the president dangerously powerful.

The Northern Home Front

In the North, the war heightened the strong differences between the Democrats and the Republicans. The Democrats won significant victories in congressional elections in the fall and winter of 1862, testifying to the depth and breadth of the opposition to Lincoln and his conduct of the war. Wealthy businessmen were eager to reestablish trade with their former Southern partners, whereas Irish immigrants wanted to end the risk of the draft and competition from freed slaves. Many citizens of Ohio, Indiana, and Illinois, whose families had come from the South, wanted to renew the Southern connections that had been broken by the war.

The Union passed its **Conscription Act** in March 1863 because disease, wounds, and desertion had depleted the ranks of soldiers faster than they could be replaced. When drafted, a man could appear for duty, hire a substitute to fight in his place, or pay a fee of $300 directly to the government. Poorer communities resented the wealthy who could avoid service. Demonstrations broke out in Chicago, Pennsylvania mining towns, Ohio, rural Vermont, and Boston. State and federal governments often paid bounties—signing bonuses—to those who volunteered. More than a few men took the bounties and then promptly deserted and moved to another locality to claim another bounty.

The opposition to the Lincoln government raised crucial issues. With the North claiming to fight for liberty, what limitations on freedom of speech and protest could it enforce? A Democratic congressman from Ohio, Clement Vallandigham, tested those limits in the spring of 1863. Hating both secessionists and abolitionists, Vallandigham refused to obey a general's orders to stop criticizing the Lincoln administration. He was arrested, tried before a military court, and sentenced to imprisonment for the rest of the war. Lincoln was dismayed by these events. He commuted Vallandigham's sentence, sending him to the Confederates in Tennessee, hoping to make Vallandigham appear a Southern sympathizer rather than a martyr to the cause of free speech. Vallandigham quickly escaped to Canada, however, where he continued his criticism. Ohio Democrats defiantly nominated Vallandigham for governor in the elections to be held in the fall of 1863. If things continued to go badly for the Union, who knew what kind of success a critic of Lincoln might find?

African American Soldiers   Although Northern civilian and military leaders remained deeply divided and ambivalent about black freedom, it became clear to everyone that black men could be of great value to the Union. In May 1863, the War Department created the Bureau of Colored Troops, charged with recruiting regiments not only in the North but among Southern slaves and free blacks as well.

African American men rushed to enlist as soon as they heard of the new black regiments. At first, black recruits found themselves restricted to noncombat roles and a lower rate of pay: $10 a month versus the $13 a month and $3.50 clothing allowance given to white soldiers. Black men, though eager to serve, protested that they could not support their families on such amounts. African Americans knew, and coveted, the rights and privileges of other Americans. They wrote petitions and appealed to higher authorities, often in the language of the Declaration of Independence and the Constitution.

Confederate officials who expected **African American soldiers** to make reluctant or cowed fighters soon discovered otherwise. In May 1863, two black regiments stormed, seven times, a heavily fortified Confederate installation at Port Hudson, Louisiana. Soon after, black soldiers found themselves on the other side of the barricades. At **Milliken's Bend**, Louisiana, they fought Confederates hand-to-hand. Northern newspapers echoed the words of praise from generals in the field: "No troops could be more determined or more daring."

Encouraged and frequently supported financially by their communities, African American men in the North went to the recruiting tables in great numbers. Black and white abolitionists alike recognized how critical military service would be to proving African Americans' entitlement to full citizenship. Frederick Douglass, the leading spokesman for black Americans, celebrated the enlistments: "Once let the black man get upon his person the brass letters, U.S.; let him get an eagle on his button, and a musket on his shoulder, and bullets in his pocket, and there is no power on earth which can deny that he has earned the right to citizenship in the United States." From Rhode Island to Ohio, black troops prepared to head south.

THE BATTLEFIELDS OF SUMMER: 1863

Everything seemed in place for a climactic culmination of the war in the summer of 1863. The Union had almost severed the western half of the Confederacy from the eastern; the Federal army had penetrated deep into Tennessee and stood on the threshold of Georgia. Nevertheless, Confederate armies maintained their morale and learned to make the most of their advantages.

Vicksburg and Chancellorsville, November 2, 1862–July 4, 1863, and May 1–5, 1863 Union leaders needed all the help they could get in early 1863. Ulysses S. Grant and William T. Sherman remained frustrated in their goal of seizing Vicksburg; William S. Rosecrans faced Braxton Bragg in Tennessee; Robert E. Lee's army had yet to be decisively defeated despite the men, resources, and determination thrown into battle against him. Lee would face General Joseph Hooker, whom Lincoln had chosen to replace Ambrose Burnside. Throughout the spring, "Fighting Joe" Hooker energized his men and repaired some of the damage to morale and readiness inflicted at Fredericksburg. But no one knew if he would be able to handle Lee.

The Northern public was especially impatient with Grant and Sherman. Grant knew the delays threatened his command. Vicksburg, heavily fortified by both geography and the Confederates, seemed most vulnerable to attack from the southeast, but to get there, Grant would have to find a way to move his men across the Mississippi River without landing them in swamps. Throughout the long, wet winter, Grant had tried one experiment after another, including digging canals. Nothing had worked.

Grant finally decided on a bold move: he would run a flotilla of gunboats and barges past Vicksburg under the cover of night to ferry his men across the Mississippi south of the city, where the land was better. The guns of Vicksburg stood 200 feet above the river, ready to fire down on any passing craft, but the Union men covered their ships' boilers with sacks of grain and bales of cotton to protect them from the shelling. Most of the boats made it through. Grant had Sherman create a diversion, confusing the Confederates, and then ferried his entire army across the Mississippi. Grant's army remained vulnerable, cut off from his allies and his major supply base, but by mid-May, Grant had fought four battles, cost the South eight thousand dead and wounded, marched 200 miles, and pinned thirty thousand Confederates within Vicksburg's fortifications.

In the same week. Grant made his landing near Vicksburg, Hooker began his attack on Lee, still based in Fredericksburg. Hooker commanded 130,000 men. Unlike Burnside, however, he intended to outsmart Lee rather than try to overwhelm him with numbers. A large Union force would sweep around Lee and attack him from

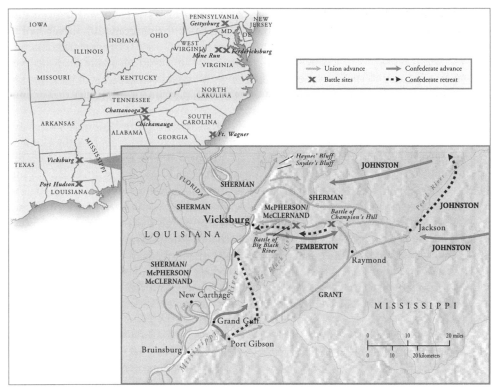

MAP 15.1 Vicksburg, April–July, 1863.

After months of frustration, Ulysses S. Grant and William T. Sherman found a way to attack Vicksburg from the south and east. Following a great struggle, the Union generals were able to take the city on July 4, 1863.

behind as another force attacked from the front. To keep from being bottled up in Fredericksburg, Lee would have to emerge from his well-entrenched defensive position. Lee met this bold move with an even bolder one: he would divide his forces and send Stonewall Jackson to attack Hooker's men from the rear, outflanking Hooker's own flanking maneuver.

On May 2, Jackson assaulted Hooker's troops near Chancellorsville. The outnumbered Confederates defeated the surprised and indecisive Hooker, achieving a major victory. Southern jubilation, though, ended the very night of this triumph, for nervous Confederate soldiers accidentally shot Stonewall Jackson while he surveyed the scene near the front lines. The surgeons removed his arm that evening and hoped that he might live.

While Jackson lay in his tent, fading in and out of consciousness, Lee managed to contain another assault on Fredericksburg and push the Union troops away from their positions. The losses had once again been staggering—thirteen thousand casualties, roughly 22 percent of the army—but Lee had overcome a larger opponent. After the last battles quieted, however, Jackson died. His death took with it Lee's most skillful general.

The Battle of Gettysburg, July 1–3, 1863

Despite his victory at Chancellorsville, Lee recognized that the Confederacy was in trouble. Rosecrans still threatened to break through Tennessee into Georgia, Grant clawed his way closer to Vicksburg, and the Union blockade drew an ever tighter net around the coast. Some of his generals urged Lee to rush with his troops to Tennessee to defend the center of the Confederacy and pull Grant away from Vicksburg. But Lee decided that his most effective move would be to invade the North again, taking the pressure off Virginia and disheartening the Union. A successful strike into the North might yet persuade Britain and France to recognize the Confederacy and give heart to Peace Democrats, Northerners who wanted to abandon the war effort.

In early June, Lee began to move up through the Shenandoah Valley into southern Pennsylvania with seventy-five thousand men. Hooker seemed confused. When, after a minor dispute, Hooker offered his resignation to Lincoln, the president quickly accepted and put General George Meade in charge. Meade had to decide how best to stop the greatest threat the Confederate army had yet posed to the North. Washington and Baltimore lay in danger, along with the cities, towns, and farms of Pennsylvania. There, the Confederate troops enjoyed taking food and livestock from the rich land. Free blacks and fugitive slaves were also seized and forced south into slavery.

Although Lee and his men moved unchecked across the Potomac and deep into Pennsylvania, they found themselves in a dangerous situation. Lee had permitted Jeb Stuart's cavalry, his "eyes," to range widely from the main army; as a result, the Confederates had little idea where the Union army was or what moves it was making. For their part, Meade and his fellow officers decided to pursue Lee, but not too aggressively, looking for a likely time and place to confront the enemy.

On June 30, units from the Confederacy and the Union stumbled over one another at a small town neither side knew or cared much about: Gettysburg. On July 1, they began to struggle for the best defensive position near the town, fighting over the highest and most protected land. It appeared at first that the Southerners had the better of the first day's battle, but as the smoke cleared, both sides could see that late in the day, the Union army had consolidated itself on the most advantageous ground. Meade's men, after fierce fighting at the ends of their line, occupied a fishhook-shaped series of ridges and hills that permitted them to protect their flanks. The second day saw the Confederates slowly mobilize their forces for assaults on those positions and launch attacks late in the afternoon. The resulting battles in the peach orchard, the wheat field, Little Round Top, and the boulder-strewn area known as the Devil's Den proved horrific—with thirty-five thousand men dead or wounded—but left the Union in control of the high ground.

Despite the Union's superior position, Lee decided on a frontal attack the next day. The Confederates hoped their artillery would soften the middle of the Union lines. The Confederates did not realize how little damage their guns had done until well-entrenched Union troops decimated waves of an attack led by George E. Pickett. Only a few Southern men made it to the stone wall that protected the Northerners, and even those Confederates quickly fell. It proved a disastrous three days for the Army of Northern Virginia, which lost twenty-three thousand men through death or wounds, about a third of its entire force. The Union lost similar numbers of men, but it had more to lose. The Northerners and their new general had fought a defensive battle; the Southern side, short of supplies and men, had gambled on an aggressive assault. Elation swept the North. "The glorious success of the Army of the Potomac has electrified all," a Northerner exulted. In the wake of Chancellorsville and Lee's apparently effortless invasion of Pennsylvania, he admitted, many Northerners "did not believe the enemy could be whipped."

The next morning, a thousand miles away, **Vicksburg** surrendered to Ulysses S. Grant. Unlike Gettysburg, where the battle had been fought in a place no one considered strategically crucial, Vicksburg held enormous tactical and psychological importance. It had been the symbol of Confederate doggedness and Union frustration. After six weeks of siege and near starvation behind the Confederate defenses, Vicksburg fell. The Mississippi River now divided the Confederacy while it tied the Union to the Gulf of Mexico.

The New York City Draft Riots, July 13–16, 1863
On the very day that Lee struggled across the Potomac to safety, riots broke out in New York City. Northern working people had complicated feelings about the war. Many of those who labored in the North's factories, mines, farms, and railroads had come to the United States during the previous fifteen years. These people, mostly Irish and Germans, volunteered in large numbers to fight for the Union cause. Between 20 and 25 percent of the Union army consisted of immigrants, the great majority of them volunteers.

Despite their patriotism for their adopted country, many of the immigrants viewed black Americans with dread and contempt. Urban labor organizations divided over Lincoln's election and over the response to secession. Many Catholic Irishmen, almost all of them Democrats, proclaimed that they had no quarrel with white Southerners and that they resented the federal government's draft. The obvious effect of inflation on the wages of workers created strong resentments as well. Working people resented those men who had enough money to hire substitutes to fight in their place. Three hundred dollars, after all, constituted half a year's wage for a workingman.

Irish immigrants despaired at the losses among Irish American units in the field. When their regiments were decimated at Fredericksburg, Gettysburg, and elsewhere, Irish people began to wonder if commanders valued their lives as highly as those of the native born. When word came—just as the draft lottery was to take place in New York City on July 11, 1863—of the twenty-three thousand men lost at Gettysburg, the fury of working people rose, and on July 13, it exploded. Mobs began by assaulting draft officials, then turned their anger on any man who looked rich enough to have hired a substitute, then on pro-Lincoln newspapers and abolitionists' homes. They assaulted any African Americans they encountered on the streets, burning an orphanage, whipping men and women, and hanging victims from city lampposts. Lincoln was sickened by accounts of the riot and a city editor despaired, "Great God! What is this nation coming to?"

The police struggled for three days to control the riot. Eventually troops (including all-Irish units) rushed from the battlefields of Pennsylvania to aid the police. The troops fired into the rioters; more than a hundred people died, and another three hundred were injured. The working people got some of what they wanted: more welfare relief, exemptions from the draft for those whose families would have no other means of support, and an exodus of black people who feared for their lives.

Ironically, a few days after the **New York City draft riots**, scores of black troops died during a bold nighttime assault on **Fort Wagner** near Charleston, South Carolina. Despite the bravery of the African Americans, the assault failed. The Confederates made a point of burying the African American soldiers in a mass grave along with their white officer, Robert Gould Shaw, intending to insult him and his memory. Instead, they elevated him to a Northern martyr. The *Atlantic Monthly* marked a change in Northern attitudes toward black soldiers: "Through the cannon smoke of that dark night, the manhood of the colored race shines before many eyes that would not see."

The Battle of Chickamauga, September 19–20, 1863

After Gettysburg, Vicksburg, and the New York riots in July, events slowed until September, when Union General William Rosecrans left Chattanooga, near the Georgia border, and began moving toward Atlanta. His opponent, Braxton Bragg, hoped to entice Rosecrans into dividing his forces so that they could be cut off. The armies confronted one another at Chickamauga Creek—a Cherokee name meaning "river of death." The Confederates took advantage of Union mistakes on the heavily wooded battlefield, inflicting harrowing damage and driving Rosecrans back into Chattanooga. The Union troops were trapped there, the Confederates looming over them on Lookout Mountain and Missionary Ridge, with few routes of escape and limited supplies. The Northerners had gone from a position of apparent advantage to one of desperation.

Lincoln, judging Rosecrans "confused and stunned" by the battle at Chickamauga, used this opportunity to put Grant in charge of all Union armies between the Appalachian Mountains and the Mississippi River. In the fall of 1863, Grant traveled to Chattanooga, where Sherman joined him from Mississippi and Hooker came from Virginia.

The Gettysburg Address, November 19, 1863

The North's victories at Vicksburg and Gettysburg aided Lincoln's popularity. The draft riots in New York City damaged the reputations of Democrats, whereas the bravery of black soldiers on the battlefields of Louisiana and South Carolina led white Northerners, particularly Union soldiers, to rethink some

Battle of Fort Wagner. *Nearly half of the 54th Massachusetts Volunteers were killed in the assault on Fort Wagner in Charleston Harbor, but their courage under fire helped convince the North to continue recruiting African American soldiers.*

(The Granger Collection, New York)

of their prejudices. In the fall of 1863, the Republicans won major victories in Pennsylvania and Ohio. Lincoln determined to make the most of these heartening events.

When Lincoln received an invitation to speak at the dedication of the cemetery at Gettysburg on November 19, he saw it as a chance to impart a sense of direction and purpose to the Union cause. The event had not been planned with him in mind, and the president was not even the featured speaker. But Lincoln recognized that a battlefield offered the most effective backdrop for the things he wanted to say.

Burial crews had been laboring for weeks on the Gettysburg battlefield. Thousands of horse carcasses had been burned; thousands of human bodies had been hastily covered with a thin layer of soil. Pennsylvania purchased 17 acres and hired a specialist in rural cemetery design to lay out the burial plots so that no state would be offended by the location or amount of space devoted to its fallen men. Only about a third of the reburials had taken place when Lincoln arrived; caskets remained stacked at the station.

Lincoln, contrary to legend, did not dash off his speech on the back of an envelope. He had reworked and polished it for several days. The "remarks," as the program put it, lasted three minutes. Lincoln used those minutes to maximum effect. He said virtually nothing about the details of the scene surrounding the twenty thousand people at the ceremony. Neither did he mention slavery directly. Instead, he spoke of equality as the fundamental purpose of the war. He called for a "new birth of freedom."

Lincoln was attempting to shift the purpose of the war from Union for Union's sake to Union for freedom's sake. He sought to salvage something from the deaths of the fifty thousand men at Gettysburg. Democratic newspapers rebuked Lincoln for his claim, arguing that white soldiers had "too much self-respect to declare that negroes were their equals." But other Northerners accepted Lincoln's exhortation as the definition of their purpose. They might not believe that blacks deserved to be included as full participants in a government of, by, and for "the people," but they did believe that the Union fought for liberty broadly conceived. As battles and years went by, the words of the **Gettysburg Address** would gain force and resonance.

Just four days after Lincoln's speech, Grant gave the North new reason to believe its ideals might triumph. On November 23, Grant's men overwhelmed the Confederates on Lookout Mountain outside Chattanooga; two days later, Union soldiers shocked the Confederates by fighting their way up the steep Missionary Ridge because Confederate artillery could not reach opponents coming up directly from below. The Union, now in control of the cities and rail junctions of Kentucky and Tennessee, had a wide and direct route into Georgia.

England and France finally determined in late 1863 that they would not try to intervene in the American war. First Britain, then France detained or sold to foreign powers warships intended for the Confederacy. The Northern public, encouraged by events on the battlefield, supported Republican candidates in the congressional elections of 1863 more vigorously than had seemed possible just a few months before.

THE WINTER OF DISCONTENT: 1863–1864

The battles of the summer had been horrific. Both sides held their victories close to their hearts and brooded over their losses. The resolve and fury of summertime faded into the bitterness and bickering of winter. As the cycle rolled around again, people steeled themselves for another bloody year of war.

Politics North and South

Lincoln hoped to end the war as soon as possible, using persuasion as well as fighting to entice white Southerners back into the national fold. In early December 1863, he issued his proclamation of amnesty and reconstruction. To those who would take an oath of loyalty to the Union, Lincoln promised a full pardon and the return of all property other than slaves. Although he excluded Confederate leaders and high officers from this offer, Lincoln tried to include as many white Southern men as possible. As soon as 10 percent of the number of voters in 1860 had sworn their loyalty to the Union, he decreed, those Southerners could begin forming new state governments. Education and apprenticeship programs would aid former slaves in the transition to full freedom. He did not provide for African American participation in these new governments of the South.

Two factors worked against acceptance of Lincoln's policy. First, Northern Republicans and much of the public overestimated the extent and depth of Southern Unionist sentiment after years of war and occupation. Second, even in areas under federal control such as Tennessee and Kentucky, guerrilla bands and raiders terrorized the local population. Elections in parts of Tennessee were blocked by irregulars. "The people are warned . . . not to hold such an Election under pain of being Arrested and Carried South for trial," one observer reported. Civilians were often caught between threats. Those who failed to aid Union forces were perceived as "enemies of mankind" with "the rights due to pirates and robbers," whereas those who actively aided the Federals were liable to find crops trampled, barns burned, and vigilante justice enacted by neighbors and guerrillas. Politics frequently offered an excuse for acting on old rivalries by murder and pillaging.

Abolitionists and their allies attacked Lincoln's reconstruction plan as far too lenient to the Rebel masters and not helpful enough for the former slaves. In the **Wade-Davis bill** of February 1864, Republican congressmen attempted to inflict more stringent conditions on former Confederates and offer more help to former slaves. They wanted to use the power of the national government to enforce a standard set of laws across the South and to require 50 percent, rather than 10 percent, of the population to swear the loyalty oath, an oath of past as well as future loyalty. They feared that too weak a plan of reconstruction would permit former slave owners and Confederates to negate much of what the war might win. Congressmen and Secretary of the Treasury Salmon P. Chase worked behind the scenes in opposition to Lincoln's plan. With an eye toward the upcoming election and the need to entice Arkansas and Louisiana to rejoin the Union, Lincoln refused to sign the Wade-Davis bill.

Although Jefferson Davis did not have to worry about his own reelection in late 1863—the Confederacy had established the presidential term at six years—he did have to worry about congressional elections. They did not go well: forty-one of the new 106 representatives expressly opposed Davis and his policies, and he held only a slight majority in the Senate. Just as Northern Democrats called for compromise and peace, so did some Southerners. When Davis took a hands-off policy, he was criticized for doing too little. When he tried to assert more control, he found himself called "despotic" by his own vice president. Editors savaged Davis as responsible for the South's worsening fortunes: "Had the people dreamed that Mr. Davis would carry all his chronic antipathies, his bitter prejudices, his puerile partialities, and his doting favoritisms into the Presidential chair, they would never have allowed him to fill it,"

The Confederacy stumbled through the winter and into the spring of 1864, desperately watching for signs that the North might be losing heart.

Prisons

Early in the Civil War, both sides had exchanged prisoners of war rather than spending men and resources to maintain prisons. Such arrangements worked well enough into 1863, but then the system began to break down. As African Americans began serving in the Union armies, Confederates decreed that any former slave captured would be executed or reenslaved, not taken prisoner. The Union refused to participate in any exchanges so long as this policy remained in effect, and Lincoln even threatened retaliation in kind against captured Confederates. Prisoners began piling up on both sides, and stories of mistreatment became more frequent and more horrifying.

Northerners became livid when they heard about conditions at the Confederate camp at Andersonville, Georgia. The camp was built early in 1864 when the Confederates decided to move prisoners from Richmond. Not only would prisoners be less likely to be rescued by Northern troops moving south but also supplies could more easily be transported by railroad away from the heavy fighting in Virginia. The camp, built for ten thousand men in an open, partly swampy field, soon became overcrowded; it held thirty-three thousand prisoners by August. Gangs of Northern soldiers controlled daily life within the prison, routinely beating and robbing new arrivals. Of the forty-five thousand men eventually held at Andersonville, thirteen thousand died from exposure, starvation, and brutality. The camp's commander, Colonel Henry Wirz, was the only Confederate official executed for war crimes after the war.

Even higher proportions died at smaller camps in North Carolina. Although Confederates held in Northern prisons were better supplied, even there, death rates reached as high as 24 percent, with rations often short and men reduced to eating rats. Overall, about 16 percent of Northern soldiers and 12 percent of Southerners died in prison. Many in the North criticized Lincoln for refusing to reinstitute exchanges, but Lincoln would not sacrifice the former slaves. Moreover, he knew that exchanges helped the soldier-starved Confederacy more than they did the North.

Union Resolve

In March 1864, Lincoln gave new direction and purpose to the Union effort by putting Ulysses S. Grant in charge of all Northern forces. Grant and Lincoln agreed that the Union had to use its superiority in materiel, manpower, and navy to attack the Confederacy on every front at once, forcing the South to decide what territory it would sacrifice. While Grant would fight in Virginia, Lincoln left **William T. Sherman** in charge in Chattanooga. Sherman would attack the railroad center of Atlanta, cutting the Gulf South off from the Upper South. The loss of Atlanta would chop the Confederacy into pieces too small to resist the Northern army.

In retrospect, the events of 1864 may appear anticlimactic. The Confederates seemed to face overwhelming odds. Yet Southerners recognized that everything turned on holding the Northerners off until the presidential election in the North. If the Southerners could inflict enough damage on the Union army, Northerners might elect someone willing to bring the war to an end through compromise. The Confederates knew too that the three-year terms of the most experienced veterans in the Union army expired in 1864. More than half of those veterans chose to leave the army, even

MAP 15.2 Grant Against Lee in Virginia, May 1864–April 1865.

The two most important generals of the war confronted one another at one brutal battle after another between May 1864 and April 1865.

though the war was not over. They would be replaced with younger, less seasoned soldiers. The Confederates also realized that Grant, new to his command, would be confronting Robert E. Lee, who was fighting with an experienced army. All things considered, it was by no means clear in 1864 that the Union would win in Virginia or win the war.

African Americans played an increasingly large role in Union plans, for more than 180,000 black soldiers enlisted just when the North needed them most. By the spring of 1864, the means of recruitment, training, and pay for these soldiers had become well established. The Confederates, however, refused to recognize the same rules of warfare for black soldiers that they acknowledged for whites. In April 1864 at Fort Pillow in western Tennessee, Confederate cavalry under the command of Nathan Bedford Forrest shot down black Union soldiers and their white commander who attempted to surrender.

With the election clock running, Grant set out in May 1864 to destroy Lee's army. The Battle of the Wilderness near Chancellorsville saw brutal fighting and horrible losses. Fire in the tangled woods trapped wounded men, burning them alive. Grant lost more men than Hooker had in the battle of the previous year, but whereas Hooker treated such losses as a decisive defeat and retreated, Grant pushed on.

The two armies fought again and again over the next two months in the fields of Virginia. The Confederates turned the Union army back to the east of Richmond and rushed up the Shenandoah Valley to threaten Washington itself. Although they failed to take the capital, Confederate raiders "taxed" Maryland towns for thousands of dollars of greenbacks and burned the town of Chambersburg, Pennsylvania, when it refused to pay $500,000. The North repulsed the invasion and dispatched Philip Sheridan to the valley to make sure the Confederates did not regroup, while Grant pinned down Lee's main force around Richmond and Petersburg, forcing the Confederates to construct ever-longer lines of earthworks to protect the Confederate capital. In an attempt to break through Lee's defenses, Pennsylvania coal miners volunteered to tunnel under the fortifications and plant explosives. Throughout July, they dug; finally, at the end of the month, they detonated a charge and blew an enormous crater in the Confederate lines. The attack that followed the explosion, however, failed. Union soldiers piled into the crater, where the rallying Confederates trapped them.

Fortunately for Lincoln, things were going better farther south. Throughout June and July, Sherman pushed relentlessly through north Georgia toward Atlanta. By the end of July, the Southern army had fallen back into Atlanta, preparing to defend it from siege. It seemed only a matter of time before the Union triumphed. But how much time? After rapidly advancing, federal troops slowed as they closed on Atlanta and many feared Sherman was "on the eve of disaster."

The Northern Election of 1864

The president had to fight off challenges even within his own party. Some Republicans considered Lincoln too radical; others considered him too cautious. Through adroit use of patronage, however, Lincoln managed to win renomination in June. The Republican Party tried to broaden its appeal to Democrats by nominating **Andrew Johnson**, a former Democrat from Tennessee, to the vice presidency.

In the meantime, the Democrats confidently moved forward. They knew that in the eyes of his critics, Lincoln had caused the war, trampled on constitutional rights, consolidated too much power, and refused to end the war when he had a chance. The Democrats intended to take full advantage of such criticisms by nominating General George McClellan as their candidate. McClellan demonstrated that a person could oppose Lincoln's political purposes of the war without being a coward or traitor. McClellan and the Democrats portrayed themselves as the truly national party, for they were determined to restore the United States to its prewar unity and grandeur. McClellan said he would end the war if the South would reenter the Union—bringing slavery with it. It was a bargain that appealed to many in the North.

Just when it appeared that the Democrats would unseat Lincoln, news from the battlefield changed everything: Sherman had swung around **Atlanta** and begun destroying the railroads that made the small city an important junction. The Confederates, afraid they would be encircled and trapped within the city, set much of Atlanta on fire and abandoned it. Sherman and his army marched into the city on September 2. Two weeks later, Sheridan attacked the Confederates in the Shenandoah Valley, systematically destroying the valley's ability to support the Southern army again.

Even with these military victories, Lincoln won only 55 percent of the popular vote. Contrary to expectations, Lincoln carried the large majority of the armies' votes. After three years of war, soldiers in the field, even those who considered themselves

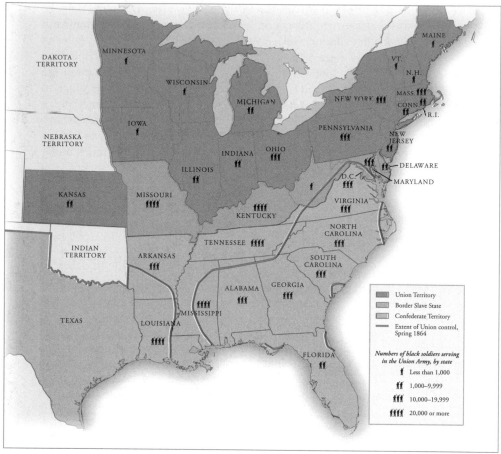

MAP 15.3 Black Soldiers in the Union Army.

African American men streamed into the U.S. Army from all across the country, but they were especially prominent in the occupied South where they had been enslaved.

loyal to McClellan, would not support the Democratic peace platform. A Vermont soldier who described himself as "a McClellan man clear to the bone" would not accept "peace by surrendering to the rebels"; instead "he would let his bones manure the soil of Virginia." Lincoln did much better in the electoral college, sweeping every state except three. The Republicans also elected heavy majorities to both houses of Congress and elected the governor and legislative majorities in all states except New Jersey, Delaware, and Kentucky.

The March to the Sea, November 15–December 21, 1864 Jefferson Davis traveled through the Lower South after the fall of Atlanta, exhorting citizens to remain defiant. A week after Lincoln's election, Sherman set out across Georgia, provisioning his army along the way, taking the war to the Southern people themselves. Such a march would be as much a demonstration of Northern power as a military maneuver: "If we can march a well-appointed army right through [Confederate] territory," Sherman argued, "it is a demonstration to the world, foreign and domestic, that we have a power which Davis cannot resist." The triumphant army of sixty thousand made its way across the state throughout the fall of 1864. Large numbers of deserters from both sides, fugitive slaves, and outlaws took advantage of the situation to inflict widespread destruction and panic. Sherman arrived at Savannah on December 21. "I beg to present to you, as a Christmas gift, the city of Savannah," Sherman buoyantly telegraphed Lincoln. Contrasting with the devastation of the South, the president's annual message to Congress outlined a portrait of a North gaining strength with "more men now than we had when the war began. . . . We are gaining strength, and may, if need be, maintain the contest indefinitely."

FROM WAR TO RECONSTRUCTION: 1865

As the war ground to a halt in early 1865, Americans had to wonder if they remembered how to share a country with their former enemies. They had to wonder, too, how different the country would be with African Americans no longer as slaves. Of all the changes the United States had ever seen, **emancipation** stood as the most profound.

War's Climax

Events moved quickly at the beginning of 1865. In January, Sherman issued **Special Field Order 15**, which reserved land in coastal South Carolina, Georgia, and Florida for former slaves. Those who settled on the land would receive 40-acre plots. Four days later, the Republicans in Congress passed the **Thirteenth Amendment**, abolishing slavery forever. Antislavery activists, black and white, packed the galleries and the House floor. Observers embraced, wept, and cheered. A congressman wrote his wife that "we can now look other nations in the face without shame."

At the beginning of February, Sherman's troops began to march north into the Carolinas. Columbia, South Carolina, was burned to the ground. Growing numbers of Confederate soldiers deserted from their armies. Lincoln met with Confederate officials at Hampton Roads on board the steamship *River Queen* to try to bring the war to an end, offering slave owners compensation for their freed slaves if the Southerners would immediately cease the war. Jefferson Davis refused to submit to the "disgrace of surrender."

At the beginning of March, Lincoln was inaugurated for his second term. Rather than gloating at the impending victory on the battlefield, Lincoln called for his fellow citizens to "bind up the nation's wounds." That same month, Congress created the Bureau of Refugees, Freedmen, and Abandoned Lands to ease the transition from slavery to freedom. Nine days later, the Confederate government, after hotly debating whether to recruit slaves to fight as soldiers if their owners agreed, finally decided to do so after Lee, desperate for men, supported the measure.

Appomattox and Assassination, April 9 and April 14, 1865

The Confederates' slave recruitment law did not have time to convert slaves to soldiers, for Grant soon began his final assault on Confederate troops in Virginia. His forces broke through Confederate entrenchments near Petersburg on April 2, and

The Copperheads

The influence of the Copperheads, peace Democrats sympathetic to the South, peaked during the summer of 1864. Although not opposed to war on principle, many Copperheads did not believe that secession was unconstitutional; others opposed emancipation. The magnitude of Grant's Virginia losses, the

THE COPPERHEAD PARTY.—IN FAVOR OF *A VIGOROUS PROSECUTION OF PEACE!*

(Library of Congress)

disaster of the Petersburg crater, and the demoralizing effects of Confederate raids into Maryland encouraged many Northerners to abandon support for the war effort in 1864. With assistance from the Confederacy, Copperheads in the Midwest laid plans to free prisoners of war and attack the North from within.

By late August, when the Democratic convention met in Chicago, Copperheads had achieved sufficient influence to insert a peace plank into the party's election platform and secure the nomination of Peace Democrat George Pendleton as McClellan's running mate. Yet the sudden reversal of Union military fortunes— Farragut's victory at Mobile Bay, Sherman's capture of Atlanta, and Sheridan's successful campaign in the Valley—renewed Northern confidence in the war. In this new atmosphere, talk of peace negotiations, which would have entailed recognizing Confederate independence, smacked of treason. Democrats struggled to distance themselves from the Copperheads, but by the time of the election, McClellan lost the popular vote and won only 21 of 233 votes in the electoral college. Soldiers, many deeply committed to the Union cause, voted overwhelmingly for Lincoln.

In this cartoon, published in 1863, poisonous copperhead snakes threaten Lady Liberty.

Richmond fell the next day. Lee hoped to lead his army to the train station at **Appomattox** Court House to resupply them, but on April 9, Grant intercepted Lee's men just short of their destination. Lee, with nowhere else to go and no other armies to come to his aid, surrendered.

A number of Confederate armies had yet to surrender and Jefferson Davis remained at large, but it was clear that the war had ended. Cities and towns across the North erupted in celebration and relief as crowds filled the streets to sing, embrace, fire salutes, and wave the flag. Southerners began to straggle home. Two days later,

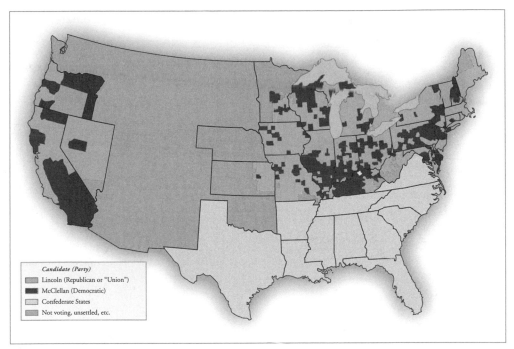

MAP 15.4 The Election of 1864.

Although Lincoln won the election of 1864, both he and McClellan enjoyed widespread popular support throughout the North. Local communities were often deeply divided in their political loyalties.

Lincoln addressed a Washington audience about what would come next for the freedmen. He admitted that Northerners differed "as to the mode, manner, and means of Reconstruction" and that the white South was "disorganized and discordant."

Lincoln did not live to take part in the planning, for he was assassinated on April 14 by **John Wilkes Booth**, a failed actor and Southern sympathizer. Booth attacked Lincoln while the president sat with Mrs. Lincoln at Ford's Theater in Washington, shooting him in the back of the head and then leaping to the stage. Lincoln never recovered consciousness and died early the next morning. Americans hearing the news were shocked. Stores and banks closed for business; bells tolled in cities throughout the North, and buildings were draped in black bunting. Anti-Southern sentiment flared in the North, and one newspaper fumed that the conspirators "have stricken down the MAN who stood forth their best intercessor before the nation . . . their finest, most forgiving friend, he who pleaded with his people to temper justice with mercy." From a beleaguered president, Lincoln had become a heroic martyr. Voicing the uncertainty of the nation, one writer asked gloomily, "And who can now tell the consequences?"

The Costs and Consequences of the War

The North lost almost 365,000 men to death and disease in the Civil War, and the South lost 260,000. Another 277,000 Northerners were wounded, along with 195,000 Southerners.

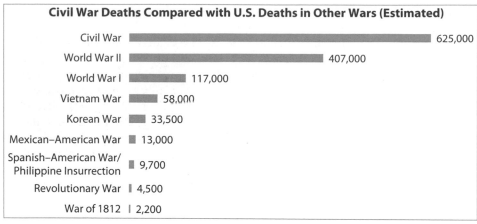

Civil War Deaths Compared with U.S. Deaths in Other Wars (Estimated)

Civil War	625,000
World War II	407,000
World War I	117,000
Vietnam War	58,000
Korean War	33,500
Mexican–American War	13,000
Spanish–American War/ Philippine Insurrection	9,700
Revolutionary War	4,500
War of 1812	2,200

FIGURE 15.1 Civil War Losses.

The Civil War exacted a horrible cost, far outstripping every other conflict in which the United States has fought.

Black Americans lost 37,000 men in the Union army and at least another 10,000 men, women, and children in the contraband camps. Widows and orphans, black and white, Northern and Southern, faced decades of struggling without a male breadwinner. Many people found their emotional lives shattered by the war. Alcohol, drug abuse, crime, and violence became widespread problems.

The Southern slave-based economy collapsed. Major Southern cities had been reduced to ash. Railroads had been ripped from the ground, engines and cars burned. Fields had turned to weeds and brush. Farm values fell by half. Livestock, tools, barns, and fences had been stolen or destroyed by the armies of both sides. Recovery was slow. In Georgia, for example, as late as 1870 the state recorded 1 million fewer pigs, 200,000 fewer cattle, and 3 million fewer acres under cultivation than in 1860. Just as damaging in the long run, lines of credit had been severed. Before emancipation, planters had used their slaves as collateral for loans. Now, with the destruction

(© CORBIS)

Abraham Lincoln. *This picture of Lincoln, taken four days before his assassination, shows the toll four years of war had taken on the fifty-six-year-old president.*

of that form of "collateral," few people outside the South were willing to loan money to planters or other investors to revive the economy.

The Civil War did not mark a sudden turn in the Northern economy, but it did accelerate processes already well under way. The nationalization of markets, the accumulation of wealth, and the consolidation of manufacturing firms became more marked after 1865. Greenbacks, bonds, and a national banking system regularized the flow of capital and spurred the growth of business. In 1862, the Republicans passed the Department of Agriculture Act, the Morrill College Land Grant Act, the Homestead Act, and the Union Pacific Railroad Act, all using the power of the federal government to encourage settlement of the West, strengthen public education, and spur economic development.

Emancipation and the South As the battles ground to a halt, slaves became former slaves. Some, especially the young, greeted freedom confidently, whereas others, especially the elderly, could not help but be wary of anything so strange, no matter how long and how much they had prayed for it. Some seized their freedom at the first opportunity, taking their families to Union camps or joining the army. Others celebrated when the Yankees came to their plantations, only to find that their owners and white neighbors retaliated when the soldiers left. Others bided their time. Some refused to believe the stories of freedom at all until their masters or mistresses called them together to announce that they were indeed no longer slaves.

Upon hearing the news, the freed people gathered to discuss their options. For many, the highest priority was to reunite their families. Such people set off on journeys in desperate efforts to find a husband, wife, child, or parent sold away in earlier years. For others, sheer survival was the highest priority. Freedom came in the late spring, barely in time to get crops in the ground. Some former slaves argued that their best bet was to stay where they were for the time being. They had heard rumors that the government would award them land. Between July and September 1865, however, those dreams died. Union officers had promised land to former slaves in Virginia, Louisiana, Mississippi, and South Carolina, but then Washington revoked the promises. The land would be returned to its former owners.

Former slave owners also responded in many different ways. Some fled to Latin America. Others tried to keep as much of slavery as they could by whipping and chaining workers to keep them from leaving. Still others offered to let former slaves stay in their cabins and work for wages. The presence of black soldiers triggered resentment and fear among former slave owners who marked the increased independence among blacks that was encouraged by "Negro troops." One slave owner believed "the people of the South are in very great danger. . . . I tell you most seriously that the whole south is resting upon a volcano."

African Americans had no choice but to compromise with white landowners. At first, in the spring of 1865, planters insisted that the former slaves work as they had worked before emancipation, in "gangs." In return for their work, they would receive a portion of the crop, shared among all the workers. Many black people chafed at this arrangement, preferring to work as individuals or families. In such places, landowners found that they had little choice but to permit black families to take primary responsibility for a portion of land. These former slaves, called "sharecroppers," provided the

Desolation of the South

After four years of war, little remained in many cities of the Confederacy. Atlanta, Columbia, and Richmond had been ravaged by fire; Vicksburg, Petersburg, and Fredericksburg had been pummeled by siege and battle. Union troops had destroyed railways, rivers were blocked by the refuse of war, and fields and farms had been stripped by the marauding troops of both sides or simply overrun by weeds. Roads, wagons, and riverboats were choked with civilian refugees,

(Library of Congress)

returning soldiers, and prisoners of war. Thousands of refugees from the countryside relied on federal aid and rations to survive. Even on farms and plantations untouched by combat, former slaves abandoned masters to seek family members and new opportunities.

DOING HISTORY ONLINE

Emancipation

After reading the accounts from Virginia (Document 10), how would you describe the Southern white reaction to emancipation? According to the newspaper article, "What Shall Become of the Freedmen" (Document 11), how did life change for freedmen?

www.cengage.com/
history/ayers/
ampassages4e

labor and received part of the crop in return. Planters, though reluctant to give up any control over the day-to-day work on their land, realized they had few choices. They possessed little cash to pay wage workers and no alternative labor.

The Bureau of Refugees, Freedmen, and Abandoned Lands—the **Freedmen's Bureau**—oversaw the transition from a slave economy to a wage economy. Its agents, approximately nine hundred for the entire South, dispensed medicine, food, and clothing from the vast stores of the federal government to displaced white and black Southerners. It created courts to adjudicate conflicts and draw up labor contracts between landholders and laborers. It established schools and coordinated female volunteers who came from the North to teach in them. Although many white Southerners resented and resisted the Freedmen's Bureau, it helped smooth the transition from slavery to freedom, from war to peace.

Black Mobilization   Black Southerners mourned the loss of Abraham Lincoln. Without his leadership, former slaves rightly worried, the forces of reaction might overwhelm their freedom. Southerners of both races watched to see what President Andrew Johnson might do.

Throughout the South, former slaves and former free blacks gathered in mass meetings, Union Leagues, and conventions to announce their vision of the new order. They wanted, above all else, equality before the law and the opportunity to vote. Their spokesmen did not demand confiscation of land or speak extensively of economic concerns in general. Let us have our basic rights before the courts and at the ballot box, they said, and we will take care of ourselves. Such concerns and confidence reflected the perspective of the conventions' leadership: former free blacks, skilled artisans, ministers, and teachers. The great mass of Southern blacks, former slaves, found their concerns neglected.

Black Southerners agreed on the centrality of two institutions: the church and the school. For generations, African Americans had been forced to worship alongside whites. For many ex-slaves, one of their first acts of freedom was to form their own churches. Before the war, forty-two thousand black Methodists in South Carolina attended biracial churches. By 1870, only six hundred mostly elderly blacks remained in those churches. People who owned virtually nothing somehow built churches across the South. A black church in Charleston was the first building raised from the ruins of the city in 1865. Those churches often served as schools as well.

CONCLUSION

The Civil War changed the United States more deeply than any other event in the nineteenth century—indeed, perhaps in all of American history. The conflict brought the deaths of more than 625,000 soldiers, a proportion of the population equivalent to 5 million people today and nearly as many as have died in all other American wars combined. Men who had been seriously wounded and disfigured would haunt the United States for generations to come, reminders of a horrific war. Children would grow up without fathers, and many young women would never find husbands.

The war, despite the blessings of Union and freedom it brought, also brought a steep price in social disorder. The Civil War saw bitter rioting in the streets in the North and the South. It saw political parties arguing over the very future of the nation. And it saw the first assassination of a president.

The Civil War triggered a major expansion of the federal government. The demands of wartime created greenbacks, the draft, and government involvement in transportation and business. It also brought a profound shift in the balance of power among the regions. Since the founding of the nation, the South had wielded influence out of proportion to its population. One president after another owned slaves, and others did the bidding of slaveholders. After Appomattox, however, the South's political domination was broken. It would be half a century before another Southern-born man—Woodrow Wilson—was elected president.

Most important, the war brought what few Americans could have imagined at the end of 1860: the immediate emancipation of 4 million enslaved people. Nowhere else in the world had so many people become free so quickly. Yet freedom emerged from the war through a circuitous route. The war began as a war for union, but as the deaths mounted and African Americans seized freedom at every opportunity, abolitionists and Republicans increasingly demanded that the war become a war to end slavery. Many white Northerners supported emancipation because it seemed the best way to end the war. Abraham Lincoln worked desperately to keep the support of both the advocates and foes of emancipation, knowing that moving too quickly would shatter the fragile support that kept him in office. The New York City draft riots and the close elections of 1863 demonstrated that many Northerners resisted the continuation of the war and its embrace of black freedom. Only Union success on the battlefield in late 1864 permitted Lincoln's reelection. His assassination made an already confused situation far more so, ending slavery and restoring the Union without a blueprint and without leadership.

CHAPTER REVIEW, 1863–1865

- African American soldiers began to enlist in great numbers.
- The Union won decisive victories at Gettysburg and Vicksburg.
- Southerners rioted in Richmond; Northerners rioted in New York City.
- The Union drove to victory in the Shenandoah Valley, in Tennessee, in Georgia, and in the Carolinas, but struggled in Virginia until the spring of 1865.
- Robert E. Lee surrendered his troops in April 1865.
- Abraham Lincoln, reelected in the winter of 1864, was assassinated in the spring of 1865.
- Four million African Americans had been freed from slavery by the passage of the Thirteenth Amendment.

◀|||| Looking Back

Chapter 15 shows that at every point in the war, both Northerners and Southerners thought the conflict might end with one more key victory by their side. Instead, each battle seemed to bring another one, even bloodier than the one that came before.

1. Did the Civil War have a turning point—a point beyond which it became clear that the United States would defeat the Confederacy? What would you identify as this point?
2. How did emancipation become a central war aim for the Union?
3. To what extent did the Confederacy collapse from within—or was it primarily overwhelmed from without?

Looking Ahead ||||▶

Chapter 16 will show that the most profound change in American history, the end of slavery, came to a nation exhausted by war and a region unprepared for freedom. Black and white, Northern and Southern, Americans struggled over the shape of the future.

1. As the war ended, what forms did it appear that Reconstruction might take? Who would control the fates of newly emancipated African Americans?
2. What did black Southerners most want and need from emancipation?

Go to the American Passages website at www.cengage.com/history/ayers/ampassages4e for additional review materials.

Reconstruction: Its Rise and Fall, 1865–1877

With the death of Abraham Lincoln in April 1865, a new president sought to reunite the nation at the end of the Civil War. The presence of Andrew Johnson in the White House took the Republican Party and the newly freed slaves in directions that shaped the way the North made policy toward the defeated South. The process became known as Reconstruction, and it has remained one of the most controversial periods in all of American history. For decades, it was thought that the Republicans did too much to transform the South. Now the consensus is that the Republicans did too little to alter what the impact of slavery had been.

Reconstruction set out to change the South and better the lives of the people, white and black, who lived there. It is one of the paradoxes of this period that these important efforts left many aspects of the southern economy in no better, and sometimes worse, shape than before Reconstruction began. A depressed economy and increased debt made sharecropping the lot of many southern farmers of both races by 1880 (see Map 16.1).

Reconstruction is often depicted as a battle among white politicians with African Americans as either pawns of more powerful forces or simply spectators while their fate was being decided. Historians now recognize that former slaves played a decisive role in building institutions and carrying on campaigns to expand their political impact in the South. The opportunity to build a multiracial society after the Civil War was a fleeting one, but it represented an important chapter in the lives of those individuals who formerly had been in bondage. To understand how the endeavor of Reconstruction rose and fell, it is necessary to turn first to Lincoln's successor, Andrew Johnson.

RECONSTRUCTION UNDER ANDREW JOHNSON, 1865–1867

In the wake of Lincoln's assassination, the nation looked to the new president for leadership. Andrew Johnson was an unknown element to most political insiders. His promise to pursue Lincoln's

CHAPTER TIMELINE

1866	Johnson vetoes Freedmen's Bureau bill • Congress passes Civil Rights Act and Freedmen's Bureau renewal over Johnson's veto • Riots in New Orleans and Memphis • Congress approves Fourteenth Amendment • Ku Klux Klan formed
1867	Congress passes Reconstruction Act and Tenure of Office Act • Constitutional conventions in Southern states • Johnson dismisses Secretary of War Stanton, triggering impeachment proceedings • First elections in South under Reconstruction Act • Alaska purchase treaty signed
1868	Andrew Johnson impeached and then acquitted • Purchase of Alaska completed • Ulysses S. Grant wins presidency
1869	Ulysses S. Grant inaugurated as president • Transcontinental railroads link up • Licensing of women lawyers begins • Fifteenth Amendment passes Congress • "Gold Corner" scheme of Jay Gould and Jim Fisk • Woman suffrage enacted in Wyoming Territory
1870	Santo Domingo annexation treaty defeated • Ku Klux Klan terror raids in the South • First Greek letter sorority (Kappa Alpha Theta) founded
1871	Ku Klux Klan Act passes Congress • Tweed Ring exposed in New York City • Chicago fire burns three and a half miles of the city
1872	Liberal Republican movement challenges Grant • Grant wins reelection over Horace Greeley
1873	Panic of 1873 starts economic depression • Salary Grab and Credit Mobilier scandals • Mark Twain and Charles Dudley Warner publish *The Gilded Age*
1874	Woman's Christian Temperance Union founded • Democrats make substantial gains in the congressional elections • Sale of typewriters begins • Chautauqua movement for summer education starts
1875	Congress passes Civil Rights Act • Smith College and Wellesley College open to provide higher education for women
1876	Sioux defeat Custer at Little Big Horn • Centennial Exposition opens in Philadelphia • Tilden and Hayes are candidates in contested presidential election
1877	Hayes declared winner of presidency after series of compromises settles disputes • Reconstruction ends

policies seemed reassuring. At this moment of national crisis, a strong hand in the White House was necessary. As it turned out, Johnson had a firm idea of how he wanted to deal with the South, but his Reconstruction policies proved neither effective nor in tune with majority opinion in the North.

This icon will direct you to interactive activities and study materials on the American Passages website: www.cengage.com/history/ayers/ampassages4e

Andrew Johnson   President Johnson wanted to attract moderates from both the North and the South to a political party that would change the nation as little as possible. Johnson had been selected to run for the vice presidency because he was a Unionist Southerner. As a result, both Northerners and Southerners distrusted him. A longtime Democrat before the crisis of the Union, Johnson maintained a limited view of government. The new president's well-known disdain for the wealthy planters of the South appealed to equally disdainful Republicans in Washington. His public statements suggested a harsh peace for the former slave owners and Confederate leaders: "*Treason* is a crime, and crime must be punished." Unlike some Republicans, however, Johnson held little sympathy for black people or for expansion of the powers of the federal government. Johnson saw himself pursuing Lincoln's highest goal, reuniting the Union. Reunification should start by winning the support of white southerners.

Johnson enjoyed a brief period to enact his vision of how to return the South to the Union. Congress was not in session at the time of Lincoln's death and would not be for seven months, so Johnson used the opportunity to implement his plan of reunion. In "Presidential Reconstruction," Johnson offered amnesty to former Confederates who took an oath of loyalty to the Union, restoring their political and civil rights and immunizing them against the seizure of their property and prosecution for treason. By 1866, Johnson granted more than seven thousand pardons to wealthy southerners and Confederate senior officers who applied individually for pardons.

Andrew Johnson.
Andrew Johnson attempted to forge a new alliance between white Northerners and white Southerners, callously abandoning black southerners in the process.

(Library of Congress)

Johnson's plans for political reunion left out any provision for black voting or participation in politics. Indeed, his plan would give the South even greater national power than it had held before because the entire African American population would now be considered individually when the number of representatives was calculated, not merely as three-fifths of a person as before the war.

White southerners could hardly believe their good fortune. The state conventions elected in 1865 flaunted their opinions of the North. Some refused to fly the American flag, some refused to ratify the Thirteenth Amendment, and some even refused to admit that secession had been illegal. Former Confederates filled important posts in state governments. Georgia elected Alexander H. Stevens, the former vice president of the aborted nation, to Congress. Even Johnson recognized that far from inaugurating new regimes led by Unionist yeoman, "there seems, in many of the elections something like defiance."

The North erupted in outrage when the new state governments enacted the so-called **black codes**, laws for controlling former slaves. The southern white legislatures granted the barest minimum of rights to black people: the right to marry, to hold property, to sue and be sued. Most of the laws decreed what African Americans could not do: move from one job to another, own or rent land, testify in court, practice certain occupations. When the members of Congress convened in December 1865, they reacted as many of their constituents did: with fury. To Northerners, even those inclined to deal leniently with the South, the former Confederates seemed to deny all the war had decided with this blatant attempt to retain racially based laws. And many Northerners blamed Johnson.

Johnson and the Radicals   It was not that most Northerners, even most Republicans, wanted the kind of policies that Radicals such as Thaddeus Stevens and Charles Sumner promoted. Stevens called for land to be seized from wealthy planters and given to the former slaves; Sumner wanted immediate and universal suffrage for blacks. But neither did Republicans want the sort of capitulation that Johnson had tolerated. "As for Negro suffrage," wrote a Chicago newspaper editor, "the mass of Union men in the Northwest did not care a great deal. What scares them is the idea that the rebels are all to be let back . . . and made a power in the government again." Moderates tried to devise plans acceptable to both sides.

The moderates sought to continue the Freedmen's Bureau. The bureau was understaffed and underfunded, but it offered some measure of hope for former slaves by mediating between whites and blacks. Its commissioner, General Oliver Howard, advocated education as the foundation for improving living conditions and prospects for blacks. By 1869, approximately three thousand schools, serving more than 150,000 students, reported to the bureau, and these numbers do not include the many private and church-funded schools throughout the South.

The bureau insisted on the innovation of formal contracts between laborer and landlord. Although these contracts infuriated southern white men, the bureau supported landowners as often as black laborers. The moderates also pushed for a civil rights bill to define American citizenship for all those born in the United States, thereby including blacks. Citizenship would bring with it equal protection under the law, though the bill said nothing about black voting. The bureau struggled against strongly held prejudice. Its Mississippi commissioner despaired of a public that failed to "conceive of the Negro having any rights at all."

Republicans supported the Freedmen's Bureau and civil rights bills as the starting point for rebuilding the nation. But Johnson vetoed both bills, claiming that they violated the rights of the states and of white southerners who had been excluded from the decision making. Republicans closed ranks to override Johnson's veto, the first major legislation ever enacted over a presidential veto.

To prevent any future erosion of black rights, the Republicans proposed the Fourteenth Amendment, which, as eventually ratified, guaranteed citizenship to all American-born people and equal protection under the law for those citizens. The amendment decreed that any state that abridged the voting rights of any male inhabitants who were over age twenty-one and citizens would suffer a proportionate reduction in its congressional representation. This clause offered white southerners the choice of acceptance of black suffrage or reduced congressional representation. It was the first constitutional amendment to use the word *male,* angering feminist abolitionists, who challenged the denial of suffrage based on sex. Johnson advised the southern states to refuse to ratify the amendment, and they promptly did so.

Throughout the second half of 1866, the North watched, appalled, as much that the Civil War had been fought for seemed to be brushed aside in the South. Not only did the southern men who met in the state conventions refuse to accept the relatively mild Fourteenth Amendment, but they fought back in every way they could against further attempts to remake the South. The spring of that year saw riots in Memphis and New Orleans in which policemen and other whites brutally assaulted and killed black people and burned their homes with little or no provocation.

It was in 1866, too, that the **Ku Klux Klan** appeared. Founded by Nathan Bedford Forrest in Tennessee, the Ku Klux Klan dedicated itself to maintaining white supremacy. The Klan dressed in costumes designed to overawe the former slaves, hiding behind their anonymity to avoid retaliation. It became in effect a military wing of the Democratic Party, devoting much of its energy to warning and killing white and black men who dared associate with the Republicans or supported black rights.

Johnson toured the country in the fall of 1866 to denounce Republicans and their policy. But even his supporters saw the tour (called the "swing around the circle") as a "thoroughly reprehensible" disaster. The voters rejected Johnson and the Democrats. Republicans won control of the governorship and legislature in every northern state. In the next Congress, Republicans could override any presidential veto. The Republicans felt they had a mandate to push harder than they had before. They had only a few months, however, until the congressional term ended in March, to decide what to do. They disagreed over the vote, land distribution, the courts, and education. Some wanted to put the South under military control for the indefinite future; others sought to return to civilian control as soon as possible. Finally, on March 2, 1867, as time was running out on the session, they passed the Reconstruction Act.

The Reconstruction Act of 1867   The **Reconstruction Act** placed the South under military rule. All the southern states except Tennessee, which had been readmitted to the Union after it ratified the Fourteenth Amendment, were divided into five military districts. Once order had been instituted, the states could proceed to elect conventions to draw up new constitutions, but those constitutions had to accept the Fourteenth Amendment and provide universal manhood suffrage. Once a majority of the state's citizens and both houses of the national Congress had approved the new constitution, the state could be readmitted to the Union.

To ensure that Andrew Johnson did not undermine the plan, which soon became known as "Radical Reconstruction," Congress sought to curb the president's power. With no threat of his veto after the 1866 elections, the Republicans could do much as they wanted. Congress decreed that it could call itself into special session. There, it limited the president's authority as commander-in-chief of the army, and in the Tenure of Office Act, it prevented him from removing officials who had been confirmed by the Senate.

Johnson, characteristically, did not accept such restrictions of his power. When he violated the Tenure of Office Act by removing Secretary of War Edwin Stanton in the summer of 1867, many in Congress decided that Johnson warranted **impeachment**. Matters stewed throughout the fall, while the first elections under the Reconstruction Act took place in the South.

Reconstruction Begins

After word of the Reconstruction Act circulated in the spring and summer, both black and white men claimed leadership roles within the Republican Party. Black Northerners came to the South looking for appointive and elective office. Ambitious black southerners, many of whom had been free and relatively prosperous before the Civil War, put themselves forward as the natural leaders of the race. Such men became the backbone of the Republican Party in black-belt districts that had a predominantly African American population.

White southerners sneered at white Northerners who supported the Republican cause, calling them "carpetbaggers." These men, according to the insulting name, were supposedly so devoid of connections and property in their northern homes that they could throw everything they had into a carpetbag (a cheap suitcase) and head south as soon as they read of the opportunities Radical Reconstruction had created. The majority of white Northerners who became Republican leaders in the South, however, had in fact moved to the region months or years before Reconstruction began. Many had been well educated in the North before the war, and many held property in the South. Like white southerners, however, the northern-born Republicans found the postwar South a difficult place in which to prosper. Black people were no more inclined to work for low wages for white Northerners than for anyone else, and southern whites often went out of their way to avoid doing business with the Yankees. As a result, when Reconstruction began, a considerable number of northerners took up the Republican cause as a way to build a political career in the South.

White southern Republicans, labeled "scalawags" by their enemies, risked being called traitors to their race and region. Few white Republicans emerged in the plantation districts because they endured ostracism, resistance, and violence. In the upcountry districts, however, former Whigs and Unionists asserted themselves against the planters and Confederates. The Republican Party became strong in the mountains of eastern Tennessee, western North Carolina, eastern Kentucky, northern Alabama, and northern Georgia. Many whites in these districts, though unwilling to join with low-country African Americans or their white leaders, struck alliances of convenience with them. Black voters and white voters generally wanted and needed different things. Blacks, largely propertyless, called for an activist government to raise taxes and provide schools, orphanages, and hospitals. Many whites, who owned land, called mainly for lower taxes.

Throughout the South, most whites watched, livid, as local black leaders, ministers, and Republicans mobilized black voters in enormous numbers in fall 1867.

Membership in Union Leagues swept the region, with local leagues assisting with labor contracts and school construction as well as political activity. An Alabama league demanded recognition of black citizenship: "We claim exactly the same rights, privileges and immunities as are enjoyed by white men—we seek nothing more and will be content with nothing less." While many white Democrats boycotted the elections, the Republicans swept into the constitutional delegate positions. Although many black men voted, African Americans made up only a relatively small part of the convention delegates. They held the majority in South Carolina and Louisiana, but much smaller proportions elsewhere. About half of the 265 African Americans elected as delegates to the state conventions had been free before the war, and most were ministers, artisans, farmers, and teachers. Over the next two years, these delegates would meet to write new, much more democratic constitutions for their states.

At the very moment of the success of the southern Republicans, however, ominous signs came from the North. Republicans were dismayed at the election returns in the North in 1867, for the Democrats' power surged from coast to coast. Many white voters thought that the Radicals had gone too far in their concern with black rights and wanted officeholders to devote their energies to problems closer to home. Racism linked Democratic appeals against blacks in the Midwest with western diatribes against the Chinese. Integrated public schools and confiscation of plantation lands for former slaves were defeated. The Republicans in Washington heard the message and began scaling back their support for any further advances in Reconstruction.

Despite these reservations, Republicans in 1867 believed that they had taken important steps toward a newer and more just society. "We have cut loose from the whole dead past," said Timothy Howe of Wisconsin, "and have cast our anchor out a hundred years." But the struggle over black rights that had begun during the Civil War was far from over. The battle shifted from the halls of Congress back to the South. There, in the decade that followed the war, blacks pursued their dreams of political equality and economic opportunity. Whites sought to preserve as many of the features of slavery as they could. Violence, brutality, election fraud, and raw economic intimidation ended the experiment in multiracial politics known as Reconstruction.

Although racial prejudices were the main cause, other forces hastened the abandonment of Reconstruction. In the mid-1870s, a severe economic depression made African American rights seem a less urgent issue. White Americans feared that the national government was becoming too powerful; a renewed commitment to localism and states' rights helped southern whites repress black aspirations. For many in the North, the hum of industry, the spread of railroads, and the rise of cities seemed more in tune with national progress than preserving the rights of former slaves.

With a western frontier to open and Native Americans to subdue, the nation retreated from the principles for which the Civil War had been fought. In the case of women's rights, for example, an initial surge of hope that women might join in the political process receded as male institutions reacted against this new movement. By the disputed presidential election of 1876, white Americans no longer wished to be involved with the fate of blacks in the South. After a decade of slow, painful withdrawal from a commitment to equality, an informal sectional compromise sealed the return of white rule to the South in 1877. That political adjustment helped structure American responses to race questions down to modern times.

FROM JOHNSON TO GRANT, 1867–1868

The struggle between the executive and legislative branches over the fate of the South continued into the second half of 1867. After Congress gathered in December 1867, sentiment for removing the president had receded, and it appeared that the president would survive for the rest of his term. Once again, however, Johnson defied Congress and precipitated a confrontation. After the Senate in January 1868 refused to accept his dismissal of Stanton, Johnson replaced him anyway. Presidential stubbornness, Republicans said, violated the Tenure of Office Act.

Emboldened by Johnson's defiance, the Republican House voted for his impeachment and leveled eleven charges against him. None of the articles of impeachment alleged violations of criminal laws; they dealt instead with Johnson's Reconstruction policies and his obstruction of Congress. The trial came in March. Two months later the Senate had failed to achieve the necessary two-thirds vote to convict Johnson. The impeachment attempt lost because moderate Republicans feared that convicting Johnson on political grounds would set a bad precedent. Moreover, Johnson himself eased up on his obstructive tactics. With the 1868 presidential election looming, why oust a man who would soon leave office? Yet Johnson did not become more conciliatory. He encouraged southern whites to resist Reconstruction and contributed to the denial of rights to African Americans that marked the 1870s. Few other presidents have done less with their historical opportunities than Andrew Johnson.

During the months of Johnson's impeachment and trial, Congress completed expansion on the North American continent with the purchase of Alaska from Russia. The Alaska purchase was a major strategic and geographic victory for the United States. Amid the controversy over the impeachment of Johnson and the upcoming presidential election, the acquisition of this northern territory did not attract great attention, however.

The Election
of 1868

The issues of the Civil War defined this presidential race. The Republicans nominated the great hero of the conflict, Ulysses S.

(HarpWeek)

Grant as Sleeping Dog.   *This Thomas Nast cartoon from* Harper's Weekly *shows the Democratic vice presidential choice, Frank Blair, as a little dog named "War" snapping at the impressive watchdog of "peace," the Republican presidential candidate, Ulysses S. Grant.*

Grant, whose popularity transcended partisanship. Republicans believed that they had selected a candidate "so independent of party politics as to be a guarantee of peace and quiet." In his official letter of acceptance, Grant said, "Let us have peace," and that phrase became the theme of the Republican campaign. The Republicans were not campaigning on any promise to expand Reconstruction or to do more for the rights of black Americans.

The Democrats turned to the former governor of New York, Horatio Seymour. Along with his running mate, Frank Blair of Missouri, Seymour relied on racial bigotry and white supremacy as the keynotes of his appeal. To win, the Democrats agreed, they had to arouse "the aversion with which the masses contemplate the equality of the negro." Seymour went out to campaign; Grant stayed home. Grant garnered 53 percent of the vote; Seymour totaled 47 percent. Although Grant carried the electoral college by a margin of 214 to 80, the signs were not good for a continuation of Reconstruction. White voters were less willing to help African Americans; whatever goals African Americans sought, they would have to achieve them on their own. The high point of post–Civil War racial reform was in the past.

The Fifteenth
Amendment
After the 1868 election, Republicans pushed for the adoption of the Fifteenth Amendment to the Constitution to finish the political reforms that Reconstruction brought. Under its terms, the federal and state governments could not restrict the right to vote because of race, color, or previous condition of servitude. Congress approved the amendment in February 1869 over Democratic opposition. The purpose of the change was to limit the legal right of the southern states to exclude African Americans from the political process. Democrats assailed it as a step toward black equality and a social revolution. In fact, the new amendment did not ensure African Americans the right to hold office, and it left untouched the restrictions that northern states imposed on the right of males to vote. Literacy tests and property qualifications remained in place in some states outside the South. State legislatures endorsed the amendment promptly and it was added to the Constitution in 1870. The adoption of the three Civil War amendments had changed the nature of the government as the administration of President Grant got under way, but American politics responded slowly to the impact of these new additions to the nation's fundamental law.

THE FIRST GRANT ADMINISTRATION, 1869–1873

Ulysses S. Grant, who came to the White House without political experience, believed that he should administer the government rather than promote new programs. "I shall on all subjects have a policy to recommend," he said in his inaugural address, "but none to enforce against the will of the people." He promised, unlike Andrew Johnson, to carry out the laws that Congress passed. Nineteenth-century Americans did not expect a president to be an activist, and neither did Grant himself. Those who hoped for a period of calm after the storms of Johnson's presidency were soon disappointed, however.

Grant's passive view of the presidency allowed Congress to play a dominant role. As a result, the executive office itself lost some of the authority Lincoln had acquired, and a generation passed before power shifted back toward the White House. Because Republicans were suspicious of strong presidents, that development aroused little protest from the governing party.

Hard choices confronted the new president. Southern Republicans begged for help from Washington to fight off resurgent Democrats. Yet many party members in the North believed that support for black aspirations seemed an electoral loser. As a result, African Americans in the South had to rely more and more on their own resources and personal courage. They made valiant efforts to involve themselves in regional politics, often at the risk of their lives.

Grant tried to stay away from partisan battles. Without a clear objective of a war before him in which victory was the goal, the president seemed confused, and he followed a shifting policy in selecting his cabinet and making appointments. He did not accept the advice of influential Republicans but depended instead on men who shared his cautious governing style. The president gave cabinet officers wide discretion to pick subordinates without worrying about their political connections. His cabinet mixed some strong appointments, such as Secretary of State Hamilton Fish, with some other individuals whose qualifications were questionable.

The South posed the most immediate problem for Grant as he learned the presidency. Playing down their racism in public statements, the Democrats argued that former Confederates should now be allowed to participate in public life. The strategy produced mixed results in 1869. Republicans did well in Mississippi and won a close race for governor in Texas. Democrats triumphed in Virginia and Tennessee. Overall, the results suggested that Republican strength was eroding as the Democrats reentered politics. Southern white Republicans and their black allies found that Washington often left them on their own to confront the resurgent Democrats. The white South waged a constant struggle to overturn Reconstruction, and the Republicans struggled to find an answer for this strategy.

A Troubled Administration

Making matters worse were allegations of scandal against the new administration. In the summer of 1869, two speculators, Jay Gould and Jim Fisk, manipulated the gold market to achieve huge profits for themselves. The price of gold rose until financial turmoil erupted on September 24, 1869. Investors who had promised to sell gold at lower prices faced ruin. Then the government sold its own gold supplies, the price of gold broke, and the market returned to its normal level. In the resulting inquiries, the public learned that some members of Grant's family had helped Gould and Fisk carry out their plan. Doubts spread about the ethical standards of Grant's presidency.

To the odor of corruption was soon added White House disarray and incompetence. The administration talked of forcing Spain to give up Cuba and then backed away from the idea. The president wanted to annex the Dominican Republic (Santo Domingo). An agent of the president worked out a treaty of annexation with Santo Domingo's rulers, and the pact was sent to the Senate. Grant pushed hard for its approval, but the Senate, fearful of the influence of speculators and lobbyists, balked. As a result, the treaty was defeated and the president embarrassed.

Grant's administration had more success with American claims for maritime losses against Great Britain. The claims were related to the *Alabama,* one of several Confederate raiders constructed in British shipyards during the Civil War. The *Alabama* had sunk numerous Union vessels. Charles Sumner, chair of the Senate Foreign Relations Committee, wanted to use the claims as leverage in an effort to acquire Canada. In 1871, the State Department worked out an amicable settlement of the issue that left Canada alone.

Grant and
Congress

The president deferred too much to Congress. In the process, congressional Republicans split on issues such as the protective tariff and the currency. The mainstream of the party believed that a tariff policy to "protect" American industries against foreign competition helped business, workers, and the party itself. A minority of Republicans called the protective policy wrong economically and a potential source of corrupt influence from the affected industries. On the currency, eastern Republicans favored the gold standard and what was known as "hard money," where every dollar was backed by an equal amount of gold. Western Republicans advocated an expansion of the money supply through paper money, or "greenbacks," and, when necessary, even the issuance of dollars backed by silver as an alternative to gold. In the Grant years, these issues loomed as large as debates about the size of the federal budget do in modern times.

Since government was still small, who held coveted jobs became a question for public dispute. Some Republicans argued that the government should follow "civil service reform," a merit system of appointing its officials. Reformers maintained that competence and nonpartisanship were better ways to staff these positions. Republicans who wanted to reduce the tariff, rely on the civil service, and treat the South with more leniency defected from the Grant administration. They formed **Liberal Republican** alliances with Democrats in such states as West Virginia and Missouri. In the 1870s, *liberal* meant someone who favored smaller government, lower tariffs, civil service, and, most important, an end to Reconstruction. If African Americans were the victims of southern violence, the liberal Republicans were willing to tolerate that result.

Grant and
His Party

With his presidency under attack, Grant turned to the Republican leaders in Congress. These politicians disliked the Liberal Republican program and its leaders. Angry Liberals threatened to bolt the party. Grant knew that he could never satisfy the demands of the Liberals on Reconstruction or the civil service. Instead, he conciliated mainstream Republicans. He dismissed dissenting cabinet officers and aligned himself with party members willing to defend Congress and the White House. Officeholders who supported Liberal Republican candidates or Democrats were fired. Despite these actions, the 1870 elections went to Grant's opponents. Liberal Republicans won races in West Virginia and Missouri. The Democrats added forty-one seats to their total in the House and picked up another six seats in the Senate. The Republicans retained control of both houses, but their position was weakening. Grant's enemies even thought he might be defeated in 1872.

The Rise of the
Klan

Mounting racial violence in the South added to the president's problems. By the summer of 1870, reports reached Washington of Klan violence against blacks and white Republicans across the South. The Klan and its offshoots, such as the Knights of the White Camelia, White Leagues, and the White Brotherhood, acted as the paramilitary arm of the Democratic Party to crush Republicanism through any means. In Tennessee a black Republican was beaten after he won an election for justice of the peace. His assailants told him "that they didn't dispute I was a very good fellow . . . but they did not intend any nigger to hold office in the United States."

Leaders of the Republican Party were hunted and killed. Four blacks died when the Klan attacked an election meeting in Alabama in October 1870. A "negro chase" in

A Cartoonist Attacks the Ku Klux Klan

The use of political cartoons to convey ideas about contemporary issues became more sophisticated after the Civil War. One of the great popular artists of the day was Thomas Nast. In the 1870s, his images attacked the refusal of southerners to grant real freedom to African Americans and the increasing reliance in the South on such terror organizations as the Ku Klux Klan and the White Leagues. Nast dramatized for his audience that southern whites, in or out of

(The Granger Collection, New York)

a hood, had the same goal: "a white man's government." These striking pictures helped sustain the Republican Party during the presidency of Ulysses S. Grant. Unfortunately for blacks in the South, neither Nast nor the white political leadership in the North persisted in their commitment to equal rights. By the end of the decade, other cartoons depicted blacks in a degrading manner in order to justify white dominance and paved the way in time for racial segregation.

South Carolina left thirteen blacks dead. A wave of shootings and brutality undermined the chances of the Republican Party to survive and grow below the Mason-Dixon line.

Breaking the Power of the Klan Viewing the wreckage of their southern parties after the 1870 elections, Republicans recognized that the Klan's terror tactics had worked to intimidate voters and demoralize their leaders. Yet the party was divided about the right answer to terror in the South. As 1871 began, the Republicans had less stomach for sending troops to the South to affect politics. As an Illinois newspaper observed, "the negro is now a voter and a citizen. Let him hereafter take his chances in the battle of life." This view represented insensitive advice to the blacks in the South who were pushing to get into politics under desperate conditions. Yet Republican leaders asked themselves whether the cost of maintaining party organizations in the South in the face of such resolute Democratic opposition justified the effort.

The violence of the Klan presented a challenge that could not be ignored. Without firm action, the Republican Party in the South might disappear. Congress adopted legislation to curb fraud, bribery, and coercion in elections. When these measures failed, the lawmakers passed the Ku Klux Klan Act of 1871, outlawing conspiracies to deprive voters of their civil rights, and banned efforts to bar any citizen from holding public office. The government also received broader powers to fight the Klan through the use of federal district attorneys to override state laws. As a last resort, military force could also be employed.

Republicans determined to end the lawbreaking and violence of the Klan. The Justice Department, established in 1870, argued that the threat the Klan posed to democratic government amounted to war. Officials in Washington mobilized federal district attorneys and U.S. marshals to institute prosecutions against the Klan. The legal offensive in 1871 brought results; in state after state, Klan leaders were indicted. Federal troops assisted the work of the Justice Department in South Carolina. The Klan was discredited as a public presence in southern politics; its violence became more covert and less visible. Although the prosecutions of the Klan showed that effective federal action could compel southern states to comply with the rule of law, sentiment in the North for such stern measures was receding. Reconstruction did not seem to be a noble crusade for human rights but part of a troubling pattern of corruption and excessive government power. With new economic issues on the political agenda, the problems of the South had to compete with the problems arising from the spread of the railroad network after the Civil War.

| Farmers and Railroads | The expansion of railroads posed new challenges for farmers in the South and West. Throughout the 1860s, two transcontinental railroads laid tracks across the country. The Union |

Pacific built westward while the Central Pacific started eastward from the West Coast. The two lines faced difficult obstacles of money and geography. The Central Pacific crossed the Sierra Nevada Mountains through rocky gorges and across treacherous rivers. Several thousand Chinese laborers did the most dangerous work: they tunneled into snowdrifts to reach their work sites and then toiled on sheer cliffs with picks and dynamite. On the Union Pacific side, more than ten thousand construction workers, many of them Irish immigrants, laid tracks across Nebraska and Wyoming.

When the two lines met at Promontory, Utah, on May 10, 1869, railroad executives drove a golden spike into the ground with a silver sledgehammer: the transcontinental lines had become a reality. Loans and subsidies from the federal government to the railroads had enabled the lines to be built quickly. The way the railroads were paid for would become a subject of scandal within a few years.

Railroad construction accelerated. In 1869, railroad mileage stood at about 47,000 miles; four years later, the total had risen to 70,268 miles. The new railroad lines employed tens of thousands of workers and extended across a far larger geographical area than any previous manufacturing enterprise. American business was starting to become much larger than any previous endeavor in the nation; that development would have important consequences. For the moment, as long as business expanded, the railroads seemed a boon to the economy.

Farmers too enjoyed postwar prosperity with higher prices for wheat and other commodities. Beneath the surface, however, tensions between agrarians and the new industries grew. In late 1867, the Patrons of Husbandry, also known as the Grange, was formed to press the case for the farmers. The Grange complained about the high mortgages the farmers owed, the prices they paid to middlemen such as the operators of grain elevators, and the economic discrimination they faced in the form of higher charges at the hands of railroads in moving their goods to market. These grievances contributed to the turbulence of politics in the 1880s and 1890s.

To balance the power of the railroads, some states created railroad commissions. In Illinois, a new constitution in 1870 instructed the legislature to pass laws establishing maximum rates for the movement of passengers and freight. The legislature set up the Illinois Railroad Commission with wide powers. Neighboring states such as Iowa, Minnesota, and Wisconsin followed the Illinois example during the next several years. Railroad companies challenged some of these laws in court, and a case testing the constitutionality of the Illinois statute worked its way toward the U.S. Supreme Court as *Munn v. Illinois*. The justices handed down their decision in 1877, as the railroad industry faced a nationwide strike.

INDIAN POLICIES

The opening of the West to railroads and the spread of farmers onto the Great Plains meant that Native Americans had to resist an encroaching white presence as had happened in the 1830s and 1850s. What had once been called "The Great American Desert" now beckoned as the home for countless farmers. The tribes that were living in the West and the Native Americans who had been displaced there in the 1830s and 1840s found their hunting grounds and tribal domains under siege.

The Peace Policy   Treatment of Native Americans after the Civil War mixed benevolence and cruelty. Grant brought more insight and respect to the issue of Native Americans than most previous presidents. His administration pursued what became known as the "peace policy." While a majority of western settlers advocated the removal or outright extermination of the Indian tribes, Grant's conciliatory approach won applause in the East.

The policy issues took shape in the years before Grant became president. Advocates of the Indians contended that the hostile tribes should be located in Dakota Territory and the Indian Territory (now Oklahoma). The government would stop treating the entire West as a giant Indian reservation. Instead, specific areas would be set aside for the Native Americans. On these "reservations," the inhabitants would learn the cultural values of white society, be taught to grow crops, and be paid a small income until they could support themselves.

Grant took up the ideas of the Indian reformers. He appointed Ely Parker, a Seneca, as commissioner of Indian affairs. Congress appropriated $2 million for Indian problems and set up the Board of Indian Commissioners to distribute the funds. Indian agents would be chosen from nominees that Christian churches provided. The peace policy blended kindness and force. If the Indians accepted the presence of church officials on the reservations, the government would leave them alone. Resistance, however, would bring the army to see that Indians stayed on the reservations. To whites, the peace policy was humane. For Native Americans, it was another in the long series of white efforts to undermine their way of life.

Slaughter of the Buffalo

The manner in which the opening of the West after the Civil War is depicted in textbooks has changed in dramatic ways during the past two decades. More attention is now given to the impact on the environment

(Kansas State Historical Society)

and on the nomadic lifestyle of the Native American residents of the Great Plains arising from the disappearance of the buffalo herds. The critical role that these animals played in sustaining the Indian way of life meant that the task of white settlers became much less dangerous when the buffalo were gone. Pictures such as this one of forty thousand hides piled up outside Dodge City, Kansas, convey a dramatic sense of the extermination of these animals. Of course, no picture can impart the odor of that many hides.

Pressures on the Indians

The 1870s brought increasing tensions. The 1870 census reported more than 2.7 million farms; ten years later, that number had risen to more than 4 million. A competition for space and resources intensified. With millions of acres under cultivation and the spread of cattle drives across Indian lands, the tribes found themselves squeezed from their traditional nomadic hunting grounds.

The systematic destruction of the buffalo herds dealt Indians another devastating blow. In the societies of the Plains tribes, the meat of the bison supplied food, and the hides provided shelter and clothes. Removal of these resources hurt the Indians economically, but the cultural impact was even greater because buffalo represented the continuity of nature and the renewal of life cycles.

The decline of the herds began during the 1860s as drought, disease, and erosion shrank their habitat. Then the demand for buffalo robes and pemmican (dried buffalo meat, berries, and fat) among whites spurred more intensive hunting. As railroads penetrated the West, hunters could send their products to customers with relative ease. More than 5 million buffalo were slaughtered during the early 1870s, and by the end of the century, only a few of these animals were alive. Conservation eventually saved the buffalo from the near extinction.

During the mid-1870s, Native Americans tried a last effort to block the social and economic tides overwhelming their way of life. By that time, Grant's peace policy had faltered as corruption and politics replaced the original desire to treat the Indians in a more humane manner. The tribes that continued to hunt and pursue their nomadic culture found unhappy whites and a hostile military in their way. The Red River War, led by Cheyenne, Kiowas, and Comanches, erupted on the southern Plain, and Indian resistance ultimately collapsed when food and supplies ran out.

The discovery of gold in the Black Hills of Dakota brought white settlers into an area where the Sioux had dominated. The Indians refused to leave, and the government sent troops to protect the gold seekers. The Indian leaders, **Crazy Horse** and **Sitting Bull**, rallied their followers to stop the army. Near what the Indians called the Greasy Grass (whites called it the Little Bighorn), Colonel **George Armstrong Custer** led a force of six hundred men in 1876. With a third of his detachment, he attacked more than two thousand Sioux warriors. Custer and his soldiers perished. The whites called it "Custer's Last Stand." The Indian victory, shocking to whites, was only a temporary success, however. The army pursued the Indians during the ensuing months. By the end of the Grant administration, the Sioux had been conquered. Only in the Southwest did the Apaches successfully resist the power of the military. Native Americans now faced cruelty, exploitation, and oppression that extended through the rest of the nineteenth century and beyond 1900. In the face of these relentless pressures from white society, Indians struggled just to survive.

WOMEN IN THE 1870S

White women during this time did not have anything that approached social or political equality with men. Amid the male-dominated public life, women struggled for some political rights, a foothold in the new industrial economy, and a way to make their voices heard about social issues. But they faced significant barriers to any kind of meaningful participation in public affairs, a condition that continued into the early twentieth century.

The debates over the adoption of the Fifteenth Amendment underscored this problem. Women had hoped that they might share in the expansion of political rights. In fact, several major advocates of woman **suffrage**, including **Susan B. Anthony**, opposed the amendment because it left women out. In Anthony's mind, black and Asian men should be barred from voting unless women had the right of suffrage as well. That put her at odds with champions of black suffrage such as Frederick Douglass.

At a meeting of the Equal Rights Association in May 1869, such differences about how to achieve suffrage produced an open break. Two distinct groups of suffragists emerged. The National Woman Suffrage Association reflected the views of Susan B. Anthony and Elizabeth Cady Stanton that the Fifteenth Amendment should be shunned until women were included. The American Woman Suffrage Association, led by Lucy Stone and Alice Stone Blackwell, endorsed the amendment and focused its work on gaining suffrage in the states. Amid this dissension, the new territory of Wyoming granted women the right of suffrage in 1869. The Wyoming legislature wanted Americans to notice their underpopulated territory, and woman suffrage was a means to that end. Nonetheless, their action represented a small step forward while the major suffrage groups feuded. A united front among suffrage advocates probably would not have made a great deal of difference in the 1870s, but the lack of cohesion was a weakness in this cause.

For women the decade of the 1870s offered both some opportunities and more reminders of their status as second-class citizens. On the positive side, educational opportunities expanded. The number of women graduating from high school stood at nearly nine thousand in 1870, compared with seven thousand men. Aware of these statistics, state universities and private colleges opened their doors to women students in growing numbers. By 1872, nearly one hundred institutions of higher learning admitted women.

Cornell University in Ithaca, New York, began accepting female applicants in 1875, and one of its first woman graduates was M. Carey Thomas, who received her B.A. in 1877. Five years later, she earned a Ph.D. at a German university. By the 1890s, she had become the president of Bryn Mawr, a woman's college outside Philadelphia. Like other women in male-dominated professions, she encountered rudeness and indifference from her masculine colleagues. She later recalled that "it is a fiery ordeal to educate a lady by coeducation."

Obtaining a degree was not a guarantee of access to professions that males controlled. Myra Bradwell tried to become a lawyer in Illinois, but the state bar association rejected her application. She sued in federal court, and in 1873 the U.S. Supreme Court decided that the law did not grant her the right to be admitted to the bar. One justice wrote that "the paramount destiny and mission of woman are to fulfill the noble and benign offices of wife and mother." That restrictive decision allowed the Illinois legislature to deny women the chance to practice law. Even though licensing of lawyers began in 1869, a year later there were only five female lawyers in the nation.

The Supreme Court also rebuffed efforts to secure woman suffrage through the courts. Virginia Minor, president of the Woman Suffrage Association of Missouri, tried to vote during the 1872 election, but the registrar of voters turned her away. She sued on the grounds that the action denied her rights as a citizen. In the case of *Minor v. Happersett* (1875), the Supreme Court unanimously concluded that suffrage was not one of the rights of citizenship because "sex has never been made one of the elements of citizenship in the United States." To gain the right to vote, women would have to amend the Constitution or obtain the right of suffrage from the states, a process that took another four decades to complete.

The Rise of Voluntary Associations

Blocked off from politics, women carved out a public space through voluntary associations. Black churchwomen established missionary societies to work in both the United States and abroad. Clubs and literary societies sprang up among white women. In New York City, women created Sorosis, a club for women only, after the New York Press Club barred females from membership. In 1873, delegates from local Sorosis clubs formed the Association for the Advancement of Women. The New England's Women's Club, located in Boston, had local laws changed during the early 1870s to allow women to serve on the Boston School Committee. Later the club founded the Women's Education Association to expand opportunities in schools and colleges. During the two decades that followed, the women's club movement put down strong roots in all parts of the nation. Soon they also found ways to exert an influence on political and cultural issues.

Despite being turned away at the polls, women made their political presence felt. Women in New York, Ohio, and Michigan protested against the sale and use of alcohol,

The War Against Drink

The temperance crusades of the 1870s against alcohol and its evils brought women into politics in an era when they could not vote in most of the nation. This cartoon links the campaign of the Women's Christian Temperance Union (WCTU) to the chivalry of the Middle Ages as the mounted women, armored in a righteous cause, destroy whisky, gin, brandy, and rum. The connection of reform with religion and patriotism gave the anti-alcohol crusade a powerful claim on middle-class sentiments. For groups whose religious creed did not bar the use of liquor, the WCTU was an intrusive force seeking to interfere with personal rights. This cartoon thus reveals

(The Granger Collection, New York)

how long what are now called "social issues" have affected the nation's politics and how they grow out of cultural and economic divisions within American society. In fact, controlling the use of alcohol has been one of the most persistent sources of social contention in the nation's history.

marching in the streets to demand that saloons and liquor dealers close down and urging drunkards to reform. Middle-class women prayed in front of bars and smashed barrels of liquor to emphasize their determination. Men joined the **temperance** movement, too, but it was the fervor of women that gave the anti-alcohol crusade new energy. "The women are in desperate earnest," said a Missouri resident who witnessed one of these campaigns.

As their protest successes grew, women sought to make their antidrink campaign more than a momentary event. In August 1874, a group of women active in the temperance cause met at Lake Chautauqua, New York and set a national meeting that evolved into the Woman's Christian Temperance Union (WCTU). Over the next five years, temperance leagues and local branches of the WCTU worked against intoxicating drink. By the end of the 1870s, a thousand unions had been formed, with an estimated twenty-six thousand members. In 1879, Frances Willard became president of the WCTU, and she took the organization beyond its original goal of temperance and into broader areas of social reform such as woman suffrage and the treatment of children. As it had before the Civil War, the campaign against alcohol revealed some of the underlying social and cultural strains of society.

Women at Work   The 1870s brought greater economic opportunities for women in sales and clerical positions in the workplace. Sales of typewriters began in 1874. E. Remington and Sons, which produced the typewriter, said in 1875 that "no invention has opened for women so broad and easy an avenue to profitable and suitable employment as the 'Type-Writer.'" By 1880, women accounted for 40 percent of the stenographers and typists in the country. These developments laid the foundation for growth in the number of female office workers during the rest of the nineteenth century.

The most typical experience of American women, however, remained toil in the fields and at home. Black women in the South labored in the open alongside their husbands who were tenant farmers or sharecroppers. They did "double duty, a man's share in the field and a woman's part at home." In the expanding cities, women worked in textile factories or became domestic servants. Many urban women also took in boarders. As a result, their intensified routine equaled that of operating a small hotel. In the daily rhythms of American society in this period, as in earlier times, the often unpaid and unrecognized labor of women was indispensable to the nation's advancement.

Middle-class women with domestic servants had some assistance, but they still did a daunting amount of work. Preparing food, washing laundry by hand, keeping the house warm before electricity, and disposing of waste all demanded hard labor. Mary Mathews, a widowed teacher in the 1870s, "got up early every Monday morning and got my clothes all washed and boiled and in the rising water; and then commenced my school at nine." Other days of the week passed in the same fashion for her and other women.

To assist women in performing these tasks, manuals about housework became popular, along with cooking schools and college courses in home economics. Catherine Beecher collaborated with her famous sister, Harriet Beecher Stowe, author of *Uncle Tom's Cabin,* in writing *The American Woman's Home* (1869). In this volume, they argued that "family labor and care tend, not only to good health, but to the highest culture of the mind." Women, they continued, were "ministers of the family state."

In the new coeducational colleges and universities, home economics programs offered instructions in operating kitchens and dining rooms efficiently. Cooking schools appeared in large cities with separate instruction for "plain cooks" and a "Ladies Class" for affluent women who sought to link "the elegancies of artistic cookery with those economic interests which it is the duty of every woman to study." Assumptions about the secondary role of women pervaded these institutions.

Not all families experienced domestic harmony. Divorce became an option in many states, and defenders of marriage moved to tighten the conditions under which marriages could be dissolved. Laws to limit the sale of birth control devices and restrict abortions reflected the same trend. The New York Society for the Suppression of Vice was formed in 1872 under the leadership of Anthony Comstock. It lobbied successfully for a national law barring information deemed obscene about birth control and abortion from being sent through the mails. Modern debate about these issues has precedents that reach back a century or more and reveal the persistence of such concerns in American history.

Although women had made some gains after the Civil War, they remained second-class citizens within the masculine political order of the period. However, that brand of politics was also coming into question as voters prepared to decide whether President Grant deserved a second term.

GRANT AND THE 1872 ELECTION

By 1872, many commentators and voters in the North were dismayed at the spectacle of national politics. "We are in danger of the way of all Republics," said one critic of the existing system. "First freedom, then glory; when that is past, wealth, vice and corruption." Restoring ethical standards was the goal of the Liberal Republicans who wanted to field a candidate against President Grant in 1872. They believed that only in that way could Reconstruction be ended and civil service reform achieved. Leading the campaign were Senator Carl Schurz, a Missouri Republican; Edwin L. Godkin, editor of *The Nation*; and Charles Francis Adams, the son of former president John Quincy Adams.

Liberals argued for smaller government and an end to the protective tariff. "The Government," wrote Godkin, "must get out of the 'protective' business and the 'subsidy' business and the 'improvement' business and 'development' business. . . . It cannot touch them without breeding corruption." But Reconstruction was their main target. They saw what happened in the South as an unwise experiment in racial democracy. In effect, black Americans in the South would have to look to whites in that region for protection of their rights and privileges.

The problem was that the Liberal Republicans did not have a good national candidate to run against Grant. Few party leaders were men with real stature. Schurz was a native of Germany and therefore ineligible to run. The race came down to Charles Francis Adams, Lyman Trumbull of Illinois, and **Horace Greeley**, editor of the *New York Tribune*. After six ballots, Greeley became the nominee. At the age of sixty-one, Greeley was an odd choice. He favored the protective tariff, unlike most reformers, and he was indifferent about the civil service. His main passion was ending Reconstruction. Once a harsh critic of the South, he had now mellowed. His personal opinions, which included vegetarianism and the use of human manure in farming, made him an eccentric to most Americans. "That Grant is an Ass no man can deny," said one Liberal in private, "but better an Ass than a mischievous idiot."

The 1872 Election   Grant was renominated on a platform that stressed the need to preserve Reconstruction: voters in the North must safeguard what they had won during the Civil War. The Democrats were in a box: if they rejected Greeley, they had no chance to win; picking him, however, would alienate southern voters who remembered Greeley's passion against the Confederacy. In the end, the Democrats accepted Greeley as their only alternative. The Liberal Republican–Democratic nominee made a vigorous public campaign, while Grant observed the tradition that the incumbent did not take part in the race personally.

The Republicans made their appeal on the issues of the war. One speaker told his audience that they could either "go vote to burn school houses, desecrate churches and violate women or vote for Horace Greeley, which means the same thing." The black leader Frederick Douglass said of the impending contest: "If the Republican party goes down, freedom goes down with it." When the voters went to the polls, the outcome was a decisive victory for Grant and his party. The president swamped Greeley in the popular vote and in the electoral tally. There were still enough Republicans in the South to enable Grant to carry all but five of the southern states in one of the last honest elections the region would see for many years. The Democrats had reached a low point behind Greeley. Worn out by the rigors of the campaign, he died in late November. The triumph was a mixed one for Grant: he remained in the White House, but scandals would soon plague his second term.

A Surge of Scandals

As the excitement of the 1872 election faded, allegations of corruption in Congress surfaced. The first controversy turned on the efforts of the Crédit Mobilier Company (named after a French company) to purchase influence with lawmakers during the 1860s. The directors of the Union Pacific had established Crédit Mobilier to build the transcontinental line. By paying themselves to construct the railroad, the participants in the venture sold bonds that were marketed at a large profit to investors and insiders. The only problem was that much of the money in effect came from the federal government through loans and guarantees.

> ### DOING HISTORY ONLINE
>
> **Grant and the Union Pacific Railroad**
>
> After reading Edward Winslow Martin's account of the Crédit Mobilier scandal (Document 14), how do you think the scandals of the Grant era affected Reconstruction policy?
>
> www.cengage.com/history/ayers/ampassages4e

To avoid a congressional probe into the company, Crédit Mobilier's managers offered leading Republicans a chance to buy shares in the company at prices well below their market value. When the lawmakers sold their shares, they pocketed the difference, the equivalent of a bribe. A newspaper broke the story in late 1872, and an investigation ensued. The probe produced a few scapegoats but cleared most of the individuals involved. Nevertheless, the episode damaged the credibility of public officials.

Another embarrassing scandal occurred in February 1873. At the end of a congressional session, a last-minute deal gave senators and representatives a retroactive pay increase. The public denounced the action as the "Salary Grab." The *Chicago Tribune* said that it was "nothing more nor less than an act of robbery." When Congress reconvened in December 1873, repeal of the salary increase sailed through both houses as politicians backtracked. These two incidents produced widespread calls for reducing government expenditures and rooting out corruption. As the humorist Mark Twain said, "It could probably be shown by facts and figures that there is no distinctly native American criminal class except Congress."

The scandals persisted throughout the remainder of Grant's presidency. Within the Treasury Department, the Whiskey Ring was exposed. Officials involved took kickbacks from liquor interests in return for not collecting federal excise taxes on whiskey. President Grant appointed a new secretary of the treasury, Benjamin H. Bristow, and told him, "Let no guilty man escape if it can be avoided." The administration also faced queries concerning the secretary of war, W. W. Belknap. For some time, Belknap's wife had been receiving cash gifts from a man who sold supplies to the army. When these ties were revealed, a congressional committee sought to start impeachment proceedings. Belknap resigned and Grant accepted his hasty departure. Few doubted Grant's personal honesty, but his cabinet selections often seemed inadequate and sometimes corrupt.

Mark Twain himself captured the spirit of the times in his novel *The Gilded Age,* published in 1873. The main character, Colonel Beriah Sellers, was an engaging confidence man who embodied the faith in progress and economic growth of the postwar years, along with a healthy amount of fraud and deceit that accompanied the rapid expansion of business. In time, the title of Twain's book came to be used for the entire era between the end of Reconstruction and the start of the twentieth century. Beneath its appealing surface, this period grappled with issues of political corruption, social disorder, and economic inequities in ways that challenged older assumptions about the role of government in society.

THE PANIC OF 1873 AND ITS CONSEQUENCES

The sense of national crisis deepened in September 1873 when the banking house of Jay Cooke and Company failed. The bank could not pay its debts or return money to its depositors and had to close. The disaster came because the bank could not market the bonds of the Northern Pacific Railroad in which it had invested heavily. As this important bank collapsed, others followed suit, businesses cut back on employment, and a downturn began. The problems rivaled similar panics that had occurred in 1819, 1837, and 1857; however, the panic of 1873 was the worst of them all.

The immediate effects of the problem lasted until 1879. In fact, an extended period of economic hard times had begun that extended through the 1890s. A hallmark of the "Great Depression," as it was then called, was declining prices for agricultural products and manufactured goods. Americans faced an economy in which falling prices placed the heaviest burdens on people who were in debt or who earned their living by selling their labor. An abundance of cheap unskilled labor proved a boon for capitalists who wanted to keep costs down. For the poor, however, it meant that they had little job security and could easily be replaced if they protested against harsh working conditions. Industrialization went forward at a substantial human cost.

The panic of 1873 occurred because of a speculative post–Civil War boom in railroad building. In 1869, railroad mileage stood at about 47,000 miles; four years later it had risen to 70,268 miles. The new railroad lines employed tens of thousands of workers and extended across a far wider geographical area than any previous manufacturing enterprise. When large railroads such as the Northern Pacific failed because of their overexpansion and inability to pay debts, the damage rippled through society. Economic activities that were dependent on the rail lines, such as car making, steel rail production, and passenger services, also fell off. Layoffs of employees and bankruptcies for businesses followed. More than ten thousand companies failed in 1878, the worst year of the depression.

The Plight of the Unemployed   Americans out of work during the 1870s had no system of unemployment insurance to cushion the shock. In some cities, up to a quarter of the work force looked for jobs without success. Tramps roamed the countryside. The conventional wisdom held that natural forces had to restore prosperity; any form of political intervention would be useless and dangerous. When President Grant proposed that the national government generate jobs through public works, the secretary of the treasury responded: "It is not part of the business of government to find employment for people."

People out of a job during the mid-1870s became desperate. Laborers in the Northeast mounted a campaign called "Work for Bread" that produced large demonstrations in major cities. The marchers asked city and state governments to pay for projects creating parks and constructing streets so jobs would be provided. In January 1874, a demonstration at Tompkins Square in New York City pitted a crowd of seven thousand unemployed laborers against police. Many marchers were arrested; others were injured in the melee.

Labor unrest crackled through the first half of the decade. Strikes marked 1874 and 1875. In Pennsylvania the railroads used their control of police and strikebreakers to put down a protracted walkout of coal miners and their supporters. Twenty alleged members of a secret society called the Molly Maguires were hanged. Conservatives feared that the nation was on the verge of revolution.

| Distress and Protest Among the Farmers | Discontent also flared in the farm belt. The price of wheat, which had stood at $1.16 a bushel in 1873, dropped to 95 cents a bushel a year later. The price of corn stood at 64 cents a bushel in 1874 but 42 cents in 1875. These changes meant substantial drops in |

farm income. As a result, farmers' land- and equipment-related debts posed an even greater burden. Faced with the economic power of the railroads and grain merchants, the farmer, said one newspaper, was alone, "confronting organized and well-equipped enemies." The Grange tried to supply political pressure about these issues, and its efforts reached Congress in 1873–1874, but little was accomplished for the next fifteen years.

| Inflationary Solutions | The decline in consumer prices and the growing burden of debt on farmers and businessmen in the South and West created pressure for laws to put more money into circulation, which |

would make debts easier to pay. The Treasury Department's decision to end the coinage of silver aroused particular anger among southern and western advocates of inflation, who called it the "Crime of 1873." Proponents of the move argued that an overabundance of silver in the marketplace required the move to a gold standard. By coining silver into money at a price above its market levels, the government was subsidizing American silver production and cheapening the currency. Opponents of the change responded that eastern bankers were setting financial policy to the detriment of farmers and debtors.

An effort to inject a modest amount of inflation into the economy came in 1875. A currency bill cleared both houses of Congress, providing some $64 million in additional money for the financial system. President Grant decided, after getting conservative advice to do so, to veto the bill in April 1875, Congress sustained his action: the government would not intervene in the deepening economic crisis. A similar reluctance to use government authority would contribute to the decline of the northern involvement with Reconstruction in the South.

THE FAILURE OF RECONSTRUCTION, 1875–1876

After the presidential election of 1872, the North's already weakened commitment to Reconstruction ebbed still more. The panic of 1873 distracted attention from the rights of black Americans. The Grant administration backed away from southern politics, and the Justice Department prosecuted fewer individuals for violations of the Enforcement Act against the Klan and pardoned some of those who had earlier been convicted of terrorist activity.

Northern support for Reconstruction eroded because of charges that the experiment in multiracial government was a failure. Liberal Republicans and northern Democrats spread racist propaganda to block the aspirations of southern blacks. The editor of *The Nation* said that black residents of South Carolina had an "average of intelligence but slightly above the level of animals." Northerners found it easier to believe that the South would be better off when whites were dominant. Black Americans should be left "to the kind feeling of the white race of the South."

A damaging setback to the economic hopes of African Americans came in 1874 with the failure of the Freedmen's Savings and Trust Company in Washington, D.C. Since its founding in 1865, the bank had managed the deposits of thousands of former slaves. It was supposed to provide lessons in thrift for its depositors. However, its manager sought larger returns by investing in speculative railroad projects. The panic of 1873 caused huge losses, and the bank failed a year later. A few customers received a portion of their savings, but most lost all their money.

The Stigma of Corruption

Corruption among southern Republican governments became a favorite theme of critics of Reconstruction. There were some genuine instances of wrongdoing, but these actions were far from widespread or typical. Moreover, the white governments that took over after Reconstruction also displayed lax political ethics and committed more serious misdeeds than their predecessors had. Nevertheless, the corruption issue gave opponents of black political participation a perfect weapon, which they used to the full. Of course, it would not have mattered if Reconstruction governments had lacked any moral flaws at all. Any government that represented a biracial community was unacceptable to white southerners.

Although participation of African Americans in southern politics increased dramatically during Reconstruction, their role in the region's public life never approached that of whites. Sixteen blacks served in Congress during the period, most only briefly, and several were unseated by white opponents. Many more held offices in the state legislatures, but even there, their numbers were comparatively modest. In 1868, for example, the Georgia legislature had 216 members, of whom only 32 were black. In only one state, South Carolina, did blacks ever hold a majority in the legislature, and they did so in only one house. One black man, P. B. S. Pinchback, served as governor of Louisiana for a little more than a month. Six African Americans held the office of lieutenant governor in the states of Louisiana, Mississippi, and South Carolina.

Two blacks served in the U.S. Senate. Hiram Revels became the first African American to enter the Senate. Elected to fill out an unexpired term, he served only one year. From 1875 to 1881, Blanche K. Bruce represented Mississippi for a full term. Thus, by the 1870s, blacks had made their presence felt in politics, but the decline of Reconstruction made that trend a short-lived one.

The Resurgence of the Democrats

The return of the Democrats as a political force further weakened support for Reconstruction. Hard economic times arising from the panic of 1873 worked against the Republicans. Discontented farmers wanted the government to inflate the currency and raise prices on their crops. Factory workers clamored for more jobs to become available. In this setting, the fate of African Americans in the South became a secondary concern. In the 1874 congressional races, angry voters turned to the Democrats, who used the issue of Republican corruption to regain control of the House of Representatives for the first time in sixteen years. The Democrats added seventy-seven seats in the House and ten seats in the Senate, in what one happy party member called a "Tidal Wave."

In the South, the revitalized Democrats "redeemed," as they called it, several states from Republican dominance. They began with Texas in 1873, then won back Arkansas the next year, and elected most of the South's members in the U.S. House of Representatives. Louisiana saw the emergence of the White League, which was determined that "the niggers shall not rule over us." In September 1874, open fighting erupted in New Orleans between armed Republicans and more than three thousand White League partisans. President Grant sent in federal troops to restore calm. In Alabama, the Democrats also relied on violence and murder to oust the Republicans. Some blacks who attempted to vote in that state's Barbour County election were shot; seven were killed and nearly seventy wounded. In view of the wide support for the Democratic Party among southern whites, honest elections would probably have produced similar results for that party at the polls; but intimidation and violence were key elements in the victories that the Democrats secured in the South in 1874.

The Democrats intended to use their control of the House of Representatives to roll back Reconstruction and prevent any further expansion of black rights. During the lame-duck congressional session of 1874–1875, Republicans, who were soon to lose power, enacted a path-breaking civil rights law that gave black citizens the right to sue in federal courts when they confronted discrimination in public accommodations such as a hotel or restaurant. The law involved a further expansion of national

MAP 16.1 Reconstruction in the South.

This map shows the times at which the states of the former Confederacy reentered the Union and then saw the Democrats regain political control. Note how quickly this process occurred for most of the southern states. The relative brevity of Reconstruction is one of the keys to why more sweeping racial change did not take place.

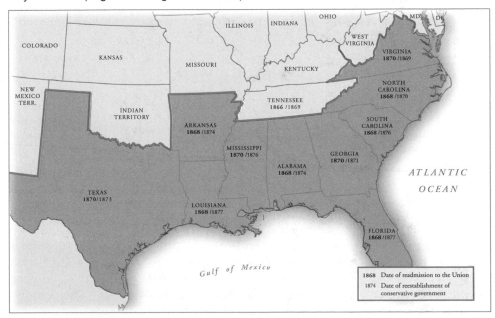

power; it remained to be seen how federal courts would rule when black plaintiffs sued to enforce their rights under the new civil rights statute.

Early in 1875, the Grant administration used troops to prevent occupation of the Louisiana state capital and illegal seizure of the state government by the Democrats in the midst of an election dispute. The action drew widespread protests from many northern Democrats and a growing number of Republicans, who said that the white South should handle its own affairs. Meanwhile, the Democrats used more violence to overturn Republican rule in Mississippi. The state's governor, Adelbert Ames, stated that he was "fighting for the Negro, and to the whole country a white man is better than a 'Nigger.'" Without a national consensus behind civil rights and Reconstruction, the fate of black Americans lay in the hands of white southerners who were determined to keep African Americans in economic, political, and cultural subjugation.

Why Reconstruction Failed
Reconstruction failed to change American race relations because it challenged long-standing racist arrangements in both the North and South. The Civil War had called these traditions into question. In the years after the fighting ended, African Americans had acted to expand their political role and take charge of their own destiny. They sought and to some degree succeeded in becoming more than passive recipients of white oppression or largesse. Then the panic of 1873, the scandals of the Grant presidency, and waning interest in black rights led white Americans to back away from an expansion of racial justice.

To help the freed slaves overcome the effects of slavery and racial bias would have involved an expansion of national governmental power to an extent far beyond what Americans believed was justified during the nineteenth century. Better to keep government small, argued whites, than to improve the lot of the former slaves in the South. As a result, black Americans experienced segregation and deepening oppression. The political gains of the Reconstruction era, especially the Fourteenth and Fifteenth amendments, remained unfulfilled promises. That failure would be one of the most bitter legacies of this period of American history.

THE CENTENNIAL YEAR, 1876

Several themes of late-nineteenth-century life intersected as the 1876 presidential election neared. The centennial of the Declaration of Independence offered citizens an opportunity to reflect on the nation's progress and unresolved social issues. The race question confronted leaders and citizens even as the passions and commitments of Reconstruction faded. The contest for the White House seemed unusually important because it would shape the direction of the country for several decades.

Marking the Centennial
As the nation's one hundredth birthday neared, the Centennial International Exhibition to be held in Philadelphia attracted public fascination. In May 1876, some 285 acres of fairgrounds held several hundred buildings crammed with exhibits, specimens, and artifacts from thirty-seven nations. The doors opened on May 10 for 200,000 spectators, including both houses of Congress, who heard a welcoming address by President Grant.

The throng poured into the building to see what had been assembled as evidence of the advance of civilization in the United States. One of the stellar attractions was the huge Corliss steam engine. Standing 40 feet tall, it weighed 700 tons. Equally alluring was the "harmonic telegraph" of **Alexander Graham Bell**, as the telephone was then called.

The complexity of American life in the 1870s was not depicted at the exhibit, however. African Americans had almost no representation. Native American cultures were displayed as "curiosities" consisting of totem poles, tepees, and trinkets. The Women's Pavilion stressed the joys of homemaking. That exhibit evoked a protest from Elizabeth Cady Stanton and Susan B. Anthony. On July 4, 1876, they read a "Women's Declaration of Independence" that contrasted their aspirations with the traditional attitudes toward women expressed at the fair. Their protest had little effect on public opinion, however.

Nearly 10 million Americans came to the fair during its run, which ended on November 10. They learned to eat bananas, and hot popcorn became a fad among city dwellers. The fair lost money, but nevertheless contributed to a growing sense of national pride and confidence. Those emotions would be tested during the bitter presidential election that dominated the second half of 1876.

The Race for the White House   A key test of the nation's institutions occurred during the disputed presidential election of 1876. The closest electoral result up to that time produced a quarrel that threatened to renew hostilities between North and South. As the election process commenced, the Democrats felt optimism about their chances to regain power for the first time since 1860. Most of the southern states would vote for the Democratic nominee; difficult economic times in the East and Midwest made voters sympathetic to the party out of power.

For its candidate, the party selected **Samuel J. Tilden**, the governor of New York. An opponent of corruption in his home state, he was regarded as a reformer even though smaller government was about all he stood for. A corporate lawyer, he believed in the gold standard, limited federal action, and restraints on spending. The Democratic platform spoke of a "revival of Jeffersonian democracy" and called for "high standards of official morality." Because Tilden was not in good health, the custom that presidential candidates did not campaign during that era worked to his advantage.

Among Republicans, there was some talk of a third term for President Grant, but the scandals of his presidency made him a liability. The front-runner for the nomination was James G. Blaine, a former Speaker of the House of Representatives. With the nomination seemingly in his grasp, Blaine came under fire for financial dealings with an Arkansas railroad while he was in the House. Despite his vigorous response to the charges, Republicans were wary of selecting him to run against Tilden.

At the national convention, Blaine took an early lead. As the balloting continued, however, his candidacy lost momentum. Instead, the Republicans selected Governor **Rutherford B. Hayes** of Ohio. Hayes had the virtues of a good military record in the Civil War and a spotless record in public office. In the campaign, the Democrats stressed Republican corruption and Tilden's honesty. In response, the Republicans relied on Reconstruction and war memories, as they had in 1868 and 1872. This rhetoric became known as "waving the bloody shirt," in memory of a Republican speaker who had held up a bloodstained Union tunic and urged voters to remember the sacrifices of the Men in Blue. Hayes saw the wisdom of this strategy: "It leads people away from hard times, which is our deadliest foe."

When the election results rolled in, it seemed at first that Tilden had won. With most of the South in his column, the Democrat had carried New York, Connecticut, and New Jersey. The electoral vote totals indicated that Tilden had won 184 votes, one short of the 185 he needed to become president. Hayes had 165 electoral votes. Three southern states, Louisiana, Florida, and South Carolina, plus a disputed elector in Oregon, were still in doubt. If they all went for Hayes, he might be in the White House.

Republican operatives moved to contest the outcome in the three undecided states. Telegrams to party members asked for evidence that African American voters had been intimidated. Honest returns from these states, Republicans argued, would show that Hayes had carried each one. The Republicans believed, moreover, that they had the advantage. In the three states they were contesting, the Republicans could rely on federal troops to safeguard state governments that were loyal to their cause. Otherwise, Democrats could simply occupy the state capitals and count the election returns their way.

The Constitution did not specify how a contested presidential election was to be resolved. Each of the states in question was submitting two sets of election returns that claimed to be official and to reflect the will of the people. The House of Representatives had the responsibility for electing a president if no one won a majority in the electoral college. At the same time, the Senate had the constitutional duty to tabulate the electoral vote. With Republicans in control of the Senate and with Democrats in control of the House, neither party could proceed without the support of the other.

To resolve the crisis, Congress created an electoral commission of fifteen members, ten from the Supreme Court. As originally conceived, the panel was to have seven Republicans, seven Democrats, and a politically independent Supreme Court justice named David Davis. Then Davis was elected to the U.S. Senate by the Illinois legislature with Democratic votes in a move to defeat a Republican incumbent. That tactic won a Senate place for the Democrats but injured Tilden's chances of prevailing in the election controversy. Davis resigned from the commission, and another member of the Supreme Court, this time a Republican, took his place. In a series of 8–7 votes along straight party lines, the electoral commission accepted the Republican returns from Louisiana, Florida, and South Carolina, and allocated the single disputed Oregon electoral vote to Hayes as well. The ruling declared that Hayes had received 185 electoral votes and Tilden 184.

Who had really been elected president in 1876? Tilden had a margin of 250,000 popular votes over Hayes and had carried sixteen states. Hayes had won eighteen states in addition to the three contested southern states. In Louisiana, Florida, and South Carolina, Tilden had received a majority of the white vote, but black Republican voters had been intimidated and terrorized to such an extent that an honest count was in doubt. Essentially the election had ended in a tie. Resolving the issue of which man would be president became an issue for the two political parties to decide.

Despite the decision of the electoral commission, the Democratic House still had to declare Hayes the winner. With the March 4, 1877, inauguration date approaching, the Democrats postponed tallying the electoral vote in an effort either to make Tilden president after March 4 or to extract concessions from the Republicans. To prevent a crisis, negotiations began among leaders from both sides to put Hayes in the White House in return for Republican agreement to end Reconstruction. The discussions were complex, involving a variety of issues such as railroad subsidies for the South, but the underlying issue was Reconstruction. If Hayes became president, the South wanted assurances that Republican rule would not be maintained through federal military

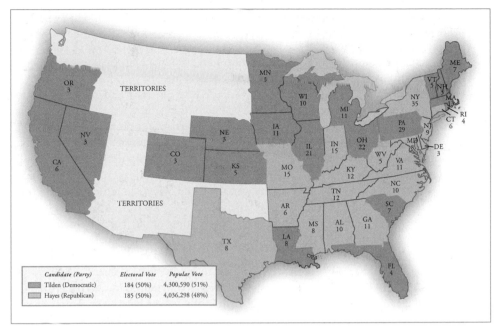

Candidate (Party)	Electoral Vote	Popular Vote
Tilden (Democratic)	184 (50%)	4,300,590 (51%)
Hayes (Republican)	185 (50%)	4,036,298 (48%)

MAP 16.2 The Election of 1876.

The presidential election of 1876 between Samuel J. Tilden for the Democrats and Rutherford B. Hayes for the Republicans turned on the votes of Florida, Louisiana, and South Carolina to produce the narrow one-vote victory in the electoral college for Hayes.

intervention. After much discussion, an unwritten understanding, which later became known as the Compromise of 1877, along these lines led Congress to decide on March 2, 1877, that Rutherford B. Hayes had been elected president of the United States.

CONCLUSION

The events that led to Hayes becoming president had great historical significance. Although the new president did not withdraw federal troops from the South, neither did he use them to keep Republican governments in power. Nor did Hayes attempt to enforce Reconstruction in the courts. Whites regained control of the South's political institutions, and black southerners remained second-class citizens with limited political and economic rights.

Several powerful historical forces produced that sad result. Pervasive racism in both the North and the South labeled African Americans as unfit for self-government. Pursuing Reconstruction into the 1880s would have involved giving to the national government more power over the lives of individual Americans than would have been tolerated in that era. Weary of Reconstruction and its moral claims, the generation of white Americans who had fought the Civil War turned their attention to other national problems. In so doing, they condemned black citizens to continued segregation and oppression.

The era of the Civil War and Reconstruction did have a positive legacy. Slavery was abolished and the Union preserved. Black Americans had demonstrated that they could fight and die for their country, help make its laws, and function as full citizens when given an honest chance to do so. The Fourteenth and Fifteenth amendments at least contained the promise of the further expansion of the rights of black Americans in the future. But for the moment the nation had missed a historical opportunity to create a more equitable, multiracial society.

As with any other postwar period, the decade between 1867 and 1877 mixed constructive changes and lamentable results. The end of the fighting released energies that produced the construction of the transcontinental railroad, a surge of industrialization, and a renewal of white settlement in the West. At the same time, Native Americans saw their way of life threatened with extinction. Political corruption infected public life, and observers lamented a general slackening of the moral tone of the nation. After economic prosperity following the war, the panic of 1873 and the hard times that ensued tested the endurance of average Americans.

Society found that women also wanted to share some of the fruits of emancipation. Campaigns for woman suffrage got under way, only to encounter adamant male resistance. Women turned to campaigns against alcohol as another means of making a political difference. In cultural realms, these were the years of Mark Twain, William Dean Howells, Henry James, and Bret Harte—American prose stylists who looked toward the creation of a national literature. Amid the discord and clamor of a society bent on economic expansion and a return to peacetime endeavors, Americans engaged problems that would carry on to the end of the century and beyond: racial justice, industrial growth, urbanization, and the proper balance between business and government. That citizens of that generation failed to solve all their difficulties is not surprising. What this chapter reveals is that they poured their energies and imagination into the task of creating a better nation in the wake of a destructive war that had shaped their lives in such a distinctive way.

CHAPTER REVIEW, 1865–1877

- The country embarked on an experiment in a multiracial democracy.
- African Americans in the South made a brave effort to participate in politics and economic life.
- Currents of racism and the opposition of white southerners doomed Reconstruction.
- Settlement of the West accelerated with the end of the Civil War and put pressure on Native American culture.
- Transcontinental railroads brought the nation together as a more cohesive economic unit.
- The panic of 1873 began a decade-long slump that brought protests from unhappy farmers and workers.
- Although they were excluded from voting, women played a significant part in public life through voluntary associations.
- By the nation's centennial in 1876, the disputed election between Hayes and Tilden marked the ebbing away of the issues of the Civil War and the eventual abandonment of Reconstruction.

◀▮▮▮ Looking Back

Reconstruction and its ultimate failure is the key theme of Chapter 16. Because the decision not to pursue racial justice had such long-range consequences for the United States, the substance of this chapter is central to an understanding of subsequent history.

1. How did the Republicans intend to reconstruct the South after the Civil War? What obstacles did they encounter?
2. How did the election of Ulysses S. Grant help or hinder the Reconstruction effort?
3. Why did Reconstruction not succeed in the South? What obstacles did white southerners place in the way of black participation in politics?
4. What defects in the national political system between 1865 and 1877 helped derail the chances of Reconstruction?
5. Which groups fully participated in making decisions about the direction of society? Which groups were either not represented or ignored?

Looking Ahead ▮▮▮▶

The next chapter takes up the process of industrialization and its effects on the economy and society. Elements in this chapter explain the rise of industrialism and set up the treatment of this issue in Chapter 17. Let's examine a few of them now.

1. What economic changes in the 1870s undercut Reconstruction and made industrialism seem more important?
2. How did the political system respond to the economic downturn of the 1870s, and how did these attitudes carry forward during the rest of the nineteenth century?
3. How did the political system then resemble modern alignments between Republicans and Democrats, and in what important ways were there differences?

Go to the American Passages website at www.cengage.com/history/ayers/ampassages4e for additional review materials.

17

An Economy Transformed: The Rise of Big Business, 1877–1887

The industrial growth that appeared in the United States after the Civil War transformed American society away from the agrarian past. These developments drew on economic and political trends that had been gathering strength during the nineteenth century. Once the process of industrialization accelerated during the 1870s and 1880s, issues and problems emerged that would dominate American life for the next century. Few other issues have influenced the nation's history more than did the spread of industry and the rise of big business in this period.

Following the Civil War, industrialism and big business intensified as railroads, petroleum, steel, and other enterprises remade the economy. Although the extent of industrialization was spotty by 1900, the overall trend toward a capitalistic economy dominated by large integrated corporations was clear. Economic change proved a benefit to some sectors of the population and traumatic to others. During the 1880s, southern and western farmers, as well as urban workers, mobilized to protest the new order. For everyone involved, the initial focus of concern became the railroads that were transforming the countryside and the economy.

RAILROADS AND A "LOCOMOTIVE PEOPLE"

The belching, noisy, indispensable railroad stood as the symbol of industrialization. One British writer noted that "the Americans are an eminently locomotive people." The completion of the transcontinental railroads underscored the energetic pace of rail development. During the 1880s, the amount of track rose steadily, reaching 185,000 miles in 1890. By that time, the United States had a more extensive railroad network than all of the European countries combined, even with Russia included.

| Creating the Railroad Network | Railroads crafted from iron and steel drew the nation together as bridges |

and tunnels swept away the obstacles of rivers and mountains. Another step toward unification was the standard gauge, or width, for all tracks. Some railroads used the standard gauge of 4 feet 8.5 inches; others relied on tracks as much as 6 feet apart. Inconsistencies meant extra equipment, higher costs, and lost time. By 1880, the standard gauge dominated, with the South the principal holdout. Then, on a single day in 1886, all southern lines converted to the standard gauge. To put all railroads on the same set of working times, the railroads established four time zones across the country in 1883. Railroads could not operate effectively when times varied from state to state, as had been the case before. Standardized time zones promoted national cohesion.

Consistency streamlined the operation of the railroads. Freight moved with greater ease through bills of lading (a statement of what was being shipped), which all lines accepted. Standard freight classifications appeared, and passenger schedules became more rational and predictable, especially after the establishment of standard time zones. With the enactment of the **Interstate Commerce Act** (1887) and the passage of other relevant legislation during the 1890s, all railroads adopted automatic couplers, air brakes, and other safety devices.

(Library of Congress)

Railroad Timetable.
The railroads imposed new standards of accuracy and precision in their operation that spilled over into daily life. This railroad timetable indicates how citizens had to conform their personal schedules to the running of the rail lines.

Railroad travel became more comfortable for passengers and more accommodating to food and other perishables. The refrigerator car preserved food for distant consumers. George Pullman pioneered the sleeping car. The railroads built huge terminals through which millions of passengers and tons of freight moved each day. These structures, symbolic of industrialism, underlined the effect of the railroad on everyday life.

More than $4 billion was invested in the railroad system by 1877. In contrast, the entire national debt of the United States government was just over $2.1 billion. To finance this huge commitment of money, the railroads drew on private investors in both the United States and Europe. An impressive amount, however, came from

This icon will direct you to interactive activities and study materials on the American Passages website: www.cengage.com/history/ayers/ampassages4e

CHAPTER TIMELINE

1877	After wages of railroad workers are reduced, national strike erupts • Desert Land Act passed
1878	Bland-Allison Act passed to buy silver • Timber and Stone Act passed
1879	Thomas Edison invents incandescent lamp • Cash register invented • Woman suffrage amendment introduced in Congress • Frances Willard becomes president of the Woman's Christian Temperance Union (WCTU) • Henry George publishes Progress and Poverty
1880	Metropolitan Museum of Art opens in New York City • James A. Garfield elected president
1881	Garfield assassinated; Chester Alan Arthur succeeds him • Boston Symphony Orchestra begins performances
1882	Chinese Exclusion Act • Standard Oil Company becomes first trust • American Association of University Women established
1883	Pendleton Civil Service Act passed • Railroads create national standard time zones • Lester Frank Ward publishes Dynamic Sociology
1884	Grover Cleveland defeats James G. Blaine for presidency • Mark Twain's The Adventures of Huckleberry Finn published
1885	Death of Ulysses S. Grant
1886	Haymarket Riot in Chicago (May 4) • Emily Dickinson dies in Amherst, Massachusetts • American Federation of Labor (AFL) formed
1887	Dawes Severalty Act passed • Interstate Commerce Act passed • Cleveland attacks tariff in annual message • First electrical streetcar service in Richmond, Virginia

government. To build the western transcontinental railroads, for example, the federal government loaned almost $65 million to the rail lines along with millions of acres of land grants. Total federal land grants to railroads exceeded 130 million acres, and state and local governments added another 49 million acres. Other state aid included loans, tax reductions, and issuing of bonds. The total amount of all such assistance approached $500 million.

By 1880 the railroad network had assumed a well-defined shape. East of the Mississippi River to the Atlantic seaboard ran four trunk (main line) railroads that carried goods and passengers from smaller towns connected by feeder (subsidiary) lines. The trunk lines were the Pennsylvania Railroad, the Erie Railroad, the New York Central Railroad, and the Baltimore and Ohio Railroad. The transcontinental lines were the Union Pacific/Central Pacific, Northern Pacific, and Southern Pacific. In the South trunk lines emerged more slowly. During the 1880s and 1890s, southern railroads built five trunk lines, including the Southern Railway and the Louisville and Nashville Railroad. These lines, interconnected and interdependent, provided Americans with cheaper, more efficient transportation to accelerate industrial expansion.

**Organizing the
Railroad Business**

Conducting their affairs on a grand scale, railroads became the first big business. Factories in a single location had fewer than a thousand workers; the railroads extended over thousands of miles and employed tens of thousands of workers. The railroads required an immense amount of equipment and facilities; no single individual could supervise it all.

New management systems emerged. Executives set up clear lines of authority. Separate operating divisions purchased supplies, maintained track and equipment, handled freight, dealt with passengers, and transmitted information. Local superintendents took care of day-to-day matters, general superintendents resolved larger policy issues, and railroad executives made the overall decisions. By the 1870s, the organizational structure of the railroads included elaborate mechanisms for cost accounting.

Railroads stimulated the national economy. From the late 1860s through the early 1890s, the railroads consumed more than half the nation's output of steel. Railroads also used about 20 percent of coal production. Their repair shops created a market for industrial workers in Midwest cities such as Chicago and Cleveland.

The United States was becoming a national economic market in which similar goods and services were available to people throughout the nation. The development of a national market also encouraged the growth of big business to meet consumer demand for canned goods, ready-made clothes, and industrial machinery. At the same time, the railroads allowed for more social and personal links among distant families

MAP 17.1 The Railroad Network, 1850–1900.

The spread of the railroad network provided a unifying force for the nation as a whole during this decade of industrial expansion.

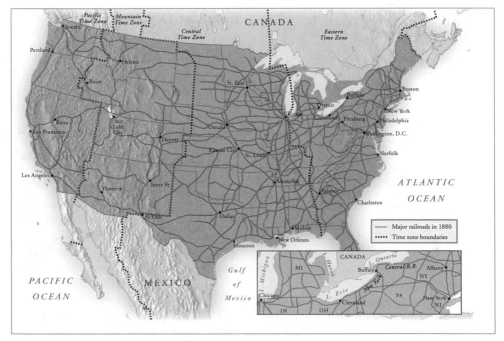

and communities. Thus, the expansion of the railroads was a key element in the dramatic changes that industrialization produced.

| The Railroad as a Social and Political Issue | As they reshaped the economy, railroads raised concerns about their impact on government and society. Land grants affected numerous communities, and railroad executives provoked controversy. Cornelius Vanderbilt of the New York Central, |

Collis P. Huntington of the Southern Pacific, and Jay Gould of the Union Pacific, among others, employed ruthless methods against competitors. Their critics called them **robber barons**, a name that came to be applied to entrepreneurs from this period in general.

Railroad leaders disliked competition. Because a railroad ran constantly and had to maintain its equipment, facilities, and labor force on a continuing basis, its operating costs were inescapable, or "fixed." To survive, a railroad needed a reliable and constant flow of freight and passengers and the revenue they supplied. One strategy was to build tracks and add lines in order to gain more business. Each new line, however, required additional business to pay off the cost of building it, so railroads waged a constant economic struggle for the available traffic.

Railroads sought to lure customers, either openly or secretly, with reduced prices. From 1865 to 1900, railroad rates declined. Some of the reduction in rates stemmed from the general deflation in prices that marked this period. Other price declines occurred because the railroads and their workers found more efficient ways to move freight and passengers.

To maintain their share of the total available business, railroads relied on secret procedures. The rebate was a discount on published rates given to a favored shipper in cash payments. Other customers had to pay the listed rate or were charged more. When faced with potentially destructive competition, the railroads engaged in price wars or tried to acquire their rivals. Railroads (and other industries) also used the pool, a private agreement to divide the available business. Working together, the railroads hoped to maintain rates at a level that ensured profits for all members of the pool.

Attractive as a means of restraining competition, pools were impossible to enforce. Their secrecy violated state laws against economic conspiracies, and weaker railroads cheated on the pool to obtain more business. Railroad men wanted the federal government to legalize pooling through legislation, an approach that was politically unpopular because it meant price-fixing and monopolies. By the mid-1880s, therefore, the larger railroads moved toward consolidation as the answer to too many railroads and too much competition.

| Regulating the Railroads | While rebates, pools, and consolidation made sense to the railroads, they angered those who traveled or shipped their goods by rail. Shippers who did not receive rebates complained. |

Railroads often charged more for a short haul than for a longer one because fewer exchanges and stops made the long haul cheaper. Because of the advantage they gave to some shippers over others, railroad rates also served the interest of cities such as Chicago or Kansas City but hurt others in the Midwest. Railroads posed dangers to the traveling public. In 1888 alone, some fifty-two hundred Americans were killed while traveling or working on the railroad, and another twenty-six thousand were injured.

Americans debated how society should treat the railroads. Few advocated government ownership to compete with private corporations. Using legislatures or courts to oversee the railroads was not popular either. Instead, Americans developed a middle way between those apparent extremes that became a hallmark of the emerging industrial society.

The answer to the railroad problem was the regulatory commission. Ideally, such a body, created by the state legislature, was composed of experts who decided issues of rates, finance, and service in a neutral, nonpartisan way. The first railroad commission had been created in New Hampshire in 1844, and four were in existence in 1861. After the war, the commission concept spread; there were twenty-eight such agencies by 1896.

There were two types of railroad commissions. One variety advised railroads of possible violations and publicized information about railroad operations. The most notable example of this form of commission was the one in Massachusetts. Critics claimed that the Massachusetts commission was weak, because it could not set rates. The second kind of railroad commission was established in Illinois in 1871. It set rates and put them into effect in 1873. Because of this authority, which other Midwest states adopted, the Illinois model became known as the strong form of the railroad commission.

During the 1870s railroads challenged the authority of these state commissions. The most important case involved Illinois, and it reached the U.S. Supreme Court in 1876. The decision in *Munn v. Illinois* (1877) declared that the state could establish a commission to regulate railroad rates. Railroads, the Court said, were "engaged in a public employment affecting the public interest." Because Congress had not yet acted to regulate interstate commerce in railroad matters, a state could make "such rules and regulations as may be necessary for the protection of the general welfare of the people within its own jurisdiction."

Despite such successes, reservations about the effectiveness of state commissions grew. Critics complained that the railroads had too much influence over the state commissions. There was some corruption, and the process of regulation was often cumbersome. Most important, the state commissions could not deal effectively with interstate railroads. In 1886, in the case of *Wabash, St. Louis, and Pacific Railway Company v. Illinois*, the Supreme Court ruled that enforcement of the Illinois law infringed on interstate commerce. Congress needed to establish a national policy for regulating the railroads.

The Interstate Commerce Act   Political and economic forces stimulated the demand for railroad regulation in the mid-1880s. Western and southern farmers lobbied for such a policy. However, their influence was less significant than that of merchants and shippers on the East Coast, who wanted a government agency to ensure that they received fair treatment from the rail companies. Some railroads preferred federal regulation to the confusion of competing state commissions, and Congress responded by passing the Interstate Commerce Act in 1887. This law set up an Interstate Commerce Commission (ICC), composed of five members that could investigate complaints of railroad misconduct or file suit against the companies. The law forbade rebates and pooling. The new regulatory agency was the first of its kind on the federal level. Despite a shaky start for the ICC in its first decade, commissions became a favored means of dealing with the problems of managing an industrial society.

BIG BUSINESS ARRIVES

The railroads were just one part of the process by which big business emerged. An acceptance of rapid change, an embrace of technology, and a growing dependence on industry became key characteristics of the United States. The days of farm and field, working by the sun and moving to the rhythm of the seasons, yielded instead to a faster paced, more hectic existence in which construction and destruction became the dominant social process.

Although the growth of the railroads laid the basis for further industrial expansion, the overall success of big business came during difficult economic times. The depression of the 1870s ebbed by 1879, but the prosperity that followed was brief. From 1881 to 1885, there was another slowdown, with numerous business failures. Two years of good times preceded another recession during 1887 and 1888. In the late nineteenth century, businesses grew larger even though prosperity was elusive.

Deflation brought about by increased productivity, a tight money supply, and an abundant labor force set the tone for business. Companies with high fixed costs, such as railroads, oil, and steel, experienced intense, constant pressure to reduce competition and avoid its impact through arrangements such as pools. In a few industries, it even seemed possible to escape competition and achieve monopoly.

John D. Rockefeller and the Emergence of Trusts Competitive forces shaped the oil industry, and **John D. Rockefeller** of Standard Oil symbolized monopoly power and economic concentration. Starting in the mid-1860s, he expanded from his base in Ohio and founded the Standard Oil Company in 1870. Despite his success in obtaining rebates from the railroads when he assured them of a dependable supply of oil to haul, Rockefeller still faced an industry with too many producers and set up Standard Oil to impose control on a chaotic business. Through rebates, other secret payments from railroads, and price-cutting, he sought to dominate his business. By the end of the 1870s, he controlled about 90 percent of the nation's oil-refining capacity and had achieved a **horizontal integration** of the oil business.

As a virtual monopoly in oil appeared, a political response followed. Under state law, Standard Oil of Ohio could not legally own stock in other oil companies or conduct its business in other states. Yet registering to do business in other states could reveal aspects of the company's business to competitors and expose it to legal challenges. In 1882, a lawyer for Rockefeller, S. T. C. Dodd, formulated a new use for an old legal device, the trust. In the common law, trustees for a widow, orphan, or an estate had wider powers than a corporation, a point that Dodd and Rockefeller exploited. Standard Oil became the first example of the trust in American business. The forty-one stockholders of Standard Oil created a board of nine trustees. In return the board held the company's stock in trust and exercised "general supervision over the affairs of said Standard Oil Companies." The trustees could select the board of directors and set policy for all Standard Oil subsidiaries in other states. In this way the trust escaped the restrictions of state laws everywhere. The term *trust* became a general label for the rise of big business.

In the late 1870s, several states passed laws that allowed corporations to own branches in other states, hold the stock of other corporations, and pursue a policy of consolidation to the extent that their industry and its conditions permitted. The "holding company" law, first enacted in New Jersey and later in Delaware, was more efficient than the trust approach. A large company simply held the stock of its sub-sidiaries. The spectacle of the trust swallowing up its rivals became ingrained in the popular imagination and produced calls on government for remedial action.

Andrew Carnegie and Steel   Almost as famous as Rockefeller was **Andrew Carnegie**, one of the few prominent businessmen of the era who rose from rags to riches. An immigrant from Scotland, he moved from telegraph clerk to private secretary of the president of the Pennsylvania Railroad. During the 1860s, he played the stock market through investments in railroading, oil, and tele-graph company securities. By 1873, however, he focused on steel. He summed up his philosophy: "Put all your good eggs in one basket, and then watch that basket."

In the 1870s, the technology of steelmaking relied on the Bessemer process of steel production in which molten pig iron was placed in a receptacle or converter and air was blown across it to remove impurities through oxidization. A flow of steel resulted in about fifteen to twenty minutes, much faster than the earlier process in which an individual "puddler" had worked the molten iron. Eventually the open-hearth method of steelmaking supplanted the Bessemer technique. In this method the iron ore was heated, and scrap metal was added to the mixture. The Bessemer process dominated the construction of steel rails; the open-hearth method proved better for heavy machinery, skyscraper beams, and other uses. By 1890, steel production had risen to 4.3 million tons annually; it would climb still more, to 10.2 million tons by 1900.

(© Rycoff Collection/CORBIS)

Industrialization.   *Industrialization was a major theme of American life in these years. This image of men working in the steel mill under intense heat and dangerous conditions captured the spirit of the decade.*

Carnegie became the dominant figure in steelmaking. "Watch the costs," he preached, "and the profits will take care of themselves." Between 1873 and 1889, Carnegie cut the cost of steel rail from $58 a ton to $25 a ton. He poured money into new equipment and plowed profits back into the business. During the 1880s, steel production at Carnegie's works rose, costs went down, and his profits grew by over $1 million annually. Carnegie sought to achieve the **vertical integration** of his steel interests, this meant controlling all the steps in the process of making steel. Carnegie acquired mines to ensure that he had raw materials, boats to move ore on rivers, railroads to carry it to his mills, and a sales force to market his many products.

Carnegie's innovations in steelmaking shaped the economy. The lower cost of steel spurred the mechanization of industry. In such industries as firearms, bicycles, and sewing machines, the use of machine tools spread technological innovations throughout the economy. Carnegie's and Rockefeller's managers broke work down into specific, well-defined tasks for each employee and made everyone in the workplace follow standardized procedures. Mass production and a continuous flow of resources into factories and of goods to the consumers were part of the larger process of industrialization that reshaped the American economy.

The Pace of Invention

Inventive Americans poured out a flood of new ideas; an average of thirteen thousand patents were issued each year during the 1870s. In the next twenty years, the annual total climbed to about twenty-one thousand. Among the new devices were the phonograph (1877), the cash register (1879), the linotype in newspaper publishing (1886), and the Kodak camera (1888). The process of innovation led to such constructive changes as the twine binder, which made harvesting straw more efficient; time locks for bank vaults; and the fountain pen.

Alexander Graham Bell and **Thomas Alva Edison** were major figures among the thousands of inventors. A Scottish immigrant from Canada, Bell wanted to transmit the human voice by electrical means. In 1876, he and his assistant, Thomas A. Watson, created a practical device for doing so: the telephone. By 1877, it was possible to make telephone calls between New York and Boston; New Haven, Connecticut, established the first telephone exchange. Soon President Hayes had a telephone installed at the White House. Long-distance service between some cities arrived in 1884.

An even more famous inventor was Thomas Alva Edison, the "Wizard of Menlo Park." Born in 1847, Edison was a telegrapher during the Civil War with a knack for making machines and devices. By the end of the 1860s, he had already patented some of his nearly eleven hundred inventions. In 1876, he established the first industrial research laboratory at Menlo Park, New Jersey. His goals, he said, were to produce "a minor invention every ten days and a big thing every six months or so." In 1877, he devised the first phonograph, although it would be another decade before he perfected it commercially. More immediately rewarding was the invention of the carbon filament incandescent lamp in 1879. Edison decided to use carbonized thread in the lamp, and it glowed for more than forty-five hours.

For the electric light to be profitable, it had to be installed in a system outside the laboratory. In 1882, Edison put his invention into operation in New York City. The area covered was about a square mile, and after a year in service there were five hundred customers with more than ten thousand lamps. Electric power caught on rapidly. Edison's system, however, relied on direct electric current for power. As the distance traveled by the current increased, the amount of usable electric power decreased. One of Edison's business rivals, George Westinghouse, discovered how to use a transformer to render electricity safe at the point where the consumer needed it. This device made possible alternating current, which could transmit higher amounts of electricity. Soon the United States was on the way to using more and more electricity in its homes and factories.

Inventions, trusts, and cost-cutting were reshaping the economy, but what of the workers who lived in this new world of industry?

AMERICANS IN THE WORKPLACE

Amid industrialization, individual Americans struggled to improve their lives as society at first resisted efforts to lessen the harmful effects of industrial growth. In 1877, there were 15 million nondomestic workers, more than half in agriculture and another 4 million in manufacturing. The economy was in the fourth year of a depression, stemming from the panic of 1873, and almost 2 million people were unemployed.

The labor force grew by more than 29 percent during the 1870s. One-fifth of the increase came from immigrants. Four out of every ten of these working immigrants were unskilled; their sweat helped the new industries expand and the cities to rise. Most of the immigrants came from northern Europe as they had before the Civil War. Irish, Germans, British, and Scandinavians made up the bulk of the newcomers. On the West Coast, Chinese immigrants built railroads and did other work that native-born citizens shunned. The expansion of the transatlantic steamship business and the aggressive work of emigration agents in Europe helped persuade many to come to the United States; hard times in Europe impelled others to make the trip. Western states and territories hoped that the new arrivals would become farmers, but the majority found work in the cities of the Northeast and Midwest. Soon distinctive ethnic communities grew up in New York, Boston, and Philadelphia.

The New Work Force Whether a worker had a skill or not, these were challenging times. Technology replaced craft skills with machines, and market pressures led businesses to limit their dependence on trained artisans. Management became more of a hierarchy. Supervisors frowned on skilled workers who sought autonomy in doing their jobs. Government supported employers and restricted the ability of workers to organize. These new policies reduced the control artisans had once exerted in the workplace. The use of apprenticeship as a way of rising in industry receded, and the work force was divided into unskilled and semiskilled employees.

Women represented another new element in the labor force. They appeared in greater numbers as teachers and office workers, and as sales clerks in the expanding department stores. Eight thousand women worked in sales in 1880; a decade later the total was more than fifty-eight thousand. Many stores preferred women, especially native-born white women, as sales clerks. Many immigrant women toiled as domestic servants, but they also found work in the sweatshops of the textile trades. For the most part, the jobs open to women were lower paid, required fewer skills, and offered less opportunity than those open to men.

Real wages for workers increased as the prices of farm products and manufactured goods fell during the deflation that lasted until the late 1890s. The hours that employees worked declined from more than sixty-five hours a week in 1860 to under sixty by 1900. Gradual though they were, these changes represented real gains.

Although workers were making progress, the industrial economy presented serious dangers to many employees. Steelworkers put in twelve hours a day, seven days a week amid the noise, heat, and hazards of the mills. In the coal mines, in the factories, and on the railroads, work was hazardous and sometimes fatal. From 1880 to 1900, some 35,000 of the 4 million workers in manufacturing died in accidents each year and another 500,000 were injured.

Workers had almost no protection against sickness, injury, or arbitrary dismissal. If an injury occurred, the courts had decided that the liability often belonged to another worker, or "fellow servant," rather than to the company that owned the factory. For a worker who was fired during an economic downturn, there were no unemployment benefits, no government programs for retraining, and little private help. Old-age pensions did not exist, and there were no private medical or retirement insurance plans. Child labor reached a peak during this period. Almost 182,000 children under the age of sixteen were at work in 1880 with no health and safety restrictions to protect them.

Workers had few ways to insulate themselves from the impact of harsh working conditions and often-cruel employers. There were sporadic attempts at labor organization and strikes throughout the nineteenth century, but unions faced legal and political obstacles. The law said that a worker and his employer were equal players in the marketplace: one buying labor for the lowest price possible, the other selling labor for as much as could be obtained. Real equality in bargaining power rarely existed. The worker had to take what was offered; the boss set the conditions of employment.

(Library of Congress)

Ruins of the Pittsburgh Round House. *The great strike of 1877 resulted in extensive violence, death and injury, and property damage. This drawing shows the ruins of the railroad round house in Pittsburgh after the rioting in that city.*

The Rise of Unions   During the 1860s and 1870s, skilled workers in cigar making, shoemaking, and coal mining formed unions. The National Labor Union (NLU), a coalition of trade unions, was established in 1866. In 1868, its leader was William Sylvis, the head of the union of craftsmen in the steel industry known as iron-puddlers. Under his direction, the NLU pursued the eight-hour day and other improvements for labor. Sylvis's death in 1869 and the dominance of middle-class social reformers in the organization eroded the influence of the National Labor Union by the early 1870s. Other union organizers would soon try again to form a national labor organization.

Because of the number of workers they employed, railroads were the first business to confront large-scale labor issues. The professional skills that engineers, firemen, brakemen, and others possessed made it more difficult for railroads to find replacements during a strike. Railroad workers joined unions based around these crafts such as the Brotherhood of Locomotive Firemen and the Brotherhood of Locomotive Engineers. "Unless labor combines," said one engineer, "it cannot be heard at all." The issue, according to one railroad executive, was, "who shall manage the road?"

A bitter railroad strike erupted during the summer of 1877. On July 1, in the middle of an economic depression, the major eastern railroads announced a 10 percent wage cut. Facing their second pay reduction in a year, railroad employees launched an unplanned protest. Strikers disrupted train traffic across Pennsylvania, West Virginia, Maryland, and Ohio. In Baltimore and Pittsburgh, strikers battled state militia. A general strike spread to Chicago, St. Louis, and other large cities. Railroad unions played a relatively small part in these walkouts, however; during the depression, their membership had declined as had their economic impact on the roads.

The governors of the states with riots called out the militia. Some militia units refused to fire on their fellow citizens. As violence spread, the Hayes administration sent in the army. Deaths ran into the hundreds; many more were injured. Faced with the overwhelming force of the government, the unrest died away. Nevertheless, the strike had touched most of the nation.

The Knights of Labor   The strike increased support for a new national labor organization: the Noble and Bold Order of the **Knights of Labor**. The Knights combined fraternal ritual, the language of Christianity, and belief in the social equality of all citizens. While advancing the cause of labor through unions and strikes where necessary, the Knights wanted government to play a larger role in protecting working people who produced goods and services for the economy. The order spoke about the "Commonwealth of Toil" and deplored "the recent alarming development of aggregated wealth." Instead it wanted "a system adopted which will secure to the laborer the fruits of his toil." By the mid-1870s, the Knights was established among coal miners in Pennsylvania. After the railroad strike, the Knights saw membership grow to nine thousand in 1879 and forty-two thousand by 1882.

The leader of the Knights was known as the grand master workman. Terence V. Powderly was elected to that post in 1879 and became the first national labor figure. The Knights grew because it had few membership requirements, and its ideology reached out to the entire working population. Its ranks embraced workers from skilled craft unions, agricultural laborers in the South, and women who were new entrants into the work force. The willingness of the Knights to include women and blacks set it apart from other unions. By 1885, the union claimed more than 100,000 members. Its message of working-class solidarity and mutual assistance among all producers appealed to many laborers.

Success brought problems of internal strain and union discipline, however. In 1885, the Knights conducted a strike against a railroad owned by Jay Gould, one of the most hated of the rail executives. They struck his Wabash, Missouri Pacific, and other lines, and achieved a form of official recognition that allowed the order to represent the company's employees in relations with management. Because it appeared that the Knights had beaten Gould, the order's popularity exploded among workers. By 1886, there were more than 700,000 members. A second walkout was called against Gould in February 1886, but this time the strike was broken through the use of police and violence against those who had walked out.

The **Haymarket Riot** in Chicago on May 4, 1886, in which anarchists were accused of throwing a bomb and sparking a deadly riot, shocked the nation. The incident grew out of a strike against the McCormick Company, which made reapers for farmers. A rally occurred, which was generally peaceful. Then, as police were dispersing the crowd, an explosion occurred in which eight police officers died. The police fired into the crowd, and eight more people died in the confusion. Police charged eight anarchists as having encouraged the bomb-thrower. The case was thin and the evidence weak. Convicted on perjured testimony and guilt by association, seven defendants received death sentences, four of which were carried out. The eighth defendant received life in prison.

As a result, the public support for labor's demands for an eight-hour workday and other concessions dried up. In fact, widespread anti-radical hysteria spread. The Haymarket episode gave new impetus to conservatives who believed that labor was receiving too many concessions. Linking organized labor with anarchism and social violence became a standard conservative tactic.

The Knights felt the shift in public attitudes the most. Although the leadership of the Knights had questioned the wisdom of strikes, business leaders and conservatives blamed them for the violence and unrest, and the union went into a permanent decline. To some workers, the failure of the Knights demonstrated the need for more violent action. Some labor leaders questioned whether the strategy of a broad, inclusive appeal and an avoidance of strikes had been wrong from the start. The shift in emphasis that followed had important long-term consequences for the history of American labor.

The American Federation of Labor One vigorous critic of the Knights of Labor was Samuel Gompers. Because a philosophy of "pure and simple unionism" had worked for his own Cigar Makers International Union, he believed that only such an approach could help labor. The son of a British cigar maker, Gompers had come to the United States in 1863. During his years of employment in the cigar trade, he decided that labor should accept corporations as a fact of life, seek concrete and limited improvements in living and working conditions, and avoid political involvements.

Late in 1886, Gompers and others organized the American Federation of Labor (AFL) whose participating unions had 150,000 members. An alliance of craft unions and skilled workers, the AFL did not try to organize the masses of industrial workers. The union opposed immigrant labor, especially of the Chinese on the West Coast, and was cool toward the idea of black members. Nevertheless, the AFL's membership rose to more than 300,000 during its first ten years, and it achieved considerable benefits for its members through judicious use of strikes and negotiations with employers. Most of the men and women who worked as unskilled labor in the nation's factories and shops, however, derived little benefit from the AFL's policies. In the minds of many middle-class Americans, that was as it should be. Unions and government involvement in the economy were, according to this way of thinking, wrong in themselves.

Social Darwinism   The political doctrine that took this stance was known as **Social Darwinism**. Charles Darwin's famous work *On the Origin of Species*, published in 1859, explained why some species survived and others became extinct. Darwin contended that a process of "natural selection" occurred in nature that enabled the "fittest" animals and plants to evolve and develop. Darwin did not attach any moral virtue to the ability of one species to survive and reproduce as a result of the process of natural selection. He was simply analyzing the workings of the world. Advocates of Darwin's ideas, such as the English writer Herbert Spencer, applied them to human existence. If the doctrine of "survival of the fittest" operated in the natural world, Spencer argued, it governed human affairs as well. Since capitalists and the wealthy represented the "fittest" individuals, it was folly to interfere with the "natural" process that produced them. "The law of the survival of the fittest was not made by man and cannot be abrogated by man," said William Graham Sumner, a leading exponent of this doctrine. "We can only by interfering with it produce the survival of the unfittest." A professor at Yale University, Sumner won a wide audience for his ideas among middle- and upper-class Americans. On the other hand, few businessmen looked to Sumner or Spencer for advice about how to succeed in the marketplace when they sought government help through tariffs and subsidies.

Social Darwinism popped up in popular culture. The rags-to-riches novels of Horatio Alger, a popular writer of the day, spread these ideas. Alger argued that men of energy and determination (the "fittest") could triumph in the competitive system even against great odds. He wrote 106 books with such titles as *Brave and Bold* and *Paddle Your Own Canoe*. The central characters were impoverished young boys who used their natural talents to gain the support of wealthy benefactors and go on to achieve riches and success. The public consumed millions of copies of Alger's books despite repetitive plots. They taught the lessons of self-reliance and personal commitment, though few corporate leaders (other than Andrew Carnegie) started at the bottom as Alger's characters did. Despite the popularity of Social Darwinism, the impact of these ideas was limited. Although many Americans applauded Social Darwinism in theory, they also tolerated considerable government intervention in the economy and social relations.

Social Darwinism attracted credible critics. One of the most famous writers on social issues of the day was Henry George. A California newspaperman, George said that the gap between the wealthy and the poor was caused by the monopoly of land by the rich and the rents that landowners charged. He expressed his ideas in *Progress and Poverty* (1879), a book that sold more than 2 million copies in the United States and more abroad. Rent, he wrote, was "a toll levied upon labor constantly and continuously," and the solution for this social ill was a "single tax" on rising land values. With such a tax, all other forms of taxation would be unnecessary. George's writings enjoyed worldwide influence. Single-tax leagues flourished in the United States, and his ideas promoted social reform

Horatio Alger Book Cover. *Horatio Alger's books, like this one in the "Luck and Pluck" series, won millions of readers with their tales of bright young boys rising through the economic system to achieve wealth and happiness.*

(The Granger Collection, New York)

among clergymen in the 1890s and early 1900s. What gave *Progress and Poverty* its major impact was the moral intensity of George's analysis of the ills of capitalist society.

Another challenge to Social Darwinism came in 1883 when a government geologist, Lester Frank Ward, published *Dynamic Sociology* in which he assailed Social Darwinism's view of evolution as applying to human society and not just to the natural world. The process of evolution did not work, he wrote, because of "the unconscious forces of nature, but also through the conscious and deliberate control by man." The idea that government should not interfere with the workings of society did not apply to its advocates: "Those who dismiss state interference are the ones who most frequently and successfully invoke it." Ward had a good point. From protective tariffs to land grants, from railroad subsidies to strike breakers, the well-off in America constantly asked government at all levels to help them with positive action. After all, the government had been a major force in promoting the development of the West at this time.

THE CHANGING WEST

The end of Indian resistance to white incursions and the economic development of the frontier brought the West into the political and social mainstream of the country. In so doing, they also contributed an enduring saga of the range cattle business and the cowboy to American folklore.

DOING HISTORY ONLINE

Westward Expansion

Examine the photos of western settlement In Ducuments 2, 3, 6, and 11. What do they suggest about the process of moving west?

 www.cengage.com/ history/ayers/ ampassages4e

The defeat of Custer at the Battle of the Little Big Horn in June 1876 was one of the final flurries of combat on the Great Plains, although some sporadic resistance continued. During 1877, the Nez Perce tribe in Oregon, led by Chief Joseph, resisted attempts to move them to a reservation. Through four months of running battles, Joseph led his band of 650 people toward Canada, but they were beaten before they could reach safety. "From where the sun now stands," said Joseph, "I will fight no more forever." The Nez Perces were sent to the Indian Territory in Oklahoma, where disease reduced their numbers before they were returned to reservations in the Northwest.

Another famous example of Native American resistance was **Geronimo**, the Apache chief in New Mexico. With a small band of followers, he left the Arizona reservation where he had been living in 1881 and raided across the Southwest for two years. After brief periods of surrender he resumed his military forays. Finally, in September 1886, confronted with the power of the army, he was persuaded to surrender once again and was exiled to Florida.

As Native American resistance ebbed, the national government shaped policy for the western tribes. Many white westerners believed that the "Indian question" could be solved only when the tribes were gone. Easterners contended that Native Americans should be assimilated into white society. Organizations such as the Indian Rights Association lobbied for these policies, and a book by Helen Hunt Jackson, *A Century of Dishonor* (1881), publicized the plight of the Native Americans. Although the eastern policies were more benevolent than the westerners' destructive motives toward the Indians, their combined efforts devastated Indian culture.

Congress passed the **Dawes Severalty Act** in 1887. Named after Senator Henry L. Dawes of Massachusetts, the law authorized the president to survey Native American reservations and divide them into 160-acre farms. After receiving their allotment, Native Americans could not lease or sell the land for twenty-five years. Any Indian who adopted "habits of civilized life" became a U.S. citizen, but most Indians did not achieve citizenship. Any surplus land after this process was finished could be sold to white settlers. For the reformers, this law pushed Native Americans toward white civilization; for the western settlers, it made Indian land available. During the next fifty years, the total land holdings of Native Americans declined from 138 million to 47 million acres. By dividing up tribal land holdings and putting Indians at the mercy of white speculators, the Dawes Act undermined the tribal structure and culture of Native Americans and simultaneously helped allow whites to start mining and cattle ranching.

The Mining and Cattle Frontier

Mining booms drew settlers to a series of bonanzas, first of gold, later of silver, and eventually of copper in territories and states such as Colorado, Montana, and the Dakotas. The mining camps became notorious for their violence and frenzied atmosphere. More than 90 percent of their inhabitants were men; most of the women were prostitutes. During the 1870s, the western mining industry came to resemble other businesses. Individual miners gradually gave way to corporations that used industrial techniques such as jets of water under high pressure to extract the metal from the ground. The ravaged land left farmers with fouled rivers and polluted fields. Some corporations, such as the Union Pacific, brought in Chinese workers to operate coal mines and other projects. In September 1885, tensions between residents of Rock Springs, Wyoming, and these Asian laborers led to a violent confrontation.

White settlement on the Great Plains during the 1880s started with the cattle ranchers, who dominated the open range in Wyoming, Colorado, and Montana. After the Civil War, ranchers in Texas found that their steers had multiplied during their absence. Enterprising cattlemen drove herds north to market at rail lines in Kansas and Nebraska. Up the Chisum and Goodnight-Loving Trails came Texas longhorns to the cattle towns of Ellsworth, Dodge City, and Abilene. Unlike the mining towns, these communities were not violent; respectable citizens quickly imposed law and order on their temporary guests.

During the late 1870s and early 1880s, cattle raising shifted from Texas to areas nearer the railroads and the Chicago stockyards. The growth of the railroad network gave ranchers access to eastern and foreign markets. Improved breeding and slaughtering practices produced beef for consumers in both the United States and Europe, and the demand grew. With cattle easy to raise in the open spaces of the West and with an efficient transportation system, entrepreneurs in New York, London, and Scotland wanted to buy cattle cheaply in the West and resell them to eastern buyers at a profit. Money poured into the West and increased the number of cattle on the ranges of Montana and Wyoming.

The life of a cowboy was not glamorous. Drudgery and routine marked ranch life. Cowboys worked fourteen-hour days, with death near if the cattle stampeded. Much of what they did—riding the line, tending sick cattle, mending fences—consisted of grinding physical labor in a harsh environment. One of every seven was African American. Former slaves from ranches in Texas or fugitives from the oppression in the South, these black cowboys gained a living but were not granted social equality. Other cowboys included Hispanics and Native Americans, and they also faced discrimination. From the Hispanic *vaqueros* and the Native Americans, other cowboys learned the techniques of breaking horses and the complex skills of managing cattle. Western development involved a subtle interaction of cultures that few whites understood.

The boom years did not last. As the ranges became overstocked in 1885 and 1886, prices for western cattle fell from thirty dollars a head to less than ten dollars. Then came the hard winter of 1886–1887 when thousands of cattle died in the blizzards. Before prices rose, investors from the East and Great Britain lost all they had. There were 9 million cows in Wyoming Territory in 1886; nine years later, that number had fallen to 3 million. The cattle industry became a more rational, routine business.

Ranchers in the West faced other challenges. Sheep raisers moved onto the range and discovered that sheep could graze more economically than cattle. Range wars between cattle and sheep growers over land and water broke out in Arizona and Wyoming. In the long run, however, sheep raising proved to be a viable business, and by 1900, there were some 30 million sheep on western ranges. Both sheep raisers and ranchers now faced competition from farmers who were moving westward.

Farming on the
Great Plains

During the 1880s, hundreds of thousands of farmers swept onto the Great Plains. Advertising by the railroad companies, touting an abundance of land, water, and opportunity, drew them from midwestern states and northern Europe. The Homestead Act of 1862 gave farmers public land, which they could use and eventually own. In practice, the 160-acre unit of the Homestead Act was too small for successful farming; a serious settler had to purchase two or three times that acreage. Nor did the Homestead Act provide the money to go west, file a claim, and acquire the machinery required for profitable farming. Few laborers in the East became homesteaders, and most of the settlers had some farming experience.

Congress complicated the land system. Cattle ranchers pushed for the Desert Land Act (1877), which allowed individuals to obtain provisional title to 640 acres in the West at twenty-five cents an acre. Before securing a title, they had to irrigate the land within three years and pay a dollar an acre more. Cowboys filed claims for their employer, threw a bucket of water onto the property, and swore that irrigation had occurred. A year later, lumber interests in the West obtained the Timber and Stone Act (1878). Directed at lands that were "unfit for cultivation" in Washington, Oregon, California, and Nevada, it permitted settlers to acquire up to 160 acres at $2.50 per acre. Lumber companies used false entries to gain title to valuable timber holdings

Most settlers obtained their land from the railroads or land companies. Congress had granted the railroads every other 160-acre section of land along their rights of way. Large tracts were closed to settlement until the railroads sold the land to farmers. From 1862 to 1900, land companies acquired almost 100 million acres from railroads or the government. Other lands had been granted to eastern states to support their agricultural colleges under the Morrill Land-Grant Act of 1862. These western holdings went into the hands of speculators who purchased the lands, as did the land of Native Americans that had been sold off to white buyers.

Farmers had to purchase their land at prices that often ranged between five and ten dollars per acre. To buy the land, the farmers borrowed from loan companies in the East and Midwest, with interest rates on the resulting mortgages as high as 25 percent annually. As long as land values rose and crop prices remained profitable, the farmers made the needed payments. When prices fell, they faced economic ruin.

Industrial growth and technological advances made farming possible in the West. Joseph Glidden of Illinois devised the practical form of barbed wire in 1873. Soon Glidden's invention came to the attention of the Washburn and Moen Company of Massachusetts, which developed a machine to produce barbed wire. By 1880, some 80 million pounds had been produced, and the price of fencing stood at ten dollars per pound. Improved plows, the cord binder for baling hay, and grain silos also aided western farming. During the 1880s, steam-powered threshers for wheat and corn-husking machines were developed.

Machines alone could not provide enough water for farming. West of the ninety-eighth meridian, which ran through the Dakotas, Nebraska, Kansas, Oklahoma, and Texas, fewer than twenty inches of rain fell annually. Efforts to irrigate the land with the waters that ran from the Rocky Mountains worked in certain areas, but the region lacked adequate rivers. Ordinary wells did not reach the waters far below the surface. Windmills offered a possible solution, but the high cost of drilling and installing a windmill made it too expensive. The most practical technique was *dry farming*, that is, cultivation using water that the land retained after rainfall.

The Harshness of Farm Life

This picture of a farm woman and her daughter collecting Buffalo chips in Kansas conveys a striking image of the emptiness of the Great Plains at the end of the nineteenth century and the ways in which settlers had to adapt to a harsh, new environment. Given the photographic equipment of this time, the two figures were posed for maximum effect—the hard-working mother with her wheelbarrow full of buffalo and cattle chips and the small daughter with her white doll. Behind them, the plains stretch endlessly away. Nonetheless, whatever its arranged qualities, the photo evokes a moment when traditional rural life met the immensity of a semiarid landscape. The crops that this woman and her husband produced then had to compete in a world market of falling prices. The farm families who experienced these challenges would be the constituency for the farm protest movement called populism that emerged in the late 1880s.

(Kansas State Historical Society)

For farm families, life on the western farms was a grind. With little wood available, shelter often consisted of a sod house made of bricks of dirt or dried sod. When it rained, the house became a mixture of mud and straw. To keep warm in the winter, the farmers burned buffalo chips (droppings) or dried sunflower plants. Grasshoppers ruined crops, animals trampled fields, and rainfall was never reliable or enough to sustain profitable farming.

The burdens of farmwork fell hardest on women. "I never knew Mama to be idle," the daughter of one farm woman recalled. The child of another farm woman remembered, "Bake day, mending day. A certain day for a certain thing. That is what I remember, those special days that my ma had." Amid the endless spaces, women labored on small plots of land, sustained by a network of friends and neighbors. Some women achieved a degree of independence in the male-dominated West. They operated farms, taught school, ran boardinghouses, and participated in politics and cultural life.

By the late 1880s, some of the western territories were ready for statehood. The territorial system had transferred eastern political ideas and values to the West and integrated settlers into the national political structure. In 1889 and 1890, Congress admitted the Dakotas, Montana, Washington, Idaho, and Wyoming into the Union.

Ranchers and settlers had overcome natural obstacles, political difficulties, and economic problems to build new societies on the Great Plains. Their efforts had created an elaborate economic and environmental system that linked the city and the country in mutually interdependent ways. By the end of the 1880s, however, the process of development stalled as farmers failed to achieve the anticipated prosperity. Crop prices fell, and the debts that settlers owed became an ever greater burden. Farm protest stirred in the West even as the same sentiments were building in the southern states.

THE NEW SOUTH?

Reconstruction ended after the 1876 election. Democrats took over state governments in South Carolina, Louisiana, and Florida. In both the North and the South, the Democrats believed that white supremacy and limited government were the basic principles of political life. The bitter memories of Radical Reconstruction and the need to maintain the South as "a white man's country" made the Democrats dominant among white southerners. Not all southerners became Democrats, however. Blacks voted Republican, as did whites in the southern mountain regions. Independents and others cooperated with Republicans against the Democrats.

The individuals who led the state governments in the South believed that they had "redeemed" the region from the mistaken Republican experiment in multiracial politics. Their policies, they claimed, lacked the corruption and waste of their Republican predecessors. In reality, the record of these politicians was worse as scandals and frauds marred the Redeemer administrations.

The Redeemers included plantation owners, a generous assortment of one-time Confederate officers, and aspiring capitalists who sought a more urban and developed South. This coalition dominated the politics of many southern states throughout the 1880s, though they could agree on only the most general (and vague) principles. Slavery had vanished, never to return, but white supremacy remained entrenched.

A key theme in the South was embodied in the phrase "the New South." Proponents of the New South argued that the region should welcome industrialization and economic expansion. An Atlanta newspaper editor named Henry Grady became the biggest backer of the idea. He thrilled northern audiences, anxious for markets and cheap labor, when he said, in 1886, that the South would soon have "a hundred farms for every plantation, fifty homes for every palace, and a diversified industry that meets the complex needs of this complex age." All over the region, steel mills, textile factories, and railroads arose.

The Industrial South Manufacturing capacity in the South grew between 1870 and 1900. In the major cotton-producing states of South Carolina, Georgia, Alabama, Mississippi, and Louisiana, capital invested in manufacturing increased about tenfold between 1869 and 1889. Southern railroads expanded during the postwar period; by 1880, there were 19,430 miles of track, double the total in 1860. Other key industries grew during this decade as well. Southern forests fell to satisfy the growing national demand for lumber. Almost 3 million board feet of yellow pine were produced in 1879 by crews working under dangerous conditions for less than a dollar a day. The region's ample deposits of iron ore stimulated the expansion of the iron and coal industries. Production of iron ore rose from 397,000 tons in 1880 to almost 2 million tons twenty years later. Birmingham, Alabama, became a center of the burgeoning southern iron industry.

Before the Civil War, tobacco had been popular as something to chew, smoke in a pipe, or use as a cigar. During the war, northern soldiers tried the variety of bright leaf tobacco grown in North Carolina, and demand for Bull Durham and other products of the area increased. During the 1880s, James Buchanan Duke developed a practical cigarette-making machine, and as production costs fell rapidly, cigarette use skyrocketed. By the end of the 1880, Duke's company made more than 800 million cigarettes annually. Americans adopted smoking as an addictive habit.

New cities and towns sprang up in the expanding South. Although industrialism led to greater prosperity, not all southerners benefited. Workers in the factories and mills bore the burden of progress: wages that were often low and conditions crude. Tobacco workers in North Carolina earned around a hundred dollars a year. In the cotton mills, an average workweek might be more than sixty hours for wages that could be as low as fifteen cents a day. Influential southerners resisted arguments against child labor, even as others tried to end the practice.

Problems of Southern Agriculture	Cotton was the money crop of the South, with 5.7 million bales produced in 1880. Growing cotton made economic sense. The crop rarely failed, caused less depletion of the soil, and brought a higher price per acre than any other alternative.

World production of cotton was increasing, however, and prices fell. Unable to bolster production to make money despite lower prices, cotton farmers were debt ridden and dependent.

Cheap labor became essential. Whites held most of the land, while blacks were forced to sell their labor. A system arose that combined **sharecropping**, tenant farming, and the "furnish merchant," who provided the farmers with the "furnish" (whatever was needed) to get them through the year. Sharecroppers received a designated proportion of their crops as their wage. The landlord or owner controlled the crop until some of it was allocated to the sharecropper. Tenant farmers owned the crop until it was sold. They then paid to the owner of the property either cash or a fixed amount of the crop. Both tenants and "croppers" depended on a local merchant for food, clothing, farm equipment, and crop supplies until their harvests were completed. To safeguard the merchant's investment, southern states passed crop lien laws that gave the merchant a claim on the crop if a farmer could not pay his debt. Thus, the farmers in the South, both black and white, were in a cycle of debt first to the landlord and then to the "furnish" merchant. In bad years the farmers did not make enough to get out of debt. With interest rates as high as 50 percent, croppers and tenants were often in a situation that resembled slavery.

The South had long lacked adequate capital, and losing the war worsened the situation. The region lacked sufficient banks to extend credit, and the national government followed policies that kept the money supply down. The South's absence of capital worsened during the 1880s.

Southern farmers believed that they faced an economic conspiracy. The furnish merchant represented the power of northern bankers, international cotton marketing companies, and industrialism. The cotton farmers tolerated these conditions because there appeared to be no other way to participate in the South's burgeoning economy. By the end of the decade, however, the problems of perpetual debt were becoming acute, and political discontent mounted. White southerners relied on one continuing advantage: they lived in a segregated society where blacks had been returned to a condition as close to slavery as the law would permit.

Segregation   Racial segregation evolved slowly but steadily across the South despite the national Civil Rights Act in 1875, which prohibited racial discrimination in public accommodations. In the *Civil Rights Cases* (1883), the Supreme Court ruled that under the Fourteenth Amendment, Congress could prohibit only state actions that violated civil rights. For individual acts of racial discrimination in restaurants, hotels, and other public places, it was up to the states to ban discrimination. Southern states chose instead to allow and encourage racial segregation as a preferred policy.

During this period, segregation lacked rigidity and legal power. In some southern states, black citizens used railroads and streetcars on a roughly equal basis with whites, but elsewhere in the region, travel facilities were segregated. Under the regimes of the Redeemers, black men voted in some numbers before 1890, retained the right to hold office, could be members of a jury, and were permitted to own weapons.

These minimal rights existed amid racial discrimination and bigotry. Black men often found their choices at the polls limited to approved white candidates, and if too many African Americans sought to cast ballots, white violence erupted. By the end of the 1880s, growing numbers of white politicians believed that blacks should be barred from the electoral process.

The fifteen years after the end of Reconstruction began with hopeful signs for African Americans in the South, but the outcome was bleak. Black families wanted to rent farms and work land for themselves rather than return to the plantation system and they believed that growing cotton in the Mississippi delta gave them a chance to participate in that region's expanding economy. The area saw an influx of blacks at the end of the 1880s as African American men competed for new jobs and the opportunity to acquire land. Sharecropping and tenant farming were also present, but in this part of the South for a brief period, there was a chance for black economic advancement. African Americans created networks of black churches and sought to educate their children.

Booker T. Washington's leadership of the Tuskegee Institute in Alabama, which began in 1881, symbolized what education and training could do. Growing up with no direct experience of slavery, a new generation of southern blacks demanded their legal rights. When older blacks warned of the possible consequences of such behavior, the younger generation answered, "We are now qualified, and being the equal of whites, should be treated as such."

Some African Americans preferred to get out of the South if they could. At the end of the 1870s, rumors spread that Kansas offered a safer haven. During 1879, some twenty thousand blacks—known as Exodusters because they were coming out of bondage as the children of Israel had in the Exodus—arrived in Kansas. More settled in the cities than actually farmed on the prairie. Hundreds of thousands of other blacks also left the South in these years.

At the end of the 1880s, white spokesmen for the South boasted of the region's progress. The South produced more cotton than ever before, towns were growing throughout the region, industries had developed, and tens of thousands of black southerners had accumulated property. Yet there were danger signs. State legislatures wrote new laws to segregate first-class railroad passengers by race. Farmers who grew more cotton each year without getting ahead organized to oppose the power of merchants and railroads. Tenants and laborers of both races seemed restless and in constant motion. Racial violence reached unprecedented levels. Southerners asked whether industrialism had brought all that much in the way of real benefits. Would the New South be any better than the Old?

LIFE AND CULTURE DURING THE 1880S

The daily rhythms of life were those of the country and the small town where most people, more than 70 percent in 1880, still resided. Of the nearly 10 million households in the nation, the most common family consisted of a husband, a wife, and their three children. The father worked in the family farm or at a job in an office or at the factory. The mother stayed at home and did the endless round of cleaning, cooking, sewing, and shopping. The children attended schools near their home or, in less prosperous families, labored to bring home income.

Prosperous Americans ate large meals. For those fortunate ones, breakfast often included fried eggs, biscuits, wheat cakes, potatoes, and steak. The afternoon and evening meals were also substantial. Among the upper classes, a fancy dinner might provide ten or eleven courses of meats, fish, salads, and starchy foods. The poor found whatever they could scrape together. These stark divisions between rich and poor were one of the enduring features of this period.

Industrialism changed the way Americans ate. Millions of tin cans made vegetables and fruits available at the twist of a can opener. In large cities, fresh meats became more accessible as the Armour meat company moved beef in iced railroad cars. Brand names told Americans that "Uneeda" biscuit, and a portly Quaker figure appeared on containers of Quaker Oats. In 1886, an Atlanta druggist, **John Pemberton**, mixed syrup extracted from the cola nut with carbonated water and called it "Coca-Cola." A year later he sold out to Asa Candler, who made *Coca-Cola* a household word.

In the homes of city dwellers, gas and electricity provided new sources of power. People who had the money to afford the newer utilities no longer had to chop and gather wood, clean fireplaces, and maintain a multitude of candles and lamps. Running water replaced water drawn by hand. Refrigeration reduced the need for daily shopping; ready-made clothing relieved housewives of constant sewing chores. Although machines lessened the burdens of the husband and children, the duties of the wife were still time-consuming. However fuel was supplied, she had to prepare the meals. Despite the availability of canned fruits and vegetables, many women did their own canning and preserving. Sewing, cleaning, and household maintenance were done without the assistance of the male members of the family. To a large extent, the wife and mother found herself alone in the house each day as the husband went to work and the children to school.

Children were educated in schools that were locally controlled and designed to instill patriotism and moral values. "We went to school to work," remembered one student, "our playing was done elsewhere." City children attended school for some 180 to 200 days a year. In rural areas, however, the demands of farm work often limited school attendance to fewer than 100 days a year. Courses included arithmetic, the

A Refreshing Pause

The continuities of American life are often best revealed in the routines of everyday existence. This advertisement for Coca-Cola attests to the enduring appeal of carbonated soft drinks to thirsty Americans and the devices advertisers have used to pitch their products. The well-dressed, respectable young woman quaffing the last drop of her Coke in the 1880s, while watching the viewer outside the ad, would become 120 years later a gyrating teenage heartthrob hawking the same brand of sugar-laden refreshment. Only the price of the drink now seems historic. In their own bubbly way, soft drinks sparkled into one of the shared experiences of Americans in an industrialized, homogenized culture. Past advertisements from the pages of newspapers and magazines are one of the best windows into how Americans lived generations ago in ways that we still recognize.

history of the United States, geography, reading, grammar, and spelling. Many students read the famous series of McGuffey's Readers, which stressed religion, obedience, and family. In the better school systems, students received instruction in Latin and at least one other foreign language; less attention was given to the sciences. For new immigrants, the school system taught the values of the dominant culture and prepared their children for citizenship.

Although only a small percentage of students attended high schools and even fewer pursued a college degree, the late nineteenth century brought rapid growth for institutions of higher learning. Wealthy businessmen created private universities such as Johns Hopkins in Baltimore (1876), the University of Chicago (1890), and Stanford in California (1891). State universities expanded in the Midwest and were created in the South. Modeled on the German educational system, these universities established academic departments and stressed research and graduate training. Higher education in the United States became increasingly professionalized.

Arts and Leisure in the 1880s Americans found an abundance of ways to entertain themselves. Appealing to a wider audience were the circuses and Wild West shows. The first three-ring circus debuted in Manhattan in 1883, and P. T. Barnum, with his "greatest show on earth," became the entertainment equivalent to the giants of industry. During the same year, William "Buffalo Bill" Cody assembled a troupe of former Pony Express riders, stagecoach robbers, and riding artists that toured the United States and Europe. Vaudeville, a form of entertainment consisting of a series of singers, comedians, and specialty acts, was a favorite of urban audiences.

Baseball dominated sports. The National League, founded in 1876, entered an era of prosperity after 1880. Baseball fans, known as "kranks," delighted in baiting the umpire. In the 1880s, many new rules were adopted, including the format of three strikes and four balls, overhand pitching, and substitutions of players. Attendance figures rose, with as many as thirty thousand people turning out for games on Memorial Day. Sunday contests were banned, as was the sale of beer at ballparks. It was a golden age for baseball.

Literate citizens found an abundance of reading. The magazines of the day, some thirty-three hundred in all, carried articles on every possible subject. Public libraries, funded in part by generous donations from Andrew Carnegie, provided easier access to the world of letters. Americans also read popular novels such as Lew Wallace's *Ben Hur* (1880), an engrossing blend of religion, ancient history, and a good story. Probably the most important literary work of the 1880s was *The Adventures of Huckleberry Finn*, written by Samuel L. Clemens ("Mark Twain") in 1884. In it, Clemens used an adventure in which a boy helps a runaway slave to create a chronicle of the nation's experience with slavery, freedom, the wonders of childhood, and the ambiguities of adult life. The most popular writer of his era, Twain captured the images of a vanishing America of Mississippi riverboats, small towns, and the social tensions that lay beneath the tranquil surface. Visual arts also fascinated Americans. Private acquisitions of paintings grew, with about 150 such collections in existence in 1880. Museums were founded in St. Louis, Detroit, and Cincinnati between 1879 and 1885, continuing a trend that had begun earlier in Boston, Philadelphia, and New York.

A symbol of the era was the Statue of Liberty in New York City, dedicated on October 28, 1886. The work of a French sculptor, Frédéric-Auguste Bartholdi, it was sponsored by a public fund-raising effort in the United States; the statue was placed on Bedloe's Island, now called Liberty Island, at the entrance to New York Harbor. Out of the campaign to raise money came the celebrated poem by Emma Lazarus that promised the "golden door" of opportunity to Europe's "huddled masses yearning to breathe free."

POLITICAL AMERICA, 1877–1887

In politics, both of the major parties sought to overcome an electoral stalemate. The Republicans won the presidency in 1876, 1880, and 1888; the Democrats triumphed in 1884 and 1892. Neither party controlled both houses of Congress on a regular basis. The Republicans had control twice, from 1881 to 1883 and 1889 to 1891; the Democrats only once, from 1893 to 1895. Outside the South, elections often were close and hard fought.

Americans lavished time on their politics. Only men took part in elections, and most of them were whites. (A few black men voted in the South.) Those who did vote turned out at a record rate: about eight out of every ten eligible voters went to the polls. Women could vote only in Wyoming and Utah. Americans listened to long speeches by candidates and read about politics in the extended stories that partisan newspapers printed.

Moral and religious values shaped how people voted and helped define which party won their support. The prohibition of alcohol, the role of religious and sectarian education in the public schools, and the observance of the Sabbath were hotly contested questions. Republicans favored government intervention to support Protestant values; Democrats thought the government should keep out of such subjects.

The most prominent national issues involved the kind of money Americans used, how the government raised revenue, and who served in the government itself. Some Americans believed that for every dollar in circulation, an equal amount of gold should be stored in the Treasury or in banks. Others contended that the government should issue more money by coining silver into currency on an equal basis with gold. Debtors favored inflation, which made their loans easier to pay; creditors liked the deflation that raised the value of their dollars. The South and West wanted inflation; the Northeast and developed portions of the Midwest preferred the existing financial system.

Other major concerns were taxation and the protective tariff. There was no federal income tax; the government raised money from excise taxes on alcohol and tobacco, and customs duties (taxes) on imported goods. The protective tariff became a hot political issue. Those who favored it believed that high customs duties protected American industry, helped workers, and developed the economy. Republicans championed the protective system; Democrats countered that tariffs raised prices, hurt consumers, and made government too expensive. The South liked the Democratic position, but Republicans found support from business and labor.

At bottom the argument was over the size and role of the national government. Should the government stimulate the economy, as the Republicans wanted, or allow natural forces to operate, as the Democrats advocated? Finally, there was the question of who should serve in government. Politicians preferred the "spoils," or patronage, system. Allocating government jobs to partisan supporters enabled them to strengthen their party. Critics of the patronage system called it a corrupt and inefficient way to choose government officials. They favored a civil service, in which individuals, chosen through competitive examinations, would administer government without being subject to partisan pressure. Civil service reformers urged Congress to write laws to reduce the power of patronage during the 1870s, but incumbents of both parties liked the existing system.

The Republicans began the period with Rutherford B. Hayes in the White House. He pushed for civil service reform and resisted pressure from Congress to base his appointments on candidates whom lawmakers favored. Hayes had promised to serve only one term. To succeed him, the Republicans nominated James A. Garfield of Ohio, and Chester Alan Arthur of New York as his running mate. The Democratic candidate was a former Civil War general named Winfield Scott Hancock. After an intense campaign that focused on the tariff issue, Garfield won by a narrow plurality in the popular vote and a larger margin in the electoral college.

On July 2, 1881, a crazed assassin shot Garfield. He died on September 19, and Chester Alan Arthur became president. Much to everyone's surprise, Arthur, who was widely regarded as a mediocrity, proved a competent chief executive. During his single term, Congress passed the Pendleton Act (1883), which created a civil service system and limited the practice of assessing campaign contributions from federal employees. The act also established rules about where and how government officials could raise campaign funds.

Arthur was a caretaker president. In 1884, the party selected its most popular figure, James G. Blaine of Maine, to run for the presidency. Questions raised about his political honesty, however, dogged him in the general election. To run against Blaine, the Democrats selected the governor of New York, Grover Cleveland. Cleveland had risen from political obscurity. The national Democrats wanted a fresh face, and the stocky Cleveland was an attractive blend of honesty, conservatism, and independence. His campaign suffered a setback when it was revealed that some years earlier, he had accepted responsibility for an illegitimate child in Buffalo. Cleveland acknowledged his part in the episode, however, and his candor defused the issue. Meanwhile, the issue of Blaine's public morality worked against the Republicans. The outcome of the election was very close, reflecting the even balance of the major parties. Cleveland carried the South, New York, New Jersey, Connecticut, and Indiana, receiving 219 electoral votes to Blaine's 182. After twenty-four years in power, the Republicans had been defeated and the Democrats had their chance to direct national policy.

Cleveland took office on March 4, 1885. During his first term, he established that his party could govern, and his political opponents gave him grudging respect. For the Democrats, however, Cleveland proved to be a mixed blessing. He was slow to turn Republican officeholders out of office, and he alienated many Democrats with his patronage policies. Still, Republicans made few gains in the congressional elections of 1886, and Cleveland seemed to have good prospects for a second term in 1888.

In December 1887, hoping to establish an issue for his reelection campaign, the president devoted his annual message to Congress (known as the State of the Union message) to tariff reform. With a surplus in the Treasury, Cleveland believed that the tariff could be reduced, leading to lower prices for consumers. The Republican reaction to Cleveland's move was one of delight. Now the 1888 election could be fought on the issue that united the Republicans and divided the Democrats.

CONCLUSION

The 1880s were lived out in the shadow of the Civil War. As one veteran, Oliver Wendell Holmes, Jr., said in 1884, "Through our great good fortunes, in our youth our hearts were touched with fire." Having experienced so much as young people, between 1877 and 1887 they sought harmony, prosperity, and stability. They pursued industrialism and its benefits with intense energy. Their achievements—in terms of railroads and factories built, inventions developed, and society transformed—were striking.

Yet the transformation of the American economy came at a cost. In 1887, deep social divisions and economic inequality characterized the United States. Regional differences remained unresolved. Industrialism had produced serious changes in the environment that would imperil the natural resources available to future generations. The animosity between capitalists and workers smoldered behind a facade of calm. The nation had yet to work out the tensions that had accompanied industrial growth. That task would be addressed in the succeeding decade in a setting in which the rise of the American city would grow to be as important a force for change as industrialism had been in the years after 1877.

CHAPTER REVIEW 1877–1887

- Railroads emerged as the first big business.
- Initial efforts were made to regulate railroads through state railroad commissions.
- Standard Oil became a monopoly in the oil business, and the new form of business, the trust, was formed.
- Andrew Carnegie turned the steel industry into a major force for economic growth.
- The merits of Social Darwinism as an ideology were debated.
- The West was opened to mining and the range cattle industry.
- Industrialization spread through the South.
- The evenly divided party system produced few policies to address the issues of industrialism effectively.

◀Ⅲ Looking Back

The focus of Chapter 17 is on the ways that industrialism affected the United States between 1877 and 1887. The ramifications of the industrializing process would have large consequences for the subsequent course of American history. Pay particular attention to how various groups in society, and specific regions of the country, responded to these new developments.

1. What conditions in the previous decade made it possible for industrialism to take hold?
2. How did cost-cutting and reducing labor expenses become a central effect of industrial growth?
3. How did the United States respond to the political problems arising from the spread of railroads?
4. In what ways was the country becoming more of a national market and economy?
5. What regions were left behind as industrialism grew?

Looking Ahead Ⅲ▶

Chapter 18 considers how cities developed in response to industrialism and looks at the ways in which the South and West reacted to the changes that agriculture was experiencing. Some of these shifts in thinking are anticipated in this chapter.

1. What pressures did industrialism place on farmers in the South and West?
2. How did the even balance of the political system prevent solutions to the economic changes of industrialism from being developed?
3. How did minorities fare during industrial growth?

Go to the American Passages website at www.cengage.com/history/ayers/ ampassages4e for additional review materials.

18

Urban Growth and Farm Protest, 1887–1893

As the United States approached its centennial in 1889, a burgeoning urban population posed growing social problems. Huge gaps between rich and poor marked the new cities. Americans sought to reconcile traditional rural values with the diversity and turbulence of the metropolis. The political system struggled to adjust to the new demands that the people of the cities posed.

The farm problems that had simmered during the early 1880s reached a crisis. In the South and West, angry farmers formed a new political organization, the People's Party. For Native Americans, African Americans, and Hispanics, the new decade emphasized their marginal status. The end of the nineteenth century saw renewed questions about the future of a nation of cities as the United States became a world power.

THE NEW URBAN SOCIETY

After **Grover Cleveland** stressed tariffs in the 1888 election, the united Republicans rallied behind their candidate, **Benjamin Harrison**, and the doctrine of tariff protection for American industries. Cleveland won the popular vote, but Harrison won the electoral tally. The Republicans also controlled both houses of Congress. With this hold on the government, the Republicans pushed an ambitious agenda of legislation. The stalemated system that had existed since the end of Reconstruction was breaking down.

During 1889 two events reflected the contrasting directions of the United States. Since the 1820s, the Five Civilized Tribes of Native Americans had lived in what is now Oklahoma. By the 1880s, however, pressure from white settlers proved irresistible in Congress. The Dawes Severalty Act of 1887 completed the process of stripping Indians of their rights. President Harrison announced that unoccupied land could be settled beginning April 22, 1889. One hundred thousand people rushed in. Within a few hours, the

CHAPTER TIMELINE

1888	Edward Bellamy publishes *Looking Backward* • Benjamin Harrison elected president over Grover Cleveland
1889	Oklahoma Territory becomes available for settlement by non-Native Americans • National Farmers Alliance and Industrial Union is organized • Jane Addams establishes Hull House in Chicago • Pan-American Congress held • First electric sewing machine marketed
1890	Congress enacts Sherman Silver Purchase Act, McKinley Tariff, and Sherman Antitrust Act • Mississippi constitutional convention establishes strict segregation laws • William Dean Howells publishes *A Hazard of New Fortunes*, a novel about the Haymarket Affair in 1886 • Republicans suffer large losses in congressional elections; Farmers' Alliance makes strong showing • National American Woman Suffrage Association set up • Battle of Wounded Knee • Daughters of the American Revolution founded • Poems by Emily Dickinson published
1891	Queen Liliuokalani comes to power in Hawaii
1892	People's party founded • Homestead strike occurs • Ida Wells-Barnett begins campaigns against lynching • Grover Cleveland defeats Benjamin Harrison in presidential election • Ellis Island opens in New York to receive immigrants
1893	Hawaiian Revolution occurs • Grover Cleveland inaugurated for second term • Mildred Hill publishes song that becomes "Happy Birthday to You" • Columbian Exposition in Chicago

"Sooners," who entered the territory early, and the "Boomers" (a general name for eager settlers) had created towns and staked out farms. The Native Americans had to make do with land that whites did not occupy.

A few months later, in August 1889, **Jane Addams** and Ellen Gates Starr founded **Hull House**, a settlement home in a Chicago neighborhood. They sought solutions to poverty, disease, and political corruption in their new residence. Hull House and Addams became famous. Her experiment reflected the view that the concentration of population in cities was "the most remarkable social phenomenon" of the nineteenth century. Jane Addams and like-minded Americans wanted to make the new cities work.

Chicago symbolized urban American since the Civil War. In 1860, Chicago had been the nation's ninth-largest city, with a population of just under 109,000. Thirty years later, Chicago held second place, with 1.1 million people. The major east–west railroads ran through the city. To the stockyards came beef cattle from the West, to its elevators grain from the prairie, and to its lumberyards wood from the forests of Wisconsin and Minnesota. After the great fire of 1871 that consumed the bulk of the city's buildings, Chicago had built the skyscrapers that gave it a distinct skyline and

This icon will direct you to interactive activities and study materials on the American Passages website: www.cengage.com/history/ayers/ampassages4e

created the ethnic neighborhoods whose residents Hull House served. With so much economic opportunity in its streets and shops, Chicago's population boomed in the late nineteenth century.

Elsewhere, urban population growth accelerated. In 1879, only nine cities had more than 100,000 inhabitants; in 1890 there were twenty-eight with populations of that size. Most of this population surge was in the Northeast and Midwest. Americans moved to the cities to escape the "hard work and no holidays" of rural life. Immigrants from Europe, many of them from cities in central and eastern Europe, remained in the large cities after they arrived. Newcomers came to Chicago and New York, worked there for months and years, and then moved on to other cities, returned to the rural areas, or, in the case of some immigrants, went back to their home country.

The Structure of the City   After 1880 American cities boomed. The horsecar gave way to electric-power cable cars in San Francisco and other hilly cities. Relying on heavy cables running on the street, these devices were clumsy, inefficient, and expensive. Electric streetcars or trolleys, powered by overhead cables and moving at ten miles an hour, soon replaced the cable system. Across the nation, urban transit electrified. To avoid traffic jams, some cities ran streetcars on elevated tracks; others went underground to create subways. The older walking city disappeared.

As their populations shifted away from their core areas, the cities used power granted by the state legislature to incorporate their suburbs into the larger metropolis. Within the center of the city, race and ethnicity determined where people lived. The more affluent residents moved far from the center to avoid the lower classes. Social and cultural ties among the city's residents loosened. Each class, racial, and ethnic group had fewer encounters with people in other sections of the city than the rise of the suburbs.

Central business districts emerged. Railroads built terminals, banks and insurance companies located their main offices downtown, and department stores anchored shopping districts. Streetcars brought customers from the suburbs to Macy's in New York, Marshall Field's in Chicago, and Filene's in Boston. In these "palaces of consumption," middle-class women shopped for attractive products. Museums, theaters, and opera houses added to the cultural resources of the industrial city.

Architects created the skyscraper for the central business district. Louis Sullivan of Chicago developed techniques for buildings to rise higher than the five to ten stories that had been the upper limits of structures. Passenger elevators, lighter walls reinforced with iron piers, and a framework of structural steel made it feasible to erect buildings with twenty to forty stories or more. The skyscrapers allowed the business district to accommodate thousands of office workers.

The numbers of people in the expanding cities strained the available living space. For the middle and upper classes, apartments were a practical answer, and apartment buildings replaced the single-family home. Poorer city residents lived in the tenement houses—six- or seven-story houses built on narrow lots. New York City had twenty thousand such structures, most of them 25 feet wide and 100 feet deep, with windows only at the front and back. During the late 1870s, after legislation mandated that at least some ventilation be provided, "dumbbell tenements," with tiny indented windows along the sides, appeared. Dozens of people lived in small, dark rooms. From the outside, the buildings looked decent, but as the novelist William Dean Howells noted, "To be

Tenement Life in the Growing Cities

Documentary photographs became a favored way of depicting social problems at the end of the nineteenth century. Photographers went into the tenements of growing cities to record the situation of urban residents. In this squalid room, four men are jammed together in filthy cicumstances on crude banks and soiled mattresses. The chances of any one of these impoverished individuals, trapped in low-wage jobs, breaking out of this kind of urban poverty was remote at best.

(The Granger Collection, New York)

DOING HISTORY ONLINE

Servicing the Urban Poor

Read the articles by Richard Croker and Ray Stannard Baker. Political machines and political bosses were a source of controversy in the 1880s and 1890s. On what grounds does Baker attack them? How does Croker defend them? Whose argument do you find more persuasive, and why?

 www.cengage.com/
history/ayers/
ampassages4e

in it, and not have the distance, is to inhale the stenches of the neglected street and to catch the yet fouler and dreadfuller poverty-smell which breathes from the open doorways."

Inside the tenement or on the teeming sidewalks, the crush of people strained water and sanitation systems. The stench of manure, open sewers, and piled-up garbage filled nostrils. Smoke from the factories and grime from machinery were everywhere. Chicago's water system struggled to work during the 1880s. Residents of Philadelphia described their water as "not only distasteful and unwholesome for drinking, but offensive for bathing purposes."

The cities expanded their facilities to supply better services. New York City created a system of reservoirs that brought water from surrounding lakes and rivers to residents. Chicago faced immense difficulties in transporting water from Lake Michigan for drinking needs and providing adequate sanitation. Park building became a priority of urban political machines and reformers alike. Although most of the new parks appeared on the outskirts of the city, away from the poorer sections, the amount of parkland in larger cities doubled during the decade after 1888.

The New Immigration

Cities grew because people flocked to them from the countryside and other nations. For the twenty years after 1870, net immigration totaled more than 7.5 million people. Unlike the immigrants from northern and western Europe who had come during the first seventy-five years of the nineteenth century, these "New Immigrants" were mainly from southern and eastern Europe. Italians, Poles, Hungarians, Russian Jews, and Czechs brought with them languages, lifestyles, and customs that often clashed with those of native-born Americans or earlier immigrants. Marrying within their own ethnic group, speaking their own language, and reading their own newspapers, they created distinctive, vibrant communities within cities.

Many newcomers first saw the United States when they entered New York Harbor. They were processed at Castle Garden at the Battery in Lower Manhattan. By the end of the 1880s, these immigration facilities had become inadequate. They were closed in 1890, and a more extensive immigrant station was opened in 1892 on **Ellis Island** in the harbor.

On Ellis Island the new arrivals were given a medical examination and questioned about their economic prospects. One often-told story was that of a German Jew confronted by an inspector who fired numerous questions at him. When finally asked his name, the man replied in Yiddish: "*Schoyn vergessen*" (I forget). The inspector heard what the words sounded like and said that "Sean Ferguson" was eligible to enter the United States.

The new arrivals labored for city construction gangs that built New York City's subways, the steel mills of Pittsburgh, and the skyscrapers of Chicago. Some men sold fruits and vegetables from pushcarts, others worked as day laborers, and increasing numbers built their own small businesses. Italian immigrant women "finished" garments for the clothing industry or made artificial flowers.

The cultural values and Old World experiences often dictated the jobs that men and women took. Italians preferred steady jobs with a dependable salary that left time for family life. Greeks joined railroad gangs where they could work in the open. Jews became shopkeepers, merchants, and peddlers, the trades that had been open to them in the anti-Semitic world of eastern Europe. Some nationalities, Bohemians and Slovaks, for example, allowed women to work as domestic servants; others, such as Jews, Italians, and Greeks, barred women from domestic work outside the home.

Ethnic neighborhoods appeared. In New York City, immigrants from Naples lived on Mott Street; Sicilians resided on Prince Street. Churches and synagogues shaped community life. Newcomers formed self-help societies to ease the transition for those who came after them: the Polish National Alliance, the Bohemian-American National Council, and the Hebrew Immigrant Aid Society, for example. They built theaters and concert halls, and created schools to educate their children. Some of the new arrivals moved away from their ethnic roots as they prospered; other immigrants soon replaced them. In the Tenth Ward of New York, the Jewish immigrant population in 1900 had a density of nine hundred people per acre, one of the highest in the world.

As the communities of immigrants grew, older residents worried about the impact of the newcomers on traditional values, and prejudice and religious intolerance flared. Editors of urban newspapers, speaking to the prejudices of their upper-class readers, called immigrants "the very scum and offal of the earth." During the 1880s, the anti-Catholic American Protective Association recruited those for whom the immigrants were a threat to Protestant religious values or a source of economic competition. Its members resolved to limit the role of Catholics in politics. These sentiments that favored "native" Americans (hence "nativist") led to calls to restrict immigration through literacy tests for entrance into the United States or quotas based on national origin.

Anti-Semitism permeated American society. In addition to the long-standing religious roots of prejudice among Christians against Jews, the struggle over inflation and deflation in monetary policy drove notions that Jewish financiers dominated world banking. Among academics, social scientists, and historians, quasi-scientific arguments arose to justify exclusion of Jews from universities and businesses.

The Urban Political Machine   Politicians in the large cities grappled with ethnicity, race, and economic class divisions. Most cities had a mayor–council form of government in which the entire population elected the mayor, and council members represented individual districts or wards. Divided, ineffective government resulted as council members traded favors and blocked legislation that hurt their districts.

Tweed Ring.
Thomas Nast used his cartoons to attack the Tweed Ring in New York City. Here Nast shows the boss talking with cronies in his headquarters about one of their corrupt plans.

200   HARPER'S

"GROSS IRREGULARITY NOT 'FRAUDULENT.'"
Boss Sweed. "To make this *look straight* is the hardest job I ever had. What made Watson go sleigh-riding?"

The urban "political machine" led by the **political boss** developed. The organization that dominated city politics consisted of an interlocking system of operations in each ward that delivered votes for their party at city and county conventions. The machine relied for its existence on the votes of the large inner-city population who turned out faithfully on election day to support the candidates whom the machine had designated.

The organization of the machine began with the ward leader who got the vote out. He supplied his employment, help in an economic crisis or brush with the law, and regularly attended the weddings, funerals, and wakes of the neighborhood. A ward leader like George Washington Plunkitt in New York or John F. "Honey Fitz" Fitzgerald in Boston was the man to see when disaster threatened. "I think that there's got to be in every ward somebody that any bloke can come to—no matter what he's done—and get help," said a Boston ward leader. "Help, you understand, none of your law and justice, but help!"

The most notorious political machine of the era was the one connected to William Magear Tweed and the "Tweed Ring" of the late 1860s in New York City. Associated with the Democratic organization known as Tammany Hall (after the name of the clubhouse where its members met), Tweed used his influence to gain lucrative city contracts for his associates and supporters.

Democratic voters in New York applauded the ring as a source of jobs and patronage. Yet, Tweed's heyday was brief. He came under assault from major newspapers for corruption, but his most effective adversary was the cartoonist, Thomas Nast. Nast's drawings depicted Tweed as the leader of a band of criminals. Revelations about tainted contracts and crooked deals brought Tweed down in the early 1870s. The conditions that assisted his rise to power still existed, though, and machines flourished in New York and other major cities.

As the big cities grew, contracts were awarded to businesses to build streets, install sewers, lay gas lines, and erect elevated trains. These projects presented abundant chances for politicians to decide how money was spent. Judgments about who built streets, parks, and sewer connections depended on payoffs and graft to the boss and his associates. The flow of money, much of it based on corruption, enabled the machine to provide the social services that people wanted.

In the public's mind, the political boss stood at the top of the machine. Careful to keep their influence out of the spotlight, these men rarely held office and managed affairs from behind the scenes through their control of the local Democratic Party. "Honest John" Kelly and Richard Croker of Tammany Hall were among the more celebrated of such leaders, but almost every major city had one. Their enemies depicted the bosses as unchallenged dictators of the city's destiny. In most cases, however, the bosses were shrewd politicians who balanced factions and interest groups in a constantly shifting political scene. The coming of industrialism had overwhelmed the old forms of city government that were based on a relatively small number of residents and a geographically limited urban area. The boss and the machine provided central direction for the city and represented an important innovation.

Reformers saw the machine as evil and graft-ridden. Members of the middle and upper classes, disturbed by the new power of the immigrants, attacked the boss and the machine as inefficient and wasteful. The boss and his allies often defeated the campaigns of the reformers because inner-city residents appreciated what the machine did for them. Reformers came and went, but the machine was always there. As George

Washington Plunkitt said, reformers "were mornin' glories—looked lovely in the mornin' and withered up in a short time, while the regular machines went on flourishin' forever, like fine old oaks."

The rank-and-file residents also knew that reformers wanted to shift power away from the lower classes. The reform program involved cutbacks in even the already minimal services that the poorer areas of the city received. On balance, the machines and bosses supplied reasonably good city government. Services were provided and economic opportunity expanded. City residents endorsed the results with their votes. Most cities had water, fire, and health services of a quality that compared with those found in the industrial nations of western Europe. In the city parks—Central Park in New York, the Boston park system, and the sprawling green spaces of St. Louis and Kansas City—the generation of the 1880s left a positive legacy to future urban residents.

The settlement houses that Jane Addams and others launched at the end of the decade improved city life. There were citizenship classes, training in cultural issues, and sports programs for local youth. Often settlement workers approached the ethnic neighborhood with arrogance and insensitivity, however. In time, though, some of these individuals gained a better understanding of the obstacles that immigrants faced. The experience in the ghettos and the streets of the cities prepared future reformers for work in subsequent campaigns. At the same time, Addams and her colleagues conveyed a strong sense of moralistic paternalism to the people they sought to serve. Their goal was to "build a bridge between European and American experiences" over which the immigrants could pass toward integration into the dominant culture. Despite this condescending attitude, the settlement house movement softened the impact of the urban experience. Still, the urbanizing process of the late nineteenth century had left the nation with accumulating social problems that would tax leaders and institutions for decades.

THE DIMINISHING RIGHTS OF MINORITY GROUPS

The rights of Native Americans, Mexican Americans, Chinese, and African Americans were at risk from repressive forces within white society. Possibilities narrowed for Americans who belonged to one of these distinct racial or ethnic minorities. In the case of Native Americans, the disastrous effects of the attitudes of whites played themselves out in tragedy.

The end of large-scale resistance to white expansion left few viable ways to protest policies that destroyed Native American traditions and confined natives to reservations or government schools. Affected by despair and hopelessness, the Plains Indians were receptive to any leaders who offered them a chance to regain their lost cultural values.

The appearance of a religious movement, the Ghost Dance, promised Plains Indians the return of their buffalo herds and an end to white domination. If the Indians performed the rituals of the dance, said a Paiute messiah named Wovoka, the Indian dead would be reborn and the whites would vanish for all time. Apprehensive whites saw the Ghost Dance as a portent of another Indian uprising.

When the army moved against the Sioux in December 1890, fighting occurred on Wounded Knee Creek on the Pine Ridge Reservation in South Dakota. Despite bitter hand-to-hand combat, the "battle" was no contest. The army's machine guns cut down the Indians; they suffered 146 dead and 51 wounded. Army losses were 25 killed and 39 wounded. The **Battle of Wounded Knee** was the last chapter in the Indian wars.

While the Indian conflicts were ebbing, social conflict involving Mexican Americans erupted in the territory of New Mexico. A major political issue was the land grants that the Spanish Crown had made. Anglo lawyers acquired title to these properties in order to assemble large landholdings of their own. Hispanic residents had grazed their cattle on communal lands that all ranchers shared. Now Anglo ranchers and settlers divided up the land with fences and sold it among themselves.

Spanish Americans tried to resist this trend by forming a secret vigilante organization, Las Gorra Blancas (The White Caps). In 1889, they cut fences and burned Anglo railroads, lumberyards, and other property. Thus, ethnic and economic tensions led to social violence in the territory as part of the resistance to the dominant power of white settlers.

Chinese immigrants came to the United States during the 1840s and 1850s to work the gold mines. They then constructed the transcontinental railroads in the 1860s. Energetic and thrifty, the Chinese soon engaged in manufacturing enterprises and farming. White Californians reacted. Laws barred the Chinese from professions in which they competed with whites, and a movement to ban Chinese immigration grew. An 1868 treaty had guaranteed free access to Chinese immigrants to the United States, but twelve years later, Washington pressured the Chinese to change the treaty to allow the regulation of Chinese immigrants. As a result, the Chinese Exclusion Act of 1882 barred Chinese entry into the United States for ten years.

Prejudice against the 104,000 Chinese in the West became more intense in these years. Congress moved to tighten restrictions on immigration. In 1889, the Supreme Court upheld the constitutionality of such laws and stated that such measures would help in "the preservation of our civilization there." Congress extended the Chinese Exclusion Act in 1892 for another ten years. By 1900, the number of Chinese living in the United States fell to 85,000. Most of the Chinese Americans resided in cities, where they established laundries, restaurants, and other small business that served members of their own community. The Chinese Benevolent Association, or "Six Companies," offered support for a Chinese culture that existed in a rich and complex setting of its own.

The Spread of Segregation

The most elaborate and sustained policy of racial separation was aimed at African Americans in the South. As blacks tried to take part in politics and seek wealth and happiness, white southerners responded with a caste structure to ensure their continued dominance.

White Americans in all parts of the nation believed that blacks were their inferiors. Reconstruction had been, in the minds of whites, a failure. Accordingly, white southerners, it was argued, should deal with the black population as they deemed best. Northern willingness to abandon the aims of the Civil War and Reconstruction was a key element in the rise of segregation.

With the tacit approval of the North, the white politicians of the South devised segregation laws to cover most spheres of human activity. Blacks were barred from white railroad cars and had to use the inferior and often shabby cars assigned to their race. Whites had their own hotels, parks, hospitals, and schools. Blacks had either to accept lesser facilities or do without them.

Informal restrictions also shaped the everyday life of blacks. African Americans were expected to step out of the way of whites, be respectful and deferential, and never, by manner or glance, to display resentment or anger. A young black man was a "boy" until he became old enough to be labeled "uncle." To call an African American person either "Mr." or "Mrs." would have implied a degree of individuality that the culture of segregation in the South could not tolerate.

Laws removed blacks from the political process. They could not serve on juries in judgment of whites. They experienced harsher penalties when convicted of a crime than white offenders. Although some blacks had voted during the 1880s, laws were passed in the next decade to make it impossible for African Americans to vote. The South took its cue from Mississippi. That state's 1890 constitutional convention required that voters demonstrate their literacy and pay a poll tax before they could cast a ballot. An illiterate man had to qualify to vote by demonstrating that he could "understand" a provision of the state constitution when it was read to him. Election judges allowed illiterate whites to vote; black voters faced complex questions about the state constitution. A poll tax had to be paid in advance and a receipt presented at the polls. These laws worked against poor whites and most blacks, who found it easier not to vote. In states like Mississippi and Louisiana, the number of registered black voters fell during the early 1890s; the number of white voters declined as well.

In addition to legal restrictions, blacks faced the constant possibility of violence. In the 1890s, an average of 187 black Americans were lynched annually. Blacks convicted of crimes were imprisoned in brutal circumstances in overcrowded penitentiaries or made to work on gangs that the state leased out to private contractors. The convict-lease system produced inmate death rates as high as 25 percent in some states.

Blacks fought the rising tide of segregation in the courts. In Louisiana, African Americans tested an 1890 law specifying that they must ride in separate railroad cars. On June 7, 1892, **Homer A. Plessy**, who was one-eighth black, boarded a train bound from New Orleans to Covington, Louisiana. He sat in the car reserved for whites, and the conductor instructed him to move to the car for blacks. He refused and was arrested. When his case came before Judge Thomas H. Ferguson, Plessy's claim that the law violated his constitutional rights was denied. The case, now known as *Plessy v. Ferguson*, was appealed to the U.S. Supreme Court. A decision was not expected for several years.

Black leaders resisted to the extent they could. The remaining African American members of southern legislatures argued against discriminatory legislation, but they were easily outvoted. A Richmond, Virginia, Democrat boasted of the tactics used to exclude blacks from elections. "It was well understood that the blacks had to be beaten by hook or by crook—they knew what to expect and they knew who was putting the thing on them but they could not prevent it." By the mid-1890s, the South was as segregated as white leaders could make it. For most blacks the constitutional guarantees of the Fourteenth and Fifteenth amendments existed only on paper. The fate of minorities had a low priority in a society where racial stereotypes infused the mind-set of a Victorian society.

A VICTORIAN SOCIETY

In the late nineteenth century, the social customs embodied in the term *Victorian* shaped how most white Americans lived. Like their counterparts in Great Britain, where Queen Victoria ruled between 1837 and 1901, these Americans professed a public code of personal behavior that demanded restraint, sexual modesty, temperate habits, and hard work. They failed to see how much the minorities in the United States also exemplified these standards, and in their own lives, white Americans often fell well short of these ideals.

The Rules of Life   Victorian morality applied to every aspect of daily life. Relations between the sexes followed precise rules. Unmarried men and women were supposed to be chaperoned when they were together. A suitor asked a woman whether he might write to her before presuming to do so. A kiss resulted in an engagement or social disgrace. Premarital sex was taboo. People married for life, mourned a dead spouse for at least a year, and showed fidelity by not remarrying. Some people flouted these guides, of course, but many followed them and the social conventions that they represented.

Once married, a couple was expected to engage in sexual intercourse only for the purpose of having children. The wife was to tame the husband's baser instincts. She was considered to be naturally pure; the husband was prey to the animalistic drives in his masculine nature. "The full force of sexual desire is seldom known to a virtuous woman," said one male writer, with the implication that women did not achieve the same pleasure in sex that men did.

In reality, of course, women's desires did not conform to these stereotypes. One mother of four in her thirties remarked that sexual relations "makes more normal people." A survey of forty-five married women, done by Professor Clelia Mosher in 1892, found that almost three-quarters of them experienced pleasure during lovemaking. Limits on the frequency of sex may have been to reduce unwanted pregnancies in a time before birth control devices became widespread.

Middle-class and upper-class men in Victorian society pursued careers out of the house, doing what a leading magazine took for its title: *The World's Work.* They spent their days at the factory or office, and the children saw them in the evening and on Sundays. Males displayed the right virtues in what was called their "character." In these classes, men might sow their "wild oats" before marriage, but after that were expected to adhere to their wedding vows. The rising number of divorces (fifty-six thousand by 1900) indicated that many did not do so. People looked the other way when men patronized prostitutes or had discreet sexual adventures outside wedlock. When it became known that a woman had followed such a course, she was disgraced.

A strict moral code governed the raising of Victorian children. Parents instilled character in their children, often by spanking or more intense physical abuse. Children were to be seen and not heard, and they were required to show respect to their elders. Discussion of sex was rare. Many women knew nothing about it until they were married.

Despite the constraints placed on children's behavior, youthful high spirits found an outlet in games and play. Entertainment was centered in the home, where families assembled to play board and card games, sing around a parlor organ or piano, and, for wealthier Americans, play croquet and lawn tennis.

On Sundays, the middle-class family went to church. Religion permeated the nation of 63 million people. In 1890, there were 145 Christian denominations with nearly 22 million members. More than 8 million people were Roman Catholics; Presbyterians, Methodists, and Southern Baptists were the major Protestant denominations. Despite fears that religious convictions were waning in the face of growing

Homestead Strike.
The Homestead strike brought violence between the steelworkers who had left their jobs and the troops sent in to break the walkout. This contemporary illustration depicts the violence that resulted.

(© Bettmann/ CORBIS)

secularism, thousands responded enthusiastically to the religious revivals that Dwight L. Moody and other celebrated evangelists conducted. Yet at the same time, Victorian ideas faced critics. Although some mainline Protestant churches assimilated the teachings of Charles Darwin without protest, other denominations contended that evolution and religion could not coexist. "The human soul shrinks from the thought that it is without kith or kin in all this wide universe," concluded an observer of the intellectual currents of the decade. The struggle about Darwinism continued over the course of the next century.

A Sporting Nation   While thinkers debated the impact of modern ideas on traditional religious verities, Americans sought relaxation and recreation in popular spectator sports. Among the upper and middle classes, football had emerged as second only to baseball in its appeal. The first intercollegiate football game occurred between Princeton and Rutgers in 1869; the modern game evolved as rules for scoring became established. Walter Camp, the unofficial coach at Yale University and the founder of the "All-American" teams, devised the line of scrimmage and the requirement that a team gain five yards in three attempts in order to retain possession of the ball. Dividing the field into five-yard squares produced the "gridiron." With regular rules came recruitment of talented athletes, charges of professionalism, and obsession with the sport among alumni. Football appealed most to those who believed that young men should demonstrate commitment to a strenuous existence in a violent game that tested their masculine courage.

Boxing had a wider appeal to all classes of society, especially because it gave ethnic groups and immigrants a chance to advance in life. Irish American boxers dominated the sport, with **John L. Sullivan** the most famous champion. Some matches were held in secret and continued for as many as seventy-five bloody rounds. The contestants did not use gloves. Gloves and formal rules appeared during the 1880s. Sullivan lost his heavyweight crown in 1892 to James J. "Gentleman Jim" Corbett in the first gloved title fight. African American fighters appeared in interracial bouts in some divisions, but white heavyweight champions observed the "color line" before 1900.

Another popular diversion was bicycling, which became a craze after 1890. At first, cycling was a sport for those who could master the brakeless "ordinary" bikes with their oversize front wheels. Then in the 1880s, the "safety" bicycle, so called because of its brakes and inflated pneumatic tires, appeared. Technology had produced a bicycle that the average person could ride in relative comfort, and the fad was on. Some 10 million bikes were in use by 1900. Cycling, which some enthusiasts said eased childbirth, led women to adopt looser garments. After the automobile appeared at the beginning of the twentieth century, the passion for bicycling receded, and memories of the craze that had marked the early 1890s faded away.

VOICES OF PROTEST AND REFORM

Bicycles were not the only craze that swept the nation at the end of the 1880s. **Edward Bellamy**, a former reporter turned novelist, published *Looking Backward: 2000–1887* in 1888. Its main character, Julian West, had gone to sleep in 1887 and woke in 2000. In the future he met Doctor Leete, who told him how the world had changed during the 113 years he had been asleep. In the new industrial order of "Nationalism," efficiency and discipline had replaced the chaos of the late nineteenth century. Citizens had purpose in their lives. Members of an industrial army, they served the state, which in turn provided them with material rewards. Bellamy's argument offered the promise of a nation organized for a common purpose in pursuit of abundance without the coercion of the government.

Bellamy became an overnight celebrity, and *Looking Backward* sold hundreds of thousands of copies. "Nationalist" clubs sprang up to spread his doctrine. The fad ebbed quickly, but Bellamy had hit a nerve in a society that was restive about industrialism. His evocation of community and cooperative action resonated in a competitive, capitalist society. Troubled individuals turned to their faith, to organization, and to political action to deal with their unease about the direction of the nation.

Religion offered one answer to the social ills of industrialism. Many clergymen had defended the inequalities of wealth and status in society. But this harsh response offended younger members of the ministry, who sought to improve society rather than to save individual souls. They rebelled against the tenets of Social Darwinism and the idea that the ills of society were the results of natural selection. Walter Rauschenbusch, a Baptist clergyman in Rochester, New York, had seen firsthand the hardship and despair that slum dwellers experienced. He believed that it was necessary to "Christianize" the social order to bring it "into harmony with the ethical convictions which we identify with Christ." The church, he wrote, must "demand protection for the moral safety of the people."

Rauschenbusch's ideas came to be known as the Social Gospel. He and other ministers went into the city to preach the Gospel to poor slum dwellers. Washington Gladden spoke out from the First Congregational Church in Columbus, Ohio, and wrote a book entitled *Applied Christianity*, which was published in 1886. "The Christian moralist," he wrote, had to tell "the Christian employer" that the wage system "when it rests on competition as its sole basis is anti-social and anti-Christian." Similar doctrines were promoted within Judaism and Catholicism. The Social Gospel contributed to the reform impulses that extended through the 1890s.

Middle-class women were leaders in the reform efforts of the 1890s. The Woman's Christian Temperance Union (WCTU) expanded its role under Frances Willard, its president from 1879 to 1899. It pursued missions to the urban poor, constructive changes in the situation of prison inmates, and protests against male-dominated politics. Prohibition thus became more than just the restriction of alcohol; for the WCTU it included a spectrum of ideas to improve society.

Women who had gained leisure time during the 1880s transformed their literary and discussion clubs into campaigns with a more ambitious agenda. A leading feminist, Charlotte Perkins Gilman, saw clubs as "the first timid steps toward social organization of these so long unsocialized members of our race." In 1890 the General Federation of Women's Clubs was founded, with a core membership of two hundred clubs and some twenty thousand women on its rolls. It sponsored cultural and educational activities for working women and homemakers. In Chicago, women's clubs supported the Legal Aid Society and other "child-saving" endeavors to help mothers raise their children in healthier settings.

The campaign to achieve woman suffrage had remained divided after the National Woman Suffrage Association and the American Woman Suffrage Association split over the Fifteenth Amendment and African American voting rights. The rift was healed through the efforts of Lucy Stone Blackwell. In 1890, the **National American Woman Suffrage Association** (NAWSA) appeared. The president was Elizabeth Cady Stanton; Susan B. Anthony succeeded her in 1892. Progress toward suffrage was slow. Elections to secure suffrage usually failed, and by the mid-1890s, only four states (Wyoming, Utah, Colorado, and Idaho) allowed women to vote. Nonetheless, NAWSA provided an important organizational foundation for future growth.

Other reform goals attracted the support of committed women. Josephine Shaw Lowell animated the Charity Organization Society, which sent "friendly visitors" into urban slums to instruct residents and "in great measure prevent the growth of pauperism." Homes were established for the impoverished mother and prostitute where she could obtain "Friends, Food, Shelter and a HELPING HAND by coming just as she is." Florence Kelley of Hull House carried the ideas of the settlement movement into the more ambitious Illinois Women's Alliance in 1892. The New York City Working Women's Society protested harsh working conditions in that city in 1890; its activities led to the formation of consumers' leagues in other cities. These diverse examples of social criticism and constructive action taught lessons about the effects of industrialism that would shape the experience of the coming generation.

LOOKING OUTWARD: FOREIGN POLICY IN THE EARLY 1890S

After decades of internal development, the nation sought a larger role in world affairs. The campaign for an expansionist foreign policy moved slowly in the face of persistent isolationism. Between 1887 and 1893, the country adopted policies that would move it toward becoming a world power.

In 1889, the United States was a weak military and diplomatic force. The army was small, with fewer than twenty-five thousand men who served in isolated posts in the West. The navy was equally insignificant. One congressman called the fleet "an alphabet of floating washtubs." Sails and wooden vessels were the rule until the 1880s when four steel ships were built.

One apparent source of support for expansion was the interest in overseas markets. In 1890, the Census Bureau announced the official closing of the frontier with the disappearance of a clear line of unsettled territory. Further expansion would have to be international. Noting the size of the nation's industrial output, business leaders and farmers worried whether the home market could consume everything that factories and farms produced. Perhaps it would become necessary to secure overseas markets to relieve the pressure. The United States still imported more than it exported; in 1887, exports stood at $810 million, imports at $967 millions. Exports fluctuated during the last quarter of the nineteenth century, but the overall trend was gradually upward. By the mid-1890s, the nation was exporting more than it imported.

The zeal for overseas markets helped feed a general enthusiasm for expansion, but the direct impact on policy was less certain. The percentage of the gross national product devoted to exports remained low. The official economic policy toward foreign trade was protectionist. Proponents of tariffs resisted efforts to lower trade barriers in order to expand overseas commerce. As a result, the sentiment for imperialism in the United States had an economic component, but the real drive for an international role had different causes.

The Roots of Imperialism

European powers scrambling to expand their empires had a powerful impact on American attitudes. As Africa and Asia became colonies and protectorates of Great Britain, Germany, France, and other countries, Americans worried about being left behind. Applying the doctrines of Social Darwinism to foreign nations, advocates of empire said that a nation that did not expand would not survive.

An expansionist leader was Captain Alfred T. Mahan of the U.S. Navy. Mahan's research into naval history led to his most important work, *The Influence of Seapower on History, 1660–1783*, published in 1890. Mahan wanted his country to seek global greatness through sea power. Only through naval bases, a powerful battleship fleet, and an aggressive foreign policy could the United States compete in a world of empires. He told policy makers that the United States should expand its foreign commerce, construct a strong navy, and acquire overseas bases. Of particular concern was a canal across Central America. Secretaries of the navy from 1889 onward listened to Mahan, as did such future leaders as Henry Cabot Lodge and Theodore Roosevelt.

The notion of Anglo-Saxon supremacy fed the new interest in foreign affairs. The Protestant minister Josiah Strong contended in *Our Country: Its Possible Future and Its Present Crisis* (1885) that "God, with infinite wisdom and skill, is training the Anglo-Saxon race for an hour sure to come in the world's future." The popular author John Fiske gave lectures on "manifest destiny." In them he predicted that "every land on the earth's surface" that was not already civilized would become "English in its language, in its religion, in political habits and traditions, and a predominant extent in the blood of its people." These statements helped make expansionism seem aligned with the nation's future.

New Departures in Foreign Policy

During the brief administration of James A. Garfield, Secretary of State James G. Blaine tried to renegotiate the Clayton-Bulwer

Treaty (1850) to give the United States control over any canal across Central America. Blaine hoped to create a pan-American system to promote stability and security in the Caribbean and South America. The end of the Garfield administration postponed any further action on pan-Americanism for almost a decade.

The gradual movement toward a greater international role continued under Presidents Chester Arthur and Grover Cleveland. Secretary of State Frederick T. Frelinghuysen pursued treaties for trade reciprocity with Mexico, Santo Domingo, and Colombia. Much as Blaine had done with South America, Frelinghuysen believed that these treaties would unite the interests of those countries with those of the United States. Congress, however, declined to act on the pacts.

Under Cleveland, the process slowed as the administration showed less enthusiasm for a canal across Nicaragua or a greater American presence worldwide. Still, the size of the navy grew during the Cleveland years. When Blaine returned to the State Department under Benjamin Harrison in 1889, the drive for an expansionist policy resumed.

Blaine sent out invitations for a conference to Latin American countries, and delegates from nineteen nations assembled in Washington on October 2, 1889, for the first International American Conference. Blaine urged the delegates to set up mechanisms for freer trade among themselves and to work out procedures for settling their regional conflicts. Unwilling to accept what seemed to be the dominance of the United States, the conference declined to pursue these initiatives. Instead, it established the International Bureau of the American Republics, which became the Pan-American Union in 1910.

Blaine persuaded his Republican colleagues in Congress to include language allowing for reciprocity treaties in the McKinley Tariff Act of 1890. A number of products were placed on the free list, including sugar, molasses, coffee, and tea; the president could impose tariffs on such items if Latin American countries did not grant the United States similar concessions on its exports. Blaine used the reciprocity clause of the McKinley Tariff to negotiate treaties with such South American countries as Argentina. U.S. exports increased, disproving the claims of critics who warned that it would stifle trade with other nations.

The Harrison administration followed a more aggressive foreign policy. Secretary of the Navy Benjamin F. Tracy urged Congress to appropriate money for a battle fleet that would not only protect the coastline of the United States but also engage enemies across the oceans. Lawmakers authorized four modern battleships, fewer than Tracy wanted but nonetheless an expansion of naval power.

The Harrison years saw greater involvement in Asia. With their eyes on potential markets for produce and crops, business leaders said that the Hawaiian Islands seemed a logical steppingstone to the Orient. Missionaries had been preaching in the islands since the 1820s; their reports fed American fascination with Hawaii. Trade relations between the United States and Hawaii had grown stronger since the reciprocity treaty, signed in 1875, gave Hawaiian sugar and other products duty-free entry into the United States. In exchange, Hawaii agreed not to grant other countries any concessions that threatened the territorial or economic independence of the island nation. The relationship was strengthened in 1887 when the treaty was renewed and the United States received the exclusive right to use the superb strategic asset of Pearl Harbor.

Within Hawaii, white immigrants and the native rulers clashed. The Hawaiian monarch, King Kalakua, had been inclined to accept closer ties between the United States and his nation. He died in 1891, bringing to power his sister, Queen Liliuokalani.

Queen Liliuokalani.
When Americans endeavored to bring the Hawaiian Islands under United States control, Queen Liliuokalani led the native Hawaiians in efforts to forestall the end of their independence. Her resistance led the Cleveland administration to block Hawaiian annexation for most of the 1890s.

(The Granger Collection, New York)

She resented the American presence in Hawaii and believed that the white minority should not dominate.

Hawaiian politics became more complex after the McKinley Tariff removed the duty-free status of Hawaiian sugar and granted bounties to American cane growers in Louisiana and beet sugar growers in the Rocky Mountain states. As the Hawaiian sugar industry slumped, economic conditions on the islands worsened. Calls for annexation arose from Americans in Hawaii and Congress in Washington.

During 1892, the Hawaiian legislature and queen argued over the presence and role of foreigners in the country. As the new year began, the queen dismissed the legislature and put in place a constitution that stripped white settlers of many of the powers they had enjoyed under the previous document. Proponents of annexation launched a revolt and called on the U.S. minister (the official representative of the United States to the islands) and the U.S. Navy. With the aid of 150 U.S. Marines, the coup succeeded. The queen capitulated and a provisional government was created. The United States agreed to a treaty of annexation with the pro-American and predominantly white rebels on February 14, 1893. It looked as if Hawaii would become a possession of the United States. Then the incoming president, Grover Cleveland, said that the treaty should not be ratified until the new administration took office. The fate of Hawaii remained in limbo.

Despite this temporary pause, American expansion during the Harrison administration was striking. The navy had grown and its mission broadened. The ties to Latin American had been extended, and the fate of Hawaii seemed to be linked to that of the United States. Harrison and Blaine had launched the nation on a path of greater overseas involvement that would continue through the 1890s. For the moment, however, internal ferment captured the nation's attention as social and political unrest flared in the heartland of the United States.

THE ANGRY FARMERS

Of all the groups that found themselves at odds with the direction of American society between 1887 and 1893, the unhappy farmers of the South and West had the greatest impact on the nation and its political system.

The election of Benjamin Harrison in 1888 and Republican control of Congress had allowed the majority party to enact a wide-ranging program of legislative activism. The key measures included the McKinley Tariff, the **Sherman Antitrust Act**, and the Sherman Silver Purchase Act. The tariff law raised rates, and the Sherman Act on silver provided for limited government purchases of the white metal. The antitrust act outlawed "combinations in restraint of trade" without providing much means to enforce the new law.

In the election of 1890, the Democrats capitalized on unhappiness with these national Republican policies, as well as a backlash against the Grand Old Party over local issues such as prohibition and laws requiring closing of businesses on the Sabbath. The new McKinley Tariff proved unpopular in the North, and in the South, Democrats used racial issues against their political rivals. The result was a Democratic victory that gave the opposition control of the House of Representatives.

The Rise of the Farmers' Alliance In the 1890 election, candidates identified with the **Farmers' Alliance** made impressive gains in the South and West. Alliance candidates won nine seats in the House and elected two U.S. senators. Their candidates dominated several southern state legislatures, and they showed strength as well in Kansas, Nebraska, South Dakota, and Minnesota.

The crisis in southern agriculture had been building for decades. As productivity increased between 1865 and 1885, the prices of farm products declined. A bushel of wheat brought almost $1.20 in 1881 but just under $0.70 a bushel in 1889. Cotton was worth almost $0.11 a pound in 1881; by 1890 that figure had fallen to $0.085 per pound.

Farmers had other grievances too. When farm prices declined, western farmers found that the debts they had run up during the 1880s were now more difficult to pay. For southern farmers, whether sharecroppers or tenants, the slide in prices meant that their debts to the "furnish merchant" also mounted up.

Railroads seemed to be villains to western and southern crop growers. High rates cut into the farmers' profits, and there were complaints that the rail lines favored manufacturers and middlemen over agrarians. The railroads wielded this power, said their critics, because they had corrupted the political process.

The system of money and banking also drew scorn. Every dollar in circulation had to have an equal amount of gold bullion behind it to keep the nation's currency on "the gold standard." Gold was stored in banks and at the U.S. Treasury. Since international gold production was static, the amount of money in circulation did not keep up with the growth in the population. The currency became deflated as the value of the dollar rose.

Wheat farmers on the Plains and cotton farmers in the South had to work harder to maintain the same level of income. The thoughts of many farmers turned to ways in which the currency might be inflated—that is, ways of putting more dollars into circulation.

The complaints of the farmers were genuine, but workable solutions were another matter. Farm prices were low because of expanding acreage under cultivation. One long-term solution was the consolidation of small farms into larger, more efficient agricultural businesses, a process that would occur later in the nation's history. But at the end of the nineteenth century, it ran counter to the widely held belief in the importance of small landowners to the health of a democratic society.

The problem of debt was equally complex. Farmers on the Plains, for example, had purchased land whose value was expected to increase, and they now faced the ruin of their ventures. Interest rates were not as high as they believed, nor were mortgage companies as tyrannical as agrarian complaints indicated. Nonetheless, the prevailing percept among farmers in the South and West was that the system took no heed of their needs or interests.

The Farmers' Alliance was formed in Texas to stop horse thieves in Lampasas County. After some early troubles, it emerged as the Texas Farmers' Alliance in 1884. Elsewhere in the South, angry farmers organized into alliances and associations that expressed their grievances. They came up with proposed solutions in a three-stage process. During the first phase, southern and western farmers looked toward cooperative action. A leader in this effort was Charles Macune, who became president of the Texas Alliance in 1886. He envisioned alliances and cooperative exchanges across the South. These institutions could provide farmers with supplies and equipment at a cost below what local merchants and retailers charged. The farmers would gain more control over the marketplace. To spread the creed of the cooperatives, the alliance sent out "lecturers" who fanned out across the region.

Cooperatives proved easier to organize than to sustain. Marketing crops at a time other than the harvest season required capital to store the crops until prices rose. The farmers lacked the money to make such a scheme work. It also proved difficult to obtain lower prices through cooperatives. A complex distribution system moved goods across the country, and that process had certain inherent costs no matter who controlled it.

Although economic success eluded the alliance between 1886 and 1890, its political power grew. The ideology of cooperative action appealed to isolated farm families. The alliance meetings brought farmers together to hear speeches, enjoy entertainment, and share experiences. The alliance thus built on collective emotion among farmers as the 1890s began.

Some members of the alliance saw African American farmers as potential allies. The Colored Farmers' National Alliance and Cooperative Union was formed in 1886. The interaction between the black alliance and its white counterpart was uneasy. Whites were usually landowners, even if impoverished ones; blacks tended to be either tenants or farm laborers. In 1891, the Colored Alliance sought to get higher wages for picking cotton. A strike for that purpose, organized by a black leader named Ben Patterson in Lee County, Arkansas, was met with violence. Fifteen of the strikers, including Patterson, were lynched, and the Colored Alliance vanished.

As farm conditions worsened during years of drought and falling crop prices, branches of the alliance gained members in the Dakotas, Nebraska, and especially Kansas. Representatives of these various organizations met in St. Louis in December 1889 to form the Farmers' Alliance and Industrial Union. The delegates agreed to leave out the word *"white"* from the organization's requirements, although state organizations in the South could exclude black members. Three key northern states, Kansas and the two Dakotas, joined the national organization.

Charles Macune offered the most important policy proposal of the conference, the subtreasury plan. Macune recognized that the major problem that confronted cotton and wheat farmers was having to sell their crops at harvest time when supplies were abundant and prices low. To surmount this obstacle, he envisioned a system of government warehouses or subtreasuries where farmers could store their crops until prices rose. To bridge the months between storage and selling, the farmers would receive a certificate of deposit from the warehouse for 80 percent of the crop's existing market value. The charge for this service would be a 1 or 2 percent annual interest rate. Farmers would wait, sell their crops for higher prices, repay the loans, and keep the resulting profits.

If a majority of wheat or cotton farmers waited until prices rose and then sold their crops, the market glut would force prices down again. The certificates that the farmers would have received for storing their crops at the subtreasury warehouses would represent another form of paper money that would fluctuate in value. Beyond that, the idea involved a large expansion of government power in an era when suspicion of federal power was still strong. To its agrarian advocates, the subtreasury seemed to be a plausible answer to the harsh conditions they confronted.

During the 1890 election, the protest movement poured its energy into speeches. In Kansas it represented an entirely new party. At a time when women took little direct part in politics, the alliance allowed female speakers to address audiences. Mary Elizabeth Lease proved one charismatic attraction with her urging to the farmers to raise "less corn and more hell." Another female attraction was Annie Diggs, who rivaled Lease in her appeal to Kansas voters.

The success of the Farmers' Alliance in the South and West led their leaders to consider mounting a third-party campaign during the next presidential election. They gathered in Ocala, Florida, in early December 1890, and their platform was known as the Ocala Demands. Their goals included the subtreasury program, abolition of private banks, regulation of transportation facilities, and the free and unlimited coinage of silver into money at a fixed ratio with gold. The issue of a third party was put off until February 1892 to allow the legislatures that had been elected with alliance support to see what they could accomplish.

As the two major parties, and especially the Democrats, fought back against the alliance, the idea of a third party gained in appeal. At a meeting of the alliance in February 1892 in St. Louis, the delegates decided to create a third party under the name the People's Party, or the Populists. They would hold their first national convention in Omaha, Nebraska, on July 4, 1892. They even had a candidate, Leonidas L. Polk of North Carolina, who was popular enough to satisfy both northern and southern farmers. When Polk died a month before the convention, the Omaha Convention chose James B. Weaver, a long-time third-party politician from Iowa, as the presidential candidate.

The party's platform took a stern view of the state of the nation. It proclaimed, that "We meet in the midst of a nation brought to the verge of moral, political, and material ruin. Corruption dominates the ballot box, the legislature, the Congress, and touches even the ermine of the bench." The specific planks endorsed the subtreasury, other reform proposals, and a new idea that was dominating the dialogue among the Populists: the free coinage of silver.

An Election Wager

By the 1890s, intense political partisanship was receding. As this Joseph Klir painting from 1892 shows, however, male voters still wagered on the outcome of election contests and paid off their bets in a most public way as the loser in this bet pulls the victor through the streets. The banners and American flags attest to the patriotic aura of the proceedings. Election betting survives today in a more electronic format through casinos and on the Internet. In private transactions, the loser simply hands over the amount of the wager. The painting thus illustrates in its own artistic way the decline in interest in politics from these late nineteenth-century rituals to the private, often individual, act of voting and celebrating the outcome that marks the twenty-first century.

(Chicago Historical Society, #CHI-03590)

By 1892, the subtreasury plan was going nowhere in Congress. As that proposal faded, the idea that inflation could be promoted by coining silver into money gained support. To expand the currency, raise prices, and reduce the weight of debt on those who owed money, silver was, the Populists argued, the best solution. The nation would base its money on two metals, gold and silver. If silver were coined into money at a ratio of 16 to 1 with gold, there would soon be ample money in circulation.

The country needed controlled inflation. However, the market price of silver stood at closer to 25 to 1, relative to gold. A policy of free coinage would lift the price of the white metal in an artificial way. If that happened, people would hoard gold, silver would lose value, and inflation would accelerate.

The **Populist Party** rejected these arguments maintaining that "money can be created by the government in any desired quantity, out of any substance, with no basis but itself." The idea of crop supports underlying the subtreasury plan and the manipulation of the money supply through the free coinage of silver would become common ideas during the twentieth century. But in 1892 they seemed radical to many Americans.

THE PRESIDENTIAL ELECTION OF 1892

Republicans and Democrats sensed that something important was happening and wondered how to respond. For the moment, the familiar routines of political life went on. The elections of 1890 had left the Republicans shocked at their losses and aware that President Harrison was not a strong candidate for reelection. Despite a last-minute challenge by James G. Blaine, Harrison was renominated as the best the Republicans could do. His party applauded the protective tariff and prepared for the Democratic onslaught.

The Democrats were confident. Their candidate was Grover Cleveland, who easily won a third nomination from his party. The platform promised lower tariffs and an end to the government spending they associated with the Republicans. Although he favored the gold standard, Cleveland kept his real views muted to conciliate Democrats in the South and West who favored inflation. In some western states, the Democrats and the Populists struck deals and "fused" their two tickets, with Cleveland getting the electoral vote and the Populists electing state candidates.

On the surface, the 1892 campaign was quiet, with the usual round of speeches about the tariff, inflation, and the role of government. The political tradition at the time said that the incumbent president should not campaign. As a result, Harrison did not make speeches. Cleveland too stayed home. The intense military-style campaigning of the post–Civil War era, with the ranks of marching men parading through the streets, was passing from the scene.

One event revealed the persisting social tensions. For workers at Andrew Carnegie's Homestead steelworks outside Pittsburgh, Pennsylvania, the summer of 1892 was a time of misery and violence. The manager of the plant, Henry Clay Frick, cut wages and refused to negotiate with skilled workers who had unionized their craft. A strike resulted, and violence broke out when detectives hired by management stormed through the town of Homestead to allow strikebreakers to retake the mills. Detectives and workers died in the ensuing battle, and state troops came in to restore order. Although the strike was broken, the walkout helped the Democrats in their appeal to labor voters disillusioned with Republicans. The **Homestead strike** seemed to many people to embody the tensions between capital and labor that industrialism had fostered.

The Populists tried to make the same argument about the struggle between agriculture and capital. James B. Weaver drew big crowds, but Democrats in the South pelted him with rotten eggs and tomatoes when he appeared. The Populists had to repel charges that they would promote a return to Reconstruction because they divided white voters. Thomas E. Watson of Georgia emerged as one of the leaders of the Populist cause. Elected to Congress in 1890, he urged black and white farmers in the South to unite against their common enemy. Democrats turned to intimidation and violence. Watson's own reelection campaign failed when the Democrats stuffed the ballot boxes against him. Other Populist candidates were counted out when the Democrats controlled the election process. When the votes in the South had been tallied, the Democrats had carried the region for Cleveland.

On the national level, Cleveland gained a second term by a decisive margin. His plurality over Harrison was almost 400,000 votes, and he won in the electoral tally with 277 votes to 145 for the Republicans. The Democrats secured control of both houses of Congress for the first time since the Civil War. Weaver carried four states and won electoral votes in three additional states for a total of 22 electoral votes. His popular vote total stood at just over 1 million.

The American economy was in trouble at the beginning of 1893. Distracting the nation from the gloomy forecasts was the prospect of a large popular spectacle that was planned in Chicago. The World's Columbian Exposition commemorated the arrival of Columbus in "The New World" four hundred years earlier. Architect Daniel Burnham and his coworkers created a series of exhibition buildings that became known as "The Great White City." The exhibition summed up the nation's achievements at the end of the nineteenth century.

To commemorate the exposition, the American Historical Association held its annual meeting in Chicago in 1893. There a young historian from the University of Wisconsin, Frederick Jackson Turner, offered a new interpretation of how the United States had changed and the challenges it faced in the immediate future. In his paper,

The Columbian Exposition.

The Columbian Exposition of 1892–1893 marked the 400th anniversary of the landing of Christopher Columbus. The "Great White City" in Chicago symbolized the progress of the nation and its technological accomplishments. The outbreak of the Panic of 1893 dulled the luster of the occasion for many Americans.

(Chicago Historical Society)

"The Significance of the Frontier in American History," Turner stressed that the availability of free land and the presence of the frontier had played a significant part in the development of democracy in the nation. He inquired about what would happen to the nation now that the possibility of free land and a new life in the West was vanishing. Turner's "frontier thesis" became a powerful and controversial explanation of the way the nation had developed.

CONCLUSION

Like many other Americans, Turner was groping to comprehend the changes that had occurred in American life since the Civil War. Industrialism, the rise of the city, and the strains of farm life all contributed to the sense of crisis that gripped the country during the 1890s. With the growth of industrialism, the towns and cities of the country swelled as residents of the rural areas and the new immigrants from Eastern Europe moved to the urban centers. As the center city and the suburbs extended beyond the old walking city of the first half of the century, transportation facilities pushed outward to provide the new population with more mobility. In the city itself, the problems of water, power, and living quarters pressed the local government for solutions. The urban machine and the city boss evolved as one means of addressing these needs.

In the farm belt of the South and West, the spread of farmland and the increased crops that followed meant that prices for farm commodities fell as production soared. With their debt burden growing and money ever harder to obtain, angry farmers turned to political action. The Farmers' Alliance and the People's Party gave voice to these sentiments and posed a threat to the two-party system. The inflationary solutions that the Populists proposed frightened middle-class Americans in the early 1890s, who saw private property as under assault. As economic hard times for the nation at large ensued, the farm protest laid the groundwork for wider-ranging social unrest.

Americans also became more conscious of their place in the world during these years. Overseas expansion seemed one way of addressing the social ills of the nation; it would mean finding new markets in Europe and Asia. A desire to share in the imperial sweep of Europe also motivated proponents of empire. A new navy and a greater diplomatic role provided the foundation for more expansive initiatives during the second half of the decade.

Despite the progress and sense of optimism that pervaded many parts of society, the country still struggled with the discrimination against minorities that was so rooted in national traditions. Segregation of African Americans in the South took hold. Advocates of this racial policy pressed forward to make it a part of every phase of southern life. For Native Americans, the transition from the 1880s to the 1890s saw the end of the Indian wars that had raged since the Europeans first invaded centuries earlier. As wards of the national government, Native Americans faced economic exploitation and efforts to break down their cultural heritage.

Industrialism, the rise of the city, and the strains of farm life all contributed to the sense of crisis that gripped the country during the 1890s. More a collection of sections than an integrated state, the United States was leaving its agrarian past for the uncertain rewards of a more industrialized, more urbanized, and more international future. Troubling signs of economic difficulties in 1891 and 1892 made citizens wonder if prosperity might disappear and the hard times of the 1870s return. Their fears were realized when the panic of 1893 changed the direction of American life.

CHAPTER REVIEW, 1887–1893

- Urban growth accelerated as big cities appeared in the wake of industrialism.
- Poverty and wealth made the city a place of contrasts and social problems.
- Urban machines arose to provide services to residents and opportunity for capitalists.
- Victorian ideas shaped middle-class attitudes as Americans sought certainty in an unstable decade.
- The nation looked outward as overseas expansion became a popular cause.
- Southern and western farmers joined together to battle low prices and the burden of debt through the Populist Party.
- The election of 1892 brought Grover Cleveland back to the White House amid growing concerns about the direction of the economy.

◀▮▮▮ Looking Back

The problems that urban and rural Americans faced in the period 1887–1893 grew out of the achievements of industrialism during the preceding decade. This chapter discusses the consequences of rapid economic change and how Americans sought to use existing institutions to respond to these developments.

1. In what ways did the growth of cities test the capacities of local governments?
2. Was the urban machine and city boss a constructive or destructive response to the changes that metropolitan areas experienced?
3. What causes underlay the economic hard times in the South and West for the nation's farmers?
4. Why did inflation seem both necessary and appropriate to those who joined the Farmers' Alliance?
5. What forces produced interest in overseas expansion around 1890? What assumptions about the world did the enthusiasm for empire reflect?

Looking Ahead ▮▮▮▶

Chapter 19 looks at the peak of farm protest during the economic depression of the 1890s. To understand what made the issues of the agrarian sector so explosive requires a good understanding of the roots of the unrest. Consider to what extent this chapter helps anticipate these issues.

1. What assumptions did Americans share about the role of government in this period? How do these premises differ (if they do) from contemporary attitudes?
2. How well equipped was the political sector to deal with the issues the Populists were advocating?
3. What attitudes about farm and city life in this period are still present in modern society?

 Go to the American Passages website at www.cengage.com/history/ayers/ampassages4e for additional review materials.

A Troubled Nation
Expands Outward,
1893–1901

D uring the 1890s, social problems that had been building
since the Civil War reached crisis proportions. An economic depression began in 1893. Americans struggled
with its effects for four years. With millions unemployed and
faith in national institutions eroding, the major political parties
confronted unhappy voters. With the majority Democrats in disarray and the Populists not a viable third party, the Republicans
emerged. The election of 1896 brought William McKinley, the
architect of Republican success, to the White House. He revitalized
the presidency after its eclipse since the death of Abraham Lincoln.
The events of these years established patterns that affected the
early decades of the twentieth century.

As the economy improved at the end of the 1890s, Americans
sought an empire in the Caribbean and the Pacific. A war with
Spain brought territorial gains and a debate about whether
overseas possessions meant fundamental change. World power
seemed both alluring and troubling at the same time. American
institutions and leaders faced the challenge of the new responsibilities. In Europe and Asia, the United States engaged problems
that persisted down to the modern era.

THE PANIC OF 1893
AND ITS EFFECTS

Grover Cleveland's second term began on March 4, 1893. In May
1893, the weakened economy collapsed into the panic of 1893.
Business had expanded during the late 1880s. In 1891 and 1892,
investors turned cautious, worried about the soundness of the
banking system and the stability of the currency. Banks failed
as depositors withdrew their funds and hoarded cash. A decline
in export trade further strained the economy. Business activity
slowed, workers were laid off, and firms cut back on production.

By the end of 1893, some six hundred banks had failed. Court-appointed receivers ran the 119 bankrupt railroads. Another fifteen thousand businesses had closed. The stock market lost hundreds of millions of dollars. Most important, by early January 1894, 2.5 million people were unemployed. The economy was functioning at only three-quarters of its capacity.

The depression fell hardest on the average workers and their families. When their jobs vanished, there were no unemployment insurance payments, no government benefits, no temporary jobs programs to bridge the gap between a living wage and poverty.

In New York City, daily newspapers distributed food, clothing, and fuel to the needy. Charitable organizations in Boston, New York, and Chicago coordinated volunteer efforts. Most well-off Americans still believed the federal government should not intervene to alleviate a depression. As a result, people slept in the parks, camped out in railroad stations, and sought food at the soup kitchens that appeared in the big cities. Angry poor people called the soup kitchens "Cleveland Cafés."

To deal with the economic slump, Cleveland proposed a simple solution: repeal the Sherman Silver Purchase Act of 1890, which specified that the government buy a fixed amount of silver each month. Cleveland argued that the law produced inflation, undermined business confidence, and caused investors to take money out of the nation's gold reserve at the Treasury Department. If the amount of the reserve fell below $100 million, the credit of the United States was in danger. In fact, the amount was largely a psychological issue and did not measure the nation's economic condition.

In August 1893, Cleveland called a special session of Congress to repeal the Sherman Act. His own party was split. Northeastern party members believed in the gold standard with religious fervor. In the South and Far West, Democrats contended that the nation needed the free and unlimited coinage of silver into money at the fixed ratio to gold of 16 to 1. By asking his party to repeal the Sherman Act, Cleveland invited Democrats to wage war against each other.

Over the protests of his party and with no tolerance of compromise, Cleveland insisted that Congress repeal the Sherman Act, and with the aid of Republican votes, he won the battle. The bill repealing the Sherman Act was signed into law on November 1, 1893.

Having blamed the Sherman Act for the depression, Cleveland waited for an economic turnaround. Although confidence in the dollar grew and the flow of gold out of the country eased, prosperity did not return. By 1894, every indicator headed downward. More railroads failed, more businesses closed, and more people were laid off to join the millions who were already unemployed.

In the 1892 campaign, the Democrats had promised to lower tariff rates. They produced a bill to lower tariff rates in the House. With only narrow control in their chamber, Senate Democrats wrote a tariff bill that pleased those hoping to help their own states. In some instances, that meant raising customs rates on key products such as sugar, coal, and iron. The law fell far short of the tariff reform that the Democrats had promised in 1892.

 This icon will direct you to interactive activities and study materials on the American Passages website: www.cengage.com/history/ayers/ampassages4e

CHAPTER TIMELINE

1893	Grover Cleveland inaugurated as president • Panic of 1893 begins four years of depression • Sherman Silver Purchase Act repealed • National League of Colored Women established
1894	Coxey's army marches on Washington • Pullman strike occurs • Republicans make major gains in elections • Radcliffe College for women opens in Cambridge, Massachusetts
1895	Booker T. Washington proposes "Atlanta Compromise" • Venezuelan crisis brings threat of war with British • Utah adopts woman suffrage • Stephen Crane's *The Red Badge of Courage* published
1896	Republicans nominate William McKinley • William Jennings Bryan receives Democratic and Populist presidential nominations • Trading stamps are offered by stores in the United States • McKinley wins presidential election • Plessy v. Ferguson decision endorses racial segregation
1897	Dingley Tariff enacted • Jell-O is introduced
1898	Battleship Maine explodes in Havana Harbor • United States and Spain go to war • Treaty of Paris ends war and United States obtains Philippines and Puerto Rico
1899	Insurrection in Philippines begins • Open Door policy toward China announced
1900	McKinley and Bryan each renominated for presidency • Republicans win presidential election • International Ladies Garment Workers Union founded

Congress finally passed the Wilson-Gorman Tariff Act in August 1894. It reduced rates on wool, copper, and lumber, and raised duties on many other items. The measure repealed the reciprocal trade provisions of the McKinley Tariff, which had aimed at opening up markets and easing the political costs of protection. To make up for lost revenues, the Wilson-Gorman bill added a modest tax on personal incomes. Disgusted with the outcome, Cleveland let the bill become law without his signature.

The Results of Hard Times

Outside Washington, as the hard times lingered, some of the unemployed took their grievances to Washington. In the Midwest, those out of work formed "Coxey's army," uniting behind Jacob S. Coxey, a businessman from Massillon, Ohio. On Easter Sunday 1894, he left for Washington with three hundred supporters to petition for a program of road building paid for by $500 million of paper money. Coxey and his son, "Legal Tender Coxey," headed the procession, which included more than forty reporters. Slowly and painfully, the "Commonweal Army of Christ" approached Washington.

Across the nation other armies rode the rails, marched through cities, and demanded jobs from the government. The climax for Coxey and his followers came on May 1, 1894, when they reached Capitol Hill and tried to present their demands to Congress. But police intercepted Coxey, clubbed him, and then arrested him for trespassing and "walking on the grass." The other armies were discouraged and dispersed, but the protests undermined the political credibility of the Cleveland administration.

Even more devastating was a major railroad strike. **George Pullman**, the developer of the railroad sleeping car, had created a model town outside Chicago where his employees were to reside in apparent comfort and serenity. Employees who lived in Pullman and worked for the Pullman Palace Car Company found that their "model" town, however, was expensive and oppressive. The prices that workers paid for services often ran 10 percent above what was charged in other communities.

When Pullman laid off employees and trimmed wages for others, he did not reduce the rents that his workers paid. As a result, in May 1894 the workers struck. They asked railroad workers across the nation not to handle Pullman's cars to help the walkout. The response from the American Railway Union (ARU) and its president, **Eugene Victor Debs**, was cautious at first. But by late June, the ARU started a sympathetic boycott and decided not to move trains with Pullman cars.

At its height, the **Pullman strike** involved 125,000 men representing twenty railroads. The commerce of the nation stalled as freight shipments backed up. The ARU did not interfere with the mails lest that action arouse the opposition of the federal government. Its economic power could not match that of the railroads' General Managers' Association, however, which had influence with Cleveland and his attorney general, Richard Olney, himself a former railroad corporation lawyer. On July 2, 1894, the president and the Justice Department obtained a court injunction to bar the strikers from blocking interstate commerce. Federal troops were ordered to Chicago.

Violence erupted as angry mobs, irate at the action of the federal government, destroyed railroad property and equipment. The strikers were not to blame for the episode; the rioters were local people. Police and National Guard troops put down the disturbance, but the public gave Cleveland and the federal government the credit. For the moment, the president regained his popularity among conservatives in both parties. His standing with ordinary voters remained low, however.

Debs went to jail for violating the court's injunction, and the U.S. Supreme Court confirmed his sentence in *In re Debs* (1895). By doing so the Court gave businesses a potent way to stifle labor unrest. If a strike began, management could seek an injunction from a friendly federal judge, jail the union leaders, and break the strike. Union power stagnated throughout the rest of the decade.

Politically, the strike divided the Democrats. The governor of Illinois, John P. Altgeld, had protested Cleveland's actions. When the president overruled him, the governor resolved to oppose the administration in 1896. Across the South and West, bitterness against the president became even more intense. Hate mail flooded into the White House, warning him of death if he crossed the Mississippi River.

1894: A Significant Election Approaching the congressional elections of 1894, the Democrats were demoralized and divided. For the Populists, however, these elections offered an excellent chance to establish themselves as a credible challenger to the two major parties. The Republicans assailed the Democrats for failing to restore prosperity. Republican speakers urged a return to the policy of tariff protection that they had pursued under Benjamin Harrison. Party leaders, such as **William McKinley**, the governor of Ohio, crisscrossed the

Midwest speaking to enthusiastic audiences. Former House Speaker Thomas B. Reed said, "The Democratic mortality will be so great next fall that their dead will be buried in trenches and marked unknown."

The Republicans prevailed in one of the most decisive congressional elections in the nation's history. The Democrats lost 113 seats in the largest transfer of power from one party to another in the annals of the two-party system. The Republicans regained control of the House of Representatives by a margin of 244 to 105. There were twenty-four states in which no Democrat won a federal office; six other states elected only one Democrat. In the Midwest, 168 Republicans and only 9 Democrats were elected to Congress.

The stalemated politics of the late nineteenth century had ended in an election that changed the nation's politics. A Republican electoral majority would dominate American politics until 1929. The decision foreshadowed a Republican victory in the presidential contest in 1896.

The Populists were disappointed with the outcome of the 1894 election. While the total vote for the Populists had increased over 1892, much of that rise occurred in the South where the Democrats then used their control of the electoral machinery to deny victory to Populist candidates. The Populist delegation in Congress went from eleven members to seven. By 1894, the Populists were identified with the free coinage of silver, which appealed to the debt-burdened South and West. For industrial workers who had to survive on a fixed or declining income, higher prices arising from this inflationary policy seemed less attractive. The Populists told each other that they would do better in 1896, but they assumed that neither the Republicans nor the Democrats would adopt a free-silver position. In fact, the Populists' failure to mount a significant challenge to the major parties during the 1894 election signaled the end of their assault on the two-party system.

THE PAIN OF HARD TIMES

The economic impact of the depression of the 1890s was profound and far-reaching. By 1894, the economy operated at 80 percent of capacity. Total output of goods and services was down by some 13 percent. Unemployment ranged between 17 and 19 percent of the work force. As the amount of money in circulation dropped, the nation experienced severe deflation. In the South, for example, cotton prices fell from 8.4 cents per pound in 1892 to 4.6 cents per pound in 1894. Since a figure of 10 cents per pound was necessary to break even, southern cotton farmers faced disaster. For people with money, their dollars bought more goods. Among those out of work and without funds, however, lower prices were little comfort when they had no money to pay for the necessities of life.

With their husbands, fathers, and sons laid off, women joined the work force in greater numbers during the decade. During the 1890s, the total number of women with jobs rose from 3.7 million to just under 5 million. They gained employment in the expanding clerical fields, where they mastered typing and stenography. Traditional occupations such as teaching and nursing also attracted more women. In the factories, Irish American, French Canadian, and Italian American women worked in textile and clothing establishments or did piecework for tobacco processors and shoemakers. In commercial food production and laundries, the number of women employees also

Child Labor in the 1890s

The spread of indus-
trialism in the late
nineteenth century
expanded jobs and
economic opportu-
nity, but social prob-
lems arose as well.
Young people found
work in factories and
small businesses, as
this photo of working
children exemplifies.
The conditions were
often primitive and
the workweek long
and demanding. Few

protections existed for children who were injured on the job, and they might
find themselves discharged for small infractions of rules or the whim of their
employer. Efforts to regulate child labor ran up against well-entrenched ideas that
work built character in the young, as well as the economic need in large families
for extra income. Photographers educated the public about the existence of these
conditions in the years 1890 to 1910, and images such as this one helped create
the popular awareness behind the political and economic reforms of this period.

grew. The earnings of these women were necessary for the survival of their families.
When the male wage earner brought home only $300 per year, and rents for a tene-
ment dwelling were as much as $200 annually, the contributions of a daughter or wife
were vital. However, the wages paid to women were as much as 40 percent below what
men earned in industrial jobs.

The depression also brought young children back into the work force. During the
1880s, the percentage of employed children between the ages of ten and fifteen had
fallen from 17 percent to 12 percent. In the next decade, the percentage rose to 18 percent. By 1900, 1.75 million children were employed. By the end of the century, thirty
states had passed child labor laws, but these were often ineffective.

Reshaping the Economy
In the economy as a whole, the depression brought important
changes. As a result of the downturn, the number of bankrupt
businesses grew, revealing an obvious economic need for
reorganization. In railroads, for example, major systems such as the Union Pacific
were in receivership. The investment banker J. P. Morgan refinanced many of these rail
lines and consolidated them to raise profits and increase efficiency. The thirty-two
railroads, capitalized at more than $100 million, controlled nearly 80 percent of the
nation's rail mileage. Shippers complained that these railroads gave larger customers

unfair advantages in the form of rebates. By the end of the decade, there were increasing pleas from the South and Midwest to revive and strengthen the Interstate Commerce Commission, whose power to oversee railroad rates had been reduced by court decisions.

In the 1890s, "finance capitalists" like J. P. Morgan challenged the dominance of the "industrial capitalists" of the 1870s and 1880s who had built large enterprises in steel, oil, and railroads. These financiers launched a wave of corporate mergers that began in 1895 and continued for a decade. An average of three hundred companies a year were merged with larger firms. Twelve hundred mergers occurred in 1899. Some states, such as New Jersey and Delaware, made it easier for firms to locate holding companies there. In New York a market for industrial stocks enabled bankers to raise capital. In the case of *U.S. v. E. C. Knight* (1895), the Supreme Court ruled that the Sherman Antitrust Act applied only to monopolies of interstate commerce and not to those solely of manufacturing. This decision made it more difficult to enforce the antitrust laws, and as a result, the government took little action against any of the mergers that occurred during the 1890s.

When the economy began to recover in 1897, the public's attention turned to the growth of large businesses and trusts. Consumers believed that it was unfair for a few men or businesses to dominate a single industry or control the price of commodities.

The depression of the 1890s aroused fear and apprehension across the country. The accepted values of earlier generations came under scrutiny as people struggled to make sense of their situation. Writers questioned whether the government should simply promote economic expansion and then allow fate to decide who prospered and who did not. For the first time, many argued that government should regulate the economy in the interest of social justice. In discussion groups in Wisconsin, at rallies of farmers in Texas, and on the streets of New York and Boston, citizens wondered whether their governments at all levels should do more to promote the general welfare.

A growing number of social thinkers suggested that additional government action was necessary. In 1894, Henry Demarest Lloyd published *Wealth Against Commonwealth,* a book that detailed what he believed the Standard Oil Company had done to monopolize the oil industry and corrupt the nation. Unimpressed with the idea of merely regulating the large corporations, Lloyd called for public ownership of many transportation and manufacturing firms.

> ### DOING HISTORY ONLINE
>
> #### Fixing the Blame for Hard Times
>
> Read Eugene Debs's address to the American Railway Union and Henry Demarest Lloyd's article, "Wealth Against the Commonwealth." Where do Debs and Lloyd lay the blame for the state of the nation's economy during the depression?
>
> www.cengage.com/ history/ayers/ ampassages4e

The economic hard times strengthened the resolve of the Social Gospel movement. The church, said Walter Rauschenbusch in 1893, should be the "appointed instrument for the further realization of that new society in the world about it." Other young people of the day echoed similar themes. Ray Stannard Baker had reported on Coxey's army for his newspaper. He told his editor that "the national blood is out of order."

The Reform Campaigns

In states such as Illinois and New York, bands of women joined together as consumers pushed for better working conditions in factories and fair treatment of employees in department stores. Social workers and charity operatives decided that the plight of the poor was not simply the fault of those in need. Better government and more enlightened policies could uplift the downtrodden. As one settlement worker put it, "I never go into a tenement without longing for a better city government."

Women's participation in the process of change was significant. Julia Lathrop and Florence Kelley worked in Illinois improving state charitable institutions and inspecting factories. Mary Church Terrell led the National Association of Colored Women, founded in 1896, in making the women's clubs in the black community a more effective force for change. **Ida Wells-Barnett** rallied African American women against lynching from her first editorials in 1892 and then joined Terrell in further campaigns against these illegal executions. The suffrage movement and the women's clubs among white middle-class women and their black counterparts slowly established the basis for additional reforms after 1900.

A leading voice for a new role for women was **Charlotte Perkins Gilman**, whose major work, *Women and Economics,* was published in 1898. Gilman advocated that women seek economic independence. The home, she argued, was a primitive institution that should be transformed through modern industrial practices lest it impede "the blessed currents of progress that lead and lift us all." Housework should be professionalized and homes transformed into domestic factories; women would then be free to pursue their own destinies, which could include social reform. Gilman's work influenced a generation of women reformers as well as future feminists.

The renewed emphasis on reform during the 1890s also affected the long-standing campaign to control the sale and use of alcoholic beverages. In 1895, the Reverend H. H. Russell established the Anti-Saloon League in Oberlin, Ohio. Its organization relied on a network of local Protestant churches throughout the nation. Unlike previous efforts to pass antiliquor laws, the league focused on a single issue: the regulation of saloons. It became a model for the kind of lobbying that would characterize reform campaigns during the first two decades of the twentieth century.

The prohibition campaigns in the South brought black women and white women together in a brief alliance to cripple what they both regarded as an important social evil. In some parts of North Carolina, for example, white women organized chapters of the Woman's Christian Temperance Union (WCTU) among black women. When white volunteers did not visit black neighborhoods, black women took over and set up their own organizations. Even as racial barriers rose in the South, black women and white women continued to work together to curb drinking until the end of the 1890s, when deteriorating race relations made it politically impossible to do so.

To counter the drive for prohibition, brewers and liquor producers created lobbying groups to match the Anti-Saloon League and the persistent militance of the WCTU. Brewing associations appeared in battleground states such as Texas to coordinate strategies in local option elections and to get "wet" voters to the polls. Antiprohibition sentiment flourished among Irish Americans and German Americans in the cities and towns of the Northeast and Midwest. The struggles over liquor often pitted the countryside dwellers against urban residents who wanted liquor to remain available.

Reform in the Cities and States

As the depression revealed social problems and political injustices, efforts at reform were made in the cities. In Detroit, Hazen Pingree had been elected mayor in 1889. During the depression, he decided that city government ought to do more than just stand by while the poor suffered. He constructed his own political machine to pursue social justice through lower utility rates and expanded government services. That brought him into conflict with the streetcar companies and utilities that dominated Detroit politics. In Chicago, a British editor, William T. Stead, visited the city for the Columbian Exposition in 1893. What he saw in the slums led him to write *If Christ Came to Chicago* in 1894. Stead contended that the city needed a spiritual and political revival. He singled out the power of the street railway operator, Charles T. Yerkes, as particularly oppressive because of the high rates and poor service his companies provided. Stead's attack led to the formation of the Chicago Civic Federation, which sought to control gambling, clean up the slums, and limit the power of men like Yerkes. Similar reform groups sprang up in Wisconsin's cities to restrain corporations that provided vital municipal services at an exorbitant cost to taxpayers.

By the mid-1890s, these examples of urban reform sparked the creation of groups to address national urban problems. The National Municipal League appeared in 1894; in the same year the First National Conference for Good City Government took place. Over the next several years reformers diagnosed the ills of American cities and recommended solutions. Out of these debates came the ideas that would flourish during the Progressive era a decade later.

As the depression worsened, citizens looked to their state governments for answers and instead found political and social problems that rivaled the plight of the cities. In Wisconsin a Republican politician, Robert M. La Follette, built a political following by attacking the entrenched organization within his own party. He called for primary elections to choose candidates for office rather than leave the decision to the politicians and their rigged meetings. After his triumphs in the **Spanish-American War**, **Theodore Roosevelt** was elected governor of New York, where he displayed his vigorous leadership skills in publicizing the activities of large corporations and using state power to conserve natural resources.

The work of reform governors and their supporters in the states led to greater reliance on experts and nonpartisan commissions in making decisions about public policy. Railroad commissions, public utility commissions, and investigative boards to oversee key industries were formed. By the end of the decade, however, observers believed that meaningful reform would come only when the federal government shaped national legislation to curb railroads and trusts engaged in interstate commerce.

Substantive Due Process and Its Critics

Among the most powerful obstacles to reform were judges who upheld business interests. The doctrine of substantive due process gave state and federal judges a way to block legislative attempts to regulate economic behavior. According to this doctrine, the due process clause of the Fourteenth Amendment did not apply only to the issue of whether the procedure used to pass a law had been fair. Judges might consider how the substance of the law affected life, liberty, and property. They could then decide whether the law was so inherently unfair that it would be unjust even if the procedures for implementing the statute were unbiased. This approach gave the judiciary the right to decide whether a law regulating business enterprise was fair to the corporation being supervised.

Judges also interpreted federal laws in ways that limited efforts to curb corporate power. The same year (1895) that the Court issued the *E. C. Knight* decision, which constrained the scope of the Sherman Antitrust Act, it also ruled in *Pollock v. Farmers' Loan and Trust Co.* that the income tax provisions of the Wilson-Gorman Tariff were unconstitutional because they were a direct tax that the Constitution prohibited. In labor cases, courts imposed injunctions to bar unions from boycotts and strikes.

A few jurists and lawyers, however, had doubts about this philosophy of favoring corporations. In Massachusetts, Oliver Wendell Holmes, Jr., had published *The Common Law* in 1881. Holmes contended that "the life of the law has not been logic; it has been experience." By this he meant that judges should not base their rulings on abstract premises and theories such as freedom of contract, but should consider the rational basis of a law in judging whether it was constitutional or not.

Conservative himself, Holmes was ready to defer to the popular will in legislative matters. If the Constitution did not prohibit a state from building a slaughterhouse or regulating an industry, his response was, "God-dammit, let them build it." In Nebraska, Roscoe Pound was evolving a similar reality-based approach to legal thinking that became known as sociological jurisprudence. Louis D. Brandeis of Massachusetts was gaining a reputation as the "People's Lawyer" who believed that the legal system should serve small businesses and consumers as well as large corporations.

Pragmatism and Realism   The philosopher William James of Harvard University developed an explanation for what political and legal reformers were trying to do. He called it *pragmatism*. James believed that truth is more than an abstract concept. Truth must demonstrate its value in the real world. "What in short is the truth's cash value in experiential terms?" James asked. To James, pragmatism meant "looking away from first things, principles, 'categories,' supposed necessities; and of looking towards last things, fruits, consequences, facts." James divided the world into tough-minded people, who based their actions on facts and pragmatic truths, and tender-minded people, who were swayed by abstractions. His philosophy emphasized self-reliance and gritty reality. It appealed to a generation of reformers who sought practical solutions to the problems they saw in their communities and the nation as a whole.

Another spokesman for reform was a University of Chicago teacher and philosopher named John Dewey. In his major work, *The School and Society* (1899), Dewey contended that schools should undertake the task of preparing students to live in a complex, industrial world. The public school must do more than transmit academic knowledge for its own sake. As an institution, it should be a means of instilling democratic values and usable skills. Education, Dewey wrote, "is the fundamental method of social progress and reform."

During the 1890s, writers and artists turned to the world around them. They preached the doctrine of realism and tried to capture the complexity of a natural world in which science, technology, and capitalism were challenging older values. William Dean Howells, a novelist, examined the impact of capitalism on workers and urban dwellers in New York City in *A Hazard of New Fortunes* (1890). During the depression, Howell's novels and essays were sharply critical of the new industrial system.

Stephen Crane depicted the ways in which the city exploited and destroyed a young woman in *Maggie: A Girl of the Streets* (1893).

Two noteworthy practitioners of literary naturalism were Frank Norris and Theodore Dreiser. Norris wrote about California railroads in *The Octopus* (1901) and about the wheat market in Chicago in *The Pit* (1903). In his Darwinian world, humanity was trapped in the impersonal grip of soulless corporations. In *Sister Carrie* (1900), Dreiser described how a small-town girl went to work in Chicago and was consumed by its temptations. These novels reached a large audience, and their depiction of characters caught in an amoral universe intensified the sentiment for reform.

By the 1890s, then, the currents that would come together as the Progressive movement of the 1900–1920 period were forming. Urban reformers, believers in the Social Gospel, politically active women, candidates angry with the established powers in their state's dominant party—all of these groups shared a pervasive discontent with the state of society. The volatile domestic and international events of the 1890s would prepare the ground for a generation of reform.

African Americans and Segregation   In addition to experiencing the economic deprivations affecting the country as a whole during the 1890s, African Americans confronted the ever-tightening grip of segregation in the South. Although blacks had made great strides in building viable communities and economic institutions since Reconstruction, white southerners disliked their advancement. Instead, whites endeavored to return African Americans to a subordinate position. The courts proved unreceptive to the pleas of blacks for equal treatment under the law.

A spokesman for blacks emerged in **Booker T. Washington**, who argued that African Americans should emphasize hard work and personal development rather

Booker T. Washington.   *Booker T. Washington was a captivating speaker who preached that African Americans must demonstrate to whites their capacity to achieve progress.*

than rebelling against their condition. Whites applauded Washington's philosophy as the proper course for blacks to take. Meanwhile, race riots and lynchings expressed the bigotry and intolerance that characterized most whites in these years.

Washington believed that African Americans must demonstrate their worthiness for citizenship through their own achievements. In 1895, he reached a national audience when he spoke at the Cotton States and International Exposition in Atlanta. His **Atlanta Compromise** told white Americans what they wanted to hear about black citizens. Accordingly, what Washington said made him the leading black figure in the United States for a generation. "In all the things that are purely social, we can be separate as the fingers," Washington proclaimed, "yet one as the hand in all things essential to mutual progress." To his fellow blacks he said, "It is at the bottom of life we must begin" to create an economic base through hard work: "Cast down your bucket where you are" and be "patient, law-abiding and unresentful." Any "agitation of questions of social equality" would be "the extremest folly."

Washington's white audience gave him an enthusiastic response, and white philanthropists funded his school, the Tuskegee Institute, generously. Behind the scenes, Washington dominated the political lives of blacks and he secretly funded court challenges to segregation. In public, however, he came to symbolize an accommodation with the existing racial system.

The Supreme Court put its stamp of approval on segregation as a legal doctrine a year later. Homer A. Plessy's appeal of the Louisiana court's decision upholding segregation of railroad cars had made its way to the Supreme Court. The court heard oral arguments in April 1896 and rendered its judgment five weeks later. By a vote of seven to one in the case of ***Plessy v. Ferguson***, the justices upheld the Louisiana law and, by implication, the principle of segregation. Writing for the majority, Justice Henry Billings Brown said that the Fourteenth Amendment "could not have been intended to abolish distinctions based on color, or to enforce social, as distinguished from political equality, or a commingling of the two races upon terms unsatisfactory to either." He rejected the argument that "the enforced separation of the races stamps the colored race with a badge of inferiority." In a dissenting opinion, Justice John Marshall Harlan responded that "our Constitution is color-blind, and neither knows nor tolerates classes among citizens." This ruling determined the legal situation of African Americans for more than half a century.

As the political rights of blacks diminished, white attacks on them increased. During the North Carolina elections of 1898, race was a key issue that led to a Democratic victory over the Populists, Republicans, and their African American allies. Once whites had won, they turned on the black-dominated local government in Wilmington, North Carolina. Several hundred whites attacked areas where blacks lived in December 1898, killing eleven people and driving residents from their homes. Lynchings in the South continued at a rate of more than one hundred per year.

Although black Americans faced daunting obstacles in the 1890s, they made substantial progress toward improved living conditions in ways that showed that they were more than simply the victims of white oppression. They founded colleges in the South, created self-help institutions in black churches, and developed pockets of well-off citizens in cities such as Washington, Boston, Baltimore, and Philadelphia. In the South black women pursued social reform in states with impressive determination.

The National Association of Colored Women sought to become, in the words of its president, Mary Church Terrell, "partners in the great firm of progress and reform." African American resistance to segregation shaped the 1890s as much as did the white drive to subjugate blacks in the South and the North.

FOREIGN POLICY CHALLENGES

Amid the political turmoil of the second Cleveland administration, foreign affairs pressed for attention. The nation stood on the verge of becoming a world power, and national leaders debated how to respond to increasing competition with powerful international rivals and the upsurge of nationalism among colonial peoples.

The first pressing issue was Hawaii. Grover Cleveland was not convinced that the revolution that had occurred in 1893 represented the will of the Hawaiian people. Holding the treaty of annexation back from the Senate, he dispatched a special commission to investigate conditions. Believing that the native population backed Queen Liliuokalani, he refused to send the treaty to the Senate and asked for restoration of the native government. The revolutionary government declined to yield power, however, and in 1894 the administration granted it diplomatic recognition.

Another foreign policy crisis occurred in 1894 when a dispute arose between Great Britain and Venezuela over the precise boundary line that separated Venezuela and British Guiana. The Cleveland administration concluded that the controversy was also a test of the Monroe Doctrine, which barred European influence in the Western Hemisphere. In 1895, the new secretary of state, Richard Olney, sent a diplomatic note to London that asserted that the United States was "practically sovereign on this continent, and its fiat is law upon the subjects to which it confines its interposition." The British responded slowly, and when their answer finally arrived, it rejected the arguments of the Cleveland administration. Newspapers talked of a possible war. The president asked Congress for the power to name a commission to decide the boundary dispute and enforce its decision. The British found themselves in a difficult position. In South Africa they were encountering problems that would eventually lead to the Boer War (1899–1902), and they had few European friends when it came to foreign policy. Accordingly they decided to arbitrate their quarrel with Venezuela through a joint Anglo-American-Venezuelan commission to resolve the dispute, and the crisis passed.

The Cuban Crisis, 1895–1896 The most dangerous foreign policy issue that confronted Cleveland stemmed from the revolution that Cubans launched against Spanish rule in February 1895. The Wilson-Gorman Tariff had increased import duties on Cuban sugar, damaging the island's economy, which depended on sugar. Rebels took to the battlefield in February 1895 seeking to oust the Spanish. Unable to defeat the rebels in direct combat, the Spanish drove the civilian population into cities and fortified areas. The "reconcentration" camps where these refugees were housed were disease-ridden and overcrowded. The architect of this harsh policy was General Valeriano Weyler, nicknamed "The Butcher" for his cruelty to the captive Cubans.

The American public took a close interest in the Cuban situation. Investments in the island, totaling about $50 million, were threatened by the conflict. Religious denominations saw the brutality and famine of the rebellion as cause for concern and perhaps direct intervention. Sensational newspapers, known as the **yellow press** because one of them carried a popular comic strip about "The Yellow Kid," printed numerous stories about atrocities in Cuba. **William Randolph Hearst**, publisher of the *New York Morning Journal,* and Joseph Pulitzer of the *New York World* were the most sensational practitioners of this kind of journalism. The Cubans also established an office in New York from which their "junta" dispensed propaganda to a receptive audience. Concern about Cuba was a significant element in the nation's foreign policy during the mid-1890s.

President Cleveland tried to enforce the neutrality laws that limited shipments of arms to Cuba. He did not recognize the Cubans as belligerents, and he informed the Spanish that they might count on the good offices of the United States in negotiating an end to the fighting. This position suited Spain, which followed a policy of procrastination to quell the revolt before the United States intervened. By the end of his administration, the president was pressing Spain to make concessions to the Cubans, but he never challenged Spain's right to exercise its sovereignty over the island. Congress prodded the president to take more aggressive action, but he refused. As a result, when the end of the Cleveland administration approached early in 1897, his policy toward Cuba had little support in the United States.

The Battle of the Standards: 1896   The foreign policy problems of the Cleveland administration stemmed in part from the weakened political situation after the 1894 elections. Preferring to work alone and wary of threats on his life, Cleveland increased the number of guards around the White House and rarely ventured out to meet his fellow citizens.

The reserves of gold were still shrinking, despite the repeal of the Sherman Silver Purchase Act in 1893. To bolster the reserves and bring in gold, the White House sold government bonds. The sale that took place in February 1895 was handled by New York banker J. P. Morgan, who made a nice profit from the transaction. Eventually there were four bond sales, which supplied needed currency for the Treasury but also further alienated Democratic advocates of inflation and free silver.

As the 1896 election approached, the Republicans, after their sweep of the 1894 election, wanted a candidate who could cash in on their likely victory. The front-runner was William McKinley of Ohio, a veteran of the Civil War, former member of Congress, and governor of Ohio from 1892 to 1896. A popular speaker, he was identified with the protective tariff. With the aid of his close friend Marcus A. Hanna, an industrialist from Ohio, McKinley became the favorite for the Republican nomination. His campaign slogan proclaimed him as "The Advance Agent of Prosperity."

McKinley won on the first ballot at the Republican National Convention in St. Louis in June 1896. The only difficult issue was gold and silver. Eastern Republicans wanted the party to endorse the gold standard. The key plank contained that language, but it also conciliated pro-silver Republicans with a promise to seek wider international use of silver. The Republicans expected to wage a tariff-centered campaign against a nominee saddled with the unpopularity of Cleveland.

Bryan and the Cross of Gold   The Democratic convention took an unexpected turn. After the elections of 1894, the free silver wing of the party dominated the South and West. By 1896, an articulate spokesman for the silver cause would appeal to many Democrats. Among the leading candidates for the nomination, however, none possessed the required excitement and devotion to silver. A young politician from Nebraska named William Jennings Bryan saw himself as the "logic of the situation." During 1895 and early 1896, he urged leaders to think of him as a possible second choice should the convention deadlock. By the time the Democratic National Convention opened in Chicago in July 1896, there was a good deal of latent support for Bryan among the delegates.

Bryan's chance came during the debate over whether the party platform should endorse silver. He arranged to be the final speaker on behalf of free silver. Bryan had a clear, musical voice that could be heard across the convention hall. The speech he gave, entitled the "Cross of Gold," became a classic moment in American political oratory. He asked the delegates whether the party would stand "upon the side of the idle holders of capital, or upon the side of the struggling masses?" His answer was simple. To those who wanted a gold standard, the Democrats would say: "You shall not press down upon the brow of labor this crown of thorns, you shall not crucify mankind upon a cross of gold." His audience was enthralled.

The next day the convention nominated Bryan for president on a free silver platform. A wave of support for Bryan swept the country, and the Republicans found their careful plans for the campaign suddenly at risk. Since the Democrats could not raise much in the way of campaign funds, Bryan decided to take his message to the voters. He prepared for an extensive nationwide campaign tour to speak on behalf of the common man, a rural nation, and the older agrarian virtues.

Bryan's nomination left the Populist Party in disarray. The Populists had delayed their national convention until after the two major parties had named their candidates, and they now faced a dilemma: if they failed to select Bryan as their candidate, they would be accused of depriving silver of any chance of victory; yet if they went along with Bryan's nomination, there would be no need for their party. With some reluctance, they ultimately decided to name Bryan as the presidential nominee and picked Thomas E. Watson as their vice-presidential choice. The Democrats refused to accept this awkward compromise; all that Watson's selection did was to confuse voters about which Bryan slate of elections they should pick.

Bryan, thirty-six-years-old, pursued the presidency with youthful energy. He traveled 18,000 miles and gave more than six hundred speeches; his audiences, estimated at a total of 3 million people, turned out to see "The Boy Orator of the Platte River." To counter Bryan, the Republicans raised between $3.5 million and $4 million from fearful corporations. The Democrats charged that the Republicans and their business allies were coercing workers to vote for McKinley. Most industrial workers voted Republican because they feared the inflationary effects of free silver. Mark Hanna, who managed McKinley's campaign, used the party's substantial war chest to distribute several hundred million pamphlets to the voters. Republican speakers took to the campaign trail; party newspapers poured out information about the merits of the tariff and the gold standard.

The key to the Republican campaign was McKinley, who stayed home in Canton, Ohio, and let the voters come to him. As the weeks passed, more than 750,000 people stood in McKinley's yard to hear his speeches about the dangers of free silver. "If the free coinage of silver means a fifty-three cent dollar, then it is not an honest dollar,"

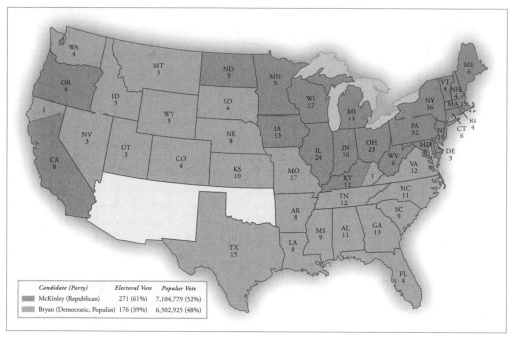

MAP 19.1 The Election of 1896.

The election of 1896 was a climax to the upheavals of the mid-1890s. Note the sectional alignment that divided the nation between the agrarian South and West, which supported William Jennings Bryan, and the industrialized East and Midwest, where William McKinley and the Republicans were strong.

McKinley said. By mid-September, the tide turned against Bryan, and there were signs that the Republicans would win in November.

The result was the most decisive outcome since the 1872 presidential contest. McKinley had a margin of 600,000 popular votes and won 271 electoral votes to 176 for Bryan. Bryan ran well in the South, the Plains states, and the Far West. McKinley dominated in the Northeast, the mid-Atlantic states, and the Midwest. Despite his appeals to the labor vote, Bryan ran poorly in the cities. Free silver might lead to inflation, an idea that had little appeal to workers on fixed incomes. McKinley's argument that the tariff would restore prosperity also took hold in the more industrialized areas of the country.

The 1896 results confirmed the outcome of the 1894 election. The Republicans had established themselves as the nation's majority party. The South remained solidly Democratic; the industrial North was Republican. The older issue of how much the government ought to promote economic expansion was giving way to the new problem of whether the government should regulate the economy so as to relieve injustices and imbalances in the way that society worked. Bryan and the Populists had suggested that government should play a larger regulatory role. The voters had chosen instead to accept the economic nationalism of the Republicans as embodied in the tariff and the gold standard.

THE WAR WITH SPAIN AND OVERSEAS EXPANSION, 1898–1899

When Grover Cleveland departed in March 1897, he left a weakened presidency. McKinley improved relations with the press, which Cleveland had ignored; he traveled extensively to promote his policies, and he used experts and commissions to strengthen the operation of the national government.

In domestic policy, McKinley persuaded Congress to enact the Dingley Tariff of 1897, which raised customs rates. He also sought, without success, to convince European nations to agree to wider use of silver through an international agreement. As a result, when the Republicans gained control of both houses of Congress after the 1898 election, the Gold Standard Act of 1900 reaffirmed that gold, and only gold, was the basis of the nation's currency. Gold discoveries in South Africa and Alaska inflated the currency by making more gold available. Returning prosperity relieved the agricultural tensions of the decade.

Spain and Cuba   McKinley faced a growing crisis in Cuba. He wanted Spain to withdraw from Cuba if its forces could not suppress the rebellion quickly. Any solution must be acceptable to the Cuban rebels. Since they would accept nothing less than the end of Spanish rule, there was little basis for a negotiated

William McKinley: The First Modern President. *William McKinley's use of his power as commander in chief, his improved relations with the press, and his mastery of Congress helped make him the first modern president.*

(Library of Congress)

settlement. During 1897, however, McKinley tried to persuade Spain to agree to a diplomatic solution. Yet, no Spanish government could stay in power that agreed to leave Cuba without a fight.

At first it appeared that the president's policy might work. In the fall of 1897 the Spanish government moved toward granting the Cubans some control over their internal affairs. Foreign policy, however, was to remain in Spanish hands. The practice of moving Cubans into reconcentration camps was abandoned. However, the situation worsened during the early months of 1898 as the rebellion persisted. On January 12, 1898, pro-Spanish elements in Cuba rioted against the autonomy program. To monitor the situation, the White House sent a warship to Havana. The battleship U.S.S. *Maine* arrived there on January 25. Spain was pleased that the United States was resuming visits that had earlier been discontinued, but the diplomatic problem continued. On February 1, Spain insisted that its sovereignty over Cuba must be preserved even if it meant resisting foreign intervention.

On February 9, 1898, newspapers in the United States published a letter written by the Spanish minister to the United States, Enrique Dupuy de Lôme, to a friend; Cuban rebels had intercepted the letter. In it, de Lôme described McKinley as "weak and a bidder for the admiration of the crowd." These insulting remarks led to de Lôme's recall and resignation. The minister's other statements revealed, however, that Spain was playing for time in its negotiations with Washington in hopes that the Americans might change their mind or that pressure from European countries would lead them to do so.

The Sinking of the Maine: February 15, 1898 On February 15, the U.S.S. *Maine* exploded in Havana Harbor, killing 260 officers and men. The cause of the blast, according to modern research, was spontaneous combustion in a coal bunker. In 1898, however, the public believed that Spain had either caused an external explosion or had failed to prevent it. McKinley established a naval board of inquiry to probe the disaster. The deadline for its report was mid-March 1898. While he waited, McKinley made military preparations and explored unsuccessfully the idea of buying Cuba from Spain.

On March 17, a Republican senator who had visited Cuba, Redfield Proctor of Vermont, told the Senate that conditions in the country were horrible. The speech swayed the public toward intervention in the war. Two days later, McKinley learned that the naval board had concluded, on the basis of the science of the time and the physical evidence, that an external explosion had caused the destruction of the *Maine*. When the report went to Congress, pressure on the president to intervene in Cuba mounted.

McKinley pushed Spain to agree to an armistice in the fighting that still raged in Cuba or to permit American mediation that would end in Cuban independence. However, the Spanish were opposed to independence for Cuba in any form. Still, McKinley was able to hold off Congress until Spain had another chance to consider its options. When a negative answer arrived from Spain on March 31, 1898, McKinley prepared to put the issue before Congress.

There was one last flurry of diplomatic activity. On April 9, Spain agreed, at the urging of its European friends, to suspend hostilities in Cuba. It was not an armistice, which would have meant formal recognition of the Cuban cause. The Spanish military commander in Cuba would determine how long the cessation of the fighting would last. There was no agreement on Cuban independence from Madrid. Thus, the Spanish had not yielded on the key demands of the United States.

McKinley sent his message to Congress on April 11, requesting presidential authority to end the fighting in Cuba through armed force if necessary. At the end of his message, the president mentioned that Spain had proposed to suspend hostilities, but he gave the idea little significance. Spain's acceptance of a suspension of hostilities did not represent a surrender to the demands of the United States. The diplomatic impasse between the two countries was unbroken.

Over the following week, Congress debated the president's request. To show that the United States had no selfish motives, the lawmakers adopted an amendment offered by Senator Henry M. Teller, a Colorado Democrat. The Teller Amendment stated that the United States did not intend to control Cuba or annex it. Yet Congress also declined to extend official recognition to the Cuban rebels to preserve freedom of action for the United States. For McKinley, the important result was a resolution authorizing him to act; this was passed on April 19, and the president signed it the following day. Spain immediately broke diplomatic relations with the United States; it declared war on April 24. Congress replied that a state of war had existed between the United States and Spain since April 21.

The Spanish–American War, 1898

The war between the United States and Spain occurred because both sides believed their cause was just. McKinley had pursued a diplomatic solution until it became clear that Spain would not agree to a negotiated settlement that would end its reign over Cuba. In the end, Spain preferred to lose Cuba on the battlefield rather than at the bargaining table.

The war began with a stunning naval victory. On May 1, 1898, Commodore George Dewey and the Asiatic naval squadron defeated the Spanish navy at Manila Bay in the Philippine Islands. The U.S. unit was in the waters of the Philippines because of war plans that had been developed in 1895 and updated as relations with Spain worsened. The goal was to hit the Spanish hard in the Philippines and thus pressure them to surrender Cuba. The triumph at Manila Bay made Dewey a national hero, but it confronted the president with new opportunities and problems in foreign policy.

To follow up on Dewey's success, the McKinley administration dispatched troops to the Philippines. The president wanted the option of acquiring the islands as a result of the war. He thought that a port in the Philippines might be enough, but he intended to maintain flexibility.

With the Philippines at stake, the Hawaiian Islands gained in strategic value. A treaty of annexation had been worked out during 1897, but the pact stalled in Congress. After the war began, the president and congressional leaders turned to a strategy of annexation by means of a legislative resolution that needed only a simple majority from Congress. Through presidential persuasion, the required votes for the resolution were obtained in July 1898, and Hawaii was annexed.

Meanwhile, U.S. policy toward the Philippines and their possible acquisition became a source of tension with Filipino leaders, notably Emilio Aguinaldo, who wanted independence. The administration instructed army and navy officers not to have any formal dealings with the Filipinos. The buildup of military strength continued, and

"Smoked Yankees" and the War with Spain

The Spanish–American War produced a surge of patriotic volunteers and enthusiasm, but the main brunt of the fighting fell to the small regular army that was ready for immediate action in Cuba. As a result, black troops played a significant, if now largely forgotten, role in the successful campaign to oust the Spanish from the Caribbean island. The picture records some of the black soldiers after a Cuban battle. American society credited white men such as Theodore Roosevelt and his Rough Riders with these victories, and African Americans were deleted from the historical record and their contributions to victory expunged. In the wake of imperialism, the nation became even more segregated. Placing a picture of black soldiers in this textbook is designed to emphasize that the American past is more complicated than the way it is often presented.

(The Granger Collection, New York)

the ambitions of the Filipinos were seen as an obstacle to American policy rather than as a legitimate expression of nationalism.

The main combat of the war took place in Cuba. The U.S. Army numbered 25,000 men, so the nation turned to volunteers. In the first wave of national enthusiasm, there were 1 million volunteers, far more than the army could handle. Eventually about 280,000 men saw active duty. Soldiers complained about shortages of ammunition and supplies and the poor quality of the food rations. The army experimented with canned beef, creating an inedible meal and a postwar controversy over the product. In the regular army, an important part of the force that fought the Spanish were the four regiments composed of African American soldiers, or the "Smoked Yankees," as the Spanish troops described them. Seasoned fighters against Indians, the black soldiers were ordered to move south and prepare to invade Cuba. On their way through the southern states, they encountered scorn, segregation, and threats.

The African American soldiers did not endure such treatment quietly. When they boarded segregated railroad cars, they sat wherever they pleased. If they saw signs that barred their presence, they took down the signs. Violence broke out between white troops and black troops in Florida, and men were killed and wounded in the exchanges of gunfire. Seeing all this, one soldier asked poignantly: "Is America any better than Spain?" Once the black regiments reached Cuba, their military contribution was significant. They earned numerous decorations for bravery, and five of them won the Congressional Medal of Honor.

Despite the bravery of the "Smoked Yankees," the Spanish–American War worsened the plight of African Americans. The ideology of imperialism that allowed whites to dominate Cubans and Filipinos also supported racial segregation in the South. McKinley's efforts to reconcile the whites of the North and South brought harmony at the expense of black Americans.

In late June, the U.S. Navy found the Spanish fleet in the harbor of Santiago de Cuba, and army detachments went ashore to engage the Spanish forces holding the city. On July 1, the army, commanded by General William R. Shafter, defeated the Spanish defenders at the Battle of San Juan Hill. Theodore Roosevelt and his volunteer regiment of Rough Riders took part in the battle. Roosevelt became a national hero on his way to the presidency, but the Rough Riders might have been defeated had it not been for the timely support they received from their black comrades.

On July 3, the navy destroyed the Spanish fleet when it tried to escape from Santiago Harbor. Negotiations for an armistice began. McKinley insisted that Spain relinquish Cuba and Puerto Rico and that the fate of the Philippines be discussed at the peace conference. Spain did not like these terms, but it had no choice but to accept them, which it did on August 12, 1898.

John Hay, soon to be McKinley's secretary of state, called it "a splendid little war." Victory had been achieved at a low cost in terms of combat deaths: 281 officers and men. However, malaria, yellow fever, and other diseases killed more than 2,500 others. A public outcry arose after the war about the condition of the army, and McKinley named a commission to investigate the leadership of the War Department and the way the war had been conducted. The commission's report led to reforms such as general staff shakeups and improved organization that strengthened the future fighting ability of the army. The war also strengthened the power of the presidency because of McKinley's expansive use of his role as commander in chief of the armed forces.

The peace conference with Spain was held in Paris. McKinley appointed a commission that included several senators who would ultimately vote on any treaty that they negotiated. The president was aware that Germany and Japan had an interest in the Philippines, and he intended for the United States to retain control of the islands rather than allow them to become the possession of the Germans or Japanese. American officials did not believe that the Filipinos could determine their own destiny; the islands would fall into the hands of a European power. Within the United States, opponents of a policy of expansion, calling themselves anti-imperialists, aroused public sentiment against the administration.

To build support for his foreign policy, McKinley made effective use of the powers of his office. During October, he toured the Midwest. Ordinarily presidents did not

(Library of Congress)

White House War Room.   *President McKinley directed the war with Spain from the White House. The "War Room" kept track of the movement of ships and men.*

take part in congressional election campaigns. However, though billed as a nonpartisan event, McKinley's tour helped Republican candidates in the 1898 congressional contest. It also gave the president an opportunity to state the case for a more expansive foreign policy. In a typical address, he told an Iowa audience that "we do not want to shirk a single responsibility that has been put upon us by the results of the war."

The Philippines was the most divisive issue at the peace conference. On October 25, 1898, the president's commissioners asked him for instructions. On October 28, he responded that he could see "but one plain path of duty, the acceptance of the archipelago." In the peace treaty signed on December 10, 1898, the United States gained the Philippines, Guam, and Puerto Rico. Spain gave up its claims to Cuba and received a payment of $20 million for what it had lost. The United States obtained legal sovereignty over the Philippines but would soon face challenges from the island's inhabitants. Opponents of imperialism tried to block acceptance of the treaty in the Senate. To win the necessary two-thirds vote, McKinley employed the power of the presidency in new and creative ways. In December, he went south to woo Democrats. He used patronage to persuade wavering senators and exerted pressure on the state legislatures, which elected senators. Believing that the Democrats would benefit if the issue was settled before the 1900 elections, William Jennings Bryan endorsed the treaty. That action divided the opposition at a key point. The Senate approved the Treaty of Paris on February 6, 1899, by a vote of 57 to 27, one more than the necessary two-thirds.

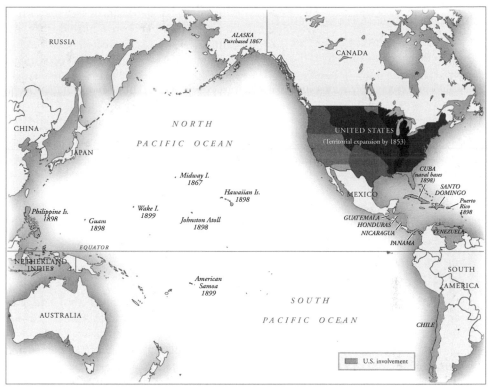

MAP 19.2 U.S. Overseas Expansion, 1867–1899.

For four decades after the Civil War the United States expanded, slowly at first and then with a rush in the 1890s. This map shows what the nation acquired and when it did so. It also indicates where the United States was involved with Latin American nations and in some instances the great European powers.

As the Senate voted, the nation knew that fighting had erupted in the Philippines between U.S. soldiers and the Filipino troops that Aguinaldo commanded. Relations between the two sides had worsened during December 1898 as it became clear that the United States did not intend to leave the islands. Although the president asserted that his nation had "no imperial designs" on the Philippines, anti-imperialists and the Filipinos were not convinced. For Aguinaldo and his supporters, it seemed that they had ousted the Spanish only to replace them with another imperial master, the United States.

During 1899, the U.S. Army defeated the Filipinos in conventional battles, and the administration sent out a commission to work out a civil government under U.S. sovereignty. However, the Filipinos turned to guerrilla tactics. Their soldiers hit selected targets and then blended back into the population. Faced with this new threat, the U.S. Army responded by killing some Filipino prisoners and torturing others to gain information. The army's purpose was not genocidal, but many soldiers and their officers violated the rules of war and government policy in brutal and inhumane ways. With revelations of these misdeeds, enthusiasm for further imperialistic adventures ebbed.

DOING HISTORY ONLINE

President McKinley Learns of the Philippine Insurrection

Based on your reading of the text and the excerpt from the diary of George B. Cortelyou, answer the following questions. Why had the Filipinos attacked the U.S. forces near Manila? What was the peace treaty to which President McKinley referred? When did the Senate approve the treaty and what part might these events have played in senatorial deliberations?

 www.cengage.com/history/ayers/ampassages4e

During the last two years of McKinley's first term, imperialism became a heated issue. An Anti-Imperialist League, created in November 1898, united the opposition against McKinley's foreign policy. Critics of expansionism charged that overseas possessions would damage the nation's democratic institutions. Some people used racist arguments to block the acquisition of lands where nonwhite populations lived. Others evoked moral concern about imperialism. A number of prominent Americans, including steelmaker Andrew Carnegie, House Speaker Thomas B. Reed, and the longtime reformer Carl Schurz, lent their voices to the anti-imperialist campaign.

Advocates of empire adapted the ideas of Social Darwinism and Anglo-Saxon supremacy to justify the acquisition of other countries. Theodore Roosevelt, Henry Cabot Lodge of Massachusetts, and their allies contended that the nation could not escape the world responsibilities that the war with Spain had brought. By 1900, Americans believed that the gains of empire should be retained and protected but not increased. The examination of the nation's goals and purposes contributed to the mood of reform and renewal that emerged at the turn of the century.

Other foreign policy issues emerged from the outcome of the war. The Teller Amendment blocked the annexation of Cuba, but the McKinley administration wanted to ensure that the island did not become a target of European intervention, most notably from Germany. A military government ran Cuba during 1899. As a civil government developed, the United States insisted on guarantees that Cuba would retain political and military ties with the country that had liberated it. The result of this process was the Platt Amendment of March 1901, which barred an independent Cuba from allying itself with another foreign power. The United States had the right to intervene to preserve stability and gained a naval base at Guantanamo in Cuba.

The acquisition of the Philippines heightened interest about the fate of China, where European powers sought to establish economic and political spheres of influence. Worried about the nation's trade with China and concerned to preserve that country's territorial integrity, the administration, through Secretary of State John Hay, issued in September 1899 what became known as the Open Door Notes. The messages asked European countries active in China to preserve trading privileges and other economic rights that gave the United States a chance to compete for markets there. The replies of the powers were noncommittal, but Hay announced in March 1900 that the other nations had accepted the U.S. position in principle. The Open Door Notes became a significant assertion of U.S. interest in China.

When antiforeign sentiment in China, especially against western missionaries, led to the Boxer Rebellion during the summer of 1900, an important test of the Open Door principle occurred. Secret associations known as the Righteous and Harmonious

Fists (hence Boxers) launched a series of attacks on westerners in China. Europeans who had taken refuge in Peking were rescued by an international force that included twenty-five hundred U.S. soldiers. President McKinley justified sending the troops into a country with which the United States was at peace as a legitimate use of his war power under the Constitution. Secretary Hay reaffirmed the U.S. commitment to the Open Door policy in a diplomatic circular to the powers that he issued on July 3, 1900. McKinley withdrew the troops rapidly after their rescue mission had been completed.

The Spanish–American War and the expansion of American commitments in the Pacific demonstrated the need for a waterway that would link the two oceans and enable the navy to conduct its growing worldwide responsibilities. The McKinley administration laid the groundwork for a canal across Central America when it renegotiated the Clayton-Bulwer Treaty of 1850 with Great Britain. That document prohibited both nations from exercising exclusive control over any future waterway. After extended negotiations with the British, a treaty was worked out in the summer of 1901.

THE 1900 ELECTION AND A NEW CENTURY

The signs seemed to point to McKinley's reelection. Prosperity had returned, and the conflict in the Philippines was being won. McKinley's vice president, Garret A. Hobart, died in November 1899. Theodore Roosevelt, the popular young governor of New York, became McKinley's running mate. To oppose McKinley, the Democrats again turned to William Jennings Bryan. Bryan made another vigorous campaign, attacking imperialism as a threat to the nation's institutions, and accusing the Republicans of being the tools of the trusts and the business community. The Democratic candidate also renewed his pleas for a free silver policy. The anti-imperialists did not trust Bryan because of his free silver views and because he had recommended approving the Treaty of Paris in 1899, but they preferred him to McKinley.

Because in that era incumbent presidents did not make speeches, McKinley allowed Theodore Roosevelt to do most of the campaigning. Bryan made so many criticisms that his campaign lacked a clear theme. McKinley increased his margin in the popular vote over what he had achieved four years earlier. The result in the electoral college was 292 for McKinley and 155 for Bryan.

McKinley gained further victories in foreign policy. Congress set up a civilian government for the Philippines when the insurrection had ended, which occurred shortly after the capture of Emilio Aguinaldo in March 1901. On May 27, 1901, the Supreme Court ruled in the *Insular Cases* that the Philippines and Puerto Rico were properly possessions of the United States but that their inhabitants had not become citizens of the country. The decision upheld McKinley's colonial policy and provided legal justification for imperialism.

Meanwhile, the president was turning his attention to two major domestic issues: the growth of big business and the issue of high tariffs. By 1901, McKinley was persuaded that some action was necessary to enforce the Sherman Antitrust Act of 1890. He had also modified his earlier support for the protective tariff and now believed that reciprocal trade treaties should be adopted that would lower duties on products entering the United States. Treaties that had been negotiated with other countries such as France and Argentina had not yet received Senate action. McKinley intended to prod the Senate to take them up at the next session, which would convene in December 1901.

As he had done to secure ratification of the treaty with Spain in 1898, he also planned to travel extensively during 1901 to raise the trade issue with the American people. That decision would bring him to Buffalo, New York, in September 1901 to make a speech about freer trade and reciprocal tariff treaties.

As the new century began, McKinley had revived the power of the presidency after the decades of congressional supremacy that followed the Civil War. He had expanded the size of the president's staff, begun to involve the press in the coverage of White House affairs, and personalized the office through his travels. In many respects, McKinley was the first modern president.

The nation saw the arrival of the twentieth century on December 31, 1900, with a mixture of confidence about what the United States had accomplished and apprehension about what the future held. The depression of the 1890s remained a vivid memory for most citizens, even with the return of prosperity after 1897. The shift in attitudes toward government and its role that had occurred during the hard times led many people to advocate programs of social reform.

With the end of the century in sight, and the experience of the war with Spain still vivid, there was a flurry of public debate about the direction of the nation. A National Social and Political Conference took place in Buffalo, New York, in 1899 that brought together Eugene V. Debs, Henry Demarest Lloyd, Samuel Gompers, and Hazen Pingree, among others. The delegates called for "equality of economic opportunity and political power." Their goals required a more activist government than had been common in the nineteenth century.

In 1900, other future advocates of change appeared. After a long political battle in Wisconsin against the leaders of the Republican Party, Robert M. La Follette finally won election as governor. His agenda looked toward changes in the way the state government functioned and more regulation of the state's railroads. Other governors in the Midwest were advancing similar concerns about the power of corporations. The pressure for reform in the states was mounting.

A devastating hurricane in Galveston, Texas, in September 1900 caused significant damage to that Texas city. Political leaders there turned to a new form of government to deal with rebuilding. Commissioners of fire, water, police, and other services replaced the older style of ward leaders. The idea of having officials tied to the workings of city departments rather than representing geographic areas would attract increasing attention after the turn of the new century.

In the academic world, a biting analysis of how Americans used the wealth that they had acquired during the process of industrialization was published. Thorstein Veblen was a professor at the University of Chicago when he wrote *The Theory of the Leisure Class* (1899). In this book he analyzed the ways in which citizens displayed their social status. Although his writings offered more diagnosis than solutions, Veblen was a provocative critic of capitalist institutions and practices at a time when his fellow citizens worried about their impact on national life.

At both ends of the economic spectrum, Americans looked to organizations to address social ills. In 1900, Italian and Jewish immigrants who worked in the clothing business in New York City united to form the International Ladies Garment Workers Union (ILGWU). The membership, predominantly female, used the ILGWU to spread the ideas of unionism to other immigrant workers and to discuss alternatives to the existing system. That would be a hallmark of progressive change. Also in 1900, the more well-to-do business leaders of the day created the National Civic Federation. Made up of representatives from organized labor, the business community, and the public, the federation sought to promote harmony between labor and capital. The issue of labor relations would become significant in the decade ahead.

CONCLUSION

The balance sheet on the achievements of the late nineteenth century was a mixed one. Optimists cited the nation's burgeoning productive capacity, the totals of steel produced and railroad tracks laid, and the impressive per capita wealth of U.S. citizens. Most of the population could read, and there were more than two thousand newspapers available covering a staggering variety of subjects. There was an equally dazzling array of magazines on the newsstands with growing numbers of illustrations of national and world events. Advertisers spent $90 million in 1900 to tempt readers to try their products.

The United States was devoted to education. There were 1,700 libraries in the nation that held more than 5,000 volumes in their collections. Almost 240,000 students attended 977 colleges and universities at the turn of the century, or a little more than 1 percent of Americans between the ages of fifteen and twenty-five. Eighty percent of these institutions admitted women to their programs, although men received four times as many degrees as women did. Below the college level, 16 million children went to public schools. The educated, literate work force that resulted was the envy of competing economies in western Europe.

On the negative side were the social problems that the nation confronted. An estimated 10 million Americans, or about 13 percent of the population, lived below the poverty line. A visitor to the United States said that half its population was "ill-housed, ill-fed, and ill-clothed." Although the often-anticipated social revolution of the 1890s had not occurred, influential leaders such as Theodore Roosevelt worried about the potential for violence and upheaval if moderate reforms did not take place. In addition, the nation faced the problems of segregation, the future of Native Americans, and the place of immigrants in American society. Americans turned to these questions with an energy that made the twenty years between 1900 and 1920 famous as an age of political reform and government regulation.

CHAPTER REVIEW, 1893–1901

- The country faced the challenge of a serious economic depression.
- Labor unrest and social dislocation proliferated.
- The Democratic Party split into competing factions and lost national power.
- The Populists failed to become a viable third party.
- The Republicans gained a national majority in the 1894 and 1896 elections.
- William McKinley revitalized the presidency.
- Tension with Spain over Cuba led to war in 1898.
- The United States acquired an overseas empire by 1900.

◀━ⅠⅠⅠ *Looking Back*

The events that dominated American life in the 1890s stemmed from problems that had been accumulating since the Civil War. This chapter discussed the political and economic systems as they confronted the effects of a major depression and the country's increasing presence on the world stage.

1. What were the options open to the government when an economic collapse occurred?
2. Why did President Grover Cleveland face the political blame for problems with business and finance that he inherited?
3. Why did the Republicans become the big winners in the politics of the 1890s?
4. How did American social commentators react to the panic of 1893 and its effects on the nation?
5. Should the United States have intervened in Cuba in 1898?

Looking Ahead ⅠⅠⅠ━▶

In the next chapter, Theodore Roosevelt takes the stage as one of the leaders of the Progressive movement of political reform. In what ways does this chapter foreshadow these developments?

1. How did attitudes change during the 1890s about the proper role of government?
2. What problems did imperialism leave to be solved after 1900?
3. How did Americans see themselves and their country as the twentieth century opened?
4. What was the position of the United States in the world in 1900?

Go to the American Passages website at www.cengage.com/history/ayers/ampassages4e for additional review materials.

20

Theodore Roosevelt and Progressive Reform, 1901–1909

On September 6, 1901, President William McKinley was shot in Buffalo, New York. A week later he died, and Vice President Theodore Roosevelt became president. The eight years that followed were part of the Progressive era. Responding to the social and economic impact of industrialism, Americans endeavored to curb the power of large businesses, improve conditions for consumers, and reform the political parties.

Citizens argued about whether government should regulate the economy and whether the power to do so should be local or national. The political party itself became controversial. Its critics contended that intense partisanship had corrupted government and weakened democracy; power therefore should be shifted toward the individual voter. Other advocates of change clamored for more voter participation by broadening the ability of citizens to propose laws, choose candidates, and overturn judicial decisions. Thus, during a time of prosperity at home and relative peace abroad, the United States experienced political ferment. The issues that Americans debated at the turn of the twentieth century would dominate the agenda of domestic policy for decades.

THE UNITED STATES AT THE START OF THE TWENTIETH CENTURY

In 1901, Americans balanced confidence about the future in a new century with worries about the direction of their society. The population stood at 76 million, up from 63 million ten years earlier.

Immigrants accelerated the population growth, with new arrivals coming at a prodigious rate: 488,000 in 1900, 688,000 in 1902, and more than 1.1 million in 1906. Like their late-nineteenth-century predecessors, the majority of these newcomers settled in the nation's growing cities.

CHAPTER TIMELINE

1901	United States Steel created • William McKinley inaugurated for second term • Theodore Roosevelt becomes president
1902	Antitrust suit filed against Northern Securities Company • Anthracite coal strike • Teddy Bear toy introduced • McClure's Magazine starts muckraking journalism
1903	Elkins Act outlaws railroad rebates • Alaska Boundary dispute settled • Panama Canal Zone acquired • Wright brothers make first successful powered flight • National Women's Trade Union League founded
1904	Roosevelt elected president; declines to run in 1908 • Roosevelt Corollary to Monroe Doctrine
1905	Niagara Movement to improve conditions for African Americans • Portsmouth Conference settles Russo-Japanese War
1906	Algeciras Conference in Morocco • President Roosevelt attacks muckrakers • Passage of Hepburn Act (railroads), Pure Food and Drugs Act, Meat Inspection Amendment
1907	Panic of 1907 • Self-contained electric clothes washer developed
1908	Henry Ford introduces Model T automobile • Election of William Howard Taft • Supreme Court upholds Oregon law limiting hours of work for women in Muller v. Oregon
1909	Taft inaugurated as president • National Association for the Advancement of Colored People (NAACP) founded • Roosevelt leaves for Africa

Most Americans still lived in rural areas or small towns with fewer than twenty-five hundred residents. Not for another twenty years would the population become more urban than rural. As the cities expanded, tensions between rural and urban areas mounted.

A Longer Life Span   People lived longer in 1900, a trend that accelerated throughout the twentieth century. Life expectancy for white men rose from forty-seven years in 1901 to almost fifty-four in 1920. For white women, the increase was from around fifty-one years in 1901 to almost fifty-five in 1920. Life expectancy for members of minority groups rose from thirty-four years in 1901 to just over forty-five in 1920.

The population was young in 1900. The median age was twenty-three; it rose to just over twenty-five by 1920. The death rate for the entire population was 17 per thousand in 1900. It fell to 13 per thousand by 1920. For infants in the Progressive era, the prospects were less encouraging. In 1915, the first year for which there are accurate numbers, almost 61 deaths were recorded for every 10,000 births; the infant mortality rate reached more than 68 deaths per 10,000 births in 1921. For nonwhite babies the

This icon will direct you to interactive activities and study materials on the American Passages website: www.cengage.com/history/ayers/ampassages4e

Immigration in the Progressive Era

Tables of historical numbers can seem dull and uninformative. In the case of these figures on immigration into the United States during the first decade of the twentieth century, the totals show a dramatic transformation in the population whose effects shaped politics, economics, and culture. The newcomers arrived primarily from southern and eastern Europe, as well as Asia, and soon put their stamp on cities as diverse as New York and San Francisco.

Vibrant immigrant communities arose. The surge produced a backlash in efforts to restrict immigration that ultimately led to cutbacks by the 1920s. But the impact of these new Americans proved lasting in the way people lived and their expectations about the role of government. A more varied, turbulent, and interesting United States came out of the process that these numbers represent.

TABLE 20.1 Immigration into the United States, 1901–1909	
1901	487,918
1902	687,743
1903	857,046
1904	812,870
1905	1,026,499
1906	1,100,735
1907	1,285,349
1908	782,870
1909	751,786

Source: *The Statistical History of the United States* (1965), p. 56.

picture was even worse: almost 106 deaths per 10,000 live births in 1915. Some positive changes occurred, however. More and more mothers gave birth in hospitals rather than at home. Improved medical techniques and the antiseptic setting of the hospitals helped reduce the incidence of infant mortality.

Children at Work The problem of child labor persisted. In 1900, more than 1.75 million children between the ages of ten and fifteen worked in the labor force. In the South, children worked in cotton mills. Conditions were so bad that reformers called the mills and their communities "the poorest place in the world for training citizens of a democracy." Abolishing child labor was a major goal of reform campaigns after 1900.

Changes in the Family In families whose children did not have to work, child rearing became more organized and systematic. Kindergartens gained popularity as a way to prepare children for school. There were five thousand in 1900 and nearly nine thousand twenty years later. The federal government held conferences on child rearing and issued booklets about infant care. Improved methods of contraception led to smaller families. In 1900, the average mother had 3.6 children, compared with 7.0 children in 1800. Attention shifted to rearing fewer children more successfully.

The status of women also changed after 1900. Some younger women delayed marriage to attend college. Yet opportunities for women to enter law, medicine, or higher education remained limited. In 1920, fewer than 1.5 percent of all attorneys were women. In 1910, there were only nine thousand women doctors, about 6 percent of all physicians. Restrictive policies on admissions to medical schools and barriers to staff positions at hospitals posed obstacles to women who sought to become doctors. Nursing and social work were more accessible to women, but women still faced condescension from men.

Women at Work   Women in factories, mills, and garment sweatshops saw little improvement in their condition as the new century began. Their workday was ten hours long, and six- and seven-day weeks were common. Men received higher pay than women; labor unions regarded women as competitors for jobs held by men. Women set up their own unions, such as the **National Women's Trade Union League**, established in 1903. They also formed the backbone of the International Ladies Garment Workers Union, which led strikes in New York City in 1910 and 1911.

Social trends altered the status of women. Their clothes became less confining and cumbersome. The full skirt was still the fashion in 1900, but soon after, petticoats and corsets disappeared. Women showed their ankles and arms in public. Some more daring young women, such as Alice Roosevelt, the daughter of President Theodore Roosevelt, smoked in public, and others used cosmetics openly. In dance halls and restaurants, young people danced the turkey trot and the bunny hug to the rhythms of ragtime.

These changes affected the institution of marriage. Fewer marriage ceremonies used the word *obey*. Women asked more of their husbands, including companionship and sexual pleasure. Government programs were instituted to encourage family

Women in a Cotton Mill.

In the South, women labored in the cotton mills of the region for long hours with low pay. Although the Supreme Court upheld the principle that a state could limit the hours that women worked in Muller v. Oregon, the decision had little effect in North Carolina where these women worked in the spinning room of the White Oak Cotton Mill in Greensboro.

(Library of Congress)

togetherness. In 1914, prodded by advocates of the traditional home (and the florist industry), Congress designated Mother's Day a national holiday.

Divorce was easier and more common than in the past. About four marriages out of every thousand ended in divorce in 1900, but in the ensuing years, the divorce rate increased three times faster than the rate of population growth. There were 56,000 divorces in 1900 and 100,000 in 1914. Slowly, attitudes toward broken marriages changed; divorces no longer brought social disgrace.

A Nation of
Consumers

In 1900, 76 million people in the United States owned 21 million horses. Some forecasters said that the automobile would replace the horse, but in 1903, only a little more than 11,000 cars were sold. During the next decade, however, Henry Ford of Dearborn, Michigan, created the Model T. Ford's goal was to use mass production techniques to sell an automobile in large numbers. By 1908, the Model T was ready, priced at about $850. Sales increased as Ford reduced the car's price. In 1908, 5,986 Model T's were sold; by 1912, the total was 78,611. The mass-produced automobile, which promoted mobility and greater access to places to shop, was a key element in the evolution of the consumer society during the Progressive era.

Standardized food products also gained popular acceptance. Asa Candler's Coca-Cola became more available when the parent company licensed bottling plants throughout the nation. There were 241 bottlers by 1905, 493 by 1910, and 1,095 a decade later. In 1912, Procter & Gamble introduced Crisco, a vegetable shortening, to sell its cottonseed oil. The company used marketing campaigns in popular periodicals, held "Crisco teas" at which clubwomen could try out their own recipes, and created cooking schools to spread awareness. By 1915, its advertising proclaimed that "Crisco is rapidly taking the place of butter and lard for cooking." Other famous brands, such as Kellogg's Corn Flakes, Uneeda Biscuit, and Kodak cameras, relied on mass advertising, billboards, and mail flyers to instill popular desire for these new and convenient consumer goods.

Advertising now permeated American culture. Newspapers and magazines gave lower rates to advertisers that bought entire pages. Billboards appealed to the new motoring public but outraged garden club members when they obscured scenic views. Advertising agencies shaped the content of product information. Men were urged to buy Gillette razors because "You Ought to Shave Every Morning." Toothbrush ads proclaimed that Americans should "keep their teeth and mouths clean." The Kodak camera was an essential part of the Christmas season as "your family historian."

To master these markets, advertisers surveyed potential purchasers. Agencies tracked customers through reports from salespeople, mail surveys, and questionnaires printed in magazines. Coca-Cola, for example, increased its advertising budget annually and in 1913 distributed 5 million metal Coca-Cola signs across the country.

Sears, Roebuck and Company led in consumer marketing. Founded in 1893, the company was the brainchild of Richard Warren Sears, who believed in low prices. Beginning with mail-order watches, Sears expanded to general merchandise that was sold in an annual catalogue. He cut prices for desirable products such as sewing machines and cream separators and soon produced record sales. Sears spent lavishly on advertising—over $1.5 million in 1902—and promised low prices, guarantees of all products and parts, and the opportunity to order merchandise without prepaying.

"Send No Money" was the Sears slogan. Volume sales at low prices built a market for Sears; the company sent out more than 1.5 million catalogues in 1902. For rural Americans, the Sears catalogue became their link to the expanding world of consumer products.

A British visitor said that the standard of American life had reached a height "hitherto unrealized in a civilized society." National income stood at $17 billion; the average American's annual per capita income of $227 was the highest in the world. Innovations promised further abundance to a prosperous population.

Despite these positive trends, citizens worried about the nation's future. The growth of big business, the spread of labor organizations, the corruption in politics, the decline of the individual in a bureaucratic society—all these trends prompted fear that older values and attitudes were under assault. For white Americans, however, the persistent issue of race and the treatment of minorities did not attract much attention during this period of reform.

THEODORE ROOSEVELT AND THE MODERN PRESIDENCY

The president during these dramatic changes in American life was Theodore Roosevelt who, at age forty-two, also was the youngest chief executive to that time. During the war with Spain, his volunteer regiment of Rough Riders had charged up Kettle Hill in Cuba against the fortified Spanish position. A national hero, he was elected governor of New York in 1898. When he criticized corporate abuses, Republican leaders exiled him to the vice presidency.

Roosevelt pledged to continue McKinley's policies. Yet the youthful and vigorous Roosevelt made news in fresh ways. He changed the official name of the president's residency to the White House and infused energy into its daily routine. His large family—he had six children—captivated the nation. The president's oldest daughter, Alice Lee, made her debut at the White House, kept a pet snake, and drove around Washington in fast cars. "I can be President of the United States or I can control Alice," Roosevelt told friends who asked him to rein in his daughter. "I cannot possibly do both."

Roosevelt decided that the president should be the "steward" of the general welfare. As long as the Constitution did not prohibit executive action, the president should stretch the limits of what was possible. Roosevelt built on McKinley's example but went further, causing the public to see the president as the focus of national authority. Roosevelt reformed college football to make it less violent, pursued simplified spelling of English (*thru* instead of *through*, for example), and waged loud, frequent quarrels with his political enemies. Like a preacher in church, he called the White House his "bully pulpit," using it to give sermons to the country about morality and duty.

The new president wanted to limit the power of big business to avoid more radical reforms from the Democrats or Socialists. He also believed that the nation had to protect its natural resources. Until he bolted in 1912, the Republican Party seemed the best means to implement Roosevelt's goals. As a result, he left the protective tariff alone and cooperated with the conservative Republicans who dominated Congress during his first term. Later, when he exerted stronger presidential power, his relations with Capitol Hill worsened.

Theodore Roosevelt was the first celebrity president. The spread of newspapers and the emergence of motion pictures enabled Americans to follow the nation's leader

Reading page

491-571

with greater attention than ever before. Roosevelt dramatized government. By using the power of his office in this way, he strengthened the presidency for future challenges.

Roosevelt and Big Business

On February 19, 1902, the Department of Justice announced a suit under the Sherman Antitrust Act (1890) against the Northern Securities Company. That firm, created in late 1901, merged major railroads in the Northwest, including the Great Northern, the Northern Pacific, and the Chicago, Burlington, and Quincy Company. The key leaders of this large company were James J. Hill and E. H. Harriman; their financing came from **J. P. Morgan**, the investment banker who had restructured the railroad network in the 1890s, and the steel companies that he represented. The merger sought to reduce destructive competition among warring railroads and make railroad rates more stable. Opposition to the merger came from states across which the company would operate, most notably in Minnesota. Farmers and business operators in the Upper Midwest feared that a giant railroad would raise rates and limit their profits, so they urged their governors to file suit against the new company in federal court. The creation of the Northern Securities Company was part of the trend toward larger economic units that had begun during the 1890s. A highly publicized case was the United States Steel Company, which had been formed in 1901. The steel merger symbolized bigness in business in the same way that the railroad combine did.

The Carnegie Steel Company dominated the industry, producing finished steel products at a lower unit cost than its rivals. For J. P. Morgan and the steel companies that he represented, Carnegie's power might make competing firms go bankrupt. The logical answer, Morgan concluded, was to buy out Carnegie and create a steel company to control the entire industry. Morgan sent an aide to see Carnegie. "If Andy wants to sell, I'll buy," said Morgan. "Go and find his price."

In a penciled note the next day, Carnegie said that the price was $480 million. Morgan paused and responded: "I accept this price." The merger was made public on March 3, 1901. Carnegie Steel joined other firms financed by Morgan such as Federal Steel and the National Tube Company. The half-billion dollars that Carnegie received for his holding was a staggering sum in an era when there was no federal income tax, no capital gains tax, and low inflation. In modern terms, Carnegie probably would have received more than $50 billion.

The new company, United States Steel, was capitalized at $1.4 billion. It had 168,000 employees and controlled 60 percent of the steel industry's productive capacity. Smaller steel companies would have to compete with the vertical integration Carnegie had achieved with the company that Morgan had acquired. Workers in steel now faced a powerful employer that could fix wage levels in any way it chose. "We have billion dollar combines," said one editor, "maneuvered by a handful of men who have never been in a plant and think of a factory as just another chip in a gigantic financial poker game."

Controlling the Trusts

Theodore Roosevelt saw business consolidation as inevitable, but he believed the federal government should not just stand by. The large corporations should not be destroyed. Firms that were socially beneficial should be encouraged; those that misbehaved should be regulated. A good firm, in Roosevelt's mind, paid its workers a decent wage, avoided labor strife, did not overcharge the public, and did not corrupt the political process. Bad corporations failed to follow these precepts. At first Roosevelt thought that publicizing the activities of corporations would be enough regulation. He soon concluded that he must establish the power of the federal government to intervene in the economy. The Northern Securities Company was unpopular, so the president acted.

Roosevelt argued that "trusts are creatures of the State, and the State not only has the right to control them, but it is in duty bound to control them wherever the need of such control is shown." In 1904, the Supreme Court ruled 5 to 4 that the Northern Securities Company violated the Sherman Act. The case reestablished the power of the national government to use the Sherman Act, which had been called into question in the 1895 case of *U.S. v. E. C. Knight.* The American public saw Roosevelt as a **trustbuster,** willing to curb the power of big business. Having established that the government was supreme, the president used trust-busting sparingly against "bad" trusts and sought to assist "good" trusts with policies that rewarded their positive behavior.

The Square Deal in the Coal Strike

Roosevelt intervened to end a strike in the coal industry during the autumn of 1902. The 140,000 members of the United Mine Workers walked off their jobs in the anthracite (hard coal) fields of Pennsylvania. The miners asked for a pay hike and for the railroads and coal operators to recognize their union. Having lost an earlier strike in 1900, management wanted to break the strike and the union. As the walkout stretched into autumn, fears grew of winter coal shortages. If voters were cold in November, the Republicans faced political losses in the 1902 congressional elections. Yet neither side in the walkout seemed prepared to yield.

As the crisis worsened, Roosevelt brought both sides to the White House in early October. Throughout a day of talks, Roosevelt urged the workers and owners to settle. The union's president, John Mitchell, agreed to arbitration, but the mine owners refused. Roosevelt responded that he might bring in the army to mine coal. Facing that threat, J. P. Morgan and Elihu Root worked out a deal in which a presidential commission was set up to look into the strike. The panel granted the miners a 10 percent pay increase, but the union was not recognized. Unlike Grover Cleveland during the Pullman strike, Roosevelt wielded presidential power to treat capital and labor on an equal basis. Roosevelt called his approach the **Square Deal.**

Roosevelt's record limited Republican losses in the congressional elections and virtually ensured the president's nomination as the Republican candidate in 1904. During the session of Congress that began in December 1902, Roosevelt endorsed the Elkins Act, which would outlaw the rebates railroads gave to favored customers. Roosevelt also called for a law to create the Department of Commerce. One of the agencies of this new department would be the Bureau of Corporations, which would publicize corporate records and indicate which businesses were behaving in the public interest. Roosevelt now had the weapons he sought to distinguish between businesses that he deemed socially good and those that behaved improperly.

Race Relations in the Roosevelt Era

On October 16, 1901, Booker T. Washington, the director of the Tuskegee Institute in Alabama and the leading African

American in the United States, dined with the president and his family at the White House. Since he had emerged as a leading advocate for African Americans during the 1890s, Washington had built a political machine among black Republicans in the South. He came to the White House to discuss the new president's nominations for patronage positions in the South. Southerners were not happy to learn that a black man had eaten with the president. A Tennessee newspaper editor called the occasion "the most damnable outrage that has ever been perpetrated by any citizen of the United States."

Roosevelt saw himself as a friend of African Americans, but his conduct indicated how much he shared white prejudices. Needing the votes of black delegates to win the Republican nomination, he defended appointing African Americans to post offices and customs houses and resisted efforts to oust them. But Roosevelt did not challenge the system of racial segregation that now permeated the nation.

For the majority of African Americans in the first decade of the twentieth century, bigotry and violence were everywhere. "Don't monkey with white supremacy," warned a Mississippi newspaper, "it is loaded with determination, gun-powder and dynamite." Eight days after Washington and Roosevelt sat down to dinner, a black man named **"Bill" Morris**, who had allegedly robbed and raped a white woman, was burned at the stake in Balltown, Louisiana. Apprehended by a mob, Morris was "taken back to the scene of his crime." No trial occurred. Instead, "pine knots and pine straw were heaped about him and over this kerosene was poured and the whole set on fire." Between seventy and eighty black citizens of the United States were lynched during each year of Roosevelt's presidency. Lynching had declined from its post–Civil War peak in the 1890s, but it still meant that these horrific events were taking place on the average of every fourth day each year.

Economic and social conditions had worsened since the passage of segregation laws in the South during the 1880s and 1890s. Nine million southern blacks lived in rural poverty. Black wage workers received much less per day and per hour than their white counterparts in the same trade. Other black men were industrial or agricultural peasants, virtual slaves who received only food and a place to sleep for their labor. "The white man is the boss," said one man. "You got to talk to him like he is the boss." Facilities for the races were supposed to be "separate but equal," but this was rarely the case in practice.

Blacks no longer voted in significant numbers. The white primary, in which only white voters could participate in the affairs of the Democratic Party, meant that African Americans had no voice in choosing those who would govern them. Blacks retained some role in the Republican Party because their votes helped to choose the delegates to the national convention. For the most part, though, the bitter comment of one African American politician summed up the situation: "The Negro's status in Southern politics is dark as Hell and smells like cheese."

When he dined with Theodore Roosevelt, Booker T. Washington demonstrated to other African Americans that he could deliver the support of white politicians. Yet to keep the president's friendship and obtain money from wealthy whites, Washington accepted segregation and the racist system it represented. Washington was doing what he had proposed in his speech in Atlanta in 1895. By the time Roosevelt became president, more militant blacks charged that Washington's methods had failed.

Their leader was **W. E. B. Du Bois**, who had received a doctoral degree from Harvard and taught sociology at Atlanta University, a black institution. After initially supporting Washington's policy, Du Bois decided that blacks had to confront

W. E. B. Du Bois and the Struggle for African American Rights

The early twentieth century saw the worst era of racial segregation in the United States as the position of African Americans and other minorities steadily deteriorated North and South.

A few voices were raised in protest. Of these, the black thinker who had the greatest impact was W. E. B. Du Bois. Pictured here in the conservative clothes and look of middle-class respectability that he favored in this phase of his life, Du Bois waged a vigorous assault on the public ideas of Booker T. Washington and the notion that blacks should accept their subordinate position. Du Bois led the intellectual efforts to repudiate the

(© Bettmann/CORBIS)

doctrine that African Americans were inferior to whites in brains and talent. His organizing efforts, especially the Niagara Conference of 1905, laid the basis for what would become the National Association for the Advancement of Colored People. His presence in this text attests to the rich history of African Americans that is too often omitted from popular accounts of the nation's development.

segregation. In *The Souls of Black Folk* (1903), he criticized Washington's method as having "practically accepted the alleged inferiority of the Negro."

In June 1905, Du Bois led a delegation of twenty-nine blacks to Niagara Falls, New York, where they called for political and social rights. The meeting denied that "the Negro American assents to inferiority, is submissive under oppression and apologetic before insult." The Niagara Conference aroused Booker T. Washington's intense opposition, but it laid the basis for more lasting protests about the worsening situation of African Americans.

Du Bois, Washington, and blacks in general found Roosevelt less sympathetic to their needs in his second term when he was no longer a candidate for the presidency. He made no public statement about a 1906 race riot in Atlanta, Georgia, in which four blacks were killed and many others injured. Later that year, he discharged without a hearing or trial the African American soldiers who were falsely accused by white residents eager to have the troops transferred of shooting up Brownsville, Texas.

As Roosevelt abandoned African Americans, their plight worsened. In August 1908, whites rioted against blacks in Springfield, Illinois, where two blacks were lynched. A tide of bigotry swept the nation that neither the president nor the national government did anything to quell. In 1909, prominent white reformers such as Oswald Garrison Villard (grandson of the abolitionist William Lloyd Garrison), Mary White Ovington, and William E. Walling met with Du Bois, Ida Wells-Barnett, and other African Americans to form the **National Association for the Advancement of Colored People (NAACP)**. They sought an end to segregation, voting rights for blacks, and equal education for all children. In an era of ethnocentrism and a struggle among the Western powers to subdue colonial peoples, this appeal for racial justice went unheeded.

Roosevelt and Foreign Policy

In foreign policy, Theodore Roosevelt wanted to complete the work left over from the Spanish–American War. Because the world was increasingly dangerous, military preparedness was a key goal. "There is a homely adage which runs," the president said, "Speak softly and carry a big stick; you will go far." By 1905, he had added ten battleships to the navy and improved its gunnery. Although Roosevelt loved to perform on the world stage without having to consult Congress, he always remembered the public's caution about overseas adventures. Except in the Philippines, where guerrilla war sputtered on, Roosevelt sent no American forces into armed combat during his presidency.

He did act in places where the power of the United States was dominant. In 1902, Germany and Great Britain used their navies to collect debts that Venezuela owed them; Roosevelt sent the U.S. Navy into the region to limit foreign involvement. Similar problems with the Dominican Republic and its debts two years later led him to pronounce the **Roosevelt Corollary** as a natural extension of the Monroe Doctrine. In his annual message in 1904, he said that "chronic wrongdoing or impotence" of Latin American nations in paying their debts might lead the United States "to the exercise of an international police power." After 1905, the United States controlled customs revenues and tax services in the Dominican Republic.

Roosevelt sought better relations with Great Britain to secure a canal across Central America. A possible flashpoint between Washington and London was the boundary between Alaska and Canada. Discoveries of gold in the Yukon region in 1896 attracted rival miners and speculators and raised the possibility of violence between Canadians and Americans. Roosevelt used an Anglo-American Commission to settle the dispute in favor of the United States.

The United States had long wanted a canal built across Central America. During the Spanish–American War, the battleship U.S.S. *Oregon* had taken two months to go from San Francisco Bay around South America to join the navy near Cuba. In the Hay-Pauncefote Treaty (1901), Great Britain gave up its rights to a canal. Congress then decided in 1902 that the best route lay across Panama. A treaty with Colombia, of which Panama was then a part, provided for a six-mile-wide canal zone, running forty miles from ocean shore to ocean shore, under American control, with a ninety-nine-year lease. The Colombians would receive a $10 million payment and $250,000

Theodore Roosevelt and the Strong Presidency

One of the key features of politics and government during the twentieth century was the rise of the strong presidency. In the process, presidents became political celebrities. The youthful vigor of Theodore Roosevelt between 1901 and 1909, particularly his keen eye for the limelight, made him the darling of cartoonists in the nation's magazines and newspapers. In this image of the gigantic president striding the isthmus of Panama between the Atlantic and Pacific oceans to build a canal, one gets a sense of how Roosevelt's larger-than-life qualities enhanced the power of his office and fixed public attention on the occupants of the White House. The dropping of the dirt from Roosevelt's shovel on the Colombian capital of Bogotá reflects as well how popular Roosevelt's disdainful treatment of the Colombians was as he made the Canal Zone a reality in 1903–1904.

(The Granger Collection, New York)

per year in rent. The U.S. Senate ratified the pact. The Colombian Senate, however, believing that the treaty infringed on their country's sovereignty and wanting more money, balked.

Within Panama, opponents of Colombian rule, who reflected the mounting spirit of Panamanian nationalism plus a desire to profit from the projected waterway, plotted revolution. Lawyers for the New Panama Canal Company lobbied for American intervention if a rebellion broke out. The uprising occurred in November 1903 amid strong signals that Roosevelt supported the revolution. The presence of American naval vessels discouraged the Colombians from putting down the rebellion. The United States recognized the new Panamanian government, as did other European and Latin American nations.

In November 1903, discussions with the representative of Panama, a Frenchman named Philippe Bunau-Varilla, led to the Hay–Bunau-Varilla Treaty, which created a ten-mile-wide zone across Panama in exchange for a $10 million payment and $250,000 annual rent. Within the Canal Zone, the United States could act as a sovereign nation, a provision that subsequent Panamanian governments resented. Construction of the canal proceeded slowly until Roosevelt put the U.S. Army in charge. Roosevelt visited Panama himself in 1906, thus becoming the first president to leave the continental United States while in office.

Building the Panama Canal cost more than $350 million, or the equivalent of several billion dollars in modern funds. Almost six thousand workers died of disease and accidents during construction. The official opening took place on August 15, 1914. Theodore Roosevelt regarded the canal as the greatest achievement of his presidency. His infringement on Colombian sovereignty, however, left bitter feelings in Latin America.

The Election of 1904 Roosevelt's domestic and foreign policy triumphs made him the favorite in the 1904 election. The Democrats turned to Alton B. Parker, a dull, conservative New York state judge. Despite last-minute Democratic charges that big business was behind the Republican campaign, Roosevelt received more than 56 percent of the vote, compared with Parker's 38 percent. The number of Americans who voted, however, was more than 400,000 below the 1900 figure. Turnout also slipped to under 65 percent of the voters in the North, compared with nearly 72 percent four years before. On election night, Roosevelt said that the three years he had served represented his first term as president. He would not be a candidate for another term in 1908. By respecting the two-term tradition, he hoped he could then embark on a campaign of reform without being accused of personal ambition to stay in office.

In his 1904 annual message, Roosevelt asked legislators to strengthen the power of the Interstate Commerce Commission to regulate the railroads. To carry out the Square Deal, the power of the federal government should be used to make all of society more just. Sensing where public opinion was going, Roosevelt caught the spirit of change that came to be called the Progressive movement. In his second term, he put the power of the modern presidency behind the new agenda for reform.

PROGRESSIVE CAMPAIGNS TO REFORM THE NATION

Responding to the growth of cities, the problems of industrialism, and fears about the nation's future, some American citizens called for political and societal reforms. The movement, termed **progressivism**, sought to expand the power of government and make politics more democratic.

Currents of Reform Progressivism occurred during a period of prosperity in which Americans saw themselves more as consumers than producers. A sense of well-being allowed middle-class citizens to address the social and economic problems that had emerged during the depression of the 1890s. After the deflation of the late nineteenth century, rising prices aroused concern about the high cost of living. Critics of the Republican protective tariff policies charged that customs duties added to inflation. Equally strong were fears of the effects of business consolidation on the smaller companies for which so many people worked. In 1909, 1 percent of firms accounted for 45 percent of manufactured goods.

DOING HISTORY ONLINE

Tainted Food and Drugs

Which group played a more important role in safeguarding the nation's food and drug supply: progressive reformers or the Congress?

 www.cengage.com/history/ayers/ampassages4e

When Americans focused on the products they bought and used, they listened when investigative reporters said that patent medicines were unsafe. The discovery that meat-packing plants and other food processors tolerated unsanitary conditions led to federal regulation in 1906. Pure food and pure drugs were so necessary, reformers argued, that businesses would have to accept more governmental intrusion than ever.

The movement for progressive reform drew on forces that had been gathering strength for two decades. Despite their diversity of goals and approaches, shared assumptions united most people who called themselves progressives.

During the years before World War I, when Europe was at peace and society seemed to be improving, men and women believed that human nature was basically good and could be made better. Government at all levels could promote a better society, and the state had a duty to relieve the ills that were a result of industrial growth.

One answer for the problems of democracy was more democracy. Proposals for a direct primary to allow voters to choose the candidates of their political parties became popular. The selection of U.S. senators should be taken away from state legislatures and given to the people. The voters themselves should have the right to decide public issues in referenda, propose laws in initiatives, and remove or recall officials or judges whose decisions offended majority sentiment in a city or state.

Another strand of progressivism sought order and efficiency. Government had become corrupt, expensive, and clumsy. Accordingly, efforts were made to improve the structure of cities and states to make them work with more economy and less confusion. The commission form of city government did away with elected aldermen from local wards and replaced them with officials who were chosen in citywide elections and assigned to a specific department such as utilities, transit, or housing. Regulatory agencies like the Federal Trade Commission and the **Interstate Commerce Commission**, staffed with experts on the industries they supervised, would see that the marketplace operated in an orderly way without partisan influences. A strong distrust of political parties animated this style of reform.

Some reformers sought programs that emphasized social control of groups and individuals. Prohibition of the use of alcohol, restriction of immigration into the United States, and efforts to shift political power in cities away from the poor and unorganized reflected a desire to compel correct behavior or restrict democracy to native-born white Americans and the "respectable" classes. These coercive aspects of reform became less attractive to later generations.

Despite these failings, progressivism made constructive changes. The regulatory agencies, direct primaries, and other programs softened the impact of an industrial social order. The principle that government was responsible for the general welfare of the nation also became well established. Reform did not attack the preeminence of democratic capitalism, but the men and women who joined the crusades for change during the era of Theodore Roosevelt wanted to improve their country, not to revolutionize it.

The Muckrakers   A group of journalists who exposed corruption and weaknesses in American society were important progressive figures. They published their revelations in numerous monthly and weekly magazines. Selling for as little as ten cents a copy, these magazines, such as *The World's Work, The American Magazine, Cosmopolitan, Everybody's Magazine, The American Review of Reviews*, and *Arena*, gained large circulations and advertising revenues. New printing techniques made these periodicals economical and profitable. More than two thousand daily newspapers gave reporters expanding opportunities to probe for scandals and scoops.

Samuel S. McClure, publisher of *McClure's Magazine*, helped launch the popular literature of exposure. By 1902, his monthly journal had attracted a wide middle-class audience for its appealing blend of fact and fiction. McClure wanted the magazine to address major issues and decided that the rise of big business and trusts provided the "great theme" he sought. He sent one of his star reporters, **Ida Tarbell**, to look into the Standard Oil Company. With Tarbell's articles ready to run in the autumn of 1902, McClure expanded on an article that another reporter, Lincoln Steffens, had written about municipal corruption in St. Louis. That essay, "Tweed Days in St. Louis," led to a series on city government in the magazine that was published under the title "The Shame of the Cities" (1904). The January 1903 issue of *McClure's* carried articles by Tarbell and Steffens, along with an essay about the anthracite coal strike by Ray Stannard Baker.

Other magazines soon followed *McClure's*. One writer called it "government by magazine." Samuel Hopkins Adams exposed fraud in patent medicines; his series contributed to the passage of the Pure Food and Drugs Act in 1906. Ray Stannard Baker wrote about unethical railroad practices; his revelations assisted President Roosevelt in his campaign for regulation. For almost five years, the popular press echoed with disclosures of this nature.

In April 1906, Theodore Roosevelt, unhappy with press attacks on the Republican party and conservative senators, used the label "muckrakers" to refer to investigative journalists. He was comparing them to a character in John Bunyan's *Pilgrim's Progress* who spent all his time raking the muck on the floor and therefore could not see heaven above him. **Muckraking** seemed to symbolize a style of reporting that emphasized only the negative, and by 1907, popular interest in it waned. While it lasted, however, muckraking gave progressivism much of its momentum. It supported the view of many reformers that once the facts of an evil situation were revealed, the political system would move to correct them.

Women and the   Women were the crucial foot soldiers of progressive reform.
Progressive Reform   Changes in the status of middle-class women gave them more
                                   time to devote to progressive causes. The settlement house movement attracted young women who were interested in social service. The number of such houses had risen steadily since the 1890s, and by 1905, there were more than two hundred of them. Jane Addams of Hull House in Chicago remained in the forefront of the movement. Other women joined Addams to promote urban-oriented reforms. Florence Kelley guided the National Consumers League. Julia Lathrop supported child labor legislation and in 1912 became the first director of the federal

Children's Bureau. In New York, Lillian Wald used the Henry Street Settlement as a base for work to improve conditions for women and children. She also cooperated with the NAACP to pursue racial justice.

Not all settlement house workers were women, but these institutions gave female reformers a supportive environment and a foundation on which to base their role in society. Women also figured in the conservation movement. In garden clubs and women's improvement clubs, they criticized the spread of billboards, dirty streets, and neglected parks in efforts they called "municipal housekeeping." Women joined the Audubon Society, the Women's National Rivers and Harbors Congress, and the Sierra Club. They saved species of birds from extinction, fought against dams and destructive logging in the West, and campaigned for more national parks.

The Continuing Fight for Women Suffrage The lack of the right to vote frustrated women, and the campaign for woman suffrage became a central concern. Once they could participate in politics, women would promote progressive causes. Carrie Chapman Catt, president of the National American Woman Suffrage Association, said that "the enfranchisement of women will be the crowning glory of democratic government." To reach that goal, however, the movement had to overcome substantial problems. In Congress, southern Democrats opposed suffrage because it might lead to votes for African Americans. Liquor interests feared that suffrage would help the prohibitionists. Within the suffrage campaign, fund-raising problems and organizational disarray limited the effectiveness of the drive for votes.

By 1910, it was evident that the strategy of pursuing a constitutional amendment at the federal level had stalled. Suffragists turned to the states, where they organized campaigns that appealed to a majority of male voters. The result was a string of victories in western states such as Washington (1910), California (1911), Oregon (1912), Arizona (1912), Kansas (1912), Montana (1914), and Nevada (1914). Although these results were gratifying, advocates of woman suffrage looked to national solutions to produce faster change. They wanted their reform to achieve what had been accomplished elsewhere in the cities and states of the nation.

Reform in the Cities Progressive reformers made their first important impact in the nation's cities. Two Ohio mayors, Samuel "Golden Rule" Jones of Toledo (1897–1903) and Tom L. Johnson of Cleveland (1901–1909), sought to change the way their cities functioned. A wealthy businessman, Johnson lowered streetcar fares and introduced an electric lighting plan to show how rates could be kept low. Jones instituted municipal ownership of the trolley system, provided higher wages for city employees than private industry did, and founded free kindergartens for Toledo's children. Some cities, such as Milwaukee, Syracuse, and Minneapolis, elected Socialist mayors during the Progressive era. These city executives pushed for the same style of clean, efficient government that their progressive counterparts advocated, and they demonstrated that Socialist politicians could govern responsibly.

More typical of urban reform across the country were efforts to change the structure of city government itself. In September 1900, a devastating hurricane hit Galveston, Texas. As they buried their seven thousand dead and surveyed the wreckage of their city, residents decided to change their form of government. The reforms became known as the commission form of city government, or in more popular use, "The Galveston Idea."

Individual commissioners, elected from the city at large rather than from geographically based wards, conducted the affairs of the police, fire, and utility departments. In that way, the influence of local politics and ward bosses was reduced. Refined in Des Moines, Iowa, in 1908, commission government was in place in 160 cities by 1911. The shift away from ward representation also restricted the power of local interests in a nonpartisan way, according to its advocates. The new approach, however, sometimes reduced the voting impact of minority groups.

Soon the commission form gave way to the city manager idea because a single, professionally trained executive was thought to be more efficient even than a group of commissioners. Under this arrangement, the city council named a nonpartisan executive who was trained to administer the city under policies that the council specified. The plan promised efficiency, cost cutting, and reduced partisan influence. Smaller and medium-sized municipalities began instituting the city manager form around 1908.

Urban reform achieved positive results in many cities. Reduction of political influence and limits on the role of partisanship did produce better government in some instances if a lack of corruption and efficiency were the only ruling criteria. However, the consequences, even with these transformations, were not always constructive. Middle-class reformers who pursued these changes often did so at the expense of residents of poorer areas of the city, who now found it harder to get a hearing from city hall. Stressing the interest of the city as a whole did not always translate into fair treatment for the less advantaged and less powerful. Perhaps on the surface the city ran with more efficiency, but the poor got fewer parks, worse services, and less criminal justice. What "better government" meant always depended on the class, ethnic, or social perspective from which these changes were viewed.

Reform in the States

As urban reformers tried to improve their cities, they often confronted barriers within state government. The constitutions of many states barred a city government from managing its own taxes, regulating its public utilities, or supervising moral behavior. By 1900, some cities had obtained "home rule," but frustrated reformers saw state governments as obstacles to change. When progressives looked at the state level, they saw corruption and business influence that resembled those they had fought locally. Reformers charged that the political party, tied to business interests, prevented meaningful improvements.

In states, progressives favored the initiative and referendum because they limited the power of political parties to shape public policy. Allowing the people to propose laws or vote on laws that had been enacted gave less authority to established political figures and institutions. The initiative and referendum first appeared in South Dakota in 1898; other western states adopted them before 1908. By 1915, twenty-one states had some form of these progressive procedures.

The direct primary spread across most of the nation by 1916; the recall was largely confined to a small number of western states. The primary was popular because it gave the power to make nominations to the voters. The recall was more controversial. Angry conservatives charged that an election to remove a judge threatened the independence of the judiciary.

Greater emphasis on the regulatory power of state government accompanied these procedural reforms. Progressives strengthened existing state railroad commissions and created new commissions to oversee public utilities and insurance companies.

Robert M. La Follette.

Progressivism drew much of its energy from reformers on the state level. Robert M. La Follette of Wisconsin was one of the most controversial. This cartoon shows what happened to Wisconsin as "Battle Bob" tamed the corporations and created a "model state." La Follette's thick hair made him a favorite of cartoonists.

(The Granger Collection, New York)

State government attracted popular and effective leaders during the twenty years after 1900. Theodore Roosevelt was a forceful executive for New York during his one term as governor. Also in New York, Charles Evans Hughes became famous for his probe of insurance companies, which gained him the governorship in 1906. Hughes increased the state's role in regulating utilities and railroads. Woodrow Wilson, elected governor of New Jersey in 1910, limited the power of corporations in that state.

The leading symbol of state reform was **Robert M. La Follette**, a Wisconsin Republican. When Republican Party leaders opposed him after he was elected governor in 1900, he launched a crusade against them. During his two terms as governor, from 1901 to 1905, he established the direct primary, regulated Wisconsin's railroads, and levied higher taxes on corporations. He forged a close relationship between the state government and faculty members at the University of Wisconsin who advised him about policy. This reliance on academic experts was called the "Wisconsin Idea."

By 1905, progressivism was moving on to the national stage. The issues that reformers faced in the states and cities now seemed to require action by the federal government. Corporations were interstate in character; only Washington could regulate them. To solve the problems of political parties, the Constitution had to be changed. To create a more moral society, progressives contended, the national government had to grant women the vote, regulate the consumption of alcohol, and limit immigration into the United States.

With growth came problems in defining what it meant to be a progressive and what aims to pursue. Where should the balance be struck between the goal of a more democratic society and that of greater efficiency? Efficiency required organization, expertise, and compulsion. Decision making should be left to the experts who knew how to regulate a railroad or a public utility. But that process enabled a well-organized interest group or lobbying campaign to exercise significant influence and sometimes corrupt the system. A major result of progressivism was more opportunities for organized groups to shape public policy.

The changes that sought to make the political process more democratic sometimes had unexpected results. Conservative groups used the initiative and referendum for their own ends. Well-funded pressure groups could employ the ballot to pursue an issue such as lower taxes or to attack an unpopular idea or group. The initiative could also reduce the electorate to deciding such issues as how long the lunch hour of a fire department might last. The direct primary did not mean that good candidates replaced bad candidates. A wealthy but less qualified candidate could circumvent the party and achieve success in the primary.

The direct election of U.S. senators, mandated through the Seventeenth Amendment in 1913, took the power of choice away from the state legislatures and gave it to the voters in each state. Candidates had to raise larger amounts of money for their campaigns, which gave an advantage to wealthy men. Meanwhile, lobbying groups simply found new channels for improper influence. One unexpected consequence of these changes was the declining popular interest in voting that became evident in the 1904 presidential election and later contests. Political parties, for all their weaknesses, had mobilized voters to come to the ballot box. The progressives never found a replacement for that function of the parties.

During the spring of 1905, however, reform was still fresh. Advocates of change believed that limited and gradual measures could improve society. With Roosevelt in the White House, they had a president who also believed that moderate reform was necessary to avoid radical transformations.

ROOSEVELT AND THE MODERN PRESIDENCY: THE SECOND TERM

In his second term, Theodore Roosevelt traveled to promote his programs, built up the bureaucratic machinery of the national government, and pushed Congress to consider a wide range of social problems, from child labor to increased taxation of the wealthy. The president attracted bright young men to Washington to join him, and under Roosevelt the nation's capital became the focus of news.

Roosevelt began his reform campaign with the railroad regulation he had promised in his 1904 annual message. Customers of railroads in the South and West complained that rates were too high. Shippers and politicians maintained that the federal government, not the railroads themselves, should determine whether a rate was fair. To do that, the Interstate Commerce Commission (ICC) should have the power to review railroad rates to ensure that they were reasonable.

Roosevelt agreed. During 1905, he spoke for his program across the South and West. The Department of Justice launched well-publicized probes to find out whether railroads were still giving rebates in violation of the 1903 Elkins Act. Roosevelt dangled the threat of revising the tariff to sway Republican leaders in the House to favor his approach. He shared information about railroad misdeeds with sympathetic reporters. When the rail companies started their own public relations effort, it backfired because the public did not believe the railroad claims.

Still, getting a bill that the White House wanted through Congress was not easy. Matters went smoothly in the House. The Hepburn bill, named after William P. Hepburn of Iowa, initiated to give the ICC greater authority over railroads and their practices, was passed in February 1906 by a vote of 346 to 7. Representatives knew that the Senate would make significant changes in their handiwork. Voting against the railroads was a political winner and offered the House members a free vote to please their constituents.

The Senate was the main obstacle. A long struggle ensued between Roosevelt and the conservative Republican leader, Nelson W. Aldrich of Rhode Island. The issue was whether the courts should have broad power to review the ICC's rulings. If courts had such authority, they could water down the law. The Senate won some victories on the issue, but the Hepburn Act was passed in late June 1906. The ICC now had the power to establish maximum rates and to review the accounts and records of the railroads. The Hepburn Act showed how a strong president could achieve a major legislative goal when he summoned public opinion to support a popular cause.

The Expansion of Regulation   There was more to Roosevelt's regulatory program than railroads. Muckrakers had revealed that patent medicines sold over the counter were usually ineffective and sometimes dangerous. Led by Dr. Harvey Wiley of the Department of Agriculture, the government conducted experiments on the purity of food that revealed that toxic chemicals made many food products unsafe. By early 1906, the clamor for reform had led to the introduction of a bill in Congress to restrict the sale of impure or adulterated food and drugs. The measure was passed by the Senate but stalled in the House of Representatives.

During the winter of 1906, thousands of Americans read *The Jungle*, a novel about the meat-packing industry in Chicago. Written by a young socialist named **Upton Sinclair**, the book depicted shocking conditions in the plants as an argument for government ownership and control of the means of production. The public ignored Sinclair's political message; they were outraged that filth endangered their meat supply.

President Roosevelt was angered as well. If the government did not take action, he feared that the socialism Sinclair favored might gain followers. The White House supported an amendment to the Agricultural Appropriation Act of 1906 that set up a federal program for meat inspection. The meat-packing industry tried to water down the bill, but the law represented a significant advance in regulatory power.

The controversy over meat inspection cleared the way for House action on the Pure Food and Drugs Act. As a result, that measure was passed on June 30, 1906. A happy president called the three regulatory laws "a noteworthy advance in the policy of securing Federal supervision and control over corporations."

To achieve that control, Roosevelt placed less emphasis on breaking up large corporations. Instead, he used the Bureau of Corporations to supervise companies that the White House deemed socially responsible. Having decided which businesses and corporate leaders met his standards of morality in the marketplace, he made private agreements with International Harvester and United States Steel. In return for letting the government examine their financial records, these companies would not be subjected to antitrust prosecutions. Firms that Roosevelt disliked, including Standard Oil, would be disciplined by federal lawsuits. Presidential power, mixed with administrative discretion, would control corporate misdeeds.

| Roosevelt and World Politics | Roosevelt displayed equal energy in the conduct of foreign affairs. He carried on secret negotiations without Congress's knowledge, broadened the nation's activities in Asia and |

Europe, and tried to educate the American people to accept a new role as a world power.

Early in 1904, war broke out when the Japanese launched a surprise attack on Russia to seize territory on the Asian mainland and dominate Manchuria. Roosevelt sympathized with Japan because he regarded the Russians as a threat to the Open Door policy in China. As the Japanese won a series of decisive victories, however, the president now favored a negotiated settlement, and he was ready to act as an intermediary when the two parties began negotiations.

Though victorious on the battlefield, Japan was financially exhausted. In April 1905, Tokyo invited Roosevelt to mediate. Roosevelt summoned the combatants to a peace conference held in Portsmouth, New Hampshire, in August, and the two nations agreed to end the conflict; the Treaty of Portsmouth was signed in September 1905. Meanwhile the Roosevelt administration recognized the supremacy of Japan over its neighbor, Korea. In turn, Japan pledged that it had no aggressive designs on the Philippines. In 1906, Roosevelt received the Nobel Peace Prize for his achievement.

In Europe, Roosevelt sought to reduce the growing tension between Germany and the other major powers, France and Great Britain, over Berlin's ambitions to play a larger role on the Continent. Roosevelt sympathized with Britain and France, but he wanted Germany and its leader, Kaiser Wilhelm II, to be reasonable. During 1905, the Germans made a major issue of French dominance of Morocco. The kaiser wanted a conference to determine Morocco's status. Roosevelt convinced Britain and France to accept a conference rather than go to war over the fate of the North African country. The president expanded the international role of the United States when he sent delegates to the Algeciras Conference. Roosevelt's efforts helped preserve the uneasy European peace for the remainder of the decade while issues loomed again with Japan in the Pacific.

| The Gentleman's Agreement | Later in 1906, the lingering problems in Japanese–American relations flared up again. Japan resented the nativist immigration policies of the United States that discriminated against |

Japanese newcomers. On the West Coast, the increasing number of Japanese workers and residents intensified nativist and racist sentiments. When the San Francisco school board segregated children of Japanese ancestry, Japan reacted angrily. Washington and Tokyo eventually worked out the "Gentlemen's Agreement" of 1907. The order of the school board was revoked, and Japan agreed to limit the number of immigrants who left that country for the United States.

To increase funding for the navy from an economy-minded Congress, Roosevelt sent the American navy's "Great White Fleet" on an around-the-world tour from 1907 to 1909. When the vessels stopped in Japan in October 1908, the reception was enthusiastic and friendly. A month later, the two nations negotiated the Root-Takahira Agreement, which called for the open door in China, the independence of that country, and preservation of the status quo in the Pacific. For the moment, the underlying rivalry between the two countries eased.

When he left office in March 1909, Roosevelt expressed pride that the United States was "at absolute peace" with the rest of the world. His policy in the Caribbean had reaffirmed the supremacy of the United States and made possible the construction of the Panama Canal. In Asia he had done his best with the limited power available to

(The Granger Collection, New York)

Great White Fleet.   *Roosevelt's Great White Fleet projected American naval power around the world at the end of his presidential administration. The ambitious voyage reflected the president's belief in the navy as the nation's first line of defense for its overseas possessions.*

him. Roosevelt's involvement in Europe had been positive, but it had not addressed the interlocking alliance systems that would lead to war in 1914.

Roosevelt's Domestic Policies   As the congressional elections of 1906 approached, the Republican Party was still dominant. Some voters were turning away from the Republicans, however, and the Democrats entered the contest with optimism. They had a new asset to help them against the Republicans: organized labor. The American Federation of Labor (AFL) had a membership of nearly 1.7 million by 1904. Its leaders hoped for legislation to limit the power of state and federal courts to block strikes through injunctions. When Republicans in Congress rejected such a program, the leader of the union, Samuel Gompers, called for the defeat of Republican candidates.

In addition to the opposition of the AFL, Roosevelt worried about the growing power of the Socialist Party and the most radical wing of the labor movement, the Industrial Workers of the World (IWW). Founded in 1905, the IWW, nicknamed the "Wobblies," criticized the AFL as timid and called for the overthrow of capitalism. The Socialist Party, under the leadership of Eugene V. Debs, also gained strength at the polls. In 1904, Debs won 400,000 votes. Roosevelt believed that his reforms were necessary to stave off more sweeping social change. During the 1906 election campaign, he sent out members of his cabinet to attack the IWW as violent and dangerous.

Despite Roosevelt's efforts, the Republicans lost twenty-six seats in the elections, but the campaign of the AFL to unseat Republicans did not do as much damage as Gompers had promised. Nevertheless, the results revealed that the Republicans had significant problems. The protective tariff divided the party: midwesterners wanted lower duties, whereas Republicans in the East would tolerate no tariff revision. Roosevelt's regulatory policies alienated party conservatives who became angry when Roosevelt regulated railroads, watched over the quality of food products, and attacked large corporations.

Conservatives believed that one branch of the government could withstand the temptations to follow Roosevelt. The judiciary, composed of judges who were usually appointed rather than elected, often ruled in a conservative manner to strike down progressive laws. In the case of *Lochner v. New York* (1905), for example, the Supreme Court overturned a New York law that limited the hours employees could work in a bakery. The Court ruled that the law infringed on the right of the bakers under the Fourteenth Amendment to get the best reward for their labor. Sometimes the justices made an exception and supported progressive laws. For example, in the 1908 case of **Muller v. Oregon**, influenced by a brief submitted by Louis D. Brandeis, they upheld an Oregon statute that limited the hours women could work. In other decisions that same year, however, the Court invalidated the Employers Liabilities Act of 1906 and curbed the power of labor unions in the Danbury Hatters case (*Loewe v. Lawlor*). Roosevelt regarded the courts not as a balance wheel for the political system but an obstacle to needed social change.

Roosevelt's campaign for the conservation of natural resources also reflected his presidential activism. He created refuges for wild birds, preserved the Grand Canyon against intrusion from development, and set aside national parks. During his first term, he worked for passage of the Newlands Reclamation Act (1902), which established a system of irrigation reservoirs in the West financed through the sale of public lands.

Roosevelt worked closely with **Gifford Pinchot** of the U.S. Forestry Service to formulate conservation policy. Neither man thought that natural resources should be locked up and saved for some indefinite future use. Instead, the national parks, coal lands, oil reserves, water-power sites, and national forests in the West should be managed by trained experts from the federal government to achieve the maximum amount of effective use. For Roosevelt and Pinchot, conservation did not mean that large corporations should be excluded from developing such resources. In fact, corporations might be the best means of exploiting resources in the wisest possible way. Conservationists who were convinced that the wilderness should be preserved rather than developed opposed the Roosevelt-Pinchot policy.

Roosevelt had alerted Americans to a serious national problem. He raised important issues about the future of timber, water, wildlife, and mineral resources. He created national parks, including Mesa Verde and Crater Lake, and established four national game preserves, fifty-one bird reservations, and 150 national forests. He could be proud of the National Monuments Act (1906) that put some important national treasures beyond the reach of development and destruction. He also convened the 1908 Governors Conference on Conservation that looked into social issues relating to natural and human resources. The president had alerted the nation to these pressing concerns in an innovative way.

DOING HISTORY ONLINE

Theodore Roosevelt: Conservationist?

Examine the documents in the modules "Theodore Roosevelt on Conservation, 1901" and "Theodore Roosevelt's African Game Trials, 1910," and consider the following question: Was Theodore Roosevelt a conservationist?

www.cengage.com/history/ayers/ampassages4e

Roosevelt's resource policies required a high degree of control by the federal government and the cooperation of large corporations. In the West, there was much resentment of programs that Washington had devised without much local support and implemented over the protests of the westerners themselves.

Roosevelt remained popular with the American people during the waning years of his administration. Among conservative Republicans, however, unhappiness with the president mounted. On Capitol Hill, party members in the House and Senate balked at Roosevelt's assertiveness. When problems in the banking industry led to the panic of 1907, a momentary collapse of the financial system and a brief recession followed. Roosevelt's Republican opponents blamed the economic troubles on his regulatory policies. To stem the danger to banks, Roosevelt agreed to let United States Steel acquire the Tennessee Coal and Iron Company, a decision that came back to affect Roosevelt after his presidency.

The issue of Roosevelt's successor became a central problem for Republicans. Hoping to see his progressive policies carried on, the president decided to support his secretary of war, William Howard Taft, whom he regarded as his natural successor. By early 1907, Roosevelt had become the real campaign manager of Taft's drive to win the Republican nomination.

During early 1908, Roosevelt endorsed more sweeping regulation of corporations, a tax on inheritances of great wealth, and compensation laws for workers. Congressional

MAP 20.1 Theodore Roosevelt: National Parks and Monuments.

Theodore Roosevelt, as a conservationist president, established National Parks and Monuments to preserve the nation's heritage. This map shows what he accomplished in both categories. Several of the National Monuments later became National Parks and thus have the date when Roosevelt established them and the date that their status changed to a park.

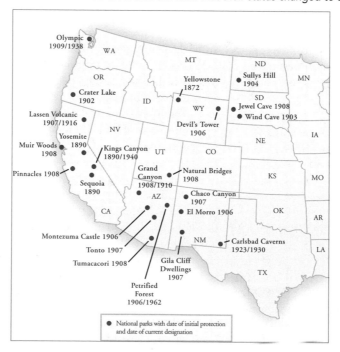

Olympic 1909/1938 — WA
MT
ND
Crater Lake 1902 — OR
Yellowstone 1872
Sullys Hill 1904 — MN
ID
SD
Lassen Volcanic 1907/1916
WY
Jewel Cave 1908
NV
Devil's Tower 1906 — Wind Cave 1903
Yosemite 1890
NE
IA
Muir Woods 1908
Kings Canyon 1890/1940 — UT
CO
Pinnacles 1908
Grand Canyon 1908/1910
Natural Bridges 1908
KS
MO
Sequoia 1890
AZ
Chaco Canyon 1907
CA
El Morro 1906
OK
AR
Montezuma Castle 1906
NM
Carlsbad Caverns 1923/1930
LA
Tonto 1907
Tumacacori 1908
Gila Cliff Dwellings 1907
TX
Petrified Forest 1906/1962

● National parks with date of initial protection and date of current designation

Republicans reacted coolly to these proposals, and relations between the White House and Capitol Hill worsened throughout 1908.

Meanwhile, Taft advanced toward the Republican nomination at the national convention in June, where he won easily on the first ballot. In their platform, the Republicans promised to revise the protective tariff at a special session of Congress shortly after the new president was inaugurated. The public assumed that any change in the tariff would lead to lower rates.

| The 1908 Presidential Election | The Democrats nominated William Jennings Bryan for the third time and were optimistic about his chances. After all, Roosevelt was not a candidate, and Taft had not been tested at the polls. In |

the early days of the campaign, Bryan ran well. Then Roosevelt threw his support behind Taft in a series of public statements (incumbent presidents still did not campaign in those days), and the Republicans won again: Taft garnered 321 electoral votes to Bryan's 162. The popular vote went solidly for Taft, although Bryan ran much better than Alton B. Parker had in 1904. The election was marked by ticket-splitting: voters cast ballots for Taft for president and Democrats for other offices. The partisan allegiances and loyalties of the late nineteenth century were breaking down.

Roosevelt had picked Taft as his successor because he was convinced that Taft would carry on with his reform policies. Shortly after the election, however, tensions developed between Roosevelt and his political heir over how the pace of reform should be managed. Taft was more conservative than Roosevelt had perceived. In addition, battles between Roosevelt and Congress flared as inauguration day approached. As Roosevelt prepared to leave office and embark on a hunting trip to Africa, the Republican Party remained divided over its future.

CONCLUSION

Theodore Roosevelt was an important president. In domestic policy, he had demonstrated how a chief executive could mobilize public opinion behind the policies of the national government. On the world stage, he had involved the nation in European and Asian affairs to preserve international stability.

Not all that Roosevelt did was positive. His handling of race relations was neither consistent nor principled, and he failed to exercise serious leadership on this troubling problem. Sometimes he flirted with excessive power in pursuit of his political enemies. He had also showed little respect for the constraints that the Constitution imposed on his office. Nevertheless, he offered an example of exciting leadership on which later presidents would build.

Theodore Roosevelt had neither caused the Progressive movement to emerge nor encouraged all of its campaigns. He had given reform a visible national leader. As a result, progressives would point to numerous successes: railroad regulation, conservation, and pure food and drug legislation. The agenda of change was still incomplete, however. For the new president, the issue was whether to extend reform or to thwart it. Meanwhile, reformers in the states debated issues of cultural and economic policy: prohibition of alcohol, woman suffrage, immigration restriction, and procedural reforms. The Roosevelt years had been exciting, but the climax of progressivism would come during the presidency of William Howard Taft.

CHAPTER REVIEW, 1901–1909

During the years when Theodore Roosevelt was president, he:

- Launched a program of government regulation.
- Attacked the trusts.
- Expanded the role of the United States in the world.

At the same time, the Progressive movement:

- Began with reform in the nation's cities.
- Expanded to deal with state issues.
- Became a national force under Roosevelt's leadership.
- Addressed such social problems as woman suffrage, child labor, and conservation of natural resources.
- Sought greater democracy and social efficiency.

◀◀◀ Looking Back

Much of what Theodore Roosevelt tried to do as president built on ideas and attitudes that were advanced during the 1890s and discussed in Chapter 19. In analyzing this chapter, you should be aware of how events such as the panic of 1893, the election of 1896, and the Spanish–American War influenced the way issues were framed after 1900.

1. How did the experience of the 1890s shape the way Theodore Roosevelt approached the presidency?
2. What obstacles did the Republican Party pose to Roosevelt's programs in the White House?
3. Was Roosevelt a progressive or conservative in his approach to government?
4. Why did conservation seem so important during the early twentieth century?
5. In your judgment, what made Roosevelt so popular?

Looking Ahead ▶▶▶

For all his accomplishments, Roosevelt left some problems for his political successors and the society to solve. In Chapter 21, you'll see how Roosevelt's mixed legacy shaped how society responded to William Howard Taft and Woodrow Wilson, very different national leaders.

1. Did Roosevelt strengthen or weaken the Republican Party during his presidency?
2. What problems arose because of Roosevelt's love of executive power and presidential discretion?
3. Was accepting big business as an accomplished fact the only way to deal with the problem of large corporations?
4. Was the United States ready to be a world power as Roosevelt envisioned?

 Go to the American Passages website at www.cengage.com/history/ayers/ ampassages4e for additional review materials.

Progressivism at High Tide, 1909–1914

21

W hen Theodore Roosevelt left office in March 1909, progressivism entered a phase of partisan upheaval. Under William Howard Taft, the Republicans split as conservatives and reformers struggled for control. The Democrats moved toward a more active role for the national government and away from state rights. The Socialists mounted a vigorous challenge from the left. For five years, it seemed as though the party system might fragment.

Political ferment revealed reform tensions. Campaigns for woman suffrage, the prohibition of alcohol, restriction of immigration, and social justice created new coalitions that sometimes followed party lines and at other times disrupted them. In the process, progressivism provoked a conservative reaction that limited the possibilities for reform.

The social and economic forces creating a consumer society also gathered strength. Henry Ford's low-priced automobile gained greater popularity, while other products of industrialism attracted more customers. Women found more opportunities for employment. For minorities, however, these years saw continuing tension and racial strife.

International strains in Europe and revolutions in Latin America and Asia made foreign policy more of a national concern than it had been since the war with Spain in 1898. Still, the outbreak of fighting in Europe during the summer of 1914 came as a shock to the United States. World war added new complexity to an already turbulent period.

TAFT'S CONSERVATIVE PRESIDENCY

Soon after **William Howard Taft** took office on March 4, 1909, Theodore Roosevelt left for his hunting safari in Africa. The hope on Wall Street, ran a joke of the day, was that a lion would do its duty. A celebrity as an ex-president, Roosevelt found that his activities were news, even across the ocean. The issues of regulation, social justice, and corporate power with which he had struggled were also on the agenda for his successor.

For Taft, Republican conservatives expected him to slow the movement toward reform. Party progressives wanted the new president to expand Roosevelt's legacy. The Republicans had promised in their 1908 platform to revise the tariff but had not specified whether rates would go up or down. The president planned to call a special session of Congress that would revise the tariff downward. Republicans waited to see what Taft would do.

A native of Cincinnati, Ohio, fifty-one-year-old Taft had been a lawyer and a federal judge before heading the Philippine Commission in 1900. He proved to be an adept colonial administrator, but Roosevelt summoned him back to the United States in 1904 to serve as secretary of war.

During Roosevelt's presidency, Taft acted as troubleshooter for the administration. When Roosevelt went on vacation, he told reporters that he felt confident because the portly Taft was in Washington "sitting on the lid." Roosevelt looked forward to a continuation of his policies under his successor, but Roosevelt had misjudged where Taft stood on a number of issues, especially the power of the presidency.

Taft was a conservative man who did not agree with Roosevelt's expansive view of presidential power. Taft believed that the president should act within the strict letter of the law and the constitutional boundaries of his office, a philosophy that was bound to disappoint Roosevelt and the progressive Republicans.

Taft also lacked Roosevelt's sure sense of public relations. He played golf at fashionable country clubs and vacationed with wealthy men at a time when riches were associated with political corruption. He quarreled with the press and often put off writing speeches until the last minute. The success he had enjoyed as a speaker during the 1908 campaign was soon forgotten as he failed to sway audiences or committed political gaffes. Taft also depended on the advice of his wife, Helen Herron Taft, in political matters, but during the spring of 1909, she had a stroke that deprived him of her emotional support.

In revising the tariff, Taft confronted the consequences of Roosevelt's postponement of the issue during his two terms. Progressive Republicans favored reductions in customs duties and a move away from protectionism. Conservatives, however, regarded the tariff as the cornerstone of Republicanism and felt that high rates were justified. To maintain Republican unity in Congress, Taft supported the reelection of conservative Joseph G. Cannon as Speaker of the House.

Once Congress assembled in March 1909, Taft asked for a new tariff law that would, as he had said in his inaugural address "permit the reduction of rates in certain schedules and will require the advancement of few, if any." In April, the House passed a tariff bill that lowered rates on sugar, iron, and lumber. It placed lumber, coal, and cattle hides on the free list. The measure was named the Payne bill after its author, Sereno E. Payne, chairman of the Ways and Means Committee. After it passed the House, the bill went to the Senate where the Republicans had sixty-one members and the Democrats thirty-one. The Republican leader, Nelson Aldrich of Rhode Island, was regarded as a virtual dictator of the Senate.

In fact, Aldrich's position was vulnerable. Among the Senate Republicans, there were seven to ten midwesterners, such as Robert La Follette of Wisconsin, Albert J.

This icon will direct you to interactive activities and study materials on the American Passages website: www.cengage.com/history/ayers/ampassages4e

CHAPTER TIMELINE

1909	William Howard Taft inaugurated as president • Enactment of Payne-Aldrich Tariff
1910	Ballinger-Pinchot controversy over conservation worsens • Roosevelt returns from Africa, announces New Nationalism • Camp Fire Girls founded • Democrats regain control of House of Representatives
1911	Triangle Fire in New York City kills 146 people • Harriet Quimby becomes first licensed woman pilot
1912	Taft defeats Roosevelt for Republican nomination • Bitter strike in Lawrence, Massachusetts • S S *Titanic* hits iceberg and sinks in North Atlantic • Roosevelt forms Progressive party • Woodrow Wilson defeats Taft and Roosevelt in presidential race
1913	Suffragettes stage large march on the day before Woodrow Wilson is inaugurated • Federal income tax adopted • Armory Show of Modern Art held in New York City • Federal Reserve System established
1914	Henry Ford announces Five-Dollar Day program • Fighting occurs at Vera Cruz in Mexico • Outbreak of First World War

Beveridge of Indiana, and Jonathan P. Dolliver of Iowa, who wanted to see lower tariffs and limits on Aldrich's power. On the other side of the debate, senators from the East and Far West insisted that goods from their states must be protected against foreign competition. Aldrich did not have a majority of votes for the Payne bill.

Aldrich had the Senate Finance Committee write a bill with eight hundred amendments, half of which raised rates back toward those of the Dingley Tariff. That move outraged progressive senators among the Republicans. During the summer of 1909, Dolliver, La Follette, and Beveridge attacked Aldrich's bill. They said that the public expected lower tariffs, and they denounced attempts to protect it. The Aldrich version finally cleared the Senate in early July by a vote of 45 to 34. Ten Republicans voted against Aldrich.

As a House–Senate conference committee hammered out the final version of the bill, both sides looked to Taft. The president used his leverage to obtain some concessions, such as lower duties on gloves, lumber, and cattle hides, but he failed to obtain reductions on wool, cotton, and industrial products. Convinced that he had gained all he could, Taft signed the Payne-Aldrich Tariff in early August 1909. The battle had split the Republicans because the tariff had not fulfilled the promises of the 1908 party platform.

Taft endorsed the new tariff during a tour of the Midwest in September. Speaking at Winona, Minnesota, he called the law "the best tariff bill that the Republican Party ever passed." Conservatives applauded his remarks, while progressives fumed over the outcome of the tariff fight. The president then refused to appoint individuals whom the progressives recommended for federal offices in their states.

The Battle over Conservation

Taft also found himself engaged in a battle that threatened to disrupt his friendship with Theodore Roosevelt. Federal government control of natural resources had been one of Roosevelt's favorite policies. His principal aide had been chief forester Gifford Pinchot. But Taft disliked Pinchot and doubted whether the policies Roosevelt had pursued were legal. The president and his secretary of the interior, Richard A. Ballinger, adopted conservation policies that conformed to existing laws and allowed less room for presidential initiative. When Ballinger opened lands for development that Pinchot had closed off to settlers and businesses, Pinchot struck back. He accused Ballinger of acting as an agent for J. P. Morgan and a syndicate trying to sell valuable coal lands in Alaska. After looking into the charges, Taft sided with Ballinger.

Pinchot leaked information about the episode to the press. In early 1910, he went even further, writing a letter of protest to a senator that the lawmaker in turn released to the public. Taft thereupon fired Pinchot for insubordination. In the ensuing controversy, a congressional probe revealed that Taft and Ballinger had not done what Pinchot had charged.

Taft seemed to be attacking a key Roosevelt policy. Roosevelt in Africa received letters from friends saying that Taft was betraying him. The former president responded that perhaps he had made a mistake in picking Taft. Washington buzzed with talk that Roosevelt might run in 1912.

The congressional session in the spring of 1910 compounded Taft's problems. Progressive Republicans joined with Democrats to restrict the power of Speaker Cannon to hold up legislation. Because Taft had supported the Speaker, this move was seen as a rebuke to the White House. Some constructive measures emerged from the session. Railroad legislation broadened the power of the Interstate Commerce Commission over the railroads. The navy was given more money, and progressives enacted a law to encourage private citizens to use federal banks located in post offices. Taft got little credit for these improvements. Progressives charged that he did more to frustrate reform than to push it.

Roosevelt's Return   Meanwhile, Theodore Roosevelt had returned to the United States in June 1910, his ears filled with Taft's alleged misdeeds. Roosevelt decided that it was up to him to get the Republican Party back on the right course. He received a tumultuous welcome when his ship entered New York Harbor. Guns boomed and fireboats shot water into the air. A crowd of 100,000 people cheered him as he rode up the streets. His popularity seemed as strong as ever.

At first, Roosevelt refrained from public quarrels with the president. Meanwhile, the Republicans' internal warfare intensified. Taft used his appointment power once again against the midwestern progressives in his party; their candidates were not nominated for positions in the federal government. Taft went even further, trying to organize loyal Republicans against reform leaders such as Dolliver, La Follette, and Beveridge. These moves failed, and the president's inability to rally support within his own party emphasized his weakness. Taft knew that his troubles with Roosevelt were growing.

Roosevelt sharpened his quarrel with Taft in a series of speeches during the summer of 1910. He called his program the **New Nationalism**. In a speech at Osawatomie, Kansas, in August, he said that "the New Nationalism regards the executive power as the steward of the public welfare." He wanted the Square Deal of his presidency to be expanded. Roosevelt said the "rules of the game" should be "changed so as to work for a more substantial equality of opportunity and reward for equally good service." He called for an income tax, inheritance taxes on large fortunes, workmen's compensation laws, and legislation to "regulate child labor and work for women." Roosevelt was advocating the modern regulatory state and wanted to achieve it as president.

In the congressional elections of 1910, the Democrats benefited from Republican discord and the desire of the public for a change in parties. The opposition gained control of the House of Representatives when the Republicans lost fifty-eight seats. In the Senate, the Republicans dropped ten seats. They still had a ten-seat majority, but the progressive Republicans often voted with the Democrats. Republicans suffered their biggest losses in the industrial East, where twenty-six Republican House members were defeated. Stressing inflation and the high cost of living, Democrats won governorships in New York, New Jersey, Ohio, and Indiana and looked forward to the presidential election of 1912.

PROGRESSIVE VICTORIES

Between 1910 and 1913 progressivism intensified, as the movement for social change gathered momentum. The reformers seemed to have public opinion behind them, and conservatives in both parties were on the defensive. The forces of reform pushed forward to achieve their policy goals.

Woman Suffrage   In April 1910, the National American Woman Suffrage Association (NAWSA) presented Congress with a petition that more than 400,000 people had signed. The document sought a constitutional

Woman Suffrage Parade Booklet, March 3, 1913.
The suffrage parade in Washington, D.C. on March 3, 1913, which produced violence against the marchers, became one of the controversial moments in the process of women receiving the vote. This image of the booklet for the march indicates the goals of the organizers.

amendment allowing women to vote. Although Congress refused to act, one suffrage worker, surprised by the number of signers of the petition, said that her cause "is actually fashionable now." Under the leadership of Anna Howard Shaw, NAWSA's membership grew. In Washington (1910), California (1911), and Arizona, Kansas, and Oregon (1912), **woman suffrage** triumphed. However, referenda to give women the vote failed in Ohio, Wisconsin, and Michigan. Within the movement, younger women, eager for results, urged the older leaders to concentrate on obtaining a constitutional amendment.

Alice Paul led the radical wing of the suffrage movement that aimed to change the Constitution. She had fought for the vote in England and now wanted to apply tactics of picketing and civil disobedience to the United States. Other women joined her, including Lucy Burns and Harriot Stanton Blatch, daughter of Elizabeth Cady Stanton. For a few years, Paul and her allies worked on NAWSA's congressional committee. On March 3, 1913, before **Woodrow Wilson** became president, Paul's supporters staged a well-publicized suffrage parade in Washington, D.C. Frustrated at the cautious tactics of NAWSA, Paul and Burns left the organization in early 1914 to form the Congressional Union. The new organization insisted that only a constitutional amendment would win the victory to gain the vote for women.

Significant obstacles to suffrage remained, however. The liquor industry feared that women who voted would support **Prohibition**. White southerners worried that if Congress enacted woman suffrage, reform might lead to efforts to safeguard black voting rights across the nation. Men saw their dominance threatened if women took part in politics. To counter these arguments, NAWSA stressed that female voting meant purer and more honest politics. The organization also played down the argument that women should have equal political rights and instead, contended that woman suffrage would offset the votes of immigrants and racial minorities in large cities. Thus, suffragists would be protecting traditional values against "alien" assaults.

> ### DOING HISTORY ONLINE
>
> **Votes for Women a Practical Necessity**
>
> Read the articles on woman suffrage. How have other progressive reform movements influenced the woman suffrage movement?
>
> www.cengage.com/history/ayers/ampassages4e

Prohibition

Efforts to restrict the use and sale of alcohol also prospered. The Anti-Saloon League had held a dominant position among prohibitionist organizations since its founding during the 1890s. Older groups, such as the Woman's Christian Temperance Union, played an important role in the crusade, but the Anti-Saloon League used interest group politics that focused on specific, targeted legislative goals. In the case of prohibition, the league sought to limit the power of the liquor industry to sell its product. At first the league sought elections to give voters in a county or state the "local option" to ban the sale of alcohol. By 1906, impatient with the slowness of the local option, the league turned to statewide elections to get the job done more quickly.

Oklahoma adopted Prohibition in 1907. By 1914, eight other states had banned the sale of alcohol. Militant prohibitionists (they were called "drys"; antiprohibitionists

Chinese Immigration on the West Coast

Immigration into the United States between 1900 and 1914 was not solely a European experience. Despite such obstacles as the Chinese Exclusion Act of 1882, Chinese Americans found ways to bring young men from their native country to the United States. This picture shows a group of such Chinese newcomers as they went through immigration. They had to demonstrate that they were being brought in as the sons or relatives of American citizens of Chinese origin. Small numbers of Japanese immigrants also entered the country during these years. Both Asian immigrant groups built prosperous lives and that development sparked white Americans' resentment of their economic success. Racial tensions persisted and led to friction between the Japanese and American governments during the presidency of Theodore Roosevelt. Sentiment on the West Coast to restrict Asian immigration remained strong into the 1920s and beyond.

(The Granger Collection, New York)

were "wets") found the state-by-state process discouraging. In 1913, prohibitionists in Congress passed the Webb-Kenyon Act, which outlawed the shipment of alcohol into dry states. Skeptical of Prohibition as a social cause, President Taft vetoed the bill, but Congress overrode him. The Anti-Saloon League's next goal was a constitutional amendment to ban the sale of alcohol in the United States.

Restriction of Immigration   The effort to restrict immigration into the United States accelerated. The flow of newcomers from southern and eastern Europe persisted. There were more than 1 million immigrants in 1910, nearly 2 million in 1913, and over a million more in 1914, before the outbreak of World War I. In addition, revolutionary upheavals in Mexico drove thousands of Hispanic immigrants into the Southwest.

Protestants wanted to keep out Catholic and Jewish newcomers. Labor unions feared that immigrants would become strikebreakers; rural residents saw urban populations growing at their expense. Prejudice against the Chinese and Japanese fed nativist sentiments on the West Coast. Diplomatic friction with Japan followed. By 1913, a bill to impose a literacy test on immigrants passed both houses of Congress. President Taft vetoed the measure, and Congress was unable to override it.

Progressive reform offered some support to the nativist and racist feelings. Since businesses favored a loose immigration policy, opposition to immigration was portrayed as a way to help workers already in the United States. A feeling that cultures from southern and eastern Europe threatened traditional values led some progressives to endorse restriction.

An incident in Atlanta, Georgia, in 1913 underlined the tensions surrounding immigration restriction. When a young factory worker, Mary Phagan, was murdered, suspicion focused on her superintendent, Leo Frank. A Jew whose parents had come from Russia, Frank was innocent, but he fell victim to anti-Semitism and fear of outsiders. As a "victim worthy to pay for the crime," he was convicted and sentenced to death. After the governor of Georgia commuted his sentence, a mob abducted and lynched him in August 1915. The episode helped to promote the rise of the Ku Klux Klan (a second version of the hooded order that had arisen during Reconstruction appeared in these years), a further testament to the xenophobia and bigotry in the age of reform.

Saving the Children Americans worried about their children's future as mass entertainment, the lure of the city, and looser attitudes about sex offered new temptations. Three organizations sprang up to address these concerns. In 1910–1911, the Boy Scouts of America, modeled on the British precedent created by Robert Baden-Powell, began training young men in loyalty and service. Boys twelve through eighteen years enrolled to receive instruction in "the military virtues such as honor, loyalty, obedience, and patriotism."

For young women, there were the Girl Scouts, founded by Juliette Low in 1912, and the Campfire Girls, founded two years earlier. These two groups prepared American girls for future domestic responsibilities. "The homemaker of tomorrow," said one Girl Scout leader, "must be made efficient in her task and happy in it." With the constructive activities that the Girl Scouts, Campfire Girls, and Boy Scouts supplied, delinquency and crime among the young would be reduced, or so their advocates maintained.

The struggle against child labor overshadowed all the other drives to improve the condition of children. In 1910, some 200,000 youngsters below the age of twelve labored in mills and factories. Attempts to limit child labor in textile firms in the South brought meager results. In 1912, the reformers succeeded in establishing the Children's Bureau within the federal government, but Congress failed to pass any legislation that directly addressed the child labor problem.

Despite the many obstacles that progressive reformers faced, they believed that the nation was making genuine gains. William Allen White, a Kansas newspaper editor and a friend

---

DOING HISTORY ONLINE

Night Scene at Indiana Glass Works

Look at the image online, and evaluate the following statement: Given the hard work they were doing, the boys in this photograph do not look neglected, ill-treated, or even unhappy to be working.

 www.cengage.com/history/ayers/ampassages4e

of many of the leading progressives, recalled that "all over the land in a score of states and more, young men in both parties were taking leadership by attacking things as they were in that day." Women, too, felt a sense of possibility that infused middle-class reform during the years before World War I.

LABOR PROTEST IN A CHANGING WORKPLACE

Conflict marked the relations between labor and capital. Bitter struggles between workers and employers occurred in the garment unions of New York, among the textile workers of Massachusetts, and in the coal mines of Colorado. American laborers measured their progress in violent and bloody confrontations against harsh conditions in the workplace.

As industrialization spread, factories and businesses expanded. In Chicago during these years, Marshall Field's department store had five thousand salespeople in its many store departments. The meatpacking firm of Swift and Company employed twenty-three thousand people in its seven plants by 1903. The Amoskeag Company textile mills in Manchester, New Hampshire, dominated the lives of its seventeen thousand employees with welfare programs and company organizations.

The nature of large corporations changed. Important companies applied scientific research techniques and social science procedures that altered the working experience of Americans. The need to develop new products led such corporations as DuPont and General Electric to emulate the example of German firms. General Electric set up links to universities that allowed scientists and engineers on their faculties to address the needs of the corporations in their research. The ties between business and education propelled economic growth for the rest of the century.

New Rules for the Workplace
Within the large factories, relationships between employers and workers became more structured and routinized. The informal dominance that the foreman had exercised during the nineteenth century gave way to bureaucratic practices. To control costs and ensure steady production, companies set up procedures for regular reporting on expenditures, centralization of purchasing and maintenance, and measurement of worker productivity.

Out of these innovations came a new way to run the factory and workplace. Frederick Winslow Taylor developed scientific management. As a mechanical engineer in the steel industry, Taylor believed that careful study of each individual task would lead to efficiency. Once the maximum amount of time to do a specific job was established, workers could be instructed on how to complete the task without any wasted motion. Stopwatches measured the speed of work down to the split second.

As a concept, Taylorism enjoyed great popularity among businesspeople. Although most employers did not adopt all of Taylor's ideas, the principle of managing factories and shops systematically took hold. Since the core of scientific management meant reducing all jobs to a set of simple steps that required little skill, workers resented practices that made them perform repetitive, routine movements all day long. Henry Ford claimed that "no man wants to be burdened with the care and responsibility of deciding things." Thus, he believed that workers welcomed freedom from mental strain. In fact, employees objected to being "reduced to a scientific formula," said one machinist.

The Limits of Paternalism   While scientific management viewed workers in a detached and bloodless way, some corporations revived paternalism through welfare and incentive programs. Lunchrooms and toilet areas were cleaned up, recreational facilities established, and plans devised for pensions and profit sharing. National Cash Register of Dayton, Ohio, was a leader in the field, along with H. J. Heinz Company, the Amoskeag Mills, and Remington Typewriter.

Yet most American workers saw only marginal improvement. Businesses used a variety of techniques to block unions and prevent workers from improving their condition. The National Association of Manufacturers (NAM) pushed for laws to outlaw the union shop (mandating membership in a union to work in the plant) in favor the "open shop," in which unions were not allowed. Blacklists of pro-union employees circulated, and new workers often had to sign contracts that barred them from joining a union. When strikes occurred, employers used nonunion labor (strikers called them "scabs") to end the walkouts. Court injunctions limited the ability of strikers to picket and organize. Violent clashes between workers and police accompanied many strikes.

Unorganized Workers   The working classes in the cities faced the ravages of inflation as prosperity and an increasing supply of gold contributed to a rising price level for consumers. While wages rose, prices accelerated at a faster rate. Many consumer products remained out of reach of the average laborer. These workers faced dangerous conditions in their factories and sweatshops. Laborers turned to strikes and unions. In New York City and Philadelphia from 1909 to 1911, the International Ladies Garment Workers Union organized workers within the shirtwaist (a woman's blouse or dress with details copied from men's shirts) manufacturing business. Twenty thousand women strikers took their grievances into the streets to demonstrate their solidarity. They wrested some concessions from their employees in the form of union shops and improved working conditions.

Many manufacturers forced their employees to work in deplorable conditions with poor ventilation, filth, and danger to the lives of those who labored. In March 1911, a fire erupted at the Triangle Shirtwaist Company on New York City's Lower East Side. As the workers fled the flames, they found locked doors to prevent them from taking breaks and no fire escape routes. The conflagration claimed 146 lives, many of them killed when they jumped to the pavement below. The **Triangle Shirtwaist fire** spurred reform efforts among politicians in the New York legislature.

Varieties of Labor Protest   Labor unions grew between 1900 and 1914. The American Federation of Labor, led by Samuel Gompers, had several million members. The politics of the AFL had not changed since the end of the nineteenth century. Its craft unions discouraged organization among industrial workers. Women employees received little support from Gompers and his allies.

The Industrial Workers of the World (IWW) appealed to the unskilled masses. Its ultimate goal was still a social revolution that would sweep away industrial capitalism. To the IWW's leadership, including William D. "Big Bill" Haywood and Elizabeth Gurley Flynn, violent strikes seemed the best way to promote industrial warfare.

Strikes in Lawrence and Ludlow   The IWW gained national attention during a strike in the textile mills of Lawrence, Massachusetts, in mid-January 1912. After the textile companies announced substantial wage reductions, the workers walked out. Haywood came to Lawrence to support the strike. The children of strikers were sent to live in other cities, a tactic that publicized the walkout and swayed public opinion to the workers' cause. On March 1, the companies granted them a pay hike. Women strikers were key participants in the victory. As one of their songs put it, they sought "bread and roses," or a living wage and a life with hope. Despite this local success, the IWW did not build a strong following in the East.

In Colorado, the United Mine Workers struck against the Colorado Fuel and Iron Company in September 1913, complaining about low wages and company camps with brutal guards. John D. Rockefeller, who controlled the coal company, asked the governor to call in the National Guard. Confrontations between soldiers and miners ended in the "Ludlow Massacre" of April 20, 1914, in which troops fired on miners in a tent city at Ludlow. Five strikers and one soldier were shot, and two women and eleven children died in the flames that broke out in the tents. Federal inquiries followed, and the workers obtained some concessions. Yet later in 1914 they were forced to end the strike without gaining union recognition.

Changes in the workplace during the Progressive period had benefited the employers far more than they had improved the lot of the people who labored in factories and shops. Some social legislation had been enacted to protect the worker from the effects of industrial accidents. The length of the working day had been reduced somewhat, for example. Unlike Great Britain or Germany, however, the United States still did not provide social insurance when a worker became unemployed, pension benefits for old age, or equal bargaining power on the job. The absence of these benefits fed the political passions that surged through the nation during the years that Taft was president. Whether it was in his view of labor relations, his attitude toward progressivism, or his conduct of foreign policy, Taft seemed out of touch with the nation's mood.

REPUBLICAN DISCORD AND DEMOCRATIC OPPORTUNITY

The Taft administration followed the broad outlines of what Roosevelt had done, but with some new labels for the effort to spread American influence in Asia and Latin America. In foreign affairs, William Howard Taft and his secretary of state, Philander C. Knox, adopted the policy of **dollar diplomacy** toward Latin America and Asia. When U.S. corporations traded and invested in underdeveloped areas of the world, peace and stability increased. Instead of military force, the ties of finance and capital would instruct countries in the wise conduct of their affairs. "The borrower is the servant of the lender," said Knox. Military intervention should be a last resort to restore order.

Latin America offered an ideal location for applying the principles of dollar diplomacy. No European countries challenged the supremacy of the United States there. In 1909, Taft and Knox induced bankers to loan money to Honduras to prevent British investors from achieving undue influence. In 1911, they compelled the government of Nicaragua to accept another loan from U.S. investors. Unfortunately for Taft, some Nicaraguans regarded the scheme as an intrusion in their affairs, and they rebelled against the government that had made the deal. The Taft administration sent U.S. Marines to Nicaragua; the resulting U.S. military presence continued for several decades, and a lasting feeling of bitterness marked relations with Latin America.

Taft and Knox also applied dollar diplomacy to China. The government wanted American capitalists to support a railroad in China, first to develop the country and then to offset Japan. Roosevelt had recognized Japanese dominance in the region; Knox challenged it economically. A syndicate of nations would lend China money to purchase existing railroads in Manchuria. The plan collapsed when the British, Russians, and Japanese rejected the idea in early 1910. Instead of promoting stability in China, Knox drove the Japanese and Russians to join forces against American interests. The Knox initiative sparked resentment in Japan, and relations between that country and the United States remained tense. Dollar diplomacy proved to be an ineffective way to achieve world influence.

A foreign policy problem closer to home emerged in 1911. Porfirio Díaz had ruled Mexico for almost forty years. American investment came because he had maintained apparent calm and stability. In fact, however, his dictatorial rule eventually erupted in a revolution. Francisco I. Madero, the leader of the rebels, came to power hoping to transform the nation. But he aroused the opposition of conservative forces, including the military, large landowners, and the Roman Catholic church. Shortly before Taft's term ended in 1913, Madero was overthrown and murdered. Mexico remained in revolutionary ferment.

Following Republican losses in the elections of 1910, Taft and Roosevelt agreed not to attack each other during the first half of 1911. Republican progressives still looked for an alternative to Taft in 1912. To placate the progressives, Taft eased Ballinger out of the cabinet and named two supporters of Roosevelt as secretary of the interior and secretary of war.

Taft's troubles with Congress persisted. He negotiated a trade agreement with Canada based on reciprocal concessions on tariffs. Neither the Democrats nor the progressive Republicans liked Canadian reciprocity because it lowered import duties on products that affected their districts. Taft pushed the agreement through Congress in mid-1911, but when Canadian voters rejected the government that had supported it, another Taft initiative died.

Next, the president's fragile friendship with Roosevelt collapsed. Unlike Roosevelt, Taft really believed in "busting" the trusts, and his Justice Department attacked large corporations. In October 1911, carrying out Taft's policy views about the wisdom of competition, the Department of Justice filed an antitrust suit against United States Steel. One of the practices that violated the law, according to the indictment, was the company's acquisition of the Tennessee Coal and Iron Company during the panic of 1907.

Since Roosevelt had approved the merger, the indictment held him up to ridicule, and he was furious. By the early part of 1912, he decided to challenge Taft for the Republican nomination. "My hat is in the ring, the fight is on, and I am stripped to the buff," he said in February 1912. The prospect of Roosevelt running for a third term as president set off a lively debate about the wisdom of that course and the dangers it might pose for the political system.

The Struggle Between Roosevelt and Taft

Throughout the spring of 1912, a bitter battle for the Republican nomination raged. For the first time, a few states held primary elections to choose delegates to the Republican convention. That change gave an obvious advantage to Roosevelt, who enjoyed more popularity than Taft among rank-and-file Republicans. As a result, he attracted a majority of these voters. Taft, however, ran strongly among party regulars (the men who held state and local offices or occupied positions in the Republican organization), who controlled the nominating conventions. As the Republican National Convention opened in Chicago, neither man had a clear majority. Several hundred delegates were contested, but the Republican National Committee awarded most of them to Taft. When the national convention upheld what the national committee had done, Roosevelt believed that Taft had stolen from him a prize that was rightfully his. Summoning his followers to leave the convention, Roosevelt denounced Taft and promised to fight on. "We stand at Armageddon and we battle for the Lord," he said. For the next two months, Roosevelt prepared to run as a third-party candidate.

The Democratic Opportunity

To exploit the disarray of their opponents, the Democrats needed a credible presidential candidate. One attractive newcomer was the governor of New Jersey, Woodrow Wilson, who had carried that staunchly Republican state by a sizable majority in 1910. Woodrow Wilson was fifty-six years old in 1912. Born in Virginia, he grew up in the South and shared its racial views. He attended Princeton University in New Jersey, studied law for a time, and then earned a doctorate in history and political science at Johns Hopkins University. He joined the Princeton faculty in 1890, was quickly recognized as an outstanding instructor, and became president of the university in 1902. After initial successes, he ran into resistance from more conservative alumni and faculty when he attacked the exclusive, fraternity-like eating clubs that dominated Princeton's social life. He resigned from the Princeton presidency in 1910 and won the New Jersey governorship in his first try at elective office.

The Wilson Candidacy

Although he was an educational innovator, Wilson had long been a conservative Democrat; political opportunity led him to champion such reform ideas as the direct primary, the initiative, and the referendum. Some Democrats preferred the moderate and less inspiring leadership of the Speaker of the House, James Beauchamp "Champ" Clark of Missouri, who endorsed lower tariffs and not much else. Wilson, Clark, and several other Democratic hopefuls fought for the nomination in primaries and state conventions.

When the national convention met in Baltimore in late June, no candidate was in sight of the two-thirds majority needed for the nomination. As a fresh face, Wilson had strong backing among the delegates as a candidate all Democrats could agree to endorse. He was free from the defeats of the past and offered the prospect of fresh ideas. After forty-six ballots, Wilson was nominated. The hopes for victory looked bright in November.

The 1912 Contenders

Once again the Socialist party selected Eugene V. Debs as its candidate. Debs had run in every election since 1900, and his total vote had increased each time. He knew that he would not be elected, but in his mind he was preparing the way for a nation that would in time turn to socialism. The party also made gains at the state and local levels. Seven hundred thousand voters supported Socialist candidates in 1910, and the following year Socialist mayors or city officials were chosen in seventy-four cities. Labor unrest seemed to be growing, especially in the Lawrence, Massachusetts, textile strike that broke out in January 1912. "Comrades," Debs cried, "this is our year."

Socialism gained followers because the party spoke to the grievances of the agricultural and working poor. Disputes within their ranks over whether to pursue reform at the ballot box or through more violent means prevented the party from offering a united front. Moreover, since he had little chance of winning, Debs did not have to frame programs with a view to carrying them out in office.

Republicans who supported Roosevelt formed the Progressive Party behind his banner and prepared to hold their first national convention. The atmosphere of the convention, which met in Chicago in August 1912, mixed the fervor of a revival meeting with the traditional backroom bargaining of other conventions. Delegates sang "Onward Christian Soldiers" as the theme of the meeting and their movement.

To woo the white South, the delegates excluded African Americans from the convention. Roosevelt defended the protective tariff and attacked reciprocity with Canada. The main financial support for the new party came from wealthy newspaper publishers and corporate executives, who liked Roosevelt's belief that big business should be accepted as a fact of economic life and regulated in the way he had discussed during his presidency.

At its core, however, the Progressive Party's endorsement of expanded social justice legislation made it more forward-looking than either the Republicans' or the Democrats'. Jane Addams and other social justice reformers joined Roosevelt's crusade for that reason. The party supported woman suffrage, limits on child labor, and a system of

Progressive Party.
The Progressive Party under Theodore Roosevelt argued that the two old parties had failed. The third-party effort appealed to votes disenchanted with the old methods of politics.

THE "OPEN ROAD"

"I suppose you know the force that is behind the new party that has recently been formed—the so-called Progressive party. It is a force of discontent with the regular parties of the United States. It is the feeling that men have gone into blind alleys and come out often enough, and that they propose to find an open road for themselves."—WOODROW WILSON
From the Journal (Boston)

"social insurance." The centerpiece of Roosevelt's New Nationalism was the proposal for an "administrative commission" that would "maintain permanent, active supervision over industrial corporations engaged in interstate commerce." Roosevelt continued his policy of distinguishing between "good trusts" that served the public interest and "bad trusts" that harmed society. Enacting Roosevelt's program involved a broadening of national authority and an expansion of the bureaucratic machinery of the federal government. The role of the president would also expand to ensure that the public's rights were protected. Roosevelt's position in 1912 looked forward to the regulatory and welfare state that emerged later in the twentieth century. Critics at the time warned that in the wrong hands, this increased national power could also threaten individual liberty.

Woodrow Wilson and the New Freedom

At first Woodrow Wilson did not plan to campaign much. As Roosevelt laid out his program, however, the Democratic nominee soon decided to confront his major rival. Wilson told the voters that only a Democratic president could govern effectively with the Democratic Congress that was certain to be elected. He then offered a program of his own to counter Roosevelt's New Nationalism. He called it the New Freedom.

As Roosevelt began his campaign, Wilson consulted with **Louis D. Brandeis**, a prominent lawyer in Boston and reformist thinker. Brandeis believed that big

MAP 21.1 The Election of 1912.

Because Democrat Woodrow Wilson faced a divided opposition in the presidential election of 1912, the result was a landslide victory in the electoral vote. Theodore Roosevelt's Progressive Party ran second, and William Howard Taft's Republicans were a distant third.

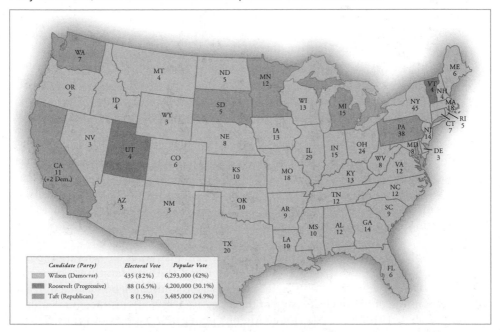

Candidate (Party)	Electoral Vote	Popular Vote
Wilson (Democrat)	435 (82%)	6,293,000 (42%)
Roosevelt (Progressive)	88 (16.5%)	4,200,000 (30.1%)
Taft (Republican)	8 (1.5%)	3,485,000 (24.9%)

business was inefficient economically and dangerous to democracy. He told Wilson that the issue Roosevelt was raising could be met with a simple question: Shall we have regulated competition or regulated monopoly? Wilson should emphasize the need for greater competition to control monopoly and call for stricter enforcement of the antitrust laws. Rather than relying on trusts and large corporations to act in a socially responsible manner, as Roosevelt contended, the government should create conditions in which competition could flourish.

As for social justice, Wilson said that he supported the goals of eliminating child labor, improving wages for women, and expanding benefits for employees, but he questioned whether the federal government should supply these benefits. In that way he appealed to progressives but also prevented southern Democrats from opposing him as an enemy of state rights (and segregation). Throughout the campaign, Wilson stressed that the tariff should be reduced to lower prices and break the link between the government and big business that the Republicans had established. The New Freedom was, like most other campaign slogans, broad and vague. It gave Wilson a mandate for action without tying his hands.

THE BEGINNING OF WILSON'S PRESIDENCY

The 1912 election was turbulent down to election day. From the outset of the campaign, it was clear that the Democrats had the electoral advantage over the divided Republicans and Progressives. Wilson received four hundred thirty-five electoral votes to eighty-eight for Roosevelt and eight for Taft. The Democrats swept Congress: they had fifty-one seats in the Senate to forty-four for the Republicans, and their margin in the House was 291 to 127. Nevertheless, Wilson was a minority president. He received about 42 percent of the popular vote. Eugene Debs won just over 900,000 popular votes, or 6 percent of the total, and Roosevelt and Taft divided the rest. Voter turnout for the election was lower than it had been in 1908.

In the White House, Woodrow Wilson was a brilliant speaker whose moral rhetoric spoke of lofty ideals. He strengthened the power of the presidency, increased the regulatory role of the national government, and led the nation to play a greater part in international affairs. Even more than Roosevelt, he had the capacity to articulate national values in effective and moving language.

With these strong qualities came important limitations. Before he became president, Wilson had suffered a series of small strokes that increased his natural stubbornness and made him reluctant to accept unwelcome advice. Although he often called for open government and sought what he called "common counsel," he kept his decisions to himself and consulted only a few friends about his policies. His righteousness and sense of personal virtue caused his political enemies to develop an intense dislike of his methods and tactics. However, when the tide of events ran with Wilson, as they did during his first term, he was a powerful leader.

Tariff Reform — Wilson lost no time in demonstrating his intention to be a strong president. He picked **William Jennings Bryan**, the leading Democrat in the country, other than Wilson himself, to be secretary of state in recognition of Bryan's leadership of the party after 1896. In his inaugural address on March 4, 1913, he spoke eloquently of the negative aspects of industrialism.

To implement his program, Wilson first asked Congress to take up the issue of the tariff, which symbolized the links between Republicans and big business. He called the lawmakers into a special session in April 1913, and to dramatize the problem, he decided to deliver his message to Congress in person. No president had done so since Jefferson had abandoned the practice in 1801, but presidential appearances before Congress became more common once Wilson resumed the technique. The move proved to be an important step in expanding presidential influence on Capitol Hill and in the nation at large.

Wilson urged the House and Senate to reduce import duties. The Democratic House responded with a measure to lower tariffs, named after Oscar W. Underwood, the chairman of the Ways and Means Committee. The Underwood bill cut duties on raw wool, sugar, cotton goods, and silks. To compensate for the revenue that would be lost, the new tariff imposed a small tax on annual incomes over $4,000 with rates increasing for those who made more than $20,000 a year. Progressives had secured ratification of the **Sixteenth Amendment** in February 1913, which made the income tax constitutional.

Democrats worried about what would happen when the Underwood bill reached the Senate. In fact, the Democrats were relatively unified in 1913, and pressure from large corporations for higher rates had eased. Only smaller businesses, fearing foreign competition, pushed hard for tariff protection. President Wilson added his voice on May 26, when he denounced the "industrious" and "insidious" lobby that was trying to weaken the drive for tariff reform. He said that he would be the people's lobbyist. It was a dramatic gesture, but not really necessary. The Democrats stuck together, lowered the duties that the House had set, and passed the bill in August by a vote of forty-four to thirty-seven. The conference committee's version of the bill passed both houses in October. Wilson signed the Underwood Tariff into law on October 3, 1913. The president and his party had demonstrated that they could provide positive leadership.

The Federal
Reserve System

Building on his momentum, Wilson turned to another important subject in June 1913. Since the panic of 1907, there had been a clear need for reform of the nation's banking system. A modern economy could not function efficiently without a central bank with the capacity to control the currency, meet the monetary needs of different sections of the country, and ensure that the money supply was adequate to the demands of the growing economy. The issue became whether private banking interests or the national government should be in charge of the central bank.

Wilson initially favored a system of private reserve banks until Secretary of State Bryan and his allies in Congress insisted that the federal government must be supreme over the reserve banks and the currency they would issue. At the urging of Louis Brandeis, Wilson accepted Bryan's ideas.

It took six months to get a banking bill through Congress. Wilson had to appease southern and western Democrats, who wanted two changes in the proposed law: expand the credit available to farmers and outlaw the practice known as interlocking directorates, in which banking officials served as directors of banks with which they competed. For reformers, such arrangements symbolized the power of finance capital. The president withstood criticism from the banking community itself and used patronage and persuasion to win over potential opponents among Democrats in the Senate.

Congress completed its action in mid-December, and Wilson signed the Federal Reserve Act on December 27. This act was one of the most important pieces of economic legislation of the first half of the twentieth century. It established the Federal Reserve Board, whose members the president appointed, and created a structure consisting of twelve reserve banks located around the country. The Federal Reserve had the power to determine the amount of money in circulation, expand or contract credit as needed, and respond to some degree to changes in the business cycle. That has proved to be an indispensable weapon for the government in managing the economy since that time.

Wilson and the Progressive Agenda
Wilson had now gone a good distance toward fulfilling his campaign pledges to reduce the tariff, reform the banking system, and deal with the problem of trusts. Early in 1914, the president asked Congress to consider trusts in a constructive spirit. Some of the legislation passed in that year followed the principles that Wilson had outlined in his campaign. The Clayton Antitrust Act (1914) endeavored to spell out precisely the business practices that restricted competition and then to prohibit them.

As time passed, Wilson came to favor the creation of a trade commission that would respond to business practices as they evolved, an idea that resembled what Theodore Roosevelt had proposed in 1912. The Federal Trade Commission was established during fall 1914. A delighted Wilson said that he had almost completed the program he had promised in his 1912 presidential campaign.

The president's statements disappointed progressives who wanted social justice legislation. Wilson did not yet believe that Washington should support the demands of progressive interest groups. He also worried about the precedent if a government used power to address specific social issues. Such a policy might lead to attacks on racial segregation in the South that Wilson supported. In fact, the Wilson administration expanded racial segregation in the federal government. The color line, Wilson told a black delegation that came to protest such policies, "may not be intended against anybody, but for the benefit of both."

When supporters of woman suffrage sought Wilson's backing in 1913 and 1914, he refused to provide it. He also opposed federal aid for rural credits, restrictions on child labor through congressional action, and Prohibition. Court decisions had subjected organized labor to the workings of the antitrust laws, and the unions wanted that policy changed through legislation. Again, Wilson declined to act. Worsening economic conditions during the spring and summer of 1914 reinforced Wilson's belief that his administration should remain conservative on social issues. He tried to reassure businesses that the administration was friendly toward them. These gestures did not appease the Republicans or their business supporters, however. There were indications that the Democrats would have a difficult time at the polls in the 1914 congressional elections.

SOCIAL AND CULTURAL CHANGE DURING THE WILSON YEARS

While politicians worked out Wilson's New Freedom programs during 1913 and 1914, social and cultural transformations proceeded. The Victorian era, with its cultural restraints, faded. Americans with a literary or artistic bent turned to the ideas of European thinkers, who emphasized greater freedom for the individual in an uncertain

The Model T Ford

Table 21.1, about Henry Ford's Model T, is a revealing look at the impact of the automobile on American society in the years preceding entry into World War I. As Ford introduced assembly-line methods into his production facility at Highland Park, Michigan, the output of cars rose steadily. The economies of scale that Ford's engineers achieved allowed them at the same time to bring down the cost to the consumer by more than half ($850 to $360) in an eight-year period. Sales rose as well, enabling Ford to finance his Five-Dollar Day program for workers and to put more capital into his productive capacity.

A careful scrutiny of the table discloses some key points about the emergence of a mass economy in the early twentieth century. Ford understood that lower costs for each unit produced greater and more dependable profits for his company. At the same time, consumers needed a secure income to afford to buy cars and other products. The information in the table thus offers a snapshot of an economy and society moving away from the industrial system of Andrew Carnegie and John D. Rockefeller, and toward the mass production, consumer-oriented system of the modern United States.

TABLE 21.1 Manufacturing and Marketing of Model T Fords, 1908–1916.

Calendar Year	Retail Price (Touring Car)	Total Model T Production	Total Model T Sale
1908	$850	n.a.	5,986
1909	950	13,840	12,292
1910	780	20,727	19,293
1911	690	53,488	40,402
1912	600	82,388	78,611
1913	550	189,088	182,809
1914	490	230,788	260,720
1915	440	394,788	355,276
1916	360	585,388	577,036

Source: From *The American System to Mass Production, 1800–1932: The Development of Manufacturing Technology in the United States*, by David Hounshell, p. 224, Table 6.1. © 1985 Johns Hopkins University Press. Reprinted with permission of The Johns Hopkins University Press.

world. Some of these principles came to be defined as modernism. In the days just before World War I, a sense of optimism and possibility filled the air.

Automobiles for a Mass Market   When Wilson went to his inauguration on March 4, 1913, he drove in an automobile, the first time a president-elect had traveled to his swearing-in by car. This action symbolized the vast changes that were making the people of the United States more mobile in their daily lives and more eager for the consumer products of an industrial society. In particular, Henry Ford's innovations in both production and marketing were bringing cars within the reach of the average middle-class American.

If Ford wanted to fulfill his dream of building "a motor car for the great multitude," he had to devise a means of producing cars continually and in even greater quantities. He borrowed the concept of the assembly line from the meatpacking industry, and his engineers adapted it to carmaking. The Ford plant covered more than sixty-five acres in Highland Park, Michigan. It featured a large belt, fed by smaller belts, that brought the chassis of the car and its windshields, tanks, batteries, and other parts together in a smoothly functioning operation. At first, it took the work force ninety-three minutes to turn out a single Model T. By 1920, the cars were coming off the line at the rate of one per minute. In 1914 the Model T cost under $500 and Ford produced more than 260,000 cars.

On January 5, 1914, Ford proclaimed that he would pay his workers five dollars for an eight-hour day. At the time the average wage worker in manufacturing made around twenty cents per hour, so Ford would be paying three times that to his employees. The announcement made headline news across the country, and Ford became a national hero. He understood that people needed to earn enough money in wages to be able to afford the cars he was making. He realized that he could make more money by selling large numbers of low-priced vehicles than he could by selling a few expensive cars. Ford thus could be described as an apostle of the emerging mass society.

The Five-Dollar Day program was also designed to head off potential unrest among Ford workers. Absenteeism and high turnover among employees hampered production schedules. In addition, unhappiness among workers might lead to the organization of unions. To offset these trends, the new program aimed at sharing profits in a way that would keep workers at their jobs. In addition, Ford developed a "Sociological Department" to instill in employees the values required for efficient mass production. Workers who were productive and cooperative received higher wages. Those who were not were discharged.

The Growing Use of Electricity   The Five-Dollar Day was an apparent sign of progress. Another was the spreading reliance on electricity. Average annual use of electricity doubled during the twenty years after 1912. New products offered homemakers the chance to ease the dull routines of domestic work. General Electric introduced the Radiant Toaster in 1912, which promised "Crisp, Delicious, Golden-Brown Toast on the Breakfast Table." The Hoover Suction Sweeper would "Sweep with Electricity for 3¢ a Week." Newer stoves and washing machines also came into use. Women could buy ready-made clothes and spend less time on the sewing that had occupied much of their day a generation earlier.

Other technological developments were still in their early stages. The Wright brothers had made the first powered flight in 1903, and technological progress in flying accelerated during the decade that followed. Harriet Quimby of the United States was the first woman to fly a plane across the English Channel. Meanwhile, the use of wireless telegraphy in marine navigation expanded. The disaster of the SS *Titanic*, which hit an iceberg in April 1912 and sank with the loss of hundreds of passengers, underlined the need for reliable radio communications for all vessels. Congress

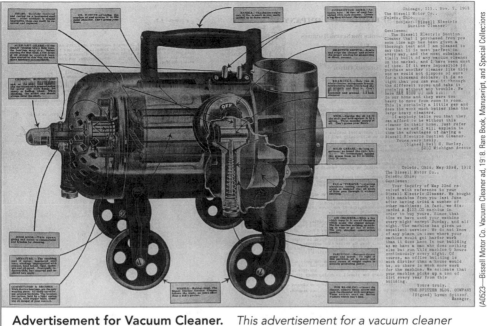

Advertisement for Vacuum Cleaner. *This advertisement for a vacuum cleaner that could be used conveniently in the home was part of the growing market for consumer appliances that reshaped American domestic life.*

enacted a bill mandating the navy to promote radio usage. Within a few years tentative steps would be taken toward broadcasting voices over the airwaves.

Artistic and Social Ferment

In 1913, the International Exhibit of Modern Art took place at the 69th Regiment Armory in New York City. Quickly dubbed "the Armory Show," it displayed the works of such European painters as Pablo Picasso and Henri Matisse. The modernist paintings, abstract and challenging, offended many critics, who attacked them in vicious terms. Nevertheless the public flocked to see the paintings, and American artists were stimulated and challenged to adopt the new forms of expression. As one critic predicted, "American art will never be the same again."

The period also produced innovative literary figures who would become even more famous during the 1920s. Reporters and novelists clustered in New York's Greenwich Village. Among them were Max Eastman, publisher of *The Masses*, a magazine that assailed conventional values and the established political system; Eugene O'Neill, a playwright; and John Reed, a radical journalist. Outside New York City, Theodore Dreiser was continuing a literary career that included *The Financier* (1912), a novel depicting a ruthless tycoon; Sherwood Anderson was a short-story author who criticized middle-class life in the nation's heartland.

Among the influential writers of the day was Walter Lippmann, a Harvard-educated commentator and social critic, who published *A Preface to Politics* (1913) and *Drift and Mastery* (1914). Lippmann sympathized with the New Nationalism of Theodore Roosevelt, and he was one of the cofounders, with Herbert Croly, of *The New Republic*,

(© Bettman/CORBIS)

Women in the Progressive Era. *Greater freedom for women in the Progressive era brought them into places previously reserved for men. These four women are drinking in the bar of a New York hotel.*

soon a leading journal of political opinion and cultural commentary. Another important critical voice was H. L. Mencken, editor of *Smart Set*, a New York magazine, in which he assailed the cultural provincialism of much of American culture.

Women sought to gain greater rights and share the freedoms that men enjoyed. In 1912, women in Greenwich Village founded a club called Heterodoxy, whose only demand was that its members "not be orthodox" in their views. In their discussions and in the public meetings they sponsored, they called their doctrine "feminism," which they defined as an attempt on the part of women to be "our whole big human selves."

Heterodoxy represented only a small proportion of American women, but cultural changes occurred even for those who did not call themselves feminists. Women's skirts had become several inches shorter since the beginning of the century, when they had reached down to the ankle. Bobbed hair became fashionable, and more women smoked openly in public. When movie stars like Mary Pickford became famous, the use of cosmetics spread as women emulated the images of feminine beauty that appeared on screen. The "flapper," with short skirts and bobbed hair, an image associated with the 1920s, actually made her appearance at about this time. The years between 1910 and 1920 saw greater opportunities for women in employment and cultural affairs than would occur in the 1920s.

Americans at Play   The ways in which Americans used their leisure time reflected a trend toward mass entertainment. Boxing was still a major sport. When Arthur John **"Jack" Johnson** became the first African American heavyweight champion in 1908, the white-controlled media clamored for a "white hope" to reclaim the title. Jackson defeated each of his white challengers in the ring, but fled the

Jim Thorpe

In the 1912 Olympic Games held in Sweden, an American athlete named Jim Thorpe captured the imagination of the nation by winning gold medals in the pentathlon and the decathlon competitions. A member of the Sac and Fox of the Woodland tribe, Thorpe had been sent to the Carlisle Indian School in Pennsylvania at age sixteen, where he was taught to adopt the ways of white Americans. There he displayed a talent for football, baseball, and track. Fame seemed to offer a way out of the economic and cultural limits that society imposed on Native Americans at that time. The feats at the Olympics added to his athletic renown, but it was revealed a few months later that he had played baseball for money, in violation of the strict Olympic rules, and he was stripped of his medals. Although he later had success in professional football and baseball, Thorpe had a troubled life on the margins of celebrity until his death in 1953 at the age of sixty-six.

country when the government accused him of transporting women across state lines for immoral purposes. In 1915, an aging Johnson lost the heavyweight title.

Baseball attained new heights of popularity. The two professional leagues had emerged, and the World Series had become an annual fall ritual to decide the "world's champion." The public avidly absorbed the ample news coverage that baseball received.

Motion Pictures and the Vaudeville Stage Motion pictures and vaudeville competed for entertainment dollars. In elaborate vaudeville houses, audiences saw such stars as Fanny Brice, Al Jolson, and Sophie Tucker in well-developed routines aimed at the whole family. A circuit of theaters gave performers a reliable market in which to perfect their craft and maintain their popularity. By the time Wilson became president, motion pictures were challenging the dominance of vaudeville. Movies were evolving from short features into stories of an hour or more. The places where patrons saw films were upgraded, while the price of admission remained reasonable. An average family of five could see a movie for less than a half dollar, which put films well within the income of even poorer Americans. Within a decade, movies emerged as the mass entertainment of the nation. They were lively and up-to-date and conveyed a sense of modern life and spontaneity that made nineteenth-century ideas appear even more dated and obsolete.

New Freedom Diplomacy

Throughout the Progressive era, domestic political and economic concerns dominated. Newspapers covered international news, and readers could follow the unfolding of European diplomacy if they wished. Isolated from the tensions of world affairs by two vast oceans, Americans allowed their elected leaders to conduct foreign policy as long as the general policies of isolation and noninvolvement with Europe were observed.

Woodrow Wilson and the World Woodrow Wilson came to the presidency without any experience in foreign policy. In fact, early in 1913 he remarked to a friend that it "would be the irony of fate if my administration had to deal chiefly with foreign affairs." Nevertheless, Wilson had definite ideas about how the nation should behave in world affairs. During his first eighteen months in the White House, Wilson applied his precepts to diplomatic problems in Asia and Latin America, situations that trained him for the greater trials he would face in World War I.

The president handled most of the business of foreign affairs himself. He appointed William Jennings Bryan as secretary of state, but he never allowed Bryan to have a significant role in shaping policy. Bryan spent some of his time making speeches about public issues and promoting international treaties of conciliation that he thought would end the threat of war. Many countries signed these treaties before the war broke out in 1914; they provided for a "cooling-off" period before countries could begin fighting.

In foreign affairs, Woodrow Wilson believed that the United States should set an example for the rest of the world because of the nation's commitment to democracy and capitalism. "Morality and not expediency is the thing that must guide us," he said in 1913.

In Asia, the Wilson administration stepped back from Taft's commitments, instructing American bankers to withdraw from the Chinese railroad consortium that Taft and Knox had sponsored. The United States also recognized the Republic of China, which had come into power following the 1911 revolution that ousted the Manchu dynasty. Wilson and the Democrats put the Philippine Islands on the road toward independence, but their efforts to counter the rise of Japanese influence in Asia proved less successful.

Wilson wanted his policy toward Latin America to be less intrusive and less dominant than Roosevelt's had been. To that end, he worked out a treaty with Colombia that apologized for Roosevelt's actions in helping to foment the Panamanian revolution in 1903–1904. The pact outraged the former president, and the Senate did not approve the treaty while Wilson was in office. Better relations with Latin America did not, in the president's mind, mean accepting governments that offended his moral values. "I am going to teach the South American Republics to elect good men," he said. That principle led him into the kinds of intervention that he would have preferred to avoid. He kept troops in Nicaragua and extracted further concessions from that country. Other military detachments went to Cuba, Haiti, and the Dominican Republic.

| The Mexican Involvement and Its Consequences | In Mexico, Wilson confronted a revolution. The Madero government, which had taken over from Porfirio Díaz in 1911, was ousted just before Wilson was inaugurated in March 1913. The man who toppled Francisco Madero was General |

Victoriano Huerta. Although most European nations quickly recognized Huerta's government, the United States did not. To win recognition from the United States, the Mexicans would have to install a government that relied on law rather than "arbitrary and irregular force."

Wilson instead threw the weight of the United States behind Venustiano Carranza, a rebel against the Huerta government, but his offers of cooperation were not accepted. If Carranza agreed to Wilson's insistence on some U.S. economic and political presence in Mexico, he would have been regarded as pro-American, a fatal weakness to the sensitive Mexican populace.

To block the flow of munitions into Mexico from the United States and Europe, Wilson had sent the navy to patrol the Gulf of Mexico. Sailors from the USS *Dolphin* went ashore at Tampico on April 9 without the necessary permission, and Mexican authorities arrested them. Released quickly and without further incident, they returned to their ship. The admiral on the scene nonetheless demanded that the Mexican authorities apologize and make a twenty-one-gun salute to the American flag. Huerta's government replied that the Mexican flag should be saluted.

The president asked Congress for authority to use force at a time when a German vessel was unloading arms on the Mexican shore. Wilson ordered troops to occupy the port of Vera Cruz. In the heavy fighting that erupted, more than a hundred Mexicans and nineteen Americans died. All the warring parties in Mexico denounced the United States. The two countries seemed on the edge of outright war.

Wilson drew back and accepted mediation. The negotiations led to the evacuation of Vera Cruz on November 14. Dependent on outside funds to pay his army, Huerta left office when his money ran out in July 1914. Carranza took power, and Wilson promptly recognized his government. A rebellion against Carranza by one of his generals would lead to further confrontations with the United States during the rest of Wilson's first term.

Revolutionary upheavals in Mexico produced an increase in immigrants from that country into the United States after 1910. A mix of social, political, and economic forces had already produced a rising number of Mexican immigrants after 1900. Although many of those immigrants returned to Mexico after working in the United States for several months, some thirty-five thousand to seventy-five thousand Hispanic immigrants stayed on each year. The dictatorial regime of Porfirio Díaz impelled political dissidents and impoverished peasants to travel north. The revolution that began in 1911 drove more Mexicans toward the U.S. border. Throughout these years, the spread of irrigation agriculture, railroads, and mining in the Southwest increased the demand for inexpensive labor. The closing off of Japanese immigration after 1907 made Mexican laborers an attractive option for Anglo businesses.

The newcomers from south of the border found work in the sugar beet fields of Colorado; in the agricultural valleys of south Texas and southern California, where they picked the lettuce and citrus fruits that grew in irrigated fields; and in the towns of Arizona and New Mexico. Other Hispanics labored for daily wages in Los Angeles,

El Paso, and San Antonio. They paved streets, built houses, and processed food for the Anglo community. Their wages were low—sometimes less than $1.25 per day.

Major centers of Hispanic life emerged in the southwestern cities. Ethnic communities sponsored mutual aid societies and established Spanish-language newspapers to ease the immigrants' adjustment to a new culture. Religious prejudice remained strong, however. When Mexican immigrants settled in San Bernadino, California, one long-time resident warned that he "might use a shotgun on these aliens if necessary." In Texas and California, segregation and poverty limited the opportunities open to Mexican Americans.

The international tension between Mexico and the Wilson administration led to periodic "brown scares" along the border. Anglo residents feared vague conspiracies to reclaim land lost by Mexico during the nineteenth century. Cross-border incursions from Mexico heightened tensions. By 1915, a violent cultural conflict that claimed hundreds of lives was in progress in south Texas. As a result of these struggles, Mexican Americans lost much of the land they held in the area. Nevertheless, Hispanics had achieved the basis for a greater presence in the United States during the twentieth century.

WORLD WAR I

By 1914, the major European nations were on edge. If one country found itself at war with another, all the other powers could be drawn into the struggle. On one side stood Germany, in the center of Europe. Its powerful industries and efficient army worried its neighbors, France and Russia. The Germans sought the international respect they believed to be their rightful due. They had built up a large navy that had fueled tensions with Great Britain. Their leader, Kaiser Wilhelm II, had erratic dreams of world influence that his generals and admirals adapted for their own expansionist purposes. The Germans had treaty links to the sprawling and turbulent nations of Austria–Hungary and the even more ramshackle regime of the Ottoman Turks. Italy had been part of the so-called **Triple Alliance** with Germany and Austria–Hungary, but these ties were frayed by 1914.

Against the Germans stood the French (who coveted territory they had lost in the Franco-Prussian War of 1871), the Russians, and, if the Germans attacked France, the British. The Russian Empire was in decay, with revolutionary sentiments just below the surface. The French feared another defeat at the hands of Germany, and the British worried about German naval strength and Berlin's plans for dominance of western Europe. All the powers had elaborate plans for mobilization in a general crisis. Once these timetables went into effect, the relentless pressure of military events would frustrate efforts at a diplomatic resolution.

World War I began in the Balkans. On June 28, 1914, the Austrian archduke, **Franz Ferdinand**, and his wife were murdered in the town of Sarajevo in Bosnia, a province of the Austro-Hungarian Empire. The Austrians soon learned that the killer had been paid by the Serbians and made harsh demands on Serbia that would have left that nation defenseless. The Germans supported their Austrian allies, with the result that the Russians came to the defense of the Serbs. Soon all the European countries were drawn into the conflict.

By early August 1914, the general war that Europeans had long feared and anticipated was under way. Germany, Austria–Hungary, and Turkey, known as the Central Powers, were fighting Great Britain, France, and Russia, now called the Allies. Italy remained neutral. Soon the guns of August began a conflagration that lasted four years and consumed the flesh and blood of a generation.

The sudden outbreak of fighting in Europe surprised Americans, even those who were well informed about world events. Although the arms race among the great powers had seemed potentially dangerous, it had been a century since a major war had involved all the major European countries. Surely, the conventional wisdom of the day said, the self-restraint and wisdom of the great nations made a destructive war unlikely. Faith in progress and the betterment of humanity, so much a part of the Progressive era's creed, made war unthinkable. When the armies marched, Americans were shocked. The world war came at a time of emotional distress for Wilson. His wife, Ellen, had died on August 6, 1914. This personal loss devastated the president, who occupied himself in dealing with the war. On the domestic political scene, the Democrats expected serious losses in the congressional elections. The Republicans had won back some of the Progressive voters who had followed Roosevelt in 1912. Until war broke out, it seemed as if politics might be returning to something resembling its normal patterns.

CONCLUSION

The Republican split between Theodore Roosevelt and William Howard Taft had opened the way for Woodrow Wilson to win the presidency in 1912, a result that produced the domestic program Wilson called the New Freedom. Progressivism thus went through several different phases during the brief period from the New Nationalism of Roosevelt to the governmental activism that Wilson embraced after 1914.

In the process, the contradictions in the reform movement emerged. Should government power be used, as Wilson suggested, to restore competitive balance in the economy without the need for constant regulation? Or, as Roosevelt argued, should the government become bigger to provide consistent supervision of the marketplace? Differences also surfaced over whether society should pursue social justice by doing more for the less fortunate. As these battles were waged, some of the energy and purpose of the reformers ebbed as conservatism made a comeback over such issues as labor's rights and higher taxes.

In the cultural realm, currents of modern thought appeared to question older Victorian values. Women became freer in their relationships with men, artists took a skeptical look at the ills of society, and race relations changed as African Americans moved out of the South. In the years before the World War, optimism about the future of humanity pervaded the United States. Some even talked of an end to war and strife among nations.

The economy took the first steps toward a consumer culture in the 1920s. Henry Ford's Model T car was priced to appeal to many more Americans. In addition, if the spirit of his salary of five dollars a day for his employees was followed, customers would also have the money to buy one. Motion pictures became the fastest growing form of popular entertainment, and visionaries spoke of making the new medium of radio available to the masses.

In foreign affairs, the United States sought greater world influence without overseas involvement. The nation remained dominant in Latin America, though the revolution in Mexico underscored how complex the role of foreign policy might become. For all of the problems of Mexico, Haiti, and Nicaragua in this period, the country saw little to worry about from the world at large. Protected by oceans from the tensions of the European countries and the ferment in Asia, the United States could, so the thinking went, follow its own destiny without the mistakes of the Old World on the other side of the Atlantic. That comfortable assumption disappeared once the guns of August fired in 1914.

That war produced a lasting change in the course of American history. As it ended the nation's isolation from world events, Americans had to confront the challenges of a world role. During the seven years that followed, Woodrow Wilson would pursue neutrality, enter the war in 1917, and see his dreams of world peace collapse in 1921. Social and political reform continued for a time and then gave way to conservatism. With all these developments, the impact of progressivism on the direction of American politics remained significant. The issues that had been identified in domestic affairs between 1901 and 1914, particularly the question of the government's role in the economy, endured.

CHAPTER REVIEW, 1909–1914

- The presidency of William Howard Taft faltered.
- The Republican Party split between Taft and Roosevelt.
- The Democrats made a comeback under Woodrow Wilson.
- Wilson's New Freedom was enacted in 1913–1914.
- Consumer culture emerged.
- Movies arose as popular entertainment.
- Progress toward the attainment of woman suffrage was made.
- Cultural ferment led to new trends in art and writing.

◀☰☰☰ *Looking Back*

The Taft–Roosevelt split that devastated the Republicans had its origins amid the issues discussed in the previous chapter. The basis for the division had been created during the last years of Roosevelt's presidency.

1. Was Theodore Roosevelt as good a politician as he thought he was?
2. How did Roosevelt and Taft differ in their view of what a president should do?
3. How did the New Nationalism represent a culmination of Roosevelt's political philosophy as president?

Looking Ahead ☰☰☰▶

The next chapter considers what happened when progressives encountered the effects of the war raging in Europe beginning in 1914. The outbreak of the conflict called into question the progressive conviction that human beings were basically good. When the United States entered the war in April 1917, some reforms were pushed forward, and some progressive issues suffered. The international problems that came out of World War I set the pattern for future disputes in the Middle East and Asia.

1. How did Woodrow Wilson view the U.S. role in the rest of the world, especially in Latin America?
2. What view of human nature did the reformers have, and why did the outbreak of World War I prove such a shock?
3. How much of a world power was the United States in 1914?
4. Why did Americans believe they could stay out of European quarrels?
5. What kind of presidential leadership did Woodrow Wilson offer to the Democrats?

Go to the American Passages website at www.cengage.com/history/ayers/ampassages4e for additional review materials.

22

Over There and Over Here: The Impact of World War I, 1914–1921

Americans wanted to keep out of the European war. Yet events in the conflict influenced domestic politics, altered the Progressive movement, and changed the fortunes of women, African Americans, and socialists. The nation's traditional values came under repeated attack as the war continued. U.S. entry into the war in April 1917 transformed the country in an even more striking fashion.

World War I brought several campaigns for social change, most notably Prohibition and woman suffrage, to national success. Yet by the time these results occurred, the movement for reform had stalled. The nation rejected an activist government, expensive programs, and efforts to improve society. When Woodrow Wilson left the White House on March 4, 1921, he gave way to Warren G. Harding, who promised a return to older values and a respite from moral uplift.

STAYING NEUTRAL IN A WORLD CONFLICT

President Wilson in August 1914 asked his fellow citizens to "be neutral in fact as well as in name" and "impartial in thought as well as in action." Long an admirer of British government and culture, Wilson himself had more sympathy for the Allies than for Germany and its wartime partners. He also believed that some kind of "association of nations" must prevent future world wars. In conducting foreign policy, however, he was as even-handed toward the two sides as any president could have been.

The War and American Public Opinion

The initial results of Wilson's neutrality decisions came in national politics. Going into the congressional elections of

568

1914, the Republicans anticipated gains in the House and Senate. The Democratic slogan became, "War in the East! Peace in the West! Thank God for Wilson!" The Republicans picked up sixty-three seats in the House, but the Democrats retained control. In the Senate, the president's party actually added five seats. The Democrats did well in the Midwest, where support for progressive reforms remained strong. As Wilson looked toward reelection in 1916, he decided to form a coalition of southern and western voters united on a platform of peace and reform. To do so, the president had to pay attention to the interest groups—union workers, farmers, and woman suffrage advocates—that he had rebuffed between 1913 and 1915. If the war stimulated the economy, the combination of peace, prosperity, and reform might reelect the president.

The British had inherent advantages in their financial ties with the United States. Economic links with Great Britain were strong, and they intensified as the war progressed. Exports to Britain and France totaled $754 million in 1914; in 1916, they stood at $2.75 billion. Meanwhile, trade with Germany, which had totaled $190 million in 1914, virtually ceased because of the British blockade. The United States could have embargoed all trade with belligerent powers, as many American supporters of Germany recommended, but that strategy would have devastated the economy.

The Germans also had strong support in the United States. The more than 5 million German Americans, most numerous in the Midwest, represented a sizable bloc of votes that usually favored Republicans. The 3 million–plus Irish Americans hated England and cheered for its enemies. Germany conducted an expensive propaganda campaign of pamphlets and newspaper advertisements. Money directed through the German-dominated brewing industry paid for the campaign. Undercutting their public relations image, however, the Germans also used espionage and sabotage to cripple the British war effort and hamper American assistance to the Allies.

The British matched German expenditures on propaganda describing the alleged atrocities of their foe. They also relied on their cultural ties with the upper classes and opinion makers in the Northeast to set forth the British case in magazines and newspapers. Over the course of the neutrality period, the British gained an ascendancy in the battle to influence American thinking.

The way the Germans waged the war hurt their cause with Americans. In the opening days of the fighting, the German army violated Belgium's neutrality, crossing that nation's borders to invade France. Confronted with a British naval blockade designed to strangle its economy and capacity to wage war, Germany turned to a new weapon, the submarine, early in 1915. In contrast to surface ships, the submarine relied on surprise attacks based on its ability to submerge. Passengers on torpedoed ships were left to drown. Submarines could not provide warnings without risk to themselves, and the Germans resisted pleas that they should do so.

Germany declared that enemy vessels would be sunk on sight, a policy many Americans regarded as a violation of the civilized rules of war. These implicit regulations said that warships should not attack merchant vessels without warning. Neither should they target innocent passengers with their tactics. Despite this aggressive strategy, Germany had only twenty-one submarines when the fighting began; these

This icon will direct you to interactive activities and study materials on the American Passages website: www.cengage.com/history/ayers/ampassages4e

CHAPTER TIMELINE

1914	Wilson declares American neutrality in World War I • President also proclaims first National Mother's Day
1915	Lusitania torpedoed with loss of 128 Americans • Wilson announces preparedness campaign • The Birth of a Nation promotes revival of Ku Klux Klan • Great Migration of African Americans continues
1916	Army pursues Pancho Villa into Mexico • Wilson wins second term over Charles Evans Hughes
1917	Wilson makes "Peace Without Victory" speech • Woman suffrage advocates arrested and jailed for picketing the White House • Germans resume unrestricted submarine campaign • United States enters world war • Military draft enacted to raise army
1918	Wilson announces "Fourteen Points" for peace settlement • American troops join in Allied drive toward Germany • First granulated soap ("Rinso") introduced • Influenza epidemic sweeps the globe and kills 20 million people • Armistice ends First World War
1919	Wilson negotiates Treaty of Versailles • Dial telephones introduced • Prohibition amendment adopted • Wilson stricken with stroke
1920	Senate defeats League of Nations for second time • Woman suffrage amendment ratified • Warren G. Harding wins presidency • Edith Wharton wins Pulitzer Prize for her novel *The Age of Innocence*
1921	Harding becomes President

new vessels could not win the war by themselves. The use of the submarine, however, put Germany in direct conflict with the United States, the leading neutral country.

The *Lusitania* Crisis On May 7, 1915, when a German submarine fired a torpedo into the British liner ***Lusitania*** off the Irish coast, the huge vessel sank quickly. Among the nearly 1,200 passengers who died were 128 Americans. To most people, this event was an atrocity, not an inescapable by-product of modern warfare. Wilson had said that Germany would be held to "strict accountability" for submarine attacks on Americans. He decided, however, that the *Lusitania* was not worth a war.

The president was applauded when he said, three days after the *Lusitania* incident, that "there is such a thing as a man being too proud to fight. There is such a thing as a nation being so right that it does not need to convince others by force that it is right." Allied sympathizers denounced Wilson's words, but the president's readiness to negotiate was generally approved.

Wilson sought an apology and a pledge to limit submarine warfare. His diplomatic response was strong enough, however, that his anti-war Secretary of State William Jennings Bryan, fearful that war might result, resigned in protest in June 1915. He was replaced by Robert Lansing, a pro-Allied diplomat. During the remainder of the summer, the Germans kept the negotiating process going without apologizing or yielding on any point.

In August, the Germans torpedoed a British liner, the *Arabic,* wounding two Americans. Wilson told the Germans privately that the United States would break diplomatic relations with them if submarine warfare continued. Still unsure whether the submarine alone could win the war, Berlin offered a conditional pledge not to make unannounced attacks on passenger liners, which defused the situation briefly. In the following year, the Germans sank thirty-seven unarmed liners.

The United States and Its World Role The neutrality issue forced Americans to consider the nation's future role in a warring world. Many groups wanted the United States to maintain its traditional posture of noninvolvement. German Americans and Irish Americans saw no need to help the British. Progressive reformers regarded war and foreign commitments as the death of reform. In the Midwest and on the Pacific Coast, peace sentiments were widespread.

Led by Theodore Roosevelt, northeastern Republicans called for military "preparedness" in the event of ultimate American entry into the war. Army and navy officials knew that they would have to expand their forces if they were to play any significant role on the Allied side. In late 1914, Wilson had blocked programs to strengthen the military defense. By the summer of 1915, however, he changed his position and sought a larger army and navy. He promised a navy "second to none" and more troops for the regular army. Many Democrats in the South and West opposed Wilson on the issue of preparedness and the increased spending that it entailed. In early 1916, the president made a speaking tour to arouse popular support for his policy.

As the debate over preparedness intensified, some opinion leaders argued that a world organization should be formed to keep the peace once the fighting stopped.

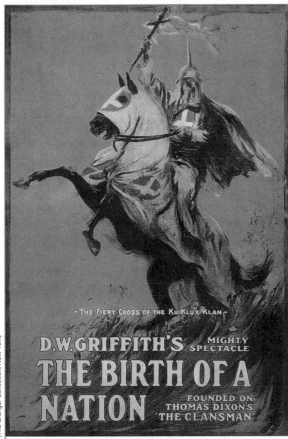

(The Granger Collection, New York)

The Birth of a Nation. *D. W. Griffith's film The Birth of a Nation was an artistic triumph with a racist theme. This poster advertising the film depicts the Ku Klux Klan as akin to medieval knights in the garb of chivalry. White audiences ignored the Klan's violent reality for African Americans.*

The League to Enforce Peace was created in June 1915, with William Howard Taft as its leader. As 1915 ended, Wilson had not yet thrown his influence behind the idea of a world organization.

SOCIAL CHANGE DURING THE PERIOD OF NEUTRALITY

During 1915, Americans flocked to theaters to see a new motion picture that depicted sensational events in the nation's past. David Wark Griffith's *The Birth of a Nation*, based on an antiblack novel by Thomas Dixon, *The Clansman*, portrayed the Reconstruction period in the South as a time when ignorant African Americans terrorized whites and made a travesty of government. An artistic triumph because it used new techniques such as flashbacks and close-ups, the movie twisted history to glamorize the Ku Klux Klan and the white South. Audiences were enthusiastic, box office records were broken, and President Wilson reportedly said: "It is like writing history with lightning." Efforts by African Americans to have the film banned were largely unsuccessful.

Inspired by the film's portrayal of the Klan, a group of white men burned a cross at Stone Mountain, Georgia, to symbolize their resurgence as a racist order. At first the revived Klan's membership remained under five thousand nationally, but the social tensions of the postwar era proved a fertile ground for organizing in the South and Midwest.

The political prospects for improved rights for blacks remained as bleak as they had been since the 1890s. The Wilson administration and the Democratic Party resisted efforts to reduce racism. After protests from blacks and a few progressives, the White House retreated from efforts to enforce segregation in the federal government, but that was a minor victory. The Supreme Court did, however, rule in the case of *Guinn v. United States* (1915) that the grandfather clause that Oklahoma used to exempt whites from a literacy test for voting was unconstitutional. That clause exempted from the literacy test whites whose ancestors had been born before a specific date. Oklahoma found other ways to register whites and restrict blacks, but the decision foreshadowed future racial progress toward greater protection of minority rights.

The Great Migration For African Americans in the South, life was still painful and burdensome. Southern agriculture experienced crippling problems. Natural disasters hit the region in the form of floods and droughts. The boll weevil, an insect that destroys cotton, undermined the farm economy. Blacks began leaving the South for cities in the North. The **Great Migration** started slowly around 1910 and then accelerated between 1914 and 1920 when more than 600,000 African Americans left the South.

The outbreak of the war played a key role in this process. As immigration from Europe ended, the labor market for unskilled workers in the North expanded. Blacks who came to the North found a better life but not a paradise. They secured work in the coal mines of West Virginia, the stockyards of Chicago, and the steel mills of Pittsburgh. Sixty thousand blacks moved to Chicago between 1916 and 1920, a 148 percent increase in its African American population. Chicago was a natural destination because so many railroads from the South passed through that major transportation hub. Similar percentage increases occurred in Pittsburgh, Cincinnati, and Detroit.

The Great Migration of African Americans to the North

The Great Migration of African Americans from the South to northern cities during the second decade of the twentieth century reshaped the nation's cities and, in time, its political, social, and cultural life. This photograph of a black family arriving in Chicago in 1916 reveals in their faces the determination and pain that the journey out of the segregated South demanded. The expressions underscore the rigors of the process, the way in which a few belongings and their best clothes prepared them for the trip, and their apprehension about the uncertain future that they faced in the North.

(Schomburg Center/Art Resource, NY)

This photograph comes from the rich collection of images of black life in the Schomburg Center for Research in Black Culture at the New York Public Library. The photographic documentation of African American life in such twentieth-century records enables history texts to do better justice to the everyday life of all Americans and the individual families of which they were a part. Thus, a simple scene of a family in search of a better life for themselves and their children becomes a symbol of a larger national quest for these values.

As their population in the North grew, blacks encountered discrimination in housing and public services, including from long-standing residents of African American communities in northern cities who looked down on the new arrivals. Nevertheless, southern blacks continued to move north in an historic population shift that reshaped the politics and culture of the nation's largest cities.

The Rise of the Movies

In 1914, a young British comedian began appearing in films for the Keystone company, a filmmaking venture in Los Angeles. Although most of his thirty-five pictures were very short, one film, *Tillie's Punctured Romance*, ran for thirty minutes. Audiences asked about the funny actor in the derby hat and little tramp costume. By 1915, the whole nation was talking about Charlie Chaplin, and a craze called "Chaplinitis" swept the land. In January 1915, Chaplin signed with Essanay Pictures for the then-huge sum of $1,250 a week. (An industrial worker made around $600 per year.) Within twelve months Chaplin moved on to the Mutual Film Corporation at $10,000 a week. Stardom had come quickly for the twenty-six-year-old actor.

After a shaky start at the beginning of the century, motion pictures had arrived as mass entertainment. There were more than ten thousand nickelodeon (charging five cents per customer) theaters by 1912, and up to 20 million Americans went to the movies regularly. Soon movies became longer, and exhibitors began constructing motion picture theaters that could seat up to five thousand customers at a show.

Although Chaplin was the most famous male performer of his time, he was not the only "star" whom the studios created during the era of the silent movie. Executives found that audiences wanted to know about the private lives of the people they saw on the flickering screens. Mary Pickford became "America's Sweetheart" in a series of roles that depicted a demure damsel in acute distress. Douglas Fairbanks used his athletic ability as the swashbuckling hero of such films as *American Aristocracy* (1916) and *Wild and Woolly* (1917). Theda Bara became the "vamp" in *A Fool There Was* (1915).

The business of making movies became concentrated in a few large studios that controlled the process of production and distribution. Because of its mild climate, Hollywood, California, emerged as the center of the picture industry. Studios like Vitagraph and Paramount dominated the making and marketing of films.

Most moviegoers lived in cities where the large theaters were located. Immigrants found that they could learn about American life at the movies. Parents worried when their children saw such films as *Women and Wine* or *Man and His Mate*. Reformers clamored for censorship boards to screen films for scenes that showed lustful images or suggested that criminals profited from their crimes.

Shifting Attitudes Toward Sex The nation's family and sexual values continued to face challenges. In 1916, one of every nine marriages ended in the divorce courts. Meanwhile, family size was decreasing. By 1920, two or three children were born to the average mother; in 1860, the average had been five or six.

Norms of sexual behavior moved away from the restrictions of the Victorian era. For women born around 1900, the rate of sexual intercourse before marriage was twice as high as it had been for women born a decade earlier. Nevertheless, the overall incidence of premarital sexual behavior remained very low in comparison with the present.

Despite the changes in sexual practices, the official attitudes of the nation remained restrictive. Homosexual relationships were outlawed, even though some college-educated women maintained "partnerships" or "Boston marriages." Laws governing the dissemination of information about birth control discouraged the use of contraception. In many states and cities it was a crime to sell condoms or distribute information about how to avoid pregnancy. A federal statute, the Comstock Law of 1873, barred the making, selling, distribution, or importation of contraceptives, as well as any transmission of birth control information through the mails. The only ground on which abortions were permitted was to save the life of the mother.

Margaret Sanger, a thirty-two-year-old home nurse and radical activist living in Greenwich Village in 1911, saw women suffering from disease and poverty because of their large number of children. Often women had many babies because they lacked knowledge about ways to limit births. In 1914, Sanger coined the term *birth control* and began publishing a periodical, *Woman Rebel.* Women, she wrote, "cannot be on an equal footing with men until they have full and complete control over their reproductive function." Indicted for sending such information through the mails, she went to Europe, consulted with experts on family planning, and returned to the United States determined to arouse support for birth control.

A year later she founded a clinic in a poor neighborhood of Brooklyn that distributed information about contraception to the female residents. The police soon closed the clinic down, and Sanger went to jail. When the case was appealed, a higher court affirmed the right of doctors to prescribe birth control devices. Sanger then organized the Birth Control League to promote her cause. Some feminists regarded birth control as a liberating idea; others saw the availability of contraceptive devices as likely to encourage promiscuity and thus promote male dominance.

THE PERSISTENCE OF REFORM

Progressive reform campaigns pressed ahead. Prohibition capitalized on anti-German sentiment to reduce the political power of the brewing industry. The end of the flow of immigrants from Europe enabled advocates of immigration restriction to gain support for tighter laws. Supporters of woman suffrage also used the war as a way of mobilizing women behind their cause.

Woman suffrage gained strength after 1914 despite serious divisions among the movement's leaders. Alice Paul and the militant Congressional Union pressed for a constitutional amendment. Their tactics included demonstrations and a direct challenge to the Democrats as the party in power. In contrast, the National American Woman Suffrage Association (NAWSA), led by **Carrie Chapman Catt** after 1915, emphasized nonpartisanship and state-by-state organization. Paul and her allies formed the National Woman's Party to defeat Wilson and the Democrats. NAWSA continued its efforts to win the right to vote in individual states, but it now sought a constitutional amendment as well. As the election approached, the momentum for suffrage seemed to be building. Even President Wilson, who had previously opposed the idea, now said that individual states could adopt woman suffrage if they wished.

The drive for Prohibition, the second major cultural reform campaign, intensified. In 1914, the Anti-Saloon League pressed for a constitutional amendment to ban the sale of alcohol. At the same time, efforts to make the states liquor-free went forward, with notable success. In 1913–1914, more than a dozen states adopted Prohibition legislation or held referenda in which the voters adopted Prohibition. Nine more states adopted such laws in 1915. Gradually prohibitionist candidates within the major parties won seats in Congress. The prohibition campaign also gained from the anti-immigrant sentiments that intensified in the nation on the eve of World War I.

Closing the Door for Immigrants   The war in Europe shut off immigration to the United States from eastern European countries. Belligerent nations needed every person within their borders to sustain the war effort. The reduced flow of new-comers did not stop the campaign to restrict immigration, however. Proponents of immigration limits contended that the eventual peace would open the door to an even greater influx of outsiders. The ethnic tensions that the neutrality debate produced heightened sensitivity about what came to be called "hyphenated Americans." Congress again passed an immigration restriction law with a literacy test in 1915, which President Wilson again vetoed.

After 1914, progressive reformers looked to the federal government for help with the agenda of social change. In the light of the results of the 1914 congressional elections, Wilson understood that he must move left to win four more years in office. Putting aside his earlier reservations about the use of national power to achieve such reforms as child labor legislation or agricultural credits for farmers, he shifted toward the progressive side. He also became more willing to use the authority of his office to push for reform.

One notable step that Wilson took was to nominate Louis D. Brandeis to the U.S. Supreme Court in January 1916. Brandeis had advised Wilson on the New Freedom, and he had won renown as the "People's Lawyer" and a foe of consolidated business enterprise. Since Brandeis was a longtime champion of reform causes and a prominent Jew, his appointment aroused intense, often anti-Semitic, feelings among conservatives. In the end he was confirmed, and Wilson's strong endorsement of him convinced progressives that the president was on their side.

During the months before the election campaign began, Wilson came out for laws to restrict child labor, promote federal loans to farmers (known as agricultural credits), provide federal aid for highway construction, and cover federal employees with workers' compensation laws. When a national railroad strike threatened in August 1916, Wilson compelled Congress to pass the Adamson Act, which mandated an eight-hour work day for railroad employees. Labor responded with strong support for Wilson's reelection bid. Meanwhile, the improving economy, driven by orders from the Allies for American products and foodstuffs, helped the Democrats.

Wilson's reelection chances hinged on the uneasy neutrality he had maintained toward the Germans and the British throughout 1916. The Republicans seemed divided between those who wished to do more for the Allies and those who either disliked overseas involvement or wished to help Germany. Wilson would benefit if he could find a middle position that combined defense of American rights with preservation of neutrality.

The president had to deal with several related wartime issues during the first half of 1916. By the end of 1915, he had obtained a German apology and indemnity for the dead Americans of the *Lusitania*. After the sinking of the *Arabic*, the Germans had also pledged not to attack passenger liners without warning. Then the United States suggested an arrangement in which the Germans would limit submarine warfare and the Allies would not arm merchant ships. When this proposal (or *modus vivendi*) collapsed because of British and German opposition, Germany resumed submarine attacks on armed shipping, whether it was belligerent or neutral, in February 1916.

On March 24, 1916, a German submarine attacked an unarmed steamer, the *Sussex*, in the English Channel. American passengers on board were injured, and another diplomatic crisis ensued. Wilson told Berlin that continued attacks on unarmed merchant vessels without warning would lead to a breaking of diplomatic ties, a prelude to U.S. entry into the war. The Germans again faced the question of whether the submarine alone could win the war. At the time, only about eighteen of their fifty-two submarines could be on patrol at any one time. With hopes of a victory on land still alive, the Germans pledged that they would not conduct attacks on merchant vessels without warning. The so-called Sussex Pledge gave Wilson a major diplomatic success because it had staved off a war that most Americans dreaded.

During these same months, Wilson also tried to arrange a negotiated settlement of the war. In December 1915, he sent his close friend, Colonel Edward M. House, to discuss peace terms with the British, French, and Germans. House's talks led to an agreement with the British foreign minister, Edward Grey, for Anglo-American mediation of the war; if the Germans rebuffed the idea, the United States would enter the war on the side of the Allies. The House-Grey Memorandum, as the agreement was called, never took effect because Wilson watered it down and the British ignored it.

During the first half of 1916, Wilson emerged as a forceful national leader. His speaking tour calling for preparedness swung public opinion behind his program to provide more weapons and personnel for the army and navy. When Congress sought to assert itself through resolutions warning Americans not to travel on the ships of the warring powers, the president pressured Congress to have the resolutions defeated on the grounds that they interfered with his power to conduct foreign policy. In May 1916, the president argued, in a speech to the League to Enforce Peace, that the major nations of the world should find a way to band together to preserve peace.

In the spring of 1916, the issue of Mexico once again grabbed the nation's headlines. The Mexican civil war had continued after the American intervention at Vera Cruz in 1914. Although Wilson did not like the regime of Venustiano Carranza, he extended diplomatic recognition to it when it became clear that Carranza had emerged as the nation's effective leader.

Then a rebel named Pancho Villa raided towns in New Mexico and Texas in 1916, killing and wounding numerous Americans. The U.S. Army under General John J. Pershing pursued him across the Rio Grande. Heedless of Mexican feelings about this intrusion on their sovereignty, the United States seemed to be headed for a war. Wilson negotiated a diplomatic settlement. Nevertheless, American troops remained in Mexico for two years, placing a continued strain on relations between the two nations.

THE 1916 PRESIDENTIAL ELECTION

The Democrats approached the 1916 election with confidence. The president's program of progressive domestic legislation was moving through Congress, the international situation appeared to have vindicated Wilson's leadership, and the economy was prosperous because of the war orders that the British and French had placed for munitions, food, and industrial products. The Republicans first had to win back the Progressives, some of whom found Wilson's reform program attractive. Eastern Republicans wanted the United States to intervene on the side of the Allies. In the Midwest, progressive Republicans and German Americans opposed a pro-Allied policy.

Theodore Roosevelt hoped to be the Republican nominee, but the Republicans turned to Supreme Court Justice **Charles Evans Hughes**. He had been a progressive governor of New York, was not scarred with the wounds of 1912, and had said little about foreign policy. A remnant of the Progressive Party nominated Roosevelt, but he declined, and the party soon disappeared. The Republicans offered assurances that they favored some domestic reforms and carefully straddled the more controversial questions of preparedness, neutrality, and loyalty of ethnic groups such as the German Americans.

For the Democrats, the excitement occurred over the party's platform and the campaign slogan that arose from it. In that document, the delegates praised Wilson's ability to preserve American neutrality. In his keynote address to the Democratic delegates, a former governor of New York, Martin Glynn, noted that Wilson had maintained neutrality. Each time he referred to this fact, the audience exclaimed, "What did we do? What did we do?" and he shouted back: "We didn't go to war! We didn't go to war!" The Democrats had their slogan: "He kept us out of war."

In the campaign that followed, Wilson employed the themes of peace, progressivism, and prosperity in his speeches. Hughes, though, had difficulty finding a way to appeal to Republicans who shared Roosevelt's position and to the German American voters who wanted the nation to stay out of the conflict. Hughes also proved to be an ineffective campaigner, although he had the benefit of a party that still attracted a majority of voters outside the South. To win, the Democrats assembled a coalition of voters in the South and West, the peace vote, women (who could vote in western and middle western states), and midwestern farmers who were happy with wartime prosperity. Wilson won one of the closest elections in the nation's history. He gained 277 electoral votes from thirty states, and Hughes won 254 electoral votes from

MAP 22.1 The Election of 1916.

The election of 1916, fought under the shadow of World War I in Europe, saw Woodrow Wilson campaign on a platform of peace, prosperity, and progressive reform. That was enough to enable the Democratic incumbent to run well in the West and compile a tight victory over Charles Evans Hughes and the Republicans.

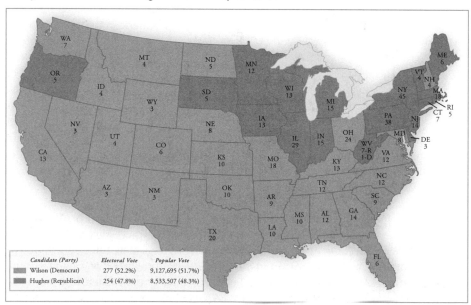

Candidate (Party)	Electoral Vote	Popular Vote
Wilson (Democrat)	277 (52.2%)	9,127,695 (51.7%)
Hughes (Republican)	254 (47.8%)	8,533,507 (48.3%)

eighteen states. The president amassed a little more than 49 percent of the vote, polling 600,000 more popular votes than Hughes did.

Wilson's Attempts to Mediate   Wilson now pressed for a negotiated settlement of the war. Relations with the British had soured during 1916 because of the way the Royal Navy and the British Foreign Office interfered with American shipping in enforcing their blockade against Germany. Meanwhile, the British were becoming more dependent on American loans and credits to pay for the supplies that they had been buying since 1914. Under the circumstances, the president believed, London might be receptive to an American mediation effort. The president also knew that pressure was rising within the German military for unrestricted use of submarines.

On December 18, 1916, Wilson asked the warring countries to state their terms for a negotiated peace. Both the British and the Germans rejected the president's offer; the solution would have to come on the battlefield. In response, Wilson addressed the U.S. Senate on January 22, 1917, in a speech that called for a "Peace Without Victory." He argued that "only a peace among equals can last," and set out a program that included plans to create a league of nations. The attitude of the warring powers was skeptical. The idea of a league of nations to prevent future wars also aroused opposition in the Senate.

American Intervention in the War   Aware that their military position in the conflict was deteriorating, the German high command decided on January 9, 1917, that only the submarine could win the war before the United States sent troops to Europe. Unrestricted submarine attacks would be resumed on February 1 to choke off supplies to Great Britain. Wilson learned of the German decision on January 31 and realized that Berlin had not been negotiating in good faith. He broke diplomatic relations on February 4. The submarine campaign began as scheduled, and American lives were lost. On February 26, the president asked Congress for authority to arm U.S. merchant ships. With peace sentiment still strong on Capitol Hill, the administration faced a tough fight to get the bill passed.

An unexpected revelation about German war aims then happened. British intelligence had intercepted and decoded a secret German diplomatic telegram to its ambassador in Mexico. The **Zimmerman Telegram**, named after the German foreign minister Arthur Zimmerman, dangled the return to Mexico of Arizona, New Mexico, and Texas as bait to entice the Mexicans to enter the war on the German side. Wilson released this diplomatic bombshell to the public on March 1, and the House promptly passed the bill to arm merchant ships. Eleven senators, led by Robert M. La Follette of Wisconsin, filibustered against the bill until Congress adjourned on March 4. In fact, Wilson could arm the ships on his own authority, which he did on March 9.

The Outbreak of Hostilities   The submarine campaign was hurting the Allies badly, and defeat seemed possible. One stumbling block to American support for the Allied cause had always been the presence of Russia on the side of the British and French. Alliance with that autocratic monarchy mocked the notion that the Allies were fighting for democratic values. When the outbreak of revolution in Russia toppled the regime of Tsar Nicholas II, it seemed to offer some hope for reform. Meanwhile, the Germans sank three American ships on March 18

The Zimmerman Telegram and Code Breaking

The use of codes and ciphers, although traditional in warfare, became more sophisticated and important during the twentieth century as radio and telegraphy developed. One of the most sensational examples of this trend came in World War I with the revelation of the Zimmerman Telegram. In that document, Germany proposed to Mexico an alliance against the United States in the event of war in 1917. British code-breakers, who had been reading German diplomatic traffic, easily intercepted the message, decoded it, and passed it on to Washington. The White House used the information to sway reluctant members of Congress to support President Wilson as war with Germany neared. Secret intelligence thus became a publicity tool as well as a military weapon. Published in the newspapers in its encoded and unbroken form, the telegram as pictured here provided a brief but elusive glimpse into a secret world that grew in importance even after the war ended.

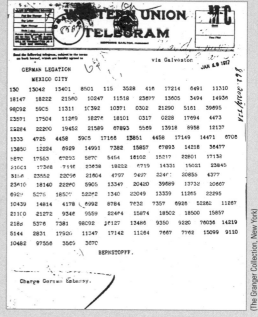

(The Granger Collection, New York)

with large losses. Wilson called Congress into special session on April 2. On a soft spring evening, the president asked for a declaration of war against Germany. "The world must be made safe for democracy," he told them. "It is a fearful thing to lead this great peaceful people into war, into the most terrible and disastrous of all wars, civilization itself seeming to be in the balance. But the right is more precious than peace." Evoking the language of the sixteenth-century German religious reformer Martin Luther, Wilson said of his nation, "God helping her, she can do no other."

Congress declared war on Germany on April 6, 1917. Although the votes were overwhelming (82 to 7 in the Senate; 373 to 50 in the House), the nation was divided. In large parts of the South and West, the public felt no need to become involved in European quarrels or to benefit eastern business interests that might profit from the fighting. Opposition to the war remained high among German Americans and Irish Americans. Dedicated reformers and Socialists saw the war as a betrayal of reform ideals.

For Wilson himself, involvement in the war seemed to be the price the nation had to pay to influence the peace settlement. His lofty rhetoric encouraged Americans to believe that a better world could be obtained through the use of military force. In that sense, the president paved the way for the later disillusion among Americans that frustrated his ambitious plans for world leadership.

A Nation at War

During World War I, the power of the federal government increased in response to the need to mobilize the populace for war. Average citizens found that they had to respond to government programs and directives in strange and unfamiliar ways, such as accepting bureaucratic rules for their businesses, listening to government propaganda, and changing their eating habits.

The government assumed that the American contribution to the war would consist of furnishing money and supplies to the Allied cause. It soon became apparent that American soldiers would have to go across the Atlantic and join in the fighting to achieve an Allied victory.

As of April 1917, the German army still occupied large portions of France seized in 1914. Meanwhile, gigantic battles occurred on the "eastern front" between the Russians, on the one hand, and the Germans and their Austrian allies, on the other. On the "western front," where the Allies and the Germans confronted each other in France, the two sides fought in elaborate trenches from which soldiers fired at each other or mounted attacks against well-fortified positions. Dug-in artillery and machine guns gave the advantage to the defense. The French suffered more than 1.4 million casualties on the western front in 1915. The Germans tried to break the will of the French at Verdun in 1916; both sides lost more than 300,000 men in the ensuing struggle. The British attacked in northern France in 1916; 60,000 men were killed or wounded in a single day's fighting. Similar carnage occurred when the British renewed their offensive on the Somme River in 1917. After the French went on the attack in 1917 with heavy casualties, their broken armies mutinied against further slaughter.

The Wilson administration did not want to raise an army through volunteer methods. A volunteer system was undependable and did not keep trained individuals at their jobs in key war industries. In May 1917, Congress adopted the Selective Service Act whereby men between the ages of twenty-one and thirty had to register for the draft with local boards that were set up to administer the program. By the end of the war 24 million young men had been registered, and about 3 million had been called into the armed forces. Another 340,000 men tried to evade the draft and became "slackers." There were also 65,000 men who claimed exemptions for religious reasons.

To command the American Expeditionary Force (AEF), Wilson selected General John J. Pershing, who had pursued Pancho Villa into Mexico. The nation was ill-prepared for war: the army had no plans for a war with Germany in western Europe, and it lacked the rifles and machine guns necessary for a modern conflict. Moreover, its staff structure was loaded with old officers who lacked initiative and experience in commanding large numbers of men.

Training the troops for warfare often reflected progressive ideals. The government endeavored to maintain the purity of troops with extensive programs to limit excessive drinking and venereal disease. The army also provided an optional opportunity to acquire inexpensive life insurance, which increased popular interest in such programs after the war. The pace of mobilization was slow. It was not until more than a year after the entry into the war that American troops reached France in substantial numbers.

While the army was being raised, the navy faced a more immediate challenge. During April 1917, German submarines sank almost 900,000 tons of Allied shipping. At that rate, half the oceangoing shipping available to the British would disappear by the end of 1917. The British had only enough food for six weeks in reserve. The American naval commander in Europe, Admiral William S. Sims, turned to convoys to escort vulnerable merchant ships across the Atlantic. American destroyers on escort duty became a key part of the strategy that eventually ended the submarine threat, and troops began to move toward Europe. The Germans did not regard troop ships as significant targets because of their belief that American soldiers lacked fighting ability. Two million men were shipped to France before the armistice was signed, and they provided the margin for an Allied victory.

The government raised a third of the money for the war, some $9 billion, through increased taxes. The remainder came from citizens who purchased **Liberty Bonds** from the government. These interest-bearing securities brought in more than $15 billion. Children were taught to save their pennies and nickels for thrift stamps. They learned a rhyme to urge them on:

> Hush little thrift stamp,
> Don't you cry;
> You'll be a war bond
> By and by.

Those who were unwilling to contribute were told that failure to buy bonds was unpatriotic and helped the Germans. In some cases, violence coerced the reluctant contributors. That happened in Texas where those who failed to sign up for Liberty Bonds were whipped. The total cost of the war to the United States exceeded $35 billion. The United States loaned more than $11.2 billion to the Allies, most of it never repaid. Yet Washington had no choice. In June 1917, one British official told his government that "if loan stops, war stops." President Wilson counted on the Allies' financial dependence on the United States as a weapon to use in achieving the goals of his postwar diplomacy.

The Allies also needed food. The British depended on supplies from their empire, which took a long time to reach Europe by ship and were vulnerable to submarine attack. Without American food, sent via convoys under the protection of the U.S. Navy, serious shortages would have impaired Allied ability to wage war. To mobilize the agricultural resources of the United States, Congress passed the Lever Act, which established the Food Administration. Wilson selected Herbert Hoover to head this new agency. A mining engineer from California, Hoover had gained international fame through his work to feed the starving people of Belgium.

Hoover asked Americans to observe "wheatless days" and "meatless days" because "wheatless days in America make sleepless nights in Germany." Women and children planted "war gardens" to raise fruits and vegetables. Higher prices induced farmers to expand their production. The wheat crop was 637 million bushels in 1917; a year later, it stood at 921 million bushels.

The campaign to conserve food boosted the effort to restrict the sale and use of alcoholic beverages. Scarce grain supplies had to be reserved for soldiers in the field and Allied populations overseas. As a wartime slogan put it, "Shall the many have food or the few have drink?" Prohibitionists argued that drink impaired the fighting ability of the armed forces and those working in defense plants. The connection of the brewing industry with German Americans also worked in favor of the prohibitionist cause.

Congress passed legislation to restrict the production of liquor, and in December 1917 the lawmakers approved the **Eighteenth Amendment**, which banned the production and sale of alcoholic beverages. All that remained was to ensure ratification of the amendment by the required number of states, a task that the Anti-Saloon League was well equipped to handle.

Managing the Wartime Economy

The president used his power to wage the war to establish the expanded bureaucracy required to manage production of war supplies and oversee their shipment to the Allies. Wilson did not seek to have government take over business. He hoped that a business–government partnership would develop naturally. However, much government encouragement and direction were needed before the business community fully joined the war effort.

The eventual record of mobilization was mixed. The United States tried to build ships and planes under the direction of government agencies. Those efforts produced at least one British-designed plane that used American-built engines, and large numbers of merchant ships were constructed in American shipyards. But Pershing's men used British and French artillery and equipment. The government had more success with expanding the production of coal, the major source of residential heating and industrial power, through the Fuel Administration. Coal prices were raised to stimulate production, and "daylight savings time" was established to reduce the use of fuel for nonmilitary purposes.

The nation's railroads became so confused during the first year of the war that immense and costly transportation snarls resulted. The armed forces insisted on immediate passage for railcars with war supplies; tie-ups of rail traffic all over the East Coast resulted. Finally the government took over the railroads in January 1918, placing the secretary of the treasury, William G. McAdoo, in charge of operations. McAdoo raised the wages of railroad workers, dropped inefficient routes, and allowed the lines to raise their rates. The tie-ups soon disappeared.

Even before U.S. entry into the war, the government had made plans for coordinating industrial production. Staffed with "dollar-a-year men" whose salaries were paid by their former companies, the War Industries Board (WIB) was supposed to make sure that the purchasing and allocation of supplies for the armed forces followed rational programs. The WIB fell well short of this standard during 1917 in such industries as munitions, airplane production, and merchant shipping. In March 1918, under pressure from Congress and Republican critics such as Theodore Roosevelt, Wilson placed Bernard Baruch, a Wall Street speculator and contributor to the Democratic Party, at the head of the WIB.

Baruch and his aides attacked needless waste in production. They standardized products, established priorities for the shipment of important goods, and set prices to encourage factories to turn out goods quickly. Simply by altering bicycle designs, the WIB saved two thousand tons of steel for war goods. Baruch had to compromise with both the powerful and politically well-connected automobile and steel industries to induce them to abandon peacetime production in favor of handling wartime orders. In the process, the industries made significant profits from their government contracts.

As one steel executive put it, "We are all making more money out of this war than the average human being ought to."

The American Federation of Labor and its president, Samuel Gompers, threw their support behind the war. In return for the government's agreement to allow unions to participate in economic policy making, Gompers and the AFL promised not to strike or to press for union shops in factories. Between 1917 and 1920, the AFL gained more than 2 million members.

Nonunion workers also benefited from the government's wartime policies. The National War Labor Board, headed by former president William Howard Taft, set standards for wages and hours that were far more generous and enlightened than those private industry had provided. A minimum wage was mandated, as were maximum hours and improved working conditions. In one plant, women saw their wages raised to almost eleven dollars per week. The government also created housing for war workers and began a system of medical care and life insurance for federal employees.

Black Americans in the War   While some blacks wanted no part of the European conflict as a conflict among their white oppressors, most African American leaders agreed with W. E. B. Du Bois that they should "forget about special grievances and close our ranks shoulder to shoulder with our own fellow white citizens." Some 367,000 black soldiers served during the war; 42,000 of them saw combat in France. Most of the African American servicemen, however, were assigned to labor battalions and supply duties. The War Department moved very slowly to commission black officers; at the end of the war there were only 1,200. Several African American units fought bravely. Others were given inadequate training and equipment, but when they performed poorly in combat, the blame was placed on their supposed inferiority. Blacks had little motivation to fight in the first place in a segregated army that represented a segregated nation. Moreover, for some blacks stationed in France, the experience of being in a country without a long tradition of racism made them impatient for greater freedom at home.

African American troops stationed in the United States faced familiar dangers. In August 1917, in Houston, Texas, black soldiers reacted to segregation and abuse by the police with attacks on the police and on white citizens that left sixteen whites and four soldiers dead. The army indicted 118 soldiers, of whom 110 were convicted by courts-martial. Nineteen black soldiers were hanged.

Racial tensions intensified elsewhere in the nation as whites and blacks confronted each other when northern cities experienced an influx of African Americans. During the summer of 1917, race riots in East St. Louis, Illinois, resulted in the deaths of forty blacks and nine whites. Forty-eight lynchings occurred in 1917 and sixty-three in 1918. Facing discrimination and violence, blacks responded with a heightened sense of outrage. Marches were held to protest the race riots. Banners called on President Wilson to "Bring Democracy to America Before You Carry It to Europe."

During the war the black migration to northern cities continued. As the African American communities in Chicago, New York, Philadelphia, and other northern cities grew, black newspapers published articles about the **"New Negro"** who did not "fear the face of day. The time for cringing is over." The repressive actions of the Wilson administration in such episodes as the Houston riot and the failure to act against lynching fed the new currents of militance among black Americans.

Women's Issues in the Great War

The leaders of the National American Woman Suffrage Association decided that identification with the war offered the surest and fastest road to achieving their goal. Carrie Chapman Catt argued that giving women the vote would enable them to offset disloyal elements at home. "Every slacker has a vote," said Catt, a vote that newly enfranchised women could counter. Members of NAWSA appeared at rallies and proclaimed that suffrage should be a "war measure" that would repay women for their contributions to the war. The National Woman's Party picketed the White House to embarrass Wilson for failing to support woman suffrage. The combined impact of these tactics led to the passage of the woman suffrage amendment in the House of Representatives in January 1918. Wilson came out in favor of the amendment just before the congressional elections of that year. The Senate still had to act, but the war had made possible the eventual victory of the campaign to give women the vote.

Woman Suffrage Picketer. *Militant proponents of woman suffrage picketed the White House in 1917–1918 to move President Wilson to support their cause. Their presence embarrassed the president and several of the picketers went to jail for their beliefs.*

(© Bettmann/CORBIS)

Beyond the success of woman suffrage, however, the war did not go on long enough to produce lasting changes in the condition of American women. Only about 400,000 more women joined the labor force; some 8 million found better-paying jobs as a result of the conflict. More than 20,000 women served in the military. The navy and the marines enlisted 13,000 of them, largely in office jobs. The army employed more than 5,000 as nurses. In industry, women were hired as drivers, farm workers, and secretaries. As soon as the war ended, though, they were expected to relinquish these jobs to returning servicemen. As a Chicago woman complained, "During the war they called us heroines, but they throw us on the scrapheap now."

Civil Liberties in Wartime

The Wilson administration mobilized public opinion to offset potential opposition to the conflict. As a result, the White

House mounted a campaign of laws, agencies, and popular spirit to arouse support for the war and to quell dissent. In doing so, however, Woodrow Wilson and the men around him abused and restricted the civil liberties of many Americans.

The government created the Committee on Public Information (CPI) on April 13, 1917, and President Wilson named George Creel, a former newspaperman, as its head. Creel called his task "the world's greatest adventure in advertising"; he saw his role as one of fusing Americans into "one white-hot mass . . . with fraternity, devotion, courage, and deathless determination." To spread its message, the CPI used pamphlets, billboards, and motion pictures such as *The American Indian Gets into the War Game*. Seventy-five thousand speakers, known as "Four-Minute Men" (because of the length of their talks), spoke to audiences throughout the nation.

Four-Minute Men asked listeners: "Do you want to take the slightest chance of meeting Prussianism here in America?" The national goal was unity, the Germans were depraved animals, and the nation was engaged in a crusade to "make the world safe for democracy." Wilson's wartime speeches described the United States as "an instrument in the hands of God to see that liberty is made secure for mankind."

The Limits of Dissent

The Wilson administration and Congress placed legislative limits on the ability of Americans to criticize the government or the war effort. The Espionage Act of 1917 curbed espionage and sabotage, and made its definitions so sweeping that they embraced even public criticism of the war and its conduct. A person who violated the law could be sentenced to twenty years in prison. The Trading with the Enemy Act, passed in October 1917, authorized the postmaster general to suspend the mailing privileges of foreign-language periodicals and newspapers that he deemed offensive to the government. Postmaster General Albert S. Burleson used that law and the Espionage Act to bar from the mail publications that he considered treasonous or seditious. In 1918, Congress passed the Alien Act, which gave the government broad powers to deport any noncitizen who advocated revolution or anarchism. Most sweeping was the Sedition Act of 1918, which prohibited "uttering, printing, writing, or publishing any disloyal, profane, scurrilous, or abusive language" about either the government or the armed forces.

DOING HISTORY ONLINE

The Propaganda War

Study the documents online, and read the section "A Nation at War" in the textbook. How did America's involvement in the war alter the relationship between the federal government and the people of the nation?

www.cengage.com/history/ayers/ampassages4e

These laws were vigorously enforced. Burleson pursued critics of the administration relentlessly. The Socialist magazine *The Masses* was barred from the mails for carrying articles claiming that "this is Woodrow Wilson's and Wall Street's War." The Justice Department was equally vigilant. People were sent to prison for saying, "Wilson is a wooden-headed son of a bitch" or remarking that this was "a rich man's war." Eugene V. Debs, the perennial Socialist candidate for president, received a ten-year prison sentence for opposing the draft and the war. The American Protective League, a volunteer organization designed to locate draft evaders, became a vigilante branch of the Justice

Department that used wiretapping, illegal searches, and other lawless techniques to find "slackers" and other opponents of the war.

Wartime Hysteria The zeal of the government to stamp out dissent was matched by private hysteria toward Germans. Sauerkraut became "liberty cabbage," hamburgers reemerged as "Salisbury steak," and some cities gave up pretzels. Speaking the German language in public was banned in half of the states by 1918, and German literary works vanished from libraries. Musicians with German names, such as the violinist Fritz Kreisler, found their careers crippled.

Some German Americans suffered more serious injuries. When they refused to buy war bonds, mobs beat them until they promised to contribute. Editorials warned: "YOUR NEIGHBOR, YOUR MAID, YOUR LAWYER, YOUR WAITER MAY BE A GERMAN SPY." Radicals, too, were the victims of mob violence. Frank Little, an organizer for the Industrial Workers of the World (IWW), was hanged from a railroad trestle in Montana for denouncing the war at a labor rally.

The Political Legacy of Repression The government had legitimate reason to be concerned about German espionage, but the repression of civil liberties during the war was excessive. President Wilson did not order cabinet officials to engage in such conduct, but he failed to keep them in check when he learned about what they were doing. The government's campaign against radicals and progressives, key areas of Wilson's coalition in 1916, undermined support for the president in domestic politics. In his eagerness to win the war, Wilson had allowed his government to destroy part of his own political base.

THE ROAD TO VICTORY

During the late winter of 1918, as American troops arrived in France, the Allies faced a dangerous military crisis. In November 1917, the communist revolution in Russia had taken that nation out of the Allied coalition and enabled the Germans to move troops to the western front. Berlin hoped to achieve victory before the Americans could reinforce the Allies. The German attack came on March 21, 1918, and it made impressive gains until the Allies held. When further attacks were made against the French in April and May, American reinforcements helped stop the assault. At battles near Chateau-Thierry and in Belleau Wood in early June, the men of the American Expeditionary Force (AEF) endured frightful losses but halted the Germans.

The Germans made one more offensive thrust in mid-July, and the British, French, and Americans repelled it as well. Counterattacks moved the Germans backward, a retreat that continued until the end of the war. In September 1918, the American army went on the offensive at the town of Saint-Mihiel near the southern end of the trenches. At the end of the month, Americans launched another thrust toward the Meuse River and the Argonne Forest. Their casualties were heavy, but the AEF pierced the German defenses to threaten key supply routes of the enemy.

Wilson's Peace Program Wilson had set out his views on peace in a major address to Congress on January 8, 1918. Using the archives of the tsarist government, the Russian communists had released secret treaties that the Allies had made before 1917 dividing up Europe and the Middle East once victory was achieved. These documents cast doubt on Allied claims that they were fighting for unselfish reasons. Wilson endeavored to shape the Allied answer and regain the diplomatic initiative.

To present the American cause in a better light, Wilson offered a peace program with fourteen specific elements that became known as the Fourteen Points. Among the key provisions were freedom of the seas, free trade, and more open diplomacy. Freedom of the seas would prevent a repetition of the submarine threat the United States had faced before entering the war. Wilson believed that secret treaties and balance-of-power diplomacy had helped bring about the war itself. The president advocated national self-determination for all nations. He meant that the borders of countries should reflect the national origins of the people who lived in a particular area. He also advocated an "association of nations" to keep the peace.

The Fourteen Points would not be easy to achieve. After four years of slaughter, Britain and France wanted to punish Germany and cripple its ability to wage war. They disliked Wilson's criticism of their war aims and his interference with European policies. For the desperate Germans, the Fourteen Points seemed much more appealing than negotiations with London and Paris. In early October, a civilian government in Germany asked Wilson to arrange an armistice based on the Fourteen Points. Working through Colonel House, the president negotiated an agreement for an end to the fighting. He also used the threat of a separate settlement with the Germans to induce the British and French to accept the Fourteen Points and attend the peace conference. The fighting ended on November 11, 1918, at 11:00 A.M.

Woodrow Wilson had achieved a diplomatic triumph with the conclusion of the armistice, but his success proved to be temporary. Even as he prepared to lead the American delegation to Paris, his domestic political base was eroding. During the war, he had proclaimed, "politics is adjourned." In fact, however, partisan battles continued, with both Wilson and his enemies using the war for their own political purposes.

The 1918 Elections Throughout the conflict, President Wilson kept the Republicans at arm's length and treated the conflict as a war for Democrats only. He did not bring Republicans into his government at the highest levels, and he attacked Republicans who opposed his policies. Meanwhile, his enemies capitalized on the unhappiness of farmers and workers over the administration's domestic programs. Midwestern farmers, for example, disliked the price controls that had been imposed on wheat. They complained that southerners in Congress had prevented similar price controls from being put on cotton. As a result, wheat farmers saw their profits held down while cotton producers did well. Progressives who had supported Wilson in 1916 recoiled from the administration's repressive tactics toward dissenters. In late October 1918, Wilson tried to stave off the defeat with an appeal to the American people to elect a Democratic Congress. The statement allowed Wilson's enemies to claim that he had been decisively repudiated when the results showed that both the House and the Senate would have Republican majorities. For a president who needed bipartisan support in the Senate for any treaty he might write at the upcoming Peace Conference in Paris, it was a major blunder.

The Paris Peace Conference

In a break with the tradition that presidents did not travel outside the country, Wilson had already decided to attend the peace conference. Despite Republican criticism, he believed that he needed to direct the negotiations himself. But his selection of delegates to accompany him showed his continuing insensitivity to bipartisanship. The five men he chose were his close allies, with only one nominal Republican among them.

Wilson did not send any senators to Paris. Had he done so, he would have had to include Senator Henry Cabot Lodge of Massachusetts, the next chairman of the Foreign Relations Committee. Wilson and Lodge hated each other. Adding to their natural political differences was an element of personality conflict. Lodge believed Wilson was dishonest and tricky; Wilson saw Lodge as a reactionary out to thwart the president's goals for humanity. If Wilson could not take Lodge, he could not invite any other senators. Unwilling to accept advice or share the credit, Wilson also declined to select other prominent Republicans such as William Howard Taft or Elihu Root.

The President in Europe

Europeans greeted Wilson with rapturous applause. When he arrived in Paris, 2 million people cheered him as he rode up the Champs-Elysées. They called him "Wilson le Juste (the Just)" and expected him to fulfill their desires for a peaceful world and for revenge against the Germans. To them, the Fourteen Points were a rhetorical device, not a statement of Wilson's real position on issues. Wilson came to believe that he could appeal to the peoples of the world over the heads of their leaders to support his program of international peace.

The other major figures at the conference were David Lloyd George, the prime minister of Great Britain, and Georges Clemenceau, the premier of France. Both men were hard-headed realists who did not share Wilson's idealism. "God gave us the Ten Commandments, and we broke them," said Clemenceau. "Wilson gives us the Fourteen Points. We shall see." Along with the prime minister of Italy, Vittorio Orlando, Wilson, Clemenceau, and Lloyd George made up the "Big Four" who directed the peace conference toward a settlement of the issues that the war had raised.

The Shadow of Bolshevism

Four years of war had left the world in disorder, and nations large and small came to Paris to have their fate decided. A striking absentee was the new Soviet Union, the communist nation that the Russian Bolsheviks had established after their successful revolution. Civil war raged in Russia between the "Reds" of communism and the "Whites," who wanted to block Bolshevik control of the nation. Meanwhile, the Bolsheviks' authoritarian leader, Vladimir Ilyich Lenin, and his colleagues wished to extend communist rule beyond Russia's borders.

In 1919, national leaders worried that the infection of communism might spread into western Europe, and they had not recognized the government in Moscow. The French and British had tried to strangle the new regime by providing financial support for its enemies and intervening militarily in some areas of Russia. Helping its allies and trying to undermine bolshevism, the United States had dispatched small detachments of troops to Siberia and Vladivostok in 1918 and 1919. The American presence in Russia became a long-standing grievance for the Soviet regime that emerged from the Bolshevik victory.

The Terms of Peace The negotiations about the terms of peace with Germany produced both victories and defeats for Wilson. He had to accept the inclusion in the treaty of a clause that assigned Germany "guilt" for starting the war in 1914. That language proved to be a source of discontent for a resurgent Germany in the 1920s and 1930s. The Germans were also assessed severe financial penalties in the form of reparations that eventually amounted to $33 billion, a provision that fueled their resentment in the 1930s.

Wilson achieved partial success in his efforts to establish self-determination in the peace settlement. He accepted Italian desire for control of the city of Fiume on the Adriatic Coast, could not block Japan from territorial gains in China, and was unable to prevent several groups of ethnic and national minorities in eastern Europe from being left under the dominance of other ruling groups, as in the case of Germans in the new nation of Czechoslovakia.

The League of Nations Wilson's main goal was establishment of the League of Nations. The league consisted of a general assembly of all member nations; a council made up of Great Britain, France, Italy, Japan, and the United States, with four other countries that the assembly selected; and an international court of justice. For Wilson, the "heart of the covenant" of the League of Nations was Article X, which required member nations to preserve each other's independence and take concerted action when any member of the league was attacked.

In February 1919, Wilson returned to the United States for the end of the congressional session. Senator Lodge then circulated a document that thirty-seven senators signed. It stated that the treaty must be amended or they would not vote for it. Such a document, signed by a number of those who agreed with it, went by the term *round robin*. This pledge had drawn enough votes to defeat the treaty unless Wilson made changes in the document. The president attacked his critics publicly, further intensifying partisan animosity.

Wilson and the Treaty of Versailles To secure changes in the treaty for the Senate, Wilson had to make concessions to the other nations at the Peace Conference when he returned to Europe. These included the imposition of reparations on Germany, the war guilt clause, and limits on German's ability to rearm. In return, Wilson obtained provisions that protected the Monroe Doctrine from league action, removed domestic issues from the league's proceedings,

(The Granger Collection, New York)

The League of Nations. *Cartoonists in the United States found Wilson's League of Nations and the political battle that ensued a natural subject.*

and allowed any nation to leave the world organization with two years' notice. The final version of the Treaty of Versailles was signed on June 28, 1919, in the Hall of Mirrors at the Palace of Versailles outside Paris. For all of its problems and weaknesses, the treaty was the closest thing to a reasonable settlement that Wilson could have obtained.

The Senate and the League

The Republicans now controlled the Senate 49 to 47, so the president could not win the necessary two-thirds majority without the votes of some of his political opponents. Some Republicans were opposed to the treaty as an infringement on American sovereignty, no matter what it said. These were the fourteen "irreconcilables"; two Democrats were also part of this group. Wilson had to seek help from the twelve "mild reservationists," who wanted only changes in the wording, and the twenty-three "strong reservationists," who sought to limit the league's power over American actions. The president could count on about thirty-five of the forty-seven Democrats in the Senate. Assuming that some of the mild reservationists would support the treaty, the Democrats had to find twenty Republican votes to gain the necessary sixty-four votes to approve the treaty.

In the political battle that ensued, Senator Lodge focused on Article X and the issue of whether Congress should be able to approve any American participation in the league's attempts to prevent international aggression. Lodge also played for time, hoping that public opinion would turn against the treaty. He had the lengthy treaty read aloud to the Senate. Meanwhile, Wilson insisted that the treaty be approved without changes or "reservations."

Wilson's Tour and Collapse

By September 1919, with the treaty in trouble, Wilson decided to take his case to the American people. Despite audience approval of his speeches, Wilson's health broke under the strain. The circulatory problems that had bothered him for years erupted. He was rushed back to Washington, where he suffered a massive stroke on October 2, 1919. His left side was paralyzed, seriously impairing his ability to govern.

The president's wife and his doctors did not reveal how sick Wilson was. The first lady screened his few visitors and decided what documents her husband would see. People at the time and historians since have argued that she acted as a kind of female president. In fact, Mrs. Wilson whom he had married in 1915 a year after the death of his first wife in 1914, did only what her ailing husband allowed her to do. But as for the nation's chief executive, Wilson was only a shell of a president, and the government drifted.

The Defeat of the League

The Senate voted on the treaty on November 19, 1919, with reservations that Lodge had included in the document. Lodge would have required Congress to approve any sanctions imposed by the league on an aggressor. When the Democratic leader in the Senate asked Wilson about possible compromises, he replied that changing Article X "cuts the very heart out of the Treaty." The Senate rejected the treaty with reservations by a vote of 39 to 55. Then the lawmakers voted on the treaty without reservations. It lost, 38 in favor and 53 against. In the end, the decision about a possible compromise with Lodge was Wilson's to make. He told Senate Democrats: "Let Lodge compromise."

FROM WAR TO PEACE

Meanwhile the nation experienced domestic upheaval. Citizens grappled with labor unrest, a Red Scare (fear of communist or "Red" subversion), a surge in prices following the end of the war, and an influenza epidemic. The postwar period was one of the most difficult that Americans had ever experienced.

The influenza epidemic began with dramatic suddenness at the end of 1918 and spread rapidly through the population. No vaccines existed to combat it; no antibiotics were available to fight the secondary infections that resulted from it. More than 650,000 Americans died of the disease in 1918 and 1919. The number of dead bodies overwhelmed the funeral facilities of many major cities; coffins filled a circus tent in Boston. Children skipping rope made the epidemic part of their song:

> I had a little bird,
> And his name was Enza;
> I opened the window,
> And in flew Enza!

The influenza pandemic receded in 1920, leaving a worldwide total of 20 million people dead. The pandemic had sapped the strength of the Allied armed forces to enforce the peace treaty, had diverted attention from important social problems, and illustrated how vulnerable humanity was to these infectious diseases.

The Waning Spirit of Progressivism   By 1919, the campaigns for Prohibition and woman suffrage were nearing their goals. Enough states had ratified the Eighteenth Amendment (the Prohibition amendment) by January 1919 to make it part of the Constitution. In October 1919, Congress passed the Volstead Act, named after its congressional sponsor, Andrew J. Volstead of Minnesota, to enforce Prohibition. Wilson vetoed the measure as unwarranted after the war had ended, but Congress passed it over his objection. The United States became "dry" on January 15, 1920. Prohibitionists expected widespread compliance and easy enforcement.

After the House passed the Nineteenth Amendment (the woman suffrage amendment) in 1918, it took the Senate another year to approve it. Suffrage advocates then lobbied the states to ratify the amendment. When the Tennessee legislature voted for ratification in August 1920, three-quarters of the states had approved woman suffrage. Women would now "take their appropriate place in political work," said Carrie Chapman Catt.

The Struggles of Labor   After the Armistice, the nation shifted from a wartime economy to peacetime pursuits with dizzying speed. The government declined to manage the changeover from a wartime to a peacetime economy. High inflation developed as prices were freed from wartime controls, and unemployment rose as returning soldiers sought jobs. The government's cost of living index rose nearly 80 percent above prewar levels in 1919, and it went up to 105 percent a year later. Unemployment reached nearly 12 percent by 1921.

Unions struck for higher wages. Seattle shipyard workers walked off their jobs, and the Industrial Workers of the World called for a general strike to support them. When sixty thousand laborers took part in the protest, the mayor of Seattle, Ole Hanson, responded with mobilization of police and soldiers that made him, in the eyes of those who agreed with him, "the Saviour of Seattle." Newspapers depicted the strike as a prelude to communist revolution.

The Reaction Against Strikes The largest industrial strike of the year occurred in the steel industry. The American Federation of Labor tried to organize all steelworkers to end the seven-day week and the twelve-hour day. In September, 350,000 steelworkers left the mills. The steel manufacturers refused to recognize the union. Strikebreakers were hired from among the ranks of unemployed blacks, Hispanics, and immigrants. The steel companies kept their factories running while they waited for the strike to be broken through police harassment and internal divisions within the unions. Conservatives attacked the radical background of one of the strike organizers, William Z. Foster. Although the strikers remained united for several months, they could not withstand the accumulated financial and political pressure from management. This first effort at a strike by an entire work force failed in early 1920.

Other strikes of the year included a walkout by coal miners and a strike by police in Boston. Inflation had hit the Boston police hard, and they struck late in 1919. When looting and other criminal acts occurred because of the absence of police, public opinion turned against the striking officers. The governor of Massachusetts, Calvin Coolidge, became a national celebrity when he said: "There is no right to strike against the public safety, by anybody, anywhere, any time." To many middle-class Americans, the social order seemed to be unraveling.

Racial tensions also flared up in the turbulent postwar atmosphere. There were frequent lynchings in the South. In the North, the tide of African American migration produced confrontations with angry whites. Rioting against blacks occurred in Washington, D.C., in June 1919. During the same summer a young black man was stoned and killed when whites found him on a Chicago beach from which African Americans had been excluded. Angry blacks attacked the police who had stood by while the killing occurred. Five days of violence followed in which thirty-eight people, most of them black, were killed and another five hundred were injured. Violent episodes roiled two dozen other cities during what one black leader called "the red summer." Racism and antilabor sentiments fed on each other during these months.

Searching for a cause of the social unrest that pervaded the nation, Americans looked to radicalism and communism. The emotions aroused by the government's wartime propaganda fueled the Red Scare of 1919–1920. About seventy thousand people belonged to one of the two branches of the Communist Party. However, the radicals' reliance on violence and terrorism inflamed popular fears. When several mail bombs exploded on May 1, 1919, and dozens of others were found in the mail, press and public called for government action.

Attorney General A. Mitchell Palmer established a division in the Justice Department to hunt for radicals; the division was headed by J. Edgar Hoover, who later became director of the Federal Bureau of Investigation. In November 1919, Palmer launched raids against suspected radicals, and a month later he deported three hundred aliens to the Soviet Union. In the process, the legal rights of these suspects were violated, and they were kept in custody, away from their families and attorneys.

Throughout the country, civil liberties came under assault. State legislatures investigated alleged subversives. Communist parties were outlawed, antiradical legislation was adopted, and Socialists were expelled from the New York legislature. Suspected members of the IWW and other groups were subjected to vigilante violence and official repression.

The U.S. Supreme Court upheld the constitutionality of most of the laws that restricted civil liberties during the war and the Red Scare. Justice Oliver Wendell Holmes, Jr., devised a means of testing whether the First Amendment had been violated. In *Schenck v. United States* (1919), he asked whether words or utterances posed "a clear and present danger" of interference with the government, the war effort, or civil order. The answer was that they had. The Court also sustained the conviction of Eugene V. Debs for speaking out against the war.

By 1920, the Red Scare lost momentum. Palmer had forecast a violent uprising on May 1, 1920, and when it did not occur, his credibility suffered. Some government officials, especially in the Department of Labor, opposed Palmer's deportation policies. Other public figures, such as Charles Evans Hughes, denounced New York's efforts against socialist lawmakers. Despite the waning Red Scare hysteria, it was during this period that police in Massachusetts arrested two anarchists and Italian aliens, Nicola Sacco and Bartolomeo Vanzetti, for their alleged complicity in a robbery and murder at a shoe company in South Braintree, Massachusetts. In a case that attracted international attention, the two were convicted and eventually executed.

Gradually the frenzy of Red hunting abated. During the Wilson administration, a dangerous precedent had been set for government interference with individual rights. The bureaucratic machinery was in place for future attempts to compel loyalty and punish dissent.

Harding and "Normalcy"

In March 1920, with Wilson ill and the government leaderless, the Senate once again took up the Treaty of Versailles with reservations. On March 19, the treaty received forty-nine votes in favor and thirty-five against, seven short of the number needed to ratify it. Wilson had said that he would not approve the pact with reservations, but the vote showed that a compromise could have been reached. Wilson hoped that the election would be a "solemn referendum" on the treaty, but that did not happen.

The Republicans had expected that Theodore Roosevelt would be their nominee in 1920, but he died on January 6, 1919, of circulatory ailments and heart problems. The Republicans turned to Senator Warren G. Harding of Ohio. A first-term senator, Harding was not a smart man, but the Republicans had had enough of intelligent candidates in Roosevelt, Taft, and Charles Evans Hughes. Harding looked like a president and had made few enemies. He had been engaged in an illicit love affair in his home town of Marion, Ohio, but that information was carefully repressed. To run with him, the convention named Governor Calvin Coolidge of Massachusetts. Harding emphasized a return to older values, which he labeled "normalcy." He called for "not heroics, but healing."

For the Democrats the nominee was Governor James M. Cox of Ohio, a moderate progressive from the party's antiprohibitionist wing, and his running mate was Franklin D. Roosevelt of New York. The Democratic candidates supported the League of Nations; the Republicans generally dodged the subject until the end of the campaign, when

Harding advocated rejection of the treaty. The issue did not have much effect. Voters wanted to turn the Democrats out of office because of anger at big government, high taxes, and labor unrest. The electorate rejected progressivism and the use of government to make society more just. They rejected the Democrats in a landslide. Harding received 16 million votes to 9 million for Cox.

CONCLUSION

The United States was a late entrant into World War I, and that conflict did not produce the revolutionary upheavals in the United States that some European nations experienced between 1914 and 1918. Nonetheless, the six years that stretched from the outbreak of the war in August 1914 to the election of Warren G. Harding as president in 1920 brought significant changes. The larger meaning of this chapter lies in the many ways that citizens faced a world in which older values and attitudes now seemed obsolete.

The war cast grave doubt on the progressive faith that human beings were good and could be made even better through democracy and reform. The millions of deaths overseas, among them more than fifty thousand American soldiers and sailors, shook the confidence of a generation in the prospect of an ever-improving future for all citizens. With these sobering revelations also came suspicions about the value of bigger government and higher taxes. By 1920, voters longed for a return to prewar certainty, or what Harding called "normalcy."

But the changes that jolted society were long lasting. The movement of African Americans from the rural South to the urban North in the Great Migration made race a more national dilemma and shifted politics for both Democrats and Republicans. Woman suffrage marked a major expansion of democracy even if newly enfranchised females did not produce a purer and more enlightened political dialogue. For a time, Americans sought to curb the problem of alcohol by an amendment to the Constitution restricting the sale and distribution of such beverages.

In the wake of World War I, the nation briefly contemplated a more active role in the world but then drew back. Woodrow Wilson's League of Nations, building on wartime idealism, seemed less attractive in the harsh light of the postwar disillusionment with attempts to make the world safe for democracy. Although there was no going back to isolation, Americans thought they could let the Old World grapple with the consequences of its mistakes.

Later developments in the twentieth century, including the rise of Nazi Germany and the challenge from the Soviet Union, would make these judgments of the World War I period seem sadly mistaken. How could these men and women not see that in the errors of their great war lay the seeds of another greater conflict a generation later? What this chapter reveals is that in the setting of their time, people buffeted by world war and profound social change embraced certainties of their past and pursued reassurance. Not knowing what their descendants would learn, they did their best in an era of upheaval and shock to deal with the world that had changed so much in just short years.

CHAPTER REVIEW, 1914–1921

- The nation grappled with how to remain neutral in a world experiencing political upheaval.
- Southern blacks moved to northern cities in what came to be known as the Great Migration.
- The movies emerged as mass entertainment.
- Woodrow Wilson was reelected in 1916.
- The United States entered the world war in April 1917.
- Government power expanded during wartime.
- The American military contributed to the Allied victory.
- The Senate debated and then rejected the League of Nations.
- The country passed through postwar trauma including the Red Scare.
- Warren G. Harding was elected president in 1920.

◀▮▮▮ Looking Back

The problems that reformers encountered after 1914 had their roots in the record of the first years of the twentieth century. Looking back on the era of Theodore Roosevelt, William Howard Taft, and the early years of Woodrow Wilson's presidency, you can see the assumptions about human nature and the role of government that foreshadowed the later problems that weakened the hold of progressivism on the American people.

1. How deeply rooted was the progressive spirit? What groups did it include, and which ones did it leave out?
2. How far did the presidents in this period want to go in changing American society?
3. Why did World War I have such a devastating effect on progressive assumptions about humanity and the world?

Looking Ahead ▮▮▮▶

In the 1920s, Americans would reject many of the accomplishments of the Progressive era and repudiate much of what reformers had contributed to government and politics. The next chapter explores whether these conservative trends went too far. What remained of value in the Progressive legacy?

1. Why did the United States adopt Prohibition as an answer to the problems of alcohol?
2. Why did woman suffrage not produce the fundamental changes in American society that its proponents expected?
3. How did Americans feel about their place in the world after the experiences of the First World War I and the struggle over the League of Nations?

Go to the American Passages website at www.cengage.com/history/ayers/ampassages4e for additional review materials.

The Age of Jazz and Mass Culture, 1921–1927

23

During the 1920s the United States became modern as the automobile and other technological developments reshaped the economy and society. The shared experiences of Americans made the nation more cohesive as citizens encountered movies, radio, and sports in common. Social attitudes toward sex and family life moved away from Victorian restraints. Young people emerged as a distinct group. Advertising made public relations a significant characteristic of the period.

After a postwar depression, the economy rebounded from 1922 to 1927. The Republican administrations of Warren G. Harding and Calvin Coolidge lowered income taxes and encouraged private enterprise. Issues of culture and morality shaped politics more than did questions of economic reform. Prohibition and the Ku Klux Klan split the Democrats.

In foreign affairs, the decade was officially a time of isolation after the rejection of the League of Nations in 1919–1920. Government policy reinforced perceptions that the United States was aloof from the world. Yet the reality was more complex and subtle. Although involvement in world affairs increased more slowly, the United States maintained a significant stake in the postwar European and Asian economies.

A MORE URBAN NATION

The census of 1920 indicated the country was on an important new course. For the first time, the government reported that more Americans lived in towns and cities with twenty-five hundred or more residents than in the countryside. The small-town and rural experience still dominated the lives of most citizens, but the trend toward urban residence was transforming the nation.

More than 10 million Americans lived in cities with 1 million people or more in 1920; that figure rose to more than 15 million by 1930. Such places as New York, Detroit, and Los Angeles saw large increases in their populations. Some 19 million people left the country for the city over these ten years. The migration of African

Americans from the South to the North continued unabated. The percentage of blacks listed as urban residents rose by nearly 10 percent between 1920 and 1930, compared with a rise of about 5 percent for whites.

For the young people who flocked to Chicago, New York, and Los Angeles, city life offered excitement and energy that farm life could not match. Within the concrete canyons and electric avenues, visitors found theaters, dance halls, and vaudeville artists that they could never hope to see in a small town. Many Americans resented the temptations of the city and associated them with foreign influences and assaults on traditional values.

Immigration Restricted After the war, more than 430,000 people sought entry to the United States in 1920, and another 805,000 came in 1921. In response, advocates of immigration restriction renewed their campaign to shut off the flow of entrants from southern and eastern Europe.

Proponents of restriction argued that the immigrants lacked the qualities of successful American citizens. Madison Grant, one of the leading advocates of immigration restriction, said that "these immigrants adopt the language of the [native-born] American, they wear his clothes, they steal his name, and they are beginning to take his women, but they seldom adopt his religion or understand his ideals."

The pressure on Congress grew. The American Federation of Labor, which feared the use of aliens as strikebreakers, added its weight to the campaign for immigration restrictions. In 1921, Congress enacted an emergency quota law that limited immigration from Europe to 600,000 people annually. Great Britain and Germany received the highest quotas. Three years later, the lawmakers passed the National Origins Quota Act, which reduced annual legal immigration from Europe to about 150,000 people, gave preference to entrants from northern European countries, and blocked Asian immigrants entirely. The quota of immigrants from each country was determined by the number of residents from these countries counted in the 1890 census.

Despite their racist premises, the new laws did not end immigration during the 1920s. After 1924, the recorded number of immigrants totaled about 300,000 annually until the Great Depression. Legal immigrants from Canada and Mexico accounted for much of that total. However, the impact on people who wished to emigrate from southern and eastern Europe was dramatic. For example, 95,000 immigrants had come into the United States from Poland in 1921; for each of the next three years, the annual total of immigrants from that country was only about 28,000.

Since the immigration law did not affect Mexicans, 500,000 newcomers from that country crossed the border during the 1920s and swelled the ranks of Americans of Hispanic ancestry. Mexicans were concentrated in California and Texas.

The Sacco-Vanzetti Case The widespread tension about immigration played a significant part in the fate of two Italian immigrants whose criminal trial became a major controversy. In 1920 a murder and robbery took place in South Braintree, Massachusetts. Nicola Sacco and Bartolomeo

This icon will direct you to interactive activities and study materials on the *American Passages* website: www.cengage.com/history/ayers/ampassages4e

CHAPTER TIMELINE

1921	Warren G. Harding becomes president • Immigration laws set quotas for eastern and southern Europeans • Sheppard-Towner Maternity and Infancy Protection Act passed
1922	Fordney-McCumber Tariff enacted • Sinclair Lewis's *Babbitt* published • Supreme Court rules minimum wage for women is unconstitutional in *Adkins v. Children's Hospital*
1923	Teapot Dome scandal • *Time* magazine starts publishing • Equal Rights amendment drafted by Alice Paul • Death of Warren G. Harding • Calvin Coolidge becomes president
1924	Coolidge wins presidential election • Nellie Tayloe Ross (Wyoming) and Miriam Amanda Ferguson (Texas) became first elected women governors
1925	Scopes trial in Tennessee over teaching of evolution • Publication of F. Scott Fitzgerald's *The Great Gatsby*
1926	Publication of Ernest Hemingway's *The Sun Also Rises* • Gertrude Ederle becomes first woman to swim across English Channel
1927	Charles Lindbergh flies the Atlantic alone • Sacco and Vanzetti executed • Babe Ruth hits sixty home runs • Henry Ford introduces Model A car • Calvin Coolidge announces "I do not choose to run" for president in 1928

Vanzetti were arrested for the crime, and their trial began in June 1921. Despite allegations that authorities had framed the two men for the crime because of their anarchist beliefs, a jury found them guilty. Numerous appeals for a new trial were made. The case soon became a focus for liberals and intellectuals convinced that **Sacco and Vanzetti** had not received a fair trial because of their foreign origin.

Over the next several years, the attorneys for the convicted defendants filed a series of appeals to overturn the verdict. The lawyers challenged the conduct of the jury, attacked the quality of the evidence against the two men, and questioned the accuracy of the identifications that various witnesses had made. None of this changed the mind of the presiding judge. By October 1924, all motions for a new trial had been denied. The defendants hired a new attorney, and a public campaign for a new trial and their release gained national attention in 1925 and 1926. Within Massachusetts, where animosity against immigrants still raged, the state government did not waver in its belief that Sacco and Vanzetti were guilty.

By 1927, the appeals process had run its course. Despite strong evidence that the two men had not received a fair trial and substantial indications that they were not guilty, the legal machinery moved them toward the electric chair with the date of the execution set for July 1927. With a worldwide campaign under way to save Sacco and Vanzetti, pressure intensified on Massachusetts officials to review the case. The governor appointed a special commission to look into the trial. After flawed and biased proceedings, the panel decided to affirm the convictions, and Sacco and Vanzetti were executed on August 23. The outcome convinced many radicals of the inherent unfairness of the American legal system.

The Ku Klux Klan   The pressures of immigration from abroad and the movement of Americans from the country to the city produced intense social strains. The most sensational and violent of these developments was the reappearance of the Ku Klux Klan. Revitalized after 1915 in the South, the Klan gained followers slowly. By 1920, however, the Klan had become a marketing device for clever promoters who used the Klan's brew of racism, anti-Catholicism, and anti-immigrant views to acquire converts. The hooded order spread into northern states as well, with a particularly large presence in Indiana. The Klan claimed that it had 3 million members in the early 1920s. The masks and sheets that members of the order wore provided an anonymity that attracted recruits in the southern countryside and in the cities of the Midwest where formerly rural residents had moved.

A secret ritual added to the Klan mystique. Members contributed a ten dollar entrance fee, called a "klecktoken." They read the Kloran and dedicated themselves to "Karacter, Honor, Duty." In time they might rise to become a King Kleagle or a Grand Goblin of the Domain. Members asked each other "Ayak," for "Are you a Klansman?" The proper reply was "Akia," meaning "A Klansman I am."

The Klan's program embraced opposition to Catholics, Jews, blacks, Asians, violators of the Prohibition laws, and anyone else who displeased local Klansmen. In their rallies, marching members carried signs that read "COHABITATION BETWEEN WHITES AND BLACKS MUST STOP." Even more than the Klan of the

Ku Klux Klan.   *The Ku Klux Klan was on the march with its message of bigotry in the early 1920s. This picture shows members of the hooded order as they paraded in Washington, D.C. The tensions that the Klan represented echoed through the entire decade.*

(© Bettmann/CORBIS)

Reconstruction era, the Klan of the 1920s based its appeal on the desire of many white Americans for a more tranquil and less confusing social order. The Klan's efforts to create such conditions made it attractive to many citizens who never wore a hood. But the Klan also contained an ugly strain of violence and vigilantism. In many states, its members lynched people they disagreed with; tortured blacks, Catholics, and Jews; and made a mockery of law enforcement.

Soon the Klan went into politics. In 1922, its members elected a senator in Texas and became a powerful presence in the legislatures of that state and others in the Southwest. In Indiana, members of the order dominated the police of the state's major cities. The Klan also wielded significant influence in the Rocky Mountain states and the Pacific Northwest.

For the Democrats, the Klan posed a difficult problem. The party was already divided over cultural issues. Southern members favored Prohibition and disliked large cities. In the North, Democrats were ethnically diverse, opposed to Prohibition, and rooted in the new urban lifestyles. The Klan intensified these tensions. Some "dry" Democrats saw the Klan as a legitimate form of political protest. The "wets" in northern cities regarded the Klan as an expression of cultural and regional intolerance. The Klan's influence peaked around 1923. As the Klan sought greater political power, the two major parties, especially the Democrats, absorbed some of the Klan's appeal and weakened its hold on the public.

The Rise of Black Militance

African Americans asserted their identity and independence in these years too. Sacrifices during World War I had made blacks impatient and resentful of the indignities of segregation. Yet white-on-black violence, such as the brutal attack on the African American area of Tulsa, Oklahoma, in 1921, persisted. A growing spirit of assertiveness and militancy appeared in the art and literature of black intellectuals. A poet named Claude McKay issued his rallying cry in 1922: "If we must die, let it not be like hogs / Hunted and penned in an inglorious spot." Instead, he concluded, "Like men we'll face the murderous, cowardly pack, / Pressed to the wall, dying, but—fighting back."

For the African Americans who crowded into the large northern cities during the Great Migration, the promise of America seemed illusory. They lived in substandard housing, paid higher rents for their apartments than whites did, and could obtain only menial jobs. The Harlem neighborhood of New York City might be "the greatest Negro city in the world," as author James Weldon Johnson called it, but it was also a place where every day, blacks saw how white society discriminated against them.

This atmosphere of dissatisfaction greeted **Marcus Garvey**, a young black man who immigrated to the United States in 1916. Garvey preached a doctrine of Pan-Africanism and promised to "organize the 400,000,000 Negroes of the World into a vast organization to plant the banner of freedom in the great continent of Africa." He worked through the Universal Negro Improvement Association (UNIA) to establish societies that were not controlled by imperialist nations. He founded his campaign on international shipping lines and newspapers that would enable blacks to travel to Africa and communicate among themselves. Rallies and conventions in New York and other cities drew up to twenty-five thousand people and raised funds for the UNIA.

Garvey's business ventures failed. The shipping lines collapsed, and the investors, mostly African Americans, lost their money. Blacks were divided in their views of the charismatic Garvey. The National Association for the Advancement of Colored People bristled when Garvey attacked its political agenda as too cautious and then met with a Klan leader. His criticisms of labor unions alienated key African American leaders such as A. Phillip Randolph of the Brotherhood of Sleeping Car Porters. Black opponents sent damaging information about Garvey's finances to the Department of Justice, and the government indicted him for mail fraud. He was convicted and went to prison in 1925. The important legacy of Garvey and the UNIA was the idea that urban blacks could band together to wield economic and political power.

Dry America:
The First Phase
The initial impact of Prohibition on the lives of Americans achieved much of what its proponents had predicted. The national consumption of alcohol declined from about two gallons per capita during the war years annually to around three-fourths of a gallon in 1921 and 1922 (Table 23.1). Alcohol use rose again during the rest of the decade but remained below pre-war levels. Alcoholism as a medical problem became less prevalent. Many hospitals closed their alcoholism wards because of a lack of patients. Contrary to later legend, Prohibition did affect drinking habits in the United States.

Yet the extent of compliance with Prohibition was spotty. Some people made their own liquor; instructions for doing so were easily obtained. In centers of "wet" sentiment, like San Francisco and Boston, the law was never enforced. Several states did not even ratify the Eighteenth Amendment. Others failed to pass state laws to support the federal legislation. Believing that compliance ought to be voluntary, Congress appropriated inadequate funds to the Treasury Department's Prohibition Bureau,

TABLE 23.1 Estimated Alcohol Consumption in the United States, 1920–1930 (Gallons per Capita)

1920	N/A
1921	0.54
1922	0.91
1923	1.07
1924	1.05
1925	1.10
1926	1.18
1927	1.12
1928	1.18
1929	1.20
1930	1.06

Source: Derived from Joseph R. Gusfield, "Prohibition: The Impact of Political Utopianism," in John Braeman, Robert H. Bremner, and David Brody, eds., *Change and Continuity in Twentieth-Century America: The 1920s* (Columbus, Ohio: Ohio State University Press, 1968), p. 275.

so there were never enough federal men to cover the nation adequately. Even when agents acted decisively, the rising number of arrests led to huge backlogs in the federal court system.

The upper classes expected the working poor to obey the Prohibition law, but they resisted any change in their own drinking practices. With a ready market for illegal liquor in the major cities, enterprising individuals moved alcohol across the border into the United States. These "rum runners" and **bootleggers** brought in shipments of alcohol from Canada and the Caribbean. Their wares were sold at illegal saloons or "speakeasies" where city dwellers congregated in the evenings.

Prohibition did not, however, create organized crime. Nor were the 1920s a decade of rising crime rates. The nation became more aware of crime as a social problem, because of the well-publicized activities of gangsters like **Alphonse "Al" Capone** and Johnny Torrio in Chicago. Prohibition offered individuals already involved in crime another incentive to tap the immense profits to be had from easing the thirst of upper-class Americans. Capone in particular devoted himself to gaining control of gambling, prostitution, and bootlegging in the Chicago area. In New York, other mobsters built up networks of criminal enterprises to provide the same services. These sensational cases undermined faith in the positive effects of Prohibition.

HARDING AS PRESIDENT

Because of the scandals associated with his administration, Warren G. Harding once was depicted as the worst president in American history. During his brief term, however, he was very popular. He surrounded himself with what he called the "Best Minds," as his selection of Charles Evans Hughes as his secretary of state, banker Andrew Mellon as secretary of the treasury, and Herbert Hoover as secretary of commerce attested. After years in which the presidency had seemed separated from the people, Harding and his wife, Florence, opened up the White House to tourists and greeted visitors from the public with evident pleasure. Throughout the country, Harding was a well-regarded president whose speeches appealed to a desire for a calmer, less activist chief executive.

The new administration pressed for a legislative program that combined some constructive reforms with a return to older Republican trade policies. The 1921 Budget and Accounting Act gave the government a more precise sense of how the nation's funds were being spent. It established an executive budget for the president, the General Accounting Office for Congress, and the Bureau of the Budget in the executive branch. The Republicans rebuilt tariff protection in an emergency law of 1921 and then wrote the Fordney-McCumber Tariff Law a year later. Reflecting the party's suspicion of a powerful national government, Treasury Secretary Mellon pushed for lower income tax rates, particularly for individuals with higher incomes.

The Harding administration stayed aloof from the League of Nations. Since the failure to ratify the Treaty of Versailles left the nation in a technical state of war with Germany, the two countries negotiated a separate peace treaty in 1921. Throughout the 1920s, Washington withheld recognition from the new Soviet Union because of fears that diplomatic relations with the Communist government might spread the bacillus of subversion. American interests turned back toward Latin America. To reduce the nation's military role in the region, the administration withdrew marines from Haiti, the Dominican Republic, and Nicaragua. Trade, and investment, expanded south of the border.

The Far East claimed a large amount of attention as Japan expanded its power in China. The United States wanted to preserve the Open Door policy and restrain Japanese influence, and it relied on diplomacy and economic pressure as its main weapons. Both nations were, however, increasing the size of their navies at this time. Congress and the administration called for a conference in which representatives of Great Britain, Japan, and the United States would meet to discuss naval issues and peace in the Far East. The United States and Great Britain arranged for such a meeting in Washington in November 1921.

The Washington Naval Conference began with a dramatic proposal by Secretary of State Hughes to scrap outright sixty battleships of all nations. He also proposed that limits be placed on the number of battleships and aircraft carriers that Japan, the United States, and Britain could build. Out of the conference came the Five Power Treaty, which provided a fixed ratio for warship construction. For every five ships the United States built, the British could also build five, and the Japanese could build three. The Japanese were not happy with the 5-5-3 arrangement, but in return they secured an American pledge not to construct defenses in such U.S. possessions as Guam and the Philippines. For a time, the naval arms race in the Pacific slowed. Although the long-range effects of the conference were modest, the episode fueled Japanese-American tensions and contributed to the grievances that Tokyo felt regarding how the Western nations treated the rising Asian power.

The Washington Conference also resulted in two other pacts: the Four Power Treaty and the Nine Power Treaty. The Four Power Treaty ended a long-standing (since 1902) alliance between Great Britain and France, and committed the United States, France, Great Britain, and Japan to respect each country's territorial possessions. In the Nine Power Treaty, the signatory nations agreed to avoid interference with China's internal affairs. The Washington Conference ended without the United States having to make commitments that entailed the risk of force or greater international involvement. In diplomacy as in domestic policy, the Harding administration seemed attuned to the desires of the country.

THE NEW ECONOMY

The postwar recession dogged the first two years of the Harding administration, and the hard times contributed to substantial Republican losses in the 1922 congressional elections. The Democrats gained seventy-four seats in the House and six in the Senate. Yet the long-range news proved beneficial for Republicans. The economy slowly picked up in 1922 and 1923, productive output returned to its 1918 levels, and employment rose. As wages climbed, discontent ebbed, and the Republicans looked forward to the 1924 presidential election with greater optimism.

The improvement in the economy's performance during 1922 began a period of unprecedented prosperity. The gross national product soared almost 40 percent, increasing from nearly $76 billion in 1922 to $97.3 billion in 1927. The per capita income of Americans went up about 30 percent during the same period. Real earnings for wage workers rose more than 20 percent, whereas hours worked declined slightly. The unemployment rate fell from 12 percent of the labor force in 1922 to 4 percent in 1927.

The Car Culture   The number of cars registered in 1920 totaled 8.25 million, while the number of trucks was 1.1 million. By 1927, there were more than 20 million cars on the roads, along with more than 3 million trucks and buses. Automobiles needed oil and gasoline to operate, steel for their frames, rubber for their tires, glass for windshields, and service businesses for dealers and drivers. For the traveler on the road, motels offered accommodations, billboards advertised attractions, and roadside restaurants provided food and diversion. The Federal Highways Act of 1921 left road construction to the states, but set national standards for concrete road surfaces and access to roads. The size of the road network grew from seven thousand miles at the end of the war to fifty thousand miles in 1927. Gasoline taxes brought in revenues for the states, enabling them to build more roads, which in turn fostered the development of suburbs distant from the old city centers.

No longer did young women and men have to carry on courtship within sight of parents and chaperones. When fathers urged their daughters not to go out driving with boys, the young women replied: "What on earth do you want me to do? Just sit around all evening?" Cars consumed a large chunk of the working family's income as Americans readily took to the practice of buying their cars on the installment plan.

For many African Americans in the South, owning a car gave them at least some mobility and escape from a segregated life. The enclosed car, initially a prestigious model, soon became standard on the road; by 1927, 83 percent of cars were of this type.

As the decade began, Henry Ford was still the most famous carmaker in the nation. His showplace was the huge factory on the Rouge River near Detroit. Sprawling across two thousand acres, the Rouge River plant employed seventy-five thousand workers to turn out the reliable, familiar Model T car. In 1921, Ford made more than half of the automobiles produced in the United States, turning out a new vehicle every ten seconds. A car cost less than $300.

The Model T was a popular car but not an attractive one. The joke was that you could get a Model T in any color, so long as it was black. Ford's failure to develop different car models opened a competitive opportunity to General Motors (GM). Although GM had been in severe financial difficulty in 1920, the DuPont family acquired the firm. They brought in Alfred P. Sloan, Jr., as chief assistant to the president. In 1923, when he became president, Sloan set up a system of independent operating divisions that produced models of Chevrolets, Buicks, and other vehicles annually. GM introduced self-starters, fuel gauges, reliable headlights, and other features that consumers liked. The constant flow of new models induced customers to want a fresh vehicle every few years. The General Motors Acceptance Corporation made it easy to acquire a car on the installment plan.

By the mid-1920s, Ford's sales fell as those of General Motors rose. Ford dealers switched to General Motors, and the used-car market undercut Ford at the other end of the price scale. Henry Ford had revolutionized American transportation before 1920. Now he was losing out because of his resistance to marketing and manufacturing innovation.

During the spring of 1927, Henry Ford ended production of the Model T and turned to the development of a new car. Within months the Model A was ready for consumers. Interest in the product was high; orders for hundreds of thousands were taken before the new model was introduced. Even though it would be months before Ford could meet the customer demand for the automobile, on December 1, 1927, the company unveiled the Model A. Like General Motors, Ford marketed the Model A through a huge advertising campaign. It also created a credit corporation, again modeled on what GM had done, to enable buyers to obtain cars on credit. The combined efforts of Ford and Sloan gave the automobile business in the 1920s the structure and style that would dominate until the start of World War II.

Electrical America   Electricity also stimulated the economy during the 1920s. By 1928, electricity drove 70 percent of factory equipment. Two-thirds of the families in towns and cities had electricity in their homes as well, stimulating demand for the electrical appliances that industry was turning out in abundance. Homemakers bought some 15 million electric irons and another 7 million vacuum cleaners. Advertisers appealed to women with descriptions of the all-electric kitchen "Where Work Is Easy!" Sales of consumer appliances were one of the major economic stimulants of the decade. The electric power industry expanded rapidly, as did the firms that made equipment for the power plants.

The diffusion of electricity facilitated the growth of radio. The first station, KDKA in Pittsburgh, went on the air in 1920. There were only four in 1922; a year later, 566 were in operation. In 1923, a New York station, WBAY, began selling time to anyone who would pay for it. Commercial radio caught on quickly. Soon announcers and performers became popular attractions. Listeners wrote to them for advice about love affairs and to praise the human contact that radios provided. In 1923, there were radios in 400,000 households.

Three years later, in 1926, the Radio Corporation of America (RCA), led by its president, David Sarnoff, established the first national network of stations, the National Broadcasting Company (NBC). Telephone wires carried the broadcast signals to stations scattered across the country. NBC consisted of two networks, the "red" and the "blue." Programming was diverse, and commercial sponsors oversaw the content of such programs as *The Maxwell House Hour* and the *Ipana Troubadours*. Radio was another element in the creation of a mass culture during the decade.

Movies in the   Each week, 100 million people went to see movies at one of the
Silent Era   twenty thousand theaters that showed silent pictures. Some
movie houses were plain and functional. Others featured expensive lobbies and plush furniture. Ticket prices were relatively low and stable, usually about fifty cents. As one college student recalled, "You learn plenty about love from the movies." Pictures shaped how young people kissed on dates, what they wore, and what they said. "I cling to my dream world woven about the movies I have seen," said another student.

From their uncertain beginnings at the turn of the century, motion picture studios had developed into large enterprises employing hundreds of people. Studio heads like Adolph Zukor of Paramount Pictures and Louis B. Mayer of Metro-Goldwyn-Mayer (MGM) controlled chains of theaters, to which they allocated the pictures they made on a rigidly controlled basis. To get a popular feature film, theater owners would have to accept the entire yearly production lineup of a major studio.

Motion picture stars were the bedrock of the business. Charlie Chaplin's popularity rose to even greater heights during the early 1920s in such films as *The Gold Rush* (1925). Other box-office attractions included Rudolph Valentino, whose sudden death in 1926 brought thousands of weeping fans, in a line stretching for eight city blocks, to his New York funeral.

To maintain its hold on the popular mind, Hollywood reacted quickly when sex scandals tarnished the industry's image early in the 1920s. The studios recruited Will H. Hays, a prominent Republican, to serve as president of the Motion Pictures Producers and Distributors Association in 1922. Hays tried to persuade moviemakers to inject more moral content into films. Skillful directors such as Cecil B. DeMille circumvented these mild warnings. He argued that the sex scenes in *The Ten Commandments* were based on biblical descriptions.

Later in the decade evidence accumulated that silent films were boring audiences, and filmmakers believed that talking motion pictures were the logical next step. Fearful that they might lose their hold on the public, the major studios agreed that none of them would make talking pictures unless they all did. One of the smaller studios, Warner Brothers, was working on a sound picture called **The Jazz Singer**. Its star was Al Jolson, who specialized in rendering popular tunes in blackface. This evocation of a racist past appealed to his listeners nostalgic for a time when white supremacy had been even more dominant than it was in the 1920s. When he ad-libbed his catch phrase, "You Ain't Heard Nothing Yet!" and sang several songs, audiences exploded with applause. Within two years, silent pictures gave way to sound, and Hollywood entered the golden era of the studio system.

Advertising
America

Advertisers developed new and effective ways to persuade Americans to acquire the products coming out of the nation's factories and workshops, and the advertising business boomed. Before World War I, the total amount spent on advertising stood at about $400 million annually. It soared to $2.6 billion by 1929. Radios brought advertising into the home, and billboards attracted the attention of millions of motorists. Advertising, said one of its practitioners, "literally creates demand for the things of life that raise the standard of living, elevate the taste, changing luxuries into necessities."

Among the products that advertising promoted was Listerine, which was said to eliminate halitosis, the medical term for bad breath. Other consumers were urged to ingest yeast at least twice a day to fight constipation and skin problems. The ingenious advertising executive Albert Lasker induced Americans to drink orange juice daily at breakfast, broke the taboo against advertising the sanitary napkin Kotex, and described Kleenex as "the handkerchief you can throw away." He also claimed Pepsodent toothpaste would remove "film" from the fortunate user's teeth.

> **DOING HISTORY ONLINE**
>
> Automotive Advertising, 1923
>
> According to the ads online, what are some of the ways in which the automobile reshaped Americans' lives?
>
> www.cengage.com/ history/ayers/ ampassages4e

The most celebrated advertising man of the decade was Bruce Barton, who wrote a biography of Jesus Christ in order to demonstrate that advertising went back to biblical times. In *The Man Nobody Knows* (1925), Barton retold the New Testament in terms that Americans of the 1920s could easily grasp. Jesus, wrote Barton, "recognized the basic principle that all good advertising is news." The twelve disciples were a model of an efficient business organization, and Jesus himself was a master salesman. "He was never trite or commonplace; he had no routine." Barton's book became a national best-seller.

The Changing Face of Agriculture

American farmers in the 1920s struggled with the problems of abundance. The introduction of mechanical tractors and tillers, like the one depicted here from North Dakota, made it possible for farmers to increase their production far beyond what had been done with horse-drawn equipment. The family watching the new machine from their horse and buggy symbolizes the transition that farmers were experiencing.

As farmers brought their cash crops in through the use of machinery, they found that success in growing wheat and other staple crops only intensified their economic dilemmas. The price of wheat, for example, plunged during the first half of the decade as a result of national and international overproduction. Small farmers learned that they could not survive in a market that favored larger enterprises with the capital to purchase modern equipment like this plow.

(© CORBIS)

Those Left Behind   Not all segments of society shared equally in the return of good times. The postwar depression hit the farm sector with devastating force. Farmers had never benefited from the upturn that marked the cities. For labor also, this was a time of retreat.

The United States still relied on farming as a key element in the economy. The 7 million families who lived on farms in 1920 did not generally enjoy the modern conveniences and appliances that had appeared in the cities. In some areas, farm life resembled that of the pioneers more than it did the city dwellers. Overproduction of crops drove down prices and led to massive harvests that could not be marketed. In the South, for example, the price of cotton was 40 cents a pound in 1920 but slid to 10 cents a pound in 1921. Wheat stood at $1.82 per bushel in 1920, sagged to $0.926 in 1924, and then recovered to $1.437 in 1925. The postwar recovery of agriculture in Europe meant that overseas markets were smaller as well. The per capita income of most farmers did not rise substantially after 1919, and there was a widening gap between what farmers earned and what city dwellers made.

To improve their lot, farmers sought higher tariff duties on imported products. They also revived the idea of farm cooperatives to market more effectively. Federal legislation to regulate the trading of grain futures and extend more credit to farmers was marginally helpful, but the underlying problem of overproduction continued.

In 1921, a plow manufacturer named George Peek proposed that American farmers ship surplus products overseas and dump them on the world market at whatever price they could obtain. The government would buy farm products at the market price and then sell them abroad. Taxes on the processing of crops would cover the cost to the government and the taxpayer. The chairs of the House and Senate Agriculture Committees introduced a bill to enact such a program in January 1924. Known as the McNary-Haugen Plan, it gained much support in the Midwest and soon commanded national attention. Critics called it price-fixing at government expense.

Labor in Retreat   After World War I, the Red Scare of 1919–1920 stalled labor's drive to organize coal mining, steel, and other industries that employed thousands of unskilled workers. In the minds of middle-class Americans, labor unions seemed identified with attacks on society itself. The number of unionized laborers dropped from nearly 5 million in 1921 to fewer than 3.5 million eight years later. The American Federation of Labor (AFL), under its president, William Green, presented only weak challenges to employers. It accepted what management called "business unionism," or the nonunion "open shop," which was labeled the "American Plan." Efforts to organize unskilled workers were abandoned.

Government and business threw up numerous obstacles to labor's interests. The U.S. Supreme Court struck down minimum wages for women in Washington, D.C. In the case of *Adkins v. Children's Hospital*, the Supreme Court ruled that the law infringed on the right of workers to sell their labor for whatever they could obtain. This "liberty-of-contract" doctrine accordingly barred Congress from passing such a law. In addition to an unsympathetic Supreme Court, unions faced opposition from the White House. When strikes occurred in railroading during 1922, the Harding administration obtained harsh court orders that effectively ended the walkouts.

Businesses used less repressive tactics as well. Some of the bigger and more enlightened firms provided what became known as welfare capitalism. General Electric, International Harvester, and Bethlehem Steel represented companies that sought to appease workers with recreational facilities, benefit plans, and sometimes even profit-sharing opportunities. Estimates indicated that as many as 4 million workers received such rewards. After the middle of the decade, however, these programs stalled as the lack of labor militancy removed the incentive to make concessions to workers. Most workers remained dependent on the goodwill of their employer for whatever job security they possessed. They could not look to the federal government for any positive assistance.

The Harding Scandals By early 1923, Harding's presidency was mired in rumors of scandal. Attorney General Harry Daugherty was a political ally of the president, but his loose direction of the Justice Department allowed corruption to flourish. Scandals also festered in the Veterans Bureau and the Office of the Alien Property Custodian.

The most serious wrongdoing involved the secretary of the interior, **Albert B. Fall**. Federal oil reserves at Elk Hills, California, and Teapot Dome, Wyoming (where the rocks vaguely resembled a teapot), were leased to private oil companies. Fall received $400,000 in loans from friends in the industry in what many interpreted as payoffs for his leasing decisions. The Teapot Dome scandal emerged in 1923–1924 after Harding died, but it established his administration's reputation as one of the most corrupt in American history.

A weak president and a poor judge of people, Harding allowed cronies and crooks to infest his administration. By 1923, he knew about the ethical problems in the Veterans Bureau, and he suspected that scandals lurked in the Department of the Interior and the Justice Department as well. During a tour of the Pacific Northwest in July 1923, the president fell ill. He died in San Francisco on August 2 of heart disease.

Keep Cool with Coolidge Harding's successor was Calvin Coolidge, the former governor of Massachusetts. Coolidge came to be viewed in Washington as a stereotypical New Englander, a man of few words. In fact, Coolidge was quite talkative in the regular press conferences that he held twice a week. Although he slept twelve hours a day, Coolidge worked hard greeting visitors and addressing the needs of those who told him their problems with the federal government. His wife, Grace, brought glamour and a sense of fun to the White House, offsetting her husband's dour personality.

Coolidge was much more committed to the conservative principles of the Republicans than Harding had been. He proclaimed that "the business of America is business," and he endorsed policies designed to promote corporate enterprise. He extended the tax-cutting policies of Treasury Secretary Mellon. The president also appointed pro-business individuals to head the regulatory agencies and departments that the progressives had established a generation earlier. Meanwhile, he removed the Harding holdovers, such as Harry Daugherty, who might prove politically embarrassing when Coolidge ran for the presidency in 1924.

Coolidge lost little time in gaining control of the Republican Party. The president used modern public relations techniques to bolster his image as an embodiment of old-time virtues of morality and frugality. Movie stars came to the White House to endorse the president and, under the leadership of the stylish Grace Coolidge, sang the campaign theme song: "Keep Cool with Coolidge."

The Discordant Democrats The Democrats hoped that the Teapot Dome scandal and other revelations of wrongdoing in the Harding years would be their ticket back to the White House. But when the Teapot Dome scandal could not be linked to anyone in the White House, the issue faded away.

Prohibition had split the Democrats between the dry faithful of the South and West, who wanted strict enforcement of the Volstead Act, and the wet residents of the large cities of the North and Midwest, who saw Prohibition as a foolish experiment. The two leading candidates for the Democratic Party nomination reflected this regional tension. William G. McAdoo represented the progressive, prohibitionist wing. Governor Alfred E. Smith of New York was a Roman Catholic who opposed Prohibition. The Democratic National Convention left the party with almost no chance of defeating President Coolidge. McAdoo and Smith deadlocked through dozens of ballots. Finally, after 103 ballots, the exhausted delegates compromised and chose a former member of Congress and Wall Street lawyer named John W. Davis.

Senator Robert M. La Follette of Wisconsin, who had been seeking the presidency for many years, became the champion of what remained of the progressive spirit and the anger of the midwestern farmers. Although he was nominated for president at a convention of the Progressive Party, he did not attend the meeting or identify himself with the party. The American Federation of Labor and the railroad unions backed La Follette, but with little money or enthusiasm.

The Republicans ignored Davis and concentrated on the alleged radicalism of La Follette and his supporters. The choice, they said, was "Coolidge or Chaos." Coolidge polled more than 15.7 million votes, more than the combined total of his two rivals. Although the Republicans retained firm control of both houses of Congress, beneath the surface, electoral trends were moving toward the Democrats. In the northern cities the party's share of the vote grew during the 1920s. If a candidate appeared who could unite the traditionally Democratic South with the ethnic voters of the Northeast, Republican supremacy might be in jeopardy.

A BLOSSOMING IN ART AND LITERATURE

While politics followed a conservative path during the 1920s, the nation's cultural life experienced a productivity and artistic success that would be unrivaled during the rest of the twentieth century. In music, drama, and literature, the decade brought forth a rare assembly of first-rate talents.

The Harlem Renaissance African American intellectual life centered in New York City. There, authors and poets lived in the black section known as Harlem. The "Harlem Renaissance" owed much to W. E. B. Du Bois's encouragement of African American writing in *The Crisis*, the journal of the National Association for the Advancement of Colored People (NAACP). In the New York of the early 1920s, the ferment associated with Marcus Garvey, the exciting nightlife, the relative relaxation of racial bigotry, and the interest of wealthy white patrons enabled a few black writers to pursue literary careers.

The Harlem Renaissance reached its peak in 1925, when a national magazine ran an article titled "Harlem: Mecca of the New Negro." In the same year, **Alain Locke's** book *The New Negro* was published. Locke argued that African Americans' "more immediate hope" depended on the ability of blacks and whites to evaluate "the Negro in terms of his artistic endowments and cultural contributions, past and prospective." Other major figures in the Renaissance were the poets Langston Hughes ("The Weary Blues"), Countee Cullen ("Do I Marvel"), **Zora Neale Hurston** (the play *Color Struck*), Claude McKay (*Harlem Shadows*), as well as the memoirist and songwriter James Weldon Johnson (*God's Trombones*). Although these writers' artistic merit was undeniable, the Harlem Renaissance did little to alter the segregationist laws and customs that restricted the lives of most African Americans.

(The Granger Collection, New York)

Zora Neale Hurston. *The Harlem Renaissance gave an opportunity for numerous black writers and poets to gain a larger audience than would have been possible even ten years earlier. One of them was the story writer and novelist Zora Neale Hurston, who wrote about the African American masses.*

The Sound of Jazz After World War I, the improvised music that came to be called jazz brought together black musicians and a few white players in Kansas City, Chicago, and New York. At the rent parties where Harlem residents raised money to pay their landlords, in the nightclubs controlled by organized crime, and in the after-hours jam sessions, jazz became a unique American art form.

The major innovators of jazz included trumpeter **Louis Armstrong** and tenor sax player Coleman Hawkins, who took the new music beyond its roots in New Orleans toward a more sophisticated style. Blues artists such as Bessie Smith and Ma Rainey sold "race records" to black and white audiences. Edward Kennedy "Duke" Ellington and Fletcher Henderson led larger orchestras that showed what jazz could accomplish in a more structured setting. The rhythms and sounds of jazz gave the 1920s its enduring title: the Jazz Age.

Writers looked at the postwar world in a critical spirit that grew out of the European ideas and a skepticism about older values. The most popular novelist of the early 1920s was Sinclair Lewis, whose books *Main Street* (1920) and *Babbitt* (1922) examined with unsparing honesty small-town life in the Midwest. His novels *Arrowsmith* (1925) and *Elmer Gantry* (1927) enhanced his reputation, but his artistic powers failed in the 1930s.

Young people devoured the work of the acidic essayist and social critic Henry L. Mencken, who wrote for the *American Mercury*. Mencken was a Baltimore newspaperman who had little time for the sacred cows of middle-class culture or, as he called them, the "booboisie." He characterized democracy as "the worship of jackals by jackasses" and said that puritanism was "the haunting fear that somebody, somewhere may be happy." Aimed more at the middle-class audience was *Time*, started in March 1923 by Briton Hadden and Henry Luce. *Time* sought to present the week's news in readable and sprightly prose.

The most influential fiction author of the decade was Ernest Hemingway, whose terse, understated prose spoke of the pain and disillusion that men had suffered during the fighting in World War I. In *The Sun Also Rises* (1926) and *A Farewell to Arms* (1929), Hemingway expressed the anguish of young Americans who had lost faith in the moral customs of their parents.

Another serious novelist of the day was **F. Scott Fitzgerald**. Like Hemingway, he, along with his wife, Zelda, captured attention as the embodiment of the free spirit of the Jazz Age. At the same time, Fitzgerald was a dedicated artist who sought to write a great novel that would ensure his fame. In *The Great Gatsby* (1925), he came as close to that goal as any other author of the time. The book chronicled how the young man Jay Gatsby sought to recapture a lost love among the aristocracy of the Long Island shore. In Gatsby's failure to win his dream, Fitzgerald, like other authors of the Jazz Age, saw the inability of Americans to escape the burdens of their own pasts.

An Age of Artistic Achievement

The list of important authors during the 1920s was long and distinguished. It included such artistic innovators as T. S. Eliot, who lived in Great Britain and whose poems such as "The Waste Land" (1922) influenced a generation of poets on both sides of the Atlantic. Novelists such as John Dos Passos, Sherwood Anderson, Edith Wharton, Willa Cather, and William Faulkner produced a body of work that delved into the lives of aristocratic women (Wharton), prairie pioneers (Cather), the working poor and middle class (Dos Passos), the residents of small towns (Anderson), and the Deep South (Faulkner).

The theater witnessed the emergence of the Broadway musical in the work of Richard Rodgers and Lorenz Hart (*Garrick Gaieties*), George and Ira Gershwin (*Lady, Be Good*), Jerome Kern and Oscar Hammerstein II (*Showboat*), and Cole Porter (*Paris*). The great age of the American popular song, inspired by the musicals, began in the 1920s and lasted for three decades. Serious drama drew on the talents of the brooding and pessimistic Eugene O'Neill as well as Elmer Rice and Maxwell Anderson.

In architecture, the innovative work of Frank Lloyd Wright had given him a reputation for artistic daring before 1920, but commercial success eluded him. American architects designed planned, suburban communities modeled on historical models from England or the Southwest. Skyscrapers and city centers such as Rockefeller Center in New York City embodied a building style that emphasized light and air. Amid the prosperity and optimism of the 1920s, it seemed that the possibilities for a lively and vibrant culture were limitless.

FUNDAMENTALISM AND TRADITIONAL VALUES

For most Americans, the literary and artistic ferment of the 1920s was part of a broader set of challenges to the older lifestyles with which they had grown up. Residents of small towns and newcomers to the growing cities sought to find reassurance in the older ways that they fondly remembered. The currents of religious and social conservatism remained dominant.

The Fundamentalist Movement

Amid the social ferment that accompanied the rise of the Ku Klux Klan, the tensions over nativism, and the reaction against modern ideas, American Protestantism engaged in a passionate debate over the proper position of Christians toward science, the doctrine of evolution, and liberal ideas. Conservative church leaders in northern Baptist and Presbyterian pulpits spoke of the dangers to faith from a society that had moved away from the Bible and its teachings. In 1920, a minister called the movement "fundamentalism" because it

The Vanishing Evangelist

In May 1926 the popular California evangelist, Aimee Semple McPherson vanished from a beach at Venice, California. More than a month later, after intense newspaper coverage of her disappearance, McPherson surfaced in Mexico with a lurid tale of being kidnapped. This sensational episode, aspects of which are still mysterious, riveted the nation's attention because McPherson had become a celebrity preacher using the modern media of the 1920s to spread her religious message. She had employed the radio with great skill to attract audiences to her brand of fundamentalist Christianity amid the culture wars of the 1920s.

McPherson was a forerunner of modern televised evangelism as she linked spectacle and piety into a product that attracted millions of followers. At the same time, she foreshadowed other ministers in the political realm with her calls to "Christianize" America. By the time she died in 1944, Aimee Semple McPherson had established herself as an important innovator in the history of conservative Protestantism and had left her mark on the nation's culture.

(Courtesy of The Bancroft Library, University of California, Berkeley)

sought to reaffirm precepts of the Christian creed such as the literal truth of the Bible and the central place of Jesus Christ in saving humanity. In California, Aimee Semple McPherson fused fundamentalism with modern media techniques and achieved national fame in so doing.

Fundamentalism had a political and social agenda as well as a religious message. On the local and state levels, believers sought to eradicate traces of modern ideas that contradicted biblical teachings. The doctrine of evolution became a special target of fundamentalist wrath. William Jennings Bryan emerged as a leading champion of the crusade. "It is better to trust the Rock of Ages," he said, "than to know the age of rocks." In a dozen state legislatures, lawmakers introduced bills to ban the teaching of evolution in public schools. The Anti-Evolution League hoped to amend the Constitution to bar the teaching of evolution anywhere in the nation. In 1924, Tennessee passed a law that prohibited the spending of public money "to teach any theory that denies the story of the Divine Creation of man as taught in the Bible."

The Scopes Trial   In 1925, a schoolteacher named John T. Scopes taught evolution in Dayton, Tennessee. The local authorities indicted Scopes, and his case came to trial. William Jennings Bryan agreed to help prosecute Scopes, and the American Civil Liberties Union brought in the noted trial lawyer Clarence Darrow for the defense. The **Scopes trial** attracted national attention, and the trial became a media circus. The judge refused to let Darrow call in scientists to defend evolution.

DOING HISTORY ONLINE

. . . And Its Discontents

Who or what groups are represented in this online section? What do some of them have in common?

 www.cengage.com/
history/ayers/
ampassages4e

Darrow summoned Bryan as an expert witness on the Bible. The two men sparred for several days. Bryan defended the literal interpretation of the Bible, but to the reporters covering the trial, he seemed to wither under Darrow's cross-examination. Sophisticated Americans regarded Bryan as a joke, but in rural America, he remained a hero. The jury found Scopes guilty and assessed him a small fine. Bryan died shortly after the trial. Although Scopes lost, to many Americans the Scopes trial signaled the end of fundamentalism; the political side of the movement did lose momentum during the late 1920s. But during the same period, fundamentalism returned to its roots. It concentrated on creating a network of churches, schools, and colleges where its doctrines could be taught to future generations. The forces underlying fundamentalism during the 1920s would remain a potent element in American culture.

Prohibition in Retreat   By the mid-1920s, the Prohibition experiment was faltering. Enforcement and compliance waned. The spread of bootlegging and its ties with organized crime meant that state and federal authorities faced an ever-growing challenge in attempting to stop the movement of illegal liquor across the Canadian border or from ships that gathered near major U.S. ports. The brewing and liquor interests called for a campaign to repeal the Eighteenth Amendment, and the Association Against the Prohibition Amendment became a strong lobbying force.

Consumption of alcohol rose to more than one gallon annually per capita by 1923 and reached almost one and one-quarter gallons three years later. With the national law on the books, the Anti-Saloon League lost some of its intensity during the 1920s. When the problems associated with drinking declined, its urgency as a social issue receded. The consensus that had brought Prohibition into existence during World War I was crumbling as the 1928 presidential election approached. As yet, however, a majority of Americans opposed outright repeal of Prohibition.

THE YOUTH CULTURE AND BIG-TIME SPORTS

During the 1920s, changes in the family gave youth more importance. Women stopped having children at a younger age, and they thus had more time to devote to their own interests. Divorce gained favor as a way of ending unhappy marriages; in 1924, one marriage in seven ended in divorce, a large increase since the turn of the century. The emphasis shifted to making marriages more fulfilling for both partners. Marriage counseling gained in popularity, as did manuals telling men and women how to achieve greater sexual gratification.

As the nature of marriage changed, the role of children in the household was also transformed. Parents were no longer regarded as the unquestioned rulers of the home. One major influence on how American children were raised was the work of the behavioral psychologist John B. Watson. He taught that by manipulating the stimuli that a child experienced, the parents could create the kind of adult they wanted. Children, he said, "are made, not born." He instructed parents to follow a system of reward and punishment to shape the character of their offspring.

The ability of parents to decide what their children should read and think came under attack from the growing pervasiveness of the consumer culture. Young people were bombarded with alluring images of automobiles, makeup, motion pictures, and other attractions. Since children no longer were so important to the wage-earning power of the family, they were given greater freedom to spend their leisure time as they deemed best. A teenager might have four to six evenings a week to spend away from home. Adolescence came to be seen as a distinct phase in the development of young Americans in which they lived within their own subculture and responded to its demands for fun, excitement, and novelty. Dating became a ritualized form of courting behavior carried on at movies, dances, and athletic events, as well as in automobiles.

More young Americans attended high school during the 1920s than ever before, and the percentage of those who went to college increased. The college experience became the model for middle-class white youth across the nation. Freed from parental supervision, college women could smoke in public, go out on dates, and engage in the latest trends in sexual activity, "necking and petting." Male students with enough income joined fraternities, drank heavily, and devoted endless amounts of time to athletic contests and dates.

The college experience for students from lower-class families, different religious backgrounds, or minority groups was less comfortable. Informal quotas limited the numbers of Jewish students admitted to Yale, Columbia, and Harvard. In the South, African Americans of college age were restricted to predominantly black institutions that struggled with fewer resources and less distinguished faculties. Poorer students at state universities and private colleges worked their way through, often performing the menial tasks that made life pleasant for their affluent peers.

Big-Time Sports During the 1920s, college football grew into a national obsession as money was poured into the construction of stadiums, the coaching staffs, and in many instances, the players themselves. Large stadiums sprang up on the West Coast and in the Midwest. The most famous football player of the era was Harold "Red" Grange of the University of Illinois. When he scored four touchdowns in twelve minutes against the University of Michigan in 1924, his picture appeared on the cover of the new *Time* magazine. After he left college, Grange joined the newly formed National Professional Football League and received $12,000 per game at the start. In contrast, the average worker in 1925 made 65 cents an hour.

Boxing attracted millions of followers. The first popular champion was William Harrison "Jack" Dempsey, who received $1 million for his fight against the French-man Georges Carpentier in 1921. To avoid confronting the leading African American contender Henry Willis, Dempsey and his manager agreed to fight James Joseph "Gene" Tunney. Tunney defeated an overconfident Dempsey in 1927 in a bout that featured the "long count." Dempsey knocked Tunney down, but then did not go promptly to a neutral corner. With the referee starting the count late, Tunney was able to get up off the canvas and knock out his rival.

Baseball: The National Sport

Of all the American sports, baseball symbolized the excitement and passion of the 1920s. The game experienced a wounding scandal in 1919 when it was revealed that members of the Chicago White Sox had conspired to fix the World Series. Although the players were ultimately acquitted of any crime, the "Black Sox" scandal cast a shadow over the game. The major league club owners hired a new baseball commissioner, Kenesaw Mountain Landis, a former federal judge, and gave him sweeping authority over the operations of baseball. Landis barred the "Black Sox" players from the game for life for having cheated, and he exercised his power vigorously to keep baseball pure.

Baseball underwent even more dramatic changes on the field because of the emergence of a new kind of player in the person of **George Herman "Babe" Ruth**. Ruth was a pitcher for the Boston Red Sox when they sold him to the New York Yankees for $400,000 in 1918. Ruth was the first of the celebrity sluggers; he belted out fifty-four home runs during the 1920 season, and fans flocked to see him perform. The Yankees decided to construct Yankee Stadium ("the House that Ruth built") to accommodate the fans who wanted to be there when Ruth connected. The Yankees won American League pennants from 1921 to 1923, and in 1923 they won the World Series. Batting averages rose in both leagues, as did attendance records. Professional baseball remained a white man's game, however; talented black players such as Josh Gibson labored in obscurity in the Negro leagues.

The peak of baseball in the 1920s came in 1927 when Babe Ruth hit sixty home runs and the New York Yankees captured the American League pennant and the World Series in four games. Their "Murderers Row" of skilled hitters produced "five o'clock lightning" that resulted in comeback victories in the day games that were organized baseball in that period. When Ruth hit his sixtieth home run in late September, commentators speculated that his record would stand for decades. The feat summed up the allure of a sports-crazy decade.

NEW ROLES FOR WOMEN

After the achievement of woman suffrage, most people expected the newly enfranchised voters to produce a genuine change in politics. It soon became apparent that women cast their votes much as men did. The possibility of a cohesive bloc of female voters evaporated. Yet while women did not change politics, they found that their place in society underwent significant transformations.

Women in Politics   Following 1923, the more militant wing of the suffragists, identified with Alice Paul and the **National Woman's Party**, advocated the equal rights amendment (ERA). The amendment stated that "men and women shall have equal rights throughout the United States and every place subject to its jurisdiction." Other female reformers, such as Florence Kelley and Carrie Chapman Catt, regarded the ERA as a threat to the hard-won legislation that protected women in the workplace on such issues as maximum hours, minimum wage, and safer conditions. These women favored an approach such as the Sheppard-Towner Act of 1921, which supplied federal matching funds to states that created programs in which mothers would be instructed on caring for their babies and safeguarding their own health. Despite the efforts of the National Woman's Party and the support of the Republicans, the ERA was not adopted.

Two states, Wyoming and Texas, elected female governors. Nellie Tayloe Ross of Wyoming was chosen to fill out the unexpired term of her husband after he died in office. Miriam Amanda Ferguson of Texas won election in 1924 because her husband, a former governor, had been impeached and barred from holding office in the state. She became his surrogate. Eleven women were elected to the House of Representatives, many of them as political heirs of their husbands. Many more won seats in state legislatures or held local offices. Eleanor Roosevelt, the wife of a rising Democratic politician in New York, built up a network of support for her causes and career among women in her party.

Social causes enlisted women who had started their careers in public life years earlier. Margaret Sanger continued to be a staunch advocate of birth control. She founded the American Birth Control League, which became Planned Parenthood in 1942. Sanger capitalized on a popular interest in "eugenics," a quasi-scientific movement to limit births among "unfit" elements of the population. The racist implications of the theory stirred only modest controversy before the rise of Nazi Germany in the 1930s. Sanger found increased support for birth control among doctors as the 1920s progressed. The greatest effect of the campaign was seen in middle-class women. The poor and minorities turned to older, less reliable methods of avoiding pregnancy and often resorted to abortions when pregnant.

The New Woman   Social feminism confronted the influence of the mass media in shaping the attitudes of women during the 1920s. Older female reformers noted sadly that their younger counterparts were likely "to be bored" when the subject of feminism came up. In their relations with men, young women of the 1920s practiced a new sexual freedom. Among women born after 1900, the rate of premarital intercourse, while still low by modern standards, was twice as high as it had been among women born a decade earlier.

Women joined the work force in growing numbers. At the beginning of the decade, 8.3 million women, or about 24 percent of the national work force, were employed outside the home. Ten years later, the number stood at 10.6 million, or 27 percent. A few occupations accounted for 85 percent of female jobs. One-third of these women worked in clerical positions, 20 percent labored as domestic servants, and another third were employed in factory jobs. Many women with factory jobs worked a full week and continued to spend many hours on household chores as well. The median wage for women usually stood at about 55 percent of what men earned for comparable jobs. At the same time women entered new professions and became celebrities. Amelia Earhart, for example, was the first woman pilot to cross the Atlantic, and emerged as the most famous woman flier of the era.

For the majority of women, however, the barriers to advancement and opportunity remained high. Poor white women in the South often worked at dead-end jobs in textile mills or agricultural processing plants. Black women found it difficult to secure nondomestic jobs in either the North or the South. When African Americans were employed to move supplies or equipment in factories, they did the heavy, menial labor that white workers shunned. In the Southwest, Hispanic women picked crops, shelled pecans, or worked as domestic servants. Labor unions rarely addressed the situation of female workers. When strikes did occur, as in New Jersey and Massachusetts during the middle of the decade, employers sometimes granted concessions—and then moved their factories to the South, where labor was cheaper and unions were weaker.

Career women faced formidable obstacles. When a woman schoolteacher married, many school districts compelled her to resign. College faculties, the medical profession, and the law had more women members than in the past, but they made it difficult for women to advance in these careers. In government, men received favorable treatment. Although many women worked outside the home out of economic necessity, they were expected to juggle their careers and domestic responsibilities. Women who were "creative" or who had "administrative gifts or business ability," said the feminist Crystal Eastman, and who also had "the normal desire to be mothers, must make up their minds to be sort of supermen."

COOLIDGE IN THE WHITE HOUSE

The inauguration of President Coolidge on March 4, 1925, was the first to be broadcast over the radio. The administration's policy goals were modest. In 1926, Coolidge asked Congress for a cut in taxes. The lawmakers responded with a measure that lowered the surtax on people who made more than $100,000 annually, reduced the estate tax to 20 percent, and eliminated the gift tax. Few married couples earned more than the $3,500 exemption, and only about 4 million Americans filed tax returns during this period. The changes in the law affected only the most affluent in the society.

The president also supported laws to oversee the expansion of the new airline industry and regulate the growing radio business. Coolidge vetoed a bill to develop the electric power potential of the Tennessee River at Muscle Shoals, Alabama, for public purposes. When Congress twice passed the McNary-Haugen Plan to assist agriculture, Coolidge vetoed it on the grounds that trying to raise crop prices through government intervention was both expensive and wrong.

Coolidge's Foreign Policy Although the United States remained out of the League of Nations and proclaimed that it would remain aloof from foreign involvements, it was not in fact an isolationist country during the 1920s. The Coolidge administration participated in foreign relations in ways that would have seemed impossible a decade earlier. Its effort to have the United States join the World Court (a part of the League of Nations whose official title was the Permanent Court of International Justice) in 1925 and 1926 collapsed when the Senate insisted on major conditions for American membership, including limits on the court's ability to issue advisory opinions on disputed issues. The government encouraged the expansion of American business around the world, and Washington used corporate executives as ambassadors and in framing monetary policy. Americans applauded U.S.

policy in Latin America, Asia, and Europe because it did not involve the use of force or the commitment of soldiers. Sentiment for peace remained strong.

In Latin America, troubled relations with Mexico, especially over control of oil reserves, persisted. The administration sent an emissary, Dwight Morrow, who mediated an agreement to protect American oil companies from further expropriation. Marines were withdrawn from Nicaragua in 1925 but were sent back a year later when civil war erupted again. American efforts to instruct the Nicaraguans in what Washington said were democratic procedures did not produce the desired results by the time the Coolidge presidency ended.

Diplomacy and Finance in the 1920s

After the decision not to join the League of Nations, U.S. interest in Europe became chiefly financial. American bankers and investors played a large part in providing the reparation payments required of Germany in the Treaty of Versailles. Because of the size of the sums they had to pay, the Germans were unable to meet their obligations without American help. In 1924, the Coolidge administration endorsed a plan that scaled back German reparations and loaned that country money to meet its debts. During the next four years, Germany borrowed almost $1.5 million from the United States. European nations in turn used the money paid to them by the Germans to buy American farm and factory products.

The Coolidge administration continued the policy of nonrecognition of the Soviet Union, but it did not object when business interests, including Henry Ford, made substantial investments there. Americans also sent large amounts of aid and food when the Soviets faced famine during the early 1920s. In China, the U.S. government watched apprehensively as revolution and civil war wracked that nation. Washington extended de facto recognition to the government of the Nationalist leader, Chiang Kai-shek, a stance that reflected the general policy of encouraging positive developments overseas without assuming any direct obligations. A symbol of that sentiment came in American support for the idea of outlawing war altogether. When the French foreign minister, Aristide Briand, proposed a mutual security agreement between his country and the United States, the State Department, under Frank B. Kellogg, proposed instead a multilateral agreement to have signatory nations renounce war. Peace groups supported the idea, and the Kellogg-Briand Pact was signed in 1928 and ratified a year later. War was not abolished, of course, but Americans in the 1920s thought it was an attainable goal. Meanwhile, they turned their attention to a stunning feat of personal daring and technological expertise.

Lucky Lindy and Retiring Cal

In 1927, two surprising events riveted the attention of Americans. The first came in May when **Charles A. Lindbergh** flew alone across the Atlantic Ocean from New York to Paris. Lindbergh did not make the first nonstop flight across the ocean; two British aviators had accomplished that feat eight years earlier, flying from Ireland to Newfoundland in 1919. By 1926, however, a $25,000 prize was offered for the first nonstop flight between New York and Paris, a distance of thirty-six hundred miles. Charles Lindbergh had been an army flier and was working as an airmail pilot for the government when he heard about the contest. He raised money from local leaders in St. Louis and other cities. He called his monoplane the *Spirit of St. Louis*. On May 10, a tired Lindbergh (he had not slept the night before) took off from Roosevelt Field in New York on his

The Heroic Lindbergh

This picture of Charles A. Lindbergh after his historic flight to Paris captures the fascination that people in the 1920s had with celebrity, science, and the cult of the individual. Although the Atlantic had been crossed in an airplane years earlier, the spectacle of Lindbergh, "the Lone Eagle," braving the elements to fly solo from New York across the ocean enthralled the public around the world. While technology made Lindbergh's accomplishment possible, Americans persuaded themselves that the flier was a hero in the mold of the frontier and the West, conquering the dangers of the unknown. Aviation also symbolized the ability of the postwar generation to extend progress in benign ways. In the next decade, the possibility of bombers carrying deadly payloads would reshape how airplanes were seen. But in the heady days of 1927, Charles Lindbergh exemplified how Americans in the 1920s wanted to see themselves—on the cutting edge of change while affirming older, traditional values.

(The Granger Collection, New York)

way to Paris. When he landed in the French capital thirty-six hours later, he was a worldwide celebrity. He received a ticker tape parade in New York City, medals from foreign nations, and a lifetime in the public eye. To the generation of the 1920s, Lindbergh's feat symbolized the ability of a single person to bend technology to his will and overcome nature. By the summer of 1927, Lindbergh was the most famous person in the United States, eclipsing even President Coolidge.

Calvin Coolidge could easily have sought another term in 1928. But he may have sensed the weaknesses in the economy that would become evident two years later. While vacationing in the Black Hills of South Dakota during the summer of 1927, the president gave reporters a simple statement: "I do not choose to run for president in 1928." This surprise announcement opened up the race for the Republican presidential nomination to other potential contenders, including the secretary of commerce, Herbert Hoover.

As 1927 ended, there were some signs that the economy was not as robust as it had been. A slight recession occurred in which wholesale prices fell nearly 4.5 percent. Production slowed, and consumer spending also dropped. Despite these warning signs, the banking system continued to expand credit, and stock market speculation persisted. For the average American, there was little concrete evidence that the boom years might be coming to a close. Calvin Coolidge was going out of public life on top with prosperity still a sure thing in the minds of most Americans with money to spend and invest.

CONCLUSION

The years between World War I and the start of the Great Depression have never lost their reputation for excitement and novelty. Bathtub gin, flappers, syncopation, and gangsters remain part of the national image of that time. Prohibition did encounter serious opposition from the upper classes, and evasion of the law was widespread. Nevertheless, liquor control did change drinking habits, so the experiment was not a complete failure.

For women the sense that the 1920s represented a new age of sexual and social liberation was rather superficial. Sexual practices did become more flexible, but marriage and family continued to be viewed as the goals toward which most women should aspire. The number of women in the workplace rose, but the percentage of women in the labor force did not change much. Politics saw an infusion of women into both major parties, but genuine equality remained elusive. The 1920s did not produce anything like the gains in political or social status that had been achieved by women during the previous decade.

In its culture, the United States went through an artistic renaissance. Literature, art, and music explored new channels and brought forth important figures whose influence remained strong through the 1930s and beyond. The works of Hemingway, Fitzgerald, and Mencken, the jazz of Ellington and Louis Armstrong, and the achievements of numerous other artists made the 1920s a high point of American artistic expression.

The 1920s brought important economic changes for many Americans. A consumer culture based on mass appeal tied middle-class society together through common experiences of driving automobiles, listening to radios, and attending films each week. The cultural response was more complex. The Ku Klux Klan, the movement for immigration restriction, and the rise of fundamentalism challenged the newer ways and revealed that the United States was still divided between the values of town and country.

While the potential for social conflict persisted, the economic good times of the decade left few avenues for effective protest and unrest. For a brief period it seemed possible that discord might vanish in a rising tide of economic growth. However, the prosperity of the 1920s did not alter the inequities between rich and poor. If the national belief in a prosperous future were to disappear, the latent strains within American life might resurface.

In retrospect, these years would come to be seen as a time of isolation from the cares and problems of the postwar world. The United States was involved overseas with its destiny linked to the economies of Europe and Asia. The American people did not, however, believe that they would have to be militarily committed to the fates of people beyond the two oceans that protected the continent. In the 1930s, that confidence would decrease as dangerous new powers arose to challenge democracy in western Europe and the Pacific. Soon the 1920s would come to be regarded as a time of lost innocence.

CHAPTER REVIEW, 1921–1927

During the 1920s, the United States became more modern because of:
- The rise of a consumer society
- The growing popularity of automobiles
- The development of radio and the motion picture industry
- The expanding use of electricity
- Greater opportunities for women in the economy

Resisting the trends toward a mass society and culture were:
- The effort to enforce Prohibition
- The rise of the Ku Klux Klan
- The growing tension between secular forces and religious fundamentalism
- Continuing discrimination against minorities

◀▥ Looking Back

The 1920s owed much to the way that the economy made the transition from war to peace between 1918 and 1921. The political effects of the same period prepared the way for Republican dominance throughout the decade. Unhappiness with the League of Nations also shaped American foreign policy.

1. What problems did Warren G. Harding confront when he took office in March 1921?
2. How did the failure of the League of Nations to gain Senate approval affect foreign policy under Harding and Coolidge?
3. What were the roots of the cultural tensions of 1920s that anti-immigration, the Ku Klux Klan, and the revolt against the city reflected?

Looking Ahead ▥▶

The key elements of the 1920s were economic prosperity, cultural change toward a more urban and cosmopolitan society, and the underlying problems that caused the Great Depression at the end of the decade. As you read, be alert for the ways in which these forces interacted to make the 1920s so important in shaping the rest of the century.

1. Although the 1920s were prosperous, not all sectors of American life shared in the bounty. Why was the depressed state of agriculture so important?
2. How solidly based was the consumer culture of the decade in economic terms?
3. How was income distributed, and what government tax policies affected that issue under Harding and Coolidge?
4. What accounted for the flowering of the arts and culture during this period? What traces of the 1920s can still be found in mass entertainment now?

Go to the *American Passages* website at www.cengage.com/history/ayers/ ampassages4e for additional review materials.

24

The Great Depression, 1927–1933

As the end of the 1920s approached, some well-off Americans viewed the future with confidence. Accepting the Republican presidential nomination in 1928, Herbert Hoover proclaimed: "We in America today are nearer to the final triumph over poverty than ever before in the history of any land." Farmers would not have shared Hoover's optimism, nor would African Americans and the poor. Among those who had benefited from the boom of the 1920s, however, the prosperity and abundance enjoyed by the fortunate seemed destined to extend into the immediate future.

Then came the shocks: first, the stock market crash in October 1929, then a severe economic depression that worsened during the early 1930s. The good times of the 1920s were replaced with bread lines, soup kitchens, and the wandering homeless. The administration of President Herbert Hoover took unprecedented actions to relieve the crisis, but nothing seemed to work. Resentment against the president, the economic system, and the wealthy grew. The specter of social revolution arose. Pressures for political change led to the election of **Franklin D. Roosevelt** in 1932.

By 1933, the Great Depression, as it came to be called, affected almost everyone in American society. It worsened the already difficult situation of the nation's farmers. For African Americans, Hispanics, and the poor, it meant even more misery and suffering than they usually faced. A generation of Americans looked to the federal government for answers to the social and economic problems they confronted.

THE STOCK MARKET CRASH OF OCTOBER 1929

At the time of the **stock market crash of 1929**, the incumbent president was Herbert Hoover. Elected in 1928 after a divisive campaign against the Democratic candidate, Governor Alfred E. Smith of New York, Hoover brought to the White House the knowledge gained from a successful career in the mining business

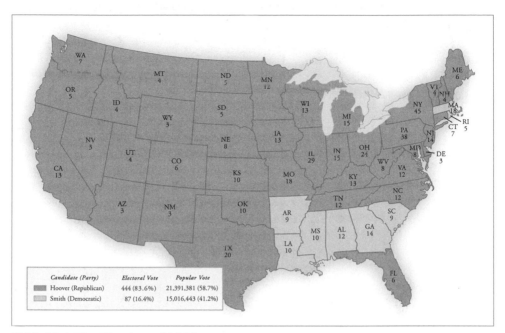

Candidate (Party)	Electoral Vote	Popular Vote
Hoover (Republican)	444 (83.6%)	21,391,381 (58.7%)
Smith (Democratic)	87 (16.4%)	15,016,443 (41.2%)

MAP 24.1 The Election of 1928.

In the election of 1928, Herbert Hoover achieved an electoral landslide and cracked the "Solid South" for the first time since Republican successes in Reconstruction. Alfred E. Smith did carry Massachusetts and Rhode Island, whose heavily Roman Catholic populations supported him. Those victories anticipated Democratic gains in the 1930s.

and in government as secretary of commerce under Warren G. Harding and Calvin Coolidge. Hoover's intense personal style and love of the limelight led Coolidge to dub him "the Boy Wonder." For the Republicans, he was the natural front-runner in 1928 once Coolidge decided not to run. In the election contest, Hoover benefited from the Americans' suspicion of Smith, a Roman Catholic, which permeated the heavily Protestant South and Midwest. Now the question was whether "the Great Engineer," as Hoover was dubbed, could become a successful president.

To the average American, the economic signs during the summer of 1929 seemed encouraging. The prices of stocks traded on the New York Stock Exchange were reaching ever-higher levels. At the beginning of 1928, for example, the industrial index of the *New York Times* was recorded at 245. Within twelve months, it had risen to 331. It soared to 452 by September 1929. Radio Corporation of America stock shot up from $85 a share to $420 a share during 1928. DuPont's stock price went from $310 to $525. A poem appeared in a popular magazine:

> Oh, hush thee, my babe, granny's bought some more shares,
> Daddy's gone out to play with the bulls and bears,

This icon will direct you to interactive activities and study materials on the *American Passages* website: www.cengage.com/history/ayers/ampassages4e

CHAPTER TIMELINE

1928	Republicans nominate Herbert Hoover as their presidential candidate • Democrats select Alfred E. Smith • Hoover elected president of the United States
1929	Stock market crash, September–October 1929
1930	Smoot-Hawley Tariff bill passed to raise tariff rates • Birds Eye frozen foods and Wonder sliced bread introduced • Democratic gains in congressional elections
1931	President Hoover declares moratorium on payment of war debts • Association of Southern Women Against Lynching starts • Japanese invade Manchuria
1932	Bonus March in Washington • Amelia Earhart makes first transatlantic solo flight by a woman • Democrats nominate Franklin D. Roosevelt who promises New Deal • Roosevelt wins landslide election victory
1933	Banks fail during first two months • Depression worsens • Roosevelt inaugurated March 4, 1933

Mother's buying on tips, and she simply can't lose,
And baby shall have some expensive new shoes!

These giddy investors would be brought up short when the market's rise came to a shuddering halt in the cataclysmic moments of the epic Wall Street downturn that persists in the folklore of capitalism as the Great Crash.

Causes of the Crash What dire alignment of negative economic forces triggered the calamity of October 1929? The decade of the 1920s had seen a wild investment fever that led all too many gullible investors into risky ventures for the allure of quick profits. In the sunshine state of Florida, where dreams of riches blossomed in the humid atmosphere, there had been an epic land boom in the middle part of this ten-year span. Asking prices for some of the most favored lots, those near the balmy waters of the subtropical Atlantic Ocean, rose to $15,000 or $20,000 a foot for acreage on the shore. When a devastating hurricane in 1926 deflated these dreams, land prices collapsed. Willing investors then badgered their brokers for other speculative opportunities that would feed the insatiable appetites for quick and profitable returns that dominated the era.

By 1927, the stock market seemed the ideal place to acquire the fast buck that Americans pursued. The issuance of Liberty Bonds during World War I had shown citizens the potential upside of stock purchases. Corporations increasingly relied on stock offerings to bring in

---

DOING HISTORY ONLINE

The Crash

Study the documents online and the sections in the textbook on "The Stock Market Crash of 1929" and "The Great Depression." What is the connection between the stock market crash and the Depression?

 www.cengage.com/history/ayers/ampassages4e

the cash to finance the growth of their businesses. Stockbrokers hawked their products with hard-sell advertising techniques developed for consumer goods from Kleenex to Fords. Finally, during the go-go years of the Harding and Coolidge presidencies, generous government tax policies allowed the super wealthy to retain money that they then poured into the coffers of brokerage firms for stock purchases. The richest Americans, by legal means, sometimes paid no income taxes at all. Five hundred families reveled in incomes of more than $1 million in 1929. Awash with funds, these opulent investors saw the stock market as a way to get even richer.

One tempting device for smaller investors was to buy stocks in what was called then, as it is now, "margin" trading. An investor purchased a stock on credit, putting up only 10 or 15 percent of the actual price. Because Wall Street sentiment believed that stock prices were headed toward even better prices in the future, a person, according to this rosy scenario, could sell the stock at a higher level, pay off the broker, and still pocket a substantial profit. Just as someone might acquire a house or a car on credit, so brokers urged their customers to invest $100 with the prospect of controlling $1,000 or more worth of stock. People borrowed money to buy on margin. In this way, a tiny investment might represent a commitment to buy several thousand dollars worth of stock. Of course, the investor could be required to provide the full price of the stock at any time. But with the market seemingly going up on a permanent basis, that risk seemed a small one.

Investors with inside knowledge manipulated a stock's price up and down in order to fleece the unwary public or, in the phrase of the market, "shear the sheep." A firm called Kolster Radio had no earnings in 1929, but insiders drove the value up to $95 before the price collapsed back to $3 a share. New companies often consisted of nothing more than schemes to issue stock assuming that the market would rise. These firms produced no goods; they were paper empires with no real value, such as Ivar Kreuger's International Match Company. Government regulation of stock issues on both the state and federal levels was very lax, and the stock exchanges themselves had few requirements for revealing the true financial status of these companies. Some of the investment trusts, as they were called, were frauds; those who put money into them lost their entire investment.

Rosy statistics and forecasts made the stock market crash of October 1929 even more of a shock. The problem began in September after stock prices reached record levels. Stock prices then declined early in the month, regained some strength, and resumed a downward drift. No abrupt collapse had occurred, and many on Wall Street, their confidence unshaken, saw these events as one of the temporary "corrections" that preceded further upward surges. A few people warned of impending problems, but they were dismissed as chronic naysayers who had been wrong before. President Hoover told his financial broker to sell off some of his holdings because "possible hard times are coming." He did not say that to the public. Most owners of stock simply waited for the rise in prices to begin again.

Then on October 24, 1929, which became known in Wall Street lore as **Black Thursday**, traders began selling stocks and found that there were few buyers. Prices collapsed, and the total number of shares traded reached 13 million, then an all-time record. Stockholders absorbed, by some estimates, a $9 billion loss in the value of their equities. During the afternoon, a banking syndicate, led by J. P. Morgan, Jr., urged investors to be calm. The syndicate bought stocks, and the market seemed to quiet. Over the weekend, the hope was that normal trading might recover.

The blow fell on October 29, when selling of stocks resumed at an even more intense rate. More than 16 million shares changed hands in a single day. Prestigious stocks such as American Telephone and Telegraph and General Electric recorded declines that wiped out large parts of their equity value. Fistfights occurred on the trading floor, and rumors of suicides swept through the exchange. The story went that when one trader checked into a hotel and asked for a room, the clerk inquired: "For sleeping or jumping, sir?" The naive optimism of the 1920s was evaporating as harsh reality came home to Wall Street.

The number of Americans who actually participated in the stock market in 1929 stood at between 1.5 million and 2 million. Most of the corporate dividends in that year went to about 600,000 stockholders whose annual incomes were above $5,000. These individuals were betting on the nation's economic future and sought to benefit from a prosperity that appeared to be permanent. The crash of 1929 wiped out many of these investors. Others cut back on their stock holdings and trimmed their personal expenditures.

The stock market collapse revealed serious underlying weaknesses in the economy. The well-to-do citizens who played the market were confident that other investors would buy their stocks at the higher price levels of the precrash period. Because of the way income was distributed in the United States, with the rich getting a far higher share than that of other segments of the population, there were not enough people in the upper brackets for that assumption to be realistic. Once wealthy investors began to sell their stocks, there were no other potential buyers to keep security prices high, and a fall in the market became unavoidable.

The consequences of the stock market's decline were striking. The prices of individual stocks underwent a sustained downward slide. Within a few months, such a high-flying issue as General Electric had dropped from $403 a share to $168. Standard Oil shares fell from $83 to $48. One index of stock prices had gone to 469.5

(Library of Congress)

Breadline. *In the wake of the Great Depression, breadlines became a common occurrence in the United States. This one was formed under the Brooklyn Bridge in New York City as desperate people waited for food.*

in September and was at 220.1 by November. During the next twelve months, the gross national product sank from nearly $88 billion down to $76 billion. The economy was slumping into a prolonged depression.

BROTHER, CAN YOU SPARE A DIME: THE GREAT DEPRESSION

Although the stock market crash represented a serious setback for the nation's economic health, the Great Depression of the 1930s that followed arose from causes more deeply rooted than just the decline in stock values of October 1929. Despite the apparent prosperity of the 1920s, the United States faced serious structural problems that combined to cause the prolonged economic downturn.

The most pervasive dilemma that the U.S. economy faced had to do with the distribution of income during the 1920s. By 1929, the 5 percent of Americans at the top income level were receiving one-third of the total annual personal income. Those who made up the lowest 40 percent of the population received about one-eighth of the available income. For an economy that depended on the purchase of consumer goods for its expansion, there were not enough people with money to buy the products that industry was turning out. The amount of spendable income that the top 1 percent of the population received rose from 12 percent in 1920 to 19 percent nine years later. That gain for the wealthy meant that there was less money for the mass of consumers to spend on the products of American factories and businesses.

Wealth was also concentrated in the hands of those with the highest incomes. More than 21 million families, or 80 percent of the national population, did not have any savings at all. The 2.3 percent of families with incomes above $10,000 a year, however, possessed two-thirds of the available savings. A consumer society had emerged, but the bulk of the consumers were unable to participate fully in the economic process. Although wealth had been more concentrated earlier in the century, the disparities of the late 1920s contributed to the onset of the Depression.

Instead of using the profits that their businesses gained from selling goods during the mid-1920s to invest in new factories or a better-paid work force, industry leaders had put their gains into the stock market or speculative ventures. Loans to New York stockbrokers, for example, went from $3.5 billion in July 1927 to $8.5 billion in September 1929. By 1927, the market for new cars and new houses began to weaken, indicating falling demand for consumer goods.

Another chronic weakness of the economy was in agriculture, a sector that never shared in the general prosperity of the 1920s. The problem of overproduction of farm goods had not been addressed, and as prices fell at the beginning of the Depression, farmers felt the effects. At the beginning of 1931, cotton stood at nine to ten cents per pound; when farmers brought in their crop in the fall, the price had skidded to under six cents a pound. When farmers could not pay off their mortgages, rural banks soon failed. The ripple of banking failures strained a banking system that the stock market crash had weakened. In the countryside, crops rotted because they could not be sold, and farmers talked of strikes and other protests.

The world economy was also fragile. The settlement of World War I had imposed heavy reparation payments on the defeated Germans. Because the Germans could not pay these sums, they borrowed from investors and banks in the United States.

In that way Americans financed the German debt payments to the victorious British and French. Those countries, in turn, could use the funds to pay off their war debts to the United States.

In 1924, the United States had reduced the burden of German war debts, and in 1929, another plan was offered that cut back further on the amount that Germany owed while establishing a payment schedule that extended the length of time for retiring the debt. These concessions alleviated the situation to some degree, but the basic problem persisted. This intricate and interlocking process hinged on the strength of the American economy. The United States, however, created tariff barriers that discouraged European imports and steered American capital toward internal economic development. When the European economies experienced difficulties themselves after 1929, the weakened structure of debts and loans soon collapsed, further damaging the economy of the United States. In fact, President Hoover would later argue that the entire Depression arose from causes beyond the borders of the United States. The debts were important in the overall situation of the world economy, but they were a contributing cause to the Depression in the United States rather than the main element in the crisis.

In 1929–1930, the United States lacked many of the government programs to lessen the cumulative effects of a depression. There was no government insurance of bank deposits. Individual banks were vulnerable to sudden demands by depositors to withdraw their money. Many banks had invested in the stock market and thereby placed their assets at risk. Other prominent bankers had embezzled some of the funds under their control to finance their investing. Among banks in general, there was little cooperation when a crisis occurred. To save themselves, stronger banks called in loans made to smaller banks, thus worsening the condition of weaker banks.

For an individual employee thrown out of work, there was no unemployment insurance. Old age pensions were also rare. Conventional economic thinking taught that the government should play a minimal role during hard times. Many people believed that the natural forces of the economy must work themselves out without the government intruding into the process. Secretary of the Treasury Andrew Mellon told President Hoover that "a panic was not altogether a bad thing" because "it will purge the rottenness out of the system." Americans who did not have Mellon's wealth and secure income were less persuaded of the therapeutic effects of hard times.

The Depression Takes Hold

The stock market crash did not cause the Depression, and for some months after the disaster on Wall Street, it seemed as though the economy might rebound without much assistance from Washington. President Hoover endeavored to strike an encouraging note when he said in late 1929, "The fundamental business of the country is sound." He conferred with leading business figures about measures to maintain public confidence, especially programs to bolster prices and wages. He asked the Federal Reserve System to facilitate business borrowing. For the moment, events seemed to be going Hoover's way. During the first several months of 1930, stock market prices recovered from their 1929 lows. In 1930, Congress enacted the Smoot-Hawley Tariff, which raised customs duties to high levels. Republicans believed that tariff protection would enable American agriculture and industry to rebound. The bill passed the Senate by a narrow margin, and despite some reservations, Hoover signed the measure on June 17, 1930.

Unemployment During the Great Depression

The dimensions of the Great Depression of the 1930s are sometimes hard to grasp in human terms. This table documenting the rise of unemployment during the late 1920s and into the early 1930s provides the raw totals of people out of work. As the numbers show, the modest unemployment of 1929 rose dramatically by 1930 and then nearly doubled a year later. The increase in the number of people out of work strained the resources of relief agencies, which were then largely private.

TABLE 24.1 Unemployment, 1927–1933

Year	Number Unemployed	Percentage of Labor Force
1927	1,890,000	4.1
1928	2,080,000	4.4
1929	1,550,000	3.2
1930	4,340,000	8.7
1931	8,020,000	15.9
1932	12,060,000	23.6
1933	12,830,000	24.9

Source: Historical Statistics of the United States, 1985, p. 73.

Mass unemployment had not been seen since the hard times of the 1890s. By 1932, the percentage of those unemployed had risen to almost 24 percent, and many other workers saw pay cuts and reductions in the hours that they spent on the job. With no unemployment insurance or organized system of government relief to tide workers over, poverty was the inescapable result. The impact of these stark numbers lingered for more than a decade on the people who found themselves the unexpected victims of this massive and prolonged economic downturn.

The Smoot-Hawley law has been blamed for the severity of the worldwide depression because it made it more difficult for European business to sell goods in the United States. The negative impact of the Smoot-Hawley Tariff has probably been overstated, relative to the other, more severe causes of the Depression. In any case, by the middle of 1930, the effects of the downturn began to be felt in many areas of government activity.

During the 1930s and afterward, many Americans would place the responsibility for the Great Depression on President Hoover and his policies. More than any previous chief executive, Hoover endeavored to use the power of his office to address the economic crisis. He favored reduction of taxes, easing of bank credits, and a modest program of public works to provide jobs. Some members of Congress opposed these ideas as too activist; others said that Hoover proposed too little. Meanwhile, the White House issued a series of confident statements to bolster public faith that the economic downturn would be brief. When the stock market turned upward briefly in 1930, for example, the president told the nation: "I am convinced we have passed the worst and with continued effort shall rapidly recover."

But as 1930 continued, it was clear that the Depression was not going away. Bank failures soared from 659 in 1929 to 1,350 a year later. Businesses were closing, investment was declining, and corporate profits were falling off. Industrial production was 26 percent lower at the end of 1930 than it had been 12 months earlier. By October

1930, 4 million people were without jobs (almost 9 percent of the labor force), and the trend worsened as each month passed. Within a year, nearly 16 percent of the labor force was out of work.

To encourage confidence, Hoover exhorted businesses to keep prices up and employees at work. Conferences with industry leaders at the White House were covered extensively in the press. These sessions were designed to show the American people that the Depression was being addressed. The president lacked the power to make corporations retain workers or to prevent price-cutting. Despite any public pledges they might offer to Hoover, corporate executives trimmed payrolls and reduced costs when it seemed necessary.

HOOVER'S PROGRAMS TO FIGHT THE DEPRESSION

The president sought to apply his principles of voluntary action to keep the banking system afloat. In October 1931, he persuaded bankers to set up the National Credit Corporation, a private agency that would underwrite banks that had failed and safeguard their depositors. Unfortunately, the management of the banks proved reluctant to acquire the assets of their failed competitors, and the experiment was a disaster.

Herbert Hoover did not view government action as an appropriate way of responding to the Depression. Instead, he believed that the traditional self-reliance and volunteer spirit of the American people provided the most dependable means of ending the economic slump. His policies promoting economic recovery and providing relief for the unemployed stemmed from that fundamental conviction. He asked Americans who had jobs to invest more in their neighbors, to spend something extra to ensure that everyone could work. He set up presidential committees to coordinate volunteer relief efforts for the unemployed. One of those committees was the President's Organization of Unemployment Relief (or POUR). Yet none of these efforts dealt with the misery that Americans faced every day as the Depression intensified.

The programs that Hoover put forward were inadequate for the size of the unemployment situation. By 1931, 8 million people were on the jobless rolls. They overwhelmed the resources of existing charitable agencies that normally provided help to the blind, the deaf, and the physically disabled. Nor were the cities and states capable of providing relief at a time when the Depression reduced their tax revenues and increased the demand for services.

In this situation, the president's informal committees for dealing with unemployment proved ineffective. The POUR program coordinated relief agencies and urged people to help their neighbors. The First Lady, Lou Hoover, long a leader of the Girl Scouts, mobilized its members for the same purpose. These efforts, commendable as they were, did little to deal with the mass unemployment that gripped the country. Yet when politicians clamored for action by the national government, Hoover remained resolutely opposed.

A symbolic event underscored the president's political ineptitude in dealing with the Depression and its effects. When drought struck the Midwest in 1930 and 1931, Congress proposed to appropriate $60 million to help the victims of the disaster buy fuel and food. Hoover accepted the idea of allocating money to feed animals, but he rejected the idea of feeding farmers and their families. One member of Congress said that the administration would give food to "jackasses . . . but not starving babies." The president accepted a compromise that spent the money without saying that some of it would be used for food. The spectacle of the president being more solicitous for animals than starving citizens was another testimony to Hoover's inability to empathize with the plight of his fellow Americans.

Everyday Life During the Depression
For most Americans after 1929, there was no single decisive moment when they knew that the economy was in trouble. A husband might find his pay reduced or his hours of work cut back. Soon families were making changes in their lifestyle, postponing purchases, and sending children out to find jobs. When a person lost a job, savings helped tide the family over until another job could be found. But as time passed and no jobs appeared, savings ran out, and the family home was put up for sale or the mortgage was foreclosed. The family slipped into the ranks of the unemployed or the poor. In a trend that became a lasting image of the Depression, men selling apples appeared on the street corners in major cities. Beggars and panhandlers became a common sight as well.

For those who were at the bottom of the economy even during boom times, the Depression presented still greater challenges. "The Negro was born in depression," said one African American. "It only became official when it hit the white man." In the South, whites seeking work took over the low-paying service jobs that African Americans had traditionally filled. Some black workers in the South encountered violence when whites compelled them to leave their jobs. Elsewhere, white laborers went on strike, insisting that African American workers be dismissed.

Women were told that they too should relinquish their jobs to men to end the unemployment crisis. Some corporations fired all their married women employees, and school districts in the South dismissed women teachers who married. Because women did the domestic and clerical tasks that men did not care to do even in hard times, the number of women employed did not decline as fast as the number of men. Nevertheless, the Depression retarded the economic progress of women.

For Native Americans, the hard times perpetuated a legacy of neglect that had endured for decades. The Bureau of Indian Affairs (BIA) did not address the many social problems that the people under its jurisdiction confronted. Nearly half the Indians on reservations had no land; the other half subsisted on poor-quality land. Poverty pervaded Indian society along with a rate of infant mortality that far exceeded the rate for the white population. Criticism of the BIA mounted, but, despite a rhetorical commitment to reform, the Hoover administration accomplished little to improve Native American life.

On the nation's farms, abundant crops could not find a market, so the produce rotted in the fields. Mortgages were foreclosed, and many former landowners fell into the status of tenant farmers as the Depression wore on. In 1929, President Hoover had persuaded Congress to pass the Agricultural Marketing Act, which created the Federal Farm Board whose purpose was to stabilize farm prices. When farm surpluses around the world swamped grain markets in 1930, it proved impossible to prevent commodity prices from falling. Talk of strikes and protests was common among farmers during 1931 and 1932. During the summer of 1932, Milo Reno, an Iowa farmer, created the

Distress on the Farm in the Great Depression

This picture of a farm being sold at auction during the Great Depression shows the culmination of the agricultural problems discussed in an earlier Picturing the Past feature in Chapter 23 (page 608). Even with the prosperity of the 1920s, farmers remained trapped in a cycle of overproduction and falling commodity prices. As the bottom dropped out of the economy in the early 1930s and deflation hit all sectors, many farmers found it impossible to pay their debts and make a living. One by one, smaller, less efficient farms went under. As farm bankruptcies spread, scenes like the one in this photograph became commonplace in rural America. The potential for violence from the resentful neighbors became so strong that armed state troopers and National Guardsmen were needed to keep order as the sales went forward. The sense of imminent anger and protest that pervades this picture was a common thread throughout American life during the hard times of the 1930s.

(© Bettmann/CORBIS)

Farmers' Holiday Association, which urged growers to hold their crops off the market until prices rose. The association put its program into verse:

> Let's call a farmers' holiday
> A holiday let's hold;
> We'll eat our ham and wheat and eggs
> And let them eat their gold.

In the Southwest, the Hoover administration, faced with growing unemployment in that region, endeavored to reduce the number of people looking for jobs with a program to send Hispanic workers and their families back to Mexico and other Latin American countries. Some eighty-two thousand Mexicans were deported, and another half-million immigrants crossed the border out of fear that they would be sent back under duress. For Hispanic Americans who stayed in the United States, relief from the government was often hard to find because of a belief that it should be limited to "Americans."

Hoovervilles.
The shantytowns where the homeless and unemployed lived became known as "Hoovervilles." Their presence on the outskirts of the large cities became a common sight as the Depression deepened.

(© Bettmann/CORBIS)

As the Depression deepened, the homeless and unemployed took to the roads and rails, looking for work or better times. Migratory workers moved through the agricultural sections of California, picking figs and grapes for whatever they could earn. Others went from city to city, finding inadequate meals at relief stations, shuffling through a breadline in some cities, stealing or begging for food in others. The homeless lived in shantytowns outside cities that were dubbed **Hoovervilles**. Soon derogatory references to the president spread throughout the nation. A pocket turned outward as a sign of distress was "a Hoover flag."

By 1931, a sense of despair and hopelessness pervaded many segments of society. People who had been out of work for a year or two had lost the energy and inner resources to rebound even if a job was available. Others began to question the nation's values and beliefs. Bread riots occurred in several cities, the Communist Party forecast that the system was toppling, and the nation's political leaders seemed out of touch with the downward trend of economic events. A popular song caught the nation's angry, restless mood:

> Once I built a railroad, made it run
> Made it race against time.
> Once I built a railroad, now its done
> Brother, can you spare a dime?

The Depression did not touch every American in the same way. Despite the economic disruptions, daily life in much of the nation went on as it always had. Families stayed together with the father holding a job, the mother running the home, and their children growing up and attending school. There might be less money to spend, but in these regions, poverty had not yet become entrenched. Breadlines and people selling apples happened somewhere else. Nevertheless, the economic uncertainty that gripped so many people contributed to a general sense of unease and doubt that permeated the early 1930s.

Mass Culture
During the
Depression

Amid the hardships of the Depression, Americans found diversions and amusements in the mass media and popular entertainment that had emerged during the 1920s. Radio's popularity grew despite the hard times. Sales of radio sets in the United States reached $300 million annually by 1933. Consumers said that their radio would be one of the last things they sold to make ends meet. The habit of listening to a favorite program was an integral part of the daily lives of many families.

Radio was becoming more commercial every year. Programming appealed to popular tastes and sought the largest available audience. Listeners preferred daytime dramas such as *One Man's Family* and *Mary Noble, Backstage Wife*, quickly dubbed "soap operas" after the detergent companies that sponsored them. With the increasing emphasis on profits and ratings, commercials became commonplace. Listeners were told:

> When you're feeling kind blue
> And you wonder what to do
> Che-e-ew Chiclets, and
> Chee-ee-er up!

The most popular radio program of the Depression years was **Amos 'n' Andy**, which portrayed the lives of two African American men in Harlem as interpreted by two white entertainers, Freeman Gosden and Charles Correll. Performed in heavy dialect, the show captured a huge audience at seven o'clock each evening. The tales of black life appealed to white stereotypes about African Americans, but they also gained an audience among blacks because the characters' experiences were comparable to those of minority listeners.

With ticket prices very low and audiences hungry for diversion from the trials of daily life, Hollywood presented a wide choice of films between 1929 and 1932. Sound movies had replaced the silent pictures of the 1920s, and escapist entertainment dominated the movie screens across the country. Audiences laughed at the Marx Brothers in *Cocoanuts* (1929) and *Monkey Business* (1931). Musicals found a ready audience, and there was a vogue for gangster films such as *Little Caesar* (1931) with Edward G. Robinson and *The Public Enemy* (1931) with James Cagney. During the early 1930s, Hollywood pressed the limits of tolerance for sexual innuendoes and bawdy themes with stars such as Mae West.

Despite the economic and social limits of the economic downturn, the cultural flowering that had begun during the preceding decade continued. In Kansas City and other midwestern cities, African American musicians were developing a new jazz style that would become known as "swing" when white musicians smoothed its hard edges to make it appealing to their audiences. The hardships of the era evoked artistic creativity and a vibrant popular culture that would dominate the entertainment scene for half a century.

A DARKENING WORLD

With the economies of the democratic nations weakened and the structure of international relations tottering, authoritarian forces around the world asserted themselves against the existing order. The democracies and the Hoover administration seemed powerless to alter the trend of events.

Herbert Hoover entered the White House with well-formulated ideas about the national role in foreign affairs. Since future wars were unlikely, he believed, it was time to pursue disarmament and let the force of world opinion maintain peace. In Latin America, the president proclaimed the **good neighbor policy**. He promised not to repeat previous U.S. interventions in the region and withdrew marines from Nicaragua and Haiti. In 1930, the State Department renounced the Roosevelt Corollary of 1904 that had asserted an American right to intervene in nations to the south. Despite outbreaks of revolutions in South America during his term, Hoover kept his word and left Latin American nations alone.

Drawing on his Quaker heritage, Hoover thought that wars were senseless and disarmament imperative. A naval conference in 1927 had brought Great Britain, Japan, and the United States to the diplomatic table. Disagreements about the size of vessels to be covered broke up the meeting. Hoover reassembled the major naval powers in London for a conference on disarmament. The London Treaty of 1930 made only a modest contribution to peace. To reduce military spending, the provisions of the Washington Conference pacts were extended for five years. The United States won parity with Britain in all naval vessels, and the Japanese gained the same result for submarines. Japan remained the dominant power in the Pacific, but there was little that the Hoover administration could do to change that reality.

As the U.S. economy deteriorated, the effects spread to Europe and further undermined the power of the democratic nations. With less money to invest, American capitalists could not lend to European governments, especially in Germany. The Smoot-Hawley tariff made it more difficult for Europeans and other importers to sell their products in the United States. International trade stagnated, and production in all industrial companies declined. In 1931, Germany and Austria endeavored to set up a customs union to deal with their common problems, but the French objected to the plan and cut off payments to banks in the two countries. In the resulting turmoil, the Creditanstaldt, Austria's central bank, collapsed. The entire structure of international banking stood on the brink of disaster.

Hoover decided that the only answer was a moratorium on the payment of war debts to give the European countries time to regain their financial stability. He declared on June 21, 1931, that the United States would observe an eighteen-month moratorium on the collection of its foreign debts. The French held back for two weeks, putting further strain on German banks. In the end, all the countries involved agreed to Hoover's initiative.

The moratorium was the only possible answer, but it came too late to stop the erosion of the international financial system. A few months later, Great Britain devalued the pound when it could no longer maintain the gold standard. (That meant that the British would no longer buy gold at a fixed price and would allow the value of the pound to fall relative to other currencies.) This step reduced the price of British products and made them more competitive in world markets. However, as other nations soon followed this course, prices began to fall worldwide as production slowed, people took money out of circulation, and economic activity began to halt.

The weakening of the democracies provided an opening for authoritarian powers eager to challenge the existing order. The first test came in the Far East. In September 1931, Japanese troops detonated a weak explosive charge under a Japanese-owned railroad in Manchuria and blamed the episode on the Manchurians. The Japanese military had fabricated the incident as an excuse for attacking Chinese positions in Manchuria. During the weeks that followed, the Japanese army invaded Manchuria and advanced deep into the countryside. They then bombed Chinese cities to deter any opposition to their effort to occupy all of Manchuria.

Frustrated by the power of the Western countries and desperate for raw materials, Japan and its military wanted to expel the foreign countries that had achieved a political and economic presence in China and the Far East. Anger at the discriminatory racial policies of the United States, Great Britain, and other European powers fed this frustration. Japan was also fearful that a resurgent China might pose a threat to Japanese ambitions and access to crucial materials for Tokyo's economy. Desire for political and economic supremacy in the Pacific completed the Japanese agenda.

A Challenge to the League of Nations   Japan's attack on Manchuria posed a threat to the League of Nations. It also confronted the United States with the problem of what to do about a clear violation of policies and treaties to which Washington was a party, such as the Open Door policy and the Nine-Power Treaty. Yet the American army was no match for Japan's, and the administration had not maintained naval strength at the levels allowed in the various treaties that had been signed during the preceding decade. In addition, Congress would not have been sympathetic to U.S. intervention in a remote foreign quarrel. For the same reason, Washington could not look to European countries. Nor could it endorse an economic boycott against Japan under the sponsorship of the League of Nations. Secretary of State Henry L. Stimson issued statements to China and Japan that proclaimed the unwillingness of the United States to recognize territorial changes in China produced by aggressive actions. This policy of nonrecognition became known as the Stimson Doctrine. The Japanese pressed ahead with their campaign to occupy Manchuria and intimidate China despite the secretary's comments.

The League of Nations criticized the Japanese policy, and Japan responded by withdrawing from the organization early in 1933. The United States and Japan were now embarked on a course that would lead to ever more bitter encounters and ultimately to all-out war.

(The Granger Collection, New York)

Japanese Invasion of Manchuria.   *When Japan invaded Manchuria in 1931, it violated a number of international agreements that it had signed. This cartoon provides an American commentary on these actions. The depiction of Japanese militarism would be a running theme in the United States throughout the 1930s and 1940s.*

Germany Moves Toward the Nazis In Germany, resentment about the Treaty of Versailles had grown during the Depression. Convinced that they had not lost the war on the battlefield (even though the German army was on the brink of collapse at the time of the Armistice in 1918), Germans wanted revenge for the restrictions placed on them in the peace settlement. They listened to the anti-Semitic, nationalistic ravings of the National Socialist Party under Adolf Hitler. Hitler's message of national power and fanatical hatred of the Jews proved intoxicating to the German people, and in 1932, he stood on the brink of obtaining power. Some Americans, insensitive to Hitler's ideology of racial oppression, even admired the policies of Hitler and the Italian dictator Benito Mussolini because they apparently offered decisive action to deal with the economic crisis. The situation of democratic governments, on the other hand, was perilous as the United States entered the third year of the Depression.

A POLITICAL OPPORTUNITY FOR THE DEMOCRATS

At the beginning of 1932, the Hoover presidency was in dire political trouble. Even his advisers were critical. One official remarked that the president "has a childlike faith in statements," and a political commentator concluded that "there seems to be no class or section where Hoover is strong." By 1932, the limits of the president's voluntary approach had become evident even to him. During the winter he supported a congressional initiative to establish the Reconstruction Finance Corporation (RFC). Congress authorized this agency to loan up to $2 billion in tax money to save banks, insurance companies, and railroads from financial collapse. The law that set up the RFC repudiated the principle of voluntary action that Hoover had been following since the Depression began. It put the federal government behind the effort to achieve economic recovery and signaled that Washington could no longer take a passive or hands-off role when the economy turned downward.

> ### DOING HISTORY ONLINE
>
> **Herbert Hoover and the Economy**
>
> Read the documents in this section. Why did the Depression so indelibly tarnish Herbert Hoover's reputation?
>
> www.cengage.com/ history/ayers/ ampassages4e

Republican problems meant opportunity for the Democrats. In their congressional programs, however, the Democrats were not much more creative than their opponents. A deep split persisted within the party over the proper role of government in dealing with the Depression. Many of the conservatives who had supported **Al Smith** would not look kindly on a candidate who wished to expand government's part in dealing with the Depression.

In the 1930 elections, the Democrats picked up eight seats in the Senate. The Republicans retained control of the upper house by only a single vote. In the House, the Democratic gain was forty-nine seats, not enough to give the Democrats a majority, although their total of 216 members put them close. Whether the Democrats could unite behind a coherent program remained an open question in Washington as the presidential election neared.

When Congress reassembled late in 1931, the Democrats had gained several other seats because of the death or retirement of four Republicans. As a result, **John Nance "Cactus Jack" Garner** of Texas became the new Speaker of the House. A crusty conservative with no fresh ideas, Garner's major proposals seemed likely to make the Depression even worse. His answer to the growing budget deficit that the Depression produced was to offer a national sales tax. Such a proposal would have hurt lower-income Americans and, by taking money out of the economy, would also have been deflationary at a time when the economy needed stimulation. Before the bill could pass the House, angry rebels in both parties killed the sales tax idea. The Democrats in Congress seemed as bereft of ideas as the Republicans for fighting the Depression.

The front-runner for the Democratic prize in 1932 was Franklin D. Roosevelt, from a wealthy branch of his family that lived on the Hudson River in Hyde Park, New York. After attending the aristocratic Groton School and Harvard University, he had studied law in New York City. In 1910, he won a seat in the New York state senate and three years later became assistant secretary of the navy in the Wilson administration. Seven years in Washington had given him a thorough introduction to the politics of that city.

Although Franklin D. Roosevelt was only a distant cousin of Theodore, his wife, Eleanor, was the former president's niece. His connection to a famous name helped Roosevelt secure the Democratic vice-presidential nomination in 1920. Although the Democrats lost, the race gave Roosevelt valuable national exposure.

In 1921, Roosevelt was stricken with polio and lost the use of his legs. For the rest of his life, he could not walk without crutches and usually used a wheelchair. The public knew of his disability, but the press did not stress his condition. Counted out of politics because of his illness, Roosevelt worked his way back into Democratic affairs during the mid-1920s and in 1928 was elected governor of New York by a narrow margin despite the Hoover landslide. Two years later, he won reelection by a huge majority.

Roosevelt shared many of the ideas of the mainstream of the Democratic Party. He believed in balanced budgets, the gold standard, and capitalism. Yet he also had an instinctive rapport with people in all segments of society, and he relished the exercise of power. His progressive views on the role of government separated him from conservatives in his party, who longed for a return to the pre-Wilsonian traditions of small government, states' rights, and minimal government involvement with the economy. Roosevelt trusted no one completely and never confided his deepest thoughts about his political destiny. Many observers judged him to be superficial and shallow.

Roosevelt's campaign got off to a strong start. His manager, James A. Farley, who had been wooing potential delegates since 1930, had mapped out a strategy to attract both big-city leaders, whose support for the Democrats had been growing, and the Solid South. As a source of ideas for his campaign, Roosevelt turned to the academic community in the Northeast. He recruited several professors from Columbia University in New York to write speeches and formulate concepts for his programs. These scholars were promptly named the **brain trust**. In his speeches, Roosevelt talked of "the forgotten man at the bottom of the economic pyramid" who was suffering from the effects of the Depression. The answer, Roosevelt said, was "bold, persistent experimentation."

As Roosevelt's campaign gathered strength, it became clear from newspaper surveys, crude polls, and the sense that the administration was faltering, that Hoover was going to lose. Other Democrats challenged the front-runner. Still angry over his 1928 defeat, which he blamed on religious bigotry, and no longer friendly with Roosevelt, Al Smith wanted another chance at the White House. He became a more active candidate as the weeks passed, and his strength in the Northeast made him a serious rival to Roosevelt. Roosevelt was clearly the choice of a majority of the Democrats, but party rules mandated that a nominee receive two-thirds of the votes of the convention delegates. If Garner and Smith teamed up against him and their delegates stood firm, Roosevelt could not win.

The Democratic National Convention opened in Chicago on June 20, 1932. The Roosevelt forces faced many difficulties during the days that followed. But when it came to the actual balloting, his opponents could not rally around anyone else. In the end, Speaker Garner decided to release his delegates to Roosevelt; his reward would be the vice-presidential nomination, which he said was "not worth a pitcher of warm piss." At the same time, the California delegation swung its support to Roosevelt on the fourth ballot.

A New Deal

In a dramatic break with the political tradition that barred candidates from appearing at a convention to accept a nomination, Roosevelt boarded a plane and flew to Chicago through stormy weather. There he delivered his speech in which he used a phrase that would become the trademark of his presidency: "I pledge you, I pledge myself to a new deal for the American people." The candidate seemed poised and self-assured, and he radiated optimism. The convention band played the new Democratic theme: "Happy Days Are Here Again." Meanwhile, the gloomy Republicans nominated Hoover and braced for defeat. As the politicians prepared for battle, the economy remained on a downward path.

The Economy in Distress

To deal with the growing budget deficit, Congress imposed new taxes in the Revenue Act of 1932. The sales tax idea had been dropped, but other levies on corporations, estates, and incomes made this the greatest peacetime increase in taxes in the nation's history. At a time when the economy needed fiscal stimulus, the tax measure drew funds out of the hands of consumers. Raising taxes in an election year added to Hoover's growing unpopularity.

The weakening of the Hoover administration and the increasing power of the Democrats led to an important change in labor policy during 1932. For many years, employers had used friendly federal judges and the power of injunctions to cripple the ability of labor unions to win strikes. The Norris-LaGuardia Act of 1932, by contrast, extended to workers "full freedom of association" in unions and labor representation, restricted the use of injunctions, and barred reliance on "yellow-dog" contracts, which prevented workers from joining unions.

As the Depression worsened during its third year, the plight of unemployed Americans deteriorated well beyond the ability of cities and states to provide aid. Congress became restive as the Reconstruction Finance Corporation extended loans to large corporations and the White House resisted legislation to help the needy and distressed. Bills were introduced to provide direct assistance to the unemployed, but a coalition of Republicans and southern Democrats blocked their passage. As news spread about how much money businesses had received from the RFC, pressure intensified for Congress to do something. The result was the Emergency Relief and Construction Act of 1932, which required states to attest that they could not raise any money themselves before federal funds were allocated to them. The law limited the kinds of construction projects that could be funded, but it represented at least a symbolic step toward a greater federal role in meeting the needs of desperate Americans in the midst of an economic crisis.

The Bonus March   During the summer of 1932, other desperate citizens sought immediate relief from the government in the form of cash. After World War I, Congress had promised war veterans cash bonuses in the form of paid-up life insurance to be disbursed in 1945. During the Hoover presidency, the needs of veterans as a group had been generously funded, and on the whole they had suffered less from the Depression than had some other groups. As the Depression worsened, however, the veterans clamored for early access to their "bonus" money. Hoover vetoed a proposal to allow veterans to borrow against the value of their bonuses in 1931, and during spring 1932, Congress decided not to authorize early payment of the bonuses.

To make their presence felt, thousands of veterans organized the Bonus Expeditionary Force, or the **Bonus Army**, which came to Washington during the summer of 1932 to listen to Congress debate the bonus proposal. They camped out in tarpaper dwellings and tents on the banks of the Anacostia River; some slept in government buildings. The authorities in Washington generally cooperated with the veterans and did what they could to provide them with food and shelter during their stay. Hoover ignored them. When it became clear that Congress was not going to help the Bonus

Bonus March Huts Burning. *Pictures of the burning huts of the Bonus Army contributed to the sense that the Hoover administration was out of touch with the American people and their needs during the election year of 1932.*

Marchers and would adjourn in mid-July 1932, the Hoover administration urged the Bonus Army to leave Washington and even allocated $100,000 to pay for the cost of sending the men home. Some of the marchers took advantage of this offer and left Washington. Others stayed on, hoping for a change in government policy.

Some officials in the Hoover administration wanted a confrontation with the marchers in order to bolster the president's reputation as a champion of law and order. On July 28, the secretary of war ordered the police to remove marchers from government buildings. When the police moved in, the veterans resisted, and fighting broke out. A police pistol went off, other officers began shooting, and soon two Bonus Marchers lay dead. The president ordered the federal troops in Washington, commanded by General Douglas MacArthur, to restore order. The general took his men, armed with tanks and machine guns, across the Anacostia River into the main camp of the Bonus Army. The veterans fled in terror as the soldiers approached. Tear gas canisters were hurled, tents were burned, and the crowd dispersed in a panic. Motion picture cameras caught MacArthur in full military regalia directing the attack, and moviegoers across the nation saw newsreels of American soldiers ousting the Bonus Army from its camp.

The Hoover administration laid the blame for the incident on the influence of communists inside the veterans' camp. There were a few communists among the veterans, but they had little influence on the protest. Law enforcement agencies found no evidence of an organized conspiracy among the marchers, and public opinion favored the veterans. "If the Army must be called out to make war on unarmed citizens," said a newspaper editor, "this is no longer America."

The 1932 Election   The economic devastation produced by the Great Depression offered groups outside the two-party system a promising chance to win votes for more radical solutions to the nation's problems. The Communists, for example, organized Unemployed Councils to stage protests against high rents and evictions of tenants. Socialists and other left-wing groups cooperated with the Communists in protest marches and petitions for relief. Efforts to organize sharecroppers and tenant farmers in the South also went forward under the sponsorship of the Communists during these years. The Communists wooed African American support when they defended the **Scottsboro boys**, a group of young black men who had been unjustly accused of raping two white women in Alabama in 1931. In 1932, some prominent intellectuals endorsed the Communist presidential campaign or supported the Socialist candidate, Norman Thomas.

For the majority of Americans who were still aligned with the two-party system, however, the only real choice lay between Roosevelt and Hoover. Many of Roosevelt's advisers told him that he did not have to campaign to win the race. Roosevelt saw the matter differently. If he ran a passive, traditional campaign, he would not persuade the voters who were looking for a change. A front-porch campaign would also have fed rumors that he could not withstand the physical rigors of the presidency. So Roosevelt crisscrossed the country, making speeches that assailed the Republican leadership and attacked Hoover's record.

Roosevelt's Campaign   Roosevelt wanted to occupy the political middle ground, and as a result his campaign speeches took a variety of contradictory positions. At times he seemed to be calling for a more activist federal government that would adapt "existing economic organizations to the service of the people." On other occasions he attacked Hoover's budget deficits and wasteful government spending. Most of Roosevelt's appeal came down to hope, confidence, and the promise of political change.

The incumbent president knew he was going to lose, but he campaigned doggedly. Hoover told the voters that the nation faced a choice between "two philosophies of government," with freedom and individual initiative the philosophy of the Republicans and socialism and regimentation the aim of the Democrats. Roosevelt countered that the country needed new ideas to get out of the Depression, although he left it unclear just what those new ideas would be. Abandoned by many of his fellow Republicans and unpopular with the voters, Hoover staggered through his lifeless campaign.

Hoover Defeated On election day, the Democratic candidate won overwhelmingly in the popular vote and scored a 472-to-59 triumph in the electoral college. His party secured almost 57 percent of the popular vote and made significant gains in Congress: ninety seats in the House and thirteen in the Senate. The election proved a major disappointment to both the Socialists and the Communists. Norman Thomas, running on the Socialist ticket, received fewer than 1 million votes. William Z. Foster, the Communist candidate, gained just over 100,000 ballots.

By 1932, politicians realized that the four-month period between the time that a president was elected and the inauguration was too long for a modern industrialized nation. A quicker transition to the incoming administration was imperative. A constitutional amendment moving the date of the inauguration to January 20 was under consideration, but the **Twentieth Amendment** would not go into effect until 1937. Meanwhile, the country faced a worsening economic crisis.

During these four months, the Depression reached its lowest point. One-quarter of the work force could not find jobs, and the relief system had failed. The gross national product, which had stood at more than $103 billion in 1929, slid to $58 billion by 1932. Wheat sold for 30 cents a bushel compared with the $3 a bushel it had brought in 1920. Farmers threatened more action to stop foreclosures of delinquent mortgages in their states. In December, hunger marchers came to Washington to ask for government aid. The growing numbers of failing banks presented a dire threat: 1,453 banks shut their doors in 1932, and political leaders feared that the nation's entire financial structure could be threatened.

Neither Hoover nor Roosevelt was able to deal with these growing problems. The defeated president believed that the cause of the Depression lay beyond the nation's borders. Wary of making commitments before taking office, Roosevelt dodged Hoover's efforts to obtain his backing. Hoover became convinced that Roosevelt cared little for the welfare of the country, whereas Roosevelt saw his defeated rival as a sore loser who was trying to win through subterfuge what he had lost at the polls.

Meanwhile, a crisis of confidence in banks gripped the country. Alarm about the banking system had been spreading since October 1932. During that month, the governor of Nevada proclaimed a twelve-day bank "holiday" to end depositor runs on banks. The news spurred depositors in other states to remove funds from their local banks. In Michigan, two banks in Detroit seemed about to fail by mid-February. Hoover tried to persuade business leaders, including Henry Ford, to place deposits in

A Bank Fails

One of the most unsettling aspects of the Great Depression was the increasing numbers of bank failures. Since there was no national system to insure bank deposits, those who had money in a financial institution were vulnerable when a bank failed or a "run" occurred as depositors sought to get out whatever money they could. With no federal authority to help banks in trouble, the collapse of one major bank could trigger a ripple effect of failures that could paralyze commerce in an entire region or state. This picture shows an anxious crowd milling about outside a bank in New York City that until this crisis had paid 4 percent interest on "thrift accounts." The sense of fear that is evident in the body language of passersby peering into the bank conveys the worry that more and more Americans felt about their financial security as the Depression continued its downward course in the early 1930s.

(© Bettmann/CORBIS)

the troubled banks. Ford was willing, but others were not. The governor of Michigan intervened and declared a bank holiday on February 14. Depositors in other states, fearing that their deposits would be frozen, tried to withdraw their money from local banks. Governors in nine other states were forced to announce bank holidays.

Hoover pressed the incoming president for immediate joint action. Roosevelt was still reluctant to tie his own hands before he took office. The days passed as February ended with no agreement on either side to do anything about the banking crisis. The two men held one last awkward business meeting on March 3 but came to no positive decisions.

As the transition of power neared, general apprehension increased. By the morning of March 4, banks in New York City, the nation's financial capital, were shutting their doors. A weary Hoover concluded in a moment of personal despair: "We are at the end of our string." Shortly before eleven o'clock, the outgoing president joined Franklin Roosevelt in a waiting limousine, and the two men drove off toward the Capitol. Roosevelt waved to well-wishers in the crowd as Hoover sat in silence. A nation mired in the worst depression in its history waited to hear what the new president would say.

CONCLUSION

The economic slump of the early 1930s was one of the most significant events in American history. It called into question faith in the brighter future that the nation promised to all. The Depression also changed the way Americans viewed the federal government. Although they retained their suspicion of intrusive national power, they expected that Washington would prevent future depressions and relieve the effects of the one that was occurring. Radical solutions that involved dismantling capitalism or redistributing income on a large scale gained relatively few adherents.

The Depression discredited the Republican Party for two decades in presidential elections. The memory of President Hoover and his failed policies was so strong that Democratic candidates ran against him for a generation. Although Hoover lived thirty years after he left the White House, his reputation never recovered.

The popular esteem for large corporations also fell dramatically during the 1930s when the public learned how their executives had profited from inside information and tax advantages. A congressional probe in early 1933 disclosed that Wall Street executives had benefited from inside information about stock market transactions. Other similar revelations followed once Roosevelt took office.

The major political and economic institutions that had governed the nation for half a century—the Republican Party and corporate power—were challenged by the force and size of the Great Depression. Industrialism had become embedded in American life, but there remained serious questions about how society ought to respond to the inequities and injustices that often accompanied industrial growth. Would the United States turn to radical solutions as European countries had done? Could democratic institutions respond to the demands of economic hardship? Franklin D. Roosevelt had now promised a "new deal" for the American people. Noon approached in Washington, and Roosevelt walked on crutches the thirty-seven painful and difficult steps from his seat to the place in front of the Capitol where he would take the oath of office.

CHAPTER REVIEW, 1927–1933

- The stock market collapsed in October 1929.
- Confidence in the economy eroded quickly.
- President Hoover's efforts to restore public confidence did not succeed.
- Existing programs to provide relief to the unemployed proved inadequate.
- Economic decline helped fuel the rise of authoritarian governments in Europe and Asia.
- By 1932 President Hoover's administration had lost political credibility.
- The election of 1932 brought the election of Franklin D. Roosevelt and the arrival of the New Deal.
- The economy stood at a low point when Roosevelt took office in March 1933.

◀|||*Looking Back*

Chapter 24 discusses the causes of the Great Depression, which were rooted in the period of World War I and projected forward into the developing economy of the 1920s. When reviewing the causes of the economic collapse, look for signs of problems that were discussed in the preceding chapter:

1. Why was the stock market crash of 1929 an important element in the nation's economic problems and yet not a decisive cause of the Depression?
2. Why was more not done to prevent the weaknesses in the economy that became apparent after 1929?
3. Why was Herbert Hoover elected in 1928? What political assets did he have that became liabilities once the Depression began?

Looking Ahead |||▶

Nothing had prepared Americans for the Great Depression, and the effects proved to be long-lasting in all aspects of life. Debate still continues over what caused the downturn and why it lasted so long. Chapter 25 focuses on what made this period so traumatic for so many citizens.

1. Why would the Depression prove to be so hard to end?
2. What structural weaknesses in the American economy did the Depression reveal?
3. Herbert Hoover said that the 1932 election presented the United States with a fundamental choice between liberty and regimentation. What did he mean by that statement?
4. Why was Hoover, who was so successful in bringing relief to millions in Belgium and the Soviet Union, unable to do the same in the United States?
5. Which deeply held beliefs of Hoover did the Depression challenge?

 Go to the *American Passages* website at www.cengage.com/history/ayers/ampassages4e for additional review materials.

25

The New Deal, 1933–1939

O n March 4, 1933, Franklin Roosevelt took the presidential oath of office in a steady, chilling rain. "Only a foolish optimist can deny the dark realities of the moment," he told the huge crowd and the millions who listened on radio. Roosevelt's voice radiated confidence and concern. "This nation asks for action, and action now," he declared. Comparing the Depression to an all-out war of survival, he vowed to ask Congress for the "broad executive power . . . that would be given to me if we were in fact invaded by a foreign foe."

Roosevelt offered few specifics. His objective was to convince a dispirited people to have faith in him and in themselves. Standing erect in his cumbersome leg braces, Roosevelt stressed four major themes: sacrifice, discipline, compassion, and hope. "The only thing we have to fear," he assured the nation, "is fear itself."

ROCK BOTTOM, WINTER 1932–1933

This fear was understandable. The winter of 1932–1933 was a time of intense suffering and despair. Unemployment reached a staggering 25 percent. Banks were failing everywhere. Food prices had collapsed, forcing farmers from their land. Roosevelt understood how deeply the Depression had shaken the country and sapped its confidence. "I have [seen] the faces of thousands of Americans," he confided to a friend. "They have the frightened look of children. . . . They are saying, 'We are caught in some thing we don't understand; perhaps this fellow can help us out.'"

Taking Charge   No peacetime president ever faced a tougher challenge, or a greater opportunity. Respected commentators were predicting the end of capitalism if the Depression hung on much longer. At the very least, Americans were desperate for change, and that meant supporting almost any initiative designed to revive the economy, feed the hungry, and put people back to work.

Roosevelt possessed neither a comprehensive plan to end the Depression nor a rigid set of economic beliefs. What he did have was the willingness to experiment, act decisively, and use the government as a powerful weapon in the struggle for economic recovery. "Take a method and try it," he liked to say. "If it fails admit it frankly and try another."

Roosevelt surrounded himself with men and women of talent, accomplishment, and wide-ranging views. His closest advisers included Republicans and Democrats, agricultural theorists and urban planners, college professors and political pros. In addition, the **New Deal** attracted thousands of young people to Washington, drawn by the opportunity to do something meaningful—and perhaps historic—with their lives.

The Bank Crisis

More than five thousand banks had failed in the United States between 1930 and 1932, wiping out countless savings accounts

Mar. 4, 1933 THE NEW YORKER Price 15 cents

(The Granger Collection, New York)

Hoover and Roosevelt. *This* New Yorker *cartoon, sketched well before the inauguration, accurately predicted feelings of both men—the glum Hoover and the exuberant Roosevelt—as they rode down Pennsylvania Avenue together on March 4, 1933.*

and stalling the nation's credit. Panicked depositors, unable to tell a good bank from a bad one, lost faith in them all, and an avalanche of withdrawals resulted. By the time Roosevelt took office, nineteen states had declared "bank holidays" (or closings) to head off a full-scale collapse.

On March 6, 1933, the president called Congress back into special session and proclaimed a national "bank holiday." Three days later, his emergency banking proposal was enacted in a matter of hours. The new law provided the federal inspection of all banks. Those with liquid assets would be allowed to reopen with a license from the Treasury Department; the others would be reorganized, if possible, or closed for good.

On March 12, Roosevelt addressed the nation in the first of his "fireside chats." About half of America's homes had radios in 1933, and the president's audience that Sunday evening was estimated at 60 million people. "I want to talk for a few minutes

This icon will direct you to interactive activities and study materials on the American Passages website: www.cengage.com/history/ayers/ampassages4e

CHAPTER TIMELINE

1933	Franklin D. Roosevelt inaugurated as president • Eighteenth Amendment is repealed, ending Prohibition • "First hundred days" of New Deal includes passage of Agricultural Adjustment Act and National Industrial Recovery Act • Adolf Hitler becomes chancellor of Germany • United States extends diplomatic recognition to the Soviet Union
1934	Senator Huey Long establishes "Share Our Wealth Society" • Labor violence erupts in major American cities • Democrats add to huge congressional majorities in midterm elections
1935	Huey Long assassinated • "Second New Deal" emerges with passage of Wagner Act and Social Security Act • Congress passes first Neutrality Act, reflecting the nation's isolationist mood
1936	FDR reelected to second term • John L. Lewis and other labor leaders break with AFL to form the CIO • Civil war erupts in Spain
1937	Roosevelt unveils "Court-packing plan" • Autoworkers stage "sit-down strike" at GM plant in Flint, Michigan • Severe economic recession begins
1938	Passage of Fair Labor Standards Act • Anti–New Deal forces make gains in midterm elections • Hitler wins major concessions from French and British leaders at Munich Conference
1939	Marian Anderson gives concert at Lincoln Memorial • German forces attack Poland after Hitler and Stalin sign a "non-aggression" pact

about banking," he began, assuring everyone that the system was now safe. The listeners believed him. In the following days, as the stronger banks reopened, deposits greatly exceeded withdrawals. By the end of March, almost $1 billion had been returned from mattresses to bank vaults. The crisis was over.

Roosevelt's handling of the bank emergency revealed his essential pragmatism. In the midst of such turmoil, he could easily have taken a more radical approach—by nationalizing the banks, for example, or instituting much tighter controls. Instead, he demonstrated that his primary mission would be to preserve capitalism, not to replace it. And that meant reforming its institutions with substantial federal aid.

The president also showed himself to be a master of communication. His ability to reach people in the radio age, to win their confidence, was perhaps his greatest gift. He would use it often in the coming years as the nation faced the twin crises of economic hardship and global war.

Extending Relief The special session of Congress lasted from March 9 to June 16, 1933, a period known as "the first hundred days." In that time, more than a dozen major bills proposed by the White House were enacted. With both the House and the Senate now under firm Democratic control, Roosevelt had little trouble getting his legislation passed. As the banking crisis ended, he moved quickly to help those too desperate to help themselves. The problem was daunting. By conservative estimates, more than 30 million Americans were now living in family units with no income at all.

FDR and Polio

Franklin Roosevelt contracted infantile paralysis, later known as polio, in 1921, at the age of thirty-nine. The disease permanently paralyzed him from the waist down. Though Americans, of course, were aware of his disability, it did not seem a part of the Roosevelt they knew. As president, FDR had an unspoken agreement with the press not to be photographed in a wheelchair or in a helpless position. The Secret Service prepared for his appearances by constructing wooden ramps and putting handgrips on the podium. When Roosevelt fell—as he did at the 1936 Democratic National Convention—the press did not report it.

(© Bettmann/ CORBIS)

The photograph here typifies what Americans saw: FDR on his feet, leaning on a cane while grasping the arm of an aide. As biographer Hugh Gallagher, himself a polio victim, has written: "Among the thousands of political cartoons and caricatures of FDR, not one shows the man physically impaired. In fact, many of them have him as a man of action—running, jumping, doing things." Some have criticized Roosevelt for hiding his disability and not doing enough to alter the popular image of the disabled. But the president believed that concerns about his health and stamina would detract from his ability to lead the nation in perilous times.

The Hoover administration had refused to consider federal payments to the jobless. As a result, state and local governments had been forced to ration what little relief they could muster. In 1932, the average weekly payment to an "out-of-work" family in New York City was $2.39. In Detroit, the figure dropped to 15 cents a day before the money ran out. Some cities were forced to limit relief to families with three or more children; others offered free food and fuel.

Roosevelt believed that relief efforts should be a local responsibility. He too worried about the cost of funding such efforts and about the consequences of giving people money that they hadn't actually earned. Yet there seemed to be no alternative. It was essential, said one of Roosevelt's advisers, to pursue "long-run" economic growth. The problem, he added, is that "people don't eat in the long run—they eat every day."

On March 21, the White House sent two major relief proposals to Capitol Hill. The first one created the **Civilian Conservation Corps (CCC)**. Based on a program that Roosevelt had implemented as governor of New York, the CCC combined the president's enthusiasm for nature with his belief in national service for the young. It provided government conservation jobs to "city boys," ages seventeen to twenty-four, in isolated camps run by the U.S. Army. The pay was thirty dollars a month, with twenty-two dollars going directly to the worker's family.

The CCC was both popular and successful. It eased unemployment a bit, lowered crime rates in the cities, and kept countless families off relief. It also helped to protect and restore the nation's environment, while teaching young men the discipline of hard work. More than half a million recruits cleaned beaches, built wildlife shelters, fought forest fires, and stocked rivers and streams.

Roosevelt's second relief measure was the Federal Emergency Relief Administration (FERA), which had a budget of $500 million to assist individual states in their efforts to help the unemployed. Hoping to spend the money as quickly and humanely as possible, Roosevelt chose **Harry Hopkins**, a former social worker who had directed New York's relief effort, to run the FERA. With boundless energy and an ego to match, Hopkins personified the New Deal's activist, freewheeling style. He became Roosevelt's closest adviser.

Most of the funding went to the jobless in the form of free food or a simple "dole." This troubled Hopkins, who understood both the need for such relief and the damage it could do. Real work "preserves a man's morale," he insisted. Knowing that Roosevelt felt the same way, he convinced the president to approve a federal work relief program for the unemployed.

With Hopkins in charge, the **Civil Works Administration (CWA)** hired more than 4 million people in a matter of months. Its aim was to create jobs and restore self-respect by handing out pay envelopes instead of relief checks. In reality, CWA workers sometimes performed worthless tasks, known as "boondoggles," such as raking leaves in huge circles or lugging shovelsful of dirt to faraway piles.

But this was only part of the story. The CWA spent much of its $1 billion budget on projects of lasting value. Its workers built airports and paved roads. They ran nursery schools and taught more than a million adults to read and write. They immunized children, served hot school lunches, and took garbage off the streets. Yet Roosevelt ended the CWA experiment after only four months, citing its spiraling costs. He expected federal job programs to be short-term experiments, nothing more. Otherwise, he warned, they will "become a habit with the country."

Conservation, Regional Planning, and Public Power   In the spring of 1933, FDR appeared to be governing the nation by himself. His proposals were so sweeping, and so easily enacted, that Congress seemed to have no independent function of its own. Never before had the White House taken such initiative on domestic legislation; never before had it been so successful.

At Roosevelt's behest, Congress created the Securities and Exchange Commission (SEC) to oversee the stock and bond markets. It established the Federal Deposit Insurance Corporation (FDIC) to insure bank deposits up to five thousand dollars. It provided funds to refinance one-fifth of the nation's home and farm mortgages. And it effectively ended Prohibition by permitting the sale of beer and wine with an alcoholic content of 3.2 percent. (The Eighteenth Amendment would be repealed on December 5, 1933.)

Some of Roosevelt's early proposals had personal roots. The Civilian Conservation Corps was one example; the **Tennessee Valley Authority (TVA)**, created in May 1933, was another. Like many other progressives, Roosevelt had a deep interest in the related issues of conservation, regional planning, and public power. Believing that poverty could be eradicated through the careful development of natural resources, he turned the Tennessee Valley into a laboratory for his most cherished ideas.

Covering seven states and forty thousand square miles, the Tennessee Valley was America's poorest region. Most of its 1 million people—mainly small farmers and sharecroppers—lived in isolated communities, without electricity, medical care, proper schooling, or paved roads. The TVA transformed this region in fundamental ways. Within a decade, sixteen huge dams and hydroelectric plants were in operation along the Tennessee River, providing flood control; cheap, abundant power; and thousands of jobs. Per capita income rose dramatically. Electric power gave local residents what millions of other Americans already took for granted: radios and refrigerators, plumbing, lights in houses and barns.

TVA was widely viewed as one of the New Deal's greatest achievements. Yet its critics included many residents of the Tennessee Valley, whose complaints reflected the changing face of reform. To their thinking, TVA displaced thousands of people, attracted low-wage factory jobs, and caused serious environmental damage. At best, they argued, it brought a measure of comfort and prosperity to a badly depressed region. At worst, it allowed distant bureaucrats to decide how local people should live.

ECONOMIC RECOVERY, SPRING 1933

With the bank crisis over and federal relief flowing to those most desperately in need, the Roosevelt administration turned to the long-term issue of providing a structure for the nation's economic recovery. In agriculture, which accounted for one-quarter of all American jobs, the problems were severe. Most farmers had been slumping badly since the 1920s. The introduction of tractors and high-grade fertilizer had made them more productive than ever before. Yet their share of the world market had declined because of high tariff walls and tough foreign competition.

If overproduction plagued American agriculture in this era, the problem facing American industry was quite the reverse. So many factories had closed their doors during the Depression that too little was being produced. The resulting unemployment caused a drop in purchasing power, which forced even more factories to shut down. Something had to be done to break this vicious cycle.

Trouble on the Land The Roosevelt administration turned first to the agricultural problems. Farmers in 1932 were earning less than one-third of their meager 1929 incomes. As food prices collapsed, there was talk of open rebellion in the heartland. Farmers blocked roads, clashed with police, and threatened to lynch any official who foreclosed a family farm. Roosevelt was sympathetic. He believed that low farm income was a leading cause of the Depression, and he needed the support of rural legislators to get his New Deal programs adopted. The proposal he sent Congress therefore incorporated the ideas of the nation's major farm interest groups. Passed in May 1933, the **Agricultural Adjustment Act** confronted the problems of overproduction and mounting surpluses that had conspired to erode farm income over the years. The act also created the Agricultural Adjustment Administration (AAA) to oversee this process.

The AAA had one clear goal in mind: to raise farm prices by encouraging farmers to produce less. The idea was no longer to win back world markets, but rather to limit domestic output in order to achieve "parity," or fair price levels, within the

United States. The act compensated farmers who voluntarily removed acreage from production. And it funded these payments through a tax on farm processors—such as flour millers, meatpackers, and cotton gin operators.

Problems quickly arose. Because spring planting was already underway, the AAA encouraged farmers to plow under a large portion of their crops. Producing less food while millions were going hungry was difficult for people to understand, but destroying food seemed particularly senseless and cruel. Secretary of Agriculture Henry A. Wallace described the process as "a shocking commentary on our civilization." Yet there seemed to be no faster way to aid the farmer's plight.

Within a year, more than 3 million farmers had signed individual contracts with the AAA. The early results were encouraging. Cotton, wheat, and corn production fell significantly as farmers cultivated fewer acres and cashed their government checks. Farm income shot up almost 60 percent between 1932 and 1935—the result of rising food prices and generous loans to those who stored their surpluses in government warehouses.

Nature played a role as well. During the 1930s, the American farm belt experienced record highs in temperature and record lows in rainfall. The Great Plains were hardest hit. Terrifying dust storms swept through Kansas, Nebraska, Colorado, Oklahoma, Texas, and the Dakotas like a black blizzard, packing gale-force winds and stripping nutrients from the soil. Cornfields were turned into sand dunes and cattle were buried alive. "This is the ultimate darkness," a Kansas woman wrote in her diary. "So must come the end of the world."

The **Dust Bowl** disaster triggered one of the largest internal migrations in the nation's history. More than 3 million people abandoned their Dust Bowl farms in the 1930s, with Oklahoma, Kansas, and South Dakota losing huge chunks of population. By one account, "The people did not stop to shut the door—they just walked out, leaving behind them the wreckage of their labors: an ugly little shack with broken windows covered by cardboard, a sagging ridgepole, a barren, dusty yard, the windmill creaking in the wind." Many set out for California, where the "fortunate" among them found work picking fruit, boxing vegetables, and baling hay. Living in hellish squatter camps, enduring disease and discrimination ("Negroes and Okies Upstairs," read a local theater sign), they moved from field to orchard in the San Joaquin and Imperial Valleys, earning pitiful wages and "going on relief."

Tenants and Landowners   The AAA helped countless farm families and ignored countless others. The large farmers got the biggest subsidies. Yet the system barely touched those at the bottom of the pile: the tenants and sharecroppers, almost one-half of the nation's white farm families and three-quarters of the black farm families. Most of them lived in desperate poverty, working the cotton fields of the rural South. Under AAA regulations, these tenants were supposed to get a fair share of the acreage reduction payments, but this rarely occurred. Few landlords obeyed the rules, and some evicted their tenants in order to take even more land out of production.

In response, tenants and sharecroppers formed their own organization, the Southern Tenant Farmers' Union (STFU), to fight for their rights. "The landlord is always betwixt us, beatin' us and starvin' us," complained a black sharecropper from Arkansas.

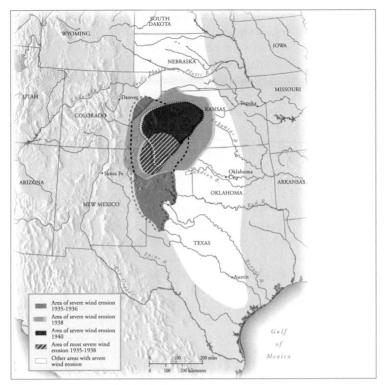

MAP 25.1 The Dust Bowl, 1936–1940.

The immense dust storms that blew through the high plains in the 1930s covered nearly 100 million acres in the hardest-hit states of Texas, Oklahoma, Kansas, Colorado, and New Mexico. The great Dust Bowl tragedy caused terrible economic hardship and a mass migration from the High Plains, with tens of thousands of displaced farmers heading west to California.

"There ain't but one way for us to get him where he can't help himself and that's for us to get together and stay together."

But this would not be easy. Tenants who joined the union were evicted from their shacks, blacklisted by employers, and denied credit at banks and stores. Union organizers were beaten and jailed, and the SFTU soon collapsed.

Conditions were no better in the Southwest and Far West, where destitute Mexican farm workers struggled to survive. Many had been brought north by American ranchers and growers seeking cheap labor in better times. Now, as the demand for workers decreased, and job competition with poor whites (including the Dust Bowl refugees) intensified, their desperation grew. Since most of these farm workers were not U.S. citizens, local governments often denied them relief. Between 1930 and 1935, moreover, the federal government deported at least 200,000 Mexicans, some of whom were longtime residents of Texas, Arizona, and California; a larger number returned to Mexico on their own. Those who stayed behind toiled for starvation wages in the fields. Like the Tenant Farmer's Union in Arkansas, their attempts to unionize were crushed by local vigilantes and police. In 1936, author John Steinbeck reported on a strike of Mexican lettuce workers near his home in Salinas, California. "The attitude of the employer," he wrote, "is one of hatred and suspicion, his method is the threat of the deputies' guns. The workers are herded about like animals. Every possible method is used to make them feel inferior and insecure."

The AAA revolutionized American agriculture. Never before had the federal government been as deeply involved in the affairs of American farmers; never before had it encouraged its citizens to produce fewer goods, not more. Although key elements of the AAA would be struck down by the Supreme Court in *United States v. Butler* (1936), the concept of federal farm subsidies continues to dominate America's agricultural policy to the present day.

Centralized Economic Planning The Roosevelt administration had an equally ambitious plan to revive the economy, reopen idle factories, and put people back to work. On June 13, 1933, Congress passed the **National Industrial Recovery Act (NIRA)** amid a flood of optimistic projections. Modeled on the industrial mobilization during World War I, the NIRA was designed as a vehicle for centralized economic planning. Roosevelt himself viewed it as the primary weapon in his crusade against the Depression. The act, he boasted, "is the most important and far reaching legislation ever enacted by the American Congress."

The NIRA created two more federal agencies: the Public Works Administration (PWA) and the National Recovery Administration (NRA). The former, with a budget of $3.3 billion, was supposed to "prime the economic pump" by providing jobs for the unemployed and new orders for the factories that produced steel, glass, rubber, cement, and heavy equipment. What made the PWA so appealing was its emphasis on private employment: workers were to be hired and paid by individual contractors, not by the federal government.

Roosevelt selected Secretary of the Interior Harold Ickes, a veteran progressive, to run the PWA. It proved to be an excellent choice. Under Ickes's leadership, the PWA constructed schools, hospitals, post offices, and sewage systems. It built the Golden Gate Bridge in San Francisco and the Triborough Bridge in New York City, the Grand Coulee Dam in Washington State, and the Boulder Dam in Colorado. No one brought more honest efficiency to government than Harold Ickes, and no one got more value for the dollar.

The key to Roosevelt's recovery program, however, was the NRA. Under the flamboyant leadership of General Hugh S. Johnson, the NRA encouraged representatives of business and labor to create codes of "fair practice" designed to stabilize the economy through planning and cooperation. Johnson's agency promised something to everyone, though not in equal amounts. Business leaders, who dominated the code-writing process, got the biggest gift of all: the suspension of antitrust laws that had dogged them for years.

In return for such generosity, these leaders agreed to significant labor reforms. Each NRA code featured a maximum hour and minimum wage provision (usually forty hours and dollars per week). Child labor was forbidden, and Section 7A of the NIRA guaranteed labor unions the right to organize and bargain collectively.

General Johnson barnstormed the country by airplane, giving speeches and lining up support. With a patriotic symbol (the blue eagle) and a catchy slogan ("We Do Our Part"), Johnson organized the biggest public spectacles of the

Child Labor in the 1930s

Few other employment issues have proved as contentious and enduring as child labor. From colonial times forward, children worked on farms and in family businesses, often alongside parents and siblings. With the coming of Industrialization, children labored in coal mines, canneries, sweatshops, and factories (like the spindle boys pictured here in a Georgia cotton mill), working long hours for pitifully low wages.

By 1900, the abolition of child labor became a powerful force in American politics, supported by progressive reformers, but opposed by many business groups. In 1918, the U.S. Supreme Court, in *Hammer v. Daggenhart*, struck down the first national child labor law. In the 1920s, a proposed constitutional amendment to end this shameful practice also fell short. But the movement gained fresh support during the Great Depression as adult unemployment rose dramatically and new technologies decreased the need for unskilled factory labor. In 1938, with FDR's blessing, Congress passed the Fair Labor Standards Act, which largely ended child labor in the United States. Three years later, a more liberal Supreme Court unanimously upheld this law. Today, child labor is again on the rise, especially among illegal aliens and school dropouts. The issue is far from resolved.

(© Horace Bristol/ CORBIS)

Depression era. In the summer of 1933, more than 250,000 New Yorkers paraded down Fifth Avenue singing:

> Join the good old N.R.A., Boys, and
>   we will end this awful strife.
> Join it with the spirit that will give
>   the Eagle life.
> Join in folks, then push and pull, many
>   millions strong.
> While we go marching to Prosperity.

Johnson signed up the big industries—coal, steel, oil, autos, shipbuilding, chemicals, and clothing—before going after the others. By the end of 1933, the NRA had 746 different agreements in place. There was a code for the mop handle makers, another for the dog food industry, and even one for the burlesque houses that determined the number of strippers in each show.

DOING HISTORY ONLINE

John L. Lewis on the NRA, 1934

Based on your reading of the document online and the "Economic Recovery" section of this chapter, what were the benefits and disadvantages of the NRA for organized labor?

 www.cengage. com/history/ayers/ ampassages4e

Before long, however, the NRA was in trouble. Small businessmen complained that the codes encouraged monopolies and drowned them in paperwork. Labor leaders charged that employers ignored the wage and hour provisions, while cracking down on union activity. And consumers blamed the NRA for raising prices at a time when their purchasing power was extremely low.

All of this was true. Because the codes were voluntary, they carried no legal weight. (Johnson naively assumed that the power of public opinion would keep potential violators in line.) The large companies obeyed them when it was in their interest to do so and ignored them when it wasn't. As a result, the codes became a device for fixing prices, stifling competition, and limiting production. This may have guaranteed a profit for some companies, but it was the wrong remedy for solving an economic crisis in which the revival of consumer spending was a key to recovery.

In 1934, General Johnson suffered a nervous breakdown, leading Roosevelt to replace him with a five-member executive board. The president seemed relieved when the Supreme Court, in *Schechter Poultry Company v. United States* (1935), struck down the NRA on the grounds that Congress had delegated too much legislative authority to the executive branch. "It has been an awful headache," Roosevelt confided to an aide. "I think perhaps NRA has done all it can do."

NEW DEAL DIPLOMACY, 1933–1934

Foreign affairs were not high on President Roosevelt's agenda. His riveting inaugural address had devoted one sentence to the entire subject. "In the field of world policy," he declared, "I would dedicate this nation to the policy of the good neighbor"—a theme already sounded by outgoing president Herbert Hoover. The United States was in turmoil, struggling through the worst economic crisis in its history. "I favored as a practical policy," said Roosevelt, "the putting of first things first."

The Soviet
Question

FDR was no isolationist. He believed deeply in the concepts of international cooperation and global security, as Americans would shortly discover. One of his first diplomatic initiatives, in November 1933, was to extend formal recognition to the Soviet Union. The move was opposed by many Americans who viewed the Soviet Union as a godless, totalitarian society bent on exporting the "communist revolution" throughout the world. But Roosevelt believed that the United States could no longer afford to ignore the world's largest nation.

The move did not pay quick dividends to either side. Trade with the Soviet Union remained low, partly because Soviet dictator Joseph Stalin was determined to make his nation self-sufficient. The Russians also ignored their promise not to spread "communist propaganda" in the United States and then refused to pay their $150 million war debt to Washington. Yet for all of these problems, relations between the United States and the Soviet Union would slowly improve in the 1930s and early 1940s as ominous world events drew them closer together. For FDR, recognition of Stalin's regime seemed less a threat than an opportunity.

The Good
Neighbor

The Roosevelt administration showed a growing interest in Latin America, where U.S. companies had billions of dollars invested in the production of foodstuffs like coffee and sugar and in raw materials such as copper and oil. Along with efforts to increase trade in this region, the United States extended the Good Neighbor Policy by affirming at the 1933 Pan-American Conference in Uruguay that no nation "has the right to intervene in the internal or external affairs of another." Shortly after, the Roosevelt administration recalled several hundred U.S. Marines stationed in Haiti and signed a treaty with Panama recognizing the responsibility of both nations to operate and defend the Panama Canal.

There were exceptions, however. In Cuba, a nation of vital economic and strategic importance to the United States, intervention was a way of life. In 1934, the State Department used its considerable leverage to help bring an "acceptable" government to power in Havana, more sympathetic to North American business interests. With a friendly new regime in place, led by Sergeant Fulgencio Batista, the United States agreed to renounce direct intervention under the Platt Amendment in return for permission to keep its huge naval base at Guantánamo Bay.

The Good Neighbor Policy faced its sternest test even closer to home. In 1934, President Lázaro Cárdenas of Mexico began a national recovery program much like FDR's New Deal. Pledging "Mexico for the Mexicans," Cárdenas attempted to nationalize the agricultural and mining properties of all foreign corporations, as required by the Mexican Constitution of 1917. Though Cárdenas promised "fair compensation" for these holdings, American and British companies demanded more than the Mexicans were willing to pay. (American oil interests wanted $262 million; the Cárdenas government offered $10 million.) Over the objections of many businessmen, the Roosevelt administration convinced Mexico to pay $40 million in compensation for foreign-owned lands it had seized and another $29 million for the oil fields.

Roosevelt's caution was understandable. The president realized that better relations with Latin America required a new approach. Moreover, with fascism rising in Europe and in Asia, the need for inter-American cooperation was essential.

CRITICS: RIGHT AND LEFT, 1934–1935

By 1934, the Depression seemed to be easing. Allthough enormous problems remained, there was less talk about the dangers of starvation, violent upheaval, or complete economic collapse. The New Deal had injected a dose of hope and confidence into the body politic. Yet as things got better, people inevitably wanted more. The spirit of unity, the shared sense of hardship and struggle, began to dissolve.

The American Liberty League and the 1934 Election   The first rumblings came from the political right. In the summer of 1934, a group of conservative business leaders formed the American Liberty League to combat the alleged "radicalism" of the New Deal. They believed that Roosevelt was leading the country down "a foreign path" by attacking free enterprise, favoring workers over employers, and increasing the power of the federal government. "There can be only one capital," said a Liberty League spokesman, "Washington or Moscow."

The league generously supported Roosevelt's political opponents in the 1934 congressional elections. But the results served only to reinforce the president's enormous popularity. Instead of losing ground—the normal pattern for the majority party in midterm elections—the Democrats picked up nine seats in the Senate and nine in the House. Few pundits could recall a more lopsided election, and some questioned the future of the Republican Party. As publisher William Allen White put it, Roosevelt had been "all but crowned by the people."

In reality, the election results were a mixed blessing for the Democrats. Most Americans approved of the New Deal. Their main criticism was that it had not gone far—or fast—enough to end the Depression. In Minnesota, for example, Governor Floyd Olsen was reelected on an independent "Farmer-Labor" ticket that advocated state ownership of utilities and railroads.

In neighboring Wisconsin, the sons of "Fighting Bob" La Follette formed a new Progressive Party that endorsed the idea of a welfare state. And in California, Upton Sinclair, author of *The Jungle*, ran for governor on a program called EPIC (End Poverty in California), which promised to hand over idle factories and farmland to the poor and unemployed. Sinclair received almost 900,000 votes in a bitter, losing effort—a sign of things to come.

"Every Man a King"   The most serious challenge to Roosevelt's leadership was offered by Louisiana's **Huey P. Long**. Known as the "Kingfish," after a strutting, smooth-talking character on the popular radio program *Amos 'n' Andy*, Long combined a gift for showmanship with ruthless ambition. On the campaign trail, he wore a white linen suit, orchid shirt, pink necktie, straw hat, and two-toned shoes. A superb orator and a master storyteller, he understood the value of the spoken word in a state where few people owned radios, read newspapers, or traveled far from home.

As governor of Louisiana, Long pushed his unique brand of southern populism. By revising the tax codes to make corporations and wealthy citizens pay more, he was able to construct new hospitals, bring paved roads and bridges to rural areas, and give free textbooks to the poor. At the same time, he built a political machine of almost totalitarian proportions. When Long vacated the governor's chair to enter the U.S. Senate in 1932, he controlled the legislature, the courts, and the civil service system of Louisiana.

"I came to the United States Senate," Long wrote, "to spread the wealth of the land among all of the people." As a Democrat, he campaigned hard for Roosevelt in 1932 and supported much of the early New Deal. But as time passed, he grew restless with the slow pace of reform. In 1934, Long proposed his own agenda, promising to "make every man a king."

Under Long's plan, no one would be allowed to earn more than $1.8 million per year or to keep a personal fortune in excess of $5 million. After confiscating this surplus, the government would provide each family with a house, a car, a radio, and an annual income of at least twenty-five hundred dollars. Veterans would get their bonus, and deserving students could attend college free of charge.

Most economists were appalled. They knew that there weren't nearly enough millionaires around to finance Long's proposal. According to one study, the government would have had to confiscate all yearly incomes above $3,000—not $1.8 million—to provide each family with $2,500. Long didn't much care about the arithmetic. "You don't have to understand it," he told his followers. "Just shut your damned eyes and believe it. That's all."

By 1935, Long's "Share Our Wealth Society" claimed 8 million members nationwide. At local meetings across the nation, his followers sang:

Every man a king, every man a king
For you can be a millionaire
But there's something belongs to
    others
There's enough for all to share.

The Radio Priest and the Pension Doctor

Long did not lack for competitors. In Royal Oak, Michigan, a working-class suburb of Detroit, Father Charles Edward Coughlin was busy leading a protest movement of his own. As the pastor of a small Catholic church, Shrine of the Little Flower, Coughlin became a towering figure in the 1930s by mixing prayer with politics in a way that touched millions—and frightened millions more.

Coughlin could be heard every Sunday on seventeen CBS radio outlets nationwide. An early Roosevelt supporter, he compared the New Deal to "Christ's Deal," assuring listeners that "Gabriel is over the White House, not Lucifer." Like Senator Long, Coughlin deplored the fact that too much wealth was concentrated in too few hands. Unlike Long, however, he blamed this evil on a tight money supply, manipulated by international bankers in London and New York.

Coughlin believed that "free silver"—the old Populist nostrum—would solve this problem and bring prosperity to all. His attacks on British bankers won him strong support in the Irish-Catholic community, and his call for monetary reform appealed to debt-ridden farmers and merchants in America's small towns. Before long, Coughlin's radio show, *Golden Hour of the Little Flower*, had more listeners (an estimated 40 million) than *Amos 'n' Andy* and *Gracie Allen*.

By 1934, the "Radio Priest" was souring on the New Deal. Angered by Roosevelt's disinterest in his "silver solution," he formed the National Union for Social Justice to challenge the president's leadership. "I glory in the fact that I am a simple Catholic priest," Coughlin declared, "endeavoring to inject Christianity into the fabric of an economic system woven upon the loom of the greedy."

A third protest movement, led by Francis E. Townsend, a retired physician living in California, offered yet another solution to the ills of the 1930s. Townsend had no desire to punish the rich, alter the money supply, or challenge the capitalist order. What disturbed him was the sight of elderly men and women sifting through garbage cans for food. In 1934, Townsend proposed a measure to revive the economy by meeting the specific needs of older Americans. It guaranteed a pension of two hundred dollars per month to those over the age of sixty who promised to stay out of the job market and spend the two hundred dollars by month's end. The pensions would be funded by a 2 percent sales tax on all "business transactions."

According to Townsend, his plan would create jobs for the young, increase the country's purchasing power, and provide security for the elderly. What he did not say was that his plan, known as Old Age Revolving Pensions Limited, was impossibly expensive. By most estimates, Townsend needed a sales tax approaching 70 percent in order to properly fund his proposal. When asked about this at a congressional hearing, the doctor replied: "I'm not in the least interested in the cost of the plan."

Neither were his followers. By 1935, more than 10 million Americans had signed petitions supporting Townsend's idea, and public opinion polls showed strong support for a government-sponsored pension plan. Townsend had unleashed a powerful new interest group, the elderly, and American politics would never be the same again.

THE SECOND NEW DEAL, 1935–1936

The American Liberty League, the victories of Floyd Olsen and the La Follette brothers, the rumblings of Long, Coughlin, and Townsend—all raised nagging problems for Franklin Roosevelt and the New Deal. Although national income in 1935 was a full 25 percent above the 1933 level, millions were still living on handouts, without much hope of a permanent job. Inside the White House, Roosevelt's key advisers were nudging him further to the left. "Boys—this is our hour," said the opportunistic Harry Hopkins. "We've got to get everything we want—a works program, social security, wages and hours, everything—now or never."

Jobs, Jobs, Jobs   In the spring of 1935, Roosevelt presented Congress with a "must" list of reforms, the so-called second New Deal. He requested—and received—$4.8 billion in work relief for the unemployed, the largest single appropriation in the nation's history. After allocating generous shares to his favorite projects, such as the CCC, Roosevelt established yet another agency, the Works Progress Administration (WPA), with Hopkins in charge, to create "jobs, jobs, jobs!"

In that task, it was very successful. At its height in 1936, the WPA employed 25 percent of the nation's entire work force. Many of these jobs, however, were low-paying and temporary so as to avoid competition with private enterprise.

The New Deal and the Arts

Among the most controversial parts of FDR's New Deal was Federal One, an experiment to provide government funding for the arts. Established under the huge Works Progress Administration, Federal One aimed to employ out-of-work professionals to help bring culture to the masses. Its Federal Theater Project performed everything from Shakespeare to puppet shows for audiences that rarely, if ever, had seen a live production before. Its Federal Arts Project produced museum exhibits, murals for public buildings (like the one pictured here in San Francisco's Coit Tower), and painting classes for the poor. Playwright Arthur Miller worked for Federal One, as did Actor Burt Lancaster, artist Jackson Pollock, and writers Saul Bellow and Richard Wright. Though some criticized these projects as wasteful and politically slanted to the New Deal (note the clean, well-fed, contented workers in the mural), they remained popular with the American public. Asked about the artwork, FDR said: "Some of it is good, some of it not so good, but all of it is native, human, eager and alive—all of it painted by their own kind in their own country."

(WPA Mural; Coit Tower, San Francisco)

Concentrating on small construction projects, the WPA built schools and playgrounds, repaired countless bridges and landing fields, and improved 650,000 miles of roads. Its National Youth Administration, inspired by Eleanor Roosevelt, provided part-time work to several million high school and college students.

Social Security   The president's "must" list included a social welfare plan that challenged the cherished concepts of voluntarism and individual responsibility. At the urging of Labor Secretary Frances Perkins, the nation's first woman cabinet member, Roosevelt proposed legislation (passed as the Social Security Act of 1935) to create a national pension fund, an unemployment insurance system, and public assistance programs for dependent mothers and children, the physically disabled, and those in chronic need. The pension was financed by a payroll tax to begin in 1937. Benefits were purposely modest—about twenty to thirty dollars per month—because Roosevelt did not intend "social security" to be the main source of personal retirement income, as it has become for many people today.

The Social Security Act had numerous defects. It excluded millions of vulnerable wage earners, such as domestics, farm workers, and the self-employed, from the pension fund. It taxed all participants at a fixed rate, forcing those with the lowest incomes to pay a far greater share of their wages into the system. Over time, the Social Security fund emerged as the country's most important and expensive domestic program.

"Class Warfare" Roosevelt had never been a strong supporter of organized labor. He felt uneasy about the tactics of labor leaders such as **John L. Lewis**, head of the United Mine Workers, who had tripled his membership (from 150,000 to almost 500,000) with an aggressive organizing campaign that declared, "The president wants you to join a union!" Roosevelt worried that labor's militant new spirit would accelerate the violent confrontations of 1934, when pitched battles erupted between striking workers and police on the streets of Minneapolis, San Francisco, and Detroit.

In the wake of these disturbances, Senator Robert Wagner of New York authored a bill to protect the rights of workers to organize and bargain collectively. His legislation filled a dramatic void, because the Supreme Court had just declared parts of the NIRA—including Section 7A regarding labor union rights—to be unconstitutional. Passed in 1935, the National Labor Relations Act prohibited employers from engaging in a wide range of "unfair labor practices," such as spying on their workers. The law also created the National Labor Relations Board (NLRB) to supervise union elections and determine the appropriate bargaining agents.

The Wagner Act revealed deep divisions within the union movement. At the American Federation of Labor's annual convention in 1935, John L. Lewis pleaded with fellow leaders to begin

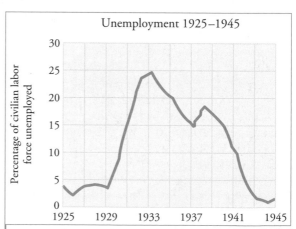

Unemployment, 1925–1945 *This chart shows the two great peaks of unemployment—the first in 1933, as FDR took office; the second (and smaller one) during the recession of 1938, when federal spending was reduced. The chart also shows the enormous impact of World War II in bringing unemployment—and the Great Depression itself—to an end.*

DOING HISTORY ONLINE

National Labor Relations Act, 1935

Read the document online. According to the act, why is this legislation needed? What is significant about this reasoning?

 www.cengage.com/history/ayers/ampassages4e

serious membership drives in the steel mills, automobile plants, and rubber factories. Lewis wanted these mass production workers to be organized by industry rather than by craft. Only then, he argued, could the power of big business be successfully confronted.

Most AFL leaders were unmoved. As representatives of skilled craftsworkers, such as masons and carpenters, they had little interest in organizing industrial unions composed largely of African Americans and ethnic groups from eastern and southern Europe. Indeed, after Lewis finished his emotional plea to the AFL convention, Carpenters' president "Big Bill" Hutcheson called him a "bastard." Lewis floored Hutcheson with a solid right to the jaw and stormed out of the convention.

Shortly after, Lewis joined with like-minded labor leaders to form the Congress of Industrial Organizations (CIO). Their goal was to create powerful unions in the larger mass production industries such as automobiles and steel. Labor's "civil war" had begun.

THE FASCIST CHALLENGE

As the 1936 presidential election approached, Americans watched events in Europe with growing apprehension. From the Soviet Union came stories about a regime that was brutalizing its people in an attempt to "collectivize" the society and stamp out internal dissent. In Germany and Italy, powerful dictators emerged, preaching race hatred and vowing to expand their nation's borders. For millions of Americans, the scene was frighteningly familiar—a replay of events that had led Europe, and eventually the United States, into the bloodiest war of all time earlier in the century.

Hitler and Mussolini Adolf Hitler became the German chancellor in January 1933, a few months before FDR was sworn in as president. Born in Austria in 1889, Hitler had moved to Bavaria as a young man and fought in the German army during World War I. Wounded and jobless, he helped form the National Socialist (Nazi) Party, one of the many extremist groups that thrived in the economic chaos of war-battered Germany. In 1923, Hitler was arrested in Munich for staging an unsuccessful coup against the Weimar government. From his prison cell, he wrote *Mein Kampf* ("My Struggle"), a rambling account of his racial theories, plans for Germany, and hatred of Jews.

As the Weimar government collapsed in the Depression, the Nazis gained strength. Millions welcomed their promise to create jobs, restore German glory, and avenge the "humiliation" of Versailles. Nazi representation in the Reichstag (parliament) rose from 12 in 1928 to 230 by 1932. A year later, Hitler became chancellor of Germany. The results were alarming. Constitutional rights were suspended and competing political parties banned. Nazi supporters held mass book-burning rallies, drove Jews from universities, boycotted their businesses, and attacked them in the streets. "Hitler is a madman," President Roosevelt told a French diplomat.

Under the Nazis, the state increased its control over industry, while leaving it in private hands. This allowed Hitler to begin a massive rearmament program, which produced badly needed jobs. By 1934, German factories were producing tanks and military aircraft. A year later, Hitler proposed a 500,000-man army and instituted the draft. In 1936, Nazi forces marched into the Rhineland—a clear violation of the Versailles treaty—and reoccupied it without firing a shot. "Today Germany," the Nazis chanted, "tomorrow the world."

Hitler had modeled himself, to some degree, after Italian dictator Benito Mussolini, the father of fascism in modern Europe. Born in 1883, Mussolini had served in the Italian army during World War I. Playing on the social unrest and economic turmoil of the postwar era, he seized national power in 1922 and proclaimed Fascismo, a merging of state and business leadership under the banner of extreme nationalism. As the supreme leader, or Duce, he preached national unity and state management (though not ownership) of Italy's industrial base. Like Hitler, he destroyed labor unions, censored the press, abolished all political parties but his own, and relied on a secret police force to silence his critics. In 1935, Italian forces invaded Ethiopia. For Mussolini, the attack was a way of restoring Italy's ancient glory. The fighting in Ethopia was brutal and one-sided, pitting Italian tanks and machine guns against local defenders armed with little more than spears and bows and arrows. At the League of Nations, Ethiopian Emperor Haile Selassie pleaded for support. The league responded by branding Italy the aggressor but sent no military help. After annexing Ethiopia in 1936, Mussolini signed a pact of friendship with Hitler, known as the Rome–Berlin Axis.

The Neutrality Acts Americans did not want to become involved in European squabbles as they had in the past. They were determined that history must not repeat itself—that American blood must not be shed again on foreign soil. There was only one way to avoid another war, most people believed, and that was to remain truly neutral in world affairs.

Although this sentiment had deep historical roots, running all the way back to George Washington, the key to understanding America's anxiety in the early 1930s was the legacy of World War I—the belief that U.S. participation had been a mistake, that America had been lured into the conflict, against its vital interests, by a conspiracy of evil men. In 1934, the U.S. Senate set up a committee, chaired by isolationist Gerald P. Nye of North Dakota, to investigate the reasons for America's involvement in World War I. The Nye committee highlighted a series of well-known facts: large banks and corporations had made huge profits during World War I by giving loans and selling arms to the various combatants. It followed, therefore, that the United States had been led into this conflict by greedy bankers and businessmen determined to protect their investments. The press dubbed them "merchants of death."

This was a simplistic explanation, to be sure. It ignored the rather tangled reality of American intervention—from submarine warfare to the Zimmermann Telegram, from President Wilson's rigid morality to the defense of neutral rights. Yet the Nye committee findings enjoyed wide popular support in a nation determined to avoid another war.

The isolationist impulse was particularly strong in the Great Plains and Upper Midwest, where populist suspicions of Wall Street and international bankers went back a long way. It attracted many Americans of German descent, who remembered their brutal treatment during World War I; of Irish descent, who opposed aid to Great Britain in any form; and of Italian descent, who viewed Mussolini as a hero in these years. Isolationism—in some cases combined with pacifism—also appealed to clergy, peace groups, and college students.

Congress responded to this public mood with legislation designed to avoid the "entanglements" that had led to American participation in World War I. The first Neutrality Act, passed after the Ethiopian invasion of 1935, empowered the president to determine when a state of war existed anywhere in the world. In that event, the president would declare an embargo on all combatants. American arms shipments would cease, and American citizens would be warned against traveling on the vessels of belligerents. In February 1936, Congress passed a second Neutrality Act, prohibiting American banks from extending loans or credits to any nation at war.

President Roosevelt did not like these bills. He believed that absolute neutrality favored powerful aggressor nations by forcing the United States to treat all sides equally. Yet FDR signed them into law for political reasons. The Neutrality Acts had wide popular support. He knew that a veto would give strong ammunition to the Republicans in the coming presidential campaign.

MANDATE FROM THE PEOPLE, 1936

As the 1936 election approached, FDR had reason for concern. Although personal income and industrial production had risen dramatically since he took office in 1933, millions were still unemployed. In addition, more than 80 percent of the nation's newspapers and most of the business community remained loyal to the Republican Party, meaning that Roosevelt's major presidential opponent could count on strong editorial and financial support.

The 1936 Election   In June, the Republicans gathered in Cleveland to nominate their presidential ticket. Herbert Hoover, anxious for another crack at Roosevelt, received a thunderous ovation. But the convention delegates, seeking a winner, not a martyr, chose Kansas governor Alfred M. Landon to head the Republican ticket, and Frank Knox, a Chicago publisher, to be the vice-presidential nominee.

Landon, a political moderate, promised "fewer radio talks, fewer experiments, and a lot more common sense." His problem was that he radiated little of the compassion and confidence that made the president so popular with the masses.

Roosevelt also faced presidential challenges from the left. Both the Communists and the Socialists ran spirited campaigns in 1936, demanding more federal aid for the poor. But Roosevelt's most serious concern—a political merger involving Coughlin, Townsend, and Long—was effectively eliminated in September 1935, when an assassin's bullet killed the Louisiana senator in Baton Rouge. To replace the charismatic Long, these dissident forces nominated William "Liberty Bill" Lemke, an obscure North Dakota congressman, to be their presidential candidate on the new Union Party ticket.

Roosevelt's political strategy differed markedly from 1932. In that campaign, he had stressed the common hopes and needs that bound people together; in 1936, he emphasized the class differences that separated those who supported the New Deal from those who opposed it. Time and again, Roosevelt portrayed the election as a contest between common people and privileged people, between compassion and greed. In his final campaign speech at New York's Madison Square Garden, he declared that the "forces of selfishness" had "met their match" in the Roosevelt administration. "They are unanimous in their hatred of me," the president thundered, "and I welcome their hatred."

On November 3, FDR crushed Landon and Lemke in the most one-sided election since 1820. The final totals showed Roosevelt with 27,752,869 popular votes, Landon with 16,674,665, and Lemke with 882,479. (The Socialist and Communist party candidates polled fewer than 300,000 votes between them.) Roosevelt won every state except Maine and Vermont, and the Democratic Party added to its huge majorities in both houses of Congress. A few days after the election, Father Coughlin announced his retirement from the radio.

African Americans and the New Deal Roosevelt's landslide victory signaled a dramatic shift in American politics. A new majority coalition had emerged. In the farm belt, Roosevelt won over long-time Republicans with federal subsidies and price supports. In the cities, he attracted workers grateful for welfare benefits and WPA jobs. And he appealed to ethnic minorities by filling many White House positions, cabinet posts, and federal judgeships with Catholics and Jews.

Adding to the president's strength was the support he received from the CIO. Describing Roosevelt as "the worker's best friend," the industrial unions campaigned tirelessly for him, and the effort paid off: FDR captured the working-class vote in 1936 by a margin of four to one.

The most striking political change, however, occurred within the nation's African

(© Bettmann/CORBIS)

African Americans Voting. *Although few blacks voted in the South during the 1930s, their growing numbers in northern cities like Chicago and New York increased their political influence within the New Deal coalition.*

American community. The steady migration of blacks to northern cities, where they could vote, increased their political power. Historically, most blacks supported the Republican Party, an allegiance that dated back to Abraham Lincoln and the Civil War. In 1932, Herbert Hoover had won an overwhelming share of their votes.

With the New Deal, however, a massive switch took place. In large part, African Americans became Democrats because the Roosevelt administration provided jobs and welfare benefits to all Americans, regardless of race. This federal assistance was especially welcome in black communities, where poverty and discrimination had long been facts of life. "The Negro was born in depression," a black leader recalled. "It only became official when it hit the white man."

By 1933, black unemployment had reached 50 percent. Fortunately, the two New Deal administrators most responsible for creating jobs were sympathetic to minority needs. At the PWA, Harold Ickes insisted that blacks receive equal pay on all construction projects. Although local officials often ignored these rules, the PWA provided thousands of jobs for African Americans, while building black schools and hospitals throughout the segregated South. At the WPA, Harry Hopkins set the same standards with somewhat better results. Blacks received a generous share of WPA work in northern cities—a testimony to both their joblessness and political clout. "Let Jesus Lead You and Roosevelt Feed You" became a rallying cry in African American churches during the election of 1936.

Many blacks viewed the New Deal as a progressive social force. They welcomed an administration that showed some interest in their struggle, and they particularly admired the efforts of first lady **Eleanor Roosevelt**, who served as the White House conscience on matters pertaining to minority rights.

Eleanor Roosevelt had a passion for public service and a deep commitment to the poor. Her interest in civil rights had been fueled in large measure by her friendship with prominent African Americans such as **Mary McLeod Bethune**, founder of Bethune-Cookman College in Florida. Born in a sharecropper's shack, the fifteenth child of former slaves, Bethune had acquainted the first lady with the special problems facing African Americans—from the scandal of lynching to the crisis in public education. In 1936, Eleanor Roosevelt recommended Bethune to head the National Youth Administration's Office of Negro Affairs.

As the New Deal's highest-ranking black appointee, Bethune presided over the administration's "black cabinet," which advised the White House on minority issues. Working together with Eleanor Roosevelt and other civil rights advocates, she helped to encourage—and monitor—the New Deal's racial progress. Much of it was symbolic. In an age of rigid segregation, Eleanor Roosevelt visited black colleges, spoke at black conferences, and socialized with black women. (She raised eyebrows by inviting Bethune to tea at the White House.) When the Daughters of the American Revolution refused to allow **Marian Anderson**, a gifted black contralto, to perform at Washington's Constitution Hall, Eleanor Roosevelt resigned from the organization. A few months later, Harold Ickes arranged for Anderson to sing at the Lincoln Memorial on Easter Sunday, 1939. An integrated audience of seventy-five thousand gathered to hear her.

Yet the good work of Eleanor Roosevelt and others could not mask larger New Deal failures in the field of civil rights. Throughout his presidency, for example, Franklin Roosevelt never attempted to challenge southern racial customs. He made no effort to break down segregation barriers or enable blacks to vote. And he

DOING HISTORY ONLINE

Letters from the "Forgotten Man" to Mrs. Roosevelt, 1934

Read the letters online. Why did ordinary people write to Mrs. Roosevelt?

  www.cengage. com/history/ayers/ ampassages4e

remained on the sidelines as federal antilynching bills were narrowly defeated in Congress. Without his leadership, not a single piece of civil rights legislation was enacted in the New Deal years.

Roosevelt argued that he could not support civil rights legislation without alienating southern Democrats, who controlled the most important committees in Congress. "They will block every bill I [need] to keep America from collapsing," Roosevelt said. "I just can't take that risk."

The president's position did not prevent blacks from supporting him in 1936. Roosevelt received 76 percent of their votes—the same total that Herbert Hoover had won four years before. On balance, African Americans viewed the New Deal as a clear improvement over the Republican past. "My friends, go turn Lincoln's picture to the wall," a black editor wrote in 1935. "That debt has been paid in full."

Popular Culture in the Depression

The economic struggles of the 1930s shaped not only the politics of American life but the culture as well. Hard times encouraged federal participation in the arts and triggered a leftward tilt among many intellectuals and writers. A flurry of "proletarian literature" emerged in the early Depression years, emphasizing the "class struggle" through stories about heroic workers resisting the exploitation of evil employers. Several important black writers—including Ralph Ellison, Richard Wright, and Langston Hughes—identified with the Communist Party because it appeared to actively support civil rights. For most intellectuals, however, the fascination with communism was fleeting. As free thinkers, they could not adjust to the party's rigid conformity or its blind support of the Soviet dictator, Joseph Stalin.

The Depression era also witnessed the spread of a popular culture born in the preceding decades. Photojournalism came of age in the 1930s with the publication of magazines such as *Life* and *Look* and the vivid imagery of government-sponsored photographers like Walker Evans and Dorothea Lange. In the comics trade, Superman (1938) demonstrated that Americans were anxious to get beyond the tame characters from the newspaper strips. He was quickly followed by comic books featuring Batman and Captain Marvel. In popular music, the "swing era" brought the jazz of African American artists to a much broader public. In radio and in movies, the changes were most dramatic and profound.

The Big Screen By the 1930s, the motion picture was the leading form of popular culture in the United States. Most Americans attended at least one movie a week; many followed the lives of their favorite stars in gossip columns and fan magazines. Theater owners attracted customers by offering inducements such as the "double feature," which dramatically increased the number of films produced during this decade. In the larger cities, movie theaters were transformed into fantasy palaces, with thick carpets, winding staircases, ushers in tuxedoes, and the twinkling lights of chandeliers. For millions, the theater became a temporary escape from the bleak realities of the Depression.

Hollywood mirrored the changing attitudes of the 1930s. It was no accident that the most popular movie of 1932, the year America hit rock bottom, was Mervyn LeRoy's *I Am a Fugitive from a Chain Gang*, the story of a decent man, unjustly convicted of a crime, who escapes from a brutal southern penal farm. In the final scene, the hero meets his former girlfriend, who asks him how he survives. From the shadows of a dark alley—representing the Depression itself—he whispers: "I steal."

Other early films from this decade, such as *Little Caesar* (1930) and *Public Enemy* (1931), focused on big city mobsters who ruthlessly shot their way to the top. Although these "bad guys" were either killed or brought to justice on screen, the public's fascination with criminal activity reached a peak in these years with the romanticizing of bank robbers (and cold-blooded murderers) like John Dillinger, Bonnie Parker and Clyde Barrow, Baby Face Nelson, and Ma Barker. All died in shoot-outs with local police or the FBI.

The evolving optimism of the 1930s—the promise of better times—was apparent in Hollywood films. The 1930s saw Fred Astaire whirling Ginger Rogers across the nightclub dance floor; Mickey Rooney courting Judy Garland in the blissfully innocent "Andy Hardy" movies; and Walt Disney raising the animated cartoon to an art form in his feature film *Snow White and the Seven Dwarfs* (1937). Wildly popular in this decade (and beyond) were the Marx brothers—Groucho, Harpo, and Chico—whose classic comedies demolished upper-class snobbery, foolish tradition, and much of the English language.

More significant were the moral dramas of director Frank Capra, including *Mr. Deeds Goes to Town* (1936), starring Gary Cooper, and *Mr. Smith Goes to Washington* (1939), with Jimmy Stewart. Both the movies and the leading men represented the virtues of heartland America, with its strong sense of decency and cooperation. Common people could be fooled by greedy bankers and selfish politicians, but not for long. Life got better when "good folks" followed their instincts.

The most memorable films of this era, *Gone with the Wind* and **The Grapes of Wrath**, showcased Hollywood's ability to transform best-selling fiction into successful movies, seen by millions who had read the novels of Margaret Mitchell, John Steinbeck, and others—and millions more who had not. Both films related the epic struggle of families in crisis, trying desperately to survive. *The Grapes of Wrath*, set in the Depression, depicts the awful conditions faced by the Dust Bowl farmers who migrated to California. True to the 1930s, it is a story of marginal people confronting economic injustice—people who stick together and refuse to give up. The hero, Tom Joad, promises his ma that "wherever they's a fight so hungry people can eat, I'll be there. Wherever they's a cop beatin' up a guy, I'll be there." Ma Joad is a source of strength and common sense. "They ain't gonna wipe us out," she insists. "Why, we're the people—we go on."

The Radio Age   Like the movie boom, the rapid growth of radio in the Depression encouraged the spread of popular culture. Politicians and public figures such as President Roosevelt and Father Coughlin used radio to great effect. So did companies seeking to mass-market their products. Organized along commercial lines in the 1920s, radio continued firmly down that path in the 1930s, with two giant firms—the National Broadcasting Company (NBC) and the Columbia Broadcasting System (CBS)—dominating the nation's airwaves.

In an odd way, the economic turmoil of the 1930s aided radio by weakening other forms of entertainment. As vaudeville failed and the infant recording industry struggled, popular performers, including Al Jolson and Jack Benny, continued their careers on the radio. For morning and afternoon fare, the networks relied on domestic dramas such as *Ma Perkins* and *Helen Trent*, which appealed to women working in the home. Often sponsored by soap and beauty companies, these programs, known as "soap operas," doled out the story line in daily fifteen-minute installments. In the evenings, as entire families gathered around the radio, the entertainment broadened to include quiz shows, talent contests, and adventure programs like *Inner Sanctum* and *The Green Hornet*. Surveys showed that the average American in the 1930s listened to more than four hours of radio each day.

Radio carried sporting events, political conventions, and the news. Millions followed the 1936 Berlin Olympics, where Jesse Owens, the African American track star, embarrassed Adolf Hitler by winning four gold medals. Two years later, the heavyweight title fight from Yankee Stadium between Joe Louis, the black champion, and Max Schmeling, the German challenger, was broadcast throughout the world. When Louis knocked out Schmeling in the first round, Americans celebrated in the streets.

Perhaps nothing better demonstrated the power of radio than the infamous "War of the Worlds" episode. On Halloween evening 1938, actor Orson Welles, star of CBS's *Mercury Theater*, did a powerful reading of the H. G. Wells novel, *War of the Worlds*, presenting it as a simulated newscast in which violent aliens from Mars land in the New Jersey town of Grovers Mills. "I can see the thing's body," sobbed a "roving reporter" at the scene. "It's large as a bear and it glistens like wet leather. That face . . . the black eyes and saliva dripping from its rimless lips." Although Welles repeatedly interrupted the program to explain what he was doing, national panic nevertheless ensued. Thousands fled their homes, believing that the Martians had wiped out the New Jersey State Police and were advancing toward New York City. Traffic came to a halt in parts of the Northeast; bus and train stations were jammed; churches overflowed with weeping families. A few commentators blamed the hysteria on world events; the rising tide of fascism in Europe made people uneasy. Everybody else blamed Welles for misusing—or at least misjudging—the power of radio. Newspaper headlines screamed: "Radio War Terrorizes U.S." and "Panic Grips Nation as Radio Announces 'Mars Attacks World.'" When the furor died down, President Roosevelt invited Welles to the White House. "You know, Orson," he joked, "you and I are the two best actors in America."

THE SECOND TERM, 1937–1940

In his second inaugural address, FDR emphasized the New Deal's unfinished business. "I see one-third of a nation ill-housed, ill-clad, ill-nourished," he declared. The president was optimistic. The election had provided him with a stunning popular mandate and with huge Democratic majorities on Capitol Hill. To Roosevelt's thinking, only one roadblock lay in his path: the Supreme Court.

A confrontation seemed inevitable. The Supreme Court was dominated by elderly, conservative justices, appointed in the Harding–Coolidge years, who despised the New Deal and worked zealously to subvert its legislation. In Roosevelt's first term, the Court had struck down the NRA, the AAA, and a series of social welfare laws.

In the coming months, it would be reviewing—and likely overturning—the National Labor Relations Act and the Social Security Act, two of the New Deal's most precious accomplishments.

Roosevelt struck first. In February 1937, without consulting Congress, he unveiled sweeping legislation to reorganize the federal court system. Under his plan, fifty new judgeships would be created by adding one judge for each sitting justice over the age of seventy who refused to retire. The Supreme Court would get a maximum of six new members, raising its total to fifteen.

The plan was legal. The Constitution sets no limits on the size of the Supreme Court; indeed, the number of justices, determined by Congress, had fluctuated between six and ten in the previous century. Roosevelt assumed that his overwhelming reelection in 1936 had given him the green light to crush all opposition to the New Deal, regardless of the source.

He was badly mistaken. Many Americans worried that his "Court-packing" plan would undermine judicial independence and threaten the balance of power among the three branches of government. As the opposition grew stronger, aides urged Roosevelt to withdraw the bill.

In the spring of 1937, the Supreme Court changed course. By votes of 5 to 4, with one moderate justice switching sides, it upheld both the Wagner Act and the Social Security Act. Then, one by one, the old conservatives decided to retire. This allowed Roosevelt—the only president in American history to make no Supreme Court appointments during his first four-year term—to fill five vacancies in the next three years. The justices he chose—especially Hugo Black, Felix Frankfurter, and William O. Douglas—would steer a more liberal course for decades to come.

Nevertheless, the Court battle emboldened Roosevelt's opponents by proving that the president could be beaten. "The New Deal," wrote one observer, "would never be the same."

Union Struggles

Away from Washington, new battles raged in the automobile plants of Michigan, the textile mills of North Carolina, and the coal fields of Kentucky as industrial workers demanded union recognition under the banner of the CIO. In perhaps the most spectacular episode, autoworkers at a General Motors (GM) plant in Flint, Michigan, went on strike inside the factory, refusing to leave. Their spontaneous technique, known as the "sit-down," spread quickly to other sites. In February 1937, GM recognized the CIO's United Automobile Workers (UAW) as the bargaining agent for its employees. Chrysler came to terms a few months later.

The victory at GM forced other employers into line. Firestone signed a contract with the CIO's Rubber Workers, General Electric and RCA with the Electrical Workers. Even U.S. Steel, an old enemy of organized labor, agreed to generous terms with the Steelworkers: union recognition, a firty-hour week, and a 10 percent wage increase.

There were some holdouts. Henry Ford hired an army of thugs to rough up union organizers and disrupt strikers on the picket lines. Republic Steel of Chicago stockpiled more weapons than did the city police department. "I won't have a contract with an irresponsible, racketeering, violent communistic body like the CIO," fumed Republic president Tom C. Girdler.

The worst violence occurred outside Republic's South Chicago mill on Memorial Day 1937. There heavily armed police battled rock-throwing strikers on the picket line. Before it ended, ten workers had been killed by gunfire, and dozens more had been injured. In the following months, Ford and Republic Steel came to terms. Under pressure from the National Labor Relations Board, they gradually accepted industrial unionism as a legitimate force in American life. With a membership approaching 3 million, the CIO had come a long way since its break with the conservative, craft-oriented American Federation of Labor a few years before.

LOSING GROUND

The Court battle and the sit-down strikes slowed the political momentum that followed FDR's reelection landslide in 1936. Further problems loomed in Europe, where fascism continued to gain strength, and in the United States, where a serious recession in 1937 eroded public confidence in the New Deal. For President Roosevelt, the road ahead appeared even more menacing than before.

Fascist Advances   Late in 1936, civil war broke out in Spain. A group of military officers, led by General Francisco Franco, attempted to overthrow the recently elected government. Because Franco represented the Falangist, or fascist elements in Spain, he received military aid from Hitler and Mussolini. On the other side, Joseph Stalin aided the government (or "loyalist") forces, which contained a large socialist and communist contingent. The war itself was brutal, with extreme cruelty on both sides. Before it ended, more than 600,000 people were killed.

The Spanish Civil War triggered strong emotions in the United States. Some Americans praised Franco as a bastion against communism and a strong supporter of the Catholic church. Others condemned him as a fascist thug, determined to

Hitler Youth.   *Hitler Youth in Germany rounding up books to be burned, including works of Thomas Mann and Albert Einstein. As Joseph Goebbels, the Nazi propaganda minister, declared: "These flames not only illuminate the final end of an old era; they also light up the new."*

overthrow a popularly elected government by force. Several thousand Americans went to Spain as part of the Abraham Lincoln Brigade, organized by the Communist Party, to fight on the Loyalist side. As Ernest Hemingway said of Franco, "There is only one way to quell a bully and that is to thrash him."

The Rising Nazi Menace

In central Europe, Hitler marched boldly toward war. Vowing to unite all German-speaking people, he moved on Austria in 1938, adding 6 million "Germans" to the Third Reich. Then he demanded the Sudetenland, a region in western Czechoslovakia where 3 million ethnic Germans lived. The Czechs possessed both a well-trained army and a defense treaty with France. As central Europe's only remaining democracy, Czechoslovakia looked to the French and British for support against the Nazi threat.

That support never came. Neither France nor England wanted a showdown with Germany. France had lost half of its male population between the ages of twenty and thirty-two during World War I. In Britain, Oxford students adopted a resolution in the 1930s declaring that they would not take up arms for their country under any circumstances. Antiwar feeling was so strong that a kind of diplomatic paralysis set in. The result was the Munich debacle of 1938.

At Munich, Prime Minister Neville Chamberlain of England and Premier Edouard Daladier of France agreed to Hitler's demand for the Sudetenland in the Munich Agreement. In return the German leader promised not to take any more territory. Daladier then pressured the Czechs to accept this dismal bargain, while Chamberlain congratulated everyone—Hitler included—for bringing "peace in our time."

The news from inside Germany was even worse. Early in 1938, the Nazis torched Munich's Great Synagogue and began the initial deportation of Jews to the infamous concentration camp at Buchenwald. On the evening of November 9—known as Kristallnacht, the "night of broken glass"—Nazi mobs burned synagogues, looted stores, and attacked Jews in cities throughout Germany. Dozens were murdered, and hundreds beaten and raped. Then the Nazis passed new laws to confiscate Jewish property, bar Jews from meaningful employment, and deprive them of ordinary liberties such as attending school and driving a car.

When word of these events reached the United States, President Roosevelt was furious. "I myself could scarcely believe that such things could occur in a twentieth century civilization," he told reporters. Roosevelt immediately called a conference of thirty-two nations to discuss plans for accepting desperate Jewish refugees from Germany, Austria, and Czechoslovakia. But no country, with the exception of small and densely populated Holland, showed a willingness to help. In the United States, a combination of anti-Semitism, isolationist sentiment, and hard times kept the "golden door" tightly shut. Most Americans did not want "foreigners" competing with them for jobs and resources in the midst of the Depression.

The result was disastrous. At a time when many Jews could have fled from Hitler, there was almost no place for them to go. Between 1935 and 1941, the United States took in an average of eighty-five hundred Jews per year—a number far below the annual German quota of thirty thousand set by the National Origins Act of 1924. Among those allowed to enter were "high-profile" Jewish refugees such as the physicist Albert Einstein.

AN END TO REFORM

Until 1937, the American economy had been making steady, if uneven, progress. National income and production finally reached 1929 levels, stock prices were climbing, and profits were up. Roosevelt now hoped to slow government spending as the business picture improved. He wanted to balance the federal budget and cut the mounting national debt.

The president knew that national recovery had been fueled by the New Deal's farm subsidies, relief programs, and public works. He was familiar with the writings of British economist John Maynard Keynes, who advocated a policy of deficit spending in hard times to spur economic growth. Yet Roosevelt had never been fully comfortable with government's expanding role. He feared that the growing national debt would generate inflation, and he worried about the effect of federal welfare programs on the recipients' initiative and self-respect.

In 1937, Roosevelt slashed funding for both the PWA and WPA, cutting almost 2 million jobs. At the same time, the new Social Security payroll tax took effect, removing billions of dollars of purchasing power from the economy. The result was recession—the most serious economic plunge of the Roosevelt years. As unemployment rose and production plummeted, the nation slipped back toward the nightmare of 1933, with breadlines and soup kitchens dotting the landscape.

In October, Roosevelt called Congress into special session. Within weeks, a $5 billion expenditure was approved for federal relief and public works. The economy responded, showing the impact of government spending once again. But the recession further weakened Roosevelt's image as a forceful leader in perilous times.

By 1938, the New Deal had clearly lost momentum. Harry Hopkins blamed it on six grinding years of Depression and reform, claiming the public was "bored with the poor, the unemployed, the insecure." Facing a more combative Congress—Republicans and conservative Democrats made significant gains in the 1938 elections—Roosevelt decided to "tread water" for a while. Among his few legislative achievements that year was passage of the Fair Labor Standards Act, which abolished child labor in most industries, and provided a minimum hourly wage (forty cents) and a maximum workweek (forty hours) to be phased in over time. Like Social Security, the act did not cover those who needed it most, such as farm workers and domestics. Yet almost a million Americans had their wages raised immediately by this law, and countless millions had their work hours shortened as well.

CONCLUSION

In responding to the enormous challenges of the Great Depression, Franklin Roosevelt's New Deal altered politics and society in fundamental ways. For the first time, the federal government provided massive assistance to the poor and the unemployed. It stabilized the banking system, protected farmers with price supports, guaranteed the rights of organized labor, and created a national pension plan. The New Deal also produced a more class-oriented Democratic Party, appealing to industrial workers, hard-pressed farmers, and urban minorities. Avoiding the political extremes that plagued other nations in the Depression era, Roosevelt steered a middle course between laissez-faire and socialism—a course that combined free enterprise and democracy with national planning and social reform.

During the New Deal years, the size and scope of the federal government increased dramatically. Facing a catastrophic depression, FDR used the presidential office, as never before in U.S. history, to extend needed relief, stimulate job growth, and regulate the economy. He became the first president to regularly fashion his own legislative agenda for Congress to consider, tilting the future balance of political power strongly in favor of the executive branch. At times Roosevelt badly overreached himself, as in his failed attempt to "pack" the Supreme Court in 1937. On the whole, though, he proved a remarkably popular and resourceful figure, using his ebullient personality, his courageous struggle with polio, and his understanding of the media, especially radio, to form a powerful bond with the people.

What the New Deal did best was to restore a sense of hope and purpose to a demoralized nation. Yet its overriding goal in these years—the promise of full economic recovery—remained elusive at best. Fearful of mounting budget deficits and ever-growing relief rolls, President Roosevelt never committed himself to the level of consistent federal spending urged by economists like John Maynard Keynes. When the New Deal ended in 1939, more than 8 million Americans were still unemployed. It would take a world war, and the full mobilization that followed, to put them permanently back to work.

CHAPTER REVIEW, 1933–1939

- The United States hit rock bottom economically as banks collapsed and millions lost their jobs.
- Congress enacted emergency legislation to provide needed relief during the "first hundred days."
- The nation slowly recovered, leading to Roosevelt's landslide reelection in 1936.
- The New Deal laid the foundation for a welfare state with programs such as social security and unemployment insurance.
- Unions won recognition following successful strikes against employers in the automobile, steel, and other industries.
- Drought and dust storms caused great damage in parts of Kansas, Nebraska, Oklahoma, Texas, and Colorado and forced tens of thousands of people to leave the region.
- Fascist aggression and Japanese militarism led to a bitter national debate regarding America's role in the world.

◄▮▮▮ Looking Back

Chapter 25 considers the impact of the Great Depression on the social, economic, and political structure of the United States. Among the key issues considered is the new relationship between the federal government and the average citizen.

1. What were the most pressing problems facing the Roosevelt administration when it came to power, and how did it address them?
2. Who were President Roosevelt's major critics, and how did they propose to deal with the Great Depression?
3. What impact did the Great Depression have on the realignment of the major political parties?
4. How did the American people view international relations in the 1930s, and what factors were responsible for the perceptions of America's role in the world?

Looking Ahead ▮▮▮►

Chapter 26 examines the impact of World War II on American society. Following the Japanese attack on Pearl Harbor, isolationist sentiment would end, the nation would mobilize its defenses, and 15 million men and women would serve in the armed forces against the Axis powers of Germany, Italy, and Japan.

1. What impact would the coming of World War II have on the economic problems facing Americans in the 1930?
2. What would happen to the powerful isolationist movement of this era?
3. Given the darkening world situation, would President Roosevelt decide to break with political precedent and run for a third presidential term?

Go to the American Passages website at www.cengage.com/history/ayers/ampassages4e for additional review materials.

The Second World War, 1939–1945

Prime Minister Neville Chamberlain's "peace in our time" lasted fewer than six months. In March 1939, the Germans marched into central Czechoslovakia. To the south, Franco's forces won a final victory in the Spanish Civil War, and Mussolini's army annexed neighboring Albania. Throughout the summer months, Nazi threats multiplied. "So long as Germans in Poland suffer grievously, so long as they are imprisoned away from the Fatherland," warned Hitler, "Europe can have no peace."

President Roosevelt declared neutrality, reflecting the clear sentiment of the American people. At the same time, he worked to mobilize the nation's defense effort and shape public opinion against the growing Nazi menace.

WAR IN EUROPE, 1939–1940

In August 1939, Hitler and Stalin stunned the world by signing a nonaggression pact. Both dictators were buying time for an inevitable showdown between their armed forces. And both had designs on Polish territory, which they secretly divided in their agreement. On September 1, German ground troops and armored divisions stormed into Poland from the west, backed by their powerful air force (Luftwaffe). Two weeks later, Soviet troops attacked from the east, reclaiming the territory that Russia had lost to Poland after World War I.

Blitzkrieg　　　　Hitler's Blitzkrieg (lightning strike) into Poland shattered the lingering illusions of Munich. Having pledged themselves to guarantee Poland's borders, England and France reluctantly declared war on Germany. The British sent a small, ill-equipped army to defend western Europe against further Nazi aggression, while the French reinforced their "impregnable" Maginot Line facing Germany. An eerie calm settled over Europe as all sides prepared for battle.

That six-month calm, known as the "phony war," ended in April 1940 when the Nazis overran Denmark and Norway. In May, they invaded Belgium, Holland, Luxembourg—and France itself. From the skies, the Luftwaffe strafed fleeing civilians and flattened cities such as Rotterdam. On the ground, German troops and armor swept through the Ardennes Forest, skirting the Maginot Line. The huge French army collapsed in disarray. Within weeks, German units had reached the French coastline, trapping the British army at Dunkirk, with its back to the sea. In early June, a flotilla of small ships from England—tugs, pleasure craft, and naval vessels—ferried 330,000 soldiers to safety. It was both a defeat and a deliverance for the British forces, who had been badly mauled but rescued from disaster.

In mid-June, as Paris fell to the advancing Nazi army, Mussolini attacked France from the south. Following the French surrender on June 22, the German Luftwaffe attacked England in force. Hitler's plan was to gain control of the skies in preparation for a full-scale invasion of the British Isles. Day and night, German planes dropped their bombs on London and other cities in a murderous attempt to break civilian morale. Day and night, the British Royal Air Force rose up to meet the Luftwaffe, with devastating effect. By early fall, Nazi air losses forced Hitler to abandon his invasion plans. "Never in the field of human conflict," said England's new prime minister, **Winston Churchill**, of the brave pilots who fought the Battle of Britain, "was so much owed by so many to so few."

A Third Term for FDR

Events in Europe shattered America's isolationist facade. Unlike Woodrow Wilson in 1914, President Roosevelt did not ask the people to be "neutral in thought as well as in action." If England fell to the Nazis, he believed, the United States would become an isolated fortress, vulnerable to attack from the air and the sea. Most Americans felt the same way. A national poll found 83 percent hoping for a British victory, 16 percent neutral, and only 1 percent supporting the Nazis.

The German Blitzkrieg increased American concerns about defense. In August 1940, President Roosevelt and Congress worked to fashion the first peacetime draft in American history, the Selective Service Act, as well as a $10.5 billion appropriation for defense. With factories now open around-the-clock to build tanks, war planes, and naval vessels, unemployment virtually disappeared. The Great Depression was over.

Building a strong defense was one thing, aiding the Allies quite another. As Michigan senator Arthur Vandenberg, a leading isolationist, put it: "I do not believe that we can become an arsenal for one belligerent without becoming a target for another." Vandenberg used World War I as his example, charging that America's support for the Allied war effort had led to its participation in the war itself. With a presidential election on the horizon, FDR would have to answer this charge.

Until the last moment, however, there was no assurance that Roosevelt would even run. No American president had ever served a third term—a taboo that reflected the public's deep suspicion of entrenched federal power.

By 1940, the picture had changed. The idea of tested presidential leadership took on added appeal. Roosevelt expected to run again. Hoping to defuse the third-term issue, he allowed himself to be "drafted" by the Democratic National Convention in

This icon will direct you to interactive activities and study materials on the American Passages website: www.cengage.com/history/ayers/ampassages4e

CHAPTER TIMELINE

1933–1945	Franklin Delano Roosevelt presidency
1939	Germany invades Poland, starting World War II
1940	Germany conquers the Low Countries and France • British Air Force beats back Luftwaffe in skies over England, preventing Nazi invasion • Selective Service Act brings first peacetime draft • Franklin Roosevelt elected to an unprecedented third term in the White House
1941	Lend-Lease Act passed by Congress • Nazi armies invade the Soviet Union • Atlantic Charter is issued • Japan attacks Pearl Harbor, bringing United States into war
1942	Japanese forces capture the Philippines • Internment of Japanese Americans begins • FDR authorizes top secret Manhattan Project to build an atomic weapon • U.S. forces land in Africa to begin Operation Torch • U.S. Navy halts Japanese advance at the Battle of Midway • Manhattan Project begins
1943	Soviets win pivotal victory over Nazis at Stalingrad • Race riot in Detroit, "zoot-suit" riots in Los Angeles • U.S. forces invade Italy • U.S. Marines capture Guadalcanal
1944	Allies launch Normandy Invasion • U.S. forces, led by General MacArthur, recapture Philippines • Roosevelt elected to fourth term • G.I. Bill passes
1945	Allied leaders discuss postwar issues at Yalta • FDR dies; Harry Truman becomes president • Hitler commits suicide days before Germany surrenders • United States captures Iwo Jima and Okinawa • Atomic bomb is successfully tested in New Mexico desert • United States drops atomic bombs on Hiroshima and Nagasaki • Japan surrenders, ending World War II • U.S. produces more than half the world's manufactured goods

Chicago, thus appearing reluctant but dutiful in the public's mind. Roosevelt selected the enigmatic Henry Wallace to be his vice-presidential running mate.

The Republicans, meeting in Philadelphia, nominated **Wendell Willkie** of Indiana for president and Senator Charles McNary of Oregon for vice president. A Wall Street lawyer and the head of a large utilities corporation, Willkie held two positions almost guaranteed to make the voters suspicious. He had never run for public office before or held an appointive government position. His political ascent was due in large part to the public relations skills of his advisers.

The 1940 campaign was dominated by foreign affairs. Although Willkie shared Roosevelt's views about the dangers of Nazi aggression, he attacked the president for moving too quickly on the European stage. Among Willkie's complaints was a controversial decision by FDR to supply England with "overage" destroyers. In the summer of 1940, Churchill had begged the United States for naval support to protect British sea lanes from Nazi submarine attacks. In September, without consulting Congress, the president sent fifty old but serviceable warships to England in return for long-term leases to British military bases in Newfoundland, Bermuda, and other parts of the Western Hemisphere. The agreement outraged isolationists, who viewed it as

Breaking Tradition: A Presidential Third Term

Franklin Roosevelt's decision to seek a third term in 1940 broke a long-standing precedent. Note the political poster here, which uses the authoritative, nonpartisan image of Uncle Sam to make this point. At that time, the Constitution set no limits on the number of terms a president could serve. In the nation's formative years, Presidents George Washington, Thomas Jefferson, and James Madison had all retired after two full terms in office, setting an informal precedent. Although former President Ulysses S. Grant had unsuccessfully sought the Republican nomination for a third term in 1880 and former President Theodore Roosevelt was defeated in his quest for a third term on the Progressive Party ticket in 1912, no sitting president had campaigned for a third term until FDR. Given the state of world affairs in 1940, the issue of a third term generated little interest; Americans were far more focused on the coming of war. When Roosevelt ran for a fourth term in 1944, Republicans raised the issue obliquely, describing the president and his advisers as "tired old men."

In 1947, a Republican-led Congress passed an amendment that limited presidents to two terms. The Twenty-Second Amendment was ratified, with little public rancor or discussion, in 1951.

Courtesy of Franklin D. Roosevelt Library

a clear violation of American neutrality. In response, Roosevelt made a public promise he would not be able to keep. "I have said this before, but I shall say it again and again and again," he told a cheering crowd in Boston. "Your boys are not going to be sent into any foreign wars."

Roosevelt defeated Willkie with ease—27 million votes to 22 million, 449 electoral votes to 82. He carried all of America's major cities, piling up impressive totals among blacks, Jews, ethnic minorities, and union members. New York Mayor Fiorello La Guardia put it well: "Americans prefer Roosevelt with his known faults to Willkie with his unknown virtues."

THE END OF NEUTRALITY, 1940–1941

Shortly after the election, Roosevelt learned that England could no longer afford the supplies it needed to fight the Nazi war machine. He responded by asking Congress for the authority to sell or lease "defense material" to any nation he judged "vital to the defense of the United States." Roosevelt compared his **Lend-Lease** proposal to the simple act of lending a garden hose to a neighbor whose house was on fire. In Europe, he said, the British desperately needed tanks, guns, and planes to extinguish the raging inferno of nazism. "We must be the great arsenal of democracy," Roosevelt declared.

Lend-Lease

Lend-Lease set off a furious national debate. In 1940, FDR's opponents organized the America First Committee to keep the nation "neutral" by defeating Lend-Lease. Supported by Henry Ford and Charles Lindbergh, it appealed to the isolationist notion that America should be prepared to defend its own territory, leaving Europe's wars to the Europeans. At times, however, the committee's message became muddled and conspiratorial, as when Lindbergh described American Jews as the "principal war agitators" behind Lend-Lease.

By 1941, Roosevelt gained the upper hand. Public opinion moved sharply against isolationism as Hitler became a more ominous threat. Polls showed a clear majority of Americans willing to risk war with Germany in order to help the British survive. In March, a $7 billion Lend-Lease bill sailed through Congress, assisted by powerful lobbying groups such as the Committee to Defend America by Aiding the Allies.

In June 1941, Hitler shattered the recent Nazi-Soviet Pact by invading the Soviet Union with more than 2 million troops. Roosevelt responded by offering Stalin immediate Lend-Lease support. The idea of aiding a Communist dictator was hard for Americans to accept. But Roosevelt stood firm, believing that wars made strange bedfellows and that Hitler must be stopped at all costs. At his insistence, the Soviets received $12 billion in aid over the next four years.

With Lend-Lease in place, Roosevelt abandoned all pretense of neutrality. To ensure that American goods reached England, he instructed the navy to protect merchant shipping in the North Atlantic sea lanes. In August 1941, Roosevelt and Churchill met aboard the USS *Augusta*, off the Newfoundland coast, to discuss their mutual aims and principles. The result was a communiqué known as the **Atlantic Charter**, which called for freedom of the seas, freedom from want and fear, and self-determination for all people. The charter would become the blueprint for the United Nations following World War II.

In the fall of 1941, Roosevelt armed America's merchant fleet and authorized U.S. destroyers to hunt German U-boats (or submarines) under a policy known as "active defense." That October, a German submarine sank a U.S. destroyer off Iceland, with the loss of a hundred American lives. In his ballad to the men who died, Woody Guthrie asked: "What were their names, tell me, what were their names? Did you have a friend on the good *Reuben James*?"

War would come shortly, but not where Roosevelt expected.

The Road to Pearl Harbor

As Hitler swept relentlessly though Europe, another power was stirring halfway around the globe. Like Germany and

Italy, Japan had become a militarist state controlled by leaders with expansionist ideas. In the 1930s, the Japanese had invaded China, routing its army, terror-bombing cities, and brutalizing civilians in the infamous "rape of Nanking," where thousands died at the hands of rampaging Japanese troops. The United States barely protested. With his focus on the Nazis, Roosevelt sought to avoid a crisis with Japan, even after its planes bombed an American gunboat, the *Panay*, on the Yangtze River in 1937, killing three sailors and injuring forty-three more.

In 1938, the Japanese unveiled their plan for empire, known as the "Greater East Asia Co-Prosperity Sphere." Viewing themselves as superior to their neighbors, they aimed to rule their region by annexing European colonies in Southeast Asia and the Western Pacific. Control of French Indochina, the Dutch East Indies, and British Malaya would provide the food and raw materials to make Japan self-sufficient and secure. Only one obstacle stood in the way—the United States.

Japan purchased the bulk of its steel, oil, heavy equipment, and machine parts from U.S. suppliers. To help prevent further Japanese expansion, the Roosevelt administration placed an embargo on certain strategic goods to Japan and moved the Pacific Fleet from San Diego to **Pearl Harbor**. The Japanese responded by negotiating a defense treaty (the so-called Tripartite Pact) with Germany and Italy. Relations steadily declined. Hitler's Blitzkrieg left defeated France and Holland unable to defend their Asian colonies. When Japan moved against Indochina in April 1941, Roosevelt retaliated by freezing all Japanese assets in the United States and blocking shipments of scrap iron and aviation fuel to Japan.

Both sides prepared for war. Military analysts expected Japan to move southwest, toward the Dutch East Indies and British Malaya, in search of needed rubber and oil. Instead, on November 26, 1941, a huge Japanese naval fleet, led by Admiral Chuichi Nagumo, headed due east into rough Pacific waters. The armada included six aircraft carriers with four hundred warplanes, two battleships, two cruisers, nine destroyers, and dozens of support vessels. Traveling under complete radio silence, the fleet was destined for Pearl Harbor, Hawaii, five thousand miles away.

On Sunday morning, December 7, 1941, Admiral Nagumo's fleet reached its take-off point, 220 miles north of Pearl Harbor. At 7:40 A.M., the first wave of Japanese warplanes appeared. The wing commander radioed back the words, "Tora [tiger], Tora, Tora," meaning that surprise had been complete. The battleship *Arizona* suffered a direct hit and went up in flames. More than twelve hundred crew members were killed. The *Oklahoma* capsized after taking three torpedoes, trapping four hundred men below deck. A second Japanese assault at 9:00 A.M. completed the carnage. All told, eighteen warships had been sunk or were badly damaged, three hundred planes had been lost, and twenty-four hundred Americans had died.

It could have been worse. The aircraft carriers *Lexington* and *Enterprise* were away from Pearl Harbor on maneuvers. And Japanese commanders made a strategic error by not launching a third air attack against the oil depots, machine shops, and repair facilities. As a result, many of the damaged warships were back in action within months.

Why was Pearl Harbor so woefully unprepared? By the fall of 1941, the United States had broken the Japanese diplomatic code, known as MAGIC. American planners knew that war was coming. On November 27, Army Chief of Staff George C. Marshall sent a warning to all American military outposts in the Pacific. "Japanese future action unpredictable," it said, "but hostile action possible at any moment."

Yet Pearl Harbor was not viewed as the likely point of attack. It was thousands of miles from Japan and supposedly well defended. The very idea of a Japanese fleet sailing so far without detection seemed utterly fantastic. At Pearl Harbor, the commanders most feared sabotage from the large Japanese population living in Hawaii. Though some Americans believed that Roosevelt secretly encouraged the Japanese attack in order to bring the United States into World War II, the truth is more mundane: the debacle at Pearl Harbor was caused by negligence and errors in judgment, not by a backroom conspiracy at the White House.

On December 8, Congress declared war against Japan. Only Montana's representative, Jeanette Rankin, dissented. (A longtime peace activist, she also had voted against President Wilson's war message in 1917.) On December 11, Germany and Italy honored the Tripartite Pact by declaring war on the United States. Almost instantly, Americans closed ranks. As Roosevelt's former enemy Senator Burton Wheeler put it, "The only thing to do now is lick the hell out of them."

Early Defeats   The attack on Pearl Harbor began one of the bleakest years in American military history. In the North Atlantic, allied shipping losses reached almost a million tons per month. On the Eastern front, Nazi forces approached the outskirts of Moscow, where Soviet resistance was fierce. In Egypt, German General Erwin Rommel's elite Afrika Korps threatened the Suez Canal.

The news from Asia was grimmer still. Following Pearl Harbor, Japan moved quickly against American possessions in the Pacific, overrunning Guam, Wake Island, and eventually the Philippines. On December 10, 1941, the Japanese attacked the British fleet off Malaya, sinking the battleship *Prince of Wales* and the cruiser *Repulse*. In the following weeks, Burma, Hong Kong, Singapore, Malaya, and the Dutch East Indies fell like dominoes to Japanese invaders. Japan now had the resources—the oil, tin, rubber, and foodstuffs—to match its appetite for empire.

For Americans, the most galling defeat occurred in the Philippines, where 100,000 U.S. and Filipino troops surrendered to the Japanese after a bloody six-month struggle. The military campaign had actually been lost on December 8, 1941, when the Japanese successfully bombed Clark Field, destroying dozens of planes based there to defend the islands. (The failure to prepare for such an attack one day after Pearl Harbor was scandalous.) Lacking air cover, the defenders retreated to the jungles of the **Bataan Peninsula**, just north of Manila. As food ran out, they ate snakes, monkeys, cavalry horses, plants, and grass. Their songs were of hopelessness and despair.

We're the battling bastards of Bataan;
No Mama, no papa, no Uncle Sam.
No aunts, no uncles, no cousins, no nieces;
No pills, no planes, no artillery pieces.
. . . And Nobody gives a damn!

In March 1942, President Roosevelt ordered the commanding officer, **General Douglas MacArthur**, to slip out of the Philippines, leaving his troops behind. The trapped defenders made their stand at Corregidor, a fortresslike island in Manila Bay. After two months of constant bombardment, General Jonathan Wainwright surrendered to the Japanese. His diseased and starving men were brutalized by their captors on the infamous Bataan Death March, an event that further fueled America's boiling hatred of Japan.

Despite these disasters, the nation remained united and confident of victory. The road ahead would be long, the challenges immense. As *Time* magazine reminded its readers, "At the end of six months of war, the U.S. has: Not yet taken a single inch of enemy territory. Not yet beaten the enemy in a single major battle. . . . Not yet opened an offensive campaign. The war, in short, has still to be fought."

THE HOME FRONT

The United States had begun to mobilize for World War II before the attack on Pearl Harbor. In 1940, following the Nazi invasion of Western Europe, Congress had enacted the first peacetime draft in American history. When war came a year later, the draft was extended for the length of the conflict. Brought together by the attack on Pearl Harbor and determined to beat back Nazi and Japanese aggression, the American people were far more unified than they had been during World War I. Six million men volunteered for military service between 1942 and 1945 and another 10 million were drafted. Deferments were severely limited, draft evasion relatively rare. The Selective Service System permitted those who opposed war on religious grounds to register as conscientious objectors, a status that permitted them to fulfill their obligation by doing nonmilitary tasks in the Army Medical Corps or by working in civilian hospitals or on selected public works projects.

On the home front, Americans vowed to outproduce their enemies and sacrifice for the "boys" at the front. "Our great strength," said a defense worker from San Diego, "is that we're all in this together."

War Production   FDR named Donald Nelson of Sears, Roebuck to run the newly created War Production Board (WPB). Nelson's main job was to oversee the transformation of American factories—to get companies such as Ford and General Motors to make tanks and warplanes instead of automobiles. To accomplish this, the federal government offered generous incentives. Antitrust laws were suspended so military orders could be filled quickly without competitive bidding. Companies were given low-interest loans to retool and "cost-plus" contracts that guaranteed them a profit. Not surprisingly, the industrial giants made out best. As the war progressed, America's top one hundred companies increased their percentage of the nation's total production from 30 to 70 percent. Ford, for example, began construction of a huge new factory in 1941, named Willow Run, to build B-24 Liberator bombers. In the next four years, it turned out 8,685 airplanes—one every sixty-three minutes.

Between 1940 and 1945, the nation's gross national product doubled, and the federal budget reached $95 billion, a tenfold increase. In the first half of 1942, the government placed more than $100 billion in war orders, requesting more goods than American factories had ever produced in a single year. The list included 60,000 planes, 45,000 tanks, 20,000 antiaircraft guns, and 8 million tons of merchant shipping. The orders for 1943 were even larger. By war's end, military spending exceeded $300 billion.

Roosevelt hoped to finance this effort without dramatically raising the national debt, which meant taxation over borrowing, a policy Congress strongly opposed. The result was a compromise that combined both of these elements. The Revenue Act of 1942 added millions of new taxpayers to the federal rolls and dramatically raised the rates paid by Americans in higher income brackets. Along with increases in corporate and inheritance rates, taxation provided about 45 percent of the war's total cost—less than Roosevelt wanted, but far more than the comparable figures for World War I or the Civil War.

Borrowing accounted for the rest. The national debt reached $260 billion in 1945, six times higher than that in 1941. The government relied on banks and brokerage houses for loans, but common people did their share. "There are millions who ask, 'What can we do to help?' " said Treasury Secretary Henry Morgenthau in 1942. "The reason I want a [war bond campaign] is to give people an opportunity to do something."

Morgenthau sold bonds in inventive ways. Hollywood stars organized "victory tours" through three hundred communities. Hedy Lamarr promised to kiss anyone who bought a $25,000 bond. Carol Lombard died in a plane crash on her way home from a bond rally. Factory workers participated in payroll savings plans by putting a percentage of their earnings into government bonds.

By 1942, the problem was no longer finding enough work for the people; it was finding enough people for the work to be done. Factories stayed open around the clock, providing new opportunities to underemployed groups such as women, blacks, and the elderly. Seventeen million new jobs were created during World War II. Wages and salaries more than doubled, due in large part to the overtime that people put in. Per capita income rose from $373 in 1940 to just over $1,000 by 1945. As a result, the United States experienced a rare but significant redistribution of wealth, with the bottom half of the nation's wage earners gaining a larger share of the pie.

Making Do

Though Americans took home bigger paychecks than ever before, they found less and less to spend them on. In 1942, Congress created the Office of Price Administration (OPA) to ration vital goods, preach self-sacrifice to the public, and control the inflation caused by too much money chasing too few goods. Gas, tires, sugar, coffee, meat, butter, alcohol—all became scarce. Most car owners were issued coupon books limiting them to three gallons of gasoline per week. Pleasure driving virtually ended, causing thousands of restaurants and drive-in businesses to close. As manufacturers cut back on cloth and wool, women's skirts got shorter, two-piece swimsuits (midriff exposed) became the rage, and men's suits no longer had cuffs. Metal buttons, rubber girdles, and leather shoes simply disappeared.

Changes on the home front could be seen through "the prism of baseball," the national game. Many wanted major league baseball suspended during the war, but Roosevelt disagreed, claiming that it united Americans and built up their morale. The 1941 season had been one of the best ever, with Ted Williams batting over 400 and Joe DiMaggio's fifty-six-game hitting streak. The next year was very different indeed. Night games were banned because of air-raid blackouts. Spring training took place in the northern cities, rather than in Florida, to cut back on travel and save fuel. Ballparks held blood drives and bond drives, and soldiers in uniform were admitted free of charge. In 1942, Detroit Tigers slugger Hank Greenberg became the first major leaguer to be drafted into the armed forces. By 1943, most of the stars were gone, replaced by men who were too old or physically unfit for duty, such as Pete Gray, a one-armed outfielder for the St. Louis Browns. In response to public concerns, FBI director J. Edgar Hoover declared that his agents had investigated the new major leaguers and found no draft dodgers among them. But recruiting ball players became so difficult that the St. Louis Cardinals placed an advertisement in *Sporting News*: "We have positions open on our AA, B, and D minor league clubs," it said. "If you believe you can qualify for one of these good baseball jobs, tell us about yourself."

OPPORTUNITY AND DISCRIMINATION

In many respects, World War II produced a social revolution in the United States. The severe labor shortage caused an enormous migration of people from rural areas to cities, from South to North, and especially to the West Coast, where so many war industries were located. With defense factories booming and 15 million people in the armed forces, Americans were forced to reexamine long-held stereotypes about women and minorities in the workplace and on the battlefield. The war provided enormous possibilities for advancement and for change. It also unleashed prejudices that led to the mass detention of American citizens, and others, on largely racial grounds.

Women and the War Effort The war brought new responsibilities and opportunities for American women. During the Depression, for example, women were expected to step aside in the job market to make way for unemployed men. A national poll in 1936 showed an overwhelming percentage of both sexes agreeing that wives with employed husbands should not work. Furthermore, the majority of employed women held poorly paid jobs as clerks and "salesgirls," or as low-end industrial workers in textile and clothing factories.

The war brought instant changes. More than 6 million women took defense jobs, half of whom had not been previously employed. They worked as welders and electricians, on assembly lines and in munitions plants. More than three-quarters of these women were married, and most were over thirty-five years old—a truly remarkable change. Some had husbands in the armed forces. (The standard monthly allotment for a serviceman's family was fifty dollars, less than half the national average.) Young mothers were not expected to work, although a sizable number did. Because the government and private industry provided little child care assistance, absenteeism and job turnover among younger women were extremely high.

The symbol of America's new working woman was **Rosie the Riveter**, memorialized by Norman Rockwell on the cover of the *Saturday Evening Post* with her overalls, her work tools, and her foot planted on a copy of *Mein Kampf*, helping to grind fascism to dust.

> All the day long whether rain or shine—
> She's a part of the assembly line—
> She's making history working for victory—
> Rosie the Riveter.

Rosie was trim and beautiful, signifying that a woman could do a man's job—temporarily—without losing her feminine charm. Advertisers played heavily on this theme. A hand-cream company praised the "flower-like skin of today's American Girl, energetically at work six days a week in a big war plant." A cosmetics ad went even further: "Our lipstick can't win the war, but it symbolizes one of the reasons why we are fighting. . . . the precious right of women to be feminine and lovely."

(Library of Congress)

Women Workers. *The labor shortages of World War II created new employment opportunities for women, most of whom were married and over thirty-five. More than six million women worked in defense industries across the country, including shipyards, munition plants, and aircraft factories.*

Although this work paid well, wage discrimination was rampant in the defense industries, where women earned far less than did men in the same jobs. Employers and labor unions rationalized such inequities by noting that men had seniority, put in more overtime, and did the "skilled" work. In 1945, female factory workers averaged thirty-two dollars per week compared with fifty-five dollars for men.

Women also were told that their work would end with the war's completion, when defense spending dropped and the veterans came home to reclaim their old jobs. Many women welcomed a return to domesticity after four years of struggle, sacrifice, and separation from a husband overseas. But a survey of female defense workers in 1944 showed that most of them—particularly married, middle-aged women—hoped to continue in their jobs.

This was not to be. Although more women than ever before remained in the labor force following World War II, the bulk of them were pushed back into lower-paying "feminized" work. Still, a foundation had been laid. As a riveter from Los Angeles recalled, "Yeah, going to work during the war made me grow up and realize I could do things. . . . It was quite a change."

The "Double V" Campaign   For millions of American blacks, the war against racist Germany and Japan could not be separated from the ongoing struggle to achieve equal rights. The *Pittsburgh Courier*, an influential African American newspaper, demanded a "Double V" campaign from the Negro community: "victory over our enemies at home and victory over our enemies on the battlefields abroad." To the cynical suggestion that minorities secretly wished for an American defeat, black heavyweight champion Joe Louis responded: "America's got lots of problems, but Hitler won't fix them."

One obvious problem was the small number of blacks employed in high-paying factory jobs. "The Negro will be considered only as janitors," stated North American Aviation, one of the nation's leading military contractors. "Regardless of their training as aircraft workers, we will not employ them." In 1941, A. Philip Randolph, president of the Brotherhood of Sleeping Car Porters, an all-Negro labor union, proposed a "March on Washington" to protest job discrimination in the defense industries and segregation of the armed forces. "We loyal Americans," he said, "demand the right to work and fight for our country." Fearing the negative publicity, President Roosevelt convinced the organizers to call off their march in return for an executive order (8802) declaring that "there shall be no discrimination in the employment of workers because of race, creed, or national origin." To facilitate the order, Roosevelt appointed the Fair Employment Practices Committee (FEPC) to "investigate complaints" and "redress grievances." With a tiny budget and no enforcement powers, the FEPC held public hearings, preached equality in the workplace—and was largely ignored.

Still, the desperate need for labor provided new opportunities for minorities. More than a million blacks migrated to the North and West during World War II, taking factory jobs in New York and California, Michigan and Illinois. Most were attracted by the higher wages and the chance to escape stifling oppression; many came from the Deep South, where the invention of the mechanical cotton picker had forced them from the land. The percentage of African Americans in the war industries reached 7.5 percent by 1944—less than their share of the population but a vast improvement over 1941. The work itself was often menial, such as cleaning factory bathrooms and sweeping the floors. Black workers had little access to the skilled, high-paying jobs, because powerful craft unions like the Machinists and the Carpenters remained lily white. But thousands of African Americans took semiskilled positions on the assembly line, which meant higher wages than ever before.

For black working women, the changes were more dramatic. On the eve of World War II, about 70 percent of them labored as servants in private homes. By war's end, that figure had fallen below 50 percent, as 400,000 black females left domestic work for the defense plants. "The war made me live better, it really did," recalled an aircraft worker who moved from rural Texas to Los Angeles. "My sister always said that Hitler was the one that got us out of the white folks' kitchen."

Where racial barriers were crossed, however, violence often followed. In Mobile, Alabama, the promotion of eleven black welders led white shipyard workers to go on a rampage through the African American community, severely beating dozens of residents. In Philadelphia, white transit workers walked off their jobs to protest the elevation of eight blacks to the rank of motorman. Their stoppage brought the city to a halt, effectively closing the vital Philadelphia Navy Yard. Moving quickly, federal officials sent eight thousand fully armed soldiers to run the buses and streetcars, and threatened to fire the strikers and draft them into the armed forces. The walkout collapsed two days later.

The worst racial violence flared in Detroit, the nation's leading war production center. With good jobs available on the assembly lines of Chrysler, General Motors, and Ford, Detroit's area wide labor force grew from 400,000 in 1940 to almost 900,000 by 1943. With the war effort receiving the government's full attention, little thought

African American Nurses in World War II

Thousands of African American women enlisted in the armed forces during World War II. Some joined the newly created Women's Army Corps, taking noncombatant positions as clerks, cooks, and drivers. Others (pictured here) served in the Army and Navy Nurse Corps, helping to evacuate casualties and staffing hospitals throughout the United States, Europe, and the Pacific theater. As with African American men, African American women were forced to serve in racially

(© Bettmann/CORBIS)

segregated units. Indeed, despite a shortage of nurses, the surgeon general issued a directive limiting the service of black nurses to "hospitals or wards devoted exclusively to the treatment of Negro soldiers." As one African American newspaper complained: "There are hundreds of young colored nurses. They are eager to serve in the Army, the Navy, the Marine Corps . . . and [possess] skills acquired through long apprenticeship in recognized hospitals. Given equal opportunity for training, the Negro nurse has no superior in any national or racial group in the world." By 1945, as the demands of war increased, African American nurses often treated wounded soldiers regardless of race.

was given to building new homes, schools, and hospitals. Indeed, state spending for health and education actually declined in Michigan during World War II. Those who arrived in Detroit, mainly poor, rural people of both races, found themselves competing for living space and social services with Detroit's established blue-collar labor force—and with each other. Half of Detroit's wartime black population lived in miserable, substandard housing, often one family to a room, with no indoor toilets or running water. Bulging public schools switched to half-day sessions. Infant mortality rates skyrocketed, and tuberculosis reached epidemic proportions.

In 1942, an angry mob in Detroit kept several black families from moving into a public housing project in a white neighborhood. The following year, a fight between whites and blacks at a municipal park sparked a race riot involving huge mobs with guns, knives, and clubs. Detroit's poorly trained police force, weakened by the departure of its best men to the armed forces, did little to stop the carnage. By the time federal troops established calm in the city, thirty-five people were dead and more than seven hundred wounded. The police shot seventeen "looters" during the riot, all of them black.

Mob violence on the West Coast involved other victims. In California, a hate campaign led by local politicians and the press blamed Mexican Americans for an alleged rise in drugs, crime, and gang warfare. In June 1943, white sailors from surrounding

"Zoot-Suit" Riots. *Police in Los Angeles take a young man to jail during the 1943 "zoot-suit" riots in which hundreds were injured and arrested.*

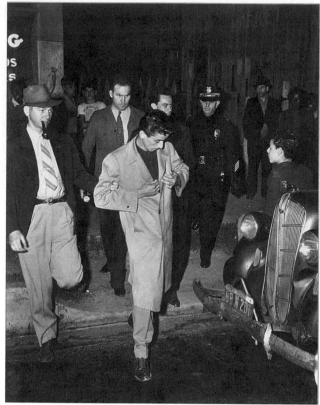

(© Bettmann/CORBIS)

naval bases roamed the Mexican districts of Los Angeles, Long Beach, Pasadena, and other cities looking for "zooters"—young Mexican Americans in ducktail haircuts wearing long jackets with wide pleated pants, pegged at the cuff. Cheered on by white crowds, the sailors became a vigilante mob—stripping the young men of their "zoot suits," cutting their hair, and beating them senseless. "Throughout the night the Mexican communities were in the wildest possible turmoil," wrote a Los Angeles reporter. "Scores of mothers were trying to locate their youngsters and several hundred Mexicans milled around the police substations and the Central jail trying to get word of the missing members of their families."

The zoot suit violence had other roots as well. Unlike the Depression era, when jobs were scarce and Mexicans were deported in large numbers, the United States now needed all the labor it could get. In 1942, the American and Mexican governments agreed to a so-called *bracero* (contract labor) program in which several hundred thousand Mexicans were brought to the United States to plant and harvest crops. In addition, the shortage of factory labor during World War II led to an influx of Hispanic workers in the shipyards and defense plants of southern California. In cities like Los Angeles, where African American and Hispanic workers arrived at a rate of ten thousand per month, crowding and competition bred resentment and fear.

To many residents of southern California, the "zooters" came to represent the Hispanic community as a whole. Rumors flew that Mexican Americans were hindering the war effort by evading the draft. In fact, the reverse was true: Mexican Americans served in numbers far greater than their percentage of the general population—350,000 out of 1.4 million—and seventeen were awarded the Congressional Medal of Honor.

Mexican Americans were integrated in the armed forces during World War II; African Americans were not. All branches except the tiny Coast Guard practiced race discrimination as a matter of course. The marines did not take blacks until 1943, when twenty thousand were recruited to unload supplies and munitions during the amphibious Pacific landings—an extremely hazardous duty that subjected them to withering artillery and sniper fire from dug-in Japanese defenders. The navy segregated blacks by occupation, with most working as food handlers, stevedores, and "mess-boys." In July 1944, a huge explosion at an ammunition depot in Port Chicago, California, killed 250 black sailors from a segregated work unit. When 50 survivors refused an order to return to work, claiming they had been singled out for these dangerous jobs on account of race, they were court-martialed, convicted of mutiny, and sentenced to prison. Following an intense publicity campaign in the Negro press, the black sailors were returned to duty.

More than 500,000 African Americans served in the army, which placed them in segregated divisions that were commanded by white officers. Because most training facilities were located in the Deep South, where the weather was mild and construction costs low, black recruits faced hostile surroundings. Racial clashes at military posts were regularly reported in the Negro press, as were the murders of black soldiers by white mobs in Arkansas, Georgia, Mississippi, and Texas.

Only one black army division saw significant combat—the 92nd Infantry in Italy. When questioned about this, Secretary of War Henry Stimson claimed that "Negroes have been unable to master efficiently the techniques of modern weapons." The truth, however, was that racial prejudice dominated the military chain of command. When given the opportunity, black units performed superbly. The 99th Air Force Fighter squadron, known as the Tuskegee Airmen, earned two Distinguished Unit Citations and shot down a dozen Nazi planes during the Anzio invasion of 1943. Escorting American bombers over Germany in 1944 and 1945, pilots of the 99th compiled a perfect record: not a single bomber under their protection was lost to enemy fire.

Such treatment fueled anger, protest, and pride. The Negro press became more assertive in the drive for equal rights. America's leading black organization, the National Association for the Advancement of Colored People (NAACP), increased its wartime membership from 70,000 to 500,000. In 1942, young activists, black and white, formed the Congress of Racial Equality to challenge segregated restaurants in Washington and Baltimore, chanting, "We die together. Let's eat together." A powerful civil rights movement was slowly taking shape.

Internment of Japanese Americans, 1942–1945   President Roosevelt was determined to avoid a recurrence of the federal repression and vigilante activity that had marred the home front during World War I. Yet the years between 1942 and 1945 witnessed the most glaring denial of civil liberties in American history. The victims included people of Japanese ancestry—citizen and noncitizen alike—living mainly on the West Coast of the United States.

On December 8, 1941, Roosevelt issued a standard executive order requiring enemy aliens to register with local police. Before long, the president lifted the enemy alien designation for Italians and Germans in the United States, but not for the Japanese. The attack on Pearl Harbor, the Bataan Death March, the fall of Hong Kong and Singapore, Wake Island and the Philippines—all sent shock waves across the United States. Although J. Edgar Hoover saw no evidence of a Japanese "threat" to American security, the public thought otherwise. *Time* magazine published an article after Pearl Harbor entitled, "How to Tell Your Friends from the Japs," which included such tips as "Japanese—except for wrestlers—are seldom fat" and "Japanese are likely to be stockier and broader-hipped than Chinese." More ominous were the words of Henry McLemore, a columnist for the *San Francisco Examiner*. "I am for the immediate removal of every Japanese on the West Coast to a point in the interior," he wrote. "Herd 'em up, pack 'em off, and give 'em the inside room in the badlands. . . . Personally, I hate the Japanese. And that goes for all of them."

More than 90 percent of the 125,000 Japanese Americans lived in California, Oregon, and Washington. (Two-thirds were citizens, or **Nisei**, born in the United States; the rest were noncitizens, or Issei, born in Japan and ineligible for naturalization under the Immigration Laws of 1882 and 1924.) Few in number, politically powerless, and less well assimilated than European ethnic groups, the Japanese in America made perfect targets. Military leaders raised the dangers of allowing them to live so close to aircraft plants and naval bases. Patriotic groups linked them to the atrocities committed by the Japanese armed forces eight thousand miles away. Local farmers and fishermen resented the economic success of these hard-working people. All wanted their removal from the West Coast.

President Roosevelt capitulated. In February 1942, he issued Executive Order 9066, giving Secretary of War Stimson the authority to designate military zones inside the United States "from which any or all persons may be excluded." A few days later, the army interpreted that order to include the entire West Coast and all people of Japanese extraction. "A Jap's a Jap," said General John DeWitt, head of the West Coast Defense Command. "It makes no difference whether he is an American citizen or not."

Roosevelt preferred a "voluntary" removal and resettlement to rural parts of the West. The problem, however, was that the Japanese Americans were unlikely to leave their homes and businesses voluntarily, and the western states were unwilling to take them. As the governor of Idaho said, "If you send them here, they'll be hanging from every tree in the state. Why not send them back to Japan? They live like rats, breed like rats, and act like rats."

In March, the president issued Executive Order 9102, establishing the War Relocation Authority. Milton Eisenhower—brother of General Dwight D. Eisenhower—became its director. Japanese internment camps were set up in the deserts of California and Arizona, the mountains of Wyoming, and the scrublands of Utah and Colorado. Japanese Americans on the West Coast were given a few weeks to sell their belongings, get their affairs in order, and report to "processing centers" at converted racetracks, ballparks, and fairgrounds. By June, 120,000 men, women, and children, most of them American citizens, reached the internment camps.

Conditions there were harsh but not brutal. Families lived together in spartan army barracks with little privacy and poor sanitation. Most worked as farm laborers. "All of Manzanar was a stockade, actually—a prison," wrote a young Japanese American

DOING HISTORY ONLINE

Civil Liberties in Wartime

Read the section on internment and refer back to the World War I section on the propaganda war (in Chapter 22). Evaluate the following statement: The federal government restricted civil liberties more during World War II than during World War I.

www.cengage.com/
history/ayers/
ampassages4e

woman of her California camp. "We were in jail. There was barbed wire all around, there were great big watch towers in the corners, and there were spotlights turned on during the night."

The Supreme Court did not intervene. In *Hirabayashi v. United States* (1943) it upheld a curfew ordinance against Japanese Americans in Seattle on the grounds that wartime conditions sometimes justified measures that "place citizens of one ancestry in a different category from others." The Court also ruled (*Korematsu v. United States*, 1944) that the evacuation of Japanese Americans was appropriate, but added (*Endo v. United States*, 1944) that the War Relocation Authority should attempt to separate "loyal" internees from "disloyal" ones, and set the loyal free.

It took almost forty years for a measure of justice to prevail. In 1981, a congressional panel concluded that the internment program had resulted from a combination of race prejudice, war hysteria, and the failure of political leadership. It had nothing to do with "military necessity," as its supporters had claimed. In 1988, Congress awarded each survivor of the internment camps $20,000 in "reparations" for the terrible wrong that had been done.

THE GRAND ALLIANCE

Most Americans saw Japan as the primary villain of World War II. Opinion polls showed the public overwhelmingly in favor of concentrating the war effort in the Pacific against a "barbaric" and "treacherous" foe. Yet President Roosevelt and his military advisers felt otherwise. To their thinking, American power should be directed against the stronger enemy—Germany. Roosevelt viewed the Nazis as the real threat to world peace, and Europe as the key battleground.

North Africa, Stalingrad, and the Second Front, 1942–1943   America's two major allies had conflicting strategies, interests, and concerns. The British did not believe in confronting Hitler with immediate, massive force. They remembered their staggering losses to the Germans during World War I, and they had felt the power of the Nazis at Dunkirk and in the London air raids. The British, moreover, had a far-flung empire to defend. Their strategy was to strike at "the soft underbelly" of the Axis in North Africa and the Mediterranean rather than to confront Hitler directly in France.

The Russians strongly disagreed. Already facing a huge Nazi force deep inside their territory, they wanted the United States and Britain to open a "second front" in western Europe so as to relieve German pressure on them in the east. That meant a major Allied invasion of France. As one American diplomat said of Soviet Foreign Minister V. M. Molotov, "He knows only four words of English—'yes,' 'no' and 'second front.'"

Though America's top military advisers leaned toward the Russian strategy, President Roosevelt favored the British approach. At present, he realized, the United States was unprepared for a full-scale invasion of Europe. But a smaller operation against Nazi forces in North Africa, as the British proposed, had the benefit of getting the United States into the war quickly on the proper scale.

To make this possible, the United States had to gain control of the ocean. In the first three months of 1942, German submarines sank almost 1 million tons of Allied shipping. The so-called wolf packs were so close to American shores that bathers on the New Jersey and Virginia coasts watched in horror as merchant ships were torpedoed. By 1943, however, technological advances in antisubmarine warfare turned the tide. The use of sonar and powerful depth charges made German U-boats more vulnerable underwater, and the development of sophisticated radar allowed American aircraft to spot and destroy them as they surfaced to recharge their batteries. More than 900 of the 1,162 German submarines commissioned during World War II were sunk or captured.

In November 1942, American troops under the command of **General Dwight D. Eisenhower** invaded the French North African colonies of Morocco and Algeria in an operation code-named TORCH. At virtually the same moment, British forces badly mauled General Rommel's army at El Alamein in Egypt, ending Nazi hopes of taking the Suez Canal. Though Hitler rushed reinforcements to North Africa, the Allies prevailed, taking enemy-held territory for the first time in the war.

In North Africa, the Allies fought and defeated twelve Nazi divisions. In the Soviet Union, the Russians were fighting two hundred German divisions along an enormous 2,000-mile front. The pivotal battle occurred at Stalingrad, a vital transportation hub on the Volga River, in the bitter winter of 1942–1943. As the Germans advanced, Stalin ordered his namesake city held at all costs. The fighting was block-to-block, house-to-house, and finally hand-to-hand. Hitler would not let his forces retreat, even after they ran out of fuel and food. Surrounded by Russian forces, overwhelmed by starvation, exposure, and suicide, the German commander surrendered on February 2, 1943.

Stalingrad marked the turning point of the European war. The myth of German invincibility was over. The Russians were advancing steadily in the east, aided by a stream of tanks, planes, food, and clothing from the United States under Lend-Lease. Now Stalin expected an Allied thrust from the west—the long-promised second front.

Churchill had other ideas. At a meeting with Roosevelt in Casablanca, he convinced the president to put off a cross-channel invasion in favor of an assault on Axis troops across the Mediterranean in Italy. Roosevelt attempted to pacify Stalin by promising to open a second front the following year and to accept nothing less than Germany's unconditional surrender. But the Soviets, having sacrificed more troops at Stalingrad than the United States would lose in the entire war, were suspicious and displeased.

The Italian campaign began in the summer of 1943. Sicily fell in a month, and Mussolini along with it. Overthrown by antifascist Italians, the Duce fled to Nazi lines in the north. The battle for Italy was intense. A young American soldier, badly injured in the campaign, wrote to his wife: "So many buddies gone and so many wounded! . . . We walked straight into death, not one man flinched or tried to save himself. I am proud to say, darling, that I was one of those brave [men.]"

The Italian campaign dragged on for almost two years, draining troops and resources for the planned invasion of France. (In April 1945, antifascists captured

Mussolini, killed him, and strung him up by his heels.) Suspicions between Stalin and his wartime allies deepened as Roosevelt and Churchill set the terms of Italy's surrender without consulting the Soviet leader. In addition, postponement of the second front gave Stalin the opportunity to gobble up much of central Europe as his troops pushed toward Germany from the east.

The three Allied leaders met together for the first time in November 1943 at the Tehran Conference in Iran. Roosevelt and Churchill promised to launch their cross-channel invasion the following spring. The future of Germany and need for a United Nations were also discussed. "We are going to get along fine with Stalin and the Russian people," Roosevelt declared.

The Normandy Invasion, June 1944   By 1944, the Allies were in complete control of the skies over western Europe and in command of the seas. Their amphibious landings in North Africa and Italy had provided valuable experience for the job that lay ahead. In April and May, General Eisenhower assembled his huge invasion force in England—3 million men, 2.5 million tons of supplies, and thousands of planes, landing craft, and escort vessels. Meanwhile, Allied aircraft pounded the Atlantic Wall, a line of German fortifications stretching hundreds of miles along the coast of France and the Low Countries.

Despite meticulous preparation, Eisenhower faced enormous risks. The Nazis had fifty-five divisions in France. To keep them dispersed and guessing, Allied intelligence spread false information about the planned invasion sites. The deceptions worked: Hitler and his generals put their strongest defense at Pas de Calais, the English Channel's narrowest point.

The massive D-Day invasion—**Operation OVERLORD**—began on the morning of June 6, 1944. Eisenhower's biggest worry was the weather. A channel storm had postponed one attempt, and another storm was predicted. Before the men left, he told them: "You are about to embark upon the Great Crusade, toward which we have striven these many months. The eyes of the world are upon you."

The invasion succeeded. With overwhelming air cover, Allied forces assaulted Normandy and dropped paratroopers behind enemy lines. The heaviest fighting took place at Omaha Beach, where U.S. Rangers scaled sheer cliffs under withering fire to silence Nazi gunners. By nightfall, 150,000 men were ashore.

Others quickly followed. Within two months, more than a million Allied troops were in France—liberating Paris in August and reaching the German border by September. With the Soviets pressing from the east, a Nazi surrender seemed only weeks away. But the Germans counterattacked in December 1944, taking British and American forces by surprise. The Battle of the Bulge was Hitler's last gasp—a failed attempt to crack Allied morale. U.S. troops took heavy casualties but stood firm. Germany lost 100,000 men and the will to fight on. Hitler committed suicide in his Berlin bunker on April 30, 1945, with Russian soldiers a few miles away. Germany surrendered a week later. The Thousand-Year Reich had lasted a dozen murderous years.

Facing the Holocaust   In the spring of 1945, Allied troops liberated the Nazi concentration camps in Poland and Germany. Ghastly pictures of starving survivors and rotting corpses flashed around the world, recording the almost inconceivable horror in which 6 million European Jews and

MAP 26.1 The War in Europe.

The U.S. military effort against German and Italian forces in World War II began in North Africa, moved to Italy, and culminated in the D-Day invasion of France in 1944. With the aid of England and other nations, the Allied forces reached Germany from the west in 1945. Meanwhile, following a tenacious defense of their homeland, Russian troops pushed deep into Germany from the east, destroying the bulk of Nazi fighting forces and playing a key role in the German surrender.

4 million others (including Poles, gypsies, homosexuals, and political dissidents) were exterminated during World War II.

To American leaders, these photos of the Holocaust produced shock but hardly surprise. Evidence of the death camps had reached the United States in 1942, yet the government had paid scant attention to the consequences. The State Department, well known for its anti-Semitism in that era, made it virtually impossible for refugees fleeing the Nazis to enter the United States. An applicant for a wartime visa had to provide the names of two American sponsors before submitting six copies of a form that measured four feet in length. As a result, only 10 percent of America's immigration quotas were met during World War II, leaving almost 200,000 slots unfilled.

President Roosevelt did not seriously intervene. Consumed by the responsibilities of leading his nation in a global war, he insisted that the best way to aid the victims of nazism was to defeat Hitler's armies as quickly as possible. His only acknowledgment of the impending disaster came in 1944, when he created the War Refugee Board, which helped finance the activities of Raoul Wallenberg, the courageous Swedish diplomat who prevented thousands of Hungarian Jews from being deported to the death camps. Had it been formed earlier and supported more firmly by the White House, the War Refugee Board might have played a major role in saving innocent lives.

The United States had other options as well. Its bombers could have attacked the rail lines leading to the death camps, as well as the gas chambers and crematoria that lay inside. The War Department avoided these targets, claiming they were too dangerous and too far away. This clearly was not true. In 1944, Allied bombers flew hundreds of missions within a thirty-five-mile radius of Auschwitz.

When liberation came to the concentration camps, the vast majority of prisoners were dead. One survivor at Dachau recalled the very moment the American troops arrived. "We were free. We broke into weeping, kissed the tank. A Negro soldier gave us a tin of meat, bread, and chocolate. We sat down on the ground and ate up all the food together. The Negro watched us, tears in his eyes."

THE PACIFIC WAR, 1942–1945

Shortly after the attack on Pearl Harbor, Admiral Isoroku Yamamoto, Japan's leading naval strategist, issued a stern private warning. "In the first six months to a year of war against the U.S. and England," he said, "I will run wild and I will show you an uninterrupted succession of victories: I must tell you that, should the war be prolonged for two or three years, I have no confidence in our ultimate victory." Yamamoto understood America's overwhelming advantage in population and productivity. What he doubted was the will of its people to fight—and win—a long, bloody struggle.

The war against Japan would be fought differently from the war against Germany. In the Pacific, the United States would do the great bulk of the Allied fighting; in Europe, that burden was shared by others, including Great Britain, and, most important, the Soviet Union. In Europe, armor and artillery were essential to the Allied victory; in the Pacific, it would be aircraft carriers and submarines. By war's end, the United States would lose 128 combatant vessels to Japanese warships and aircraft but only 29 to German fire. The Japanese surrender in 1945 would end the largest naval war in history.

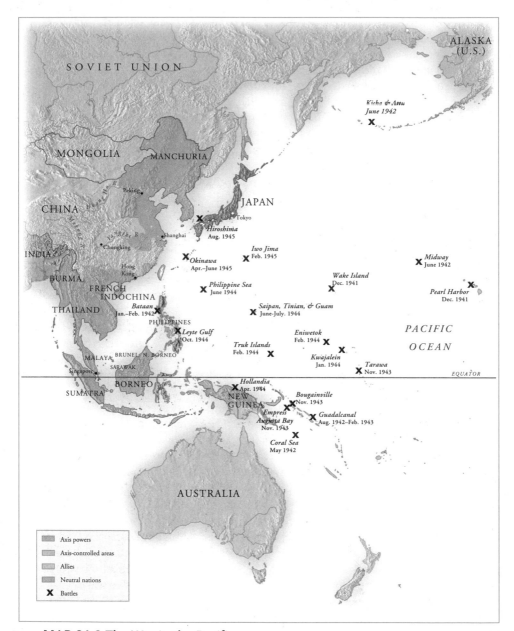

MAP 26.2 The War in the Pacific.

Following Pearl Harbor, the Japanese attempted to set up an impregnable defense line across the Pacific. But the stunning American naval victory at Midway Island in 1942 allowed U.S. forces to move west toward Japan, successfully clearing Japanese-held islands in brutal combat. By 1944, the American bombing campaign against Japan itself was fully underway. The dropping of two atomic bombs in August 1945 helped bring the war to a close.

Turning the Tide, May–June 1942   The Japanese hoped to create an impregnable defense line in the Pacific. Their strategy included new conquests, such as Australia, and a naval thrust against the U.S. carrier fleet. Yet two key engagements in the spring of 1942 shattered Yamamoto's illusion about American will power and naval strength. On May 7, a task force led by two American carriers—the *Lexington* and *Yorktown*—held its own against a larger Japanese force at the Battle of the Coral Sea, just north of Australia. Though the "Lady Lex" was sunk, heavy Japanese losses saved Australia from invasion or certain blockade.

A month later, the two sides clashed again. Admiral Yamamoto brought a huge fleet to **Midway Island**, a thousand miles west of Hawaii, to flush out and destroy the American carrier fleet. But the U.S. Navy, having broken the Japanese military code, was well aware of his intentions. In a three-day battle, brilliantly commanded by Rear Admiral Raymond A. Spruance, the Americans sank four Japanese carriers (losing the *Yorktown*) and shot down 320 planes. Japan would never fully recover from this beating.

Closing in on Japan   After Midway, the United States followed a two-pronged plan of attack. Admiral Chester Nimitz was to move west from Hawaii toward Formosa, while General Douglas MacArthur was to come north from Australia toward the Philippines, with their forces combining for an eventual assault on Japan. The Pacific theater would see no massed land battles like Stalingrad or the Bulge. The fighting would be sporadic but brutal, involving air attacks, naval duels, and amphibious landings by U.S. Marines on selected Japanese-held islands. It would be "a war without mercy," with bitter racial hatreds on both sides.

The first American offensive occurred at Guadalcanal, a small tropical island in the Solomons, off New Guinea, in August 1942. For six months, American marines waged a desperate campaign in swamps and jungles, battling intense heat, malaria, dysentery, infection, and leeches, as well as the Japanese. When the island was finally secured in February 1943, General MacArthur began a "leapfrog" campaign across New Guinea to the Philippines, attacking some islands while bypassing others. By 1944, Manila was in his sights.

In the central Pacific, Admiral Nimitz was moving west, ever closer to Japan. In November 1943, the marines assaulted Tarawa, a tiny strip of beach in the Gilbert Islands, incurring three thousand casualties in a successful three-day assault. Next came the Marshall Islands; the Marianas—Guam, Tinian, and Saipan—followed. Control of the Marianas, only twelve hundred miles from Tokyo, placed major Japanese cities within range of America's new B-29 bombers. The battle for Saipan raged through June and July 1944. The Japanese defenders fought, quite literally, to the last man. Worse, thousands of Japanese civilians on the island committed suicide—a preview, some believed, of what lay ahead in Japan.

The end seemed near. In October 1944, MacArthur returned to the Philippines in triumph, while an American naval force destroyed four Japanese carriers at the Battle of Leyte Gulf, outside Manila. To the north, American troops took the island of Iwo Jima in brutal combat and then attacked Okinawa, less than four hundred miles from Japan. Admiral Nimitz assembled a huge force for the invasion—180,000 troops, most of his carriers, and eighteen battleships. The Japanese had an army of 110,000 on Okinawa, the final barrier to the homeland itself.

Flag Raising at Iwo Jima

No other image from World War II remains as meaningful to Americans as Joe Rosenthal's Pulitzer Prize~–winning photograph of the "Flag Raising at Iwo Jima," an enduring symbol of courage and victory that would be memorialized in James Bradley's best-selling book, *Flags of Our Fathers*.

Of the six marines who planted Old Glory on that barren hilltop in February 1945, three would soon be killed; among the survivors was Ira Hayes, a Native American from the Pima Reservation in Arizona. So riveting was this photo that

(Library of Congress)

Hayes was ordered back to the United States, where he toured the country in a series of war bond rallies, embarrassed by the attention and longing to return to his platoon.

More than forty thousand Native Americans served in the armed forces during World War II, the first conflict in which they were eligible for the draft. Conscription went smoothly on most reservations, and enlistment rates, driven by poverty as well as patriotism, were extremely high. Unlike African Americans, who were forced into segregated units, Native Americans fought alongside whites in all branches of the armed services. Proud of their reputation as warriors, Native Americans also played a role in gathering intelligence behind enemy lines. Navajo Code Talkers transmitted vital information in their native tongue, a code the Japanese couldn't break. By 1945, more than a third of all Native Americans between the ages of eighteen and fifty had left Indian land permanently for the armed forces and war-related jobs.

Ira Hayes returned to the Pima Reservation. Forgotten now, haunted by painful memories, without a job or an education, he fell into a life of alcoholism and despair. In 1954, he froze to death in an irrigation ditch, at the age of thirty-three. He was buried at Arlington National Cemetery with full military honors.

The battle took three months, from April through June 1945. Waves of Japanese kamikaze (suicide) planes attacked the Allied fleet, inflicting terrible damage. American troops suffered a casualty rate of 35 percent, the highest of the war. Seven thousand were killed on land and five thousand at sea, and forty thousand were wounded. The Japanese lost fifteen hundred kamikazes and virtually all of their soldiers. These appalling losses would be a factor in America's decision to use atomic weapons against Japan.

A CHANGE IN LEADERSHIP, 1944–1945

In November 1944, the American people reelected Franklin Roosevelt to an unprecedented fourth presidential term. Roosevelt defeated Republican Thomas Dewey, the moderate forty-two-year-old governor of New York. The president's handling of the war was not an issue in the campaign. Dewey hammered away at problems on the home front, such as food shortages, gas rationing, squalid housing for war workers, and government "red tape." Roosevelt campaigned as the war leader, urging voters "not to change horses in midstream." To bolster his chances, Democratic Party leaders removed the increasingly unpopular Vice President Henry Wallace from the ticket and replaced him with **Senator Harry S Truman** of Missouri.

The Yalta Accords   When Truman visited the White House to plan campaign strategy with Roosevelt, he was appalled by the president's feeble condition. In February 1945, with Germany near collapse, an exhausted FDR met with Churchill and Stalin at Yalta, in southern Russia, to lay the groundwork for peace and order in the postwar world. On several issues, agreement came easily. The Russians promised to enter the Pacific war after Germany's defeat in return for territorial concessions in the Far East. The three leaders also blessed the formation of a new international body, to be known as the United Nations.

But agreement on the larger issues proved elusive. The Soviet Union had suffered staggering losses at German hands. At least 20 million Russians were dead or wounded; thousands of towns, factories, and collective farms had been destroyed. From Stalin's perspective, the Soviets deserved more than simple gratitude for their role in defeating the great bulk of Hitler's army. They needed the means to rebuild their nation and protect it from further attacks.

Stalin hoped to ensure Soviet security through the permanent partition of Germany. And he demanded huge reparations from the Germans—at least $20 billion—with Russia getting half. Furthermore, Stalin had no intention of removing Soviet troops from the lands they now controlled in eastern Europe. In both world wars, Germany had marched directly through Poland to devastate the Russian heartland. Stalin would not let this happen again.

Roosevelt and Churchill had other ideas. Both men viewed a healthy, "de-Nazified" Germany as essential to the reconstruction of postwar Europe, and both feared the expansion of Soviet power into the vacuum created by Hitler's defeat. The British also claimed a moral stake in Poland, having declared war on Germany in 1939 to help defend the Poles from the Nazi assault. To desert them now—to permit a victorious Stalin to replace a defeated Hitler—smacked of the very appeasement that had doomed Allied policy a decade before. Few believed that the Polish people would pick Stalin or communism if given a free choice.

The **Yalta Accords** created a legacy of mistrust. The parties agreed to split Germany into four "zones of occupation"—American, Russian, British, and French. Berlin, deep inside the Soviet zone, also was divided among the Allies. Yet the vital issue of reparations was postponed, as were plans for Germany's eventual reunification. At Roosevelt's urging, Stalin accepted a "Declaration for a Liberated Europe" that promised "free and unfettered elections" in Poland and elsewhere at some unspecified date. But these words did not mean the same thing in Moscow as in the West. An American adviser accurately described the agreement as "so elastic that [Stalin] can stretch it all the way from Yalta to Washington without ever technically breaking it."

In the weeks following Yalta, Roosevelt's optimism about Soviet–American relations seemed to fade. Pledges of free elections in Europe were ignored. The Yalta Accords did not prevent Stalin from ordering the murder of political dissidents in Romania and Bulgaria and the arrest of anticommunist leaders in Poland. His ruthlessness seemed to highlight the unpleasant truth that America had little or no influence in the nations now occupied by Soviet troops. "We can't do business with Stalin," FDR complained privately. "He has broken every one of the promises he made at Yalta."

Truman in Charge   On April 12, 1945—less than two months into his fourth term—FDR died of a massive stroke at his vacation retreat in Warm Springs, Georgia. The nation was shocked. Roosevelt had been president for twelve years, leading the people through the Great Depression and World War II. "He was the one American who knew, or seemed to know, where the world was going," wrote *Life* magazine. "The plans were all in his head."

The new president was largely unknown. Born on a Missouri farm in 1884, Harry Truman had served as an artillery officer in World War I before jumping into local politics in Kansas City. Elected to public office in the 1920s with the aid of Tom Pendergast, a crooked Democratic boss, Truman walked a fine line between efficient service to his constituents and partisan loyalty to a corrupt political machine. Fair and honest himself, Truman went about the business of building better roads and improving public services while ignoring the squalor of those who put him in office.

Working for the Pendergast machine got Truman elected to the U.S. Senate in 1934. Still, the label of "machine politician" would plague him for years. It was hard to earn respect as a legislator when the newspapers kept referring to him as "the senator from Pendergast."

Truman did not inspire immediate confidence in his ability to fill Roosevelt's giant shoes. Small in stature, with thick glasses and a high-pitched midwestern twang, he seemed thoroughly ordinary to all but those who knew him best. As vice president, he was largely excluded from the major discussions relating to foreign policy and the war. After taking the presidential oath of office, Truman turned to reporters and said, "Boys, if you ever pray, pray for me now."

As expected, Truman received conflicting advice. A number of FDR's confidants, including Henry Wallace, urged him to keep the wartime alliance alive by accommodating Russia's economic needs and security demands. But others, such as Averell Harriman, U.S. ambassador to the Soviet Union, prodded Truman to demand Russia's strict compliance with the Yalta Accords. The new president did not want a confrontation with Stalin. He still hoped for Soviet help in ending the Pacific war and building a lasting peace. Yet the more Truman learned about events in Poland and eastern Europe, the angrier he became. Ten days after taking office, he confronted Soviet Foreign Minister V. M. Molotov at the White House, claiming that Russia had ignored the Yalta Accords and warning him that economic aid to Russia would never get through Congress so long as this attitude persisted. When Truman finished, Molotov told him, "I've never been talked to like that in my life." "Carry out your agreements," Truman shot back, "and you won't get talked to like that."

In July 1945, Truman left the United States aboard the USS *Augusta* for his first face-to-face meeting with Stalin and Churchill at Potsdam, near Berlin. The three leaders agreed on a number of important issues, including the terms of peace for defeated Germany and public trials for Nazi war criminals. "I can deal with Stalin," Truman wrote in his diary. "He is honest—but smart as hell."

His optimism didn't last long. The conference was halted for several days by the stunning defeat of Winston Churchill's Conservative Party in the British parliamentary elections. Churchill returned to England, replaced by the new Labour prime minister, Clement Attlee. When the talks resumed, Stalin brushed aside Truman's concerns about Poland and eastern Europe, and Truman rebuffed Stalin's attempt to claim reparations from the western zones of occupation in Germany. The conference ended on a chilly note. There seemed little doubt that Russia would remain in the lands it now controlled, and that Germany would remain divided for some time to come.

The Atomic Bombs, August 1945   One of Truman's first decisions concerned the use of atomic weapons. As the United States took control of the island chains east of Japan in 1944, a ferocious bombing campaign of the Japanese home islands took place. In March 1945, three hundred American B-29s led by Major General Curtis LeMay firebombed Tokyo, killing 100,000 people, leaving 1 million homeless and destroying much of the city. These raids were particularly devastating because Japan had few planes left to defend its densely populated areas. In the following months, conventional (nonatomic) bombings pounded Japan's major cities.

Shortly after taking office, President Truman was told about the atomic bomb by Secretary of War Stimson, who called it "the most terrible weapon ever known in human history." The decision to build this bomb had been made by President Roosevelt in response to reports from refugee scientists, such as Germany's Albert Einstein, that the Nazis were already at work on one. The American effort, known as the Manhattan Project, included top-secret facilities in Hanford, Washington; Oak Ridge, Tennessee; and Los Alamos, New Mexico, to design and construct this bomb, and produce the fissionable material for an atomic explosion.

At President Truman's direction, an Interim Committee was formed to advise him about the bomb. Chaired by Henry Stimson, the committee recommended the use of atomic weapons against Japan, without warning, as soon as they became available. Another group, the Target Committee, chose four major cities—Hiroshima, Kokura,

Niigata, and Nagasaki—based on their strategic importance and the fact that each of them, unlike Tokyo, was untouched by war. On July 16, 1945, the atomic bomb was successfully tested near Alamogordo, New Mexico. The explosion, equivalent to fifteen thousand tons of dynamite, was visible two hundred miles away. Truman learned of the test while attending the Allied Summit meeting in Potsdam. He immediately issued a public ultimatum to the Japanese, calling on them to surrender unconditionally or face "prompt and utter destruction."

A number of top scientists on the Manhattan Project objected. Having urged one president to build the atomic bomb to counter Germany, they now found themselves begging another president not to use it against Japan. These scientists were joined by other civilian and military officials, who argued that Japan already was close to surrender and that use of the bomb would trigger a dangerous arms race with the Russians.

But Truman held firm, believing that the bomb would save American and Japanese lives by ending the war quickly. On the morning of August 6, 1945, a B-29 named **Enola Gay** dropped an atomic bomb over Hiroshima, incinerating the industrial city and killing at least 100,000 people. (Thousands more would die of radiation effects, a problem poorly understood by scientists at that time.) Three days later, a B-29 named *Bock's Car* dropped a second atomic bomb on Nagasaki, with much the same effect. On August 14, the Japanese asked for peace.

Though Americans overwhelmingly supported these bombings, the decision remains controversial to this day. Some believe that Truman dropped the bomb to scare the Russians in Europe and keep them out of the Asian war. Others think the decision was based on racism and revenge. Still others argue that the United States should have made it clear to the Japanese that the terms of "unconditional surrender" did not mean that their emperor would have to be removed. For all the controversy, however, one inescapable fact remains: Japanese leaders could not bring themselves to surrender until two atomic bombs had been dropped.

World War II formally ended on September 2, 1945, when the Japanese signed the document of surrender aboard the battleship *Missouri* in Tokyo Bay. More than 25 million soldiers and civilians died in the struggle (see Table 26.1). Speaking from

TABLE 26.1 World War II Casualties

Country	Battle Deaths	Wounded
U.S.S.R.	6,115,000	14,012,000
Germany	3,250,000	7,250,000
China	1,324,516	1,762,006
Japan	1,270,000	140,000
Poland	664,000	530,000
United Kingdom	357,116	369,267
United States	291,557	670,846
France	201,568	400,000
Italy	149,496	66,716

Source: Information Please Almanac (Boston: Houghton Mifflin Co., 1988).

the deck of the Missouri that day, General MacArthur issued a warning for the new atomic age. "We have had our last chance," he said. "If we do not devise some greater and more equitable system, Armageddon will be at our door."

CONCLUSION

In many ways, World War II was to Americans of the mid-twentieth century what the Civil War had been to Americans of the mid-nineteenth century: a watershed event, defining the course of history for generations to come. When the war erupted in Europe in 1939, there seemed little chance that the United States would become involved. Bitter memories of World War I and its aftermath still prevailed. More concerned by the lingering effects of the Great Depression than by the growing menace posed by Germany, Italy, and Japan, the American people seemed relieved by President Roosevelt's campaign pledge in 1940 that "your boys are not going to be sent into any foreign war."

When war did come with the Japanese bombing of Pearl Harbor, the nation quickly came together. The United States had been attacked, and virtually everyone understood the evil of the enemies the country now faced. The war shattered the illusion that Americans could remain separate from the world's problems. In leading the Grand Alliance against Axis aggression, the United States took on the full responsibilities of a global power. In doing so, it served notice that America's influence on world affairs would be substantial in the postwar era, whether in containing the spread of communism, constructing a nuclear arsenal, spending billions in foreign aid, or rebuilding the battered economies of Western Europe and Japan. The days of isolationism were gone for good.

World War II had an equally profound impact on domestic affairs. It ended the Great Depression, created full employment, and increased mean family income an astonishing 25 percent. It demonstrated the ability of an ethnically diverse nation to unite in a just cause, though racial segregation remained in place and basic civil liberties, in the case of Japanese Americans, were tragically denied. And it opened new opportunities for women and minorities in the workplace, although full economic and political equality in the United States remained a dream unfulfilled. In 1945 Americans looked to the future with cautious optimism—proud of their accomplishments and yearning for better times.

CHAPTER REVIEW, 1939–1945

- Nazi Germany invaded Poland on September 1, 1939, unleashing World War II.
- Roosevelt won an unprecedented third term in 1940 by vowing to keep the country out of war.
- The Japanese attack on Pearl Harbor plunged the nation into World War II.
- Heavy war production brought the Great Depression to an end.
- Married women joined the labor force in record numbers, taking jobs normally reserved for men.

- Allied forces in the North Atlantic Theater stormed the beaches of France in 1944, following heavy fighting in North Africa and in Italy.
- Roosevelt, Stalin, and Churchill met at Yalta in 1945 to map strategy for the postwar world.
- Vice President Harry S Truman became president following the death of FDR in April 1945.
- Germany surrendered a month later, following the suicide of Adolf Hitler and the Allied assault on Berlin.
- Japan surrendered in August 1945, following the dropping of two atomic bombs.

◀◀◀ *Looking Back*

Chapter 26 examines both the way in which the United States fought World War II and the great changes that occurred in domestic and international affairs.

1. How did America mobilize for war? What changes took place on the home front that aided the war production?
2. How lasting and substantial were the gains made by women and minorities during the war?
3. How well did the Grand Alliance work, what strategies were employed to keep it together, and what problems arose regarding the interests of the different parties?

Looking Ahead ▶▶▶

Chapter 27 looks at American society following World War II, tracing the impact of the war on foreign and domestic affairs, from the Cold War to the baby boom to the growth of suburbia.

1. What decisions were made, or avoided, during World War II that had a direct impact on the diplomatic problems facing the United States and the Soviet Union in the coming years?
2. How difficult would it be for America's 15 million veterans to readjust to civilian life following the war?
3. Would the tremendous wartime prosperity in the United States be maintained once the conflict was over?

Go to the American Passages website at www.cengage.com/history/ayers/ampassages4e for additional review materials.

Postwar America, 1946–1952

Henry R. Luce was a man of grand visions and powerful views. One rival dubbed him "Lord of the Press" because his publishing empire included *Time, Life,* and *Fortune,* among other mass circulation magazines. In February 1941, Luce composed an editorial prodding the American people to accept their new role as citizens of "the strongest and most vital nation in the world." The time had come, he insisted, to exert "the full measure of our influence, for such purposes as we see fit" in the dawning "American Century."

The belief in America's destiny was as old as the country itself. Yet the challenges of World War II had turned this rhetoric into reality by placing the United States at the very center of the international stage. Old empires lay in ruins; an atomic era had begun. Only the United States seemed to possess the combination of military strength, economic resources, and political stability to rebuild a world battered by war.

RECONVERSION, 1946

The United States faced two major problems following World War II. The first concerned relations with the Soviet Union. Would the two nations be able to maintain the Grand Alliance, or would their obvious differences about the shape and direction of postwar Europe degenerate into conflict, and possibly war? The second problem related to the domestic economy. Many Americans feared that the Great Depression might return after World War II as defense spending dropped and factory jobs disappeared. In the months following Japan's surrender, the federal government cancelled more than $30 billion in military contracts, forcing 800,000 layoffs in the aircraft industry alone. Could the United States handle the difficult reconversion from a wartime to a peacetime economy? Or would it slip back into the dark days of joblessness, poverty, and despair?

The Veterans Return President Truman's first job was to bring the soldiers home. Twelve million Americans were still in uniform in 1945, most of them young men, ages eighteen to thirty-four, who had experienced the dual hardships of economic depression and war. Their dream was to return home quickly and get on with their lives. One soldier put his feelings in a poem:

> Please Mr. Truman, won't you send us home?
> We have captured Napoli and liberated Rome.
> We have licked the master race.
> Now there's lots of shipping space.
> So, won't you send us home.

This pressure brought results. Within a year, the number of men and women in the armed forces had dropped to 3 million, despite the growing Soviet threat.

For many GIs, these were anxious, difficult times. The divorce rate shot up dramatically in 1945, reflecting the tensions of readjustment to civilian life. A major housing shortage, brought on by the absence of home building during World War II, made things even worse. Washington, D.C., reported 25,000 homeless veterans, Chicago more than 100,000. North Dakota veterans took to living in converted grain bins. One serviceman complained: "You fight a damn war and you finally come home and everybody slaps you on the back and tells you what a wonderful job you did . . . but when it comes to really doing something, then nobody's home."

In fact, assistance for returning veterans had received careful attention from the wartime Congress, which passed the popular Servicemen's Readjustment Act in 1944. Known as the GI Bill, it provided almost $20 billion for various programs in the decade following World War II. The social and economic effects of this legislation were enormous. The GI Bill fueled a nationwide construction boom by providing long-term, low-interest mortgages to veterans, plus a two thousand dollar bonus toward the purchase of a new home. Furthermore, it allowed former soldiers to fulfill the dream of a college degree, thereby expanding the system of higher education as never before. In 1947, for example, more than half of the thirty thousand students at the University of Minnesota were veterans of World War II. Older, more serious, and determined to make up for lost time, they formed the nucleus of America's expanding white-collar workforce in the prosperous years ahead.

(Library of Congress)

Veterans Attending College. *The GI Bill of 1944 expanded and democratized higher education as never before.*

This icon will direct you to interactive activities and study materials on the American Passages website: www.cengage.com/history/ayers/ampassages4e

CHAPTER TIMELINE

1946	Dr. Spock publishes *Common Sense Book of Baby and Child Care* • Republicans capture both houses of Congress
1947	Truman Doctrine is unveiled • Marshall Plan is implemented • Jackie Robinson breaks baseball's color line
1948	Harry Truman upsets Thomas Dewey in tight presidential race • Whittaker Chambers confronts Alger Hiss
1949	Soviet Union successfully tests an atomic bomb • China falls to the Communists
1950	Senator Joe McCarthy charges that Communists have penetrated the State Department • Korean War begins
1951	General Douglas MacArthur is relieved of his command in Korea
1952	Richard Nixon delivers dramatic Checkers speech • Dwight Eisenhower is elected president

Lurching Toward Prosperity

The fear of another economic depression in the United States did not last long. The increase in federal spending for veterans helped to offset the decrease in defense spending. And a surge of consumer demand held out the promise of prosperity based on peace. For the past five years, Americans had worked overtime in offices and factories, banking their paychecks, buying savings bonds, and dreaming of the day when cars, appliances, prime beef, and nylon stockings would reappear in the nation's stores and showrooms. Between Pearl Harbor and the Japanese surrender, the public had accumulated an astonishing $140 billion in savings and liquid securities, and the average weekly wage had almost doubled, from $24.20 to $44.30. "I'm tired of ration books and empty shelves," said one factory worker. "I'm ready to spend."

But factories could not change from fighter planes to automobiles overnight. Reconversion took time. With the demand for consumer goods far outpacing the supply, President Truman hoped to keep inflation in line by extending wartime price controls. His plan met strong opposition from the business community, which lobbied hard to "strike the shackles from American free enterprise." In June 1946, controls were lifted and prices shot up. The cost of meat doubled in two weeks, leading the *New York Daily News* to quip:

PRICES SOAR, BUYERS SORE
STEERS JUMP OVER THE MOON

Not surprisingly, the labor movement took a militant stance. Since higher prices meant a drop in real wages, the United Automobile Workers (UAW) demanded an average pay hike of 33 cents an hour from General Motors in 1946, from $1.12 to $1.45. When the corporation offered a 10-cent hourly raise, the union struck for 113 days, eventually settling for 18 cents. Shortly after, the UAW and the auto companies agreed to a cost-of-living adjustment (COLA) clause in future contracts.

The country was soon plagued by a wave of strikes. When two railroad brotherhoods threatened a work stoppage designed to shut down the country's rail service, President Truman signed an executive order seizing the railroads. "If you think I'm going to sit here and let you tie up this whole country," he told union leaders, "you're crazy as hell." A few weeks later, the United Mine Workers (UMW) went on strike, forcing power stations and factories to close for lack of fuel.

In response, President Truman went on the radio to demand that the miners return to work at once. They did, coaxed along by a federal court injunction that led to $3.5 million in damages against the UMW. For Truman, these victories came at a heavy cost. Not only did he offend large parts of the labor movement, he also appeared incapable of governing a nation wracked by consumer shortages, labor strife, soaring inflation, and an approaching cold war.

In November 1946, the Democratic Party suffered a crushing defeat at the polls. Campaigning against the ills of reconversion ("Had Enough?") and the president's alleged incompetence ("To Err Is Truman"), the Republicans gained control of the Senate and the House for the first time since 1928. When the Truman family returned to Washington from a campaign trip on election eve, no one showed up to greet them. The train station was deserted. "Don't worry about me," the president told his daughter, Margaret. "I know how things will turn out and they'll be all right."

AFFLUENCE AND ANXIETY

The pain and sacrifice of the Great Depression and World War II led most Americans to yearn for both emotional security and material success. As expected, the family grew in importance, providing a sense of comfort and stability to people after years of separation and loss. Along with the focus on families came a changing middle-class culture, based on suburban living, a **baby boom**, an emphasis on more traditional sex roles, and an explosion of consumer goods. In the coming years, the nation's unprecedented prosperity would be measured by the increased size and abundant possessions of its thriving middle class.

The Postwar American Family
One of the songs made popular by returning American veterans was titled, "I've Got to Make Up for Lost Time." Beginning in 1946, the United States experienced a surge in marriage rates and birthrates, following record lows in the Depression decade. The young adults (ages eighteen to thirty) of this era became the most "marrying" generation in American history, with 97 percent of the women and 94 percent of the men taking marriage vows. By 1950, the age of marriage for American women had dropped below twenty, another record, and the percentage of divorces, initially high among returning veterans, reached an all-time low.

The baby boom was equally dramatic. The number of children per family in the United States jumped from 2.6 in 1940 to 3.2 by decade's end. Birthrates doubled for a third child and tripled for a fourth, as the American population grew by 20 million in the 1940s. At a time when access to birth control information was rapidly increasing, U.S. population growth rivaled not England's but rather India's.

These spiraling marriage and birthrates went hand in hand with a shift back to more traditional sex roles following World War II. Actress Ann Sothern exemplified the reordering of domestic priorities when she advised women, shortly before Japan's surrender, to begin "planning our house—our perfect house" and to think about the nursery. "I know a lot of men are dreaming of coming back not only to those girls who

A Medical Miracle

Medical research in post–World War II America moved at a dramatic pace. Life expectancy had climbed from forty-nine years in 1900 to sixty-eight years by 1950. There were several reasons for this, including a healthier diet, cleaner food and water, and stricter personal hygiene. But much of it owed to the marketing of "wonder drugs" capable of obliterating a wide range of bacteria without poisoning the human body. In 1941, two British scientists, Howard Florey and Ernst Boris Chain, refined Alexander Fleming's previous discovery of penicillin by purifying the compound and then encouraging drug companies in the United States and England to mass-produce it for public use. Penicillin became the first true antibiotic; hailed as "the most glamorous drug ever invented," it treated everything from deadly pneumonia to the common sore throat, saving millions of lives.

No medical problem seemed beyond the scope of the laboratory anymore. Indeed, researchers now appeared within sight of a most improbable goal: a planet free of deadly infectious disease. "Will such a world exist?" a scientist asked. "We believe so." In our current world of AIDS, Ebola virus, and avian influenza, one marvels at the arrogance of these words. Infectious disease remains a remarkably adaptive foe. For medical researchers, the battle goes on.

waved goodbye to them," she added. "They are dreaming of coming back to the mothers of their children and the least we can do as women is to try to live up to some of these expectations." Indeed, one of the most popular wartime advertisements showed a mother in overalls about to leave for the factory. She is at the door when her little daughter asks: "Mother, when will you stay home again?" And she responds: "Some jubilant day, mother will stay home again doing the job she likes—making a home for you and daddy when he gets back."

Quite naturally, this emphasis on family life strengthened long-held prejudices against married women holding full-time jobs outside the home. As a result, the gains made in female employment during World War II largely disappeared. Returning veterans reclaimed millions of factory jobs held by women and minorities. The female labor force dropped from a wartime high of 19 million in 1945 to less than 17 million by 1947. On the Ford and General Motors assembly lines, the percentage of women plummeted from 25 to 6 percent. Although many women gladly returned to their former domestic lives, the vast majority, according to postwar surveys, hoped to keep their jobs. "I'd stay if they wanted me to," said a female aircraft worker, "but without taking a man's place from him."

The social pressures on women were enormous. A host of "experts" asserted that women belonged in the home for their own good as well as the good of society—that women needed to be housewives and mothers in order to be fulfilled. In their 1947 best-seller, *Modern Women: The Lost Sex*, Marynia Farnham and Ferdinand Lundberg noted that "all mature childless women are emotionally disturbed" and that "the pursuit of a career is essentially masculine." Furthermore, these experts claimed that returning veterans needed special love and attention after so many years away from home.

The concept of mothering as central to the postwar family was further popularized by Dr. Benjamin Spock, whose *Common Sense Book of Baby and Child Care* (1946) became the standard reference for parents of the baby-boom generation. While most reviewers noted Spock's relaxed, more permissive attitude toward child rearing, another message came through as well. Women must be the primary caregivers, Spock insisted. It was their role to shape the infant into a normal, happy adult. For Spock and countless others, a man's success was measured by his performance in the outside world, a woman's success by her skills in raising well-adjusted children. As feminist author Betty Friedan recalled, "Oh, how Dr. Spock could make me feel guilty!"

The emphasis on traditional sex roles also affected female education. World War II had opened up new opportunities for women in science, engineering, and medicine. For the first time in history, women constituted a majority of the nation's college graduates. But the return of male veterans, combined with the educational benefits provided them by the GI Bill, reversed these temporary gains. At Cornell University, for example, women comprised 50 percent of the wartime classes but only 20 percent of the postwar classes. More significant, the percentage of college women who graduated fell from 40 percent during World War II to 25 percent by 1950.

The steepest declines occurred in professional education. Engineering colleges, which doubled their enrollments to more than 200,000 by 1946, accepted fewer than 1,300 women, with more than half of these schools accepting no women at all. Female enrollments in medical schools dropped from a high of 15 percent during World War II to 5 percent by 1950. A study of medical students in this era showed deep prejudice among men and self-limiting attitudes among women. The majority of men, believing they made better doctors than women did, thought that women should face tougher admission standards. The majority of women, insisting that marriage was more important than a career, claimed they would cut back their hours, or even stop working, to meet their family obligations. On campuses across the nation, educators struggled to find the proper curriculum for female students. The ideal, said one college president, was to enable women "to foster the intellectual and emotional life of her family and community"—to fill the American home with proper moral values and good cooking.

Before long, the postwar American woman became the nation's primary consumer. Between 1946 and 1950, Americans purchased 21 million automobiles, 20 million refrigerators, 5.5 million electric stoves, and more than 2 million dishwashers. This consumer explosion resulted from a combination of factors: the baby boom, the huge savings accumulated during World War II, the availability of credit, and the effectiveness of mass advertising in creating consumer demand. The average American now had access to department store charge accounts and easy payment plans with almost no money down. In 1950, the Diner's Club introduced America's first credit card. "Buy Now, Pay Later," urged General Motors, and most people obliged.

Ironically, this new consumer society led millions of women back into the labor force. By 1950, more women were working outside the home than ever before. The difference, however, was that postwar American women returned to low-paying, often part-time employment in "feminine" jobs such as clerks, salespeople, secretaries, waitresses, telephone operators, and domestics. Working to supplement the family income and help finance the automobile, the kitchen appliances, the summer vacation, the children's college tuition, American women earned but 53 percent of the wages of American men in 1950—a drop of 10 percent since the heady years of "Rosie the Riveter" during World War II.

Suburbia   No possession was more prized by the postwar American family than the suburban home. In 1944, fewer than 120,000 new houses were built in the United States, a figure that rose to 900,000 by 1946 and 1.7 million by 1950. More than 80 percent of these new houses were built in suburban areas surrounding established cities. While prosperity and population growth produced the need for more housing, the rush to suburbia was accelerated by a flood of federal mortgage money and a revolution in the building of affordable, single-family homes.

The GI Bill provided the cash to bolster demand. With mortgage money now available, the housing shortage quickly disappeared. Leading the way were builders like William Levitt, who purchased several thousand acres of farmland in Hempstead, New York, twenty-five miles east of Manhattan, for the mass production of private homes. Levitt modeled his operation after Henry Ford's automobile assembly plants. His building materials were produced and precut in Levitt factories, delivered by Levitt trucks, and assembled by Levitt work crews, each performing a single task such as framing, pouring concrete, or painting window shutters. In good weather, Levitt workers put up 180 houses a week. The typical dwelling— a solid, two-bedroom Cape Cod style, with a kitchen–dining room, living room with fireplace, single bath, and expansion attic—sold for $7,900. When completed, **Levittown**, Long Island, contained 17,000 houses, plus dozens of parks, ball fields, swimming pools, churches,

DOING HISTORY ONLINE

The Six Thousand Houses That Levitt Built, 1948

Read the article online along with the section on Suburbia in the textbook. Imagine that you are a newly married World War II veteran or someone married to a soldier just returned from the war in 1947. Would you want to live in Levittown? Why or why not?

 www.cengage.com/ history/ayers/ ampassages4e

Levittown, Long Island. *The GI bill helped fuel the boom in suburban housing after World War II, with communities like Levittown, New York, springing up across the country.*

and shopping areas for the 82,000 residents. Levitt followed his Long Island venture with similar towns in Pennsylvania and New Jersey.

City dwellers were attracted by Levittown's good schools, safe streets, and open space. The idea of owning one's home, moreover, was a central part of the American dream. But what stood out to others was the sameness of Levittown—a place where people lived in similar houses, accumulated similar possessions, and conformed to similar rules. Levitt salesmen restricted their communities to white applicants, who then signed pledges saying they would not resell their homes to blacks. As late as the 1960s, the percentage of African Americans living in the three Levittown developments was well below 1 percent, a figure that represented most suburban areas nationwide. Furthermore, Levittown appeared to reinforce the traditional family roles of postwar America, with mothers caring for their children while fathers commuted long distances to work.

THE SOVIET THREAT

Relations between the United States and the Soviet Union were moving swiftly downhill. The failure to find common ground on a host of vital issues—from "free elections" in Poland to the German payment of reparations—raised anger and suspicion on both sides. Soviet leaders now viewed the United States as largely indifferent to the security needs of the Russian people, and American leaders increasingly portrayed the Soviet Union as a belligerent force in the world, bent more on expanding its empire than on defending its territory. Relations would worsen in the coming years, as the Soviets tightened their grip in Eastern Europe and successfully tested an atomic bomb in 1949. The Grand Alliance was over; the Cold War had begun.

Containment

Within hours of Germany's surrender, President Truman had signed an executive order ending Lend-Lease aid to the Allies. Though Truman reversed himself under a storm of criticism, Congress abolished Lend-Lease following Japan's surrender in August 1945. A few months later, the United States gave England a low-interest $3.75 billion loan and ignored a similar request from the Russians.

In February 1946, Stalin delivered a major address predicting the collapse of capitalism and the dawn of a communist world. The following month, with Truman at his side, former Prime Minister Churchill told an audience at Westminster College in Missouri that Russia had drawn an **Iron Curtain** across Europe. The West must unite against Soviet expansion, Churchill said, adding that "God had willed" the atomic bomb to Britain and America so as to ensure their ultimate triumph over this totalitarian foe.

A more compelling rebuttal to Stalin's speech came from a forty-two-year-old foreign service officer stationed at the U.S. embassy in Moscow. In an 8,000-word telegram, George F. Kennan laid out the doctrine of **containment** that would influence American foreign policy for the next twenty years. According to Kennan, Russia was an implacable foe, determined to expand its empire and undermine Western democratic values. America must be patient, Kennan believed. It must define its vital interests and then be prepared to defend them through "the adroit and vigilant application of counterforce at a series of constantly shifting geographical and political points."

Kennan's "long telegram" arrived in Washington at the perfect time. Poland and Eastern Europe were now lost causes; there seemed little that the United States could do to change their dismal fate. The objective, Truman believed, was to block communist expansion into new areas vulnerable to Soviet influence and control. "Unless Russia is faced with an iron fist and strong language another war is in the making," he predicted. "I am tired of babying the Soviets."

The Truman Doctrine and the Marshall Plan

The new trouble spot appeared to be the Mediterranean, where the Soviet Union was demanding territorial concessions from Iran and Turkey, and where communist-led guerrillas were battling the Greek government in a bloody civil war. Early in 1947, Great Britain, the traditional power in that area, informed the United States that it could no longer provide military and economic assistance to Greece and Turkey. Exhausted by World War II, Britain urged the United States to maintain that aid in order to prevent further Soviet expansion.

At a White House meeting six days later, **General George C. Marshall**, the new secretary of state, presented the case for American aid to congressional leaders from both parties. When Marshall's soft-spoken approach failed to rally the meeting, his assistant, Dean Acheson, took over. In sweeping terms, Acheson portrayed the future of Greece and Turkey as a test case of American resolve against Soviet aggression. If Greece fell to the communists, Acheson warned, other nations would follow "like apples in a barrel infected by one rotten one." When he finished, Republican Senator

Arthur Vandenberg of Michigan summed up the feeling in the room. "Mr. President," he said, turning to Harry Truman, "if you will say that to Congress and the country, I will support you and I believe most members will do the same."

On March 12, 1947, the president offered his **Truman Doctrine** before a joint session of Congress and a national radio audience. In the current crisis, he began, "every nation must choose between alternative ways of life." One way guaranteed "individual liberty" and "political freedom," the other promoted "terror" and "oppression." In a world of good and evil, Truman declared, it "must be the policy of the United States to support free peoples who are resisting attempted subjugation by armed minorities or by outside pressures."

Some critics noted that the regimes in Greece and Turkey were a far cry from the democratic ideals that the president lauded in his speech. Others worried that the Truman Doctrine would lead the United States into an expensive, open-ended crusade against left-wing forces around the globe. Yet most Americans supported Truman's position, and Congress allocated $400 million in military aid for Greece and Turkey.

On June 5, 1947, at the Harvard University commencement, Secretary of State Marshall unveiled a far more ambitious proposal known as the European Recovery Plan, or the **Marshall Plan**. The danger seemed clear: without massive economic aid, European governments might collapse, leaving chaos in their wake. "Our policy is not directed against any country or doctrine," Marshall said, "but against hunger, poverty, desperation, and fear."

Several weeks later, seventeen European nations, including the Soviet Union, met in Paris to assess their common needs. But the Soviets walked out after a few sessions, forcing nations like Poland and Hungary to leave as well. The Soviets balked at the idea of divulging critical information about their economy to outsiders. And they surely feared that massive American aid would tie them and the nations they now controlled to a capitalist orbit that might undermine the communist system.

Truman was not sorry to see them leave. He realized that Congress would not look favorably on the prospect of spending billions of dollars to reconstruct a country that seemed so brutal to its neighbors and so threatening to the United States. With the Russians and their satellites out of the picture, the remaining European nations prepared an agenda for economic recovery that came to $27 billion, a huge sum. After six months of bitter debate, Congress reduced that figure by about half. The largest expenditures went to Britain, Germany, and France.

The Marshall Plan proved a tremendous success. By creating jobs and raising living standards, it restored economic confidence throughout Western Europe and curbed the influence of local Communist Parties in Italy and France. Furthermore, the Marshall Plan increased American trade and investment in Europe, opening vast new markets for U.S. goods. As President Truman noted, "Peace, freedom, and world trade are indivisible."

The rising prosperity in Western Europe was matched by growing repression in the East. Stalin moved first on Hungary, staging a rigged election backed by Russian troops. Next came Czechoslovakia, where the Soviets toppled a coalition government led by Jan Masaryk, a statesman with many admirers in the West. A few days later, Masaryk either jumped or was pushed to his death from an office window in Prague. Against this ominous background, President Truman proposed legislation to streamline the nation's military and diplomatic services. Passed as the National Security Act of 1947, it unified the armed forces under a single Department of Defense, created the National Security Council (NSC) to provide foreign policy information to the president, and established the Central Intelligence Agency (CIA) to coordinate intelligence gathering abroad. While providing the White House with vital information in a number of Cold War crises, the CIA would face criticism in the coming years for illegally spying on American citizens and attempting to overthrow governments viewed as hostile to the United States.

LIBERALISM IN RETREAT

In foreign affairs, President Truman could count on strong bipartisan support. Republican legislators had joined with Democrats to endorse early Cold War initiatives like the Truman Doctrine and the Marshall Plan. But the president had no such luck on domestic issues. For one thing, the widening rift with Russia produced a growing concern about the influence of communists and their "sympathizers" inside the federal government. For another, the president's attempt to extend the liberal agenda through ambitious social and economic legislation—known as the "Fair Deal"—met with stiff resistance in Congress after 1946. As one Republican leader put it: "We have to break with the corrupting idea that we can legislate prosperity, legislate equality, legislate opportunity."

The Cold War at Home
The Iron Curtain that descended on Europe had a tremendous psychological impact on the United States. Americans were fearful of communism and frustrated by the turn of global events. The defeat of fascism had not made the world a safer place. One form of totalitarianism had been replaced by another. The result was an erosion of public tolerance for left-wing activity, spurred on by prominent government officials like Attorney General Tom Clark, who warned that communists were "everywhere" in the United States—"in factories, offices, butcher shops, on street corners, in private businesses, and each carries with him the germs of death for society."

In fact, the American Communist Party was far weaker in 1947 than it had been a decade before, and its numbers were dwindling by the day. Yet that did not stop President Truman from establishing a Federal Loyalty-Security Program for the first time in American history. Truman acted, in large part, to keep congressional conservatives from fashioning an even tougher loyalty program. The one he put in place called for extensive background checks of all civilian workers in the federal bureaucracy. The criteria for disloyalty included everything from espionage to "sympathetic association" with groups deemed "subversive" by the attorney general.

The congressional assault on domestic subversion was led by the **House Un-American Activities Committee (HUAC)**. Formed in the 1930s to investigate Nazi propaganda in the United States, HUAC had been revived after World War II as a watchdog against communist propaganda. Among its more visible members was a young congressman from southern California named Richard M. Nixon. In 1947, HUAC launched a spectacular investigation of the motion picture industry, alleging that "flagrant Communist propaganda films" had been produced during World War II on the specific orders of President Roosevelt. The committee subpoenaed a number of pro-communist writers and directors, who angrily refused to answer questions about their political beliefs and associations. Known as the "Hollywood Ten," these individuals were cited for contempt, sent to jail, and "blacklisted" from working in the entertainment industry, a practice that became increasingly common in the late 1940s and 1950s. HUAC also heard from a host of "friendly" Hollywood witnesses, including movie stars Gary Cooper, Ronald Reagan, and the dapper Adolphe Menjou, who declared: "I am a witch-hunter if the witches are Communists. I am a Red-baiter I would like to see them all back in Russia."

The following year brought HUAC even more publicity. A witness named Whittaker Chambers, then a senior editor for *Time* magazine, claimed to have once been part of a "Communist cell" in Washington that included Alger Hiss, a former government official who had advised President Roosevelt in foreign affairs. Hiss denied Chambers's allegations in testimony before HUAC a few days later. When Chambers repeated the charge on a national radio broadcast, Hiss sued him for libel.

Chambers struck back hard, producing dozens of classified State Department documents from the 1930s that, he claimed, Hiss had stolen and passed on to the Russians. Suddenly the ground had shifted to espionage, a more serious charge. The evidence—known as the "Pumpkin Papers" because Chambers had briefly hidden it in a pumpkin patch on his Maryland farm—included five rolls of microfilm and summaries of confidential reports Hiss had written in longhand or typed on a unique typewriter he once owned. In December 1948, a federal grand jury indicted Hiss for perjuring himself before HUAC. (The ten-year statute of limitations on espionage had just run out.) The first trial ended in a hung jury; the second one sent Hiss to jail.

The guilty verdict sent shock waves through the nation. If Alger Hiss was a traitor, some wondered, how many just like him were still loose in the Truman administration, working secretly to help the Soviet Union win the Cold War. This question would come to dominate American politics over the next several years.

The Domestic Agenda   The Republican landslide of 1946 appeared to signal the decline of American liberalism. In the following months, the Republican Congress brushed aside President Truman's proposals for national health insurance and federal aid to education, and passed major legislation, known as the Taft-Hartley Act, to curb the power of organized labor. Taft-Hartley generated strong public support, given the crippling strikes of the previous year. In 1947, organized labor was at the height of its influence, with 15 million members nationwide. More than 35 percent of all nonagricultural workers belonged to a union, the highest total ever reached in the United States.

To counter the threats of powerful unions like the United Mine Workers, Taft-Hartley gave the president authority to impose an eighty-day "cooling-off" period to prevent strikes that threatened the national interest. More important, the bill outlawed the closed shop, a device that forced workers to join a union at the time they were hired, and it encouraged the states to pass "right-to-work" laws that made union organizing more difficult. Although Truman strongly opposed Taft-Hartley, the Republican Congress easily overrode his veto.

Truman also confronted the issue of racial discrimination by forming a special task force on civil rights. Its final report included a series of bold recommendations, such as the desegregation of the armed forces and the creation of a special division within the Justice Department devoted solely to civil rights. Truman endorsed these recommendations, although his personal feelings about them were mixed. As a political leader, he had to balance the interests of two distinct Democratic Party voting blocs: southern whites and northern blacks. As an individual, he believed that all citizens deserved political rights and equal opportunity, yet he felt uncomfortable with the notion of social equality for African Americans, as did most other white people of that era. Addressing the NAACP's national convention in 1947—the first American president to do so—Truman spoke out strongly against prejudice and hate. "The only limit to a [person's] achievement," he declared, "should be his ability, his industry, and his character."

**Breaking the
Color Line**

Truman's statement seemed particularly appropriate in 1947. On April 15, Major League baseball broke its long-standing "color line" in an opening day game at Brooklyn's Ebbets Field. "History was made here Tuesday afternoon," reported the *Pittsburgh Courier*, an African American newspaper, "when smiling **Jackie Robinson** trotted out on the green-swept diamond with the rest of his Dodger teammates."

Baseball had been all-white for generations. Blacks played in the so-called Negro Leagues. Poorly paid, they often barnstormed from town to town, taking on local teams in exhibitions that combined great baseball with crowd-pleasing entertainment. The top players— pitcher Leroy "Satchel" Paige, catcher Josh Gibson, infielder George "Cool Papa" Bell—were as good as, if not better than, the top Major League stars. Hall of Fame pitcher Walter Johnson claimed that Gibson "can do everything. He hits the ball a mile. He catches so easy he might as well be in a rocking chair. Throws like a rifle. Too bad this Gibson is a colored fellow."

The vast majority of Major League owners opposed integration. Branch Rickey of the Brooklyn Dodgers was an exception. Mixing deep religious values with shrewd business sense, Rickey insisted that integration was good for America, for baseball, and for the Dodgers. "The Negroes will make us winners for

DOING HISTORY ONLINE

Jackie Robinson and the Negro Leagues, 1948

Read the documents online. How does the document on The Decline of the Negro Leagues, 1948, relate to the others in this unit?

www.cengage.com/
history/ayers/
ampassages4e

Jackie Robinson. *Breaking the color line in Major League baseball in 1947, Jackie Robinson led the Brooklyn Dodgers to six pennants and a World Series victory in his brilliant career.*

AP Photos

years to come," he said, "and for that I will happily bear being called a bleeding heart and a do-gooder and all that humanitarian rot."

To break the color line, Rickey selected Jack Roosevelt Robinson, twenty-seven years old, a man of tremendous talent and pride. The son of sharecroppers and the grandson of slaves, Robinson moved from rural Georgia to Pasadena, California, where his athletic skills earned him a scholarship to UCLA. A letterman in four sports—baseball, football, basketball, and track—he also won tournaments in tennis and golf. Drafted into the army during World War II, Robinson fought bigotry at every turn. As a second lieutenant in a segregated tank unit, he was court-martialed for insubordination, but acquitted, after refusing to move to the rear of an army bus. Honorably discharged in 1944, he joined the Kansas City Monarchs, a Negro League team, as a shortstop at four hundred dollars a month. On a road trip to Oklahoma, teammate Buck O'Neill recalled, Robinson personally broke the color line at a local filling station by demanding to use the rest room. When the attendant refused, Robinson told him: "Take the hose out of the tank. If we can't go to the rest room, we won't get gas here." Startled, the attendant replied: "Well, you boys can go to the rest room, but don't stay long."

Rickey met secretly with Robinson in the fall of 1945. Talent was not an issue. Robinson was hitting .385 for the Monarchs and stealing bases by the bunch. What most concerned Rickey was Robinson's temper. How would he react to racial slurs, pitches thrown at his head, runners sliding into him spikes first? For three hours, Rickey grilled Robinson about the need for absolute self-control. "Do you want a ballplayer who's afraid to fight back?" Robinson asked. "I want a ballplayer with enough guts not to fight back," Rickey answered. "You will symbolize a crucial cause. One incident, just one incident, can set it back twenty years." "Mr. Rickey," Robinson replied, "if you want to take this gamble, I will promise you there will be no incident."

Robinson kept his word, enduring segregated hotels, racial insults, even death threats against his family. His pioneering effort caught the public's fancy, and huge crowds followed him everywhere. Chicago, Cincinnati, Philadelphia, Pittsburgh, St. Louis—all set attendance records when Robinson appeared, with black fans leading the way. As one writer put it, "Jackie's nimble/Jackie's quick. Jackie's making the turnstiles click." By season's end, Robinson had led the Dodgers to the National League pennant and won designation as Rookie of the Year.

But the struggle was far from over. It would be another decade before all Major League teams accepted integration. Yet the efforts begun by Branch Rickey and Jackie Robinson helped change the face of America by democratizing its "National Game." Looking back on the events of 1947, sportswriter Jimmy Cannon recalled a side of Robinson that captured both his courage and his pain. He was, said Cannon, "the loneliest man I have ever seen in sports."

Man of the People As the 1948 presidential election approached, Harry Truman seemed a beaten man. His relations with Congress were stormy and unproductive, especially in domestic affairs. The press, remembering the elegant and fatherly FDR, portrayed Truman as too small for the job. Likely supporters deserted him in droves. In December 1947, a band of left-wing Democrats formed the Progressive Citizens of America, with an eye toward the coming election. Their leader was Henry Wallace, the former vice president and secretary of commerce, whom

Truman had fired for criticizing the administration's firm stance toward the Soviet Union. Wallace opposed both the Truman Doctrine and the Marshall Plan. Though he had no hope of winning the presidential election in 1948, his Progressive Party seemed likely to split the Democratic vote.

Some urged Truman not to run. A number of Democratic leaders suggested other presidential candidates, including General Dwight D. Eisenhower. The *New Republic*, a favorite of liberals, ran the front cover headline: "Harry Truman Should Quit." The Democrats convened in Philadelphia, where the heat was oppressive and tempers grew short. When word reached the convention that Eisenhower was unavailable, "Boss" Frank Hague of Jersey City threw down his cigar. "Truman," he mumbled. "Harry Truman, oh my God!"

Left with no alternative, the delegates nominated Truman for president and Alben Barkley, the popular but aging Senate majority leader from Kentucky, for vice president. Barkley had strong ties to the South. Yet even he could not prevent the convention from dividing along sectional lines when northern liberals, led by Mayor Hubert Humphrey of Minneapolis, demanded the endorsement of Truman's civil rights initiatives. "The time has arrived," said Humphrey, "for the Democratic party to get out of the shadow of states' rights, and walk forthrightly into the bright sunshine of human rights."

The passage of a strong civil rights plank led many southern Democrats to walk out of the convention. Two days later, waving Confederate flags and denouncing Harry Truman, they formed the States' Rights (Dixiecrat) party at a gathering in Birmingham, Alabama. The Dixiecrats chose governors Strom Thurmond of South Carolina and Fielding Wright of Mississippi to be, respectively, their presidential and vice-presidential candidates. Their platform demanded "complete segregation of the races."

Divided into three camps, the Democratic Party appeared hopelessly overmatched. Not only did President Truman face Henry Wallace on his left and Strom Thurmond on his right, but the national Republican ticket of New York Governor Thomas E. Dewey for president and California Governor Earl Warren for vice president was the strongest in years. Truman's campaign strategy was to portray himself as a common people's president, protecting the voters and their hard-earned New Deal benefits from a heartless Republican assault. To highlight these differences, he called a special session of Congress to demand passage of an eight-point program that included civil rights, public housing, federal aid to education, a higher minimum wage, and storage facilities for farmers. When the Republican Congress refused to act, calling Truman's move a "publicity stunt," the president lambasted the Republicans as selfish politicians, interested only in the rich.

Truman also used his presidential power in significant ways. He showed support for the new state of Israel by offering it political recognition and economic assistance. He issued his promised executive order desegregating the armed forces. And he forcefully confronted Stalin in a showdown over Germany and Berlin.

In June 1948, Russian troops blockaded West Berlin to protest the merging of the French, British, and American occupation zones into the unified nation of West Germany. The city lay deep inside Soviet-controlled territory. With all roads and rail lines through East Germany now closed to allied traffic, its future seemed bleak. Truman ruled out force to break the blockade because American troops were greatly outnumbered. Instead, he and his advisers decided to supply West Berlin from the air.

In the coming months, American and British pilots made close to 300,000 flights into the city, delivering food, fuel, and medical supplies. By the time the Russians called off their blockade, Berlin, the former Nazi capital, had become the symbol of resistance to communist oppression.

Truman could see his fortunes rising as the 1948 campaign progressed. Crisscrossing the nation by train, he drew huge, friendly crowds at each whistle stop. To shouts of "Give 'em hell, Harry!" he ripped into the "do-nothing" Republican Congress and its "plans" to dismantle Franklin Roosevelt's work. "This is a crusade of the people against the special interests," Truman repeated, "and if you back me up we're going to win."

The experts didn't think so. Opinion polls showed Dewey with a substantial lead. On election eve, the staunchly Republican *Chicago Tribune* carried the now-famous mistaken headline: "Dewey Defeats Truman."

In fact, Truman won the closest presidential contest since 1916, collecting 24.1 million votes to Dewey's 22 million, and 303 electoral votes to Dewey's 189. Strom Thurmond captured 1.1 million votes and four southern states under the Dixiecrat banner, and Henry Wallace won no states and barely a million votes. Ironically, the three-way Democratic split appeared to help Truman by allowing him to speak out forcefully against Soviet expansion and aggressively court African American voters in the pivotal northern industrial states. In the end, the people chose Truman's frank, common appeal over Dewey's stiff, evasive demeanor. The New Deal coalition had held for another election.

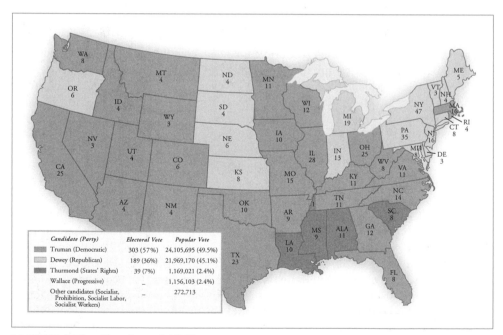

Candidate (Party)	Electoral Vote	Popular Vote
Truman (Democratic)	303 (57%)	24,105,695 (49.5%)
Dewey (Republican)	189 (36%)	21,969,170 (45.1%)
Thurmond (States' Rights)	39 (7%)	1,169,021 (2.4%)
Wallace (Progressive)	–	1,156,103 (2.4%)
Other candidates (Socialist, Prohibition, Socialist Labor, Socialist Workers)	–	272,713

MAP 27.1 The Election of 1948.

The presidential election of 1948 is considered one of the greatest upsets in American political history. Because there were four significant candidates, two running on third-party tickets, the victor, President Truman, captured a majority of the electoral votes without actually winning a majority of the popular vote.

THE COLD WAR INTENSIFIES, 1949–1953

Truman had little time to savor his victory. In the summer of 1949, an American spy plane returned from a flight over the Soviet Union with photographs revealing strong traces of radioactive material. The conclusion was obvious: Russia had exploded an atomic device. Combined with alarming new developments in Asia, the loss of America's atomic monopoly served to heighten global tensions in the coming months while dramatically increasing the fear of communism at home.

The Fall of China and the Creation of NATO, 1949 President Truman broke the news in a one-sentence statement to the press: "We have evidence an atomic explosion occurred in the USSR." Domestic reaction was severe. Ever since Hiroshima, Americans had been taught to depend on nuclear superiority in the Cold War and to believe that Russia, a supposedly backward nation, could not possibly develop an atomic bomb before the mid-1950s, if ever. That could mean only one thing: espionage. The Soviets, it appeared, had stolen the biggest secret of all.

The news from China was equally grim. Following World War II, Chiang Kai-shek and his Nationalist (Kuomintang) forces had renewed their offensive against the communist forces of Mao Tse-tung. Chiang counted heavily on American support. He believed that his fight against communism, his powerful friends in Congress, and his image as China's savior would force the Truman administration to back him at all costs.

Chiang was mistaken. The president and his advisers were far less interested in Asia than they were in Western Europe. They were not about to be trapped into an open-ended commitment in the Far East. From 1946 to 1949, the United States gave Chiang's government about $2 billion in military aid—enough, it was hoped, to satisfy Chiang's American friends without seriously affecting the more important buildup in Europe.

As civil war raged in China, Chiang's forces met defeat after defeat. Much of the American weaponry that fleeing Nationalist troops discarded would end up in communist hands. In August 1949, the State Department issued a 1,054-page "White Paper on China," conceding that the world's largest country was about to fall to the communists. "The unfortunate but inescapable fact," said Dean Acheson, the new secretary of state, "is that the ominous result of the civil war in China was beyond [our] control." Though Acheson was correct, his White Paper sounded more like an excuse than an explanation. Americans were bewildered. How well did "containment" really work when more than 600 million people were "lost" to communism?

Determined to prevent further communist expansion elsewhere, the United States joined with eleven West European nations to create the **North Atlantic Treaty Organization (NATO)** in 1949. The treaty was extremely significant; in promising to support fellow NATO members in the event of Soviet attack, it formally ended America's long tradition of avoiding entangling alliances abroad. A year later, Secretary of State Acheson and Paul Nitze, his deputy, produced a secret document known as National Security Council Paper 68 (NSC 68), which advocated the use of military force to stop communist aggression throughout the world. According to NSC 68, the United States should act in concert with other nations wherever possible, but alone if need be.

The document called for an unprecedented peacetime increase in military spending—from $13 billion to $50 billion per year—and for the construction of a huge new "thermo-nuclear device," the hydrogen bomb. Though Truman never showed this document to Congress, it became, in Acheson's words, "the fundamental paper" governing America's defense policy in the coming years.

War In Korea, 1950–1953   On June 25, 1950, troops from Communist North Korea invaded anti-communist South Korea with infantry, armor, and artillery in a massive land assault. Korea had been arbitrarily divided by Russian and American troops at the end of World War II. In 1948, an election to unify Korea had been cancelled when the Soviets refused to allow UN observers north of the dividing line at the thirty-eighth parallel. A stalemate thus developed, with Kim Il Sung, the Communist dictator of North Korea, and Syngman Rhee, the anti-communist dictator of South Korea, making daily threats to "liberate" each other's land.

The North Korean attack put great pressure on President Truman. His administration had treated the Rhee government with indifference, removing American combat troops from Korea in 1949 and implying that Korea itself was not vital to the free world's security. Yet here was a classic case of aggression, Truman believed. To ignore it was to encourage it elsewhere—and to turn away from NSC 68.

There were political considerations too. If the president did nothing, he would only reinforce the Republican charge that his administration was "soft" on communism. Thus, Truman moved quickly, proposing a UN resolution that offered "such assistance to South Korea as may be necessary to repel armed attack." (The Russians, boycotting the Security Council to protest the UN's refusal to seat Communist China, were unable to cast a paralyzing veto.) A week later, without consulting Congress, Truman dispatched ground troops to South Korea.

Following two months of backward movement, UN forces under the command of General Douglas MacArthur took the offensive. In September 1950, MacArthur outflanked the enemy with a brilliant amphibious landing at Inchon, on South Korea's west coast. By October, UN troops had crossed the thirty-eighth parallel in pursuit of the routed North Korean army. As the public listened in amazement, MacArthur spoke of having his men "home before Christmas."

There were ominous signs, however. First, by sending troops into North Korea, President Truman and the United Nations had gone beyond their original mandate to defend South Korea from outside aggression. Second, General MacArthur appeared oblivious to the possibility that Communist China might enter the war. As UN forces drove north, they captured scores of Chinese Communist troops near the Yalu River that divided North Korea and Manchuria. On November 5, the Chinese attacked—300,000 strong—pushing MacArthur's startled army back toward the thirty-eighth parallel. In the following weeks, American army and marine units fought their way through mountain blizzards and a wall of Chinese infantry to form a defense line just south of the thirty-eighth parallel. Although disaster had been averted, the nation was shocked by what *Time* magazine described as "the worst military setback the United States has ever suffered."

By March 1951, the Communist offensive had stalled. UN forces pushed ahead to the thirty-eighth parallel, where the two sides faced each other in a bloody standoff.

Not surprisingly, General MacArthur called for an escalation of the war. Killing Chinese soldiers was not enough, he argued, for replacements could always be found. MacArthur recommended a naval blockade of China's coast, massive bombing of its factories and power plants, and an invasion of the Chinese mainland by the forces of Chiang Kai-shek.

This plea for an expanded war was understandable. MacArthur, like most other Americans, believed in the concept of total victory. His message, quite simply, was that the lands surrendered to the Communists by weak-kneed civilians like Truman and Acheson could be recaptured through the full exercise of American military power.

The president saw things differently. Any attempt to widen the war, he realized, would alarm other UN participants and perhaps bring Russia into the conflict. The Soviets might send troops to the Asian front or put pressure on Western Europe. Furthermore, Russia's involvement raised the threat of nuclear attack. As General Omar Bradley noted, MacArthur's strategy was the very opposite of the one proposed by President Truman and the Joint Chiefs of Staff. "So long as we regard the Soviet Union as the main antagonist and Western Europe as the main prize," he said, "it would involve us in the wrong war, at the wrong place, at the wrong time, and with the wrong enemy."

Despite repeated warnings from the president, MacArthur refused to keep his views to himself. The final blowup came in April 1951 when Republicans in Congress released a letter that MacArthur had sent them from the battlefield that criticized Truman's refusal to meet force "with maximum counterforce," and ended with the oft-quoted phrase: "There is no substitute for victory." Furious at such insubordination, the president relieved MacArthur of his command.

MacArthur returned to the United States a genuine folk hero, a man who symbolized old military values in a world complicated by the horrors of nuclear war. Cities across the nation burned President Truman in effigy. Letters to the White House ran twenty-one to one against MacArthur's firing. On Capitol Hill, angry representatives placed some of the telegrams they received into the *Congressional Record*: "Impeach the Imbecile" and "We Wish to Protest the Latest Outrage by the Pig in the White House." Harry Truman's old standard—"If you can't stand the heat, stay out of the kitchen"—had never been more strenuously tested.

McCarthyism and the Election of 1952

On a bleak February evening in 1950, a little-known politician delivered a speech about "Communist subversion" in the federal government to a Republican women's club in Wheeling, West Virginia. "I have here in my hand," Senator **Joseph R. McCarthy** of Wisconsin told his audience, "a list of 205 Communists that were made known to the secretary of state and who are still working and shaping the policy of the State Department." The message was clear: America, the strongest nation on earth, was losing the Cold War to the evil forces of communism because the U.S. government was filled with "traitors" like **Alger Hiss** who wanted the communists to win.

McCarthy's charges remain controversial to this day. His supporters see him as an honorable patriot, spreading the alarm like a latter-day Paul Revere. His detractors, a far larger group, view McCarthy as a fearmonger who divided the nation and destroyed

The Blacklist

As the Cold War heated up in the late 1940s, a number of powerful sources in and out of government charged that communists and their sympathizers were polluting the nation's entertainment industry—radio, television, and movies—with subversive propaganda.

Fearful of an angry public reaction, industry leaders agreed to check the political backgrounds of their employees. This led to the blacklisting of dozens of entertainers who were denied work for allegedly supporting the communist cause. The most influential blacklist of this era, Red Channels (pictured), demonstrates the "guilt by association" technique often used by Red hunters of this era, who made accusations against people based on their connection, however fleeting, with groups deemed "communist" or "un-American." Compiled by three former FBI agents, Red Channels included the names of conductor Leonard Bernstein, composer Aaron Copeland, actress Lena Horne, and more than a hundred others. Much of the information was erroneous. In the late 1950s, a Texas broadcaster named John Henry Faulk exposed the sordid nature of Red Channels by successfully suing its publisher for libel. The final blow came in 1960 when a major Hollywood studio hired the blacklisted writer Dalton Trumbo to do the screenplay for the hit movie *Spartacus* under his own name. "The blacklist was a time of evil," Trumbo observed. "None of us—right, left, center—emerged from that long nightmare without sin."

numerous reputations and careers. Indeed, the current edition of *Webster's New World Dictionary* defines "McCarthyism" as "the use of indiscriminate, often unfounded accusations" to suppress the rights of others.

The Rise of Joe McCarthy

Wisconsin's junior senator was an erratic politician, known for his reckless ambition and raucous behavior. He knew little about communists in government or anywhere else. But the newspapers printed his charges, and the public was aroused. McCarthy had struck a nerve in the country, rubbed raw by Soviet aggression in Europe, the Communist victory in China, the Alger Hiss case, and the news of the Russian atomic bomb. As Americans searched for explanations, McCarthy provided the simplest answer of all. The real enemy was not in Moscow, he thundered, but rather in Washington, D.C.

McCarthy's charges of treason in high places made him an instant celebrity. Prominent Republicans, sensing the political benefits of the "Communist issue," rallied to his side. Senator Robert Taft of Ohio, known as "Mr. Republican," privately dismissed McCarthy's charges as "nonsense." Yet he told McCarthy to keep punching—"if one case doesn't work, try another."

President Truman viewed McCarthy as a shameless publicity hound who would say anything to make headlines. He was right about the senator yet helpless to stop him. The fear of communism kept growing, aided by the outbreak of war in Korea. Air raid drills became the order of the day, with school children taught to dive under their desks and shield their eyes against atomic blasts. In New York City, school officials distributed metal "dog tags." "If a bomb gets me in the street," a first-grader explained, "people will know what my name is." In Washington, a typical real estate ad read: "Small farms—out beyond the atomic blasts." Mayor Mike DiSalle of Toledo, Ohio, tried to calm worried residents by joking that he would build large neon signs directing communist pilots to Cleveland and Detroit.

McCarthy's attacks grew bolder. As the 1952 presidential campaign approached, he called George C. Marshall a traitor, mocked Dean Acheson as the "Red Dean of fashion," and described President Truman as a drunkard, adding, "the son-of-a-bitch ought to be impeached." Yet party colleagues continued to encourage McCarthy, viewing him as the man who could turn public anxiety and distrust into Republican votes.

"I Like Ike"

By 1952, Harry Truman's public approval rating had dropped to 23 percent—the lowest ever recorded by an American president. The *New Republic* called him "a spent force politically" and urged him to withdraw from the coming presidential campaign. In March, Truman announced he would not seek reelection.

> ### DOING HISTORY ONLINE
>
> **Undercover in the Communist Party, 1951**
>
> Read the article online along with the section on McCarthyism in the textbook. Why did the Communist Party target the steel industry, as Mary Markward said it did in her congressional testimony?
>
> www.cengage.com/ history/ayers/ ampassages4e

The most impressive Democratic candidate, Governor Adlai Stevenson of Illinois, had earned a reputation as a liberal reformer. Eloquent and witty, he appealed to both party regulars and the liberal intelligentsia, much as FDR had. Stevenson had his handicaps, including a recent divorce and a past friendship with Alger Hiss. The Democrats nominated him for president on the third convention ballot. Senator John Sparkman of Alabama, a Fair Dealer and a segregationist, was given the vice-presidential nod.

The battle for the Republican presidential nomination was in many ways a battle for control of the Republican Party. The moderate wing, represented by Governor Thomas Dewey of New York and Senator Henry Cabot Lodge, Jr., of Massachusetts, was committed to internationalism and to many New Deal reforms. The conservative wing, led by Senator Robert Taft of Ohio, was suspicious of the New Deal and wary of America's expanding global commitments, especially the defense and reconstruction of Europe. Beyond

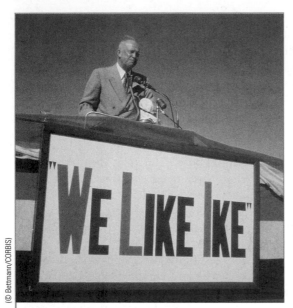

"We Like Ike." *America liked Ike, who won a smashing victory at the polls in 1952, ending twenty years of Democratic party rule.*

these views was a yearning for the past, for the pre-Depression days when government was smaller, cheaper, and less intrusive.

Senator Taft, the son of former President and Chief Justice William Howard Taft, had earned the respect of his colleagues and the plaudits of Washington reporters, who voted him "best senator" in 1949. On many domestic issues, such as public housing, Taft was more flexible than his conservative supporters. Yet he too feared that a powerful commitment to Western Europe could lead the United States into another world war.

Only one man stood between Taft and the Republican nomination, and he was a powerful opponent. In 1948, the leaders of both major political parties had begged him, unsuccessfully, to enter their presidential primaries. "I don't believe a man should try to pass his historical peak," said General Dwight D. Eisenhower. "I think I pretty well hit mine when I accepted the German surrender in 1945." Yet his moderate Republican supporters, believing that Eisenhower alone could defeat Taft for the presidential nomination, convinced the general that people wanted him, the country needed him, duty called once again.

Eisenhower, sixty-one years old, was raised in Abilene, Kansas, a prairie town west of Topeka. He attended schools with no lights or plumbing and earned his diploma while working the night shift in a dairy. In 1911, the young man, nicknamed Ike, won an appointment to the U.S. Military Academy at West Point. After graduating near the middle of his class, Eisenhower married Mamie Dowd, the daughter of a Denver businessman, and began his swift climb through the ranks. In the 1930s, he served as chief aide to General Douglas MacArthur, recalling: "Oh, yes, I studied dramatics under him for seven years." In 1941, he moved to the War Department and helped plan the D-Day invasion of France. His work was so outstanding that President Roosevelt named him Commanding General, European Theater of Operations, a promotion that jumped him over hundreds of officers with greater seniority.

It turned out to be one of the best decisions of World War II. Eisenhower commanded history's most successful coalition force—American, British, French, Polish, and Canadian troops—with courage, diplomacy, and skill. He was brilliant at handling people and reconciling the most diverse points of view. In the following years, Eisenhower served as army chief of staff, president of Columbia University, and commander of NATO forces.

The Republican convention nominated Eisenhower on the first ballot. Most delegates did not believe he would make a better president than Taft, simply a better candidate. Eisenhower defused the bitter feelings of conservatives by selecting Richard Nixon to be his running mate and accepting a party platform that accused the Democrats of shielding traitors in high places and bungling the Korean War.

On the campaign trail, General Eisenhower talked about leadership and morality, while Senator Nixon attacked from below. Traveling by train on the "Look Ahead Neighbor Special," Eisenhower visited more than two hundred cities and towns. At every stop, he introduced Mamie, praised America, bemoaned the "mess in Washington," and promised to clean it up. Then the whistle sounded and the train pulled away to the chants of "I Like Ike."

On September 28, 1952, the *New York Post*, a pro-Democratic newspaper, broke the biggest story of the campaign: "Secret Rich Men's Fund Keeps Nixon in Style Far Beyond His Salary." The Nixon fund of eighteen thousand dollars, donated by a group of California supporters, had never been a secret; it had been used for routine political expenses; and it was similar to those of other politicians. Nixon responded by blaming the "Reds" for his troubles. "The Communists, the left-wingers, have been fighting me with every smear," he declared. "They did it yesterday. They tried to say I had taken the money."

The campaign ground to a halt. On September 23, Nixon went on national television to explain his side of the story. To an audience estimated at 55 million, he spoke about his boyhood, his family, his war record, his finances, and his admiration for General Eisenhower. He explained how the fund worked, asked the American people to support him, and then described the one gift he would never return. It was, said Nixon, "a little cocker spaniel dog and our little girl named it Checkers. And you know the kids love that dog and I just want to say that we're going to keep it."

The reaction was volcanic. More than 2 million phone calls and telegrams poured into Republican offices across the country. They were followed by millions of letters, running 300 to 1 in Nixon's favor. Eisenhower had no choice but to keep his running mate on the ticket. The "Checkers speech" saved Nixon's career.

It also demonstrated the emerging power of television in national affairs. In the campaign's final weeks, the Republican Party ran dozens of twenty-second TV spots for Eisenhower, who used the ads to soothe voter anxiety about his views on popular New Deal welfare programs. "Social security, housing, workmen's compensation, unemployment insurance—these are things that must be kept above politics and campaigns," he said. "They are rights, not issues." The general also vowed that if elected, he would visit Korea "to help serve the American people in the cause of peace."

Stevenson tried to ridicule the announcement. "If elected," he replied, "I shall go to the White House." But few Americans were amused. On November 4, Eisenhower overwhelmed Stevenson—33.9 million votes to 27.3 million and 442 electoral votes to 89. Eisenhower became the first Republican in decades to crack the Solid South, winning four states and coming close in several others. He did well in cities, where ethnic voters, concerned about the rise of communism in Europe, deserted the Democrats in droves. Nearly 25 percent of Eisenhower's total came from men and women who had supported Harry Truman in 1948.

Some observers spoke of a new Republican era, but this was not the case. Almost everywhere, Eisenhower ran well ahead of his ticket. Although the Republicans managed to gain a slim majority in Congress, they did so by riding the general's coattails to victory.

CONCLUSION

Even before World War II ended, American planners, confident of victory, could sense the troubles that lay ahead. They saw big problems looming in foreign affairs, from the threat of Soviet expansion to the reconstruction of Western Europe. And they worried about the impact of peace on the nation's wartime economic boom. What would happen when defense spending dropped and factory jobs disappeared? Was it possible that the United States might slip back into the nightmare of the 1930s, when millions were hungry and unemployed?

The economic worries proved groundless. The war had created a near full-employment economy, leaving Americans with a great pile of disposable income—and a powerful urge to spend. Congress, meanwhile, passed the Servicemen's Readjustment Act (the GI Bill), designed to help returning soldiers as well as to bolster the economy by encouraging veterans to go to college and buy a new home. The economy took off, fueled by a baby boom, a rush to suburbia, and an explosion of consumer goods. The postwar years were among the most prosperous in U.S. history.

Things did not go as smoothly in foreign affairs. The reconstruction of Japan and Western Europe proved remarkably successful. At the same time, however, relations with the Soviet Union began a downward spiral as the two remaining superpowers entered into a Cold War punctuated by military threats and a growing arms race. One foreign policy crisis followed another: Soviet domination of Eastern Europe, the fall of mainland China to communism, and the North Korean invasion of South Korea. By 1950 the threat of international communism seemed as ominous to the American people as the threat of nazism had been a decade before.

Life in the postwar United States was marked by a combination of affluence and anxiety. Following two decades of economic depression, world war, and cold war, Americans wanted a leader who would steer a moderate course in domestic and foreign affairs: a leader who would heal partisan wounds without turning back the clock and who would end the conflict in Korea without widening it or compromising the nation's honor. In 1952, Dwight D. Eisenhower seemed to be the one.

CHAPTER REVIEW, 1946–1952

- The United States moved from a wartime to a peacetime economy.
- Returning veterans received generous education and housing benefits under the GI Bill.
- A tremendous surge in marriage and birth rates spurred a rush to suburbia.
- Soviet–American relations deteriorated as the iron curtain descended over Eastern Europe.
- A symbolic step toward racial justice occurred with the integration of Major League Baseball in 1947.
- The Alger Hiss case heightened fears of Soviet espionage in the United States.
- Harry Truman's surprise reelection in 1948 kept the New Deal coalition intact.
- The Korean War raised fears of a widening conflict with Communist China and a nuclear confrontation with the Soviet Union.
- Dwight Eisenhower's victory in 1952 ended two decades of Democratic control of the executive branch.

◀▬ꜰꜰꜰ *Looking Back*

Chapter 27 looks at the United States in the post–World War II years, following one of the defining moments in its history. Key points are the baby boom, the growth of suburbia, and the beginning of the Cold War.

1. What accounted for the worsening of relations between the Soviet Union and the United States?
2. Why did the wartime prosperity continue, and greatly increase, following World War II? What factors accounted for this?
3. Why did Harry Truman defeat Thomas Dewey for the presidency in 1948? Why did so many pundits think Dewey would win?
4. What impact did the case of Alger Hiss have on the rise of Senator Joseph R. McCarthy? What else was responsible for the popular support that McCarthy received?

Looking Ahead ꜰꜰꜰ▬▶

Chapter 28 examines the united states in the 1950s, a time of continued economic prosperity and material comfort, on the one hand, and a time of enduring cold war tensions and momentous racial stirrings, on the other.

1. What were the major problems Dwight Eisenhower would face in assuming the presidency?
2. Was it possible that a new administration in Washington would be better able to deal with international problems than the old one, especially problems relating to the Cold War?
3. Would the prosperity of the early postwar era last into the future, and would it expand to include the poorest groups in society?

Go to the American Passages website at www.cengage.com/history/ayers/ ampassages4e for additional review materials.

28 The Eisenhower Years, 1953–1960

The United States at the middle of the twentieth century was far different from the nation we live in today. The **Cold War** was at its height, U.S. soldiers were dying in Korea, and communism seemed a formidable foe. The American population of 153 million contained a small and declining number of foreign born, the result of strict immigration quotas installed in the 1920s. Most blacks still lived in the South, where racial segregation was the law. Blue-collar workers outnumbered white-collar workers, and labor unions, led by charismatic figures like John L. Lewis and Walter Reuther, were at the height of their power. Major League baseball had only sixteen teams, none west of St. Louis. There were no supermarkets or shopping malls, no motel chains or ballpoint pens. Television was just beginning, rock music still a few years away. More than half of the nation's farm dwellings had no electricity. It cost three cents to mail a letter and a nickel to buy a Coke.

Marriage rates were at an all-time high, and divorce rates kept declining. In 1954, *McCall's* magazine used the term *togetherness* to describe American family life, with shared activities such as Little League, car rides, and backyard barbecues. Though more women worked outside the home in 1950 than in 1944, the height of World War II, they did so mainly to supplement the family income, not to seek full-time careers. In the growing cult of motherhood, fulfillment meant meeting the needs of others. Feminism was described in psychology books as a "deep illness," entirely out of place.

America at mid-twentieth century saw an acceleration of postwar trends. As 40 million people moved to the suburbs, the large cities declined in population, political power, and quality of life. Racial lines remained rigid, with census data showing the suburbs to be more affluent than the cities they surrounded—and 98 percent white. Automobile sales skyrocketed, creating whole new industries to service American travelers. Inventions poured forth, from the computer to the polio vaccine. And a new president was elected to guide the country through these anxious, demanding times.

A NEW DIRECTION, 1953

Dwight Eisenhower entered the White House on a wave of good feeling. His lack of political experience appeared to be an asset after the turmoil of the Truman years. Americans trusted Eisenhower's judgment and admired his character. They believed that his enormous skills as a military leader would serve him equally well as president of the United States.

Modern Republicanism

Yet few Americans knew where Eisenhower stood on important domestic or international issues. His presidential campaign in 1952 had been intentionally vague. He described himself as a moderate, using the term "modern Republicanism" to define his political approach.

Eisenhower filled his cabinet with prominent business leaders. For secretary of defense, he chose Charles E. ("Engine Charlie") Wilson, former president of General Motors, who proclaimed at his confirmation hearing that "what was good for our country was good for General Motors, and vice versa." For secretary of the treasury, Eisenhower selected George Humphrey, a fiscal conservative who believed in smaller government and less federal spending. Eisenhower had no intention of dismantling popular New Deal programs such as social security or unemployment insurance, and he supported a significant hike in the minimum hourly wage, from seventy-five cents to a dollar. Yet wherever possible, he worked to balance the budget, trim government expenditures, and stimulate private enterprise. "I'm conservative when it comes to money," Eisenhower claimed, but "liberal when it comes to human beings."

In his first year as president, federal spending and federal income taxes were both cut by 10 percent. Eisenhower also opposed expansion of such popular but expensive federal programs as price supports for farmers and cheap public power from government dams and electric plants. In perhaps his most controversial early move, the president strongly supported passage of the Tidelands Oil Act, which transferred coastal oil land worth at least $40 billion from the federal government to the states. Critics, fearing the exploitation of these vital reserves by a few giant corporations, described "Tidelands" as the "most unjustified giveaway program" of the modern era.

A Truce in Korea

One member of Eisenhower's cabinet, Secretary of State John Foster Dulles, stood above the rest. The son of a minister and grandson of a former secretary of state, Dulles trained from his earliest days to serve God and country. Most observers found him arrogant, stubborn, and sour. Yet Eisenhower respected his secretary as a tough, knowledgeable adviser who willingly took the heat for actions the president himself had formulated. "I know what they say about Foster—dull, duller, Dulles—and all that," Eisenhower told a friend. "But the [critics] love to hit him rather than me."

The president's first priority in foreign affairs was to end the Korean conflict. Though willing to accept the same terms that Truman had proposed—two Koreas,

This icon will direct you to interactive activities and study materials on the American Passages website: www.cengage.com/history/ayers/ampassages4e

1953	Truce ends fighting in Korea • Soviet dictator Joseph Stalin dies
1954	Supreme Court issues school desegregation ruling in *Brown v. Board of Education* • U.S. Senate censures Joseph McCarthy
1955	Bus boycott begins in Montgomery, Alabama • Elvis Presley signs with RCA Records • Brooklyn Dodgers finally win World Series
1956	Federal Highway Act passed, forging massive interstate highway system • Hungarian Revolution and Suez crisis strain U.S.–Soviet relations • Eisenhower easily reelected
1957	Russians launch *Sputnik* • Federal troops sent to enforce school integration order in Little Rock
1958	U.S. manned space program begins
1959	Fidel Castro leads successful revolution in Cuba • Soviet Premier Nikita Khrushchev visits United States
1960	American U-2 spy plane shot down over Soviet Union • John F. Kennedy elected president

North and South, divided at the thirty-eighth parallel—Eisenhower demanded a prompt resolution. To speed this process, Dulles apparently warned the Communist Chinese (through diplomatic channels in India) that the United States would not rule out the use of atomic weapons if the Korean stalemate dragged on.

The impact of this "nuclear threat" is difficult to gauge. The Chinese Communists probably viewed Eisenhower, a military leader, as a more dangerous foe than Harry Truman. Yet huge Communist battlefield losses, coupled with the sudden death of Joseph Stalin, helped spur the peace process. In July 1953, a truce was signed that stopped the fighting without formally ending the war. More than 50,000 Americans were killed and 103,000 were wounded in Korea. The Pentagon estimated that 2.4 million civilians died or were seriously injured in the three years of terrible fighting, along with 850,000 troops from South Korea, 520,000 from North Korea, and 950,000 from Communist China.

THE COLD WAR AT HOME AND ABROAD, 1953–1954

When Republicans took control of Congress and the White House in 1953, the "communist issue" gained center stage. On Capitol Hill, 185 of the 221 House Republicans applied for duty on the House Un-American Activities Committee, where Chairman Harold Velde of Illinois vowed to hunt down communists like "rats." At the White House, President Eisenhower promised both a crackdown on "subversives" in government and a "New Look" in military affairs, designed to streamline American forces for the continuing struggle against "worldwide Communist aggression."

The Hunt for "Subversives" Shortly after taking office, President Eisenhower issued an executive order that extended the scope of the Federal Loyalty

Searching for "Reds" in Government

The search for communists in government became one of the key political issues of the early Cold War era. This cartoon gives the impression that communists were rampant in the federal bureaucracy in the 1950s and that Uncle Sam was adept at the tough but vital job of weeding them out. Was this perception correct? Recent evidence—gleaned from newly opened Soviet security archives and a supersecret American code-breaking project known as Venona—suggests that communist espionage in government was indeed a serious problem during the late 1930s and World War II and that among those Americans who spied for the Soviet Union was Alger Hiss (pages 799–800). The new

(Culver Pictures)

evidence, however, does not support the sensational charges of Senator Joseph R. McCarthy and others that hundreds of communists were still at work in the federal government in the 1950s. Indeed, it appears that such penetration declined dramatically after World War II, due, in large part, to the careful scrutiny of the FBI. In 1953, the time of this cartoon, the Eisenhower administration announced that 1,456 federal employees had been fired under the Federal Loyalty Program. It turned out, however, that the vast majority were released for offenses such as alcoholism, malingering, and alleged homosexuality. Almost none was dismissed for reasons pertaining to disloyalty.

Security Program. A few months later, he announced that 1,456 federal workers had been fired as "security risks," including "alcoholics," "homosexuals," and "political subversives." The most controversial security case involved J. Robert Oppenheimer, the distinguished physicist who directed the Manhattan Project during World War II. Oppenheimer's prewar association with left-wing radicals was widely known. He had been checked and rechecked by the FBI, cleared and recleared by the Atomic Energy Commission until 1953, when the Eisenhower administration suspended his top security clearance. Many believed that Oppenheimer's troubles resulted from his public opposition to the building of the hydrogen bomb—a charge the administration vigorously denied.

   In Congress, the Red-hunting fervor was even more intense. The Senate assault was led by Joseph McCarthy, newly appointed chairman of the Committee on Government Operations and its powerful Subcommittee on Investigations. Filling key staff positions with ex-FBI agents and former prosecutors like Roy M. Cohn, an abrasive young attorney from New York, McCarthy looked for "Communist influence" in the State Department and other government agencies. His hearings did not uncover many communists. They did, however, ruin numerous careers, undermine worker morale, and make the United States look fearful in the eyes of the world. Not surprisingly, Republican criticism of McCarthy began to build. After all, he was now attacking a federal bureaucracy controlled by his own party.

Many expected Eisenhower to put the senator in his place. But the new president was slow to respond, believing that a brawl with McCarthy would divide Republicans into warring camps and seriously demean the presidential office. Time and again, he told his aides: "I just will not—I refuse to get into the gutter with that guy."

Eisenhower changed his mind after McCarthy's subcommittee, spearheaded by Roy Cohn, began to investigate charges that a "Communist spy ring" was operating at Fort Monmouth, New Jersey, home of the Army Signal Corps. Army officials responded that Cohn was harassing the service in order to win preferential treatment for a close friend and part-time McCarthy staffer named G. David Schine, who had recently been drafted into the army. Early in 1954, the Senate agreed to investigate these conflicting allegations. Furious at the attacks on his beloved army, Eisenhower privately urged Republican Senate leaders to televise the hearings. The president wanted the American people to see McCarthy in action, and it proved to be a shrewd move. For thirty-six days, the nation watched the senator's frightening outbursts and crude personal attacks. The highlight of the hearings came on June 9, 1954, when army counsel Joseph Welch sternly rebuked McCarthy for his menacing behavior, asking: "Have you no sense of decency, sir? Have you left no sense of decency?" The spectators burst into applause.

A few months later, the Senate censured McCarthy for bringing that body "into dishonor and disrepute." The vote was 67 to 22, with only conservative Republicans opposed. Many believed that McCarthy's censure was linked to the easing of Cold War tensions at home. The Korean War was over, and Stalin was dead. For McCarthy, things came apart at a wicked rate of speed. Reporters and colleagues ignored him, and his influence disappeared. Unable to get his message across, McCarthy spent his final days drinking in private. He died of liver failure in 1957, virtually alone, at the age of forty-eight.

Brinksmanship and Covert Action   Like Truman before him, President Eisenhower supported the containment of communism through military, economic, and diplomatic means. But he took a different approach, which he called the "New Look." It was fruitless to match the communists "man for man, gun for gun," he reasoned. The Korean stalemate showed the folly of that approach. In place of conventional forces, the United States must emphasize "the deterrent of massive retaliatory power." This meant using America's edge in nuclear weapons and long-range bombers to best advantage.

The New Look allowed Eisenhower to cut defense spending by 20 percent between 1953 and 1955. The number of men and women in uniform went down each year, and the production of atomic warheads dramatically increased. Secretary of State Dulles viewed the New Look as a way to intimidate potential enemies with the implied threat of atomic attack. He called this "brinksmanship," claiming that "the ability to get to the verge without getting into the war is the necessary art."

Critics, however, saw brinksmanship as a dangerous game. Intimidation meant little, they warned, if the United States did not intend to back up its words. Was Eisenhower willing to consider atomic weapons as a viable option in every international crisis? If not, he undermined America's credibility; if so, he risked nuclear destruction. To increase his flexibility in foreign affairs, the president needed other options as well.

In 1953, Eisenhower appointed Allen Dulles, younger brother of the secretary of state, to head the Central Intelligence Agency (CIA). Dulles emphasized "covert action" over intelligence gathering—a change the president fully endorsed. Most of the CIA's new work was cloaked in secrecy, and much of it was illegal. Covert action became one of Eisenhower's favorite foreign policy tools.

Iran was a case in point. In 1953, the new government of Mohammed Mossadegh nationalized the British-controlled oil fields and deposed the pro-Western shah of Iran. The United States, believing Mossadegh's government to be pro-communist, feared for its oil supplies in the Middle East. President Eisenhower thus approved a CIA operation that toppled Mossadegh and returned the young shah to power. A few months later, Iran agreed to split its oil production among three Western nations, with American companies getting 40 percent, British companies 40 percent, and Dutch companies 20 percent. The grateful shah told the CIA: "I owe my throne to God, my people, my army, and to you."

In 1954, the CIA struck again, forcing the overthrow of Guatemala's democratically elected president, Jacobo Arbenz Guzman. Guatemala was one of the world's poorest nations. Its largest employer and landholder, the American-owned United Fruit Company, controlled much of the Guatemalan economy. After taking office, Arbenz supported a strike of banana workers on United Fruit plantations, who were seeking wages of $1.50 a day. Far more provocative, however, was a new law, known as Decree 900, which expropriated millions of acres of private property for the use of landless peasant families. Under this law, the Arbenz government offered United Fruit $1.2 million for 234,000 acres of its land—a figure based on the absurdly low tax assessments given United Fruit in the past.

The company had powerful allies in the United States. Numerous government officials, including both Dulles brothers, were linked to United Fruit through their previous corporate positions. Defending the company's interests came naturally to them, and the idea of expropriating American property smacked of "communist thinking." If Arbenz succeeded, they reasoned, the notion could spread across Latin America like wildfire.

Eisenhower moved quickly, authorizing the overthrow of Arbenz by Guatemalan exiles trained at CIA bases in Honduras and Nicaragua. The small invasion force, backed by CIA pilots, tore through Arbenz's poorly equipped army. The American press, meanwhile, accepted the Eisenhower–Dulles account that Guatemalan liberators had ousted a dangerous, pro-communist regime with minimal American help. In the following months, the new government of General Carlos Castillo Armas established a military dictatorship, executed hundreds of Arbenz supporters, and returned the expropriated lands to United Fruit.

Events in Indochina (or Vietnam) did not turn out as well for the American interests. Following World War II, nationalist forces in that French colony, led by **Ho Chi Minh**, a popular Marxist leader, began an armed struggle for independence.

The United States, viewing Ho (incorrectly) as a puppet of Moscow, supported French attempts to crush the Vietnamese resistance, known as the Vietminh. By 1953, American military aid to France in the Indochina conflict totaled nearly $3 billion.

It failed to turn the tide. The Vietminh grew stronger. In 1954, Ho's forces surrounded twelve thousand elite French troops at an isolated garrison called Dien Bien Phu. Facing sure defeat, the French appealed to the United States for help. After an agonizing debate with Pentagon and State Department officials—which included the possibility of using nuclear weapons—President Eisenhower refused to commit American ground troops or air support to save Dien Bien Phu. On May 7, 1954, the battered garrison surrendered, effectively ending French rule in Vietnam.

At peace talks in Geneva, Switzerland, the two sides agreed to a cease-fire and a temporary partition of Vietnam at the seventeenth parallel, with French troops moving south of that line and Vietminh forces moving north. Free elections were scheduled for 1956, at which time the French were to fully withdraw. The United States refused to recognize the Geneva Accords. Eisenhower and Dulles were not about to acquiesce in a unified Vietnam under the leadership of Ho Chi Minh, the certain winner in the proposed election of 1956. The U.S. plan, therefore, was to prevent that election, while creating a permanent anti-communist government in South Vietnam supported by American economic and military aid.

To Eisenhower, the survival of South Vietnam became the key to containing communism in Asia. He described the so-called **domino theory** at a press conference about Indochina in 1954. "You have a row of dominoes set up," he began. "You knock over the first one, and what will happen to the last one is a certainty that it will go over quickly. So the possible consequences of the loss [of Vietnam] are just incalculable to the free world."

THE CIVIL RIGHTS MOVEMENT, 1954–1955

The 1950s witnessed enormous gains in the struggle for minority rights. In federal courts and in cities throughout the South, African Americans struggled to eradicate the system of racial segregation that denied them dignity, opportunity, and equal protection under the law. Though the Eisenhower administration proved far less sympathetic to the cause of civil rights than the Truman administration had been, the movement for racial justice took on a power and a spirit that would transform the nation in the coming years.

Brown v. Board of Education   In September 1953, Chief Justice Fred Vinson died of a heart attack, requiring President Eisenhower to make his first appointment to the U.S. Supreme Court. Eisenhower offered the position to California Governor Earl Warren, who won prompt Senate approval. Far more liberal than Eisenhower on social issues, Warren would sometimes anger the president in the coming years, but rarely lose his respect.

The major issue facing the Supreme Court in 1953 was civil rights. For more than a decade, a group of talented African American attorneys had been filing legal challenges to segregated public facilities in the South, hoping to erode the "separate but equal" doctrine of *Plessy v. Ferguson*. Led by Thurgood Marshall and William Hastie of the NAACP's Legal Defense Fund, these attorneys targeted specific areas, such

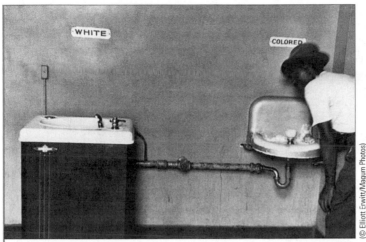

Segregation in the South. *Jim Crow was a way of life in the South, where public and private facilities ranging from hospitals to restaurants to cemeteries were racially segregated by law.*

as professional education (law, medicine, teaching), to establish precedents for the larger fight.

This strategy worked well. In 1950, the Supreme Court stretched the *Plessy* doctrine to its limits in two lawsuits brought by the NAACP. In *Sweatt v. Painter*, the Court ruled that Texas authorities must admit a black applicant to the all-white state law school in Austin because they had failed to provide African Americans with a comparable facility, thereby violating the equal protection clause of the Fourteenth Amendment. And in *McLaurin v. Oklahoma*, the Court struck down a scheme that segregated a black student within that state's graduate school of education, forcing him to sit alone in the library and the lecture halls in a section marked "Reserved for Coloreds."

With these victories, the NAACP took on the larger challenge of racial segregation in the nation's public schools. Unlike *Sweatt* and *McLaurin*, which involved a small number of adult students, the new cases touched millions of children, white and black, in twenty-one states and the District of Columbia. By 1953, five separate lawsuits had reached the Supreme Court, including *Brown v. Board of Education of Topeka*.

Brown involved a Kansas law that permitted cities to segregate their public schools. With NAACP support, the Reverend Oliver Brown sued the Topeka school board, arguing that his eight-year-old daughter should not be forced to attend a Negro school a mile from her home when there was a white public school only three blocks away. The Supreme Court was badly divided. Several justices supported the *Plessy* doctrine; others argued that it fostered racial inequality. Believing racial segregation to be both unconstitutional and morally wrong, Chief Justice Warren insisted that the Supreme Court speak in a powerful, united voice against this evil. Anything less, he reasoned, would encourage massive resistance in the South.

On May 17, 1954, the Supreme Court overturned *Plessy v. Ferguson* in a stunning 9–0 decision, written by Warren himself. Relying on the studies of social scientists such as Kenneth Clark, the chief justice claimed that racial segregation had a "detrimental effect" on black children by making them feel inferior to whites. "In the field of public education the doctrine of 'separate but equal' has no place," he stated. "Separate educational facilities are inherently unequal."

The Supreme Court put off its implementation guidelines (known as *Brown II*) for a full year, hoping to let passions cool in the South. *Brown II* required local school boards to draw up desegregation plans with the approval of a federal district judge. But there were no timetables, and the wording was intentionally vague. Integration should proceed, it said, "with all deliberate speed."

White southern reaction was intense. "You are not required to obey any court which passes out such a ruling," Senator James O. Eastland of Mississippi told his constituents. "In fact, you are obligated to defy it." Violence flared across the South. "In one school district after another," wrote an observer, "segregationists staged the same drama: forcing young blacks to enter a school by passing rock-throwing white mobs and white pickets shouting 'Nigger,' 'Nigger,' 'Nigger.'" The Ku Klux Klan came alive in the 1950s, and new groups like the White Citizens' Council were formed to defend segregation and the "southern way of life."

Many Americans looked to the White House for guidance about civil rights. But Eisenhower had little to say about the issue, partly because he personally opposed the "forced integration" of the races. When asked at a press conference if he had any advice for the South on how to handle the *Brown* decision, Eisenhower replied: "Not in the slightest. The Supreme Court has spoken and I am sworn to uphold the constitutional processes in this country; and I will obey."

The Montgomery Bus Boycott

The battle over public school integration was but one of many such struggles in the South during this era. Some were fought by attorneys in federal courtrooms; others involved ordinary men and women determined to challenge the indignities of racial segregation and second-class treatment in their daily lives. "Nothing is quite as humiliating, so murderously angering," said one African American, "as to know that because you are black you may have to walk a half mile farther than whites to urinate; that because you are black you have to receive your food through a window in the back of a restaurant or sit in a garbage-littered yard."

The black people of Montgomery, Alabama, had experienced such treatment for years. Known as "the cradle of the Confederacy," Montgomery enforced segregation and racial etiquette in meticulous detail. Blacks always tipped their hats to whites, always stood in the presence of whites unless told to sit, and always addressed whites with a title of respect. ("Boss," "Sir," and "Ma'am" were most common.) Restrooms, drinking fountains, blood banks, movie theaters, cemeteries—all were separated by race. It was illegal for whites and blacks to play checkers together on public property or to share a taxi cab. On the local buses, blacks paid their fares in the front, got off the vehicle, and entered the "colored section" through the rear door. They also had to relinquish their seats to white passengers when the front section filled up.

On December 1, 1955, a simple yet revolutionary act of resistance occurred on a crowded Montgomery bus. **Rosa Parks**, a forty-two-year-old black seamstress and member of the local NAACP, refused to give up her seat to a white. The bus driver called the police. "They got on the bus," Parks recalled, "and one of them asked me why I didn't stand up. I asked him, 'Why do you push us around?' He said, '. . . I don't know, but the law is the law and you're under arrest.'"

News of Parks's defiance electrified the black community. Within days a boycott of Montgomery's bus system was begun, organized by local clergymen and the Women's Political Council, the black alternative to the all-white League of Women Voters. Calling themselves the Montgomery Improvement Association (MIA), they chose a young minister named **Martin Luther King, Jr.**, to lead the struggle for open seating in public transportation, a small but highly symbolic step.

King, twenty-six years old, was a newcomer to Montgomery. He was selected in part because his youth and vocation made him less vulnerable to economic and political pressure from whites. The son of a well-known Atlanta pastor, King earned his college degree at Morehouse and his doctorate at Boston University's School of Theology before heading south with his new wife, Coretta Scott King, to serve as pastor of Montgomery's Dexter Avenue Baptist Church in 1954. Dr. King was familiar with the works of Gandhi and Thoreau, and he viewed mass action and nonviolent resistance as essential weapons in the war against racial injustice.

King rallied the black community with the eloquent passion of his words. "There comes a time when people get tired," he told a packed rally after Rosa Parks's arrest. "We are here this evening to say to those who have mistreated us so long that we are tired—tired of being segregated and humiliated, tired of being kicked about by the brutal feet of oppression. We have no alternative but to protest."

King's reputation soared. He kept the movement together despite police harassment and the firebombing of his home. Blacks in Montgomery formed car pools to get people to their destinations. The churches raised money for fuel, and black-owned garages did repair work free of charge. Many people rode bicycles or simply walked for miles. The **Montgomery bus boycott** nearly bankrupted the city bus system and badly hurt the white merchants downtown. Mother Pollard, bent with age, inspired the movement with her simple remark: "My feets is tired, but my soul is rested."

In November 1956, the federal courts struck down the Alabama law requiring racial segregation in public transportation. A month later, blacks sat in the front of the Montgomery buses without incident. The boycott, lasting 381 days, demonstrated both the power of collective action and the possibility of social change. In 1957, Dr. King joined with other black ministers and civil rights activists to form the Southern Christian Leadership Conference (SCLC), an organization devoted to racial justice through peaceful means. "Noncooperation with evil," King declared, "is as much a moral obligation as is cooperation with good."

THE GOLDEN AGE OF TELEVISION

In the 1950s, social commentators analyzed a host of new issues in American life. Some worried about the struggle between individuals and organizations, the apparent quest for security over adventure, the monotony of modern work. A few focused on the supposed emptiness of suburban living, the growing cult of domesticity among women, the changing standards of success. Yet what struck virtually all critics and commentators in the 1950s was the impact of television on American life—an impact that altered politics, news gathering, consumer tastes, and popular culture in truly revolutionary ways.

The Magic Box   When World War II ended, there were seventeen TV sets in the United States. The late 1940s saw major changes in television technology, such as the use of coaxial cable and the introduction of color. In 1949, a TV set appeared for the first time in the Sears, Roebuck catalogue—$149.95 "with indoor antenna." A year later, Americans were buying twenty thousand television sets a day. The two most popular shows of that era were Milton Berle's *Texaco Star Theater* and Ed Sullivan's *Toast of the Town*. Berle, a physical comedian, seemed perfect for a visual medium like TV. His fast-paced humor relied on sight gags instead of verbal banter. The press called him "Mr. Television."

Sullivan, a former gossip columnist, was awkward and unsmiling on camera. What made him unique was his ability to provide fresh entertainment to Americans of all tastes and ages. Sullivan's Sunday night variety show, mixing opera with acrobats, ran for twenty-three years on CBS. His guests included Elvis Presley, Dean Martin and Jerry Lewis, pianist Van Cliburn, dancer Rudolf Nureyev, singer Lena Horne,

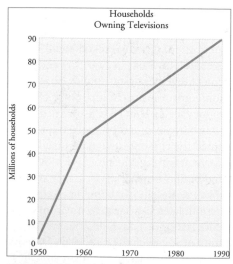

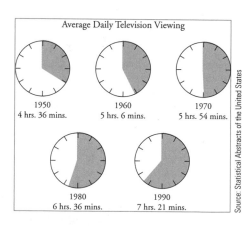

Source: Statistical Abstracts of the United States

FIGURE 28.1 The Television Revolution, 1950–1990.

As television became commonplace in the 1950s, TV viewing altered the nature of American politics and culture. Average daily television viewing has increased in each decade, with Americans now spending almost half their waking hours with their sets turned on.

and the Beatles. "Ed Sullivan will last," said pianist Oscar Levant, "as long as other people have talent."

Television's potential was impossible to ignore. In 1951, an obscure Tennessee politician named Estes Kefauver became a national figure by holding televised hearings into organized crime. Senator Kefauver grilled prominent mobsters like New York's Frank Costello as 25 million viewers watched in amazement. The TV cameras perfectly captured Costello's discomfort by focusing for several minutes on his jittery, sweat-soaked hands.

Nixon's "Checkers speech" and the Army–McCarthy hearings further highlighted the impact of television in the political arena. Above all, however, TV possessed the power to sell. In 1950, local stations, desperate for programming, aired a series of old *Hopalong Cassidy* movies starring an obscure cowboy-actor named William Boyd. Within months, "Hopalong Cassidy" clothing and six-guns were in frantic demand, grossing $30 million before the craze died out. Walt Disney struck gold with his three-part series on Davy Crockett, which aired nationally in 1954. Millions of children wore coonskin caps to school. There were Davy Crockett shirts and blankets, toothbrushes and lunch boxes. One department store chain sold twenty thousand surplus pup tents in less than a week by printing "Davy Crockett" on the flap.

By 1954, three national networks were firmly in place. As the major radio powers, ABC, CBS, and NBC held a decided advantage over potential competitors in technology and talent. Indeed, these networks filled their early airtime by moving popular radio programs like *Jack Benny, Burns & Allen*, and *Amos 'n' Andy* over to TV. The faster television grew, the more its schedule expanded. Important advertisers signed on, sponsoring entire programs such as *Kraft Television Theater* and *Motorola Playhouse*. This, in turn, provided work for hundreds of performers at a time when the motion picture industry was losing ground to television. New York City, the early center of TV production, became a magnet for young actors and writers like Paul Newman, Sidney Poitier, Joanne Woodward, Rod Serling, Neil Simon, and Mel Brooks.

Some critics called this era the "golden age" of television. They pointed to the high quality of plays and dramas, the original comedy of Sid Caesar and Jackie Gleason, and the powerful documentaries of Edward R. Murrow on *See It Now*. Yet by 1955, this "golden age" was largely over. The networks abandoned most live broadcasts in favor of filmed episodes, with Hollywood quickly replacing Manhattan as television's capital. Popular new shows like *Dragnet* and *I Love Lucy* showed the advantages of film over live TV. Production was less demanding. Errors could be corrected, scenes could be shot at different locations, and episodes could be shown more than once, creating additional revenues.

Many television shows of the 1950s reflected both the yearnings and stereotypes of American society. Popular comedies such as *Father Knows Best, Ozzie and Harriet*, and *Leave It to Beaver* portrayed the charmed lives (and minor problems) of middle-class white families in the suburbs. Mother was a housewife. Dad held a pressure-free white-collar job. The kids were well adjusted and witty. Money was never a problem. No one stayed angry for long. "You know, Mom," said Beaver Cleaver, "when we're in a mess, you kind of make things seem not so messy." "Well," June Cleaver replied, "isn't that sort of what mothers are for?"

Married women in TV sitcoms did not work outside the home. Their husbands would not permit it. This rule even applied to childless couples like Ralph and

Alice Kramden of *The Honeymooners*, one of television's rare programs about urban, working-class people. Furthermore, single women in sitcoms rarely took their jobs seriously. Like Eve Arden in *Our Miss Brooks* and Ann Sothern in *Private Secretary*, they spent most of their time hunting for a husband.

Though racial minorities almost never appeared in these sitcoms, they did play major—if stereotypical—roles in two or three popular shows of the 1950s. There was *Beulah*, the big-hearted domestic in a white suburban household, and *Rochester*, the wisecracking butler on the Jack Benny Show. Above all, there was *Amos 'n' Andy*, an adaptation of the popular radio show created by two white men, Freeman Gosden and Charles Correll, that featured an all-black cast. The NAACP angrily denounced *Amos 'n' Andy* for portraying blacks as "clowns" and "crooks," but others praised the performers for transforming racist stereotypes into "authentic black humor."

The Quiz Show Scandals   No other event raised more concerns about the control and direction of commercial television in the 1950s than the quiz show scandals. Quiz shows were a throwback to the radio era; they appeared early on television but did not generate much interest until Revlon cosmetics produced a "big money" version called *The $64,000 Question*, which aired on CBS in June 1955.

The rules were simple. After choosing a topic, such as science or baseball, the contestant fielded questions that began at $64 and doubled with each correct answer. At the $16,000 plateau, the contestant entered a glass "isolation booth." The show drew the highest ratings in TV history—a whopping 85 percent audience share—when contestants went for the $64,000 question. Meanwhile, Revlon's annual sales rose from $34 million to $86 million, and its stock jumped from $12 to $20 a share.

Before long, the airwaves were flooded with imitations. In 1956, *The $64,000 Question* lost its top rating to NBC's *Twenty-One*, which pitted two competitors in a trivia contest structured like the blackjack card game. The stakes grew ever larger. Charles Van Doren, a handsome English instructor at Columbia University, won $129,000 on *Twenty-One* and became an instant national hero.

His good fortune did not last long. In 1959, a grand jury investigation revealed that numerous quiz show contestants had been given the questions in advance. It turned out that both *The $64,000 Question* and *Twenty-One* were rigged, with players coached about every detail of their performance.

President Eisenhower condemned the "selfishness" and "greed" of the perpetrators. Yet there was nothing illegal about these shows. Indeed, some sponsors defended them as a form of entertainment, akin to professional wrestling or a ghostwritten book. As public anger mounted, however, Congress passed legislation to prevent the rigging of TV quiz shows, and the networks promised to regulate themselves. *The $64,000 Question, Twenty-One*, and other big money game shows quickly left the air.

The quality of television did not improve. New programs became clones of each other—bland sitcoms or violent westerns and crime dramas. Advertising now consumed 20 percent of television airtime, with more money spent making commercials than producing the shows themselves. One study in the 1950s estimated that an American youngster spent eleven thousand hours in the classroom through high school and fifteen thousand hours in front of TV. Another concluded that adults spent more time watching television than working for pay. There were complaints that television tended to isolate people and to shorten their attention spans. Nobody needed to concentrate for more than a half-hour—and not very hard at that.

As television expanded, other media outlets declined. Mass circulation magazines such as *Look* and *Collier's* folded in the 1950s, and newspaper readership went way down. Movie attendance dropped, and radio lost listeners, forcing both industries to experiment in order to survive. Hollywood tried Cinemascope, Technicolor, 3-D glasses, drive-in movies, and big budget spectacles like *The Ten Commandments* and *Ben Hur*. Radio moved from soap operas and big band music to "hip" disc jockeys spinning rock 'n' roll. Nevertheless, television was now king. People watched the same programs in Boston and San Diego, in rural hamlets and in cities, in rich areas and in poor. America's popular culture, consumer needs, and general information—all came increasingly from TV.

YOUTH CULTURE

In the 1950s, a distinctive teenage culture emerged, rooted in the enormous prosperity and population growth that followed World War II. America's young people were far removed from the grim events of the previous two decades. Raised in relative affluence, surrounded by messages that undermined traditional values of thrift and self-denial, these new teenagers were perceived as a special group with a unique subculture. They rarely worked, yet their pockets were full. By 1956, the nation's teenage market topped $9 billion a year. The typical adolescent spent as much on entertainment as had the average family in 1941.

A New Kind of Music   Nothing defined these 13 million teenagers more clearly than the music they shared. In the 1940s, popular music was dominated by the "big bands" of Glenn Miller and Tommy Dorsey, the Broadway show tunes of Rodgers and Hammerstein, and the mellow voices of Bing Crosby, Frank Sinatra, and the Andrews Sisters. These artists appealed to a broad white audience of all ages. Other forms of popular music—bluegrass, country, rhythm and blues—were limited by region and race.

But not for long. The huge migration of rural blacks and whites to industrial centers during World War II profoundly altered popular culture. The sounds of "race" music, "hillbilly" music, and gospel became readily available to mainstream America for the first time. Record sales tripled during the 1950s, aided by technological advances like the transistor radio and the 45 rpm vinyl disc (or "single"). The main consumers were young people, who acquired new tastes by flipping the radio dial.

In 1951, a Cleveland, Ohio, record dealer noticed that white teenagers at his store were "going crazy" over the songs of black rhythm and blues artists like Ivory Joe Hunter and Lloyd Price. He told a local disc jockey named **Alan Freed**, who decided to play these records on the air. Freed's new program, *The Moondog Party*, took Cleveland by storm. Soon Freed was hosting live shows at the local arena to overflow crowds. Pounding his fists to the rhythm, chanting "go man, go," Freed became the self-proclaimed father of rock 'n' roll.

"I'll never forget the first time I heard his show," a writer recalled. "I couldn't believe sounds like that were coming out of the radio." Freed understood the defiant, sensual nature of rock 'n' roll, the way it separated the young from everyone else.

It was their music, played by their heroes, set to their special beat. Indeed, rock's first national hit, "Rock Around the Clock," by Bill Haley and the Comets, became the theme song for *Blackboard Jungle*, a movie about rebellious high school students set to the throbbing rhythms of rock 'n' roll.

The Rise of Elvis

Haley's success was fleeting. He didn't generate the intense excitement or sexual spark that teenagers craved. As Haley faded, a twenty-one-year-old truck driver from Memphis exploded onto the popular music scene. His name was Elvis Presley; the year was 1955.

Born in rural Mississippi, Presley was surrounded by the sounds of country music, gospel, and blues. As a teenager in Memphis, he listened to WDIA—"the Mother Station of Negroes"—and frequented the legendary blues clubs along Beale Street. The music moved him deeply, providing both spiritual force and physical release.

Memphis was also home to Sun Records, a label with strong southern roots. Owned by Sam Phillips, Sun recorded white country singers like Johnny Cash and black bluesmen such as B. B. King. What Phillips most wanted was an artist who combined these two sounds instinctively, without appearing artificial or forced. "If I could find a white man who had the Negro sound and the Negro feel," Phillips said, "I could make a million dollars."

Presley was that man. Signing with Sun Records in 1954, he took the region by storm. The press described his unique style as "a cross between be-bop and country" and "a new hillbilly blues beat." It wasn't just the sound. Tall and handsome, with long sideburns and slicked-back hair, Presley was a riveting performer, combining little-boy shyness with enormous sexual charisma. A fellow artist described young Presley on tour:

> This cat came out in red pants and a green coat and a pink shirt and socks, and he had this sneer on his face. And he stood behind the mike for five minutes, I'll bet, before he made a move. [Meanwhile] these high school girls were screaming and fainting and running up to the stage, and then he started to move his hips real slow like he had a thing for his guitar.

When Presley became too big to handle, Sun Records sold his contract to RCA in 1955 for thirty-five thousand dollars, a sizable amount at that time. Before long, he was a national sensation. His early hits topped the charts in popular music, country, and rhythm and blues—the first time that had ever occurred. In less than a year, Elvis recorded eight number-one songs and six of RCA's all-time top twenty-five records. When he appeared on *Ed Sullivan*, the cameras carefully shot him from the waist up. The ratings were extraordinary. "I want to say to Elvis and the country," Sullivan told his audience, "that this is a real decent, fine boy."

Young Elvis was modest and polite. He didn't smoke or drink or use drugs. He was so devoted to his parents that friends laughingly described him as a mama's boy. Yet his exaggerated sexuality on stage made him the target of those who believed that rock 'n' roll was a vulgar and dangerous assault on America's youth. "Popular music," wrote one television critic, "has reached its lowest depths in the grunt and groin antics of Mr. Presley."

Such criticism served only to enhance Presley's stature in the teenage world. And his success led the major record companies to experiment more aggressively with black rhythm and blues. At that time, white "cover artists" still were used to record toned-down versions of "race" music for white teenage audiences. In 1954, Big Joe Turner's legendary "Shake, Rattle, and Roll" did not make the popular charts, but Bill Haley's cover version became a number-one hit. Turner began:

Well you wear low dresooo
The sun comes shinin' through
I can't believe my eyes
That all of this belongs to you.

Haley sang:

You wear those dresses
Your hair done up so nice
You look so warm
But your heart is cold as ice.

In 1956, rock music reached a milestone when **Little Richard**'s sensual recordings of "Long Tall Sally" and "Rip It Up" outsold the "sanitized" versions sung by Pat Boone, America's leading white cover artist.

There was more to rock 'n' roll, of course, than Elvis Presley and rhythm and blues. Teenagers adored the sweet sounds of the Everly Brothers, the lush harmony of the Platters, and the clean-cut innocence of Ricky Nelson. Furthermore, jazz and folk singing retained a healthy following, as did popular artists like Sinatra, Perry Como, and Nat "King" Cole. Nevertheless, the music that defined this era for most Americans, and for teenagers in particular, was hard-edged rock 'n' roll. It was the car radio blasting Presley's "Hound Dog," Chuck Berry's "Maybellene," and Little Richard's "Tutti Frutti" on a carefree Saturday night. A wop bop a lu bop a lop bam boom!

The Beat Generation

Whatever else might be said about Elvis Presley and other rock heroes, they loved the system that made them millionaires. Elvis spent lavishly. His first royalties were used to purchase three new homes and matching Cadillacs for his parents, though his mother didn't drive. Material rewards were the standard by which Presley, and countless others, measured their success.

The Beat movement was different. Composed of young writers and poets based mainly in San Francisco and New York, it blossomed in the mid-1950s as a reaction against mainstream standards and beliefs. The word "beat" described a feeling of emotional and physical exhaustion. The Beats despised politics, consumerism, and technology. They viewed American culture as meaningless, conformist, banal. Their leading poet, Allen Ginsberg, provided a bitter portrait of generational despair in *Howl* (1955).

The Beats linked happiness and creativity with absolute freedom. Their model was Dean Moriarty, the hero of Jack Kerouac's *On the Road* (1957), an autobiographical novel about the cross-country adventures of Kerouac and his friends finding adventure and renewal (not to mention sex and drugs) beyond the confines of middle-class life. *On the Road* became both a national best-seller and a cult book on America's college campuses. In a sense, Kerouac and Presley had something important in common: both appealed to young people who seemed dissatisfied with the apparent blandness of American culture.

CRISES AND CELEBRATION, 1955–1956

In September 1955, President Eisenhower suffered a heart attack while vacationing in Colorado. The news raised obvious questions about his present and future course. At age sixty-five, Eisenhower was one of the oldest presidents in American history. How quickly would he recover, if at all? Who would guide the nation in his absence?

Eisenhower spent the next four months recovering in the hospital and at his Gettysburg farm. Fortunately, the fall of 1955 was a time of political tranquility, with Congress out of session, no bills to sign or veto, and no crises looming on the international scene. The president stayed in close contact with his advisers as he slowly regained his health. Returning to the White House early in 1956, he announced his plan to seek reelection. The public was vastly relieved. As columnist James Reston noted, Eisenhower was more than a president; he was "a national phenomenon, like baseball."

Conquering Polio   The president's full recovery was not the only positive health news of 1955. On a far larger front, a medical research team led by Dr. Jonas Salk, a virologist at the University of Pittsburgh, announced the successful testing of a vaccine to combat poliomyelitis, the most frightening public health problem of the postwar era. More than fifty thousand polio cases were reported in 1954, mostly of children who took sick during the summer months. The disease produced flulike symptoms in most cases, but a more virulent form, which entered the central nervous system, led to paralysis and sometimes death. Not surprisingly, the epidemic produced a national panic. Cities closed swimming pools and beaches; families cancelled vacations, boiled their dishes, and avoided indoor crowds. Children were warned against jumping in puddles, drinking from water fountains, and making new friends.

The March of Dimes became America's favorite charity, raising millions to find a vaccine for polio and to finance the care of patients through therapy, leg braces, and iron lungs. Determined to provide immediate protection against the disease, Dr. Salk tested his polio vaccine on several million schoolchildren in 1954. "It was the largest peacetime mobilization of its kind," wrote one observer, "one in which the mothers of America rose up to save, in many cases, their own children."

The testing proved extremely successful. The federal government approved the polio vaccine in 1955, touching off emotional public celebrations. "People observed moments of silence, rang bells, honked horns, blew factory whistles, drank toasts, hugged children, attended church." By 1960, fewer than a thousand new polio cases were reported in the United States.

Interstate Highways The nation's confidence soared even higher with passage of the Federal Highway Act of 1956, which authorized $25 billion in new taxes on cars, trucks, and gasoline for the construction of forty thousand miles of interstate roads over the next ten years. The huge highway network, linking all cities with more than fifty thousand people, allowed a driver to travel the continent uninterrupted, save stops for food and gas. Eisenhower viewed this project as both a convenience to motorists and a boost to the economy. The president also linked good highways to Cold War events, warning that cities must be evacuated quickly in the event of nuclear war.

America's Dream Car

The decade following World War II marked the height of America's love affair with the automobile. Each year's sales proved better than the last; in 1955 alone, more than 7 million cars rolled off the nation's assembly lines. This dramatic growth was not shared equally, however. As the 1950s progressed, the "Big Three" automakers— General Motors, Ford, and Chrysler—took over the market as the poorly funded "independents" disappeared: Kaiser and Willys in 1955, Nash and Hudson in 1957, Packard in 1958. As this advertisement demonstrates, the American automobile of the postwar era became ever more powerful and luxurious, representing not just a means of transportation but a status symbol as well. Indeed, General Motors produced five different cars with five distinct images: Chevrolet for "hoi polloi," Pontiac for "the poor but proud," Oldsmobile for "the comfortable but discreet," Buick for "the striving," and Cadillac (pictured here) for "the rich." Yet even the cheaper models came with a V-8 engine, automatic transmission, air-conditioning, tail fins, miles of chrome, and whitewall tires. Around 1957, a series of small, economical European imports, led by the Volkswagen "beetle," arrived to compete with America's overdesigned, gas-guzzling behemoths. The battle was on.

Happy Resolution for a Happy New Year!

Cadillac

Courtesy of The Advertising Archives

The Highway Act spurred enormous economic growth. Improved roads meant higher oil revenues, soaring car sales, more business for truckers, and greater mobility for travelers. The so-called highway trade took off. Ray Krock opened his first McDonald's in 1955 in Des Plaines, Illinois, a suburb of Chicago. In Memphis, Kemmons Wilson unveiled the first Holiday Inn, featuring a restaurant, a swimming pool, and clean, air-conditioned rooms with free TV. Before long McDonald's golden arches and Holiday Inn's green neon lettering were among the most recognizable logos in America.

Opposing the Highway Act of 1956 was akin to opposing prosperity, progress, and national defense. A few social critics like Lewis Mumford expressed concern about the deterioration of urban centers, the stink of auto pollution, and the future of interstate rail service, but they were drowned out by the optimistic majority. As the prestigious *Architectural Forum* noted, America's new highway system was "the greatest man-made physical enterprise of all time with the exception of war."

Hungary and Suez   In the fall of 1956, at the height of the presidential campaign, foreign affairs took center stage. From central Europe came a dangerous challenge to the Eisenhower–Dulles rhetoric about liberating nations from communist oppression. From the Middle East came a crisis that pitted the United States against its most loyal allies: Israel, England, and France.

Following Stalin's death in 1953, Russian leaders called for "peaceful coexistence" between the Communist bloc and "differing political and social systems." In 1956, Soviet Premier **Nikita Khrushchev** stunned the Twentieth Communist Party Congress in Moscow by denouncing Stalin's brutality and hinting at a relaxation of the Soviet grip on central and eastern Europe.

The reaction was predictable. Protests flared throughout the Soviet bloc, demanding an end to Russian rule. In Warsaw, angry crowds sacked the Communist Party headquarters, and in Budapest street battles escalated into full-scale civil war.

The Hungarian revolt put Eisenhower on the spot. In 1952, his campaign rhetoric had blasted the Democrats for being "soft" on communism. From 1953 forward, his administration had vowed to "roll back" the communist wave, not simply to contain it. Now the time had come to put words into action by supporting the anti-communist freedom fighters in Hungary. Yet Eisenhower refused to send American troops, or even to airlift supplies to the resisters, for fear of starting an all-out war with the Soviet Union. In October 1956, Russian tanks and troops stormed into Budapest to crush the revolt.

At the very moment of the Hungarian revolt, another crisis erupted in the Middle East, a region of growing interest and concern to the United States. Although American policy supported the new state of Israel, it also recognized the strategic importance and economic power of Israel's Arab neighbors. In 1952, a young Egyptian military officer named Gamal Abdel Nasser had dramatically altered Middle Eastern politics by overthrowing the corrupt regime of King Farouk. As an Arab nationalist, Nasser steered a middle course between the Cold War powers, hoping to play off one side against the other. To the Egyptian people, he promised both the destruction of Israel and an end to British control of the Suez Canal.

The United States tried to woo Nasser with economic aid. It even agreed to finance his pet project, the Aswan Dam, a huge hydroelectric plant on the Nile River. But trouble arose in 1956 when Secretary Dulles withdrew the Aswan offer to protest Egypt's recognition of Communist China. Unable to punish the United States directly, Nasser did the next best thing by seizing the Suez Canal.

The move could not be ignored. In 1955, Nasser had blockaded the Gulf of Aqaba, Israel's sole outlet to the Red Sea. Now he controlled the waterway that linked western Europe to its oil supply in the Middle East. On October 29, 1956, Israeli armor poured into the Sinai, routing Egyptian forces. Two days later, French and British paratroopers landed near Alexandria and easily retook the Suez Canal.

Eisenhower immediately condemned this invasion. At the very least, he believed, the attack undermined Western interests in the Middle East by forcing Egypt and other Arab states closer to the Soviet bloc. Privately, the White House pressured

England, France, and Israel to withdraw. Publicly, the United States supported a UN resolution that denounced the invasion and called for negotiations regarding the canal. On November 6, a cease-fire was signed, ending the crisis but not the ill will.

Events in Hungary and Suez came in the midst of Eisenhower's 1956 reelection campaign. Expecting an easy victory, the president worried most about picking the proper running mate, a critical choice given his advanced age and questionable health. Eisenhower did not believe that Vice President Nixon was the best person to lead the nation in a crisis. "I've watched Dick a long time and he just hasn't grown," Ike told an aide. "So I just haven't honestly been able to believe that he is presidential timber."

In a private meeting, Eisenhower urged Nixon to trade in his vice-presidential hat for a cabinet post. Yet when Nixon resisted, the president backed down, fearing a backlash within Republican ranks. In November 1956, Eisenhower and Nixon trounced the Democratic slate of Adlai Stevenson and Senator Estes Kefauver by almost 10 million votes, a margin of victory even wider than in 1952. Nevertheless, the Democrats easily retained their majorities in both houses of Congress, demonstrating that Eisenhower, who accepted New Deal reforms as a permanent part of American life, remained far more popular than the political party he led.

A SECOND TERM, 1957–1960

Eisenhower returned to office on an optimistic note. Events in Hungary and the Middle East faded momentarily from view. *Time* magazine even praised the president for his moderation "in time of crisis and threat of World War III." The economy was strong; unemployment was low. The nation seemed confident, prosperous, and secure.

Confrontation at Little Rock These good feelings did not last long. Throughout the South, opposition to the *Brown* decision was spreading, with some white southerners interpreting Eisenhower's virtual silence on the issue as a sign that he supported their resistance to integrated schools. In 1956, more than one hundred congressmen from the former Confederate states issued a "Southern Manifesto" that vowed to resist court-ordered integration "by all lawful means." A year later, in Little Rock, Arkansas, Governor **Orval Faubus** triggered the inevitable confrontation between national authority and "states' rights" by defying a federal court order to integrate the all-white Central High School. First the Arkansas National Guard, and then a crowd of angry whites, turned away the nine black students.

As televised scenes of mob violence in Little Rock flashed around the world, President Eisenhower finally, but firmly, took command. Vowing to use "the full power of the United States . . . to carry out the orders of the federal court," he nationalized the Arkansas Guard and dispatched a thousand fully equipped army paratroopers to surround the high school and escort the black students to their classes. The soldiers remained for months, though peace was quickly restored. Ironically, Dwight Eisenhower became the first president since Reconstruction to protect the civil rights of African Americans through the use of military force.

Sputnik and Its Aftermath On October 4, 1957, the Soviet Union launched *Sputnik I* (or "traveling companion"), the first artificial satellite, weighing less than two hundred pounds. The admiral in charge of America's satellite program dismissed *Sputnik I* as "a hunk of iron almost anybody could launch." But a month later, the Russians orbited *Sputnik II*, an eleven-hundred-pound capsule with a small dog inside.

The news provoked anger and dismay. Americans had always taken for granted their technological superiority. Even the Soviet atomic bomb was seen as an aberration, most likely built from stolen U.S. blueprints. But *Sputnik* was different; it shook the nation's confidence and wounded its pride. The feeling grew that America had become complacent in its affluence and that danger lay ahead. "The time has clearly come," said an alarmed senator, "to be less concerned with the depth of the pile of the new broadloom or the height of the tail fin of the new car and to be more prepared to shed blood, sweat, and tears."

The nation's educational system came under withering fire. Critics emerged from every corner, bemoaning the sorry state of America's schools. In an issue devoted to the "Crisis in Education," *Life* magazine followed a sixteen-year-old Russian student and his American counterpart through a typical high school day. Alexi took difficult courses in science and math. He spoke fluent English, played chess and the piano, exercised vigorously, and studied four hours after class. Stephen, meanwhile, spent his day lounging through basic geometry and learning how to type. The students around him read magazines like *Modern Romance* in their English class. No one seemed to study. The end result, warned the *Life* editors, was a generation of young Americans ill equipped "to cope with the technicalities of the Space Age."

The embarrassments continued. In December 1957, millions watched on television as the U.S. Navy's much-publicized Vanguard rocket caught fire on takeoff and crashed to the ground. (The press dubbed it "Flopnik.") A month later, the army launched a ten-pound satellite named *Explorer I* aboard its new Jupiter rocket. Determined to calm public fears, President Eisenhower insisted that the United States was well ahead of the Soviet Union in nuclear research and delivery systems. But the people thought otherwise, especially after the Russians orbited a third satellite weighing almost three thousand pounds.

In fact, however, Eisenhower was correct. His own information, not available to the public, made two vital points. First, the Russians needed more powerful missiles because the warheads they carried were heavier and cruder, owing to inferior technology. Second, the Soviets did not have enough intercontinental ballistic missiles to counter America's huge lead in manned nuclear bombers. Put simply, the United States was in no real danger of being outgunned.

Eisenhower got this information from the CIA's U-2 spy planes, which crossed the Soviet Union at seventy thousand feet. The U-2 flights were both secret and illegal, a clear violation of Russian air space. But the cameras on board, capable of picking up license plate numbers in the Kremlin's parking lot, provided American intelligence with a detailed picture of the Soviet war machine. Of course, the president could not speak candidly about Russian military power without also admitting the existence of these U-2 flights.

This was an awful dilemma. Critics now demanded expensive crash programs for weapons research, missile construction, and community fallout shelters to protect against nuclear attack. Eisenhower vigorously opposed these programs, claiming that they undermined economic prosperity and threatened the "very values we are trying to defend." Using his exalted stature as general and war hero, he battled hard—and

The Kitchen Debate

This famous photograph of Soviet Premier Nikita Khrushchev and Vice President Richard Nixon squaring off in their impromptu "Kitchen Debate" in Moscow in 1959 demonstrates that the Cold War had a cultural component that went beyond military confrontation. Standing nose-to-nose in a "model" American kitchen, the two leaders argued about the merits of Western consumer culture. Khrushchev saw America's love affair with "gadgetry" as a sure sign of capitalist laziness and decay.

Looking grumpily at the array of gleaming appliances, he asked: "Don't you have a machine that puts food in your mouth and pushes it down?" But Nixon, known as a militant anti-communist, won praise for responding to Khrushchev that it was "better to compete in the relative merits of washing machines than in the strength of rockets." The Cold War would continue for years, but for the moment, the battlefield seemed a far different place.

© Elliott Erwitt/ Magnum Photos

successfully—to keep military budgets stable during these years. Defense spending increased from $38 billion in 1957 to $41 billion in 1960, a tiny jump after inflation.

Still, the impact of *Sputnik* did not quickly disappear. For the first time, Americans started to view their educational system in terms of national security. This meant greater emphasis on science, mathematics, and foreign language study. In 1958, Congress passed the National Defense Education Act, which funded high school programs in these fields and college scholarships for deserving students. That same year, Eisenhower reluctantly endorsed the creation of the National Aeronautics and Space Administration (NASA), in response to overwhelming public pressure.

END OF AN ERA

In November 1958, the Democrats won a smashing victory in the off-year elections, increasing their majorities in the House (282–153) and the Senate (62–34) to the largest level since 1936. *Sputnik* was partly responsible for this landslide, but so too was an economic recession in 1957 that lingered for the next two years. Determined to avoid the inflationary risks of increased federal spending, Eisenhower did little to counter a steady rise in unemployment and a sharp (if temporary) decline in the annual rate of economic growth.

There were optimistic signs, however. In the summer of 1959, Vice President Nixon visited Moscow at Khrushchev's invitation to open a trade show featuring consumer products from Russia and the United States. Several weeks later, Khrushchev accepted President Eisenhower's invitation to visit the United States. Khrushchev toured an Iowa farm and an IBM plant near San Francisco. At a Hollywood studio, he watched the filming of *Can-Can* and then, offended by the skimpy costumes, launched into a diatribe against capitalist "pornography." When his trip to Disneyland was canceled for security reasons, Khrushchev was furious. "What's wrong?" he yelled. "Do you have rocket launching pads there? Or have gangsters taken hold of the place?"

The trip ended on a hopeful note with a visit to the presidential retreat at Camp David, where Khrushchev and Eisenhower spent two days in leisurely conversation. They announced that Eisenhower would visit the Soviet Union in 1960 following a summit meeting of world leaders in Paris. The main issues, they agreed, were nuclear disarmament and the future of Berlin.

The summit meeting was a disaster. As he left for Paris in May 1960, Eisenhower learned that a U-2 spy plane was missing. A few days later, Khrushchev revealed that an American aircraft had been shot down deep inside the Soviet Union. Assuming that the pilot was dead, Eisenhower falsely described the U-2 as a weather research plane that had veered off course during a routine flight over Turkey. But Khrushchev then produced the pilot, **Francis Gary Powers**, frightened but very much alive.

At the summit, Eisenhower took full responsibility for the incident but refused to apologize. Indeed, he justified the U-2 flights by insisting that Soviet espionage inside the United States was rampant and that U-2 photographs were essential to America's defense, given the closed nature of Russian society. In response, Khrushchev turned the summit into a tirade against Western "banditry," adding that Eisenhower was no longer welcome on Soviet soil.

The failure at Paris deeply wounded the president. In his "farewell address" to the people, he warned that years of Cold War tensions were sapping America's strength and concentrating too much power in the hands of "a military-industrial complex." Speaking boldly, at times sadly, he urged the people to be on guard against militarism and greed and to reject a "live for today" mentality. At risk, the president concluded, was "the loss of our political and spiritual heritage."

The Election of 1960

Who would lead the United States into the next decade? Unlike the predictable Eisenhower landslides of 1952 and 1956, the election of 1960 generated drama from the start. Both major candidates were tough, hard-driving campaigners. Both were born in the twentieth century—a political first—and both entered Congress in 1946 after serving as junior naval officers during World War II. But the similarities ended there.

Richard Nixon, the forty-seven-year-old vice president, grew up in modest circumstances. His Quaker parents ran a small grocery store in Whittier, California, near Los Angeles, where Nixon worked as a boy. Neighbors and classmates recalled him as serious and socially ill at ease. After graduating from Whittier College and Duke Law

School, he married Patricia Ryan in 1940 and obtained his naval commission the following year.

Nixon's political rise was dramatic. As a new Republican congressman, he played a major role in the Alger Hiss case and then won a U.S. Senate seat in 1950 after accusing his Democratic opponent of being "soft on communism." As vice president from 1953 to 1960, Nixon emerged as the Republican Party's most aggressive defender.

John Kennedy took a different path to power. Born to wealth and privilege, he grew up in Boston, attended the finest private schools, and graduated from Harvard. His self-made millionaire father, Joseph P. Kennedy, served as ambassador to England under Franklin Roosevelt. Preaching competition and excellence, Joseph Kennedy expected his oldest son, Joe Jr., to become the first Catholic president of the United States. When Joe Jr. died in combat during World War II, the torch was passed to John Kennedy, the next oldest son. In 1943, John barely escaped death himself after his PT boat was rammed by a Japanese warship in the South Pacific. Elected to Congress in 1946 and to the Senate in 1952, Kennedy did not excel as a legislator. In constant pain from his war wounds, he underwent delicate spinal surgery and then was diagnosed with Addison's disease, an adrenal malfunction that required daily doses of cortisone. While recuperating, Kennedy won the Pulitzer Prize for *Profiles in Courage*, an intriguing book, written almost entirely by his staff, about politicians who took brave but unpopular positions on the great issues of their time.

In 1956, Kennedy ran a close second to Estes Kefauver for the Democratic Party's vice-presidential nomination. "You know, if we work like hell the next four years," Kennedy told an aide, "we will pick up all the marbles." Healthy once again, he traveled the country with his glamorous wife, Jacqueline, to line up presidential support. The crowds they drew were so large and adoring that reporters used the word *charisma* to describe the growing Kennedy mystique.

The Republican convention nominated Richard Nixon on the first ballot. As expected, Nixon chose a moderate easterner, Henry Cabot Lodge, Jr., of Massachusetts, to be his vice-presidential running mate. The Democratic convention was more dramatic. Also winning a first ballot victory, Kennedy surprised almost everyone by selecting Senator Lyndon Johnson, a long-time rival, for the vice-presidential slot. As a Texan with liberal instincts, Johnson was expected to help Kennedy in the South without hurting him in the North. "The world is changing," Kennedy proclaimed in his acceptance speech. "We stand today on the edge of a New Frontier."

Kennedy Campaign Button. *John F. Kennedy would become the second Catholic and the youngest candidate to run for president on a major party ticket.*

(© David J. & Janice L. Frent Collection/CORBIS)

The two candidates were evenly matched. Nixon campaigned on the eight-year Eisenhower record, reminding Americans that their nation was prosperous and at peace. Kennedy attacked that record without criticizing the popular Eisenhower by name. Portraying the United States as stagnant in a changing world, he promised new leadership "to get the country moving once again."

Kennedy had two main hurdles to overcome: religion and inexperience. No Roman Catholic had ever been elected president, a fact underscored by the crushing defeat of Al Smith in 1928. Religion became an open issue in the 1960 campaign after a group of Protestant ministers issued a statement questioning Kennedy's fitness to govern on the grounds that Roman Catholicism was "both a church and a temporal state." Kennedy confronted this issue in a powerful speech to a Baptist audience in Texas. Vowing to uphold the constitutional separation of church and state, he added: "If this election is decided on the basis that 40,000,000 Americans lost their chance of being president on the day they were baptized, then it is the whole nation that will be the loser in the eyes of history."

Kennedy's other hurdle—inexperience—was removed in a series of televised debates with Nixon that marked the beginning of modern presidential campaigns. The first debate had the greatest impact, as more than 80 million Americans watched on

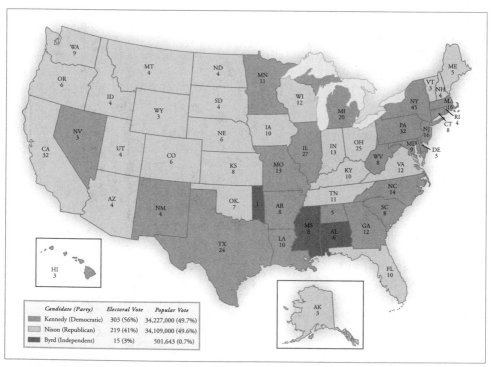

Candidate (Party)	Electoral Vote	Popular Vote
Kennedy (Democratic)	303 (56%)	34,227,000 (49.7%)
Nixon (Republican)	219 (41%)	34,109,000 (49.6%)
Byrd (Independent)	15 (3%)	501,643 (0.7%)

MAP 28.2 The Election of 1960.

In winning one of the closest presidential contests in American history, John F. Kennedy barely kept the Democratic New Deal coalition together. Several key factors were at work in this election, including the impact of the first televised presidential debates, the Catholic issue, and the suspicion of voter fraud in the key states of Texas and Illinois.

television or listened on radio. Though both candidates spoke well, the difference lay in cosmetics and style. The handsome, well-groomed Kennedy radiated confidence and charm. Nixon, by contrast, seemed awkward and pale. The hot TV lights made him sweat profusely, smudging his makeup. Those who heard the debate on radio scored it a draw. Those who saw it on television thought Kennedy the clear victor.

Kennedy won the election with 303 electoral votes to Nixon's 219. Yet the popular vote was the closest since 1888, with Kennedy getting 34,227,000 (49.7 percent) and Nixon 34,109,000 (49.6 percent). A swing of several thousand votes in Texas and Illinois, where suspicions of ballot fraud were rampant, would have given the election to Nixon. Kennedy did well among traditional Democrats (minorities, urban dwellers, the working class), and swept the Catholic vote, yet polls showed his religion costing him dearly in rural Protestant areas. Kennedy suspected that television won him the White House, and he may have been correct. The four debates, and a flood of prime-time advertisements, appeared to influence voters as never before.

CONCLUSION

Americans often look back nostalgically to the 1950s. These years were far more tranquil than the war-torn 1940s or the Depression-scarred 1930s. The Korean War ended in 1953, and the Cold War thawed a bit with the death of Joseph Stalin, Russia's brutal dictator. There would be other foreign policy crises in the 1950s, in Suez and Hungary, in Guatemala and Lebanon, but U.S. soldiers would not be dying in faraway lands. The ugliness of McCarthyism would recede as well with the Senate's condemnation of Joseph McCarthy in 1954. The Roosevelt–Truman years had come to a close, yet the New Deal legacy remained largely undisturbed. Dwight Eisenhower accepted the idea that government must provide a safety net for its citizens. And he too pledged to contain communist expansion around the globe.

The 1950s saw an explosion of mass culture, from the coming of commercial television to the birth of rock and roll. A national highway system was constructed, spurring the boom in automobiles and connecting the nation as never before. The widespread use of wonder drugs, such as penicillin and a successful polio vaccine, gave hope for a future in which laboratory science would make life healthier for humankind.

The 1950s also witnessed *Brown v. Board of Education*, perhaps the most significant Supreme Court decision of the post–Civil War era. The African American communities of Montgomery and Little Rock helped awaken America to the long-standing injustice of racial segregation, and new leaders emerged with innovative strategies to carry on the fight.

As the 1950s ended, however, nagging questions remained. Would prosperity and racial justice ever reach into the far corners of the land? Would the civil rights movement retain its momentum and nonviolent stance? Would the nation's expanding Cold War military commitments drain its economic strength—and moral authority? Would the lure of materialism and consumerism undermine precious national values? These questions would dominate the American agenda in the tumultuous years ahead.

CHAPTER REVIEW, 1953–1960

- The 1953 truce in Korea eased Cold War tensions and ended an increasingly unpopular war.
- The civil rights movement gained dramatic momentum with *Brown v. Board of Education*, the Montgomery bus boycott, and the school integration crisis in Little Rock.
- The condemnation of Senator McCarthy cooled passions surrounding the volatile issue of domestic subversion.
- A distinct youth culture emerged, fueled by the postwar baby boom.
- The launching of *Sputnik* in 1957 raised concerns that the United States was falling behind the Soviet Union in the critical fields of science and technology.
- Senator John F. Kennedy was elected president in 1960 by a razor-thin margin, returning the White House to Democratic control.

◀ⅢⅢ *Looking Back*

Chapter 28 examines the promise and prosperity of the United States in the 1950s—a time of great medical and technological advances, the growth of commercial television, an exploding youth culture, and great legal advances and burgeoning movements in the struggle for equal rights.

1. What ideological principles and personal qualities defined the Eisenhower presidency? Why did this presidency seem to fit the national mood so well?
2. How did the spread of commercial television both define and reflect the cultural values of post–World War II America?
3. Why did the Soviet launching of *Sputnik* have such a profound effect on U.S. society? Why did it cause so much national soul searching and self-reflection?
4. How did the combination of legal victories and local protests combine to fuel the civil rights movement of the 1950s?

Looking Ahead ⅢⅢ▶

Chapter 29 considers the turbulent times that followed the relative tranquility of the 1950s, showing the connections between these periods and following the political and cultural events that so badly divided the nation.

1. Did the narrow election victory of John F. Kennedy in the 1960 presidential election send a signal that Americans wanted a change of political course? If so, what sort of change did they have in mind?
2. Would it be possible to build on the major civil rights victories of the 1950s and fulfill the promises of Reconstruction almost a century before—the promises of voting rights, economic opportunity, and equal protection under the law?
3. Would the Cold War with the Soviet Union continue to dominate international relations, and would it expand into other regions of the world?

Go to the American Passages website at www.cengage.com/history/ayers/ampassages4e for additional review materials.

The Turbulent Years, 1960–1968

The 1960s opened on an ambivalent note. The gross national product reached $500 billion for the first time, yet talk of economic recession was in the air. The darkest days of McCarthyism were over, yet the fear of communism remained. The development of new products and technologies bred optimism, yet the spread of new weapons caused alarm.

Hints of protest and trouble had begun to appear. In Greensboro, North Carolina, four black college students who sat down at a Woolworth lunch counter and were denied service refused to leave. Word of their defiance triggered sit-in protests across the South, with demonstrators bravely confronting Jim Crow. Half a world away, supporters of North Vietnam's Communist ruler, Ho Chi Minh, announced the formation of a National Liberation Front to overthrow the anti-Communist government of President Ngo Dinh Diem in South Vietnam. Diem didn't seem concerned. With U.S. support, he boasted, his forces would quickly subdue these "Vietcong" [Vietnamese Communists] and bring peace to his land.

EARLY TESTS, 1961

The 1960 election was a landmark event in American political history. At age forty-three, John Kennedy became the first Catholic president, the youngest candidate to win a presidential election, and the first president to be born in the twentieth century. His inauguration on January 20, 1961, seemed to herald a new era of idealism and change. Kennedy declared: "Ask not what your country can do for you; ask what you can do for your country."

Idealism and Caution The new administration appeared to mirror these words. Young people converged on Washington with a fervor reminiscent of the early New Deal years. Public service became a badge of honor. Kennedy's White House staff included fifteen Rhodes scholars and numerous Ivy League professors. The new secretary of state, Dean Rusk, came from the Rockefeller Foundation; the new defense secretary, Robert McNamara, left the presidency of the Ford Motor Company to help "streamline" the nation's armed forces. Kennedy chose his younger brother Robert to become attorney general. Under Jacqueline Kennedy's direction, the White House became a center for the arts, with performances by cellist Pablo Casals and the American Shakespeare Festival Theatre.

Despite the lofty rhetoric and the fanfare, Kennedy took a measured approach to his early presidential duties, particularly in domestic affairs. For one thing, he lacked the huge popular mandate given to previous first-term presidents such as Franklin Roosevelt in 1932 and Dwight Eisenhower in 1952. For another, he worried about his relations with a Congress in which conservative Republicans and southern Democrats held the balance of power.

Several of Kennedy's early initiatives were in the New Deal tradition. He worked successfully to increase social security benefits and to raise the minimum wage from $1 to $1.25. More important, however, was the defeat of his $2.3 billion education bill for school construction and higher teachers' salaries, which raised nagging questions about the federal role in education. Would funds be given to racially segregated public schools or to private religious schools? Amid the confusion, the education bill died in committee.

In other areas, the new administration achieved success. By executive order, Kennedy launched the Peace Corps in March 1961. Directed by the president's brother-in-law R. Sargent Shriver, the Peace Corps sent thousands of American volunteers to underdeveloped nations to provide educational and technical assistance. With a tiny budget, it became one of Kennedy's great triumphs, showcasing American idealism and know-how throughout the world. Within three years, almost ten thousand volunteers were at work in forty-six countries, teaching school, staffing hospitals, and planting new crops.

Even more popular, though far more expensive, was the space program. Unlike Eisenhower, who opposed a costly "race to the moon with Russia," the new president viewed an American victory in this contest as essential to national prestige. Setting the goal of a manned moon landing "before this decade is out," Kennedy convinced a skeptical Congress to allocate billions of dollars for space research and rocketry, a training program for astronauts, and a mission control center in Houston.

The space race captivated the world. In April 1961, Soviet cosmonaut Yuri Gagarin orbited the globe in less than two hours. A month later, Commander Alan Shepard rocketed three hundred miles from Cape Canaveral in a suborbital flight, and in February 1962, Lieutenant Colonel **John Glenn** orbited the earth three times aboard *Friendship 7* before touching down in the Caribbean. Glenn became a national hero, with tickertape parades and a televised address before a joint session of Congress.

The Bay of Pigs

Kennedy inherited his first crisis from the previous administration. As president-elect, he was told of a secret plan, personally approved by Eisenhower, to overthrow the new Marxist government of **Fidel Castro** in Cuba. The plan called for several hundred anti-Castro exiles, trained and equipped by the CIA, to invade Cuba and trigger an anti-Communist revolution.

This icon will direct you to interactive activities and study materials on the American Passages website: www.cengage.com/history/ayers/ampassages4e

CHAPTER TIMELINE

1961	Bay of Pigs invasion fails • East Germany erects Berlin Wall • Peace Corps established
1962	Cuban missile crisis sparks nuclear confrontation • War on Poverty is formulated • Students for a Democratic Society (SDS) is organized
1963	Martin Luther King, Jr., delivers "I Have a Dream" speech at Lincoln Memorial • United States and Soviet Union sign treaty banning above-ground nuclear tests • President Kennedy is assassinated • Lyndon B. Johnson becomes president
1964	Congress passes Gulf of Tonkin Resolution • Freedom Summer voting rights campaign begins in Mississippi • Congress passes landmark Civil Rights Act • President Johnson elected by record margin
1965	American ground troops sent to Vietnam, escalating commitment • Race riot erupts in Watts, Los Angeles • Congress passes Voting Rights Act • Malcolm X assassinated
1966	Black Panthers organized in California • U.S. combat deaths in Vietnam increase tenfold to 6,664 • Antiwar protests spread to major state universities
1967	Race riots erupt in Detroit, Newark, and other cities • Thousands gather in Haight-Ashbury, San Francisco, for "summer of love"
1968	Communists launch Tet offensive in South Vietnam • President Johnson announces he will not seek reelection • Martin Luther King, Jr., is assassinated in Memphis • Robert Kennedy is assassinated in Los Angeles • Richard Nixon is elected president

Kennedy endorsed the plan. He believed that Castro set a dangerous example by aligning Cuba with the Soviet Union, and he had promised to "get tough" with Castro during the 1960 campaign. He could not easily back down now.

On April 17, 1961, a brigade of fifteen hundred waded ashore at the **Bay of Pigs**, on Cuba's southern coast. Nothing went as planned. The landing site had sharp coral reefs and swampy terrain, making it hard to unload supplies and move out from the beaches. Local workers quickly spotted the invaders, and news of their arrival sparked no popular uprising against Castro. Kennedy refused to lend vital air and naval support to the brigade in a futile attempt to hide America's role in this disaster. More than a hundred invaders were killed, and the rest were captured. After reviewing the events with his advisers, Kennedy took a walk on the White House lawn. It was "the first time in my life," a friend recalled, "that I ever saw tears come to his eyes."

The Bay of Pigs fiasco left a troubled legacy. On the one hand, it angered other Latin American governments and drove Castro even closer to the Russian embrace. On the other, it fueled Kennedy's interest in covert operations and his desire to control them more directly. After removing long-time CIA director Allen Dulles, the president approved a top-secret program, code-named Operation Mongoose, to topple the Cuban government and assassinate its leaders. Its plans included the destruction of Cuba's vital sugar crop and a box of exploding cigars for Castro.

Most important was the public reaction. Rather than hurting Kennedy, the incident marked him as a man of action, willing to take chances in the war against communism. His popularity soared. "It's just like Eisenhower," he quipped. "The worse I do the more popular I get."

The Berlin Wall   In June 1961, Kennedy met with Soviet leader Nikita Khrushchev in Vienna. Khrushchev tried to bully the new president, threatening to give East Germany full control over road and rail access to West Berlin, in violation of previous guarantees. Berlin was an embarrassment to Khrushchev. The prosperous western sector stood as a model of democratic capitalism behind the Iron Curtain. Each day, more than a thousand refugees from the Communist side poured into West Berlin. At this rate, East Germany would lose most of its skilled workers to the West.

Kennedy met the challenge, declaring that North Atlantic Treaty Organization (NATO) forces would defend the city at all costs. To emphasize this point, the president tripled draft calls, mobilized reserve units, and requested $3 billion in additional defense appropriations, which Congress quickly granted. The crisis ended in August 1961. As the world watched in amazement, workers in East Berlin constructed a wall of barbed wire and concrete around the western edge of their city, sealing off East Berlin, and eventually all of East Germany, from the non-communist world. In a tactical sense, Khrushchev achieved his objective of stopping the East German exodus to the West. In a larger sense, the wall became an admission of failure—a monument to freedom denied.

The Freedom   Kennedy's first domestic crisis occurred in the field of civil
Riders   rights. An integrationist at heart, the president wanted change
                    to come slowly, without the mass protests and violent incidents that had made headlines around the world. He worried, too, that White House support for immediate desegregation would cost him the goodwill of powerful southerners in Congress.

In 1961, the Congress of Racial Equality (CORE) announced plans to test a recent Supreme Court decision, *Boynton v. Virginia*, which prohibited racial segregation in bus terminals, train stations, and airports engaged in interstate transportation. CORE's objective, said its national director, was "to provoke the southern authorities into arresting us and thereby prod the Justice Department into enforcing the law of the land." In May, thirteen "freedom riders"—seven blacks and six whites—left Washington on a Greyhound bus bound for New Orleans. At each stop, they ignored the "white" and "colored" signs that hung by the toilets, lunch counters, and waiting rooms in defiance of federal law. Trouble erupted in Anniston, Alabama, when their bus was firebombed by a white mob. As the passengers struggled outside, they were beaten with fists and clubs.

When the violence continued in Montgomery and Birmingham, Alabama, Attorney General Robert Kennedy urged CORE to end the **freedom rides**, claiming that they embarrassed President Kennedy on the eve of his summit with Premier Khrushchev. "Doesn't the attorney general know," a black Alabaman responded, "that we've been embarrassed all our lives?"

As new freedom riders arrived to replace the wounded, the Kennedy administration sent in federal marshals to protect them. It had no choice, given the violent scenes that flashed across the nation's television sets each night. In September 1961, the federal government banned interstate carriers from using any terminal that segregated the races. After months of bloody struggle, the freedom riders prevailed.

The New Economics	Despite his increasing focus on civil rights, President Kennedy considered the economy to be his top domestic concern. Economic growth in the Eisenhower years had been steady but

increasingly slow. Real wages for an average family rose a remarkable 20 percent in the 1950s, but a series of recessions toward the end of Eisenhower's second term prompted both a drop in factory production and a rise in unemployment. By the time Kennedy took office, more Americans were out of work than at any other time since the end of World War II.

In 1962, Kennedy unveiled an economic program that differed sharply from the spending model of the New Deal and Fair Deal. Instead, he proposed a major tax cut for consumers and businesses, designed to stimulate purchasing power and encourage new investment. What worried him was the specter of inflation as the economy heated up.

To prevent this, Kennedy lobbied business and labor leaders to respect the wage and price guidelines his administration recommended to keep inflation in check. The Teamsters, Auto Workers, and Steel Workers all agreed to modest wage hikes in 1962 with the understanding that their employers would not raise prices. Two weeks later, however, U.S. Steel, the nation's third largest corporation, announced a whopping price increase of six dollars a ton, leading other steel companies to do the same.

Kennedy used his influence to roll back the price increase. Within days, the Justice Department threatened to investigate antitrust violations in the steel industry, and the Defense Department announced that it might not purchase steel from the "price-gouging" offenders. The steel companies gave in. Kennedy had won a major victory in his battle against inflation, although his rough tactics aroused deep anger in the business community. Nevertheless, the economy prospered in the early 1960s, achieving low unemployment, stable prices, and steady growth.

SOCIAL AND POLITICAL CHALLENGES, 1962

Before long, President Kennedy's political caution began to ease. A year of trial and error led him to take more confident stands in certain areas, such as U.S.–Soviet relations and the push for civil rights. As events unfolded in 1962, the president faced challenges in familiar places—the Deep South and the waters off Cuba. This time, the stakes were much higher.

The Battle for Ole Miss	In the fall of 1962, a federal court ordered the admission of James Meredith, a black air force veteran, to the all-white University of Mississippi, known as Ole Miss. Governor Ross

Barnett led the opposition. A virulent racist, who claimed that "God made the Negro different to punish him," Barnett had kept a previous black applicant from entering Ole Miss by having him committed to a mental hospital. Now Barnett invoked the doctrine of interposition—a throwback to antebellum times—by warning that Mississippi would ignore all federal rulings in order to keep segregation in place.

Kennedy responded to Barnett's challenge by dispatching several hundred federal marshals to Ole Miss. They were met by a well-armed mob, more than two thousand strong. In the riot that followed, two people were killed and hundreds were injured, including twenty-eight marshals hit by gunfire. Like Eisenhower during the Little Rock crisis, Kennedy rushed in troops and federalized the state Guard. With twenty-three thousand soldiers on campus—five times the student population—Meredith registered for classes under army bayonets. The battle at Ole Miss was over; the larger struggle for Mississippi lay ahead.

The Missiles of October   In October 1962, the world faced the most dangerous confrontation of the entire Cold War. It began with rumors, confirmed by **U-2** spy plane photos, that the Soviets were deploying intermediate-range ballistic missiles in Cuba. Speed was essential, Kennedy believed, for the missiles would become operational in less than a month. In fact, newly declassified documents have shown that a number of these Soviet missiles, carrying warheads nearly the size of the Hiroshima bomb, were already operational in Cuba—a reality of which Kennedy and his advisers were completely unaware.

Castro's need for security was understandable. In addition to Operation Mongoose, the Kennedy administration had imposed an economic embargo on Cuba and engineered its expulsion from the Organization of American States. At Castro's urging, the Soviet Union sent thousands of military advisers to Cuba, as well as defensive missiles to shoot down invading planes. Yet the deployment of offensive weapons, capable of reaching Chicago or Washington with nuclear warheads, was an alarming escalation designed to tip the balance of terror in Moscow's favor.

Kennedy convened an executive committee (known as ex-Comm) to provide a suitable response. Some ex-Comm members recommended immediate air strikes to take out the missile bases. Others, including **Robert Kennedy**, proposed a naval quarantine of Cuba, in which ships suspected of carrying military cargo to Cuba would be boarded and searched. The president carefully studied both options before choosing the latter. A quarantine shifted the burden of responsibility to Khrushchev while allowing both sides to seek a solution short of war.

On October 22, 1962, Kennedy addressed the nation on television. After describing the quarantine, he demanded that Russia remove the missiles and warned that any missile fired from Cuba would be regarded "as an attack by the Soviet Union on the United States," requiring a "full retaliatory response." American forces went on full alert. A U-2 plane over Cuba was shot down, and its pilot killed. The entire world watched anxiously as Communist-bloc vessels in the Caribbean inched closer to U.S. warships enforcing the quarantine.

On October 26, Kennedy received an emotional note from Khrushchev suggesting a settlement: Russia would remove its missiles if the United States pledged never to invade Cuba. Before the president could respond, however, a second note arrived from Khrushchev demanding that the United States also remove its Jupiter missiles along the Soviet border in Turkey.

Robert Kennedy devised a solution. Respond to the first note, he said, and ignore the second one. On October 27, the president vowed not to invade Cuba if the missiles were removed. In private, meanwhile, Robert Kennedy assured Soviet ambassador Anatoly Dobrynin that the Jupiter missiles would be removed from Turkey in the near future.

On October 28, Khrushchev accepted the deal. The Soviet premier had badly miscalculated the stern American reaction to the placement of offensive missiles in Cuba, though his restraint in the crisis helped to lead to a peaceful solution. Khrushchev soon left office in disgrace, and Kennedy's reputation soared. For two weeks in October, the world had seemed headed for nuclear war.

That fact alone seemed to sober both sides. In July 1963, a direct telephone link, known as the "hot line," was established between the White House and the Kremlin. In August, the United States and Russia joined with ninety other nations to sign the Treaty Banning Nuclear Weapons Tests in the Atmosphere, in Outer Space, and Under Water. The treaty did not prevent underground testing or provide for on-site inspection, and several emerging atomic powers, such as France and China, refused to take part. Yet a first step had been taken to cleanse the environment of radioactivity—a symbolic step on the road to a safer world.

Trouble in Vietnam   President Kennedy came away from the missile crisis with greater confidence in his ability to manage foreign problems. His primary goal, in military terms, was to replace the Eisenhower–Dulles doctrine of "massive retaliation" with a "flexible response" policy that would maximize his options in any foreign crisis. The plan called for a buildup in nuclear missiles, conventional ground troops, and Special Forces such as the "Green Berets." Not surprisingly, the defense budget rose rapidly in the Kennedy years. The armed forces added ten Polaris submarines, 200,000 ground troops, and four hundred Minutemen missiles, giving the United States a sizable advantage over Russia in nuclear weapons.

Malcolm Browne/AP Photo

Buddhist Protests.   *Quang Duc, a Buddhist monk in Saigon, burned himself to death in June 1963 to protest the crackdown on Buddhists by South Vietnamese President Ngo Dinh Diem. The Buddhist protests helped bring down the Diem government later that year.*

When Kennedy entered the White House, fewer than a thousand American military advisers were stationed in South Vietnam. Like Eisenhower, Kennedy hoped to formalize Vietnam's temporary partition at the seventeenth parallel by turning the South Vietnamese regime of Ngo Dingh Diem into a military power capable of defending itself against attacks from Ho Chi Minh's Communist government in the North.

Kennedy welcomed the challenge. U.S. Special Forces were dispatched to train South Vietnam's army, along with CIA personnel to direct covert operations and economic experts to supervise the aid programs intended to stabilize Diem's regime. Among the worst problems, it turned out, was Diem himself. Educated in the United States, a Catholic in a largely Buddhist land, Diem had little in common with the people he ruled. The South Vietnam he envisioned did not include the vital measures, such as land reform and religious toleration, that were needed to keep him in power.

In 1963, protests erupted in Saigon and other South Vietnamese cities over Diem's autocratic rule. The Buddhists held mass demonstrations against religious oppression, with several monks setting fire to themselves. As the protests escalated, army units attacked Buddhist temples and arrested their priests, sparking even greater protests from the Buddhist majority.

That fall, Diem was overthrown in a military coup engineered by South Vietnam's top generals. American officials knew about the coup but did nothing to stop it. To their surprise, the generals murdered Diem and his brother, Ngo Dinh Nhu, after taking them prisoner on the palace grounds.

By that time, sixteen thousand American "advisers" were stationed in South Vietnam. For Kennedy, the struggle had become a test of will against "Communist aggression." Yet the president also worried that the use of American troops created a dangerous momentum of its own. "It's like taking a drink," he said. "The effect wears off and you have to take another."

THE RIGHTS REVOLUTION: EARLY STEPS

In the early 1960s, the fires of social and political protest slowly came alive. In 1962, as James Meredith challenged the wall of segregation at Ole Miss, a thirty-five-year-old Mexican American named **Cesar Chavez** moved to Delano, California, with his wife and eight children. A naval veteran of World War II, Chavez toiled in the plum orchards and strawberry fields of central California before turning to community organizing. With unshakable conviction, he aimed to better the lives of impoverished migrant farm laborers by uniting them under a single banner—the black Aztec eagle of the fledgling United Farm Workers of America.

The year 1962 also witnessed the publication of two pathbreaking books about the underside of modern society: Michael Harrington's *The Other America* and Rachel Carson's *Silent Spring*. Carson, a marine biologist, exposed the contamination of wildlife, water supplies, and farmland by pesticides such as DDT. Her book helped revive America's naturalist movement. In 1963, two more seminal works appeared: **Betty Friedan's** *The Feminine Mystique*, which spurred the struggle for women's rights, and James Baldwin's *The Fire Next Time*, which warned of the growing racial divide. "To be a Negro in this country and to be relatively conscious," wrote Baldwin, "is to be in a rage all the time."

Poverty in America

In an era of increased abundance and consumerism, it was easy to forget that not everyone in the United States shared the country's great wealth and prosperity. This painful truth became the subject of a pathbreaking book, *The Other America*, by socialist author Michael Harrington, in 1962. Harrington estimated that more than 40 million people—almost one-quarter of the nation's population—lived in an "economic underworld" of joblessness, marginal wages, hunger, and despair. He emphasized that poverty could be found in every corner of the nation— among whites and blacks, natives and immigrants, rural folk and city dwellers. The picture here is from Appalachia, one of the regions highlighted in Harrington's book. It demonstrates the author's point that poverty is "a culture, an institution, a way of life" passed from one generation to the next. The powerful response to Harrington's book led to a vast array of social programs popularly known, in the words of President Lyndon Johnson, as the War on Poverty.

© Joffre Clark/ Black Star/

From Birmingham to Washington By 1963, racial injustice in America was a central issue. Birmingham, Alabama, became the new battleground, as a coalition of civil rights groups, led by Martin Luther King's Southern Christian Leadership Conference, attempted to break down the walls of discrimination in a city where African Americans had few economic opportunities or political rights. Birmingham was so rigidly segregated that a book featuring black rabbits and white rabbits eating together was removed from city libraries and a campaign was underway to banish "Negro music" from "white" radio stations.

Dr. King hoped to integrate Birmingham with a series of nonviolent protests codenamed "Project C," for confrontation. There were sit-ins at lunch counters, kneel-ins at white churches, and voter registration marches to city hall. Boycotts were organized to protest the all-white hiring practices of downtown department stores. Birmingham authorities cracked down hard. Led by Commissioner Eugene ("Bull") Connor, city police dispersed the protesters—many of them schoolchildren—with attack dogs and high-pressure fire hoses.

Dr. King was among the hundreds arrested for violating local court orders against marching and picketing. From his jail cell, he defended the morality of civil disobedience, noting that "segregation statutes are unjust because segregation distorts the soul." President Kennedy offered firm support. After dispatching federal troops to Birmingham, he assisted in an agreement that integrated the city's lunch counters and department stores. At that very moment, however, Governor George C. Wallace—proclaiming "Segregation Now! Segregation Tomorrow! Segregation Forever"—vowed to block the admission of two black students to the University of Alabama by "standing in the schoolhouse door." When federal marshals arrived, Wallace dramatically stepped aside.

The president's decisive action in Alabama signaled a major change. Viewing civil rights for the first time as a moral issue, Kennedy delivered a moving appeal for justice on national television. "One hundred years have passed since President Lincoln freed the slaves," he said, "yet their heirs, their grandsons, are not fully free. . . . And this nation, for all its hope and all its boasts, will not be fully free until all its citizens are free." Later that evening, civil rights activist Medgar Evers was assassinated outside his Jackson, Mississippi, home by a member of the Ku Klux Klan.

In June 1963, Kennedy sent Congress one of the most sweeping civil rights bills of the twentieth century. The bill, which prohibited discrimination in employment, federally assisted programs, and public accommodations such as restaurants and hotels, caused a furor on Capitol Hill. Southern legislators accused the president of "race mixing," and others, including Senator Barry Goldwater of Arizona, criticized him for abusing the "property rights" of business owners. As the bill's momentum stalled, a number of civil rights groups led by A. Philip Randolph, long-time president of the Brotherhood of Sleeping Car Porters, announced a "March on Washington for Jobs and Freedom."

On August 28, 1963, more than 200,000 people gathered at the Lincoln Memorial in the largest civil rights demonstration ever held on American soil. They listened to the spirituals of Mahalia Jackson, locked arms in solidarity as Joan Baez sang "We Shall Overcome," the anthem of the civil rights struggle, and rose in thunderous applause to the final words of Martin Luther King's now legendary address, "I Have a Dream."

Feminist Stirrings   The civil rights movement always possessed a strong female strain. From Rosa Parks in Montgomery to Ella Baker of the Southern Christian Leadership Conference, women played a prominent role in the struggle for black equality. By 1963, the spirit of these protests created a sense of determination that sparked other movements, such as women's rights.

The revival of feminism in the 1960s seemed long overdue. More than four decades after winning the vote, American women still played a minor role in government affairs. In 1963, there were no women governors, cabinet officers, or Supreme Court justices. The U.S. Senate contained one female member, Margaret Chase Smith of Maine.

Discrimination also pervaded the workplace. Although more women were working outside the home than ever before, they were increasingly concentrated in low-paying service and clerical jobs despite their rising level of education. Fewer than 4 percent of the nation's lawyers and 1 percent of the top business executives were female. As a result, full-time working women earned about 60 percent of the income of men.

These inequities were highlighted in 1963 by the final report of the Presidential Commission on the Status of Women. Led by Eleanor Roosevelt (who had died in 1962) and Esther Peterson, an assistant secretary of labor, the commission detailed a wide range of problems, including job discrimination, unequal wages, lack of child care, and legal restrictions that prevented women in some states from sitting on juries or making wills. In direct response, President Kennedy issued an executive order banning sex discrimination in federal employment. A few months later, Congress passed the Equal Pay Act of 1963, requiring employers to provide equal wages to men and women who did the same work.

Even more important in terms of the emerging women's movement was the publication of *The Feminine Mystique*. In the opening chapters, Betty Friedan described "the problem that has no name": the emptiness felt by middle-class women who sacrificed their dreams and careers to become the "happy homemakers" of suburban America. Blaming educators, advertisers, and government officials for creating a climate in which femininity and domesticity went hand in hand, Friedan concluded that "we can no longer ignore that voice in women that says: 'I want something more than my husband and my children and my home.'"

The Feminine Mystique became an instant best-seller because it voiced the unspoken feelings of so many women. Their unhappiness was not caused by individual neuroses, Friedan argued, but rather by a set of cultural values that oppressed women while pretending to improve their lives.

TRAGEDY AND TRANSITION

By the fall of 1963, the fast pace and rapid changes of the new decade were leaving their mark. A growing economy, an emerging rights revolution, an expanding war in Southeast Asia, a frantic race to the moon—each would serve to reshape the fabric of American life in the years ahead. First, however, tragedy intervened.

Dallas In late November 1963, John and Jacqueline Kennedy traveled to Texas on a political tour. The 1964 presidential race was approaching, and Texas, which had narrowly supported the Kennedy–Johnson ticket three years before, could not be taken for granted. After greeting friendly crowds in Fort Worth, the Kennedys took a motorcade through Dallas, with the bubble-top of their limousine removed on a warm and cloudless day. Along the route, people waved from office buildings and cheered from the sidewalks. As the procession reached Dealy Plaza, shots rang out from the window of a nearby book depository. President Kennedy grabbed his throat and slumped to the seat. Texas Governor John Connally was wounded in the back, wrist, and leg. The motorcade raced to Parkland Hospital, where the president was pronounced dead.

John F. Kennedy in Dallas. *Moving through the streets of Dallas, President Kennedy's limousine headed toward Dealy Plaza—and tragedy—on November 22, 1963.*

Within hours, the Dallas police arrested a twenty-four-year-old suspect named **Lee Harvey Oswald**. Two days later, Oswald was shot and killed in the basement of Dallas police headquarters by Jack Ruby, a local nightclub owner with a shady past. These shocking events led many Americans to conclude that Oswald was innocent or that he did not act alone. Dozens of theories surfaced about the Kennedy assassination, blaming leftists and rightists, Fidel Castro and the Mafia, the Ku Klux Klan and the CIA. The most logical theory, that a deranged man had committed a senseless act of violence, did not seem compelling enough to explain the death of a president so young and full of life.

Few other events in the nation's history produced so much bewilderment and grief. Charming and handsome, a war hero with a glamorous wife, Kennedy seemed the ideal president for the electronic political age. The media likened his administration to Camelot, a magical place that symbolized courage, chivalry, and hope. His tragic death added the further dimension of promise unfulfilled.

The reality was rather different, of course. Kennedy's 1,037 days in office were marked by failures as well as successes, and his leadership was more decisive in foreign policy than it was in domestic affairs. Since his death, moreover, evidence of his extramarital affairs and other personal shortcomings have raised legitimate questions about his character and morality. Still, the president's final months were his most productive by far. The Test Ban Treaty offered hope for a safer world, and a new civil rights bill had been sent to Capitol Hill. There is also the suggestion—disputed by some—that Kennedy was rethinking his position on Vietnam. "If I tried to pull out completely now," he told Senator Mike Mansfield, "we would have another Joe McCarthy red scare on our hands, but I can do it after I'm reelected."

The trip to Dallas shattered those hopes and plans.

LBJ

Within hours of the assassination, **Lyndon Baines Johnson** took the presidential oath of office aboard *Air Force One*, with his wife, Lady Bird, and Jacqueline Kennedy standing at his side. As the nation mourned its fallen leader, President Johnson vowed to continue the programs and policies of the Kennedy administration. "All I have," he told a special session of Congress, "I would gladly have given not to be standing here today."

Lyndon Baines Johnson—known as LBJ—bore little resemblance to the president he replaced. Born in the Texas hill country in 1908, Johnson came from a different region, a lower social class, and an older political generation. After graduating from a public college, he worked in the Washington office of a Texas congressman before returning home to become state director of the National Youth Administration, a New Deal agency that provided work-study funds for needy students. The experience strengthened his confidence in the government's ability to improve people's lives. Johnson described Franklin Roosevelt, his mentor and role model, as "like a daddy to me."

In the following years, Johnson won a seat in Congress, served as a naval officer during World War II, and became a U.S. senator in 1949. (His margin of victory, a mere eighty-seven votes, earned him the nickname "Landslide Lyndon.") Elected Senate majority leader by his Democratic colleagues in the 1950s, Johnson worked efficiently with the Eisenhower White House to craft important legislation on defense spending, highway construction, and civil rights.

LBJ lacked the good looks and regal charm of John Kennedy. He seemed crude and plodding by comparison, with his heavy drawl, cowboy boots, and earthy language. Yet few people in Washington knew more about the political process—how things really got done. Johnson recognized the true pockets of power. He knew when to flatter, when to bully, and when to bargain. Incredibly ambitious and hardworking—he survived a near-fatal heart attack in 1955—Johnson entered the White House with three decades of political experience under his belt.

| Tax Cuts and Civil Rights | The new president moved quickly to restore public confidence through a smooth transition of power. To calm mounting suspicion of conspiracy, he appointed a seven-member commission, |

headed by Chief Justice Earl Warren, to investigate the Kennedy assassination and issue a report. To provide stability in the executive branch, he convinced Secretary of State Dean Rusk, Secretary of Defense Robert McNamara, and other key officials to remain at their jobs. Where Kennedy had proclaimed, "Let us begin," Johnson added, "Let us continue!"

One of his first acts as president was to work for the tax cut that Kennedy had supported. To please fiscal conservatives in Congress, Johnson agreed to slash the federal budget. He believed that lower taxes would spur economic growth and lower unemployment, thereby increasing federal revenues down the road. In February 1964, Johnson signed a measure that cut taxes by $10 billion over the next two years.

The economy responded. With more money available for investment and consumption, the gross national product shot up 7 percent in 1964 and 8 percent the following year, and unemployment fell below 5 percent for the first time since World War II. Furthermore, the economic boom generated even greater federal revenues, just as Johnson had predicted.

Within weeks after taking office, the president met with Martin Luther King, Jr., and other black leaders to assure them of his commitment to civil rights. In his heart, Johnson considered segregation to be an immoral system that retarded an entire region's advancement. "He felt about the race question much as I did," a Texas friend recalled, "namely that it obsessed the South and diverted it from attending to its economic and educational problems."

The civil rights bill had strong public backing outside the South. In February, the House of Representatives easily approved it by a vote of 290 to 130, but the bill hit a wall in the Senate, where southern opponents used the filibuster to prevent its passage. The bill's success depended on a vote for cloture, ending debate, which required the agreement of two-thirds of the Senate. Working together, Senators Hubert Humphrey (D, Minnesota) and Everett Dirksen (R, Illinois) gathered bipartisan support. The Senate voted for cloture on June 10, 1964 (ending a seventy-five-day filibuster), and passed the bill the following afternoon. Described by the *New York Times* as "the most far-reaching civil rights [legislation] since Reconstruction days," it withheld federal funds from segregated public programs, created the Equal Employment Opportunity Commission, and outlawed discrimination in public accommodations, such as theaters, restaurants, and hotels. Furthermore, a last-minute lobbying effort by Senator Margaret Chase Smith and other women's rights supporters added another category—sex—to the clause in Title VII that prohibited employment discrimination based on race, creed, or national origin. What seemed like a minor addition became a powerful asset to working women in the future.

President Johnson signed the bill into law on July 2, 1964. Though compliance came slowly, the Civil Rights Act marked a vital turning point in the struggle for equal rights. Quoting Victor Hugo, Senator Dirksen declared that "no army can withstand the strength of an idea whose time has come."

Landslide in 1964   LBJ entered the 1964 presidential campaign on a tidal wave of popularity and goodwill. His early months in office were blunder free. The nation prospered, Vietnam appeared as a distant blip on the screen, and the only war on Johnson's public agenda was the one against poverty, which he promised to wage—and win—after his expected victory at the polls.

The summer of 1964, however, offered signs of trouble to come. In Mississippi, an attempt to register black voters by local activists and northern college students met violent resistance from white mobs. On June 21, three volunteers—James Chaney, Andrew Goodman, and Michael Schwerner—disappeared after inspecting the ruins of a firebombed black church. Because Goodman and Schwerner were northern whites, the incident made the front pages of newspapers across the country. Five weeks later, FBI agents found three bodies buried in an earthen dam. The civil rights workers had been murdered by local Klansmen and police, seven of whom were eventually convicted and sent to jail.

Racial tensions that summer were not confined to the South. In July, a confrontation between residents and police officers in Harlem led to several nights of arson and looting. The trouble was followed by disturbances in the black neighborhoods of Philadelphia, Pennsylvania; Paterson, New Jersey; and Rochester, New York. At the Democratic National Convention in Atlantic City, moreover, the race issue took center stage. Although the nomination of President Johnson and Senator Humphrey, his running mate, went smoothly, a floor fight erupted over the seating of two rival Mississippi delegations—one composed of state party segregationists, the other representing the biracial Mississippi Freedom Democratic Party (MFDP).

Led by **Fannie Lou Hamer**, the twentieth child of illiterate sharecroppers, the MFDP spoke for the disenfranchised black majority in Mississippi. "I was beaten till I was exhausted," Hamer told the national convention. "All of this on account we

Voters as Consumers in a New Television World

By 1964, the use of television for political advertising was on the rise. But negative TV spots, so common in election campaigns today, were still relatively rare. All that changed, however, with an ad (shown here) produced for the Democrats by Doyle Dane Bernbach, one of America's largest advertising firms, which portrayed Republican presidential candidate Barry Goldwater as a dangerous extremist who could easily plunge the world into nuclear war. By following the individual frames, one can see a little girl innocently pulling the petals from a daisy. As she reaches the number nine, an adult voice begins a reverse countdown for the launching of an atomic device. At zero, the girl's face is engulfed by a huge mushroom cloud. The ominous voice-over appears under the final three frames. Ironically, the notorious "Daisy Ad" aired only once on television; the Democrats pulled it after the Republicans filed a formal complaint with the Fair Campaign Practices Committee. But news programs showed the ad over and over again, sending the message into millions of American homes.

"Ten, nine, eight, seven . . .

six, five, four, three . . .

two, one . . .

These are the stakes. To make a world in which all of God's children can live . . .

or to go into the dark. We must either love each other or we must die . . .

VOTE FOR PRESIDENT JOHNSON ON NOVEMBER 3.

The stakes are too high for you to stay home."

wanted to register, to become first class citizens. If the Freedom Democratic party is not seated now, I question America."

Johnson hoped to compromise. Acting through Senator Humphrey, he offered the Freedom Party two voting delegates and the promise of a fully integrated Mississippi delegation at future national conventions. The compromise pleased no one. Hamer rejected it as a "token" gesture, and several white Mississippi delegates left Atlantic City in a huff.

At the Republican National Convention in San Francisco, the simmering feud between moderates and conservatives boiled over, with delegates shouting down opponents with catcalls and boos. After bitter debate, the convention chose Senator Barry Goldwater of Arizona for the presidential nomination and Representative William Miller of New York for the vice-presidential spot. In a defiant acceptance speech, Goldwater promised a "spiritual awakening" for America, adding: "Extremism in the defense of liberty is no vice. Moderation in the pursuit of justice is no virtue."

Goldwater opposed "big government" in domestic affairs but supported large military budgets to deter "Communist aggression." His Senate record included votes against social security increases, the Nuclear Test Ban Treaty of 1963, and the Civil Rights Act of 1964. In contrast to Goldwater, President Johnson came across as the candidate of all Americans, with promises galore. "We're in favor of a lot of things and we're against mighty few," he said.

Even in foreign affairs, his least favorite subject, Johnson appeared confident and controlled. In August 1964, two U.S. Navy destroyers, the *Maddox* and *C. Turner Joy*, engaged several North Vietnamese torpedo boats in the Gulf of Tonkin. The truth about this incident—Did a battle really occur? Who fired first? What were American warships doing in these waters?—was overshadowed by Johnson's dramatic response. First he ordered U.S. planes to bomb military targets deep inside North Vietnam. Then he requested—and received—a congressional resolution authorizing the president to "take all necessary measures" to repel "further aggression."

The Gulf of Tonkin Resolution gave Johnson the authority he would need to escalate the Vietnam War. During the 1964 campaign, however, he assured voters that nothing could be further from his mind. "We don't want American boys to do the fighting for Asian boys," he declared. "We don't want to get tied down in a land war in Asia."

The election was never in doubt. Johnson won 61 percent of the popular vote (43 million to 27 million) and forty-four of the fifty states (486 electoral votes to Goldwater's 52). His lopsided margin of victory allowed the Democrats to increase their substantial majorities in both houses of Congress.

For Republicans, however, the news was not all bad. The election returns showed that a new coalition was forming in their ranks, with the party gaining strength among middle-class white voters in the South and Southwest. Furthermore, Goldwater attracted thousands of young recruits who were determined to reshape the Republican Party along more conservative lines. For these legions, 1964 was a beginning rather than an end.

THE GREAT SOCIETY, 1964–1965

President Johnson viewed his landslide victory as a mandate for change. Anxious to leave his mark on history, he spoke of creating "a great society" for Americans in which the "quality of our goals" exceeded the "quantity of our goods," a society in which poverty, ignorance, and discrimination no longer existed, and the spirit of "true community" prevailed.

Declaring War on Poverty   The centerpiece of Johnson's expansive vision was his War on Poverty, a concept that President Kennedy and his aides had explored shortly before his death. To maintain continuity, Johnson named R. Sargent Shriver, one of Kennedy's brothers-in-law, to coordinate the numerous programs created by the Economic Opportunity Act of 1964, including the Job Corps, the Neighborhood Youth Corps, and Volunteers in Service to America (VISTA), a domestic service program modeled on the Peace Corps.

The most controversial aspect of the War on Poverty was its emphasis on community action, which encouraged neighborhood groups to play an active role in federally funded projects. Some initiatives, such as food stamps and Head Start, a preschool enrichment program, proved very successful. Others were cited for waste and fraud. Of greatest lasting impact, it appeared, was the increase of minority participation in local affairs.

Poverty did decline dramatically in this era—the result of an expanding economy as well as federal programs aimed directly at the poor. In 1960, more than 40 million Americans (20 percent of the population) lived beneath the poverty line; by 1970, that figure had dropped to 24 million (12 percent). For all of its problems, the much maligned and seriously underfunded War on Poverty achieved a fair measure of success.

Health Care and Immigration Reform The Great Society included a mixture of original programs and borrowed ideas. A kind of infectious optimism gripped Washington. Nothing seemed politically impossible with Lyndon Johnson in charge.

Health care was a good example. When Johnson took office in 1963, a majority of older Americans were without health insurance, one-fifth of the nation's poor had never visited a doctor, and the infant mortality rate showed no signs of declining, despite the introduction of lifesaving vaccines. Johnson believed that medical care for the poor and the elderly was an essential part of the Great Society. Yet the idea of federal involvement raised fundamental questions about the role of government in a free enterprise system. The American Medical Association (AMA) and private insurers strongly opposed such intervention, calling it "socialized medicine."

After months of intense lobbying, Congress passed the landmark legislation, known as Medicare and Medicaid, that Johnson requested. Medicare provided federal assistance to the elderly for hospital expenses and doctors' fees, and Medicaid extended medical coverage to welfare recipients through matching grants to the states. Both programs grew rapidly, reaching 40 million Americans by 1970. Though supporters pointed with pride to statistics showing both an increase in life expectancy and a drop in infant mortality, critics noted the exploding federal costs, the gaps in coverage, and the inferior quality of health care to the poor. Few government programs proved more controversial and expensive to maintain than Medicare and Medicaid, and none would prove more difficult to reform.

The Great Society also included a new immigration law, passed in 1965. Though vitally important to the nation's future, it went largely unnoticed at the time. In one bold sweep, the Immigration Act removed the national origins quotas, as well as the ban on Asians, which dated back to 1924. Although it set a ceiling of about 300,000 immigrants per year, the law permitted the family members of American citizens (both naturalized and native born) to enter the United States without limit.

The impact was dramatic. Prior to 1965, Europe accounted for 90 percent of the new arrivals to the United States; after 1965, only 10 percent. By the mid-1970s, a majority of legal immigrants came from seven Asian and Latin American countries: Korea, Taiwan, India, the Philippines, Cuba, the Dominican Republic, and Mexico.

THE EXPANDING WAR, 1965–1966

Lyndon Johnson inherited a rich agenda from the Kennedy White House, including the War on Poverty and the push for civil rights. But nothing proved as important, or damaging, to his presidency as the conflict in Vietnam. When Johnson assumed office, there were fewer than 20,000 American "advisers" in that divided country. Within three years, that number had risen to almost 500,000, with no end in sight. Vietnam quickly became Johnson's war—and ultimately his nightmare.

Point of No Return Vietnam was part of a larger containment effort that had guided American foreign affairs since the end of World War II. Like Presidents Truman, Eisenhower, and Kennedy, LBJ based his commitment to Vietnam on a series of powerful assumptions, such as saving "democracy" in Asia, halting the spread of communism, and maintaining America's credibility around the globe. It hardly mattered that South Vietnam was neither a democracy nor the victim of an international communist plot. What did matter was the need for strength and staying power in a world crisis—the belief that a defeat for the United States anywhere would undermine its standing everywhere.

Johnson understood the political stakes. "I am not going to lose Vietnam," he said. His plan was to pressure the communist enemy in a measured fashion that would neither alarm the American public nor divert resources from his cherished domestic programs. The Gulf of Tonkin Resolution gave him the authority to move forward. The Vietcong attack at Pleiku provided the motive.

Pleiku, a market town in the central highlands of South Vietnam, was home to a military airstrip guarded by American Special Forces. In February 1965, a Vietcong mortar barrage killed eight Americans and wounded more than a hundred. Several days later, U.S. warplanes began the massive bombing of North Vietnam. Known first as Operation Rolling Thunder, the air strikes hit targets checked personally by President Johnson, who boasted that "they can't even bomb an outhouse without my approval." The problem, however, was that air power had little impact on North Vietnam's ability to wage war. The bombings killed thousands, flattened factories and power plants, and ravaged the economy, yet the flow of communist troops and supplies into South Vietnam never stopped.

In March 1965, two marine battalions arrived at the huge new U.S. Air Force base in Da Nang, raising the American troop total in South Vietnam above 100,000. By December, troop levels reached 184,000, and they rose each month thereafter. Draft calls zoomed from 100,000 in 1964 to 340,000 by 1966, leading millions of young men to seek student deferments or to join the National Guard in the hope of avoiding combat in Vietnam.

By 1965, at least half of South Vietnam was controlled by Vietcong or North Vietnamese troops. The new South Vietnamese government of General Nguyen Van Thieu appeared more stable than previous ones, but its army was no match for the well-disciplined Communist soldiers. As Johnson saw it, American forces would defend South Vietnam until its people were ready to defend themselves. "We will not be defeated," the president vowed. "We will not withdraw."

American strategy in Vietnam had both a military and political objective: to wear down the enemy with superior firepower and to "win the hearts and minds" of the South Vietnamese people. Neither proved successful. North Vietnam, a nation of 19 million, continued to field a large army despite enormous casualties, while the Vietcong provided able support. Fighting on native soil, these soldiers waged relentless, often brutal war against a "foreign aggressor" and its "puppets" inside South Vietnam. Between 1965 and 1966, U.S. combat deaths rose tenfold, from 636 to 6,664.

Americans fought bravely, and morale at this point remained high. Yet the very nature of the war alienated these soldiers from the people they had come to defend. It would have been trying, under the best of circumstances, to distinguish between innocent civilians and Vietcong. Unfamiliar with the language and culture of Vietnam, Americans increasingly viewed everyone as the enemy. Each village appeared as "a dark room full of deadly spiders," a soldier recalled.

American planners tried numerous strategies to isolate the Vietcong. Most included the movement of peasant populations from their ancestral lands to "strategic hamlets" or to cities unprepared for the arrival of thousands of homeless refugees. Between 1960 and 1970, the percentage of South Vietnamese living in urban areas jumped from 20 to 43 percent. In these bulging cities, jobs were scarce, prostitution flourished, and families split apart.

Those who remained in the countryside faced terror from all sides: North Vietnamese mortar attacks, Vietcong assassination squads, and American assaults from the air. U.S. planes and helicopters defoliated the fields and forests with chemical sprays and pounded suspected enemy strongholds with bombs and napalm (jellied gasoline). In one of the most telling remarks of the war, an American officer explained his mission bluntly: "We had to destroy this town in order to save it."

Early Protests   Even as President Johnson escalated the war in 1965, he expected the Great Society to move freely ahead. A "rich nation" like the United States, he declared, "can afford to make progress at home while meeting its obligations abroad."

For a time, his domestic agenda remained impressive. Fueled by the immense economic prosperity of 1965 and 1966, the Great Society added the Education Act, which extended federal aid to public and private schools, and the Model Cities Act, which provided funds to upgrade housing, health services, crime prevention, and parks. In addition, LBJ reaffirmed his commitment to civil rights by appointing the first African American Supreme Court justice, Thurgood Marshall, and the first African American cabinet member, Robert Weaver, to head the new Department of Housing and Urban Development (HUD).

The momentum did not last. The first rumblings of antiwar protest came from the college campuses, where a new group, calling itself **Students for a Democratic Society (SDS)**, was gaining ground. Formed in 1962, SDS issued a "Declaration of Principles" that denounced "racism" and "militarism," among other evils, and promised a new politics based on socialist ideals. Limited at first to elite colleges and major state universities, such as Harvard, the University of California at Berkeley, and the University of Wisconsin, the organization expanded in direct proportion to the war itself.

The early student leaders called their movement the "New Left." Some of them, known as "Red-diaper babies," were the children of "Old Left" radicals from the 1930s and 1940s. Others came from the burgeoning civil rights movement. Impatient and idealistic, they identified with the "revolutionary" movements of the emerging Third World. To their eyes, Fidel Castro and Ho Chi Minh were positive forces in history, representing a fundamental shift in power from the privileged elites to the struggling masses. Not surprisingly, Vietnam became the New Left's defining issue—a symbol of popular resistance to America's "imperialist" designs.

Early in 1965, antiwar students and faculty at the University of Michigan held the nation's first "teach-in" to discuss the consequences of escalation in Vietnam. The idea spread rapidly from campus to campus—with the University of Maine's teach-in attracting three hundred people and Berkeley's drawing more than twelve thousand. On Easter Sunday, a crowd of thirty thousand attended the first major antiwar rally in Washington, sponsored by SDS.

THE RIGHTS REVOLUTION: CENTER STAGE

The national mood of unity and reconciliation that followed President Kennedy's assassination in November 1963 did not last much beyond the landslide election of 1964. The war in Vietnam created divisions that grew wider by the year. Americans became more skeptical of their leaders and less likely to believe official explanations of events.

Voting Rights   Following passage of the landmark Civil Rights Act of 1964, the struggle for racial justice moved to the next battleground: voting rights in the Deep South. The campaign was already under way in places like Selma, Alabama, where local activists, facing intense white resistance, asked Martin Luther King, Jr., and his Southern Christian Leadership Conference for support.

The Selma demonstrations began early in 1965. Local blacks marched daily to the courthouse, where Sheriff Jim Clark—wearing a huge button with the single word NEVER—used force to turn them away. Thousands were arrested, beaten with clubs, and shocked with cattle prods for attempting to register with the local election board. In March, Dr. King decided to lead a protest march from Selma to Montgomery, the state capital, fifty miles away. "We are demanding the ballot," he declared.

On March 9—known as Bloody Sunday—a contingent of Sheriff Clark's deputies and Alabama state police attacked the marchers, sending seventeen to the hospital. Hundreds of civil rights leaders, entertainers, politicians, and clergy rushed to Selma to lend their support, but the violence continued. James Reeb, a Unitarian minister from Boston, was beaten to death by a gang of whites, and Viola Luizzo, a civil rights activist from Michigan, was shot and killed by the Klan.

On March 15, President Johnson made a special trip to Capitol Hill to urge passage of a new voting rights bill. In the most eloquent speech of his career, Johnson said:

> What happened in Selma is part of a larger movement which reaches into every section and state of America. It is the effort of Negroes to secure for themselves the full blessing of American life.
>
> Their cause must be our cause, too. Because it is not just Negroes, but really it is all of us who must overcome the crippling legacy of bigotry and injustice.
>
> And we shall overcome.

The Watts Explosion

Five days later, on August 11, a riot erupted in Watts, a black section of Los Angeles, triggering the worst urban violence since World War II. The **Watts riot** began with the arrest of a black motorist by a white highway patrolman. A crowd gathered, police reinforcements arrived, and several arrests were made. As word of the incident spread, several thousand people—mostly young men—rampaged down Crenshaw Boulevard, looting stores, burning buildings, and overturning cars. The violence flared each evening for a week. It took fourteen thousand National Guardsmen to restore order. At least thirty-four people were killed, a thousand injured, and four thousand arrested, with property damage estimated at $200 million.

News of the Watts riot shocked President Johnson. "We simply hadn't seen the warnings," recalled Attorney General Ramsey Clark. "We had looked at [civil rights] as basically a southern problem, but . . . in fact the problems of the urban ghettos [were much worse]."

Times had changed. By 1965, almost half of America's black population lived outside the South, mostly in large cities, and Watts epitomized the conditions of day-to-day urban life. Good housing was scarce. As black neighborhoods became overcrowded, residents wishing to move elsewhere were trapped by racial discrimination. Inferior schools hampered upward mobility. Two out of three adults in Watts lacked a high school education, and one in eight was illiterate. Watts had the highest unemployment rate, and lowest income level, of any Los Angeles neighborhood except Skid Row. Two hundred of 205 policemen assigned to Watts were white. Crime was rampant, public services poor. "The sewers stank in the summer, there was not enough water to flush toilets, not enough pressure to fight fires," said one Watts resident. "The social fabric just couldn't stand the strain."

The riot was a spontaneous event, not a planned act of destruction. In the next three years, hundreds of northern black neighborhoods would explode. The worst riots, in Newark and Detroit, would begin, as Watts did, with an incident between local blacks and white police.

Most African Americans deplored the riots and took no part. Yet a competing vision, far different from the one preached by Dr. King, was gathering strength in the black community. As he walked the streets of Watts after the riot, King met a group of youths shouting, "We won!" He asked how anyone could claim victory in the face of such violence and destruction. "We won," a young man answered, "because we made them pay attention to us."

DOING HISTORY ONLINE

The Voting Rights Act, 1965

Read the document online. Lyndon Johnson was the strongest advocate of civil rights to occupy the White House in the twentieth century. Why, then, did the northern ghettos suffer through four years of summer race riots, when angry and disaffected African Americans took to the streets to dramatize their demands for change?

 www.cengage.com/ history/ayers/ ampassages4e

Black Power

By the mid-1960s, Dr. King's leadership in the civil rights movement was increasingly under attack. Younger African

Black Voter Registration

Black voter registration in the South was one of the great accomplishments of the civil rights movement. Spurred by the Selma demonstrations, President Johnson signed the Voting Rights Act on August 6, 1965, which abolished discriminatory practices such as the literacy test, and authorized federal examiners to register voters, instead of relying on the individual states. As this table demonstrates, the act profoundly altered the political landscape of the South.

Within months of its passage, more than 2 million black southerners were registered to vote. Most supported the Democratic Party of Presidents John F.

(LIBRARY OF CONGRESS)

(continued)

Americans, in particular, seemed reluctant to follow his course. At a 1966 rally in Mississippi, a recent Howard University graduate named Stokely Carmichael brought this issue to a head. Just released from jail for leading a peaceful civil rights protest, Carmichael vented his anger as a clearly uncomfortable Dr. King sat behind him on the stage. "This is the twenty-seventh time I've been arrested," Carmichael shouted, "and I ain't going to jail no more. The only way we gonna stop them white men from whuppin' us is to take over. What we gonna start saying now is '**Black Power.**'" The crowd took up the chant: "Black Power! Black Power! Black Power!"

Black Power became a symbol of African American unity in the mid-1960s, stressing group strength, independent action, and racial pride. In local communities, black activists lobbied school boards to add African American history and culture to the curriculum. On college campuses, black students pressed administrators to speed up minority recruitment, establish black studies programs, and provide separate living quarters—a demand that alarmed integrationists, black and white. In the political arena, Carl Stokes of Cleveland and Richard Hatcher of Gary, Indiana, became the first African Ameri-

(continued)

Kennedy and Lyndon Johnson, which had endorsed the cause of civil rights. At the same time, however, white southerners deserted the Democrats and moved overwhelmingly into the Republican Party. In the 1968 presidential election, (see Map 29.3) Democratic candidate Hubert Humphrey would win only one southern state, beginning a trend of Republican dominance in the South that has lasted, with few notable exceptions, to the present time.

TABLE 29.1 Black Voter Registration

State	1960	1966	Percentage Increase
Alabama	66,000	250,000	278.8
Arkansas	73,000	115,000	57.5
Florida	183,000	303,000	65.6
Georgia	180,000	300,000	66.7
Louisiana	159,000	243,000	52.8
Mississippi	22,000	175,000	695.4
North Carolina	210,000	282,000	34.3
South Carolina	58,000	191,000	229.3
Tennessee	185,000	225,000	21.6
Texas	227,000	400,000	76.2
Virginia	100,000	205,000	105.0

Source: U.S. Bureau of the Census, *Statistical Abstract of the United States: 1982–83* (103d ed.) Washington, D.C., 1982.

can mayors of northern cities by combining hard work with racial solidarity. Across the nation, black men and women donned African clothing, took on African names, and wore their hair unstraightened in an "Afro" style. "Black Is Beautiful" became a powerful slogan in this era, as did, "Say it loud, I'm black and I'm proud," by soul singer James Brown.

To militants like Stokely Carmichael, Black Power meant a political separation of the races. His position reflected a generational split between "old" civil rights groups such as the NAACP, which viewed racial integration as the key to black advancement, and "new" movement groups like Carmichael's Student Nonviolent Coordinating Committee (SNCC), which began to exclude whites. "Black people," said Carmichael, "must be seen in positions of power doing and articulating for themselves."

The separatist impulse had deep roots in the African American community. Its renewed strength in the 1960s was due in large part to a black nationalist movement that appealed to young people in the bleakest neighborhoods of urban America. "There is a different type of Negro emerging from the 18- to 25-year-old bracket," said a black leader in Watts. "They identify with Malcolm X's philosophy."

Malcolm X was the most popular and controversial Black Muslim leader of the 1960s. Born Malcolm Little, he joined the Nation of Islam while serving a prison term for robbery and adopted the "X" to replace "the white slave-master name which had been imposed upon my paternal forebears by some blue-eyed devil." The Nation of Islam was a black nationalist group, organized in Detroit in 1931, which preached a doctrine of self-help, moral discipline, and complete separation of the races. Its code of behavior, based on the rejection of racist stereotypes, stressed neatness, abstinence, and a firm division of male and female roles. Black Muslims were forbidden to smoke, drink alcohol, or have sex outside marriage. "Wake up, clean up, and stand up," their motto declared.

Created by Elijah Poole, who renamed himself Elijah Muhammad, the Black Muslims were strongest in the urban ghettos, where their membership reached upward of 100,000, with a far larger mass of sympathizers. Assigned by Elijah Muhammad to a temple in Harlem, Malcolm X became a charismatic figure to young black men, in particular, with his bold statements about the impact of white injustice on black self-esteem. "The worst crime the white man has committed," he said, "is to teach us to hate ourselves."

Malcolm X also preached self-defense, saying that blacks must protect themselves "by any means necessary" and that "killing is a two-way street." Such rhetoric made it easy to label the entire Black Muslim movement as extremist and to construe its message as one of violence and hate.

Malcolm X created a public furor by describing the assassination of President Kennedy as an instance of "the chickens come home to roost." Expelled from the Nation of Islam by Elijah Muhammad, he traveled to Mecca on a spiritual pilgrimage and discovered, to his surprise, the insignificance of color in Islamic thought. This led him to form a rival Muslim group, the Organization of Afro-American Unity, which emphasized black nationalism in a manner that did not demonize whites. Assassinated in 1965 by followers of Elijah Muhammad, Malcolm X became a martyr to millions of African Americans, some praising his militant call for self-defense, others stressing his message of self-discipline and self-respect.

Occasionally Black Power became a vehicle of rage and racial revenge. SNCC chairman H. Rap Brown, for example, urged a crowd in Cambridge, Maryland, to "burn this town down," adding: "Don't love the white man to death, shoot him to death." And some went beyond rhetoric by forming groups like the Black Panthers to take their grievances to the streets.

Founded in 1966 by an Oakland, California, ex-convict named Huey Newton, the Panthers provided a violent alternative to other black movements of this era. Portraying themselves as opponents of a "racist-capitalist police state," the Panthers demanded the release of all blacks from prison and the payment of "slave reparations" by whites.

Adept at self-promotion, the Panthers won modest support in black neighborhoods through their community work. With perhaps five thousand members nationwide, most in the San Francisco Bay area, they ran food banks, health clinics, and preschool programs in rundown city neighborhoods. At the same time, however, Newton and his aides routinely engaged in extortion, drug dealing, and other criminal acts. Heavily armed, wearing black clothing and dark sunglasses, the Panthers became a feared enemy—and primary target—of law enforcement, including the FBI. At least twenty-eight members and eleven policemen were killed in shoot-outs and ambushes between these forces.

"Sisterhood
Is Powerful"

The rights revolution of the 1960s included demands for sexual, as well as racial, equality. Both the Equal Pay Act of 1963 and the Civil Rights Act of 1964 were important steps in the battle against gender discrimination, yet progress had been slow. In the fall of 1966, a band of activists formed the National Organization for Women (NOW) to speed the pace of change.

At NOW's first convention, the three hundred delegates elected Betty Friedan president. Never radical, NOW pursued its major goals—passage of an equal rights amendment and sexual equality in the workplace—through political means. Its leaders took pains to portray NOW as an organization for women, not of women, and it welcomed male support.

NOW grew slowly. Its membership in 1970 totaled fifteen thousand—mostly white, middle-aged, and middle class. Yet NOW's impact on the emerging women's movement was enormous, both in what it represented and what it seemed to lack. For many younger women, raised in the affluence of suburban America, the resurgence of feminism went beyond the fight for political and economic equality. What attracted them was the call for female solidarity—the power of sisterhood—in the larger struggle for sexual liberation.

Some of these women were veterans of the civil rights movement. Others were active in the antiwar protests on college campuses. Although deeply committed to these causes, they discovered that sexism—the assumption of male superiority—also existed in organizations devoted to justice and equal rights. Thus, women found themselves thankful for the skills and self-confidence they had developed, yet resentful of their expected roles as cooks, secretaries, and sexual objects. When asked what positions women filled in his organization, Stokely Carmichael brought roars of male laughter by noting: "The position of women in SNCC is prone."

Determined to confront sexism on all fronts, these "new feminists" developed strategies and communities of their own. As women's liberation emerged in the mid-1960s, feminist study groups appeared, along with feminist newspapers, health clinics, and bookstores. The more radical elements, viewing men as the enemy, denounced marriage as "legal whoredom" and regarded the nuclear family as a form of female slavery. While rejecting such notions, mainstream feminists also struggled with the dilemma of how to achieve greater power and fulfillment in a male-dominated culture.

The new feminism met immediate resistance—and not only from men. Surveys of American women in the 1960s showed both a growing sensitivity to issues of sex discrimination and a strong distaste for "women's lib." Most housewives expressed pride in their values and experiences and resented the "elitism" of the feminist movement—the implication that outside employment was more fulfilling than housework or that women degraded themselves by trying to appear attractive to men. As the country artist Tammy Wynette sang: "Don't Liberate Me, Love Me." A long and difficult struggle lay ahead.

The Counterculture The emerging radicalism of America's youth in the 1960s had both a cultural and political base. Bound together with civil rights, women's rights, and the antiwar protests was a diffuse new movement, known as the counterculture, which challenged traditional values. To many young people, the counterculture symbolized personal liberation and generational strength—a break with the humdrum, hollow world of adults.

In 1965, a San Francisco journalist used the term "hippie" to describe a new breed of rebel—passionate, spontaneous, and free. Many wore their hair long and dressed in jeans and sandals. Like the Bohemians of the early 1900s and the Beats of the 1950s, they defined themselves as opponents of the dominant culture, with its emphasis on competition, consumerism, and conformity, an alienation so brilliantly portrayed in Mike Nichols's film *The Graduate* and Paul Simon and Art Garfunkel's "Sounds of Silence." Some young people joined communes, explored ancient religions, or turned to the occult. But far more pervasive were the sexual freedom, the vital new music, and the illegal drug use that marked these turbulent times.

The counterculture did not begin the sexual revolution of the 1960s. That process was already under way, fueled by the introduction of oral contraceptives in 1960, the emergence of a women's rights movement, and a series of Supreme Court decisions that widened public access to sexually explicit material. The counterculture played a different but equally important role by challenging conventional morality at every turn.

The results were dramatic. When the Beatles took America by storm in 1964, their chart-busting songs included "I Want to Hold Your Hand," "She Loves You," and "Please, Please Me." Marijuana use, a federal crime since 1937, was rare in middle-class society, and lysergic acid diethylamide (LSD) was largely unknown. By 1967, however, the Beatles were imagining "Lucy in the Sky with Diamonds" (LSD) and wailing, "Why Don't We Do It in the Road!"

The counterculture spread inward through America from the East and West coasts. In Cambridge, Massachusetts, a Harvard researcher named Timothy Leary became the nation's first psychedelic guru by promoting LSD as the pathway to heightened consciousness and sexual pleasure. In San Francisco, author Ken Kesey (*One Flew over the Cuckoo's Nest*) and his Merry Pranksters staged a series of public LSD parties, known as acid tests, that drew thousands of participants in 1966. Wearing wild costumes, with painted faces, the revelers danced to the sounds of Jerry Garcia and his Grateful Dead.

To much of the public, San Francisco became synonymous with the counterculture. Acid rock flourished in local clubs like the Fillmore West, where Jimi Hendrix ("Purple Haze"), Steppenwolf ("Magic Carpet Ride"), and the Jefferson Airplane ("White Rabbit") celebrated drug tripping in their songs. In 1967, more than seventy-five thousand young people migrated to San Francisco's Haight-Ashbury district to be part of the much publicized "summer of love." The majority of arrivals, studies showed, were runaways and school dropouts with no means of support. By summer's end, Haight-Ashbury was awash in drug overdoses, venereal disease, panhandling, and prostitution.

At first the national media embraced the counterculture as a "hip" challenge to the blandness of middle-class suburban life. Magazines as diverse as *Time* and *Playboy* doted on every aspect of the hippie existence, and the Levi-Strauss corporation used acid rockers to promote its new line of jeans. Hollywood celebrated the counterculture with films such as *Easy Rider*, about two footloose drug dealers on a motorcycle tour of self-discovery, and *I Love You, Alice B. Toklas*, in which a dull lawyer becomes a fun-loving hippie after accidentally taking hashish. The smash hit of the 1968 Broadway season was the rock musical *Hair*, depicting a draft evader's journey through the pleasure-filled Age of Aquarius.

Yet most young people of the 1960s experienced neither the nightmare of Haight-Ashbury nor the dream world of *Hair*. Millions of them remained on the margins of the counterculture, admiring its styles and sounds while rejecting its revolutionary mantra. And millions more entered adulthood without the slightest sign of protest or alienation. Indeed, some commentators spoke of a serious intragenerational split in this era, pitting young people who accepted, or aspired to, America's middle-class promise against more radical young people who did not.

A DIVIDED NATION, 1968

As 1968 began, **General William Westmoreland**, commander of U.S. forces in Southeast Asia, offered an optimistic assessment of the Vietnam War. In his view, American and South Vietnamese (ARVN) troops were gaining strength and confidence as the fighting progressed.

The Tet Offensive   Four days later, seventy thousand Communist troops assaulted American and ARVN positions throughout South Vietnam. Their lightning offensive, begun on the lunar New Year holiday of Tet, took Westmoreland by surprise. In Saigon, Vietcong units reached the American embassy before being driven back. After capturing Hue, one of South Vietnam's oldest cities, Communist soldiers murdered thousands of civilians and dumped their bodies into a mass grave.

As a military operation, the **Tet offensive** clearly failed. Using their overwhelming firepower, American and ARVN forces inflicted frightful casualties on the enemy. In the three-week battle to recapture Hue, more than 5,000 Communist soldiers were killed, along with 400 ARVN troops and 150 American marines. Vietcong losses were so severe that the brunt of the ground fighting after Tet would have to be shouldered by North Vietnamese troops.

(National Archives)

Young Marine.   *Although U.S. troops inflicted heavy casualties on the Vietcong and the North Vietnamese during the Tet offensive of 1968, the intensity of the fighting shocked the American public and increased public criticism of the war.*

In psychological terms, however, the Tet offensive marked a turning point in the war. The sheer size of the Communist attacks, their ability to strike so many targets in force, made a mockery of Westmoreland's optimistic claims. Reporting from Saigon after the Tet offensive, Walter Cronkite, America's most popular television journalist, claimed that a military victory was nowhere in sight. At best, Cronkite predicted, "the bloody experience of Vietnam is to end in a stalemate."

A stalemate was exactly what Americans feared most. The Tet offensive accelerated Johnson's political decline. His approval rating dropped from 48 to 36 percent, with most Americans expressing skepticism about official claims of military progress in Vietnam. Columnist Art Buchwald compared LBJ to General Custer at the Little Big Horn, and the prestigious *Wall Street Journal* warned that "the whole war effort is likely doomed."

The President Steps Aside As Lyndon Johnson pondered his political future, the memory of Harry S Truman was fresh in his mind. In 1952, Truman had decided not to seek reelection after losing the New Hampshire Democratic presidential primary to Senator Estes Kefauver of Tennessee. The main issue then was the stalemate in Korea. In 1968, LBJ faced a spirited challenge in New Hampshire from Senator Eugene McCarthy of Minnesota. The main issue now was the stalemate in Vietnam.

McCarthy's presidential campaign reflected the deep divisions within Democratic Party ranks. The "peace faction," led by younger activists, hoped to "dump Johnson" by mobilizing antiwar sentiment against him in key primary states. Hundreds of college students arrived in New Hampshire to work for the McCarthy campaign. Long hair and beards were taboo; well-scrubbed volunteers in sports coats and dresses ("be clean for Gene") canvassed house to house. "These college kids are fabulous," one Democratic leader remarked. "They knock at the door and come in politely, and people are delighted."

The New Hampshire results sent shock waves through the political system. McCarthy came within a whisker of defeating President Johnson in the Democratic primary. Polls showed McCarthy winning the support of "hawks" who demanded victory in Vietnam, as well as "doves" who wanted to pull out at once.

Four days later, Robert Kennedy entered the presidential race. As the former attorney general and a current U.S. senator from New York, he was both a critic of the Vietnam War and a champion of minority causes, especially in the field of civil rights. Millions saw "Bobby" as the keeper of Camelot, the heir to his fallen brother's legacy.

On March 31, President Johnson announced his political retirement in a stunning televised address: "I shall not seek, and I will not accept, the nomination of my party for another term as your President." A few weeks later, Vice President Hubert Humphrey entered the presidential race as the "regular" Democratic candidate, endorsed by Johnson himself. Humphrey's strategy was to line up delegates without contesting Kennedy or McCarthy in the volatile state primaries, where his chances of winning were slim.

A Violent Spring Early in April, Martin Luther King, Jr., traveled to Memphis to support a strike of city garbage workers for better wages and conditions. His social vision was ever expanding, as he challenged Americans to

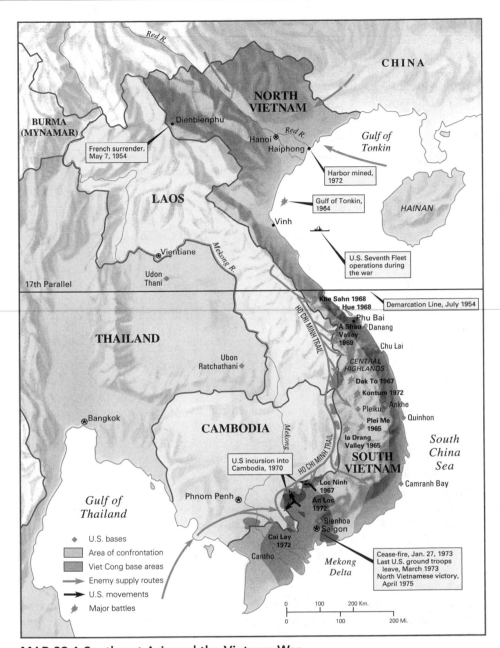

MAP 29.1 Southeast Asia and the Vietnam War.

To prevent communists from coming to power in Vietnam, Cambodia, and Laos in the 1960s, the United States intervened massively in Southeast Asia. The interventions failed, and the remaining American troops made a hasty exit from Vietnam in 1975, when the victorious Vietcong and North Vietnamese took Saigon and renamed it Ho Chi Minh City.

DOING HISTORY ONLINE

Martin Luther King and Economic Justice, 1966

Read the document online. Why did Martin Luther King, Jr., turn his attention to issues other than civil rights in the late 1960s?

www.cengage.com/ history/ayers/ ampassages4e

confront the "interrelated" evils of racism, militarism, and poverty. In 1968, Dr. King's projects included a "Poor People's March on Washington" and a "moral crusade" to end the war in Vietnam.

On the evening of April 3, King delivered a passionate sermon at a Memphis church. Demanding justice for the poor and the powerless, he seemed to sense the danger he was in. "I've been to the mountaintop," he cried. "I may not get there with you, but I want you to know that we as a people will get to the promised land." The following night, King was shot by James Earl Ray, a white racist, as he stood on the balcony of the Lorraine Motel. He died instantly, at the age of thirty-nine.

News of Dr. King's death touched off riots in African American communities from Boston to San Francisco. At the White House, President Johnson proclaimed a day of national mourning. Forty-five people died in these national riots, including twenty-four in Washington, D.C.

Among the presidential candidates, Robert Kennedy seemed closest to the message of Dr. King. Centering his campaign on the connection between domestic unrest and the Vietnam War, Kennedy visited migrant labor camps, Indian reservations, and inner-city neighborhoods to highlight the problems of disadvantaged Americans and the work to be done. He also supported the labor strike of Cesar Chavez and his National Farm Workers against the grape growers in central California.

Chavez, a military veteran, had grown up on an Arizona farm before moving to California in the 1940s. Married, with children, he

(© 1976 Bob Fitch/Tak Stock)

Cesar Chavez. *In the 1960s, Cesar Chavez became the public voice of migrant workers who toiled in the fields and orchards across the United States. He asked Americans to support the cause by boycotting products from growers who opposed attempts to unionize these workers.*

devoted his life to social causes, first in the barrios of San Jose and then in the fields and orchards where migrant laborers, many of them women and children, toiled in desperate conditions. Though Chavez rose from poverty and Robert Kennedy was born into privilege, the two became friends. Both men were close to forty years old, both were devout Catholics, and both admired the nonviolence of King and Gandhi in the struggle for justice and social change. As Kennedy campaigned in California, the grape strike was entering its third year. To protest the stalemate and the growing violence on both sides, Chavez began a fast that continued for twenty-one days. He ended it, in poor health, by breaking bread with Senator Kennedy at a Mass of thanksgiving. Despite enormous media coverage, and a national boycott of table grapes, the strike dragged on.

In June 1968, Kennedy took a major step toward the Democratic presidential nomination by defeating Eugene McCarthy in the delegate-rich California primary. That night, after greeting supporters at a Los Angeles hotel, Kennedy was shot and killed by a deranged Arab nationalist named Sirhan Sirhan. The nation went numb. Who could have imagined the horror of four national leaders—John F. Kennedy, Malcolm X, Martin Luther King, Jr., and Robert F. Kennedy—all dead at the hands of assassins?

The Chicago Convention	Throughout the spring of 1968, a coalition of antiwar groups prepared for a massive peace demonstration at the Democratic National Convention in Chicago. Originally expecting

500,000 people, the organizers dramatically lowered their estimates following the withdrawal of President Johnson in March and the murder of Senator Kennedy in June. Furthermore, Mayor Richard Daley made it clear that protesters were not welcome in his city. Fearing serious bloodshed at the Democratic convention, Senator McCarthy urged young demonstrators to stay away.

There was reason for concern. The continued military buildup in Vietnam had created a violent cycle of protest and response at home. That spring, thousands of young men burned their draft cards in public; some were beaten by angry crowds. Demonstrators tried to block troop trains and army induction centers, leading to bloody clashes with police. At Columbia University, students from SDS took over several buildings and trashed them to protest "war-related" research on campus. Hundreds were arrested, a general strike followed, and the university closed down for the semester.

Chicago resembled a war zone in August 1968, with six thousand army troops, five thousand National Guardsmen, and hundreds of Chicago riot police patrolling the streets. Denied permits to rally in public places, the protesters—perhaps four thousand strong—gathered in a park opposite the Hilton Hotel, where many Democratic party leaders were staying. Conflict was inevitable. Radical speakers from SDS and the Black Panthers harangued the crowd. Abbie Hoffman and Jerry Rubin, founders of the Youth International ("Yippie") Party, held workshops on LSD production and then chose a pig as their candidate with the slogan: "They nominated a president and he eats the people. We nominate a president and the people eat him."

On the evening of August 28, the demonstrators tried to march to the convention arena. As millions watched on television, the police moved in with clubs and mace, while National Guardsmen fired tear gas at the crowd. Hundreds were badly beaten, including reporters and bystanders, in what investigators later described as a "police riot." Even so, the blame did not rest entirely with one side. "We were not just innocent people who were victimized," Abbie Hoffman admitted. "We came to plan a confrontation."

News of the street violence shocked the Democratic convention. From the podium, Senator Abraham Ribicoff of Connecticut condemned "the Gestapo tactics on the streets of Chicago." His remark set off booing, cursing, and wild applause. Television cameras caught a furious Mayor Daley hurling ethnic insults at Ribicoff and telling the "lousy mother_____" to "go home."

The shaken delegates chose Hubert Humphrey and Senator Edmund Muskie of Maine to be their presidential and vice-presidential nominees. A staunch liberal, Humphrey exemplified the New Deal Democratic tradition of Roosevelt, Truman, Kennedy, and LBJ. His great weakness in 1968 was his loyal (if reluctant) support for Johnson's handling of the war. To many Americans, Humphrey endorsed the very policies that had divided the nation and left the Democratic Party in disarray.

Nixon's the One   Meeting in Miami, the Republicans faced a much simpler task. The Goldwater defeat of 1964 opened the door for candidates with broader political appeal, such as **Richard Nixon**. Having lost a bruising election for president in 1960 and another for governor of California in 1962, Nixon kept his fortunes alive by marketing himself as both a devoted Republican and an experienced public figure. After choosing him on the first ballot in 1968, the delegates selected Governor Spiro T. Agnew of Maryland to be his vice-presidential running mate.

Nixon campaigned as the spokesman for America's "silent majority"—the people who worked hard, paid their taxes, went to church, obeyed the law, and respected the

MAP 29.2 The Election of 1968.

In a bitterly fought three-way contest for the presidency, held against the backdrop of a nation badly split by the Vietnam War, Richard Nixon won a razor-thin victory with 43 percent of the popular vote.

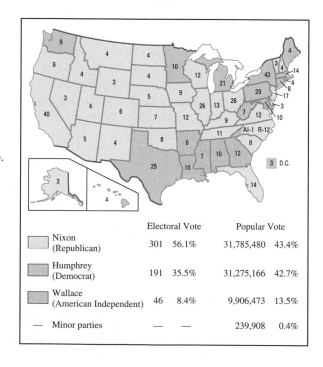

		Electoral Vote		Popular Vote	
	Nixon (Republican)	301	56.1%	31,785,480	43.4%
	Humphrey (Democrat)	191	35.5%	31,275,166	42.7%
	Wallace (American Independent)	46	8.4%	9,906,473	13.5%
—	Minor parties	—	—	239,908	0.4%

flag. In a nation grown weary of urban riots and campus demonstrations, he vowed to make "law and order" his number one domestic priority and to bring "peace with honor" to Vietnam.

For the first time since 1948, the presidential campaign attracted a serious third-party candidate, Governor George Wallace of Alabama. An ardent segregationist, Wallace showed surprising strength in white working-class areas of the North and West, where issues such as rising crime rates and draft deferments for college students were vital concerns. In blunt, sometimes explosive language, Wallace lashed out at "liberal judges," "welfare cheats," and "pot-smoking freaks in their beards and sandals."

Early opinion polls showed Nixon far ahead of Humphrey, with Wallace running a strong third. Yet the gap closed considerably in the campaign's final weeks when President Johnson ordered a temporary bombing halt in North Vietnam, and millions of Democratic voters, fearful of a Nixon presidency, returned to the party fold. On election day, Nixon won 43.4 percent of the votes and 301 electoral votes, to 42.7 percent and 191 for Humphrey, and 13.5 percent and 46 for Wallace.

CONCLUSION

Few other decades in American history have provided more drama and tragedy than the 1960s. What began with such hope and promise soon gave way to deep suspicion and despair, as Americans reeled from one crisis to another.

Most Americans welcomed the vibrancy of President Kennedy as they had welcomed the steadiness of President Eisenhower eight years before. They applauded Kennedy's call for young people to get involved in public service, as well as his tough stance against international communism, especially during the Cuban missile crisis of 1962. In truth, Kennedy's record in domestic affairs was relatively thin. Lacking a large electoral mandate and facing stiff congressional opposition, Kennedy moved cautiously in civil rights and federal spending for social programs. His assassination in 1963 left a deeply grieving nation to ponder the legacy of a leader who died so young—and with so much left undone.

Using the memory of this fallen president and retaining most of his key advisers, Lyndon Johnson pressed forward in both domestic and foreign affairs. He crafted legislation that produced landmark advances in civil rights and the War on Poverty, while continuing the escalation of America's military commitment to an independent, anti-Communist South Vietnam. As Johnson soon discovered, however, the war in Vietnam undermined his domestic programs and created deep skepticism about the truth of his claims that the war was being won—or was worth the cost. The shocks of 1968, beginning with Johnson's decision not to seek reelection, continuing with the assassinations of Dr. Martin Luther King, Jr., and Robert F. Kennedy, and culminating in the riotous Democratic National Convention in Chicago, left Americans reeling and alarmed.

To a large degree, Richard Nixon rode the political whirlwind that swept America in 1968. His margin of victory against Hubert Humphrey was nearly as narrow as his margin of defeat against John Kennedy in 1960. Yet the combined total for Nixon and Wallace in 1968—almost 57 percent—signaled a major swing to the right. The radical protests of the 1960s had fueled an inevitable backlash against the liberal party in power. The Great Society lay in ruins. The Nixon years had begun.

CHAPTER REVIEW, 1960–1968

- The Cuban missile crisis was settled peacefully in 1962, ending the most serious nuclear confrontation of the Cold War.
- The war in Vietnam entered public consciousness in 1963, as the number of American military advisers increased and the government of South Vietnam was overthrown in a military coup.
- President Kennedy's assassination in Dallas threw the nation into mourning and brought Lyndon Johnson to the Oval Office.
- Following a landslide victory in 1964, Johnson unveiled plans to create a "great society" modeled after the social programs begun during the New Deal.
- The expanding war in Vietnam pushed Johnson's ambitious domestic agenda to the side.
- Johnson decided not to seek reelection amid growing antiwar protests and racial violence in America's cities.
- The assassinations of Dr. King and Senator Robert Kennedy combined with violent events during the National Democratic Convention to stun the nation in 1968.
- Richard Nixon was elected president, vowing to end the war in Vietnam while restoring "law and order" at home.

◄ ▌▌▌ Looking Back

Chapter 29 examines the impact of the rights revolution, the Vietnam War, and the cultural struggles in the United States during the 1960s, one of the most challenging and bitterly divisive periods in recent history:

1. What accounts for the enduring popularity of President John F. Kennedy? Was it his policies, his vision, or were other factors at work as well?
2. In what ways did the assumptions of U.S. leaders regarding communist expansion remain fixed in the 1960s, and in what ways did they change? Was Lyndon Johnson a prisoner to assumptions that went back to the early days of the Cold War?
3. What impact did the movement for racial equality have on other so-called rights movements in the 1960s? In what ways did the civil rights struggle itself change in this decade?

Looking Ahead ▌▌▌ ►

Chapter 30 considers the consequences of the tumultuous events of the 1960s. The nation would wrestle with President Nixon's strategy to withdraw U.S. troops from Vietnam and, in an amazing turn of events, watch the president become embroiled in the greatest political scandal in U.S. history.

1. Would a nation as bitterly divided as the United States begin to heal its wounds with a new president at the helm, a president who vowed "to bring the American people together"?
2. Would the "rights revolution" of the 1960s continue to gain momentum in the coming years, and how would its impact be felt in the courts and in the political arena?
3. Was it possible to rekindle interest in the core programs of the Great Society, or would Americans move away from the ideas and proposals that had defined domestic liberalism since the New Deal Era?

Go to the American Passages website at www.cengage.com/history/ayers/ampassages4e for additional review materials.

Crisis of Confidence, 1969–1980

R ichard Nixon had been in politics for most of his adult life. As a congressman, a senator, and a vice president, he thrived on controversy and kept moving ahead. Bitter defeats in the presidential election of 1960 and the California gubernatorial race of 1962 did not diminish his ambition or ruin his dreams. On the morning after his presidential victory in 1968, Nixon addressed a nation battered by racial turmoil, urban violence, generational conflict, political assassinations, and continuing war. Vowing to unite the country and restore confidence in its institutions, he recalled a campaign stop he had made in the little town of Deshler, Ohio, where teenager held up a sign reading, "Bring Us Together." That message, he assured his listeners, "will be the great objective of this administration . . . to bring the American people together." The tragic presidency of Richard Nixon was under way.

AMERICA UNITED AND DIVIDED

The new era began with optimistic signals and improbable events. For a time, the dark days of 1968 were pushed aside by the miracles of 1969. In January, the New York Jets, led by "Broadway" Joe Namath, the nation's most celebrated bachelor, won the Super Bowl by crushing the heavily favored Baltimore Colts. In October, the New York Mets, once regarded as the worst team in Major League baseball history, defeated the Baltimore Orioles in a World Series that left millions of Americans screaming, "Ya gotta believe!" Sandwiched between these events were two enormous spectacles, each affecting the nation in a very different way.

The Miracles of 1969   In the summer of 1969, NASA fulfilled John F. Kennedy's bold promise to land a man on the moon "before this decade is out." The lunar mission culminated eight years of extraordinary progress and awful failure, including the 1967 *Apollo 1* disaster in which three astronauts died on the launch pad when their capsule exploded in flames. On July 16, astronauts Neil Armstrong, Edwin "Buzz" Aldrin, and Michael Collins began their 286,000-mile lunar mission—*Apollo 11*—from Cape Kennedy aboard the command vessel *Columbia*. As they neared their destination, Armstrong and Aldrin entered the Eagle, a fragile moon module, for the final descent. On July 20, before a television audience of 500 million people, Neil Armstrong put his foot on the lunar surface and said: "That's one small step for man, one giant leap for mankind."

Armstrong and Aldrin spent twenty-one hours on the moon. A television camera beamed back pictures of the men gathering samples, measuring temperature (234 degrees Fahrenheit in sunlight, 279 below zero in darkness), and planting a small American flag. As they rocketed back to Earth, the astronauts provided breathtaking pictures of the world from 175,000 miles away. "No matter where you travel," Armstrong joked, "it's nice to get home."

Other moon missions followed, including the dramatic rescue of *Apollo* 13 in 1970. Americans marveled at the skill and bravery of these astronauts without fully understanding the scientific value of their missions. By studying lunar rocks and photographs, geologists learned that the earth and the moon were formed at the same time—about 4.6 billion years ago—and that both had been pounded for millions of years by a hail of comets, asteroids, and meteorites that helped reshape their outer crust. The moon missions spurred the growth of computer technology and led to numerous product advancements, from fireproof clothing to better navigation systems for jetliners.

A month after the moon landing, national attention shifted to an earthly extravaganza, the **Woodstock** Music and Art Fair, on a six-hundred-acre dairy farm in the Catskill Mountains northwest of New York City. Billed as an "Aquarian Exposition," Woodstock fused rock music, hard drugs, free love, and antiwar protest into three days of mud-splattered revelry. Expecting a crowd of perhaps 100,000—a ridiculously low estimate for a pageant that included Janis Joplin, Jimi Hendrix, Joan Baez, the Grateful Dead, and Jefferson Airplane, among others—the organizers were overwhelmed by the response. More than 400,000 people showed up, knocking down the fences and ticket windows, creating mammoth traffic jams, gobbling up the available food and water, bathing nude in cattle ponds, and sharing marijuana and LSD.

Some news reports breathlessly portrayed the event as a cultural watershed. One magazine called Woodstock "the model of how good we will all feel after the revolution." In truth, the long weekend at Max Yasgur's farm was far less than that. The vast majority at Woodstock were middle-class students and workers, not cultural dropouts or political revolutionaries. "They would always keep something of Woodstock in their hearts," wrote one perceptive observer, "but that would be while they were making it in the system, not overthrowing it."

What survived Woodstock were the new attitudes of young people toward personal expression, political activism, and, in some cases, dangerous excess. These things did not die out in the 1970s, though they took rather different forms. The mellow portrait of Woodstock soon gave way to the ugly spectacle of Altamont, near San Francisco, where a rock concert featuring the Rolling Stones turned into a bloodbath, with one man beaten to death. In 1970, drug and alcohol addiction claimed the lives of Janis Joplin and Jimi Hendrix. For many young people, the age of innocence was over.

 This icon will direct you to interactive activities and study materials on the American Passages website: www.cengage.com/history/ayers/ampassages4e

CHAPTER TIMELINE

1969	Neil Armstrong sets foot on the moon • Woodstock rock festival attracts 400,000 people • First antiwar "moratorium" attracts huge crowds nationwide
1970	U.S. troops invade Cambodia • College students killed by National Guard at Kent State and by local police at Jackson State • Environmentalists celebrate first Earth Day
1971	Pentagon Papers released • My Lai massacre is exposed
1972	President Nixon visits mainland China • Watergate break-in occurs • Nixon wins reelection in a landslide
1973	Congress investigates spreading Watergate scandals • Vice President Spiro Agnew resigns after pleading no contest to income tax evasion • Supreme Court legalizes abortion in *Roe v. Wade* • War in Middle East leads to Arab oil embargo and energy crisis
1974	Facing impeachment, President Nixon resigns • Gerald Ford becomes president, issues blanket pardon • Violent antibusing protests in Boston
1975	South Vietnam falls • United States and Soviet Union sign human rights pledge in Helsinki Accords
1976	Jimmy Carter elected president
1977	Carter signs Panama Canal treaties
1978	Israel and Egypt sign Camp David Accords • Supreme Court rules on affirmative action in Bakke case
1979	Crisis at Three Mile Island nuclear plant • Militant students storm American embassy in Iran, taking hostages • Soviet troops invade Afghanistan
1980	U.S. boycotts Olympic Games in Moscow • Ronald Reagan elected president

Vietnamization   In order to bring America together, Richard Nixon would have to end its military involvement in Vietnam. During his inaugural parade on January 20, 1969, Nixon heard the chants of antiwar protesters as his limousine made its way from the Capitol to the White House. The next morning he was handed the weekly American casualty figures from Vietnam: 85 killed, 1,237 wounded—a chilling reminder, he wrote, of the war's "tragic cost."

Within weeks, Nixon unveiled a plan, known as **Vietnamization**, to end America's participation in the war. It called for the gradual replacement of U.S. troops by well-trained and supplied South Vietnamese soldiers—a process that included the deployment of American air power and the intensification of peace efforts aimed at getting American and North Vietnamese troops out of South Vietnam. From Nixon's perspective, Vietnamization represented the best solution to a dreadful dilemma. He refused to abandon Vietnam. "I will not," he repeated, "be the first President of the United States to lose a war." Yet he could not continue a conflict that cost 14,600 American lives and $30 billion in 1968 alone.

Vietnamization did not work well on the battlefield, as time would show. But it did have the advantage of substituting Asian casualties for American ones, which made it popular in the United States. In June 1969, President Nixon announced that 25,000 American combat troops were being withdrawn from Vietnam—the first stage of a pullout to be completed by late 1972.

Confrontation at Home

Despite Vietnamization and troop withdrawals, the antiwar movement retained considerable force. On November 15, 1969—"Mobilization Day"—hundreds of thousands of people attended rallies in New York, Boston, San Francisco, Washington, and other cities to demand the immediate removal of all American troops from Vietnam. Some considered the war immoral; others viewed it as a lost cause that was ripping the nation apart. To show his contempt for the protests, President Nixon made a point of listing his schedule that afternoon, which included several hours of watching the Washington Redskins on television.

In March 1970, the White House announced the withdrawal of 150,000 more combat troops over the coming year. The nation's leading antiwar group, the Vietnam Moratorium Committee, responded by closing its national office. But a month later, in a startling development, the president told the nation that American troops had just invaded Cambodia to disrupt enemy supply lines that ran through that country along the so-called Ho Chi Minh Trail. "We are a strong people," he said, "and we shall not be defeated in Vietnam."

Nixon misjudged the public reaction. The idea of expanding the war under any circumstances brought protesters back into the streets. At **Kent State University** in Ohio, several thousand students rampaged through the business district and clashed with local police. That evening, Kent State's ROTC building went up in flames, leading the governor to send in the National Guard. The troops were ordered to prevent students from gathering in large blocs—an ironic twist, since a noontime rally was planned to protest the guard's presence. On May 4, the guardsmen confronted five hundred students at the rally, where rocks and bottles were thrown from a distance and tear gas was lobbed in return. Suddenly, without warning, a group of guardsmen fired their rifles at the crowd, killing four and wounding nine others.

Word of the shootings touched off campus protests nationwide. Reserve Officers Training Corps (ROTC) buildings were attacked, and governors in sixteen more states called out the National Guard. Many colleges shut down for the semester, canceling final exams and mailing diplomas to the graduates. Surveys showed a clear majority of Americans approving of the National Guard's response at Kent State and supporting forceful measures against those who challenged government authority through unlawful, or even disrespectful, behavior. Many blue-collar workers fumed at the sight of draft-deferred, middle-class students protesting the war from the safety of a college campus while their own sons and brothers were slogging through the jungles of Vietnam. That rage turned to violence in New York City, when several hundred construction workers charged into an antiwar rally and severely beat the demonstrators and onlookers with hammers, pipes, and fists. A week later, President Nixon invited the leader of New York's construction workers' union to the White House, where the two men exchanged gifts and compliments.

Tragedy at Jackson State

In May 1970, news of the American incursion into Cambodia led to massive protests on college campuses. Six students died in separate incidents at **Kent State** in Ohio and **Jackson State University** in Mississippi. The incidents, though very different, were lumped together in the press as disturbances against the war. In fact, the troubles at Jackson State were racially motivated. Jackson, the capital of Mississippi, was rigidly segregated, and students at the all-black college had clashed repeatedly with the all-white police force and highway patrol. On the night of May 14, following a series of rock-throwing episodes, the police fired more than 150 rounds into a dormitory, killing two students and wounding a dozen more. This chilling photo shows the violent police reaction. In comparison to Kent State, the Jackson State incident got little publicity, leading some to conclude that the death of black students was less important to mainstream America than the death of whites.

(© Bettmann/CORBIS)

The violence continued in fits and spurts. Left-wing radicals bombed the headquarters of Mobil Oil, IBM, and other pillars of the "imperialist war machine." At the University of Wisconsin, the late-night bombing of a science center that housed a military research laboratory left one graduate student dead. In New York City, three radicals accidentally blew themselves to bits while mixing explosives. And in Chicago, a splinter group of the dormant Students for a Democratic Society attempted to "trash" the downtown business district in a final assault on the "ruling class." Three hundred looters and window smashers were arrested.

My Lai and the Pentagon Papers The news from Vietnam was equally grim. Reports surfaced about a massacre of civilians by U.S. troops at the village of My Lai, a suspected Vietcong stronghold, in 1968. Encountering no resistance, an infantry unit led by Lieutenant William Calley methodically executed the villagers and dumped their bodies into a mass grave. A number of the women were raped; at least two hundred people, many of them children, were murdered. Evidence of these atrocities was ignored by field commanders until a soldier not connected with the incident sent letters to the Pentagon and the press.

Most Americans considered My Lai an aberration. Yet the public reaction to Lieutenant Calley's court-martial verdict (guilty) and sentence (life imprisonment) in 1971 raised the very issues that had divided Americans since the war began. Some believed that Calley acted out of frustration after seeing so many of his fellow soldiers killed. Others blamed a society—as one GI put it—that "forced these kids to die in a foreign land for a cause it refused to defend at home." Letters poured into Washington opposing the conviction. "Free Calley" signs appeared on car bumpers, in store win dows, even in churches. Following numerous appeals and a case review by President Nixon, Calley was paroled in 1974.

The My Lai incident raised nagging questions about the fitness of American troops as the war dragged on. By all accounts, U.S. soldiers had fought superbly under trying circumstances until 1969. But the stepped-up troop withdrawals and rising antiwar protests served to isolate those who remained in Vietnam. Drug use increased dangerously. Racial tensions flared, as did violent attacks on officers, known as "fraggings," in which disgruntled soldiers used hand grenades as weapons. Some men ignored direct orders to fight. They were reluctant to risk their lives for a cause that appeared all but lost.

Within weeks of Calley's court-martial, another crisis erupted with publication of the Pentagon Papers, a secret report of the decision-making process that led to American involvement in Vietnam. Commissioned in 1967 and containing numerous classified documents within its seven thousand pages, the report was made public by Daniel Ellsberg, a former intelligence officer who had turned against the war. Ellsberg gave a copy to the *New York Times*, which printed the first installment on June 13, 1971.

The report focused mainly on the Kennedy–Johnson years. Yet Nixon viewed Ellsberg's behavior as a threat to his own presidency as well. He feared that continued leaks of classified material might reveal damaging information about current policies, such as the secret bombing of Cambodia. As a result, the White House sought a court injunction to halt further publication of the Pentagon Papers on grounds that national security was at stake. The Supreme Court rejected this argument, however, ruling 6 to 3 that suppression violated First Amendment guarantees.

Nixon did not give up the fight. Obsessed by the Ellsberg incident, he authorized the creation of a special White House unit, known as the "Plumbers," to "stop security leaks and investigate other sensitive matters." In a tape-recorded conversation on September 18, 1971, Nixon demanded that "the roughest, toughest people [get] to work on this." A few weeks later, the Plumbers carried out their first assignment: burglarizing the office of Ellsberg's psychiatrist in an attempt to gather embarrassing information. Nixon's top domestic adviser, John Ehrlichman, casually informed the president that other "little operations" were planned. "We've got some dirty tricks underway," he said. "It may pay off."

Activism, Rights, and Reform

Political and social activism did not end with the 1960s, as the environmental movement and the antiwar protests clearly showed. While the angry, media-centered radicalism of groups like SDS and the Black Panthers largely disappeared, the movements for women's rights and minority rights remained very much alive, bringing progress and backlash in their wake.

Expanding
Women's Rights

On August 26, 1970, feminist leaders organized a nationwide rally to mark the fiftieth anniversary of the Nineteenth Amendment, which had given women the right to vote. Thousands showed up with signs ranging from "Sisterhood Is Powerful" to "Don't Cook Dinner — Starve a Rat Today." The speeches focused on equality for women in education and employment, the need for reproductive freedom, and passage of the **equal rights amendment** (ERA), an idea first proposed in 1923.

The revived women's movement was already making strides. In 1969, feminist protests forced a number of the nation's best colleges, including Yale and Princeton, to admit women, and the military academies soon followed suit. During the 1970s, female graduates from the nation's law schools rose from 5 to 30 percent of each class and at medical schools from 8 to 23 percent. Yet the number of women elected to public office or promoted to high management positions lagged far behind, and the wages of full-time working women remained well below those of men.

The women's movement had many voices and a wide range of ideas. Nothing better illustrated this diversity than the outpouring of books and magazines that provided an alternative to older publications such as *Good Housekeeping* and *Ladies' Home Journal*, which focused on motherhood, domesticity, and consumerism as the primary female roles. Handbooks like *Our Bodies, Ourselves* (1971) and *The New Woman's Survival Catalogue* (1972) sold millions of copies by combining a new feminist ideology, based on professional achievement and personal freedom, with medical and psychological strategies for good health. A flood of best-sellers emerged—Kate Millett's *Sexual Politics* (1969) and Germaine Greer's *The Female Eunuch* (1970) among them—contending that women could never experience fulfillment within the traditional confines of marriage and family life. In 1972, three scholarly journals devoted to women's studies appeared, as did the Berkshire Conference on the History of Women.

Women's March for Equality. *"Women's March for Equality" moves down New York's Fifth Avenue.*

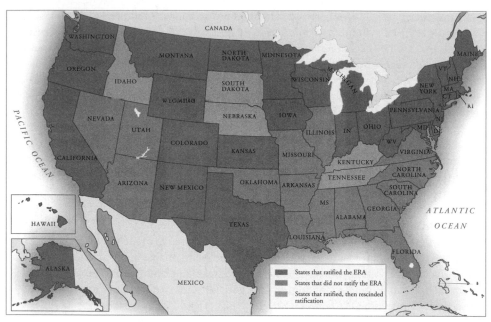

MAP 30.1 The Struggle for the Equal Rights Amendment.

When Congress endorsed the ERA, its ratification by three quarters of the states seemed certain. But opposition mounted quickly, and supporters were never able to reach the magic number of thirty-eight. From a high of thirty-five states, the number fell to thirty, as five states rescinded ratification. A look at the map shows that much of the opposition to ERA was centered in the South and in rural states.

That same year marked the publication of *Ms.*, the first feminist magazine to attract a mass circulation. A sampling of its articles showed how dramatically times had changed: "Raising Kids Without Sex Roles," "Women Tell the Truth About Their Abortions," and "Do Feminists Do It Better?"

Minority Power   The political and cultural upheavals of the 1960s had produced a "rights consciousness" that spread dramatically as the decade progressed. For many groups, 1969 was a pivotal year, marking their emergence on the national scene. That summer, for example, a routine police assault against homosexuals at the Stonewall Inn in Manhattan's Greenwich Village produced a most uncommon response. For the first time the patrons fought back, triggering several days of rioting and protest against the harassment of homosexuals. The "Stonewall riot" led to the formation of the Gay Liberation Front, which began the movement to encourage group solidarity within the homosexual community and confront openly the prejudice that gay men and women had suffered, in fearful silence, for so many years. "We reject society's attempt to impose sexual roles and definitions of our nature," announced the Gay Liberation Front. "We are stepping outside these roles and simplistic myths. We are going to be who we are."

In 1969, Mexican American activists in Texas formed **La Raza Unida**, a political party devoted to furthering Chicano causes and candidates through the ballot. This new party, which spread to several southwestern states, reflected the growing demand for political power and cultural self-determination within the Hispanic community, which had grown from 3 million in 1960 to more than 9 million a decade later. The increase, consisting mainly of Cuban Americans and Puerto Ricans on the nation's East Coast and Mexican Americans throughout the West provided unique opportunities for change.

On September 16, 1969, Mexican American students across the Southwest boycotted classes to celebrate ethnic pride (or "Chicanismo") on Mexico's Independence Day, while a group at the University of California at Berkeley, shouting "Brown Power," staged a sit-in to demand a program in Chicano studies. (Within a few years, more than fifty universities would have such a program.) Furthermore, political leverage by Hispanic groups spurred Congress to improve conditions for migrant farm workers, many of whom were Mexican American, and to provide federal funding for bilingual education, a much-debated concept that soon included the right of non-English-speaking students to schooling in their native language. Mexican Americans were also elected to the U.S. House of Representatives in Texas and California, the U.S. Senate in New Mexico, and the governorships of Arizona and New Mexico.

In the fall of 1969, several dozen Native Americans took over Alcatraz Island, an unoccupied former federal penitentiary in San Francisco Bay, to publicize the claims and grievances of a younger, more militant generation. "It has no running water; it has inadequate sanitation facilities; there is no industry; there are no health care facilities," said one protest leader, comparing the rocky island to a typical Indian reservation. The group spent nineteen months on Alcatraz, symbolically offering to buy it for "$24 in glass beads and red cloth."

The protest signaled a change in the American Indian community. By any measure, Native Americans were the single most deprived group in the United States, with an unemployment rate ten times higher and a life expectancy twenty years lower than the national average. In the late 1960s, a new group known as American Indian Movement (AIM), inspired by the black freedom struggles, began to preach a philosophy of "Red Power" that rejected the "assimilationist" policies of their elders. In 1972, AIM supported a march on Washington—named the Trail of Broken Treaties—that ended with a group of protesters barricading themselves inside the Bureau of Indian Affairs and wrecking much of the building. A year later, AIM militants seized the South Dakota village of Wounded Knee on the Pine Ridge Sioux Reservation, site of an infamous massacre by federal troops in 1890, to highlight both the squalid conditions there and the "broken promises" that stripped Native Americans of their independence and their land. Two Indians were killed in the seventy-one-day standoff with federal agents.

This pressure took political and legislative forms as well. In 1970, the federal government returned forty-eight thousand acres of sacred land to the Taos Pueblo of New Mexico, beginning a cautious policy of negotiation that grew significantly in the coming years. In addition, the Nixon administration targeted minority aid programs for Native Americans living in urban areas, and Congress added funding through the Indian Education Act of 1972. Nevertheless, the alarming rates of suicide, alcoholism, and illiteracy among Native American children continued throughout the 1970s and beyond—a clear warning of how much remained to be done.

Black Capitalism and Civil Rights   Richard Nixon took office at a crucial juncture in the campaign for civil rights. The epic struggles of the 1950s and early 1960s had formally abolished de jure (legal) segregation in public schools and public accommodations—a remarkable achievement—yet serious problems remained. The vast majority of southern children still attended all-white or all-black schools in defiance of *Brown v. Board of Education*, and the situation was little better in the North and West, where de facto segregation in housing and employment kept most neighborhood schools rigidly segregated by race. Furthermore, although the percentage of middle-class African Americans increased substantially in the 1960s, the rate of black unemployment remained twice the national average, and male joblessness in urban areas sometimes reached 40 percent. This meant a deepening economic split within the African American community, with almost half the black families enjoying middle-class status and an equal percentage living below the poverty line in run-down, unsafe, segregated neighborhoods where jobs were scarce and single women increasingly raised children on their own.

Civil rights did not rank high on Nixon's domestic agenda. Because most blacks voted Democratic—Hubert Humphrey got 95 percent of their votes in 1968—the president owed them no political debt. On the contrary, he hoped to create a "new Republican majority" by winning over white working-class Democrats, North and South, who feared that minorities were getting too much attention from the federal government.

Nixon's boldest civil rights initiatives related to business and employment. In 1969, he created the Office of Minority Business Enterprise, noting that "people who own their own homes and property do not burn their neighborhoods." Over the next three years, the federal government tripled its assistance to minority enterprises through grants and low-interest loans. More controversial was the administration's proposal to bring black workers into the high-wage, "lily-white" construction industry. Known as the Philadelphia Plan, it required the construction unions—carpenters, electricians, and the like—to set up goals and timetables for hiring black apprentices on government-sponsored projects.

On the emotional issue of public school integration, the president took a more cautious approach. Hoping to win white political converts in the South, he supported the efforts of Mississippi officials in 1969 to postpone court-ordered school integration, while firmly opposing efforts to deny federal funding to segregated schools. When told that Justice Department officials were planning to speed up school integration, the president warned them to "knock off this crap," adding: "Do what the law allows you and not one bit more." As a result, the battle shifted back to the courts, especially the U.S. Supreme Court, where major changes were now under way.

The Burger Court   In 1969, Chief Justice Earl Warren stepped down from the bench. The seventy-seven-year-old Warren had submitted his resignation in 1968, expecting President Johnson to choose a suitably liberal replacement. But problems arose when Johnson nominated his close friend Abe Fortas, an associate justice on the Supreme Court, to become the new chief justice. Senate conservatives organized a filibuster to deny Fortas the post; then a brewing scandal over his finances forced Fortas to resign from the Court. This gave incoming President Nixon the luxury of appointing two Supreme Court justices at once.

The first choice went smoothly. The Senate quickly confirmed Judge Warren E. Burger, a moderate northern Republican, to replace Warren as chief justice. But Nixon's other nominee, Judge Clement Haynsworth, a conservative from South Carolina, ran into trouble when Senate liberals raised questions about his antagonism toward civil rights and organized labor. Fifteen Republicans joined forty Democrats to reject

Haynsworth—a rare event for the Senate, which had not defeated a Supreme Court nominee since the days of Herbert Hoover.

Stung by the vote, President Nixon nominated another southerner, Judge G. Harrold Carswell, whose general qualifications and civil rights record were far inferior to Haynoworth's. He was rejected as well. A few weeks later, the Senate unanimously confirmed Nixon's third choice, Judge Harry Blackmun of Minnesota. And the president got to make two more Supreme Court nominations the following year when Justices Hugo Black and John Marshall Harlan retired. His selections—William Rehnquist, a prominent Arizona conservative, and Lewis Powell, a distinguished Virginia attorney—were easily confirmed.

The Burger Court proved more independent than most people, including Nixon, had expected. Among other decisions, it upheld publication of the Pentagon Papers and struck down "capricious" state laws imposing the death penalty, thereby halting capital punishment for almost two decades (*Furman v. Georgia*, 1972). In addition, the Burger Court held that state laws prohibiting abortion were unconstitutional because they violated a woman's "right to privacy" under the Fourteenth Amendment (***Roe v. Wade***, 1973). Justice Blackmun's majority opinion permitted a state to outlaw abortion in the final three months of pregnancy, noting, however, that the life and health of the mother must be considered at all times. The following year, almost 1 million legal abortions were performed in the United States.

The Burger Court also confronted segregation in the public schools. Its unanimous ruling in *Swann v. Charlotte-Mecklenburg Board of Education* (1971) served notice that controversial methods like "forced" busing could be used as legal remedies to achieve racial balance. Though millions of youngsters rode buses to school each day, the idea of transporting children to different neighborhoods in the name of racial integration fueled parental anger and fear. Opinion polls showed that whites overwhelmingly opposed forced busing and that African Americans, though by a smaller margin, also disapproved. For many black parents, busing simply obscured the problems of neglect that had plagued their school districts for years.

Violence sometimes followed. In Boston, a court-ordered plan in 1974 to bus white schoolchildren to Roxbury, a poor black neighborhood, and black children to South Boston, a poor white neighborhood, led to mob action reminiscent of Little Rock, Arkansas, in 1957. Buses were stoned, black students were beaten, and federal marshals rushed in to protect them. Ironically, the schools in both neighborhoods were in awful condition, unlike the wealthy suburban Boston schools, which were not included in the desegregation plan. All too often, forced busing became a class issue, involving poorer people of all races.

NEW DIRECTIONS AT HOME AND ABROAD

Like John F. Kennedy, President Nixon cared more about foreign policy than about domestic affairs. "All you need," he mused, "is a competent Cabinet to run the country at home." As a moderate Republican in the Eisenhower mold, Nixon endorsed the basic outlines of the modern welfare state, which included social security, unemployment insurance, a minimum wage, the right to unionize, and health care for the elderly. Yet Nixon also understood—and exploited—the public's growing concern that the Great Society era had tilted too far in favor of poor people and minority groups. Convinced that Americans were fed up with wasteful government programs and angry street demonstrations, he tried to find, in his words, a domestic "middle ground."

Rethinking Welfare   President Nixon moved cautiously on the domestic front. His immediate goals were to implement a revenue-sharing plan that sent more tax dollars back to the states and localities and to simplify the welfare system, making it more efficient and less expensive. Revenue sharing, designed to limit the power of the national government, was a modest success. Congress passed legislation transferring $30 billion in federal revenue over five years—less than Nixon wanted but more than state and local governments had received in the past. Welfare reform proved a much harder sell. Here the president looked to domestic adviser Daniel P. Moynihan, a social scientist whose controversial writings on poverty and family breakup in the African American community reflected a shifting emphasis from equal rights, which focused on constitutional guarantees, to equal opportunity, which stressed socioeconomic gains. Everyone agreed that the current welfare system—Aid to Families with Dependent Children (AFDC)—was seriously flawed. Its programs lacked accountability, and the payments varied widely from state to state. At Moynihan's urging, President Nixon offered an alternative to AFDC, known as the Family Assistance Plan (FAP).

The new plan proposed a complete overhaul of the welfare system. Instead of providing a host of costly services, the government would guarantee a minimum annual income to the poor, beginning at sixteen hundred dollars for a family of four, with additional funding for food stamps. The individual states were expected to subsidize this income, and able-bodied parents (excepting mothers of preschool children) were required to seek employment or job training. Not surprisingly, FAP ran into withering criticism. Liberals complained that sixteen hundred dollars was unreasonably low, while conservatives opposed the very concept of a guaranteed annual income.

To his credit, Nixon did not trim needed programs as his own plan went down to defeat. On the contrary, he supported Democratic-sponsored measures in Congress to increase food stamp expenditures and provide automatic cost-of-living adjustments (COLAs) for social security recipients to help them keep up with inflation. Although Nixon did not care to publicize this achievement, he became the first president since Franklin Roosevelt to propose a federal budget with more spending for social services than for national defense.

Protecting the   On April 22, 1970, millions of Americans gathered in schools,
Environment   churches, and parks to celebrate Earth Day, an event sponsored by environmental groups like the Sierra Club to educate people about the ecological problems afflicting the modern world. Begun a few years earlier, following the appearance of Rachel Carson's book *Silent Spring*, the environmental movement gained strength after a series of well-publicized disasters, such as the chemical fire that ignited Cleveland's Cuyahoga River, the giant oil spill that fouled the beaches of Santa Barbara, and the "death" of Lake Erie by farm runoff and factory waste. The dire predictions of scientists about population growth, poisoned food and water, endangered species, and air pollution added fuel to the cause. As biologist Barry Commoner noted in his best-selling 1971 book, *The Closing Circle*, "our present course,

if continued, will destroy the capability of the environment to support a reasonably civilized human society."

At first, President Nixon showed little interest in environmental problems. Indeed, his administration accidentally marked Earth Day by approving a project that raised serious ecological concerns, the eight-hundred-mile Alaskan oil pipeline. Yet Nixon soon considered environmentalism to be a powerful force—one that cut across class, racial, and political lines. Unlike many other issues, it gave the appearance of uniting Americans against a common foe.

Moving quickly, his administration banned the use of DDT in the United States and stopped production of chemical and biological weapons, though not the plant defoliants or napalm used in Vietnam. More significant, the White House supported a bipartisan effort to establish the Environmental Protection Agency (EPA) and pass the Clean Air Act of 1970 and the Endangered Species Act of 1973.

These were notable achievements. The Clean Air Act set strict national guidelines for the reduction of automobile and factory emissions, with fines and jail sentences for polluters. The Endangered Species Act protected rare plants and animals from extinction. Congress also passed the Water Pollution Control Act over Nixon's veto in 1972. The law, mandating $25 billion for the cleanup of America's neglected lakes and rivers, was too costly for the president, though it proved effective in bringing polluted waters back to life. The EPA, meanwhile, monitored the progress of these laws and required environmental "impact studies" for all future federal projects.

Though Americans readily agreed about the need for clean air, pure water, and protecting wildlife, the cost of doing these things did not fall equally on everyone's shoulders. Auto manufacturers warned that the expense of meeting the new emission standards would result in higher car prices and the layoff of production workers. Loggers in the Northwest angrily accused the EPA of being more interested in protecting a few forest birds than in allowing human beings to earn a living. A common bumper sticker in Oregon read: "If You're Hungry and out of Work, Eat an Environmentalist." Could strategies be devised to protect jobs and the environment simultaneously? Could American corporations effectively compete with foreign companies that did not face such restrictions? Should the United States abandon atomic power, offshore oil drilling, and other potential threats to the environment at a time when the demand for energy was rapidly increasing? Protecting the environment raised serious questions for the future.

DOING HISTORY ONLINE

Endangered Species Act, 1973

Read the document online. What possible reasons were there for Richard Nixon, a Republican, to decide to sign the Endangered Species Act, a piece of legislation promoted by liberals and environmental groups that typically were allied with the Democratic Party?

www.cengage.com/
history/ayers/
ampassages4e

A New World Order

Richard Nixon loved the challenge of foreign affairs. The secrecy, intrigue, and deal making fascinated him in ways that domestic matters never could. Determined to control foreign policy even more rigidly than previous presidents had, Nixon bypassed the State Department in favor of the National Security Council (NSC), based in the White

House itself. To direct the NSC, he chose **Henry Kissinger**, a German refugee and Harvard political scientist. In Kissinger, the president found the perfect match for his "realistic" view of foreign affairs in which hard assessments of the national interest took precedence over moral and ideological concerns.

Both men agreed that America's bipolar approach, based on the containment of Soviet communism, no longer made sense. They wanted a more flexible policy that recognized the growing strength of Western Europe, Communist China, and Japan. They believed that the United States could no longer afford to police the world in every skirmish or to finance an arms race that grew more dangerous—and expensive—with each passing year. The Nixon–Kissinger approach meant talking with old enemies, finding common ground through negotiation, and encouraging a more widespread balance of world power.

This innovative thinking, however, did not extend to all parts of the globe. The president still viewed Fidel Castro as a mortal enemy and openly encouraged the CIA to undermine the democratically elected, left-wing government of Chilean president Salvadore Allende, who was overthrown and apparently murdered by right-wing military forces in 1973. "I don't see why we have to allow a country to go Marxist just because its people are irresponsible," Henry Kissinger argued. In Latin America, at least, the New World Order appeared strikingly similar to the old one.

The China Opening In one sense, Richard Nixon seemed an odd choice to strip away years of rigid Cold War thinking in foreign affairs. He was, after all, a rough-and-tumble anti-communist known for his bitter attacks on State Department officials during the McCarthy years. Yet that is what made his new initiatives all the more remarkable. Nixon's skill in foreign affairs lay in his ability to seize opportunities in a rapidly changing world. One of his first moves was to take advantage of the widening rift between Communist China and the Soviet Union.

The United States at this time did not even recognize Communist China. Since 1949, American policy considered the anti-Communist regime on Taiwan the legitimate government of mainland China. There were some who believed that only a politician with Nixon's Red-hunting credentials would dare to change this policy after so many years. No one could seriously accuse this president—as he had accused so many others—of being "soft on communism."

Nixon wanted a new relationship with China for several reasons. The trade possibilities were enormous. Better relations also increased the chances of a peace settlement in Vietnam, while strengthening America's bargaining position with the Soviet Union, which feared any alliance between Washington and Beijing. Most of all, Nixon realized that China must now be recognized as a legitimate world power. The United States could no longer afford to ignore this reality.

Nixon worked behind the scenes, knowing that Americans considered China the "most dangerous" nation on earth. The first public breakthrough came in 1971, when an American table tennis team was invited to China for an exhibition tour. Meanwhile, Henry Kissinger secretly visited Beijing to plan a summit meeting between Chinese and American leaders. President Nixon hinted at his future plans in a remarkable magazine interview. "If there is anything I want to do before I die," he said, "it is to go to China."

Nixon arrived there on February 22, 1972—the first American president ever to set foot on Chinese soil. For the next eight days, the world watched in amazement as he walked along the Great Wall and strolled through the Forbidden City. "The Chinese Army band played 'America the Beautiful' and 'Home on the Range,'" wrote the *New York Times*. "President Nixon quoted Chairman Mao Zedong approvingly, used his chopsticks skillfully, and clinked glasses with every Chinese official in sight."

The trip ended with a joint statement, known as the Shanghai Communiqué, that promised closer relations between the two countries in trade, travel, and cultural exchange. Each nation agreed to open a legation (a small staff office that ranks below an embassy) in the other's capital city, beginning the process of diplomatic recognition that would take seven more years to complete. The most important issues, such as human rights and nuclear proliferation, were tactfully ignored. And the most controversial issue—the future of Taiwan—demonstrated the deep rift that still existed. Communist China asserted its claim to the island, demanding that American troops on Taiwan be removed. The United States called for a "peaceful solution" to the "Taiwan question" and promised to reduce its forces as "tensions" in the region declined. Still, the historic significance of Nixon's visit overshadowed the problems that lay ahead. "We have been here a week," he declared. "This was the week that changed the world."

Détente

Three months later, the president traveled to Moscow for a summit meeting with Soviet leader Leonid Brezhnev. A master of timing in foreign affairs, Nixon believed that his successful trip to China, coupled with a faltering Russian economy, would make the Soviets more likely to strike a serious deal with the United States. The key issues were arms control and increased trade. Both sides possessed huge atomic arsenals that cost billions of dollars and increased the chances of catastrophic war. The Russians desperately needed grain, heavy equipment, and technical assistance; American farmers and manufacturers saw new markets for their goods.

The Moscow Summit further enhanced the Nixon–Kissinger record in foreign affairs. On May 22, 1972, the United States and the Soviet Union signed the Strategic Arms Limitation Treaty (SALT) that limited the number of long-range offensive missiles (ICBMs) and an antiballistic missile (ABM) agreement that froze the production of these missiles for the next five years. No one believed that the arms race was now over. Yet these initial treaties, committing the superpowers to the principle of arms reduction, represented a stunning breakthrough in Soviet–American relations.

The economic agreements were less successful. Though U.S.–Soviet trade more than tripled over the next three years, the greatest increase came in a single wheat deal with American farmers and grain dealers that caused a temporary shortage in the United States. Not surprisingly, American consumers fumed at the idea of shipping low-priced wheat to a foreign country while bread prices rose dramatically at home.

Nevertheless, the Moscow Summit provided a solid foundation for **détente**, with both sides pledging to reduce world tensions and coexist peacefully. As President Nixon left Moscow, he noted the differences between the Soviet leaders he faced in 1959, when he was vice president, and the ones who endorsed détente. The current leaders, he wrote, "do not have as much of an inferiority complex as was the case in

Khrushchev's period. But they still crave to be respected as equals, and on this point I think we made a good impression."

FOUR MORE YEARS?

After a full term in office, Richard Nixon could look back on a record of notable achievement. Relations with Cold War opponents like the Soviet Union and Communist China had dramatically improved as détente replaced confrontation. Although the Vietnam War continued, the steady withdrawal of American troops meant fewer casualties and an end to the draft. Even the economy looked better, with unemployment and inflation under control.

The Landslide of 1972   Nixon's Democratic challengers faced an uphill battle. From the political right, Governor **George Wallace** of Alabama continued the presidential odyssey he began in 1968, when he had captured five southern states as a third-party candidate. Campaigning this time as a Democrat, Wallace won wide support among white working-class voters for his opposition to forced busing and his attacks on "welfare cheats." After winning the Democratic presidential primary in Florida and running a close second in Wisconsin, Wallace was shot and paralyzed by a would-be assassin, ending his presidential quest.

A few weeks later, on June 17, 1972, five men were arrested while burglarizing the Democratic National Headquarters at the **Watergate** complex in Washington, D.C. Four of them were Cubans who had worked previously for the CIA; they were led by James W. McCord, the security director for Richard Nixon's Committee to Re-Elect the President, known as CREEP. Supervising from a nearby hotel, and later arrested, were two presidential aides—Gordon Liddy and E. Howard Hunt—who belonged to the newly created "Plumbers" unit. Responding to the break-in, Nixon assured the public that no one "presently employed" in his administration was involved "in this very bizarre incident," adding: "What really hurts is if you try to cover it up."

At the Republican National Convention in Miami, the delegates enthusiastically renominated the Nixon–Agnew team. The Democratic race, however, proved far more contentious. The candidates included Hubert Humphrey, the 1968 presidential nominee; Senator **George McGovern** of South Dakota, the favorite of younger, more liberal Democrats; and Representative Shirley Chisholm of New York, the first African American to seek the presidential nomination of a major political party.

The Democratic National Convention, meeting in Miami Beach, reflected the party reforms that followed the bloody "siege of Chicago" in 1968. The changes were dramatic, with the percentage of female delegates increasing from 13 to 38 percent, blacks from 5 to 15 percent, and those under thirty years old from 3 to 23 percent. Moreover, these new delegates embraced the causes of numerous "out groups" in society, such as homosexuals, migrant workers, and the urban poor. Deeply committed to the "rights revolution" of the 1960s, they proposed a major redistribution of political power and cultural authority in the United States.

The delegates chose George McGovern for president and Senator Thomas Eagleton of Missouri for vice president. The campaign faced trouble from the start. Reporters learned that Senator Eagleton had been hospitalized in the past for mental depression and fatigue, twice undergoing electroshock therapy. At first, McGovern stood by his running mate, but as criticism mounted, he replaced Eagleton with former Peace Corps director Sargent Shriver. Appearing weak and opportunistic, McGovern dropped further in the polls.

Far more damaging was the lack of unity within Democratic ranks. Many of McGovern's key positions, such as amnesty for draft resisters, liberalization of marijuana laws, and greater welfare benefits for the poor, offended moderate and working-class Democrats, who believed their party had moved too far to the left. On election day, Nixon overwhelmed McGovern, carrying every state but Massachusetts and winning 61 percent of the popular vote.

Yet Nixon's landslide victory was more limited than it appeared. Ticket splitting flourished in 1972, with the Democratic Party easily retaining control of Congress. Thus, legions of Democratic voters rejected McGovern's message without deserting the party itself. Furthermore, the percentage of eligible voters who cast ballots in presidential elections continued to fall, from 62 percent in 1964, to 61 percent in 1968, to 56 percent in 1972. This suggested a growing alienation from the political process—and a hint of the protest to come.

Exit from Vietnam   Richard Nixon's impressive reelection victory seemed a sure sign that passions were cooling and better times lay ahead. The president's first task was to end the Vietnam conflict on honorable terms and secure the release of American prisoners of war. But the key to any settlement, Nixon understood, was the future security of South Vietnam. What would happen after U.S. troops left that country? Would the American sacrifice be in vain?

In the spring of 1972, North Vietnam had mounted a major offensive in the South, gambling that Nixon's concern about the coming presidential election would prevent the United States from responding. The offensive failed miserably, however, when Nixon ordered massive bombing raids against North Vietnam. Following his reelection that fall, the president increased these air assaults in order to force a peace settlement with the North.

"These bastards," said Nixon, "have never been bombed like they're going to be bombed this time." In late December 1972, American B-52s filled the skies over Hanoi and Haiphong, dropping more tonnage than all American planes had dropped in the previous two years. The damage done to North Vietnam was staggering: harbors, factories, railway lines, storage facilities, and sometimes adjoining neighborhoods were destroyed. Moreover, where only one B-52 had been lost in combat throughout the entire war, fifteen were shot down in these so-called Christmas bombings.

On January 27, 1973, an agreement was signed in which the United States agreed to withdraw its remaining troops from Vietnam in return for a North Vietnamese promise to release all American prisoners of war. Nixon also vowed to "respond in full force" if North Vietnam attacked South Vietnam in the future. The United States, he proclaimed, had achieved "peace with honor" at last.

What Nixon got, in reality, was an American exit from Vietnam that left the vulnerable South Vietnamese government at the mercy of its communist opponents. Despite his pledge, the United States could respond to future treaty violations only with air power; sending troops back into combat was now unthinkable. The agreement ended American involvement without guaranteeing South Vietnam's long-term survival.

The American public expressed relief at the settlement but little jubilation. The war had divided the country, raised suspicions about government to dangerous levels, and drained billions of dollars from vital domestic programs. More than 50,000 U.S. soldiers were killed in Vietnam and 300,000 were wounded. At least 1 million Asians died, and more would perish in the coming years. As the *New York Times* noted, "There is no dancing in the streets, no honking of horns, no champagne."

Public attention soon shifted to the return of 587 American POWs. Many had spent up to seven years in North Vietnamese jails, and some had been tortured. "We are honored to have the opportunity to serve our country under difficult circumstances," said their senior officer as his plane touched down on American soil. That very day, former President Lyndon Johnson died in his sleep. "His tragedy—and ours," Senator Edmund Muskie stated, "was the war."

Watergate and the Abuse of Power As 1973 began, Richard Nixon's public approval rating stood at a remarkable 68 percent. With Vietnam behind him, the president appeared ready to launch a successful second term. Yet all that ended in April when the Watergate burglars pleaded guilty to minor charges of theft and wiretapping in order to avoid a public trial. Suspecting a cover-up, federal judge John Sirica convinced the lead burglar, James McCord, to admit that high-ranking White House officials were involved in planning the break-in. This startling confession, combined with the investigative stories of *Washington Post* reporters Bob Woodward and Carl Bernstein, turned the Watergate affair into front-page news.

During the spring of 1973, President Nixon reluctantly appointed Harvard Law School professor Archibald Cox as an independent prosecutor in the Watergate case. The Senate formed a special investigating committee chaired by seventy-three-year-old Sam Ervin of North Carolina, who modestly described himself as "a simple country lawyer." Under Ervin's careful direction, the committee heard sworn testimony from present and former Nixon aides about a "seamless web" of criminal activity designed to undermine the president's critics and political opponents. In meticulous detail, John Dean, the former White House counsel, implicated Nixon himself in a plan to ensure the silence of the imprisoned burglars by paying them "hush money."

Nixon denied any involvement in Watergate, claiming that he had been too busy running the nation to bother with the day-to-day workings of his reelection campaign. Many Americans—and most Republican leaders—took Nixon at his word. As House minority leader **Gerald R. Ford** of Michigan declared, "I have the greatest confidence in the president and am absolutely positive he had nothing to do with this mess."

In July, White House aide Alexander Butterfield stunned the Ervin committee by revealing that Nixon had secretly recorded his Oval Office conversations since 1971. Sensing that the true story of presidential involvement in the Watergate scandal could now be uncovered, Judge Sirica, special prosecutor Cox, and chairman Ervin all demanded to hear the relevant tapes. But Nixon refused to release them, citing executive privilege and the separation of powers. When Cox persisted, Nixon ordered Attorney General Elliot Richardson to fire him. Richardson and his top deputy refused, leading to their swift removal. These dramatic developments, known as the "Saturday Night Massacre," produced angry calls for Nixon's impeachment.

There was trouble for the vice president as well. In 1973, a Baltimore grand jury looked into allegations that Spiro Agnew, while governor of Maryland, had accepted illegal payoffs from building contractors. After first denying these charges, the vice president resigned his office and pleaded nolo contendere (no contest) to one count of income tax evasion. He received three years' probation plus a ten-thousand-dollar fine.

Under the Twenty-fifth Amendment, adopted in 1967, the president is obligated to nominate a vice president "who shall take the office upon confirmation by a majority vote of both houses of Congress." To bolster his declining fortunes, Nixon chose the well-respected Gerald Ford, who was quickly confirmed. But the president ran into more trouble when the Internal Revenue Service (IRS) disclosed that he owed $500,000 in back taxes from 1970 and 1971; Nixon had paid less than $1,000 in each of these years. Responding emotionally, Nixon told a press conference, "I am not a crook."

By this point, however, public confidence in Nixon had disappeared. The testimony of John Dean, the Saturday Night Massacre, the resignation of Spiro Agnew, the embarrassing IRS disclosures—all cast doubt on the president's fitness to lead. A Gallup poll taken in November 1973 showed Nixon's public approval had dropped to 27 percent. In desperation, the president released transcripts of several Watergate-related conversations (but not the tapes themselves), claiming that they cleared him of wrongdoing. Many thought otherwise. The transcripts contained ethnic and racial slurs, vulgar language (with "expletives deleted"), and strong hints of presidential involvement in a cover-up.

Nixon's refusal to release the tapes reached a climax in July 1974, when the House Judiciary Committee debated charges of presidential impeachment before a national television audience. Led by chairman Peter Rodino of New Jersey and the eloquent Barbara Jordan of Texas, the committee approved three charges—obstruction of justice, abuse of power, and contempt of Congress—at the very moment that a unanimous Supreme Court ordered Nixon to comply with Judge Sirica's subpoena for the Watergate tapes. On August 5, the president released the material that sealed his fate. Although they provided no evidence that Nixon knew about the Watergate burglary in advance, the tapes showed him playing an active role in the attempt to cover up White House involvement in the crime.

Faced with certain impeachment and removal, Richard Nixon became the first president to resign from office. In a tearful farewell to his staff on August 9, he preached the very advice that he himself was incapable of following. "Always remember," he said, "those who hate you don't win unless you hate them. And then you destroy yourself."

What were the lessons of Watergate? For one thing, Americans learned again that the system of checks and balances put in place by the founding fathers had done its job well. Lawbreaking at the highest level was exposed. A president had resigned his office in disgrace, and the government had moved forward without a hitch, showing both the wisdom of the Constitution and the power of our laws. Still, had not it been for the tenacity of reporters Woodward and Bernstein, the intuition of Judge Sirica, and the disclosure of the secret White House tapes, the scandal known as Watergate may never have been exposed.

Someone else had helped as well. For more than thirty years, Woodward and Bernstein had shielded the identity of their most crucial source in the Watergate story, promising to reveal his name only after his death. But in 2005, a ninety-one-year-old former FBI official named W. Mark Felt stepped forward to claim credit for his role.

"I'm the guy they used to call 'Deep Throat,'" he declared. Woodward and Bernstein quickly admitted it was true. The biggest remaining mystery of Watergate had finally been put to rest.

OPEC and the Oil Embargo

In the midst of the Watergate scandal, a serious crisis erupted over the nation's energy needs. On October 6, 1973—the Jewish high holiday of Yom Kippur—Egypt and Syria attacked Israel from two sides. After some hesitation, the United States backed Israel, a long-time ally, by airlifting vital military supplies. American aid proved essential in helping Israel repel the attack, and the Organization of Petroleum Exporting Countries (OPEC), led by Saudi Arabia and other Arab nations, responded by halting oil shipments to the United States, Western Europe, and Japan.

The oil embargo created an immediate panic, though the problem had been building for years. As the U.S. economy flourished after World War II, its energy consumption soared. Americans, barely 6 percent of the world's population in 1974, used more than 30 percent of the world's energy. Furthermore, as the expense of exploring and drilling for domestic oil increased, the United States turned to foreign suppliers, especially in the Middle East. Between 1968 and 1973, America's consumption of imported oil tripled from 12 to 36 percent.

This reliance on foreign sources left the United States extremely vulnerable to the OPEC embargo. No other nation was more dependent on fossil fuels, and no nation had been more wasteful. As the cold weather set in, President Nixon warned that "we are heading toward the most acute shortage of energy since World War II." In response, the government reduced highway speed limits to 55 miles per hour, lowered thermostats in office buildings to 68 degrees, approved daylight savings time in winter, eased environmental restrictions on coal mining, and pushed the development of nuclear power. Across the nation, stores and factories closed early, families dimmed their Christmas lighting, and northern colleges canceled their midwinter semesters. Long lines formed at the gas stations, which were closed on Sundays to conserve precious fuel.

The oil embargo ended in April 1974, but the impact lingered on. Energy costs rose dramatically, even as supplies returned to normal, because OPEC tripled its price. A gallon of gas in the United States rose from 30 cents (before the embargo) to 75 cents and more. Consumers faced soaring inflation, and manufacturers confronted higher production costs. Some regions, such as the automobile- and steel-producing Midwest, were particularly hard hit; other areas, like the energy-producing Sunbelt, gained in population and political influence.

Above all, the energy crisis shook the foundations of the American dream. For three decades, a booming economy had produced a standard of living unparalleled in terms of material comfort, home ownership, and access to higher education. American culture thrived on the assumption of upward mobility—that the nation's children would do better than their parents had done. But after 1973, that assumption was in peril.

Prosperity could no longer be taken for granted. Following the oil embargo, average weekly earnings in the United States (adjusted for inflation) stopped growing for the first time in thirty years. So too did worker productivity. The increased cost of energy, combined with spiraling federal deficits and aggressive foreign competition in manufacturing and technology, made the American economy more vulnerable than before.

OPEC Oil Embargo. *The OPEC oil embargo of 1973–1974 left Americans high and dry at the gas pumps.*

(© 1998 Dennis Brack/Black Star)

GERALD FORD IN THE WHITE HOUSE

Vice President Gerald Ford, a former football star at the University of Michigan who had served honorably for two decades in the U.S. House of Representatives, seemed the ideal figure to restore public confidence in the presidency. As a Republican Party loyalist, he had opposed most of Lyndon Johnson's Great Society legislation while strongly supporting the war in Vietnam. Yet even Ford's political opponents praised his decency, his integrity, his humble, straightforward ways. After the charisma of John Kennedy, the explosive energy of Lyndon Johnson, and the divisive appeals of Richard Nixon, Americans were ready, it appeared, for a leader with common values and an ordinary touch. As the new president joked, "I'm a Ford, not a Lincoln."

The Watergate Legacy

Gerald Ford entered the White House at a pivotal time. He inherited a situation in which the legislative branch of government, emboldened by the disasters of Watergate and Vietnam, appeared anxious to restore its former authority by cutting the executive branch down to size. In 1973, for example, Congress passed the War Powers Act that required the president to notify Congress within forty-eight hours about the foreign deployment of American combat troops. If Congress did not formally endorse that action within sixty days, the troops would be withdrawn. In addition, Congress passed the Freedom of Information Act, which gave the American people unprecedented access to classified government material.

The Senate also held a series of spectacular hearings into the abuses and criminal activity of executive intelligence agencies such as the FBI and the CIA. The public learned that FBI agents had routinely harassed, blackmailed, and wiretapped prominent Americans such as Martin Luther King, Jr., and CIA operatives had engaged in illegal drug experiments, money laundering, and bungled assassinations of world leaders like Fidel Castro. These revelations led President Ford to create a monitoring device known as the Intelligence Oversight Board. But Congress, with fresh memories of the Watergate cover-up, formed a permanent watchdog committee to investigate such behavior on its own.

Ford too fell victim to the Watergate morass. During his vice-presidential confirmation hearing in 1973, he had gone on record against a possible presidential pardon for Richard Nixon. "I do not think the public would stand for it," he declared. Yet in September 1974, President Ford reversed his earlier position by granting Nixon a "full, free, and absolute pardon" for all crimes he "may have committed" during his term in office. Ford hoped that a presidential pardon would finally put the "national nightmare" of Watergate to rest.

In fact, the opposite occurred. By appearing to place one man above the law, Ford saw his own public approval rating plummet from 72 to 49 percent. What bothered many Americans was the fact that Ford had granted the pardon without demanding contrition in return. Richard Nixon barely apologized for Watergate. He never admitted his crimes. For Gerald Ford, the pardon was an act of mercy, but others wanted justice as well.

The Fall of South Vietnam

In October 1974, at a secret conclave outside Hanoi, the leaders of Communist North Vietnam prepared their final plans for the conquest of South Vietnam. Their main concern was the United States. Would it respond "in full force" to Communist violations of the 1973 peace accords? The North Vietnamese did not think so. "Having already withdrawn from the South," they reasoned, "the United States could hardly jump back in."

Their assessment was correct. The North Vietnamese launched a massive assault in March 1975, overwhelming South Vietnamese forces near the demilitarized zone (DMZ). As North Vietnamese troops advanced, a mixture of chaos and panic gripped South Vietnam, with thousands of soldiers deserting their units and masses of civilians clogging the highways in desperate flight. Ignoring a plea from President Ford, Congress refused to extend emergency aid to South Vietnam. On April 23, Ford acknowledged the obvious. The Vietnam War, he said, "is finished as far as America is concerned."

Saigon fell to the Communists on April 29. The televised images of Americans desperately boarding the last helicopters from the embassy grounds seemed a painful yet fitting conclusion to our nation's longest war. "What we need now in this country,"

Fall of South Vietnam. *The fall of South Vietnam to the Communists in April 1975 brought America's longest military conflict to an end.*

said a solemn Henry Kissinger, "is to put Vietnam behind us and to concentrate on problems of the future."

This was easier said than done. The humiliating collapse of South Vietnam raised serious questions about the limits of American military power. For those most deeply affected—the veterans of Vietnam—the collapse raised personal questions about the meaning of their sacrifice to the nation and to themselves. With the exception of the POWs, these veterans received no public tributes, no outpouring of thanks. Congress passed no special "GI Bill" to pay for their college tuition, to help them find employment, or to finance their new homes. Some Americans condemned the veterans for serving in an "immoral war"; others blamed them for participating in the nation's first military defeat. "The left hated us for killing," said one dejected veteran, "and the right hated us for not killing enough."

The vast majority of Vietnam veterans expressed pride in their military service and a willingness to fight there again. Most of them adjusted well to civilian life, although a sizable minority (one out of six, according to the Veterans Administration) suffered from posttraumatic stress disorder, substance abuse, and sometimes both. In addition, some veterans claimed that their exposure to Agent Orange, a toxic herbicide used to defoliate the jungles of Vietnam, had produced high rates of cancer, lung disease, and even birth defects in their children. After more than a decade of controversy, Congress passed legislation that extended benefits to Vietnam veterans with medical conditions linked to Agent Orange.

Public sentiment softened over time. Opinion polls by the late 1970s showed that most Americans considered the Vietnam veteran to be both a dutiful soldier and the victim of a tragic war. In 1982, the Vietnam Veterans Memorial, a dramatic wall of black granite with the names of fifty-eight thousand Americans who died or were missing in that war, was unveiled on the Mall in Washington, D.C. Attracting large, respectful crowds, the memorial affords recognition for the sacrifices of all who served in Vietnam.

Stumbling Toward Defeat   The pardon of Richard Nixon and the fall of South Vietnam served to erode much of the goodwill that had accompanied Gerald Ford's early days in office. The president also faced a bleak economic picture, darkened by spiraling energy costs, in which unemployment and inflation reached their highest levels in years. "The state of the union," Ford admitted in 1975, "is not good."

The president and the Congress disagreed about the best medicine for the economic slump. The Republican Ford, believing that a balanced federal budget was the key to cutting inflation, proposed sizable cuts in government programs and a voluntary citizens' campaign to curb rising prices, which he called "Whip Inflation Now" (WIN). The Democratic Congress called for increased federal spending to spur the economy and lower unemployment by creating new jobs. Although Ford vetoed more than sixty bills during his brief tenure in office, Congress overrode the president to increase social security benefits, fund public works projects, and raise the minimum wage.

In foreign affairs, Ford tried to maintain the policy of détente begun by Nixon and Kissinger, who remained as secretary of state. But unlike Nixon, the new president worried conservatives with his alleged weaknesses as a negotiator. Of particular concern was the Helsinki Accord of 1975, which pledged the United States and the Soviet Union, among other nations, to recognize the Cold War boundaries dividing Eastern and Western Europe and to respect human rights within their borders. Many Americans were dismayed by the formal acceptance of Soviet domination over nations such as Poland and East Germany; many more were skeptical about any Russian promise regarding human rights. "I am against this agreement," said former Governor Ronald Reagan of California, "and I think all Americans should be against it."

Even Ford's occasional successes left controversy in their wake. In 1975, for example, communists in Cambodia seized the American merchant ship *Mayaguez* in international waters off the Cambodian coast. The president responded with a daring rescue mission in which forty-one U.S. Marines were killed and forty-nine were wounded, although it turned out that the Cambodians had already released the *Mayaguez* and its crew. Though Ford received some criticism for not consulting Congress before sending troops into action, most Americans, applauded his decisive action. "It was wonderful," declared Senator Barry Goldwater. "It shows we've still got balls in this country."

The Election of 1976   Gerald Ford dreamed of winning the White House in his own right. Yet unlike previous incumbents, who normally breezed through the presidential nominating process, Ford faced a serious challenge in 1976 from Ronald Reagan and the Republican Right. Reagan's polished presence and outspoken conservatism played well against Ford's reserved manner and middle-of-the-road approach. With great fanfare, Reagan portrayed Ford as a weak president, unable to tame a Democratic Congress or to confront the Russians at Helsinki. In his sharpest attack, Reagan blasted Ford for opening negotiations aimed at reducing American control of the Panama Canal. "We built it, we paid for it, it's ours," Reagan thundered, "and we should tell [Panama] that we are going to keep it."

Though Reagan battled Ford to a draw in the state primaries, the president won a narrow victory at the Republican National Convention in Kansas City by agreeing to support a party platform sympathetic to the Reagan forces. The platform condemned both the Helsinki agreement and the Panama Canal negotiations and endorsed constitutional amendments to legalize school prayer and prohibit abortions. For vice president, the Republican delegates selected Senator Bob Dole of Kansas, a tough campaigner with conservative views.

Because Ford appeared so vulnerable in 1976, the Democratic race for president attracted a very large field. Among the candidates was a little-known former governor of Georgia named **James Earl ("Jimmy") Carter, Jr**. Few observers took him seriously at the start, and the voters asked, "Jimmy who?" When **Jimmy Carter** told his mother that he intended to run for president, she replied, "President of what?" Yet Carter ran an effective, well-financed campaign, portraying himself as a political outsider who was untainted by the arrogance and corruption of Washington.

Carter struck the right pose for the post-Watergate era. A deeply religious man who promised voters, "I will never lie to you," he combined the virtues of small town America with the skills of the modern corporate world. Born in Plains, Georgia, in 1924, Carter attended local schools, graduated with distinction from the U.S. Naval Academy, and spent seven years as a naval officer working on nuclear submarines. Following the death of his father in 1953, Carter returned to Plains to run the family's farm supply and peanut business. As the company prospered, he turned to politics, winning a state senate seat in 1962 and the Georgia governorship eight years later. Known as a "new South" politician, Carter supported progressive causes and reached out to black constituents through his concern for civil rights.

Meeting in New York City, the Democratic National Convention chose Carter for president and Senator Walter Mondale of Minnesota for vice president. Carter ran a safe campaign that fall, avoiding controversial issues while claiming that America was no longer "strong" or "respected" in the world. The media, meanwhile, caught Ford in a series of bumbling accidents—banging his head on a car door, tumbling down the steps of an airplane, crashing on the ski slopes, whacking spectators on the golf course with his tee shots—that made him look clownish and inept. Before long, the comedian Chevy Chase was beginning almost every episode of *Saturday Night Live* by taking a terrible tumble in the role of Gerald Ford. And the president only made things worse for himself with a series of embarrassing verbal blunders, such as his insistence during the televised debate with Carter that "there [was] no Soviet domination of Eastern Europe." By election day, many Americans viewed Ford as a decent man, doing his best in a job that appeared to overwhelm him.

Still, the race was very close. Carter won 40.8 million votes, Ford 39.1 million. The electoral count was 297 to 240. Carter swept the entire South (except for Virginia) and the key industrial states of Ohio, Pennsylvania, and New York. Ford did well in the West, carrying every state but Texas. Polls showed Carter with large majorities among both minority voters and working-class whites who had rejected McGovern in 1972. In this election, at least, the New Deal coalition held firm.

Jimmy Carter became the first president from the Deep South in more than a century, signifying that region's increased strength—and acceptance—in the national arena. Furthermore, his election witnessed the growing importance of state primaries in the nominating process as well as the influence of the new Fair Campaign Practices Act of 1974. The law provided federal funds to the major candidates ($22 million each in this election); it also established limits on personal contributions and a stricter accounting of how funds were disbursed. The result, as the 1976 election amply displayed, was a longer, more expensive presidential campaign season, with television advertising playing an ever larger role.

The Ford–Carter election continued the downward trend in voter turnout, from 55.7 percent in 1972 to 54.4 percent in 1976. Polls showed a growing sense of apathy and disillusionment among the American people, a loss of connection with politics as a positive force in their lives. As one bumper sticker put it, "Don't Vote. It Only Encourages Them!"

THE CARTER YEARS

The new Democratic administration began with promise and hope. President-elect Carter took the oath of office as Jimmy (not James Earl) Carter before leading the inaugural parade on foot down Pennsylvania Avenue dressed in a simple business suit. Determined to be a "people's president," Carter surrounded himself with populist symbolism—giving fireside chats in a sweater and blue jeans, attending town meetings from New Hampshire to New Mexico, and staying overnight in the homes of ordinary Americans. "We must have a new spirit," he declared. "We must once again have full faith in our country—and in one another."

Civil Rights in a New Era
As governor of Georgia, Jimmy Carter had opened the doors of government to minorities. As president, he did much the same thing. Women, African Americans, and Hispanics were appointed to federal positions in record numbers as judges, ambassadors, and White House aides. Women, for example, filled three of Carter's cabinet-level positions and numerous other policy-making roles. In addition, Carter's wife, Rosalyn, greatly expanded the role of first lady by serving as a key adviser to the president and representing him on diplomatic missions.

Although Carter strongly supported civil rights and gave special attention to the plight of minorities in the inner cities, the momentum for racial change in the 1970s had shifted from the executive branch to the federal courts. During Carter's term, the issue of affirmative action took center stage in *University of California Regents v. Bakke* (1978). Allan Bakke, a thirty-eight-year-old white man, was denied admission to the University of California medical school at Davis. He sued on the grounds that his test scores exceeded those of several black applicants who were admitted under a policy that reserved sixteen of one hundred spots for minorities in each entering class. The policy amounted to "reverse discrimination," Bakke charged, and thus violated his right to equal protection under the law. The case raised a fundamental conflict between the government's obligation to treat all citizens equally regardless of race and its responsibility to help the long-suffering victims of racial discrimination enter the mainstream of American society. In a 5-to-4 ruling, the Supreme Court struck down the medical school's quota policy as a violation of Bakke's constitutional rights. But it held that universities might consider race as a factor in admission "to remedy disadvantages cast on minorities by past racial prejudice."

The *Bakke* decision began a passionate debate over affirmative action that continues to this day. Opponents considered it to be a racially divisive policy as well as a dangerous step away from the American tradition of individual rights. Why penalize innocent whites, they argued, for the sins of their ancestors? But supporters of affirmative action viewed it as the surest way to remedy discrimination, past and present. "In order to get beyond racism, we must take race into account," wrote Justice Thurgood Marshall. "There is no other way."

Human Rights and Global Realities   President Carter knew little about foreign affairs. His political career had been spent entirely on state and local concerns. Yet he viewed his inexperience as an asset, freeing him from worn-out thinking and stale ideas. He believed that a fresh approach to foreign affairs would move America beyond the "big power" rivalries of the Cold War era. What America needed, he thought, was a foreign policy that stressed democracy and human rights—in short, the idealism of the United States.

Carter scored some impressive successes. Emphasizing human rights in Latin America, he withdrew American support for the military dictatorship in Chile, cut off aid to the repressive Somoza regime in Nicaragua, and encouraged the governments of Brazil and Argentina in their halting steps toward democracy. Carter also presented the Senate with a treaty that relinquished American control over the Panama Canal by the year 2000 and a second one that detailed American rights in the Canal Zone thereafter. Both treaties provoked fierce national debate; both passed the Senate by a single vote.

Carter's greatest triumph occurred in the Middle East. In 1977, Egyptian President Anwar Sadat stunned the Arab world by visiting Israel to explore peace negotiations with Prime Minister Menachem Begin. Their discussions were cordial but fruitless, for neither man seemed willing to take the risks that peace demanded. When the talks broke down, Carter invited Sadat and Begin to his presidential retreat at Camp David in Maryland. For two weeks in September 1978, Carter shuttled between the cabins of the two Middle Eastern leaders, patiently working out the details of a "peace process" between Egypt and Israel that other nations might later join.

The **Camp David Accords** led to a historic treaty the following year. Egypt agreed to recognize the state of Israel, which previously had been unthinkable for an Arab nation, and Israel pledged to return the captured Sinai Peninsula to Egypt. The treaty did not consider other vital issues, such as the fate of displaced Palestinians and the future of Israeli-held Arab territory in Gaza and the West Bank. Yet few could deny the enormity of what had transpired or the pivotal role played by President Carter in bringing it about.

Economic Blues   Early success in foreign affairs, however, could not mask Carter's problems with the troubled economy. During the 1976 presidential campaign, candidate Carter had focused on high inflation (6 percent) and unemployment (8 percent) that gripped the United States. Combining these figures into a "misery index" of 14, he had promised the American people immediate relief.

Anwar Sadat and Menachem Begin. *Anwar Sadat and Menachem Begin shake hands at Camp David, Maryland, as Jimmy Carter, who brought the men together, smiles in the background.*

Carter's program to stimulate the economy depended on a mixture of tax cuts, public works, and employment programs—a kind of "pump priming" reminiscent of Franklin Roosevelt's New Deal. The Democratic-controlled Congress responded sympathetically by funding large public works projects, reducing taxes by $30 billion, and raising the minimum wage from $2.30 to $3.35 over a five-year span. The good news was that unemployment dropped to 6 percent by 1978; the bad news was that inflation rose to 10 percent—and kept climbing.

Carter changed his approach. Creating jobs took a backseat to the problem of runaway inflation. Unlike Richard Nixon, who fought this problem by implementing wage and price controls, Carter tried to attack inflation by tightening the money supply (through higher interest rates) and controlling the federal deficit. This meant reduced government spending, a turnabout that alienated the Democratic Congress. Moreover, Carter's new policies appeared to increase unemployment without curbing inflation—the worst of both worlds. Before long, the "misery index" stood at 21.

This was not all Carter's fault, of course. The decline of American productivity, the growth of foreign competition, and the surging cost of imported oil had plagued the nation for some time. In 1977, Carter offered a substantive plan for the energy crisis, which he described as "the moral equivalent of war." (Critics called it "meow.") The plan arrived on the heels of the worst winter in modern American history, a season of blizzards, record low temperatures, and arctic winds. Based mainly on conservation—or reduced energy use—it ran into immediate opposition from oil companies, gas producers, the auto industry, and others who advocated the increased production of fossil fuels and the deregulation of prices. "This country didn't conserve its way to greatness," a Texas oil man complained. "It produced its way to greatness."

The National Energy Act, passed in November 1978, did little to reduce America's energy consumption or its reliance on foreign oil. Carter's original plans to stimulate conservation efforts were overshadowed by incentives to increase domestic energy production through tax breaks for exploration, an emphasis on alternative sources (solar, nuclear, coal), and the deregulation of natural gas. The law did not address, much less solve, the nation's fundamental energy problems—as Americans would soon discover.

The Persian Gulf   In January 1979, a chain of events unfolded that shook the nation's confidence and shattered Jimmy Carter's presidency. The year began with the overthrow of America's dependable ally, Shah Riza Pahlavi of Iran; it ended with the United States appearing helpless and dispirited in the face of mounting challenges at home and abroad.

On a visit to Iran in 1977, President Carter had described it as "an island of stability in one of the most troubled areas in the world." Iran was vital to American interests, as both an oil supplier and a bastion against Soviet influence in the Middle East. Thousands of American workers and their families lived in Iran, and thousands of Iranian students attended college in the United States. Ironically, President Carter's concern for human rights did not extend to Iran, where the army and secret police used widespread torture and repression to keep the shah and his ruling elite in power.

The Iranian Revolution was led by Ayatollah Ruhollah Khomeini, an exiled cleric, and his devoted followers. Their aim was not to set up a democracy, but rather to form a fundamentalist Islamic state. When demonstrations paralyzed Iran, the shah fled his country, leaving the religious fundamentalists in control. One of Khomeini's first moves was to end oil shipments to "the Great Satan" America, thus allowing other OPEC countries to raise their prices even more. In the United States, long gas lines reappeared, and the price reached an incredible a dollar per gallon.

With Americans reeling from months of bad news, President Carter went on national television to speak partly about the energy crisis, but mostly about a "crisis of confidence" that struck "at the very heart and soul and spirit of our national will." His address was remarkably candid. Rather than assuring anxious Americans that they had nothing to fear or trying to rally them with

Anti-American Demonstration.   *Iranian students stormed the American Embassy in Tehran in 1979, taking dozens of hostages. Unable to negotiate their release, President Carter approved a secret rescue mission that ended in disaster.*

(© Henri Bureau/Sigma/CORBIS)

ringing phrases about honor and duty, the president spoke of a nation in trouble, struggling with the values of its cherished past. In place of "hard work, strong families, and close-knit communities," he said, too many Americans "now worship self-indulgence and consumption. Human identity is no longer defined by what one does but by what one owns."

Having passionately diagnosed the illness, Carter provided no cure. The "crisis of confidence" deepened. In October, the deposed shah of Iran, suffering from cancer, was allowed to enter the United States for medical treatment. This decision, which Carter viewed as a simple humanitarian gesture, produced an explosive backlash in Iran. On November 4, militant students stormed the American embassy in Tehran, taking dozens of American hostages and parading them in blindfolds for the entire world to see. The militants demanded that the United States turn over the shah for trial in Iran. Otherwise the Americans would remain as captives—and perhaps be tried, and executed, as spies.

Carter had almost no leverage with these militants, who were supported by Khomeini himself. His attempts to settle the crisis through the United Nations were ignored by Iran. His orders to embargo Iranian oil and suspend arms sales were empty gestures because other nations refused to do the same. The remaining options—freezing Iran's assets in American banks or threatening to deport Iranian students from the United States—did nothing to change the fate of the hostages in Tehran.

For a time, the American people rallied behind their president. Carter's approval rating jumped from 30 to 61 percent in the first month of the crisis. Yet Carter grasped what many others did not: there was no easy solution to the hostage standoff. "It would not be possible, or even advisable," he warned, "to set a deadline about when, or if, I would take certain acts in the future." As the nation waited, public patience grew thin.

> ### DOING HISTORY ONLINE
>
> #### American Hostages in Iran, 1979
>
> Read the accounts online. John Limbert and Bill Belk tell different stories about being taken hostage at the American embassy in Iran. Why do their accounts differ so much?
>
> www.cengage.com/ history/ayers/ ampassages4e

The year ended with yet another nasty surprise. In December, Russian soldiers invaded neighboring Afghanistan to quell a revolt led by Muslim fundamentalists against the faltering pro-Soviet regime. The invasion ultimately backfired; fanatical resistance from Afghan fighters turned the country into a graveyard for Russian troops. Determined to act boldly in the light of the continuing Iran hostage crisis, Carter cut off grain shipments to the Soviet Union and cancelled America's participation at the upcoming Summer Olympic Games in Moscow—a boycott that many nations chose to ignore. More significant, he announced a "Carter Doctrine" for the Persian Gulf, warning that "outside aggression" would "be repelled by any means necessary, including military force." By 1980, the Cold War was heating up again. Afghanistan and its aftermath had dealt a serious blow to détente.

Death in the Desert As President Carter and the American people staggered through the repeated shocks of 1979, one issue dominated the national agenda: the fate of the hostages in Iran. The crisis took on symbolic

Three Mile Island

By the mid-1960s, nuclear power had emerged as a viable alternative to fossil fuels—a cheaper, cleaner, and virtually inexhaustible energy source for the future. As the number of commercial nuclear power plants increased, so too did their size. Among the largest was Three Mile Island (pictured) in the Susquehanna River near Harrisburg, Pennsylvania. Though a growing environmental movement in the 1970s had raised safety concerns regarding these huge facilities, and Hollywood had recently produced a box office smash, *The China Syndrome*, about a nuclear power plant disaster, the dangers still seemed remote. Then, in March 1979, a mechanical failure at Three Mile Island threatened to blanket the surrounding countryside with radioactive fallout, and thousands fled their homes. Though engineers were successful in stabilizing the damaged reactor, the looming white stacks of Three Mile Island came to symbolize the tremendous risks associated with nuclear power. There are just over one hundred nuclear power plants in the United States today; almost all were constructed before the awful scare at Three Mile Island.

(© Bettmann/CORBIS)

importance as an example of America's declining power in the world: its inability to defend its citizens, its vital interests, its national honor. The television networks flashed nightly pictures of the hostages on humiliating public display in Tehran while frenzied crowds shouted "Death to Carter" and "Down with the United States." In Washington, meanwhile, the president met regularly with the families of the hostages and worked tirelessly to find a diplomatic solution. But this seemed all but impossible, because the Iranians were not interested in a quick settlement. Reluctantly, Carter ordered a secret mission to free the hostages by force.

The result was disastrous. In April 1980, American commandos reached the Iranian desert, where two of their helicopters were disabled by mechanical problems. Another hit a U.S. cargo plane, killing eight members of the rescue mission. The commandos departed without ever getting close to the hostages in Tehran. To make matters worse, the Iranians proudly displayed the burned corpses for television crews. Most Americans blamed the president for the debacle. What little remained of Jimmy Carter's credibility disappeared that fateful day in the Iranian desert.

CONCLUSION

The United States in 1980 was an uneasy land. The social upheavals of the 1960s and 1970s had fostered anxiety as well as progress. The movement for civil rights, so certain in the era of bus boycotts, lunch counter sit-ins, and voting rights marches, was now deeply divided over issues such as forced busing and affirmative action. So, too, the struggle for women's rights generated fierce controversy over abortion, sex roles, workplace equality, and the ERA. On the economic front, Americans faced a world of new troubles—a world of stagnant incomes, rising unemployment, mounting trade deficits, and skyrocketing inflation. No longer were young people guaranteed the prospect of moving a rung or two above their parents on the ladder of success. For millions, the American dream was now on hold.

Above all, the nation appeared momentarily to lose confidence in its leaders and its goals. Watergate, OPEC, the fall of South Vietnam, the near disaster at Three Mile Island, the Iran hostage crisis, the bungled rescue attempt—all seemed to reflect a loss of national purpose, authority, and prestige. As the 1980 election approached, many Americans looked back into the past with a deep sense of nostalgia, hoping for someone to rescue the country and restore the American dream.

CHAPTER REVIEW, 1969–1980

- The spectacular moon landing in 1969 gave a weary and divided nation a welcome reason to celebrate.
- The rights revolution took on even greater momentum as movements for women's rights and minority rights expanded dramatically in universities, the workplace, and the courts.
- Following a string of remarkable successes, including a path-breaking visit to Communist China and a lopsided reelection victory, President Nixon became the first president to resign his office following revelations of his involvement in the Watergate scandal.
- The collapse of South Vietnam in 1975 ended one of the longest, most divisive chapters in American military history and raised troubling questions about the soundness of U.S. foreign policy in the Cold War era.
- Following decades of unprecedented growth, the American economy entered a period of uncertainty and decline, marked by lower productivity, soaring energy prices, higher interest rates, and runaway inflation.
- The Iran hostage crisis marked a new direction in U.S. relations with the Islamic world.

◄▌▌▌ Looking Back

Chapter 30 examines the political, economic, and psychological impact of the Watergate scandal, the OPEC oil embargo, the fall of South Vietnam, and other crises on the American people and their vision of the future.

1. What impact did the "rights revolution" of the 1960s have on political events in the 1970s? What role did the federal courts play in this process?
2. What were the defining features of the Watergate affair? Why is it considered to be the most significant, and potentially dangerous, political scandal in U.S. history?
3. Though Americans most remember the Iran hostage crisis, the United States achieved some notable successes in foreign policy during the 1970s. What were these successes, and how were they achieved?

Looking Ahead ▌▌▌►

Chapter 31 looks at the so-called Reagan Revolution: the attempt by a new president, with a different political philosophy, to restore national confidence and redirect the nation along more conservative lines.

1. How would President Reagan deal with the economic problems facing Americans in this era?
2. How would he differ from previous presidents in his dealings with the Soviet Union and in his personal view of international communism and the Cold War?
3. Was it possible to narrow the social and cultural divisions that had plagued the United States in the 1960s and 1970s, or would they continue to widen over time?

Go to the American Passages website at www.cengage.com/history/ayers/ampassages4e for additional review materials.

31

From Reagan to Clinton, 1981–1995

The presidency of **Ronald Reagan** defined the decade of the 1980s. His efforts to redirect the nation toward a smaller and less activist government aroused bitter controversy. After two decades of "failed presidencies," Reagan's consecutive presidential terms contributed to a mood of renewed optimism that endured until he left office. The ensuing administration of George H. W. Bush and the first years of William Jefferson "Bill" Clinton's presidency dealt with the legacy of Reagan and his impact on the nation.

During this period the Soviet Union collapsed, and the Cold War ended. This peaceful transition was an important contribution of the Reagan and Bush administrations. The end of that challenge to American interests revealed other tensions in the world arising from the Middle East, where terrorism became a weapon of choice for those opposed to the policies of the United States.

While the economy boomed during the 1980s, the federal government's budget deficits and the national debt increased. Rich Americans became richer, and the gulf between the affluent and the poor widened. Under the pressures of global economic change, American businesses became more efficient and less unwieldy. The price, however, was a loss of jobs in many key industries as American workers faced the trauma of "downsizing." The administration of George H. W. Bush faltered as a result. The next president, Bill Clinton, faced political discontent when he raised taxes in 1993 to address the nation's fiscal problems. The outcome for the Democrats was loss of control of Congress. For the Republicans, they emerged with strong majorities in both houses of Congress after the 1994 election.

THE REAGAN REVOLUTION

Ronald Wilson Reagan became president of the United States as the oldest man to assume the nation's highest office. Born in Illinois in 1911, he had been an actor and television personality. Disillusioned with the political liberalism of his youth, he switched to the Republicans and was elected governor of California in 1966.

CHAPTER TIMELINE

1981	Ronald Reagan inaugurated as president • Iranian-held hostages freed from captivity • Sandra Day O'Connor appointed to the Supreme Court • President Reagan survives assassination attempt • AIDS outbreak begins in United States
1982	Severe economic recession grips nation • Democrats make gains in congressional elections
1983	President Reagan proposes Strategic Defense Initiative (SDI) • Social security reforms adopted • United States invades Grenada
1984	Geraldine Ferraro becomes first female vice presidential candidate of a major party • Macintosh computer introduced • Ronald Reagan reelected
1985	Rock Hudson dies of AIDS • Gramm-Rudman-Hollings Act adopted • Reagan administration begins negotiations with Iran that lead to Iran-Contra scandal
1986	Tax Reform Act passed • *Challenger* space shuttle explodes • Immigration Reform Act adopted • Democrats regain control of Senate in elections • Iran-Contra scandal erupts
1987	United States and Soviet Union pursue arms control • Iran-Contra hearings held
1988	Democrats nominate Michael Dukakis to run for president • Antidepressant drug Prozac introduced • George H. W. Bush elected president
1989	United States invades Panama to capture Manuel Noriega • Berlin Wall comes down • Chinese kill demonstrators in Tiananmen Square • In *Webster v. Reproductive Health Services*, Supreme Court upholds right of states to limit abortion access
1990	George H. W. Bush abandons "no new taxes" pledge • Iraq invades Kuwait • Americans with Disabilities Act passed
1991	Iraq defeated in Gulf War • Clarence Thomas nominated to and confirmed for Supreme Court • Soviet Union collapses
1992	Ross Perot becomes third-party candidate for president • William Jefferson Clinton and Al Gore form the Democratic presidential ticket • Clinton and Gore win the presidential contest
1993	Siege of Branch Davidians at Waco, Texas, ends in fiery incident • Congress narrowly passes Clinton's economic program
1994	Republicans regain control of House of Representatives for the first time in forty years

Reagan's blend of conservative rhetoric and a sunny disposition made him a favorite among conservatives in the 1970s. He lost a race for the Republican presidential nomination to Gerald Ford in 1976 but became the party's nominee four years later with George H. W. Bush as his running mate.

This icon will direct you to interactive activities and study materials on the American Passages website: www.cengage.com/history/ayers/ampassages4e

The Election of 1980

The 1980 presidential campaign took place in the shadow of an ongoing crisis involving fifty-two American hostages who had been seized in Iran during the revolution against the shah. The plight of the hostages helped Jimmy Carter fend off the challenge of Senator Edward M. Kennedy of Massachusetts for the Democratic presidential nomination. A failed military attempt to rescue the hostages in April 1980 undercut Carter's standing with the voters and made his nomination a hollow prize. During the campaign, Reagan assailed Carter's record on the economy and national defense. The president fired back that Reagan was a dangerous and unreliable political extremist. In a televised debate between the two men in late October 1980, Reagan asked viewers: "Are you better off" than in 1976?

Reagan and the Republicans won the election with 44 million ballots for Reagan to 35 million for Carter and 5.7 million for third-party candidate John Anderson. In the electoral college, Reagan garnered 489 votes and Carter 49. The Republicans regained control of the Senate, picking up twelve seats from the Democrats.

Reagan in Office

Reagan said: "We must balance the budget, reduce tax rates, and restore our defenses." Reagan's long career in Hollywood had given him a skill in conveying his views that won him the title of "**The Great Communicator**." His use of humor, especially when he stressed his own foibles,

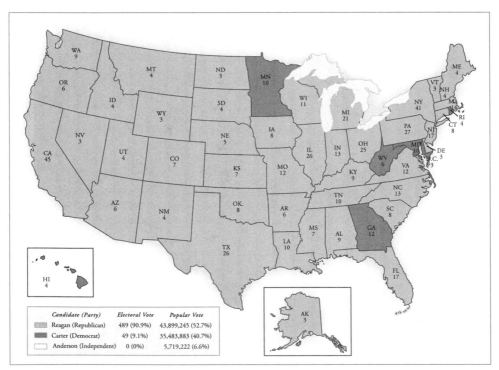

Candidate (Party)	Electoral Vote	Popular Vote
Reagan (Republican)	489 (90.9%)	43,899,245 (52.7%)
Carter (Democrat)	49 (9.1%)	35,483,883 (40.7%)
Anderson (Independent)	0 (0%)	5,719,222 (6.6%)

MAP 31.1 The Election of 1980

The election map reveals the repudiation of Jimmy Carter and his administration in 1980 and the swing to the right that put Ronald Reagan in the White House. Carter's economic record and the foreign policy problems of the late 1970s left him without an effective national political base.

was deft; it reinforced his rapport with his fellow citizens. He exuded a degree of optimism about his country, sincerity about his positions, and confidence in the rightness of his views that made him a masterful politician during his first six years as president.

At the same time, Reagan knew very little about the actual operation of the federal government and displayed scant curiosity about such matters. He read very few of the documents that crossed his desk and watched movies when he should have been reading position papers. As a friend put it, "He lived life on the surface where the small waves are, not deep down where the heavy currents tug." Many commentators said that Reagan played the role of president better than any incumbent since Franklin D. Roosevelt because of his previous experience as a film star. After the glow of the performance faded, there remained the question of whether the president had done more than walk through his job.

Reagan in Office. *Ronald Reagan conveyed a sense of strong presidential leadership through images like this one that depicted him as an American icon.*

(© David J. & Janice L. Frent Collection/CORBIS)

As Reagan started his administration, the Republicans controlled the White House and the Senate, where they commanded a 53 to 46 majority. Democrats remained the majority in the House of Representatives, 242 to 190. In 1980, the inflation rate was over 12 percent, the unemployment rate was above 7 percent, and the prime interest rate had soared to almost 20 percent. The national debt had reached $908 billion. In Reagan's view, "The most important cause of our economic problems has been the government itself."

The administration embraced traditional Republican suspicion of government spending and added to it an aggressive reduction in federal income taxes. The term "supply-side economics" became shorthand for what this program promised to do: the government should lower income and corporate tax rates to give private business and individual taxpayers more money to spend. The predicted surge in productive economic activity would result in an increase in tax revenues, which would prevent large budget deficits.

Carrying Out the Reagan Agenda The release of U.S. hostages in Iran on January 20, 1981, removed that troublesome issue. When Reagan was shot on March 30, 1981, the would-be assassin's bullet came closer to ending his life than the public knew. The president's courage and good humor in this moment of crisis increased his popularity and added to the reservoir of goodwill that he commanded.

A second event that helped Reagan was his handling of a strike by the Professional Air Traffic Controllers Organization (PATCO). As government employees, the controllers could not legally strike, and the president fired them when they refused to heed a back-to-work order. The message for the nation was that the White House would be tough on organized labor.

During the first half of 1981, a coalition of Republicans and "boll weevil Democrats" (southern and western conservatives) pushed through legislation that trimmed tax rates by 25 percent over three years. The administration sought budget cuts for a number of discretionary social programs (ones where payments to recipients were not mandated in law) to advance the president's goal of a balanced budget by 1984. Although the budget act, passed in the House on June 25, 1981, promised future reductions in spending, during its first year it provided only $16 billion in immediate cuts. That was $200 billion less than would have been required to achieve a real step toward a balanced budget.

The president declined to make cuts in what he termed "the social safety net": social security, Medicare, veterans' benefits, Head Start, and school lunch programs. The practical result was that almost half of the federal budget was placed beyond the reach of congressional budget-cutting efforts.

The Reagan administration also increased defense spending. Reagan believed that the nation's military establishment had been neglected during Carter's presidency. In 1979, however, the Democratic Congress and the administration had begun a long-range program to build up American military power, and the Reagan White House expanded on that initiative. During the Ford–Carter years, defense budgets had been less than $200 billion annually. Under Reagan, the Pentagon budget rose to nearly $300 billion per year by 1985.

The outcome of modest cuts in social programs and entitlements, sharp hikes in defense spending, and a reduction in tax rates was a growth in the government deficit to $128 billion by 1982. The ballooning federal deficits continued throughout the Reagan era, producing a surge in the national debt. The goal of a balanced budget in 1984 vanished quickly. The huge deficits drove economic policy for the decade that followed, and future generations were left with a massive debt to fund and pay off.

Deregulation

In his inaugural address, President Reagan proclaimed: "In this present crisis, government is not the solution to our problem; government is the problem." As part of his response to a large, intrusive government, Reagan advocated an extensive program of deregulation to lessen the government presence in the private sector.

The Reagan administration pursued a new course in environmental policy. Secretary of the Interior James G. Watt, a conservative who disliked all restrictions on public lands in the West, sought to open new areas for oil drilling, cut back on the acquisition of land for national parks, and put in place other bureaucrats eager to reduce the amount of environmental regulation that the government conducted.

The most spectacular and disastrous example of deregulation occurred in 1982, when Congress and the White House lifted restrictions from the savings and loan industry. During a time of high inflation and rising interest rates, savings and loan institutions had difficulty earning a profit because of the low rates of interest they were allowed by law to pay on their deposits. In 1980, Congress increased federal insurance coverage to $100,000 per account and enabled savings and loan companies to offer even higher interest rates. These measures did not, however, increase the profits on the money that the thrift institutions loaned. Partly in response to lobbying by the industry and the large campaign contributions that lawmakers received, Congress decided to deregulate these companies and allow them to invest in higher risk assets, including commercial real estate, fine art, and, in some instances, speculative or fraudulent ventures.

The Reagan administration also cut back on the number of banking and regulatory examiners. With federal deposit insurance guaranteeing that they would be bailed out, savings and loan operators plunged into ventures that were risky and often illegal. In 1983 and 1984 the banking and savings and loan businesses had made bad loans, created poorly financed individual companies, and featured corrupt operators who were looting their firms.

By the early 1980s, social security, the most popular New Deal program, had reached a funding crisis. During the 1970s, Congress and the Nixon administration had established a system of cost-of-living adjustments (COLAs) that raised benefits for social security recipients as the rate of inflation rose (known as indexing). Indexing of benefits caused the cost of social security to soar as the population aged and more people received social security checks. But efforts to trim COLAs seemed futile because tinkering with social security benefits guaranteed electoral defeat for anyone who tried it.

President Reagan learned that lesson in the spring of 1981 when the administration proposed a cut in benefits for early retirees (those who would begin receiving benefits at age sixty-two). When the initiative was announced, gleeful Democrats assailed it, and Republicans in Congress deserted Reagan. In December 1981, the president appointed a bipartisan panel to address long-range funding of the retirement program. The plan, announced after the 1982 elections, raised payroll taxes to pay for social security, taxed some of the benefits of people over age sixty-five who had high incomes, and put off providing for the long-term viability of the system.

DOING HISTORY ONLINE

Reaganomics

Read the section on "The Reagan Revolution" in the textbook and consider the documents online to answer the following question: Why were some conservatives not concerned about the large deficits that resulted from Reagan's economic policies?

 www.cengage.com/history/ayers/ampassages4e

REAGAN AND FOREIGN POLICY

In 1983, Reagan called the Soviet Union "an evil empire" and said that the Cold War was a struggle between "right and wrong and good and evil." In dealing with the Soviets, then, the president insisted arms agreements be based on the principle of "trust but verify." He was convinced that the United States could outspend the Soviet Union in an arms race. Faced with an aging and incompetent Soviet leadership between 1981 and 1985, the White House avoided any summit meetings during that period.

This stern language did not rule out flexibility. Early in the new administration the president lifted the grain embargo that President Carter had established when the Soviet Union invaded Afghanistan in 1980, a move that pleased American wheat farmers. Reagan also stated that a nuclear war could not be won and should never be fought. Although the new White House team did not like the SALT II Treaty to limit the number of nuclear missiles that Carter had negotiated, it largely observed the pact's provisions.

Rivalry with the Soviet Union The rivalry between the two superpowers flared in Central America. The Reagan administration believed that the victory of the Sandinistas, a pro-Communist faction in Nicaragua in 1979 represented a serious threat to U.S. interests in the region, especially in neighboring El Salvador. By late 1981, the United States was underwriting a rebellion against the Sandinista regime led by a faction called the **Contras.** Although President Reagan likened the anti-Sandinistas to the patriots of the American Revolution, in 1982 the Democratic House of Representatives adopted an amendment that sought to block funds from being used to oust the Sandinistas.

Reagan and his administration paid a political price for the policies of the first two years. A severe recession continued until almost the end of 1982. Although Reagan argued that the recession would soon end, the Republicans suffered a setback at the polls in the congressional elections. The Democrats gained twenty-seven seats in the House but the Republicans maintained their dominance in the Senate. Nevertheless, President Reagan again urged his fellow Republicans to "stay the course."

Shortly after the election the economy picked up steam, stimulated by the Reagan tax cuts. The inflation rate declined and unemployment receded. As the recovery gained strength, so did Reagan and his party. Adding to the president's popularity was the U.S. invasion of the Caribbean island of Grenada in October 1983. Fearing that radicals close to Fidel Castro and Cuba were about to turn Grenada into a Soviet base (an unlikely outcome), the administration launched a powerful invasion force that secured control of the island after a brief struggle.

The war in Nicaragua was not going well for the Contras, and El Salvador was experiencing atrocities from right-wing death squads that murdered their opponents and left-wing insurgents sympathetic to Nicaragua. In 1984, Congress adopted a second, more restrictive, amendment to prevent the government from aiding the Contras.

Contras in Central America.
The Reagan administration sponsored a group in Nicaragua against the Sandinista regime that became known as the "Contras."

(© Susan Meiselas/Magnum Photos)

In the Middle East, Reagan's hopes of producing a lasting peace between Israel and its neighbors were also frustrated. The administration did not stop Israel from invading Lebanon in June 1982, and U.S. Marines were sent into the region as part of a multinational peacekeeping force. American involvement in Lebanon's turbulent politics led to the death of 239 marines when a terrorist bomb blew up a barracks in 1983. The marines were withdrawn, and terrorists concluded that the United States would not stand firm in a crisis.

Strategic Defense Initiative In March 1983, the most significant defense policy initiative of the first Reagan term came when the president announced the **Strategic Defense Initiative (SDI)**. Reagan envisioned a system of weapons, based in space, that would intercept and shoot down Soviet missiles before they could reach the United States. An appealing vision on the drawing board or in animated versions for television, SDI confronted immense technical problems that made it unlikely that it could be deployed for years. Critics promptly dubbed it "Star Wars" after the hit movie and questioned its technical rationale. For Reagan, the program represented an answer to the problem of relying on nuclear deterrence to stave off war between the superpowers. He pressed forward with SDI over the objections of his political opponents and the displeasure of the Soviet Union, whose leaders knew that their faltering economy could never duplicate SDI if the Americans ever achieved it.

SOCIAL TENSIONS OF THE 1980S

The possibility of nuclear war was only one of the threats to the American people that contributed to the societal tensions. New medical challenges loomed for Americans, and they confronted as well sweeping changes in technology that would transform lives. Computers and the Internet would begin to reshape communications. Meanwhile, the rise of the religious Right would reveal tensions about fundamental beliefs that would ripple through American history for decades. But first came the specter of AIDS.

The Challenge of AIDS In the early Reagan years Americans learned of a new and deadly disease that scientists called AIDS (for acquired immune deficiency syndrome). The source of the virus was in Africa, and it first appeared in the United States in 1981. The virus ravaged the immune system of its victims, and there was no known cure. Most of those infected were doomed to an inevitable and painful death. By 1989 confirmed AIDS deaths had reached thirty-seven hundred in the United States.

The virus spread within the population through the exchange of bodily fluids. Mothers who were infected passed the condition on to their children; infected blood was transferred during transfusions. The most vulnerable groups were drug addicts, bisexuals, and homosexuals. During the first half of the decade, the spread of AIDS and fears about the fatal prognosis for those who had the disease seemed to be confined to the homosexual community. Later, largely through the sharing of needles for drug injection and unsafe sexual practices, AIDS appeared among heterosexuals, especially in low-income communities. The Reagan administration resisted attempts to distribute condoms to those at high risk for AIDS.

The sudden emergence of the AIDS epidemic was only one of the rash of social and cultural developments of the early 1980s. The nation experienced the initial stages of a revolution in communications and culture that altered American society.

The Personal Computer   In 1981, International Business Machines (IBM) announced that it would market a computer for home use. Recognizing the potential impact of such a product, two young computer software writers proposed to develop the operating system for the new machine. Bill Gates and Paul Allen of Microsoft adapted an existing software program and transformed it into DOS (disk operating system), which ran the hardware created by IBM. Important changes followed throughout the decade, including the Lotus 1-2-3 spreadsheet program in 1982, Microsoft Windows in 1983, and the Apple Macintosh computer in 1984. After January 1983, sales of personal computers rose from twenty thousand annually to more than half a million per year. People found that they could publish books from their desktops, trace financial accounts, make travel reservations, and play a wide assortment of computer games. Growing out of the Advanced Research Projects Agency of the Pentagon was a network of computers founded in 1969. As computer users and researchers exchanged messages over this and other networks in the late 1970s and early 1980s, the National Science Foundation promoted what became known as the Internet as an overall network bulletin board. Usenet groups and e-mail became more common as the 1980s progressed.

The Rise of Cable Television   In 1981, a new network appeared on cable television. Music Television (MTV) presented around-the-clock videos of rock performers aimed at a teenage audience. At about the same time, Ted Turner launched the Cable News Network (CNN) and a related programming service, Headline News, which presented the news in half-hour segments twenty-four hours a day. As cable television expanded during the 1980s, the dominance of the three major television networks (ABC, CBS, and NBC) gave way to a dizzying array of programming that offered viewers such all-sports channels as Entertainment Sports Programming Network (ESPN), all-country-music channels such as Country Music Television (CMT), and several services showing first-run movies. Another popular leisure-time activity was casino gambling that several states adopted at the end of the 1980s.

The American Family in the 1980s   The American people responded to new and troubling changes in the family and its place in society during Reagan's presidency. In 1981, the number of divorces stood at nearly 1.2 million annually, the highest rate ever. At the same time, the number of births to unmarried women rose dramatically during the 1970s. With these developments came a marked increase in the number of single-parent families, which rose from 3.8 million in 1970 to 10.5 million by 1992. The impact of this trend was especially evident among African Americans: by the end of the 1980s, more than 60 percent of all African American families were single-parent families.

The erosion of the traditional family translated into economic hardship for many children of single-parent homes. In 1983, the Bureau of the Census reported that 13 million children under age six were growing up in poverty. Much of the government's spending on efforts to alleviate poverty was directed at the elderly, so by the end of the 1980s, they received from the federal government eleven times the amount spent to address the needs of children.

One major area of concern for families was the state of the public schools. A series of high-profile national studies suggested that American education was "a disaster area." Students did not receive instruction in the skills needed to succeed in a complex and competitive world. Parents complained that their children had to do little homework, were graded too easily, and often graduated from high school without marketable skills. By 1983, another national survey, *A Nation at Risk*, said that the country faced dire consequences if public education did not undergo sweeping reform.

As families felt the effects of these economic and social changes, Americans responded with contradictory approaches. On the one hand, sexual mores became more tolerant. On the other, efforts to recapture "traditional family values" animated many groups on the conservative end of the political spectrum. The boundaries that had governed the depiction of sexual behavior in the movies and on television relaxed in significant ways during the 1980s. On prime-time television, viewers could hear language and see sexual intimacy depicted in a fashion that would have been unthinkable a few years earlier. Materials that previous generations would have considered pornographic now seemed to be readily available, even to children and teenagers.

The Religious Right

A major force in pressing for older cultural values and a return to the precepts of an earlier time was the political power and votes of evangelical Christians. One manifestation of the clout was the **Moral Majority**, an organization founded by the Reverend Jerry Falwell of Virginia in 1979. Falwell tapped into the expanding base of evangelicals in denominations such as the Southern Baptist Convention. The Moral Majority assailed abortion, homosexuality, rock music, and drugs.

Throughout the 1980s, evangelical Christianity permeated American politics. On cable television, viewers tuned in to Pat Robertson's *700 Club* on the Christian Broadcasting Network that Robertson had founded. Other ministers such as Jim Bakker with his *PTL* (Praise the Lord) program and the fiery evangelist Jimmy Swaggart commanded sizable audiences. Though both Bakker and Swaggart eventually ran afoul of the law for fraud (Bakker) and sexual misadventures (Swaggart), their message resonated in many areas of the nation.

The volatile issue of abortion spurred the rise of the Christian Right. Following the Supreme Court decision in *Roe v. Wade* (1973), the number of abortions in the United States stood at 1.5 million per year. Foes of abortion, most notably in the Roman Catholic church and among evangelical Protestants, asserted that the unborn baby was a human being from the moment of conception and entitled to all the rights of a living person. To reduce the number of abortions and to overturn the *Roe* decision, the "right-to-life" forces, as they called themselves, pressured lawmakers to cut back on the right of abortion and to enact restrictive laws.

The antiabortion forces, impatient with legislative action, believed in more direct tactics. They conducted picketing and boycotts of abortion clinics in the 1980s and arranged for massive public demonstrations. Operation Rescue tried to prevent patients from entering abortion clinics. Other protesters turned to bombing of

The 1984 Summer Olympics

Few other events of the 1980s evoked the spirit of the decade more than the Summer Olympic Games held in Los Angeles, California, from July 28 to August 12, 1984. Angry about the boycott of their games in 1980, the Soviet Union and its allies did not participate. The Los Angeles Games had almost everything else that American society wanted. There was the symbol of the games (Sam the Olympic Eagle), theme music by the popular composer John Williams, a tidy profit of $200 million for the event itself, and opening ceremonies with President Ronald Reagan. Extensive coverage from the NBC television network produced a bonanza in the ratings as viewers enjoyed a series of American triumphs from track and field to basketball. The Olympics fed into the revived sense of national purpose that the Reagan administration had done so much to evoke in an election year. More important, the games illustrated how sports, popular culture, and the mass media shape national attitudes about celebrity, recreation, and the role of the individual in a mass society.

(AFP/Getty Images)

buildings that housed clinics and assassination of doctors. The Republican Party became largely antiabortion in its policies and programs. The Democrats were equally committed to what was called "a woman's right to choose" or a "prochoice" position.

THE 1984 PRESIDENTIAL ELECTION

At the beginning of 1984, Reagan's popularity rating stood at 55 percent. The Democratic base in the South was disappearing as former members of that party defected to the Republicans. The president had made substantial gains among what were known as "Reagan Democrats," people who shared the president's social conservatism and disliked the pro–civil rights stances of the Democrats. Even the patriotic pageantry of the Summer Olympics in Los Angeles boosted the president's standing. Reagan's only apparent vulnerability was his age.

Democrats experienced staggering problems in finding a plausible candidate. In the end former vice president **Walter Mondale** of Minnesota turned back the challenge of **Jesse Jackson**, the first credible African American candidate to seek the nomination of a major party, and Senator Gary Hart of Colorado, to lock up the nomination. Mondale came under intense pressure to select a woman as his running mate, and he agreed to the selection of Representative Geraldine Ferraro of New York.

After a stumble in the first of two televised debates, Reagan rebounded in the second appearance with Mondale. When a questioner asked him about his age, the president replied that he would not allow age to be an issue. "I am not going to exploit, for political purposes, my opponent's youth and inexperience," he said. Reagan won by a landslide. He carried forty-nine of the fifty states; Mondale narrowly won his home state and swept the District of Columbia. The president collected 59 percent of the popular vote. The Republicans retained control of the Senate; the Democrats lost seats in the House but maintained their dominance of that chamber.

REAGAN'S SECOND TERM

The economic boom of the mid-1980s that bolstered Reagan's reelection fostered an atmosphere of moneymaking and social acquisitiveness. Top executives received staggering annual salaries. Wall Street experienced a "merger mania" in which corporations acquired competitors through hostile takeovers.

The youth culture reflected the spirit of materialism that permeated the 1980s. In the centers of technological change on the East and West coasts, the press proclaimed the emergence of the "young urban professionals," dubbed "yuppies" by the media. These individuals had cosmetic surgery to retain a young look, took expensive vacations, and purchased costly sports equipment. Self-indulgence seemed to be a hallmark of young people.

Yet a sobering moment in the frenetic decade came on January 28, 1986, when the space shuttle *Challenger* exploded, and all seven crew members perished in the disaster. The event happened live before a shocked audience that watched the spacecraft lift off normally and then explode a few seconds later into a mass of wreckage.

An official investigation followed while the shuttle fleet was grounded. Its proceedings revealed that the space program had grown overconfident about its procedures. Slipshod technology had contributed to the tragedy, but the incident did not undermine the public's faith in scientific progress and material abundance.

Toward Better Relations with the Soviet Union Soviet–American relations entered a new phase when **Mikhail Gorbachev** came to power. Aware of the weaknesses in his society and its economy, Gorbachev pursued a more conciliatory policy toward the West while trying to implement a restructuring of Soviet society that came to be known as *perestroika* (broadly defined as "restructuring"). He announced reductions in the deployment of Soviet missiles and said that the Soviet Union wanted to be part of Europe, not an opposing ideology. He and Reagan agreed to hold a summit conference in Geneva in

The *Challenger* Disaster. *The Challenger disaster in which all the astronauts perished shocked the nation who saw it happen on live television.*

AP Photos

November 1985. Although not much was achieved at the meeting, the two leaders liked each other and met again at Reykjavik, Iceland, in October 1986. There they attempted to outdo each other in calling for reductions in the number of nuclear weapons, with the president even offering to rid the world of all such weapons. Again there were no substantive results, but the experience indicated that a genuine arms agreement might be possible. Both the president and Nancy Reagan hoped to crown Reagan's second term with an arms control treaty that would establish his historical reputation as a peacemaker.

The Iran-Contra Affair

In November 1986 the American public learned that the United States had sold arms to the Islamic regime in Iran that had sponsored terrorist activities for most of the 1980s. Within a month the revelation came that money obtained from the arms sales had been used to support the Nicaraguan Contras in violation of congressional amendments barring the practice.

In 1985, members of the National Security Council (NSC) became convinced that the release of American hostages held in Lebanon could be secured if the United States sold arms to Iran. National security adviser Robert McFarlane believed that alleged "moderates" in Iran (those presumed to be more sympathetic to the West) would use their political influence to free hostages if American weapons were forthcoming. The evidence that such moderation existed in Iran was largely fanciful. The Iranians could use weapons in their bitter war with Iraq, which had been going on since 1982. Since disclosure of this new policy would have outraged Americans and provoked congressional investigations, the president's approval of arm sales was kept secret.

The actual shipment of weapons to Iran was carried out by Israel, with the United States replacing the transferred munitions. Unfortunately, the Iranians accepted the antitank and antiaircraft missiles but released only three hostages. In the course of the arms deals, however, the transactions generated profits. A member of the NSC staff, Marine Colonel **Oliver North**, had what he later called a "neat idea": profits from the sale of weapons to Iran should be used to support the Contras in Nicaragua. Although North maintained that his actions did not break the law, they violated congressional directives barring the provision of aid to the Contras. Moreover, the use of funds without legislative approval was illegal. In addition, a privately financed, unaccountable, and clandestine foreign policy operation was well outside constitutional limits.

News of the scandal leaked out in October 1986 when the Sandinistas shot down one of the planes taking weapons to the Contras and a captured crew member revealed the Central Intelligence Agency's links to the operation. Early in November, news of the arms-for-hostages deal surfaced in the Middle East. The reports did not affect the congressional elections in which the Democrats regained control of the Senate for the first time in six years and retained their majority in the House as well. On November 13, 1986, the president told the American people: "We did not—repeat, did not—trade weapons or anything else for hostages, nor will we." He maintained this position even though it conflicted with the known facts.

Attorney General Edwin Meese conducted a slow, ineffective probe of what had happened. In late November, conclusive proof of the diversion of money to the Contras came out. The president fired Oliver North and accepted the resignation of John Poindexter, McFarlane's successor as national security adviser and one of the central figures in what the press was now calling the **Iran-Contra scandal**.

Reagan appointed the Tower Commission, named after its chair, former Senator John Tower of Texas, to look into the White House's role in the scheme. The House and Senate created a joint committee to examine the policy and its execution. The lawmakers soon decided to grant immunity to many of the involved individuals in exchange for their testimony. That decision hampered the task of the special counsel, Lawrence Walsh, who was named to consider whether specific laws had been violated.

Although everyone concerned professed a desire to get to the bottom of the scandal, there was little inclination, even among Democrats, to see Ronald Reagan impeached for his role in it. His second term had only a year and a half to run, and many Washington insiders questioned whether it would be good for the country to have another president driven from office in disgrace.

The Tower Commission, for its part, chastised the president for an inept "management style" that allowed his subordinates to lead him into the scandal. On March 4, 1987, Reagan said that he accepted the commission's findings and reiterated that he had not intended to trade arms for hostages. His poll ratings rose, and once again the public responded to his leadership.

North and the other participants were indicted by Lawrence Walsh and convicted for some of their misdeeds, including perjury, mishandling government moneys, and other crimes. Because Congress had granted them immunity, however, higher courts overturned their convictions on the ground that the trials had been influenced by what had been heard in the congressional proceedings.

Whatever the legalities of the Iran-Contra affair, it demonstrated the weaknesses of Reagan's handling of foreign policy. Reagan had failed to ask hard questions about the arms-for-hostages proposals and had allowed erratic subordinates like North to mishandle the nation's foreign policy.

Remaking the Supreme Court: The Nomination of Robert Bork
One of the Reagan administration's major goals was to make the federal judiciary more conservative. The White House succeeded in doing so in the lower courts because, during eight years in office, Reagan nominated more than half the members of the federal judiciary. In July 1981, Reagan named the first woman to be appointed to the Court, **Sandra Day O'Connor** of Arizona. The president did not have another opportunity to appoint a justice until Chief Justice Warren Burger resigned in 1986. Reagan elevated Justice William Rehnquist to replace Burger and named Antonin Scalia, a federal appeals court judge, to take the seat that Rehnquist vacated.

In June 1987, after the Democrats had regained control of the Senate, Justice Lewis Powell resigned, and President Reagan named Robert Bork, another federal appeals court jurist, to replace him. During a long career as a legal writer before becoming a judge, Bork had taken many controversial stands on divisive issues. He had opposed the decision in *Roe v. Wade* (1973) that established a woman's right to have an abortion, and he had questioned other decisions in the areas of privacy and civil rights. The nomination galvanized Democrats in the Senate, the civil rights movement, and women's groups in a campaign to defeat Bork.

The judge's admirers claimed that his enemies had distorted his record, but his foes were able to depict Bork as a conservative ideologue outside the mainstream of American judicial thinking. Bork's performance before the Senate Judiciary Committee failed to counteract the negative public opinion that his opposition had generated. In October 1987, Bork was defeated when fifty-eight senators voted against him. Anthony Kennedy was nominated and confirmed to the Court early in 1988.

Reagan and Gorbachev: The Road to Understanding
The Iran-Contra affair produced changes in Reagan's administration that prepared the way for genuine foreign policy achievements. Former Senator Howard Baker became Reagan's chief of staff, Frank Carlucci was named secretary of defense, and Lieutenant General **Colin Powell** served as the national security adviser. These more pragmatic operators encouraged Reagan to seek further negotiations with the Soviets. By late 1987, negotiators for the two sides had agreed to remove from Europe intermediate-range missiles with nuclear warheads. Gorbachev came to Washington in December 1987 for the formal signing of the pact. Seven months later, Reagan went to Moscow to meet Gorbachev in an atmosphere of hope and reconciliation. Tensions between the two countries eased as the Soviets pulled out of Afghanistan and indicated that they no longer intended to stir up international problems. The improvement in the superpower rivalry helped Reagan regain some of his popularity with the American people as his administration neared its end.

THE 1988 PRESIDENTIAL ELECTION

With Ronald Reagan ineligible to seek a third term, the Republican Party had to pick his successor, and Vice President George Bush soon emerged as the front-runner. **George H. W. Bush** came from an aristocratic New England background but had moved to Texas after combat service in the navy during World War II. Elected to the House of Representatives in 1966, he stayed for two terms and made a losing bid for the Senate in 1970. Service in the Ford administration as envoy to China and director of the Central Intelligence Agency added to his impressive roster of government posts. He ran against Reagan for the Republican nomination in 1980 and became the vice-presidential choice despite doubts among conservatives about his allegiance to their cause. Bush's superior organization and strength in the South enabled him to defeat Senator Robert Dole of Kansas.

At the Republican convention in New Orleans, Bush's major decision involved the issue of deficits and taxes. In his acceptance speech, he predicted that Democrats in Congress would pressure him to raise taxes. He promised to reject all such proposals. "Read my lips," was his answer to Democrats. "No new taxes!"

The Democratic Choice   With Reagan no longer a candidate, Democrats believed that they now had a chance to retake the White House. Out of the field of several candidates, Massachusetts Governor Michael Dukakis emerged as the best-financed and best-organized contender. Dukakis emphasized his family's Greek immigrant background and stressed his success in stimulating the Massachusetts economy during the 1980s. Democrats paid less attention to his tepid personality and lackluster abilities as a campaigner. When the Democratic convention ended, Dukakis had a strong lead in the public opinion polls.

The Republicans raised questions about Dukakis that undermined his lead. The most penetrating of these issues had to do with prison furloughs that Massachusetts law granted to jailed criminals. In one case, a black convict named William Horton had been released on furlough, then fled Massachusetts and committed a rape in another state. The Republicans and their surrogates used the "Willie" Horton case in powerful television commercials to demonstrate what they viewed as Dukakis's ineptitude as governor, but the racial dimensions of the incident were also evident. Bush won the election with a solid margin in the electoral vote, though the Democrats retained control of Congress.

The Reagan Legacy   Even before Ronald Reagan left office, the debate about the impact of his presidency began. His partisans proclaimed the "Reagan Revolution" had transformed American attitudes toward government. They also assigned him a major role in winning the Cold War. Critics pointed to the huge federal budget deficits and growing national debt that persisted throughout the 1980s, blamed Reagan for policies that had widened the gap between rich and poor, and pointed out that he had failed to address serious urban problems.

Both Reagan's admirers and his enemies overstated his influence on American history. By the early twenty-first century, the nation still seemed to want a smaller government in theory and more government services in practice. Reagan had halted the expansion of the welfare state, but that would probably have occurred in any event by the 1980s. Reagan certainly deserved some credit for the decline of the Soviet Union, though that nation's internal difficulties were more significant than the actions of the United States at the end of the Cold War. Reagan's most enduring legacy was the burgeoning federal debt. Although Congress appropriated the money, he set national priorities, and his spending for defense went well beyond affordable levels. Reagan proved that big spenders could come in conservative as well as liberal models.

THE BUSH SUCCESSION

George H. W. Bush pledged to carry on Reagan's policies, but promised to do so in a more humane and judicious manner. He spoke of a "kinder, gentler" nation and government that would carry out conservative programs with less harshness than had marked the Reagan years. Foreign affairs interested the new president much more than did shaping policy on health care, the environment, or social policy. He had an effective foreign policy team. His secretary of state, James A. Baker, was a close friend and an adroit power broker; the national security adviser, Brent Scowcroft, and the chair of the Joint Chiefs of Staff, General Colin Powell, executed the president's policies with skill and efficiency. The collapse of communism in 1989–1990, the challenge of Iraqi expansionism in the Middle East, and the shaping of a new role for the United States gave the Bush administration's foreign policy makers much to do.

The first half of the Bush administration went very well. The president relished the art of governing and approached his job by engaging in a frenzy of activity. His press conferences demonstrated his command of information in a way that Reagan had never displayed. The public became used to seeing Bush jogging, entertaining numerous visitors to the White House, and rushing around the country from one event to another.

As time passed, however, questions arose about the purpose behind all this frenetic exertion. Bush spoke of the need to set larger goals for his presidency. He called it, in the abrupt shorthand that he often employed, "the vision thing." The phrase came into general use in discussions of whether Bush wanted to accomplish anything as president or simply wished to occupy the nation's highest office.

Bush's Domestic Policy   The president and his chief of staff, John Sununu, had no intention of breaking new ground in domestic affairs. They wanted to accomplish whatever they could without violating the campaign pledge of "no new taxes." Much to the dismay of Republican conservatives, Bush went along with Democratic legislation such as the Clean Air Act and the Americans with Disabilities Act, which involved a growth in the federal bureaucracy and expanded regulations. Any legislation that he did not like, such as an increase in the minimum wage, he vetoed. During the first three years of his presidency, Congress failed to override any of Bush's twenty-eight vetoes.

On some domestic issues, Bush favored exhortation over government programs. He promised to be the "education president" but left most of the responsibility for changes in the system to the states and localities. The Bush administration continued the "war on drugs" that Richard Nixon had begun, with emphasis on stopping the inflow of narcotics to the United States rather than reducing the demand for them among the population. An overall decline in drug use enabled the administration to claim victory for its strategy.

By 1989, however, the Bush administration had to deal with another major domestic issue. The deregulated savings and loan industry had a major collapse that left the taxpayers with a $500 billion cost to bail out depositors for the failed institutions. Congress established the Resolution Trust Corporation to sell off the assets of the failed banks and savings and loans and to obtain as much money as possible from their sale.

The Continuing AIDS Crisis

Both funding for research on AIDS and public awareness of the disease increased during the Bush years. Congress created the National Commission on AIDS in 1989, and federal government funds for treatment and research rose to over $2 billion by 1992. Still, the number of new cases continued to increase, reaching 45,603 in 1992 and 83,814 a year later. Total deaths from AIDS in the United States numbered 198,000. However, opinions regarding what to do about the epidemic remained polarized. AIDS activists wanted more money for research and greater cultural tolerance for those afflicted with the disease. Conservatives like Senator Jesse Helms of North Carolina contended that most AIDS victims were homosexuals who had brought their condition on themselves through their own behavior.

Foreign Policy Successes, 1989–1990

At the end of 1988, Gorbachev had told the United Nations that the nations of Eastern Europe were free to determine their own destiny without Soviet interference. During 1989, the old order in Eastern Europe crumbled. Poland held free elections, Hungary allowed its borders to open, and East Germany eased barriers to travel to West Germany. By the end of 1989, the Cold War seemed to be over, with the United States the clear winner. In Nicaragua, voters ousted the unpopular Sandinista government in 1990.

The Bush administration handled these developments carefully. Mindful of the nuclear weapons in the hands of the Soviet military, the president avoided gloating over the success of the West. The trend in favor of the United States continued into 1990 as Gorbachev, in February, renounced the Communist Party's monopoly over political power. The White House faced hard choices about which leader to support as rivals to Gorbachev emerged during 1990, particularly the new president of the Russian Republic, Boris Yeltsin.

One country where the administration's foreign policy encountered difficulty was China. Student protests during the spring of 1989 led to a brutal crackdown on demonstrators in Beijing's **Tiananmen Square.** The spectacle of students being killed and wounded, as well as the repressive policies of the Chinese government, produced an

AIDS

P R E V E N T I O N

UNIVERSITY OF CALIFORNIA, BERKELEY · STUDENT HEALTH SERVICE

(Library of Congress)

AIDS Poster. *The AIDS epidemic was frightening to many Americans during the 1980s as warnings about the deadly nature of the disease proflierated.*

outcry in the United States. However, Bush believed that it was important to maintain good relations with the Chinese leaders, so the administration's response to the events of June 1989 was muted and cautious.

Closer to home, the Bush administration took more decisive action toward Panama's strongman ruler, Manuel Noriega. Corrupt and deeply involved in the international narcotics trade, Noriega had been on the U.S. payroll for many years as an informant on drug matters. In 1989, his dictatorial regime refused to adhere to the results of national elections. The White House sent additional troops to Panama and called for an uprising against Noriega. For his part, Noriega declared a state of war on American military personnel and ordered that their families be captured and tortured.

In late December, the United States launched an invasion that quickly overcame the Panamanian army. Noriega eluded capture for a few embarrassing days until he sought refuge in a Vatican embassy. In early 1990, he surrendered to the Americans and in 1992 was tried and convicted of drug trafficking in a federal court in Florida.

By the spring of 1990, President Bush's pledge of "no new taxes" had become ingrained in the minds of the American people. Conservative Republicans expected him to adhere to the commitment in spite of the desire of the Democratic majorities in Congress to raise taxes as a means of dealing with the budget deficit. In 1989, the president worked out a strategy with Congress that provided for budget savings. Bush also wanted to lower the tax rate on capital gains, but that legislation became stalled in the Senate. With the budget deficit growing, however, the Democrats did not see how spending cuts alone could reduce it. Having suffered setbacks in the 1988 elections, the Democrats were not going to propose tax increases unless President Bush agreed to them.

During early 1990, there were signs that the economy had begun to slow down. The gross domestic product had grown slowly in 1989, there had been a slight loss in manufacturing jobs, and producer prices had risen. With a weakening economy, a budget stalemate posed dangers for both parties, and neither side wanted to face the implications of serious budget cuts.

Negotiations between the president and congressional Democrats continued until, on June 26, 1990, Bush announced that dealing with the deficit problem might have to include "tax revenue increases." Republicans reacted with fury. Although the reversal of "no new taxes" may have made economic and political sense to those close to Bush, the president had squandered much of the trust that the American people had placed in him in 1988.

Iraq and Kuwait   Foreign policy events soon overshadowed the political fallout from the broken tax pledge. On August 2, 1990, the Iraqi army of Saddam Hussein invaded the oil-rich kingdom of Kuwait and seized it within a few days. Suddenly the oil supplies of the United States and the industrialized world faced a new and ominous threat from the Iraqi dictator. Bush's response and the war that followed restored his popularity temporarily and seemed at the time to make his reelection a certainty.

During the 1980s, Iran and Iraq had fought a brutal and costly war that had drained the human and material resources of both countries. The United States had not taken sides in the conflict, hoping that the two countries, both of which were hostile toward the United States, would exhaust each other. Once the war ended, however, the Bush administration had pursued a conciliatory policy, allowing Iraq to purchase heavy machinery and paying little attention to its efforts to build a nuclear bomb and acquire weapons of mass destruction. During the spring of 1990, the American ambassador in Baghdad had informed Hussein that the United States took "no position" on Iraq's dispute with Kuwait. In fact, the Iraqis regarded Kuwait as part of their nation.

When Iraqi military units rolled into Kuwait, Bush decided that the takeover must be resisted. "Iraq will not be permitted to annex Kuwait," he told Congress. Heavy economic sanctions were put into effect. More important, in Operation Desert Shield, the United States deployed American troops in Saudi Arabia to deter Hussein from attacking that country. Behind the scenes, the administration had already decided that if necessary, it would use military force to oust the Iraqis from Kuwait.

For the remainder of 1990, the Bush administration moved military forces into Saudi Arabia. The end of the Cold War meant that the United States had the support of the Soviet Union in isolating Iraq from the rest of the world and therefore had much greater freedom of action than would have been the case even two years earlier.

The Budget Battle On the domestic side, the budget issue remained unsettled until the president and the Democratic leadership worked out a deficit reduction plan in September 1990. Republicans in the House of Representatives lobbied against the plan, which was defeated a few days later. Intense negotiations between the White House and Capitol Hill produced a deficit reduction agreement at the end of October that involved both tax increases and spending cuts. Angry Republicans charged that Bush had capitulated to the opposition. The Republicans went into the fall elections in a divided and unhappy mood. Their losses were modest—eight seats in the House and one in the Senate—but the conservative faithful continued to smolder with anger against Bush.

War in the Persian Gulf After the elections, Bush stepped up the pressure on Saddam Hussein to leave Kuwait. The United Nations Security Council agreed to the use of armed force against Iraq if Kuwait had not been freed by January 15, 1991. As the diplomatic options faded, Congress insisted on a vote over whether American troops should go into combat in the Middle East. The result, on January 12, 1991, was a victory for the president, although the margin in the Senate was only five votes. Five days later, Operation Desert Storm began.

In a devastating series of strikes, the allied coalition bombed the Iraqi army into submission. The most that Hussein could do in retaliation was to send missiles against Israel in hopes of fracturing the coalition. The Iraqi ruler also set Kuwaiti oil wells on fire and dumped oil into the Persian Gulf. None of these actions, however, posed a serious threat to the buildup of the allied armies.

The second phase of Desert Storm began on February 24, 1991, with a huge assault of American and allied troops against the weakened Iraqi defenders. A series of encircling maneuvers ousted the Iraqis from Kuwait with huge losses in troops and equipment. Estimates of the number of Iraqi soldiers killed ranged as high as 100,000. American deaths totaled 148, including 11 women. Within one hundred hours, the ground phase of the war ended in a complete victory on the battlefield for the anti-Iraq forces. President Bush decided not to press for Hussein's removal from power, a decision that was later criticized, and key units of the Iraqi army were left intact to

Victory in the Gulf War

The war in the Persian Gulf produced striking images of victory such as the one below of a U.S. soldier standing on top of a military vehicle. President George H. W. Bush and others proclaimed that the coalition triumph had erased "the Vietnam Syndrome" from American life. The hundred-hour war played well on television, and Bush's popularity soared for a time. The failure to end the rule of Saddam Hussein, however, meant that the apparent military success was incomplete. In the dozen years that followed, Hussein reemerged as a threat, and by 2003 the second war in the Persian Gulf occurred. A picture that seemed to mark an American victory when it was taken thus became a testament to a continuing problem with terrorism and nations such as Iraq that resisted the will of the international community.

(© Peter Turnley/CORBIS)

fight again against their own people. The Bush administration warned that an effort to oust Hussein would have fractured the coalition and raised the prospect of a protracted war against an Iraqi resistance.

Victory in the Gulf War sent Bush's popularity soaring to record levels; he received approval ratings of nearly 90 percent in some polls. The nation basked in the glow of military success, which seemed to end the sense of self-doubt that had persisted since the Vietnam War. Bush's reelection seemed assured. Major figures in the Democratic Party decided not to challenge Bush in 1992.

Yet the political dividends from Bush's military triumph did not last long. Hussein bounced back from his defeat to reassert his power in Iraq and, despite United Nations inspections, rebuilt his nation's economy. Other international problems troubled the White House during 1991. In Russia, Gorbachev faced a coup designed to bring hardliners back into power. A rival of Gorbachev, Boris Yeltsin, led demonstrations against the plotters in Moscow and their coup, which then failed. The Soviet Union collapsed, and its component nations broke apart. Yeltsin consolidated his power with promises of economic reform and put himself in a position to succeed Gorbachev. With the demise of the Soviet Union, the major threat of the Cold War had ended, but the instability in Eastern Europe posed new threats to world peace.

One area of turmoil was Yugoslavia, where the Communist government had long suppressed historic rivalries among Serbs, Croats, Bosnians, and other nationalities. Tensions between Christians and Muslims added to the dangerous potential of the situation. Civil war broke out in 1991 as Serbs battled Croats, Slovenes, and Bosnians. The Bush administration recognized Bosnia as an independent nation and thus became involved in a Balkan struggle whose problems spilled over into the next presidency.

The Battle over the Clarence Thomas Nomination

Like Ronald Reagan, George H. W. Bush wanted to continue the conservative trend that the Supreme Court had been following since the 1970s. That goal seemed even more important in the light of the Court's ruling in *Webster v. Reproductive Health Services* (1989), whereby the justices decided in a 5–4 ruling that states could set limits on the ability to obtain an abortion. Any change in the Court could affect that volatile controversy. When the liberal justice William Brennan retired in 1990, the president named David Souter of New Hampshire to succeed him. Confirmation by the Senate came easily because no one was quite sure where Souter stood on abortion.

The next nomination, in 1991, led to one of the most sensational confirmation struggles in the nation's history. When Justice Thurgood Marshall retired, many wondered whether Bush would name an African American to succeed him. The president selected **Clarence Thomas**, a Reagan appointee to the federal bench who had long opposed such programs as affirmative action.

Thomas's qualifications for the Supreme Court were modest, but he seemed to be on the way to easy confirmation until it was revealed that a black law professor at the University of Oklahoma, **Anita Hill**, had accused Thomas of sexual harassment when she had worked for him at the Equal Employment Opportunity Commission during the early 1980s. Her charges led to dramatic hearings in which Hill laid out her allegations and Thomas denied them. A national television audience watched the hearings in fascination. In the end, the Senate voted 52 to 48 to confirm Thomas, who proved to be an intense advocate of conservative positions.

DOING HISTORY ONLINE

The New World Order

Based on the documents online, write a thesis paragraph that articulates the principles that guided American foreign policy during the George H. W. Bush presidency

www.cengage.com/history/ayers/ampassages4e

AN ANGRY NATION

Meanwhile, no strong Democratic candidates had emerged to challenge Bush, who had the support of most Republicans, although there were rumblings of opposition among conservatives. It seemed probable, however, that Bush would be renominated and would then defeat whomever the Democrats put up against him. After twelve years of Bush and Reagan, the Republican coalition seemed in solid control of the nation's politics and its policy agenda.

When the Republicans made such optimistic assumptions, they failed to notice that the American people were anxious and fearful as the 1990s began. Major corporations had cut their payrolls to reduce costs in what became known as "downsizing." Large firms like IBM, Procter & Gamble, and Chrysler Corporation trimmed their payrolls dramatically, and IBM reduced its workforce by 100,000. Other businesses moved production facilities overseas in search of lower labor costs. The economy created millions of jobs, but many of them were low-paying service jobs. Multinational corporations became a focus of voter anger, as did the specter of immigrants taking jobs away from native-born Americans.

Although the Gulf War had lifted President Bush's popularity, his poll ratings receded from those lofty levels during 1991 and then dropped further. The president seemed to many Americans to have little awareness of their problems and hopes. Nonetheless, he survived a challenge from within the Grand Old Party and secured renomination. His Democratic opponent was the governor of Arkansas, **William Jefferson ("Bill") Clinton**.

Clinton aroused conflicting passions. He was a young, attractive, southern governor who campaigned as a "New Democrat" with a strong civil rights record. He had supported education and economic growth in Arkansas. Critics charged that he was a womanizer who had also evaded the draft during the Vietnam War. His business dealings also raised questions.

Racial rioting in Los Angeles during the spring of 1992 underscored the tense nature of national attitudes. Sparked by the acquittal of Los Angeles police officers on trial for beating **Rodney King**, a black suspect in their custody, the violence showed that passions over race smoldered while the nation's political leadership ignored these problems.

Many citizens, especially Republicans, looked for an alternative to a Bush–Clinton matchup. A Texas computer billionaire named Ross Perot seemed a plausible alternative. Plainspoken and tough-talking, the feisty Perot argued that professional politicians lacked the will to engage the nation's problems. Announcing his candidacy on talk show host Larry King's national call-in television program, Perot shot up in the polls.

Soon a grass-roots movement had Perot on the ballot in every state. He led Bush and Clinton in the polls. He did not say how he would fix the budget deficit and clean up Washington; he would just do so. As the media investigated his previous record in business and politics, evidence of erratic and silly behavior surfaced. He monitored the private lives of his employees; some called him "Inspector Perot." His poll numbers tanked. Just before the Democratic National Convention, Perot withdrew from the race.

The 1992 Election Campaign   Bill Clinton received a boost when Perot left the campaign. The Arkansas governor selected Senator Albert Gore of Tennessee as his running mate. The presence of two southerners on the national ticket defied political wisdom, but the voters liked the youthful and energetic Democratic team. Clinton's lead in the polls widened before the Republicans held their convention in August.

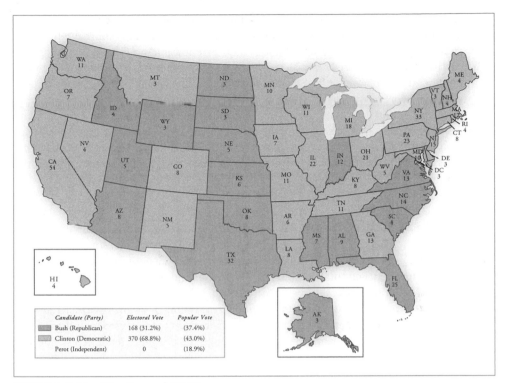

Candidate (Party)	Electoral Vote	Popular Vote
Bush (Republican)	168 (31.2%)	(37.4%)
Clinton (Democratic)	370 (68.8%)	(43.0%)
Perot (Independent)	0	(18.9%)

MAP 31.2 The Election of 1992

This map shows the ability of Bill Clinton to capitalize on the discontent with George H. W. Bush and the Republicans to achieve a landslide electoral victory. Because Clinton received only 43 percent of the votes, however, Republicans soon questioned his legitimacy as president.

The Republicans renominated Bush amid an atmosphere in which the conservative social agenda dominated. In a fiery speech, Patrick Buchanan, a conservative commentator, declared a cultural war to reclaim America from liberals, immigrants, and homosexuals. He assailed Hillary Clinton as well. The spectacle added to Bill Clinton's support, especially with women voters in the nation's suburbs.

Perot came back into the race in October 1992 and participated in the debates with Clinton and Bush. Voter interest in the election was high. Bush closed the gap somewhat during the final weeks of the campaign, but the Perot candidacy split the Republican base in many states. The result was a Clinton–Gore victory. Perot made the best popular showing of any third-party candidate but won no electoral votes. The Democrats continued their control of Congress, but the Republicans gained one Senate seat and picked up fourteen members of the House. A notable feature of the 1992 election was the addition of three female members to the U.S. Senate. Pundits dubbed it "the year of the woman."

The Difficult Opening of the Clinton Presidency Clinton's presidency faltered even before he took office. As one of his first announced priorities, the president-elect indicated that he intended to lift the long-standing ban against declared homosexuals serving in the armed forces. After much debate within the military, the Clinton administration adopted a "Don't Ask, Don't Tell" approach in which gay personnel would not be asked about their orientation and should not be openly homosexual. This stance contradicted Clinton's electoral appeal as a moderate rather than liberal Democrat. Meanwhile, the right wing of the Republicans began an assault on the president and his wife that would continue for the next four years.

After Clinton was inaugurated, an armed confrontation between agents of the Bureau of Alcohol, Tobacco, and Firearms and members of the **Branch Davidian** religious sect outside Waco, Texas, in April 1993 led to the fiery deaths of many of the Davidians. Opponents of gun control and the federal government contended that the Clinton administration envisioned dictatorial rule. That fear on the far right further sparked discontent with the new president.

Clinton's Domestic Agenda　　During his first two years, Bill Clinton achieved several domestic objectives at a high political cost. With the barest of voting margins in the House and Senate, he secured adoption of an economic package that combined tax increases and spending cuts to lower to the deficit for 1993 to $255 billion and for 1994 to $203 billion. Republicans depicted Clinton as returning to a traditional Democratic strategy of raising taxes, and they predicted economic calamity ahead. Clinton responded that the burden of higher levies fell only on the wealthiest Americans. Although the economy remained strong and the nation was prosperous throughout 1993 and 1994, the Republicans won the political argument against the Democratic tax legislation.

Clinton pursued the cause of freer world trade when he advocated passage of the North American Free Trade Agreement (NAFTA), which cleared Congress in late 1993. The trade agreement split the Democrats, and approval came with the help of Republican votes. In late 1994, the White House also secured congressional endorsement of the General Agreement on Tariffs and Trade among nations engaged in international trade (GATT) in a lame-duck session of the Democratic Congress. Again, Republican votes were central to this administration victory.

The Failure of Health Care Reform　　The major domestic goal of the new administration was reform of the nation's system of health care. Nearly 40 million citizens did not have health insurance, and the costs of medical care were rising at an alarming rate. In a dramatic expansion of the responsibilities for first ladies, the president asked Hillary Clinton to head the task force to prepare a health care plan within one hundred days. Working throughout 1993, Hillary Clinton's planners produced a health care blueprint in September. It envisioned health alliances to emphasize managed care, asked Americans to pay more to consult private physicians, and expanded to coverage to include all citizens.

The plan soon became the target of attacks from Republicans and the insurance companies as too bureaucratic, complex, and costly. The insurance industry used effective television ads of a mythical couple named "Harry and Louise" discussing the alleged drawbacks of the Clinton plan. Despite the intense lobbying efforts of Hillary Clinton, the "Clinton Health Plan," as it was known, had few friends in Congress. Republicans denied that any serious health care reform was needed and refused to present alternatives of their own. The drumbeat of opposition from the insurance industry took its toll on public opinion. By 1994 the health care issue had become a major liability for the Clinton White House.

Clinton's Political Troubles Despite his domestic accomplishments, President Clinton's popular approval ratings remained low, often below 50 percent of the electorate. From the political right, the president and his wife stirred dislike that bordered on outright hatred. Republicans charged that the Clintons were socialists bent on entrenching homosexuals, bureaucrats, and atheists in power. When an aide to the president, Vincent Foster, committed suicide during the summer of 1993, right-wing talk show hosts circulated wild and unfounded rumors that Foster had been murdered at the instructions of the president and his wife.

Hillary Clinton Testifying on Health Care. *Hillary Clinton took first lady activism to a more involved level. She testified before Congress on behalf of her health care plan in 1993.*

More serious were the charges of financial improprieties and ethical lapses that dogged the Clintons from their years in Arkansas. Investments that they had made in an Arkansas real estate venture on the Whitewater River became entangled with the failed savings and loan firm run by business associates of the Clintons, James and Susan McDougal. Federal investigators grew interested in these transactions, and in 1993 press reports disclosed that the Clintons could be named as potential witness and even targets of an investigation. Accusations soon surfaced that an effort at a cover-up had been mounted from the White House. The all-purpose label for these and other related scandals was "Whitewater." As subsequent investigations revealed, the allegations about their finances had little basis in fact, but an impression of corruption provided a useful weapon to their enemies.

The charges against the Clintons led to the appointment of an independent counsel, or special prosecutor, in 1994. When the first counsel, Robert Fiske, concluded that Vincent Foster's death was a suicide, angry conservatives had him replaced with another counsel, Kenneth Starr, a former federal judge and Bush administration lawyer.

Personally embarrassing to President Clinton were allegations that he had sexually harassed an Arkansas state employee, Paula Corbin Jones, in 1991. Jones filed a civil law suit in the spring of 1994 in which she claimed that then Governor Clinton had made unwanted sexual advances in a hotel room, including exposing himself to her.

The president's lawyers attempted to have the suit delayed until after the end of his administration on the grounds that such litigation disrupted his ability to carry out his official duties.

Clinton and the World

Bill Clinton came into office with his mind concentrated on domestic issues, and, as a result, his foreign policy got off to a rocky start. He faced a complex set of circumstances in early 1993. The United States was heavily involved around the globe—Haiti, Bosnia, and Somalia—but the Bush administration had not linked these to any kind of coherent structure other than George H. W. Bush's vague references to a "New World Order."

Clinton's first year produced a number of foreign policy problems that created an image of a president out of his depth on the world stage. In October 1993, eighteen American servicemen died in a raid in Somalia that included television footage of crowds dragging the body of an American pilot through the streets. The White House also suffered a setback in Haiti after a peacekeeping force was repulsed by angry inhabits of the islands.

The main foreign policy dilemma of these initial months was Bosnia. With United Nations peace-keeping troops, predominantly British and French, on the ground, the military options for Clinton were limited because the first targets of retaliation would be the allied troops. Working through the United Nations also proved frustrating for the White House. Tensions rose between Washington and its allies throughout 1993 over the proper course of action in the Balkans.

In less publicized ways, the administration had some accomplishments on the world stage. It obtained the withdrawal of Russian troops from the Baltic Republic of Estonia in 1994. Clinton also brokered peace negotiations among Ireland, Great Britain, and the Irish Republican Army's political arm Sinn Fein ("Ourselves Alone"). In the Middle East, State Department negotiators facilitated talks between Yasir Arafat of the Palestine Liberation Organization and Prime Minister Yitzhak Rabin of Israel that led to a celebrated handshake on the White House lawn. The United States intervened in Haiti in 1994 and produced the ouster of the military rulers as a prelude to a more democratic government.

The perception that Clinton was ineffective in foreign policy exacerbated his political troubles at home. During his first two years in office, the president's popularity ratings fell, his hold on the country remained weak, and there was speculation that he would be another one-term president. On the Right, the determination to oust Clinton in 1996 gathered momentum.

THE REPUBLICAN REVOLUTION: 1994

By 1994, the cumulative effect of the charges against the president and a Republican resurgence from the setback of 1992 transformed the political scene as the congressional elections approached. In the House of Representatives, the Republicans chose as their next leader their ideological champion, **Newton** ("Newt") **Gingrich** of Georgia. An adroit political tactician, the burly, rumpled Gingrich used the television coverage of Congress that began in the late 1970s (called C-SPAN) to broadcast his ideas to a national constituency. His militancy contributed to a partisan intensity in the House,

The Republican Revolution of 1994

The Republican takeover of Congress in 1994 was orchestrated by Newt Gingrich of Georgia, pictured here with his fellow GOP House candidates on September 27, 1994. The use of striking visuals such as the blue background for the "Contract with America" slogan and the American flags that the candidates wave attest to the influence of television on how political campaigns are marketed. The provisions of the contract had also been poll-tested with focus groups to ensure the maximum electoral popularity.

This photograph shows how American politics in the 1990s had become a series of visually alluring, highly staged productions designed not to address substantive issues but to evoke a desire response from viewers. The Republicans in 1994 proved far more adept at turning the techniques of show business and Hollywood to their advantage than did their Democratic rivals.

John Duricka/AP Photos

and he achieved the ouster of Speaker Jim Wright from office for financial misconduct in 1991. Conservative members of the House rallied to Gingrich's campaign.

To dramatize their appeal, Gingrich and the Republicans offered **A Contract with America** as their election platform. Composed of proposals tested in focus groups for their popularity with the voters, the contract promised action on a balanced budget amendment, term limits for Congress members, and making legislators obey the regulations they applied to society. All of these measures and others would be acted on within the first one hundred days of a Republican victory. As the elections began, the Republicans found their poll numbers rising and the Democrats in retreat, as the prospect of regaining control of the House became a real possibility for the first time in forty years.

On election night, the Republicans swept to victory. They had 235 seats in the House to 197 for the Democrats, and they controlled the Senate by a margin of 53 to 47. Newt Gingrich became Speaker of the House and Robert Dole the majority leader. The elections immediately prompted predictions that President Clinton's prospects for regaining the White House in 1996 were bleak. More important, conservatives now believed that they had a genuine chance to reshape the nation according to their vision of a proper society. In short, they would, so they said, prove that the election of Clinton had been only a fluke in the movement for conservative ascendancy that began with the election of Ronald Reagan in 1980.

CONCLUSION

The Reagan–Bush years began with a national mood of apprehension and fear about the future. Twelve years of Republican rule saw the end of communism, victory in the Gulf War, and the return of economic prosperity in the 1980s. Yet for all the rhetoric about "morning in America" under Reagan and "a New World Order" under George H. W. Bush, the reality did not add up to the sunny prospects that the triumph over communism was supposed to bring. In 1992, the nation turned to a younger politician from the baby-boom generation, Bill Clinton. His first two years proved a series of setbacks, and the result was the election of a Republican Congress. In the period of political polarization that ensued, the American people experienced even greater economic prosperity in the 1990s until the threat of terrorism and the looming crisis of climate change imposed even greater challenges on the United States and its future.

CHAPTER REVIEW, 1981–1995

- The United States incurred large budget deficits.
- The nation embarked on a program to build up national defense.
- Computers became an integral part of the economy and communication system.
- There was increasing political polarization over issues such as abortion.
- The Cold War drew to a close with a total victory for the United States and its allies.
- The Middle East emerged as an even more crucial foreign policy challenge during the first Iraq war.
- The United States moved to the right during the presidencies of Ronald Reagan and George H. W. Bush.
- The election of Bill Clinton produced further social tension.
- The Republicans regained control of Congress.

⬅ ॥ *Looking Back*

Chapter 31 examines the impact of the Ronald Reagan, George H. W. Bush, and Bill Clinton administrations in the context of the 1980s and early 1990s. A key point in the chapter is the nation's rightward shift in political terms and the consequences of that change for foreign policy and domestic priorities.

1. What problems confronted the new Reagan administration in 1981 as a result of the events of the Carter administration?
2. What was the international position in economic, political, and military terms relative to the Soviet Union in the early 1980s?
3. In what ways did Ronald Reagan change the role of the president? Which of his achievements have proved the most enduring and which the most controversial?
4. What were the most significant cultural and economic changes Americans experienced during the 1980s and early 1990s?
5. Was the first Iraq war as much of a victory as it was portrayed at the time?
6. How did Bill Clinton benefit from a mood for change and then suffer political reverses because of that same mood?

Looking Ahead ॥➡

The concluding chapter of the book considers the administrations of Bill Clinton and George W. Bush. The problem of terrorism, which was barely on the national agenda as this chapter comes to an end, will arise as a central concern of domestic and foreign policy as we assess the current situation in the United States.

1. How did the dislike for Bill Clinton on the Right shape the way politics evolved during the 1990s?
2. What economic choices did the people of the United States have to make in the mid-1990s as a result of the actions taken between 1981 and 1995?
3. Why were policy makers, the media, and the people generally slow to grasp the dangers of terrorism?
4. How did the legacy of Ronald Reagan affect the politics of the 1990s?
5. Has the second Iraq war made the United States more or less safe?

Go to the American Passages website at www.cengage.com/history/ayers/ampassages4e for additional review materials.

32

A Conservative Nation in a Globalizing World, 1995–2008

INTRODUCTION

The years that followed the Republican takeover of Congress in 1994 produced a series of disturbing shocks for the American people. After Bill Clinton won reelection in 1996, a personal scandal involving his sexual behavior led to his impeachment and acquittal in 1999. The disputed presidential election of 2000 strained the nation's political institutions. In the next year, the terrorist attacks of September 2001 ushered in wars in Afghanistan and Iraq that dominated policy making in foreign affairs. Ominous warnings about the potentially devastating effects of global climate change indicated that human civilization itself was at risk, perhaps within a decade.

The presidential administration of George W. Bush, elected as the embodiment of compassionate conservatism and the tradition of Ronald Reagan and his father, prosecuted the wars against terrorism with initial success abroad and political gains at home. By the eve of the 2008 election, however, the president was weakened, and his administration was in disarray. In the process, the institutions of democratic government had been strained and in some areas broken. As candidates in both parties prepared to face the voters in November 2008, a deteriorating economy compounded the challenges before the American people. The electorate confronted the question of whether the conservative policies of George W. Bush and his presidency had protected the nation from harm or created greater threats abroad and economic instability at home.

RACE, ETHNICITY, AND CULTURE WARS IN THE 1990S

While Washington watched the 1994 elections with great intensity, Americans spent more time that autumn transfixed by a sensational murder trial.

The O. J. Simpson
Trial

On June 12, 1994, Nicole Brown Simpson, the estranged ex-wife of professional football star and Heisman Trophy–winner Orenthal James "O. J." Simpson, was brutally murdered at her home. Nearby lay the corpse of Ronald Goldman, an acquaintance and restaurant employee. Police suspicions soon focused on O. J. Simpson, whose Ford Bronco had blood that could be traced to the crime scene and who had apparently left physical evidence of his presence there.

The nation was polarized about Simpson's guilt or innocence. Most white Americans believed that the strong evidence pointed to Simpson as the killer. Many black Americans talked of a police conspiracy to frame the former football star and associated his prosecution with earlier examples of racial injustice.

These opinions solidified during the protracted trial that began on January 29, 1995, and ended with Simpson's acquittal on October 3. Televised daily on the Cable News Network and Court TV and covered in excruciating detail, the trial played out as a racially charged drama that became a national obsession. The Simpson trial became one of the first indicators of how cable television fixated on events that boosted audience ratings while leaving more pressing social questions unexplored. Not required to supply news as were the broadcast channels, cable networks could emphasize the lurid and sensational. Over the next decade, cable television would refine the lessons learned from the Simpson case into techniques that diverted its audiences from hard issues of war and peace and thus ill-served the nation.

The Simpson case ended in an acquittal for the defendant in a result that further split public opinion. Black audiences cheered the verdict as it was announced. Whites watching on television expressed dismay. The national debate intensified as commentators divided along racial lines about the significance of Simpson's acquittal.

The Culture Wars

The Simpson trial took place in the context of an ongoing national debate. What should the United States do about racial injustice and the presence of diverse minority groups within the existing culture? These arguments soon broadened into discussions about **multiculturalism**, gay rights, and religious values.

Since the 1960s, a major weapon in promoting the equality of blacks and other minorities has been the policy of affirmative action in employment, higher education, and government contracts. The stated purpose of these initiatives was to remedy past discrimination and provide minorities with greater opportunities for advancement. The Supreme Court ruled in the late 1970s that race could be employed in university admissions when the goal was to achieve diversity in the student body.

Unhappiness with affirmative action as a policy led some states, such as California with Proposition 209, to pass a referendum that abolished programs for affirmative action. In the *Hopwood v. Texas* case (1996), a federal circuit court overturned the affirmative action plan of the University of Texas Law School, noting that any effort by the university to promote affirmative action was unconstitutional. Texas adopted a plan to admit the top 10 percent of graduating high school students, irrespective of their race or ethnicity, to its state universities. That allowed students from predominantly

This icon will direct you to interactive activities and study materials on the American Passages website: www.cengage.com/history/ayers/ampassages4e

CHAPTER TIMELINE

1995	Murrah Federal Building bombed in Oklahoma City • Dayton Peace Accords bring shaky peace to Bosnia • Federal government shutdown occurs
1996	Hillary Rodham Clinton is subpoenaed before grand jury • Robert Dole is Republican nominee for president • Clinton reelected president
1997	Federal budget deficit falls dramatically • Balanced budget agreement reached • Supreme Court rules that case of Clinton v. Jones can proceed while Clinton is president
1998	Scandal involving Monica Lewinsky and Clinton breaks • Clinton testifies before grand jury and admits to "inappropriate relationship" with Lewinsky • House starts impeachment inquiry against Clinton • Democrats make House gains in congressional elections
1999	Clinton acquitted after impeachment trial • War in Serbia launched by NATO
2000	Disputed election results in Florida end in Supreme Court ruling that George W. Bush is president
2000	Hillary Rodham Clinton elected to the U.S. Senate
2001	Congress passes Bush's tax cut • Terrorist attack occurs on September 11 • War in Afghanistan
2002	Republicans regain control of Senate and dominate all branches of government
2002	Former President Jimmy Carter receives Nobel Peace Prize
2003	*Columbia* space shuttle explodes, killing all seven astronauts • United States invades Iraq and topples regime of Saddam Hussein • Mister Rogers dies
2004	United States faces persistent insurgent resistance in Iraq • George W. Bush reelected president over Democrat John Kerry
2005	Chief Justice John Roberts confirmed as his replacement • Iraqi resistance continues • Hurricane Katrina devastates New Orleans and Gulf Coast
2006	Democrats retake Congress
2007	Steroids scandal rocks baseball • Subprime mortgage crisis begins
2008	NBER declares recession • Barack Obama elected president • Iraq withdrawal planned

minority schools in the state to gain access to the university systems such as the University of Texas and Texas A&M University. Even though the Supreme Court overruled the *Hopwood* decision in 2003 in the case of *Grutter v. Bollinger,* the larger problem of affirmative action and its consequences remained unsolved during the first decade of the twenty-first century.

A new front in the culture wars opened. These tensions affected the academic world in the debate about the concept of multiculturalism. In the 1980s, American academic institutions sought to open up the study of history and literature to a wider range of cultural and social experiences among groups not previously included in the American past. Addressing gender, class, and racial concerns, multiculturalism sought to draw attention to such issues as the role of black soldiers in the Civil War, Japanese Americans in World War II internment camps, and women in the American Revolution. Western civilization courses on many campuses gave way to world history, and a greater emphasis was placed on the rich cultural experience of Hispanics, Asians, and Muslims.

By the early 1990s, however, multiculturalism had come under attack from enemies on the Right. Conservatives such as Lynne Cheney, the wife of the vice president under George W. Bush, and David Horowitz, a 1960s radical who had moved rightward, accused its proponents of enforcing what was called "political correctness," an insistence on conforming to liberal or radical views on race and gender. The critics of multiculturalism argued that the academic Left used the movement to balkanize society into warring ethnic groups, limited free speech on campus, and repudiated the whole tradition of Western culture. While some of the criticisms of multiculturalism did identify areas of exaggeration and overstatements, the attackers overdramatized isolated incidents and inflated small errors into larger trends. By the end of the 1990s, passions about multiculturalism had cooled as other cultural issues such as the Clinton impeachment drew popular attention, but tensions in other areas of society remained volatile, especially over the issue of gay rights.

The efforts of gays and lesbians to attain political and social equality within the United States were met with a strong counteroffensive from conservatives who regarded homosexuals as a threat to the nation's values. In the 1990s, homosexuals contended that they should have the right to marry (that is, same-sex marriage) just as heterosexuals did. Identifying their campaign with the civil rights movement of the 1960s, gay groups wanted attacks on those who were openly homosexual to be classified as hate crimes.

FIGURE 32.1 Hispanic Population in U.S., 1930–2006

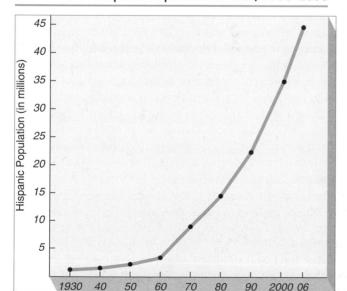

Hispanics Enter Politics

The shifting nature of the population in the United States began a slow but important change in the nation's politics in the 1990s as ethnic diversity became more pronounced. One of the most important groups in this process was Americans of Hispanic origin. In the states of the Southwest and the Far West, Hispanics made their presence felt at the polls, as candidates and as voters. This picture, taken in California during the 1990s, offers visual evidence of the rising importance of Hispanic candidates in that state. A decade later, both major parties were competing vigorously for the expanding vote that Hispanics represented. In the initial phase, the Democrats had an advantage over their Republican rivals. These election signs also attest to the ways in which the American political system accommodated to the tide of immigration that occurred in the 1990s. More than just advertisements for individual candidates, election posters and signs can, if watched carefully, measure subtle changes in the way Americans conduct their political activities.

Conservative groups assailed homosexuality as a sin or a disease. Christian groups ran elaborate advertising campaigns to persuade homosexuals to abandon their lifestyle and seek religious redemption. Gay groups countered that being a homosexual is neither a lifestyle nor a choice. Periodic acts of violence directed against gays spurred calls for federal legislation to prevent such actions. Passions surrounding the issue intensified during the first decade of the twenty-first century as efforts to ban same-sex marriages included a proposed constitutional amendment to outlaw such unions. From their enhanced political power after the elections of 1994, Republicans found such "wedge" issues as homosexuality an important contribution to their rise to greater dominance in American politics.

THE REPUBLICANS IN POWER

The new Republican majorities in Congress went to work in January 1995 with great energy to implement their "Contract with America." Laboring long hours at the start, they enacted a measure to make the regulations they imposed on Americans apply to Capitol Hill as well. The Republicans also pushed for a balanced budget amendment to the Constitution. Meanwhile, President Clinton accepted some of the Republican ideas in his State of the Union message and praised his own record on the economy.

The pace of the "Republican Revolution" remained hectic into the spring of 1995. Although the balanced budget amendment failed by a single vote in the Senate, Congress did pass a law to restrict itself from making the states enforce regulations without supplying the necessary funds to do so. Clinton approved the "unfunded mandates" measure on March 22, 1995. The Republicans failed, however, to pass a constitutional amendment imposing term limits on members of Congress. By April, Republicans proclaimed that they had enacted most of the contract within the hundred days they had set for themselves.

Domestic Terrorism in Oklahoma City Then an act of political terrorism shifted the political landscape. On April 19, 1995, an explosion ripped through the Alfred P. Murrah Federal Building in Oklahoma City, killing 168 people inside. Two suspects, Timothy McVeigh and Terry Nichols, were quickly arrested and identified as sympathetic to an extremist "militia" movement that sought the violent overthrow of the government of the United States. The public learned that small groups of militia met secretly in the countryside to practice guerrilla warfare tactics against the day when the ZOG (Zionist Occupation Government) in Washington would precipitate the final confrontation on behalf of the United Nations and the "New World Order." The glare of publicity revealed that the militia movement, though violent and dangerous, commanded only a small cadre of followers.

The aftermath of the **Oklahoma City bombing** enabled President Clinton to regain a position of trust and confidence with the American people. He went to Oklahoma City in the wake of the tragedy and participated in the ceremony of national mourning for the victims. Clinton's speech on that occasion struck a resonant note of national healing and identified the president with the broad political center of the country. The two suspects, McVeigh and Nichols, were both tried and convicted for their roles in the bombing. McVeigh was executed in 2001.

The Republicans Falter Republican overreaching also contributed to the president's rebound in the polls during the remainder of 1995. As the Republicans in Congress sought to roll back environmental legislation and reduce government regulations on business, the White House assailed them for endangering the gains that the nation had made in clean air and clean water. Clinton threatened to veto legislation that cut back on environmental spending and money for education. He cast his first veto as president in June 1995 when he turned down a Republican spending measure that would have trimmed more than a billion dollars from education funding.

Troubles dogged Clinton during 1995, especially the long-running **Whitewater** saga, which saw congressional committees probe the scandal in detail. Despite the best efforts of Republican lawmakers, the inquiry did not turn up evidence that would incriminate the president or his wife in wrongdoing. The special prosecutor, **Kenneth Starr**, continued his investigations with indictments and convictions of several Arkansas political and business figures, but that effort also yielded nothing to embarrass the Clintons directly.

Srdjan Ilic/AP Photos

Madeleine Albright in Bosnia. *The major architect of Clinton's foreign policy in his second term was Secretary of State Madeleine Albright, shown in a 1997 visit to American troops in the Balkans.*

Clinton Resurgent: Bosnia and the Government Shutdowns

The big political winner in the second half of 1995 continued to be President Clinton. Against all the critics who charged that his policy in Bosnia and Hercegovina would lead to an American involvement and a military disaster, the president succeeded by the end of the year in producing a cease-fire in the conflict and an independent Bosnia. The price was the presence of American ground troops in the Balkans, but even that risky commitment did not lead to the disaster that so many had anticipated. The opportunity for a cease-fire emerged out of a complex series of events during the summer and fall of 1995. In July, a Bosnian Serb offensive imperiled several cities that were regarded as "safe havens" for refugees from the fighting. Helped by arms that had come in from Muslim countries, Croatian and Bosnian forces launched a counterattack against the Serbs. At the end of August, Clinton authorized air strikes against the Bosnian Serbs. Within a week, a tentative peace agreement was declared, and a month later a cease-fire was reached. The United States then brokered peace negotiations in Dayton, Ohio, which produced a settlement. American and NATO troops were dispatched to help enforce the peace agreement.

Clinton Out Duels the Republican Congress

Despite the intervention in the Balkans, the main focus of American politics remained on the running battle between President Clinton and the Republicans in Congress. As budget negotiations over spending cuts that the Republicans wanted and the White House did not produced no result toward the end of 1995, some of the more confrontational members of the GOP majority in the House called for a concerted effort to shut down the government as a way of pressuring the White House to agree to their position. They assumed that Clinton lacked the resolve to withstand a closing of the government. Anger and resentment fueled the Republican outrage. Speaker Newt Gingrich felt especially aggrieved because he believed that Clinton had humiliated him. On a flight back from Israel after the funeral of Israeli leader Yitzhak Rabin, Gingrich thought he had been kept in the back of *Air Force*

One deliberately. Like his GOP colleagues, he distrusted the president and his motives.

The Republican strategy backfired. Two government shutdowns occurred, a brief one in November and a second that lasted for twenty-one days from mid-December 1995 into early January 1996. Rather than blaming the president for the deadlock, as the Republicans had anticipated, the public put the responsibility on the Republicans for the government closures that among other consequences affected tourists in Washington and at popular national parks. In early 1996, the Republicans realized that the protracted shutdown was hurting their cause. They sent President Clinton, as he wrote in his memoirs, "two more continuing resolutions that put all federal employees back to work, though they still didn't restore all government services." By January 6, 1996, the government had resumed normal operations.

While President Clinton had the upper hand in the national political arena, the long-running Whitewater saga took an ugly turn for Hillary Rodham Clinton in the early days of January 1996. Billing records from Hillary Clinton's former law firm in Arkansas, sought by the special prosecutor in 1994, turned up in the White House. Kenneth Starr, the Whitewater prosecutor, subpoenaed Mrs. Clinton to testify before his Washington grand jury. Her appearance marked the first time that a first lady had testified in a criminal proceeding while her husband was in office. She spent four hours before the grand jury panel, but no results followed from her testimony. In fact, all of the probes into the Clinton's financial affairs resulted in no actions against the couple. That aspect of the president's personal conduct proved a dry hole for the Republicans.

As the 1996 election approached, Republicans still believed that Clinton was destined to be a one-term president. In 1995, the party had explored the possibility that General Colin Powell, an African American and former chair of the Joint Chiefs of Staff, might seek the White House. After he made clear that he would not run, Senator Robert Dole of Kansas became the presumed front-runner. A decorated World War II veteran and a gifted lawmaker, Dole had run in 1988 against George H. W. Bush for the GOP prize but had lost badly. At age seventy-two, the senator also had to overcome the age problem, his reputation as a strident partisan, and the perception that he would be the easiest target for a resurgent Clinton. An indifferent speaker at best, Dole campaigned in a frenetic but often unfocused manner. He was not a good organizer, and friends worried about his ability to sustain a national presidential campaign.

Dole faced a number of challengers to his candidacy as 1996 began, but he won the key South Carolina primary on March 2. Successive victories brought the Kansas senator within sight of the nomination by April 1996. The early victory left the Dole campaign broke and unable to counter Clinton's advertising until after the Republican National Convention in late summer, when Dole received federal matching funds as the official Republican nominee. To jump-start his lagging candidacy, Dole tried a sensational gesture and resigned his Senate seat in June to campaign as a man without office or Washington power. He remained behind in the polls.

| Welfare and Other Reforms in Congress | With the election approaching and polls showing their standing with the public in jeopardy, the Republican majority on Capitol Hill relied on such tested issues for their base as reform of the welfare system. After the GOP passed such a bill, Clinton |

vetoed the measure. As the president sought to deprive his rivals of an election-year success, a compromise proposal came out of Congress at the end of July. The bill produced sweeping changes in caring for the poor. In place of the long-standing Aid for Dependent Children (AFDC) program, lawmakers established a system of block grants to the individual states. The federal responsibility to provide for the poverty-stricken, adopted during the New Deal and expanded in succeeding decades, ended. The measure also specified that legal immigrants into the United States would not be eligible for benefits during their first five years of residence. The legislation fulfilled Clinton's 1992 campaign promise to "end welfare as we know it," but it left many Democrats unhappy with the direction of their party.

The waning days of the Congress saw other accomplishments that gave the president issues on which to run and allowed the Republican Congress to rebut the charges that it was unable to act constructively. In August, lawmakers enacted a raise in the minimum wage in two steps to $5.15 per hour. It was the first hike since 1991 and came after intense Republican opposition. Responding to the continuing public unhappiness with immigration problems, Congress included in its spending legislation funds for new personnel for the Immigration and Naturalization Service, the hiring of additional Border Patrol agents, and more severe penalties for bringing in illegal aliens. Republicans failed to get language that would have barred public education to the children of illegal immigrants. The achievements of Congress undercut Dole's argument that Clinton was not an effective leader.

CLINTON WINS A SECOND TERM, 1996–1997

Mindful of their public relations disaster in Houston in 1992 when commentator Pat Buchanan emphasized moralism and values issues, the Republicans sought to reassure voters that they were an acceptable and inclusive alternative to the Democrats. Their problem remained, however, of making Senator Dole an exciting and charismatic figure who could compete with Clinton, an adroit and skilled campaigner. Dole launched his preconvention offensive with the promise of a 15 percent tax cut over a three-year period. Reflecting the sentiment within the party for what was known as a "flat tax," an income tax at a low rate for all citizens, he advocated a "fairer, flatter tax." His scheme envisioned fewer brackets and fewer deductions but did not explain where necessary revenues would be found. To Democratic charges that his proposal would "blow a hole in the deficit," Dole responded by saying that he would propose prudent spending cuts to find the $548 billion needed to offset his tax reductions. For Dole, long a champion of a balanced budget, the tax cut proposal represented an eleventh-hour conversion to the supply-side ideology of the Reagan wing of his party.

The second daring maneuver came when Dole announced that he had asked former Congressman Jack Kemp of New York to be his running mate. A favorite of conservatives, Kemp had long endorsed tax cuts and was perceived to be popular among African American voters because he had proposed enterprise zones that would bring business and employment to blighted areas. In many respects, the choice was an odd one because Kemp brought little electoral strength to the ticket. The Republicans had no hopes of carrying New York State, for example. Kemp was also an indifferent campaigner, but at the convention, his selection lifted the spirits of the Republican delegates who saw Dole trailing badly in the polls.

Midway between the conventions of the major parties came the meeting of the Reform Party that Ross Perot had established as the vehicle for his second presidential candidacy. Perot won the nomination easily. Yet he had not captured the public's imagination as he had in 1992. Perot's hope was to elbow his way into the presidential debates against Clinton and Dole, but despite efforts to use the federal courts to gain access, Perot had to watch from the sidelines.

With a commanding lead in the public opinion polls, President Clinton enjoyed a harmonious convention when the Democrats met in Chicago in late August. The platform stressed centrist themes and spoke of a "New Democratic party." Clinton and Vice President Gore were renominated, and the president promised four more years of prosperity and moderate reform in what he called his last election campaign.

During September 1996, the campaign unfolded as though Clinton and the Democrats were certain winners. Despite some fluctuations, the lead over Dole in the polls remained strong. The two presidential debates did not attract the attention that had characterized the 1992 debates, and Dole failed to crack Clinton's armor with attacks on his character and administration scandals. By the middle of October, optimistic Democrats predicted a landslide for the president and a good chance that the party might recapture the House and Senate from the Republicans.

Then newspaper reports appeared about improprieties and possible crimes in the fund-raising for the Democratic Party and the Clinton campaign. Money had flowed into the president's campaign war chest from Asian sources, and possible links to the People's Republic of China and Indonesian businesses emerged. Every day as the campaign wound down, new revelations of questionable campaign contributors and dubious funding sources followed. The lead for the Democratic congressional candidates eroded, and even some slippage occurred for President Clinton. Rather than a triumphal march, the waning days of the 1996 election saw Clinton and his party staggering toward the finish line under a severe cloud of scandal.

A Mixed Result   The Democratic ticket won 379 electoral votes and 49 percent of the popular vote to 41 percent (159 electoral votes) for Dole and Kemp. Ross Perot and the Reform Party took 8 percent of the popular vote and no electoral votes. Clinton's electoral coalition included California (to which he had devoted attention all during his first term), New York, Illinois, Michigan, and Ohio. The president also carried two staunchly Republican states—Florida and Arizona. However, he still fell short of a popular majority.

Although Dole had lost badly, the Republicans gained some consolation out of the election results. Despite a heavy assault from organized labor and Democratic congressional candidates, the Republicans retained control of both houses of Congress. In the House, the Republicans had a diminished majority of only ten seats. The Republicans picked up two Senate seats for a 55 to 45 margin over the Democrats. Because they needed sixty votes to block a Democratic filibuster, the Republicans would have to compromise with their opponents to get any legislation passed. The stage was set for another scenario of divided government to which the nation had become accustomed since the late 1960s.

An Ambitious   For a president who had come into office promoting domestic
Foreign Policy   issues, Clinton seemed to relish the international stage during

his fifth year in office. He pushed hard for the North Atlantic Treaty Organization to add members from former Communist states in Eastern Europe and saw his vision fulfilled when Poland, Hungary, and the Czech Republic were added to the alliance in March 1999. To overcome Russian opposition to expansion of NATO, the United States and its allies told Moscow in May 1997 that neither nuclear weapons nor large numbers of combat forces would be placed on the soil of the new member states. That publicly placated the Russians.

In other areas of foreign policy, the world's trouble spots remained volatile. The situation in Bosnia, though improved since the Dayton Agreement, still pitted Serbs, Croats, and Bosnians against each other despite the uneasy peace that American troops in NATO helped maintain. As for the Middle East, tensions between Palestinians and Israelis worsened amid sporadic terrorist violence. The Clinton administration pressed both sides for more movement to implement peace, but progress was elusive. Throughout the world, there were rumblings about Islamic terrorism, but that seemed to most Americans, in and out of government, an improbable threat.

An Economic Boom Throughout 1997, the American economy roared into high gear. Unemployment fell to 4.8 percent, and inflation no longer seemed a problem. With jobs plentiful and prices stable, a sense of economic optimism pervaded the nation and kept Clinton's job approval ratings around the 60 percent mark.

Adding to the euphoria was the apparent end of the budget deficit problem that had shaped politics for so many years. Surging tax revenues meant that red ink started to disappear. The 1997 budget deficit was only $25 billion, the lowest since 1974, and 1998 promised the unheard of: a budget surplus. As a result of these trends, Congress and the president worked out a balanced budget agreement in May that was signed into law on August 5. Clinton proclaimed: "The sun is rising on America again." Politicians believed they could look forward to budget surpluses for years to come. This success relied on using the money in the Social Security Trust Fund to offset other spending, but elected officials played down this budgetary sleight-of-hand in their public comments. Few realized at the time that many of the revenue statements of the corporations in the "New Economy" were fraudulent.

The Rise of the Internet A major force in driving the economic expansion of the 1990s was the rise of the Internet and the World Wide Web. These changes reshaped the way Americans got their news and communicated with each other. The development of browsers that could read the hypertext markup language (HTML) facilitated this process during the first half of the decade. In 1996, 18 million people, or about 9 percent of the population, were accessing the Internet on a regular basis. A year later the figure stood at 30 million adults. By 1998, 20 percent of all American households had Internet access. Within three years that figure had risen to almost 51 percent. By 2007, a Pew Research poll found that the number of Americans with access to the Internet was over 76 percent.

Dominating the new field were such corporations as America Online, which provided connections for 30 percent of all Internet users in the country in 1996. Other businesses sought consumers on the Web through specific Web pages or by purchasing advertising space on popular websites. Some new firms, such as the bookseller Amazon.com, saw their common stock value soar in 1998 because of the potential growth of their markets. A dot-com boom ensued in which investors poured money into what was seen as the latest hot Internet-related stock. The economic boom of the 1990s depended to a large extent on this expectation on ever-rising Internet profits. The effects of this economic expansion, including rising government revenues, a diffusion of new jobs, and a sense of well-being, helped President Clinton offset the political troubles that threatened to overtake him during the last two years of his administration.

CLINTON EMBATTLED

The political result of these favorable economic events was a good year for President Clinton that left him popular and Democrats optimistic about regaining control of the House in 1998. The major setback of the year came when the Supreme Court ruled 9–0 on May 27, 1997, in *Clinton v. Jones* that the sexual harassment lawsuit against the president could go forward while he was in office. Other problems dogged Clinton. Congressional probes on the 1996 campaign scandal indicated that the president and Vice President Al Gore had played a larger role in raising money for their campaigns from wealthy donors than they had earlier admitted. Kenneth Starr's Whitewater investigation moved along without major indictments but still posed a potential threat to the White House.

The Monica Lewinsky Scandal — Then in mid-January 1998, a stunned nation learned that a former White House intern and then employee named Monica Lewinsky had been involved in a sexual relationship with President Clinton during her employment. Once the news broke, Clinton asserted that he had not had sex with Lewinsky. For seven months, he reiterated that version of events. Meanwhile, Kenneth Starr investigated whether Clinton had lied under oath in the Paula Jones case when he said he had not had sex with Lewinsky, whether he had obstructed justice, and whether he had asked others to lie on his behalf. This sordid spectacle absorbed vast amounts of television news coverage throughout 1998.

Clinton's denials and strategy of delay worked in the short run. His poll numbers remained high, and Starr's popularity sagged. In the end, however, abundant evidence emerged that Clinton and Lewinsky had had sexual contact. On August 17, 1998, Clinton acknowledged "inappropriate" conduct with Lewinsky when he testified before Starr's Washington grand jury from the White House. That night he told the nation the same thing in a four-and-a-half-minute speech that was widely regarded as a low point of his presidency.

A few weeks later, Starr sent a report to the House of Representatives alleging that there were grounds for impeaching Clinton for lying under oath, obstruction of justice, abuse of power, and other offenses. The House Judiciary Committee recommended that an **impeachment** inquiry commence, and the House voted to authorize a probe after the 1998 elections.

The Monica Lewinsky scandal and its fallout left Clinton a wounded president. He retained the ability to achieve foreign policy successes such as a deal he brokered between Israelis and Palestinians in October 1998. With Clinton's resiliency as a politician, a rebound during his last two years was possible. But his tactics and conduct in handling the Lewinsky matter had cost him dearly in terms of his political capital with the American people.

The 1998 Elections The Republicans entered the 1998 election season with high ambitions to build on their majorities in the House and Senate. In the Senate, they hoped to reach sixty Republicans, which would enable them to end Democratic filibusters. After Clinton's speech on August 17, it seemed as if a Republican rout was in the offing. Alienated Democrats were predicted to stay home, and energized Republicans would flock to the polls to rebuke Clinton.

Instead, the Republicans overplayed their hand. Their moves to impeach Clinton awakened the Democrats and produced a backlash among voters who were still favorable to Clinton. On November 3, 1998, the Democrats in the House actually gained five seats, not enough to regain control but an amazing feat in the sixth year of a two-term presidency. Republican control of the House narrowed to 223–211, a thin majority. In the Senate, the two parties battled to a draw, with the Republicans holding the same 55–45 edge that existed when election day dawned. Two significant Republican victories came in Florida and Texas, where the two sons of George H. W. Bush, Jeb Bush in Florida and **George W. Bush** in Texas, were elected governors. For George W. Bush, his reelection made him the prospective front-runner for the Republican presidential nomination in 2000.

Clinton Impeached and Acquitted Despite the results of the congressional elections, Republican leaders in Congress pressed ahead with the impeachment of President Clinton. In December the House Judiciary Committee, on a nearly party-line vote, sent four articles of impeachment to the full House. That body adopted two articles of impeachment charging President Clinton with perjury in his grand jury testimony in August 1998 and with obstruction of justice in trying to hide his relationship with Monica Lewinsky from members of his staff, and the Starr probe. But when the Senate opened its trial in mid-January, it soon became evident that the forty-five Democrats would not vote for conviction and a two-thirds majority to convict and remove the president did not exist.

President Clinton's popularity with the public remained high, and his State of the Union address on January 19, 1999, drove his poll ratings still higher. He was acquitted on both counts when the Senate voted on February 12, 1999. On the perjury count, the total was forty-five Republican senators voting to convict the president and all forty-five Democrats as well as ten Republicans voting for acquittal. On the second article involving obstruction of justice, the Senate split evenly, with fifty Republican votes for conviction and forty-five Democrats and five Republicans voting for acquittal. William Jefferson Clinton remained in office, a wounded chief executive with two years left on his second term.

The impeachment episode reflected the intense emotions that Clinton had provoked during his time in the White House. To the Republicans and other Americans on the right, he was an illegitimate president, twice elected by a minority of voters through trickery and deceit, who had committed crimes in office that warranted his removal. To the remainder of the country, some 65 percent according to most polls, he was a president who, while probably guilty of the offenses with which he was charged, was performing well in office and should not be removed.

During the weeks following the end of the impeachment trial, pundits forecast that Clinton's poll ratings would drop once the crisis was over. That did not happen as the economy remained prosperous and the Dow Jones Industrial Average hovered around 10,000. In late March 1999, NATO began airstrikes against the Serbian government to stop "ethnic cleansing" of the Albanians near Kosovo. Despite the warning of Clinton's critics, the air campaign ended in success for the NATO forces. The nation turned to the impending presidential contest. In the economy there were signs of a slowdown as the excesses of the dot-com revolution, including speculation and falsified corporate profits ended the bubble of the late 1990s.

THE DISPUTED PRESIDENTIAL ELECTION OF 2000: BUSH VERSUS GORE

The Republican front-runner was Governor George W. Bush of Texas, the son of the former president. Elected governor in 1994 and reelected in 1998, the Texan announced his bid for the presidency in mid-1999 and soon amassed a campaign treasury that ultimately reached more than $100 million. Bush promised that he would be "a compassionate conservative" who would "change the tone" in Washington after the partisan discord of the Clinton era. He advocated a $1.6 trillion tax cut and promised to reform the educational system. Bush lost the New Hampshire primary to Senator John McCain of Arizona, but then won a number of primaries to lock up the delegates needed to control the national convention in Philadelphia.

For his running mate, Bush chose Richard "Dick" Cheney, a former House member and secretary of defense in the administration of Bush's father. Cheney headed the vice-presidential selection committee for Bush and ended up recommending himself. Long convinced that the presidency had lost too much power because of Watergate and congressional assertiveness, Cheney intended to increase executive power. He also shared the views of Republican intellectuals who called themselves "neoconservatives." These writers, including William Kristol and Paul Wolfowitz, contended that the United States should exercise military might in the Middle East to oust Saddam Hussein from power. This end could be achieved, they argued, at little cost to the United States, and the resulting victory would persuade the rest of the region to become both democratic and more accepting of the existence of Israel. Neoconservatives saw Clinton as timid and weak in foreign policy, and they longed to reestablish American supremacy.

Albert Gore easily won his party's nomination but had problems separating himself from the scandals of the Clinton years. He also faced a hostile press corps that focused on every lapse to paint Gore as indecisive and opportunistic. Gore emerged from the Democratic convention behind Bush but closed the gap during September 2000. The election hinged on the three presidential debates.

Although neither candidate did well, Bush exceeded the low expectations that media pundits set for him. Gore was better on substance but was labeled arrogant and condescending. As a result, the race remained tight down to the election. As the votes were counted, the Republicans retained control of the House of Representatives, and the Senate split evenly with 50 Democrats and 50 Republicans. Gore led in the presidential popular vote, but no candidate had an electoral majority. It became clear that the state of Florida would determine the result because its 25 electoral votes would push either of the two candidates past the 271 electoral votes needed. State officials put Florida in the Bush column by fewer than 600 ballots. Gore's forces noted irregularities and flawed ballots in several Democratic counties and sought a recount in those areas.

The Bush camp insisted that the result favoring its man should be final, and charges of fraud, manipulation, and political pressure flashed back and forth throughout November. Finally, the case of *Bush v. Gore* reached the U.S. Supreme Court in mid-December. On the key issue of whether the decision of the Florida Supreme Court ordering a statewide recount should be upheld, the Court ruled 5–4 in favor of Bush in a decision that many commentators dubbed both hasty and partisan. Gore accepted the outcome as final and conceded the election.

THE PRESIDENCY OF GEORGE W. BUSH

In office, Bush continued to act as permanent campaigner who used the devices of the modern media age to present an image of a strong chief executive. He pushed through Congress a series of tax cuts that, the White House said, were designed to assist the struggling economy. The budget surplus of the 1990s soon disappeared as a brief recession followed the end of the dot-com bubble. Record debt became one continuing legacy of the Bush era.

Like Richard Cheney, Bush believed that the presidency had become weakened, and his administration acted to reassert executive authority. They did so largely by

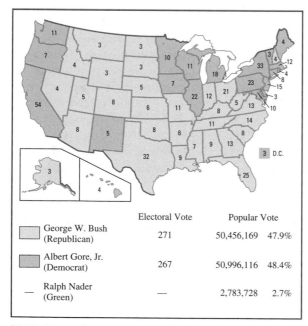

	Electoral Vote	Popular Vote	
George W. Bush (Republican)	271	50,456,169	47.9%
Albert Gore, Jr. (Democrat)	267	50,996,116	48.4%
Ralph Nader (Green)	—	2,783,728	2.7%

MAP 32.1 The Presidential Election of 2000.

The map of the 2000 election reflects the closeness of the electoral vote. Note the extent to which the voters were distributed into a pro-Gore coalition on the coasts and a pro-Bush coalition in the interior of the nation, with some key exceptions in the Midwest and the Far West. A comparison with the presidential election of 1896 (see Map 19.1) gives an interesting sense of how partisan alignments changed during the twentieth century.

ignoring traditional restraints on presidential power and in many cases flouting the Constitution. The president disregarded congressional laws of which he disapproved and claimed unfettered right to govern as he deemed best. Secrecy and deceit became hallmarks of the Bush era. Unfortunately, the search for absolute power did not include comparable competence on the part of the president. Bush was not a hard worker. He governed more through intuition than through substance, and he longed to be out of Washington. In foreign and domestic policy, the Bush White House mixed arrogance with ineptitude.

Meanwhile, Vice President Cheney functioned as a coexecutive who sought additional presidential power to conduct surveillance of Americans, pursue a foreign policy in which allies counted for little, and make policy in secret. The vice president soon overshadowed the secretary of state, Colin Powell, and the national security adviser, Condoleezza Rice. He proved to be an inept policy maker who believed his own propaganda regarding how easy an invasion of Iraq would be.

September 11, 2001, and After One issue, international terrorism, had not been of central concern to most Americans during the 1990s. A bombing of the World Trade Center in New York City in 1993 had not shaken the nation out of its indifference to the threat. Other attacks on American embassies in Africa in 1998 and a similar assault on the destroyer USS *Cole* in Yemen in October 2000 had not brought the issue home. The name of the leader of one terrorist group—**Osama bin Laden**—was largely unknown to the average citizen, even though bin Laden, a fundamentalist Muslim of Saudi Arabian origin, sought the violent end of American influence in the Middle East from his base in Afghanistan. Even a frightening report from a prestigious commission in February 2001 warning of a likely terrorist attack on American soil did little to disturb the lack of alertness that

Ground Zero. *The pictures of Ground Zero where the World Trade Center collapsed became a powerful symbol of the damage the attacks of September 11 had inflicted on the United States and its standing in the world.*

pervaded the government and the mass media. President Bush received a briefing on August 6, 2001, that bin Laden was planning an attack somewhere inside the United States, but no sense of imminent danger showed in White House actions.

On the morning of **September 11, 2001**, two hijacked jetliners slammed into the twin towers of the World Trade Center in New York City. Both buildings collapsed into flames and rubble, and almost three thousand people died. A third airliner crashed into the Pentagon, leaving another two hundred people dead. A fourth plane fell to the ground in rural Pennsylvania after the passengers attacked the hijackers. All air traffic was grounded for several days, consumer spending slumped, and the weakened economy slipped into recession.

This devastating attack on American soil, for which Osama bin Laden and his terrorist network, Al Qaeda, took credit, rattled the nation's morale as it became clear that the terrorists sought nothing less than the destruction of the United States itself. President Bush promised a "war on terrorism" and launched air strikes and ground troops into Afghanistan to fight its Taliban regime that harbored bin Laden. He rejected any thought of seeking national unity in his government and instead saw the terrorism crisis as a chance to confirm Republican dominance with the voters. Soon the Taliban government had been toppled and Al Qaeda disrupted, but American forces remained in Afghanistan into 2008 as the Taliban resisted the presence of outside troops.

The Dilemma of Iraq

Bush administration targeted Saddam Hussein and his government in Iraq as the main focus of the antiterrorist effort. The White House argued that Iraq was linked to Al Qaeda, but the evidence for such a connection was thin. Convinced that the invasion of Iraq was necessary both to topple a tyrant and spread democracy in the Middle East, the Bush administration issued warnings that weapons of mass destruction could be used against the United States. This policy led Washington, in the words of a British official, to see that intelligence was "fixed" (or manipulated) around the policy of invading Iraq.

Preparations for war accelerated during 2002 while the White House sought diplomatic support for efforts to curb Hussein and the alleged weapons of mass destruction he possessed. By the autumn of 2002, a United Nations resolution calling on Hussein to admit inspectors had been passed. Hussein said that his government would agree to the resolution, but his previous flouting of the inspections process made the United States suspicious. The administration moved toward war as 2002 ended. The director of the Central Intelligence Agency, George Tenet, responded to a question from President Bush about where weapons of mass destruction existed in Iraq by saying it was "a slam dunk" that they were present.

The terrorist threat validated George W. Bush as a national leader, and his popularity rose to unprecedented high levels. The administration pushed through Congress the **Patriot Act** of October 26, 2001, which gave broad powers to the federal government to combat terrorism, even at the price of some constitutional guarantees on civil liberties. A year later Congress established the Homeland Security Department on November 25, 2002. The new agency included the Federal Emergency Management Agency (FEMA) despite warnings of the bureaucratic danger of making FEMA part of this unwieldy department. In the congressional elections of 2002, the Republicans, using a strong organization and ample campaign contributions, rode Bush's campaigning and the public confidence in his leadership to victory. Security issues affected the voters more than did the faltering economy and the Democratic emphasis on domestic problems. The GOP regained control of the Senate and widened its majority in the House. As 2003 began, the president and his party seemed poised to enact their conservative agenda.

Meanwhile, preparations for war with Iraq intensified. Secretary of State Colin Powell argued the case for war in a speech to the United Nations in February 2003. Powell's calm, direct presentation convinced many skeptics that Iraq and Saddam Hussein did indeed possess destructive weapons. Although there were doubters at the time, only after the war began did it become apparent that Powell's speech rested on faulty, misleading, and fabricated evidence.

Dissatisfied with the work of the United Nations weapons inspectors, which found no weapons of mass destruction, the United States had failed to obtain a second United Nations resolution authorizing force. The strong opposition of the international community to an American invasion of Iraq, combined with diplomatic setbacks by the Bush White House, left Washington frustrated. The Bush administration, along with its only major ally, Great Britain, decided that an attack on Saddam Hussein's brutal regime could not be delayed. The Bush administration, from Vice President Cheney to Secretary of Defense Donald Rumsfeld, expected a swift victory of the fighting on the order of what had occurred during the ground war in the Gulf in 1991. An invasion force of around 145,000 men seemed enough to White House planners even though some generals recommended two or three times that number. Vice President Cheney said that "significant elements" of Hussein's military force were "likely to step aside" once war began. In this mood of confidence about victory, President Bush told the military "let's go" on March 19, 2003, and the war commenced.

Once launched, the powerful offensive of the American-led coalition swept through Iraq in a dramatic three-week campaign that left the United States in military control of the nation. Saddam Hussein was either dead or in hiding, the major officials of Iraq were captured, and the symbols of Hussein's rule had been destroyed. On May 1, 2003, President Bush declared the major combat phase of the war at an end.

Convinced that they would win an easy victory, the Bush administration had not made plans for the occupation of Iraq. Soon they faced an insurgent movement that resisted the American presence through car bombs, improvised explosive devices that blew up under the lightly armored U.S. vehicles, and guerrilla attacks. By early 2008, almost four thousand American troops had been killed and thousands more wounded. Estimates of Iraqi deaths mounted into the hundreds of thousands. No weapons of mass destruction were found, and inspectors concluded that Hussein had abandoned these efforts after his 1991 defeat. Political efforts to provide a new government for Iraq continued well into 2008.

THE EROSION OF THE BUSH PRESIDENCY, 2005–2008

Angry Democrats looked for a winning presidential candidate in 2004 without success. The election pitted Senator John F. Kerry of Massachusetts against President Bush in a bitterly contested race. Kerry had a war record in Vietnam that was supposed to

The Legacy of Katrina

In late August 2005, Hurricane Katrina hit the city of New Orleans and the Mississippi Coast with devastating force. Large areas of the city were flooded, hundreds perished, the population was dispersed, and the life of New Orleans permanently changed. Three years after the tragedy, the residents

of New Orleans still struggle with the effects of the storm. Promises of government assistance in rebuilding and reconstruction have proved more illusion than reality. This picture of a home impacted by the force of Hurricane Katrina underscore the impact of this calamitous storm on a great American city. The failure of government and politics to deal in a satisfactory manner with the impact of the hurricane is one of the most sobering aspects of these events.

insulate him from attacks on his patriotism. Instead the Republicans argued that his achievements were bogus, reports that the credulous news media repeated without careful checking. As a result, Bush still seemed the stronger leader in the public mind. Bush won a majority of the popular vote and secured 286 electoral votes to 252 for Kerry. The Republicans picked up seats in both the House and the Senate, and they spoke of a mandate for their conservative philosophy during the four years to come.

Bush's second term, however, got off to a rocky start. The president misjudged the meaning of the election. He mounted an intense effort to change social security from an entitlement program to one where individuals would manage private accounts with investments in stocks and bonds. Bush claimed that this shift would produce greater returns for individuals. Critics responded that the social security system was not in crisis, private accounts were risky investments, and the president was trying to implement long-term conservative plans to destroy this popular New Deal program.

The war in Iraq, with no end in sight and persistent American casualties each month, became a political liability for the president. Revelations about torture of Iraqi captives in the Abu Ghraib prison near Baghdad undermined the nation's moral standing. An intense debate began about the value of torture as a means of extracting information from prisoners. Bush's poll ratings slipped in the summer of 2005 into the 40 percent range, their lowest levels for his time in office up until then.

In August 2005, Hurricane Katrina hit the Gulf Coast, devastating large portions of Alabama, Mississippi, and Louisiana. When the levees in New Orleans broke, low-lying areas of the Crescent City became flooded, with hundreds of people dead and large parts of the city uninhabitable. Television viewers across the country saw citizens of New Orleans crowded into the Superdome in horrible conditions, while others clung to rooftops until Coast Guard rescue helicopters could reach them. The social order of the city seemed to have broken down during those desperate days.

Despite ample warnings of the dangers to the city of a Category 4 hurricane and forecasts of where Katrina would hit as landfall approached, city, state, and federal governments performed badly in the crisis. The actions of the federal government represented the greatest shortfall in actual results. President Bush had named inept cronies to head the **Department of Homeland Security** and FEMA, and those two arms of the national government were late, slow, and inefficient in meeting the challenges of the crisis. A terrible disaster worsened because of the shoddy reaction of Washington and the Bush administration. The president's apparent insensitivity to the disaster compounded the damage to his reputation. Once the image of a decisive leader was shattered, he proved incapable of regaining the trust of the American people.

Throughout 2006, Republicans were on the defensive in Congress. Polls suggested that voters wanted a change of leadership. The Republican leaders in the House did not cut federal spending as conservatives had promised, and they increased expenditures to record levels. There was no legislative oversight of the executive branch, especially about the increasingly unpopular war in Iraq as casualties among American soldiers and Iraqi civilians mounted. Revelations of corruption among Republican lawmakers further eroded support for the majority. By the fall of 2006, it was evident that the Democrats were poised to make gains in the House of Representatives. Few pundits believed, however, that the Democrats could regain control of the Senate.

A SOCIETY IN CRISIS

Five years into the new century, Americans argued over social and cultural divisions with ever greater intensity. Conservatives pushed forward against what they deemed a secular, irreligious liberal establishment. Liberals felt beleaguered and under siege from religious fundamentalists. Issues of immigration, science, marriage, and economics posed severe challenges to the nation's institutions. Individuals living in the United States, citizens and noncitizens alike, complained that the news and entertainment media were reluctant to address these matters lest they interfere with the pursuit of ratings and profits.

By 2006, the networks and cable television, owned by large corporations and entertainment conglomerates, shaped the way Americans obtained information about everything from sports to politics. These giant corporations emphasized trivial and transient events in their programming and made their political views known even in ostensibly "straight" news reporting. Fox News, which started operations in 1997, behaved as an arm of the Republican Party. Cable News Network (CNN) imitated Fox, with indifferent success. Commentators on the air acted as partisans rather than reporters. Since complex issues required air time to explain and bored the average viewer, these questions rarely received more than occasion mentions.

As a counterweight to these forces, individuals on the Internet created websites (known as weblogs) on which they could express their opinions about current events and a host of other subjects. These **bloggers** gained influence as their sites proliferated. In 2003–2004, for example, they propelled Vermont Governor Howard Dean into a brief lead for the Democratic nomination before he gave way to John Kerry. On the Left, such sites as Eschaton, Daily Kos, Talking Points Memo, and Firedog Lake became popular. Talking Points Memo, organized by Josh Marshall, played a large role in the success of the Democrats in the run-up to the 2006 elections as it exposed Republican scandals in and out of Congress. On the Right, Instapundit and National Review Online (NRO) gained popularity.

The Immigration Debate
Throughout the 1990s and the first decade of the new century, the question of the role of immigrants, both legal and illegal, roiled American politics and culture. Legal immigrants, most of whom were Hispanics and Asians, totaled almost 600,000 per year during the early 1990s. Estimates of the number of illegal immigrants each year ranged from 300,000 to half a million. In the 1990s, the Immigration and Naturalization Service forecast that there might be as many as 13 million immigrants coming to the United States over the next decade.

Debate about the value and cost of this wave of immigrants escalated during the mid-1990s. Studies demonstrated that immigrants, both legal and illegal, contributed more to society in taxes and productivity than they consumed from government services, but the mere increased presence of Hispanics and Asians, the so-called browning of America, produced political conflict, especially in California. In 1994, California voters adopted in an election landslide Proposition 187, a ballot initiative that barred illegal immigrants from receiving state benefits in education and health. After its adoption, court challenges delayed its implementation, but by 1996, the governor ordered many of its provisions into effect. On the national scene, Congress debated immigration restrictions as it decided what to do about reform of the welfare system. The crosscurrents over immigration persisted over the next ten years, with politicians pressed to take action. So volatile was the issue that little constructive could be done either to stem the flow of illegal immigrants or to assimilate the people who came to the United States legally, seeking a better life.

By 2005, the immigration issue had once again claimed national attention. The estimates of 11 to 12 million people in the country illegally had proven to be accurate. In states along the border with Mexico, especially Arizona, groups opposed to immigration proposed the building of fences to stop the flow of entrants into the United States. By 2008 a fence was actually in the process of construction. Corporations that relied on less expensive labor from undocumented immigrants resisted legislation that imposed penalties for employing illegal immigrants. Both sides asked Congress to take action in 2006 and 2007, but the partisan division on the immigration question prevented passage of any bill.

Cable news channels, especially CNN with a commentator named Lou Dobbs, ran repeated stories about the misdeeds, real and less credible, of illegal immigrants. Within the Republican Party, contenders for the party's 2008 presidential nomination filled their speeches with calls for tougher penalties against illegal immigration, which they believed would resonate with the base of the party. In fact, candidates who were the most strident fared less well in the early primaries. Nonetheless, the Republicans risked losses among Hispanic voters, who generally supported a path to citizenship for

Immigration Demonstration. *As evidence of their growing political muscle, immigrant groups staged large demonstrations to show their presence and resistance to restrictive immigration policies.*

(© J. Emilic Flores/CORBIS)

undocumented workers. As the 2008 election developed, surveys confirmed that the immigration issue might not be as salient politically as the media coverage suggested. However, as the economy slipped into a possible recession in January 2008, the immigration question retained the potential to regain its power to polarize opinion.

The Persistence of Native American Activism

Out of the headlines that dominated the national media during the first decade of the twenty-first century, the descendants of the original inhabitants of North America maintained a tradition of resistance that had existed since the end of the Indian wars during the 1880s and 1890s through the confrontations of the 1970s. Native Americans, faced with such challenges as a suicide rate among young people ten times higher than the national average, have sought to use both legal means and high-profile publicity to alert the nation and the rest of the world to their legitimate grievances. The National Congress of American Indians sued in federal court alleging that the Indian Trust Fund, created under the Dawes Act of 1887, had been depriving Indians of their payments for decades. Claims could reach, they said, more than $137 billion.

While some Indians saw large revenues from casino gambling, others struggled with poverty, disease, and neglect. A symbolic act in 2007 underscored the depth of Native American anger. Representatives of the Lakota Sioux officially repudiated the treaties the tribe had signed with the United States in 1851 and 1868. The next step was to secure international recognition for the Lakota Nation within the borders of the United States. While such a result was improbable, the protest attracted international attention and reminded the country that the issues that Native Americans had raised abut their conditions were far from resolved.

Redefining the
Right to Marry

A cultural issue that aroused strong feelings along the political spectrum was the prospect of gays and lesbians being granted the right to marry their partners and achieve the legal and civil privileges that heterosexual couples enjoyed. In Canada and several European countries, such rights already existed. Religious conservatives regarded this change as a violation of divine law and opposed legislation or court decisions to include homosexuals in marriage law. Gays lobbied through such organizations as the Human Rights Campaign in states such as Massachusetts, whose Supreme Court ruled in 2005 that same-sex marriages could occur, and elsewhere for an equal status under the law for their unions.

While the opponents of same-sex marriages were vocal and intense, the long-term trend seemed to be in the direction of this shift in attitudes toward marriage. Younger Americans, familiar with gays because of people they knew and the television programs that portrayed homosexual characters, tended to be more tolerant and less upset by same-sex unions. In the years after 2001, this issue ebbed and flowed as a matter of public concern. During the early part of the decade, Republicans used referenda on gay marriage as a way to increase the turnout of conservatives during the 2002 and 2004 elections. Polling indicated by 2008 that gay marriage had less salience in this regard.

Battles over
Evolution

Conservatives criticized the teaching of evolution with as much intensity as they attacked gay marriage. The cultural battles that had been raging over evolution since the 1920s intensified after 2001. On the right, such lobbying groups as the Discover Institute pushed creationism as an alternative explanation for human origins. The doctrine taught that a divine power had made the universe through what was called "intelligent design." Proponents of this creed contended that the design of the universe could be explained only by a purposeful creator. Creationists lobbied to have their position given equal status with evolution and succeeded in Kansas and Texas. When a school board in Dover, Pennsylvania, adopted an intelligent design curriculum, however, opponents took the board to court. A judge ruled against intelligent design in a setback to the larger movement. As the debate revealed, Americans remain polarized about science and its implications.

Economic Troubles
in the New Century

During the opening years of the Bush presidency, after the economic expansion of the late 1990s, the country experienced a mild recession that ended in November 2001. To counter the effects of the downturn, the Federal Reserve System had made credit easier through low interest rates and a growth in the money supply. The tax cuts of the first Bush term added to the stimulus that the economy received. These policies facilitated a boom in housing as new construction and home resales leaped ahead. Homeowners became convinced that the value of their dwellings would always rise. In such circumstances, many borrowers took out large loans without a corresponding income to make payments. They bet instead on the appreciation they would receive when the value of their home rose. Lenders at the same time extended credit on generous initial rates ("teaser loans") to many individuals. Mortgage lenders packaged these loans with other loans and sold them to banks and financial institutions. State and federal regulators paid little attention to these practices. Since these loans did not have the worth of those made by "prime lenders," they were dubbed "subprime" loans in the financial industry.

As long as housing prices rose across the country, few problems seemed evident. When in 2007 the housing market softened and foreclosures accelerated, the dubious quality of these subprime loans became evident as banks and lenders incurred staggering losses. Early in 2008, the financial giant Citibank reported losses of $10 billion. Bank of America sought to acquire Countrywide, a major lender, after that firm went into virtual bankruptcy. Other major financial institutions from Merrill Lynch to J. P. Morgan banks wrote down billions of dollars in bad loans.

By early 2008, the housing crisis had spilled over into the large economy. With billions of dollars in bad loans unlikely ever to be paid, the financial system revealed fundamental weaknesses. Fears of a recession mounted, and the Federal Reserve System in a surprise action cut interest rates by three-quarters of a percent in mid-January 2008. Forecasters warned that the impending recession could be long and deep. Congress responded with legislation to put money into the hands of consumers with tax rebates, but critics questioned whether that move would stave off the looming economic trouble. Because of the importance of the American economy in a world in which **globalization** was an increasingly important fact of life, markets in other countries also seemed shaky as 2008 began. After eight years of conservative economic policies under George W. Bush, the United States was now confronted with a huge national debt, a shrunken manufacturing base, and an economy without the resources needed for a quick rebound to prosperity.

The Climate
Change Crisis

For more than a century, scientists had predicted that the accumulation of carbon dioxide that human civilization produced would likely result in the warming of the globe. As a U.S. senator in 1992, Albert Gore, Jr., had written *Earth in the Balance* pointing out this phenomenon and its dangerous consequences. Over the next decade and a half, more evidence of global warming accumulated as glaciers melted, ice sheets shrank in the Arctic and Antarctic, and sea levels rose. A scientific consensus emerged that **climate change** was occurring and that humanity was primarily responsible for what was taking place. Dire forecasts told of more catastrophic events if prompt steps were not taken to reduce the extent of carbon emissions in the atmosphere.

The United States, a major source of carbon emissions from cars, industry, and agriculture, proved reluctant to take any significant steps in the crisis. The Kyoto Treaty of 1999, which sought some steps against climate change, encountered overwhelming opposition in the Senate and then outright rejection from the Bush administration. The White House aligned itself with those who denied that any crisis existed or that the activities of humanity could alleviate the phenomenon.

A 2006 documentary firm produced and narrated by former vice president Gore, *An Inconvenient Truth*, presented the case for action against climate change and received an Academy Award in 2007. By that year, panels of scientists said that action had to be taken within a decade to stave off the most damaging effects of global warming on agriculture, sea levels, and weather. Other scientists indicated that these projections were too optimistic and that the very existence of human civilization was in jeopardy. The truth about the impact of climate change was likely to determine the future of society in the United States and for civilization itself.

THE 2006 ELECTION AND AFTER

The congressional elections of 2006 did produce a Democratic majority in the House of Representatives. That in turn led to the election of the first women Speaker of the House of Representatives, Nancy Pelosi. In the Senate, the Democrats won all the contested seats possible to achieve a narrow two-vote majority. Harry Reid of Nevada became the new majority leader. Polls indicated that the Democratic intention to scale down or end the war in Iraq had much to do with the Democratic victory.

President Bush drew an opposite conclusion. He accepted the recommendation of conservative advisers than an increase, or "surge," of American forces in Iraq would reduce the violence in that country and promote political reconciliation among the warring factions. Throughout 2007, the American military did achieve a lowering of the resistance to the occupation and eventually a fall off in American monthly troop deaths to around twenty-five per month at the end of the year. However, the Iraqis did not take the political steps the surge was designed to promote. By the spring of 2008, troop reductions would have to occur because of a shortage of American forces. The prospect of an end to the Iraq war seemed more distant than ever. Some Republicans, such as presidential candidate John McCain, forecast that American soldiers might still be in Iraq for fifty to one hundred years.

The 2008 presidential election began early in 2008. Senator John McCain of Arizona emerged as the presumptive Republican nominee by early March. His age (he would be seventy-two in 2009) and ties to corporate lobbyists were his minuses; his reputation as a "maverick" lawmaker gave him appeal to moderates. On the Democratic side, Senator Barack Obama of Illinois and Senator Hillary Clinton of New York became the final two contenders in a hotly contested race. By June, though their totals in the popular vote were very close, Obama had a clear lead in delegates and seemed poised to become the party's nominee at the Democratic National Convention in August.

DOING HISTORY ONLINE

Barack Obama

Read online about Barack Obama's remarks at the 2004 Democratic convention.

1. What themes from this 2004 speech on behalf of John Kerry recurred in Obama's presidential campaign in 2008?
2. What part does a sense of hope and possibility play in Obama's evocation of the America he sees in the future?
3. To what extent is the speech partisan in nature? How often does he mention the Democratic Party as an organization?

 www.cengage.com/history/ayers/ampassages4e

CONCLUSION

The 2008 presidential election would be an important one for the people of the United States for whom great challenges now remained. The nation had come far since its colonial beginnings, with significant accomplishments and sobering defeats. Yet the issues now transcended those of the past. Could its people find a way to survive amid the dangers of terrorism, economic decline, military overreach, and, most of all, the mounting threat of global climate change? The capacity of the society to engage and solve these issues would determine the direction of the American passage in the twenty-first century.

Steven Senne/AP Photos

John McCain. *Senator John McCain of Arizona emerged from a crowded Republican field to become the nominee of his party during the spring of 2008. His credentials as a Vietman war hero, foe of pork-barrel spending, and reputation as a maverick were seen as assets that would enable him to overcome questions about his age at 72 years old and fears on the party's right that he was not conservative enough.*

(© Andrew Gombert/epa/CORBIS)

Hillary Clinton and Barack Obama. *Senator Hillary Clinton of New York and Senator Barack Obama of Illinois fought a spirited duel for the Democratic nomination during the spring of 2008. With a superior organization and support from the party establishment, Obama gained enough delegates to assure his nomination at the Democratic convention in August. As the first African-American candidate of a major party, he opened up a narrow lead over Republican John McCain during the summer.*

CHAPTER REVIEW, 1995–2008

- Political turmoil and partisanship characterized public life.
- Racial, ethnic, and cultural tensions continued unabated.
- The rise of the Internet and a growing reliance on computers changed the way people did business and communicated.
- Bill Clinton was impeached and acquitted.
- George W. Bush was elected president in 2000.
- The attacks of September 11, 2001, brought the threat of domestic and foreign terrorism to the forefront of Americans' consciousness.
- A prolonged war in Iraq dragged on.
- Global climate change threatened the existence of civilization

◄▌▌▌ Looking Back

The years between 1995 and 2008 have become contested terrain in the polarized politics of the modern United States. The two most recent presidents, Bill Clinton and George W. Bush, aroused intense feelings for and against them. The emphasis on personality and character that dominated politics also diverted attention from the serious problems that the nation faced as the threat of terrorism and environmental disasters arose.

1. Where does Bill Clinton fit within the recent history of the Democratic Party?
2. Why did terrorism not receive more attention during the 1990s?
3. How did the conservatism of George W. Bush resemble or differ from previous conservative presidencies?
4. In what ways has terrorism altered the nature of the American government?
5. What are the most serious historical challenges the next president will face?

Looking Ahead ▌▌▌►

This is the last chapter of the book, and so these questions are not for further reading. Think about these issues as you ponder the sweep of American history and what could occur during your lifetime as the national passage moves on.

1. What will it take to deal with the challenge of terrorism?
2. What should the United States do to resolve the conflict while at the same time preserving its democratic heritage?
3. How different will American society be in twenty-five years because of the developments between 1995 and 2008?
4. Should optimism or pessimism be the dominant theme in evaluating the future of the United States in the light of the history you have just finished reading?

Go to the American Passages website at www.cengage.com/history/ayers/ampassages4e for additional review materials.

Appendix A: The Declaration of Independence

THE UNANIMOUS DECLARATION OF THE THIRTEEN UNITED STATES OF AMERICA

When in the Course of human events it becomes necessary for one people to dissolve the political bands which have connected them with another, and to assume among the Powers of the earth, the separate and equal station to which the Laws of Nature and of Nature's God entitle them, a decent respect to the opinions of mankind requires that they should declare the causes which impel them to the separation.

We hold these truths to be self-evident, that all men are created equal, that they are endowed by their Creator with certain unalienable Rights, that among these are Life, Liberty and the pursuit of Happiness. That to secure these rights, Governments are instituted among Men, deriving their just Powers from the consent of the governed. That whenever any Form of Government becomes destructive of these ends, it is the Right of the People to alter or to abolish it, and to institute new Government, laying its foundation on such principles and organizing its Powers in such form, as to them shall seem most likely to effect their Safety and Happiness. Prudence, indeed, will dictate that Governments long established should not be changed for light and transient causes; and accordingly all experience hath shewn, that mankind are more disposed to suffer, while evils are sufferable, than to right themselves by abolishing the forms to which they are accustomed. But when a long train of abuses and usurpations, pursuing invariably the same Object evinces a design to reduce them under absolute Despotism, it is their right, it is their duty, to throw off such Government, and to provide new Guards for their future security. Such has been the patient sufferance of these Colonies; and such is now the necessity which constrains them to alter their former

Text is reprinted from the facsimile of the engrossed copy in the National Archives. The original spelling, capitalization, and punctuation have been retained. Paragraphing has been added.

Systems of Government. The history of the present King of Great Britain is a history of repeated injuries and usurpations, all having in direct object the establishment of an absolute Tyranny over these States. To prove this, let Facts be submitted to a candid world.

He has refused his Assent to Laws, the most wholesome and necessary for the public good.

He has forbidden his Governors to pass Laws of immediate and pressing importance, unless suspended in their operation till his Assent should be obtained; and when so suspended, he has utterly neglected to attend to them.

He has refused to pass other Laws for the accommodation of large districts of people, unless those people would relinquish the right of Representation in the Legislature, a right inestimable to them and formidable to tyrants only.

He has called together legislative bodies at places unusual, uncomfortable, and distant from the depository of their Public Records, for the sole Purpose of fatiguing them into compliance with his measures.

He has dissolved Representative Houses repeatedly, for opposing with manly firmness his invasions on the rights of the People.

He has refused for a long time, after such dissolutions, to cause others to be elected; whereby the Legislative Powers, incapable of Annihilation, have returned to the People at large for their exercise; the State remaining in the mean time exposed to all the dangers of invasion from without, and convulsions within.

He has endeavoured to prevent the Population of these States; for that purpose obstructing the Laws for Naturalization of Foreigners; refusing to pass others to encourage their migrations hither, and raising the conditions of new Appropriations of Lands.

He has obstructed the Administration of Justice, by refusing his Assent to Laws for establishing Judiciary Powers.

He has made Judges dependent on his Will alone, for the tenure of their offices, and the amount and payment of their salaries.

He has erected a multitude of New Offices, and sent hither swarms of Officers to harass our People, and eat out their substance.

He has kept among us, in times of peace, Standing Armies without the Consent of our legislatures.

He has affected to render the Military independent of and superior to the Civil Power.

He has combined with others to subject us to a jurisdiction foreign to our constitution, and unacknowledged by our laws; giving his Assent to their Acts of pretended Legislation:

For Quartering large bodies of armed troops among us:

For protecting them, by a mock Trial, from Punishment for any Murders which they should commit on the Inhabitants of these States:

For cutting off our Trade with all parts of the world:

For imposing Taxes on us without our Consent:

For depriving us in many cases, of the benefits of Trial by Jury:

For transporting us beyond Seas to be tried for pretended offences:

For abolishing the free System of English Laws in a neighbouring Province, establishing therein an Arbitrary government, and enlarging its Boundaries so as to render it at once an example and fit instrument for introducing the same absolute rule into these Colonies:

For taking away our Charters, abolishing our most valuable Laws, and altering fundamentally the Forms of our Governments:

For suspending our own Legislatures, and declaring themselves invested with Power to legislate for us in all cases whatsoever.

He has abdicated Government here, by declaring us out of his Protection, and waging War against us.

He has plundered our seas, ravaged our Coasts, burnt our towns, and destroyed the lives of our people.

He is at this time transporting large Armies of foreign Mercenaries to compleat the works of death, desolation and tyranny, already begun with circumstances of Cruelty and perfidy scarcely paralleled in the most barbarous ages, and totally unworthy the Head of a civilized nation.

He has constrained our fellow Citizens taken Captive on the high Seas to bear Arms against their Country, to become the executioners of their friends and Brethren, or to fall themselves by their Hands.

He has excited domestic insurrections amongst us, and has endeavoured to bring on the inhabitants of our frontiers, the merciless Indian Savages, whose known rule of warfare, is an undistinguished destruction of all ages, sexes and conditions.

In every stage of these Oppressions We have Petitioned for Redress in the most humble terms: Our repeated Petitions have been answered only by repeated injury. A Prince, whose character is thus marked by every act which may define a Tyrant, is unfit to be the ruler of a free People.

Nor have We been wanting in attentions to our British brethren. We have warned them from time to time of attempts by their legislature to extend an unwarrantable jurisdiction over us. We have reminded them of the circumstances of our emigration and settlement here. We have appealed to their native justice and magnanimity, and we have conjured them by the ties of our common kindred to disavow the usurpations, which, would inevitably interrupt our connections and correspondence. They too have been deaf to the voice of justice and of consanguinity. We must, therefore, acquiesce in the necessity, which denounces our Separation, and hold them, as we hold the rest of mankind, Enemies in War, in Peace Friends.

We, therefore, the Representatives of the United States of America, in General Congress, Assembled, appealing to the Supreme Judge of the world for the rectitude of our intentions, do, in the Name, and by Authority of the good People of these Colonies, solemnly publish and declare, That these United Colonies are, and of Right ought to be Free and Independent States; that they are Absolved from all Allegiance to the British Crown, and that all political connection between them and the State of Great Britain, is and ought to be totally dissolved; and that, as Free and Independent States, they have full Power to levy War, conclude Peace, contract Alliances, establish Commerce, and to do all other Acts and Things which Independent States may of right do. And for the support of this Declaration, with a firm reliance on the protection of divine Providence, we mutually pledge to each other our Lives, our Fortunes and our sacred Honor.

Appendix B: The Constitution of the United States of America

We the People of the United States, in Order to form a more perfect Union, establish Justice, insure domestic Tranquility, provide for the common defence, promote the general Welfare, and secure the Blessings of Liberty to ourselves and our Posterity, do ordain and establish this Constitution for the United States of America.

Article I

Section 1   All legislative Powers herein granted shall be vested in a Congress of the United States, which shall consist of a Senate and House of Representatives.

Section 2   The House of Representatives shall be composed of Members chosen every second Year by the People of the several States, and the Electors in each State shall have the Qualifications requisite for Electors of the most numerous Branch of the State Legislature.

No Person shall be a Representative who shall not have attained to the Age of twenty five Years, and been seven Years a Citizen of the United States, and who shall not, when elected, be an Inhabitant of that State in which he shall be chosen.

Representatives and direct Taxes[1] shall be apportioned among the several States which may be included within this Union, according to their respective Numbers, which shall be determined by adding to the whole Number of free Persons, including those bound to Service for a Term of Years, and excluding Indians not taxed, three fifths of all other Persons.[2] The actual Enumeration shall be made within three Years after the first Meeting of the Congress of the United States, and within every subsequent Term of ten Years, in such Manner as they shall by Law direct. The Number of Representatives shall not exceed one for every thirty

Text is from the engrossed copy in the National Archives. Original spelling, capitalization, and punctuation have been retained.

Thousand, but each State shall have at Least one Representative; and until such enumeration shall be made, the State of New Hampshire shall be entitled to chuse three; Massachusetts eight; Rhode Island and Providence Plantations one; Connecticut five; New York six; New Jersey four; Pennsylvania eight; Delaware one; Maryland six; Virginia ten; North Carolina five; South Carolina five; and Georgia three.

When vacancies happen in the Representation from any State, the Executive Authority thereof shall issue Writs of Election to fill such Vacancies.

The House of Representatives shall chuse their Speaker and other Officers; and shall have the sole Power of Impeachment.

Section 3   The Senate of the United States shall be composed of two Senators from each State, chosen by the Legislature thereof, for six Years; and each Senator shall have one Vote.[3]

Immediately after they shall be assembled in Consequence of the first Election, they shall be divided as equally as may be into three Classes. The Seats of the Senators of the first Class shall be vacated at the Expiration of the second Year, of the second Class at the Expiration of the fourth Year, and of the third Class at the Expiration of the sixth Year, so that one third may be chosen every second Year; and if Vacancies happen by Resignation, or otherwise, during the Recess of the Legislature of any State, the Executive thereof may make temporary Appointments until the next Meeting of the Legislature, which shall then fill such Vacancies.[4]

No Person shall be a Senator who shall not have attained to the Age of thirty Years, and been nine Years a Citizen of the United States, and who shall not, when elected, be an Inhabitant of that State for which he shall be chosen.

The Vice President of the United States shall be President of the Senate, but shall have no Vote, unless they be equally divided.

The Senate shall chuse their other Officers, and also a President pro tempore, in the Absence of the Vice President, or when he shall exercise the Office of President of the United States.

The Senate shall have the sole Power to try all Impeachments. When sitting for that Purpose, they shall be on Oath or Affirmation. When the President of the United States is tried, the Chief Justice shall preside: And no Person shall be convicted without the Concurrence of two thirds of the Members present.

Judgment in Cases of Impeachment shall not extend further than to removal from Office, and disqualification to hold and enjoy any Office of honor, Trust or Profit under the United States: but the Party convicted shall nevertheless be liable and subject to Indictment, Trial, Judgment and Punishment, according to Law.

Section 4   The Times, Places and Manner of holding Elections for Senators and Representatives, shall be prescribed in each State by the Legislature thereof, but the Congress may at any time by Law make or alter such Regulation, except as to the Places of chusing Senators.

The Congress shall assemble at least once in every Year, and such Meeting shall be on the first Monday in December, unless they shall by Law appoint a different Day.[5]

Section 5   Each House shall be the Judge of the Elections, Returns and Qualifications of its own Members, and a Majority of each shall constitute a Quorum to do Business; but a smaller Number may adjourn from day to day, and may be authorized to compel the Attendance of absent Members, in such Manner, and under such Penalties as each House may provide.

Each House may determine the Rules of its Proceedings, punish its Members for disorderly Behaviour, and, with the Concurrence of two thirds, expel a Member.

Each House shall keep a Journal of its Proceedings, and from time to time publish the same, excepting such Parts as may in their Judgment require Secrecy; and the Yeas and Nays of the Members of either House on any question shall, at the Desire of one fifth of those Present, be entered on the Journal.

Neither House, during the Session of Congress, shall, without the Consent of the other, adjourn for more than three days, nor to any other Place than that in which the two Houses shall be sitting.

Section 6   The Senators and Representatives shall receive a Compensation for their Services, to be ascertained by Law, and paid out of the Treasury of the United States. They shall in all Cases, except Treason, Felony and Breach of the Peace, be privileged from Arrest during their Attendance at the Session of their respective Houses, and in going to and returning from the same; and for any Speech or Debate in either House, they shall not be questioned in any other Place.

No Senator or Representative shall, during the Time for which he was elected, be appointed to any civil Office under the Authority of the United States, which shall have been created, or the Emoluments whereof shall have been encreased during such time; and no Person holding any Office under the United States, shall be a Member of either House during his Continuance in Office.

Section 7   All Bills for raising Revenue shall originate in the House of Representatives; but the Senate may propose or concur with Amendments as on other Bills.

Every Bill which shall have passed the House of Representatives and the Senate shall, before it become a Law, be presented to the President of the United States; If he approve he shall sign it, but if not he shall return it, with his Objections to that House in which it shall have originated, who shall enter the Objections at large on their Journal, and proceed to reconsider it. If after such Reconsideration two thirds of that House shall agree to pass the Bill, it shall be sent, together with the Objections, to the other House, by which it shall likewise be reconsidered, and if approved by two thirds of that House, it shall become a Law. But in all such Cases the Votes of both Houses shall be determined by yeas and Nays, and the Names of the Persons voting for and against the Bill shall be entered on the Journal of each House respectively. If any Bill shall not be returned by the President within ten Days (Sundays excepted) after it shall have been presented to him, the Same shall be a Law, in like Manner as if he had signed it, unless the Congress by their Adjournment prevent its Return, in which Case it shall not be a Law.

Every Order, Resolution, or Vote to which the Concurrence of the Senate and House of Representatives may be necessary (except on a question of Adjournment) shall be presented to the President of the United States; and before the Same shall take Effect, shall be approved by him, or being disapproved by him shall be repassed by two thirds of the Senate and House of Representatives, according to the Rules and Limitations prescribed in the Case of a Bill.

Section 8   The Congress shall have power To lay and collect Taxes, Duties, Imposts and Excises, to pay the Debts and provide for the common Defence and general Welfare of the United States; but all Duties, Imposts and Excises shall be uniform throughout the United States;

To borrow Money on the credit of the United States;

To regulate Commerce with foreign Nations, and among the several States, and with the Indian Tribes;

To establish an uniform Rule of Naturalization, and uniform Laws on the subject of Bankruptcies throughout the United States;

To coin Money, regulate the Value thereof, and of foreign Coin, and fix the Standard of Weights and Measures;

To provide for the Punishment of counterfeiting the Securities and current Coin of the United States;

To establish Post Offices and post Roads;

To promote the Progress of Science and useful Arts, by securing for limited Times to Authors and Inventors the exclusive Right to their respective Writings and Discoveries;

To constitute Tribunals inferior to the supreme Court;

To define and punish Piracies and Felonies committed on the high Seas, and Offences against the Law of Nations;

To declare War, grant Letters of Marque and Reprisal, and make Rules concerning Captures on Land and Water;

To raise and support Armies, but no Appropriation of Money to that Use shall be for a longer Term than two Years;

To provide and maintain a Navy;

To make Rules for the Government and Regulation of the land and naval Forces;

To provide for calling forth the Militia to execute the Laws of the Union, suppress Insurrections and repel Invasions;

To provide for organizing, arming, and disciplining, the Militia, and for governing such Part of them as may be employed in the Service of the United States, reserving to the States respectively, the Appointment of the Officers, and the Authority of training the Militia according to the discipline prescribed by Congress;

To exercise exclusive Legislation in all Cases whatsoever, over such District (not exceeding ten Miles square) as may, by Cession of particular States, and the Acceptance of Congress, become the Seat of the Government of the United States, and to exercise like Authority over all Places purchased by the Consent of the Legislature of the State in which the Same shall be, for the Erection of Forts, Magazines, Arsenals, dock-Yards, and other needful Buildings;—And

To make all Laws which shall be necessary and proper for carrying into Execution the foregoing Powers, and all other Powers vested by this Constitution in the Government of the United States, or in any Department or Officer thereof.

Section 9   The Migration or Importation of such Persons as any of the States now existing shall think proper to admit, shall not be prohibited by the Congress prior to the Year one thousand eight hundred and eight, but a Tax or duty may be imposed on such Importation, not exceeding ten dollars for each Person.

The Privilege of the Writ of Habeas Corpus shall not be suspended, unless when in Cases of Rebellion or Invasion the public Safety may require it.

No Bill of Attainder or ex post facto Law shall be passed.

No Capitation, or other direct, Tax shall be laid, unless in Proportion to the Census or Enumeration herein before directed to be taken.

No Tax or Duty shall be laid on Articles exported from any State.

No Preference shall be given by any Regulation of Commerce or Revenue to the Ports of one State over those of another: nor shall Vessels bound to, or from, one State, be obliged to enter, clear, or pay Duties in another.

No Money shall be drawn from the Treasury, but in Consequence of Appropriations made by Law, and a regular Statement and Account of the Receipts and Expenditures of all public Money shall be published from time to time.

No Title of Nobility shall be granted by the United States: And no Person holding any Office of Profit or Trust under them, shall, without the Consent of the Congress, accept of any present, Emolument, Office, or Title, of any kind whatever, from any King, Prince, or foreign State.

Section 10   No State shall enter into any Treaty, Alliance, or Confederation; grant Letters of Marque and Reprisal; coin Money; emit Bills of Credit; make any Thing but gold and silver Coin a Tender in Payment of Debts; pass any Bill of Attainder, ex post facto Law, or Law impairing the Obligation of Contracts, or grant any Title of Nobility.

No State shall, without the Consent of the Congress, lay any Imposts or Duties on Imports or Exports, except what may be absolutely necessary for executing its inspection Laws: and the net Produce of all Duties and Imposts, laid by any State on Imports or Exports, shall be for the Use of the Treasury of the United States; and all such Laws shall be subject to the Revision and Controul of the Congress.

No State shall, without the Consent of Congress, lay any Duty of Tonnage, keep Troops, or Ships of War in time of Peace, enter into any Agreement or Compact with another State, or with a foreign Power, or engage in War, unless actually invaded, or in such imminent Danger as will not admit of delay.

Article II

Section 1   The executive Power shall be vested in a President of the United States of America. He shall hold his Office during the Term of four Years, and, together with the Vice President, chosen for the same Term, be elected, as follows:

Each State shall appoint, in such Manner as the Legislature thereof may direct, a Number of Electors, equal to the whole Number of Senators and Representatives to which the State may be entitled in the Congress: but no Senator or Representative, or Person holding an Office of Trust or Profit under the United States, shall be appointed an Elector.

The Electors shall meet in their respective States, and vote by Ballot for two Persons, of whom one at least shall not be an Inhabitant of the same State with themselves. And they shall make a List of all the Persons voted for, and of the Number of Votes for each; which List they shall sign and certify, and transmit sealed to the Seat of the Government of the United States, directed to the President of the Senate. The President of the Senate shall, in the Presence of the Senate and House of Representatives, open all the Certificates, and the Votes shall then be counted. The Person having the greatest Number of Votes shall be the President, if such Number be a Majority of the whole Number of Electors appointed; and if there be more than one who have such Majority, and have an equal Number of Votes, then the House of Representatives shall immediately chuse by Ballot one of them for President; and if no Person have a Majority, then from the five highest on the List the said House shall in like Manner chuse the President. But in chusing the President, the Votes shall be taken by States, the Representation from each State having one Vote; A quorum for this Purpose shall consist of a Member or Members from two thirds of the States, and a Majority of all the States shall be necessary to a Choice. In every Case, after the Choice of the President, the Person having the greatest Number of Votes of the Electors shall be the Vice President. But if there should remain two or more who have equal Votes, the Senate shall chuse from them by Ballot the Vice President.[6]

The Congress may determine the Time of chusing the Electors, and the Day on which they shall give their Votes; which Day shall be the same throughout the United States.

No Person except a natural born Citizen, or a Citizen of the United States, at the time of the Adoption of this Constitution, shall be eligible to the Office of President, neither shall any Person be eligible to that Office who shall not have attained to the Age of thirty five Years, and been fourteen Years a Resident within the United States.

In Case of the Removal of the President from Office, or of his Death, Resignation, or Inability to discharge the Powers and Duties of the said Office, the Same shall devolve on the Vice President, and the Congress may by Law provide for the Case of Removal, Death, Resignation or Inability, both of the President and Vice President, declaring what Officer shall then act as President, and such Officer shall act accordingly, until the Disability be removed, or a President shall be elected.[7]

The President shall, at stated Times, receive for his Services, a Compensation, which shall neither be encreased nor diminished during the Period for which he shall have been elected, and he shall not receive within that Period any other Emolument from the United States, or any of them.

Before he enter on the Execution of his Office, he shall take the following Oath or Affirmation:—"I do solemnly swear (or affirm) that I will faithfully execute the Office of President of the United States, and will to the best of my Ability, preserve, protect and defend the Constitution of the United States."

Section 2   The President shall be Commander in Chief of the Army and Navy of the United States, and of the Militia of the several States, when called into the actual Service of the United States; he may require the Opinion, in writing, of the principal Officer in each of the executive Departments, upon any Subject relating to the Duties of their respective Offices, and he shall have Power to grant Reprieves and Pardons for Offences against the United States, except in Cases of Impeachment.

He shall have Power, by and with the Advice and Consent of the Senate, to make Treaties, provided two thirds of the Senators present concur; and he shall nominate, and by and with the Advice and Consent of the Senate, shall appoint Ambassadors, other public Ministers and Consuls, Judges of the supreme Court, and all other Officers of the United States, whose Appointments are not herein otherwise provided for, and which shall be established by Law; but the Congress may by Law vest the Appointment of such inferior Officers, as they think proper, in the President alone, in the Courts of Law, or in the Heads of Departments.

The President shall have Power to fill up all Vacancies that may happen during the Recess of the Senate, by granting Commissions which shall expire at the End of their next Session.

Section 3   He shall from time to time give the Congress Information of the State of the Union, and recommend to their Consideration such Measures as he shall judge necessary and expedient; he may, on extraordinary Occasions, convene both Houses, or either of them, and in Case of Disagreement between them, with Respect to the Time of Adjournment, he may adjourn them to such Time as he shall think proper; he shall receive Ambassadors and other public Ministers; he shall take Care that the Laws be faithfully executed, and shall Commission all the Officers of the United States.

Section 4   The President, Vice President and all civil Officers of the United States, shall be removed from Office on Impeachment for, and Conviction of, Treason, Bribery, or other high Crimes and Misdemeanors.

Article III

Section 1   The judicial Power of the United States, shall be vested in one supreme Court, and in such inferior Courts as the Congress may from time to time ordain and establish. The Judges, both of the supreme and inferior Courts, shall hold their Offices during good Behaviour, and shall, at stated Times, receive for their Services, a Compensation, which shall not be diminished during their Continuance in Office.

Section 2   The judicial Power shall extend to all Cases, in Law and Equity, arising under this Constitution, the Laws of the United States, and Treaties made, or which shall be made, under their Authority;—to all Cases affecting Ambassadors, other public Ministers and Consuls;—to all Cases of admiralty and maritime Jurisdiction;—to Controversies to which the United States shall be a Party;—to Controversies between two or more States;—between a State and Citizens of another State;[8]—between Citizens of different States,—between Citizens of the same State claiming Lands under Grants of different States, and between a State, or the Citizens thereof, and foreign States, Citizens or Subjects.

In all Cases affecting Ambassadors, other public Ministers and Consuls, and those in which a State shall be Party, the supreme Court shall have original Jurisdiction. In all the other Cases before mentioned, the supreme Court shall have appellate Jurisdiction, both as to Law and Fact, with such Exceptions, and under such Regulations as the Congress shall make.

The Trial of all Crimes, except in Cases of Impeachment, shall be by Jury; and such Trial shall be held in the State where the said Crimes shall have been committed; but when not committed within any State, the Trial shall be at such Place or Places as the Congress may by Law have directed.

Section 3   Treason against the United States, shall consist only in levying War against them, or in adhering to their Enemies, giving them Aid and Comfort. No Person shall be convicted of Treason unless on the Testimony of two Witnesses to the same overt Act, or on Confession in open Court.

The Congress shall have Power to declare the Punishment of Treason, but no Attainder of Treason shall work Corruption of Blood, or Forfeiture except during the Life of the Person attainted.

Article IV

Section 1 Full Faith and Credit shall be given in each State to the public Acts, Records, and judicial Proceedings of every other State. And the Congress may by general Laws prescribe the Manner in which such Acts, Records and Proceedings shall be proved, and the Effect thereof.

Section 2 The Citizens of each State shall be entitled to all Privileges and Immunities of Citizens in the several States.

A Person charged in any State with Treason, Felony, or other Crime, who shall flee from Justice, and be found in another State, shall on Demand of the executive Authority of the State from which he fled, be delivered up, to be removed to the State having Jurisdiction of the Crime.

No Person held to Service or Labour in one State, under the Laws thereof, escaping into another, shall, in Consequence of any Law or Regulation therein, be discharged from such Service or Labour, but shall be delivered up on Claim of the Party to whom such Service or Labour may be due.

Section 3 New States may be admitted by the Congress into this Union; but no new State shall be formed or erected within the Jurisdiction of any other State, nor any State be formed by the Junction of two or more States, or Parts of States, without the Consent of the Legislatures of the States concerned as well as of the Congress.

The Congress shall have Power to dispose of and make all needful Rules and Regulations respecting the Territory or other Property belonging to the United States; and nothing in this Constitution shall be so construed as to Prejudice any Claims of the United States, or of any particular State.

Section 4 The United States shall guarantee to every State in this Union a Republican Form of Government, and shall protect each of them against Invasion; and on Application of the Legislature, or of the Executive (when the Legislature cannot be convened) against domestic Violence.

Article V

The Congress, whenever two thirds of both Houses shall deem it necessary, shall propose Amendments to this Constitution, or, on the Application of the Legislatures of two thirds of the several States, shall call a Convention for proposing Amendments, which, in either Case, shall be valid to all Intents and Purposes, as Part of this Constitution, when ratified by the Legislatures of three fourths of the several States, or by Conventions in three fourths thereof, as the one or the other Mode of Ratification may be proposed by the Congress; Provided that no Amendment which may be made prior to the Year One thousand eight hundred and eight shall in any Manner affect the first and fourth Clauses in the Ninth Section of the first Article; and that no State, without its Consent, shall be deprived of its equal Suffrage in the Senate.

Article VI

All Debts contracted and Engagements entered into, before the Adoption of this Constitution, shall be as valid against the United States under this Constitution, as under the Confederation.

This Constitution, and the Laws of the United States which shall be made in Pursuance thereof; and all Treaties made, or which shall be made, under the Authority of the United States, shall be the supreme Law of the Land; and the Judges in every State shall be bound thereby, any Thing in the Constitution or Laws of any State to the Contrary notwithstanding.

The Senators and Representatives before mentioned, and the Members of the several State Legislatures, and all executive and judicial Officers, both of the United States and of the several States, shall be bound by Oath or Affirmation, to support this Constitution; but no religious Test shall ever be required as a Qualification to any Office or public Trust under the United States.

Article VII

The Ratification of the Conventions of nine States, shall be sufficient for the Establishment of this Constitution between the States so ratifying the Same.

Done in Convention by the Unanimous Consent of the States present the Seventeenth Day of September in the Year of our Lord one thousand seven hundred and Eighty seven and of the Independence of the United States of America the Twelfth. In witness whereof We have hereunto subscribed our Names,

Articles in Addition to, and Amendment of, the Constitution of the United States of America, Proposed by Congress, and Ratified by the Legislatures of the Several States, Pursuant to the Fifth Article of the Original Constitution.

Amendment I[9]

Congress shall make no law respecting an establishment of religion, or prohibiting the free exercise there-of; or abridging the freedom of speech, or of the press; or the right of the people peaceably to assemble, and to petition the Government for a redress of grievances.

Amendment II

A well regulated Militia, being necessary to the security of a free State, the right of the people to keep and bear Arms shall not be infringed.

Amendment III

No Soldier shall, in time of peace, be quartered in any house, without the consent of the Owner, nor in time of war, but in a manner to be prescribed by law.

Amendment IV

The right of the people to be secure in their persons, houses, papers, and effects, against unreasonable searches and seizures, shall not be violated, and no Warrants shall issue, but upon probable cause, supported by Oath or affirmation, and particularly describing the place to be searched, and the persons or things to be seized.

Amendment V

No person shall be held to answer for a capital or otherwise infamous crime, unless on a presentment or indictment of a Grand Jury, except in cases arising in the land or naval forces, or in the Militia, when in actual service in time of War or public danger; nor shall any person be subject for the same offence to be twice put in jeopardy of life or limb; nor shall be compelled in any criminal case to be a witness against himself, nor be deprived of life, liberty, or property, without due process of law; nor shall private property be taken for public use, without just compensation.

Amendment VI

In all criminal prosecutions, the accused shall enjoy the right to a speedy and public trial, by an impartial jury of the State and district wherein the crime shall have been committed, which district shall have been previously ascertained by law, and to be informed of the nature and cause of the accusation; to be confronted with the witnesses against him; to have compulsory process for obtaining witnesses in his favor, and to have the Assistance of Counsel for his defence.

Amendment VII

In suits at common law, where the value in controversy shall exceed twenty dollars, the right of trial by jury shall be preserved, and no fact tried by a jury, shall be otherwise reexamined in any Court of the United States, than according to the rules of the common law.

Amendment VIII

Excessive bail shall not be required, nor excessive fines imposed, nor cruel and unusual punishments inflicted.

Amendment IX

The enumeration in the Constitution, of certain rights, shall not be construed to deny or disparage others retained by the people.

Amendment X

The powers not delegated to the United States by the Constitution; nor prohibited by it to the States, are reserved to the States respectively, or to the people.

Amendment XI[10]

The Judicial power of the United States shall not be construed to extend to any suit in law or equity, commenced or prosecuted against one of the United States by Citizens of another State, or by Citizens or Subjects of any Foreign State.

Amendment XII[11]

The Electors shall meet in their respective States and vote by ballot for President and Vice-President, one of whom, at least, shall not be an inhabitant of the same State with themselves; they shall name in their ballots the person voted for as President, and in distinct ballots the person voted for as Vice-President, and they shall make distinct lists of all persons voted for as President, and of all persons voted for as Vice-President, and of the number of votes for each, which lists they shall sign and certify, and transmit sealed to the seat of the government of the United States, directed to the President of the Senate;—The President of the Senate shall, in the presence of the Senate and House of Representatives, open all the certificates and the votes shall then be counted;—The person having the greatest number of votes for President, shall be the President, if such number be a majority of the whole number of Electors appointed;

and if no person have such majority, then from the persons having the highest numbers not exceeding three on the list of those voted for as President, the House of Representatives shall choose immediately, by ballot, the President. But in choosing the President, the votes shall be taken by states, the representation from each state having one vote; a quorum for this purpose shall consist of a member or members from two-thirds of the states, and a majority of all the states shall be necessary to a choice. And if the House of Representatives shall not choose a President whenever the right of choice shall devolve upon them, before the fourth day of March next following, then the Vice-President shall act as President, as in the case of the death or other constitutional disability of the President.—The person having the greatest number of votes as Vice-President, shall be the Vice-President, if such number be a majority of the whole number of Electors appointed, and if no person have a majority, then from the two highest numbers on the list, the Senate shall choose the Vice-President; a quorum for the purpose shall consist of two-thirds of the whole number of Senators, and a majority of the whole number shall be necessary to a choice. But no person constitutionally ineligible to the office of President shall be eligible to that of Vice-President of the United States.

Amendment XIII[12]

Section 1　Neither slavery nor involuntary servitude, except as a punishment for crime whereof the party shall have been duly convicted, shall exist within the United States, or any place subject to their jurisdiction.

Section 2　Congress shall have power to enforce this article by appropriate legislation.

Amendment XIV[13]

Section 1　All persons born or naturalized in the United States, and subject to the jurisdiction thereof, are citizens of the United States and of the State wherein they reside. No State shall make or enforce any law which shall abridge the privileges or immunities of citizens of the United States; nor shall any State deprive any person of life, liberty, or property, without due process of law; nor deny to any person within its jurisdiction the equal protection of the laws.

Section 2　Representatives shall be apportioned among the several States according to their respective numbers, counting the whole number of persons in each State, excluding Indians not taxed. But when the right to vote at any election for the choice of electors for President and Vice-President of the United States, Representatives in Congress, the Executive and Judicial officers of a State, or the members of the Legislature thereof, is denied to any of the male inhabitants of such State, being twenty-one years of age, and citizens of the United States, or in any way abridged, except for participation in rebellion, or other crime, the basis of representation therein shall be reduced in the proportion which the number of such male citizens shall bear to the whole number of male citizens twenty-one years of age in such State.

Section 3　No person shall be a Senator or Representative in Congress, or elector of President and Vice-President, or hold any office, civil or military, under the United

States, or under any State, who, having previously taken an oath, as a member of Congress, or as an officer of the United States, or as a member of any State legislature, or as an executive or judicial officer of any State, to support the Constitution of the United States, shall have engaged in insurrection or rebellion against the same, or given aid or comfort to the enemies thereof. But Congress may by a vote of two-thirds of each House, remove such disability.

Section 4   The validity of the public debt of the United States, authorized by law, including debts incurred for payment of pensions and bounties for services in suppressing insurrection or rebellion, shall not be questioned. But neither the United States nor any State shall assume or pay any debt or obligation incurred in aid of insurrection or rebellion against the United States, or any claim for the loss or emancipation of any slave; but all such debts, obligations, and claims shall be held illegal and void.

Section 5   The Congress shall have the power to enforce, by appropriate legislation, the provisions of this article.

Amendment XV[14]

Section 1   The right of citizens of the United States to vote shall not be denied or abridged by the United States or by any State on account of race, color, or previous conditions of servitude—

Section 2   The Congress shall have power to enforce this article by appropriate legislation.

Amendment XVI[15]

The Congress shall have power to lay and collect taxes on incomes, from whatever source derived, without apportionment among the several States, and without regard to any census or enumeration.

Amendment XVII[16]

The Senate of the United States shall be composed of two Senators from each State, elected by the people thereof, for six years; and each Senator shall have one vote. The electors in each State shall have the qualifications requisite for electors of the most numerous branch of the State legislatures.

When vacancies happen in the representation of any State in the Senate, the executive authority of such State shall issue writs of election to fill such vacancies: *Provided,* That the legislature of any State may empower the executive thereof to make temporary appointments until the people fill the vacancies by election as the legislature may direct.

This amendment shall not be so construed as to affect the election or term of any Senator chosen before it becomes valid as part of the Constitution.

Amendment XVIII[17]

Section 1   After one year from the ratification of this article the manufacture, sale, or transportation of intoxicating liquors within, the importation thereof into, or the exportation thereof from the United States and all territory subject to the jurisdiction thereof for beverage purposes is hereby prohibited.

Section 2   The Congress and the several States shall have concurrent power to enforce this article by appropriate legislation.

Section 3   This article shall be inoperative unless it shall have been ratified as an amendment to the Constitution by the legislatures of the several States, as provided in the Constitution, within seven years from the date of the submission hereof to the States by the Congress.

Amendment XIX[18]

Section 1   The right of citizens of the United States to vote shall not be denied or abridged by the United States or by any State on account of sex.
  Congress shall have power to enforce this article by appropriate legislation.

Amendment XX[19]

Section 1   The terms of the President and Vice-President shall end at noon on the 20th day of January, and the terms of Senators and Representatives at noon on the 3rd day of January, of the years in which such terms would have ended if this article had not been ratified; and the terms of their successors shall then begin.

Section 2   The Congress shall assemble at least once in every year, and such meeting shall begin at noon on the 3rd day of January, unless they shall by law appoint a different day.

Section 3   If, at the time fixed for the beginning of the term of the President, the President elect shall have died, the Vice-President elect shall become President. If a President shall not have been chosen before the time fixed for the beginning of his term, or if the President elect shall have failed to qualify, then the Vice-President elect shall act as President until a President shall have qualified; and the Congress may by law provide for the case wherein neither a President elect nor a Vice-President elect shall have qualified, declaring who shall then act as President, or the manner in which one who is to act shall be selected, and such person shall act accordingly until a President or Vice-President shall have qualified.

Section 4   The Congress may by law provide for the case of the death of any of the persons from whom the House of Representatives may choose a President whenever the right of choice shall have devolved upon them, and for the case of the death of any of the persons from whom the Senate may choose a Vice-President whenever the right of choice shall have devolved upon them.

Section 5   Sections 1 and 2 shall take effect on the 15th day of October following the ratification of this article.

Section 6   This article shall be inoperative unless it shall have been ratified as an amendment to the Constitution by the legislatures of three-fourths of the several States within seven years from the date of its submission.

Amendment XXI[20]

Section 1   The eighteenth article of amendment to the Constitution of the United States is hereby repealed.

Section 2   The transportation or importation into any State, Territory, or possession of the United States for delivery or use therein of intoxicating liquors, in violation of the laws thereof, is hereby prohibited.

Section 3   This article shall be inoperative unless it shall have been ratified as an amendment to the Constitution by conventions in the several States, as provided in the Constitution, within seven years from the date of the submission hereof to the States by the Congress.

Amendment XXII[21]

No person shall be elected to the office of the President more than twice, and no person who has held the office of President, or acted as President, for more than two years of a term to which some other person was elected President shall be electesd to the office of the President more than once.

But this Article shall not apply to any person holding the office of President when this Article was proposed by the Congress, and shall not prevent any person who may be holding the office of President, or acting as President, during the term within which this Article becomes operative from holding the office of President or acting as President during the remainder of such term.

Amendment XXIII[22]

Section 1   The District constituting the seat of Government of the United States shall appoint in such manner as the Congress may direct:

A number of electors of President and Vice President equal to the whole number of Senators and Representatives in Congress to which the District would be entitled if it were a State, but in no event more than the least populous State; they shall be in addition to those appointed by the States, but they shall be considered, for the purposes of the election of President and Vice President, to be electors appointed by the State; and they shall meet in the District and perform such duties as provided by the twelfth article of amendment.

Section 2   The Congress shall have power to enforce this article by appropriate legislation.

Amendment XXIV[23]

Section 1   The right of citizens of the United States to vote in any primary or other election for President or Vice President, or for Senator or Representative in Congress, shall not be denied or abridged by the United States or any State by reason of failure to pay any poll tax or other tax.

Section 2   The Congress shall have power to enforce this article by appropriate legislation.

Amendment XXV[24]

Section 1   In case of the removal of the President from office or of his death or resignation, the Vice President shall become President.

Section 2   Whenever there is a vacancy in the office of the Vice President, the President shall nominate a Vice President who shall take office upon confirmation by a majority vote of both Houses of Congress.

Section 3   Whenever the President transmits to the President pro tempore of the Senate and the Speaker of the House of Representatives his written declaration that he is unable to discharge the powers and duties of his office, and until he transmits them a written declaration to the contrary, such powers and duties shall be discharged by the Vice President as Acting President.

Section 4   Whenever the Vice President and a majority of either the principal officers of the executive department or of such other body as Congress may by law provide, transmit to the President pro tempore of the Senate and the Speaker of the House of Representatives their written declaration that the President is unable to discharge the powers and duties of his office, the Vice President shall immediately assume the powers and duties of the office of Acting President

Thereafter, when the President transmits to the President pro tempore of the Senate and the Speaker of the House of Representatives his written declaration that no inability exists, he shall resume the powers and duties of his office unless the Vice President and a majority of either the principal officers of the executive department or of such other body as Congress may by law provide, transmit within four days to the President pro tempore of the Senate and the Speaker of the House of Representatives their written declaration that the President is unable to discharge the powers and duties of his office. Thereupon Congress shall decide the issue, assembling within forty-eight hours for that purpose if not in session. If the Congress, within twenty-one days after receipt of the latter written declaration, or, if Congress is not in session, within twenty-one days after Congress is required to assemble, determines by two-thirds vote of both Houses that the President is unable to discharge the powers and duties of his office, the Vice-President shall continue to discharge the same as Acting President; otherwise, the President shall resume the powers and duties of his office.

Amendment XXVI[25]

Section 1   The right of citizens of the United States, who are eighteen years of age or older, to vote shall not be denied or abridged by the United States or by any State on account of age.

Section 2   The Congress shall have power to enforce this article by appropriate legislation.

Amendment XXVII[26]

No law, varying the compensation for the service of the Senators and Representatives, shall take effect, until an election of Representatives shall have intervened.

NOTES

1. Modified by the Sixteenth Amendment.
2. Replaced by the Fourteenth Amendment.
3. Superseded by the Seventeenth Amendment.
4. Modified by the Seventeenth Amendment.
5. Superseded by the Twentieth Amendment.
6. Superseded by the Twelfth Amendment.
7. Modified by the Twenty-fifth Amendment.
8. Modified by the Eleventh Amendment.
9. The first ten amendments were passed by Congress September 25, 1789. They were ratified by three-fourths of the states December 15, 1791.
10. Passed March 4, 1794. Ratified January 23, 1795.
11. Passed December 9, 1803. Ratified June 15, 1804.
12. Passed January 31, 1865. Ratified December 6, 1865.
13. Passed June 13, 1866. Ratified July 9, 1868.
14. Passed February 26, 1869. Ratified February 2, 1870.
15. Passed July 12, 1909. Ratified February 3, 1913.
16. Passed May 13, 1912. Ratified April 8, 1913.
17. Passed December 18, 1917. Ratified January 16, 1919.
18. Passed June 4, 1919. Ratified August 18, 1920.
19. Passed March 2, 1932. Ratified January 23, 1933.
20. Passed February 20, 1933. Ratified December 5, 1933.
21. Passed March 12, 1947. Ratified March 1, 1951.
22. Passed June 16, 1960. Ratified April 3, 1961.
23. Passed August 27, 1962. Ratified January 23, 1964.
24. Passed July 6, 1965. Ratified February 11, 1967.
25. Passed March 23, 1971. Ratified July 5, 1971.
26. Passed September 25, 1789. Ratified May 7, 1992.

Index

Note: Page numbers with f indicate a Figure or photograph